APA Handbook of

Research Methods in Psychology

APA Handbooks in Psychology

APA Handbook of
Research Methods in Psychology

VOLUME 1

Foundations, Planning, Measures,
and Psychometrics

Harris Cooper, *Editor-in-Chief*
**Paul M. Camic, Debra L. Long, A. T. Panter,
David Rindskopf, and Kenneth J. Sher**, *Associate Editors*

American Psychological Association • Washington, DC

Published by
American Psychological Association
750 First Street, NE
Washington, DC 20002-4242
www.apa.org

To order
APA Order Department
P.O. Box 92984
Washington, DC 20090-2984
Tel: (800) 374-2721; Direct: (202) 336-5510
Fax: (202) 336-5502; TDD/TTY: (202) 336-6123
Online: www.apa.org/pubs/books/
E-mail: order@apa.org

In the U.K., Europe, Africa, and the Middle East, copies may be ordered from
American Psychological Association
3 Henrietta Street
Covent Garden, London
WC2E 8LU England

AMERICAN PSYCHOLOGICAL ASSOCIATION STAFF
Gary R. VandenBos, PhD, *Publisher*
Julia Frank-McNeil, *Senior Director, APA Books*
Theodore J. Baroody, *Director, Reference, APA Books*
Kristen Knight, *Project Editor, APA Books*

Typeset in Berkeley by Cenveo Publisher Services, Columbia, MD

Printer: Maple-Vail Book Manufacturing Group, York, PA
Cover Designer: Naylor Design, Washington, DC

Library of Congress Cataloging-in-Publication Data

APA handbook of research methods in psychology / Harris Cooper,
editor-in-chief.
    v. cm.
  Includes bibliographical references and index.
  Contents: v. 1. Foundations, planning, measures, and psychometrics—
v. 2. Research designs : quantitative, qualitative, neuropsychological,
and biological—v. 3. Data analysis and research publication.
   ISBN-13: 978-1-4338-1003-9
   ISBN-10: 1-4338-1003-4
   1. Psychology—Research—Methodology—Handbooks, manuals, etc. 2.
Psychology—Research—Handbooks, manuals, etc. I. Cooper, Harris M. II.
American Psychological Association. III. Title: Handbook of research
methods in psychology.
   BF76.5.A73 2012
   150.72′1—dc23
                        2011045200

British Library Cataloguing-in-Publication Data
A CIP record is available from the British Library.

Printed in the United States of America
First Edition

DOI: 10.1037/13619-000

Contents

Volume 1: Foundations, Planning, Measures, and Psychometrics

Editorial Board

About the Editor-in-Chief

Harris Cooper, PhD, received his doctoral degree in social psychology from the University of Connecticut in 1976. From 1977 to 2003, he served on the faculty at the University of Missouri and currently serves as professor and chair in the Department of Psychology and Neuroscience at Duke University in Durham, North Carolina.

Dr. Cooper's research interests follow two paths: The first concerns research synthesis and research methodology. His book, *Research Synthesis and Meta-Analysis: A Step-by-Step Approach* (2010) is in its fourth edition. He is the coeditor of the *Handbook of Research Synthesis and Meta-Analysis* (2nd ed., 2009). In 2007, Dr. Cooper was the recipient of the Frederick Mosteller Award for Contributions to Research Synthesis Methodology given by the Campbell Collaboration. In 2008 he received the Ingram Olkin Award for Distinguished Lifetime Contribution to Research Synthesis from the Society for Research Synthesis Methodology.

In 2007–2008, Dr. Cooper chaired the American Psychological Association's (APA's) committee that developed guidelines for information about research that should be included in manuscripts submitted to APA journals. He recently authored the book *Reporting Research in Psychology: How to Meet Journal Article Reporting Standards* (2011) published by APA. He is cocreator of the Study Design and Implementation Assessment Device, an instrument for assessing the correspondence between the design and conduct of social science research and its ability to draw inferences about causal relationships. In 2007, Dr. Cooper was appointed to membership on the National Academy of Sciences's Standing Committee on Social Science Evidence for Use: Improving the Quality and Utility of Social Science Research.

Dr. Cooper is also interested in the application of social and developmental psychology to education policy issues. In particular, he studies the relationship between time and learning. Whereas most people think of issues relating time to learning in terms of how time is spent *in* school (class time, instructional time, time-on task), Dr. Cooper's work zooms *out* from school time. He focuses on issues related to the school day and school calendar (extended school days and years, summer school, year-round calendars, summer learning loss) and academic-related contexts children find themselves in outside the school day (doing homework, afterschool programs, tutoring).

Dr. Cooper served as editor for the *Psychological Bulletin* from 2003 through mid-2009. He was chair of the APA Council of Editors in 2006 and was a member of the APA committee that revised the APA *Publication Manual.*[1] Since 2009, he has served as the chief editorial advisor for APA's journal publishing program. In this role he assists the editors of APA's more than 30 journals and mediates disputes between editors and authors and between authors and authors.

[1]American Psychological Association. (2010). *Publication Manual of the American Psychological Association* (6th ed.). Washington, DC: Author.

Contributors

Alan C. Acock, PhD, Department of Human Development and Family Sciences, Oregon State University, Corvallis

Leona S. Aiken, PhD, Department of Psychology, Arizona State University, Tempe

Chana K. Akins, PhD, Department of Psychology, University of Kentucky, Lexington

Terrance L. Albrecht, PhD, Karmanos Cancer Institute, Department of Family Medicine and Public Health Sciences, Wayne State University, Detroit, MI

Corinne Allen, Department of Psychology, Rice University, Houston, TX

David M. Amodio, PhD, Department of Psychology, New York University, New York

Ananda B. Amstadter, PhD, Virginia Institute for Psychiatric and Behavioral Genetics, Virginia Commonwealth University, Richmond

Robert Andersen, PhD, Department of Sociology, University of Toronto, Toronto, Ontario, Canada

Russell J. Bailey, Department of Psychology, Brigham Young University, Provo, UT

Roger Bakeman, PhD, Department of Psychology, Georgia State University, Atlanta

Michael Bamberg, PhD, Department of Psychology, Clark University, Worcester, MA

Amanda Baraldi, MA, Department of Psychology, Arizona State University, Tempe

Michael T. Bardo, PhD, Center for Drug Abuse Research Translation, Department of Psychology, University of Kentucky, Lexington

Chris Barker, PhD, Department of Clinical, Educational, and Health Psychology, University College London, London, England

William Howard Beasley, PhD, Department of Pediatrics, University of Oklahoma Health Sciences Center, Oklahoma City

Steven M. Boker, PhD, Department of Psychology, University of Virginia, Charlottesville

Niall Bolger, PhD, Department of Psychology, Columbia University, New York, NY

Dorret I. Boomsma, PhD, Department of Biological Psychology, VU University, Amsterdam, the Netherlands

Michael Borenstein, PhD, Biostat, Inc., Englewood, NJ

Virginia Braun, PhD, Department of Psychology, The University of Auckland, Auckland, New Zealand

Antony Bryant, PhD, School of Information Management, Faculty of Information and Engineering Systems, Leeds Metropolitan University, Leeds, England

Chelsea Burfeind, BA, Department of Psychology, University of North Carolina, Chapel Hill

Jerome R. Busemeyer, PhD, Department of Psychological and Brain Sciences, Indiana University, Bloomington

Paul M. Camic, PhD, Department of Applied Psychology, Canterbury Christ Church University, Tunbridge Wells, England

Luis M. Carcoba, MD, PhD, Department of Psychiatry, El Paso Psychiatric Center, Texas Tech University Health Sciences Center, El Paso

Elizabeth J. Carroll, School of Psychology, Fairleigh Dickinson University, Teaneck, NJ

Andrew Causey, PhD, Department of Humanities, History, and Social Sciences, Columbia College, Chicago, IL

Dianne L. Chambless, PhD, Department of Psychology, University of Pennsylvania, Philadelphia

Kathy Charmaz, PhD, Department of Sociology, Sonoma State University, Rohnert Park, CA

JeeWon Cheong, PhD, Department of Psychology, University of Pittsburgh, Pittsburgh, PA

Larry Christensen, PhD, Department of Psychology, University of South Alabama, Mobile

P. Niels Christensen, PhD, Department of Psychology, Radford University, Radford, VA

Jeffrey A. Ciesla, PhD, Department of Psychology, Kent State University, Kent, OH

Victoria Clarke, PhD, Department of Psychology, Faculty of Health and Life Sciences, University of the West of England, Bristol, England

David A. Cole, PhD, Department of Psychology and Human Development, Vanderbilt University, Nashville, TN

Jessica L. Combs, MS, Department of Psychology, University of Kentucky, Lexington

Harris Cooper, PhD, Department of Psychology and Neuroscience, Duke University, Durham, NC

Stefany J. Coxe, MA, Department of Psychology, Arizona State University, Tempe

Patrick J. Curran, PhD, Department of Psychology, University of North Carolina, Chapel Hill

Kim Daniloski, Department of Marketing, Virginia Polytechnic Institute and State University, Blacksburg

Mark D'Esposito, MD, Helen Wills Neuroscience Institute, University of California, Berkeley

Adele Diederich, PhD, School of Humanities and Social Sciences, Jacobs University Bremen, Bremen, Germany

John F. Dovidio, PhD, Department of Psychology, Yale University, New Haven, CT

Susan E. Embretson, PhD, School of Psychology, Georgia Institute of Technology, Atlanta

Monica Fabiani, PhD, Beckman Institute and Psychology Department, University of Illinois at Urbana–Champaign

Xitao Fan, PhD, Faculty of Education, University of Macau, Macao, China

Fred M. Feinberg, PhD, Stephen M. Ross School of Business, University of Michigan, Ann Arbor

Lesley K. Fellows, MD, CM, DPhil, Montreal Neurological Institute, McGill University, Montreal, Quebec, Canada

Suzannah J. Ferraioli, PhD, BCBA-D, Center for Autism Research, Children's Hospital of Philadelphia, Philadelphia, PA

Emilio Ferrer, PhD, Department of Psychology, University of California, Davis

Christiane Fiege, Dipl-Psych, Institute of Education, Center for Educational Science and Psychology, Eberhard-Karls-Universität Tübingen, Tübingen, Germany

Michelle Fine, PhD, The Graduate Center, City University of New York, New York

Brian P. Flaherty, PhD, Department of Psychology, University of Washington, Seattle

Madeline Fox, **Doctoral Candidate,** The Graduate Center, City University of New York, New York

Adam L. Fried, PhD, Center for Ethics Education, Fordham University, Bronx, NY

Xiaohong Gao, PhD, ACT, Inc., Iowa City, IA

Christian Geiser, DPhil, Department of Psychology, Arizona State University, Tempe

Kurt F. Geisinger, PhD, Buros Center for Testing, Department of Educational Psychology, University of Nebraska, Lincoln

Richard Gonzalez, PhD, Department of Psychology, University of Michigan, Ann Arbor

Nisha C. Gottfredson, PhD, Center for Developmental Epidemiology, Duke Medicine, Durham, NC

Arthur C. Graesser, PhD, Department of Psychology and Institute for Intelligent Systems, University of Memphis, Memphis, TN

Gabriele Gratton, MD, PhD, Beckman Institute and Psychology Department, University of Illinois at Urbana–Champaign

Dale Griffin, PhD, Sauder School of Business, University of British Columbia, Vancouver, British Columbia, Canada

Kevin J. Grimm, PhD, Department of Psychology, University of California, Davis

William M. Grove, PhD, Department of Psychology, University of Minnesota, Minneapolis

Eddie Harmon-Jones, PhD, School of Psychology, University of New South Wales, Sydney, Australia

Deborah J. Harris, PhD, ACT, Inc., Iowa City, IA

Heather Hayes, MS, School of Psychology, Georgia Institute of Technology, Atlanta

Gary T. Henry, PhD, Department of Public Policy, University of North Carolina, Chapel Hill

Karen Henwood, PhD, Cardiff School of Social Sciences, Cardiff University, Cardiff, Wales

Ursula Hess, PhD, Department of Psychology, Humboldt University, Berlin

David C. Hoaglin, PhD, Independent Consultant, Sudbury, MA

Steven D. Hollon, PhD, Department of Psychology, Vanderbilt University, Nashville, TN

Rick H. Hoyle, PhD, Department of Psychology and Neuroscience, Duke University, Durham, NC

Masumi Iida, PhD, School of Social and Family Dynamics, Arizona State University, Tempe

James Jaccard, PhD, Department of Psychology, Florida International University, Miami

Deborah A. Kashy, PhD, Department of Psychology, Michigan State University, East Lansing

Ken Kelley, PhD, Department of Management, Mendoza College of Business, University of Notre Dame, Notre Dame, IN

Cara J. Kiff, MS, Department of Psychology, University of Washington, Seattle

Reinhold Kliegl, PhD, Department of Psychology, University of Potsdam, Potsdam, Germany

George P. Knight, PhD, Department of Psychology, Arizona State University, Tempe

Karestan C. Koenen, PhD, Department of Epidemiology, Mailman School of Public Health, Columbia University, New York, NY

Parvati Krishnamurty, PhD, NORC at the University of Chicago, Chicago, IL

Michael J. Lambert, PhD, Department of Psychology, Brigham Young University, Provo, UT

Sean P. Lane, MA, Department of Psychology, New York University, New York

Jean-Philippe Laurenceau, PhD, Department of Psychology, University of Delaware, Newark

Lisa Lee, PhD, NORC at the University of Chicago, Chicago, IL

Frederick T. L. Leong, PhD, Department of Psychology, Michigan State University, East Lansing

Lannie Ligthart, PhD, Department of Biological Psychology, VU University, Amsterdam, the Netherlands

Steven J. Luck, PhD, Center for Mind and Brain and Department of Psychology, University of California, Davis

Maike Luhmann, PhD, Department of Psychology, University of Chicago, Chicago, IL

Brent J. Lyons, Doctoral Candidate, Department of Psychology, Michigan State University, East Lansing

David P. MacKinnon, PhD, Department of Psychology, Arizona State University, Tempe

Anna Madill, PhD, Institute of Psychological Sciences, University of Leeds, Leeds, England

Randi C. Martin, PhD, Department of Psychology, Rice University, Houston, TX

David Matsumoto, PhD, Department of Psychology, San Francisco State University, San Francisco, CA

Scott E. Maxwell, PhD, Department of Psychology, University of Notre Dame, Notre Dame, IN

Henry May, PhD, Graduate School of Education, University of Pennsylvania, Philadelphia

John J. McArdle, PhD, Department of Psychology, University of Southern California, Los Angeles

Richard McCleary, PhD, School of Social Ecology, University of California, Irvine

David McDowall, PhD, School of Criminal Justice, The University at Albany, Albany, NY

James S. McGinley, MA, Department of Psychology, University of North Carolina, Chapel Hill

Robert E. McGrath, PhD, School of Psychology, Fairleigh Dickinson University, Teaneck, NJ

Danielle S. McNamara, PhD, Department of Psychology and Institute for Intelligent Systems, University of Memphis, Memphis, TN

Tyler M. Moore, MA, MSc, Department of Psychology, University of California, Los Angeles

John B. Nezlek, PhD, Department of Psychology, College of William and Mary, Williamsburg, VA

Nicole R. Nugent, PhD, Bradley/Hasbro Children's Research Center and Division of Behavioral Genetics, Rhode Island Hospital, and Department of Psychiatry and Human Behavior, Alpert Medical School of Brown University, Providence, RI

Sangeeta Panicker, PhD, American Psychological Association, Washington, DC

A. T. Panter, PhD, L. L. Thurstone Psychometric Laboratory, University of North Carolina, Chapel Hill

Carolyn M. Pearson, MS, Department of Psychology, University of Kentucky, Lexington

Louis A. Penner, PhD, Karmanos Cancer Institute, Department of Family Medicine and Public Health Sciences, Wayne State University, Detroit, MI, and Research Center for Group Dynamics, University of Michigan, Ann Arbor

Mary Ann Pentz, PhD, Institute for Health Promotion and Disease Prevention Research, University of Southern California, Los Angeles

Angela G. Pirlott, Doctoral Candidate, Department of Psychology, Arizona State University, Tempe

Nancy Pistrang, PhD, Department of Clinical, Educational, and Health Psychology, University College London, London, England

Jonathan Potter, PhD, Discourse and Rhetoric Group, Department of Social Sciences, Loughborough University, Loughborough, England

Rumi Kato Price, PhD, MPE, Department of Psychiatry, Washington University School of Medicine, St. Louis, MO

Jon Prosser, PhD, School of Education, University of Leeds, Leeds, England

Vicenç Quera, PhD, Department of Behavioral Science Methods, University of Barcelona, Barcelona, Spain

Kenneth A. Rasinski, PhD, Department of Medicine, University of Chicago, Chicago, IL

Roger Ratcliff, PhD, Department of Psychology, The Ohio State University, Columbus

Maika Rawolle, DPhil, Lehrstuhl für Psychologie, Technische Universität München, München, Germany

Keith Rayner, PhD, Department of Psychology, University of California, San Diego

Paula Reavey, PhD, Department of Psychology, Faculty of Arts and Human Sciences, London South Bank University, London, England

Charles S. Reichardt, PhD, Department of Psychology, University of Denver, Denver, CO

Ulf-Dietrich Reips, PhD, IKERBASQUE, Basque Foundation for Science, and iScience Group, Faculties for Engineering and for Psychology and Education, University of Deusto, Bilbao, Spain

Steven P. Reise, PhD, Department of Psychology, University of California, Los Angeles

David Rindskopf, PhD, City University of New York Graduate Center, New York

Shireen L. Rizvi, PhD, Graduate School of Applied and Professional Psychology, Rutgers, the State University of New Jersey, Piscataway

Garry Robins, PhD, Department of Psychological Sciences, University of Melbourne, Victoria, Australia

Joseph Lee Rodgers, PhD, Department of Psychology, University of Oklahoma, Norman

Mark W. Roosa, PhD, School of Social and Family Dynamics, Arizona State University, Tempe

Hannah R. Rothstein, PhD, Department of Management, Zicklin School of Business, Baruch College–City University of New York, New York

Christian C. Ruff, PhD, Laboratory for Social and Neural Systems Research, University of Zurich, Zurich, Switzerland, and Institute of Neurology, University College London, London, England

Margarete Sandelowski, PhD, RN, FAAN, School of Nursing, University of North Carolina, Chapel Hill

Anja Schiepe-Tiska, School of Education, Technische Universität München, München, Germany

Neal Schmitt, PhD, Department of Psychology, Michigan State University, East Lansing

Oliver C. Schultheiss, DPhil, Department of Psychology and Sport Sciences, Friedrich-Alexander University, Erlangen, Germany

Dennis J. L. G. Schutter, PhD, Department of Experimental Psychology, Helmholtz Institute, Utrecht University, Utrecht, the Netherlands

Daniel Serrano, PhD, Vedanta Research, Inc., Chapel Hill, NC

William R. Shadish, PhD, School of Social Sciences, Humanities, and Arts, University of California, Merced

Pnina Shinebourne, PhD, School of Health and Social Sciences, Middlesex University, London, England

Fiona Shirani, PhD, Cardiff School of Social Sciences, Cardiff University, Cardiff, Wales

Patrick E. Shrout, PhD, Department of Psychology, New York University, New York

Laura M. Simonds, PhD, Department of Psychology, University of Surrey, Guildford, England

Gregory T. Smith, PhD, Department of Psychology, University of Kentucky, Lexington

Jonathan A. Smith, PhD, Department of Psychological Sciences, Birkbeck University of London, London, England

Paul T. Sowden, PhD, School of Psychology, University of Surrey, Guildford, England

Karin Sternberg, PhD, Sternberg Consulting, LLC, and Oklahoma State University, Stillwater

Robert J. Sternberg, PhD, Oklahoma State University, Stillwater

David W. Stewart, PhD, School of Business Administration and The A. Gary Anderson Graduate School of Management, University of California, Riverside

Rolf Steyer, PhD, Institute of Psychology, Friedrich-Schiller-Universität Jena, Jena, Germany

Brett G. Stoudt, PhD, John Jay College of Criminal Justice, City University of New York, New York

Brian D. Stucky, PhD, RAND Corporation, Santa Monica, CA

Kristynn J. Sullivan, Doctoral Candidate, School of Social Sciences, Humanities, and Arts, University of California, Merced

Louis G. Tassinary, PhD, JD, Department of Visualization, Texas A&M University, College Station

Fetene B. Tekle, PhD, Department of Methodology and Statistics, Tilburg University, Tilburg, the Netherlands

Paul ten Have, PhD, Department of Sociology and Anthropology, University of Amsterdam, Amsterdam, the Netherlands

María Elena Torre, PhD, Public Science Project, The Graduate Center, City University of New York, New York

Roger Tourangeau, PhD, Survey Research Center, University of Michigan, Ann Arbor, and Joint Program in Survey Methodology, University of Maryland, College Park

James T. Townsend, PhD, Department of Psychological and Brain Sciences, Indiana University, Bloomington

Teresa A. Treat, PhD, Department of Psychology, University of Iowa, Iowa City

Adriana J. Umaña-Taylor, PhD, School of Social and Family Dynamics, Arizona State University, Tempe

Jeffrey C. Valentine, PhD, Department of Educational and Counseling Psychology, University of Louisville, Louisville, KY

Gary R. VandenBos, PhD, American Psychological Association, Washington, DC

Fons J. R. van de Vijver, PhD, Tilburg School of Social and Behavioral Sciences, Tilburg University, Tilburg, the Netherlands

Trisha Van Zandt, PhD, Department of Psychology, The Ohio State University, Columbus

Paul F. Velleman, PhD, Department of Statistical Sciences, Cornell University, Ithaca, NY

Jeroen K. Vermunt, PhD, Department of Methodology and Statistics, Tilburg University, Tilburg, the Netherlands

Richard J. Viken, PhD, Department of Psychological and Brain Sciences, Indiana University, Bloomington

Scott I. Vrieze, Doctoral Candidate, Department of Psychology, University of Minnesota, Minneapolis

Stanley Wasserman, PhD, Department of Psychological and Brain Sciences and Department of Statistics, Indiana University, Bloomington

David Watson, PhD, Department of Psychology, University of Notre Dame, Notre Dame, IN

Stephen G. West, PhD, Department of Psychology, Arizona State University, Tempe

Keith F. Widaman, PhD, Department of Psychology, University of California, Davis

Leland Wilkinson, PhD, Department of Computer Science, University of Illinois at Chicago, and SYSTAT, Inc., Chicago, IL

Carla Willig, PhD, Department of Psychology, City University London, London, England

Michael Windle, PhD, Department of Behavioral Science and Health Education, Emory University, Atlanta, GA

Bianca C. Wittmann, PhD, Department of Psychology, Justus Liebig University Giessen, Giessen, Germany

Ting Yan, PhD, NORC at the University of Chicago, Chicago, IL

Brian T. Yates, PhD, Department of Psychology, American University, Washington, DC

Robert K. Yin, PhD, COSMOS Corporation, Bethesda, MD

Series Preface

The *APA Handbook of Research Methods in Psychology* is the fourth publication to be released in the American Psychological Association's latest reference line, the *APA Handbooks in Psychology*™ series. The series comprises multiple two- and three-volume sets focused on core subfields, and sets will be issued individually over the next several years. Some 20 are currently envisioned, with more than half already commissioned and in various stages of completion. Additionally, several handbooks on highly focused content areas within core subfields will be released in conjunction with the series.

Thus, the *APA Handbooks in Psychology* series now joins APA's three critically acclaimed, award-winning, and best-selling dictionaries—the *APA Dictionary of Psychology* (2006), the *APA Concise Dictionary of Psychology* (2008), and the *APA College Dictionary of Psychology* (2009)—as part of a growing suite of distinguished reference literature.

Each handbook set is formulated primarily to address the reference interests and needs of researchers, clinicians, and practitioners in psychology and allied behavioral fields. A secondary purpose is to meet the needs of professionals in pertinent complementary fields (i.e., by content area), be they corporate executives and human resources personnel; physicians, psychiatrists, and other health personnel; teachers and school administrators; cultural diversity and pastoral counselors; legal professionals; and so forth. Finally, the entire series is geared to graduate students in psychology who require well-organized, detailed supplementary texts, not only for "filling in" their own specialty areas but also for gaining sound familiarity with other established specialties and emerging trends across the breadth of psychology.

Under the direction of small and select editorial boards consisting of top scholars in the field, with chapters authored by both senior and rising researchers and practitioners, each reference set is committed to a steady focus on best science and best practice. Coverage focuses on what is currently known in the particular subject area (including basic historical reviews) and the identification of the most pertinent sources of information in both core and evolving literature. Volumes and chapters alike pinpoint practical issues; probe unresolved and controversial topics; and present future theoretical, research, and practice trends. The editors provide clear guidance to the "dialogue" among chapters, with internal cross-referencing, demonstrating a robust integration of topics that leads the user to a clearer understanding of the complex interrelationships within each field.

With the imprimatur of the largest scientific and professional organization representing psychology in the United States and the largest association of psychologists in the world, and with content edited and authored by some of its most respected members, the *APA Handbooks in Psychology* series will be the indispensable and authoritative reference resource to turn to for researchers, instructors, practitioners, and field leaders alike.

Gary R. VandenBos, PhD
APA Publisher

Introduction: Objectives of Psychological Research and Their Relations to Research Methods

The American philosopher Charles Peirce (1839–1914) claimed that we use five different ways to decide what we believe is true about our world (Feibleman, 1969). First, we believe some things are true because authorities we trust tell us so. Sometimes, we know these authorities personally, such as our parents and teachers. Sometimes, they are very distant from us, such as the writers of ancient religious texts. Other times, authorities are less far removed but still not personally known, for example, the authors in a handbook on research methods.

Second, we know things are true because we have heard them repeated many times. Peirce called this the *method of tenacity*, or the *a priori method*. Here, something is believed because it has always been believed (longevity) or because we have heard it repeated over and over again. We could include in this method the common sense adages with which we are all familiar, such as "birds of a feather flock together" or "a stitch in time saves nine."

Third, we observe or experience things ourselves and our senses tell us they are true. The sun warms things up, for example.

Fourth, we know that some things are true because they can be logically derived; they are the product of rational analysis. Without getting into the formalities of logical deduction, if a trusted authority tells us that "all males have an Adam's apple," and we observe a men's intercollegiate fencing match, then logic dictates we believe that these fencers have Adam's apples under their masks.

The problem with each of these first four methods of knowing is that they are fallible. Two trusted authorities can disagree, suggesting that one (at least) must be wrong. Tenacious beliefs can lead us astray because conditions change over time, or what seems like common sense is not so sensible after all (remember, in addition to birds of a feather flocking together "opposites attract," and although a stitch in time may be frugal, "haste makes waste"). Our senses can deceive us, for example, through the application of different frames of reference, as demonstrated by optical illusions. Are the soccer balls in Figure 1 the same size?

Finally, a logical deduction is based on the validity of the premises, which may be wrong. Or, the logic itself may be faulty even though the premises are true, as when we affirm the

My sincerest thanks go to the five associate editors of this handbook, Paul M. Camic, Debra L. Long, A. T. Panter, David Rindskopf, and Kenneth J. Sher. Without their conscientious assistance, this handbook could not have happened; they deserve equal billing with me as editors. They also provided feedback on this introduction, although any mistakes remain my doing. Thanks also go to Kristen Knight, APA project editor, for her diligence and organizational efforts.

DOI: 10.1037/13619-001

FIGURE 1. Optical illusion involving
two balls of the same size. From http://
www.123opticalillusions.com/pages/sphere-
size-illusion.php

consequent ("All male fencers have an Adam's apple" and "Spencer has an Adam's apple" therefore "Spencer is a fencer").

Peirce's final method of knowing was the scientific method. We can think of the scientific method as a combination of observation and rational analysis, or observation using a set of logical rules that should lead to veridical conclusions about the world. Peirce expected the scientific method to lead to knowledge that was exactly the same for every person, uninfluenced by idiosyncratic frames of reference. He held out the hope for truly objective knowledge.

THE FLAWED BUT SELF-CRITICAL NATURE OF SCIENTIFIC INVESTIGATION

Peirce's grand vision for science, especially when applied to the social and behavioral sciences, is viewed by many in the 21st century as naive, at best. Vigorous debate prevails about whether knowledge is ever attainable without being infused with the theory of the observer (Godfrey-Smith, 2003; Kuhn, 1996). And studies that turn the methods of science on itself (the sociology of science) suggest that even when the search for objective knowledge is a desirable (and an obtainable) goal, the scientific process, in practice, is still replete with appeals to authority, idiosyncratic observation, and failures of rationality (Merton, 1957; Shadish & Fuller, 1994).

Perhaps it is best, then, to thank Peirce for having pointed out potential flaws in the ways that we acquire knowledge. And, although his belief in the existence of objective truth is open to debate, he argued that the application of rationally derived rules to observation was a self-correcting system. Over time, he asserted, by putting the claims of our authorities, observations, tenacious beliefs, and logical deductions to repeated empirical testing (with further observation and rational analysis), our erroneous beliefs would be replaced by *truer* ones.

The view of rational analysis as self-correcting captures only a secondary characteristic of the scientific method, in our case, the scientific study of thought, feeling, and behavior. At the heart of the scientific ethos is the notion of critical analysis. That is, a scientific posture requires that we be skeptical of *any* truth claim, no matter from where it comes, even from science itself. Scientists test ideas in multiple ways from multiple perspectives with the *failure to disprove* after rigorous testing as the goal of their efforts.

Let's use Figure 1 to construct an example. In an ideal world, a scientist says,

> My observation suggests that the upper ball is larger than the lower ball. Now, let's try to prove that my observation is wrong.[1] As a public demonstration, I will use my thumb and forefinger to measure the diameter of the lower ball; then, holding my hand steady, I will move my measurement to the upper ball.

The measurement would suggest that the balls were roughly equal in diameter. Another scientist might then point out that my thumb and forefinger could not be held perfectly steady and suggest a ruler be used. The ruler would still suggest that the balls were equal in diameter. The process might continue with progressively more precise and careful measurement. Eventually, the observing scientists would come to agree that the balls were indeed the same size. Then, they would turn their attention to discovering why their eyes had deceived them. And, as plausible evidence accumulated about *why* the reliance on simple observation was flawed (perhaps gathered by conducting experiments that manipulate the angle of the converging walls or the shadows in Figure 1), confidence in our conclusion about the state of nature, or the laws of visual perception, will grow.

A self-critical posture requires that truth claims never be believed with absolute certainty, only with greater or lesser certainty. This is what is most unique and, I think, exciting about the scientific posture. It is also one tenet that binds the chapters in this handbook. All of the chapter authors would agree that psychological scientists must take a critical stance toward what they call "knowledge."

SCIENCE AND DEMOCRACY

There is more to admire in this self-critical stance to knowledge acquisition. Timothy Ferris (2010) claimed that science is inherently antiauthoritarian because of its skeptical stance. In fact, he claimed that science and liberal democracy, that is, a social system that values human rights and freedom of action, go hand in hand. One cannot flourish without the other. He wrote,

> The very process of doing first-rate science—of making important discoveries rather than merely refining old ideas—depends on unfamiliar and unpopular ideas being freely promulgated, discussed, and in some instances accepted. The fact that millions of people today are open to new ideas and skeptical about political and intellectual authority is largely due to the rise of science. (2010, p. 4)

---

[1] To be more precise, in the tradition of null hypothesis testing the scientist might say, "I propose an alternative to the hypothesis that the two balls have equal diameter. I propose that the upper ball is larger. Now, let's try to reject the equal diameter hypothesis."

So, I would add another attribute shared by the authors of chapters in this handbook: open-mindedness. At the same time that scientists accept no truth claim uncritically they also turn no idea away prima facie, on its first appearance.

Maintaining this posture of "open-minded skepticism" is no easy feat. Finding the proper balance between foregoing prejudgment and embracing doubt, while holding in abeyance our only-too-human desire for certainty (and for *our* certainties to be deemed the correct ones), is the scientist's principal challenge. And psychological scientists have a particularly difficult task. They must hold to open-minded skepticism while studying their own species in contexts in which they themselves act. Unlike the physicist who can remain relatively detached from the behavior of atoms, psychological scientists can have a personal stake in what they discover about human nature, the good and the bad. So, is open-minded skepticism impossible? Perhaps. Flawed in its execution? More often than not. Worth the effort? Certainly.

In the pages of this handbook, you will find descriptions of many techniques that psychologists and others have developed to help them pursue a shared understanding of why humans think, feel, and behave the way they do. These are the tools that we use to conduct our rational analyses.

THE HANDBOOK'S ORGANIZATION

Organizing the chapters of this handbook was a huge challenge. Psychology's methods defy simple categorization because of their cross-disciplinary (and subdisciplinary) heritages. Many methods presented are similar to one another on some dimensions but far apart on others. So deciding which dimensions to prioritize has nontrivial implications for where a method appears. In addition, prioritizing some dimensions over others can border on arbitrary and be based on oversimplified characterizations of any methodology's capacities for guiding discovery. Many methods can be used for more than one purpose. We have tried to put these "Swiss Army knives" of methodology in the toolbox compartment of their most frequent use. In addition, traditions of use within subdisciplines dictated that some methods appear close together, even if grouping them defied the logic of our dimensional analysis. And, some methods are so unique that they were hard to place anywhere. These methods are no less important because of their singularity; indeed, if they are the only way to answer a question, their uniqueness can make them especially valuable.

So, as you scan the table of contents and contemplate our choices for clustering and ordering the presentation of methods, I am certain that you will be perplexed by some of our choices. Other schemes could fit equally well, or better. Below, I try to capture the high-order dimensions that informed our placement of chapters, beginning with those that relate to the earliest decisions that a researcher makes when choosing methods.

FINDING THE METHOD THAT FITS THE QUESTION

There is an old joke in which a person is searching the ground beneath the halo of a streetlight. A stranger emerges from the dark and asks, "What are you looking for?"

"My car keys," replies the searcher.

The stranger sees nothing under the light and inquires, "Where did you lose them?"

"Over there," says the searcher pointing down the street.

The stranger asks, "So why are you looking here?"

"Because this is where the light is," the searcher explains.

Clearly, this searcher's method does not fit the objective. Similarly, psychological researchers must choose methods that fit the research question that they want to answer, not the method that is available or that they know best. No matter how luminous a method is, if the questions it can answer do not correspond to the knowledge sought, the researcher will remain in the dark.

You could think of this handbook as a collection of streetlights. Each method contained herein is meant to help you shed light on thought, feeling, and behavior over a different expanse and from a different angle. As I alluded to, another frequent metaphor compares research methods with a toolbox. Here, methodology provides the hammers, screwdrivers, wrenches, and rulers that psychological researchers use when they ply their trade.

You will read repeatedly in the chapters that follow that your first task as a psychological researcher is to pick the method best suited to answer the question that motivates you. You will be told not to search where the light is or bang a nail with a screwdriver. Instead, you will learn to choose the method that best answers your question. It is the hope of the contributors that this handbook will expand the topics that you can illuminate and increase the size of your toolbox. We hope to provide you with new ways to answer old questions as well as to raise new questions, perhaps ones you did not realize could be asked.

At the broadest level, when choosing a method you make decisions about (a) what data or measurement techniques will best capture the thoughts, feelings, and behaviors that interest you; (b) what research design best fits the question that you want to answer; and (c) what strategies for data analysis best match the characteristics of your design and measurements. The simplest choice for organizing the presentation of material is the temporal sequence in which you will make these decisions. This is roughly what we have done. So, the earliest chapters in Volume 1, Parts I and II, address the broadest questions related to research designs. These involve both (a) which research designs are most appropriate for which question and (b) how to think about the ethicality and feasibility of the designs that address your question and the measures available to you. Next, the chapters in Volume 1, Parts III and IV, describe the types of data that psychologists most often collect and how to determine whether the measurement techniques that you might choose are the best ones for your purpose. In Volume 2, Parts I through Part VI, the chapters return to issues of research design and present for your consideration a panoply of options, further divided along more nuanced distinctions in their objectives (discussed in the section Interpretive Inquiry, Description, and Causal Explanation). Chapters on techniques for data analysis follow in Volume 3, Part I, again with special attention to the fit between design, measurement, and analysis. Finally, issues and choices you must consider when you write up your research to share with the community of psychologists are discussed in the handbook's concluding chapters, in Volume 3, Part II.

MEASUREMENT METHODS AND PSYCHOMETRICS

After you have a good grasp of your research question and the general design of your study you need to choose the means of measuring the variables of interest to you. You must answer the question: "What measures best capture the variables of interest?" Volume 1, Parts III and IV of the handbook help you consider your choices and pick the measure that best answers your question.

Units of Analysis

As a science matures, it adopts, adapts and invents new techniques for looking at the world. Certainly, the ruler that we used to examine the optical illusion in Figure 1 was not invented for that purpose alone; we noted its relevance to our problem and commandeered it for our cause. And, as you look at the contents of Volume 1, Parts III and IV, it will be obvious to you that this handbook describes an enormous array of rulers. Some of these rulers were invented by psychologists, but many were invented for other purposes to study phenomena of interest in other disciplines.

It is possible to think of the sciences as falling along a continuum that distinguishes them according to the size of the things that they study or their unit of analysis or investigation. So chemists, generally speaking, study things that are physically smaller than the things studied by biologists, whose units of study often are smaller than those studied by psychologists, whose units often are smaller than those studied by sociologists. Of course, the overlap in topics of interest is great, so at the margins the distinction between disciplines breaks down; it becomes difficult, if not impossible, to identify where one scientific discipline ends and the next begins. A psychologist who studies group identity is more likely to share an intellectual heritage with many sociologists than with a psychologist who studies the role of neurotransmitters in depression, whose work may be more akin to that of a neurobiologist.

Along with a blurring at the margins of disciplines comes the transfer of measurements and methods between disciplines. Not surprisingly then, in this handbook, you will find measurement techniques (as well as research designs and statistical techniques) with histories that locate their roots in numerous fields of study, including economics, political science, sociology, anthropology, neurobiology, and genetics. This is a good thing for our discipline. Psychologists have come to recognize that a complete picture of any phenomenon requires that it be examined through multiple methods, applying multiple lenses and rulers. To fully understand schizophrenia, for example, psychological scientists might need to survey its prevalence in a population; examine family dynamics; observe, interview, and test individuals with the disorder; and conduct brain scans and map genes.

Because of psychology's interdisciplinary range, the array of methods covered in this handbook is daunting. But the variety of methods that psychologists use is indicative of our discipline's strength and vitality. The authors of the handbook chapters are motivated by a search for answers; no parochialism here. They share the belief that their own method of choice cannot develop a complete picture of the world or, really, any discrete phenomenon in it. Rather, each method supplies a small piece of the puzzle. It is only when the puzzle pieces are fit together that a complete picture emerges.

Volume 1, Part III of the handbook offers many different techniques of measurement. The sections are roughly organized according to the size of their unit of analysis. It begins with the largest units and proceeds to the smallest. So, Section 1 presents techniques that measure peoples' overt individual behavior, which are typically available for others to view. Sections 2 and 3 largely describe measures for which people provide verbal or written data about what they are thinking, what they are feeling, or how they behave. Sections 4, 5, and 6 reduce the unit of analysis even further, to psychophysical and psychophysiological measures and then to measures that are biological in nature.

The chapters in Volume 1, Part IV, help you answer a second question about your measures: "How well does your chosen measure represent the variable that interests you?" This question again requires you to consider fit, but now between a concept, or latent variable, and the means that are used to measure it. Put simply, the variables involved in psychological research need to be defined in two ways, conceptually and operationally. *Conceptual* definitions describe qualities of the variable that are independent of time and space and can be used to distinguish events that are and are not instances of the concept. For example, a conceptual definition of *aggression* might be "behavior intended to cause pain or harm." Conceptual definitions can differ in breadth, that is, in the number of events that they capture. So, if the terms *pain* and *harm* are interpreted broadly, then *aggression* could include verbal as well as physical acts.

To relate concepts to concrete events, a variable must also be operationally defined. An *operational* definition is a description of the observable characteristics that allows us to determine whether a behavior or event represents an occurrence of the conceptual variable. So, an operational definition of *aggression* might include "shouting, or vocalizations above a specified decibel level" if verbal aggression is included but not so if only physical harm is included. The chapters in Volume 1, Part IV, present the criteria and many of the techniques that psychological researchers use to assess whether a measure is a good fit for a construct.

The Value of Multiple Operations

As you think about measures for a study, it is important to keep in mind that it is generally a good idea to include more than one operationalization of the constructs that interest you. Webb, Campbell, Schwartz, Sechrest, and Grove (1981) set out arguments for the value of having multiple operations to define the same underlying construct. They defined *multiple operationism* as the use of many measures that share a conceptual definition "but have different patterns of irrelevant components" (1981, p. 35). Having multiple operations of a construct has positive consequences because

> once a proposition has been confirmed by two or more independent measurement processes, the uncertainty of its interpretation is greatly reduced. . . . If a proposition can survive the onslaught of a series of imperfect measures, with all their irrelevant error, confidence should be placed in it. (Webb et al., 1981, p. 35)

Of course, Webb and colleagues were quick to point out that our confidence in a finding is first and foremost accomplished by "minimizing error in each instrument and by a reasonable belief in the different and divergent effects of the sources of error" (p. 35) across the measures that we include.

An example will show how this works. Suppose in a study you measure aggression between two people in three different ways: by unobtrusively observing participants' physical contact, by self-reported desire to harm one another, and by taking a physiological measure of arousal (one from Volume 1, Part III, Section 1; one from Section 2; and one from Section 5). You can be fairly confident that these measures do not share irrelevant sources of error. Observed behaviors might be open to misclassification (a slap on the back might be coded as an act of aggression but really be one of friendship), but self-reports and physiological arousal less so. Self-reports are more open to responding in a socially desirable manner than unobtrusive observations or physiological measures. People become aroused by both love and hate but rarely self-report hate when love is the answer.

Now suppose your study was meant to test the hypothesis that the likelihood of aggression is related to state anxiety. If all three of your measures revealed similar predicted relations to measures of state anxiety or responded similarly to manipulations meant to increase state anxiety (say, the sounding of an alarm),[2] this would allow you to rule out the irrelevant influences (misinterpretation by observers, social desirability, etc.) on your three aggression measures as the cause of the relation. If results are inconsistent across operations, having the three measures allows you to speculate on what the important differences between operations might be.

There is another benefit to including multiple operations in research. Predictions are often made from theories on the basis of presumed causal processes that include multiple steps, or causal linkages. These are the focus of causal modeling studies (Volume 2, Part III), and they also pertain to other research designs. So we might speculate that hearing an alarm increases state anxiety by increasing uncertainty and physiological arousal. In turn, uncertainty and arousal increase the likelihood of aggression. By including a measure of arousal in your study, along with observed and self-reported aggression measures, your study also tests this mediating mechanism.

Of necessity, the chapters in Volume 1, Part III, present their array of measurement methods largely as discrete choices. And, in Volume 1, Part IV, the methods for appraising a measure's fit with the construct of interest largely address the adequacy of each measure separately. But as you design a study, you should not think that you must choose one measure or another. Instead, when you consider which measure best captures your construct of interest, remember that no measure is perfect. And, to the extent reasonable, the more measures—that do not share the same imperfections and that test more than one linkage if a causal chain is hypothesized—the better.

INTERPRETIVE INQUIRY, DESCRIPTION, AND CAUSAL EXPLANATION

To choose the research design that best fits your research question, you need to consider some questions about your research aims. First, you need to consider the following: Are you seeking to (a) undertake an interpretive inquiry, (b) provide a description of an event, or (c) develop a causal explanation for the event or relation that interests you? The handbook begins with three examinations (including this Introduction and Chapters 1 and 2) that help you understand the differences between these types of questions and then, in Volume 2, map specific research designs onto specific research questions.

Interpretive Research

To choose between interpretive or descriptive research, you must also answer the question: Do you want to uncover the impetus to thoughts and actions that exist for the actors themselves or do you have your own theory or perspective to guide your data collection? Carla Willig (Chapter 1 in this volume) helps you decide whether your question naturally fits in the former category, suggesting an interpretive inquiry designs. She suggests that qualitative research designs are most appropriate when interpretation is your goal or when your question falls into one of these categories:

- What does something feel like?
- How is something experienced?
- How do people talk about something and with what consequences?
- How do people make sense of an experience? How do they construct its meaning? What does this allow them to do or not to do? To feel or not to feel?
- How does a particular event unfold? How is this experienced by participants in the event? What may be its consequences? For them and for others?

[2]Of course, multiple measures of state anxiety are as desirable a feature of your study as multiple measures of aggression.

Willig makes the point that these approaches to psychological research are most appropriate when the researchers do not want to impose their own (or someone else's) theory or perspective on the thoughts, feelings, or actions of the people that they are studying. Rather, the researchers want to uncover the impetus to behavior that exists for the actors themselves. Cultural anthropologists refer to this as using an *emic* approach to describing behaviors and (conscious or unconscious) beliefs.

Qualitative designs (detailed in Volume 2, Part I) use a range of data, including spoken or written narratives from interviews and informal conversations; archival data contained in public records and private diaries; and visual data from photographs, film, and video. Although these data are often obtained from a relatively few participants, large-scale, primarily quantitative, studies have increasingly employed a range of qualitative methods to explore a diverse range of questions. In thinking about what qualitative research can be used for, Camic, Rhodes, and Yardley (2003, pp. 8–12) have suggested the following: exploration and theory development; situated analysis; holistic analysis of complex, dynamic, and exceptional phenomena; analysis of subjective meaning; analysis of the aesthetic dimensions of experience; and relational analysis and reflexivity. It is increasingly acceptable for psychological researchers to employ both qualitative and quantitative methods.[3]

It is also possible to take an *etic* approach to research, or to answer (b) to our question. In these studies, the researchers' theories and beliefs are applied to the situations that they study. These forms of descriptive research often focus on a few specific characteristics of events or individuals chosen a priori by the researcher. Participants are then sometimes broadly sampled.

Causal Explanatory Research

If your answer to the first question was (c), that you were seeking a causal explanation for an event or relation, then you will be looking for a different type of research design. When an investigator is in search of a causal connection, research cannot be undertaken without some theoretical underpinning. Sometimes the theory is explicit, sometimes implicit, but it is always there. Theory tells us what variables to focus on as potential causes and effects, or how to divide the world into meaningful chunks.

Even with a theory to guide you, however, coming to a firm conclusion that one event has caused another may be more problematic than it seems at first.[4] In fact, "How do we know a cause when we see one?" is a question that has vexed philosophers of science for centuries. To understand why, we need to digress into a bit of science history.

The Scottish philosopher David Hume (see *A Treatise on Human Nature*, 1739–1740/1978), set out the dilemma for us (and, some would say, led social scientists astray; see Maxwell, 2004). Hume argued that for something to be considered a cause: (a) The cause and the effect had to happen together, (b) the cause had to occur before the effect, and (c) there had to be a *necessary connection* between the two events. Agreeing on whether Hume's first two conditions prevail is relatively straightforward. A researcher needs to show that Events A and B co-occur more often than would be expected by chance (although chance, being the iffy thing it is, implies that we can never make this determination with certainty). The temporal sequence of events is typically observable with a high degree of reliability (although sometimes events

---

[3]For an interesting take on the similarities and differences between quantitative and qualitative approaches, see Shweder (1996): "The true difference between the approaches is not over whether to count and measure but rather over what to count and measure, and over what one actually discovers by doing so" (p.179).

[4]See Cooper (2007) for my first presentation of this material on Hume (1739–1740/1978).

occur nearly simultaneously, and sometimes effects, in psychology at least, are caused by the anticipation of other events).

Hume's (1739–1740/1978) third condition presents the greatest challenge to researchers in search of causes. Hume argued that we can never know with perfect certainty that the event we are calling the cause was the necessary connection that caused the effect. A thought experiment will clarify his claim. Suppose I placed my coffee cup on the edge of my desk and my elbow slid into a book that then knocked the cup to the floor. What caused the coffee cup to fall? If we were to ask a group of people who observed the event to independently identify the cause of the spill, we would be confronted with multiple nominations. Most observers would say "the book" or "your elbow," but the more playful in the group might nominate "a gust of air" or even perhaps "a poltergeist." Are they wrong? Can you prove it *conclusively*?

Hume (1739–1740/1978) asserted that events happen in an unending flow and that even designating where one event ends and the next begins is subjective, that is, requires a prior theory or perspective that is supplied by the observer.[5] Therefore, he claimed, whenever we identify a *cause*, it remains possible to argue for other causes in two ways. First, we can identify another event that takes place *between* the asserted cause and effect. So, if I claim my elbow caused the coffee cup to fall, you can counterclaim that it was the book that provided the necessary connection. Yet another observer (especially a physicist) could claim *gravity* was the cause. After all, without gravity, the coffee cup would have remained suspended in air. Events preceding my errant elbow might also be viable alternate nominations—it was my writing deadline that caused me to be sitting at my desk.

Second, Hume (1739–1740/1978) argued that causal systems are open to outside influences. That is, an outside event can enter the claimed causal sequence. The "gust of air" or "poltergeist" explanation for my coffee spill would be outside "an elbow-book-gravity-spill" causal system. Could an invisible mischievous spirit have knocked the cup just a nanosecond before the book hit it?

If we accept Hume's (1739–1740/1978) argument that we never know causes with complete certainty, then how are we to proceed to answer the question, "What events cause other events to happen?" Shadish and Sullivan (Chapter 2 in this volume) present the strategies that three influential scientists—drawn from social science, statistics, and computer science—have offered for how evidence can be mapped onto causal claims so as to make the claim more or less plausible. Each strategy has implications for how data will be collected and analyzed. Oversimplifying, these strategies suggest that if causal explanation is what you seek, you next must answer the question, "Are you interested in (a) testing the implications of a causal model or (b) manipulating a possible cause to see whether it has the presumed effect?" Depending on where your interest lies, you would choose either a design that involves causal modeling or a manipulation of experimental conditions.

Causal modeling.   Research designs that propose and test causal models and do not involve experimental manipulations could be categorized as *quantitative descriptive research*. Researchers who use modeling approaches play out the *implications* of different causal assumptions and therefore produce results that bear on the plausibility of causal relations (Neimark & Estes, 1967). This is especially true of researchers who build and test structural equation models. Shadish and Sullivan (Chapter 2 in this volume) point out that causal models are often intended to provide an exhaustive description of a network of linkages,

---

[5]Note how this harkens back to the criticisms of Peirce.

which when coupled with certain assumptions (this is where Hume's, 1739–1740/1978, ghost haunts us) imply causal relationships.

Typically (and again oversimplifying), the modeling approach begins when researchers propose a sequence of interconnections that they believe captures the underlying causes of thought, feeling, or behavior. Then, they use one of numerous approaches to see how well the model and the data fit. They examine the co-occurrence of events in a multivariate, temporally sequenced framework. So, for example, I might propose that the sales of research methods handbooks are caused by (a) the editor's level of compulsiveness, which affects (b) the level of expertise of those chosen to be associate editors. Next, the expertise of the associate editors affects (c) who is chosen to be chapter authors. Then, the expertise of the chapter authors influences (d) the audience's perception of the value of the book and, finally, (e) their decision to buy the handbook.

Rodgers (2010) viewed the ascendance of mathematical and statistical modeling in psychology as nothing less than a (quiet but much needed) epistemological revolution. For one thing, most causal models focus on multivariate and temporally sequenced descriptions of behavior. These are typically more complex, and more complete, than the descriptions that you might find tested in many other approaches to studying causal relationships. Also, users of the modeling approach are less interested in testing a model against a null hypothesis ("Is this model better than no model at all?") but rather against an alternative model ("Is this model better than another proposed model?"). So, my model of handbook sales might be compared with one in which the publisher's advertising budget was also included.

Experimental and quasi-experimental designs.   When researchers control aspects of the experimental situation by the purposive manipulation of an event, typically they do so to identify a cause-and-effect relation between one or a few presumed causes and one or a few effects rather than to investigate a complex and comprehensive model.

Designs are called *experimental* when they involve purposive manipulation of different conditions within the study. In this case, a study is conducted to isolate and draw a direct link between one event (the cause) and another (the effect). In studies that employ random assignment of participants to conditions, both the introduction of the event and who is exposed to it are controlled by the researchers (or other external agents), who then leave the assignment of conditions to chance. This approach is the best we have to ensure that on average the groups will not differ before the purposive manipulation. Therefore, we can be most confident (but not completely confident) that any differences between the conditions that we have created were caused by the manipulation, rather than preexisting differences between the participants in one condition from those in another.[6]

Designs with purposive manipulations can also be quasi-experimental. Here, the researchers (or some other external agents) control the introduction of the experimental manipulation but do not control precisely who may be exposed to it. In these designs, the researchers must find ways other than random assignment to equate participants in the various conditions so as to render less plausible the notion that preexisting differences between participants can explain any differences that they find on the outcome measures (the effects).

---

[6]But we can never be completely certain that the characteristic of the manipulation that we claim is causal was the productive element because our experimental and comparison conditions can be viewed as differing on many characteristics. Hume's ghost again.

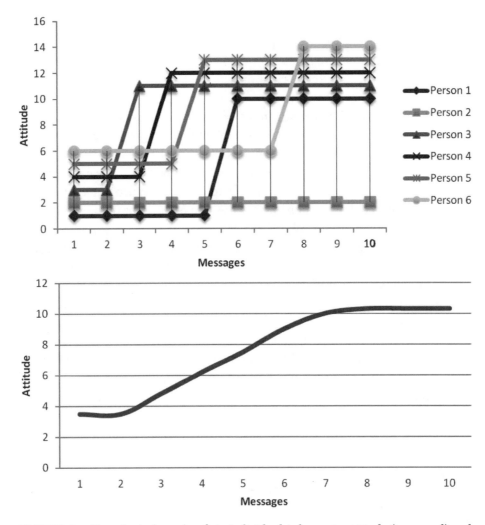

FIGURE 2. Hypothetical graphs of six individuals' change in attitude (top panel) and group-averaged attitudes of those six people (bottom panel) toward energy conservation after viewing 10 proconservation messages with different themes.

Individual-Change and Group-Difference Research

Before your quest for a research design can move from the general to the specific, you must also answer the question, Are you interested in understanding (a) how an individual (or more generally, a single unit) behaves or changes over time or (b) what makes one group different from another group, on average? Let me give an illustration that demonstrates why this distinction is so important.

We know that sometimes learning, understanding, or cognitive change comes to a person as a sudden "aha" experience (Kounios & Beeman, 2009). The person gets it pretty much all at once, and a noticeable change in thinking becomes immediately evident and remains thereafter. Different people may have aha experiences after different numbers of exposures to an event or stimulus. For example, the top panel of Figure 2 displays the scores of six hypothetical people on a questionnaire regarding their perception of the need for energy conservation. The imaginary participants were exposed to 10 proconservation messages in the same sequence.[7] Each message highlighted a different reason for conserving energy—

[7]You would not want to do this in a real experiment because it confounds the particular stimuli with the order. In this imaginary scenario, you must assume that order has no influence, so that differences between people are due to the message.

health threats from pollution, global warming, reduced costs, energy independence, and so on. On the basis of the data in this figure, the best description of how a person's perspective on the need for conservation changed would be to say,

> Each person experienced a cognitive change on viewing a particular message, after which his or her perspective became noticeably more proconservation and remained so. But the message that precipitated the change was different for different people, and some people never changed at all.

The bottom panel of Figure 2 provides a graph of how the same data look if they are averaged across the six people. A much different picture emerges. Looking at this graph, if you were to *assume* the group average effect accurately reflected what was happening to each individual person, you would say, "After the second exposure, each person gradually changed their perspective on conservation after viewing each message. After eight exposures, no additional change took place." Clearly, this would be an incorrect characterization of the process occurring at the level of the individual person. That said, the group-averaged data could be used to describe how change occurred for the group as a whole, as a single unit. Thus, the correct interpretation of the group-averaged data would be to say, "When a group was exposed to proconservation messages, the group average attitude changed gradually after the second exposure, but there was no additional change after eight exposures." This would be an accurate description of how the group behaved over exposures, but it would not adequately describe any single member within the group.

Whether you are interested in the individual or group-averaged effect depends on the context in which your question is being asked. Sometimes the group average does represent the behavior of a single unit. So the bottom panel of Figure 2 is a description of, say, how one city's perspective might be described if the 10 messages were weekly programs aired on a local television channel. Then, the city becomes the unit, not the individuals who populate it. If your problem focuses on understanding how individual units change over time, then the top panel of Figure 2 provides you with six replications of the phenomena of interest. The bottom panel is irrelevant to your question. If your focus is on how a group average changes over time, the bottom panel provides you with one instance of this and the top panel is irrelevant.

Summary of Design Considerations

Figure 3 lays out the relations between the four questions about a research question. The figure needs to be read from both the top and the bottom to arrive at the designs in the middle. This is because two questions, those about interpretive, descriptive, or explanatory research (at the top) and single-unit versus differences-between-groups-of-units research (at the bottom), are independent of one another. Which of the two other questions you answer depends on how you answer the question about interpretation, description, or explanation. A theory-discovery or theory-specified approach is available to you once you have decided that your question is interpretive or descriptive. If your question is explanatory, it is theory driven by definition, but you must decide whether the question involves modeling the causal implications of the theory or estimating its causal effect via an experimental manipulation.

The handbook uses the answers to these questions to organize the chapters on research design found in Volume 2. Interpretive research designs that emphasize a qualitative approach are detailed in Part I. Most of these designs also focus on questions that involve describing the current state or change in an individual unit of interest or a small sample.

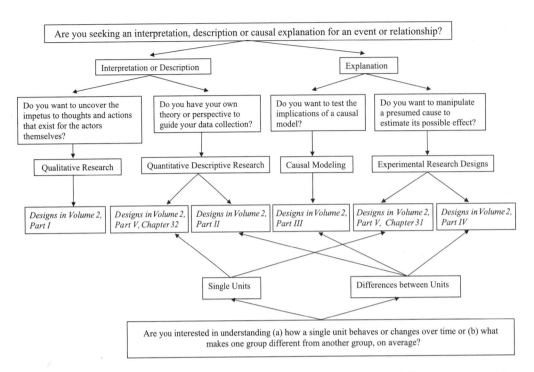

FIGURE 3. Relations between research questions, research designs, and the organization of parts in the *APA Handbook of Research Methods in Psychology*.

Volume 2, Parts II through VI, introduces designs that emphasize an etic (or theory-specified), more quantitative approach to research. Volume 2, Part II, presents issues in sampling for quantitative studies. Although the techniques described herein will be of interest to all researchers, they would be of special interest to those who are conducting descriptive research. So, for example, if you are collecting data on the impact of growing up in a single-parent home, this section will assist you in planning your strategy for sampling respondents, help you consider issues you will encounter in collecting data from participants over time, and help you determine how you might use the Internet. Volume 2, Part III, focuses on designs that build and test the implications of causal models. You will find here approaches that differ in the type of data that they employ (sometimes even simulated data) and in the assumptions that are made as part of the data analysis (e.g., Bayesian modeling). Volume 2, Part IV, focuses on research with experimental manipulations, in which participants are deliberately treated differently. Section 1 of Part IV distinguishes these designs depending on how participants were assigned to their experimental conditions. Section 2 of Part IV describes many of the unique problems that psychologists face when they conduct experimental research in applied settings.

In Volume 2, Part V, designs are introduced that focus on theory-testing questions, rely heavily on quantification, and are used to study change in individual units. These designs all require multiple measurements of the same dependent variable(s) over a period of time. They can be used to study change that is either (a) naturally occurring, for example, as when a researcher wants to describe how a person's cognitive abilities change as they age, or (b) purposively manipulated, as when a researcher examines an older adult's cognitive ability before and after an intervention that is meant to improve memory. The designs in Volume 2, Part VI, are labeled "Neuropsychology" and "Biological Psychology." Here you will find designs for theory-driven research that derive largely from the more biological end of psychology's family tree.

QUANTITATIVE DATA ANALYSIS

Once you have chosen your design and measures, the next question you must answer is, "What data analysis procedure corresponds to your research design and the characteristics of your measures?" Volume 3, Part I, presents a compendium of your options for analysis. Section 1 presents different techniques that you can use to get to know your data as a whole. Special attention is paid to discovering distributional or other characteristics of data (e.g., outliers, missing values) that might dictate your approach to analysis or that might need to be addressed before your more substantive analysis should proceed. Section 2 presents some approaches to describing your data and techniques that you might use to communicate your findings to others.

Volume 3, Part I, Sections 3 to 5, presents both basic and advanced techniques for analyzing and interpreting social and behavioral science data. The chapters are organized first according to the number of dependent or outcome measures in the analysis. In Section 3 you will find methods that are used when you want to relate a single dependent or outcome variable (e.g., self-reported aggression) to one or more independent or predictor variables (e.g., state anxiety, age, sex).

In Volume 3, Part I, Section 4, statistical techniques are presented that apply to studies involving, in their most basic case, a single outcome or criterion measure that has been measured more than once, over time. So, if the chapter on "Issues in Collecting Longitudinal Data" (Volume 2, Chapter 16) is of interest to you, you will likely find an analytic strategy here that meets your needs. However, if your data involve a single participant with multiple measures over time, your analytic choices are covered in Volume 2, Part V, along with your design choices.

The methods in Volume 3, Part I, Section 5, pertain to data analyses in which you have many measures and make no distinction between which variables are independent or dependent, predictor or criterion. Most frequently, these techniques are used to uncover the abstract, or latent, variables that underlie a set of observed, or manifest, variables. For example, we might use an exploratory factor analysis to determine the number of factors underlying a multi-item measure of aggression or a confirmatory factor analysis (on the same instrument) to test the theory that the tendency toward physical and verbal aggression are independent (i.e., knowing how likely people are to hit you tells you nothing about how likely they are to call you a nasty name). Within Volume 3, Part I, Sections 3 to 5, you will also find a distinction in analytic choices depending on whether they pertain to (a) variables that are measured continuously or (b) variables that place people (or other units) into classes. Some of these techniques take into account the categorical nature of variables in your analyses, whereas others help you to discover what these categorical distinctions among respondents might be.

So, to find the chapters of greatest interest to you in these sections, first you will need to answer three questions: (a) Does your research problem distinguish independent or predictor variables from dependent or outcome variables? (b) Are your variables measured over time? (c) Are your variables continuous or categorical, either in how they are conceptualized or how they are measured? Of course, in many instances your answers to these questions will be complex. Within the same study, for example, you might want to reduce the number of dependent variables by constructing a composite (e.g., factor analyze the observation, self-report, and physiological measures of aggression) and then use the composite in a regression analysis (one dependent variable) with multiple indicators. Or, you will have some continuous and some class variables. As you read the chapters, you will find that one great advance in statistical science has been the recent development of sophisticated techniques that permit the integrated analysis of data that vary in their characteristics and the number of variables involved.

Volume 3, Part 1, Section 6, presents methods for studies that take into account (and capitalize on) the interdependence of responses from multiple participants who are in interaction with one another. The units of analysis can be anywhere from a dyad (e.g., a husband and wife) to a large group (e.g., a sports team, workers in an office). Because the responses of individuals in these networks are dependent on the responses of others, the data analysis strategy must take this into account. Equally important, sometimes the research question focuses on the nature of the interdependence.

Finally, in Volume 3, Part I, Section 7, you will find two chapters that present some of the special issues that arise, and some special statistical techniques that are used, when researchers reanalyze or integrate data that was collected by others. In one instance, secondary data analysis, you work with raw data that might have been collected for another purpose (e.g., crime rates and climate data in cities are used to test the relation between temperature and aggression). In the other instance, meta-analysis (the statistical results of previous research) becomes the raw data in a quantitative research synthesis.

Effect Sizes, or Relation Strength, and Their Interpretation

The chapters in Volume 3, Part I, look remarkably different from those that would have appeared in such a work a generation ago, far more so than the other parts of the handbook. Before the past 2 decades, testing the null hypothesis was the gold standard for drawing inferences about whether data revealed significant relations. More recently, the exclusive use of null hypothesis significance testing has become controversial, with some arguing that the practice should be abandoned entirely (Cohen, 1994). An American Psychological Association (APA) task force recommended that researchers need to ask of their data not only, "Are these variables related, yes or no?" but also "How much of a relationship is there?" (see Wilkinson & APA Task Force on Statistical Inference, 1999).

Prominent among the methods used to describe data is the estimation and interpretation of effect sizes, or "*the degree* to which the phenomenon is present in the population" (Cohen, 1988, p. 9). With the coming of age of effect size estimation came the importance of understanding the difference between statistical significance and *clinical* or *practical* significance. The latter requires extrastatistical interpretation of the data. To assess practical significance, researchers (and others) must wrestle with the question of how strong a relation needs to be before it can be deemed meaningful or important (see Cooper, 2008).

The answer to this question will always depend on the context in which the research takes place. Cohen (1988) has suggested some general definitions for small, medium, and large effect sizes in the social sciences. In defining these adjectives, he compared different average effect sizes that he had encountered across disciplines in the behavioral sciences. However, Cohen did not intend his labels to serve as guides for the *substantive* interpretation of relations by social scientists. Rather, he intended his rules to assist with power analyses in planning future studies, a very different objective. Using Cohen's definitions to interpret the substantive importance of an effect size misapplies his work and should be abandoned.

In fact, there is no fixed scale for the substantive interpretation of the size of a relation, and there is no substitute for knowing the research context of the specific question. Here is a simple example. Assume that we have the results of a study that evaluated an intervention that was conducted with 200 participants, 100 each in the intervention and control condition, and a dichotomous measure of success or failure. Using Cohen's definitions, an increase in success rate from 45% in the control condition to 55% in the intervention condition would be considered a small effect (equivalent to $r = .10$ explaining 1% of the variance). However, what if this effect was found on a measure of "suicides among previous attempters" and the intervention was access to a hotline? Personally, I would not be inclined to label this effect *small*, practically speaking. However, if the study measured whether previous suicide attempters did or did not endorse the statement "life is worth living" after a year of daily psychotherapy "small effect" certainly would come to my mind.

In this example, I tried to demonstrate that the interpretation of effect sizes rests heavily on (a) the intrinsic value placed on the outcome variable (how valuable is even a small difference?) and (b) the cost of the intervention. Also, when interpreting the magnitude of effects, it is informative to use contrasting elements that are closely related to the topic at hand. For example, what other interventions have been used to prevent suicide among previous attempters? If the hotline and several other interventions have been tried and found to have no effect, suddenly the daily therapy effect starts to look larger, worth pursuing further.

Effect sizes also need to be interpreted in relation to the methodology used in the primary research. So, studies with more intensive treatments (e.g., more frequent therapy sessions), more sensitive research designs (within-subject vs. between-subject), and measures with less random error can be expected to reveal larger effect sizes, all else being equal.

Although null hypothesis testing is not ignored, the contents of this handbook clearly demonstrate the shifting of emphasis from "yes or no?" to "how much?" questions. In all of the chapters on data analysis, you will find a primary emphasis on estimating and interpreting the magnitude of relations.

Sharing Results

The final part of the handbook includes two chapters that discuss the process of writing up your research and getting it published. The chapter by Sternberg and Sternberg (Chapter 26 in Volume 3) gives broad advice about the style and content of a research report, how to organize your writing, and how to pick a journal. The chapter by VandenBos (Chapter 27 in Volume 3) introduces the publication process, or what happens to papers after they are submitted.

The question you must answer with regard to reporting your research is: "What do readers need to know about your study so they can (a) evaluate its trustworthiness; (b) replicate it, if they wish; and (c) use it along with other studies to synthesize research on your topic?" Note that this question uses the word *need* rather than the word *want* that I used in all the previous questions posed. This is because the standards for reporting research have become considerably more detailed in the past decade. This is especially true since the publication of the sixth edition of the APA's *Publication Manual* (APA, 2010). The *Publication Manual* now contains tables and figures containing the Journal Article Reporting Standards (or the JARS) that summarize the information editors, reviewers, and readers will expect to see in your report.

Why are reporting standards needed? Two developments in psychology—indeed, in all the behavioral, social, and medical sciences—have led to an increased emphasis on complete research reporting. First, social science evidence is being increasingly used in public policy decision making. This use places new importance on understanding how research was conducted and what it found (APA Presidential Task Force on Evidence-Based Practice, 2006). Policymakers and practitioners who wish to make decisions that are informed by scientific evidence want to know how reliable the information they are considering is and in what context the data were collected. This dictates that research reports be comprehensive in their descriptions of methods and results.

Second, psychological scientists studying basic processes have found that as evidence about specific hypotheses and theories accumulates, greater reliance is being placed on syntheses of research, especially meta-analyses (see Valentine, Volume 3, Chapter 25, this handbook). Psychologists who use meta-analysis summarize findings, but they also use variations in research methods to find clues to the variables that might mediate differences in findings. These clues emerge by grouping studies on the basis of distinctions in their methods and then comparing their results. For example, a meta-analyst might group studies of the relation between state anxiety and aggression depending on what type of aggression measure was used: observation, self-report, or physiological. What are the implications if only one type of measure reveals a relation? This synthesis-based evidence is then used to guide the next generation of problems and hypotheses to be studied in new data collections. Meta-analysis requires detailed descriptions of what you have done. Without complete reporting of methods and results, the utility of your study is diminished.

Table 1 reproduces the first table from the JARS that is presented in the *Publication Manual* (APA Publications and Communications Board Working Group on JARS, 2008). It summarizes information that is recommended for inclusion in all reports of psychological research. Many of the themes that I have touched on in this chapter are reflected in the items. Because there are so many research designs used by psychological scientists, Table 1 contains only a brief entry regarding the type of research design. Two other tables currently included in the JARS (but not reproduced here) provide reporting standards for research designs involving experimental manipulations using either random or nonrandom assignment. This modular feature of the JARS makes it possible for other research designs to be added to the standards by adding new modules, so that eventually all of the designs contained in this handbook can have JARS modules associated with them.

In Cooper (2011), I included a brief introduction to each item listed in the JARS as well as an explanation of why it was deemed important for inclusion. The bottom line is that without complete reporting, the value of your study for the users of your findings will be diminished.

CONCLUSION

"Introductions" to edited works are required to address what the chapters that follow have in common as well as how the differences between chapters are to be understood. Writing such a chapter for a handbook as broad in scope as this one has required that I touch on similarities at lofty levels of abstraction, such as the methods by which people know things and the relation of science to democracy.

But I have been able as well to uncover some very down-to-earth examples of similarities in the chapters. For example, as I have noted several times, a principle shared by all of the authors is that the research methods you choose should be appropriate to answer the question that you pose. This dictum seems almost too obvious to state. Let us not fool ourselves, however. The opposing desire to use the tool you know even if it's not a perfect fit is often hard to resist. Hopefully, this handbook will expand your toolbox so that this latter approach loses its appeal.

Describing the differences between chapters and how they can be understood has presented an equally formidable challenge. It was easy to begin with the sequence of method choices—assessing the ethics and feasibility of different approaches, then choosing measures,

TABLE 1

Journal Article Reporting Standards (JARS): Information Recommended for Inclusion in Manuscripts That Report New Data Collections Regardless of Research Design

Paper section and topic	Description
Title and title page	Identify variables and theoretical issues under investigation and the relationship between them
	Author note contains acknowledgment of special circumstances:
	Use of data also appearing in previous publications, dissertations, or conference papers
	Sources of funding or other support
	Relationships that may be perceived as conflicts of interest
Abstract	Problem under investigation
	Participants or subjects; specifying pertinent characteristics; in animal research, include genus and species
	Study method, including:
	Sample size
	Any apparatus used
	Outcome measures
	Data-gathering procedures
	Research design (e.g., experiment, observational study)
	Findings, including effect sizes and confidence intervals and/or statistical significance levels
	Conclusions and the implications or applications
Introduction	The importance of the problem:
	Theoretical or practical implications
	Review of relevant scholarship:
	Relation to previous work
	If other aspects of this study have been reported on previously, how the current report differs from these earlier reports
	Specific hypotheses and objectives:
	Theories or other means used to derive hypotheses
	Primary and secondary hypotheses, other planned analyses
	How hypotheses and research design relate to one another
Method	
Participant characteristics	Eligibility and exclusion criteria, including any restrictions based on demographic characteristics
	Major demographic characteristics as well as important topic-specific characteristics (e.g., achievement level in studies of educational interventions), or in the case of animal research, genus and species
Sampling procedures	Procedures for selecting participants, including:
	The sampling method if a systematic sampling plan was implemented
	Percentage of sample approached that participated
	Self-selection (either by individuals or units, such as schools or clinics)
	Settings and locations where data were collected
	Agreements and payments made to participants
	Institutional review board agreements, ethical standards met, safety monitoring
Sample size, power, and precision	Intended sample size
	Actual sample size, if different from intended sample size
	How sample size was determined:
	Power analysis, or methods used to determine precision of parameter estimates
	Explanation of any interim analyses and stopping rules
Measures and covariates	Definitions of all primary and secondary measures and covariates:
	Include measures collected but not included in this report
	Methods used to collect data

(Continued)

TABLE 1   (*Continued*)

	Methods used to enhance the quality of measurements:
	Training and reliability of data collectors
	Use of multiple observations
	Information on validated or ad hoc instruments created for individual studies, for example, psychometric and biometric properties
Research design	Whether conditions were manipulated or naturally observed
	Type of research design; provided in Table 3 are modules for:
	Randomized experiments (Module A1)
	Quasi-experiments (Module A2)
	Other designs would have different reporting needs associated with them
Results	
Participant flow	Total number of participants
	Flow of participants through each stage of the study
Recruitment	Dates defining the periods of recruitment and repeated measurements or follow-up
Statistics and data analysis	Information concerning problems with statistical assumptions and/or data distributions that could affect the validity of findings
	Missing data:
	Frequency or percentages of missing data
	Empirical evidence and/or theoretical arguments for the causes of data that are missing, for example, missing completely at random (MCAR), missing at random (MAR), or missing not at random (MNAR)
	Methods for addressing missing data, if used
	For each primary and secondary outcome and for each subgroup, a summary of:
	Cases deleted from each analysis
	Subgroup or cell sample sizes, cell means, standard deviations, or other estimates of precision, and other descriptive statistics
	Effect sizes and confidence intervals
	For inferential statistics (null hypothesis significance testing), information about:
	The a priori Type I error rate adopted
	Direction, magnitude, degrees of freedom, and exact p level, even if no significant effect is reported
	For multivariable analytic systems (e.g., multivariate analyses of variance, regression analyses, structural equation modeling analyses, and hierarchical linear modeling) also include the associated variance–covariance (or correlation) matrix or matrices
	Estimation problems (e.g., failure to converge, bad solution spaces), anomalous data points
	Statistical software program, if specialized procedures were used
	Report any other analyses performed, including adjusted analyses, indicating those that were prespecified and those that were exploratory (though not necessarily in level of detail of primary analyses)
Ancillary analyses	Discussion of implications of ancillary analyses for statistical error rates
Discussion	Statement of support or nonsupport for all original hypotheses:
	Distinguished by primary and secondary hypotheses
	Post hoc explanations
	Similarities and differences between results and work of others
	Interpretation of the results, taking into account:
	Sources of potential bias and other threats to internal validity
	Imprecision of measures
	The overall number of tests or overlap among tests, and
	Other limitations or weaknesses of the study
	Generalizability (external validity) of the findings, taking into account:
	The target population
	Other contextual issues
	Discussion of implications for future research, program, or policy

a research design, statistical techniques, and ending with research reports—although we know that in practice these choices are never as linear as they appear in books.

Bringing an equally linear order to the array of research designs, measurements, and analytic techniques available to psychological scientists was the most difficult task. Different approaches to psychological research begin with different epistemic assumptions and then travel through subdisciplines with different traditions. Like the species that we study, the methods used by psychological scientists defy simple categorization. But this is a good thing (even if it causes trouble for us editors). After all, if science is humankind's greatest achievement (and I think it is), then isn't turning the lens of science on ourselves the ultimate expression of our uniqueness?

Harris Cooper
Editor-in-Chief

References

American Psychological Association. (2010). *Publication manual of the American Psychological Association* (6th ed.). Washington, DC: Author.

American Psychological Association, Presidential Task Force on Evidence-Based Practice. (2006). Evidence-based practice in psychology. *American Psychologist, 61,* 271–283.

American Psychological Association, Publications and Communications Board Working Group on Journal Article Reporting Standards. (2008). Reporting standards for research in psychology: Why do we need them? What might they be? *American Psychologist, 63,* 839–851.

Camic, P. M., Rhodes, J. E., & Yardley, L. (2003). Naming the stars: Integrating qualitative methods in psychological research. In P. M. Camic, J. E. Rhodes, & L. Yardley (Eds.), *Qualitative research in psychology: Expanding perspective in methodology and design* (pp. 3–15). Washington, DC: American Psychological Association.

Cohen, J. (1988). *Statistical power analysis for the behavioral sciences.* Hillsdale, NJ: Erlbaum.

Cohen, J. (1994). The earth is round ($p < .05$). *American Psychologist, 49,* 997–1003.

Cooper, H. (2007). *Evaluating and interpreting research syntheses in adult learning and literacy.* Cambridge, MA: National Center for the Study of Adult Learning and Literacy.

Cooper, H. (2008). The search for meaningful ways to express the effects of interventions. *Child Development Perspectives, 2,* 181–186.

Cooper, H. (2011). *Reporting research in psychology: How to meet journal article reporting standards.* Washington, DC: American Psychological Association.

Feibleman, J. K. (1969). *An introduction to the philosophy of Charles S. Peirce.* Cambridge, MA: MIT Press.

Ferris, T. (2010). *The science of liberty.* New York, NY: HarperCollins.

Godfrey-Smith, P. (2003). *Theory and reality: An introduction to the philosophy of science.* Chicago, IL: University of Chicago Press.

Hume, D. (1978). *A treatise on human nature.* Oxford, England: Oxford Press. (Original work published 1739–1740)

Kounios, J., & Beeman, M. (2009). The aha! experience. The cognitive neuroscience of insight. *Current Directions in Psychological Science, 18,* 210–216.

Kuhn, T. S. (1996). *The structure of scientific revolutions* (3rd ed.). Chicago, IL: University of Chicago Press.

Maxwell, J. A. (2004). Causal explanation, qualitative research, and scientific inquiry in education. *Educational Researcher, 33,* 3–11.

Merton, R. K. (1957). Priorities of scientific discovery. In N. Storer (Ed.), *The sociology of science: Theoretical and empirical investigations* (pp. 635–659). Chicago, IL: University of Chicago Press.

Niemark, E. D., & Estes, W. K. (1967). *Stimulus sampling theory.* San Francisco, CA: Holden-Day.

Rodgers, J. L. (2010). The epistemology of mathematical and statistical modeling. *American Psychologist, 65,* 1–12.

Shadish, W. R., & Fuller, S. (Eds.). (1994). *The social psychology of science.* New York, NY: Guilford Press.

Shweder, R. A. (1996). Quanta and qualia: What is the "object" of ethnographic research? In R. Jessor, A. Colby, & R. A: Shweder (Eds.), *Ethnography and human development: Context and meaning is social inquiry* (pp. 175–182). Chicago, IL: University of Chicago Press.

Webb, E. J., Campbell, D. T., Schwartz, R. D., Sechrest, L., & Grove, J. B. (1981). *Nonreactive measures in the social sciences.* Boston, MA: Houghton Mifflin.

Wilkinson, L., & APA Task Force on Statistical Inference. (1999). Statistical methods in psychology journals: Guidelines and explanations. *American Psychologist, 54,* 594–604.

PART I

PHILOSOPHICAL, ETHICAL, AND SOCIETAL UNDERPINNINGS OF PSYCHOLOGICAL RESEARCH

Philosophical Issues for Research in Psychology

CHAPTER 1

PERSPECTIVES ON THE EPISTEMOLOGICAL BASES FOR QUALITATIVE RESEARCH

Carla Willig

This chapter reviews and clarifies the various ways in which qualitative researchers approach the creation of knowledge. Qualitative research can take many forms. Within the general rubric of qualitative research, we can find a wide range of activities that are driven by different goals, deploy different research strategies, and generate different kinds of insights. This means that although all qualitative research shares some important attributes (and these will be identified in the next section), it also is characterized by fundamental differences in epistemological orientation. In other words, qualitative researchers can take a range of different positions in relation to questions about the nature and status of any knowledge claims that may be made on the basis of their research. This chapter maps out the range of epistemological positions available to qualitative researchers and discusses the implications for the way in which qualitative research is conducted and evaluated.

The chapter is structured as follows: In the first section, we are reminded of the nature and purpose of qualitative research in general. We identify the most important characteristics of qualitative research, those which are shared by all forms of qualitative research (see the section What Is Qualitative Research?). In the second section, we discuss the different strands within the qualitative research endeavor. Here, we focus on the different types of knowledge that can be generated on the basis of different approaches to qualitative enquiry (see the section Differences Among Qualitative Approaches). In the third section, we introduce the various epistemological frameworks that underpin these different approaches

(see the section Epistemological Frameworks). In the last section, we discuss their implications for the evaluation of qualitative research (see Evaluation).

WHAT IS QUALITATIVE RESEARCH?

Qualitative research is primarily concerned with meaning. Qualitative researchers are interested in subjectivity and experience. They want to understand better what their research participants' experiences are like, what they mean to them, how they talk about them, and how they make sense of them. Qualitative researchers try to capture the quality and texture of their research participants' experiences and aim to understand the implications and consequences of those experiences, for participants and for other people. Qualitative research addresses the following types of questions:

- What does something feel like? For example, a qualitative researcher might want to find out what it is like to be the only man in an all-female workplace.
- How is something experienced? For example, we may want to conduct qualitative research into the experience of being made redundant.
- How do people talk about something and with what consequences? For example, we may analyze naturally occurring conversations about housework and explore subject positions available to men and women within this.
- How do people make sense of an experience? How do they construct its meaning? What does

DOI: 10.1037/13619-002
APA Handbook of Research Methods in Psychology: Vol. 1. Foundations, Planning, Measures, and Psychometrics, H. Cooper (Editor-in-Chief)

this allow them to do or not to do? To feel or not to feel? For example, a qualitative study could explore the ways in which people who have been injured in a road traffic accident make sense of this experience and how this allows them to position themselves in relation to the accident.

- How does a particular (social or psychological) event unfold? How do participants experience the event? What may be its consequences? For them or for others? For example, we may want to find out how the end of an intimate relationship comes about, how those involved experience such an ending, what *breaking up* means to them, and how it may shape their views of future relationships.

Qualitative research does not, and cannot, answer questions about relationships between variables or about cause-and-effect relationships. Qualitative research is concerned with the description and interpretation of research participants' experiences. It tends to prioritize depth of understanding over breadth of coverage, and as such, the knowledge it generates tends to be localized and context specific. Qualitative researchers do not aim to generalize their findings to general populations and they do not aim to develop predictive models of human behavior. Instead, qualitative researchers tend to work in a *bottom-up* fashion, exploring in depth relatively small amounts of data (e.g., a small number of semistructured interviews, an individual case, or a set of documents relating to a specific event), working through the data line by line. As a result, any insights generated on the basis of qualitative analysis tend to be context specific and are not generalizable to general populations.

Common features of qualitative research include the following:

- **Presents findings in everyday language.** Because qualitative research aims to capture and convey the meanings research participants attribute to their experiences and actions, research findings tend to take the form of verbal accounts. Such qualitative accounts may vary in the extent to which they are descriptive or interpretative, in the extent to which they utilize expert discourse (such as psychological terminology), and in the

extent to which they deploy poetic language or a prose style. Qualitative research findings, however, tend *not* to be represented by numbers or equations, they do *not* involve statistical calculations, and they do *not* draw conclusions about probabilities of occurrences or covariations of phenomena within a population.

- **Views meaning in context.** Qualitative researchers are concerned with how individual research participants make sense of specific experiences within particular contexts. This means that any meanings identified are specific to the context within which they are constructed and deployed by the participants. For example, to understand what it means to somebody to get married, we need to know something about the individual's life history and their social and cultural context as well as their situation at the time of the interview. Qualitative research, therefore, tends not to draw conclusions about what something might mean in general. Indeed, from a qualitative perspective, it is questionable whether such generalized meanings do, in fact, exist.

- **Incorporates researcher reflexivity.** Qualitative researchers' concern with meaning and interpretation means that they need to pay particular attention to the ways in which their own beliefs, assumptions, and experiences may shape (both limit and facilitate) their reading of qualitative data. For example, whether the researcher has personal experience of the phenomenon under investigation is important and the nature of the experience (or indeed its absence) needs to be thought about as it inevitably will frame the researcher's approach to the topic. Researcher reflexivity ought to be an integral part of any qualitative study because meaning is always *given* to data and never simply identified or discovered within it.

- **Studies the real world.** Qualitative research is concerned with participants' life experiences, which means that ideally qualitative data ought to be collected *in situ*, that is, where and when the experiences of interest actually take place. Such naturally occurring data include tape recordings of conversations in real-life contexts, such as homes, workplaces, or over the telephone, as well as video recordings of social interactions such as those at football matches, pubs, or clubs. Because collecting naturally occurring data is not always ethically or practically possible, however, a lot of qualitative data takes the form of transcripts of semistructured interviews with people who have agreed to talk about their experiences. Either way, whether in situ or in the form of description and reflection after the event, qualitative data always are concerned with real life, that is, with events and experiences that take place irrespective of whether the researcher studies them. Experimentation has no place in qualitative research (unless the aim is to study the experience of taking part in an experiment).

■ **Is primarily inductive.** Unlike hypothetico-deductive research, qualitative research does not set out to test hypotheses derived from existing theories. On the contrary, most qualitative research deliberately brackets the researcher's theoretical knowledge to allow novel insights and understandings to emerge from the data. As such, most qualitative research aspires to an inductive model of knowledge generation. Exceptions to this do exist, however, and these are in the section Differences Among Qualitative Approaches. Also, most if not all qualitative researchers recognize that pure induction is an impossibility given the role of the researcher in the research process and that without some kind of theoretical lens data collection and analysis cannot take place. The challenge to the qualitative researcher is to enable the data set to speak for itself (as far as possible) and to surprise the researcher rather than to simply confirm or refute his or her expectations.

DIFFERENCES AMONG QUALITATIVE APPROACHES

Drisko (1997) developed Glaser's (1992) analogy of qualitative research as a "family of approaches" by suggesting that "in this family there are some close relations, some distant relations, some extended kin, some odd cousins, and a few nasty divorces." Differences between qualitative approaches to research can go deep and some varieties of qualitative

research methodology are incompatible with one another. The various formal philosophical and epistemological positions available to qualitative researchers are mapped out in the section Epistemological Frameworks. In this section, we prepare the ground by identifying the major points of tension around which the family of qualitative research organizes itself. These points of tension include (a) the role of theory, (b) description versus interpretation, (c) realism versus relativism, and (d) politics.

The Role of Theory

As indicated in the section What Is Qualitative Research? although most qualitative research adopts an inductive model of knowledge generation, some qualitative approaches also include a deductive element. For example, grounded theory methodology involves a process of testing emerging theoretical formulations against incoming data, thus moving between developing and testing theory as the research progresses toward saturation. For example, a researcher may want to understand what caused a fight between rival fans at a football match. The researcher begins the research with no assumptions about what happened and she or he begins by interviewing bystanders, witnesses, and participants in the fight. Preliminary analysis of the data generates a hypothesis about what triggered the event and the researcher returns to the field and conducts further interviews with particular individuals to test the hypothesis and to develop it into a coherent account of how the fight came about. In this case, the theory that is being tested is the emergent theory that has been conceived on the basis of an inductive process and does not involve the application of preexisting theoretical perspectives.

Alternatively, approaches such as psychoanalytic case studies draw on existing theoretical frameworks (such as Freudian or Kleinian theories) to account for the manifest content of the data. For example, the researcher may attribute theory-driven meanings to an interviewee's behaviors during the interview and conclude that the interviewee's long pauses, hesitations, and incomplete sentences signify resistance to acknowledging underlying feelings, such as anger or anxiety. In these cases, theory is imported from outside of the study into the research. Another example of deliberate and purposeful importing of theory into qualitative research is provided by critical approaches, such as Marxist or feminist analyses, whereby a preestablished perspective is applied to interpret the data (see Drisko, 1997). Imported theoretical perspectives supply a lens through which the data can be read, thus generating insights into particular dimensions of experience that have been identified as being of interest to the researcher or as being important for social or political reasons long before the data have been collected.

Description Versus Interpretation

Qualitative approaches also vary in the extent to which they aspire to move beyond the data and to interpret what is being presented. That is to say, they vary in the extent to which they take data "at face value." Some qualitative approaches, such as descriptive phenomenology, stay close to research participants' accounts of their experience as the aim of such research is to capture, clarify, and represent the quality and texture of those experiences. Here, analyzing data means paying close attention to what is being said by the participant, grasping and distilling its meaning, and systematically representing it to others. In descriptive approaches to qualitative research, meaning is found in the text itself or, as Kendall and Murray (2005) put it, "the meaning of any story is embodied in that story" (p. 749).

Other approaches, such as interpretative phenomenology, aspire to go further and to give meaning to participants' experiences beyond that which the participants may be able or willing to attribute to it. In other words, even without the application of a particular theory to the data (see the section What Is Qualitative Research?), it is possible to extract meanings that are not immediately obvious to even the person who has produced the account (i.e., the research participant). For example, existential themes such as fear of death or fear of meaninglessness may be expressed only indirectly and by way of analogy in the research participant's account, yet an interpretative analysis may conclude that they underpin and, indeed, give a deeper meaning to the account.

These two positions (descriptive vs. interpretative) are sometimes referred to as "hermeneutics of meaning recollection" (descriptive) and "hermeneutics of suspicion" (interpretative; see Langdridge, 2007, Chapter 4, on Ricoeur and hermeneutics; see also Giorgi, 1992, for a discussion of the differences between interpretative science and descriptive science).

Realism Versus Relativism

Qualitative researchers need to think carefully about the status of the products of their research and the sorts of claims they wish to make on the basis of them. They need to ask themselves to what extent their research aims to shed light on reality (i.e., on how things are in the world) and to what extent they are simply trying to offer reflections that may (or may not) be of use to others who are trying to make sense of their own and others' experiences. In other words, does their research aim to hold up a mirror to reflect reality as it is or is the purpose of their research to provide a space within which to engage with and reflect on a particular experiential phenomenon? Discussions about realism and relativism in qualitative research are complicated by the fact that both the status of the data (as realist or relativist) *and* the status of the analysis of the data (as realist or relativist) need to be established. It is important to recognize that these are two distinct but equally important considerations that easily can get confused or conflated.

To start with the status of the data, qualitative researchers can take a realist position that takes data (such as research participants' accounts) at face value and treats them akin to witness statements, that is to say, as a description of events that actually took place in the real world. From such a position, the researcher would take great care to ensure that the data collected are accurate and truthful by ensuring that the conditions under which accounts are produced are favorable (e.g., that participants feel safe and nondefensive, and that nothing will prevent them from opening up and telling the truth). Alternatively, the researcher can adopt a relativist position in relation to the status of the data, which means that research participants' accounts are of interest *not* because they inform the researcher about what is actually going on in the world (e.g., what really happened to the participant), but rather because they tell the researcher something about how the participants are constructing meaning in their lives. In such a case, the researcher is not concerned with the truth value of what participants are telling him or her; instead, the aim of the research is to generate rich and detailed accounts that will enable the researcher to gain a better understanding of the participant's meaning-making activities.

Moving on to the status of the analysis, again, two broad positions are available to the researcher: a realist position that aspires to the production of accurate and valid knowledge about what is going on, either in the social world, in terms of (a) events that are taking place in this world (this is in line with the realist position on the status of the data) *or* (b) actions that research participants are taking when they construct meaning (this is in line with the relativist position on the status of the data). In both cases, the researcher's (metaphorical) task is to hold up a mirror to accurately reflect what is going on either in the world out there, or inside the mind of the research participant. This means that it is possible to adopt a realist position (i.e., holding up the mirror) in relation to relativist data (i.e., the research participant's constructions). Such a position claims that the researcher can accurately and truthfully represent the participant's subjective world (i.e., their constructions of meaning). Alternatively, the research can adopt a relativist position in relation to the analysis. This would mean abandoning any truth claims regarding the analytic insights produced, arguing instead that what is being offered is the researcher's reading of the data, which tells us just as much (or more) about the researcher (and his or her meaning-making activities) as it does about the participants or indeed about the social world. It could be argued that a very fine line exists between this type of research and the sorts of activities that an artist may engage in.

Politics

Qualitative research can have an explicitly political dimension in that some qualitative researchers are motivated by a desire to give voice to otherwise underrepresented or oppressed social groups.

Indeed, feminist scholars were instrumental in introducing and promoting qualitative research methods in psychology. Because qualitative research tends to be bottom-up (allowing the voices of research participants to be heard) and because it tends to be inductive (avoiding the imposition of existing concepts and categories), qualitative research can be used as part of an empowerment agenda. Qualitative research also can be practiced in an egalitarian, participatory, and collaborative way (such as in action research or some types of ethnography in which the research participants set the agenda and shape the direction of the research), thus allowing the researcher to challenge established power relations between (expert) researchers and (naïve) research participants.

More interpretative versions of qualitative research (see the section Differences Among Qualitative Approaches) adopt a more conventional "knowing" stance, embracing the role of an expert who, as a result of familiarity with the relevant psychological literature, may be able to understand the participants better than they can understand themselves. For example, Hollway and Jefferson's (2000) approach to qualitative analysis was based on the premise that people "may not know why they experience or feel things in the way that they do [and] are motivated, largely unconsciously, to disguise the meaning of at least some of their feelings and actions" (p. 26). Thus, qualitative researchers have a range of options regarding the political orientation of their research activities. Although qualitative research often is associated with a liberal, egalitarian social agenda, not all qualitative research adopts this perspective.

EPISTEMOLOGICAL FRAMEWORKS

The previous section demonstrated that qualitative researchers can adopt a wide range of positions regarding the meaning and status of the kind of knowledge their research generates (or, indeed, regarding the extent to which the production of knowledge is possible or desirable in the first place). Epistemological positions are characterized by a set of assumptions about knowledge and knowing that provide answers to the question "What and how can we know?" Paradoxically, although we tend to think about research as being about finding answers to questions through some form of systematic process of empirical enquiry, the starting point of any research project is, in fact, a set of assumptions that themselves are not based on anything other than philosophical reflection. This is inevitable, and it is important that researchers are aware of, clear about, and prepared to acknowledge and *own* their epistemological position. This is not always easy because the most fundamental assumptions we make about the world are often unacknowledged and implicit; that is, we take them for granted. This section maps out the range of epistemological positions available to qualitative researchers and discusses their relationships with one another. It also suggests ways in which researchers can identify and clarify their own assumptions.

Perhaps the easiest way for a researcher to access the assumptions she or he makes is to ask him- or herself a series of questions (see also Willig, 2008, Chapter 1), such as the following:

■ What kind of knowledge do I aim to create?
■ What are the assumptions that I make about the (material, social, and psychological) world(s) that I study?
■ How do I conceptualize the role of the researcher in the research process? What is the relationship between myself and the knowledge I aim to generate?

The remainder of this section looks at the range of possible answers to these three questions and provides examples of research designs informed by the epistemological positions indicated by such answers. Positions and their concomitant designs will be grouped into three broad approaches that are characterized by the type of knowledge they aim to create: (a) realist knowledge, (b) phenomenological knowledge, and (c) social constructionist knowledge (see Figure 1.1 for a summary).

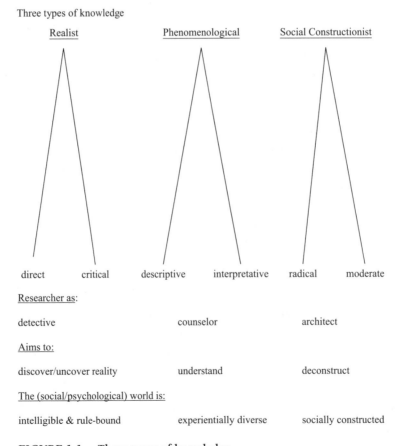

FIGURE 1.1. Three types of knowledge.

Realist Knowledge

Qualitative researchers can use qualitative methods of data collection and analysis to obtain a rich, accurate, detailed, and comprehensive picture of (some aspects of) the social world or of human psychology. The type of knowledge sought in this case aspires to capture and reflect as truthfully as possible something that is happening in the real world and that exists independently of the researcher's, and indeed the research participants', views or knowledge about it. The sorts of things a researcher who aspires to generate this type of (*realist*) knowledge might study include social processes (e.g., what happens when a new member joins an established reading group or what happens when an organization implements a new equal opportunities policy?) and psychological mechanisms or processes (e.g., how a person who suffers from panic attacks plans a journey on public transport or how people who lost a parent at an early age approach intimate relationships).

The assumption underpinning this type of research is that certain processes or patterns of a social or psychological nature characterize or shape the behavior or the thinking of research participants, and these can be identified and conveyed by the researcher. This means that the researcher assumes that the (material, social, psychological) world she or he investigates potentially can be understood, provided that the researcher is skilled enough to uncover the patterns, regularities, structures, or laws of behavior that characterize it and that generate the social or psychological phenomena we witness (and that constitute one's data). The researcher can succeed or fail in this process, which means that the researcher aspires to generate valid and reliable knowledge about a social or psychological phenomenon that exists independently of the researcher's awareness of it. As such, this type of research is characterized by a discovery orientation (see Madill, Jordan, & Shirley, 2000). The role of the researcher in this situation is akin to that of a detective who uses his or her skills, knowledge, and experience to uncover hitherto hidden facts and who, through his or her labor, makes what appeared puzzling or mysterious intelligible. The kinds of methods used by qualitative researchers who aim to produce this type of (realist) knowledge include

(realist versions of) ethnography and grounded theory methodology as well as such varieties of interpretative analysis as psychoanalytic approaches (but these methods also can be used from within a less realist epistemological framework, which is discussed in the section Varieties of Realist Knowledge).

Phenomenological Knowledge

Alternatively, qualitative research can aim to produce knowledge about the subjective experience of research participants (rather than about the social or psychological patterns or processes that underpin, structure, or shape such subjective experiences, as realist knowledge does). In this case, the researcher aspires to capture something that exists in the world (namely, the participants' feelings, thoughts, and perceptions—that is, their experiences); however, no claim is being made regarding its relationship with other facets of the world or indeed regarding the accuracy of the participants' accounts of their experiences (e.g., whether a phenomenological account of an embodied experience such as anger or anxiety matches up with objective physiological measures such as blood pressure or galvanic skin response). Such research aims to understand experience (rather than to discover what is "really" going on). In other words, it does not matter whether what a research participant describes is an accurate reflection of what happened to him or her or a fantasy; instead, the type of knowledge the researcher is trying to obtain is *phenomenological* knowledge—that is, knowledge of the quality and texture of the participant's experience. For example, a researcher might want to find out what it is like to be living with a diagnosis of psychosis or how a participant experiences the process of going through a divorce. Finding that a participant experiences herself as "rejected by the whole world," for example, constitutes phenomenological knowledge irrespective of whether the participant really is being rejected by everyone she encounters.

The task of the researcher in this type of research is to get as close as possible to the research participant's experience, to step into that person's shoes, and to look at the world through his or her eyes, that is to say, to enter his or her world. Here, the role of the researcher is similar to that of the *person-centered counselor* who listens to the client's account of his or her experience empathically, without judging and without questioning the external validity of what the client is saying. This means that the researcher assumes that there is more than one *world* to be studied. This is because researchers who seek this type of knowledge are interested in the experiential world of the participant (rather than the material, social, or psychological structures that may give rise to particular experiences—for example, the biochemical changes associated with psychosis or the social processes that can give rise to stereotyping); what appear to be the "same" (material, social, psychological) conditions (e.g., a divorce, a diagnosis, an accident) can be experienced in many different ways, and this means that there are potentially as many (experiential) worlds as there are individuals. A researcher who attempts to generate this type of knowledge asks, "What is the world like *for this participant*?" (rather than "What is the world like and what is it about the world that makes a particular experience possible?"). The kinds of methods used by qualitative researchers who aim to produce this type of (phenomenological) knowledge, unsurprisingly, tend to be phenomenological methods (such as interpretative phenomenological analysis or descriptive phenomenology, but note that phenomenological methods engage with the process of interpretation in a variety of ways that are discussed in the section Varieties of Phenomenological Knowledge later in this chapter).

Social Constructionist Knowledge

Finally, a qualitative researcher can adopt a much more skeptical position in relation to knowledge and argue that what is of interest is not so much what is really going on (realist approach to knowledge) or how something is actually experienced by participants (phenomenological approach) but rather how people talk about the world and, therefore, how they construct versions of reality through the use of language. Here, the type of knowledge aspired to is not knowledge about the world or knowledge about how things are (experienced) but rather knowledge about the process by which such knowledge is constructed in the first place. This

means that questions about the nature of social and psychological events and experiences are suspended and instead the researcher is concerned with the social construction of knowledge. Because language plays such an important part in the construction of knowledge, qualitative researchers who adopt a *social constructionist* orientation to knowledge generation tend to study discourses and the ways in which they are deployed within particular contexts. For example, a researcher might analyze the language used in policy documents about antisocial behavior to understand how the phenomenon of concern—"antisocial behavior"—is constructed within these documents and how the discourses used in the documents position those who are constructed as the targets of proposed interventions.

Such an approach to research is based on the assumption that all human experience is mediated by language, which means that all social and psychological phenomena are constructed in one way or another. It also means that all knowledge about the world and experience of the world is very much socially mediated and that individual experiences are always the product of internalized social constructions. In other words, when participants are telling the researcher about their experiences, they are not seen to be giving voice to an inner reality (as in phenomenological research) or to be providing information about social or psychological processes (as in realist research); instead, the researcher is interested in how socially available ways of talking about the phenomenon of interest (i.e., discourses) are deployed by the participant and how these may shape the participant's experience. Here, the role of the researcher is to draw attention to the constructed nature of social reality and to trace the specific ways in which particular phenomena are constructed through discourse and to reflect on the consequences of this for those who are affected (that is to say, who are "positioned") by these social constructions. As such, the role of the researcher is akin to that of an architect who looks at the phenomenon of interest with a view to how it has been constructed and from what resources and materials. The most commonly used method to produce this type of (social constructionist) knowledge is discourse analysis (of which there are several versions, including discursive psychology, Foucauldian discourse analysis, and critical discourse analysis); however, other methods such as narrative analysis and memory work also can be used.

Within these three basic approaches to conceptualizing the types of knowledge sought by qualitative researchers, each theme has variations (usually in the form of more or less radical versions). In the following section, we identify a variety of positions within each approach to knowledge generation.

Varieties of Realist Knowledge

Realist aspirations to knowledge generation range from what is sometimes referred to as naive to more critical varieties. *Naive realist* approaches are characterized by the assumption that a relatively uncomplicated and direct relationship exists between what presents itself (the data, the evidence) and what is going on (the reality we want to understand). In other words, we assume that the data more or less directly represent (mirror, reflect) reality. For example, if we wanted to find out how people make decisions about whether to have an HIV antibody test and we interviewed individuals who recently made such a decision, a naïve realist approach would dictate that we take participants' accounts at face value and that we accept that their accounts constitute accurate descriptions of how they made their decision. The task of the researcher, therefore, would be (a) to ensure that participants feel safe and comfortable enough to provide the researcher with accurate and detailed accounts and (b) to analyze the accounts in such as way as to produce a clear and systematic model of the decision-making process (or the variety of pathways for decision making if that is what the accounts indicate).

To call such research "naive realist" is to belittle it. The label *naive* does imply a criticism, and it is unlikely that a researcher would ever willingly describe their own research as naïve realist—even if he or she subscribed to the assumptions about knowledge generation that are associated with this label. Also, some very valuable research aims to "give voice" to otherwise-marginalized individuals and communities and is underpinned by the assumption that what participants are telling the researcher about their experiences (e.g., of suffering,

of exploitation, of oppression) reflects a social reality that needs to be exposed, acknowledged, and understood. Again, to call such research "naive" is to disparage and devalue research that clearly does have its uses and significance. Perhaps a less value-laden term such as *direct* realism would be preferable.

Critical realist approaches to knowledge generation differ from the more direct (or naive) version in that they are formed on the basis of the assumption that although the data can tell us about what is going on in the real (i.e., material, social, psychological) world, it does not do so in a self-evident, unmediated fashion. In other words, a critical realist approach does not assume that the data directly reflect reality (like a mirror image); rather, the data need to be interpreted to provide access to the underlying structures that generate the manifestations that constitute the data. For example, if we carry out a participant observation of the social rituals and practices that characterize life within a particular community, the data we collect (in the form of recordings of observations, conversations, interviews, documents, and photographs which capture life in the community, perhaps) would provide us with information about what members of the community do, how they relate to one another, and how they structure and manage their social life. However, the data would not tell us, directly and explicitly, what it might be (e.g., historically or politically) that drives, shapes, and maintains these structures and practices. To understand this, we need to move beyond the data and draw on knowledge, theories, and evidence from outside the particular study and use these to account for what we have observed. For instance, a community's history, its relations with neighboring communities or particular geographic conditions may help the researcher explain why people do what they do.

Crucially, from a critical realist standpoint, it is not necessary (in fact, we would not usually expect) that research participants be aware of the underlying mechanisms or conditions that inform their overt behaviors and experiences. Research informed by psychoanalytic theory is a good example of critical realist research in that it is assumed that the underlying (in this case, psychological) structures that generate the manifest, observable phenomena (behaviors, symptoms, dreams, slips of the tongue, etc.) are not necessarily accessible to those who experience them (i.e., the research participants, the patients). This assumption, however, does not mean that such structures are not "real." Critical realist research can vary in the extent to which it proclaims the existence of underlying structures and mechanisms with anything approaching certainty. Some researchers have presented their analyses with caution and the proviso that the interpretations offered are just that—interpretations that represent possibilities rather than certainties (e.g., Frosh & Saville-Young, 2008). Others have taken a much more knowing stance and present their analyses as insights into how things (actually, really) are (e.g., how people function psychologically or how communities are formed; see Hollway & Jefferson, 2000).

Varieties of Phenomenological Knowledge

All phenomenological knowledge aspires to increase the researcher's understanding of research participants' experience. As such, phenomenological knowledge is *insider knowledge*—that is, a knowledge that attempts to shed light on phenomena through an understanding of how these phenomena present themselves in or through experience; that is to say, how they appear to somebody within a particular context. Differences exist, however, in the extent to which phenomenological knowledge bases itself on the researcher's interpretation of research participants' experience. This means that phenomenological approaches to knowledge generation range from descriptive to interpretative varieties. *Descriptive phenomenology* is very much concerned with capturing experience "precisely as it presents itself, neither adding nor subtracting from it" (Giorgi, 1992, p. 121). Descriptive phenomenology does not aim to account for or explain the experience or to attribute meanings to it that are imported from outside of the account of the actual experience. In other words, it does not go beyond the data. For example, a descriptive phenomenologist might be interested in the phenomenon of being surprised. To better understand this phenomenon, the researcher might conduct a series of semistructured interviews with individuals who recently have experienced a surprise (such

as winning a prize, being invited on an unexpected holiday, or receiving a letter from a long-lost friend). The analysis of the interviews would aim to generate an understanding of what characterizes the experience of being surprised; in other words, the researcher would want to know what it is that people experience when they are surprised—for instance, the person may experience a sense of a loss of control, of ambivalence, or of uncertainty about how to respond, and perhaps also feelings of joy and excitement. We do not know what characterizes the experience until we have conducted a phenomenological analysis of the data and, as a descriptive phenomenologist, we should not allow our experiences, expectations, and assumptions regarding the experience of surprise to inform our analysis of the data. The end product of a descriptive phenomenological study would be an account of the structure of the phenomenon of being surprised that is formed entirely on the basis of participants' accounts of their experiences.

By contrast, *interpretative phenomenology* does not take accounts of experience "at face value" in the same way; instead, interpretative phenomenologists do move beyond the data in that they step outside of the account and reflect on its status as an account and its wider (social, cultural, psychological) meanings. As Larkin, Watts, and Clifton (2006) put it in their discussion of interpretative phenomenological analysis, such interpretative analysis "positions the initial 'description' in relation to a wider social, cultural, and perhaps even theoretical, context. This second-order account aims to provide a critical and conceptual commentary upon the participants' personal 'sense-making' activities" (p. 104). For example, an interpretative phenomenologist might want to explore the experience of women who have tried and failed to conceive with the help of in vitro fertilization. The researcher would start the research process in much the same way as a descriptive phenomenologist and conduct semistructured interviews with women who recently have had this experience. The next step (still in line with descriptive phenomenology) would be to engage with the interview transcripts with the aim of entering the participant's world, understanding what it has been like for the participants to go through the experience, and producing a description of the experience that captures its quality and texture, and that portrays its structure and essence.

The interpretative phenomenologist acknowledges that understanding the participant's experience presupposes a process of making sense of the participant's account in the first place; in other words, the researcher needs to give meaning to the account to understand it. Therefore, through a hermeneutic circle of giving and recovering meaning, the researcher is intimately implicated in making sense of the participant's account of a failure to conceive a child. In a further interpretative move, the researcher may contextualize the participants' experience by reflecting on the social and economic structures within which women in our culture experience reproduction, or the social and cultural expectations and norms that prevail at the time of data collection. The aim of such reflection would be to make (further) sense of participants' experiences and to understand better how such experiences are made possible by the context within which they occur.

Descriptive and interpretative versions of phenomenological research therefore differ in their approach to reflexivity. Although descriptive phenomenologists believe that it is possible to produce descriptions that capture and comprehend the phenomenon as it presents itself, interpretative phenomenologists argue that it is not, in fact, possible to produce a pure description of experience in any case and that description always involves a certain amount of interpretation. At the most basic level, it is argued, one's choice of words shapes the meaning of what they are trying to convey and this means that, inevitably, the researcher adds meaning to the data.

Varieties of Social Constructionist Knowledge

By way of contrast with realist approaches, the social constructionist perspective is often described as *relativist*. It is relativist in the sense that it questions the "out-there-ness" of the world and it rejects the idea that objects, events, and even experiences precede and inform our descriptions of them. Indeed, it rejects the notion of description altogether and replaces it with that of construction. Social

constructionism is relativist in the sense that it conceptualizes language as a form of social action that constructs versions of reality; here, it is discourse that constructs reality rather than reality that determines how we describe or talk about it. More or less radical strands of social constructionism exist, however, and not all social constructionist researchers would describe themselves as relativists. This means that social constructionist approaches to knowledge production can range from *radical* to more *moderate* versions. Research that is concerned with the ways in which speakers within a particular social context strategically deploy discursive resources to achieve a particular interactional objective may be conducted from a radical relativist position. Such a position demands that the researcher abandons any ambition to gain access to the participants' inner experience or indeed to understand how they make sense of their experience. Instead, the researcher assumes that participants will construct different versions of reality (i.e., of their experiences, their histories, their memories, their thoughts and feelings) depending on the social context within which they find themselves and the stake that they have in this context.

In other words, from a radical social constructionist perspective, there is nothing outside of the text. Reality is what participants are constructing within a particular interaction through discourse. This reality does not survive the context within which it has been constructed, as a different reality will be constructed to suit the next context. This means that the radical version of social constructionism foregrounds the variability and flexibility of accounts. It aims to understand how and why discursive objects and positions are constructed in particular ways within particular contexts and it explores the consequences of such constructions for those who are using them and those who are positioned by them (i.e., the speakers in a conversation). For example, a researcher might be interested in how people who have decided to commence psychotherapy introduce themselves to their new psychotherapist and how they explain why they are there. To obtain suitable data, the researcher would need to obtain recordings of first sessions of a number of therapist–client dyads. These recordings would be transcribed and then analyzed. The aim of the analysis would be to identify the ways in which the participants in the sessions deploy discursive resources and with what consequences. For instance, the researcher might observe that some clients begin by pointing out that they had waited until they had reached the "end of their tether" before making the appointment. The researcher might observe that by doing this, clients position themselves within a moral discourse and construct themselves as deserving of help because they have tried very hard to sort out their own problems before asking for help. Clients may also disclaim an (undesirable) identity, perhaps that of a needy person, by emphasizing that they have never sought help before and that their present visit to the therapist was an exceptional event. In this way, clients might position themselves as responsible adults whose help-seeking is not a sign of weakness or of psychopathology.

The important thing to remember is that a radical social constructionist researcher would not be interested in the validity of these accounts—indeed, he or she would not believe in the relevance or even the possibility of establishing these accounts' validity. In other words, it is irrelevant whether clients really are seeking help for the first time or whether they really are (or feel) weak, strong, or needy. The point of social constructionist research is to examine localized, context-specific discursive productions (e.g., of the self as "adult," as "strong," "normal," or "deserving") and their action orientation and consequences within the specific context. In other words, the radical social constructionist researcher would be interested only in the particular reality constructed for the purposes of a specific conversation.

By contrast, more moderate (that is to say, less relativist) approaches to social constructionist research would want to go beyond the study of localized deployments of discursive resources and make connections between the discourses that are used within a particular local context and the wider sociocultural context. For example, the researcher might be interested in exploring contemporary therapy culture more generally, looking at self-help texts; television shows that reference psychotherapy; and "problem pages" in newspapers and magazines, where experts answer letters from troubled readers.

Having identified dominant discourses surrounding psychotherapy in the 21st century, the researcher might then explore the ways in which such discourses position people (e.g., as damaged by their past, as in need of expert help, as responsible for working through their issues) and with what consequences (e.g., as a society, we may expect individuals to invest in their mental health and well-being). By grounding discourses in social, cultural, economic, and material structures, more moderate social constructionist researchers are making reference to something outside of the text. They invoke a reality that preexists and indeed shapes the ways in which individuals construct meaning within particular contexts. This means that the moderate social constructionist position has an affinity with the *critical realist* position (see the section Varieties of Realist Knowledge). Although radical social constructionists emphasize people's ability to play with discursive resources and to use them creatively to construct the social realities that suit their needs at a particular moment in time, moderate social constructionists are more concerned with the ways in which available discourses can constrain and limit what can be said or done within particular contexts.

Figure 1.1 provides a summary of what characterizes the three different types of knowledge that qualitative researchers can aim to produce. In this chapter, I have kept the use of specialist (philosophy of science) terminology to a minimum and instead have focused on a description of the assumptions (about the nature of knowledge, about the world, about the role of the researcher) that underpin and characterize the three approaches and that define their differences. I have argued that what matters is that we ask the right questions about a study (i.e., What kind of knowledge is being produced? What are the assumptions that have been made about the world that is being studied? What is the role of the researcher in the research process?) and that these answers will help us to identify (and make explicit) its epistemological foundations. I would argue that how we then label a particular epistemological position is of secondary importance as long as we are clear about its parameters. Those who are familiar with the qualitative research methodology literature will be aware that, as Ponterotto (2005) has pointed out, numerous classification schemas in the literature aim to classify approaches to qualitative research in meaningful and helpful ways and that use terminology lifted from the philosophy of science. For example, we find references to "modernisms, postmodernism, social constructionism and constructivism" (Hansen, 2004); "positivism, postpositivism, constructivism-interpretivism, and critical-ideological" approaches (Ponterotto, 2005); and "positivism, postpositivism, critical theory, constructivism, and participatory" approaches (Guba & Lincoln, 2005).

Such classification schemas often are developed within the context of formulating a critique of quantitative research in cases in which qualitative (often referred to as "new paradigm") approaches are contrasted with quantitative (often characterized as *positivist* and *postpositivist*) approaches. Such critiques are important in their own right, but it is not necessarily helpful to present classifications of qualitative epistemologies within such a context. A preoccupation with contrasting quantitative with qualitative perspectives can lead to a homogenizing of qualitative research and a lack of attention to the differences between qualitative approaches. As a result, we often find representations of both quantitative and qualitative perspectives that lack sophistication and differentiation and that (despite the use of erudite terminology) actually simplify and sometimes even caricature both perspectives. Often, a simple dichotomy between a positivist (old paradigm) quantitative perspective and a constructivist (new paradigm) qualitative perspective is constructed (and this usually positions the former as flawed and in need of replacement by the latter; see also Shadish, 1995, for a discussion of common errors and misrepresentations in epistemological debates in the social sciences). The problem with such dichotomous classifications is that they do not acknowledge the full range of qualitative epistemologies that, as indicated, can reach from naive (or better, direct) realism to radical social constructionism. In other words, not all qualitative research is constructivist, not all of it is relativist, and not all of it is interpretivist. Furthermore, as discussed in the section Differences Among Qualitative Approaches, references to these terms do not mean anything until we have

clarified whether we are applying them to describe the status of the data (e.g., as descriptions of reality, as witness statements, as individual constructions, as social constructions, etc.) or to the status of our analysis (as accurate knowledge of reality, as an interpretation, as a construction, as an artistic production, etc.).

EVALUATION

How can we assess the quality and value of a particular piece of qualitative research? Given that qualitative research is concerned with meaning, and given that it usually takes the form of descriptions or interpretations of research participants' context-specific experiences, it follows that the criteria traditionally used to evaluate quantitative research (i.e., reliability, representativeness, generalizability, objectivity, and validity) are not applicable to qualitative research. Does this mean that qualitative research cannot, or should not, be evaluated? Does it mean that in qualitative research "anything goes"? Opinion is divided on this subject, with some qualitative researchers (e.g., Forshaw, 2007) rejecting the whole notion of "method" in qualitative research (and with it any aspirations to "rigor"), proposing that the aim of qualitative research ought to be to produce ideas that resonate with readers and that generate debate rather than to produce insights that claim to have some validity or even truth value. It follows that it is not meaningful to assess the value of qualitative research in terms other than its creativity and originality.

Others (myself included; see Willig, 2007, 2008) disagree with this argument, proposing instead that qualitative research involves a process of systematic, cyclical, and critical reflection whose quality can be assessed. Like everything else in qualitative research, however, evaluation is not a simple or a straightforward matter. This is because the criteria we use for evaluating a qualitative study must be informed by the study's epistemological position. In other words, to be able to evaluate a study's contribution to knowledge in a meaningful way, we need to know what it was the researchers wanted to find out and what kind of knowledge they aimed to generate. Several authors have compiled lists of generic criteria for evaluating qualitative research (e.g., Elliott, Fischer, & Rennie, 1999; Henwood & Pidgeon, 1992; Yardley, 2000) and although some overlap exists between these, as I have argued elsewhere, "it is clear that authors approach the question of evaluation from the particular standpoint afforded by their own preferred methodological approach" (Willig, 2008, p. 152).

I concur with Madill et al. (2000) and Reicher (2000), who have argued that no such thing as a unified qualitative research paradigm exists and, therefore, that the criteria we use to evaluate qualitative studies need to be tailored to fit the particular methodology they are meant to appraise. For example, Madill et al. proposed that *objectivity* (i.e., the absence of bias on the part of the researcher) and *reliability* (i.e., the extent to which findings have been triangulated) are criteria that can be applied meaningfully to evaluate realist research, whereas from a radical constructionist point of view, any criteria that are concerned with the accuracy or authenticity of accounts would be meaningless. Instead, to evaluate such studies, we would need to assess their *internal coherence* (i.e., the extent to which the analytic narrative "hangs together" without internal contradictions), to establish *deviant case analysis* (i.e., the extent to which the limits of the applicability of the analytic insights have been identified), and *reader evaluation* (i.e., the extent to which the study is perceived by its readers to increase their insights and understanding). Finally, an evaluation of what Madill et al. described as *contextual constructionist* research (and that is compatible with the phenomenological perspective identified in this chapter) requires scrutiny of the study's use of reflexivity and the extent to which it explores (and ideally theorizes) the relationship between accounts (i.e., both the participants' accounts, that is to say the data as well as the researcher's analytic account) and the context(s) within which these have been produced. Finlay and Gough (2003) proposed that different "versions of reflexivity" reflect different epistemological orientations so that

> for some, reflexivity is celebrated as part of our essential human capacity, while

for others it is a self-critical lens. Some researchers utilize reflexivity to introspect, as a source of personal insight, while others employ it to interrogate the rhetoric underlying shared social discourses. Some treat it as a methodological tool to ensure "truth," while others exploit it as weapon to undermine truth claims. (p. x)

This means that reflexivity can be used in different ways and for different purposes. For example, for a *direct realist* researcher, reflexivity can be a way of acknowledging and bracketing off personal expectations and assumptions so that they do not make their way into the analysis and distort (or even silence) the participant's voice that is trying to make itself heard. By contrast, an interpretative phenomenological researcher may draw on his or her own thoughts and feelings about what the participant is saying to uncover meanings within it that are not immediately obvious to the participant. Finally, a radical social constructionist researcher can use reflexivity to trace the ways in which his or her own contributions to the conversation with the participant have positioned the participant and how this may have shaped the interview.

Again, these differences have implications for the evaluation of a qualitative study in that the use of reflexivity within the design of the study needs to be assessed in its own terms. In other words, we need to ask whether reflexivity has been used in a way that is compatible with the epistemological orientation of the study and whether the use of reflexivity within the study's design has met its own objectives. From our discussion of evaluation so far, it should have become clear that to make meaningful evaluation possible, a study's author needs to clearly identify the study's epistemological position. Therefore, the most important criterion for evaluating qualitative research ought to be *epistemological reflexivity* (i.e., the extent to which a study clearly and unambiguously identifies its epistemological stance) as this is a precondition for any further evaluation. Indeed, Madill et al. (2000) concluded that "qualitative researchers have a responsibility to make their epistemological position clear, conduct their research in a manner consistent with that position, and present their findings in a way that allows them to be evaluated appropriately" (p. 17).

CONCLUSION

The aim of this chapter is to review and clarify the various ways in which qualitative researchers approach the production of knowledge. It has been suggested that qualitative researchers can aim to produce three types of knowledge and these were given the labels *realist*, *phenomenological*, and *social constructionist*. Each of these types of knowledge was shown to be formed on the basis of different answers to questions about the nature and status of knowledge claims, the assumptions the researcher makes about the social and psychological worlds she or he is studying, and the role of the researcher in the research process. It was proposed that different methods of data collection and analysis are required to generate the different types of knowledge, and that the evaluative criteria we use to assess the value and quality of a qualitative study may differ depending on the type of knowledge the study aspires to produce. To develop these epistemological arguments and to clearly distinguish among the three positions, we have foregrounded their differences. In this concluding section, I return to the bigger picture and reflect on the ways in which the three approaches complement one another. Each research project is motivated and driven by a research question that specifies which aspect or dimension of social or psychological reality the study aims to shed light on. No study ever seeks to simply study (the meaning of) life as such or to understand the world in general. Even realist research only ever seeks to establish the truth about something in particular rather than simply the truth. In addition, every study will have to work within a set of practical constraints (such as available time and finances, for example) which set limits to what it can aspire to find out.

All this means that even the most carefully designed study can never achieve more than to shed light on one small part of a much bigger whole. It could be argued, therefore, that the three types of knowledge identified in this chapter, rather than

constituting alternative visions of what valid or useful knowledge should look like, are simply providing three different angles from which to view human experience. They shed light on three different aspects of human experience. From this point of view, qualitative research is about attempting to discover new aspects of a totality that never can be accessed directly or captured in its entirety.

Cohn (2005) referred to this as the "amplification" of meaning. To illustrate this way of thinking, and to illustrate what amplification of meaning may involve, let us imagine a researcher who wants to understand what happens when someone is diagnosed with a terminal illness. First, the researcher might want to listen to first-person accounts of this experience. To this end, she conducts semistructured interviews with a number of participants who have had this experience. Her aim is to shed light on the experience of receiving a terminal diagnosis. At this point, the researcher adopts a realist approach, taking the accounts at face value. She produces a thematic analysis that aims to capture and systematically represent how the participants experienced the process of being given their diagnosis. She identifies a number of interesting patterns in relation to the ways in which participants were treated by medical staff and perhaps also in the ways in which the participants' loved ones responded to the situation. The research could end here, having produced some useful and important insights.

Let us assume that the researcher has the time and motivation to continue with the research. Let us also assume that the researcher had noticed that, despite their many shared experiences with medical staff and loved ones, the participants gave quite different meanings to their illnesses. She also noticed that this seemed to inform the participants' sense of themselves as a terminally ill patient and how they felt about their illness. To better understand these differences, the researcher arranges further interviews with the participants, this time using a phenomenological approach to explore their subjective experience in greater depth. This phase of the research generates a further set of themes, this time capturing the existential dimensions of the experience of being diagnosed with a terminal illness and the range of existential meanings that can be given to such an experience. Again, the research could end at this point. Let us assume, however, that the researcher is still willing and able to continue with her project. She reflects on the fact that all the participants included references to the question of responsibility (for the illness) and that many of them grappled with issues around blame (for the illness) in their accounts. She decides that she wants to find out more about this and adopts a social constructionist approach, focusing on the use of discourses of individual responsibility within the context of terminal illness. She returns to the data (both sets of interviews) and analyzes them again, this time using a discourse analytic approach. To contextualize her participants' use of discourse in their constructions of meaning around their terminal diagnosis, the researcher analyzes newspaper articles and television documentaries about terminal illness and compares the discursive constructions used in those documents with those deployed by the participants.

Much more could be done to shed further light on the experience of being diagnosed with a terminal illness, but let us take pity on our hypothetical researcher and stop here. It remains for us to conclude that, rather than being mutually exclusive, realist, phenomenological, and social constructionist forms of knowing can be thought of as providing access to different aspects of our social and psychological world(s) and that our choice of which one(s) to mobilize within the context of a particular research project is a question of knowing what we want to know on this particular occasion.

References

Cohn, H. W. (2005). Interpretation: Explanation or understanding. In E. van Deurzen & C. Arnold-Baker (Eds.), *Existential perspectives on human issues. A handbook for therapeutic practice* (pp. 221–226). Basingstoke, England: Palgrave Macmillan.

Denzin, N. K., & Lincoln, Y. S. (Eds.). (2005). *The Sage handbook of qualitative research* (3rd ed.). Thousand Oaks, CA: Sage.

Drisko, J. W. (1997). Strengthening qualitative studies and reports: Standards to promote academic integrity. *Journal of Social Work Education, 33*, 185–197.

Elliott, R., Fischer, C. T., & Rennie, D. L. (1999). Evolving guidelines for publication of qualitative research studies in psychology and related fields. *British Journal of Clinical Psychology, 38*, 215–229. doi:10.1348/014466599162782

Finlay, L., & Gough, B. (Eds.). (2003). *Reflexivity: A practical guide for researchers in health and social sciences.* Oxford, England: Blackwell.

Forshaw, M. J. (2007). Free qualitative research from the shackles of method. *The Psychologist, 20*, 478–479.

Frosh, S., & Saville-Young, L. (2008). Psychoanalytic approaches to qualitative psychology. In C. Willig & W. Stainton Rogers (Eds.), *The Sage handbook of qualitative research in psychology* (pp. 109–126). London, England: Sage.

Giorgi, A. (1992). Description versus interpretation: Competing alternative strategies for qualitative research. *Journal of Phenomenological Psychology, 23*, 119–135. doi:10.1163/156916292X00090

Glaser, B. (1992). *Basics of grounded theory analysis.* Mill Valley, CA: Sociology Press.

Guba, E. G., & Lincoln, Y. S. (2005). Paradigmatic controversies, contradictions, and emerging influences. In N. K. Denzin & Y. S. Lincoln (Eds.), *The Sage handbook of qualitative research* (3rd ed., pp. 191–215). Thousand Oaks, CA: Sage.

Hansen, J. T. (2004). Thoughts on knowing: Epistemic implications of counselling practice. *Journal of Counseling and Development, 82*, 131–138.

Henwood, K. L., & Pidgeon, N. F. (1992). Qualitative research and psychological theorising. *British Journal of Psychology, 83*, 97–111. doi:10.1111/j.2044-8295.1992.tb02426.x

Hollway, W., & Jefferson, T. (2000). *Doing qualitative research differently: Free association, narrative and the interview method.* London, England: Sage.

Kendall, M., & Murray, S. A. (2005). Tales of the unexpected: Patients' poetic accounts of the journey to a diagnosis of lung cancer: A prospective serial qualitative interview study. *Qualitative Inquiry, 11*, 733–751. doi:10.1177/1077800405276819

Langdridge, D. (2007). *Phenomenological psychology: Theory, research and method.* London, England: Pearson Prentice Hall.

Larkin, M., Watts, S., & Clifton, E. (2006). Giving voice and making sense in interpretative phenomenological analysis. *Qualitative Research in Psychology, 3*, 102–120. doi:10.1191/1478088706qp062oa

Madill, A., Jordan, A., & Shirley, C. (2000). Objectivity and reliability in qualitative analysis: Realist, contextualist and radical constructionist epistemologies. *British Journal of Psychology, 91*, 1–20. doi:10.1348/000712600161646

Ponterotto, J. G. (2005). Qualitative research in counselling psychology: A primer on research paradigms and philosophy of science. *Journal of Counseling Psychology, 52*, 126–136. doi:10.1037/0022-0167.52.2.126

Reicher, S. (2000). Against methodolatry: Some comments on Elliott, Fischer and Rennie. *British Journal of Clinical Psychology, 39*, 1–6. doi:10.1348/014466500163031

Shadish, W. R. (1995). Philosophy of science and the quantitative-qualitative debates: Thirteen common errors. *Evaluation and Program Planning, 18*, 63–75. doi:10.1016/0149-7189(94)00050-8

Willig, C. (2007). Qualitative research: The need for system. [Letter to the editor]. *The Psychologist, 20*, 597.

Willig, C. (2008). *Introducing qualitative research in psychology* (2nd ed.). Maidenhead, England: McGraw Hill Open University Press.

Yardley, L. (2000). Dilemmas in qualitative health research. *Psychology and Health, 15*, 215–228. doi:10.1080/08870440008400302

CHAPTER 2

THEORIES OF CAUSATION IN PSYCHOLOGICAL SCIENCE

William R. Shadish and Kristynn J. Sullivan

Causal inference is central to psychological science. It plays a key role in psychological theory, a role that is made salient by the emphasis on experimentation in the training of graduate students and in the execution of much basic and applied psychological research. For decades, many psychologists have relied on the work of Donald Campbell to help guide their thinking about causal inference (e.g., Campbell, 1957; Campbell & Stanley, 1963; Cook & Campbell, 1979; Shadish, Cook, & Campbell, 2002). It is a tribute to the power and usefulness of Campbell's work that its impact has lasted more than 50 years. Yet the decades also have seen new theories of causation arise in disciplines as diverse as economics, statistics, and computer science. Psychologists often are unaware of these developments, and when they are aware, often struggle to understand them and their relationship to the language and ideas that dominate in psychology. This chapter reviews some of these recent developments in theories of causation, using Campbell's familiar work as a touchstone from which to examine newer work by statistician Donald Rubin and computer scientist Judea Pearl.

Campbell received both his bachelor's degree in psychology and doctorate in social psychology, in 1939 and 1947 respectively, from the University of California, Berkeley. The majority of his career was spent at Northwestern University, and most of his causal inference work was generated in the 1950s, 1960s, and 1970s. Much of the terminology in psychological discussions of causation theory, such as *internal and external validity* and *quasi-experiment*, can be credited to Campbell. In addition, he invented quasi-experimental designs such as the regression discontinuity design, and he adapted and popularized others. The theory he developed along with his many colleagues is the most pervasive causation theory in the fields of psychology and education. As a result, he is one of the most cited psychologists in these fields.

Rubin also received a bachelor's degree in psychology from Princeton University in 1965, followed by a doctorate in statistics from Harvard in 1970. He briefly worked at the University of Chicago and the Educational Testing Service, but then returned to Harvard as a statistician. His work on causal inference occurred later than most of Campbell's. Rubin's theory is followed more in other fields, such as statistics and economics, and is relatively unknown within psychology. He is, however, responsible for many novel contributions to the field of statistics, such as the use of multiple imputation for addressing missing data (e.g., Little & Rubin, 2002). He is one of the top 10 most cited statisticians in the world.

Pearl received a bachelor's degree in electrical engineering from the Technion in Israel in 1960, a master's degree in physics from Rutgers University in 1965, and a doctorate in electrical engineering from the Polytechnic Institute of Brooklyn in 1965. He worked at RCA Research Laboratories on superconductive parametric and storage devices and at

This research was supported in part by Grant R305U070003 from the Institute for Educational Sciences, U.S. Department of Education. Parts of this work are adapted from "Campbell and Rubin: A Primer and Comparison of Their Approaches to Causal Inference in Field Settings," by W. R. Shadish, 2010, *Psychological Methods, 15*, pp. 3–17. Copyright 2010 by the American Psychological Association. The authors thank Judea Pearl for extensive comments on earlier versions of this manuscript.

DOI: 10.1037/13619-003

Electronic Memories, Inc., on advanced memory systems. He then joined the School of Engineering at UCLA in 1970, where he is currently a professor of computer science and statistics and director of the cognitive systems laboratory. His work on causal inference is of slightly more recent vintage compared with that of Campbell and Rubin, with roots in the 1980s (Burns & Pearl, 1981; Pearl & Tarsi, 1986) but with its major statements mostly during the 1990s and later (e.g., Pearl, 2000, 2009a, 2010a). Not surprisingly given his background in engineering and computer science, his work—at least until recently—has had its greatest impact in fields like cognitive science, artificial intelligence, and machine learning.

The three models share nontrivial common ground, despite their different origins. They have published classic works that are cited repeatedly and are prominent in their spheres of influence. To varying degrees, they bring experimental terminology into observational research. They acknowledge the importance of manipulable causes. Yet they also have nontrivial differences. Campbell and Rubin, for example, focus most heavily on simple descriptive inferences about whether A caused B; Pearl is as concerned with the mechanisms that mediate or moderate that effect. Campbell and Rubin strongly prefer randomized experiments when they are feasible; such a preference is less apparent in Pearl. These three theories, however, rarely have been compared, contrasted, combined, or even cross-referenced to identify their similarities and differences. This chapter will do just that, first by describing each theory in its own terms and then by comparing them on superordinate criteria.

A PRIMER ON THREE CAUSAL MODELS

It is an oversimplification to describe the broad-ranging work of any of these three scholars as a model. The latter implies a compactness, precision, and singular focus that belies their breadth and depth. At the core of each of these approaches, however, a finite group of terms and ideas exists that is its unique key contribution. Therefore, for convenience's sake in this chapter, we refer to Campbell's causal model (CCM), Pearl's causal model (PCM), and Rubin's causal model (RCM), the latter being a commonly used acronym in

the literature (e.g., Holland, 1986). In this chapter, PCM and CCM are convenient counterpoints to that notation, intended to facilitate contrasts. These abbreviations also allow inclusive reference to all those who worked on CCM, PCM, and RCM. For instance, parts of CCM were developed by Cook (e.g., Cook, 1990, 1991; Cook & Campbell, 1979), parts of RCM by Rosenbaum (e.g., Rosenbaum, 2002), and parts of PCM by Tian (e.g., Tian & Pearl, 2000). Accordingly, references to these acronyms in this chapter refer to the models rather to Campbell, Rubin, or Pearl themselves.

Campbell's Causal Model

The core of CCM is Campbell's validity typology and the associated threats to validity. CCM uses these tools to take a critical approach to the design of new studies and critique of completed studies that probe causal relationships. CCM's work first appeared as a journal article (Campbell, 1957), then as a greatly expanded book chapter (Campbell & Stanley, 1963), and finally as a reprint of that chapter as a freestanding book (Campbell & Stanley, 1966) that was revisited and expanded in book form twice over the next 4 decades (Cook & Campbell, 1979; Shadish et al., 2002) and elaborated in many additional works.

At its start, CCM outlined a key dichotomy, that scientists make two general kinds of inferences from experiments:

- Inferences about "did, in fact, the experimental stimulus make some significant difference in this specific instance" (Campbell, 1957, p. 297).
- Inferences about "to what populations, settings, and variables can this effect be generalized" (Campbell, 1957, p. 297).

Campbell labeled the former inference *internal validity* and the latter *external validity*, although he often interchanged the term *external validity* with *representativeness* or *generalizability*.

Later, the dichotomy was expanded into four validity types (Cook & Campbell, 1979; Shadish et al., 2002):

- *Statistical conclusion validity*: The validity of inferences about the correlation (covariation) between treatment and outcome.

- *Internal validity*: The validity of inferences about whether observed covariation between A (the presumed treatment) and B (the presumed outcome) reflects a causal relationship from A to B, as those variables were manipulated or measured.
- *Construct validity*: The validity with which inferences are made from the operations in a study to the theoretical constructs those operations are intended to represent.
- *External validity*: The validity of inferences about whether the observed cause-effect relationship holds over variation in persons, settings, treatment variables, and measurement variables.

These validity types give CCM a broad sweep both conceptually and practically, pertinent to quite different designs, such as case studies, path models, and experiments. The boundaries between the validity types are artificial but consistent with common categories of discourse among scholars concerned with statistics, causation, language use, and generalization.

Threats to validity include the errors we may make about the four kinds of inferences about statistics, causation, language use, and generalizability. These threats are the second part of CCM. Regarding internal validity, for example, we may infer that results from a nonrandomized experiment support the inference that a treatment worked. We may be wrong in many ways: Some event other than treatment may have caused the outcome (the threat of history), the scores of the participants may have changed on their own without treatment (maturation or regression), or the practice provided by repeated testing may have caused the participants to improve their performance without treatment (testing). Originally, Campbell (1957) presented eight threats to internal validity and four to external validity. As CCM developed, the lists proliferated, although they seem to be asymptoting: Cook and Campbell (1979) had 33 threats, and Shadish et al. (2002) had 37. Presentation of all threats for all four validity types is beyond the scope of the present chapter as well as unnecessary to its central focus.

The various validity types and threats to validity are used to identify and, if possible, prevent problems that may hinder accurate casual inference. The focus is on preventing these threats with strong experimental design, but if that is not possible, then to address them in statistical analysis after data have been collected—the third key feature of CCM. Of the four validity types, CCM always has prioritized internal validity, saying first that "internal validity is the prior and indispensable condition" (Campbell, 1957, p. 310) and later that "*internal validity* is the *sine qua non*" (Campbell & Stanley, 1963, p. 175). From the start, this set Campbell at odds with some contemporaries such as Cronbach (1982). CCM focuses on the design of high-quality experiments that improve internal validity, claiming that it makes no sense to experiment without caring if the result is a good estimate of whether the treatment worked.

In CCM, the strategy is to design studies that reduce "the number of plausible rival hypotheses available to account for the data. The fewer such plausible rival hypotheses remaining, the greater the degree of 'confirmation'" (Campbell & Stanley, 1963, p. 206). The second line of attack is to assess the threats that were not controlled in the design, which is harder to do convincingly. The second option, however, is often the only choice, as in situations in which better designs cannot be used for logistical or ethical reasons, or when criticizing completed studies. With their emphasis on prevention of validity threats through design, CCM is always on the lookout for new design tools that might improve causal inference. This included inventing the regression discontinuity design (Thistlethwaite & Campbell, 1960), but mostly extended existing work, such as Chapin's (1932, 1947) experimental work in sociology, McCall's (1923) book on designing education experiments, Fisher's (1925, 1926) already classic work on experimentation in agriculture, and Lazarsfeld's (1948) writings on panel designs. CCM now gives priority among the nonrandomized designs to regression discontinuity, interrupted time series with a control series, nonequivalent comparison group designs with high-quality measures and stable matching, and complex pattern-matching designs, in that order. The latter refer to designs that make complex predictions in which a diverse pattern of results must occur, using a study that may include multiple nonrandomized designs each with different presumed biases: "The more numerous and independent the ways in which the experimental effect is demonstrated, the less numerous and less plausible any singular rival invalidating hypothesis becomes" (Campbell & Stanley, 1963, p. 206).

This stress on design over analysis was summed up well by Light, Singer, and Willett (1990): "You can't fix by analysis what you bungled by design" (p. viii). The emphasis of the CCM, then, is on the reduction of contextually important, plausible threats to validity as well as the addition of well-thought-out design features. If possible, it is better to rule out a threat to validity with design features than to rely on statistical analysis and human judgment to assess whether a threat is plausible after the fact. For example, for a nonrandomized experiment, a carefully chosen control group (one that is in the same locale as the treatment group and that focuses on the same kinds of person) is crucial within the CCM tradition. Also called a focal local control, this type of selection is presumed to be better than, for example, a random sample from a national database, such as economists have used to construct control groups. Simply put, in the CCM, design rules (Shadish & Cook, 1999).

Lastly, remember that Campbell's thinking about causal inference was nested within the context of his broader interests. In one sense, his work on causal inference could be thought of as a special case of his interests in biases in human cognition in general. For example, as a social psychologist, he studied biases that ranged from basic perceptual illusions to cultural biases; and as a meta-scientist, he examined social psychological biases in scientific work. In another sense, CCM also fits into the context of Campbell's evolutionary epistemology, in which Campbell postulated that experiments are an evaluative mechanism used to select potentially effective ideas for retention in the scientific knowledge base. Although discussions of these larger frameworks are beyond the scope of this article, it is impossible to fully understand CCM without referencing the contexts in which it is embedded.

Rubin's Causal Model

Rubin has presented a compact and precise conceptualization of causal inference (RCM; e.g., Holland, 1986), although Rubin frequently has credited the model to Neyman (1923/1990). A good summary is found in Rubin (2004). RCM features three key elements: units, treatments, and potential outcomes. Let Y be the outcome measure. $Y(1)$ would be defined as the potential outcome that would be observed if the unit (participant) is exposed to the treatment level of an independent variable W ($W = 1$). Then, $Y(0)$ would be defined as the potential outcome that would be observed if the unit was not exposed to the targeted treatment ($W = 0$). Under these assumptions, the potential individual casual effect is the difference between these two potential outcomes, or $Y(1) - Y(0)$. The average casual effect is then the average of all units' individual casual effects. These are potential outcomes, however, only until the treatment begins. Necessarily, once treatment begins, only $Y(1)$ or $Y(0)$ can be observed per unit (as the same participant cannot simultaneously be given the treatment and not given the treatment). Because of this factor, the problem of casual inference within RCM is how to estimate the missing outcome, or the potential outcome that was not observed. These missing data sometimes are called *counterfactuals* because they are not actually observed. In addition, it is no longer possible to estimate individual causal effects as previously defined [$Y(1) - Y(0)$] because one of the two required variables will be missing. Average causal effect over all of the units still can be estimated under certain conditions, such as random assignment.

The most crucial assumption that RCM makes is the stable-unit-treatment-value assumption (SUTVA). SUTVA states that the representation of potential outcomes and effects outlined in the preceding paragraph reflect all possible values that could be observed in any given study. For example, SUTVA assumes that no interference occurs between individual units, or that the outcome observed on one unit is not affected by the treatment given to another unit. This assumption is commonly violated by nesting (e.g., of children within classrooms), in which case the units depend on each other in some fashion. Nesting is not the only way in which SUTVA's assumption of independence of units is violated, however. Another example of a violation of SUTVA is that one person's receipt of a flu vaccine may affect the likelihood that another will be infected, or that one person taking aspirin for a headache may affect whether another person gets a headache from listening to the headache sufferer complain. These violations of SUTVA imply that each unit no longer has only two potential outcomes that depend on whether they receive treatment or no treatment. Instead, each unit has a set of potential outcomes depending on what treatment condition they receive as well as what treatment condition other participants receive. This set of potential outcomes grows exponentially as the number of treatment conditions and participants increase. Eventually, the number of potential outcomes will make computations impossibly complex. For example, consider an experiment with just two participants (P1 and P2). With SUTVA, P1 has only two potential outcomes, one if P1 receives treatment [$Y(1)$] and the other if P1 receives the comparison condition [$Y(0)$]. But without SUTVA, P1 now has four potential outcomes, $Y(1)$ if P2 receives treatment, $Y(1)$ if P2 receives the comparison condition, $Y(0)$ if P2 receives treatment, and $Y(0)$ if P2 receives the comparison condition. If the number of participants increases to three, the number of potential outcomes assuming SUTVA is still two for each participant, but without SUTVA it is eight. With the number of participants that are characteristic of real experiments, the number of potential outcomes for each participant without SUTVA is so large as to be intractable. In addition, even if no interference occurs between the units, without SUTVA, we may have to worry that within the ith unit, more than one version of each treatment condition is possible (e.g., an ineffective or an effective aspirin tablet). SUTVA, therefore, is a simplification that is necessary to make causal inference possible under real-world complexities. Under these same real-world complexities, however, SUTVA is not always true. So, although the assumption that units have only one potential outcome in fact may be an essential simplification, it is not clear that it is always plausible. Most readers find SUTVA as well as the implications of violations of SUTVA, to be one of the more difficult concepts in RCM.

Also crucial to RCM is the assignment mechanism by which units do or do not receive treatment. Although it is impossible to observe both potential outcomes on any individual unit, random assignment of all units to treatment conditions allows for obtaining an unbiased estimate of the population causal effect, by calculating the average causal effect of the studied units. Randomly assigning units to groups creates a situation in which one of the two possible potential outcomes is missing completely at random. Formal statistical theory (Rubin, 2004) as well as intuition state that unobserved outcomes missing completely at random should not affect the average over the observed units, at least not with a large enough sample size. Any individual experiment may vary slightly from this statement because of sampling error, but the assumption is that it generally will be true. When random assignment does not occur, the situation becomes more complex. In some cases, assignment is not totally random, but it is made on the basis, in whole or in part, of an observed variable. Examples of this include regression discontinuity designs, in which assignment to conditions is made solely on the basis of a cutoff on an observed variable (Shadish et al., 2002), or an experiment in which random assignment occurs in conjunction with a blocking variable. These types of assignment are called ignorable because although they are not completely random, potential outcomes still are unrelated to treatment assignment as long as those known variables are included in the model. With this procedure, an unbiased estimate of effect can be obtained. In all other cases of nonrandom assignment, however, assignment is made on the basis of a combination of factors, including unobserved variables. Unobserved variables cannot be specifically included in the model, and as such, assignment is nonignorable, which makes estimating effects more difficult and sometimes impossible.

The assignment mechanism affects not only the probability of being assigned to a particular condition, but also how much the researcher knows about outside variables affecting that probability. Take, for example, an experiment in which units are assigned to either a treatment or a no-treatment condition by a coin toss. The probability of being assigned to either group is widely understood to be $p = .50$; and, in addition, it is intuitively understood that no other variables (e.g., gender of the participant) will be related systematically to that probability. In RCM, the assignment probabilities are formalized as propensity scores, that is, predicted probabilities of assignment to each condition. In practice, randomized experiments are subject to sampling error (or unlucky randomization) in which some covariates from a vector of all possible covariates X (measured or not) may be imbalanced across conditions (e.g., a disproportionate number of males are in the treatment group). In those cases, the observed propensity score is related to those covariates and varies randomly from its true value (Rubin & Thomas, 1992).

When a nonrandom but ignorable (as defined in the previous paragraph) assignment mechanism is used, the true propensity score is a function of the known assignment variables. In this situation, X takes on a slightly different meaning than it did in a randomized experiment. For example, in a regression discontinuity design, participants are assigned to conditions on the basis of whether they fall above or below a cutoff score of a specific assignment variable. In this situation, X must contain that assignment variable in addition to any other covariates the researcher is interested in measuring. According to Rubin (2004), designs in which covariates in X fully determine assignment to conditions are called *regular designs*. When assignment is nonrandomized and not controlled, as in observational studies, regular designs form the basis of further analysis. Ideally, in these designs, X would contain all the variables that determined whether a unit received treatment. In practice, however, those variables are almost never fully known with certainty, which in turn means that the true propensity score is also unknown. In this situation, the propensity score is estimated using methods, such as logistic regression, in which covariates are used to predict the condition in which a unit is placed. RCM suggests rules for knowing what constitutes a good propensity score, but much of that work is preliminary and ongoing. Good propensity scores can be used to create balance over treatment and control conditions across all observed covariates that are used to create the propensity scores (e.g., Rubin, 2001), but this alone is not sufficient for bias reduction. The strong ignorability assumption, a critical assumption discussed in the next paragraph, also must be met.

RCM then uses propensity scores to estimate effect size for studies in which assignment is not ignorable. For example, in nonrandom designs, propensity scores can be used to match or stratify units. Units matched on propensity scores are matched on all of the covariates used to create the propensity scores, and units stratified across scores are similar on all of the included covariates. If it can be correctly argued that all of the variables pertinent to the assignment mechanism were included in the propensity score calculation, then the strongly ignorable treatment assignment assumption has been met, and RCM argues that assignment mechanism now can be treated as unconfounded, as in random assignment. The strongly ignorable treatment assignment assumption is essential, but as of yet, no direct test can be made of whether this assumption has been met in most cases. This is not a flaw in RCM, however, because RCM merely formalizes the implicit uncertainty that is present from the lack of knowledge of an assignment in any nonregular design. Furthermore, RCM treats the matching or stratification procedure as part of the design of a good observational study, rather than a statistical test to perform after the fact. In that sense, creating propensity scores, assessing their balance, and conducting the initial matching or stratification are all essential pieces of the design of a prospective experiment and ought to be done without looking at the outcome variable of interest. These elements are considered to be part of the treatment, and standard analyses then can be used to estimate the effect of treatment. Again, RCM emphasizes that the success of propensity score analyses rests on the ignorability assumption and does provide ways to assess how sensitive results might be to violations of this assumption (Rubin, 2001).

After laying this groundwork, RCM moves on to more advanced topics. For example, one topic deals with treatment crossovers and incomplete treatment implementation, combining RCM with econometric instrumental variable analysis to deal successfully with this key problem if some strong but often plausible assumptions are met (Angrist, Imbens, & Rubin, 1996). Another example addresses getting better estimates of the effects of mediational variables (coming between treatment and outcome, caused by treatment and mediating the effect; Frangakis & Rubin, 2002). A third example deals with missing data in the covariates used to predict the propensity scores (D'Agostino & Rubin, 2000). Yet another example addresses how to deal with clustering issues in RCM (Frangakis, Rubin, & Zhou, 2002). These examples provide mere glimpses of RCM's yield in the design and analysis of studies investigating causal links.

As with Campbell, knowledge of the larger context of Rubin's other work is necessary to fully understand RCM. Rubin's mentor was William G. Cochran, a statistician with a persistent and detailed interest in estimation of effects from nonrandomized experiments. Rubin's dissertation reflected this interest and concerned the use of matching and regression adjustments in nonrandomized experiments. This mentorship undoubtedly shaped the nature of his interests in field experimentation. Rubin is also a pioneer in methods for dealing with missing data (e.g., Little & Rubin, 2002; Rubin, 1987). His work on missing data led him to conceptualize the randomized experiment as a study in which some potential outcomes are, by virtue of random assignment, missing completely at random. Similarly, that work also led to the use of multiple imputation in explaining a Bayesian understanding of computing the average causal effect (Rubin, 2004).

Pearl's Causal Model

PCM provides a language and a set of statistical rules for causal inference in the kinds of models that variously are called path models, structural equation models, or causal models. In the latter case, the very use of the word causal has been controversial (e.g., Freedman, 1987). The reason for this controversy is that statistics, in general, has not had the means by which to move to safe causal inferences from the correlations and covariances that typically provide the data for causal models, which often are gathered in observational rather than experimental contexts. Statistics did not have the means to secure causal inference from a combination of theoretical assumptions and observational data. PCM is not limited to observational data, but it is with observational data that its contributions are intended to provide the most help. Good introductions to PCM have been provided by Morgan and Winship (2007), Hayduk et al. (2003), and Pearl (1998, 2010b), on which this

presentation of PCM relies heavily. For convenience given the number of new terms introduced in PCM, Table 2.1 summarizes some of the common terms in PCM and path analysis to clarify their overlap; readers familiar with path analysis may benefit from reading that table before continuing. New terms are italicized in text on first use.

PCM often works with graphs called *directed acyclic graphs* (DAGs). DAGs look like graphs that are common in path analysis, although they differ in important ways. The principles of PCM are based on nonparametric structural equation models (SEMs), augmented with ideas from both logic and graph theory. Yet PCM differs in important ways from SEM. Most implementations of SEM are parametric and require knowledge of the functional form of the relationships among all the variables in the model. PCM is nonparametric, so that one only need specify the relationships in the model, not whether the relationship between nodes is linear, quadratic, cubic, and so forth. PCM falls back on parametric modeling only when the nonparametric formulation of high dimensional problems is not practical. DAGs are Markovian, that is, they are acyclic in cases in which all the error terms in the DAG are jointly independent. PCM does not rely on these restrictions in many cases, however, when it allows correlation among error terms in the form of bidirected arrows or latent variables. DAGs may not include cycles (i.e., paths that start and eventually end at the same node). DAGs and PCM more generally do not assign any important role to the kinds of overall goodness-of-fit tests common to SEM, noting that support for a specific causal claim depends mostly on the theoretical assumptions embedded in the DAG that must be ascertained even if the model fits the data perfectly.

The starting point in PCM is the assertion that every exercise in causal analysis must commence with a set of theoretical or judgmental causal assumptions and that such assumptions are best articulated and represented in the form of directed acyclic graphs (DAGs). Consider Figure 2.1, for example. The letters each identify an observed random variable, called a *node*, represented by the solid black dot (•). A single-headed arrow like that going from X to Y indicates the direction of a

TABLE 2.1

Novel and Related Terms in Pearl's Causal Model and Path Analysis

Pearl's causal model	Path analysis	Discussion
Node	Variable	Probably synonymous.
Edge	Path	An edge is always one arrow, which may be unidirected or bidirected, whereas a path in both Pearl's causal model and path analysis is a consecutive sequence of edges or arrows connecting two variables.
Directed edge	Direct path	Probably synonymous, both are represented as straight arrows from one variable to another representing the direction of presumed causal effect.
Bidirected edge	Curved path with arrowhead on each end	A bidirected edge is the usual curved path where a common but unobserved node causes both nodes where the arrowheads point.
Directed acyclic graphs (DAGs)	Path models, structural equation models, causal models	DAGs look very much like path models. However, DAGs are mostly nonparametric They are called Markovian if all error terms are jointly independent and no paths start and eventually end at the same node. They are semi-Markovian if errors are dependent (shown as bidirected edges).
Parent, grandparent, ancestor, child, descendent		These terms have no equivalent terms in path analysis, but they do have the obvious equivalent cases in path models. They refer to particular kinds of relationships among nodes in DAGs specifying various kinds of degrees of separation of nodes. Terms like exogenous, endogenous and mediating variables in path models may sometimes meet the definition of these terms in DAGs.
Collider		Another term with no equivalent specific term in path models. A collider is a node that is a mutual direct descendent of two (or more) nodes in a DAG, and, if conditioned on, creates spurious association between these nodes.
d-separation	Vanishing partial correlation	d-separation (directional separation) is a graphic test for determining when any two sets of nodes in a DAG are statistically independent after controlling for a third set.
Back-door path		A back-door path from X to Y is a path from X to Y that includes a directed edge pointing directly at X from an ancestor of X. No equivalent term exists in path analysis, but such paths would be identified by Wright's (1921) rules as a path contributing to the covariation between X and Y.
Back-door criterion		A graphic test for determining when causal effects can be estimated consistently by controlling for a set of covariates in the DAG.
Fork of mutual dependence		In a DAG, a set of edges where a third variable C causes X and Y. No equivalent path analysis term exists.
Inverted fork of mutual causation		In a DAG, a set of edges where X and Y both cause C, which is therefore a collider. No equivalent path analysis term exists.
$do(x)$ operator		This operator replaces the random variable X in a DAG with a constant x that is a specific value of X such as x_1 = received treatment or x_0 = did not receive treatment. It also removes all arrows pointing to X and, thus, mimics experimental control. No equivalent path analysis term.

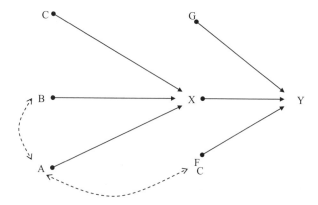

FIGURE 2.1. A directed acyclic graph. From *Counterfactuals and Causal Inference* (Figure 1.1), by S. L. Morgan and C. Winship, 2007, Cambridge, England: Cambridge University Press. Copyright 2007 by Cambridge University Press. Adapted with the permission of Cambridge University Press.

presumed causal relationship from one node to another and is called a *directed edge*. Curved, dashed, double-headed arrows like that between A and B, called *bidirected edges*, indicate that a common but unobserved node causes both nodes that appear where the arrowheads point. A *path* is a consecutive sequence of edges, whether directed or bidirected, connecting two variables. If an arrow exists between X and Y in Figure 2.1, with the obvious hypothesis that X causes Y, then X is a *parent* of Y, and Y is the *child* of X. Causes of parent variables are *grandparents*, so A, B, and C are grandparents of Y in Figure 2.1. All direct and indirect causes of a variable are its *ancestors*, and all variables that receive direct or indirect effects of a variable are its *descendents*. A mutual direct descendent of two (or more) variables is called a *collider*. Both X and Y in Figure 2.1 are colliders resulting from A, B, C, and F, G, X, respectively. The intuition is that the effects of A, B, and C collide at X. A is also a collider because it descends from both the common cause of A and B, and the common cause of A and F, represented by the bidirected edges in the DAG.

The assumption that all error terms (not shown explicitly in the DAG) are independent permits one to predict conditional dependencies between any sets of nodes in the model using a graphic test called *d-separation*. If any two variables in a DAG are

d-separated (directional separation), then they must be statistically independent after controlling for one or more other variables. In Figure 2.1, for example, A and Y are d-separated controlling for X and F because no paths remain to get from A to Y; but controlling only for X does not result in d-separation because the path $A - F - Y$ remains a permissible path from A to Y. Less obvious, d-separation of two variables can be thwarted by controlling for their mutual causal descendent(s), for example, controlling for a collider directly descended from them. Indeed, observing a common consequence of two causes can produce a relationship between those causes even if they originally were independent. Controlling for the descendant of just one of the two variables, however, will not induce that relationship.

The logic of d-separation generates empirically testable hypotheses about the conditional independencies that would have to hold between any two variables of interest (sometimes called *focal* variables). Two variables that are d-separated in a DAG should have a zero partial correlation when controlling for the covariates that block all paths between the two variables—in the previous example, the partial correlation between X and Y controlling for A. The researcher can use the logic of *d*-separation to identify, before gathering data, a set of empirically testable hypotheses that are implied by the model and, when data are gathered, apply those test to validate or refute the model. Once tested, PCM decides whether the causal assumptions embedded in the model are sufficient to yield an unbiased causal claim. Calling this the identification phase, Pearl (2010a) has said that it "is the most neglected step in current practice of quantitative analysis" (p. 108). So using the logic of d-separation is itself independent of any empirical test.[1]

In addition to identifying the testable implications of a given causal structure, PCM can also tell which variables in this DAG must be observed and included in the analysis to estimate a causal relationship between any two variables, say, X and Y. This can be done in PCM in three nonexhaustive ways. The first is to find a set of observed covariates that block (i.e., *d*-separate) all *back-door paths* from X to Y, that is, a

[1]The next four paragraphs delve into technical details about d-separation and may be skipped by readers with no interest in those details.

path from X to Y that includes a directed edge pointing directly at X from an ancestor of X. In Figure 2.1, the paths $X - A - F - Y$ and $X - B - A - F - Y$ are back-door paths. The directed edge from X to Y is not a back-door path because it contains no directed edge pointing to X. One can identify a causal effect from X to Y by conditioning on observed variables that block each back-door path, in cases in which conditioning is done using standard control methods as stratification, matching, or regression with those variables. Conditioning on such variables in the graph is equivalent to satisfying the requirement of "strong ignorability" in the RCM (Pearl, 2009a, pp. 341–344).

Pearl (2000, 2009a) defined a variable or set of variables Z to block a back-door path if

1. the back-door path includes a mediational path from X to Y ($X \rightarrow C \rightarrow Y$), where C is in Z, or
2. the back-door path includes a *fork of mutual dependence* ($X \leftarrow C \rightarrow Y$), that is, where C causes X and Y, and C is in Z, or
3. the back-door path includes an *inverted fork of mutual causation* ($X \rightarrow C \leftarrow Y$), where X and Y both cause C, and neither C nor its descendents are in Z.

The latter requirement means that Z cannot include a collider that happens to be on the back-door path unless Z also blocks the pathways to that collider. According to these requirements, the back-door paths from X to Y are blocked by conditioning on variables F or B A. Stratifying on A alone would not do because the backdoor path $X - B - A - F - Y$ will remain unblocked.

The second strategy is to use an instrumental variable for X to estimate the effect of X on Y. In Figure 2.1, C is an instrument because it has no effect on Y except by its effect on X. Economists frequently use this approach, and it assumes the effect of C on X and X on Y are both linear. The latter assumption holds if C and X are dichotomous (e.g., a treatment dummy variable) and Y is at least interval-scaled, both of which often hold in many observational studies. The estimate of the causal effect of X on Y is then the ratio of the effect of C on Y and X on Y. A problem would occur, however, if a directed edge from C to G is introduced into Figure 2.1. This

violates the definition of an instrument by creating a new back-door path from X to Y through C and G. The causal estimate from X to Y, however, still can be obtained by using C as an instrument while at the same time conditioning on G to block the back-door path—which also illustrates that these three strategies for estimating causal effects can be combined.

The third strategy is illustrated in Figure 2.2 where M and N have no parents other than X, and they also mediate the causal relationship between X and Y. The effect of X on Y can be estimated even if variables A and F are unobserved, and the backdoor path $X - A - F - Y$ remains unblocked. One estimates the causal effect of X on M and N, and then of M and N on Y, stratifying on X, and then combining the two estimates to construct the desired effect of X on Y. This can be done because M and N have no parents other than X in this DAG, so the effect of X on Y is completely captured by the mediators M and N.

PCM introduces the mathematical operator called $do(x)$ to help model causal effects and counterfactuals. The operator $do(x)$ mimics in the model what the manipulation of X can do in, say, a randomized experiment—that is, it can remove all paths into X. This operator replaces the random variable X in a DAG with a constant x that is a specific value of X such as x_1 = received treatment or x_0 = did not receive treatment. For instance, if we set X in Figure 2.1 to x_0, Figure 2.3 would result. Now

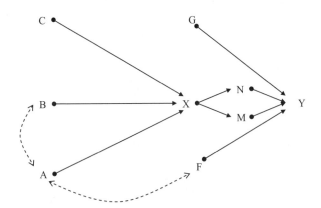

FIGURE 2.2. A DAG with a mediating mechanism that completely accounts for the causal effect of *X on Y*. From *Counterfactuals and Causal Inference* (Figure 1.2), by S. L. Morgan and C. Winship, 2007, Cambridge, England: Cambridge University Press. Copyright 2007 by Cambridge University Press. Adapted with the permission of Cambridge University Press.

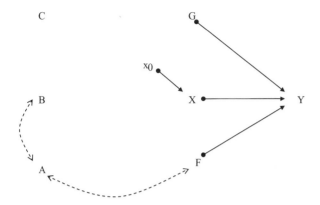

FIGURE 2.3. A DAG figure from Figure 2.1 with a *do(x)* operator.

X is independent of all the variables that previously were its ancestors (A, B, and C), and no back-door paths exist. By comparing how results vary when setting x_1 versus x_0, PCM can emulate the effect of an intervention and express that effect mathematically, in terms of the (known and unknown) distributions that govern the variables in the graph. If that effect can be expressed in terms of observed distributions, the effect is *identifiable,* that is, it can be estimated without bias. Furthermore, the *do(x)* operator in PCM does not require that X be manipulable. It can stand for a manipulable treatment, or a nonmanipulable treatment, such as gender, or the gravitational constant (Pearl, 2010a).

Three other points are implied by the preceding discussion. First, estimating causal effects does not require conditioning on all available variables; in many examples, a subset of these variables will suffice. In the case of an ancestral collider variable, conditioning should not be done. PCM provides rules for knowing which variables are sufficient, given the DAG, and which would be harmful. Second, when more than one of these three strategies can be applied to a given DAG, similar estimates from them may bolster confidence in the estimated effect conditional on the DAG. Third, the creation of a DAG leads to an explanatory model of causation, that is, a more elaborate depiction of the conditions under which, and mechanisms by which, X causes Y. So the DAG facilitates discussions among scientists to refine assumptions and confirm or refute their scientific plausibility. Morgan and Winship (2007), Hayduk et al. (2003), and Pearl (2000,

2009a, 2010a) have extensively elaborated these basic strategies and many other more complex examples.

PCM potentially enables the researcher to do many tasks. We have assumed the researcher is interested in only two focal variables, X and Y in our example; but the researcher may be interested in the causal effects of more than one pair of focal variables. For each pair of focal variables, the back-door paths, descendants, and control variables may differ, so in principle, the task becomes logistically more complex as more pairs of focal variables are of interest. Still, the DAG provides this information succinctly without having to remodel things from scratch when the focus changes. When the data are available, the researcher need not test the entire model at once, as is currently practiced, but rather can focus on the empirical implications of the model, keeping track of which tests are relevant to the target quantity, and which tests are more powerful or costly. A given causal claim might pass all the suggested tests, or some of them, or might not be testable for others. Hayduk et al. (2003) suggested that these tasks eventually will benefit from computer programs to conduct the tests and keep track of the results. Such programs are as yet in their infancy (Pearl, 2000, pp. 50–54; Scheines, Spirtes, Glymour, & Meek, 1994; Shipley, 2000, p. 306).

The most crucial matter in PCM is the creation of the DAG. The results of most of the logic and empirical tests of a DAG, and their implications for causal conclusions, depend on the DAG containing both the correct nodes and the correct set of edges connecting those nodes. These assumptions, in various disguises, must be made in every causal inference exercise, regardless of the approach one takes; hence the importance of making them explicit and transparent. This universal requirement is emphasized in numerous variants in PCM. For instance, in the process of discussing the relationship between PCM and Wright's (1921) work on path analysis, Pearl (2010a) said, "Assuming of course that we are prepared to defend the causal assumptions encoded in the diagram" (p. 87). Still later in the same paper he said, "The lion's share of supporting causal claims falls on the shoulders of untested causal assumptions" (p. 35), and he regretted the current tendency among propensity score analysts to "play down the cautionary note concerning the required admissibility of *S*" (p. 37). PCM asks researchers to do the homework necessary to create a plausible DAG during the design of the data-gathering study, recognizing, first, that this is likely to be a long-term iterative process as the scientific theory bolstering the DAG is developed, tested, and refined, and, second, that this process cannot be avoided regardless if one chooses to encode assumptions in a DAG or in many other alternative notational systems.

ANALYSIS OF THE THREE MODELS

We have now described the basic features of CCM, RCM, and PCM, and we move on to further compare and contrast the three models. Specifically, we address several of the models' core characteristics, including philosophies of causal inference, definitions of effect, theories of cause, external validity, matching, quantification, and emphases on design versus analysis. Finally, the chapter concludes with a discussion of some of the key problems in all these models.

Philosophies of Causal Inference

RCM, CCM, and PCM have casual inference as their central focus. Consistently, however, CCM is more wide-ranging in its conceptual and philosophical scope; whereas RCM and PCM have a more narrow focus but also a more powerful formal statistical model. CCM courses widely through both descriptive and normative epistemological literature (Campbell, 1988; Shadish, Cook, & Leviton, 1991). This includes philosophy of causal inference (Cook & Campbell, 1986); but Campbell's epistemological credentials extend quite diversely into sociology of science, psychology of science, and general philosophy of science. For example, in the sociology of science, Campbell has weighed in on the merits of weak relativism as an approach to knowledge construction; in psychology of science, he discussed the social psychology of tribal leadership in science; and in the philosophy of science, Campbell coined the term *evolutionary epistemology* (Campbell, 1974) and is considered a significant contributor to that philosophical literature. Campbell's extensive

background in various aspects of philosophy of science thus brought an unusual wealth and depth to his discussions of the use of experiments as a way in which to construct knowledge in both science and day-to-day life.

CCM's approach to causation is tied more explicitly to the philosophical literature than RCM or PCM. For example, Cook and Campbell (1979) described their work as "derived from Mill's inductivist canons, a modified version of Popper's falsificationism, and a functionalist analysis of why cause is important in human affairs" (p. 1). CCM explicitly acknowledges the impact on Cook and Campbell's thinking of the work of the philosopher John Stuart Mill on causation. For instance, the idea that identifying a causal relationship requires showing that the cause came before the effect, that the cause covaries with the effect, and that alternative explanations of the relationship between the cause and effect are all implausible relates clearly to Mill's work. The threats to validity that CCM outline reflect these requirements. The threats to internal validity include Mill's first temporal requirement (ambiguous temporal precedence) and the remaining threats (history, maturation, selection, attrition, testing, instrumentation, regression to the mean) are examples of alternative explanations that must be eliminated to establish causation. CCM also acknowledges the influence of Mill's Methods of Experimental Inquiry (White, 2000). Certain design features are direct offshoots of this influence. For instance, CCM thinks about experimental methods not as identifying causes but rather eliminating noncauses (PCM sees this as a key feature of a DAG, as well), it acknowledges the distinct differences between casual inference from observation and casual inference by intervention, and it agrees that experimental inquiry methodology must be tailored to previous scientific knowledge as well as the real-world conditions in which the researcher is operating.

From philosopher Karl Popper (1959), CCM places the idea of falsifying hypotheses in a crucial role. Specifically, the model advises the experimenter to gather data that force causal claims to compete with alternative explanations epitomized by the threats to validity, complementing Mill's idea of eliminating noncauses. Ideally, of course, CCM advocates designing studies that avoid validity threats in the first place; but, if that is not possible, CCM advises researchers to collect data about variables other than the treatment that might have caused the effect. The application of this falsification logic is uneven in practice, but good examples exist (Duckart, 1998; Reynolds & West, 1987). Even with well-designed and executed studies, CCM recognizes that researchers can quite easily create doubts as to whether threats to validity actually exist. For this reason, CCM is skeptical about the results of any one study; instead encouraging research programs in which studies are designed out of various theoretical biases. Perhaps more important, CCM invites criticisms by rivals who do not agree with the causal conclusions and who therefore may be situated in a better position to offer compelling counter explanations for individual study findings.

Lastly, CCM ties the human development of understanding of casual inferences to evolutionary pressures and natural selection. Such processes reward those who could perceive macrolevel causes in their environments (e.g., large predators), and who recognize the value of manipulations, such as starting fires or making weapons in response to such causes (Cook & Campbell, 1979). The general context for scientific casual inference is situated within this framework of the natural human activity of making casual inferences. CCM strongly stresses the influence of social psychological factors on construction of scientific knowledge (Campbell, 1984, 1988). It is a deeply psychological theory of how scientists as human beings make causal inferences, especially in nonrandomized designs. The theory has as much in common with the social psychology of Heider (1958) as with the philosophies of Mill and Popper (Cordray, 1986).

RCM is less intimately tied with the formal philosophical literature. The common reference to RCM as a counterfactual theory of causation (e.g., Dawid, 2000; Holland, 1986; Morgan & Winship, 2007; Winship & Morgan, 1999) is an important exception. A counterfactual is a condition that would occur if an event in the world was different than in reality. Under a counterfactual theory, causal statements are also counterfactual statements because the effect of a cause or treatment is the difference between what actually happened to the person who received the cause (the fact), and what would have happened to that person had they not received the cause (the counterfactual). Lewis (1973) credited the 18th-century Scottish philosopher David Hume with the first clear statement of a counterfactual theory of causation:

> We may define a cause to be *an object followed by another, and where all the objects, similar to the first, are followed by objects similar to the second*. Or, in other words, *where, if the first object had not been, the second never had existed*. (Hume, 1748/1963, Section VII)

The last sentence of Hume's statement is a counterfactual claim, but Hume did not further develop counterfactual causation, focusing instead on a more positivist analysis (Cook & Campbell, 1979). Since this first mention, other philosophers have developed counterfactual theories (Collins, Hall, & Paul, 2004).

Despite the frequent referent to RCM as a counterfactual theory, Rubin (2005) preferred not to characterize it as such. He preferred to conceptualize the theory using a potential outcome language. From this view, all potential outcomes could be observed (in principle) until treatment is assigned. Some can be observed after assignment, but by definition, counterfactuals never can be observed. RCM assumes the possibility of observing any of the potential outcomes. Despite their seemingly contradictory properties, potential outcomes and counterfactuals are not at odds. The RCM potential outcomes analysis is a formal statistical model, not a philosophy of causation like the counterfactual theory. So rather than an opposing theory, RCM is a statistical model of effects that is consistent with a counterfactual philosophy of causation. When potential outcomes are not observed in an experiment, they become counterfactuals.

RCM also has features of falsification, but these features are a much weaker component than in CCM. For example, hidden bias analysis is used to falsify claimed effects by estimating how much bias (resulting from unmeasured variables) would have to be present before the effect's point and confidence interval changed. However, although this provides a change point, it does not tell whether hidden bias actually exists within the study. This can be an important point, as illustrated in a study described by Rosenbaum (1991) that seemed invulnerable to hidden biases. The study caused assignment probabilities ranging from .09 to .91; these probabilities cover almost the full range of possible nonrandom assignments (random assignment into two conditions with equal sample sizes would use a true probability of .50, to put this into context). According to Rosenbaum (1991), later research showed that a larger bias probably existed. In addition to bias assessment, propensity score analysis includes an examination of balance over groups after propensity score adjustment. If the data set is still extremely unbalanced, it is possible that the researcher will conclude that causal inference is not possible without heroic assumptions. This is a falsification of the claim that a causal inference can be tested well in the specific quasi-experiment. But these are minor emphases on falsification as compared with CCM, which is centrally built around the concept.

Although on the surface the philosophical differences between CCM and RCM appear quite numerous, practically no real disagreement results. For example, both models emphasize the necessity of manipulable experimental causes and advise against easy acceptance of proposed casual inference because of the fallibility of human judgment. It also is possible that they would agree on topics CCM addresses but RCM fails to mention. For instance, Cook and Campbell (1979) ended their discussion of causation with eight claims, such as "the effects in molar causal laws can be the results of multiple causes" (p. 33), and "dependable intermediate mediational units are involved in most strong molar laws" (p. 35). Although the specific statistical emphasis of RCM is not likely to have generated those claims, it is also unlikely that the model would disagree with any of them. Conversely, RCM philosophical writings are not extensive enough to generate true discord between the models.

The methodological machinery of PCM makes little explicit reference to philosophies of causation, but closer inspection shows both knowledge and use of them. The epilogue of Pearl (2000), for example, briefly reviewed the history of philosophy of causation, including Aristotle, David Hume, Bertrand Russell, and Patrick Suppes. Similarly, PCM acknowledges specific intellectual debts to Hume's framing of the problem of extracting causal inferences from experience (in the form of data) and to philosophical thinking on probabilistic causation (e.g., Eells, 1991). The most commonly cited philosophers in his book come mostly from the latter tradition or ones related to it, including not only Ellery Eels and Patrick Suppes but also Nancy Cartwright and Clark Glymour.

Where PCM differs most significantly from CCM and RCM is in its much greater emphasis on explanatory causation (the causal model within which X and Y are embedded) than descriptive causation (did X cause Y?). This is not to say PCM is uninterested in the latter; clearly, all the rules for d-separation and $do(x)$ operators are aimed substantially at estimating that descriptive causal relationship. Rather, it is that the mechanism PCM uses to get to that goal is quite different from RCM or CCM. The latter idealize the randomized experiment as the method to be emulated given its obvious strength in estimating the direct effect of X on Y. PCM gives no special place to that experiment. Rather, PCM focuses on developing a sufficiently complete causal model (DAG) with valid causal assumptions (about what edges are not in the model, in particular). In some senses, this is a more ambitious goal than in RCM or CCM, for it requires more scientific knowledge about all the variables and edges that must be (or not be) in the model. At its best, this kind of model helps to explain the observed descriptive causal relationship. Those explanations, in turn, provide a basis for more general causal claims, for they ideally can specify the necessary and sufficient conditions required for replicating that descriptive causal relationship in other conditions.

Possibly the most important difference in the philosophies of these three models is the greater stress on human (and therefore scientific) fallibility in CCM. Paradoxically, CCM is skeptical about the possibility of performing tasks it sometimes requires to generate good causal inferences. Humans are poor at making many kinds of causal judgments, prone to confirmation biases, blind to apparent falsifications, and lazy about both design and identifying alternative explanations. Yet when CCM's first line of defense, strong methodology and study design, either fails or is not practical to use, the next plan of attack often relies strongly on the above judgments to identify threats. Fallible human judgment is used to assess whether the identified threats have been rendered moot or implausible. This approach is especially true in weaker nonrandomized experiments. Because of the weight placed on human judgment, CCM argues that the responsibility to be critical lies within the community of scholars rather than with any one researcher, especially a community whose interests would lead them to find fault (Cook, 1985). As technology advances, tools such as propensity score analysis or DAGs sometimes can make it possible to substitute more objective measures or corrections for the fallible judgments.

Neither RCM nor PCM share the sweeping sense of fallibility in CCM. Yet they are self-critical in a different way. They focus less on the sense of fallibilism inherent in scientific work (as all scientists are also humans) and more on continually clarifying assumptions and searching for tests of assumptions. This results in many technical advances that reduce the reliance that CCM has on human judgment. For example, RCM emphasizes the importance of making and testing assumptions about whether a data set can support a credible propensity score analysis. PCM stresses the importance of careful and constant attention to the plausibility of a causal model. As of yet, however, the suggestions of PCM and RCM address only a fraction of the qualitative judgments made in CCM's wide-ranging scope.

Ironically, these senses of fallibilism are perhaps the hardest features of all three models to transfer from theory into general practice. Many are the researchers who proudly proclaimed the use of a quasi-experimental design that Campbell would have found wanting. Many are the researchers who use propensity score analysis with little attention to the plausibility of assumptions like strong ignorability. And many more may cite PCM as justification

for causal inferences without the caveats about the plausibility of the model. As Campbell (1994) once said, "My methodological recommendations have been over-cited and under-followed" (p. 295).

Definition of Effect

One of RCM's defining strengths is its explicit conceptual definition of an effect. In comparison, CCM never had an explicit definition of effect on a conceptual level until it adopted RCM's (Shadish et al., 2002). This is quite a substantial lapse given the centrality of finding the effects of causes within CCM. Implicitly, CCM defined effect using the counterfactual theory that RCM eschews in favor of the potential outcomes definition. The implicit definition governing CCM is most clearly outlined in Campbell's (1975) article "Degrees of Freedom and the Case Study," in which he addressed causal inference within a one-group pretest–posttest design. He supported using this type of design to infer effects only when substantial prior knowledge exists about how the outcome variable acts in the absence of the intervention, or in other words, with confident knowledge of the counterfactual.

Other than this example, however, CCM has treated effects as differences between two facts rather than two potential outcomes. For example, instead of thinking of it as the difference between what happened and what could have happened within one unit, CCM conceptualizes effects as what happened to the treatment group when compared with what happened to the control group, or what happened before treatment versus what happened posttreatment. This is not so much a conceptual definition of what effects are or should be in general as it is a computation to find observed differences. The computation worked reliably only in randomized experiments, and with other designs, it was considered valid only to the extent that the researcher was confident the quasi-experiment ruled out plausible alternative explanations, as randomized experiments can. In both models, then, the randomized experiment is upheld as the gold standard in design. RCM does so by building propensity score logic for nonrandomized studies on the basis of what is known about "regular" designs (Rubin, 2004), and CCM does so by acknowledging, as Campbell (1986) noted, that "backhandedly, threats to internal validity were, initially and implicitly, those for which random assignment did control" (p. 68). CCM reaches the correct counterfactual only if those threats are implausible, and in this sense, threats to internal validity are counterfactuals. They are things that might possibly have happened if the treatment units had not received treatment. They are not all possible counterfactuals, however, as neither model has any way of fully knowing all possible counterfactuals.

Despite the fact that CCM has now incorporated RCM's definition of effect into its model, this is probably not enough. For example, CCM discusses why random assignment works (Shadish et al., 2002, Chapter 8), utilizing several explanations that are all partly true, but all of which might be better presented in the context of the potential outcomes model. Hypothetically then, CCM could present RCM's potential outcomes model, and then easily transition into how randomized experiments are a practical way in which to estimate the average causal effects that the model introduces on a conceptual level. Rubin (2005) has done the work for randomized experiments, and he and others have done the same for many nonrandomized experiments (e.g., Angrist & Lavy, 1999; Hahn, Todd, & Vand er Klaauw, 2001; Morgan & Winship, 2007; Rubin, 2004; Winship & Morgan, 1999).

PCM's definition of effect relies on solving a set of equations representing a DAG to estimate the effect of $X = x$ on Y, or more technically, to "the space of probability distributions on Y" (Pearl, 2000, p. 70), using the $do(x)$ operator. Practically, this calculation most likely would be expressed as a regression coefficient, for example, from a SEM. This approach is more similar to how CCM would measure an effect than to RCM's definition of an effect. Yet PCM points out that it also can estimate a causal effect defined as the difference in the effect between the model where $X = x_0$ and $X = x_1$. The latter is neither a potential outcome nor a counterfactual definition of effect in RCM's sense because it is made on the basis of the difference between two estimates, whereas counterfactuals and potential outcomes cannot always be observed.

Most of CCM's approach to estimating effects could otherwise adopt the DAGs and associated

logic as a way of picturing effect estimation in their wide array of experimental and quasi-experimental designs. Probably the same is true of RCM. What most likely prevents such adoption is skepticism about two things. First, both RCM and CCM prefer design solutions to statistical solutions, although all three causal models use both. Second, both RCM and CCM have little confidence that those who do cause-probing studies in field settings can create an accurate DAG given the seemingly intractable nature of unknown selection biases. In their discussion of SEM, for example, Shadish et al. (2002) repeatedly stress the vulnerability of these models to misspecification. This remains one of the most salient differences between PCM on the one hand and RCM and CCM on the other.

Theory of Cause

Of the three approaches, CCM has paid far more attention to a theory of cause than either RCM or PCM. This may occur for different reasons in PCM versus RCM. In the case of RCM, its focus on estimating effects in field settings requires practically no attention to the nature of causes: "The definition of 'cause' is complex and challenging, but for empirical research, the idea of a causal effect of an agent or treatment seems more straightforward or practically useful" (Little & Rubin, 2000, p. 122). In the case of PCM, its origins in mathematics, computer science, and graph theory may have given it a context in which causes were more often symbols or hypothetical examples than the kinds of complex social, educational, medical, or economic interventions in the real world that motivated RCM and CCM. If experiments really are about discovering the effects of manipulations, and if one's theory of causal inference is limited to experimental demonstrations that measure the effect, then this rudimentary definition of cause is possibly all that is needed. Even if it is not necessary, a more developed theory of cause still can be quite useful in understanding results.

The only knowledge we have about cause in an experiment often may be the actions the researcher took to manipulate the treatment. This is quite partial knowledge. CCM aspires to more, which is reflected specifically in the development of construct validity for the cause. For example, Campbell

(1957) stated that participant reactivity to the experimental manipulation is a part of the treatment; and he emphasized that experimental treatments are not single units of intervention, but rather multidimensional packages consisting of many components: "The actual *X* in any one experiment is a specific combination of stimuli, all confounded for interpretive purposes, and only some relevant to the experimenter's intent and theory" (p. 309). Cook and Campbell (1979) elaborated a construct validity of causes. Later work in CCM adopted Mackie's (1974) conception of cause as a constellation of features, of which researchers often focus on only one, despite the fact that all of the causes may be necessary to produce an effect (Cook & Campbell, 1986; Shadish et al., 2002). Furthermore, CCM stresses the necessity of programs of research to identify the nature and defining characteristics of a cause, using many studies investigating the same question, but with slight variations on the features of the causal package. This method will reveal some features that are crucial to the effectiveness of the causal package, whereas others will prove irrelevant.

To some extent, Campbell's interest in the nature of cause is a result of the context in which he worked: social psychology. Experiments in social psychology place high importance on knowing about cause in great detail because pervasive arguments often occur about whether an experimental intervention actually reflects the construct of interest from social psychology theory. By contrast, the highly abstract nature of PCM has not required great attention to understanding the cause; and applied experiments of the kind most common to RCM tend to be less theoretically driven than experiments in social psychology. But even those applied experiments could benefit from at least some theory of cause. For example, in the late 1990s, a team of researchers in Boston headed by the late Judah Folkman reported that a new drug called endostatin shrank tumors by limiting their blood supply (Folkman, 1996). Other respected researchers could not replicate the effect even when using drugs shipped to them from Folkman's lab. Scientists eventually replicated the results after they traveled to Folkman's lab to learn how to properly manufacture, transport, store, and handle the drug and how to inject it in the right location at

the right depth and angle. An observer called these contingencies the "in-our-hands" phenomenon, saying, "Even we don't know which details are important, so it might take you some time to work it out" (Rowe, 1999, p. 732). The effects of endostatin required it to be embedded in a set of conditions that were not even fully understood by the original investigators and still may not be understood in the 21st century (Pollack, 2008).

Another situation in which a theory of cause is a useful tool is when considering the status of causes that are not manipulable. Both CCM and RCM agree that nonmanipulable agents cannot be causes within an experiment. CCM and PCM both entertain hypotheses about nonmanipulable causes, for instance, of genetics in phenylketonuria (PKU), despite the fact that the pertinent genes cannot be manipulated (Shadish et al., 2002). RCM is less clear on whether it would entertain the same ideas. This leads to debates within the field about the implications of manipulability for RCM and, more broadly, for the field of causal inference (Berk, 2004; Holland, 1986; Reskin, 2003; Woodward, 2003). Morgan and Winship (2007) made two points about this. First, it may be that RCM might not apply to causes that are not capable of being manipulated, because it is impossible to calculate an individual causal effect when the probability of a person being assigned to a condition is zero. Second, the counterfactual framework built into RCM encourages thinking about nonmanipulable causes to clarify the nature of the specific causal question being asked to specify the circumstances that have to be considered when defining what the counterfactual might have been. This is more complicated and ambiguous when dealing with nonmanipulable causes. For example, is the counterfactual for a person with PKU a person who is identical in every aspect except for the presence of the genetic defect from the moment it first appeared? Or, does it include a person with every other result that the genetic defect could result in, such as the diet commonly used to treat PKU? PCM and CCM would consider all versions of these questions to be valid. PCM, for example, might devise multiple DAGs to represent each of the pertinent scenarios, estimating the causal effect for each.

So CCM has a more functionally developed theory of cause than either PCM or RCM. This probably speaks again to the different goals the models have. CCM aspires to a generalized casual theory, one that covers most aspects (such as general cause theory) of the many kinds of inferences a researcher might make from various types of cause-probing studies. RCM has a much more narrow purpose: to define an effect clearly and precisely to better measure the effect in a single experiment. PCM has a different narrow purpose: to state the conditions under which a given DAG can support a causal inference, no matter what the cause. None of the three theories can function well without a theory of the effect; and all three could do without much theory of cause if effect estimation were the only issue. But this is not the case.

Causal Generalizations: External and Construct Validity

CCM pays great attention to generalizability in the form of construct and external validity. Originally (e.g., Campbell, 1957; Campbell & Stanley, 1966), CCM merely identifies these concepts of generalization as important ("the desideratum"; Campbell & Stanley, 1966, p. 5), with little methodology developed for studying generalization except the multi-trait–multimethod matrix for studying construct validity (Campbell & Fiske, 1959). Cook and Campbell (1979) extended the theory of construct validity of both the treatment and the outcome, and identified possible alternatives to random sampling that could be used to generalize findings from experiments. Cook (1990, 1991) developed both theory and methodology for studying the mechanisms of generalization, laying the foundation for what became three chapters on the topic in Shadish et al. (2002; Cook, 2004). Over the course of the 50 years this work spans, the theory and methodology have become more developed. For example, meta-analytic techniques now play a key role in analyzing how effects vary over different persons, locations, treatments, and outcomes across multiple studies. Another important technique is identifying and modeling casual explanations that mediate between a cause and an effect; as such, explanations contextualize knowledge in a way that makes labeling and transferring the effect across conditions easier.

RCM has made contributions to meta-analysis and meditational modeling, both conceptual (e.g., Rubin, 1990, 1992) and statistical (e.g., Frangakis & Rubin, 2002; Rosnow, Rosenthal, & Rubin, 2000), but the model rarely overtly ties these methods to the generalization of causes. One notable exception is Rubin's (1990, 1992) work on response surface modeling in meta-analysis. This work builds from the premise that a literature may not contain many or any studies that precisely match the meta-analyst's methodological or substantive question of interest. Rubin's approach to this problem is to use the available data from literature to project results to an ideal study that may not exist in literature but that would provide the test desired in a perfect world. This is a crucial form of external validity generalization; however, it has been little developed either statistically (Vanhonacker, 1996) or in application (Shadish, Matt, Navarro, & Phillips, 2000; Stanley & Jarrell, 1998).

PCM has little to say explicitly about generalizations of any sort. To the extent that CCM is correct in its claim that causal explanation is a key facilitator of causal generalization, the DAGs in PCM are useful tools for the task if they are used to generate and test such explanations. An example might be the use of DAG technology to generate and test explanatory models of, say, causal mediation within randomized experiments. In addition, researchers who have a DAG and a data set against which to compare it can manipulate the operationalizations of the DAG to test various hypotheses that might bear on some generalizations. The logic would be similar to that of the $do(x)$ operator, in which case the researcher fixes some variable to the value dictated by the desired generalization, for example, limiting the gender variable first to males and second to females, to test whether a treatment effect varies by gender.

Neither RCM nor CCM have been overly successful in translating their respective ideas and theory concerning causal generalizations into practical applications. This lack of success might be the result of the emphasis that is put on internal validity throughout applied scientific thinking and funding. An exception to this general rule is again meta-analysis, which has seen increased use and funding over the years. The increase in meta-analysis cannot be directly credited to RCM or CCM, however. Rather, the increase seems to be focused on getting better effect size estimates instead of the more generalization-relevant exploration of how effects vary over person, treatment, or other study characteristics. In fact, a perusal of thousands of systematic reviews in the Cochrane Collaboration Library confirms that many meta-analyses include few or no tests of moderators that could be used for the latter aim, and these reviews report only the overall effect size for the intervention. The assumption among applied researchers seems to be that knowledge about causal generalization emerges fairly organically from programs of research and occasional reviews of them. Researchers appear to feel little need for active guidance on the topic.

By contrast, the kinds of explanatory models that PCM encourages are, in many respects, the heart of basic scientific theory. Scientists pursue those theories in multiple ways, from programs of research that explore moderators and mediators one at a time experimentally, to meditational models consistent with PCM. The main question would be whether the particular methods that PCM recommends are perceived by that community as having sufficiently novel and useful suggestions to warrant the effort to adopt them. The jury is still out on that question, perhaps not surprising given that PCM is the newest of the three theories.

Quantification

Both PCM and RCM are much more thorough and successful in quantification than CCM. After all, Rubin is a statistician and Pearl is a computer scientist with an appointment in statistics. RCM has generated the highly quantitative potential outcomes model, pays careful attention to statistical assumptions, and has created statistical tools to improve effect estimation such as propensity scores and hidden bias analysis as well as other methodological developments, such as the use of instrumental variable analyses in the presence of partial treatment implementation (Angrist et al., 1996). PCM has generated a theory of causal modeling with roots in mathematics, graph theory, and statistics, a theory that aspires to be the most general integration of the available quantitative approaches to causal inference.

On the surface, it may not appear that CCM is quantitative given its more broad theoretical focus, but this is a bit deceiving. Few of the many students coming out of the tradition were quantitative (Brewer & Collins, 1981; Campbell, 1988), but notable exceptions have included Reichardt and Gollob (1986) and Trochim and Cappelleri (1992). Although Campbell himself was not a statistician, he successfully collaborated with the statisticians of his day for much of his work on specific methodology, such as regression discontinuity design (Cook, 2007) and the multitrait–multimethod matrix (Boruch & Wolins, 1970). The multitrait–multimethod matrix is not really a part of CCM, but regression discontinuity designs certainly are, and both lines of research are still pursued in the 21st century. In addition, CCM has attracted the attention of both statisticians and economists (Meyer, 1995; Meyer, Viscusi, & Durbin, 1995), although that attention often is critical (e.g., Cronbach, 1982; Rogosa, 1980).

Perhaps it is a more accurate assessment to say that CCM is quantitative on issues on the periphery of the CCM tradition. That is, CCM has given little attention to how to quantify matters that concern its validity typology, threats to validity, or how design features can be used to reduce the plausibility of threats. Fortunately, the omission of statistical applications within the theoretical framework is at least partially remediable. For example, much work has been done to quantify the effects of attrition on bias in randomized experiments, both within and outside of the CCM tradition (e.g., Deluccchi, 1994; Shadish, Hu, Glaser, Kownacki, & Wong, 1998; Shih & Quan, 1997; Verbeke & Molenberghs, 2000; Yeaton, Wortman, & Langberg, 1983). In addition, some work exists that quantifies the effects of testing threats to internal validity and outlines specific ways in which CCM could be more quantitative (Braver & Braver, 1988; Reichardt, 2000; Reichardt & Gollob, 1987; Solomon, 1949). Other research has been done to quantify CCM and join analysis to design, including the work by Winship and Morgan (1999) and Haviland, Nagin, and Rosenbaum (2007), which uses multiple pretests to improve inferences in nonrandomized designs. Clearly, CCM needs to begin to incorporate these developments more explicitly.

Quantification of CCM can only go so far because many issues concerning causation are more qualitative than quantitative. For example, one threat to internal validity is history, that is, an event not part of treatment occurred at the same time as treatment and was actually responsible for part or all of the observed effect. Another is the threat of instrumentation, for instance, a change in the instrument used to assess outcome across data points in a time-series design (Neustrom & Norton, 1993). It is difficult to see how to include a covariate in a propensity score analysis that detects or adjusts for such threats, or to build those variables into a DAG. In addition, DAGS and propensity scores do little to assess threats to construct or external validity, and they are not designed to detect cases in which the qualitative and quantitative inferences differ, as when quantitative analysis suggests a treatment is effective, but an ethnographer identifies serious problems with it (Reichardt & Cook, 1979). It is possible that the qualitative features of CCM eventually might be quantifiable in a grand statistical theory of causal inference. The breadth that this would necessarily cover makes it implausible that this will be developed in the near future. For this reason, the heavy focus of RCM and PCM on quantification necessitates that only a small subsection of casual theory is covered in these models. The parts that have been successfully quantified are the pieces connected most closely to the measurements of effects. These contributions are important but not sufficient on their own to assist the cause-probing researcher in all the pertinent tasks.

Design and Analysis

Both RCM and especially CCM have a preference for strong designs, in particular randomized experiments, whenever possible. Except for matching designs, however, RCM focuses on analysis, and CCM focuses more on design. The best example of this difference is regression discontinuity design. Thistlethwaite and Campbell (1960) invented the design, but a statistical proof of the design was not published until Rubin (1977; an earlier unpublished proof was provided by Goldberger, 1972). Similarly, when time series are discussed in the RCM tradition (e.g., Winship & Morgan, 1999), such work focuses entirely on analysis, whereas Campbell's treatment of the subject is much more design oriented. For example, CCM discusses such variations as adding a control group or nonequivalent dependent variable and using repeated and removed treatments, negative treatments, or staggered implementation across locations, which are aimed at increasing the confidence about any of the conclusions drawn about effects.

In most cases, these divergent emphases are quite complementary. CCM is strong on design and broad conceptual issues, but it lacks analytic sophistication as well as practical tools that move conclusions about confidence in effects from the qualitative to the quantitative realm when using a nonrandomized design. Conversely, RCM is strong on analysis, but some researchers utilize the statistical procedures without implementing careful design first, as both models would advocate. Yet the strengths of both models are essential: Good design makes for better analytic results, and better analyses can improve a potentially lower yield from a weak design. Examples of this are evident in the field; for instance, it is clear that tools like propensity scores can be used to remedy the reliance of CCM on qualitative judgments by scientists who often are not good at identifying and ruling out alternative casual explanations. Caution is necessary to implement the tools that RCM makes available, however. It can be tempting for scientists to take the lazy way out of difficult design issues and run less well-designed studies, hoping that the analytic tools can be used to fix bungled design.

RCM, like most statistical approaches to causation, appears to value design most when it contributes to a quantitative result (e.g., an effect size, confidence interval, or significance test). CCM expands on this approach and models how to use information even if it is only possible to do so in a qualitative fashion. For example, propensity score adjustment is an excellent tool to deal with a subset of threats to internal validity, namely, the selection threat and perhaps also maturation and regression, as special forms of selection bias. In this instance, the quantitative adjustment may be used to improve inferences about treatment effects. However, propensity score analysis does not address the internal validity threats of history, testing, or instrumentation, despite the fact that all of these can produce a spurious effect. CCM accounts for this qualitatively and thus raises these concerns in a way that RCM does not. It would be best to have a way to quantify these concerns as well, but as of yet, neither CCM nor RCM has done so.

One noticeable exception to RCM's general preference for analysis exists in the method of matching. Both CCM and RCM have considered the method of matching carefully, as it is frequently used as a seemingly plausible method for creating comparable groups when random assignment is not feasible. Until recently, CCM has maintained a generally skeptical stance toward matching in nonrandomized experiments, as evidenced in such comments as "the two groups have an inevitable systematic difference on the factors determining the choice involved, a difference which no amount of matching can remove" (Campbell, 1957, p. 300). The best-developed early study of this issue in CCM is that of Campbell and Erlebacher (1970), who analyzed the pernicious effects of matching on effect estimation in a study by Cicirelli and Associates (1969) concerning the effectiveness of the early Head Start program. The latter group of researchers presented startling results: that a matched group of children who did not receive the intervention performed better than the Head Start children. In response, Campbell and Erlebacher (1970) showed how the results actually could be due to a combination of selection bias on the true underlying variables and measurement unreliability. These problems together could have caused the groups to regress in opposite directions, thereby creating an inflated and invalid negative estimate of the treatment effect. This latter interpretation was supported by a reanalysis of the original data (Magidson, 1977). This event firmly embedded a general skepticism toward matching within the CCM tradition. More recently, however, CCM has relaxed the overarching skepticism and supported the use of matching on variables that are stable and reliable, such as achievement scores, aggregated to the school level and across years of pretest data (e.g., Millsap et al., 2000), and well-developed propensity scores.

Through the development of propensity scores, RCM has revived matching along with similar designs, such as stratification (Rubin, 2006). Because propensity scores are created by combining several covariates, they are more likely to be more stable and more reliable than the individual variables of which they consist. In this way, their use converges with the instances laid out by CCM in which matching is acceptable practice. The kinds of stable matching variables CCM originally endorsed were fairly uncommon, however, whereas propensity scores are more easily available. In addition, matching across propensity scores has clearer theoretical rationales for creating better estimates of effect. Despite this, in practice, results as to whether propensity scores actually do create better estimates seem to be mixed (Dehejia & Wahba, 1999; Glazerman, Levy, & Myers, 2003). Studies addressing this question with arguably better methodology, however, appear to be more optimistic (Luellen, Shadish, & Clark, 2005; Shadish, Clark, & Steiner, 2008; Shadish, Luellen, & Clark, 2006). Even in this latter group, however, propensity scores appear to be quite sensitive to how missing data in the covariates (that make up the score) are handled, quality of pretest covariate measurement might be more important than the specific statistics used to generate propensity scores, and research so far does not show a strong advantage of propensity scores over ordinary regression in reducing bias (e.g., Cook, Steiner & Pohl, 2009; Steiner, Cook, & Shadish, in press; Steiner, Cook, Shadish, & Clark, in press). Clearly, however, much more work needs to be done to identify the conditions under which one can be fairly confident that matching consistently reduces, rather than increases, bias.

Designs like randomized or nonrandomized experiments receive little attention in PCM, so it is difficult to know where PCM fits into this discussion. Nowhere in PCM does one find the granting of any special status to randomized experiments in estimating effects, although one might deduce from its discussion of the analogy between a *do*(*x*) operator and the physical operation of random assignment that PCM acknowledges the advantages of randomization for making causal estimation in a DAG easier to do. Discussions of randomized experiments in PCM tend to characterize them as a restricted paradigm because causal questions are much broader than can be addressed by a randomized experiment.

Most of the prose in PCM is aimed at analysis, or at the conceptual work that goes into creating a DAG and a defensible causal claim before the analysis. That conceptual work might be considered a form of design in the same way that RCM considers attention to balancing tests before estimating effects to be a form of design. That is, both should occur without knowledge of the outcome analysis and should aim to set up the conditions to be met before a valid analysis of effects should occur. This is a much weaker form of design than present in CCM. Yet as a general conceptual structure, PCM can be adapted to any design and to the use of propensity score analysis and matching.

PCM has less enthusiasm for the kind of empirical comparisons of randomized to adjusted nonrandomized experiments that RCM and CCM have used to test, for example, whether propensity score adjustments in nonrandomized experiments yield the same answer as a parallel randomized experiment. Pearl (2010a) has noted that such tests provide no logical or mathematical proof of the similarity of the two methods and depend greatly on the particular context (setting, intervention, units, outcome measures, and perhaps even time) in which the study was run. Not surprisingly, then, we are aware of no empirical comparisons of effect estimates from randomized experiments versus an analysis based in PCM.

DISCUSSION

Discussing the relative merits of CCM, RCM, and PCM is made more difficult by substantial differences in terminology across the three theories. For example, imagine that CCM wishes to assess whether PCM or RCM give the same priority to internal validity that CCM does. Neither PCM nor RCM much mention that phrase, nor any of the other validity types and pertinent threats. Similarly, RCM's SUTVA is obtuse to many readers (Rubin, 2010; Shadish, 2010), with authors sometimes combining discussions of SUTVA with discussions of CCM's validity types in ways that perhaps neither RCM nor CCM would recognize or endorse (e.g.,

Dawid, 2000, p. 414; Oakes, 2004, p. 1943). And PCM has adopted a different language for talking about causation, so that the familiar terms in path analysis or structural equation modeling as used in CCM or RCM need translation into PCM terms that are not always cognates—a directed edge is not the same thing as a path, and not all structural equation models are directed acyclic graphs. These are, then, different models for approaching causation, and it is doubtful that any scholar has a sufficient grasp of all three to compare and evaluate them with full accuracy. In the present case, we are far more familiar with CCM than the other two models, and we are especially new to PCM. Still, the effort must be made to advance the interdisciplinary theory of causation that seems to be emerging in the past few decades.

One start to the comparison is to speculate about the key problems in each of the three models. Although the next three paragraphs will describe the problems in terms unique to each model, we will conclude that the problems all have a similar root—they are all limited in one way or another by the state of knowledge about the key variables and the relationships among them. Starting with CCM, its concepts yield the broadest approach to causation of the three models. In particular, the attention to issues of construct and external validity are unmatched in the other two theories. Its key problem is its general lack of quantification, a point made by Rosenbaum (1999) in response to Shadish and Cook's (1999) early effort to compare parts of CCM to RCM. Threats to validity are central to CCM, for instance, yet CCM does not offer compelling quantitative ways to show how those threats affect an inference. Attrition is a good example, in part because it is a threat for which some quantitative work has been done (e.g., Deluccchi, 1994; Shadish et al., 1998; Shih & Quan, 1997; Verbeke & Molenberghs, 2000; Yeaton et al., 1983). Measuring attrition is simple; but CCM has no canonical method for showing what attrition rates result in a more or less accurate descriptive causal inference in a given study. Especially as applied in practice, many researchers simply note the amount of attrition that is present, and if it exceeds a subjectively formulated percentage, they allow that attrition may be a problem. Lack of quantification is to some degree inevitable in CCM given the breadth of its concepts, but it also results from a failure of many researchers within the CCM tradition even to try to generate such answers.

With RCM, two key problems emerge. One is the pivotal role of the strong ignorability assumption, an assumption that so far cannot be tested within RCM yet that is absolutely central to the success of the methods that RCM suggests for observational studies. We have made only small steps in understanding how to select pretest covariates that might meet this condition (e.g., Cook et al., 2009; Steiner, Cook, & Shadish, in press; Steiner, Cook, Shadish, & Clark, in press). PCM asserts that it has completely solved this problem in theory, to the maximum extent allowed by available scientific knowledge, yet the available knowledge in many practical endeavors is so scant that we are skeptical whether one can take full advantage of this solution. The second problem is its failure, at least until recently, to give sufficient attention to the design of good observational studies. Most of the early examples that RCM gave relied on observational data sets that already has been gathered by other researchers for other purposes, with RCM doing a secondary analysis to try to improve the accuracy of the effect estimate. Only in the past few years has RCM begun to write about the importance of good prospective design of observational studies: both the use of better design elements like carefully selected control groups, and the deliberate development of measures of the selection process through such means as interviewing participants and providers to discover and accurately describe those processes (Rubin, 2007, 2008).

Two key problems also emerge with PCM. The first is the necessity in PCM of knowing that the DAG is correct, for otherwise the results of the logical and empirical tests in PCM may be incorrect. A mature research topic sometimes may be confident of the key variables and the relationships among them, especially if the problem is investigated in a closed system with a limited number of variables known to be relevant. Some parts of cognitive science might approximate these conditions, for example. The applied causal questions of most interest to RCM and CCM, however, almost certainly do not do so. As a corollary, then, PCM's approach to strong

ignorability also relies on correct specification of the DAG, with the same implications of an incorrect DAG for the accuracy of the test. The second problem is the paucity of examples of practical applications of PCM. This may in part be what Imbens (2010) referred to when he said,

> My personal view is that the proponents of the graphical approach . . . have not demonstrated convincingly to economists that adopting (part) of their framework offers sufficient benefits relative to the framework currently used by economists. (p. 47)

Morgan and Winship (2007) have provided some examples, but their book so thoroughly mixes RCM and PCM that the benefits specific to PCM are not necessarily transparent. Indirect evidence of the potential usefulness of PCM is the fact that many economists and social scientists use structural equation models that are closely related to DAGs, despite lingering difficulties in interpreting their causal content (difficulties that PCM claims to have eliminated).

One common theme across the problems in all three theories is that despite the different ways that each theory has approached causal inference, in observational studies, one must make assumptions of some sort to make progress. With CCM, it is the assumption that the researcher has ruled out threats to validity (alternative explanations for the effect); with RCM, it is the assumption that strong ignorability holds; and, with PCM, it is the assumption that the DAG is correct. In all three, of course, one can use data or logic or experience to probe the validity of these assumptions, measuring some of the threats to see whether they remain plausible, showing that one obtains balance with propensity scores, or showing that the DAG is consistent with the observed data or past research. But these are profoundly fallible probes, they only test parts of the relevant assumptions or are only weakly related to the assumption, and they are incapable in principle of proving the assumptions are valid. With observational studies, we have no free lunch, no royal road to valid effect estimation.

PCM claims to offer some visibility from this treacherous road. For example, it claims that a recent proof of the completeness of the "*do*-calculus" (Shpitser & Pearl, 2008) implies that no method can do better than PCM, given the same uncertainty about the science underlying a problem. For PCM, Halpern's (1998) proof that RCM and PCM are logically equivalent, differing merely in emphasis and convenience, further implies that an informative comparison between the two should examine separately each phase of the inference process (as was done in Pearl, 2010b). PCM aims to demonstrate the benefit of a hybrid strategy whereby scientific knowledge is articulated via graphs, and algebraic derivations are pursued in RCM notation. But this is difficult to do correctly.

Herein lies a dilemma. PCM requires knowledge of two things: (a) the right set of variables and (b) the right model of the relationship between those variables. For many or perhaps nearly all applications that might be characterized by such terms as program evaluation or applied quasi-experimentation or cognates, most researchers regard the first task as nearly hopeless given how unknown selection bias typically is. To aspire to the second task if the first one is hopeless seems not only doubly hopeless but also more time-consuming than the benefits likely will warrant. This suggests a complementary interpretation to that of Imbens (2010), that a failure to adopt PCM to these applied problems reflects a justifiable skepticism about the value of the additional work.

RCM's program of research seems aimed at the first of these two tasks in hopes that its tools like propensity score adjustment might be able to do good enough in making correct causal assessments from observational data. Consider, for example, recent empirical efforts to understand the conditions under which statistical adjustments of quasi-experiments can be made to match findings from randomized experiments (e.g., Cook, Shadish, & Wong, 2008; Cook et al., 2009; Dehejia & Wahba, 1999; Glazerman et al., 2003; Shadish et al., 2008; Steiner, Cook, & Shadish, in press; Steiner, Cook, Shadish, & Clark, in press). One might think of such studies as a program of research conducted on the basis of induction. Such studies take existing suggestions for improving causal estimates, such as propensity score analysis or the use of DAG methods, and test those suggestions empirically. No single test of this kind can escape its context, so any generalizations from

one such a study would be extremely speculative. But a program of research of this kind, where multiple investigators vary many key features of the study (persons, settings, times, treatments, outcomes, etc.), has the potential to produce an empirical basis for making inductive hypotheses about what does and does not work in generating accurate causal estimates. Given the problem of induction (that we may never know if we will observe a falsifying instance), such results never can be logically conclusive. Indeed, we cannot rule out the possibility that the program will fail to identify any useful hypotheses. If such a program were to be successful, however, it would help us to understand the conditions under which we might be able to create causal estimates that are good enough (accurate enough by some criterion to be agreed on by the community of scholars), albeit not optimal. This is a different approach from PCM's provision of a causal logic that allows the researcher to deduce causal inferences from a given set of conditions, a more challenging task but one that eventually might lead to a solution more likely to be optimal if it could be successful.

CCM falls in between the other two models in its approach to this dilemma, but probably with more affinity to RCM than PCM. On the one hand, CCM always has allowed that if you fully know the specification of the selection process and measure that process perfectly, then the researcher can use methods like structural equation modeling to generate accurate causal estimates. Adding the benefits of PCM's approach to this claim would probably strengthen CCM's understanding and explication of the conditions under which this can be done. On the other hand, CCM shares the skepticism of RCM about being able to solve PCM's second task. Ultimately, CCM prefers advocating stronger experimental and quasi-experimental design approaches that are less formalized and more reliant on fallible but inevitable plausibility judgments; and CCM takes the inductive program of research as its best current hope for solving the applied causal inference problems of most interest to CCM and RCM.

We can give two reasonable responses to these reservations, however. First, we must make the effort to do both tasks if we really want to advance scientific and practical understanding of what works. After all, if we do not try to model the relationships among variables in a serious way now, then when should we do so? Should we wait for the inductive program to reach its limits or fail? Should we pursue both inductive and deductive tasks simultaneously, and if so, what incentive is there for applied researchers to take on the harder task? Surely, however, we should not simply abandon the second task just because it is harder to do both tasks than just the first.

The second reasonable response is that PCM has identified some specific conditions under which adjusting for certain pretest variables, whether in propensity scores or ordinary regression, can increase bias of causal estimates. The most salient of them is the collider variable, a variable that is a mutual direct descendent of two (or more) variables, which if controlled can increase bias. A second example is certain uses of instrumental variables that might also increase bias (Pearl, 2009b). A useful project would be to begin to identify and catalog such conditions, probably separately for each substantive area of interest. The project is formidable because knowing that a variable is an instrument or a collider depends on knowing the relationships among variables. But the project is probably not impossible to begin.

Most likely, we need multiple approaches to solving these difficult causal inference issues. We need the inductivist investigators who use results from many studies to create a theory of when tools like propensity score analysis might help. We need the deductivist investigators who will create the SEMs and DAGs that better embody the goals of science involving creation of better scientific theories about the phenomena we study. Who will do each kind of research will no doubt depend on many factors, including but not limited to a researcher's perception of whether the knowledge base in a field is mature enough to support strong model development and whether the perceived payoff of investing resources into doing each task compared with the alternatives is worth the effort.

Elsewhere we have described other gaps in RCM and CCM (Shadish, 2010). PCM helps fill some but not all of those gaps. One was that CCM and RCM both focus primarily on field experimentation. PCM may connect a bit better to laboratory experimentation in which tight experimental control and careful attention to theoretically based construction of causal models might make a DAG more likely to be plausible. A second gap was that RCM and CCM both focus somewhat more on the simple descriptive inference that A caused B, and less so on the explanatory mediators and moderators of the effect. Again PCM attends more to the latter as a by-product of the construction of a valid DAG. A third gap is that all of these three theories devote far more attention to finding the effects of known causes than to finding the unknown causes of known effects. PCM has put the most effort of the three into creating fully developed theories of causes of effects, including attribution, regret, explanation, and other counterfactual relationships (see Pearl, 2009a, Chapters 9 and 10). The latter is often the province of epidemiology, especially retrospective case control studies. Perhaps a further iteration of this comparison of theories of causation might include the work of James Robins, and epidemiologist and biostatistician whose work might help fill this gap (e.g., Robins, Hernan, & Brumback, 2000).

What is encouraging about all these developments, however, is the possible emergence of a truly interdisciplinary theory of causation applied to the conduct of social science (Imbens, 2010). Many economists and statisticians have begun to use the common terminology supplied by the potential outcomes model in RCM to talk about causation (e.g., Angrist et al., 1996). Statisticians have begun to write much more about the importance of good design and pretest measurement to the statistical adjustments they suggest (Rubin, 2007, 2008). Psychologists have begun to incorporate analytic models from RCM into their work (Shadish et al., 2002, 2008). Sociologists have combined RCM and PCM in a synthesis that also includes more extensive discussion of good design (Morgan & Winship, 2007). Because of the sheer number of disciplines involved, and the many terminological differences across PCM, CCM, and RCM (and others), the going is slow and the progress is incremental, measured in decades. But progress it is, and a shared theory of causal inference that moves beyond CCM, RCM, and PCM does now indeed seem feasible.

References

Angrist, J. D., Imbens, G. W., & Rubin, D. B. (1996). Identification of causal effects using instrumental variables. *Journal of the American Statistical Association, 91*, 444–455. doi:10.2307/2291629

Angrist, J. D., & Lavy, V. (1999). Using Maimonides' rule to identify the effects of class size on scholastic achievement. *The Quarterly Journal of Economics, 114*, 533–575. doi:10.1162/003355399556061

Berk, R. A. (2004). *Regression analysis: A constructive critique.* Thousand Oaks, CA: Sage.

Boruch, R. F., & Wolins, L. (1970). A procedure for estimation of trait, method, and error variance attributable to a measure. *Educational and Psychological Measurement, 30*, 547–574.

Braver, M. C. W., & Braver, S. L. (1988). Statistical treatment of the Solomon Four-Group design: A meta-analytic approach. *Psychological Bulletin, 104*, 150–154. doi:10.1037/0033-2909.104.1.150

Brewer, M. B., & Collins, B. E. (Eds.). (1981). *Scientific inquiry and the social sciences: A volume in honor of Donald T. Campbell.* San Francisco, CA: Jossey-Bass.

Burns, M., & Pearl, J. (1981). Causal and diagnostic inferences: A comparison of validity. *Organizational Behavior and Human Performance, 28*, 379–394. doi:10.1016/0030-5073(81)90005-2

Campbell, D. T. (1957). Factors relevant to the validity of experiments in social settings. *Psychological Bulletin, 54*, 297–312. doi:10.1037/h0040950

Campbell, D. T. (1974). Evolutionary epistemology. In P. A. Schilpp (Ed.), *The philosophy of Karl Popper* (pp. 412–463). La Salle, IL: Open Court.

Campbell, D. T. (1975). "Degrees of freedom" and the case study. *Comparative Political Studies, 2*, 178–193.

Campbell, D. T. (1984). Toward an epistemologically relevant sociology of science. *Science, Technology, and Human Values, 10*, 38–48.

Campbell, D. T. (1986). Relabeling internal and external validity for applied social scientists. In W. M. K. Trochim (Ed.), *Advances in quasi-experimental design and analysis* (pp. 67–77). San Francisco, CA: Jossey-Bass.

Campbell, D. T. (1988). *Methodology and epistemology for social science: Selected papers* (E. S. Overman, Ed.). Chicago: University of Illinois Press.

Campbell, D. T., & Erlebacher, A. E. (1970). How regression artifacts can mistakenly make compensatory education programs look harmful. In J. Hellmuth (Ed.), *The Disadvantaged Child: Vol. 3. Compensatory education: A national debate.* New York, NY: Bruner/Mazel.

Campbell, D. T., & Fiske, D. W. (1959). Convergent and discriminant validation by the multitrait-multimethod matrix. *Psychological Bulletin, 56*, 81–105. doi:10.1037/h0046016

Campbell, D. T., & Stanley, J. C. (1963). Experimental and quasi-experimental designs for research on teaching. In N. L. Gage (Ed.), *Handbook of research on teaching* (pp. 171–246). Chicago, IL: Rand McNally.

Campbell, D. T., & Stanley, J. C. (1966). *Experimental and quasi-experimental designs for research.* Chicago, IL: Rand McNally.

Chapin, F. S. (1932). The advantages of experimental sociology in the study of family group patterns. *Social Forces, 11*, 200–207. doi:10.2307/2569773

Chapin, F. S. (1947). *Experimental designs in sociological research.* New York, NY: Harper.

Cicirelli, V. G., & Associates. (1969). *The impact of Head Start: An evaluation of the effects of Head Start on children's cognitive and affective development: Vol. 1. A report to the Office of Economic Opportunity.* Athens: Ohio University and Westinghouse Learning Corporation.

Collins, J., Hall, E., & Paul, L. (Eds.). (2004). *Causation and counterfactuals.* Cambridge, MA: MIT Press.

Cook, T. D. (1985). Postpositivist critical multiplism. In L. Shotland & M. M. Mark (Eds.), *Social science and social policy* (pp. 21–62). Newbury Park, CA: Sage.

Cook, T. D. (1990). The generalization of causal connections: Multiple theories in search of clear practice. In L. Sechrest, E. Perrin, & J. Bunker (Eds.), *Research methodology: Strengthening causal interpretations of nonexperimental data* (pp. 9–31) (DHHS Publication No. PHS 90–3454). Rockville, MD: Department of Health and Human Services.

Cook, T. D. (1991). Clarifying the warrant for generalized causal inferences in quasi-experimentation. In M. W. McLaughlin & D. C. Phillips (Eds.), *Evaluation and education: At quarter-century* (pp. 115–144). Chicago, IL: National Society for the Study of Education.

Cook, T. D. (2004). Causal generalization: How Campbell and Cronbach influenced my theoretical thinking on this topic, including in Shadish, Cook, and Campbell. In M. Alkin (Ed.), *Evaluation roots: Tracing theorists' views and influences* (pp. 88–113). Thousand Oaks, CA: Sage.

Cook, T. D. (2007). "Waiting for life to arrive": A history of the regression-discontinuity design in psychology, statistics and economics. *Journal of Econometrics, 142*, 636–654. doi:10.1016/j.jeconom.2007.05.002

Cook, T. D., & Campbell, D. T. (1979). *Quasi-experimentation: Design and analysis issues for field settings.* Chicago, IL: Rand McNally.

Cook, T. D., & Campbell, D. T. (1986). The causal assumptions of quasi-experimental practice. *Synthese, 68,* 141–180.

Cook, T. D., Shadish, W. R., & Wong, V. C. (2008). Three conditions under which experiments and observational studies produce comparable causal estimates: New findings from within-study comparisons. *Journal of Policy Analysis and Management, 27,* 724–750. doi:10.1002/pam.20375

Cook, T. D., Steiner, P. M., & Pohl, S. (2009). How bias reduction is affected by covariate choice, unreliability, and mode of data analysis: Results from two types of within-study comparisons. *Multivariate Behavioral Research, 44,* 828–847. doi:10.1080/00273170903333673

Cordray, D. W. (1986). Quasi-experimental analysis: A mixture of methods and judgment. In W. M. K. Trochim (Ed.), *Advances in quasi-experimental design and analysis* (pp. 9–27). San Francisco, CA: Jossey-Bass.

Cronbach, L. J. (1982). *Designing evaluations of educational and social programs.* San Francisco, CA: Jossey-Bass.

D'Agostino, R., Jr., & Rubin, D. B. (2000). Estimation and use of propensity scores with incomplete data. *Journal of the American Statistical Association, 95,* 749–759. doi:10.2307/2669455

Dawid, A. P. (2000). Causal inference without counterfactuals. *Journal of the American Statistical Association, 95,* 407–448. doi:10.2307/2669377

Dehejia, R., & Wahba, S. (1999). Causal effects in non-experimental studies: Re-evaluating the evaluation of training programs. *Journal of the American Statistical Association, 94,* 1053–1062. doi:10.2307/2669919

Deluccchi, K. L. (1994). Methods for the analysis of binary outcome results in the presence of missing data. *Journal of Consulting and Clinical Psychology, 62,* 569–575. doi:10.1037/0022-006X.62.3.569

Duckart, J. P. (1998). An evaluation of the Baltimore Community Lead Education and Reduction Corps (CLEARCorps) Program. *Evaluation Review, 22,* 373–402. doi:10.1177/0193841X9802200303

Eells, E. (1991). *Probabilistic causality.* New York, NY: Cambridge University Press. doi:10.1017/CBO9780511570667

Fisher, R. A. (1925). *Statistical methods for research workers.* London, England: Oliver & Boyd.

Fisher, R. A. (1926). The arrangement of field experiments. *Journal of the Ministry of Agriculture, 33,* 503–513.

Folkman, J. (1996). Fighting cancer by attacking its blood supply. *Scientific American, 275,* 150–154. doi:10.1038/scientificamerican0996-150

Frangakis, C., & Rubin, D. B. (2002). Principal stratification in causal inference. *Biometrics, 58,* 21–29. doi:10.1111/j.0006-341X.2002.00021.x

Frangakis, C. E., Rubin, D. B., & Zhou, X.-H. (2002). Clustered encouragement designs with individual noncompliance: Bayesian inference with randomization, and applications to advanced directive forms. *Biostatistics (Oxford, England), 3,* 147–164. doi:10.1093/biostatistics/3.2.147

Freedman, D. A. (1987). As others see us: A case study in path analysis. *Journal of Educational Statistics, 12,* 101–128. doi:10.2307/1164888

Glazerman, S., Levy, D. M., & Myers, D. (2003). Nonexperimental versus experimental estimates of earnings impacts. *The Annals of the American Academy of Political and Social Science, 589,* 63–93. doi:10.1177/0002716203254879

Goldberger, A. S. (1972). *Selection bias in evaluating treatment effects: Some formal illustrations* (Discussion Paper 123–72). Madison: University of Wisconsin, Institute for Research on Poverty.

Hahn, J., Todd, P., & Van der Klaauw, W. (2001). Identification and estimation of treatment effects with a regression-discontinuity design. *Econometrica, 69,* 201–209. doi:10.1111/1468-0262.00183

Halpern, J. Y. (1998). Axiomatizing causal reasoning. In G. F. Cooper & S. Moral (Eds.), *Uncertainty in artificial intelligence* (pp. 202–210). San Francisco, CA: Morgan Kaufmann.

Haviland, A., Nagin, D. S., & Rosenbaum, P. R. (2007). Combining propensity score matching and group-based trajectory analysis in an observational study. *Psychological Methods, 12,* 247–267. doi:10.1037/1082-989X.12.3.247

Hayduk, L., Cummings, G., Stratkotter, R., Nimmo, M., Grygoryev, K., Dosman, D., . . . Boadu, K. (2003). Pearl's D-Separation: One more step into causal thinking. *Structural Equation Modeling, 10,* 289–311. doi:10.1207/S15328007SEM1002_8

Heider, F. (1958). *The psychology of interpersonal relations.* New York, NY: Wiley.

Holland, P. W. (1986). Statistics and causal inference. *Journal of the American Statistical Association, 81,* 945–970. doi:10.2307/2289064

Hume, D. (1963). *An enquiry concerning human understanding.* LaSalle, IL: Open Court Press. (Original work published 1748)

Imbens, G. W. (2010). An economist's perspective on Shadish (2010) and West & Thoemmes (2010). *Psychological Methods, 15,* 47–55.

Lazarsfeld, P. F. (1948). The use of panels in social research. *Proceedings of the American Philosophical Society, 92,* 405–410.

Lewis, D. (1973). *Counterfactuals.* Cambridge, MA: Blackwell.

Light, R. J., Singer, J. D., & Willett, J. B. (1990). *By design: Planning research in higher education.* Cambridge, MA: Harvard University Press.

Little, R. J. A., & Rubin, D. B. (2000). Causal effects in clinical and epidemiological studies via potential outcomes: Concepts and analytic approaches. *Annual Review of Public Health, 21,* 121–145. doi:10.1146/annurev.publhealth.21.1.121

Little, R. J. A., & Rubin, D. B. (2002). *Statistical analysis with missing data* (2nd ed.). New York, NY: Wiley.

Luellen, J. K., Shadish, W. R., & Clark, M. H. (2005). Propensity scores: An introduction and experimental test. *Evaluation Review, 29,* 530–558. doi:10.1177/0193841X05275596

Mackie, J. L. (1974). *The cement of the universe: A study of causation.* Oxford, England: Oxford University Press.

Magidson, J. (1977). Toward a causal model approach for adjusting for preexisting differences in the nonequivalent control group situation. *Evaluation Quarterly, 1,* 399–420. doi:10.1177/0193841X7700100303

McCall, W. A. (1923). *How to experiment in education.* New York, NY: Macmillan.

Meyer, B. D. (1995). Natural and quasi-experiments in economics. *Journal of Business and Economic Statistics, 13,* 151–161. doi:10.2307/1392369

Meyer, B. D., Viscusi, W. K., & Durbin, D. L. (1995). Workers' compensation and injury duration: Evidence from a natural experiment. *The American Economic Review, 85,* 322–340.

Millsap, M. A., Chase, A., Obeidallah, D., Perez-Smith, A. P., Brigham, N., & Johnston, K. (2000). *Evaluation of Detroit's Comer Schools and Families Initiative: Final REPORT.* Cambridge, MA: Abt Associates.

Morgan, S. L., & Winship, C. (2007). *Counterfactuals and causal inference.* Cambridge, England: Cambridge University Press.

Neustrom, M. W., & Norton, W. M. (1993). The impact of drunk driving legislation in Louisiana. *Journal of Safety Research, 24,* 107–121. doi:10.1016/0022-4375(93)90005-8

Neyman, J. (1990). On the application of probability theory to agricultural experiments: Essay on principles. Section 9. *Statistical Science, 5,* 465–480. (Original work published 1923)

Oakes, J. M. (2004). The (mis)estimation of neighborhood effects: Causal inference for a practicable social epidemiology. *Social Science and Medicine, 58,* 1929–1952. doi:10.1016/j.socscimed.2003.08.004

Pearl, J. (1998). Graphs, causality, and structural equation models. *Sociological Methods and Research, 27,* 226–284. doi:10.1177/0049124198027002004

Pearl, J. (2000). *Causality: Models, reasoning, and inference.* New York, NY: Cambridge University Press.

Pearl, J. (2009a). *Causality: Models, reasoning, and inference* (2nd ed.). New York, NY: Cambridge University Press.

Pearl, J. (2009b). *On a class of bias-amplifying covariates that endanger effect estimates* (Technical Report R-356). Retrieved from http://ftp.cs.ucla.edu/pub/stat_ser/r356.pdf

Pearl, J. (2010a). The foundations of causal inference. *Sociological Methodology, 40,* 74–149. doi:10.1111/j.1467-9531.2010.01228.X

Pearl, J. (2010b). An introduction to causal inference. *The International Journal of Biostatistics, 6.* doi:10.2202/1557-4679.1203

Pearl, J., & Tarsi, M. (1986). Structuring causal trees. *Journal of Complexity, 2,* 60–77. doi:10.1016/0885-064X(86)90023-3

Pollack, A. (2008, January 28). Judah Folkman, researcher, dies at 74. *New York Times.* Retrieved from http://www.nyt.com

Popper, K. R. (1959). *The logic of scientific discovery.* New York, NY: Basic Books.

Reichardt, C. S. (2000). A typology of strategies for ruling out threats to validity. In L. Bickman (Ed.), *Research design: Donald Campbell's legacy* (Vol. 2, pp. 89–115). Thousand Oaks, CA: Sage.

Reichardt, C. S., & Cook, T. D. (1979). Beyond qualitative versus quantitative methods. In T. D. Cook & C. S. Reichardt (Eds.), *Qualitative and quantitative methods in evaluation research* (pp. 7–32). Newbury Park, CA: Sage.

Reichardt, C. S., & Gollob, H. F. (1986). Satisfying the constraints of causal modeling. In W. M. K. Trochim (Ed.), *Advances in quasi-experimental design and analysis* (pp. 91–107). San Francisco, CA: Jossey-Bass.

Reichardt, C. S., & Gollob, H. F. (1987). Taking uncertainty into account when estimating effects. In M. M. Mark & R. L. Shotland (Eds.), *Multiple methods for program evaluation* (pp. 7–22). San Francisco, CA: Jossey-Bass.

Reskin, B. F. (2003). Including mechanisms in our models of ascriptive inequality. *American Sociological Review, 68,* 1–21. doi:10.2307/3088900

Reynolds, K. D., & West, S. G. (1987). A multiplist strategy for strengthening nonequivalent control group designs. *Evaluation Review, 11,* 691–714. doi:10.1177/0193841X8701100601

Robins, J. M., Hernan, M. A., & Brumback, B. (2000). Marginal structural models and causal inference in epidemiology. *Epidemiology (Cambridge, Mass.), 11,* 550–560. doi:10.1097/00001648-200009000-00011

Rogosa, D. (1980). A critique of cross-lagged correlation. *Psychological Bulletin, 88,* 245–258. doi:10.1037/0033-2909.88.2.245

Rosenbaum, P. R. (1991). Discussing hidden bias in observational studies. *Annals of Internal Medicine, 115,* 901–905.

Rosenbaum, P. R. (1999). Choice as an alternative to control in observational studies: Rejoinder. *Statistical Science, 14,* 300–304.

Rosenbaum, P. R. (2002). *Observational studies* (2nd ed.). New York, NY: Springer-Verlag.

Rosnow, R. L., Rosenthal, R., & Rubin, D. B. (2000). Contrasts and correlations in effect size estimation. *Psychological Science, 11,* 446–453. doi:10.1111/1467-9280.00287

Rowe, P. M. (1999). What is all the hullabaloo about endostatin? *Lancet, 353,* 732. doi:10.1016/S0140-6736(05)76101-8

Rubin, D. B. (1977). Assignment to treatment group on the basis of a covariate. *Journal of Educational Statistics, 2,* 1–26. doi:10.2307/1164933

Rubin, D. B. (1987). *Multiple imputation for nonresponse in surveys.* New York, NY: Wiley.

Rubin, D. B. (1990). A new perspective. In K. W. Wachter & M. L. Straf (Eds.), *The future of meta-analysis* (pp. 155–165). New York, NY: Sage.

Rubin, D. B. (1992). Meta-analysis: Literature synthesis or effect-size surface estimation? *Journal of Educational Statistics, 17,* 363–374. doi:10.2307/1165129

Rubin, D. B. (2001). Using propensity scores to help design observational studies: Application to the tobacco litigation. *Health Services and Outcomes Research Methodology, 2,* 169–188. doi:10.1023/A:1020363010465

Rubin, D. B. (2004). Teaching statistical inference for causal effects in experiments and observational studies. *Journal of Educational and Behavioral Statistics, 29,* 343–367. doi:10.3102/10769986029003343

Rubin, D. B. (2005). Causal inference using potential outcomes. *Journal of the American Statistical Association, 100,* 322–331. doi:10.1198/016214504000001880

Rubin, D. B. (2006). *Matched sampling for causal effects.* New York, NY: Cambridge University Press.

Rubin, D. B. (2007). The design versus the analysis of observational studies for causal effects: Parallels with the design of randomized trials. *Statistics in Medicine, 26,* 20–36. doi:10.1002/sim.2739

Rubin, D. B. (2008). For objective causal inference, design trumps analysis. *Annals of Applied Statistics, 2,* 808–840. doi:10.1214/08-AOAS187

Rubin, D. B. (2010). Reflections stimulated by the comments of Shadish (2010) and West and Thoemmes (2010). *Psychological Methods, 15,* 38–46. doi:10.1037/a0018537

Rubin, D. B., & Thomas, N. (1992). Characterizing the effect of matching using linear propensity score methods with normal covariates. *Biometrika, 79,* 797–809. doi:10.1093/biomet/79.4.797

Scheines, R., Spirtes, P., Glymour, C., & Meek, C. (1994). *Tetrad II: Tools for causal modeling, User's manual.* Hillsdale, NJ: Erlbaum.

Shadish, W. R. (2010). Campbell and Rubin: A primer and comparison of their approaches to causal inference in field settings. *Psychological Methods, 15,* 3–17. doi:10.1037/a0015916

Shadish, W. R., Clark, M. H., & Steiner, P. M. (2008). Can nonrandomized experiments yield accurate answers? A randomized experiment comparing random to nonrandom assignment. *Journal of the American Statistical Association, 103,* 1334–1344. doi:10.1198/016214508000000733

Shadish, W. R., & Cook, T. D. (1999). Design rules: More steps towards a complete theory of quasi-experimentation. *Statistical Science, 14,* 294–300.

Shadish, W. R., Cook, T. D., & Campbell, D. T. (2002). *Experimental and quasi-experimental design for generalized causal inference.* Boston, MA: Houghton Mifflin.

Shadish, W. R., Cook, T. D., & Leviton, L. C. (1991). *Foundations of program evaluation: Theories of practice.* Newbury Park, CA: Sage.

Shadish, W. R., Hu, X., Glaser, R. R., Kownacki, R. J., & Wong, T. (1998). A method for exploring the effects of attrition in randomized experiments with dichotomous outcomes. *Psychological Methods, 3,* 3–22. doi:10.1037/1082-989X.3.1.3

Shadish, W. R., Luellen, J. K., & Clark, M. H. (2006). Propensity scores and quasi-experimentation. In R. R. Bootzin & P. McKnight (Eds.), *Strengthening research methodology: Psychological measurement and evaluation* (pp. 143–157). Washington, DC: American Psychological Association. doi:10.1037/11384-008

Shadish, W. R., Matt, G. E., Navarro, A. M., & Phillips, G. (2000). The effects of psychological therapies under clinically representative conditions: A meta-analysis. *Psychological Bulletin, 126,* 512–529. doi:10.1037/0033-2909.126.4.512

Shih, W. J., & Quan, H. (1997). Testing for treatment differences with dropouts present in clinical trials—A composite approach. *Statistics in Medicine, 16,* 1225–1239. doi:10.1002/(SICI)1097-0258(19970615)16:11<1225::AID-SIM548>3.0.CO;2-Y

Shipley, B. (2000). A new inferential test for path models based on directed acyclic graphs. *Structural Equation Modeling, 7,* 206–218. doi:10.1207/S15328007SEM0702_4

Shpitser, I., & Pearl, J. (2008). What counterfactuals can be tested. In *Proceedings of the 23rd conference on uncertainty in artificial intelligence* (pp. 352–359). Vancouver, British Columbia, Canada: AUAI Press.

Solomon, R. L. (1949). An extension of control group design. *Psychological Bulletin, 46,* 137–150. doi:10.1037/h0062958

Stanley, T. D., & Jarrell, S. B. (1998). Gender wage discrimination bias: A meta-regression analysis. *The Journal of Human Resources, 33,* 947–973. doi:10.2307/146404

Steiner, P. M., Cook, T. D., & Shadish, W. R. (in press). On the importance of reliable covariate measurement in selection bias adjustments using propensity scores. *Journal of Educational and Behavioral Statistics.*

Steiner, P. M., Cook, T. D., Shadish, W. R., & Clark, M. H. (in press). The importance of covariate selection in controlling for selection bias in observational studies. *Psychological Methods.*

Thistlethwaite, D. L., & Campbell, D. T. (1960). Regression-discontinuity analysis: Alternative to the ex post facto experiment. *Journal of Educational Psychology, 51,* 309–317. doi:10.1037/h0044319

Tian, J., & Pearl, J. (2000). Probabilities of causation: Bounds and identification. In C. Boutilier & M. Goldszmidt (Eds.), *Proceedings of the 16th conference on uncertainty in artificial intelligence* (pp. 589–598). San Francisco, CA: Morgan Kaufmann.

Trochim, W. M. K., & Cappelleri, J. C. (1992). Cutoff assignment strategies for enhancing randomized clinical trials. *Controlled Clinical Trials, 13,* 190–212. doi:10.1016/0197-2456(92)90003-I

Vanhonacker, W. R. (1996). Meta-analysis and response surface extrapolation: A least squares approach. *The American Statistician, 50,* 294–299. doi:10.2307/2684923

Verbeke, G., & Molenberghs, G. (2000). *Linear mixed models for longitudinal data.* New York, NY: Springer.

White, P. A. (2000). Causal attribution and Mill's methods of experimental inquiry: Past, present and prospect. *British Journal of Social Psychology, 39,* 429–447. doi:10.1348/014466600164589

Winship, C., & Morgan, S. L. (1999). The estimation of causal effects from observational data. *Annual Review of Psychology, 25,* 659–706.

Woodward, J. (2003). *Making things happen: A theory of causal explanation.* New York, NY: Oxford University Press.

Wright, S. (1921). Correlation and causation. *Journal of Agricultural Research, 20,* 557–585.

Yeaton, W. H., Wortman, P. M., & Langberg, N. (1983). Differential attrition: Estimating the effect of crossovers on the evaluation of a medical technology. *Evaluation Review, 7,* 831–840. doi:10.1177/0193841X8300700607

Ethical and Professional Considerations in Conducting Psychological Research

CHAPTER 3

ETHICS IN PSYCHOLOGICAL RESEARCH: GUIDELINES AND REGULATIONS

Adam L. Fried

Ethical decision making in psychological research requires knowledge of the rules and regulations governing its practices as well as the ability to identify and resolve complex ethical conflicts. Psychologists have a professional responsibility to act in ways that maximize benefits of research and minimize harms, to promote trust in the research process and in the results of science, to engage in honest and truthful scientific practices, to distribute the benefits and burdens of science evenly between all persons, and to design and implement research procedures that recognize and respect individual differences.

Investigators engage several resources when approaching ethical questions, including professional logic and the advice of colleagues, managers, and institutional representatives. To competently conduct psychological research, researchers also must possess a reasonable understanding of the purpose and application of state and federal regulations, laws, and other rules governing research; institutional research rules; and professional guidelines and enforceable standards governing research. Researchers also much have the ability to use these resources to engage in ethical decision making and the resolution of complex dilemmas. Although an understanding of these resources is integral to ethical decision making in the responsible conduct of research, they are sometimes insufficient to adequately resolve certain complex questions. Rather than offering a final answer, these resources may be better viewed as tools for the thoughtful researcher to use in resolving ethical questions.

Research involves a pursuit of knowledge that often contributes to the betterment of society by informing practice, policy, and services. Researchers who work with human participants must balance the goals of maintaining standards of good science while also protecting the welfare and promoting the autonomy of participants. Although these goals may be seen as competing and potentially at odds, they need not and should not be. Certain frameworks (such as relational ethics) can provide investigators with methods to conceptualize ethics-in-science decision making so that these goals can work in concert to promote the ideals of good science.

The atrocities of the Nazi war crimes as well as other high-profile research studies that have resulted in substantial harm to particularly vulnerable participants (such as the Tuskegee syphilis study [Brandt, 1978] and the Willowbrook hepatitis study [Rothman & Rothman, 1984]) have contributed to an erosion of public trust in the biomedical and behavioral sciences. More recently, important questions about the integrity of the research enterprise have been raised through highly publicized potential conflicts of interest among investigators, institutions, and corporations. Institutions, regulatory bodies, and professional associations have responded to these developments by creating and enforcing rules that prevent or resolve ethical conflicts in the scientific community. These historic and recent examples underscore the critical importance of competent ethical decision making and planning.

This chapter provides an introduction to ethical issues and resources in psychological research with human participants, including an overview of federal regulations, institutional oversight, and

DOI: 10.1037/13619-004
APA Handbook of Research Methods in Psychology: Vol. 1. Foundations, Planning, Measures, and Psychometrics, H. Cooper (Editor-in-Chief)

professional guidelines, and discusses major concepts in research ethics related to the planning and execution of behavioral research (more information about issues related to research dissemination can be found in Volume 3, Chapter 27, this handbook). This chapter also discusses approaches to science-in-ethics decision making when addressing novel ethical questions and challenges in which standard regulations and professional guidelines may offer incomplete solutions.

FEDERAL REGULATIONS: HISTORY AND SCOPE

The history of regulations governing research often is traced back to the Nuremberg Code (1949), which was enacted after the public learned of the atrocities associated with the work of Nazi scientists during World War II. The Nuremberg Code introduced several important principles governing research with human subjects, including informed consent procedures and the right of participants to withdraw participation.

Following the Nuremberg Code, the Declaration of Helsinki of the World Medical Association (1964/2008) elaborated on points contained in the Nuremberg Code and included topics such as non-therapeutic biomedical research with human participants. Finally, the Belmont Report (National Commission for the Protection of Human Subjects of Biomedical and Behavioral Research, 1979) provided the basis for federal biomedical and behavioral research regulations. In addition to a brief discussion of the Belmont Report, two other important federal regulations and laws will be discussed as they relate to research in the next sections: the Code of Federal Regulations and the Health Information Portability and Accountability Act of 1996.

The Belmont Report

The National Commission for Protection of Human Subjects of Biomedical and Behavioral Research was created through the National Research Act of 1974. The commission's charge was to identify and summarize the basic ethical principles to guide investigators conducting biomedical and behavioral research, with the resulting document known as the Belmont Report (National Commission for the Protection of Human Subjects of Biomedical and Behavioral Research, 1979).

Divided into three main sections, the Belmont Report laid the foundation for regulations and professional guidelines governing biomedical and behavioral research. Notably, the Report (a) distinguished between the goals and methods of research and professional practice; (b) highlighted the foundational ethical principles guiding human subjects research, including Respect for Persons, Beneficence, and Justice (these principles are discussed as they apply to psychological research in the section describing the American Psychological Association [APA] *Ethical Principles of Psychologists and Code of Conduct* (the Ethics Code; APA, 2010); and (c) identified and described three basic requirements of research: informed consent procedures, risk–benefit analysis, and participant selection and recruitment, which focused on issues of justice in terms of bearing the burdens of research and enjoying the benefits of science. From the Belmont Report, the federal regulations for research were born.

Code of Federal Regulations

The U.S. Department of Health and Human Service (DHHS) has codified regulations governing research with human subjects in the United States in its *Code of Federal Regulations* (CFR) Title 45, Part 46: Protection of Human Subjects (DHHS, 2001). This portion of the code is divided into several parts, with sections describing general rules and principles and institutional review board registration procedures, and sections governing biomedical and behavioral research with specific vulnerable populations (such as children, prisoners, pregnant women, human fetuses, and neonates). The Office of Human Research Protections (an office within the DHHS) monitors institutions (who, in turn, monitor the investigators) to ensure compliance with federal regulations. For example, in most studies, adverse reactions to study methods must be reported to their institution's review board, which, in turn, may be required to report to the Office of Human Research Protections for monitoring and possible investigation. More information about CFR rules and designations are discussed in the section Institutional Oversight.

Health Information Portability and Accountability Act

In response to the increasingly common practice of electronic transfer of health-related data among health care professionals, and in an effort to increase patient access to health-related records, the U.S. Congress enacted the Health Information Portability and Accountability Act of 1996 (HIPAA). This law has significant effects on records privacy and disclosure, the electronic transmission of data, and data security for both practice and research.

HIPAA governs protected health information (PHI), or individually identifiable health data, among covered entities (which includes health plans and health care providers, employers, and health care clearinghouses). Data that are completely deidentified; do not relate to the past, present, or future health of an individual; and are not created or received by a covered entity are not considered PHI.

HIPAA affects certain types of research, which is defined as "the systematic investigation, including research development, testing, and evaluation, designed to develop or contribute to generalizable knowledge" (DHHS, 2001). Researchers who are covered entities and collect or store PHI have specific obligations under the HIPAA, including providing participants with a description of their privacy rights and how their data are used and implementing procedures to ensure that data are secure and that only authorized representatives have access to these records. For example, investigators should be aware that for HIPAA-covered research, participants may be able to access certain types of health records under this law. Investigators may be able to temporarily deny access to these records while the research is ongoing, but only if the participant has agreed to this during the consent process. Furthermore, participants may be able to access these records once the research is complete. In most cases, for PHI data to be created, used, or disclosed for research purposes, a signed authorization (for the limited use of the research project) must be executed by the individual or personal representative.

Investigators should be aware that HIPAA rules have implications for children, adolescents, and those who have legal authority to act on behalf of minors (Fisher, 2004). In most cases, the legal guardian (known as the *personal representative* for the person who lacks legal authority to make health care decisions) is considered the authorized decision maker for the party.

INSTITUTIONAL OVERSIGHT

In addition to federal regulations, many institutions may enact and enforce institutional rules governing research, often coordinated by the institutional review board (IRB). The overall aim of an IRB is to protect the rights and welfare of research participants. To accomplish this aim, the IRB reviews, evaluates, approves, and oversees research protocols submitted by investigators within their particular institution to ensure compliance with the institutional and federal rules related to the practice of research.

Submitting Protocols to the IRB

Applications to the IRB (which are submitted by investigators) typically include background and overview of the study (including research aims), recruitment procedures, description of participants (including inclusion and exclusion criteria), methods of data collection, confidentiality procedures, potential risks and benefits to the participant, detailed procedures for monitoring and reporting any adverse reactions, and the informed consent form. The IRB chair or committee, which often is composed of a variety of professionals from the institution, and a community representative who is not officially affiliated with the institution, review the application. If warranted, the chair or committee asks the investigator(s) to attend a meeting of the IRB committee to answer questions raised by members of the committee or to clarify areas of concern. The IRB may then approve the protocol, request that the investigator make revisions, or deny the application and provide the investigator with the reasons for the denial (Bankert & Amdur, 2005).

Formal approval from a research review committee or board (such as an IRB) is required in most cases, and under the APA Ethics Code (APA, 2010), investigators are responsible for determining whether such approval is required from their institution (Standard 8.01, Institutional Approval). Certain types of research may qualify as exempt from IRB review (i.e., certain types of research on normal education practices). It is recommended, however, that researchers avoid making this determination alone, and in fact many institutions require their IRBs to make this decision (Prentice & Oki, 2005). Under the National Research Act of 1974, investigators whose research is funded by federal monies must seek approval from their institution's IRB before initiating any research. In addition, institutions may require all studies considered to be research (including those not funded by federal monies) to be submitted for IRB review.

Once a protocol is approved, the IRB has no further role in the research. The IRB is charged with overseeing the research, and investigators who do not comply with their IRB's rules or procedures risk their research being suspended or terminated by the institution. IRBs also require periodic reviews of the research protocols. For example, informed consent forms often are approved only for a limited period of time (e.g., 1 year), after which the investigator(s) must apply for renewal of the project from the IRB.

Minimal Risk Research

Minimal risk is a classification of research that is described in federal regulations as involving procedures that are commensurate with activities encountered in daily life or routine physical or psychological examinations (45 C.F.R. § 46.102i). Minimal risk classifications (or minor increase over minimal risk) group research protocols in terms of risk to participants and may provide a justification for IRBs to approve certain types of research with no prospect for direct benefit with certain vulnerable populations, allow researchers to submit protocols under expedited review procedures, or waive informed consent procedures.

IRBs traditionally make the determination of whether a research protocol meets minimal risk criteria, although tremendous variability may exist in terms of how and which procedures are classified as minimal risk across IRBs (Shah, Whittle, Wilfond,

Gensler, & Wendler, 2004). At least a portion of this variability may be due to difficulty applying the language used in the federal regulations defining the level of risk associated with minimal risk (those "ordinarily encountered in daily life or during the performance of routine physical or psychological examinations or tests"; DHHS, 2001, 45 C.F.R. § 46.102i) as well as the definition of minor in the *minor risk over minimal risk* category, as confusion may arise with regard to applying the "daily life" standard relatively (i.e., compared with other individuals similar to the target participant group) or uniformly (i.e., comparing the risks to a healthy individual living in a safe environment; Fisher, Kornestsky, & Prentice, 2007; Kopelman, 2004).

PROFESSIONAL GUIDELINES FOR PSYCHOLOGICAL RESEARCH: THE APA ETHICS CODE

The Ethics Code (APA, 2010) provides guidance and specific rules for psychologists and students who are engaged in related professional tasks, including research. In its effort to merit public trust, establish the integrity of the profession, and regulate the professional behaviors of those in the field, the Ethics Code represents a collective agreement among psychologists on the profession's moral principles as well as the enforceable standards related to the work of psychologists.

The Ethics Code (APA, 2010) includes five principles that are applicable to the professional work of psychologists. These principles do not represent specific rules or enforceable policies related to professional conduct but rather are aspirational in nature and frame the values that psychologists, in their everyday work, strive to fulfill. The enforceable standards (which articulate the rules that psychologists are to follow) are derived from five basic principles, which are described in the following sections as they apply to research activities.

Principle A. Beneficence and Nonmaleficence

This principle recognizes that psychologists aspire to maximize good results and minimize harms in the context of their work. Psychologists promote the welfare of others by attempting to prevent potential harms that may result from participation in a professional activity. If harms cannot be prevented or already have occurred, psychologists have a duty to minimize negative consequences and to remedy harms when possible. The principle of Beneficence and Nonmaleficence applies not only to those with whom the professional works directly (such as research participants) but also to broader groups, such as organizations, institutions, and society at large.

Principle B. Fidelity and Responsibility

Psychologists engage in behaviors that merit the trust of those with whom they work as well as the public in general, and they recognize that behaviors contrary to these principles threaten the integrity of the profession. This principle of Fidelity and Responsibility reflects the integral role of trust in the successful discharge of psychological activities. For example, individuals who consent to participate in research on potentially illegal activities, such as drug use, trust psychologists to hold to their promises of confidentiality. Researchers who behave in an unethical manner violate their responsibilities and obligations to participants, society, and science in general, and they harm the integrity of the profession.

Principle C. Integrity

To promote and maintain the integrity of the profession, psychologists must be honest in the scientific practice of psychology. This requires openness and truthfulness with the individuals with whom they work (e.g., research participants, IRBs, funding agencies) as well as accuracy in the planning, implementation, and dissemination of scientific results. For example, the Ethics Code (APA, 2010) includes strict rules mandating psychologists to report research findings in an honest and truthful fashion, and not to plagiarize or otherwise misrepresent the work of others as their own.

Principle D. Justice

Psychologists must take steps to provide all individuals with fair and equitable treatment, and appropriate access to the benefits of science. As such, investigators ensure that the burdens and risks of research are not borne exclusively by any one group

or individual, but rather are distributed equally. Similarly, the benefits of scientific developments and breakthroughs should not be limited to certain groups. For example, many randomized treatment research protocols include provisions to provide the investigative treatment to the control group if shown to be effective or successful.

Principle E. Respect for People's Rights and Dignity

This principle reflects psychologists' commitment for respect of the rights of all individuals to privacy and self-governance and requires that psychologists recognize and respect individual differences in such ways that minimize vulnerabilities and maximize strengths. For example, colearning techniques and researcher consultation (discussed in the section Community Consultation and Colearning Procedures) with prospective participant groups and communities help investigators develop scientific aims and research procedures that are sensitive to the research population and specific study context (Fisher, 2002; Fisher & Fried, 2010; Fisher & Fyrberg, 1994; Fisher & Masty, 2006; Fisher & Wallace, 2000).

APA STANDARDS

In addition to the five aspirational principles, the Ethics Code (APA, 2010) includes 10 sets of enforceable standards, each describing an area of professional conduct. The next sections highlight some major areas and standards that are particularly relevant for research with human subjects. The following is not meant to be an exhaustive summary and the reader is advised to consult the ethics code in its entirety.

Informed Consent

Informed consent is one of the most fundamental concepts in the responsible conduct of biomedical and behavioral research. As reflected in federal regulations and professional guidelines, valid informed consent procedures demonstrate science's respect for the self-determination of research participants to make informed, rational, and voluntary decisions about participation, while also protecting vulnerable populations from participation decisions that may be harmful or lead to exploitation. Respect for participant autonomy and regard for human welfare are critical components to the scientific enterprise.

Aforementioned historical incidents, such as the Tuskegee syphilis study (Brandt, 1978) and the Willowbrook hepatitis study (Rothman & Rothman, 1984), have contributed to an erosion of public trust in science in general, and, specifically, trust in investigators' methods. Over the past several decades, a remarkable paradigm shift has occurred in the participant–investigator relationship, from a paternalistic approach in which scientists and professionals often influenced participation decisions to one that emphasizes and respects the autonomous decision-making abilities of participants (Fisher, 2009). To that end, informed consent procedures are seen as a way to ensure that participants make informed, voluntary, and rational decisions with respect to participating in a particular study.

Informed consent for behavioral and biomedical research must meet three main requirements. First, consent must be informed, which requires that important and relevant aspects of the research project must be communicated to the participant in a manner that can be readily understood by participants, including relevant research procedures, time and duration of participation, methods of confidentiality, types of scientific methods employed, methods of assignment (e.g., experimental and control groups), and purpose of the research. The second requirement is that consent must be voluntary and participation in a study must not be unduly coerced. The third requirement for valid informed consent is that it be rational such that participants understand and appreciate the research-related information being presented (including the risks and benefits of participation), and apply this information to their situation to include a risk–benefit analysis in making and communicating a decision about participation (Appelbaum & Grisso, 1995).

Informed nature of consent. To make a truly informed decision about participating in an activity, relevant information about the activity must be communicated to participants. Participants therefore are entitled to be informed of all relevant aspects of

a particular study that would reasonably be expected to influence their decision to participate (Fisher, Hoagwood, & Jensen, 1996), including the following: a statement describing the purpose and procedures of the study (including expected duration of participation), foreseeable risks and benefits, confidentiality procedures and the limits of these, any compensation or other types of incentives for participation, that the study involves research, the voluntary nature of participation (and any consequences for withdrawal of participation), and the investigator's contact information. To avoid possible coercion and participant misinterpretations, federal regulations (45 C.F.R. § 46.116) require that the language of the informed consent process be understandable to the participants, including attention to primary language and education levels of the participant. For example, when creating an informed consent form for a research project with developmentally disabled adults, the investigators should consider consulting with disability professionals to select language and format that are commensurate with the participants' education and ability levels. Finally, participants must be afforded an opportunity to ask relevant questions about the research and have them answered by research staff.

The following sections briefly outline some common components of the informed consent process. The nature and emphasis of each consent concept will differ on the basis of the type of study and the specific research populations. For example, nonintervention research traditionally involves no probability of direct benefit to the participant, whereas participants may personally gain or be assisted through participation in intervention research; therefore, the informed consent process for these types of protocols may differ in key ways, including the types of information provided and the aspects and considerations in the voluntary nature of participation. Readers are encouraged to consult additional sources for clarification about informed consent procedures specific to their own projects.

Risks and benefits. The CFR requires researchers minimize research risks to participants (45 C.F.R. § 46.111(a)(1)) and ensure an adequate balance of research risks and benefits (45 C.F.R. § 46.1119(a)(2)). The informed consent process is an opportunity for researchers to communicate the benefits and risks of participation in an open and honest manner, and provides the participant with sufficient information to autonomously weigh the risks and benefits in a meaningful way to assist their participation decision. Possible benefits of research projects may vary depending on the type of study and the participant, and may include benefits (such as experimental treatments or psychological and psychosocial assessments) that may not be readily available outside of the research setting. For example, some studies, such as those that include an intervention component, may represent the possibility of considerable benefit to participants that have disorders or conditions for which few empirically supported treatments are available. Other studies, such as survey or observational research, may represent little direct benefit to the participant (aside from a possible altruistic benefit the participant may derive from contributing to the scientific study of a particular phenomenon or condition). With respect to the former, researchers must be careful to address potential misperceptions about the nature of the research and potential outcomes related to the intervention. For example, therapeutic misconceptions (i.e., the belief that group assignment or experimental treatment decisions are based on the individual treatment needs of a particular participant; Appelbaum, Roth, Lidz, Benson, & Winslade, 1987) may be common in certain types of intervention research. In addition, participants may either over- or underestimate the research benefits and risks, known as *therapeutic misestimation* (Horng & Grady, 2003). These misperceptions can be addressed by describing in detail the experimental nature of the intervention, clarifying the known benefits and risks of the intervention, and clarifying that it is unknown whether the intervention will be of benefit to the particular condition.

Research risks also vary considerably, depending on the nature of the study and its methods. Almost all research represents some potential risk, such as iatrogenic effects of treatments, breaches of confidentiality, or possible negative reactions to research procedures or subject matter. For example, investigators conducting research that surveys the incidence and nature of trauma should consider including a statement that participation in this project may elicit negative memories or emotions related to past traumatic events. In addition, researchers should be prepared to address immediate or future negative reactions resulting from participation (discussed further in the section Research Debriefing). The nature of these risks must be clearly articulated to participants along with an estimation of the likelihood of these occurrences as well as the possible effects, if known.

Confidentiality. Relevant information about confidentiality associated with the specific research project must be described clearly to prospective participants before any data collection (Standard 4.02, Discussing the Limits of Confidentiality; APA, 2010). For example, a psychologist conducting survey research over the Internet should inform prospective participants about the relevant limits of confidentiality using this medium of data collection, such as threats of third-party viewing of data (APA, 2010; Fisher & Fried, 2003) as well as the methods used to maintain data security (e.g., password-protected computers, firewalls, data encryption). Methods of maintaining data security for non-Internet research also should be communicated, such as the use of a participant coding system, secure storage of data, and deidentifying data sets.

Researchers should consult state and federal laws regarding mandated reporting and duty-to-warn requirements, such as in the cases of child or elder abuse or specific threats of harm to a third party, and communicate such requirements to prospective participants. For example, research psychologists conducting psychotherapy trials may be held to the same duty-to-warn requirements as practicing psychologists in nonresearch settings when provided information by clients that meets the state or local reporting law criteria (Appelbaum & Rosenbaum, 1989). Additional information about confidentiality in research settings is addressed in the section Confidentiality.

Randomized group assignment. Intervention research that involves the use of experimental treatments to determine either the efficacy of a particular treatment or the comparative benefit of an experimental intervention against another treatment requires that the researcher inform prospective participants about specific details related to group assignment (Standard 8.02b, Informed Consent to Research; APA, 2010). For example, the use of a control group in a randomized trial requires the researchers to inform participants about (a) the possibility that they will not be assigned to the treatment group and may be placed in the control group, (b) the nature of random assignment, (c) the nature of the intervention and control groups (e.g., no-treatment, placebo, wait-list), and (d) the benefits and risks of assignment to each group (Standard 8.02b, Informed Consent to Research; APA, 2010). In addition, investigators should ensure clinical equipoise between the two conditions, meaning that there is no established clinical or empirical superiority between the comparative and the intervention treatment (Freedman, 1987; Rothman & Michael, 1994).

Participant compensation and possible costs.

Investigators should clarify the nature and type of compensation offered (if any) to individuals in exchange for participation in a study. The informed consent process should indicate clearly any conditions or prerequisites for receiving the compensation (e.g., all study materials must be completed in their entirety for the participant to be eligible for compensation) and compensation for partial participation (if any). In addition, any costs (including out-of-pocket expenses) that may be incurred by the participant (or their insurance), such as fees associated with tests, assessments, and treatments as well as the research-related expenses that will be covered by the researchers or sponsors, also should be discussed clearly (Hunt, 2005). Participant compensation will be further discussed in the section Inducements for Research Participation.

The voluntary nature of informed consent.

Voluntary consent has been viewed as an essential component in the protection of participant welfare and rights (Freedman, 1975) and is a second requirement for valid informed consent. That is, participants should not be unduly influenced to participate in research, such as through unfair or coercive compensation. Inducements that far

exceed or otherwise are not commensurate with the research requirements and making adjunct treatments or other services that ordinarily would be provided to the individual contingent on research participation are examples of situations that may threaten the voluntary nature of consent. Research with particularly vulnerable populations, such as prisoners, the chronically mentally ill, the poor, or the intellectually disabled, require that investigators be particularly sensitive to unanticipated or unintentional sources of coercion and consider instituting additional procedures to ensure that participation is completely voluntary.

During the informed consent process, the nature and purpose of the assessments and interventions should be clarified, with attention given to potential differences between research and treatment. The consent process should include information about potential consequences related to the decision to decline or withdraw participation, especially when participants are recruited in certain service-provision settings, such as counseling and treatment centers or social services agencies. This type of design may present a potentially coercive situation in which a participant may not adequately distinguish between voluntarily participating in research and receiving professional services. Such confusion may lead to the erroneous belief that the provision of psychological services is contingent on the individual's participation in research (Fisher & Goodman, 2009), especially if the person conducting the research is also providing or involved in the provision of services. In such cases, the investigator has an added responsibility to ensure that the two roles (and differences between the two) as well as the extent to which participation in the research project will be distinguishable from the other services participants already or are entitled to receive, are clearly communicated and that participants understand that refusal to participate or withdrawal of participation will not result in a reduction or disruption of services or other negative consequence (Fisher, 2009; Fisher et al., 2002).

For example, a researcher conducting an anonymous study of substance abuse symptoms secondary to depression in an outpatient psychotherapy clinic specializing in mood disorders should make clear the nature of the assessments (paper-and-pencil self-report), the purpose (to assess symptoms of substance abuse to better understand the relationship between substance abuse and depression), the nature of confidentiality (anonymous data collection), the use of such information (only for research purposes and will not be communicated to the client's primary therapist nor associated with the client's treatment records), and that declining to participate in the research will in no way affect the services the participant is currently or may be eligible to receive at the treatment center.

Inducements for research participation and the voluntary nature of consent.

Psychologists often offer incentives and compensation (such as gift certificates, cash, tangible goods, and class credit) in recognition of the participants' value (or to offset the cost) of the time and effort spent as a participant in a study. Researchers who offer inducements must make sometimes-difficult determinations about what type and level of compensation is fair so as to not undervalue participation, but also to avoid coercing participation, especially among vulnerable populations.

Payments to research participants has long been a controversial topic, and questions have been raised about the degree to which payments unduly influences the decision to participate in a study (Macklin, 1981). Concerns exist that participants may lie or conceal information to meet inclusion criteria for a particular study if the inducements are excessive (Fisher, 2009), potentially leading to harm to participants or others, or providing inaccurate or misleading knowledge that may partially invalidate the results of a particular study.

For some research designs, professional services (such as assessment and/or treatment) are provided as compensation for participant time and effort. In these cases, researchers must make clear the exact nature of the services being offered (including limitations) and the terms of the exchange (i.e., if the participant must complete all aspects of data collection or is entitled to receive services if they complete only part; Standard 8.06, Offering Inducements for Research Participation; APA, 2010). Furthermore, participants also must be provided with information

about the right to decline or withdraw participation, and be provided with referrals and alternative affordable services, if available and appropriate.

Payment in-kind.

Arguments for and against participant compensation in forms other than cash (known as *payment in kind*), such as goods or certificates in exchange for goods, continue to be debated. On the one hand, cash money may represent a significant decisional influence on those with limited financial means, perhaps unintentionally coercing participation in research in which they otherwise would not have participated without such incentive (Grady, 2001). On the other hand, researchers who actively avoid compensating with cash because of concerns about what participants may do with the money (e.g., procure illegal drugs, gamble) may be hindering participant autonomy by a priori deciding that cash is not appropriate for the participant. In addition, alternatives to cash may not be seen as being of equal value in terms of compensation (Schonfeld, Brown, Weniger, & Gordon, 2003). Finally, the use of incentives in lieu of cash may unintentionally communicate certain judgments toward participants or have other negative effects. For example, research has suggested that participants may find that research that purposely provides alternative incentives in lieu of cash to be denigrating and offensive (Oransky, Fisher, Mahadevan, & Singer, 2009).

Required university-based research and the voluntary nature of consent.

Some education institutions (e.g., colleges and universities) require participation in research studies as part of the curriculum, as a component of a specific class (such as an introductory psychology course), or to obtain extra credit. Such experiences may provide students with a first-hand learning experience about the nature of research and participation. Institutions that require research participation must be sensitive to the possibility that students may not wish to participate in the research being offered by the institution at the time, or in research in general. Therefore, to avoid possible coercion and exploitation, the APA Ethics Code (Standard 8.04b, Client/Patient, Student, and Subordinate Research Participants; APA, 2010) requires that students be given a nonresearch choice that is equitable in terms of time and effort to participation in a research study. These may include attending a related education lecture or completing a writing assignment.

The rational nature of informed consent.   The final requirement of informed consent is that the decision to participate in research must be rational. That is, the participant must have the capability to understand the relevant information about the research study and evaluate the pros and cons of participating (as it relates to his or her particular situation) to arrive at a well-reasoned participation decision. These considerations become particularly relevant when working with individuals who have certain clinical disorders (such as schizophrenia), children and adolescents, and individuals with intellectual disability, as their capacity to comprehend the information necessary to arrive at a rational participation decision may be particularly vulnerable. As such, informed consent procedures with these at-risk groups may pose special challenges to the rational understanding of relevant research procedures and rights.

To ensure rational consent, investigators must determine participant consent capacity. This determination can be complex, as researchers attempt to balance the goals of protecting participant welfare by preventing ill-informed decisions that may be harmful or exploitative with the aim of preserving autonomy. Psycholegal standards used in the determination of consent capacity have been proposed by Appelbaum and Grisso (1995) and include that the individual (a) understands the purpose, procedures, and basic informed consent information relevant to the study; (b) appreciates the risks and benefits of participation in the specific research as it will affect him or her personally; (c) is capable of weighing the risks and benefits of participation in the study to make the best decision for that participant; and (d) is capable of communicating a decision about participation.

Informed consent with vulnerable populations. The informed consent process with vulnerable and at-risk populations often presents novel and unique ethical dilemmas. Individuals who have poor or questionable consent capacity should be provided

with resources and protections against ill-informed decisions that may result in harmful consequences (Delano, 2005). For example, investigators may consider instituting alternative research procedures to address possible capacity vulnerabilities, such as altering the informed consent process to increase comprehension (e.g., reading the information to participants, using language that is easier to understand, repeating consent information throughout the study, assessing their comprehension throughout the process), developing advanced research directives, or appointing surrogate decision makers (DuBois, 2007).

Informed consent for clinical research with psychiatric or impaired populations.   Many recent and historic research studies that have been seen as abusive and harmful have included vulnerable populations who lack adequate decision-making skills. Individuals with decisional impairments (including conditions that actually or reasonably would be expected to compromise cognitive functioning related to decision making) present researchers with unique questions about the appropriateness of standard informed consent procedures. Children and adolescents with psychiatric disorders represent especially vulnerable populations, in which developmental levels or psychiatric symptoms (or a combination thereof) may impair their ability to adequately understand or voluntarily consent or assent to participation (Hoagwood, 2003).

The presence of a psychiatric disorder or intellectual disability does not in and of itself necessarily render a participant unable to provide valid informed consent. For example, research with psychiatric populations suggests that the presence of a psychiatric disorder (Carpenter et al., 2000), the severity of the condition (Carpenter et al., 2000; Palmer et al., 2005), or hospitalization history (Kovnick, Appelbaum, Hoge, & Leadbetter, 2003) may be individually poor indicators of consent capacity, because significant variation exists within these characteristics (Fried & Fisher, 2008). In addition, research by Fisher, Cea, Davidson, and Fried (2006) that assessed the ability of adults with intellectual disabilities to provide informed consent (based on Appelbaum & Grisso's, 1995, four psycholegal standards) found that, on average, adults with mild intellectual disabilities performed as well as adults without intellectual disability on several indexes of consent comprehension.

Informed consent for research with children and adolescents. Children have the right to expect that they will be treated fairly and their interests will be protected by researchers (Fisher, 2009). Investigators should be aware that research with children and adolescents often is guided by specific laws, regulations, and guidelines that may differ from those governing research with adults. Aside from the fact that most children and adolescents may not independently legally consent to participation in a research study, many do not have the cognitive skills to independently weigh the risks and benefits of participation, making their ability to provide rational and voluntary consent questionable (Bruzzese & Fisher, 2003; Fisher, 2009; Fisher & Masty, 2006). To protect children and adolescents from potentially making harmful decisions with regard to research participation, when informed consent is mandatory, regulations and professional codes of conduct, in most cases, require consent from a legally authorized party. Certain exceptions exist, such as when the research project has been approved by an IRB to dispense with informed consent or when seeking consent from a guardian may pose a risk or otherwise not be in the best interests of the child. In such cases, researchers should consider alternative consent methods, such as the appointment of a consent advocate or representative to ensure that participants' rights and welfare are protected (Fisher, 2004).

Parental consent does not guarantee that children will not be exposed to potentially damaging methods or material (Fisher & Rosendahl, 1990). In addition to formal consent from parents, the APA Ethics Code (Standard 3.10b, Informed Consent; APA, 2010) requires that researchers provide child and adolescent participants with relevant information about the prospective study when appropriate so that they may make a decision (assent or dissent) about participation. In most cases, a child's decision against participating in research should be respected (exceptions may include certain types of clinical

research for which the study may represent an opportunity for treatment for an otherwise relatively untreatable condition or disorder).

Investigators also should be aware of what Fisher (2005) has described as the *assent paradox*, in which key aspects of the research (such as the risks and benefits, the voluntary nature of participation, and their right to withdraw without penalty) are explained to children, but they may not fully understand or believe that their participation is voluntary and they are free to withdraw at any time. It is also important to remember that although children and adolescents may lack the cognitive ability to provide truly informed consent, methods and techniques can be used to improve consent capacity (Abramovitch, Freedman, Henry, & Van Brunschot, 1995; Bruzzese & Fisher, 2003; Tymchuk, 1992). Researchers who are considering conducting research with children and adolescents should familiarize themselves with the appropriate informed consent literature to design consent procedures that are respectful of both areas of comprehension strength and weakness (Fisher et al., 2006; Fisher & Fried, 2010; Fisher & Ragsdale, 2006; Fried & Fisher, 2008).

Researchers also should be aware that school-based research may be governed by a number of federal regulations, laws (e.g., Family Educational Rights and Privacy Act of 1974; Protection of Pupil Rights Amendment of 2004), and professional guidelines. Some child and adolescent researchers use *passive consent* methods in schools and other settings, in which legal guardians are given information about an upcoming study and must alert the school or researchers if they object to their child participating in the research. This practice is controversial, and it has been argued that it violates the spirit and intent of informed consent (Fisher, 2004; Hicks, 2005). Passive consent procedures are generally not considered consistent with federal regulations or the APA Ethics Code (APA, 2010) except in specific circumstances, such as when the IRB has granted a waiver of guardian consent (in which case researchers may still inform a guardian of the research before his or her child participates) or when research meets Standard 8.05, Dispensing With Informed Consent for Research (Fisher, 2009).

Waiver of informed consent. Certain types of research may qualify for a waiver of informed consent under federal regulations (DHHS, 2001) and the APA Ethics Code (APA, 2010). Under current federal guidelines, research must meet four criteria for an IRB to consider waiving informed consent procedures: (a) The research represents minimal risk (as described, a type of research category used in federal research regulations that is synonymous with everyday occurrences, such as normal tasks associated with school or work, physician check-ups, or employment assessments) and therefore is not expected to cause significant physical or emotional distress or harm; (b) waiver of the informed consent will not negatively affect the rights and welfare of participants; (c) the waiver is necessary to feasibly complete the research; and (d) information about the study will be provided to participants whenever feasible and appropriate.

Any waiver of informed consent must be granted by an IRB or other research review group, which will complete a risk–benefit analysis with respect to the proposed research and waiver, and then determine whether the study meets the appropriate criteria (Elliot, 2006). Researchers should note that even if an IRB grants a waiver of informed consent, the board still may require the researcher to implement debriefing procedures. Standard 8.05, Dispensing with Informed Consent (APA, 2010) specifies the types of research in this category, which includes certain studies conducted in schools; research designs in which personal and otherwise-identifiable information is not associated with research data (and cannot be linked), such as anonymous or naturalistic designs; certain types of archival research; and certain analyses of job or organizational effectiveness (in which the employment status of the individual would not be at risk and confidentiality is protected).

Deception Research

Investigators engage in deception when they either deliberately misinform or purposely do not provide a participant with information that might reasonably be expected to affect their decision to participate in a research study (Fisher, 2005; Fisher & Fyrberg, 1994; Sieber, 1982). Deception research has been and continues to be a controversial method of scientific inquiry because of the delicate balance of risks and benefits inherent in the design. On the one hand, deception research has the potential to generate valuable and beneficial knowledge that otherwise would be unattainable with research that uses non-deceptive techniques. On the other, it has been argued that deception research violates the autonomy and self-determination of individuals and may harm the integrity of the relationship between participant and investigator (Sieber, 1982).

In effect, deception research deprives the individual of the ability to make a truly informed decision about participation because the individual has not been given a priori the correct or comprehensive information about the purpose or nature of the study (Fisher, 2009; Sieber, 1982). Because of the unique and potentially significant risks associated with deception research (compared with nondeceptive techniques), the APA Ethics Code (APA, 2010) requires that research that employs deceptive techniques must demonstrate that (a) the use of such methods are "justified by the study's significant prospective scientific, educational, or applied value" (p. 11) and (b) nondeceptive techniques and methods are not scientifically practical or appropriate. With respect to this final condition, Fisher (2009) has noted that researchers who elect to use deceptive techniques over nondeceptive alternatives because of time, effort, or cost considerations may be in violation of this standard. In addition to the scientific requirements, the APA Ethics Code (APA, 2010) prohibits deceptive techniques when the research would cause physical pain or significant emotional discomfort or distress.

One frequent question in deception research is whether and when participants should be told about deceptive techniques (commonly referred to as *dehoaxing*). The APA Ethics Code (APA, 2010) requires that participants be informed of any deceptive techniques "as early as is feasible" (p. 11), which provides the researcher with some leeway in terms of timing. Although it is certainly preferable to inform participants about the use of deceptive techniques at the end of their research participation, the scientific validity of certain studies may be compromised if other prospective participants are informed about the nature and purpose of the techniques (i.e., through word of mouth from past participants). For this reason, the Ethics Code permits psychologists to wait until the end of data collection to inform participants of the use of deceptive techniques.

It is important to distinguish between debriefing (which is required in most research protocols and provides individuals with information about the study after participation, whether or not deceptive techniques have been used) and dehoaxing (which applies to deceptive techniques). Reactions to dehoaxing techniques can range from participants experiencing embarrassment, discomfort, and anger to participants verbalizing an understanding of the scientific need for the research to employ deceptive techniques (Fisher & Fyrberg, 1994).

Psychologists must take steps to desensitize participants or alleviate potentially negative reactions following dehoaxing. Sieber (1983) recommended that dehoaxing techniques should address potential participant mistrust and lost confidence in scientific research as well as provide the individual with a feeling of satisfaction about their participation by conveying the social or scientific benefits of the research project.

Researchers should be aware and prepare for the possibility that many participants may not reveal negative reactions to the researcher at the time of dehoaxing or debriefing (Fisher & Fyrberg, 1994) and, therefore, techniques should address potentially delayed or long-lasting negative reactions. Finally, the APA Ethics Code (APA, 2010) requires that once participants learn of the deceptive techniques used in the study, they be given the option to withdraw their data from analysis.

Research Debriefing

Standard 8.08, Debriefing (APA, 2010) requires that researchers debrief participants after most studies by providing them with relevant information about the study and giving them an opportunity to ask questions (either immediately after the study or at a later date, by providing contact information). Debriefing also offers an opportunity for the researcher to address any harm that may have occurred as a result of participation in the study. This may be especially important in certain types of clinical research,

research with children and vulnerable populations, and research that taps emotionally provocative subject matter, such as trauma.

Unlike dehoaxing, debriefing techniques apply to all types of research and provide an opportunity to correct any misconceptions or erroneous beliefs about the study or their participation (APA, 2010). In certain studies, debriefing may significantly compromise the scientific validity of a study or harm participants (e.g., eliciting negative feelings, such as embarrassment, anxiety or stress, or anger). This is particularly common with children, who may lack the ability to understand the purpose of research or the nature of the procedures (Fisher, 2009; Sieber, 1983). Similar to the determination of when it is appropriate to dispense with informed consent, the decision to exclude or otherwise alter standard debriefing procedures should be done only in consultation with an institution's IRB or research review group.

It is important for investigators to remember that their responsibility to participants does not end with the completion of data collection. Rather, researchers must be committed to preventing or minimizing harm that may result from participation in the study (Keith-Spiegel & Koocher, 1985) and consider that participants may not disclose harms during the debriefing session (Fisher & Fyrberg, 1994).

Confidentiality

Protecting confidentiality reflects not only the fidelity and responsibility that exist toward the people with whom researchers work, but also exemplifies respect for people's rights to autonomy and privacy. Promises of confidentiality help to ensure that participants feel secure in providing honest and accurate answers to research questions and participate fully in study-related tasks. Without such confidentiality methods, participants may fear or experience significant types of harm, including embarrassment, and emotional, legal, financial, or social harm, depending on the nature of the data and breach.

Methods to ensure confidentiality are required in both federal regulations (DHHS, 2001) and professional guidelines governing research. For example, 45 C.F.R. § 46.111 requires that institutional approval for research cannot be granted without adequate methods to protect confidential data (when appropriate), such as methods to maintain security, coding, storage, and disposal. In addition, the APA Ethics Code (APA, 2010) includes several standards with respect to confidentiality and disclosures (see Standard 4.01, Maintaining Confidentiality; Standard 4.04, Minimizing Intrusions on Privacy; and Standard 4.05, Disclosures). The applicability of such regulations and standards will depend on the type of research being conducted. For example, researchers collecting data via the Internet or other such medium may employ specific and unique methods for maintaining confidentiality (such as firewall protection or data encryption) that may differ significantly from those used in other research data collection mechanisms, such as those used in audio or video observational data or paper-and-pencil surveys. Researchers should consult relevant literature, professional guidelines, and their IRB about appropriate methods of maintaining data security and confidentiality.

As indicated in the section Informed Consent, researchers may be mandated to disclose certain information learned during the research process. Knowing when it is necessary to disclose confidential information may not always be clear, especially when research concerns potentially illegal and dangerous behaviors, such as alcohol and drug use, possibility of suicide, and violence.[1] In general, investigators should prepare for the types of disclosures and reports that they may have to make as it relates to their areas of research. This would include researching the federal, state, and local laws and the institutional regulations governing disclosures and reporting as well as identifying local community agencies and health care facilities that could be used as referral sources (Fisher & Goodman, 2009). For example, researchers who propose to study levels of personal anger and frustration among full-time caretakers of elderly family members should consult local, state, and federal laws (as well as with colleagues and their IRB) to determine any elder abuse and neglect reporting requirements and procedures. Researchers should include such information in the informed consent process as well as information about low-cost counseling resources, respite services, and relevant support groups.

Researchers who are collecting data on potentially sensitive information should consider applying for a *certificate of confidentiality* (Public Health Service Act, Section, 301(d), 42 U.S.C. Section 241(d)) before the commencement of data collection. The certificate, offered by National Institutes of Health and other DHHS agencies, protects the investigator (and those associated with data collection) from being compelled (either by law enforcement, subpoena, or otherwise) to produce identifiable research data that may expose a research participant to potential harm (e.g., legal or financial). (See http://nih.gov/grants/policy/coc/ for additional information about certificates of confidentiality.) Researchers should be aware that the certificate of confidentiality does not absolve them of mandatory reporting requirements, such as in the case of child abuse. Furthermore, as a matter of policy, DHHS staff may request access to research data that otherwise is protected by the certificate of confidentiality. The intent, scope, and limitations of the certificate of confidentiality should be communicated clearly to prospective participants during the informed consent process.

Conflicts of Interest

Attention to conflicts of interest in biomedical and behavioral research has increased in recent years. Conflicts of interest are potentially harmful when a researcher or reviewer's professional judgment or decision making is influenced by some other interest (e.g., professional advancement, financial gain, commercial interests). Investigators who conduct studies without disclosing potentially significant conflicts of interests risk the integrity of the profession by tingeing research results with a degree of uncertainty and doubt about the degree to which (if at all) the conflict or potential conflict (such as ties with a private or corporate sponsor or institution) may have influenced the planning, collection, interpretation, or dissemination of the research data.

---

[1]See Fisher and Goodman (2009) for an excellent discussion of confidentiality and disclosure procedures in nonintervention research with dangerous and illegal behaviors.

Such conflicts also have the potential to threaten the public's trust in science (Goldner, 2000). Examples of potential conflicts of interest in biomedical and behavioral research may include certain industry-sponsored research and financial or employment relationships between the investigator or research institution and a company, institution, or group that may have some interest in the outcome of a particular study.

As a result of increased attention to these issues, regulatory and professional bodies have begun to address conflicts of interest more directly. For example, the APA Ethics Code included a new standard solely about conflicts of interest (Standard 3.06, Conflict of Interest, APA, 2010) in its 2002 revision that focuses on conflicts that may impair the professional work of a psychologist or have the potential to harm or exploit those with whom they work. The APA Task Force on External Funding also published recommendations with respect to conflicts of interest in research, practice, and education (Pachter, Fox, Zimbardo, & Antonuccio, 2007).

Relational Approaches to Research Ethics

Relational approaches to ethical decision making frame research aims and procedures as a product of the association between the investigator and participant in the research context. Such approaches encourage moral discourse between participant and investigator to construct optimal scientific methods and adequately resolve ethical questions (Fisher, 1999; Fisher & Fried, 2010; Fisher & Goodman, 2009; Fisher & Masty, 2006; Fisher & Ragsdale, 2006). Two relational ethics methods are briefly discussed: (a) goodness of fit and (b) community consultation and colearning procedures.

Goodness of fit. Goodness-of-fit approaches frequently have been used to shape informed consent procedures with populations with questionable consent capacity. Rather than exclusively focusing on consent vulnerabilities associated with the specific population, a goodness-of-fit approach views consent capacity interactively in terms of the participant and research context and seeks to explore methods of modifying the research process and environment to increase capacity (Fisher, 2003; Fisher

& Fried, 2010; Fisher & Goodman, 2009; Fisher & Masty, 2006; Masty & Fisher, 2008). For example, research with individuals with intellectual disabilities requires careful consideration with regard to the appropriateness of standard informed consent procedures within the specific scientific context, as standard informed consent methods may lead to harm or exploitation because of weaknesses in consent comprehension (Fisher, Cea, Davidson, & Fried, 2006). A goodness-of-fit approach would include consideration of alternative methods to ensure that consent is informed, voluntary, and rational, such as reviewing consent capacity research conducted with similar populations, assessing the consent capacity of participants, simplifying the consent language, using multimedia methods to present consent information, employing educational tools to enhance consent capacity, and including other individuals in the consent process to provide guidance to participants (such as family members, consent advocates, or consent surrogates; Fisher, 2003; Fried & Fisher, 2008).

Community consultation and colearning procedures. Another set of relational ethics methods used by researchers working with human participants is colearning and community consultation, which recognizes that certain types of research designs and procedures may represent differing levels of risk, depending on the population (Fisher & Fried, 2010). According to this perspective, individuals may hold certain views toward research (including reactions, attitudes, and perspectives about scientific motives and methods, and researchers) that may have serious implications for the methods used by researchers and the type and level of protections instituted. Therefore, according to a relational ethics approach, to adequately shape research methods to the specific research–participant environment, investigators must learn more about the population from their participants and communities (Fisher, 2002; Fisher & Fried, 2010; Fisher & Fyrberg, 1994; Fisher & Masty, 2006; Fisher & Wallace, 2000). Consultation with participant communities represents a valuable opportunity for researchers to gain support for the proposed study and enhance trust among participants (Fisher et al.,

2002; Hoagwood, 2003; Melton, Levine, Koocher, Rosenthal, & Thompson, 1988). Such methods may be especially important for traditionally disenfranchised communities who may distrust not only the motives of investigators but also the methods of the scientific enterprise in general (Fisher & Wallace, 2000).

Research with vulnerable or impaired populations requires careful and thoughtful consideration on the part of investigators. Even well-intentioned scientists can unknowingly cause harm through their work, such as through the use of culturally insensitive research tools or dissemination methods that stigmatize groups of people or communities. Although participant perspectives can never replace or override the investigator's responsibility to conduct ethically sound and scientifically valid research, community consultation can provide investigators with important knowledge to contribute to selection and implementation of optimal research procedures (Fisher & Fried, 2010).

CONCLUSION

The responsible conduct of research with human participants often requires investigators to engage in sometimes-challenging ethical decision making in response to complex dilemmas, irrespective of the type of research and participants or the level of experience of the researcher. Psychologists often engage federal regulations, state and local laws, IRBs, and the APA Ethics Code (APA, 2010) to inform their professional behaviors. Although these resources provide guidance with respect to planning, executing, and disseminating research, at times they may appear to be in conflict with each other or may be silent on certain issues, without a clear resolution. Such situations require psychologists to engage in a decision-making process that both respects the welfare, rights, and autonomy of participants while also preserving the scientific integrity of the research and fulfilling the investigator's obligations and professional responsibilities. Effective science-in-ethics decision making, while informed by these resources as well as the moral compass of the investigators, advice of colleagues, and guidance of IRBs, often requires consideration of how the research environment interacts with participant views, strengths, and vulnerabilities. Relational ethics may provide a helpful framework for scientists to shape research methods and practices to the specific research situation.

References

Abramovitch, R., Freedman, J. L., Henry, K., & Van Brunschot, M. (1995). Children's capacity to agree to psychological research: Knowledge of risks and benefits and voluntariness. *Ethics and Behavior, 5*, 25–48. doi:10.1207/s15327019eb0501_3

American Psychological Association. (2010). *Ethical principles of psychologists and code of conduct (2002, Amended June 1, 2010)*. Retrieved from http://www.apa.org/ethics/code/index.aspx

Appelbaum, P. S., & Grisso, T. (1995). The MacArthur Treatment Competence Study: Mental illness and the competence to consent to treatment. *Law and Human Behavior, 19*, 105–126. doi:10.1007/BF01499321

Appelbaum, P. S., & Rosenbaum, A. (1989). *Tarasoff* and the researchers: Does the duty to protect apply in the research setting. *American Psychologist, 44*, 885–894. doi:10.1037/0003-066X.44.6.885

Appelbaum, P. S., Roth, L. H., Lidz, C. W., Benson, P., & Winslade, W. (1987). False hopes and best data: Consent to research and the therapeutic misconception. *The Hastings Center Report, 17*, 20–24. doi:10.2307/3562038

Bankert, E. A., & Amdur, R. J. (Eds.). (2005). *Institutional review board: Management and function* (2nd ed.). Sudbury, MA: Jones & Bartlett.

Brandt, A. M. (1978). Racism and research: The case of the Tuskegee syphilis study. *Hastings Center Magazine*, 21–29.

Bruzzese, J. M., & Fisher, C. B. (2003). Assessing and enhancing the research consent capacity of children and youth. *Applied Developmental Science, 7*, 13–26. doi:10.1207/S1532480XADS0701_2

Carpenter, W. T., Jr., Gold, J. M., Lahti, A. C., Queern, C. A., Conley, R. R., Bartko, J. J., . . . Appelbaum, P. S. (2000). Decisional capacity for informed consent in schizophrenia research. *Archives of General Psychiatry, 57*, 533–538. doi:10.1001/archpsyc.57.6.533

Delano, S. J. (2005). Research involving adults with decisional impairment. In E. A. Bankert & R. J. Amdur (Eds.), *Institutional review board: Management and function* (2nd ed., pp. 373–377). Sudbury, MA: Jones & Bartlett.

Department of Health and Human Services. (2001). Title 45: Public Welfare, Part 46, *Code of Federal Regulations, Protection of Human Subjects*. Washington, DC: U.S. Government Printing Office.

DuBois, J. (2007). *Ethics in mental health research: Principles, guidance, and cases.* New York, NY: Oxford University Press.

Elliot, M. M. (2006). Research without consent or documentation thereof. In E. A. Bankert & R. J. Amdur (Eds.), *Institutional review board: Management and function* (2nd ed., pp. 216–221). Sudbury, MA: Jones & Bartlett.

Fisher, C. B. (1999). Relational ethics and research with vulnerable populations. In *Reports on research involving persons with mental disorders that may affect decision making capacity* (Vol. 2, pp. 29–49). Rockville, MD: National Bioethics Advisory Commission.

Fisher, C. B. (2002). Participant consultation: Ethical insights into parental permission and confidentiality procedures for policy relevant research with youth. In R. M. Lerner, F. Jacobs, & D. Wertlieb (Eds.), *Handbook of applied developmental science* (Vol. 4, pp. 371–396). Thousand Oaks, CA: Sage.

Fisher, C. B. (2003). A goodness-of-fit ethic for informed consent to research involving persons with mental retardation and developmental disabilities. *Mental Retardation and Developmental Disabilities Research Reviews, 9,* 27–31. doi:10.1002/mrdd.10052

Fisher, C. B. (2004). Informed consent and clinical research involving children and adolescents: Implications of the revised APA Ethics Code and HIPAA. *Journal of Clinical Child and Adolescent Psychology, 33,* 832–839. doi:10.1207/s15374424jccp3304_18

Fisher, C. B. (2005). Deception research involving children: Ethical practice and paradox. *Ethics and Behavior, 15,* 271–287. doi:10.1207/s15327019eb1503_7

Fisher, C. B. (2009). *Decoding the ethics code* (2nd ed.). Thousand Oaks, CA: Sage.

Fisher, C. B., Cea, C., Davidson, P., & Fried, A. L. (2006). Capacity of persons with mental retardation to consent to participation in randomized clinical trials. *The American Journal of Psychiatry, 163,* 1813–1820. doi:10.1176/appi.ajp.163.10.1813

Fisher, C. B., & Fried, A. L. (2003). Internet-mediated psychological services and the APA ethics code. *Psychotherapy: Theory, Research, Practice, Training, 40,* 103–111. doi:10.1037/0033-3204.40.1-2.103

Fisher, C. B., & Fried, A. L. (2010). Ethical issues and challenges in applied research in child and adolescent development. In V. Malhomes & C. Lomanoco (Eds.), *Applied research in adolescent development* (pp. 131–152). London, England: Taylor & Francis.

Fisher, C. B., & Fyrberg, D. (1994). Participant Partners: College students weigh the costs and benefits of deceptive research. *American Psychologist, 49,* 417–427. doi:10.1037/0003-066X.49.5.417

Fisher, C. B., & Goodman, S. J. (2009). Goodness-of-fit ethics for nonintervention research involving dangerous and illegal behaviors. In D. Buchanan, C. B. Fisher, & L. Gable (Eds.), *Research with high-risk populations: Balancing science, ethics, and law* (pp. 25–46). Washington, DC: American Psychological Association. doi:10.1037/11878-001

Fisher, C. B., Hoagwood, K., Boyce, C., Duster, T., Frank, D. A., Grisso, T., . . . Zayas, L. H. (2002). Research ethics for mental health science involving ethnic minority children and youth. *American Psychologist, 57,* 1024–1040. doi:10.1037/0003-066X.57.12.1024

Fisher, C. B., Hoagwood, K., & Jensen, P. (1996). Casebook on ethical issues in research with children and adolescents with mental disorders. In K. Hoagwood, P. Jensen, & C. B. Fisher (Eds.), *Ethical issues in research with children and adolescents with mental disorders* (pp. 135–238). Hillsdale, NJ: Erlbaum.

Fisher, C. B., Kornetsky, S. Z., & Prentice, E. D. (2007). Determining risk in pediatric research with no prospect of direct benefit: Time for a national consensus on the interpretation of federal regulations. *The American Journal of Bioethics, 7,* 5–10. doi:10.1080/15265160601171572

Fisher, C. B., & Masty, J. K. (2006). Community perspectives on the ethics of adolescent risk research. In B. Leadbeater, T. Reicken, C. Benoit, M. Jansson, & A. Marshall (Eds.), *Research ethics in community-based and participatory action research with youth* (pp. 22–41). Toronto, Ontario, Canada: University of Toronto Press.

Fisher, C. B., & Ragsdale, K. (2006). A goodness-of-fit ethics for multicultural research. In J. Trimble & C. B. Fisher (Eds.), *The handbook of ethical research with ethnocultural populations and communities* (pp. 3–26). Thousand Oaks, CA: Sage.

Fisher, C. B., & Rosendahl, S. A. (1990). Risks and remedies of research participation. In C. B. Fisher & W. W. Tryon (Eds.), *Ethics in applied developmental psychology: Emerging issues in an emerging field* (pp. 43–59). Norwood, NJ: Ablex.

Fisher, C. B., & Wallace, S. A. (2000). Through the community looking glass: Re-evaluating the ethical and policy implications of research on adolescent risk and psychopathology. *Ethics and Behavior, 10,* 99–118. doi:10.1207/S15327019EB1002_01

Freedman, B. (1975). A moral theory of informed consent. *The Hastings Center Report, 5,* 32–39. doi:10.2307/3561421

Freedman, B. (1987). Equipoise and the ethics of clinical research. *The New England Journal of Medicine, 317,* 141–145. doi:10.1056/NEJM198707163170304

Fried, A. L., & Fisher, C. B. (2008). The ethics of informed consent for research in clinical and abnormal psychology. In D. McKay (Ed.), *Handbook of research methods in abnormal and clinical psychology* (pp. 5–22). Thousand Oaks, CA: Sage.

Goldner, J. A. (2000). Dealing with conflicts of interest in biomedical research: IRB oversight as the next best solution to the abolitionist approach. *The Journal of Law, Medicine, and Ethics, 28*, 379–404.

Grady, C. (2001). Money for research participation: Does it jeopardize informed consent? *The American Journal of Bioethics, 1*, 40–44. doi:10.1162/152651601300 169031

Hicks, L. (2005). Research in public schools. In E. A. Bankert & R. J. Amdur (Eds.), *Institutional review board: Management and function* (2nd ed., pp. 341–345). Sudbury, MA: Jones & Bartlett.

Hoagwood, K. (2003). Ethical issues in child and adolescent psychosocial treatment research. In A. E. Kazdin & J. R. Weisz (Eds.), *Evidence-based psychotherapies for children and adolescents* (pp. 60–75). New York, NY: Guilford Press.

Horng, S., & Grady, C. (2003). Misunderstanding in clinical research: Distinguishing therapeutic misconception, therapeutic misestimation, and therapeutic optimism. *IRB: Ethics and Human Research, 25*, 11–16. doi:10.2307/3564408

Hunt, K. M. (2005). Explaining the cost of research participation. In E. A. Bankert & R. J. Amdur (Eds.), *Institutional review board: Management and function* (2nd ed., pp. 236–240). Sudbury, MA: Jones & Bartlett.

Keith-Spiegel, P., & Koocher, G. P. (1985). *Ethics in psychology: Professional standards and cases.* New York, NY: Crown.

Kopelman, L. (2004). Minimal risk as an international ethical standard in research. *Journal of Medicine and Philosophy, 29*, 351–358.

Kovnick, J. A., Appelbaum, P. S., Hoge, S. K., & Leadbetter, R. A. (2003). Competence to consent to research among long-stay inpatients with chronic schizophrenia. *Psychiatric Services, 54*, 1247–1252. doi:10.1176/appi.ps.54.9.1247

Macklin, R. (1981). "Due" and "undue" inducements: On paying money to research subjects. *IRB: Ethics and Human Research, 3*, 1–6. doi:10.2307/3564136

Masty, J., & Fisher, C. (2008). Ethics of treatment and intervention research with children and adolescents with behavioral and mental disorders. *Ethics and Behavior, 18*, 139–160. doi:10.1080/1050842080 2063897

Melton, G. B., Levine, R. J., Koocher, G. P., Rosenthal, R., & Thompson, W. C. (1988). Community consultation in socially sensitive research: Lessons from clinical trials of treatments for AIDS. *American Psychologist, 43*, 573–581. doi:10.1037/0003-066X.43.7.573

National Commission for the Protection of Human Subjects of Biomedical and Behavioral Research. (1979). The Belmont Report: Ethical principles and guidelines for the protection of human subjects in research. In B. Steinbock, J. D. Arras, & A. J. London (Eds.), *Ethical issues in modern medicine* (6th ed., pp. 738–745). New York, NY: McGraw-Hill.

Nuremberg Code. (1949). *Trials of war criminals before the Nuremberg military tribunals under Control Council Law No. 10* (Vol. 2, pp. 181–182). Washington, DC: U.S. Government Printing Office. Retrieved from http://ohsr.od.nih.gov/guidelines/ nuremberg.html

Oransky, M., Fisher, C. B., Mahadevan, M., & Singer, M. (2009). Barriers and opportunities for recruitment for nonintervention studies on HIV risk: Perspectives of street drug users. *Substance Use and Misuse, 44*, 1642–1659.

Pachter, W. S., Fox, R. E., Zimbardo, P., & Antonuccio, D. O. (2007). Corporate funding and conflicts of interest. A primer for psychologists. *American Psychologist, 62*, 1005–1015. doi:10.1037/0003-066X.62.9.1005

Palmer, B. W., Dunn, L. B., Appelbaum, P. S., Mudaliar, S., Thai, L., Henry, R., . . . Jeste, D. V. (2005). Assessment of capacity to consent to research among older persons with schizophrenia, Alzheimer disease, or diabetes mellitus. *Archives of General Psychiatry, 62*, 726–733. doi:10.1001/archpsyc.62.7.726

Prentice, E. D., & Oki, G. (2005). Exempt from Institutional Review Board review. In E. A. Bankert & R. J. Amdur (Eds.), *Institutional review board: Management and function* (2nd ed., pp. 93–96). Sudbury, MA: Jones & Bartlett.

Rothman, D. J., & Rothman, S. M. (1984). *The Willowbrook Wars.* New York, NY: Harper & Row.

Rothman, K. J., & Michaels, K. B. (1994). The continued unethical use of placebo controls. *New England Journal of Medicine, 331*, 394–398.

Schonfeld, T. L., Brown, J. S., Weniger, M., & Gordon, B. (2003). Research involving the homeless: Arguments against payment-in-kind (PinK). *IRB: Ethics and Human Research, 25*, 17–20. doi:10.2307/3564602

Shah, S., Whittle, A., Wilfond, B., Gensler, G., & Wendler, D. (2004). How do institutional review boards apply the federal risk and benefit standards for pediatric research. *JAMA, 291*, 476–482. doi:10.1001/ jama.291.4.476

Sieber, J. E. (1982). Deception in social research I: Kinds of deception and the wrongs they may involve. *IRB: Ethics and Human Research, 4*, 1–5. doi:10.2307/3564511

Sieber, J. E. (1983). Deception in social research III: The nature and limits of debriefing. *IRB: Ethics and Human Research, 5*, 1–4. doi:10.2307/3564511

Tymchuk, A. J. (1992). Assent process. In B. Stanley & J. E. Sieber (Eds.), *Social research on children and adolescents* (pp. 128–139). Newbury Park, CA: Sage.

World Medical Association. (2008). *Declaration of Helsinki: Ethical principles for medical research involving human subjects.* Retrieved from http://www.wma.net/en/30publications/10policies/b3 (Original work published 1964)

CHAPTER 4

ETHICS AND REGULATION OF RESEARCH WITH NONHUMAN ANIMALS

Chana K. Akins and Sangeeta Panicker

The terms *research ethics* and *research regulation* often are used synonymously. On the one hand, loose usage of these two terms can be problematic—it can lead to loss of focus and thoughtless adherence to the letter of the law rather than the spirit of the law (regulation). On the other hand, it emphasizes the important relationship between the ethical principles that undergird the conduct of research and regulations that have evolved in response to a perceived need for oversight of the research enterprise.

Although the ethics of research with nonhuman animals is more complicated than the ethics of research with human participants, it also is more straightforward. When viewed within the framework of individual rights and freedoms, the ethics of conducting research with species incapable of providing consent may be regarded as problematic. It can be argued, however, that imposing such a human-centered framework on other species is inappropriate.

Dess and Foltin (2004) have provided a structure for discussing the ethics of research with nonhuman animals in their chapter titled "The Ethics Cascade." They proposed a series of questions to help teachers promote civil dialogue with students about the ethics of nonhuman animal research. The questions begin by addressing broad issues, such as who is the arbiter of morality, and gradually become more

focused on specific issues, such as the ethics of selecting one method over another comparable one.

As evidenced by the long history of biomedical and behavioral research with nonhuman animals[1] and the continuously evolving regulatory oversight mechanisms for such research, it is clear that we as a society have decided that conducting research with such animals has value and is ethically defensible and responsible. That being the case, what are our ethical obligations to our nonhuman animal research subjects? Conducting research with nonhuman animals is a privilege that society grants scientists—how should this privilege be respected and preserved?

CONTRIBUTIONS OF PSYCHOLOGICAL RESEARCH WITH NONHUMAN ANIMALS

Psychological research with nonhuman animals has played a significant role in advancing our understanding of processes of learning, memory, perception, motivation, and emotion. It also has contributed to the development of treatment for various clinical disorders, such as anxiety, schizophrenia, Alzheimer's disease, depression, phobias, learning disabilities, and addiction. Furthermore, such research has benefited nonhuman animals, such as in the development of programs to reestablish populations of endangered or threatened species. Carroll and

---

[1]Readers should note the use of the term *animal* throughout this chapter. As Hodos and Campbell (1990) pointed out, evolution is not linear with humans as the most perfectly evolved. Rather, evolution is branching, with *Homo sapiens* being only one of the more recently evolved limbs. Referring to laboratory animals as *infrahuman* or tacitly removing humans from the category of animals (as in the phrase *humans and animals*) has struck many behavioral scientists as inappropriate (Dess & Chapman, 1998; Poling, 1984). Therefore, we use the term *nonhuman animals* to recognize this logic.

DOI: 10.1037/13619-005
APA Handbook of Research Methods in Psychology: Vol. 1. Foundations, Planning, Measures, and Psychometrics, H. Cooper (Editor-in-Chief)

Overmier (2001) reviewed numerous contributions of psychological research using nonhuman animals, including the development of behavioral therapies to alleviate chronic pain, therapeutic drugs, and biofeedback-based therapies.

Many problems studied by psychologists involve trying to find causal relations among variables as they relate or contribute to psychological disorders. Some causal relations are not easily studied in humans. Research often needs to be conducted in controlled settings, and this is difficult, if not impossible, to do with humans. Therefore, another benefit of using nonhuman animals in psychological research is that the environment can be controlled and variables can be manipulated to clarify casual relations.

Researchers are legally and ethically required to consider the possibility of alternatives to using nonhuman animals. A literature search for alternatives such as tissue culture and computer simulations must be conducted before receiving approval to use animals for research purposes. Often, fundamental research questions cannot be addressed with these alternatives because the answers can be found only by studying intact organisms. Plants are not a viable alternative because they do not contain a nervous system. Tissue cultures might be used to study cellular processes, but how these processes operate in live organisms cannot be studied without an intact organism. Computer simulations are becoming more and more sophisticated; however, they require knowledge obtained from live behaving organisms and cannot be used to generate new information about behavior. Although these alternatives continue to become more advanced, they are nowhere near adequate substitutes for the use of nonhuman animals in psychological research.

With regard to the number of animals used for research purposes, about 90% of laboratory animals used in studies of psychology are rodents and birds, and only about 5% are nonhuman primates. Dogs and cats rarely are used in psychological research (American Psychological Association [APA], Committee on Animal Research and Ethics, 1996b). Furthermore, the number of animals used in research is small relative to the number of animals used for other purposes. In 2008, the U.S. Department of Agriculture's (USDA) Animal and Plant Health Inspection Service (APHIS) reported that the number of animals used for research remained at about 1 million, whereas more than 10 billion animals were used for food, and the latter number continues to increase.

ANIMAL RIGHTS VERSUS ANIMAL WELFARE: WHAT IS THE DIFFERENCE?

Most people believe that nonhuman animals should be afforded protections. Significant differences exist, however, in the goals and tactics of individuals and organizations who subscribe to animal rights ideology versus those who believe in animal welfare. It is important that the public understand these differences. Animal rights advocates generally oppose all activities that they believe involve the exploitation of animals, including, but not limited to, raising and slaughtering livestock for human or animal consumption, hunting, zoos, guide dogs for the disabled, search and rescue dogs, and the practice of owning pets. They also condemn any and all use of animals in research for human benefit. In contrast, animal welfare advocates endorse the responsible use of animals to satisfy certain human needs and also believe that humans have an obligation to treat animals humanely. Animal welfare advocates believe that humans are responsible for providing animals with basic needs, including food, water, shelter, and health, and ensuring that they do not experience unnecessary suffering.

Concern for Animal Welfare in the Laboratory

Many opponents to the use of animals in laboratory research believe that scientists may be lax about animal care or that they may go so far as to neglect animals in their care for the benefit of their research. Contrary to this belief, researchers not only are morally and ethically responsible for the care of the animals being used in their laboratories but also must provide adequate care to conduct good science. Animals that experience pain, discomfort, and other stress are likely to experience behavioral and physiological changes that may increase the variability of experimental results and introduce confounds.

In the event that some research requires that animals experience pain or discomfort, scientists are obligated to justify it and to minimize its extent.

As the debate about what the most humane treatment is for animals in the laboratory continues, regulations for animal care in laboratory research have increased. Although the increase in regulations is welcomed by some, particularly those who are opposed to the use of animals to benefit humans in any form, others believe that the increase in regulations might impede the progress of science—science that would not only benefit humans, but nonhuman animals as well. As regulations for animal care in laboratory research become increasingly stringent, the motivation behind increasing these regulations has become increasingly questionable. Often those leading the charge for increasing regulatory restrictions on research with nonhuman animals are entities that believe any and all research with nonhuman animals is unethical and should be abolished.

Many individuals also question whether these regulations are established on the basis of actual knowledge about the needs of nonhuman animals or on the basis of what humans consider might be comfortable for animals. For example, federal regulations require that animals be placed in a pain category (pain categories are discussed more in the following section), implying that they are experiencing pain and distress when they are food deprived. Certainly, too much food deprivation may result in distress and possibly even pain. Some empirical research, however, suggests that animals that are food deprived, to a certain degree, are perhaps healthier than those that are allowed to feed freely (Poling, Nickel, & Alling, 1990) because animals in the wild typically do not have free access to food whenever they choose. In contrast, laboratory animals that are not food deprived are allowed to eat as much food as they choose. These animals may gain excess weight and be more susceptible to poor health compared with those that experience more limited and natural food intake. This example suggests that animal care regulations should be considered carefully using specific knowledge about different species and their needs rather than basing decisions on human assumptions about what is most comfortable for animals.

Research Oversight With Nonhuman Animals

Research with nonhuman animals has multiple levels of oversight, many of which are overlapping. The original Laboratory Animal Welfare Act (AWA), also known as the Pet Protection Act, was passed by Congress in 1966 and was intended to prevent the theft of pet dogs and cats and their subsequent sale for research purposes. The current AWA includes the original law and several amendments passed by Congress in 1970, 1976, 1985, and most recently in 2002. APHIS is mandated by the AWA to oversee animal welfare for animals that are covered under the act. Research animals that are covered under the AWA regulations include warm-blooded animals with the exceptions of rats (of the genus *Rattus*), mice (of the genus *Mus*), and birds bred for the purpose of research.

The Public Health Service (PHS) policy differs from the AWA in that it covers all vertebrates and applies to all institutions that receive PHS funding. The PHS Office of Laboratory Animal Welfare (OLAW) oversees the care and use of vertebrate animals at these institutions and requires these institutions to file an Animal Welfare Assurance with OLAW stating how they will comply with PHS policy. The assurance is reviewed and approved by OLAW and holds the institution directly accountable. It represents a commitment that the institution will comply with the PHS policy, with the *Guide for the Care and Use of Laboratory Animals* (the *Guide*; Institute for Laboratory Animal Research [ILAR], 2011), and with the animal welfare regulation. A sample Animal Welfare Assurance can be found on the National Institutes of Health website (http://grants.nih.gov/grants/olaw/sampledoc/dlass60.rtf).

Both USDA regulations and PHS policy require that each facility where research with animals is conducted establish an Institutional Animal Care and Use Committee (IACUC) to provide oversight. At a minimum, the IACUC must include a veterinarian, a practicing scientist experienced in animal research, a person whose primary concerns are in nonscientific areas, and a person who is unaffiliated with the institution except as a member of the IACUC. The IACUC is charged with determining whether activities involving animals that occur at the institution are in accordance with the regulations.

In accordance with OLAW, the IACUC is federally mandated to perform the following responsibilities:

- Review the institution's program for humane care and use of animals at least every 6 months.
- Inspect all of the institution's animal facilities at least once every 6 months.
- Prepare reports of the IACUC evaluations and submit the reports to the institutional official. The reports must distinguish significant deficiencies from minor deficiencies. If program or facility deficiencies are noted, the reports must contain a reasonable and specific plan and schedule for correcting each deficiency.
- Review concerns involving the care and use of animals at the institution.
- Make written recommendations to the institutional official regarding any aspect of the institution's animal program, facilities, or personnel training.
- Review and approve, require modifications in (to secure approval), or withhold approval of activities related to the care and use of animals.
- Review and approve, require modifications in (to secure approval), or withhold approval of proposed significant changes regarding the use of animals in ongoing activities.
- Be authorized to suspend an activity involving animals.

It is important for investigators to understand that the IACUC has the authority to suspend an activity (protocol) that it previously approved. Suspension of an activity is a matter of ensuring institutional compliance, and it typically is done only when a researcher is conducting an activity with animals that has not received prior approval. It is the investigator's responsibility to seek approval (usually by submitting a new protocol or an amendment) for any new animal-use activity before conducting it.

HOW TO GET APPROVAL FOR ANIMAL USE: THE IACUC PROTOCOL

Before any project involving the use of animals may begin, all animal use activities must be documented in a protocol and be reviewed and approved by the IACUC. A sample proposal application for animal research can be found on the National Institutes of Health website (http://grants.nih.gov/grants/olaw/sampledoc/oacu3040-2.rtf). Following submission of a protocol, the IACUC typically assigns a designated reviewer and a veterinarian from the committee to conduct the review. The regulations, however, allow an opportunity for every IACUC member to request discussion of a protocol at a convened committee meeting.

The IACUC protocol application requires sufficient information about the project to evaluate whether the proposed activities comply with the regulations. The first part of the protocol application involves writing a nontechnical synopsis that should describe the project in layperson's language and address the use of animals in the project. Investigators are asked to list all internal and external funding sources related to the proposed studies. Federal policies require the IACUC to confirm that vertebrate animal studies that are described in grants coincide with descriptions in IACUC protocols.

Another key feature of the protocol review is adequate justification for the use of animals and for the number of animals being requested. Russell and Burch (1959) originally proposed the three Rs: replacement, reduction, and refinement. *Replacement* refers to whether animal use can be replaced by computer modeling, cell cultures, or with a phylogenetically lower species. As discussed, these alternatives typically are not likely to replace animal usage in psychological research. Nevertheless, adequate justification for not using these alternatives is required in the protocol. *Reduction* refers to reducing the number of animals necessary to satisfy the experimental objectives. Investigators are required to justify the number of animals requested and provide evidence for why this number is necessary for the proper interpretation of the results. A statistical power analysis is an acceptable way to justify the number of animals needed for an experiment. If a power analysis is not possible, a citation of previous research is acceptable. *Refinement* refers to utilizing methods to minimize pain and distress. Typically, this involves justifying the use of invasive techniques or the nonalleviation of potentially painful procedures with analgesics or other pain-relieving drugs. Investigators are expected to conduct a literature search to ensure that they are not duplicating the proposed research, that alternatives are not suitable for replacing animals in their experiments, and that they are using the least painful procedures without detracting from the scientific merit of the experiments.

The protocol application requires investigators to describe any expected adverse consequences that the animals may experience as a result of the procedures, such as loss of appetite, postoperative discomfort, or pain at an injection site. The investigator is asked to describe how animals will be monitored. This allows the veterinary staff to be preemptive of any adverse consequences and address them promptly when they arise.

PAIN CATEGORIES AND PAIN AND DISTRESS

As defined by animal welfare regulations, the USDA uses specific Humane Animal Use Categories. There is no Category A. Category B generally is restricted to animals used solely for breeding or holding purposes. These are animals that are not being experimentally manipulated. One example of this might be observing an animal in the wild without manipulating it or its environment. Animals assigned to Category C are on research, testing, or education protocols in which they are not subjected to more than slight or momentary pain or distress. Animals receiving routine procedures such as blood collection would fall in this category. Animals used in teaching, research, surgery, or tests involving pain or distress for which appropriate anesthetic, analgesic, or tranquilizing drugs are used are assigned to Category D. An essential component of any Category D protocol is the inclusion of an appropriate treatment (anesthesia, analgesia, euthanasia, etc.) to prevent, reduce, or eliminate the pain and distress. Animals that are typically assigned to Category E are used in teaching, experiments, research, surgery, or tests involving pain or distress in which the use of anesthetic, analgesic, or tranquilizing drugs would adversely affect the interpretation of the results. An explanation of the procedures that produce pain or distress in these

animals and the reasons such drugs will not be used must be provided to and approved by the IACUC. Category E animal use protocols are controversial and receive increased IACUC, USDA, and PHS scrutiny. The basic premise of a Category E animal use protocol is that although pain and distress potentially could be relieved, the investigator has chosen not to do so because it would interfere with the proposed research and invalidate the results.

USDA regulations define a *painful procedure* as "any procedure that would reasonably be expected to cause more than slight or momentary pain or distress in a human being to which that procedure was applied." The IACUC is required to determine whether the investigator has considered alternatives to potentially painful or distressful procedures. When the potential for pain or distress exists, researchers are expected to carefully monitor animals and relieve the pain or distress whenever possible. This may be accomplished by administration of anesthetics or analgesics. By regulation, a specific scientific justification must be provided whenever anesthetics or analgesics are withheld, which might be necessary when the drugs would interfere with the interpretation of experimental data.

Relatively few animals that are used in research are assigned to Pain Category E. In their Animal Care Annual Report of Activities (USDA, 2008), APHIS reported that of about 1 million animals used in research that are covered under AWA, only about 8% were assigned to Pain Category E. According to their estimates, the majority of animals used in research are assigned to categories with either no pain or momentary pain.

MAINTAINING IACUC APPROVAL AND STAYING IN COMPLIANCE

Federal laws require that IACUCs perform annual reviews of animal studies. These reviews request the number of animals used in the past year and any unanticipated problems that were encountered while conducting the research. If an investigator fails to submit an annual report, the IACUC may inactivate the protocol until one is submitted. An investigator cannot conduct animal research on that particular protocol until it is reactivated.

In addition to annual protocol reviews to ensure that investigators comply with the care and use of animals, institutions have established procedures for individuals to report concerns about animal care and use or other noncompliance issues. Typically, the names and phone numbers of contact persons are placed within the area where animal research is conducted. If the person reporting the incidence wishes to remain anonymous, this typically is granted. If the incidence that is reported involves an animal welfare issue or a human safety concern, the institution may take immediate action, including suspension of the research activity and notification to the appropriate officials. If an activity is suspended, the incident and the actions taken by the committee are reported to APHIS and any agency funding that activity. In the event that immediate action is not required, the IACUC typically forms a subcommittee made up of IACUC members who then determine the course of action and whether further investigation is necessary. If the subcommittee decides that further investigation is needed, they will gather information and complete a report that includes supporting documentation, such as records, a summary of the concerns as they relate to the regulations, and a course of action. The IACUC reviews this report and then may request additional information, determine that no evidence or basis for the concern exists, or determine that the concern is valid. If allegations of animal mistreatment or protocol noncompliance are verified, the IACUC can apply sanctions. Examples of potential sanctions include monitoring the individual or testing that involves animals, mandating specific training to avoid future incidents, or temporarily or permanently revoking the investigator's privilege to conduct research with animals.

THE ROLE OF OTHER ORGANIZATIONS

In addition to local, state, and federal laws, many institutions have deemed it important to demonstrate a higher level of accountability than is required by law by voluntarily receiving accreditation from the Association for the Assessment and Accreditation of Laboratory Animal Care International (AAALAC). AAALAC is a private nonprofit organization that sets the gold standard for laboratory animal care and guides research facilities seeking to ensure that they provide the best conditions for their research animals. The organization promotes high-quality and humane animal care in research and education. Accreditation by AAALAC is viewed as evidence that the institution's animal care facilities comply with federal codes applicable to animal research and *also* are taking extra steps to achieve excellence in animal care and use. Once accredited, institutions are inspected every 3 years to determine whether they may retain their accreditation. Every laboratory in the institution using animals must meet the criteria and pass inspection, and all animal care procedures and oversight procedures are reviewed. Although AAALAC accreditation is not required to demonstrate humane care of animals in research facilities, it is growing in popularity. Currently, more than 800 animal care and use programs in 32 countries have earned AAALAC accreditation.

Part of the National Research Council, the ILAR is another key player in the humane care and use of laboratory animals. It functions as a part of the National Academies to provide independent, objective advice to the federal government, the scientific community, and the public. Using the principles of the three Rs (refinement, reduction, and replacement) as a foundation, it evaluates and disseminates information on issues related to the ethical use of animals in scientific research. ILAR has produced numerous publications, including the *Guide* (2011), *Occupational Health and Safety in the Care and Use of Research Animals* (1997), *Recognition and Alleviation of Pain in Laboratory Animals* (2009), and the *ILAR Journal*.

Although not directly involved in the oversight of research with nonhuman animals, the organization Public Responsibility in Medicine and Research plays an important role in regulating such research at the local institutional level. It is the leader in educating IACUC staff and members on compliance with federal regulations and policies on the protection of research subjects—both people and other animals. It also influences public policy and promotes dialogue and debate. To date, the organization has 3,500 members and is a valuable resource to anyone concerned with the issue of research ethics.

Professional organizations also may play a role in governing animal research activities. For example, the APA's Committee on Animal Research and Ethics has a resource titled *Guidelines for Ethical Conduct in the Care and Use of Animals* (APA, 1996a) that recommends procedures for psychologists who use animals in their research. Anyone who publishes in APA journals is required to conduct their research with animals in accordance with these guidelines. The APA guidelines are based on the federal policies as well as the *Guide* (ILAR, 2011).

HELPFUL RESOURCES FOR INVESTIGATORS

The *Guide* adheres to PHS Policy on humane care of and use of laboratory animals. The *Guide* was developed by the scientific community and produced by the ILAR (2011). The purpose of the *Guide* is to promote the humane care of animals used in biomedical and behavioral research and teaching. The Animal Welfare Act Regulations (AWARs) include detailed husbandry standards that must be followed for the species covered. The PHS Policy refers to the AWARs, but also specifically to the *Guide. Guidelines for the Care and Use of Mammals in Neuroscience and Behavioral Research* (ILAR, 2003) covers best practices in neuroscience research and includes behavioral methods to study brain functions.

Recent advances in the scientific understanding of pain and distress have resulted in ILAR updating its 1992 report on the recognition and alleviation of pain and distress in laboratory animals. The update resulted in the publication of two separate reports: *Recognition and Alleviation of Distress in Laboratory Animals* (2008) and *Recognition and Alleviation of Pain in Laboratory Animals* (2009).

OUR RESPONSIBILITY AS RESEARCHERS

As stewards of the nonhuman animal research enterprise, researchers have a dual obligation to ensure the humane care and treatment of laboratory animals, and to gain and maintain public trust in the enterprise. To achieve this goal, researchers need to ensure that the public has an appreciation for the value of research with nonhuman animals in psychology. It is critical to counteract misinformation about research that is perpetrated by entities that are against the use of nonhuman animal research, purely on ideological grounds. To that end, students from elementary school to graduate school need to be educated about how nonhuman animal research, whether basic or applied, has made and continues to make valuable contributions to improving the lives of people and other animals.

Maintaining public support also requires responsible use of resources. New regulations often make the conduct of such research more difficult, more time consuming, and more expensive. New regulations should be accompanied by increased protection of the welfare of the research animal. The research community should work with regulatory agencies toward ensuring science-based regulations and policies that more effectively protect the welfare of these animals while also ensuring the responsible use of resources (especially public funding) for scientifically and ethically sound research that could improve lives.

References

American Psychological Association, Committee on Animal Research and Ethics. (1996a). *Guidelines for ethical conduct in the care and use of animals.* Retrieved from http://www.apa.org/science/leadership/care/guidelines.aspx

American Psychological Association, Committee on Animal Research and Ethics. (1996b). *Research with animals in psychology.* Retrieved from http://www.apa.org/research/responsible/research-animals.pdf

Animal Welfare Act, Pub. L. 89-544, U.S.C. Title 7, §§ 2131–2156 (1966).

Carroll, M. E., & Overmier, J. B. (Eds.). (2001). *Animal research and human health: Advancing human welfare through behavioral science.* Washington, DC: American Psychological Association. doi:10.1037/10441-000

Dess, N. K., & Chapman, C. D. (1998). "Humans and animals"? On saying what we mean. *Psychological Science, 9,* 156–157. doi:10.1111/1467-9280.00030

Dess, N. K., & Foltin, R. W. (2004). The ethics cascade. In C. K. Akins, S. Panicker, & C. L. Cunningham (Eds.), *Laboratory animals in research and teaching: Ethics, care, and methods* (pp. 31–39). Washington, DC: American Psychological Association.

Hodos, W., & Campbell, C. G. G. (1990). Evolutionary scales and comparative studies of animal cognition.

In R. P. Kenser & D. S. Olton (Eds.), *The neurobiology of comparative cognition* (pp. 1–20). Hillsdale, NJ: Erlbaum.

Institute for Laboratory and Animal Research. (1992). *Recognition and alleviation of pain and distress in laboratory animals*. Washington, DC: National Academies Press.

Institute for Laboratory Animal Research. (1997). *Occupational health and safety in the care and use of research animals*. Washington, DC: National Academies Press.

Institute for Laboratory Animal Research. (2003). *Guidelines for the care and use of mammals in neuroscience and behavioral research*. Washington, DC: National Academies Press.

Institute for Laboratory Animal Research. (2008). *Recognition and alleviation of distress in laboratory animals*. Washington, DC: National Academies Press.

Institute for Laboratory Animal Research. (2009). *Recognition and alleviation of pain in laboratory animals*. Washington, DC: National Academies Press.

Institute for Laboratory Animal Research. (2011). *Guide for the care and use of laboratory animals* (8th ed.). Washington, DC: National Academies Press.

Poling, A. (1984). Comparing humans to other species: We're animals and they're not infrahumans. *The Behavior Analyst, 7,* 211–212.

Poling, A., Nickel, M., & Alling, K. (1990). Free birds aren't fat: Weight gain in captured wild pigeons maintained under laboratory conditions. *Journal of the Experimental Analysis of Behavior, 53,* 423–424. doi:10.1901/jeab.1990.53-423

Russell, W. M. S., & Burch, R. L. (1959). *The principles of humane experimental technique*. London, England: Methuen.

U.S. Department of Agriculture, Animal and Plant Health Inspection Service. (2008). *Animal care annual report of activities: Fiscal year 2007*. Retrieved from http://www.aphis.usda.gov/publications/animal_welfare/content/printable_version/2007_AC_Report.pdf

Cultural and Societal Issues in Conducting Psychological Research

CHAPTER 5

CROSS-CULTURAL RESEARCH
METHODS

David Matsumoto and Fons J. R. van de Vijver

The study of culture has blossomed into one of the most important areas of research in psychology. Articles involving cultural variables appear more today than ever before in mainstream journals in developmental, clinical, personality, and social psychology as well as in many specialty journals. Theorists are increasingly incorporating culture as an important variable in their theories and models of psychological processes.

Psychological scientists can take many methodological approaches to the study of the relationship between culture and psychological processes, and an in-depth review of all of these methodologies is beyond the scope of this chapter. Instead we focus here on culture–comparative research, in which two or more cultural groups are compared on some psychological variables of interest. This method is the methodological backbone supporting the growth of cultural science in psychology, regardless of the theoretical approach or perspective one adopts in understanding cultural influences on mind and behavior. Differences used to exist between those who called themselves cross-cultural psychologists and cultural psychologists, with the former basing most of their work on cross-cultural comparison and the latter arguing that such comparisons were unwarranted (Greenfield, 1997; Shweder, 1999). For example, early cultural psychologists argued that constructs such as emotion, intelligence, or morality were inherently linked to specific cultures, and that these constructs could not be understood, explained, or studied outside of their specific cultural contexts, thus rendering cross-cultural

comparisons of those constructs invalid. Today, however, even those who call themselves cultural psychologists clearly use cross-cultural research methods as the method of choice when conducting research. The phenomenological and interpretive approach of the early days has given way to more quantitative data collection methods, such as testing and experimentation (e.g., Heine et al., 2001; Kitayama, Mesquita, & Karasawa, 2006; Markus, Uchida, Omoregie, Townsend, & Kitayama, 2006).

Cross-cultural comparisons offer many potential advantages. They test the boundaries of knowledge and stretch the methodological parameters under which such knowledge is created and vetted in psychology. They highlight important similarities and differences across cultures. They bring researchers in disparate and divergent cultures together for a common cause. Their findings promote international and intercultural exchange, understanding, and cooperation. They contribute to a broader and deeper understanding of human behavior and the mind. And they inform theories that accommodate both individual and cultural sources of variation (Berry, Poortinga, Segall, & Dasen, 2002).

There are risks and liabilities as well, the foremost of which is the production of cultural knowledge that is incorrect because of flawed methodology. Cross-cultural research brings with it a host of methodological issues that go much beyond monocultural studies, from issues concerning translation, measurement equivalence, sampling, data analytic techniques, and data reporting. To be sure,

DOI: 10.1037/13619-006
APA Handbook of Research Methods in Psychology: Vol. 1. Foundations, Planning, Measures, and Psychometrics, H. Cooper (Editor-in-Chief)

85

good cultural science (empirical research contributing to systematic knowledge about culture and its relationship to psychological processes) is first and foremost good science, and many concepts that ensure the methodological rigor of any quality scientific enterprise are applicable to cross-cultural research as well. It is also important to be knowledgeable about issues and problems that are unique to cross-cultural studies, however, because the risk of producing cultural knowledge that is incorrect or not replicable is too great if these methodological pitfalls are not understood and addressed.

Cross-cultural research also brings with it ethical issues and challenges, many of which are quite similar to those faced when conducting monocultural research (Pack-Brown & Braun Williams, 2003). Many ethical considerations that researchers must make—regardless of whether they are conducting a multinational study or a simple study using a convenience sample of U.S. college students—are somewhat universal. Thus, we refer interested readers to the *Ethical Principles of Psychologists and Code of Conduct* (the Ethics Code; American Psychological Association [APA], 2010), which outline five ethical principles for the conduct of psychologists: Principle A, Beneficence and Nonmaleficence; Principle B, Fidelity and Responsibility; Principle C, Integrity; Principle D, Justice; and Principle E, Respect for People's Rights and Dignity.

This chapter introduces readers to the methodological issues that need to be addressed when conducting cross-cultural research and to the ethical issues unique to cross-cultural research. Consequently, we divide the chapter into two parts. With regard to method, many resources are available to readers that discuss the issues raised in much greater depth; thus, we consider the material only briefly. With regard to ethics, few resources are available; thus, we consider our work a living document, the start and definitely not the end of a dialogue on this issue.

METHODOLOGICAL ISSUES

Bias and Equivalence

Bias and *equivalence* are key terms in the methodology of cross-cultural studies. Bias refers to differences in a measurement instrument that do not have exactly the same meaning within and across cultures (Poortinga, 1989). A cross-cultural study shows bias if differences in measurement outcomes (categorizations or scores) do not correspond to cross-cultural differences in the construct purportedly measured by the instrument. If scores are biased, individual differences within a culture (*within-culture differences*) do not have the same meaning as cultural differences (*between-culture differences*). For example, scores on a coping questionnaire that show bias may be a valid measure of coping if they are compared within a single cultural group, whereas cross-cultural differences identified on the basis of this questionnaire may be influenced by other factors, such as translation issues, item inappropriateness, or differential response styles. Differences resulting from bias are not random, but rather are systematic. A replication of a study with a biased instrument in similar samples will show the same biased results.

Equivalence refers to the level of comparability of measurement outcomes. For example, do diagnostic categories have the same meaning across cultures? Is obsessive–compulsive disorder identical across the cultures studied? Do persons from different cultures with the same diagnosis suffer from the same clinical syndrome? Do scores on personality scales have the same meaning within and between cultures? Bias threatens the equivalence of measurement outcomes across cultures, and it is only when instruments are free of bias that measurement outcomes are equivalent and have the same meaning within and across cultures.

Bias and equivalence are two sides of the same coin. Cross-cultural equivalence requires the absence of biases, and the presence of cross-cultural bias always results in some form of inequivalence. Nonetheless, research on cross-cultural bias and equivalence tends to highlight different issues and a joint consideration of bias and equivalence provides a more comprehensive view of how valid cross-cultural comparisons can be made.

Bias. Bias signals the presence of nuisance factors (Poortinga, 1989). If scores are biased, their psychological meaning is culture or group dependent and group differences in assessment outcomes need to be accounted for, at least to some extent, by auxiliary psychological constructs or measurement artifacts (see Table 5.1 for an overview). Bias is not an inherent characteristic of an instrument but arises in the application of an instrument in at least two cultural groups. As a consequence, an instrument is not inherently biased, but it may become so when scores from specific cultural groups are compared.

We discuss three of the major types of bias: *construct, method,* and *item bias. Construct bias* can be caused by incomplete overlap of construct-relevant behaviors, and this leads to construct inequivalence. An empirical example can be found in Ho's (1996) work on *filial piety,* defined as a psychological characteristic associated with being "a good son or daughter." The Chinese conception, which includes the expectation that children should assume the role of caretaker of elderly parents, is broader than the corresponding Western notion. An inventory of filial piety based on the Chinese conceptualization covers aspects unrelated to the Western notion, whereas a Western-based inventory will leave important Chinese aspects uncovered. Construct bias can be caused by differential appropriateness of the behaviors associated with the construct in the different cultures.

Method bias is a label for all sources of bias resulting from factors often described in the methods section of empirical papers. Three subtypes of method bias are distinguished here, depending on whether the bias comes from the sample, administration, or instrument. *Sample bias* is more likely to jeopardize cross-cultural comparisons when the cultures examined differ in many respects; a large cultural distance often increases the number of alternative explanations that need to be considered. For example, a sample from the West African tribe of Burkina Faso is likely to be quite different than a sample of U.S. undergraduates (Tracy & Robins, 2008), and cultural differences are easier to obtain because of these sample differences. *Administration method bias* can be caused by differences in the procedures or mode used to administer an instrument. For example, when interviews are held in respondents' homes, physical conditions (e.g., ambient noise, presence of others) are difficult to control. Respondents are more prepared to answer sensitive

questions in a self-completion mode than in a face-to-face interview. *Instrument bias* is a common source of bias in cognitive tests, and this bias refers to systematic cultural differences in the meaning of the items in an instrument that confound cross-cultural comparisons. Piswanger (1975) administered a figural inductive reasoning test to high school students in Austria, Nigeria, and Togo (educated in Arabic). The most striking findings were the cross-cultural differences in item difficulties related to identifying and applying rules in a horizontal direction (i.e., left to right). This was interpreted as a bias because of the different directions in writing Latin-based languages as opposed to Arabic.

Closely related to instrument bias is *item bias,* which refers to anomalies at the item level and also is called *differential item functioning* (Camilli & Shepard, 1994; Holland & Wainer, 1993). According to a definition that is widely used in education and psychology, an item is biased if respondents with the same standing on the underlying construct (e.g., they are equally *intelligent*) do not have the same mean score on the item because of different cultural origins. Item bias can arise in various ways, such as poor item translation, ambiguities in the original item, low familiarity or appropriateness of the item content in certain cultures, and the influence of culture-specific nuisance factors or connotations associated with the item wording. Gomez, Burns, and Walsh (2008) examined behaviors associated with oppositional defiance disorder. Australian, Malaysian Malay, and Malaysian Chinese parents had to rate their children on behaviors such as "is touchy," "argues," and "blames others." The item about being touchy was more prevalent among Malaysian parents in comparison to the other items. The authors interpreted this difference as a consequence of the lower tolerance of deviant behavior by Malaysian parents compared with Australian parents.

Equivalence. We describe here four hierarchically nested types of equivalence. *Construct inequivalence* refers to constructs that lack a shared meaning, which precludes any cross-cultural comparison. In the literature, claims of construct inequivalence can be grouped into three broad subcategories, which differ in the degree of inequivalence (partial

---

TABLE 5.1

Overview of Types of Bias and Ways to Deal With It

Type and source of bias	How to deal with it?

Construct bias

■ Only partial overlap in the definitions of the construct across cultures	■ Decentering (i.e., simultaneously developing the same instrument in several cultures)
■ Differential appropriateness of the behaviors associated with the construct (e.g., skills do not belong to the repertoire of one of the cultural groups)	■ Convergence approach (i.e., independent within-culture development of instruments and subsequent cross-cultural administration of all instruments)
■ Poor sampling of all relevant behaviors indicative of a construct (e.g., short instruments)	■ Consult informants with expertise in local culture and language[a]
■ Incomplete coverage of the relevant aspects/facets of the construct (e.g., not all relevant domains are sampled)	■ Use samples of bilingual participants[a]
	■ Conduct local pilot studies (e.g., content analyses of free-response questions)[a]
	■ Nonstandard instrument administration (e.g., "thinking aloud")[a]

Method bias

■ Incomparability of samples (e.g., differences in education and motivation)[b]	■ Cross-cultural comparison of nomological networks (e.g., convergent-discriminant validity studies, and monotrait–multimethod studies)
■ Differences in administration conditions, physical (e.g., noise) or social (e.g., group size)[b]	■ Connotation of key phrases (e.g., similarity of meaning of key terms such as "somewhat agree")
■ Ambiguous instructions for respondents or guidelines for research administrators[b]	■ Extensive training of interviewers and administrators
■ Differential expertise of administrators[c]	■ Detailed manual/protocol for administration, scoring, and interpretation
■ Tester, interviewer, and observer effects (e.g., halo effects)[c]	■ Detailed instructions (e.g., with adequate examples and/or exercises)
■ Communication problems between respondent and interviewer (in the widest sense)[c]	■ Include background and contextual variables (e.g., education background)
■ Differential familiarity with stimulus materials[c]	■ Gather collateral information (e.g., test-taking behavior or test attitudes)
■ Differential familiarity with response procedures[d]	■ Assessment of response styles
■ Differential response styles (e.g., social desirability, extremity tendency, and acquiescence)[d]	■ Conduct test–retest, training, or intervention studies

Item bias

■ Poor translation or ambiguous items	■ Judgmental methods (e.g., linguistic and psychological analysis)
■ Nuisance factors (e.g., items may invoke additional traits or abilities)	■ Psychometric methods (e.g., differential item functioning analysis)
■ Cultural specifics (e.g., differences in connotative meaning and/or appropriateness of item content)	

Note. From *Cross-Cultural Research Methods in Psychology* (pp. 23–24), by D. Matsumoto and F. J. R. van de Vijver (Eds.), 2011, New York, NY: Cambridge University Press. Copyright 2011 by Cambridge University Press. Reprinted with permission.
[a]Also used for dealing with method bias. [b]Sample bias. [c]Administration bias. [d]Instrument bias.

or total). The first and strongest claim of inequivalence is found in studies that opt for a strong emic, relativistic viewpoint, which argues that psychological constructs are inextricably tied to their natural context and cannot be studied outside this context. Any cross-cultural comparison is then erroneous as psychological constructs are cross-culturally inequivalent. Some previous writers have argued, for example, that certain aspects of morality—for example, definitions of morality and its domains, concepts of justice, and so on—are inextricably bound with culture, and thus cannot be understood outside of a specific cultural context and thus cannot be compared across cultures (Miller, 2001; Shweder, 1999).

A second subcategory is exemplified by psychological constructs that are associated with specific cultural groups, such as culture-bound syndromes (e.g., *taijin kyofusho,* a Japanese concept referring to an intense fear that one's body is discomforting or insulting for others by its appearance, smell, or movements).

The third subcategory is empirically based and found in cross-cultural studies in which the data do not show any evidence for comparability of construct across cultures; inequivalence is the consequence of a lack of comparability of scores cross-culturally. For example, Van Haaften and van de Vijver (1996) administered Paulhus's Locus of Control Scale measuring intrapersonal, interpersonal, and sociopolitical aspects among various groups of illiterate Sahel dwellers. The three aspects could not be identified in factor analysis in any group.

Structural or functional equivalence refers to whether or not an instrument administered in different cultural groups measures the same construct(s) in all the groups. In operational terms, this condition requires identity of underlying dimensions (factors) in all groups, that is, whether the instrument shows the same factor structure in all groups. Examinations of the items loading on each of the scales of the five-factor model of personality, for example, are attempts at demonstrating structural equivalence (McCrae et al., 2000). Functional equivalence as a specific type of structural equivalence refers to identity of nomological networks (i.e., relationships with other constructs). A questionnaire that measures, say, openness to new cultures shows functional equivalence if it measures the same psychological constructs in each culture, as manifested in a similar pattern of convergent and divergent validity (i.e., nonzero correlations with presumably related measures and zero correlations with presumably unrelated measures).

Tests of structural equivalence are applied more often than tests of functional equivalence.

The reason is not statistical or technical. With advances in statistical modeling (notably path analysis as part of structural equation modeling), tests of the cross-cultural similarity of nomological networks are straightforward. However, nomological networks are often based on a combination of psychological scales and background variables, such as socioeconomic status, education, and sex. In the absence of a guiding theoretical framework, the use of psychological scales to validate other psychological scales can lead easily lead to an endless regress in which each scale used for validation has to be validated.

Metric or *measurement unit equivalence* refers to whether the measurement scales of instruments have the same units of measurement, but a different origin (e.g., Celsius and Kelvin scales in temperature measurement). This type of equivalence assumes interval- or ratio-level scores (with the same measurement units in each culture). Measurement unit equivalence applies when a source of bias shifts the scores of different cultural groups differentially, but it does not affect the relative scores of individuals within each cultural group. For example, social desirability and stimulus familiarity influence questionnaire scores more in some cultures than in others, but they may influence individuals within a given cultural group in a similar way. When the relative contribution of both bias sources cannot be estimated, the interpretation of group comparisons of mean scores remains ambiguous.

Finally, *scalar* or *full score equivalence* assumes both an identical interval or ratio scale and an identical scale origin across cultural groups. Only in the case of scalar (or full score) equivalence can direct cross-cultural comparisons be made; this is the only type of equivalence that allows for the conclusion that average scores obtained in two cultures are different or equal. Beuckelaer, Lievens, and Swinnen (2007) examined the equivalence of a global organizational survey measuring six work climate factors as administered across 25 countries. Using structural equation modeling, the authors found scalar equivalence only for comparisons of English-speaking countries and metric equivalence for the other countries.

A Taxonomy of Cross-Cultural Studies

Three dimensions can be used to classify the research questions raised in cross-cultural research (and hence, cross-cultural studies; van de Vijver, 2009). The first dimension refers to the presence or absence of *contextual factors* in a research design. Contextual factors may involve characteristics of the participants (such as socioeconomic status, education, and age) or their cultures (such as economic development and religious institutions). From a methodological perspective, contextual factors involve any variable that can explain, partly or fully, observed cross-cultural differences (Poortinga, van de Vijver, Joe, & van de Koppel, 1987). Including such factors in a study will enhance its validity and help rule out the influence of biases and inequivalence because an evaluation of their influence can help to (dis)confirm their role in accounting for the cultural differences observed. For example, administering a measure of response styles can evaluate to what extent cross-cultural differences on extroversion are influenced by these styles.

The second dimension involves the distinction between *exploratory* and *hypothesis-testing* studies. Exploratory studies attempt to increase our understanding of cross-cultural differences by documenting similarities and differences. Most often these involve simple, quasi-experimental designs in which two or more groups are compared on some target variable(s) of interest. Researchers tend to stay "close to the data" in exploratory studies, whereas hypothesis-testing studies make larger inferential jumps by testing theories of cross-cultural similarities and differences. Unfortunately, the validity of these inferential jumps is often threatened by cross-cultural biases and inequivalence. The methodological strengths and weaknesses of exploratory and hypothesis-testing studies mirror each other. The main strength of exploratory studies is their broad scope for identifying cross-cultural similarities and differences, which is particularly important in under-researched domains of cross-cultural psychology. The main weakness of such studies is their limited capability to address the causes of the observed differences. The focused search of similarities and differences in hypothesis-testing studies leads to more substantial contribution to theory development and explicit attempts to deal with rival explanations, but it is less likely to discover interesting differences outside of the realm of the tested theory. These studies are likely to involve experiments manipulating key variables considered to be the active cultural ingredients that produce differences in the first place, or unpackaging studies, which involve such variables as covariates or mediators in quasi-experimental design.

What is compared across cultures is addressed in the third dimension. A distinction is made between *structure-* and *level-oriented studies*. The former involve comparisons of constructs (is depression conceptualized in the same way across cultures?), their structures (can depression be assessed by the same constituent elements in different cultures?), or their relationships with other constructs (do depression and anxiety have the same relationship in all countries?). The latter involve the comparisons of scores (do individuals from different cultures show the same level of depression?). Structure-oriented studies focus on relationships among variables and attempt to identify similarities and differences in these relations across cultures. From a methodological perspective, structure-oriented studies are simpler than level-oriented studies, which usually are more open to alternative interpretations. For example, suppose that a neuroticism questionnaire has been administered in two countries and that the two countries differ in extremity scoring (i.e., the use of the extreme values on the scale). If all the items are phrased in the same direction (which is often the case in personality measurement), cross-cultural differences in extremity scoring will be confounded with valid differences in neuroticism. As a consequence, cross-cultural differences in means are difficult to interpret. As long as extremity scoring affects only the item means and leaves item correlations and covariances unchanged, the factor structure, which often is examined in structure-oriented studies, will not be affected.

Studies with cultural groups that have a large cultural distance from each other are likely to be more threatened by biases and inequivalence. Studies that do not include contextual factors, which are designed to evaluate hypotheses and advance a theory, and that target level-oriented cultural differences also are more threatened by biases and inequivalence.

Researchers can deal with the various issues of bias and inequivalence both before they start their research (a priori procedures) and after data have been collected (a posteriori procedures). These are not either–or alternatives; optimally, researchers can and should apply both procedures. In the following sections, we discuss the various issues that can be addressed within these two groups of procedures.

A Priori Procedures

Identifying the research question. By far the most important part of any study, cross-cultural or not, is knowing what research questions to ask. Because cultural differences are relatively easy to obtain, especially the greater the cultural distance between the groups being compared, researchers should remember that the purpose of conducting research is to contribute to a body of knowledge (the literature), and any consideration of research designs starts first with a comprehensive and functional knowledge of that literature so that one understands what gaps in the knowledge exist and what research questions should be addressed to contribute to that knowledge. It happens all too often that researchers exclusively focus on designing the methodology of a study without considering adequately what research question should be addressed. Sophisticated statistical techniques and elegant research designs cannot salvage studies that are not novel or insightful.

Designing cross-cultural studies. Understanding why any study is to be conducted leads to questions about how to conduct it, which is a discussion in the realm of research methodology. Questions related to the taxonomy apply in this case as well: Is the study exploratory in nature, or hypothesis testing? Does it or should it include contextual variables? And is it structure oriented or level oriented? No one study can do everything, and in our opinion, it is better to do something of limited scope very well than to conduct a study that addresses too much not so well at all.

With regard to studies that are designed to document cultural differences, it is important to keep in mind that the field has gone much beyond the need to merely document differences between two or more cultures on any psychological variable. Indeed,

because of cultural distance, it is fairly easy to document differences on something, provided the cultures being compared are disparate enough. Instead, one of the major challenges that cross-cultural researchers face today concerns how to isolate the source of such differences, and to identify the active cultural (vs. noncultural) ingredients that produced those differences. It is in the empirical documentation of those active cultural ingredients that cross-cultural research designs need to pay close attention to.

Researchers need to pay attention to a number of theoretical and empirical issues (see Matsumoto & Yoo, 2006, for a more complete discussion). For example, is the source of the differences to be explained cultural or not? Examining these questions forces researchers to have a definition of what is culture and to find ways of objectively measuring it. Once the active cultural ingredients that produce differences are identified, a level-of-analysis issue arises. Cultural variables exist on the group and individual levels. Studies can be entirely on the individual or cultural level, or can involve a mixture of the two in varying degrees with multiple levels. Different variables at different levels of analysis bring with them different theoretical and methodological implications, and require different interpretations back to the research literature. When individual-level cultural variables are incorporated in a study, researchers need to distinguish between them and noncultural variables on the individual level, such as personality. Certainly a variable is not cultural just because a researcher says so; a well thought-out rationale is needed that is based in theory and on data that support the identification and distinction of such variables.

Another question that researchers must face in designing studies concerns their theoretical model of how things work. A commonly held view is that culture produces differences in a fairly top-down manner, a theoretical bias held by many. But how do we know that to be true, and more important, how does one demonstrate that empirically? It may very well be that individual-level psychological processes and behavior produce culture in a bottom-up fashion, or that both top-down and bottom-up processes occur simultaneously. Regardless of how one believes things are put together, researchers should adopt research design strategies that are commensurate with their beliefs and models.

Unpackaging studies. Once researchers isolate the active cultural ingredients that produce differences, a variety of methodologies are available to test them, including unpackaging studies and experiments. Each has its own risks and benefits. We discuss unpackaging studies in a little more depth.

Cross-cultural research is largely based on quasi-experimental designs, and as such, when differences are found, it is impossible to draw conclusions about the source of those differences. Despite that fact, cross-cultural scientists often do draw those conclusions, with little or no empirical justification, and thereby commit an ecological fallacy (Campbell, 1961). In the realm of cultural science, when researchers attribute the source of observed differences in a quasi-experimental design to culture, this mistaken inference has been termed the *cultural attribution fallacy* (Matsumoto & Yoo, 2006). One way to address this limitation in quasi-experimental designs is to include variables in the data collection that operationalize meaningful dimensions of culture and then empirically test the degree to which those variables account for those differences. Such variables are called context variables, and quasi-experimental designs that include context variables are known as unpackaging studies. Bond and van de Vijver (2011) have discussed at length the nature of these studies, and how unpackaging variables can be included in cross-cultural research. Statistical techniques now exist (e.g., mediation analyses) that allow researchers to empirically justify the degree to which the unpackaging variables included account for cultural differences. An example can be found in a study by Singelis, Bond, Sharkey, and Lai (1999), in which they demonstrated that cultural differences in ability to be embarrassed could be explained by independent versus interdependent self-construals. Regardless of whether one conducts unpackaging studies or experiments, once a basic paradigm is adopted, researchers need to deal with the nitty-gritty of the science, including sampling, translation, measurement bias and equivalence, data analysis, and the like.

Dealing with language and translations. One of the major issues that faces cross-cultural researchers concerns how to deal with language, especially in terms of the instruments and procedures of a study. Of all the methodological issues that face cultural scientists, none is more unique to cross-cultural research than the fact that cross-cultural studies often require the collection of data in two or more linguistic groups. As such, issues concerning equivalence between the languages used in the study become of paramount importance. Even if words are translated into different languages, the resulting translations many not be equivalent to the originals. Elsewhere, Hambleton and Zenisky (2011) described 25 criteria with which to evaluate the adequacy of translations done for cross-cultural research, spanning such topics as general translation questions, item format and appearance, grammar and phrasing, passages and other item-relevant stimulus materials, and cultural relevance or specificity. The evaluation sheet offered to readers is an especially useful tool for researchers.

Sampling. When doing cross-cultural work, it is impossible to just access participants from the local introductory psychology participant pool. Thus, another way in which issues concerning equivalence and bias affect cross-cultural work is sampling. Indeed, it is easy for samples across cultures to differ on many demographic characteristics, and these demographics often confound any observed differences; thus, conclusions about observed differences on psychological variables may need to be interpreted in terms of relevant background characteristics, such as differences in education instead of cultural differences. Boehnke, Lietz, Schreier, and Wilhelm (2011) discussed issues concerning sampling on both the individual and cultural levels, and provided guidelines for researchers that allow for empirically justified conclusions to be drawn, while at the same time being sensitive to the particular needs and issues associated with samples from different cultures.

Designing questions and scales. Another way in which people of different cultures may differ is in the use of response scales. Although early cross-cultural research viewed different cultural biases in the use of scales as nuisance variables that needed to be controlled, theoretical and empirical perspectives today view such biases as potentially important aspects of culture and personality (Smith, 2004). Johnson, Shavitt, and Holbrook (2011) discussed these issues, paying close attention to concerns about socially desirable responding, acquiescence, and extreme responding, and provided useful guidelines and suggestions for cultural scientists.

A Posteriori Procedures

Because measurement equivalence is such an important issue in cross-cultural research, researchers comparing cultures on measures need to take steps after the data are collected to ensure this equivalence. Multiple data analytic methods can be used to investigate and establish structural equivalence in the structure- and level-oriented studies (Fischer & Fontaine, 2011; Sireci, 2011). For structural-oriented studies, techniques include multidimensional scaling, principal component analysis, exploratory factor analysis, and confirmatory factor analysis; for level-oriented studies, techniques include delta plots, standardization, Mantel-Haenszel, item response theory, likelihood ratio tests, and logistic regression.

Cross-cultural studies typically involve data at multiple levels, which inherently are nested (e.g., data from individuals with specific personalities collected in specific situations, within specific cultures located in specific ecologies). These kinds of multilevel data allow for the possibility of analyzing the relationship between data at different levels, allowing researchers to document empirically the associations between ecological, cultural, individual, and situational variables and individual-level means or relationships among variables. In recent years, techniques for analyzing multilevel data have blossomed; these techniques can be used if data are available from a large number of cultures. In particular, multilevel random coefficient models may be appropriate for handling the types of nested data in cross-cultural research, providing numerous statistical advantages over statistical techniques based on ordinary least squares analyses. We encourage researchers to take advantage of such techniques (see Nezlek, 2011).

Because cross-cultural data typically exist on multiple levels, researchers can examine structural relationships among psychological phenomena not only on the individual level, which is the traditional approach, but also on the cultural level. Relationships among variables on the individual level may or may not be the same on the cultural level, and researchers need to analyze data at these levels separately. A positive correlation on the basis of ecological level data can be positive, negative, or zero when individual-level data are analyzed. The classic work in this field is Robinson's (1950) study, which demonstrated that even though a small, positive correlation (0.118) existed between foreign birth and illiteracy when individual-level data were analyzed, strong negative correlations were obtained when data were aggregated across individuals by region (–0.619) or state (–0.526). Similar types of differences in findings have been obtained in many other areas.

One of the biases in the thinking of cross-cultural psychologists is the focus on finding differences and the primacy of significance testing. Nothing is wrong with documenting differences, but an exclusive or even primary focus on differences can easily blur a balanced treatment of both cross-cultural differences and similarities, and cultural scientists should be interested in both. And, it is easy to obtain statistically significant results in cross-cultural research today because of the relative ease with which researchers can obtain large sample sizes, and because statistical significance is directly proportional to sample size. Statistical significance, however, does not necessarily reflect practical importance in the real world; two or more cultural means may be statistically different from each other but may not really reflect important differences among the individuals of those cultures. To aid in the determination of more empirically justified interpretations of data, we encourage researchers to supplement their interpretations of findings on the basis of inferential statistics with appropriate measures of effect size. Matsumoto and colleagues (Matsumoto, Grissom, & Dinnel, 2001; Matsumoto, Kim, Grissom, & Dinnel, 2011) have identified several measures of effect size that may be especially useful in cross-cultural research, including confidence intervals, the standardized difference between two sample means, probability of superiority, eta squared, and partial omega squared. Interpretations of the significance of cross-cultural differences always should be made on the basis of the appropriate effect size estimates.

ETHICAL ISSUES IN THE DESIGN OF CROSS-CULTURAL RESEARCH

As with all properly structured and internally reliable research, issues related to design are fundamental and must be considered before contact is initiated with human participants and data are collected. One of the biggest ethical dilemmas facing cross-cultural researchers today is the potential for the findings from their studies to be used to vindicate stereotypes (overgeneralized attitudes or beliefs) about cultural groups. In our view, vindication is quite different than testing the accuracy of stereotypes. The latter involves researchers' conscious knowledge of stereotypes and their efforts to test the validity and boundaries of these stereotypes; presumably, such conscious knowledge also would inform researchers of the need to be aware of their potential influence on the process of research. Vindication refers to researchers' ignorance of such stereotypes, and thus their potential lack of awareness of how these stereotypes may affect their decisions about research unconsciously. It is incumbent on researchers to understand this ignorance and to utilize research designs that can minimize the possibility of it affecting decisions. We begin an exploration of these issues by discussing the limitations related to interpretations from cross-cultural comparisons.

Potential Dangers of Cross-Cultural Research

When conducting cross-cultural research, researchers believe that differences exist between the cultures (which is why they are conducting the study in the first place), and they conduct their studies to demonstrate that those differences actually do exist. But we forget that just doing so may have important consequences, and these consequences may be associated with possible ethical dilemmas, because those very differences that are documented can be used to help perpetuate stereotypes. It is fairly easy, for example, to take research findings documenting differences between Americans and South Koreans, or European Americans and African Americans, and make statements that overgeneralize those findings to all members of those groups, essentially pigeonholing individuals into social categories and applying those findings to everyone in that group. That is, cross-cultural research (or more precisely, the incorrect application and interpretation of cross-cultural data) can be used to ignore the large degree of individual differences that exist in human behavior, and cross-cultural researchers need to be aware of this potential when designing their studies.

The findings from cross-cultural comparisons also can be used to oppress members of certain groups. A good example is the apartheid regime in South Africa. Tests designed in the Western Hemisphere were administered to different cultural groups without any consideration for the massive education, cultural, and linguistic differences in the population (Meiring, van de Vijver, Rothmann, & Barrick, 2005). After the abolishment of apartheid in 1994, many Blacks in the country treated psychological testing with suspicion because it had become associated with the justification of their unfair treatment in society. The interpretation of African American differences in intelligence also has spurred a great debate on such issues in the past 40 years (Jacoby, Glauberman, & Herrnstein, 1995; Jensen, 1969). Researchers thus need to be aware that findings could be used in these ways and have the obligation of taking active steps to avoid misuse of their findings. This obligation starts with asking the right research questions, ensuring the tempered and nuanced interpretation of these findings in their writings, and incorporating information not only about between- but also about within-group differences in their data (e.g., through the use of appropriate effects size statistics and interpreting data in relation to these statistics; Matsumoto et al., 2001; Matsumoto, Kim, et al., 2011). This obligation also extends to correcting misinterpretations of one's findings by other researchers who cite one's research.

Overgeneralization of findings is especially easy in quasi-experimental designs that do not include contextual variables that can unpack the nature and source of cultural differences. As mentioned, these designs facilitate researchers in committing the cultural attribution fallacy. It is important for studies to document meaningful differences among cultures, but it is also important for researchers to be aware of the limitation of such designs in being able to contribute to knowledge about the source of such differences. For precisely these reasons, cross-cultural researchers should consider designs that go beyond the mere documentation of differences and that attempt to isolate the active cultural ingredients that make up the source of differences, either through experimentation or unpackaging studies.

ETHICAL ISSUES REGARDING THEORIES AND HYPOTHESES TO BE TESTED

One issue that cross-cultural researchers need to face is the question of whether their research question is worthy enough of being studied. Just because a question can be asked does not necessarily mean that it should be. This issue is especially salient when considering having a vulnerable population unwittingly involved in an experiment—not all participants around the world are recruited and participate in research in the same way as those recruited in the United States. As with all research, it is always necessary to consider whether the risk involved to the participants is worth the potential knowledge to be gained by the study.

Informed Consent

In the United States, it is impossible to conduct research involving human participants without first receiving approval from an institutional review board (IRB). IRB guidelines require researchers to obtain consent from participants before collecting most types of data. Most countries have procedures and prescriptions that are less elaborate than those in the United States In fact, in some places outside of the United States, not only is submitting a research proposal for review unnecessary but obtaining consent from human participants is unnecessary as well. This raises ethical dilemmas for researchers: Do we obtain consent from participants in cultures in which it is not necessary to obtain consent, or even frowned upon? Will all participants

understand the concept of *consent* in the same way? What does *consent* mean in different cultures and who is authorized to give and obtain *consent*? Furthermore, if we *do* obtain consent from our participants, how do we obtain it? Many participants in many cultures likely will view consent documents with skepticism or fear. Will they understand such a process, and feel comfortable about giving consent?

Regardless of whether obtaining consent is necessary, we believe that researchers should strive to ensure that (a) informed consent is obtained and understood by participants, (b) invasion of privacy is minimized, and (c) consent is obtained only in a manner that minimizes coercion or undue influence. How can this process be done in a culturally competent manner?

In our experience, many of the same consent procedures can be utilized around the world, if delivered in a skilful and culturally competent manner by the research team. This manner involves the truthful and honest description of the procedures of the study, and its risks and benefits, combined with a genuine interest in the participant and his or her welfare. If written consent is required, forms need to be translated in a competent and culturally appropriate manner. Involving cultural informants as collaborators or experimenters can help to ensure that researchers are making the most diligent of efforts in this difficult ethical area of research. Moreover, cultural informants can evaluate what kind of information should be emphasized; for example, consent forms can contain abstruse legalese that may be useful to define the rights and duties of the parties but that is not meaningful when dealing with participants with a low level of education. Informed consent issues are more likely to arise if a Western institution sponsors a study and the IRB of the country that provides the money and the IRB of the country in which the study is conducted do not have similar requirements regarding approvals.

Recruitment

In the United States, participants in most psychology studies are recruited from an undergraduate psychology participant pool, mostly from introductory psychology classes, who view descriptions of studies and sign up voluntarily and of their free will.

In many cases, this process is administered by software that can be accessed by any computer connected to the Internet. Participants have minimal intervention by anyone else asking for their participation. Participation in research is a process well known to students in many U.S. universities.

In other countries and cultures, however, this is not necessarily the case. Many countries do not have an undergraduate participant pool as in the United States. Thus, different procedures often are required to recruit participants. In many instances, course instructors request that their students participate. In many situations, however, students may feel compelled to participate in a study that they otherwise would not choose of their own volition because of the perceived status of the researcher or possible ramifications for noncompliance to the requesting instructor. This compelling force may border on coercion or undue influence (which may lead to uninterested students) and presents an ethical dilemma. Researchers should avoid any recruitment procedures that involve actual or perceived coercion to participate in the studies.

Sensitive Topics

When conducting cross-cultural research, it is important to be aware of the fact that some topics and issues are sensitive to study and raise interesting ethical problems for researchers (Trimble & Fischer, 2005). We mention three of these topics to raise awareness: sex and sexuality, human rights issues, and deception.

Sex and sexuality. The United States and much of Western and Northern Europe are cultures in which sex and sexuality issues can be discussed relatively openly and freely in everyday discourse. For that reason, conducting research on sex and sexuality is relatively easier in these cultures. In many other cultures of the world, however, these topics are taboo, especially among youth or women. Thus, researchers must exercise caution when conducting research on these topics in cultures in which they are taboo. Cross-cultural differences in scores on items or scales measuring sex-related topics may not be difficult to find, but they are hard to interpret.

In some cultures of the world, homosexuality is a severe taboo, punished in some societies by social isolation, physical punishment, and in some cases even death. A researcher studying homosexuality in such cultures may be subject to the same kinds of repercussions, which strongly prohibits the generation of much useful research information about homosexuality in those cultures. Additionally, it would be difficult for individuals to volunteer to participate in such studies for fear of their safety and lives. In such cultures, added anxiety may exist that the research project itself is part of an organized activity, either by activist groups or government, to identify homosexual individuals. Such concerns exist not only for people who live in those cultures but also for individuals who emigrate to other countries; they may still fear for their lives. Thus, for the same reasons, it may be difficult to conduct such a study on homosexual immigrants in the United States. We have conducted such studies (Mireshghi & Matsumoto, 2006), and they do raise interesting and important questions concerning recruitment and consent.

Even if issues concerning sex and sexuality are not a direct focus of the study, they may be indirectly related because of questions concerning these issues on standard personality questionnaires. For example, two items on the Intercultural Adjustment Potential Scale, a scale designed to assess the potential to adjust to a multicultural environment (Matsumoto, Yoo, & LeRoux, 2007), are "sex education is a good thing" and "when a man is with a woman he is usually thinking of sex." Despite the fact that these and many other items are designed to indirectly tap personality constructs and are imbedded within literally tens or hundreds of other items, they may be taboo in certain cultures. We have conducted studies in which cultural informants have reviewed the items and recommended or required deletion of a number of these questions as well as questions that ask about attitudes toward such things as drugs in our protocols.

Human rights issues. Cultures differ considerably on many practices and issues that U.S. citizens often find difficult to understand and even offensive. These include abortion attitudes and practices, circumcision or female genital mutilation, and the punishment of women accused of premarital sex or extramarital affairs. (Conversely, many cultures find U.S. attitudes and practices offensive as well.) These are important social issues that are worthy of study and documentation; yet, as with issues concerning sex and sexuality, they may be taboo and difficult if not impossible to study in other cultures, and even within the United States.

Another consideration is the track record of countries in which researchers wish to work with regard to human rights issues. Many countries have been accused of human rights violations, and how these violations have been and are dealt with, in some cases, may form part of an important context within which research may occur. It behooves researchers to know about these issues and to gauge the degree to which they may affect the research and findings and whether it is wise to do the research in the first place.

Deception. Deception is used in many studies in the United States, and when it is used, it must gain IRB approval so that its use does not introduce undue risks to the participants. Participants must be fully debriefed about deception at the end of the study and must give their informed consent to use the data. Complex and important checks are placed on the use of deception in the United States. In countries without IRBs, however, it becomes easier to conduct research that involves deception. Such ease comes with the greater obligation to exercise caution. We do not believe that all research involving deception should be banned outright in countries without an IRB procedure, but we do believe that such research needs to be conducted with additional care and caution. This care should be taken by engaging cultural informants as collaborators who can gauge the necessity of the deception, by enacting procedures that ensure the full debriefing of the participants, and by obtaining consent to preserve individual participant integrity.

METHODS, SENSITIVITY, OR ETHICS?

The topics we raise in this section blend together issues concerning methodology, cultural sensitivity, and ethics. Studying sensitive topics in a culturally insensitive manner is likely to yield invalid results, thus posing a methodological dilemma. It also has the potential to treat participants and cultures in a disrespectful manner, and this, too, is an ethical problem. To be sure, we do not argue for a ban on research on sensitive topics. We do, however, suggest that such research must be undertaken with care, precision, and sensitivity for the topics studied in regard to the cultures in question.

Cultural Biases in Interpretations

Just as culture can bias formulation of the research questions in a cross-cultural study, it also can bias the ways researchers interpret their findings. Most researchers will inevitably interpret the data they obtain through their own cultural filters, and these biases can affect their interpretations to varying degrees. For example, if the mean response for Americans on a rating scale is 6.0 and the mean for Hong Kong Chinese is 4.0, one interpretation is that the Americans simply scored higher on the scale. Another interpretation may be that the Chinese are suppressing their responses and avoiding using the extremes of the scale. This type of interpretation is common. But how do we know the Chinese are suppressing their responses? What if it is the Americans who are exaggerating their responses? What if the Chinese mean response of 4.0 is actually more correct, and the American response is inaccurate? What if we surveyed the rest of the world and found that the overall mean was 3.0, suggesting that both the Chinese and the Americans inflated their ratings? In other words, the interpretation that the Chinese are suppressing their responses is made on the basis of an implicit assumption that U.S. data are correct and that we can use our cultural frame to interpret the results.

Whenever researchers make a value judgment or interpretation of a finding, it is always possible that this interpretation is bound by a cultural bias. Interpretations of good or bad, right or wrong, suppressing or exaggerating, important or not important are all value interpretations that may be made in a cross-cultural study. These interpretations may reflect the value orientations of the researchers as much as they do the cultures of the samples included in the study.

As researchers, we may make those interpretations without giving them a second thought—and without the slightest hint of malicious intent—only because we are so accustomed to seeing the world in a certain way. As consumers of research, we may agree with such interpretations when they agree with the ways we have learned to understand and view the world, and we often will do so unconsciously and automatically.

Cultural Informants

The involvement of cultural informants, at least on the level of advisors and at best on the level of collaborators, is a must in cross-cultural research. Cultural informants and collaborators should be engaged from the beginning of any study, providing needed advice and guidance about whether to conduct the study, the appropriateness of the theory and hypotheses to be tested, and the adequacy and appropriateness of the research design.

The involvement of cultural informants can help to avoid cultural bias in interpreting results, such as those described thus far. We strongly encourage researchers to seek out such informants or collaborators at the earliest stages of their studies and to work collaboratively with them throughout the research process. Most scientific organizations such as the APA have guidelines or criteria for authorship, and we encourage researchers to ensure that informants contribute their share of intellectual material to the research to gain authorship.

Confidentiality

In the United States, we have many rules, regulations, and guidelines concerning the need to maintain confidentiality of any data sources. Such rules do not exist in many other countries, and many other collaborators or cultural informants may not be aware of such needs or procedures. Even though a country may not have such rules or regulations, data need to be kept confidential, and access should be given only to the research team. Many participants in many other countries may worry about who has access to their data, especially if they have made statements about issues that are politically, socially, or morally sensitive in their cultures. Some data have to be smuggled out of a country because of this worry. Clearly, participants in research should be free of such anxiety concerning the use of their data when they provide it and afterward, and researchers should take extra precautions to ensure that this is indeed the case.

Impact of Research on the Community

A focus on the ecology of individual participants in research and designing research and interventions at the community level suggest a long-term commitment to the locale as part of the research process. So-called one-shot or safari approaches to community-based research should be discouraged, including the low probability that such an approach would leave a positive effect after the project ends or the grant money runs out. Researchers doing work in other countries and cultures should be attuned to how research can make positive impacts on the lives in the community because many other countries do not have the reciprocal cycle of access benefit that exists in the United States.

Research also must avoid actions, procedures, and interactive styles that violate local customs and understandings of the community. Our goals are for understanding and learning to occur—not cultural faux pas because of our lack of education of another culture. Incidences of this nature can be tempered by positive learning interaction with a cultural expert and individual research of customs and norms. At every phase of research, including the consent process, sensitivity and attention should be given to the cultural *ethos* and *eidos* of the community.

CONCLUSION

In this chapter, we have discussed basic issues concerning cross-cultural research methodology and ethical issues concerning cross-cultural psychological research with regard to design, sampling, sensitive issues, and dealing with data. Undoubtedly, we have raised more questions than provided answers. In many cases, the answers for many of the issues raised reside in local cultural communities and not in a one-size-fits-all approach to the professional and ethical conduct of research in different cultures. Our purpose has been first and foremost to raise awareness of the complex issues that face cross-cultural researchers. Thus, these issues should serve as the start, not end, of a dialogue concerning cross-cultural research methodology.

References

American Psychological Association. (2010). *Ethical principles of psychologists and code of conduct (2002, Amended June 1, 2010)*. Retrieved from http://www.apa.org/ethics/code/index/aspx

Berry, J. W., Poortinga, Y. H., Segall, M. H., & Dasen, P. R. (2002). *Cross-cultural psychology: Research and applications* (2nd ed.). New York, NY: Cambridge University Press.

Beuckelaer, A., Lievens, F., & Swinnen, G. (2007). Measurement equivalence in the conduct of a global organizational survey across countries in six cultural regions. *Journal of Occupational and Organizational Psychology, 80*, 575–600. doi:10.1348/096317907X173421

Boehnke, K., Lietz, P., Schreier, M., & Wilhelm, A. (2011). Sampling: The selection of cases for culturally comparative psychological research. In D. Matsumoto & F. J. R. van de Vijver (Eds.), *Cross-cultural research methods in psychology* (pp. 101–129). New York, NY: Cambridge University Press.

Bond, M. H., & van de Vijver, F. J. R. (2011). Making scientific sense of cultural differences in psychological outcomes: Unpackaging the magnum mysteriosum. In D. Matsumoto & F. J. R. van de Vijver (Eds.), *Cross-cultural research methods in psychology* (pp. 75–100). New York, NY: Cambridge University Press.

Camilli, G., & Shepard, L. A. (1994). *Methods for identifying biased test items*. Thousand Oaks, CA: Sage.

Campbell, D. T. (1961). The mutual methodological relevance of anthropology and psychology. In F. L. Hsu (Ed.), *Psychological anthropology* (pp. 333–352). Homewood, IL: Dorsey.

Fischer, R., & Fontaine, J. R. J. (2011). Methods for investigating structural equivalence. In D. Matsumoto & F. J. R. van de Vijver (Eds.), *Cross-cultural research methods in psychology* (pp. 179–215). New York, NY: Cambridge University Press.

Gomez, R., Burns, G. L., & Walsh, J. A. (2008). Parent ratings of the oppositional defiant disorder symptoms: Item response theory analyses of cross-national and cross-racial invariance. *Journal of Psychopathology and Behavioral Assessment, 30*, 10–19. doi:10.1007/s10862-007-9071-z

Greenfield, P. M. (1997). Culture as process: Empirical methods for cultural psychology. In J. W. Berry, Y. H. Poortinga, & J. Pandey (Eds.), *Handbook of cross-cultural psychology: Vol. 1. Theory and method* (pp. 301–346). New York, NY: Allyn & Bacon.

Hambleton, R. K., & Zenisky, A. L. (2011). Translating and adapting tests for cross-cultural assessments. In D. Matsumoto & F. J. R. van de Vijver (Eds.), *Cross-cultural research methods in psychology* (pp. 46–74). New York, NY: Cambridge University Press.

Heine, S. J., Kitayama, S., Lehman, D. R., Takata, T., Ide, E., Leung, C., & Matsumoto, H. (2001). Divergent consequences of success and failure in Japan and North America: An investigation of self-improving motivations and malleable selves. *Journal of Personality and Social Psychology, 81*, 599–615. doi:10.1037/0022-3514.81.4.599

Ho, D. Y. F. (1996). Filial piety and its psychological consequences. In M. H. Bond (Ed.), *The handbook of Chinese psychology* (pp. 155–165). New York, NY: Oxford University Press.

Holland, P. W., & Wainer, H. (Eds.). (1993). *Differential item functioning*. Hillsdale, NJ: Erlbaum.

Jacoby, R., Glauberman, N., & Herrnstein, R. J. (1995). *The bell curve debate: History, documents, opinions*. New York, NY: Times Books.

Jensen, A. R. (1969). How much can we boost IQ and scholastic achievement? *Harvard Educational Review, 39*(1), 1–123.

Johnson, T., Shavitt, S., & Holbrook, A. (2011). Survey response styles across cultures. In D. Matsumoto & F. J. R. van de Vijver (Eds.), *Cross-cultural research methods in psychology* (pp. 130–176). New York, NY: Cambridge University Press.

Kitayama, S., Mesquita, B., & Karasawa, M. (2006). Cultural affordances and emotional experience: Socially engaging and disengaging emotions in Japan and the United States. *Journal of Personality and Social Psychology, 91*, 890–903. doi:10.1037/0022-3514.91.5.890

Markus, H. R., Uchida, Y., Omoregie, H., Townsend, S. S. M., & Kitayama, S. (2006). Going for the gold: Models of agency in Japanese and American contexts. *Psychological Science, 17*, 103–112. doi:10.1111/j.1467-9280.2006.01672.x

Matsumoto, D., Grissom, R., & Dinnel, D. (2001). Do between-culture differences really mean that people are different? A look at some measures of cultural effect size. *Journal of Cross-Cultural Psychology, 32*, 478–490. doi:10.1177/0022022101032004007

Matsumoto, D., Kim, J. J., Grissom, R. J., & Dinnel, D. L. (2011). Effect sizes in cross-cultural research. In D. Matsumoto & F. J. R. van de Vijver (Eds.), *Cross-cultural research methods in psychology* (pp. 244–272). New York, NY: Cambridge University Press.

Matsumoto, D., & Yoo, S. H. (2006). Toward a new generation of cross-cultural research. *Perspectives on Psychological Science, 1,* 234–250. doi:10.1111/j.1745-6916.2006.00014.x

Matsumoto, D., Yoo, S. H., & LeRoux, J. A. (2007). Emotion and intercultural communication. In H. Kotthoff & H. Spencer-Oatley (Eds.), *Handbook of applied linguistics: Vol. 7. Intercultural communication* (pp. 77–98). Berlin, Germany: Mouton de Gruyter.

McCrae, R. R., Costa, P. T., Ostendorf, F., Angleitner, A., Hrebickova, M., Avia, M. D., . . . Smith, P. B. (2000). Nature over nurture: Temperament, personality, and life span development. *Journal of Personality and Social Psychology, 78,* 173–186. doi:10.1037/0022-3514.78.1.173

Meiring, D., van de Vijver, F. J. R., Rothmann, S., & Barrick, M. R. (2005). Construct, item, and method bias of cognitive and personality tests in South Africa. *South African Journal of Industrial Psychology, 31,* 1–8.

Miller, J. G. (2001). Culture and moral development. In D. Matsumoto (Ed.), *Handbook of culture and psychology* (pp. 151–170). New York, NY: Oxford University Press.

Mireshghi, S., & Matsumoto, D. (2006). *Cultural attitudes toward homosexuality and their effects on Iranian and American homosexuals.* Manuscript submitted for publication.

Nezlek, J. (2011). Multilevel modeling. In D. Matsumoto & F. J. R. van de Vijver (Eds.), *Cross-cultural research methods in psychology* (pp. 299–347). New York, NY: Cambridge University Press.

Pack-Brown, S. P., & Braun Williams, C. (2003). *Ethics in a multicultural context.* Newbury Park, CA: Sage.

Piswanger, K. (1975). *Interkulturelle Vergleiche mit dem Matrizentest von Formann* [Cross-cultural comparisons with Formann's Matrices Test]. Unpublished doctoral dissertation, University of Vienna, Vienna, Austria.

Poortinga, Y. H. (1989). Equivalence of cross-cultural data: An overview of basic issues. *International Journal of Psychology, 24,* 737–756.

Poortinga, Y. H., van de Vijver, F. J. R., Joe, R. C., & van de Koppel, J. M. H. (1987). Peeling the onion called culture: A synopsis. In C. Kagitcibasi (Ed.), *Growth and progress in cross-cultural psychology* (pp. 22–34). Berwyn, PA: Swets North America.

Robinson, W. S. (1950). Ecological correlations and the behavior of individuals. *American Sociological Review, 15,* 351–357. doi:10.2307/2087176

Shweder, R. A. (1999). Why cultural psychology? *Ethos, 27*(1), 62–73. doi:10.1525/eth.1999.27.1.62

Singelis, T., Bond, M., Sharkey, W. F., & Lai, C. S. Y. (1999). Unpacking culture's influence on self-esteem and embarassability. *Journal of Cross-Cultural Psychology, 30,* 315–341. doi:10.1177/0022022199030003003

Sireci, S. G. (2011). Evaluating test and survey items for bias across languages and cultures. In D. Matsumoto & F. J. R. van de Vijver (Eds.), *Cross-cultural research methods in psychology* (pp. 216–243). New York, NY: Cambridge University Press.

Smith, P. B. (2004). Acquiescent response bias as an aspect of cultural communication style. *Journal of Cross-Cultural Psychology, 35,* 50–61. doi:10.1177/0022022103260380

Tracy, J. L., & Robins, R. W. (2008). The nonverbal expression of pride: Evidence for cross-cultural recognition. *Journal of Personality and Social Psychology, 94,* 516–530. doi:10.1037/0022-3514.94.3.516

Trimble, J., & Fischer, C. (2005). *The handbook of ethical research with ethnocultural populations and communities.* Newbury Park, CA: Sage.

van de Vijver, F. J. R. (2009). *Types of cross-cultural studies in cross-cultural psychology.* Unpublished manuscript.

Van Haaften, E. H., & van de Vijver, F. J. R. (1996). Psychological consequences of environmental degradation. *Journal of Health Psychology, 1,* 411–429. doi:10.1177/135910539600100401

CHAPTER 6

RESEARCH WITH UNDERRESEARCHED POPULATIONS

Mark W. Roosa, George P. Knight, and Adriana J. Umaña-Taylor

Despite significantly large numbers of people living in poverty in the United States (U.S. Census Bureau, 2001a) and the rapid growth in racial and ethnic minority populations (U.S. Census Bureau, 2001b), psychological research with these populations is in its infancy (McLoyd, 2006). Nevertheless, this research is essential so that (a) theories can be made more universal or new ones developed, (b) researchers and practitioners can be better prepared to serve these populations in schools and social service agencies as well as provide appropriate and effective mental health services, and (c) policymakers can have the information needed to better meet the needs of these groups. Progress in the quality of research on underresearched populations (e.g., racial or ethnic minority groups or people living in poverty)[1] has been somewhat limited by overreliance on methods and procedures developed for middle-class European Americans that may not be as informative with other populations. In addition, until recently, it was difficult to locate information about effective methods specifically for the study of underresearched groups (Knight, Roosa, & Umaña-Taylor, 2009).

Quantitative research typically is defined as the systematic collection of data for description or hypothesis testing with the goal of generalizing from a sample to a population (e.g., Beins, 2004). Too often the notion of systematic data collection has been interpreted as using invariant procedures with each research participant. In practice, the use of

invariant procedures has resulted in several sources of bias in research that may escape the attention of many psychological researchers. For instance, several studies are described as having nationally representative samples while being limited to participants who are English speakers (e.g., AddHealth [Bearman, Jones, & Udry, 1997] and the National Comorbidity Survey-Replication [Kessler & Marikangas, 2004]). Because a significant portion of some minority groups are relatively recent immigrants and may have difficulty understanding or speaking English (U.S. Census Bureau, 2003), these samples are not representative of the population. The representativeness of these samples may be further compromised because of the use of a single recruitment method. Urban and low-income populations, in which ethnic and racial minority populations are overrepresented, may be less likely to respond to common research recruitment procedures (e.g., Capaldi & Patterson, 1987; Gallagher-Thompson et al., 2006). Another common source of bias from the use of invariant procedures emerges from the assumption that measures of psychological constructs developed with college student or middle-class European American samples are equally reliable and valid for all other ethnic, racial, income, or language groups (whether or not measures are translated into other languages). Items used to measure common psychological constructs, for example, self-esteem (Michaels, Barr, Roosa, & Knight, 2007) and perceived neighborhood quality

[1]For convenience, we use the term *underresearched populations* throughout this chapter whenever we refer generically to research with racial or ethnic minority or low-income populations. Whenever research or advice is more specific, we refer to the specific population to which it applies.

DOI: 10.1037/13619-007
APA Handbook of Research Methods in Psychology: Vol. 1. Foundations, Planning, Measures, and Psychometrics, H. Cooper (Editor-in-Chief)

(Kim, Nair, Knight, Roosa, & Updegraff, 2009), may convey different psychological meanings or have different scaling properties for various ethnic, racial, income, or language groups. Therefore, the use of invariant procedures can threaten both the internal validity (e.g., when measures are not equally reliable or valid across groups) and external validity (e.g., when the subsample representing one group is not as representative of that group as the subsample representing another group) of research.

From the beginnings of psychological research, studies focused overwhelmingly on middle-class, European American participants (Cauce, Ryan, & Grove, 1998). Even as recently as a few decades ago, few researchers would have been concerned about methodological issues associated with studying underresearched populations because few ethnic or racial minority or low-income individuals were included in psychological research (Knight, Roosa, & Umaña-Taylor, 2009). When other demographic groups were included or became the focus of psychological research, a common assumption was that methods and measures developed with middle-class European American samples were appropriate to use with all other groups. For several reasons this scenario has improved in recent years (McLoyd, 2006). First, the U.S. Census Bureau (2004) caught people's attention when they estimated that, collectively, minorities will constitute the majority of the U.S. population by 2050. Second, there has been a growing awareness of significant health disparities across ethnic and racial as well as income groups that often were overlooked in the past (U.S. Department of Health and Human Services, 2001). Finally, the National Institutes of Health (NIH) now require NIH-funded projects to include minority group members as participants whenever possible or to provide a compelling justification when they are excluded. Therefore, researchers now are much more likely to include significant numbers of racial and ethnic minorities in their research or to conduct research that focuses on a single specific ethnic or racial minority group (i.e., ethnic homogeneous research). To improve the quality of psychological research that includes or focuses on underresearched populations, researchers need to pay attention to the appropriateness of applying common research methods to these populations and, where necessary, adopt or develop new procedures. In this chapter, we provide a brief primer on three critical methodological issues that affect much of the research on underresearched populations: (a) improving the representativeness of samples from these populations; (b) effectively translating measures and research protocols into other languages when targeted populations include immigrants; and (c) determining the equivalence of measures across race and ethnicity, income, or language.

RECRUITMENT

There are many reasons why common recruitment processes may not be as effective or efficient for underresearched populations as for the majority population (see Knight, Roosa, & Umaña-Taylor, 2009, for a more detailed review). First, with lower rates of college attendance in low-income and many ethnic and racial minority populations (U.S. Census Bureau, 2004), members of underresearched populations may be less likely to understand what research is, its purposes or potential benefits, or how participation might contribute to the common good. Similarly, underresearched populations may have less reason to trust research institutions because of a lack of familiarity with the research process. Middle-class populations are more likely to have attended college and thereby to be exposed directly and indirectly to psychological research. Information gained from this exposure likely reduces fears and suspicions about research participation and increases the likelihood that they see the goal of research as a social good. This exposure probably increases their likelihood of participating in research when invited compared with less informed individuals (Word, 1977; Yancey, Ortega, & Kumanyika, 2006).

But middle-class ethnic and racial minority individuals, particularly African Americans and American Indians, may be reluctant to participate in research if they are aware of studies that have mistreated members of their populations or grossly misrepresented them in previous research (e.g., Manson, Garroute, Goins, & Henderson, 2004; Nelson, 2001). For instance, research on minority populations commonly has used comparative research designs that focus on low-income members of the group and compares them with middle-class European Americans (e.g., Cauce, Coronado, & Watson, 1998). This approach often has resulted in the use of a deficit perspective to formulate hypotheses or explain research findings. A deficit perspective typically (a) criticizes racial and ethnic minorities (or draws negative inferences about characteristics of the group) when a difference emerges between minority and majority group members; (b) focuses on race, ethnicity, or culture as the explanation for group differences that emerge; (c) ignores the strengths of the minority group; or (d) overlooks diversity (on multiple dimensions such as culture, income, and education) within the minority group.

Recruitment of racial and ethnic minorities also may be undermined because of the discrimination these groups have experienced in interactions with the larger society (e.g., Katz et al., 2006; Norton & Manson, 1996). In addition, efficient recruitment of underresearched populations is complicated because a significant portion of many minority groups are immigrants with limited English language ability (U.S. Census Bureau, 2004). Language issues may make it difficult or impossible for recent immigrants to understand recruitment processes conducted exclusively in English or to complete questionnaires or interviews in English. Additionally, low-income populations, among which ethnic and racial minorities are overrepresented, have greater residential mobility than the general population, making them more difficult to locate for recruitment. Finally, low-income individuals or families are less likely to have working telephones at any given time or to be accessible via e-mail (e.g., Knight, Roosa, & Umaña-Taylor, 2009).

Despite such challenges, researchers can do several things to make recruitment more efficient and generate more representative samples of underresearched populations depending on the history of the group and local conditions. For most groups, recruitment will be more productive if the process is designed to be consistent with the language (including vocabulary), values, and lifestyles of targeted individuals (e.g., Dumka, Lopez, & Carter, 2002; Sue, Fujino, Hu, Takeuchi, & Zane, 1991). At a

concrete level, recruitment within groups that include immigrants means that recruiters need to be fluently bilingual and all recruitment and study materials need to be available in targeted individuals' preferred language. Equally important, recruiters also need to be culturally competent; that is, they must be familiar with the values, interaction patterns, and communication styles of potential participants and capable of applying these skills in the recruitment process. This includes, for example, understanding when to communicate at a personal level (e.g., making comments about a targeted individual's children), knowing how to communicate in a respectful manner with each generation in a household, and being able to decipher informal signals regarding power relationships in a household (Knight, Roosa, & Umaña-Taylor, 2009). For many groups, recruitment may be more effective if it can be done via personal, particularly face-to-face, contact (Dumka, Garza, Roosa, & Stoerzinger, 1997; Maxwell, Bastani, Vida, & Warda, 2005). For individuals who have not been exposed to research, face-to-face contact provides an opportunity to make decisions about whether the recruiter or researcher is someone to trust. These same individuals may feel more confident about making a decision to participate if researchers extend the recruitment process to include an educational piece that explains what research is, why many consider it to be a public good, and exactly what participation would mean to the targeted individual or family. For many groups, personal interaction is culturally valued, considered a means of expressing respect for one another, and a means of determining whether one wants to do business with the other party (Skaff, Chesla, Mycue, & Fisher, 2002).

In addition to the common approach of appealing to potential participants' sense of altruism, other incentives may be important to getting a commitment to participate from members of underresearched populations. First and foremost, for applied studies, researchers should consider appealing to the value of collectivism that generally is stronger among underresearched populations than among the middle-class majority (Knight, Roosa, & Umaña-Taylor, 2009). Being asked to take part in an activity that can potentially benefit one's community or racial or ethnic group is a powerful incentive for many. Financial incentives also can be effective recruitment tools as long as they are offered in a timely manner (e.g., at the time of the interview or other research procedure) and are easily used by persons who may not have bank accounts or social security numbers (e.g., cash, debit cards, or gift cards instead of checks; Roosa et al., 2008).

Recruitment may be particularly challenging with groups that have been abused or misrepresented in previous research, that long have been the target of discrimination from the larger society, or that have had difficult relations with their surrounding communities or with the research institution. In such cases, researchers should consider developing collaborations or partnerships with the group or with respected agencies or individuals who serve, work with, or are part of the targeted population (e.g., Beals et al., 2005; Dumka et al., 2002). Bringing members of the targeted research population or their representatives into the research process can reduce suspicions about researchers held by members of the targeted group, increase researchers' credibility, and break down other barriers to participation in research. These partnerships can take many forms, including having members of the targeted group or their representatives as advisors to the researchers, as recruiters for the project, or as other research staff. It is also possible to establish more extensive partnerships with members of the targeted group such as via community-based participatory research (CBPR; see Volume 2, Chapter 11, this handbook).

In CBPR, the targeted population is an equal partner in the research enterprise from the problem formulation to development and implementation of methods to interpretation of results (Beals et al., 2005; Manson et al., 2004). CBPR is costly in terms of researchers' time throughout the process but particularly at the beginning when trust is being developed, methods of communication are being established, and rules governing the partnership are being negotiated. CPBR, however, may provide researchers with a level of access to and cooperation from members of the targeted population not possible through other means.

When research focuses on racially and ethnically sensitive issues such as discriminatory experiences

in the community, recruitment as well as the quality of data obtained may benefit from matching potential participants and research staff on race and ethnicity (Fulton et al., 2002; Gallagher-Thompson et al., 2006). Contrary to common belief, however, there is no apparent advantage to such matching in most research conditions (Sue et al., 1991). The most important personal characteristic of research staff may be that they are familiar with, comfortable with, and respectful toward the values and lifestyles of potential participants and can demonstrate that respect and comfort in their interactions (i.e., they are culturally competent; Knight, Roosa, & Umaña-Taylor, 2009). For example, a middle- or upper-class African American may not be the best choice for a recruiter for a study that includes large numbers of low-income inner-city African Americans, unless that individual has considerable previous experience interacting with this population. Similarly, a fourth-generation Chinese American might not be the best choice to recruit newly arrived low-income Chinese immigrants.

A final consideration for recruiting more representative samples of underresearched populations is the often-overlooked task of carefully defining the target population. It is important for researchers to have clear definitions of group membership that are conceptually consistent with the research questions being pursued. It is equally important that corresponding eligibility criteria are used to screen potential participants (e.g., Roosa et al., 2008). For instance, what kinds of research questions can be appropriately addressed with research designs that focus on Asian Americans as a whole versus a specific Asian American subgroup (e.g., Japanese Americans, Cambodian Americans)? Can the tremendous diversity within broadly defined groups such as Asians, Latinos, or American Indians be overlooked and these groups treated as homogenous without sacrificing research validity? Similarly, what definition of low income or poverty makes most sense for a specific research question (Roosa, Deng, Nair, & Burrell, 2005)?

Without careful attention to these and similar questions about group membership, both the internal and external validity of research that includes or focuses on underresearched populations can be undermined. For instance, suppose that a researcher wanted to test the hypothesis that American Indian elementary school children prefer learning through small group activities more than their European American peers because of group cultural differences on the collectivism–individualism dimension. The researcher recruits students into the study in an urban school district with a large American Indian population and assigns them to groups on the basis of their official racial classification in school records (or on the basis of children's self-reports). To the degree that the parents of children in this study are from different racial and ethnic heritages, especially the American Indian–European American combination, the independent variable (child race) will be compromised, reducing the validity of research results. Given the specific research question chosen, the researcher needs to carefully decide how to operationalize race and how to classify children with parents from two racial or ethnic groups, or whether to include such children in the study at all (Roosa et al., 2008).

Similarly, because of the simple operationalization of child race, the external validity of this study also may be compromised. To the degree that there are mixed racial or ethnic marriages in either group, the results may not generalize well to the two groups the researcher intended to study. This will be particularly true to the extent that children in either group have one American Indian parent and one European American parent because these children likely have received some socialization from both cultural groups. Furthermore, to the extent that variation exists among American Indian tribes on adherence to collectivism and to the extent that the sample has representatives from tribes at opposite ends of the collectivism–individualism continuum, the results may not generalize well to any one tribe. A more detailed definition of the independent variable (e.g., children from American Indian tribe X and European American children) and more careful operationalization of group membership (e.g., eligibility criteria such as American Indian children must be from families in which both parents are enrolled members of tribe X) would greatly improve both the internal and external validity for a study like this one.

An example of how to put much of this advice on recruitment into practice comes from a study of cultural and contextual influences on the development of Mexican American children (Roosa et al., 2008). To represent the diversity of contextual influences on children's development, the research team began by sampling school communities (i.e., attendance boundaries of elementary schools) in a large metropolitan area. This resulted in 47 economically and culturally different communities represented by public, parochial, and charter schools. To assist with the recruitment process, the research team recruited prominent representatives of the Mexican American community as members of a community advisory board. This board provided advice on several methodological aspects of the study (including the selection of school communities) and allowed their names to be used on recruitment materials.

Partnerships were formed with each school to implement the recruitment process; schools generally are respected and trusted institutions in the Latino community providing support for recruitment. Recruitment involved sending materials home in English and Spanish with each fifth-grade child in the selected schools. These materials explained that the study would focus on Latino families and described what participation would involve. In addition, these materials explained that results of the study would be used to guide the development of programs to help Latino children at home, at school, or in the community in the future. In addition, parents were told that each person who met eligibility criteria and agreed to be interviewed would receive $45 cash. Recruitment materials directed parents who were interested in the study or wanted more information about it to provide contact information so that members of the research team could talk to them about the study and answer their questions. All Latino parents who returned recruitment materials were contacted by bilingual members of the research team, usually by telephone, and the study was explained in more detail. All interviewers were culturally competent, most had extensive experience with the Latino community, and about 75% were bilingual. Parents who were interested in being considered for the study were given a screening interview to determine whether they met eligibility criteria. Because of the researchers' interest in the influence of culture on children's adaptation, families were eligible only if both of the target child's biological parents were of Mexican origin and there were no obvious adult socialization influences from other cultures in the child's home (e.g., stepfathers from another ethnic group). More than 70% of families that met all eligibility criteria completed in-home interviews. Descriptive analyses showed that the resulting sample was similar to the local Mexican American population according to U.S. Census data, and diverse in terms of language, nativity, education, income, and quality of residential community. This study and others like it demonstrate that despite many challenges, it is possible to recruit members of ethnic and racial minority or low-income groups efficiently and to obtain diverse and reasonably representative samples of these groups (e.g., Beals et al., 2005; Dumka et al., 1997).

TRANSLATION OF MEASURES

The growing interest in research with members of ethnically diverse populations in the United States, many of whom speak a language other than English, makes translation of measures and research protocols an important topic. Because many under-researched populations include substantial proportions of immigrants, measures often have to be translated into other languages to make participation in the research endeavor feasible for some individuals. Unfortunately, poor quality translations can interfere with scientific inferences because inaccuracies in translation introduce error in scores, which in turn can influence observed findings (Wang, Lee, & Fetzer, 2006).

Conceptual and semantic equivalence are necessary to make valid comparisons across ethnic groups, compare subsets of individuals (e.g., more versus less acculturated), or examine relations among constructs within a linguistically diverse ethnic group. Lack of conceptual equivalence occurs when one language version of a measure assesses a specific psychological construct and a different language version of the same measure assesses a somewhat different construct. This may happen when the targeted concept is meaningful in one language but

not the second (Kristjannson, Desrochers, & Zumbo, 2003). Semantic equivalence, however, pertains to the mapping of meanings across languages (Kristjansson et al., 2003) and is achieved when ideas expressed in one language are accurately conveyed in a second language. Unlike conceptual equivalence, which is more focused on the measure as a whole (i.e., scale level), semantic equivalence is determined at the item level. Lack of semantic equivalence occurs if items are poorly translated (van de Vijver & Tanzer, 2004), which is likely when translators attempt a literal translation rather than a semantically equivalent or meaningful translation.

Approaches to Translation

There are a number of strategies for translating measures (see Knight, Roosa, & Umaña-Taylor, 2009, for a detailed review). One of the most commonly used strategies is the *back-translation approach*, in which the measure is translated from the source language into a target language by one bilingual person, the new version is translated back into English by a second bilingual person, and then the two English versions are compared. The person translating back to the source language should not be familiar with the original version of the measure (Wang et al., 2006). A variation of this strategy is the *double translation–double back-translation* approach, which involves two translators each producing independent translations of a measure, having a third person create a revised translated version by comparing the two translated versions and resolving any issues between them, and finally having two additional translators do independent back translations of the revised translated version (Kristjansson et al., 2003).

A limitation of the back-translation approach is that a comparison of the original and the back translation could suggest equivalence (i.e., items read as exactly identical), but this could be the result of translators using a shared set of adaptation rules (see, e.g., discussion of *frame switching* later in this section), or the translation having retained inappropriate aspects of the source-language measure, such as the same grammatical structure, which made it easy to back-translate word for word into the same item (Hambleton, 2004).

Another strategy, *forward translation*, involves translating the source language version into the target language and having a group of bilinguals scrutinize the source and target language versions (Hambleton & Li, 2005). This allows judgments to be made directly about the equivalence of the source and target language versions, not by examining a back-translated version. The main weakness, however, is that a high level of inference is being made by translators (Hambleton, 2004), all of whom are bilingual and may be making insightful guesses based on their knowledge of both languages—knowledge that the monolingual participants for whom the measure is being developed will not have.

The use of bilingual translators is not ideal for two reasons. First, bilingual translators likely have more formal education, may be differentially fluent in the ethnic language, and may have had more experience with the constructs and terminology used in behavioral research than target participants who are monolingual. Bilingual translators also may be less aware of linguistic nuances of the ethnic language and of local usage of cultural constructs that pervade the daily lives of target participants. These differences may lead to a lack of equivalence of the translated measure and the original language version because the translators are different from the monolingual participants who would complete the measures of interest.

Second, research focused on the phenomenon of *frame switching* among bicultural or bilingual persons (Hong, Morris, Chiu, & Benet-Martinez, 2000; Ramírez-Esparza, Gosling, Benet-Martinez, Potter, & Pennebaker, 2006) suggests that some bilinguals may internalize information from two cultures in a manner that might interfere with a functional capacity to perform conceptually or semantically equivalent translations. For instance, cultural priming manipulations have been shown to influence expressions of values, causal attribution styles, and identity orientations among bicultural participants in research. Thus, the bicultural person responds in a manner consistent with the ethnic culture when exposed to external cues of that culture and in a mainstream manner when exposed to mainstream cues. If the language being spoken or written serves as a strong cultural prime, it can activate (or make

cognitively accessible) the system of knowledge that is associated with that specific culture and interfere with the translation process without the bilingual translator's awareness. Therefore, when bilingual persons review the original and its translation, they may make sense with the particular cultural meaning system that is active for them at the time. Monolingual research participants, for whom translated measures are being created, will not likely have this dual cultural frame of reference and almost certainly not to the same degree as bilinguals.

A final approach for translation is to utilize a review team or committee to evaluate the translation at various steps of the process. The team can (a) translate the source language version into the target language, (b) evaluate the translated items to determine whether they are meaningful for the target population in the target language, and (c) recommend changes to the original items or translated items to obtain semantic equivalence (Knight, Roosa, & Umaña-Taylor, 2009). This approach assists with establishing semantic equivalence because each translator may come up with a different translation of a particular expression and, as a team, the group can work together to determine the most appropriate meaningful translation. The disadvantages of this approach are primarily the time and costs that it entails.

Finally, within these various strategies, some researchers follow the practice of decentering, which involves making changes to both the source and target language versions of a measure until they are equivalent. Researchers who engage in this process view the source and target language versions of measures as equally open to modification (Prieto, 1992). An advantage of decentering is that equivalence may be easier to achieve once researchers are willing to accept changes in the original version. Decentering can be disadvantageous, however, if the original instrument has a history of use in the original language with accepted norms or cutoffs that can be used for comparative purposes. Because decentering could alter the psychological construct being assessed in the original version of the measure if this version has extensive changes, caution should be used in adopting this approach.

Selecting Translators

Aside from determining *how* to translate measures, researchers must also spend considerable time selecting *who* will serve as translators. In selecting translators, it is important to consider national origin and geographic region because of the considerable variability in dialects and common vocabulary within languages. In addition to differences in accent and intonation, some words have different meanings for different groups who share a language and other words may not exist for one cultural group, whereas they may be commonly used by another. It also is important to carefully consider socioeconomic status (SES). If translators and back-translators share the same SES background, and it is different from target participants' SES, the back-translated version may be equivalent to the original, but the target language version may not be meaningful for members of the population who will complete the measure (Wang et al., 2006). Scholars also recommend considering the following characteristics when selecting translators: familiarity with both languages and both cultures, knowledge of the construct being assessed, and knowledge of test construction (Geisinger, 1994; Hambleton & Li, 2005). Translators with these characteristics are unlikely to share certain demographic characteristics with certain participants, such as those with lower education levels (as discussed in the Approaches to Translation section earlier in this chapter). Thus, a diverse translation team is essential.

Piloting Translated Measures to Assess Equivalence

Scholars agree that pilot testing of translated measures is necessary to provide a rigorous assessment of the conceptual and semantic equivalence of language versions (Kristjansson et al., 2003; Wang et al., 2006). An important factor to consider is the language ability of participants involved in pilot testing. If measures are piloted with bilingual participants, findings may not be generalizable to a target population that includes a significant number of monolingual persons because bilingual participants have additional cognitive skills (Hambleton & Li, 2005). If measures are piloted on monolingual participants, then pilot subjects closely mirror much of the target population and there is no concern regarding

generalizability to the population of interest. Pilot testing with monolingual participants will identify translation problems, such as reliance on the grammar of the source language, which may escape the attention of people who are fluently bilingual.

GENERAL RECOMMENDATIONS

The strategy that researchers use when translating research instruments and protocols depends largely on the purpose of their research. For example, if the goal of the research is cross-ethnic comparison, conceptual equivalence must be established first to ensure that the measure being translated to a different language for a different cultural group is assessing a construct that is meaningful to that population (Hambleton, 2004). This may be less of a problem when researchers are studying a construct within one cultural group (e.g., Mexican-origin families in the United States), but issues of semantic equivalence may be more important because items must reflect a similar meaning across different language versions of the measure. Thus, before attempting any translation, researchers must consider the types of equivalence that are most relevant to their research as well as the translation strategies that will be most appropriate, given their goals.

Furthermore, it is critical to take into account specific characteristics of the target population when selecting a translation team and participants for pilot testing of instruments. For quantitative research, selecting translators and participants who mirror the characteristics of the target population, although costly, will significantly increase the generalizability of the measure to the intended population. For qualitative research, this strategy will help to ensure that the questions being asked of research participants are meaningful in the target language and that the translated data represent an accurate depiction of participants' beliefs and experiences (see Knight, Roosa, & Umaña-Taylor, 2009, for a detailed discussion of translation strategies for qualitative research).

Measurement Equivalence

Measures developed in White middle-class European American samples are commonly used in research on ethnic minority or economically disadvantaged samples. Researchers often do not consider the validity or reliability of the measures for these underresearched populations, or they do not consider how the internal and external validity of the research may be affected by using measures that originally were developed and normed on a different population. If the measurement plan does not ensure that measures of the target variables produce scores with equivalent meanings across race and ethnicity, income, or language groups, the observed relations may misrepresent causal relations. Take, for example, a study examining the socialization of collectivistic values across multiple cultural groups. If the measure of collectivism values did not assess collectivism equivalently across groups, the observed group similarities or differences most likely would misrepresent the causal sequences in this socialization process. This measurement problem represents a serious threat to the validity of the research. Therefore, greater attention to *measurement equivalence* (i.e., the degree to which a measure assesses the same variable in the same way across groups) is needed to obtain valid results.

Fortunately, there has been substantial development in the empirical procedures used to evaluate measurement equivalence (e.g., Camilli & Shepard, 1994; Labouvie & Ruetsch, 1995; Widaman & Reise, 1997), particularly as it applies to measures administered to participants from quite different segments of a broad population as well as to measures that have been translated (see Knight, Roosa, & Umaña-Taylor, 2009; Millsap & Kwok, 2004; and Widaman & Reise, 1997, for more detailed descriptions of these analytical procedures). In addition, scholars have described how the lack of measurement equivalence can lead to alternative explanations of observed findings (Knight, Roosa, Calderón-Tena, & Gonzales, 2009). Specifically, the absence of measurement equivalence can bias the results of studies that engage in comparisons across groups as well as when one is comparing subgroups within a broader group. In addition, the absence of measurement equivalence can bias findings when a researcher is primarily interested in examining the

relations among constructs within an ethnic or racial group or a socioeconomic group that is linguistically diverse (e.g., comparing means between immigrant Latinos who completed a measure in Spanish and their U.S.-born counterparts who completed the same measure in English). Finally, using a measure that was developed in research with middle-class European Americans in a study of a culturally different population can produce misleading results if measurement equivalence was not determined before the study even if the researcher is not making comparisons with other groups. In this case, the targeted variable (e.g., self-esteem, parent–child conflict) might have a different meaning or require different indicators or items in the targeted sample than in the samples used to develop the measure.

Evaluating the equivalence of a measure across groups requires analyses focused on the functioning of the items (or observations) on that measure as well as the functioning of the total score created from those items or observations. The creation of a good measure starts with theory that specifies the nature of the variable to be measured in the population in which it will be used. That is, knowledge of the population in which the measure is going to be used is instrumental in identifying the indicators of the variable *as they exist in the population being studied*. Theory also describes how the variable to be measured relates to other variables *in the population of interest*. A good measure produces a total score that is related to other variables as the theory specifies for the population being studied, and such a measure is then believed to have *construct validity* in that population.

Factorial Invariance

The evaluation of the functioning of the *items* on a measure across language, ethnic, race, or income groups can be accomplished through the examination of factorial invariance. Factorial invariance can be examined through the use of confirmatory factor analysis (see Volume 3, Chapter 18, this handbook).[2] Confirmatory factor analysis uses the correlations among the scores for the items on the

---

[2]A number of similar analytical procedures have been provided in the literature. In addition, some authors have recommended the use of item response theory approaches to evaluate the similarity of item functioning across groups (see Knight, Roosa, & Umaña-Taylor, 2009, for more detail).

measure to determine the degree to which these items are measuring the same factor or variable. If the same set of items or observations forms a factor within each group, the measure has *configural invariance*. When configural invariance exists, one can conclude that the items are measuring the same target variable in each group. If the factor loadings for each item are equal across groups, then the measure has *metric invariance*. If, in addition to equal factor loadings, the item intercepts are equal across groups, the measure has *strong invariance*. Finally, if in addition to equal factor loadings and intercepts the unique error variances for each item are equal across groups, then the measure has *strict invariance*. Strict invariance means that a particular score on each individual item (e.g., 3 on a Likert-type scale of 1 to 5) has the same meaning for each group. At all levels of invariance, a partially invariant model may be obtained if some, but not all, of the item features (e.g., factor loadings, intercepts, unique variances) of the factor structure are equivalent across groups (Byrne, Shavelson, & Muthén, 1989).

White, Umaña-Taylor, Knight, and Zeiders (in press) examined the factorial invariance of each of three subscales (i.e., exploration, resolution, and affirmation) of an English-language version and a Spanish-language translated version of the Ethnic Identity Scale (EIS; Umaña-Taylor, Yazedjian, & Bámaca-Gómez, 2004) in a sample of Mexican American youths. The Exploration subscale focuses on the degree to which individuals have explored their ethnic identity by doing such things as reading books or other materials that have taught them about their ethnicity. The Resolution subscale focuses on the degree to which individuals have resolved the meaningfulness of their ethnicity to their sense of self. The Affirmation subscale assesses the degree to which individuals feel positive about their ethnic group membership. White et al. demonstrated that the factor loadings, item intercepts, and unique variances for each item on the Exploration and Resolution subscales were equivalent across language versions. Confirmatory factor analysis models that constrained factor loadings, item intercepts, and unique variances for each Exploration item and each Resolution item to be equal across language versions produced nonsignificant chi-square difference and practical fit indexes similar to those produced by models that allowed these item characteristics to be different across language versions. Hence, the individual items on both the Resolution and Exploration subscales appeared to assess the respective ethnic identity dimension to the same degree across language versions. On the basis of these findings White et al. concluded that item-level and scale-level analyses focused on mean-level differences between English- and Spanish-speaking Mexican American adolescents on exploration and resolution would be justified.

In contrast, the sequence of unconstrained and constrained confirmatory factor analyses of the Affirmation subscale of the EIS suggested less than strict factorial invariance across language versions. These analyses indicated that although the factor loadings for each item on the Affirmation subscale were equivalent across language versions of the measure, the item intercepts were only modestly similar across language versions. Furthermore, the tests of strict invariance indicated that the unique error in measurement associated with each item differed substantially between the English and Spanish versions of the Affirmation subscale. Also noteworthy, factor loadings were generally lower for the Affirmation items than for the Exploration or Resolution items, perhaps because most of the Affirmation items were reverse worded. The failure to achieve strict invariance for this subscale suggests that a given score on the English and Spanish versions of this measure does not likely indicate the same degree of Affirmation. Put differently, a 3 on the English version does not necessarily correspond to a 3 on the Spanish version. Hence, White et al. (in press) concluded that analyses of mean differences using different language versions are uninterpretable because the values are not equivalent across groups.

Construct Validity Equivalence

If strict invariance is achieved according to the previous steps, the equivalence of the construct validity relations of the variable or factor score can proceed. The equivalence of construct validity relations of the target measure across groups is established by examining the cross-group similarities of the slopes and intercepts of the relations between the scores from the target measure and scores on measures of theoretically related constructs (see Knight, Roosa, & Umaña-Taylor, 2009). Equivalence in slopes can be tested by comparing the fit indexes for a multigroup structural equation model in which the slopes are unconstrained and allowed to be different across groups to a model that constrains slopes to be identical across groups.[3] As in the multigroup confirmatory factor analysis models, the adequacy of model fit is determined by examining the significance of the chi-square difference test and the differences in the practical fit indexes (e.g., comparative fit index, root-mean-square error of approximation, and standardized root-mean-square residual) across models. If the fit of the constrained slope model is satisfactory, and the fit indexes are not substantially different between the constrained and unconstrained slope models, similar comparisons are made between models that allow the intercepts of the relations among constructs to vary with a model that constrains the intercepts to be identical across groups. If comparisons of these hierarchically arranged structural equation models suggest that the slopes and intercepts are equal across groups, construct validity equivalence exists. Once again, partial construct validity equivalence may occur if the measure of the target construct is similarly related to some construct validity variables but not others.

White et al. (in press) also examined the construct validity equivalence of the English- and Spanish-translated version of the EIS subscales. Their examination of construct validity equivalence was conducted on the basis of the expectation that the three ethnic identity subscales should be related similarly across language versions to ethnic pride, Mexican American cultural values, family social support, and active coping. Both the Exploration and Resolution subscales were significantly and positively related to each of these variables as expected. Furthermore, the comparison of the fit of the constrained and unconstrained models indicated that the slopes and intercepts of these construct validity relations were the same for the English language and

Spanish language versions of these EIS subscales. Hence, any given score on either the Exploration or Resolution subscales indicates the same degree of the respective ethnic identity dimension regardless of which language version of the EIS is completed.

For the Affirmation subscale of the EIS, the pattern of construct validity relations was somewhat different. Although the slopes of relations between the Affirmation subscale and each construct validity variable were similar across language versions, affirmation was positively related only to ethnic pride and active coping. Unexpectedly, family support was not significantly related to affirmation, and Mexican American cultural values were negatively related to affirmation. Furthermore, the intercepts of the relations between the Affirmation subscale and several construct validity variables were consistently and significantly higher among youths completing the English-language version of the EIS. Given these results, it is not likely that any given affirmation score reflects the same degree of positive feelings about the ethnic group across language versions. Thus, White et al. (in press) produced evidence that the Affirmation subscale of the EIS should not be used for either mean comparisons between groups or for testing relations among variables in samples in which both the English and Spanish versions of the measure were used. On the basis of factorial invariance and construct validity invariance results, White et al. concluded that reverse-worded items in the Affirmation subscale may have been problematic among the early adolescent Mexican American sample regardless of language version, but that this difficulty may have been greater in the Spanish version.

Unfortunately, scientifically sound judgments regarding the equivalence of a measure across groups are difficult despite recent advances in analytical methods (e.g., Knight, Roosa, & Umaña-Taylor, 2009). Complete factorial invariance and construct validity equivalence may be difficult to establish. Perhaps more important, there may be variables and ethnic or income groups for which identical factor structures and construct validity

---

[3]One could also test for differences in the slopes and intercepts of the relation of the target measure scores to theoretically related variables using hierarchical multiple regression and similar logic (see Aiken & West, 1991).

relations may not reasonably be expected. That is, specific differences may exist in the functioning of individual items or relations of total scale scores to other variables that represent true differences in the nature of the target variable across groups (e.g., Kim et al., 2009; Michaels et al., 2007). As noted, the identification of indicators of a variable is made on the basis of the theoretical characterization of that variable in the group to whom the measure will be administered. If there are sound reasons to expect selected items to function differently across groups, then somewhat different factor loadings, item intercepts, or unique variances may be necessary to attain measurement equivalence. For example, an item assessing the frequency of suicidal thought may be appropriate on a scale measuring depression. Variability may be lower in responses to this item in one ethnic or economic group because of a religious prohibition against such behavior. In this case, the item may have a somewhat different factor loading across groups because of the difference in variance of the responses.

Similarly, the construct validity expectations for any particular variable are formed on the basis of the theoretical characterization of these relations to other variables in the group to whom the measure will be administered. Most often, available theory suggests that the indicators of a variable, and the expected relations to other variables, are identical across groups (although these assumptions may not have been tested). In some cases, our best and most informed theory suggests some subtly different features of the underlying construct across groups. For example, harsh parenting and restrictive control may be an adaptive parenting strategy for ethnic and economically disadvantaged youths who live in a community with high rates of violent behaviors, whereas this may represent an overly controlling quality of parental behavior in a safer middle-class neighborhood. If so, then one would expect parental control to relate differently to mental health outcomes in samples of children from relatively risky environments compared with those from safer environments.

Hence, the need to rely on theory regarding indicators of a variable, and the relation of the variable of interest to other variables, in the population being studied has important implications for the findings one would expect in factorial invariance and construct validity analyses. In some situations one might expect limited differences in factor structure or construct validity relations, and corresponding evidence of partial factorial invariance or partial construct validity equivalence. Indeed, in such situations, partial factorial invariance or partial construct validity equivalence that conforms closely to the expectations of informed theory actually would represent the most appropriate evidence of measurement equivalence.

Most empirical research on the equivalence of measures has occurred in studies that have used translated measures (e.g., White et al., in press). In part, this has occurred because the argument for potential differences in measures across languages is more obvious and straightforward than in other cases. Other research, however, has demonstrated the importance of examining measurement equivalence in studies of samples that are diverse in terms of race, ethnicity, culture, or income groups (e.g., Michaels et al., 2007). Common psychological constructs such as self-esteem can have different meanings for different groups or play different roles in their development or adjustment. Given the huge volume of studies that have made comparisons across race, ethnicity, culture, or income groups (e.g., Cauce et al., 1998), much more attention needs to be given to measurement equivalence.

CONCLUSION

Psychological research that includes or focuses on underresearched populations will continue to increase in response to changes in the demography of the U.S. population in the coming years. This new research should solidify the generalizability of some theories, contribute to changes in others, and improve the quality of services available to these populations. In this chapter, we provided an introduction to three essential steps in the research process that need to be applied more commonly in studies with underresearched populations. Obtaining more representative samples of underresearched populations, ensuring that measures are available to potential research participants in their preferred language, and ensuring that the measures we use are appropriate for and equivalent across populations will greatly improve the quality of research on these populations. The three essential research processes covered in the chapter are not, however, the only improvements that need to be made in studies with underresearched populations. Other topics that deserve the attention of researchers include (a) effective retention processes for longitudinal and intervention studies, (b) methods for creating or adapting interventions to be culturally attractive and competent for underresearched populations, and (c) ways to meet the ethical requirements of research with underresearched populations (see Knight, Roosa, & Umaña-Taylor, 2009, for a review). Finally, although the research processes described and recommended in this chapter represent the state of the art at this time, it is clear that there has been little systematic research on how to improve the validity of research with underresearched populations. The quality of research with underresearched populations could improve dramatically with more systematic approaches to determine exactly what methods work best with exactly which underresearched populations.

References

Aiken, L. S., & West, S. G. (1991). *Multiple regression: Testing and interpreting interactions*. Newbury Park, CA: Sage.

Beals, J., Manson, S. M., Whitesell, N. R., Mitchell, C. M., Novins, D. K., Simpson, S., . . . & American Indian Service Utilization, Psychiatric Epidemiology, Risk and Protective Factors Project Team. (2005). *The American Journal of Psychiatry, 162*, 1713–1722. doi:10.1176/appi.ajp.162.9.1713

Bearman, P. S., Jones, J., & Udry, J. R. (1997). *The National Longitudinal Study of Adolescent Health: Research design*. Retrieved from http://www.cpc.unc.edu/projects/addhealth/design

Beins, B. C. (2004). *Research methods: A tool for life*. New York, NY: Pearson Education.

Byrne, B. M., Shavelson, R. J., & Muthén, B. (1989). Testing for the equivalence of factor covariance and mean structures: The issue of partial measurement invariance. *Psychological Bulletin, 105*, 456–466. doi:10.1037/0033-2909.105.3.456

Camilli, G., & Shepard, L. A. (1994). *Methods for identifying biased test items*. Thousand Oaks, CA: Sage.

Capaldi, D., & Patterson, G. R. (1987). An approach to the problem to recruitment and retention rates for longitudinal research. *Behavioral Assessment, 9*, 169–177.

Cauce, A. M., Coronado, N., & Watson, J. (1998). Conceptual, methodological, and statistical issues in culturally competent research. In M. Hernandez & M. Isaacs (Eds.), *Promoting cultural competence in children's mental health services* (pp. 305–329). Baltimore, MD: Brookes.

Cauce, A. M., Ryan, K. D., & Grove, K. (1998). Children and adolescents of color, where are you? Participation, selection, recruitment, and retention in developmental research. In V. C. McLoyd & L. Steinberg (Eds.), *Studying minority adolescents: Conceptual, methodological, and theoretical issues* (pp. 147–166). Mahwah, NJ: Erlbaum.

Dumka, L., Garza, C., Roosa, M. W., & Stoerzinger, H. (1997). Recruiting and retaining high risk populations into preventive interventions. *The Journal of Primary Prevention, 18*, 25–39. doi:10.1023/A:1024626105091

Dumka, L. E., Lopez, V. A., & Carter, S. J. (2002). Parenting interventions adapted for Latino families: Progress and prospects. In J. M. Contreras, K. A. Kerns, & A. M. Neal-Barnett (Eds.), *Latino children and families in the United States: Current research and future directions* (pp. 203–231). Westport, CT: Praeger.

Fulton, P. S. J., Tierney, J., Mirpourian, N., Ericsson, J. M., Wright, J. T., & Powel, L. L. (2002). Engaging Black older adults and caregivers in urban communities in health research. *Journal of Gerontological Nursing, 28*, 19–27.

Gallagher-Thompson, D., Rabinowitz, Y., Tang, P. C. Y., Tse, C., Kwo, E., Hsu, S., . . . Thompson, L. W. (2006). Recruiting Chinese Americans for dementia caregiver researcher: Suggestions for success. *The American Journal of Geriatric Psychiatry, 14*, 676–683. doi:10.1097/01.JGP.0000221234.65585.f9

Geisinger, K. F. (1994). Cross-cultural normative assessment: Translation and adaptation issues influencing the normative interpretation of assessment instruments. *Psychological Assessment, 6*, 304–312. doi:10.1037/1040-3590.6.4.304

Hambleton, R. K. (2004). Issues, designs, and technical guidelines for adapting tests into multiple languages and cultures. In R. K. Hambleton, P. Merenda, & C. Spielberger (Eds.), *Adapting educational and psychological tests for cross-cultural assessment* (pp. 3–38). Mahwah, NJ: Erlbaum.

Hambleton, R. K., & Li, S. (2005). Translation and adaptation issues and methods for educational and psychological tests. In C. L. Frisby & C. R. Reynolds (Eds.), *Comprehensive handbook of multicultural school psychology* (pp. 881–903). New York, NY: Wiley.

Hong, Y.-Y., Morris, M., Chiu, C., & Benet-Martinez, V. (2000). Multicultural minds: A dynamic constructivist approach to culture and cognition. *American Psychologist, 55,* 709–720. doi:10.1037/0003-066X.55.7.709

Katz, R. V., Kegeles, S. S., Kressin, N. R., Green, B. L., Wang, M. Q., James, S. A., . . . Claudio, C. (2006). The Tuskegee Legacy Project: Willingness of minorities to participate in biomedical research. *Journal of Health Care for the Poor and Underserved, 17,* 698–715. doi:10.1353/hpu.2006.0126

Kessler, R. C., & Marikangas, K. R. (2004). The National Comorbidity Survey Replication (NCS-R): Background and aims. *International Journal of Methods in Psychiatric Research, 13,* 60–68. doi:10.1002/mpr.166

Kim, S. Y., Nair, R., Knight, G. P., Roosa, M. W., & Updegraff, K. A. (2009). Measurement equivalence of neighborhood quality measures for European American and Mexican American families. *Journal of Community Psychology, 37,* 1–20. doi:10.1002/jcop.20257

Knight, G. P., Roosa, M. W., Calderón-Tena, C. O., & Gonzales, N. A. (2009). Methodological issues in research on Latino populations. In F. Villaruel, G. Carlo, M. Azmitia, J. Grau, N. Cabrera, & J. Chahin (Eds.), *Handbook of U.S. Latino psychology* (pp. 45–62). Los Angeles, CA: Sage.

Knight, G. P., Roosa, M. W., & Umaña-Taylor, A. (2009). *Studying ethnic minority and economically disadvantaged populations: Methodological challenges and best practices.* Washington, DC: American Psychological Association. doi:10.1037/11887-000

Kristjansson, E. A., Desrochers, A., & Zumbo, B. (2003). Translating and adapting measurement instruments for cross-linguistic and cross-cultural research: A guide for practitioners. *CJNR: Canadian Journal of Nursing Research, 35,* 127–142.

Labouvie, E., & Ruetsch, C. (1995). Testing the equivalence of measurement scales: Simple structure and metric invariance reconsidered. *Multivariate Behavioral Research, 30,* 63–70. doi:10.1207/s15327906mbr3001_4

Manson, S. M., Garroute, E., Goins, R. T., & Henderson, P. N. (2004). Access, relevance, and control in the research process: Lessons from Indian country. *Journal of Aging and Health, 16,* 58S–77S. doi:10.1177/0898264304268149

Maxwell, A. E., Bastani, R., Vida, P., & Warda, U. S. (2005). Strategies to recruit and retain older Filipino-American immigrants for a cancer screening study. *Journal of Community Health, 30,* 167–179. doi:10.1007/s10900-004-1956-0

McLoyd, V. C. (2006). The legacy of *Child Development*'s 1990 special issue on minority children: An editorial retrospective. *Child Development, 77,* 1142–1148. doi:10.1111/j.1467-8624.2006.00952.x

Michaels, M. L., Barr, A., Roosa, M. W., & Knight, G. P. (2007). Self-esteem: Assessing measurement equivalence in a multi-ethnic sample of youth. *The Journal of Early Adolescence, 27,* 269–295. doi:10.1177/0272431607302009

Millsap, R. E., & Kwok, O.-M. (2004). Evaluating the impact of partial factorial invariance on selection in two populations. *Psychological Methods, 9,* 93–115. doi:10.1037/1082-989X.9.1.93

Nelson, R. M. (2001). Nontherapeutic research, minimal risk, and the Kennedy Krieger lead abatement study. *IRB: Ethics and Human Research, 23,* 7–11. doi:10.2307/3563898

Norton, I. M., & Manson, S. M. (1996). Research in American Indian and Alaska Native communities: Navigating the cultural universe of values and process. *Journal of Consulting and Clinical Psychology, 64,* 856–860. doi:10.1037/0022-006X.64.5.856

Prieto, A. J. (1992). A method for translation of instruments to other languages. *Adult Education Quarterly, 43,* 1–14. doi:10.1177/0741713692043001001

Ramírez-Esparza, N., Gosling, S. D., Benet-Martinez, V., Potter, J. P., & Pennebaker, J. W. (2006). Do bilinguals have two personalities? A special case of cultural frame switching. *Journal of Research in Personality, 40,* 99–120. doi:10.1016/j.jrp.2004.09.001

Roosa, M. W., Deng, S., Nair, R., & Burrell, G. L. (2005). Measures for studying poverty in family and child research. *Journal of Marriage and Family, 67,* 971–988. doi:10.1111/j.1741-3737.2005.00188.x

Roosa, M. W., Liu, F., Torres, M., Gonzales, N., Knight, G., & Saenz, D. (2008). Sampling and recruitment in studies of cultural influences on adjustment: A case study with Mexican Americans. *Journal of Family Psychology, 22,* 293–302. doi:10.1037/0893-3200.22.2.293

Skaff, M. K., Chesla, C., Mycue, V., & Fisher, L. (2002). Lessons in cultural competence: Adapting research methodology for Latino participants. *Journal of Community Psychology, 30,* 305–323. doi:10.1002/jcop.10007

Sue, S., Fujino, D. C., Hu, L., Takeuchi, D. T., & Zane, N. W. S. (1991). Community mental health services for ethnic minority groups: A test of the cultural responsiveness hypothesis. *Journal of Consulting and Clinical Psychology, 59,* 533–540. doi:10.1037/0022-006X.59.4.533

Umaña-Taylor, A. J., Yazedjian, A., & Bámaca-Gómez, M. (2004). Developing the Ethnic Identity Scale using

Eriksonian and social identity perspectives. *Identity: An International Journal of Theory and Research, 4,* 9–38. doi:10.1207/S1532706XID0401_2

U.S. Census Bureau. (2001a). *The Black population: 2000: Census 2000 brief.* Washington, DC: U.S. Department of Commerce, Economics and Statistics Administration.

U.S. Census Bureau. (2001b). *Poverty in the United States: 2000* (Current Population Reports). Washington, DC: U.S. Department of Commerce, Economics and Statistics Administration.

U.S. Census Bureau. (2003). *Language use and English-speaking ability: 2000* (Census 2000 Brief). Washington, DC: U.S. Department of Commerce, Economics and Statistics Administration.

U.S. Census Bureau. (2004). *Census Bureau projects tripling of Hispanic and Asian populations in 50 Years; non-Hispanic Whites may drop to half of total population.* Washington, DC: U.S. Department of Commerce, Economics and Statistics Administration.

U.S. Department of Health and Human Services. (2001). *Mental health: Culture, race, ethnicity* (Supplement to report of the Surgeon General). Rockville, MD: U.S. Department of Health and Human Services. Retrieved from http://mentalhealth.samhsa.gov/cre/default.asp

van de Vijver, F. J., & Tanzer, N. K. (2004). Bias and equivalence in cross-cultural assessment: An overview. *European Review of Applied Psychology/Revue Européenne de Psychologie Appliquée, 54,* 119–135.

Wang, W. L., Lee, H. L., & Fetzer, S. J. (2006). Challenges and strategies of instrument translation. *Western Journal of Nursing Research, 28,* 310–321. doi:10.1177/0193945905284712

Widaman, K. F., & Reise, S. P. (1997). Exploring the measurement invariance of psychological instruments: Applicants in the substance use domain. In K. J. Bryant, M. Windle, & S. G. West (Eds.), *The science of prevention: Methodological advances from alcohol and substance abuse research* (pp. 281–324). Washington, DC: American Psychological Association. doi:10.1037/10222-009

White, R. M. B., Umaña-Taylor, A. J., Knight, G. P., & Zeiders, K. H. (in press). Language measurement equivalence of the Ethnic Identity Scale with Mexican American early adolescents. *The Journal of Early Adolescence.*

Word, C. O. (1977). Cross cultural methods for survey research in Black urban areas. *Journal of Black Psychology, 3,* 72–87.

Yancey, A. K., Ortega, A. N., & Kumanyika, S. K. (2006). Effective recruitment and retention of minority research participants. *Annual Review of Public Health, 27,* 1–28. doi:10.1146/annurev.publhealth.27.021405.102113

PART II

PLANNING RESEARCH

CHAPTER 7

DEVELOPING TESTABLE AND IMPORTANT RESEARCH QUESTIONS

Frederick T. L. Leong, Neal Schmitt, and Brent J. Lyons

The purpose of this chapter is to provide guidance on developing testable and important research questions. We begin with a section that explores the process of developing a research question. This section discusses the issue of how research ideas are generated, judgments about ideas that are worth studying, and how new ideas or areas of research are developed. We propose a multifaceted approach to addressing these issues and we make recommendations to facilitate this process. In the second section of the chapter, we explore how to generate research questions that are important, linking these suggestions to specific recommendations, such as the need to understand the research literature and having a good sense of the real-world implications. We also discuss the likely sources of less important research ideas and provide examples related to validity generalization and structural equation modeling (SEM) approaches. In the third and final section, we review suggestions from several top researchers to address the issue of how to formulate testable research questions with special reference to experimental research that seeks to discover new effects, extending those effects and identifying moderators and mediators of such effects. We also focus on the centrality of identifying, evaluating, and selecting psychometrically sound psychological tests for research within the differential psychology tradition.

DEVELOPING A RESEARCH QUESTION

Deriving a Research Question

Developing a research question is a multifaceted process, and inspiration for research ideas can come from a variety of sources, including, but not limited to, personal interests; personal and societal problems; other people (e.g., colleagues, professors); and printed materials such as journal articles, textbooks, and news articles. Different researchers exhibit a wide variance in research topics they find interesting; Leong and Muccio (2006) compared preference in research questions to preferences in music and food. Many psychologists study human behavior that has become meaningful to them through their own personal experiences. Personal observation is a key source of ideas as individuals attempt to make sense of their lives (Daft, 1983). Researchers are encouraged to introspect and, at first, to be their own subject (Campbell, Daft, & Hulin, 1982). Specifically referring to researchers who study the workplace, Daft (1983) stated that organizations are so rich in people, stimuli, and experiences that anyone who looks around will find enough puzzlements to last for a productive career. African American social psychologists may study stereotypes and prejudice on the basis of their experiences of racial discrimination. A clinical psychologist who has lived abroad may be interested in exploring differences in cultural manifestations of schizophrenia. Or, an organizational psychologist who has struggled to balance the demands of an academic career with the needs of her or his family may ask questions about work–life balance.

One important feature of a research question is that it makes a significant and innovative contribution to the psychological literature (Petty, 2006). Developing a research question that makes a significant

DOI: 10.1037/13619-008
APA Handbook of Research Methods in Psychology: Vol. 1. Foundations, Planning, Measures, and Psychometrics, H. Cooper (Editor-in-Chief)

contribution can be a large task involving extensive reviews of literature and communication with other researchers (examples of such strategies are discussed in the following section), but innovation is largely initiated by a creative idea. Many of the most innovative ideas are the most creative and unexpected (Daft, 1983).

In a chapter outlining cognitive strategies researchers can use to find a research question, Leong and Muccio (2006) suggested a variety of idea generation resources and techniques that can be used to develop creative ideas. For example, by brainstorming, researchers can generate a list of research ideas and then select those ideas that are feasible, supported by research in the area, and motivating. Additionally, researchers can create mental maps to enhance individual creativity and inspire innovative research questions (for an overview of concept mapping, see Novak, 2004). Concept maps help individuals arrange and characterize their knowledge in unique ways, highlighting novel links between knowledge concepts that can be used to provide a solution to a problem (Ausubel, 1963, as cited in Novak, 2004). Leong and Muccio also recommended the Martian perspective as an idea-generation strategy: By looking at the world as an outsider, as "a Martian who just landed on earth" (p. 25) researchers can develop ideas that have not been thought of by others.

In addition to cognitive strategies, the real world offers many resources to aid in creative idea development. Media outlets (e.g., radio, television, newspapers, Internet blogs, and discussion boards) and novels are filled with creative ideas, revealing problems that may require research to aid in their resolution. For example, negative backlash in the news directed toward Mormons following the passage of California's Proposition 8, that overturned legalized gay marriage (e.g., see Gorski, 2009) may encourage psychologists to ask questions about stereotypes and prejudice directed toward members of the Church of Jesus Christ of Latter-Day Saints and other religious groups. Or, recent news about global warming and climate change may encourage psychologists to ask questions about how people can be influenced to adopt more environmentally friendly behaviors (e.g., see Price, 2009).

Beyond individual cognitive techniques and real-world reflection, idea generation requires collaboration. Innovation comes from exposing oneself to a variety of other people and ideas; researchers cannot simply sit alone in their offices and ponder research without considering feedback from others (Campbell et al., 1982). Multiple researchers have diverse sets of experiences and perspectives on addressing issues; thus, collaboration increases the likelihood that new ideas will be discovered.

Researchers are encouraged to utilize interpersonal strategies to accrue the benefits of collaboration in developing research questions. Professors are excellent sources for research ideas because they are knowledgeable about discrepant research findings and gaps in the literature (Cone & Foster, 1993). In addition to professors, researchers who work in applied settings (e.g., school psychologists employed by school boards to test for children's learning disabilities, or organizational psychologists employed in human resources departments of large organizations who design and implement selection systems) are valuable sources of research ideas specific to issues with which they may struggle and that the academic community has not yet addressed.

Attending conventions and conferences provides researchers with ample opportunity to talk to other researchers about their ideas and gain feedback helpful for the idea development process. To capitalize on the vast diversity of expertise present at conferences, Leong and Muccio (2006) recommended that conference attendees listen to presentations and talk to people who have shared interests and also talk to people from different subfields to learn how they approach similar issues in different ways. Generally speaking, increasing interdisciplinary contact allows researchers to learn different perspectives and to increase the potential for innovative research ideas.

Printed sources are invaluable for generating research ideas. The most important and relevant printed sources are primary scientific journal articles (Johnson & Christensen, 2008). Without conducting a thorough literature review of scientific journals in a domain of research, researchers will not know whether their question is innovative or worthwhile. Reading every published journal article about a research topic is an unrealistic and probably unnecessary task. Browsing through recent editions of journals in an area of research will provide a sense of the current issues with which researchers of that domain are concerned or struggling. Additionally, each field of interest has specific journals that are highly regarded and publish a field's most exciting and well-done research; perusing through the table of contents and abstracts of recent editions of highly regarded journals will provide a sense of the types of questions the subfield finds interesting and innovative. Beyond specific subfields, however, leading journals in psychology publish high-impact studies that have relevance to a variety of psychological subfields, such as *Psychological Science*, *Psychological Review*, and *Psychological Bulletin*.

Beyond primary sources of research ideas, research ideas can come from secondary sources of information, such as textbooks. Authors of textbooks on psychological research methods have highlighted their value in developing research questions for students (e.g., Gravetter & Forzano, 2009; Heffernan, 2005; Mertens, 2010). Information in secondary source materials is a summarized version of the information found in primary source materials. With a goal of disseminating primary source information, secondary sources are helpful for researchers who know little about a topic area and can provide a good general overview of a domain of interest. Textbooks, however, provide only a general review of a topic area and often cite studies that are several years old, neither providing enough information for an in-depth understanding of a specific research topic nor addressing more current concerns of the research community. Thus, textbooks can offer mainly a source of inspiration or a stepping stone to guide the search for a research idea to more particular and current scientific journal articles. The journal articles cited in the textbook may be the first place to look when attempting to break into a new domain of interest. Conference proceedings are published conference submissions and provide a current overview of specific topics of which a community of researchers are concerned. Consensus papers are reports that provide up-to-date data that can identify concerns of the general population. For example, the Society for Human Resource Management (SHRM, 2008) conducted a "Religion/Spirituality in the Workplace (Faith at Work) Survey" of U.S. employees to examine how organizations accommodate religion in the workplace. Responses to this survey indicated that a majority of employees feel their organizations do not accommodate their religious beliefs and, until recently, psychologists have done little to explore the role of religion in a work context. Although unpublished, theses and dissertations are scientific studies that are widely available and often have extensive literature reviews, providing a good sense of the breadth and depth of topics that are being explored by other young researchers.

In the past decade, accessing printed sources has become effortless with the help of online databases. Computer databases, such as PsycINFO, provide access to numerous primary and secondary resources. Considering the unlimited potential of personal observation, creative strategies, and interpersonal collaboration, and the vast amount of resources available to help develop a research question, the question still holds: What type of research question is worth developing?

What Questions Are Worth Asking?

The research training that most psychologists receive does not explicitly teach students how to identify the *right* research question to ask. For the most part, training to be a researcher reflects a more traditional approach to scientific analysis (Daft, 1983). In undergraduate psychology classes or graduate-level research methods seminars, students learn about scientific rigor, experimental control, planning for and removing uncertainties that could upset the research design, and so on. This traditional approach assumes that researchers know a substantial amount about the phenomenon under investigation. Petty (2006) guessed that more than 90% of what is written in textbooks and scientific journals about conducting research concerns the way a study should be designed and the appropriate ways to analyze the data; relatively little has been written about deciding what to investigate. We also can apply Leong and Muccio's (2006) food and music analogy to the diversity in perceptions among researchers of the qualities of worthy research questions, but agreement is evident that research questions should be innovative (Daft, 1983; Petty, 2006) and should contribute to a conversation among researchers regarding the particular phenomenon of interest (Daft, 1985; Huff, 2009).

According to Daft (1983), significant discoveries in science required researchers to go beyond the safe certainty of precision in design: If we understand the phenomenon well enough to entirely predict and control what happens, why study it at all? Daft agreed with Thomas (1974; cited in Daft, 1983) that "good basic research needs a high degree of uncertainty at the outset, otherwise the investigator has not chosen an important problem" (p. 540).

Although research design is important to ensure the validity of inferences that can be drawn from a particular study, according to Daft, the myth that successful research comes out as predicted, more than anything else, restricts the discovery of new knowledge in research. An innovative research question may be one that generates ambiguity about the outcomes in the study. Researchers should ask questions based on ambiguity, rather than certainty, having in mind the probability of an outcome(s); innovation is often uncontrollable. Asking a question based on ambiguity is not the same as having no predictions at all. Research that is based solely on the question "What will happen to X if I manipulate Y?" is rarely of theoretical or empirical importance. Rather, the best questions are based on the possibility of achieving answers that can discriminate between theories, each of which makes a different prediction.

In addition to innovation, research questions also need to be relevant to the concerns of the academic community. The development of knowledge and new ideas that are of interest to the academic community cannot occur in isolation (Campbell et al., 1982): Ideas also need to make sense to others for them to have meaning. Huff (2009) described research as a conversation between scholars interested in exploring a related phenomenon. The goal of research is to develop explanations of research findings and Huff defined this process as theory development: "Theories are generalized explanations that draw from and facilitate comparison and analysis of empirical observations" (p. 44).

The nature of the theoretical contribution appears to be a key factor in the success of many research studies. Daft (1985) conducted an analyses of top reasons why submitted journal articles were rejected from highly regarded journals in the field of organization sciences: More than 50% of articles were rejected because they lacked a theory that provided a foundation for asking the research question and for interpreting the results. According to Daft (1985), theory is the story behind the variables; it is the explanation as to why the variables are related. Without theory, a research study makes no contribution to the story of an academic community's conversation (Daft, 1985; Huff, 2009). To aid in theory construction, Daft (1985) has recommended that authors think of each variable in a research study as a character in a story. First, researchers should fully describe each character and then describe how and why those characters interact with one another. Research is storytelling (Daft, 1983); the *why*, not the data, is the contribution to knowledge.

Research questions should be uncertain in their outcomes and contribute to the theoretical concerns of the academic community. Determining the innovation and theoretical contribution of a research question may require researchers to use some of the strategies outlined for developing a research question. After generating an idea and before conducting the research study, Petty (2006) recommended that researchers check their research idea by reviewing the literature and asking for feedback from other scholars apart from the conversation to which they hope to contribute. In the next section, we explore in more detail how we believe important research questions are generated.

GENERATING IMPORTANT RESEARCH QUESTIONS

Beyond the broad overview provided in the section Developing a Research Question, we believe three elements are critical in ensuring that we consider important research ideas: (a) knowledge of the research and theoretical literature; (b) concern about practical problem or implications of basic theoretical research; and (c) integrating concerns about practical problems, research literature, and theory.

Knowledge of the Research and Theoretical Literature

A notion exists that scientific breakthroughs occur as a function of someone having a sudden insight or eureka experience. Archimedes supposedly exclaimed "Eureka!" (meaning "I found it!"), when he discovered a method to determine the purity of gold. Although the spontaneity of his discovery is what has been transmitted to our generation over the hundreds of years since, it is unlikely that this discovery occurred without extensive effort and thought as to how one might accomplish Archimedes's goal. A more likely sequence of events involves a process of long work and thought, such as that provided in the cases of several twentieth-century discoveries documented in the popular book *Outliers* (Gladwell, 2008). Gladwell (2008) acknowledged the role of opportunity and the good fortune of being at the right place at the right time, but he asserted that something like 10,000 hours of intense practice or effort is required for someone to become truly expert at an endeavor and have the insight to make real breakthrough discoveries. He cited the cases of Bill Gates, the Beatles, and other groups and individuals who had some level of native ability but whose true insight or accomplishments were recognized only after extended practice. Researchers are most likely to have real insight into seemingly intractable issues when they have studied a phenomenon and the related context for a long period of time.

Concern About Practical Problems or Implications of Basic Theoretical Research

Breakthroughs also require a sense of the real-world implications of a research idea. Great ideas usually are generated as a function of concern about some applied problem, a puzzling laboratory research finding, or inconsistencies in theoretical explanations of some finding. We think all these sources involve questions about how the world really works. Psychology provides many examples. The first test of intelligence (Binet & Simon, 1904) was developed to provide Parisian schoolchildren appropriate education opportunities. To help the U.S. government with the classification of thousands of Army recruits, Yerkes (1921) helped the Army develop a group test of ability. More recently, Schmidt and Hunter (1977) developed one version of meta-analysis to show that measured ability and job performance relationships generalized across situations, removing the need in some cases to conduct validation studies of a specific test before using it. A finding that jury size was related to the incidence of hung juries (Kerr, MacCoun, & Kramer, 1996) grew out of a challenge to the court that convicted a defendant with only 10 jurors as opposed to the more traditional 12 jurors. A change in the way eyewitnesses to crimes are instructed in lineups came from decision-making research by Wells (2008) that showed how instructions to pick the person who committed a crime without warning that the perpetrator might not be present led to many false identifications. Cognitive psychologists have conducted the basic research on eyewitness accuracy, but the increased attention given to some highly publicized cases of mistaken identity led to further research and appropriate practical changes in the manner in which lineups were conducted. In this case, it is not clear what came first (i.e., research or applied problem), but it is almost certain that some cognitive psychologist was curious about the ability of an eyewitness to make accurate identifications in a police lineup or some similar situation. Curiosity about the frequency of brutality in jails led Zimbardo (1972) to demonstrate the conditions in which most *normal* adults would engage in similar behavior. An attempt to understand the role of physical contact in child development led to studies of attachment in monkeys (Harlow, Harlow, & Suomi, 1971), similar work in humans, and to the development of attachment theory as well as many thousands of additional studies. These are but a few of the many examples in the field in which psychologists or others were curious about an everyday problem, sought to understand a major social issue, or were curious about the generalizability of basic laboratory research that had minimal or nonobvious applied implications when first conducted. This curiosity or need led to research questions and, in some instances, to major programs of research as well as new theories of human behavior.

Integrating Concerns About Practical Problems, Research Literature, and Theory

Our view is that important ideas arise from theoretical insight but only when it is based on a thorough knowledge of the existing literature and a curiosity about some seemingly inexplicable research finding or an important applied problem. Practical problems provide the motivation or impetus to grapple with a problem; the research literature provides the basic knowledge and often the relevant questions; theory provides the basis for an integration of the knowledge about a problem in a way that allows generalizable new knowledge or insight to emerge. Einstein's theory of general relativity is sometimes viewed as the biggest leap of scientific imagination in history, but Einstein came to his formulations by observing that gravity was equivalent to acceleration, motion affected measurements of time and space, and therefore that gravity also must affect time and space metrics. So, for example, proximity to the gravitational pull of the sun changes the speed of a clock ticking, which means that the angles of a triangle no longer equal 180 degrees.

Likely Sources of Ideas for the Novice Investigator

For a person relatively new to an area of study, a number of other sources of research ideas are available. Some authors, as may be true for most college professors, develop ideas as a result of class discussions or student questions. For example, a student question about how cross-validated multiple correlations compared with formula estimates of cross-validated multiple correlation led to a Monte Carlo simulation, the results of which were subsequently published in *Psychological Bulletin* (Schmitt, Coyle, & Rauschenberger, 1977). In the context of a discussion about interviewer decision making in the employment interview, another student asked about how applicants made decisions in an interview. This led to a study of the decision making of interviewees at a student placement center (Schmitt & Coyle, 1976). Any faculty member who conducts a graduate seminar or a research reading group certainly can cite similar instances in which student discussions of a research study lead to ideas for additional research. Of course, the students in these classes and seminars have access to the same discussions, as do the professors, and likewise should be alert to good ideas that interest them.

Another useful practice on the part of those engaged in some project is to set aside time for research discussions. Sometimes the planned research or project becomes so time-consuming or the project and data collection is relatively well laid out so that those executing the project do not have time to consider what they are doing and what questions they might be able to answer if they examined the data somewhat differently or if they collected additional data. In these discussions, it has been useful to provide members with specific assignments (e.g., come up with at least one new idea for data collection or analysis) with the obligation that they indicate why those data might be interesting. Minutes of these discussions are taken and posted on a common website, and these ideas or projects are followed up in subsequent discussions. Many of the social science–psychology projects are so large and costly that investigators should use them to examine multiple questions simultaneously. Without some specific time devoted to the generation of additional ideas, these projects are unlikely to be articulated or executed.

Another source of ideas on which to build research is to read carefully the discussion sections of journal articles in an area of interest. Quite often the authors include a future research section or outline what they believe to be the theoretical or practical implications of their work. These discussions can be a rich source of ideas for new studies that build on the author's work. Again, you need to understand the study being described and know the research area well if you are to evaluate the authors' ideas and develop a new study that adds to a research area as opposed to a study that simply tweaks some aspect of the original study.

A great deal of research in psychology is correlational, and it almost always involves multiply determined complex phenomena. Thus, it certainly is likely that research findings often can and should be moderated or mediated by additional variables. To have insight into these possibilities, knowledge of the research and theory in the subject area has no substitute. Without that knowledge, suggested moderators or mediators often will reflect naiveté and actually already may have been investigated. When moderators or mediators suggest a different theoretical explanation of an area of research, they can have a great impact on a field. Decomposition of the impact of multiple mediators on a dependent variable that reflect different theoretical orientations are likely to be of broad interest and importance. This suggestion is similar to Wicker's (1985) suggestion that researchers consider the context of their research; map out how it fits into a larger domain (e.g., the act of leaving an organization fits in a general process of withdrawal) or how the behavioral domain in which one is interested compares with another behavioral domain (e.g., risks taken in one's sexual behavior compared with risks driving a car or at a gambling casino).

Psychological Examples

Psychological investigators in other disciplines likely will have other examples of theoretical breakthroughs, but we think the work on validity generalization (Schmidt & Hunter, 1977, 1998) and SEM (Jöreskog, 1970) provides illustrations of our three major points discussed in the previous section, Generating Important Research Questions. Schmidt and Hunter (1977, 1998) knew the personnel selection literature well. They observed that tests of cognitive ability often were correlated with measures of job performance but recognized that the correlations varied greatly and occasionally were not significant statistically and near zero. At the time in the history of personnel selection during which Schmidt and Hunter were considering these issues, conventional practice involved the revalidation of tests of cognitive ability in each organization and each job for which their use as selection criteria might be proposed. Schmidt and Hunter also knew the literature on the stability of individual differences indicated that little change seemed to occur in the relative level of individuals on ability measures across the life span. This suggested that the variability in validity coefficients observed in past research might have an alternative explanation. What they knew about these various literatures—and what was well established regarding sampling theory in the field of statistics—stimulated their development of meta-analysis and

validity generalization as well as their demonstration that individual difference constructs were important across a wide array of organizational situations. A great deal of the variability that was observed in validity coefficients in studies of personnel selection could be explained by sampling error. When one accounted for sampling error, the credibility interval around large values of the estimated population validity was quite small, indicating that one could expect sizable relations between estimates of ability and job performance in most, if not all, job situations.

The development and use of SEM has changed data analyses in a broad array of scientific disciplines, including psychology. In developing this approach to data analysis, Jöreskog (1970) used knowledge of classical measurement theory and the impact of unreliability on the magnitude of observed relations. He also knew that the parameters estimated in regression equations failed to provide the relevant information (a) when the observed variables were partly a function of measurement error, (b) when interdependence or simultaneous causation existed among the observed response variables, and (c) when important explanatory variables were missing from the equations. Jöreskog's solution was to combine the issues of measurement (what are the latent variables or constructs underlying a set of observed variables?) and the specification of relations among the latent variables. The mathematical solution as embodied in a variety of software packages (e.g., MPLUS, LISREL, AMOS, EQS) has revolutionized data analyses in the social and behavioral sciences and virtually every article in some journals involves a report using SEM. The insights central to this development came from an appreciation for the deficiencies of data analysis, the problems of inference associated with regression analysis, and the need to draw more appropriate inferences about the relations among theoretical constructs.

These two examples are likely not the result of any of the idea-generation methods we mentioned in the previous section but rather the result of long-term efforts that produced a level of understanding that few other researchers could bring to bear on the issues in which they were interested. In these latter cases (e.g., development of meta-analysis and SEM), some might argue that these are examples of problems in the methods of research that led to innovations. We feel that these were insights into research that came out of a deep understanding of how research was conducted and led to thousands of subsequent studies by the authors and others. The same process seems to be involved in both examples: recognition of a problem, long-term investigation and deep understanding of the phenomena being studied, and the resultant novel insight that subsequently has generated many studies of refinement to the methods and the application of the methods to a wide array of research domains.

Role of New Methods of Inquiry

Technological improvements in our methods of measurement contribute to the range and sophistication of the research questions that we can evaluate. Jöreskog's (1970) SEM would have been virtually impossible before the advent of computers, which allow for the computational algorithms that enable estimation of SEM parameters. In the 21st century, neuroscientists are investigating many hypotheses about the relation between brain activity and behavior. Many of these hypotheses could not be evaluated without the use of electrophysiological and neuroimaging techniques. Likewise the links among genetics, illness, and behavior are greatly facilitated by the technology that allows scientists to map the human genome. Computer simulations and computer modeling allows scientists to explore the implications of their theories and research findings for large systems that never might be investigated using empirical research methods. In all these instances and more, technology allows for the confirmation and disconfirmation of theories and prior research results and opens up new research avenues. To be maximally effective in generating and investigating new research ideas, we must be conversant with a wide range of research methods or have access to a research team that provides such expertise.

We believe that the generation of novel research ideas has three elements. First, basic knowledge about a field (or multiple fields) of inquiry has no substitute. Second, important ideas usually are generated as a function of some practical need or some curiosity about an unexplained laboratory or real-world observation. The research process itself is a constant source of new ideas. Third, the knowledge of extant theories concerning a phenomena and the degree to which they can or cannot handle various empirical data will facilitate the identification of theoretical deficiencies and stimulate new insight, both practical and theoretical.

We have described several ways for early career investigators to identify tractable research questions. We also have acknowledged the importance of technology that allows us to collect new types of data. In the next section, we describe how to determine whether an important idea can be translated into a testable research question.

FORMULATING TESTABLE RESEARCH QUESTIONS

Wicker (1985) quoted Galton's observation that "the roadways of our minds are worn into very deep ruts" (p. 1094) to illustrate the point that we tend to think in repeated and routinized channels that run counter to new ideas and perspectives. Wicker distilled his recommendations into four sets of strategies as follows:

(a) Researchers should play with ideas through a process of selecting and applying metaphors, representing ideas graphically, changing the scale, and attending to process; (b) Researchers should consider contexts. They can place specific problems in a larger domain, make comparisons outside the problem domain, examine processes in the settings in which they naturally occur, consider the practical implications of research, and probe library resources; (c) It is important for researchers to probe and tinker with assumptions through such techniques as exposing hidden assumptions, making the opposite assumption, and simultaneously trusting and doubting the same assumption; and (d) Finally, it is vital that researchers clarify and systematize their conceptual frameworks. They should scrutinize the meanings of key concepts, specify relationships among concepts, and write a concept paper. (p. 1094)

There has been a long-standing discussion and philosophical debate regarding the problems associated with operationalism in psychology (e.g., Bickhard, 2001; Feest, 2005). For example, Grace (2001) pointed to the error of experimental psychologists in the 1930s when he accepted the proposition that "a theoretical construct was scientifically valid given a set of operations" (p. 67), which was too simplistic and prone to biases. This error was corrected by the adoption of the position of multiple or convergent operationalism. Without getting into the details of this philosophical debate, we agree with Grace (2001) that operationalism in psychology has value and that "the use of operational definitions facilitates clarity in communication and helps scientists to formulate empirical test of theories" (p. 67). In identifying research questions that are important and testable, it is essential to recognize the value of multiple and convergent ways of addressing the question. Only through a process of triangulation and multiple methodologies available to psychological science (such as the multitrait–multimethod approach described by Cronbach & Meehl, 1955) would we be making significant progress in advancing our science.

The advice provided by Wicker (1985) bears careful study because it provides guidance in using this multiple and convergent approach to the operationalization of our research questions. For example, related to his suggestion to "consider contexts," he also recommended placing specific problems in a larger domain. To achieve this richer and context-sensitive operationalization of our research questions, Wicker recommended that

> once the domain has been defined, the next step is to identify the major factors or influences that bear on the topic. Each of the major factors can then be analyzed into its components or attributes, and a systematic classification scheme can be developed. By examining all logical combinations of attributes, investigators can

plan research to cover appropriate— perhaps neglected—aspects of the problem. (p. 1096)

Wicker's (1985) suggestions to consider context, including attending to process, making comparisons outside the problem domain, examining the process in naturally occurring settings, and considering the practical implications of the research, are all valuable strategies in a multiple and convergent approach to operationalizing.

Consistent with the idea of multiple and convergent operationalization, Wicker's (1985) suggestions also illustrate the value of using different approaches to identifying important and testable research questions. The multiple strategies suggested by Wicker remind us of the need to move beyond the quantitative–qualitative schism. For example, Anastasi (1958) indicated many years ago that continuing debates between nature and nurture contributions to intelligence were counterproductive and most reasonable psychologists recognize that both nature and nurture are important. Instead, Anastasi proposed that the more important question was how nature and nurture interacted to influence behavior. In identifying important research questions that are worth pursuing, we need to recognize the value and contributions of both quantitative and qualitative approaches. As such, we recommend the use of mixed methods in research, consistent with the view of multiple and convergent operationalism. Such an integrated approach avoids the artificial dichotomies within the field, helping researchers to achieve both rigor and relevance challenges and to bridge the research–practice gap (i.e., research that has limited implications for the practice of psychology and practice that is not based on research evidence).

Wicker's (1985) final set of strategies included clarifying and systematizing our conceptual frameworks, pointing to the value of approaching operationalization as model building. By scrutinizing key concepts, specifying the relations among them and writing a concept paper to explain the model, researchers increase their chances of selecting testable (and testworthy) research questions that will be refined into important and significant questions.

The concept paper, which often is used by funding agencies as a screening tool, is highly valuable in helping researchers articulate and refine their research ideas into concise problem statements. The practice of preparing a concept paper not only helps the reader get an idea of the importance of the proposed study as well as its practicality, but also forces the researcher to think clearly about the research problem. Because the concept paper is repeatedly reviewed and revised by the investigator in an iterative fashion, it also enables the researcher to think about how the proposed study adds to the scientific knowledge base.

Similarly, Petty (2006) outlined strategies for formulating research questions that are particularly relevant to the current issue of operationalization and testability. Beginning with the observation that "deciding what to study is the single most important step in the research process and the one (unfortunately) on which there is the least formal guidance" (p. 466), Petty noted the importance of pursuing one's interests to ensure persistence and success. Another important observation from Petty is that the type of research questions that researchers tackle may vary with the stage of their career. For example, an early career investigator may not want to pursue a longitudinal study that involves years of data collection before analyses can begin. On the basis of his personal experience and program of research, Petty offered four specific strategies: (a) Discover a new effect, (b) extend an established effect, (c) demonstrate the mediation of an established effect, and (d) demonstrate moderation of an established effect.

Petty's (2006) first strategy for conducting significant and important research involves discovering a new effect. Discovery is the holy grail for researchers; it is exciting and has important career benefits (the effect may even be named for the researcher—e.g., the Stroop effect); however, it is likely to be achieved by senior and advanced researchers because discovery requires an in-depth knowledge of existing theories and research to discover new and important effects. Petty has provided personal examples of discovery; in addition, a series of biographies in *The Undaunted Psychologist: Adventures in Research* (Brannigan & Morrens, 1993) provide

interesting personal accounts of how leading psychology researchers came to discover new effects.

Petty's (2006) second strategy—extending an effect—is appropriate for beginning researchers. Like the first strategy, it requires the creativity and openness described by Wicker (1985). Having become familiar with an area of research, it is important for investigators to transport constructs or established effects into new areas. Many significant contributions in the field have been achieved by extending an effect to new domains and new problems. As Petty noted, however, it is critical that these extensions apply to "important judgments, behaviors, stimuli, and population groups rather than to unimportant ones" (p. 468). To ensure that extensions are made to important questions, researchers may need to use some of the approaches outlined in the section Generating Important Research Questions earlier in this chapter, such as research discussions and carefully studying the discussion sections of journal articles. Other approaches to ensuring importance of one's extension include attending conferences and departmental colloquia and studying critical reviews of the literature, such as those published in the *American Psychologist, Psychological Review, Psychological Bulletin,* and *Psychological Science.*

In addition to discovering a new effect and extending an effect, Petty (2006) proposed two strategies that are related to theory development. He recommended demonstrating the mediation of an established effect, arguing that the strategy is central to theory building in psychology. By studying why variables have the impact that they do and by studying the ways in which variables relate and influence each other, researchers can make significant contributions to the field. Indeed, a common criticism received from journal reviewers of research manuscripts is that the investigators selected an important research topic but failed to address the underlying mechanisms that may account for their effect. For example, in a study of depression, a researcher may find that African American patients, relative to European American patients, exhibit different rates of recovery in treatment as a function of a pre- and postdesign assessment. The discovery of race-related differential recovery rates is important, but it is more important to determine what mechanism within the treatment accounts for this mental health disparity.

Petty (2006) suggested that researchers need to "specify the underlying mechanism responsible for your effect and then conduct research in which you try to measure this process and see if it is responsible" (p. 469). A review of the literature as well as observations from discussions of clinical cases conferences may suggest that cultural mistrust is an important mechanism that could be responsible for lower levels of therapeutic alliance among African American than among European American patients, which, in turn produced differential recovery rates. Using Petty's strategy, the investigator might design a study that includes a pre- and postassessment of cultural mistrust and therapeutic alliance. Using structural equations modeling, the investigator might find that the degree of therapeutic alliance mediates the relation between cultural mistrust and recovery rates. This explanation is likely a much more significant contribution to the field than the empirical observation of mental health disparity.

Petty's (2006) final strategy for identifying important questions to pursue in one's program of research involves demonstrating how an established effect is moderated by another variable (or variables). Essentially, the moderation strategy involves developing a model in which the established effect is proposed to hold "for certain kinds of people or in certain kinds of situations, but not in others" (Petty, 2006, p. 471). Staying with our previous example, once the investigator has demonstrated that cultural mistrust and therapeutic alliance appears to be the mechanism that leads to poorer outcomes for African American than European American patients, the investigator might suspect that not all African Americans will exhibit the same cultural mistrust in treatment. Indeed, our familiarity with the literature suggests that cultural or racial identity may moderate this effect. By developing and adding a measure of acculturation for African Americans (Obasi & Leong, 2009), the investigator could go on to discover that African Americans with low levels of acculturation exhibit the highest level of cultural mistrust and the lowest level of therapeutic alliance.

Moreover, these patients may be the ones who show the poorest recovery rates.

Wicker (1985) suggested that it is important to play with ideas, to examine the research area within context, and to question our research assumptions. Much in the same way, Petty (2006) offered specific recommendations to discover new effects, extend an effect, and check for mediation and moderation of an effect. Whereas Petty's advice for arriving at testable and important research questions is valuable, it is primarily presented from the perspective of experimental research, but similar ideas can be used to develop and test models in other substantive areas of psychology. For those who conduct research in other subdisciplines of psychology (e.g., individual differences, longitudinal), an important prerequisite for operationalizing your research question is to select or construct psychometrically sound tests and measures. Just as experimental research is evaluated in terms of the quality of the experimental method and manipulations, research in these other areas is evaluated in terms of the quality of the operationalization of the construct. In this regard, the selection of well-validated and psychometrically sound tests and measures is crucial. Cronbach (1957) articulated differences between experimental and differential psychology and possible areas for integration. In the latter approach to psychology, accurate and reliable measures of individual difference variables, such as personality traits, are necessary for high-quality research.

In conducting research within the differential psychology tradition, it is essential to identify, evaluate, and select the best psychological tests and measures to operationalize one's research questions. One useful strategy is to select psychological tests that have been commercially published. Using this strategy in operationalizing research questions has advantages and disadvantages. The advantages are that most tests are psychometrically well validated, often provide national norms for comparisons, and allow for defensible cross-study comparisons. Companies that publish these texts usually select only those that have a strong research foundation. The profits from these tests allow the companies to generate additional research in support of their tests, especially to norm and restandardize them. Therefore, selecting commercially published tests can provide confidence in the reliability and validity of the measures used in research studies.

Many psychometrically sound and well-validated tests do not end up in commercial companies, and researchers often have to select from noncommercially published tests. The disadvantages to using commercially published tests include the costs to acquire copies of these tests and to pay for their scoring, increasing the cost of doing research. (Many companies provide discounts when their tests are used for research, rather than applied, purposes.) In addition, some commercial tests, such as the Strong Interest Inventory, have proprietary scoring algorithms that are not released to the investigators. For these protected tests, it may be somewhat difficult to examine directly the psychometric properties of the instrument and to examine items via factor analyses. The costs associated with commercial tests may discourage or prevent some investigators from using them, especially investigators with low research budgets (e.g., graduate students, investigators in developing countries). An increasing number of noncommercial versions of commercially available tests with good psychometric properties are available. For example, the International Personality Item Pool (Goldberg, 1999) is a viable and no-cost alternative to the NEO Personality Inventory—Revised measure of the Big Five factor model of personality developed by Costa and McCrae (1992). More recently, Armstrong, Allison, and Rounds (2008) developed public-domain marker scales for the RIASEC (realistic, investigative, artistic, social, enterprising, conventional), a measure of the Holland model of career interests, as an alternative to the Strong Interest Inventory, Self-Directed Search, and Vocational Preference Inventory, all of which are published commercially.

Using only existing or commercially published tests also involves an assumption or element of trust that the original constructor of the test has operationalized the construct appropriately and that the items in the measure are representative of the domain of interest. Researchers often use an existing set of items with little or no consideration for the context in which they are used, the wording of the items, and their appropriateness (or potential obsolescence) across different groups or changing circumstances faced by a group. A careful and critical reading of the items in an instrument actually may suggest researchable questions that will reevaluate or refocus thinking in an area of research. Suggestions and evaluations of existing instrumentation may represent a research question worthy of pursuit.

CONCLUSION

In an article providing advice to new researchers, Mayer (2008) quoted Nobel Prize winner Santiago Ramon Cajal's (1897/1999) book *Advice for a Young Investigator*: "Master technique and produce original data; all the rest will follow" (p. ix). In this chapter, we have summarized some useful techniques in developing important and testable research questions. In addition to Cajal's advice regarding the need to master technique and produce original data, we have discussed an important antecedent, namely, motivation. Researchers who investigate the necessary and sufficient conditions for the development of expertise have found that a basic requirement is approximately 10 years of intense deliberate practice (Ericsson & Charness, 1994; Ericsson, Krampe, & Tesch-Romer, 1993). Curiosity, drive, dedication, perseverance, and other related motives are therefore essential in the development of expertise as a researcher. We have provided some suggestions and recommendations regarding techniques for developing important and testable research questions, but you will need the motivation to master those techniques. For this reason, we end by emphasizing again the importance of selecting research problems and questions that you are passionate about and care deeply for to provide the necessary motivation to become an expert.

Earlier in the chapter, we recommended that you review some of the personal stories of leading psychological scientists and their research careers in *The Undaunted Psychologist: Adventures in Research* (Brannigan & Morrens, 1993). Many of these stories provide interesting accounts of the variety of motives that have led these scientists to pursue their program of research and become experts in their field. Indeed, Brannigan and Morrens (1993) were motivated to edit the book on the basis of their "frustrations with current textbooks that, albeit unintentionally, lead students to believe that research is a dry, humorless activity devoid of adventure and fun" (p. xi). In reading these stories, you will find that many of these scientists were captivated, excited, and stimulated by the research questions that they pursued. You also will find that many of them encountered problems, barriers, and setbacks, but they kept going and persisted in their scientific adventures. Research is highly complex, full of challenges, and often daunting. The underlying theme in the stories from these undaunted psychologists is that each had a strong, personal motivation for pursuing a research question and persisting in the "mastering of techniques and producing original data" (Cajal, 1897/1999, p. ix). We encourage you to select research questions and problems that will similarly motivate you to become undaunted psychological scientists.

References

Anastasi, A. (1958). Heredity, environment, and the question "How?" *Psychological Review, 65*, 197–208. doi:10.1037/h0044895

Armstrong, P. A., Allison, W., & Rounds, J. (2008). Development and initial validation of brief public domain RIASEC marker scales. *Journal of Vocational Behavior, 73*, 287–299. doi:10.1016/j.jvb.2008.06.003

Bickhard, M. H. (2001). The tragedy of operationalism. *Theory and Psychology, 11*, 35–44. doi:10.1177/0959354301111002

Binet, A., & Simon, T. H. (1904). Méthodes nouvelles pour le diagnostic du niveau intellectuel des anormaux [New methods for diagnosing the intellectual level of abnormal]. *L'Année Psychologique, 11*, 191–244. doi:10.3406/psy.1904.3675

Brannigan, G. B., & Morrens, M. R. (1993). *The undaunted psychologist: Adventures in research.* New York, NY: McGraw-Hill.

Cajal, S. R. (1999). *Advice for a young investigator* (N. Swanson & L. W. Swanson, Trans.). Cambridge, MA: MIT Press. (Original work published 1897)

Campbell, J. P., Daft, R. L., & Hulin, C. L. (1982). *What to study: Generating and developing research questions.* New York, NY: Sage.

Cone, J. D., & Foster, S. L. (1993). *Dissertations and theses from start to finish: Psychology and related fields.* Washington, DC: American Psychological Association.

Costa, P. T., Jr., & McCrae, R. R. (1992). *Revised NEO Personality Inventory (NEO PI-R) and NEO Five-Factor Inventory (NEO FFI): Professional manual.* Odessa, FL: Psychological Assessment Resources.

Cronbach, L. J. (1957). The two disciplines of scientific psychology. *American Psychologist, 12*, 671–684. doi:10.1037/h0043943

Cronbach, L. J., & Meehl, P. E. (1955). Construct validity in psychological tests. *Psychological Bulletin, 52*, 281–302.

Daft, R. L. (1983). Learning the craft of organizational research. *The Academy of Management Review, 8*, 539–546.

Daft, R. L. (1985). Why I recommend that your manuscript be rejected, and what you can do about it. In P. Frost & L. L. Cummings (Eds.), *Publishing in the organizational sciences* (pp. 164–182). Homewood, IL: Richard D. Irwin.

Ericsson, K. A., & Charness, N. (1994). Expert performance: Its structure and acquisition. *American Psychologist, 49*, 725–747. doi:10.1037/0003-066X.49.8.725

Ericsson, K. A., Krampe, R. T., & Tesch-Romer, C. (1993). The role of deliberate practice in the acquisition of expert performance. *Psychological Review, 100*, 363–406. doi:10.1037/0033-295X.100.3.363

Feest, U. (2005). Operationism in psychology: What the debate is about, what the debate should be about. *Journal of the History of the Behavioral Sciences, 41*, 131–149. doi:10.1002/jhbs.20079

Gladwell, M. (2008). *Outliers.* New York, NY: Little, Brown.

Goldberg, L. R. (1999). A broad-bandwidth public-domain personality inventory measuring the lower-level facets of several five-factor models. In I. Mervielde, I. Deary, F. De Fruyt, & F. Ostendorf (Eds.), *Personality psychology in Europe* (Vol. 7, pp. 7–28). Tilburg, the Netherlands: Tilburg University Press.

Gorski, E. (2009). *Leader likens anti-Mormonism to southern racism in the 60's.* Retrieved from http://www.usatoday.com/news/religion/2009–10-15-mormon-gay_N.htm

Grace, R. G. (2001). The pragmatics of operationalism: A reply. *Theory and Psychology, 11*, 67–74. doi:10.1177/0959354301111006

Gravetter, F. J., & Forzano, L. B. (2009). *Research methods for the behavioral sciences* (3rd ed.). Belmont, CA: Wadsworth Cengage Learning.

Harlow, H. F., Harlow, M. K., & Suomi, S. J. (1971). From thought to therapy: Lessons from a primate laboratory. *American Scientist, 59*, 538–549.

Heffernan, T. M. (2005). *A student's guide to studying psychology* (3rd ed.). New York, NY: Psychology Press.

Huff, A. S. (2009). *Designing research for publication.* Thousand Oaks, CA: Sage.

Johnson, B., & Christensen, L. (2008). *Educational research: Quantitative, qualitative, and mixed approaches* (3rd ed.). Thousand Oaks, CA: Sage.

Jöreskog, K. G. (1970). A general method for analysis of covariance structures. *Biometrika, 57,* 239–251.

Kerr, N. L., MacCoun, R., & Kramer, G. P. (1996). Bias in judgment: Comparing individuals and groups. *Psychological Review, 103,* 687–719. doi:10.1037/0033-295X.103.4.687

Leong, F. T. L., & Muccio, D. J. (2006). Finding a research topic. In F. T. L. Leong & J. T. Austin (Eds.), *A guide for graduate students and research assistants* (2nd ed., pp. 23–40). Thousand Oaks, CA: Sage.

Mayer, R. E. (2008). Old advice for new researchers. *Educational Psychology Review, 20,* 19–28. doi:10.1007/s10648-007-9061-4

Mertens, D. M. (2010). *Research and evaluation in education and psychology: Integrating diversity with quantitative, qualitative, and mixed methods.* Thousand Oaks, CA: Sage.

Novak, J. D. (2004). *The theory underlying concept maps and how to construct them.* Retrieved from http://uwf.edu/jgould/ConceptMappingIntro.pdf

Obasi, E. M., & Leong, F. T. L. (2009). Psychological distress, acculturation, and mental health seeking attitudes with people of African descent in the United States: A preliminary investigation. *Journal of Counseling Psychology, 56,* 227–238. doi:10.1037/a0014865

Petty, R. E. (2006). The research script: One researcher's view. In F. T. L. Austin & J. T. Austin (Eds.), *Psychology research handbook: A guide for graduate students and research assistants* (2nd ed., pp. 465–480). Thousand Oaks, CA: Sage.

Price, M. (2009). *Changing minds to prevent climate change.* Retrieved from http://apagsgradpsych.apa.org/monitor/2009/10/climate-change.aspx

Schmidt, F. L., & Hunter, J. E. (1977). Development of a general solution to the problem of validity generalization. *Journal of Applied Psychology, 62,* 529–540. doi:10.1037/0021-9010.62.5.529

Schmidt, F. L., & Hunter, J. E. (1998). The validity and utility of selection methods in personnel Psychology: Practical and theoretical implications of 85 years of research findings. *Psychological Bulletin, 124,* 262–274. doi:10.1037/0033-2909.124.2.262

Schmitt, N., & Coyle, B. W. (1976). Applicant decisions in the employment interview. *Journal of Applied Psychology, 61,* 184–192. doi:10.1037/0021-9010.61.2.184

Schmitt, N., Coyle, B. W., & Rauschenberger, J. (1977). A Monte Carlo evaluation of three estimates of cross-validated multiple correlation. *Psychological Bulletin, 84,* 751–758. doi:10.1037/0033-2909.84.4.751

Society for Human Resource Management. (2008). *Religion and corporate culture: Accommodating religious diversity in the workplace.* Alexandria, VA: Author.

Wells, G. L. (2008). Theory, logic, and data: Paths to a more coherent eyewitness science. *Applied Cognitive Psychology, 22,* 853–859. doi:10.1002/acp.1488

Wicker, A. W. (1985). Getting out of our conceptual ruts. *American Psychologist, 40,* 1094–1103. doi:10.1037/0003-066X.40.10.1094

Yerkes, R. M. (Ed.). (1921). *Memoirs of the National Academy of Sciences: Vol. 15. Psychological examining in the United States Army.* Washington, DC: U.S. Government Printing Office. doi:10.1037/10619-000

Zimbardo, P. G. (1972). Pathology of imprisonment. *Society, 9*(6), 4–8.

CHAPTER 8

ACCESSING RELEVANT LITERATURE

Hannah R. Rothstein

Accessing the research literature is an important early step in any scientific activity. In fact, searching for and reviewing research literature may be the *most common* scientific activities, because they occur both at the beginning of any new data collection effort and at the core of a stand-alone research synthesis. There are many reasons to search a research literature. Cooper (2009) and others (cf. Hart, 2001) have noted literature reviews can serve many different purposes and can vary considerably in length and detail. Some literature searches result in lengthy stand-alone documents, whereas others account for one short section of a paper describing new primary research. Still others are conducted to inform the searcher about the state of the science in a particular area and are not intended to lead directly to a paper of any kind. Some have the goal of integrating the existing literature in a field; others attempt to provide the chronology of research developments on a topic, to criticize past research, or to identify the central issues in an area. Reviewers may attempt to be neutral or to unabashedly support a particular point of view; they may try to cover all the literature or only part of it. Reviews target different audiences—some aim their work at scholars, others at practitioners or policymakers, and still others at the general public. Although the approach to searching for literature I will discuss originally was developed with stand-alone research syntheses in mind, its principles and processes will be useful to those who are conducting a literature search to educate themselves before undertaking a new research project, to those preparing the introduction section of a journal article or the first part of a thesis or dissertation, and to those researchers whose primary purpose is to summarize, integrate, or critique a body of evidence. The approach can be implemented whether or not the searcher's intention is to produce a written report of the search. Virtually anyone interested in minimizing bias while searching for and retrieving research literature will benefit from using the systematic methods described in this chapter. When the term reviewer is used in this chapter, the reader should keep in mind that it refers to any individual who is attempting to search for, retrieve, digest, summarize, or evaluate literature on a topic of interest, not just for those preparing a stand-alone review. Most of the chapter will be directed to researchers who are getting ready to write an introduction to a new primary study, but it is also intended for researchers whose primary goal is to produce a research synthesis. Additionally, I will provide guidance to individuals whose main goal is to *critically read* a research literature, such as a graduate student preparing for a comprehensive exam, or a clinician who is interested in evidence-based practice.

I begin with a description of the characteristics and shortcomings of the traditional search for literature and contrast these with the characteristics of a methodologically rigorous literature search. I discuss the extent to which the latter depend on the scope and purpose of the search. After that, I discuss the importance of planning in the literature search process, and describe the major components of this activity. Next, I focus on conducting literature

DOI: 10.1037/13619-009
APA Handbook of Research Methods in Psychology: Vol. 1. Foundations, Planning, Measures, and Psychometrics, H. Cooper (Editor-in-Chief)

searches, and include suggestions for avoiding bias in the selection of studies and in the selection of tools for searching as well as for identifying appropriate search terms when preparing search strategies for use with electronic databases. This is followed by a discussion of sources of potentially relevant literature in addition to electronic databases, and why it is important that they be included in a search. Finally, I describe how to document literature searches and their results.

THE LITERATURE SEARCH AS A SCIENTIFIC ACTIVITY

Despite its ubiquity, the search for literature generally has been exempt from the standards of science governing the other steps leading to the production of new research. Over the past 30 years, however, the search for relevant literature has been recognized as a key element in the research enterprise and the exemption of the literature search from scientific standards gradually has been revoked. When the traditional model of searching for literature has been appraised using common standards of research quality, researchers found it to be seriously flawed (Cooper, 1982, 2009; Jackson, 1980). Rather than being guided by a focused question or by a hypothesis, most searches for literature revolve around a diffuse question or a general topic. Rather than being conducted on the basis of an explicit plan for locating and selecting studies for review, the traditional literature search takes an informal and sometimes-haphazard approach, listing neither the sources to be searched nor an explanation of the basis on which particular studies or findings will be included or excluded. Rather than describing the specific information that is being sought, or how it is to be extracted from the retrieved studies, the procedures for summarizing what the studies say remain out of public view. Just as we would not give much credibility to the results and conclusions of other data collection efforts that were missing a clearly formulated research question, lacked information about sampling and data collection procedures, and failed to explain how the data were analyzed, we also should not give credence to the results of literature searches that were conducted in just this way.

In the 1980s, researchers began to formulate an approach to searching a research literature in accord with the principles of good science (Cooper, 1982; Light & Pillemer, 1984). This approach to searching emphasizes the use of clear-cut, transparent, and replicable procedures to limit bias during the assembly of relevant studies on a topic. It is guided by a clearly defined research question or problem; formulates, in advance of the search, the inclusion and exclusion criteria that will be used to appraise the relevance of studies; examines a variety of sources; and documents all information retrieval activities.

To those readers who are familiar with research synthesis, these procedures will seem familiar, because they also are the first steps in a systematic review. A full systematic review, however, is guided by prespecified criteria for the critical evaluation, integration, and presentation of information from the studies addressing a particular question as well as by the criteria for searching for, retrieving, and selecting potentially relevant studies. As this chapter focuses on *accessing* the relevant literature, it deals only with the systematic procedures that have to do with searching for and retrieving literature; selecting studies for inclusion; and, to a limited degree, extracting relevant information from included studies. More information about how to integrate and present findings may be found in Volume 3, Chapter 25, this handbook and in many books about systematic reviews and research synthesis (cf. Cooper, Hedges, & Valentine, 2009; Higgins & Green, 2008; Littell, Corcoran, & Pillai, 2008; Petticrew & Roberts, 2005).

Characteristics of a Methodologically Rigorous Literature Search

American Psychological Association's (APA) *Thesaurus of Psychological Index Terms* (2007) defines a literature review as a survey of previously published material (http://psycnet.apa.org/index.cfm?fa= subjects.thesaurus). Although I take issue with the limitation imposed by the term *published*, it is useful to use this description when considering how to conduct a scientifically credible search for literature. In this section, I review the features that influence the validity of surveys and note their applicability to literature searches and reviews.

In its "What Is a Survey?" series, the Survey Research Methods Section of the American Statistical Association (n.d.) noted that a survey rather than a census is used when it is neither possible nor feasible to collect information from the entire population. The association described the key features of a "bona fide" survey as follows: (a) If the intention is to be able to draw conclusions about the population, the sample must not be selected haphazardly or in a biased fashion; (b) it should not be designed to produce predetermined results; (c) the objectives of the survey should be as specific, clear-cut, and unambiguous as possible; (d) the information collected from the sample of respondents should be standardized so that the same questions are asked of all members of the sample; and (e) the size of the sample should be determined by the purposes of the survey. The association further noted that the planning stage is probably the most important because if the concepts being studied are not clearly defined or if the questions are ambiguously phrased, the resulting data cannot be trusted. Finally, they noted that the availability of resources needs to be taken into account when planning the project.

The same features are desirable in a bona fide survey of a research literature. Researchers often wish to draw inferences about an entire body of scientific knowledge, although it is highly unlikely that all of the relevant research on a topic will be uncovered by their search. Thus, the question of sampling, and specifically of selection bias, has to be addressed by the literature searcher. Although surveyors of research literature do not have the luxury of drawing probability samples in which the likelihood of each study's chance of being selected for the review is precisely known, steps can be taken to minimize bias in the identification and selection of studies for review. Even if a searcher espouses a particular point of view, a survey of the literature should not be conducted to produce predetermined results, but rather should objectively represent study findings. An important means of protecting against drawing predetermined conclusions is to create transparent rules for the inclusion or exclusion of studies before the actual screening process begins. The development of these rules will be made easier to the degree that the objectives of the search are as

specific, clear-cut, and unambiguous as possible. For example, the question, "What is the effect of social support on women's likelihood of experiencing postpartum depression?" provides more direction for a search than the question, "What factors during pregnancy influence postpartum mental health?" Similarly, using a standardized coding guide to extract information from the studies considered relevant will help ensure that the same information is asked of each study. This coding guide will reduce the chances that the information was selectively elicited to confirm the reviewer's expectations. Although reviewers are entitled to their opinions, they are not entitled to their own facts.

The planning stage of a search of literature is so important that two major organizations producing systematic reviews, the Cochrane and Campbell Collaborations, actually require fully written protocols before a review may be started (Higgins & Green, 2008; Littell et al., 2008). A protocol for a literature search associated with the introduction to a new data collection is unlikely to be necessary, but it is a good idea to include a detailed plan for the literature search in the protocol that will guide the new study.

Although literature reviews vary considerably along several dimensions, the requirement that you (be able to) communicate explicitly and precisely the choices that you made at key points in the course of your search holds across all the variations. A clearly defined purpose, unambiguous rules for the inclusion or exclusion of studies, explication of the procedures used to search for relevant studies, a list of sources searched, a list of studies (ultimately) selected for inclusion in the review, and a clear description of methods used to extract and integrate the information from those studies will increase the information value and scientific contribution of any literature search or review.

What *will* vary by the purpose of review is the acceptability of the choices you make. For example, the legitimacy of specific strategies used to search for studies and the criteria for including or excluding studies will differ depending on your purpose and on the nature of the literature being reviewed. Similarly, the extent to which the documentation of the choices is expected to be part of the review or retained by you as part of as a research log will vary depending on the scope of your review and on your intended audience. For example, a stand-alone review should extensively document as part of the review the choices made during the literature search, whereas an introduction-section review might include only some of these choices, with the remainder being retained by the searcher in a log. Similarly, a review intended for other scholars generally will be expected to include more documentation than a review intended for a general audience.

PLANNING THE LITERATURE SEARCH

The planning part of the search and retrieval process includes developing and refining the research question, producing a list of eligibility criteria, and assessing and allocating the resources available for conducting the search.

Defining the Question

A search for relevant literature should be based on a well-defined and clearly formulated research question. The more clearly your question is framed, the easier it will be for you to (a) decide what is relevant and (b) generate criteria for selecting studies to include. A clear statement of the research's purpose will provide, for both you and your readers, a standard that can be used in judging whether the aims of the literature search were achieved. In addition, decisions about how much time, effort, and money to invest in the search process should depend on the question the research addresses as well as on the resources that are available to you. A well-formulated research question will identify the key variables and relationships that will be the focus of the literature search. Your decisions regarding acceptable conceptual and operational definitions of these variables and about the nature of the relationship of interest (e.g., descriptive, correlational, or causal), in turn, will guide your decisions about what evidence is appropriate (or inappropriate) for inclusion.

The PICO (population, intervention, comparator, and outcome) approach is a popular tool for formulating answerable research questions and for guiding a literature search meant to precede a new study on treatment effectiveness or other studies

using experimental and quasi-experimental methods. An example of a well-formulated question for the introductory review that precedes a study of the effectiveness of a reading intervention might be, "What is the improvement in reading ability (*outcome*) for middle-school students who are reading below grade level (*population*) who receive one-on-one after-school tutoring in reading (*intervention*) compared with those who participate in an after-school remedial reading class (*comparator*)?" Additional clarification of each of the PICO elements (e.g., frequency and duration of the tutoring, the grades included in middle school) as well as specification of the study design (e.g., randomized or cluster-randomized experiments) will further illuminate the type of studies relevant to the new study and therefore appropriate to be reviewed in its introductory section.

The PICO formulation may be adapted for use with studies posing questions about correlational relationships, that is, those incorporating observational research designs. For this purpose, PICO becomes an acronym for population, independent variable, conditions/setting, and outcome variable. An example of the PICO formulation for a study on the relationship between sleep disorders and depression could be, "How strongly are sleeping disturbances (*predictor variable*) related to cognitive symptoms of depression (*criteria*) among college students (*population*) during final examination week (*condition/setting*)?" In some cases, the conditions/setting component will not be so narrowly specified.

In psychology, many variables are complex and multifaceted, and even clearly focused research questions involving the same variables can be posed either broadly or narrowly. The breadth or narrowness of the question that the research is intended to answer should influence the scope of the literature search that provides the context for the new study.

Developing Eligibility Criteria

The criteria used to include or exclude a study from a literature review should follow logically and directly from the research question. They should be defined explicitly before the literature search begins, although it is sometimes necessary to modify them during the search if studies with unanticipated features are encountered. If you do add new criteria during the search, you need to be careful not to be influenced by study results or by personal biases. Explicit eligibility criteria will enable knowledgeable readers to reach their own conclusions about specific studies that the researcher included or ignored.

Most eligibility criteria relate to types of participants, characteristics of the predictor, characteristics of the independent variable or intervention, and characteristics of the outcome or dependent variable. You may derive these directly from the PICO formulation, if you used one to structure your research question. Other commonly used eligibility criteria are the setting in which the research was conducted and features of the study design. For example, if your study is on the effectiveness of an intervention, you may decide to limit your discussion of previous work to studies that used randomized controlled experiments. Exhibit 8.1 illustrates some of the eligibility criteria from a study of stress management interventions (Richardson & Rothstein, 2008). As the example shows, in addition to defining what conditions a study must meet to be *included* in a review, you may define specific *exclusion* criteria as well.

Assessing and Allocating Resources

One of the most common mistakes made by researchers starting a literature search is underestimating the time and effort it takes to conduct a thorough search and to retrieve and screen potentially relevant studies. You can easily introduce unintentional biases in the selection of studies for inclusion if you do not dedicate sufficient human and financial resources to the search. Inadequate resources can lead to abbreviated searches; casually chosen search criteria; use of only those databases and other search tools that are easily accessible, easy to use, or free; ignoring alternate disciplines when the research question is multidisciplinary; and including only published studies (which generally are not representative of the literature as a whole).

Although the time required will vary depending on the objectives and scope of the project, if you are planning to conduct a comprehensive search, it is reasonable to allocate several weeks to several months for the search, retrieval, and critical evaluation of what has been retrieved (Hart, 2001). When the purpose of the literature search is a full-blown systematic review and meta-analysis, the typical time frame for searching (often by a team rather than a single individual) may be up to 6 months. If your goal is to produce a general overview of a topic and your search will be limited to accessible materials such as those identifiable through electronic databases and available electronically or those available at your local campus library, it may be possible to complete the search within a few days. It is important for you to remember that this type of search is more likely to produce a biased set of materials than a more comprehensive search; however, the purpose of your research project will affect how important it is to be comprehensive. In those cases in which minimization of bias is a primary concern, you must supplement electronic searches of bibliographic databases with a variety of other types of searches. In this situation, the time and effort you need to expend may increase considerably, and you should ensure that the costs of additional search and retrieval activities are budgeted for appropriately.

One of the most valuable and frequently overlooked resources is the expertise of information specialists, such as librarians. Research librarians have much to offer anyone embarking upon a literature review. A librarian is likely to have greater familiarity than you do with the content of specific databases

---

Exhibit 8.1.
An Example of Eligibility Criteria From a Review on Stress Management Interventions at Work

A study had to meet all of the following criteria to be included:
- Evaluate a primary or secondary stress management intervention (i.e., employee assistance programs were excluded)
- Include participants from the working population (i.e., studies involving students were excluded) who were not already diagnosed as having a major psychiatric disorder (e.g., depression or posttraumatic stress) or stress-related somatic disorder (e.g., hypertension)
- Use random assignment to treatment and control conditions
- Be written in English and conducted after 1976

(and thus their relevance to your investigation) and the way information is indexed within each database. In addition, librarians are likely to be more familiar with potentially valuable sources of information other than electronic databases and to know how to access them. Librarians are helpful in acquiring materials that have been located during a search as well as in costing, keeping records of, and supervising searches. The net result is that literature retrieval will be more efficient and productive and less biased if a librarian is involved. I strongly recommend that you work closely with a librarian or other information retrieval specialist from the beginning of your project. This collaboration takes on heightened importance when search tools are being chosen; search strategies are being formulated; and decisions are being made about what sources to search, what search terms to use, and how to combine them.

CONDUCTING THE SEARCH

The objective of any systematic search is to be as thorough as possible, given the resources available. This means attempting both to maximize the coverage of the search and to minimize biases, so that as many as possible of the studies potentially relevant to the question of interest, both published and unpublished, are retrieved. It is not wise for you to limit your search to published studies, as those studies often are a biased sample; that is, they generally are not representative of all the literature relevant to the research question. And, as has often been pointed out, if the sample of studies retrieved is biased, the results of the review are compromised (Egger, Davey Smith, & Altman, 2000; Rothstein, Sutton, & Borenstein, 2005). Published studies are more likely to contain significant results and stronger effects than other studies; thus, a review conducted only on the basis of published studies may reach more positive conclusions than the literature as a whole. Although some reviewers have argued that published journal articles are of higher quality than other sources of information (cf. Keel & Klump, 2003; Weisz, Weiss, Han, Granger, & Morton, 1995), others have suggested that this view is unwarranted, arguing that publication has as much, or more, to do with the individual researcher's

incentive to publish than it does with the quality of the research (cf. Grayson, 2002; Grayson & Gomersall, 2003), or that the peer-review system in academic journals is unreliable or biased and does not provide quality control (cf. Jefferson, Rudin, Brodney Folse, & Davidoff, 2006). In short, limiting a review to published papers is more likely to introduce bias than to serve as a quality control, and in most cases, publication status is not an appropriate eligibility criterion. Sources of information other than published studies (the so-called grey literature) are suggested in the section Going Beyond Electronic Databases later in this chapter.

Conducting a Preliminary Search

Researchers should conduct a preliminary search before beginning their main search. The preliminary search serves two purposes. First, it is a means to get a basic sense of the literature on the topic of interest and of the areas in which the greatest yield of studies likely will be found (so that you can concentrate your search efforts there). Second, it serves as a source of search terms for each of the key concepts in your research question, and it will help you to assess whether searching on specific terms is likely to yield relevant studies.

To develop a list of search terms, it is worthwhile to consult both standard reference tools, such as subject encyclopedias and subject thesauri (e.g., the *Encyclopedia of Psychology*, the *Dictionary of Education*), and specialized thesauri for specific databases (e.g., the *Thesaurus of Psychological Index Terms* for PsycINFO, the *Thesaurus of ERIC* [Education Resources Information Center] *Descriptors*, the U.S. National Library of Medicine Medical Subject Headings [MeSH] for searching Medline). During your preliminary search, you should try to locate previous reviews on the question of interest and, if you do not already have the information, to identify the key researchers in the area as well as the studies conducted by these researchers. It may be worthwhile at this point to conduct a citation search of the key researchers to identify other studies that have been conducted on your topic. The results of the preliminary searches can serve as the basis for estimating the number of studies on the topic. The studies retrieved during these searches can serve as a standard against which to test the usefulness of the initially selected search terms for locating potentially relevant studies. This test can be conducted by entering the search terms into a search engine accessing a database that is known to contain the standard studies and noting the proportion of the results that are identified in the same way. Should this test show that the initial search terms locate an undesirably low proportion of the known studies, you should modify your search terms.

Conducting the Main Searches

The main searches should be designed to locate as many as possible of the primary studies that are potentially relevant to your research question. This is likely to be challenging and time-consuming. You will need to make decisions about the information retrieval tools (including print and online) to be accessed, for what time period, and whether the search will include specifications related to country, language, or discipline. This is not an easy task, particularly given the multidisciplinary and global nature of many questions posed by psychologists. A review on a topic related to stress management, for example, might require searching literatures in psychology, medicine, nursing, business, and education. In a systematic review on stress management interventions by Richardson and Rothstein (2008), an electronic search of six databases (Academic Search Premier, British Library Direct, Dissertation Abstracts, ERIC, ABI Inform Global, and PsycARTI-CLES) was performed. These databases were chosen to obtain studies from different countries in a broad range of research fields, including social sciences, health care, and education, and, in fact, each of the databases contained studies that were not found in any of the other databases.

Although identification and retrieval of studies exclusively by electronic searching of bibliographic and full-text databases is rarely, if ever, sufficient to locate all relevant research, it is likely that you will locate the majority of primary studies this way, either by means of bibliographic databases that contain a citation and an abstract for a document or in full-text databases. Thus, it makes sense for you to begin by working with electronic databases. Although PsycINFO is an excellent starting point, it

is unlikely to contain all of the relevant material on any question of interest to psychologists. Other key databases to consider include CINAHL (Cumulative Index to Nursing and Allied Health Literature), ERIC, Education Abstracts, Medline, ProQuest Dissertations and Theses, SocINDEX, and SSRN (Social Science Resource Network). These databases include at least some foreign language or nonjournal material (such as theses and dissertations, conference proceedings, books or book chapters) and older material (e.g., PsycINFO journal coverage begins with materials published in 1806, and ProQuest Dissertations and Theses contains citations to dissertations conducted as far back as the early 1600s). Most include, or link to, databases containing full-text versions of much of their indexed material. A more extensive list of databases and similar resources frequently found useful by social and behavioral researchers conducting literature searches may be found in Reed and Baxter (2009), Rothstein and Hopewell (2009), and in the Wikipedia article on academic databases and search engines (http://en.wikipedia.org/wiki/List_of_academic_databases_and_search_engines). Remember that several popular databases have undergone recent name changes and that this trend likely will continue as database publishers compete, combine, and modify their holdings. If you cannot find a database that you have heard of, check to see whether it now exists under a different name. Multiple databases can be accessed simultaneously through search engines such as EBSCOhost.

The major challenge in searching multiple databases is that each database has its own unique subject term index (*thesaurus*), its own rules for searching (*syntax*), and its own way of displaying records (cf. Harris, 2005). An added complication is that some of these vary not only by database but also within databases, by search engine, and by database vendor. You should keep this in mind when attempting to transfer the knowledge gained from working with one database to your search of a different database or when using a megasearch engine like the EBSCOhost.

To ensure that a high proportion of relevant documents will be retrieved (*high recall*), you must be prepared to retrieve a greater number of irrelevant documents (*lower precision*) than may be found using typical search strategies. The best search strategies tend to be constructed using a combination of controlled vocabulary (or thesaurus) terms that are used to index documents in a given database and natural language (or free text) keywords that can be found in document titles or abstracts or other searchable fields. As Wade, Turner, Rothstein, and Lavenberg (2006) have noted, the creation of an effective search strategy requires that the following questions be addressed:

- What are the key concepts to be searched?
- What are the natural language terms that represent these concepts?
- What are the related terms for these key concepts?
- Are these key concepts represented differently in different disciplines?
- How are these key concepts represented in the controlled vocabulary within each database?

You will not be able to answer these questions fully without consulting the thesaurus for each database. The *Thesaurus of Psychological Index Terms* (APA, 2007), which contains the controlled vocabulary terms for APA's database PsycINFO (and its subsidiary databases PsycARTICLES, PsycBOOKS, PsycCRITIQUES, and PsycEXTRA), is available in hard copy. APA's own database access platform, PsycNET, as well some outside vendors for these databases also provide an online thesaurus. APA provides many online help and training resources for researchers interested in using PsycNET databases to search for literature. A good place to start is the quick reference guide (http://www.apa.org/pubs/databases/training/psycnet.pdf), which has easy-to-follow instructions about using the advanced search mode to search any of the five PsycNET databases. Other useful sources for instruction on how to conduct searches are chapters in the *Handbook of Research Synthesis and Meta-Analysis, Second Edition* (Cooper et al., 2009) on scientific communication and literature retrieval by White (2009) and on using reference databases by Reed and Baxter (2009). *Doing a Literature Search* (Hart, 2001) is a good reference for beginners, although some of its information is outdated.

Many small, specialized social science databases contain material that the larger databases do not. Many of these databases, however, do not make use of controlled vocabulary or thesauri, and the indexing in some of those that do have these features has been found to be haphazard or inconsistent (Grayson & Gomersall, 2003). In these cases, you will need to rely exclusively on natural language searches. This makes the search process time-consuming and inefficient, but the potential yield of such searches can make them invaluable if you have the resources to dedicate to this activity.

Once you have identified the search terms, you need to combine them into search statements or search strings. Exhibit 8.2 provides an illustration of how the search terms were combined into search statements for a literature search on stress management interventions (Richardson & Rothstein, 2008) and how the statements were varied by database. We were able to use a single search statement for our searches of the Academic Search Premier, British Library Direct, ERIC, and PsycARTICLES databases; when the same procedure was followed for the Dissertations Abstract database, it yielded no results

---

Exhibit 8.2.
Search Statements by Database

Academic Search Premier, British Library Direct, ERIC, and PsycARTICLES
Line 1: employee OR work OR management
AND
Line 2: stress OR wellness
AND
Line 3: program* OR intervention OR prevention

Dissertation Abstracts
Line 1: worksite AND stress AND management
AND
Line 2: program OR intervention OR prevention

ABI Inform Global
SU (employee or work or management) AND ((stress or wellness) w/2 (program* or intervention or prevention)) AND CC (9130 or 5400).

Note. SU = subject; w/2 = within two words of; CC = classification codes (for research or experiments).

and we modified our search statement. For the ABI Inform Global database, we supplemented our search terms with specific classification codes and entered them in a different format.

The most important considerations at this stage include how to make use of Boolean operators (AND, OR, NOT), truncation or wildcards (to find variants of word forms), proximity operators (to indicate that results are to be returned only when the search terms occur within a certain number of words of each other), and delimiters (to limit the search to specific publication years, document types, or study characteristics). It is critically important that you consult each database's help features to ensure that you are using these operators correctly in each case. Use of the wrong Boolean operator, truncation symbol, proximity operator, or delimiter can drastically affect the number and relevance of studies that are returned. For example, a keyword search of PsycINFO (using the PsycNET platform) for *employee* AND *stress* AND *prevention* returned 39 results, whereas a keyword search for *employee* OR *stress* AND *prevention* returned 1,106. Restricting the latter search to quantitative studies by using a methodology delimiter produced 135 results.

It is particularly frustrating to most searchers that these important symbols and operators are not standardized. Small differences among databases, search engines, and vendors in truncation symbols, proximity operators, and delimiters can lead to large differences in study yield. For example, the important truncation symbol that allows the searcher to locate variant forms of a root word may be indicated by a question mark (?), an asterisk (*), a pound sign (#), or a dollar sign ($), depending on the database. Additionally, some databases or vendors use one symbol to replace a single letter and a different symbol to replace multiple letters. Exhibit 8.3 illustrates some of the hazards involved in using truncation symbols. Similar hazards accompany the use of proximity symbols and delimiters.

As of this writing, the database PsycINFO is available through APA's own database platform PsycNET and through several other vendors. The same search of PsycINFO or PsycARTICLES via different platforms and vendors often yields different results, sometimes dramatically so. For example,

---

Exhibit 8.3.
Hazards in Using Truncation Symbols

Extreme truncation produces irrelevant results
vis* might find vision and visual, but also visa, visitation, and vista

Use of different symbols to mean the same thing in different databases
In database 1 psychol* finds psychologist, psychology, psychological
In database 2 psychol? finds psychologist, psychology, psychological

Use of different symbols to replace single or multiple letters in some databases
char* might find char, chars, chart, or charm
char? might find char, chars, chart, charm, charisma, charismatic, or character

---

when I conducted a keyword search of PsycINFO for *employee* AND *stress* AND *prevention* using the EBSCO platform, 21 citations were returned; alternately, the same search in PsycINFO using PsycNET yielded 39 citations.

GOING BEYOND ELECTRONIC DATABASES

In addition to electronic searching of databases, a thorough search for literature generally will include many or all of the following: hand searching of key journals, checking reference lists and citation searching, contacting researchers, examining conference proceedings, using the World Wide Web, and (for some questions) checking research registers. The latter five are good sources of noncommercially published literature, sometimes called *grey* or *fugitive* literature. The pros and cons of using each of these sources are discussed in the following sections.

Hand Searching Journals

A hand search involves an issue-by-issue search of a journal. Targeted hand searching of specific journals that are thought to have a high likelihood of publishing potentially relevant articles can be used to deal with problems caused by poor indexing and incomplete database coverage. But hand searching is a labor-intensive and time-consuming endeavor. Every discipline has journals that may contain relevant studies but that are not indexed by database producers. Additionally, because of the incidence of indexing errors, not all articles that are indexed in a database are retrievable from those databases. This is analogous to the problem of mislabeling a file, or misfiling a labeled file, and thus being unable to retrieve it from the filing cabinet. The evidence suggests that relying only on electronic searching will result in many potentially relevant studies being missed, even when they are present in a database. Turner et al. (2003), for example, found that an electronic search missed about two thirds of the known randomized experiments identified by an online manual search of the same journal (*Journal of Educational Psychology*) for the same years. They also reported similar findings in other research in education and health care. The specific research question (e.g., its complexity and how widespread across disciplines the literature is likely to be), the purpose of the search (e.g., stand-alone research synthesis, introduction to a new primary study, or personal learning), and the available resources (e.g., time and money) should be your prime considerations if you are trying to decide whether a hand search is warranted.

Searching Reference Lists and Citations

Searching reference lists of previously retrieved primary studies and literature reviews is generally an effective and resource-efficient method of identifying potentially relevant literature. This method, also called the *ancestry approach* or *snowballing*, requires that you review the reference sections of all retrieved articles for additional possibly relevant studies and retrieve any new material. This process continues for several cycles until no new possibly relevant references are found. In addition to scanning the reference lists of relevant articles, you can use electronic citation search engines to identify additional studies. Examples include the Science Citation Index, the Social Sciences Citation Index, and Social SciSearch, which are available through ISI Web of Knowledge (http://www.thomsonisi.com) and SCOPUS (http://www.scopus.com).

Contacting Researchers

Research centers and experts are another important source of information. Contacting researchers who are active in a field, subject specialists, and both for-profit and nonprofit companies that conduct research (e.g., the pharmaceutical industry medical device companies, test publishers, consulting firms, government and nongovernment agencies) can be important means of identifying ongoing or completed but unpublished studies. Retrieving these studies once they have been identified is a separate task, and it is widely acknowledged that requests for information about a study are not always successful (cf. Rothstein & Hopewell, 2009).

Examining Conference Proceedings

Conference proceedings are a good source of potentially relevant studies. These proceedings contain studies that may not be published in a journal, and their abstracts generally are not included in electronic databases. Evidence suggests that quite often, conference papers remain unpublished for reasons having nothing to do with the quality of the research (Rothstein & Hopewell, 2009). Some conference proceedings are available electronically from professional society websites, and others may be issued on compact discs or on paper. Many conferences do not publish proceedings, thus requiring a search of the conference program and subsequent contact with the abstract authors to obtain studies of interest. Using conference proceedings as a source increases the potential pitfall of duplication bias, with reports of the same study being reported in different conference proceedings, or in both the conference proceedings and in a journal. The review author can take steps, however, to reduce this risk (cf. Wood, 2008). For example, you can examine reports on the same topic that share one or more coauthors to assess the degree of similarity in study characteristics, sample size, and reported effects across the set of reports. If after this examination you are unable to decide whether they are duplicates or independent results, it is a good idea to ask the corresponding author.

Searching the Internet

The Internet is an increasingly important source of information about ongoing and completed research, particularly that which has not been formally published. Sources of potentially relevant literature that are mainly reachable by Internet searching include the following: websites of colleges and universities and their faculty, major libraries, professional societies, federal or national government agencies, state and local government authorities, nonprofit research organizations and foundations, advocacy groups, and corporations. Despite the popularity of Internet searches, little is known about whether searching the Internet (other than Google Scholar) is a generally useful means of identifying additional studies.

Using Research Registers

For some questions, particularly those related to health care, research registers can be a valuable source of potentially relevant studies. Such registers include national registers like the National Research Register in the United Kingdom (http://www.doh.gov.uk/research/nrr.htm) as well as numerous local and specialty registers. The World Health Organization (WHO) has created an International Clinical Trials Registry Platform through which information about the results of many clinical trials worldwide may be available (http://www.who.int/ictrp).

Exhibit 8.4 illustrates the yield of included studies from various sources for the Richardson and Rothstein (2008) systematic review.

Documenting Your Search

It is important that you carefully document the search tools, search terms, and search strategies

---

Exhibit 8.4.
Sources of Included Studies From Richardson and Rothstein (2008)

Total number of articles included in the review = 38

19 articles were from an earlier meta-analysis on the same topic

13 additional articles (of an initial return of 942 potentially relevant studies) from electronic searches of six databases

4 additional articles from contacting other researchers

2 additional articles (of 24 potentially relevant ones) from a search of the reference lists of previously identified articles (snowball search)

0 articles from websites devoted to stress research

---

you used as well as the eligibility criteria that were applied in screening studies for inclusion. The information should be specific enough so that the search and the inclusion and exclusion of studies are reproducible using the information provided in the review (or made available upon request to you, when external constraints do not permit this information to be provided in full in the review). Full and precise documentation is needed to allow readers to see what is (and is not) covered, to allow replication or updating, and to help you keep track of your search. For this last reason, it is a good idea to maintain a list of excluded studies along with the reasons for their exclusion to have available to interested readers.

Whether it is for your own purposes, or to be able to let others appraise your search, it is necessary for you to keep accurate, consistent, and clear records of what was done and what was found at each stage of the search. Specialized bibliographic management software (also called reference management software or citation management software) can be of great assistance in managing parts of this task. Popular commercial products include Endnote, Reference Manager, and Refworks, but free software such as Zotero (http://www.zotero.org) and Mendeley (http://www.mendeley.com) also is available.

CONCLUSION

The initial premise of this chapter was that searching for scientific research literature is itself a research activity and therefore should be conducted according to the basic scientific principles of transparency, replicability, and avoidance of bias. Most social science researchers are not fully aware of the degree to which traditional literature searches fall short of scientific standards. I hope that this chapter will increase awareness of the need for rigor in literature search process. The specific practices I have described in this chapter are likely to continue to change as the amount of empirical research increases and as the information retrieval industry and its technology continues its rapid evolution.

References

American Psychological Association. (2007). *Thesaurus of psychological index terms* (11th ed.). Washington, DC: Author.

American Statistical Association. (n.d.). *What is a survey?* Retrieved from http://www.whatisasurvey.info

Cooper, H. (1982). Scientific guidelines for conducting integrative research reviews. *Review of Educational Research, 52,* 291–302.

Cooper, H. (2009). *Research synthesis and meta-analysis: A step-by-step approach* (4th ed.). Thousand Oaks, CA: Sage.

Cooper, H., Hedges, L. V., & Valentine, J. C. (Eds.). (2009). *The handbook of research synthesis and meta-analysis* (2nd ed.). New York, NY: Russell Sage Foundation.

Egger, M., Davey Smith, G., & Altman, D. G. (2000). *Systematic reviews in health care: Meta-analysis in context.* London, England: British Medical Journal Books.

Grayson, L. (2002). *Evidence based policy and the quality of evidence: Rethinking peer review* (Working Paper 7). London, England: ESRC UK Centre for Evidence Based Policy and Practice. Retrieved from http://www.evidencenetwork.org

Grayson, L., & Gomersall, A. (2003). *A difficult business: Finding the evidence for social science reviews* (Working Paper 19). London, England: ESRC UK Centre for Evidence Based Policy and Practice. Retrieved from http://www.evidencenetwork.org

Harris, M. R. (2005). The librarian's roles in the systematic review process: A case study. *Journal of the Medical Library Association, 93,* 81–87.

Hart, C. (2001). *Doing a literature search: A comprehensive guide for the social sciences.* London, England: Sage.

Higgins, J. P. T., & Green, S. (Eds.). (2008). *Cochrane handbook for systematic reviews of interventions.* Chichester, England: Wiley. doi:10.1002/9780470712184

Jackson, G. (1980). Methods for integrative reviews. *Review of Educational Research, 50,* 438–460.

Jefferson, T., Rudin, M., Brodney Folse, S., & Davidoff, S. (2006). *Editorial peer review for improving the quality of reports of biomedical studies.* Available from the Cochrane Database of Methodology Reviews (Article No. MR000016).

Keel, P. K., & Klump, K. L. (2003). Are eating disorders culture-bound syndromes? Implications for conceptualizing their etiology. *Psychological Bulletin, 129,* 747–769. doi:10.1037/0033-2909.129.5.747

Light, R. J., & Pillemer, D. B. (1984). *Summing up: The science of reviewing research.* Cambridge, MA: Harvard University Press.

Littell, J. H., Corcoran, J., & Pillai, V. (2008). *Systematic reviews and meta-analysis.* New York, NY: Oxford University Press. doi:10.1093/acprof:oso/9780195326543.001.0001

Petticrew, M., & Roberts, H. (2005). *Systematic reviews in the social sciences: A practical guide.* Chichester, England: Wiley-Blackwell.

Reed, J. G., & Baxter, P. M. (2009). Using reference databases. In H. Cooper, L. V. Hedges, & J. C. Valentine (Eds.), *The handbook of research synthesis and meta-analysis* (2nd ed., pp. 73–101). New York, NY: Russell Sage Foundation.

Richardson, K. M., & Rothstein, H. R. (2008). The effects of worksite stress management intervention programs: A systematic review. *Journal of Occupational Health Psychology, 13,* 69–93. doi:10.1037/1076-8998.13.1.69

Rothstein, H. R., & Hopewell, S. (2009). Grey literature. In H. Cooper, L. V. Hedges, & J. C. Valentine (Eds.), *The handbook of research synthesis and meta-analysis* (2nd ed., pp. 103–125). New York, NY: Russell Sage Foundation.

Rothstein, H. R., Sutton, A. J., & Borenstein, M. (Eds.). (2005). *Publication bias in meta-analysis: Prevention, assessment, and adjustments.* Chichester, England: Wiley.

Turner, H., Boruch, R., Petrosino, A., de Moya, D., Lavenberg, J., & Rothstein, H. (2003). Populating an international register of randomized trials in the social, behavioral, criminological, and education sciences. *Annals of the American Academy of Political and Social Science, 589,* 203–223. doi:10.1177/0002716203256840

Wade, C. A., Turner, H. M., Rothstein, H. R., & Lavenberg, J. G. (2006). Information retrieval and the role of the information specialist in producing high-quality systematic reviews in the social, behavioural and education sciences. *Evidence and Policy, 2,* 89–108. doi:10.1332/174426406775249705

Weisz, J. R., Weiss, B., Han, S., Granger, D., & Morton, T. (1995). Effects of psychotherapy with children and adolescents revisited: A meta-analysis of treatment outcome studies. *Psychological Bulletin, 117,* 450–468. doi:10.1037/0033-2909.117.3.450

White, H. (2009). Scientific communication and literature retrieval. In H. Cooper, L. V. Hedges, & J. C. Valentine (Eds.), *The handbook of research synthesis and meta-analysis* (2nd ed., pp. 51–71). New York, NY: Russell Sage Foundation.

Wood, J. (2008). Methodology for dealing with duplicate study effects in a meta-analysis. *Organizational Research Methods, 11,* 79–95. doi:10.1177/1094428106296638

CHAPTER 9

OBTAINING AND EVALUATING RESEARCH RESOURCES

Louis A. Penner, Terrance L. Albrecht, and John F. Dovidio

This chapter is about obtaining and evaluating the resources needed to support research. We divide the chapter into two broad sections. The first discusses external support, resources that come from outside a researcher's home institution; the second discusses internal support, resources that come from within the institution. The first section of this chapter is informed by our experiences in submitting grants to the National Institutes of Health (NIH) and the National Science Foundation (NSF) and our service as members or chairs of the panels that review grant applications. The second section is informed by our experiences as department chairs, by Albrecht's experience in a leadership position at a publicly supported medical research institute, and by Dovidio's experience at a privately supported institution with an education and research mission.

EXTERNAL SUPPORT

External support usually comes in the form of a grant from the federal government or a private foundation. For a host of reasons, including diminished financial support and concerns about institutional reputations, external support for research has become increasingly important in the past 5 to 10 years. This trend is likely to continue. Just a few years ago, many institutions expected new faculty to *pursue* outside funding; now many expect faculty to *obtain* funding by the time they stand for tenure.

Furthermore, most comprehensive research universities now view internal support as venture capital expended in the interest of obtaining external support. Reflecting this increased concern with external research support, we spend the majority of this chapter discussing the processes associated with obtaining external support for research.

We bring two distinct perspectives to this chapter. Penner and Albrecht spent many years in traditional academic departments, but they currently are employed in a setting that is still somewhat unusual for psychologists and other behavioral scientists. They are both professors in a medical school, and their place of employment is a large cancer hospital and research institute. Their research is primarily problem based and focuses almost exclusively on health issues. In contrast, Dovidio is employed in a traditional psychology department at a comprehensive research university. Although much of his research addresses social problems (e.g., racism), it is somewhat theoretical in character and focuses on other topics as well as health issues. Thus, Penner and Albrecht primarily seek funding from the NIH, and Dovidio is somewhat more likely to seek support from the NSF. These federal agencies have different goals and missions; thus, they are interested in different kinds of applications. Our discussion of external funding includes separate descriptions of how to obtain funding from NIH and NSF. Because of space limitations, we do not discuss other federal agencies

The preparation of this chapter was partially supported by grants to the first and second authors from the National Cancer Institute (NCI R01 CA75003-03, 5U01CA114583-02, R21 CA139369, and 1 R01 CA138981-01) and to the third author from the National Science Foundation (R01-0613218) and the National Institutes of Health (R01HL0856331-0182). The contents of this chapter reflect the views of the three authors and have not been reviewed or endorsed by any official of either the National Institutes of Health or the National Science Foundation.

DOI: 10.1037/13619-010

that fund basic and applied research, such as the Centers for Disease Control and Prevention, the Department of Defense, and private foundations such as the Robert Wood Johnson Foundation. The different missions and structures of the organizations make obtaining funds from private foundations different from obtaining funds from federal agencies, but the principles that make a proposal competitive are similar. Readers who are interested in private sources of funding can refer to the following sources of information: (a) the Foundation Center (http://www.fconline.foundationcenter.org) and (b) Miner and Associates (http://www.minerandassociates.com).

For most psychologists, the major sources of external support will be either the NIH or the NSF. The NIH is part of the U.S. Department of Health and Human Services; the NSF is funded directly by Congress. Both spend much of their budgets to support extramural research—that is, research that is conducted at universities, academic medical centers, and other institutions that are physically, administratively, and fiscally separate from the federal government. The rationale for federal agencies providing funding to individuals at research institutions around the country is to support research and development at a national level without having to maintain a laboratory infrastructure or to directly employ personnel to complete research projects.

National Institutes of Health

NIH is the largest source of federal funds for extramural research. The current budget for NIH is about $31 billion a year (NIH, n.d.); in comparison, the budget for NSF is about $7 billion (NSF, 2010a). About 80% of NIH's $31 billion is dedicated to extramural research conducted by scientists in about 3,000 institutions in the United States and abroad. In terms of resources for research, NIH is the proverbial "800-pound gorilla in the room."

The mission and organization of NIH. In its mission statement, NIH asserts that its mission "is science in pursuit of fundamental knowledge about the nature and behavior of living systems and the application of that knowledge to extend healthy life and reduce the burdens of illness and disability" (NIH, 2010a). NIH's goals relevant to this mission are to

"foster fundamental creative discoveries" that help to protect and improve the nation's health, "expand the knowledge base in medical and associated sciences," and "develop, renew, and maintain scientific resources" that will help to fight disease. NIH funding for extramural research is clearly consistent with its mission.

There are 24 institutes and centers within NIH, each of which funds extramural research. Although the institutes and centers are the source of the funding, one of the core principles of the NIH is that individual scientists must have complete freedom to develop and conduct their research work (Scarpa, 2006). In practical terms, this means that the process of reviewing grant applications is, with a few exceptions, not done by the institutes and centers but rather by a separate entity within NIH: the Center for Scientific Review (CSR). The CSR is structurally and organizationally independent of the institutes and centers. Thus, a researcher who seeks NIH funding usually is dealing with two quite separate parts of NIH. One is a program office, which is the part of an institute or center that develops or implements institute goals and missions, solicits research applications, oversees the institute's research portfolio (i.e., the grants that it currently funds), and makes decisions about which applications ultimately should be funded. The other part is the CSR, which coordinates grant reviews.

NIH centers and programs. An organizational chart of the 24 NIH institutes and centers is presented in Figure 9.1. As the names suggest, each institute and center focuses on some kind of health problem. Most, if not all, institutes and centers have several areas of research that they fund, and these areas are divided into programs. For example, the National Cancer Institute (NCI; the largest institute within NIH, with a 2010 budget of $5.1 billion; see http://www.cancer.gov) has nine programs that provide extramural funding. The people who administer these programs and carry out their research missions are called *program officers* or *directors*. They provide information about the areas of research in which an institute or center is interested. This is done through *announcements*.

NIH makes two general kinds of announcements: program announcements (PAs) and requests for

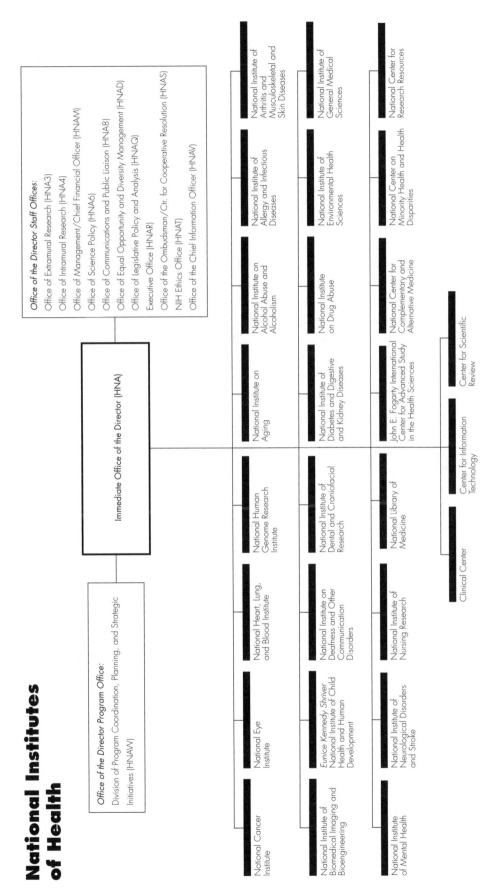

FIGURE 9.1.   The organizational structure of the National Institutes of Health (2010f).

applications (RFAs). The former are fairly broad and comprehensive. No money is specifically set aside to fund these projects; they are funded from the institute's overall annual budget. A PA represents a statement of current research interests by an institute or center. Most applications to NIH are individual investigator-initiated research applications; nonetheless, investigators must identify in their application a PA to which they are responding.

PAs provide important information and guidance about which kinds of applications are most likely to be funded. Funding at NIH is a three-step process. First, an institute or center agrees to sponsor an application. Second, a grant application must undergo scientific review, it must be judged competitive enough to be evaluated by a review panel, or *study section*, and then it must be favorably reviewed. The third step occurs when the institute funds an application. The number of applications to NIH has more than doubled in the past 10 years (Zerhouni, 2006); however, the NIH budget has not kept pace; thus, there are many more applications that receive good scores than an institute can support. In 2008, about 56,700 applications were reviewed by NIH; of those, about 15,000 were funded. (Not all applications to NIH are reviewed.) If two applications receive similarly strong scores and are very close to the cutoff for funding, the one with aims and goals that are closest to those of a program within an institute will, quite reasonably, stand a better chance of being approved for funding than the other. PAs tell an investigator what those aims and goals are.

In a *program announcement review* (PAR) money is set aside and applications are reviewed by special panels of experts in the area of the announcement. The PAR differs from all the other kinds of announcements in that an application is reviewed by a panel appointed by the institute that issues it rather than the CSR.

RFAs are somewhat similar to PARs in that they are accompanied by funds that are specifically set aside for the research and the applications submitted for these RFAs are reviewed by special panels. RFAs usually are issued for research in quite specific and well-defined areas and have specific program objectives. RFAs cannot be revised or resubmitted (unlike

investigator-initiated applications, which may be revised and resubmitted for a second review; National Institute of Mental Health, 2009).

Thus, for most researchers, the first point of contact with NIH should be with program officers or program directors (for our purposes the terms can be used interchangeably). Researchers typically contact these individuals because they have seen an announcement inviting proposals on a particular topic and want to explore the institute's interest in their application. Alternatively, researchers may have an idea for an application and want to see whether it fits with an institute's current research interests. Colleagues of ours who have been successful in receiving support from NIH have somewhat mixed views of the value of these consultations with program directors. Among some colleagues, the major reservation is that program priorities and interests are not necessarily communicated to review panels; or, if they are communicated, the people who conduct the actual reviews might not agree with these priorities and interests. Thus, the views of a program officer are of some value in getting an application funded, but many other factors are also involved.

We have found that program officers are especially helpful in telling you that their program is not interested in the kind of research you want to do. This information can save researchers considerable time and effort. Program officers can also direct researchers to other programs within NIH that are more suitable for the potential proposal. This type of information is extremely important because a grant will not be considered for review unless an institute sees it as part of its purpose or mission and agrees to sponsor it. Thus, some guidance on the kinds of research a program is looking for is quite useful. The best way to determine this is to have an initial dialogue with a program officer or director before the submission of an application.

Once an application is submitted, the abstract is circulated to relevant programs within all institutes and centers. It is sometimes the case that more than one institute or center will be interested in and sponsor an application. But, as noted, if no institute expresses interest, an application will not be reviewed.

Program directors can provide valuable advice on how to sculpt an application so that it conforms to an institute's interests. If an institute is interested in an application, program directors will follow it through the review process. Most scientific review meetings are attended by several program representatives in person or on the phone, and these representatives track the progress of high-interest applications. These representatives are prohibited from participating in the meeting or telling an applicant anything about the reviews, but they may be able to give an applicant some general feedback on how one might address problems in an unsuccessful application. Program officers can help researchers navigate the application process and, in certain instances, can help a researcher get funded.

As we have discussed, many scored applications are not funded and must be resubmitted for a second review. There is, however, a mechanism to obtain support for research that is not initially funded, without resubmitting it. A program officer plays a critical role in this mechanism, called *funding by exception*. At the end of a fiscal year, some institutes may have money left over for additional extramural funding. If so, they have a formal process for deciding which additional applications will receive funding. Program officers identify applications that they think are important or interesting, and then at a formal meeting they present these applications to a review panel that determines which applications will be funded by exception. These are applications with scores that put them close to the funding cutoff and either are quite exciting to program staff or fit extremely well with a program's mission or goals. Obviously, the probability of obtaining funding by exception increases dramatically if a program officer is familiar with an application and thinks an institute should fund this kind of research.

NIH grant mechanisms. In this section, we consider the different types of grant programs available from NIH. We restrict our review to those programs intended to fund research that addresses one relatively circumscribed research problem rather than programs that fund training programs or large research efforts that involve several independent research projects. Although NIH provides

predoctoral funding and postdoctoral fellowships, we only consider research grants for people who hold faculty lines or equivalent positions. Thus, we are primarily discussing investigator-initiated research applications.

The kind of support most commonly sought by senior investigators is a *Research Project Grant*, commonly called an *R01* (NIH, 2010g) This is an investigator-initiated project with a current budgetary cap of $500,000 a year in direct costs and typically is funded for 3 to 5 years. *Direct costs* are those that are needed to carry out the proposed research; they include researchers' and staff salaries, the cost of equipment, payment to participants, travel, and the like. In addition to direct costs, there are *indirect costs*. These are costs that a principal investigator's (PI's) home institution charges to administer and support the grant. Indirect costs are computed as a percentage of direct costs. Each institution has its own indirect costs rate, and this rate is not counted against the $500,000 per year limit. The $500,000 limit is important. If an application exceeds this limit, even by as little as a dollar or two in a single year, it must receive special approval at least 5 weeks before submission and will be reviewed by a special panel.

An R01 application typically is built on an established research program, which has already produced some promising results. Without strong preliminary findings that provide the empirical evidence and thus the foundation for an R01 application, it is extremely unlikely that it will be funded. Furthermore, reviewers must believe that the proposed research in an R01 application can be successfully completed. Many R01s include interventions, but this is not a requirement. As we discuss later in the section Review Criteria, strong theory and methodology, the potential for significant contributions to theory or clinical practice, and the quality of a research team carry much more weight than the specific approach that is taken in the application. That is, more descriptive theory-building applications may not get funded as often as applications that involve theory testing or interventions, but they do get funded.

A second mechanism is *Exploratory/Developmental Research Grant Award*, known as an *R21*. This grant mechanism provides initial funding for highly innovative and perhaps somewhat risky projects. These are considered to be high-risk/high-payoff projects that may lead to a breakthrough in a particular area or result in novel techniques, agents, methodologies, models, or applications that will affect biomedical, behavioral, or clinical research (NIH, 2010c). R21s do not need to include pilot data or preliminary data, as is the case with an R01. However, our practical experience is that R21s that include some, even minimal, pilot data often fare better than R21s without such data. R21s are currently for 2 years and carry a $275,000 total limit in direct costs.

The NIH *Small Grant Program*, or *R03* funding mechanism, is for small projects and pilot studies that can be carried out in a relatively short period of time with limited resources (NIH, 2010h). They are currently given for 2 years with a total limit of $100,000. They are viewed as laying the groundwork for future R01 and R21 applications. R03s are intended for promising new investigators who can conduct the research with quite limited resources or already have the resources available to conduct the research. For example, Albrecht and Penner's research group collects video recordings of medical interactions. Two of the junior faculty members in this group have had successful R03 applications that proposed research on these archival recordings. Not all NIH institutes and centers accept R03s, and some institutes and centers accept them only in response to specific funding announcements (NIH, 2010h).

Another research funding mechanism is the *Academic Research Enhancement Award* (*AREA*), or *R15* mechanism (NIH, 2010e). The purpose of this award is to stimulate research at educational institutions that provide training for a significant number of the nation's research scientists but that have not yet been recipients of major NIH support. The award provides funding for small-scale new or ongoing research projects, including pilot research projects; development, testing, and refinement of research techniques; secondary analysis of available data sets; and similar kinds of research projects. The AREA program is intended to strengthen the research environment at these institutions and to provide exposure to research for students who might want to pursue a career in the biomedical

sciences (NIH, 2010e). To be eligible for this award, an applicant's university or school or college within a university cannot have received more than $6 million dollars in federal funding in "four of the last fiscal years."

The final category of awards includes the *Career Development* or *K Awards* (NIH, 2010d). There are a large number of different types of K Awards. Their primary goal is to support released time for recipients to pursue their research activities. The K Awards can go to researchers at any stage of their careers, from new researchers trying to establish their program of research to senior researchers with large and productive established laboratories. Specific K Awards differ greatly in the amount and duration of support. (Interested readers may visit http://grants.nih.gov/training/careerdevelopmentawards.htm for more information about K Awards that would be most appropriate for them.)

Scientific review. As discussed, the NIH review process is intended to be totally independent of the institutes and centers that fund the research. There is, of course, some disagreement about whether this is the best way for NIH to operate because, as also mentioned, the projects that a scientific review panel believes are important may not be the ones that an institute is interested in funding. For the foreseeable future, however, this is the way that NIH will solicit, review, and fund research applications.

Once an application has an institute sponsor, it is assigned to a study section, which typically includes 20 or more researchers. They are "recognized authorities in their field . . . [who are already] PIs [principal investigators] on a project comparable to those being reviewed" (CSR, 2009). A large number of study sections span the range of basic, clinical, social, and biobehavioral health research (CSR, 2010). Although assignment to a study section is made by the CSR, applicants can look at the list of study sections and the rosters of their members and suggest a specific study section in a cover letter that accompanies a grant application. Sometimes these suggestions are followed; sometimes they are not.

After identifying any conflicts of interest among the section members, the scientific review officer, who runs the panel, assigns each application to three or four reviewers who are members of the study section panel. Ideally, the assignments are given on the basis of a reviewer's expertise in the area of the application.

In their initial evaluations, the reviewers independently rate each application on "overall impact" and five other discrete criteria (see explanations in the following sections). A week or so before their study section's meeting, reviewers electronically submit their ratings and written comments relevant to each criterion to the CSR. The individual reviewers do not know how other reviewers have rated the application when they submit their evaluations. The scores and comments are posted on a reviewer website a few days before the meeting, and reviewers are encouraged to look at the other reviewers' scores and written evaluations.

At the study section meetings, applications are reviewed within grant categories (i.e., R01, R21). Within those categories, the order in which they are reviewed is determined by the preliminary ratings of overall impact that are averaged across the independent reviewers. Each reviewer presents his or her initial ratings, the primary reviewer discusses the application, and then the other reviewers present their evaluations. Other members of the study section make comments or ask questions. The reviewers then are asked for their ratings again. Following this, all members of a section rate the overall application. The average of these ratings is the application's "impact" or "priority" score. Typically, after about half of the applications in a category have been discussed and final ratings have been assigned, the scientific review officer or panel chair asks the members of the study section whether they want to stop reviewing in this category or whether a member thinks any individual applications also should be reviewed. Any application then can be reviewed. If none is proposed for review, the review process in that category ends. Only applications that are discussed and rated by the entire panel receive priority or impact scores, which are later converted to percentiles (see following section).

The *rating criteria* system that is used to evaluate and score applications changed in the fall of 2009. At the time that this chapter is being written, the

new system has been used in two review cycles. It is certainly possible that it may be modified somewhat by the time this volume is published. Thus, we strongly urge readers to ensure that the information provided here is accurate and up-to-date at the time of their application.

Applications are rated on overall impact and on five individual review criterion. Each criterion is presented in the following paragraphs; the descriptions come directly from documents prepared by NIH for applicants and reviewers (NIH, 2010b).

Overall impact addresses the question, "What is the likelihood that this project conducted by these investigators in their environment, with this level of innovation and the proposed approaches, will have a sustained powerful influence on the research field?" (NIH, 2010b). The rating of overall impact is *not* an average of the other ratings. Rather, it is a distinct criterion evaluated on the basis of a reviewer's assessment of the application after a consideration of the other review criteria that may be relevant to a specific application. The remaining criteria, in the order in which they rated, are significance, investigators, innovation, approach, and environment:

The rating of *significance* is determined by the answer to the following question:

> Does the project address an important problem or a critical barrier to progress in the field? If the aims of the project are achieved, how will scientific knowledge, technical capability, and/or clinical practice be improved? How will successful completion of the aims change the concepts, methods, technologies, treatments, services, or preventative interventions that drive this field? (NIH, 2010b)

The rating of significance assumes that the project will be successfully completed.

The criteria for evaluating *investigators* relate to the following question: "Are the PD [project director]/PIs, collaborators, and other researchers well suited to the project?" (NIH, 2010b). The evaluations of investigator qualifications for new or early stage investigators focus primarily on their training and experience. For established investigators, the issue is whether they have demonstrated an ongoing record of accomplishments that have advanced their field.

Reviewers also rate proposals on *innovation*. The questions are as follows:

> Does the application challenge and seek to shift current research or clinical practice paradigms by utilizing novel theoretical concepts, approaches or methodologies, instrumentation, or interventions? Are the concepts, approaches or methodologies, instrumentation, or interventions novel to one field of research or novel in a broad sense? (NIH, 2010b)

Another aspect of evaluation is the *approach* adopted in the proposal:

> Are the overall strategy, methodology, and analyses well-reasoned and appropriate to accomplish the specific aims of the project? Are potential problems, alternative strategies, and benchmarks for success presented? If the project is in the early stages of development, will the strategy establish feasibility and will particularly risky aspects be managed? (NIH, 2010b)

In addition, reviewers assess the research *environment*. This evaluation involves asking, "Will the scientific environment in which the work will be done contribute to the probability of success? Are the institutional support, equipment and other physical resources available to the investigators adequate for the project proposed?" (NIH, 2010b). Will the project benefit from unique features of the scientific environment, subject populations, or collaborative arrangements?

Reviewers use a 9-point rating scale to assess overall impact and on each of the five criteria. Ratings of 1 through 3 are reserved for applications likely to have a *high impact*; 4 through 6, for *medium impact*; and 7 through 9 a *low impact*. Within these three groupings, applications are differentiated in terms of strengths and weaknesses.

In addition, the reviewers evaluate the potential risk and the adequacy of protections against these risks as well as the inclusion of women, minorities, and children. If the application is a resubmission, reviewers also comment on how well or poorly the application addresses the previous review. After the final round of scores is recorded for an application, the reviewers can, if they wish, comment on the proposed budget and amount of time that is allocated for the project. These aspects are discussed after the scoring process is concluded because budget concerns are not included in the scoring decisions. Beyond identifying any specific budgetary concerns, reviewers are explicitly prohibited from commenting on whether a project should be funded or an amount of funding.

Ratings by individual reviewers are restricted to whole numbers on the 1-to-9 scales, but, of course, average scores across reviewers are likely to contain decimals. To make things simpler, the scores are multiplied by 10. Then the raw scores for those applications that were discussed and scored by a study section (remember, about half of the applications that are received by a study section may not be discussed or scored) are converted to percentiles on the basis of the scores given to other applications in the same category during the past three rounds of reviews. If a study section reviews more than 25 R01 applications, then its scores are the basis for the *percentiling*. If the section reviews fewer than 25 R01 applications, then the scores of all study sections are used as the basis for the percentiling.

It is the percentile score that determines whether an application is eligible for funding by an institute or center. The percentile that is eligible for funding will differ across centers. For example, the 20th percentile (better than 79% of the scored applications) might make an application eligible at one institute, but it may need to be at the 10th percentile at another institute to be eligible for funding. Funding is not guaranteed, however, even if your application receives a very good percentile score. An institute has the option of not funding an eligible application because it does not fit with its mission, goals, or priorities. So, a good percentile score is a necessary but not sufficient condition for funding. Further information on the scoring process can be found at the *Scoring System and Procedure* (NIH, 2010i) website provided in the reference section of this chapter.

The application. Nearly all applications to NIH are now submitted electronically (instructions for electronic submission can be found at http://era.nih.gov/ElectronicReceipt/submit_app.htm). The form for most electronic submissions is the new SF424; the old PHS 398 is used for paper submissions. The NIH provides specific information about the new application format at their website (http://grants.nih.gov/grants/funding/424/index.htm#inst).

In this chapter, we do not discuss how to prepare a budget for an NIH application or related administrative issues because these issues are beyond our expertise and because institutions vary greatly in how they prepare budgets and the level of support they provide for grant applications. These aspects of a grant application are extremely important and often require knowledge and expertise not possessed by the typical academic researcher. Thus, we urge researchers who are preparing applications to establish contact early in the process with their institution's Office of Sponsored Research, grants specialists, or department that deals with preparing and managing grant applications. Applications are not submitted by principal investigator (PIs), but rather by their institutions. Grant awards are made to the institution not to the PI. Several stages of institutional approval typically are required, so researchers should allow ample time before the NIH submission deadline for review and approval within their institution.

In the SF424 form, three narrative sections directly address the overall impact and the significance, innovation, and approach criteria. These are the project description or abstract, specific aims, and research strategy.

The *abstract* is a short summary (30 lines or less) of the proposed project. It is likely to be what program officers read when deciding whether they will sponsor an application and almost certainly one of the first things that a reviewer will read.

The *specific aims* section is similar to the abstract but longer (one page, single spaced) and more detailed. It always is read by the reviewers, and this is where the applicant must be especially persuasive about the scientific or clinical value of the project. In the specific aims section, applicants should clearly identify the problem or issue that the grant addresses and make a persuasive case for the importance of studying it. In this section, the investigators provide the aims or goals of the project (i.e., state what the grant will accomplish) and present specific research hypotheses related to the purpose of the study and its aims (Russell & Morrison, 2010). Conventional wisdom is that if an applicant has not sold an application in the abstract and specific aims, it is unlikely that it will find support from an institute or receive a favorable evaluation from the reviewers.

The major portion of the new grant application is the *research strategy* section. This portion of an application now has serious page limitations (e.g., 12 pages for an R01; six pages for a R21). The sections of the research strategy parallel the new review criteria. Specifically, they include (a) significance: "Explain the importance of the problem or critical barrier to progress in the field that the proposed project addresses"; (b) innovation: "Explain how the application challenges and seeks to shift current research or clinical practice paradigms"; and (c) approach: "Describe the overall strategy, methodology, and analyses to be used to accomplish the specific aims of the project. . . . Include how the data will be collected, analyzed, and interpreted" and "discuss potential problems, alternative strategies, and benchmarks for success anticipated to achieve the aims" (NIH, 2010j).

There are no established guidelines for how long each of the three sections should be, and the application format is still quite new, so we think that it would be premature to offer specific advice as to the length of these sections. R01 applications previously allowed for 25 pages for the research narrative, and conventional wisdom was that they needed to be as detailed as possible, with every *i* dotted and *t* crossed. It is currently less clear what will be the best strategy in preparing the new applications. NIH's intention was to improve the quality of the review process (and reduce the load on reviewers) by limiting the amount of background detail and focusing on conceptual, and especially operational, issues relevant to the proposed project. The first round of reviews with the new format will occur about 6 months after this chapter is being written; thus, any strategic tips that we might provide could turn out to be quite wrong. On the basis of our experiences as applicants and reviewers, however, we offer a few general suggestions.

Only about 50% of applications will be reviewed, and only a small percentage of those will receive a fundable score (when translated into percentiles). Moreover, only one resubmission is now allowed. This is unlike a journal article, where a request to revise and resubmit is a fairly encouraging evaluation. Thus, the amount of preparation and editing that is needed for an application far exceeds that which normally is done for a journal article. An application needs to be carefully read by as many people as possible and carefully proofread before submission. As one fellow reviewer said about a typo-filled application, "If they are this sloppy with the application, how will they carry out the actual research?"

The application needs to stand on its own. By this we mean that an applicant should not assume that the reviewers will know who they are or, more important, be familiar with the problem of interest, the research approach one is taking, or the way in which data will be analyzed. We have been extremely impressed with the care and thought displayed by members of study sections, but the simple fact is that the assigned reviewers, although they are accomplished researchers, may not be accomplished in the specific area of your application. Like everyone else who has submitted an application, we have railed about the ignorance and biases of our reviewers, but the truth is that if a reviewer is confused about the importance of a project or does not understand the research approach an applicant has taken, that is the applicant's problem, not the reviewer's fault.

One strategy that we use to address this problem, which is also recommended by many program officers at NIH, is to present a theoretical or conceptual model early in the application, and, when possible, provide a diagram of the model (Jeffrey, 2009; Reid & Kobrin, 2009). Readers who are interested in further specific advice on writing a successful application should consult with the office of sponsored research at their institution or locate grant-writing workshops at their own or other institutions.

There are no sections of the application with the specific labels *investigators* and *environment* that are elements of the rating criteria. Nevertheless, parts of

the application do speak to these two criteria. The qualifications of investigators are probably most directly addressed in the individual biosketches that are a required part of an application and the sections on key personnel and personnel justification. In the previous application format, one could provide information on the PI and coinvestigators in the preliminary studies section. The new application does not have a section specifically devoted to preliminary studies. But it is suggested that the project director's and PI's preliminary studies, data, or experience pertinent to this application be included in the approach section. This provides yet another opportunity to present information about the prior work of the investigators, information that would seem especially important for new and early stage investigators. The environment criterion is addressed by responses to sections in the application on facilities and other resources and equipment sections, and it is advisable to address briefly any salient aspects of the environment in the approach section, as well.

In addition to the information that is provided in these 12 pages, the application also has sections on protecting participants from possible risks; the inclusion of women, minorities, and children (NIH considers participants under 20 to be children); and planned enrollment (i.e., how many men and women from different racial or ethnic groups). This information is not used in scoring, but it is considered during reviews. Problems with these sections may result in a *hold* (a formal delay in funding) being placed on the funding of an application. Removal of a hold requires an extensive explanation of why the hold is not justified or how the problems will be addressed. It is not a foregone conclusion that all holds will be removed or removed soon enough to have the grant begin in a timely manner.

As we have pointed out, fewer than half of the initial investigator-initiated applications to NIH will be scored, and many fewer than that will receive a score that makes them eligible for funding. Thus, most applicants will have to do a resubmission (formerly called an *amended version*). Remember, NIH now allows only one resubmission. The critical aspect of a resubmission is the introduction to the resubmitted application. This is a one- to three-page document (depending on the grant mechanism) in which the PI addresses the specific concerns of the reviewers. To best prepare an introduction, (a) present all of the reviewers' concerns as close to verbatim as possible, (b) address each point by clearly explaining what you did in response to that concern, and (c) refer the reader to the specific text in the new application. Obviously, if the reviewer misunderstood something or overlooked some material, one should clarify where the material is located. There is little point, however, in arguing with reviewers or refusing to make changes that easily could be made. You may feel that you stuck to your guns, but this feeling will not fund your research. The purpose of the introduction is to show how responsive you are to the reviewers' suggestions. Indeed, a section in the reviewers' form asks them to comment on the resubmission.

Obtaining funding. The percentage of NIH applications that are funded can vary substantially across institutes and centers. As we have said several times, funded applications will be those that are sponsored by an institute that receive a very good percentile score. A very good percentile score, however, does not automatically guarantee that an application will be funded. The final step is review by a council or panel within the sponsoring institute. In most instances, institutes fund projects in the order of their priority scores, but they are not required to do so. This is another place in which program officers can be quite valuable. They usually can tell you what percentile score is fundable in their institute or program and alert you to any problems that might exist with your application. The councils' decisions usually occur within a month or so of the time one receives scores on his or her application. The transfer of funds to your institution can take several months. Most important, do not expect that your application will be funded at the level you requested. For a variety of reasons, such as guidelines within NIH, seemingly inflated budgets, or a desire to fund more proposals, grants are supported at funding levels less than what was originally requested.

The National Science Foundation

NSF, created by Congress in 1950, is the second largest U.S. government research funding agency, next to NIH. As we have reported, NSF's annual budget is much smaller than that of NIH, but in the 2010 fiscal year, NSF received a much larger proportional increase than did NIH (6.7% vs. 2.3%). In addition, with an annual budget of about $7 billion, the NSF is a major funding source for research scientists. NSF funds about 20% of all federally supported basic research conducted by U.S. colleges and universities. It annually supports approximately 200,000 scientists, engineers, educators, and students in the United States and around the world.

The mission and organization of NSF. The stated mission of NSF is "to promote the progress of science; to advance the national health, prosperity, and welfare; to secure the national defense" (NSF, 2010c). Whereas the various institutes within NIH often have specific applied health-related missions, NSF emphasizes basic research—that is, research that addresses fundamental theoretical issues, but that may not have an immediate practical impact. It is a major source of funding in mathematics, computer science, and the social sciences. NSF also supports "'high risk, high pay off' ideas, novel collaborations, and numerous projects that may seem like science fiction today, but which the public will take for granted tomorrow" (NSF, 2009). The mandate of NSF does not include medical fields of research directly, but it does include basic research in the physical, natural, and behavioral sciences that are relevant to health and medicine. NSF receives more than 42,000 proposals per year and funds approximately 20% of these projects.

NSF includes seven directorates that represent several different disciplines. These directorates are (a) biological sciences (molecular, cellular, and organismal biology, environmental science); (b) computer and information science and engineering (fundamental computer science, computer and networking systems, and artificial intelligence); (c) engineering (bioengineering, environmental systems, civil and mechanical systems, chemical and transport systems, electrical and communications systems, and design and manufacturing); (d) geosciences (geological, atmospheric, and ocean sciences); (e) mathematical and physical sciences (mathematics, astronomy, physics, chemistry, and materials science); (f) education and human resources (science, technology, engineering, and mathematics education at every level); and (g) social, behavioral, and economic sciences (neuroscience, management, psychology, sociology, anthropology, linguistics, and economics).

One can electronically search for the kinds of projects that NSF is interested in funding by using The Find Funding function on the NSF website (http://www.nsf.gov/funding). In addition, NSF often has program solicitations that encourage the submission of proposals in specific topics of interest. Solicitations are usually more focused than program announcements, and normally apply for a limited period of time.

NSF grant mechanisms. Researchers most commonly seek support from NSF for specific research projects, analogous to R01 grants from NIH. In general, NSF awards are often smaller in scope than NIH awards—in total funding, in the number of years supported, and in the kind of support provided (e.g., teaching release in some programs). The nature of NSF research awards are otherwise comparable to those of NIH, although the specific types of research projects that are funded will differ because of the agencies' different missions.

The CAREER Program at NSF supports basic research activities among researchers at various stages of their career and in a range of professional contexts. The CAREER Program supports the early development of academic faculty as both educators and researchers and is intended to foster the integration of research and education components of a faculty career. These awards are akin to the K Awards from NIH.

In addition, NSF has a specific program for supporting research among faculty who teach at "predominantly undergraduate" colleges. *Research in Undergraduate Institutions* (RUI) grants support (a) individual and collaborative research projects, (b) the purchase of shared-use research instrumentation, and (c) opportunities for faculty at these colleges to work with NSF-supported researchers at other institutions. Each of the NSF directorates supports RUI activities. These awards are somewhat similar to the R15 awards from NIH.

NSF also supports undergraduate and graduate education directly. *The Research Experience for Undergraduates* (REU) program supports active and meaningful involvement in research by undergraduate students in any of the areas normally funded by NSF. REU grants are awarded to initiate and conduct projects that engage a number of students in research from the host institutions and as well as other colleges. NSF also provides graduate research fellowships for outstanding graduate students and the directorate for Social, Behavioral, and Economic Sciences (SBE) offers minority postdoctoral research fellowships.

All funding opportunities within NSF are announced on the NSF website (http://www.nsf.gov) and on the Grants.gov website (http://www.grants.gov). Proposals to NSF must conform to the procedures and format outlined in the *Grant Proposal Guide* (NSF, 2010b). Contact with NSF program personnel before proposal preparation and submission is permitted and encouraged. Proposals normally are submitted electronically.

Merit review. NSF grants that conform to the guidelines for applications proceed to the merit review stage. The grant proposals are sent to outside reviewers who have relevant expertise on the topic. Reviewers are asked to evaluate the proposal on two criteria: intellectual merit and broader impact. *Intellectual merit* is an evaluation of the importance of the proposed activity "to advancing knowledge and understanding within its own field or across different fields," and judgments of the extent to which the project is "well conceived and organized" and explores "creative, original, or potentially transformative concepts" (NSF, 2002). Intellectual merit also incorporates an assessment of the investigator's qualifications for successfully conducting the research.

The second criterion, *broader impact*, is the extent to which the project promotes "teaching, training, and learning"; broadens "the participation of underrepresented groups (e.g., gender, ethnicity, disability, geographic, etc.)"; enhances the infrastructure for research and education; produces results that can "be disseminated broadly to enhance scientific and technological understanding"; and benefits society (NSF, 2002). Each reviewer (normally three) makes a summary rating on a 5-point scale (1 = *excellent*, 2 = *very good*, 3 = *good*, 4 = *fair*, 5 = *poor*).

Following the initial reviews, proposals are evaluated by standing NSF panels, which are composed of scholars who, as a group, have the expertise that is necessary to evaluate the range of projects submitted to a particular program. The panel reads the external reviewers' comments on an application before it begins its review process. One panel member with highly relevant expertise is assigned to be the primary panel reviewer, who submits an individual assessment before the panel meets; another is asked to be the secondary panel reviewer. For the panel meetings, the primary reviewer prepares a brief synopsis and recommendation for the proposal. The secondary reviewer provides supplementary remarks. Proposals that receive a rating of "very good" or higher from at least one reviewer are discussed by the entire panel.

At the end of the panel discussion of a proposal, the primary and secondary reviewers propose a classification for funding (high, moderate, or low) or do not recommend funding. (Note how this differs from NIH in which reviewers are explicitly prohibited from discussing funding.) One panel member is assigned the role of recording and summarizing key elements of the panel evaluation and feedback. When all of the proposals have been discussed, panel members are given the opportunity to propose a reclassification of any proposal and to prioritize projects within each category of support. The comments and rankings of the review panel are recommendations to the program officer; the panel does not make the funding decisions.

The program officer for NSF considers the recommendation and discussions of the review panel, but also may include other factors, such as the transformative potential of the project or particular program objectives, in making funding decisions. The program officer evaluates projects in light of previously funded projects. Whereas the panel review focuses on the merits of each proposal individually, the program officer adopts a broader perspective on how a specific project is related to other projects that currently are being funded. After scientific, technical,

and programmatic review, and after consideration of appropriate factors, the program officer makes a funding recommendation to the division director. If the division director concurs, the recommendation is submitted to the Division of Grants and Agreements for award processing. Like NIH grants, NSF grants include both direct costs and indirect costs, computed on the basis of an existing agreement between the PI's institution and the government.

Proposals. As was the case with our discussion of NIH applications, we discuss only the narrative portions of a NSF proposal. The proposal must contain a project summary; it is more similar to the specific aims portion of a NIH application than an abstract. It must speak to the two NSF merit review criteria—intellectual merit of the proposed activity and broader impact. It also needs to include a statement of objectives and methods to be used. It cannot exceed one page.

The other major portion of the proposal is the project description, which can be up to 15 pages in length (although brevity is encouraged). Overall, the NSF project description is somewhat less structured than the NIH research approach section. In the project description, however, the PI needs to clearly explain the proposed work, its expected significance, its relation to present knowledge in the field, and its relation to the PI's current and future research. It should describe the general plan of work, including the broad design of activities to be undertaken, and, when appropriate, include a clear description of the experimental methods and procedures that will be used. Despite differences in the NSF and NIH application formats, the guidelines for writing an attractive application (e.g., making sure it can stand on its own, presenting a model) generally apply to both agencies.

Like the NIH review process, the application must include biosketches of major research personnel. A proposal that is declined by NSF may be resubmitted, but only after it has been substantially revised, and it must directly address concerns made by the previous reviewers (NSF, 2010b). As is the case with NIH applications, the PI can expect that successful applications will be awarded less money than the amount initially requested.

INTERNAL RESOURCES

Now we turn to a consideration of the kinds of internal resources needed to support productive research activities. As noted, all three authors have served as department chairs; Albrecht currently is an associate center director at a medical research institute, and Dovidio was a university provost. As part of our roles in these positions, we spent considerable time evaluating what kinds of resources faculty members need to successfully carry out their research programs and then trying to obtain such resources. These experiences inform this section of the chapter.

We take a broad perspective on the different kinds of resources that are needed to support a productive research program. One of the realities of psychology in the 21st century is that research psychologists' needs probably vary more now than at any time in the history of the discipline. Thus, it would be absurd to make statements about specific kinds of resources when some psychologists need questionnaires and appropriate computer software for data analysis, others need an animal colony and a surgical suite, and still others use neuroimaging devices. Thus, we describe some important internal resources, but we will not be specific in this regard. We consider two general types of support. One is one-time-only support, typically provided as start-up funds at the beginning of employment. The other is ongoing support that will facilitate researchers' abilities to attract external funding.

Start-Up Funds

For most psychologists, the most significant allocation of internal resources will be a one-time award of start-up funds when they first join the faculty at their institution. Correctly deciding what resources to ask for can be a difficult task for senior faculty who are moving from one institution to another; but it can be a serious or even overwhelming task for junior faculty who are taking their first permanent position. We briefly review some of the resources that we believe should be considered when requesting internal support for one's research program. We offer three general pieces of advice. First, do not assume that every resource that you had at your prior institution will be available in your new position. Second, be honest and realistic in asking for the start-up funds that you need. It is important to understand that you and the institution in which you secured your new position are both invested in your success. Hiring someone but not giving him or her resources to succeed is a bad institutional investment. In addition, as we mentioned, start-up funds are a form of venture capital that permit researchers to conduct the kinds of preliminary studies that make grant applications more compelling. At the same time, it would be institutionally irresponsible to commit resources unnecessarily, particularly in the current economic climate. Thus, in asking for resources, you need to strike a delicate balance between being assertive and protecting your ability to conduct research and not appearing to be (or actually being) avaricious and greedy. Third, get a written commitment from the institution to provide the agreed-on resources. You can consider several types of resources in start-up discussions. These resources include space, equipment, computers and computer software, research assistants, access to research participants, and human subjects review.

Irrespective of the nature of one's research program, a researcher needs *space* that is specific to his or her research program. The need for space is not restricted to laboratories in which participants are involved in experiments, or to laboratories that require wet labs or use complex equipment to observe and record physiological responses. Even researchers who conduct questionnaire studies need space for several reasons. One is that faculty with a significant teaching responsibility need a place where they can plan studies, develop study materials, and analyze their results without significant or frequent interruptions, and to store data and other confidential documents. Faculty members who conduct their research out of the same office where they meet with students, interact with colleagues, and engage in other nonresearch activities frequently can be interrupted, and this is not conducive to a productive research program. Moreover, it is not fair to students if they believe that the faculty member is preoccupied with research rather than attending to their concerns. In addition, the confidentiality of data may be compromised. Ideally, space should include offices for one's research assistants. This gives them a sense of identification with the research team, the opportunity to informally and formally exchange research ideas, and to participate in research meetings easily.

The question of whether researchers should have dedicated space to run their own experiments is a difficult one. As former department chairs, we constantly confronted the problem that single researchers, even productive ones, actually conduct experiments in their assigned space a relatively small percentage of the time. If one's research does not require special equipment that cannot be easily moved, then we would urge consideration of common research space for experiments that could be shared by several researchers. Each researcher who shares the space would have dedicated office space for the research team. This arrangement, of course, is not possible or advisable for laboratories that conduct experiments that require dedicated space because of extensive equipment safety concerns or concerns about protecting the rights of participants.

In addition to space, many laboratories require specialized equipment to conduct research successfully. Such equipment may include sophisticated video recording systems, freezers for storing biological specimens, physiological recording equipment, or a host of other devices. Obviously, one needs to be sure that the necessary equipment is provided, but it is advisable to inquire about purchasing procedures at the institution (e.g., how many different entities must approve a purchase and whether purchases can be made on an institutional credit card), vendor restrictions, and other issues that may affect how easily and quickly a piece of equipment can be purchased. Accompanying the issue of purchasing specialized equipment is whether personnel within the institution can properly install and maintain the equipment or whether such services are provided by outside contractors.

It seems rather obvious that researchers need computers and computer software to carry out their research program. The question is not whether to request such equipment but how much to request and who pays for it. Research grants often support computers that are necessary for data acquisition but are not needed for more general research use.

Before requesting a certain number of computers for a lab, find out whether any resources are provided independently from grants and start-up funds. For example, an office computer may not be automatically given to all new faculty members; it may have to be purchased with start-up funds.

Computer software is a related resource. Almost all research facilities either provide computer software to their faculty or have licenses that permit the purchase of such software, but not all institutions support the same software and there are substantial differences in how the software is purchased. For example, some institutions pay for an overall site license for SPSS, and researchers have free access to it. Other institutions require that individual faculty purchase new SPSS software each year.

One must also consider the level of technical support for hardware and software. The critical issue is the organizational arrangement for providing support. Is information technology (IT) support centralized, or does each unit within the entire organization have its own IT and hardware support staff? The latter will almost always be more accessible, but when the staff are local, it might be advisable to inquire about their experience and the depth and breadth of their expertise.

It is almost impossible to have a productive research laboratory without research assistants. In most instances, faculty members are provided with some resources to employ such assistants, but they also must recruit assistants from different sources. In evaluating this resource, one must consider the skill and expertise of the people in various employment pools. As an obvious example, if the institution does not offer postgraduate degrees, then one will have to use undergraduates in his or her laboratory or recruit assistants from other postgraduate institutions in the area. Irrespective of the source of assistants, one must consider how easy it is to recruit them (e.g., does the institution offer course credit for research assistants?) and any hidden costs (e.g., does a graduate student's employer have to cover the student's tuition?).

If one conducts research with humans, the participant pool is an important resource. This is true whether potential participants are students at an educational institution or patients at a medical facility. Almost all colleges and universities allow research with their undergraduate students, but they may differ as to whether research experience is required or optional, the quality of the system used to recruit participants in research projects, and how many students are available for research. For example, if one is at a commuter school, a large percentage of students may be working full or part time and may not be available for research participation outside of their class hours. Medical institutions may differ greatly in terms of how easy or difficult it is to access patients for research, especially research that is not medical and does not produce clinical benefits for the patients. Also, in most instances in which research is conducted within a medical facility, physicians are also participants in the research. Institutions may differ greatly about the norms with regard to physicians agreeing to be research participants.

One critical aspect of behavioral research in medical settings is regulations for approaching patients under the requirements of the Health Insurance Portability and Accountability Act of 1996 (HIPAA; see Barnes & Kulynych, 2003). One of the major provisions of HIPAA is that only people with clinical relationships with patients can directly approach them and recruit them for research. If followed to the precise letter of HIPAA, this creates an enormous barrier in access to patients. There are legal and ethical ways to address to the HIPAA regulations without having all contact with patients mediated through clinical staff, but it is something that a researcher needs to examine carefully when considering establishing a laboratory in a medical setting.

Any institution that receives federal funding and conducts research must have some sort of institutional review of the research to ensure that it complies with relevant federal (and sometimes state) rules for the appropriate and ethical conduct of research with humans and other animals. We only consider research with humans because animal research requirements are beyond our expertise. (More information about research with nonhuman animals can be found in Chapter 4 of this volume.) The mechanism for review of human research is the institutional review board (IRB). Without the board's approval, the research cannot be conducted. Although IRBs generally attempt to conform to a widely accepted set of principles, the procedures, emphases, and interpretations of IRBs vary substantially across institutions. Thus, it is important for researchers to examine and to understand the policies and practices of an institution's IRB.

In addition to start-up funding, which is normally a one-time commitment of funds, institutions often have ongoing programs to support research. These programs generally provide seed money for pilot projects that can lead to successful external grants. In addition, institutions can provide support for attempts to obtain external support in a number of other ways.

Resources to Facilitate External Support

As we suggested in the first section of this chapter, applying for external support requires considerable help from one's home institution. Institutions vary greatly, however, in how much help they provide before an application is submitted and the way that they work with a PI after an application is awarded. In an era in which external support is expected of most faculty members, it is critical for faculty to evaluate what kinds of resources are provided to those seeking grants and to those who receive them. An applicant with good preaward support has some significant advantages over one with poor preaward support. For instance, some institutions have support staff devoted to helping researchers develop budgets and prepare proposals in appropriate formats for submission. The absence of good postaward administrative support makes it difficult to carry out a funded research project.

Institutions also vary substantially in the degree to which and ways in which they encourage and support new research initiatives. Many institutions have small-grant programs that support new research initiatives and pilot projects. This funding is a form of venture capital, often tied to the expectation that recipients will follow up their internal grant by submitting a long-term proposal to an external agency for funding. Researchers who rely on external support for their research should consider what the institution's policies and practices are on cost sharing (a situation in which the institution contributes some portion of the costs that are necessary to conduct a research project, which will not be reimbursed by the external sponsor of the project), bridge funding (support to pay for continuing a research project after one grant ends and another begins), and overhead rebate (a percentage of the indirect costs that researchers may receive for scholarly activities). Finally, institutions are sometimes willing to negotiate a lower than normal overhead rate to demonstrate strong institutional support for a grant application and PI. In addition, some RFAs may set a budget cap on the total costs that the PI can request to support a grant. In this instance, total costs include indirect costs. The institution might reduce the indirect rate that it normally charges so that the amount of the direct costs that can be requested is larger.

CONCLUSION

We believe that this chapter will be useful to researchers who do not have a great deal of experience in obtaining external and internal support for their research. No magic formulae or insider tips guarantee success. No amount of familiarity with the NIH or NSF funding processes will make up for a poor conceptualization of a research problem or an unclear exposition of the research plan. To paraphrase an old joke, there are three secrets to success in obtaining external funding: hard work, hard work, and hard work. And a critical part of the hard work is persistence. Few, if any, readers of this chapter will receive funding for an initial application. Thus, the critical question is what will they do if they have not been funded? If researchers resubmit their application and the project still is not funded, what then will they do? The same application with some changes cannot be submitted again, but related research projects that approach the question of interest in a different manner are possible. Thus, it may take several different attempts before one obtains external funding. In sum, obtaining external funding often involves a long process of establishing a worthwhile program of research, seeking support for this research, constructively dealing with failure to receive funding, and then finding new and creative ways to improve the probability that the next application will be funded. It is our strong belief that despite the time and effort required, seeking external funding is a worthwhile endeavor.

It is somewhat easier, at least initially, to obtain internal support for one's research. Continuing support, however, requires awareness of the same three secrets mentioned above. Start-up packages are used to attract promising faculty members, but they are not the proverbial free lunch. Faculty who receive large start-up packages or internal grants but do not produce by publishing and attracting external support are unlikely to continue to receive internal support.

Finally, some people may criticize the recent push for external funding at most research institutions as an inherent threat to high-quality research; we do not agree with this criticism. One can do good research on important problems and attract external funding. The researcher must, of course, not let the pursuit of funding diminish or compromise the quality of the science. We believe that this is not only possible, but in many instances, presenting one's research ideas for external evaluation likely will improve their quality. Seeking external (or internal) support for one's research is an important and necessary part of psychological research efforts in the 21st century.

References

Barnes, M., & Kulynych, J. (2003). *HIPAA and human subjects research: A question and answer reference guide.* Media, PA: Barnett Educational Services.

Center for Scientific Review. (2009). *About CSR.* Retrieved from http://cms.csr.nih.gov/AboutCSR

Jeffrey, D. (2009, May). *Writing a seamless grant application.* Paper presented at the New Investigator Workshop, National Cancer Institute, Washington, DC.

National Institute of Mental Health. (2009). *Requests for applications.* Retrieved from http://www.nimh.nih.gov/research-funding/grants/requests-for-applications.shtml

National Institutes of Health. (2010a). *About NIH.* Retrieved from http://www.nih.gov/about

National Institutes of Health. (2010b). *Enhancing peer review at NIH.* Retrieved from http://enhancing-peer-review.nih.gov/restructured_applications.html

National Institutes of Health. (2010c). *Exploratory/developmental research grant award (R21).* Retrieved from http://grants.nih.gov/grants/funding/r21.htm

National Institutes of Health. (2010d). *K kiosk information about NIH career development awards.* Retrieved from http://grants.nih.gov/training/careerdevelopmentawards.htm

National Institutes of Health. (2010e). *NIH academic research enhancement award (AREA) grants (R15)*. Retrieved from http://grants.nih.gov/grants/funding/area.htm

National Institutes of Health. (2010f). *NIH organization*. Retrieved from http://www1.od.nih.gov/oma/manualchapters/management/1123/nih.pdf

National Institutes of Health. (2010g). *NIH research project grant program (R01)*. Retrieved from http://grants.nih.gov/grants/funding/r01.htm

National Institutes of Health. (2010h). *NIH small grant program (R03)*. Retrieved from http://grants.nih.gov/grants/funding/r03.htm

National Institutes of Health. (2010i). *Scoring system and procedure*. Retrieved from http://grants2.nih.gov/grants/peer/guidelines_general/scoring_system_and_procedure.pdf

National Institutes of Health. (2010j). *SF424 (R&R) application and electronic submission information*. Retrieved from http://grants.nih.gov/grants/funding/424/index.htm

National Institutes of Health. (n.d.). *Enacted appropriations for FY 2008–FY 2010*. Retrieved from http://officeofbudget.od.nih.gov/pdfs/FY11/FY%202010%20Enacted%20Appropriations.pdf

National Science Foundation. (2002). *NSF proposal processing and review*. Retrieved from http://www.nsf.gov/pubs/2002/nsf022/nsf0202_3.html

National Science Foundation. (2009). *What we do*. Retrieved from http://www.nsf.gov/about/what.jsp

National Science Foundation. (2010a). *FY 2010 budget request*. Retrieved from http://www.nsf.gov/about/budget/fy2010/index.jsp

National Science Foundation. (2010b). *Grant proposal guide*. Retrieved from http://www.nsf.gov/publications/pub_summ.jsp?ods_key=GPG

National Science Foundation. (2010c). *NSF at a glance*. Retrieved from http://www.nsf.gov/about/glance.jsp

Reid, B., & Kobrin, S. (2009, May). *Common flaws in initial applications*. Paper presented at the New Investigator Workshop, National Cancer Institute, Washington, DC.

Russell, S. W., & Morrison, D. C. (2010). *The grant application writer's workbook*. Los Olivos, CA: Grant Writers' Seminars and Workshops.

Scarpa, T. (2006, May). *Challenges and opportunities in peer review*. Paper presented at Orientation for Study Sections Chairs, National Institutes of Health, U.S. Department of Health and Human Services, Houston, TX.

Zerhouni, E. A. (2006, November 17). NIH in the post-doubling era: Realities and strategies. *Science, 314,* 1088–1090. doi:10.1126/science.1136931

CHAPTER 10

PSYCHOLOGICAL MEASUREMENT: SCALING AND ANALYSIS

Heather Hayes and Susan E. Embretson

In any scientific discipline, theories are developed, tested, and cultivated for the purposes of understanding and predicting a phenomenon. To study the phenomenon, its primary characteristics and properties must be identified and defined in a manner conducive to measurement. Measurement has been defined in a number of ways, focusing on the object itself or its properties (Campbell, 1920; Russell, 1903; Stevens, 1946). For the purpose of this chapter, *measurement* refers specifically to the *properties* of an object or phenomenon rather than the object itself (Torgerson, 1958). For example, in physics, we are not necessarily interested in measuring subatomic particles but rather their mass, charge (positive, negative), and so on. The object of study in psychological sciences is people, and their properties of interest are inherently more complex and multidimensional. For example, observable properties often require specific, *operational* definitions; *aggression* may be defined as the intent to harm someone, either physically (e.g., hitting) or verbally (e.g., yelling or shouting insults). As we argue here, however, operational definitions are more conducive to narrowly defined observable properties, not latent phenomena such as cognitive processes, intelligence, or personality. The aggression example is probably best conceived as a latent trait.

Thus, in psychology we are not interested in measuring people per se but rather their psychological qualities or properties. These we refer to as *variables*. As such, the numbers that arise from measurement reflect the presence or magnitude of an object property and establish for us a scale of measurement and a range of values that reflect an object-related variable of interest. In other words, measurement is a system of rules for assigning numbers to the variable of interest such as developing a yardstick for assessing an object's (or respondent's) properties (variables). This process is critical to the social and behavioral sciences, as no substantive theory regarding how certain psychological properties interact or affect one another can be tested without first understanding the mathematical properties of values used to represent these variables (Michell, 1990). As stated in Michell (1997),

> Measurement always presupposes theory: the claim that an attribute is quantitative is, itself, always a theory and that claim is generally embedded within a much wider quantitative theory involving the hypothesis that specific quantitative relationships between attributes obtain. Because the hypothesis that any attribute (be it physical or psychological) is quantitative is a contingent, empirical hypothesis that may, in principle, be false, the scientist proposing such an hypothesis is always logically committed to the task of testing this claim whether this commitment is recognized or not. (p. 359)

Moreover, the object of measurement is crucial. Measurements can refer to properties of a respondent, a stimulus (e.g., specific features of a visual display, cognitive task, or test item) to which the respondent responds or reacts, or the intersection of

DOI: 10.1037/13619-011
APA Handbook of Research Methods in Psychology: Vol. 1. Foundations, Planning, Measures, and Psychometrics, H. Cooper (Editor-in-Chief)

these two objects as manifested as a response-focused measure. Thus, as elaborated on in the section Focus of Measurement and Testing, scales not only vary in terms of the relationships among values but also can be constructed for a variety of variable types—respondent, item, or the item response.

Related to the latter focus of scaling, a unique issue emerges in psychological science and testing—namely, the latent nature of many psychological properties, such as cognitive ability and motivation. Given the added complexity of measuring a variable that cannot be observed directly, operational definitions are difficult to construct and are largely inappropriate. Rather, a proxy for latent variable is constructed as a set of item scores that, hypothetically, statistically correlate with one another sufficiently to warrant a common, underlying factor that accounts for or explains all of the variance among item scores. Thus, establishing a reliable and valid system of measurement and assignment of value is crucial to adequately study latent psychological phenomena. As will be shown in the section Impact of Scale Level on Statistical Inferences in Latent Trait Measurement, *latent* psychological variables and the method of measuring and comparing these variables are particularly limited by the scales of measurement that are used—more so than for observed data (McDonald, 1999). Specifically, the extent to which a measurement scale reflects real numbers (arguably

defined as continuous or quantitative in nature) determines the extent to which these values can be mathematically manipulated to study the relationships among variables (Stevens, 1946; Townsend & Ashby, 1984). In other words, the type of analysis used to investigate the relationships among psychological properties needs to be aligned with the scale of measurement underlying these properties. Inappropriate analysis of data, given its scaling properties, can result in misleading conclusions, particularly for latent variable data (McDonald, 1999; Townsend & Ashby, 1984).

MEASUREMENT SCALES: REAL NUMBERS AND LEVELS OF MEASUREMENT

In psychology, the most well-known and frequently cited taxonomy of measurement scales is that of Stevens (1946). Alternative taxonomies have emerged (e.g., see Coombs, 1950; Torgerson, 1958). Indeed, it is arguable whether Stevens's taxonomy is appropriate, and, as demonstrated later in the section Theory and Measurement Paradigms, its validity has been disputed by several researchers (e.g., Gaito, 1980; Lord, 1953; and see Michell, 1986, 1990). Nevertheless, his taxonomy and ideas provided a basis for the development of further, modern measurement theory (Townsend & Ashby, 1984), and thus discussion of this taxonomy follows.

TABLE 10.1

Scale Levels

Axiomatic properties		Scale level	Permissible transformations	Permissible statistics
1	Either $a = b$ or $a \neq b$	Nominal	Isomorphic	Mode; contingency coefficient; chi-square
2	If $a = b$ then $b = a$			
3	If $a = b$ and $b = c$ then $a = c$			
4	If $a > b$ then a not $\leq b$	Ordinal	Monotonic	Median; Spearman correlations; interquartile range
5	If $a > b$ and $b > c$ then $a > c$			
6	$a + b = b + a$	Interval	Linear	Mean; standard deviation; Pearson correlations
7	If $a = c$ and $b = d$ then $a + b = c + d$			
8	$(a + b) + c = a(b + c)$			
9	$a + 0 = a$	Ratio	Ratio	Mean; standard deviation; Pearson correlations
10	If $a = c$ and $b > 0$ then $a + b > c$			

Stevens's (1946) taxonomy consists of four scale levels that differ from one another primarily in the number of axioms that hold for the numerical values of variables and, subsequently, the extent to which these differentially scaled values can be examined and mathematically manipulated (McDonald, 1999; Torgerson, 1958). These scale levels are shown in Table 10.1. Although the taxonomy has 10 axioms, they can be narrowed down to four categories on the basis of mathematical relations among the values within the scaled variable: (a) identity, (b) order, (c) additivity, and (d) null or origin (Hölder, 1901; McDonald, 1999).

Nominal Scale

The nominal scale of measurement is the most basic of the four levels. Scales at this level fulfill Axioms 1, 2, and 3. On the basis of these axioms, two objects measured on a nominal scale can be compared only in terms of whether they fall into the same or different categories (equality and inequality, respectively). In terms of variable representation, values take the form of exhaustive and mutually exclusive categories. Examples of observed nominal variables include gender, ethnicity, and treatment type as well as other properties for which a respondent belongs to only one of the available categories. Some latent variables are also categorical (e.g., Piaget's theory has several variables measuring conservation, and on each variable a respondent would either be a conserver or nonconserver, or possibly would be in a third category called *transitional*).

Given the equivalency rule and the limited information provided by this type of scale, comparisons among respondents on a variable such as personality type are relatively simplistic. Specifically, the most we can observe of data in which values are scaled as a nominal variable is two or more homogeneous groups or classes of individuals. That is, within nominal categories, there is no variance of numerical values. For example, all respondents in a given category (e.g., females, treatment group, personality type) are interpreted as being equivalent to one another in terms of the psychological property value, but all the individuals in one category are different (in value) from respondents in another category (e.g., males are different from females).

Nominal variables are described as *qualitative* in the sense that the variables reflect qualities, rather than amounts of a characteristic.

Nevertheless, the limited information results in greater flexibility when attempting to transform variable values. In fact, numbers need not be involved until coding is needed for multiple regression or other statistical models (e.g., Cohen, Cohen, West, & Aiken, 1983).

Ordinal Scale

Number values that meet the requirements of Axioms 4 and 5 (in addition to the identity axioms) can be classified as an ordinal level of measurement (see Table 10.1). These relationships among values are more complex than those of meeting the identity requirement because values can be ordered along a continuum, where the continuum corresponds with the property of interest. Thus, a dominance relation is established among any three distinct values *a*, *b*, and *c*, where *c* dominates (or is higher in value) than *b*, which in turn dominates *a*. Values of variables measuring physical objects dominate one another in some observable manner. For example, the length of rod A exceeds that of rod B when the two rods are placed side by side. The Moh's Hardness Scale has a range from 1 (*the softest mineral is talc*) to 10 (*the hardest mineral is diamond*). Hardness was determined on the basis of the extent to which each increasingly hard mineral scratched its predecessor. Examples of ordinal-scaled variables in psychology include attitudes and personality when item responses involve a Likert scale (i.e., an item that might range from 1 for *strongly disagree* to 5 for *strongly agree*).

The ordinal scale differs from the nominal scale primary in that categories are ordered in the former. The size of the difference between any given contiguous values is unknown. As a result of the latter characteristics of values at an ordinal level of measurement, transformation of variable values is more restricted than that of nominal variable values. Specifically, the transformation must preserve the ordering of values across respondents or objects. This is called a *monotonic transformation*. Ordinal scales, however, are somewhat flexible because the original values can be squared, can be logged, or can apply any operation that is monotonic (order pre-serving) without violating the relationship between any two values.

Interval Scale

Interval scales conform to Axioms 6, 7, and 8 (see Table 10.1). With these relational properties, one may ascertain the intervals between any given set of variable values. More specifically, the *distance* (i.e., differences) between values can be ordered such that the distance between any two numerical values is greater than, equal to, or less than the dif-ference between any other two values. Thus, num-bers that achieve additivity can be mathematically manipulated by combining, concatenating, or add-ing them to one another. However, there is no fixed origin or natural zero on the continuum for an inter-val scale. Rather, an origin is chosen arbitrarily. For example, temperature measured by Fahrenheit and Celsius have arbitrary zeros—the zero or origin is different for Fahrenheit than for other methods of measuring temperature. Norm-referenced testing in psychology is another example of interval measure-ment because an arbitrary zero is defined to be the average score for the entire set of respondent scores.

Given the additional information gleaned about the relations among values on an interval scale of measurement—namely, order of values and distance between each set of values—transformations of original values are more limited in flexibility than for ordinal and nominal variable values. Specifi-cally, only linear transformations preserve the interval-level information in the data and, there-fore, are permissible. For example, if variable x is to be transformed to variable y, the following equation (with constants a and b) would be appropriate: $y = ax + b$. If $a = 2$ and $b = 1$, and your data contain the following set of x values: 5, 4, 2, and 3, then linearly transformed y values would be 11, 9, 5, and 7, respectively. (In particular, note that many common test scores are scaled using linear transformations so that measure-ments have *nice* values for means and standard deviations. Examples include SAT and Graduate Record Examination (GRE) scores, which are scaled to have a mean of 500 and standard devia-tion of 100, and IQ scores, scaled to have a mean

of 100, and typically a standard deviation of 15, 16, or 20.

Ratio Scale

Relations among variable values at the ratio scale level contain the richest quantitative information. Numbers with an underlying ratio scale demonstrate all 10 axioms and lie along the real, continuous number line. In particular, a natural and absolute zero is part of the scale, thus providing a true, fixed origin about which all other values vary. Any move-ment (or variation) of a given value or number from this origin occurs in units of one. The greater the distance from the origin, the greater the property value because of a greater accumulation of unit dis-tances from the origin. For additivity relations, on the other hand, there is no true zero; rather, a zero is assigned arbitrarily whereas other values are adjusted with respect to it. For ratio scales, numeri-cal values can be multiplied and divided as well as added and subtracted as in the case of interval-level data. Examples of ratio scaled physical properties include weight, height, and age.

Substantially more variety in mathematical and statistical modeling can be performed on this type of data because of the extensive information available. This issue will be elaborated on when considering appropriate statistical techniques for values given differences in scale level. For now, it is worth noting that the advantage of greater information is accom-panied by a greater restriction in transformation methods compared with the previous scale levels. Namely, the original value (x) can be multiplied only by a constant (c) to create a transformed (y) value: $y = cx$. If $c = 2$, and a set of x values are 5, 8, 2, and 4, then the transformed y values would be 10, 16, 4, and 8.

Scale Level and Psychological Data

Given that the four scale levels differ in the amount of information available about a variable—in which case real numbers containing a fixed, natural origin, additivity, and ordinal axiomatic properties contain the most information—the types of inferential statis-tical tests that can be performed on data vary. Para-metric tests are considered more appropriate for interval- and ratio-level data, whereas nominal and ordinal data are best approached with nonparametric tests (the impact of scale type on inferential statistics are elaborated in the section Permissible Statistics). Thus, an important issue is whether commonly used psychological measures and tasks meet the requirements of at least the interval scale level. For example, counts of behaviors, in terms of reported incidents in some defined context, or number of items passed or endorsed on a test, are quite commonplace as psychological data. If the purpose of collecting the data relates only to the specifically defined context or to the specific test, raw counts could be regarded as ratio scaled because there is a natural zero for respondents who never exhibit the behavior or get all items wrong. It is rare that such specific contexts are of interest in psychology. That is, typically the task context or test is assumed to represent a broader domain of behavior, and the purpose is to generalize from the specific task to the broader domain. That is, responses are presumed to depend on a latent variable that represents a tendency to respond in a certain way to the broader domain of interest. Although behavior counts may be regarded as ratio scale, most psychological data are interpreted as depending on latent variables, which probably are not linearly related to a specific behavioral count. Thus, most observed psychological data probably achieve only ordinal scale properties.

FOCUS OF MEASUREMENT AND TESTING: WHAT IS BEING SCALED?

To this point in the chapter, the object of interest—that which manifests or implicitly possesses some psychological property being measured—has primarily been respondents. Indeed, the main focus of latent trait measurement (and the testing industry) is to locate a respondent somewhere along the continuum of a theoretical latent trait, such as attitudes, personality, aptitudes, and cognitive abilities. This approach to scaling is referred to as *subject centered* (Torgerson, 1958), in which case *subject* is synonymous with *respondent.*

A second focus of scaling includes the very stimuli that are used to score a respondent's latent trait level—test items or survey statements. More broadly

defined, this stimulus-centered focus encompasses other forms of physical, observable stimuli that are used in perceptual and cognitive psychological research (Torgerson, 1958). Statements in an attitude survey can be compared on a property independent of the respondent's self-perceived attitude. In this latter method, the focus of measurement shifts from respondents to stimuli, where differences between respondents are assumed to be error variance. For example, in a visual search task, the object arrays differ from one another in difficulty on the basis of the similarity of the target object to the surrounding, distractor objects. These studies typically are designed to compare performance (i.e., speed of locating target object in the array) between groups that differ as a function of the difficulty of the arrays. Subsequently, analyses of variance (ANOVAs) are used to test the effect of array difficulty on performance, where within-group variance (i.e., among the individuals within the group) is anticipated to be near zero.

Finally, a third focus of scaling is known as *response centered* (Torgerson, 1958). It is the most complex method, entailing the scaling of both respondents and items on the same property, or variable, such as the latent trait, extraversion, or attitude toward gun use. More specifically, both respondent and items are placed on the same latent trait continuum and the distance or difference between a respondent and an item on that continuum predicts the likelihood that a respondent endorses an item (or the extent of endorsement, in the case of Likert-type responses). A more in-depth description of these scaling foci appears in the section Respondent-Centered Focus, emphasizing the difference among them in how scale levels are tested and achieved.

Respondent-Centered Focus

The respondent-centered method is well known and has been used widely in the testing industry. For example, in norm-referenced testing, a goal is to compare respondents on the latent trait of interest, on the basis of their scores relative to a population mean (Crocker & Algina, 1986; McDonald, 1999). In some cases, information is used to compare individuals with one another or to predict success in an educational or organizational context. Historically, respondent-centered measurement and scaling has been based in classical test theory (CTT), in which the emphasis is on a total score (Gulliksen, 1950; Lord & Novick, 1968). In the following,

$$X_p = T_p + e_p, \tag{1}$$

X_p is the observed test score of respondent p, T is respondent p's true score (i.e., a respondent's average score calculated on the basis of that particular respondent's distribution of scores if he or she took the test an infinite number of times), and e is random error that dilutes the expression of respondent p's true score. In this model, it is assumed that error is distributed normally with a mean of zero and that the correlation between error and true scores is zero. CTT statistics, such as the proportion of respondents who pass or endorse an item (p values), item–total correlations, and test reliability (Cronbach's α) are sample specific. Even generalizability theory, which is a generalization of CTT, is based on the need for multiple samples to establish reliability (in its various forms; Crocker & Algina, 1986).

Although item statistics such as p values and biserial correlations are useful in selecting items for a test form, item properties are not included in the basic model in Equation 1. In other words, CTT methods disregard variability among items along the property of interest; and, thus, score patterns (i.e., across items) such that two respondents may have equal total test scores even if, between these two respondents, different items were answered correctly (i.e., different response patterns between respondents). The primary interest concerns total score differences between respondents, not differences between items. Differences among item-level properties are treated as error and homogeneity among test items is preferred (Gulliksen, 1950). For example, if the purpose of the test is to maximize distinctions between respondents in the sample, items can be selected to maximize individual differences (i.e., maximizing the variance of total scores). In this case, items should be selected to have p values within the range from .4 to .6, and item–total score correlations should be high. The impact of item properties on test variance is an important derivation in CTT (see Crocker & Algina, 1986).

More important, however, there is no specific model or simple method of testing for assumptions regarding the scaling properties of test scores with respect to the latent trait. Instead, CTT assumes that optimal scale properties are obtained when normal distributions of total scores are produced, which can be obtained through item selection. Furthermore, the psychometric quality of the test for measuring the intended latent trait is established by research that includes studies of the test's reliability and validity (Crocker & Algina, 1986; Sijtsma & Junker, 2006).

Stimulus-Centered Focus

In contrast to the respondent-centered approach, stimulus-centered methods aim to locate stimuli on a unidimensional continuum representing the variable of interest. Multidimensionality (i.e., differences among stimuli on multiple properties, simultaneously) will not be discussed at length, but refer to Torgerson (1958) for more extensive information, particularly with respect to multidimensional scaling.

The stimulus-centered approach was developed in the latter half of the 19th century by psychophysicists studying perception. Their goal was to quantify the relationship between a stimulus (e.g., lights, tones, weights) property and human perception (visual, auditory, tactile, and so on). Although these observable properties can be scaled via more precise methods (weight with a scale, sound via wavelengths, length via rulers), psychophysicists such as Weber and Fechner were interested in the psychological aspects of these properties—namely, our perception and distinction level of stimuli as a function of their value on a psychological property of interest (brightness, loudness or pitch, heaviness). For example, a series of lights is presented in pairs, and the respondent is asked, "Which is brighter?"

To determine the smallest difference between two values that can be reliably detected by human senses, an index or unit of measurement was initially sought by psychophysicists such as Weber and Fechner. The result of these efforts is called *just noticeable differences* (JND). For perspective, the relative strength of two stimuli is considered equal if either stimulus is chosen 50% of time. JND was defined as a 75% accuracy rate—halfway between chance and perfect accuracy. Weber further specified, via Weber's (1834/1948) law, that incremental increases in strength of stimuli properties are accompanied by a proportionate increase in the magnitude of a respondent's discrepancy in the sensory perception of the two stimuli values (McDonald, 1999). Thus, JNDs were considered psychological equal units in the scaling of stimulus properties, implying that values are based on an interval scale. Fechner (1860/1948) then postulated a log relationship between stimuli property values and sensory perception. In the latter case, values are not equally spaced along the psychological continuum, but interval properties still can be determined.

Stimulus-centered measurement was extended to latent trait and individual differences variables—specifically, attitudes—by Thurstone (1927). For example, the seriousness of a crime such as arson relative to other crimes such as smuggling or murder could be established by having a group of respondents make pairwise comparisons for all crimes in the set, or by having respondents sort each crime into ordered categories that differed in seriousness level (Thurstone, 1927). As a result, these crimes can be ordered along a continuum of *crime seriousness*. These techniques are applicable to the measurement of a variety of attitudes (e.g., use of abortion, nuclear weapons). In attitude measurement,

stimuli are statements (or items) that differ from one another along a latent, theoretical "attitude toward nuclear weapons" continuum that ranges from negative (against use of nuclear weapons) to positive (pronuclear weapons). Moreover, each statement is accompanied by a response format with which a respondent can indicate his or her level of agreement (with the statement). The response format for each item is either dichotomous or ordered category (i.e., Likert). Either way, the scale for the set of items was hypothesized to be interval.

Thurstone (1927) developed procedures for testing whether values assigned to a set of statements conform to interval scaling on the basis of his laws of comparative judgment (for dichotomously scored items) and categorical judgment (for ordered category items responses). An overview of the analytic steps involved in these procedures follows. An extensive summary of the method can be found in Torgerson (1958) and Bock and Jones (1968).

Although attitude statements or stimuli theoretically can be located on a continuum of the property of interest, the process of confirming (and, in a sense, observing) the item locations depends on a sample of judges (or respondents). In other words, variance is likely (across judges or within respondents) in the rating of an item along the continuum or the sorting of an item into one of a series of ordered categories. As a result, the true location of

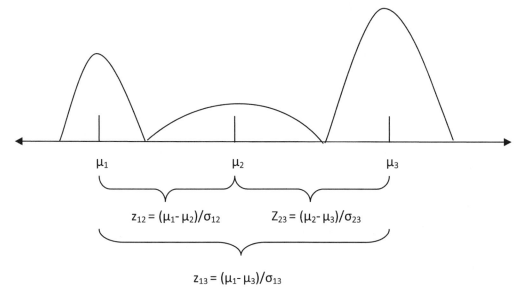

$$z_{12} = (\mu_1 - \mu_2)/\sigma_{12}$$

$$Z_{23} = (\mu_2 - \mu_3)/\sigma_{23}$$

$$z_{13} = (\mu_1 - \mu_3)/\sigma_{13}$$

FIGURE 10.1. Discriminal distributions.

an item (i) on the continuum (see Figure 10.1) is its observed mean (μ_i). The variance around this mean (σ_i^2) is viewed as error in judgment. The distance between μ_1 and μ_2, or any pair of items, also varies across judges, resulting in a normal distribution of discriminal differences and an accompanying standard deviation of differences, for example, σ_{12}. However, this information must be derived from empirical data in the form of judgment ratings or rankings via a set of equations associated with the law of comparative judgment (or the law of categorical judgment, which is an extension of the latter).

The law of comparative judgment can be represented in the following model:

$$S_1 - S_2 = z_{12} * \sqrt{\sigma_1^2 + \sigma_2^2 - 2r\sigma_1\sigma_2}, \qquad (2)$$

where S_1 and S_2 reflect the psychological (scale) values of statements 1 and 2; z_{12} is the normal deviate corresponding to the proportion of judgments in which statement 1 is rated higher, or stronger, than statement 2 on the attitudinal continuum (when 1 is greater than 2, this value is positive; when 1 is less than 2, this value is negative; when 1 and 2 are equal, this value is 0); σ_1 is the discriminal dispersion of statement 1, and σ_2 is the discriminal dispersion of statement 2; and r is the correlation (or dependency) between the discriminal dispersions of statements 1 and 2 within the same respondent (or group of judges). In its present form, the equation is insoluble because of insufficient information with which to estimate parameters. Therefore, Torgerson (1958) has offered a series of simplifying conditions. For example, the r is typically set to 0, as different paired comparisons (discriminal processes) are assumed to be independent (e.g., comparisons for different item pairs are not dependent on one another because of an underlying consistent bias in the judging process such as leniency, severity, or ambivalence). In latent trait measurement, this phenomenon is referred to as *local independence* (Lord & Novick, 1968).

The remainder of the process for deriving discriminal differences involves a series of computations in which z scores are obtained. Pairwise judgments of stimulus dominance is created by the proportion of judges (p) who rate a given item above

every other item, or above a given category threshold. Z scores are then obtained for each nondiagonal element in the probability matrix by its location on a cumulative normal distribution: for example, when two items representing attitude toward abortion are judged as being located on the same point, $p_{12} = .50$ and $z_{12} = .00$. In other words, "abortions should be allowed in certain cases" may be perceived as equivalent to "if a woman's life is in danger, she should be allowed to have an abortion." But, if "abortions should be allowed in certain cases" is compared with a less supportive, negative view of abortion (e.g., "Abortions should never be allowed in any cases"), p_{12} will equal a lower number such as .25, in which case $z_{12} = -.68$. Or if "abortions should be allowed in certain cases" is compared with a stronger, positive view of abortion (e.g., "abortions should be allowed in all cases"), p_{12} may equal .75, in which case $z_{12} = .68$. Thus, the greater the perceived distance between two items (attitude toward abortion), the further the item moves from the center of the continuum representing the property of interest.

As depicted in Figure 10.1, and consistent with the model portrayed in Equation 1, the discriminal differences between each pair of statements are additive, given the interval scale theoretically underlying the statement values. Thus, $z_{13} = z_{12} + z_{23}$. Because our example has three items, three equations will be used to determine the location (mean) of statements [e.g., for items 1 and 2: $z_{12} = (\mu_1 - \mu_2)/\sigma_{(1-2)}$]. To solve this set of equations, for which the available parameter information is insufficient, the origin and units of measurement must be fixed. This may be done by setting μ_1 to 0 and, in certain simplifying conditions (see Torgerson, 1958), setting the discriminal variances among items to be equal (i.e., equal distances between each pair of items), or approximately equal (given a linear change from one variance to another, using a constant value that is assumed to be small). In other words, the 0 point on the scale is arbitrary, meaning that the psychological properties of the attitude statements cannot be described by a ratio scale; it is whether the values achieve an interval scale that is of interest in the laws of comparative and categorical judgments.

These observed z scores contain error in judgment (i.e., variance in discriminal differences across judges), however, so additivity may not be sufficiently attained. Thus, the true differences between statements on a property must be approximated by estimating values, which then can be compared (via least squares) to determine the degree to which an interval scale underlies the data. As part of this process, a matrix of theoretically true z' values is produced by reducing error in the original z value matrix by averaging the column values (on the basis of the number, n, of judgments—i.e., judges or times one judge rates a pair of items). These latter values then can be compared with the initial z values to determine the degree of approximation and appropriateness of treating the observed values as interval in scale.

Response-Centered Focus

The response-centered approach differs from the previous two approaches in that both the item and respondents are placed on the same psychological continuum and scaled with respect to each other. Thus, the entire scaling procedure now becomes more complex, both theoretically and statistically. For example, two respondents—one who is high on extraversion, the other low—will exhibit a different response pattern for the same set of items that are manipulated such that they vary along the psychological property of extraversion. Thus, it is now the response patterns across a set of items that is central to the process of scaling respondents. Conversely, if we have a set of respondents for whom extraversion levels vary, then items can be scaled on the basis of how the respondents differ in their response patterns across items.

Similar to stimulus-centered methods, but different from the CTT approach to respondent-centered methods, the response-centered approach contains a variety of specific models and equations that can be used to test the scaling properties of respondents and items. These models can be categorized as either deterministic or probabilistic on the basis of how error in prediction is treated. Deterministic models include an error term to account for variance in response patterns not explained by either the respondent or item properties. Thus, the goal with these error-free models, which are not expected to be observed or necessarily occur in nature, is to determine the extent to which values based on this perfect scale approximated real, observed data. Con-

versely, probabilistic models directly incorporate error in the prediction model, allowing for comparison in fit among statistical models (on the basis of a decrease in error across compared models).

Deterministic models. Two well-known deterministic models are those of Guttman (1950) and Coombs (1950). These two techniques differ primarily in how the discriminal process is theorized to occur. Namely, in the Guttman model, the respondent is more likely to endorse an item as the distance between respondent and item increases such that the latter surpasses the former; thus, it is a cumulative model, similar to that of Thurstone's (1927) laws of judgment. For example, when measuring "attitude toward abortion," a respondent may be confronted with the following statement: "Abortions should only be allowed when the mother's life is in danger." If the Guttman model more closely approximates the data, then respondents will disagree with the statement because it is too strong (i.e., the respondent believes abortions should be allowed in more cases). An unfolding model (e.g., Combs, 1950), in contrast, assumes a proximity-based process whereby a respondent is more likely to endorse an item that is located close to his or her position and thus will disagree with an item from either below or above. For example, given the abortion attitude statement, a respondent may disagree from above or below. In the latter case, the attitude is too strong; the respondent is more likely to agree with the statement "Abortions should be allowed in more cases." In the former case, the attitude statement is viewed as too weak in comparison with one's own beliefs. These respondents more likely would endorse the statement "Abortions should never be allowed under any circumstances." These, and more basic, aspects of the models are discussed, in turn.

Recent models (Mokken, 1971; van Schuur, 2003) are accompanied by a series of steps in which the ordering of respondents and items can be examined visually. For example, in the Guttman model, a trace line (see Figure 10.2) or item characteristic curve (ICC; see Figure 10.5) is constructed to describe the joint impact of respondent and item on response likelihood for an item response. Visually, an ICC is a plot for which the horizontal axis is the

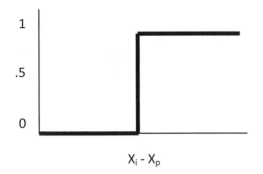

FIGURE 10.2. Trace line for Guttman scale model.

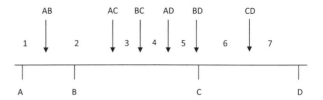

FIGURE 10.3.   Category thresholds and person-type regions.

latent variable or trait continuum, and the vertical axis is the probability of a response (correct in the case of abilities, agreement in the case of opinions, and so on). The direct comparison between respondent and item value is made on the former. Specifically, an ICC demonstrates that the discrepancy in value between respondent and item predicts the likelihood that a respondent will get a test item correct. Next, the degree to which observed data approximates the model can be tested. On the basis of this theoretical model, the likelihood of endorsing an item is either zero or one. In other words, given the distance between respondent and item on the psychological continuum, the threshold for endorsing an item versus not—that is, the slope of the prediction line—is abrupt. If a respondent's location exceeds that of the item, the likelihood of item endorsement is 100% (the respondent will endorse the item), but it is 0% otherwise; if the respondent is located below the item, he or she will not endorse the item. In other words, the location of the respondent, relative to item, perfectly predicts the response.

The Guttman model only assumes ordinal-level measurement for respondents and items. This assumption can be tested visually using a scalogram or mathematically by calculating the coefficient of reproducibility. For the former, the steps differ, somewhat, for dichotomous versus multiple category response. First, category thresholds, or dichotomous items, do not define space and continuum but rather are used to divide the stimulus space into segments (see Figure 10.3). A, B, C, and D represent midpoints, or means, for four dichotomously scored items, stimuli, or multiple ordered categories within an item. For example, when measuring weight, item

(or category response) A might represent 5 to 10 kg, B is 10 to 20 kg, C is 20 to 40 kg, and D is more than 40 kg. If the values represent the amount of verbally aggressive behavior, defined as the number of times a respondent yells at another respondent, A might be less than 2 times per day, B is between 2 and 3 times a day, C is between 3 and 4 times a day, and D is 5 or more times per day. All double-digit letters (e.g., AB, BC, etc., located above the continuum) are midpoints between two item or stimulus points on the continuum (e.g., AB is the midpoint between items A and B). As soon will be explained, these latter midpoint values are useful for determining the discriminal differences in pairs of items or stimuli and determine a set of response patterns, given a respondent's location within the numbered regions.

Once the items or stimuli are constructed to vary from low to high on a psychological property, a respondent is confronted with each stimulus and asked to rate the degree of match between the stimulus (item) and themselves. The response-centered approach represents a different basis for item ordering than the stimulus-centered approach; namely, the ordering of items represents the ease with which the items are endorsed or passed. In the stimulus-centered approach, the responses represent judgments about the stimuli and hence may be regarded as a relatively more objective and focused evaluation of the stimulus properties, although this point is debatable (McDonald, 1999; Torgerson, 1958).

Given n items with a dichotomous response format, there are 2^n possible response patterns. If a five-point Likert scale were involved, there would be 5^n possible response patterns. If items and respondents are scalable with respect to each other, only $n + 1$ of these patterns will occur. As can be seen in Figure 10.3, these permissible patterns are associated with the number of category thresholds, and the distribution of respondents who fall into each of these $n + 1$ groups or classes. Remaining patterns are inconsistent with the theory surrounding the latent trait and are regarded as *errors*, although, overall, some inconsistencies in patterns are expected. Mathematically, the scalability of items and respondents can be tested via coefficient of reproducibility:

$$C = 1 - \frac{\# \, total \; errors}{total \, \# \; of \; items * total \; number \; of \; respondents}, \quad (3)$$

which translates into the number of patterns allowable versus the number of perfect scale patterns. In general, a coefficient value of .90 is considered acceptable for an ordinal scale (Torgerson, 1958). Regrettably, there is a lack of statistical procedures for comparing fit between models, similar to a change in chi-square or log-likelihood.

Coombs's (1950) unfolding model is also deterministic and involves rank ordering preferences for stimuli or items in terms of the proximity of the stimuli or item to the respondent's perceived self-standing on the same psychological continuum. According to this model, however, respondents can disagree with an item from either above or below, depending on his or her location relative to the item. Similar to Figure 10.3, item locations can be broken down into regions with midpoints between category thresholds. If there are seven regions, there are seven groups of individuals with distinct group-specific response patterns. In other words, ordering of items now depends on the location of the respondent (see Figure 10.4), where the joint scale folds at the location of the respondent to determine ordering of items. For example, in Figure 4, respondent x_p is in Region 2, which exhibits the BACD pattern. The absolute difference between item points is not known but is relative (e.g., AB vs. CD). Thus, this

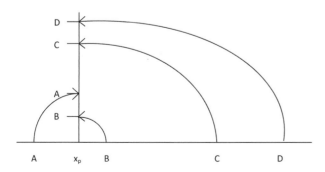

FIGURE 10.4. Folding of items around persons.

scale is considered to lie somewhere between ordinal and interval (Coombs, 1950).

Probabilistic models. Probabilistic response-centered models typically fall into the category of item response theory (IRT) models (i.e., latent trait theory; see Embretson & Reise, 2000; McDonald, 1999). Similar to the Guttman model, emphasis is placed on the correspondence between response patterns and the location of respondents and items along a psychological continuum, and this relationship can be visually represented as an ICC. More to the point, however, observed, manifest variables (item performance, endorsement, accurate response, etc.) can be used to infer and locate items and respondents on a unidimensional latent trait continuum (hence its synonymy with latent trait theory). IRT models are accompanied by a series of assumptions such as local independence (much like when the correlations among paired-item comparisons are set to zero in Thurstone's, 1927, models). The probabilistic IRT model diverges from that of Guttman in that error is accounted for in the model by changing the mathematical expression to be the probability of endorsing the item. In other words, because error is inherent in the model, the relationship between respondent-item distance and responses can take various forms that do not mirror a step function (e.g., approximations of linear, normal ogive, logistic, etc.; Lord & Novick, 1968). In Figure 10.5, three ICCs are shown—one for each of three items. The general form of the relationship between trait level and item response is the same for all items (logistic), but the parameters of the relationship such as slope and item location, or difficulty, differs across items. Moreover, IRT models and associated *hypothesized* ICCs may represent a cumulative versus an ideal-point, unfolding relationship between respondent–item distance and responses (Roberts & Laughlin, 1996). Perhaps the simplest, probabilistic response-centered model is the Rasch (1960) model:

$$P(X_{is} = 1 \mid \theta_s, \beta_i) = \frac{\exp(\theta_s - \beta_i)}{1 + \exp(\theta_s - \beta_i)}. \quad (4)$$

The left-hand side of Equation 4 for the Rasch model refers to the probability of respondent s endorsing (or accurately responding to) item i; the

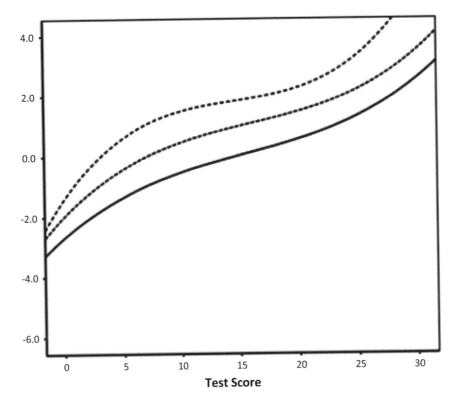

FIGURE 10.5.   Item characteristics curve.

right-hand side shows how this probability depends on the difference between the respondent's trait location (θ_s, often called *ability* even though that is not appropriate in all contexts) and the location of item i on the same latent trait continuum (β_i, called *item difficulty* for cognitive tests). In fact, the precise distance, or interval, between respondent and item along the latent trait continuum can be estimated and is used to predict a respondent's response to the item. In other words, unlike previous response-centered models, the Rasch model entails at least interval-level respondent scores. This unique property of Rasch models can be derived from Luce and Tukey's (1964) theory of conjoint measurement, in which an outcome variable (the item response) is an additive function of two other variables (in this case, the item and respondent values). As a result, the data that are well described by the Rasch model contain a wealth of information on both the items and respondents, and the widest variety of statistical analyses can be applied to these data when testing a hypothesis.

Another interesting and unique feature of Rasch (1960) models is the invariant meaning of respondent and item calibrations, a property referred to as

specific objectivity. That is, it can be shown that for any pair of trait level scores, say θ_1 and θ_2 the difference in log odds for solving *any* item β_i is given by the simple difference in the trait levels as follows:

$$\ln[P(X_{i1}=1)/(1-P(X_{i1}=1)] \\ - \ln[P(X_{i2}=1)/(1-P(X_{i2}=1)] = \theta_1 - \theta_2. \quad (5)$$

This relationship is often shown as justifying interval-level scale properties of trait levels when scaled as θ_s in the Rasch (1960) model. Conversely, for any pair of items, it can be shown that the difference in log odds that *any* respondent will respond positively is the difference in their difficulty values. Also, these same relationships can be shown in ratio form by taking the antilogs, which can be taken as a specific meaning of ratio scale properties. That is, suppose that ξ_1 and ξ_2 are the antilogs of θ_1 and θ_2, respectively. In this case, the ratio of Respondent 1 to Respondent 2 for the odds of passing (or endorsing) *any* item is given as the simple ratio of their trait scores as follows:

$$[P(X_{i1}=1)/(1-P(X_{i1}=1)]/[P(X_{i2}=1)/(1 \\ -P(X_{i2}=1)] = \xi_1/\xi_2. \quad (6)$$

Because the ratio of the trait scores for two respondents, ξ_1/ξ_2, applies to any item, the scores have a ratio scale interpretation. Suppose that the antilog of item difficulties in the Rasch (1960) model, are used to scale items, such that $\eta_i = exp\beta_i$. The ratio of two rescaled item difficulties, η_1 and η_2, indicates the relative odds that the item will be passed or endorsed by any respondent, as follows:

$$[P(X_{2s} = 1) / (1 - P(X_{2s} = 1))] = \eta_1/\eta_2. \qquad (7)$$

Specific objectivity is a property that is unique to the Rasch (1960) IRT model. When educational or psychological tests are scaled with other latent trait models, however, such as the two-parameter (2PL) or three-parameter (3PL) logistic models, items still can be compared with other items without relying on population-specific, contextual information (i.e., as in norm-referenced measurement). The relationships will not apply directly to any item but will be modified by the additional parameters in the IRT model.

The response-centered approach has some interesting relationships to the stimulus-centered approach. Specifically, both the stimulus- and response-centered approaches use a model or set of equations to test the validity of the scale level, or scalability of items with respect to respondents and vice versa. Thus, in the response-centered approach, respondent information is improved upon relative to CTT-based approaches by considering respondent locations with respect to item-level, rather than test-level, information. Also, Thurstone's (1927) laws of comparative and categorical judgments and Lord's (1952) probabilistic response-focused models both emphasize discriminal processes with a cumulative, dominance component (Bock & Jones, 1968). The former establishes differences between items on a property. For example, Item 1 is judged as stronger on a property than Item 2, which is stronger than Item 3. So, Item 1 dominates both Items 2 and 3. The latter series of comparisons emphasizes the dominance of a respondent over an item (see Sijtsma & Junker, 2006). Thus, when latent traits are of interest, Thurstone's approach is consistent with, and could have evolved easily into the modern test theory approach—namely, IRT. The common scaling of respondents and items in psychometrics was affected much later by the theoretical approaches of Lord (1953) and Rasch (1960).

PERMISSIBLE STATISTICS: MATCHING ANALYSIS WITH VARIABLE TYPE

A heavily debated topic in psychological measurement concerns what statistical analysis procedures are permissible given the scale level of the data. When Stevens (1946, 1951) developed his hierarchical taxonomy of scale levels, he also prescribed the statistical tests appropriate for each given level (see Table 10.1). Essentially, limitations for how values of a particular scale can be transformed are extended to the type of inferential statistics that can be performed. For example, parametric statistics (e.g., *t* tests, Pearson correlations, regression, etc.) rely on information such as means and standard deviations and, thus, are appropriate for interval and ratio-scaled data. Nominal and ordinal data, on the other hand, do not demonstrate a continuous equal-interval range and, thus, should be examined using nonparametric statistics such as chi-square and Spearman's rank correlation, respectively.

Although most scientists would agree with the restrictions on nominal scaled data (but see Lord, 1953), there is disagreement regarding the treatment of data as a function of its scale level. Specifically, this debate centers on two issues: (a) the basic theory underlying these restrictions—namely, the measurement paradigm and (b) related to this, the empirical implications for statistical inferences when an interval scale–latent variable is measured with ordinal scores.

Theory and Measurement Paradigms

According to Michell (1990), there are three measurement paradigms: operational, classical, and representational. In operational and classical paradigms, the relevance of Stevens's (1951) prohibitions on statistical treatment of ordinal data is contested. In these paradigms, science is viewed as the study of our numerical operations and not the study of a reality that is thought to lie beyond them. In other words, scores are measurements simply because they are reasonably consistent numerical assignments that result from a precisely specified operation. Moreover, even though nominal data are not quantitative but rather represent identity (e.g., football jersey numbers), researchers have argued that statistical analysis typically used for more quantitative scales such as ordinal, interval, and ratio can be used. For example, football number data do not know what mathematical operations are allowable; rather, they are numbers and therefore appear computable (Lord, 1953). Thus, it can be argued that there is no relation between measurement scales and appropriate statistical procedures. As commented by Townsend and Ashby (1984), "Just exactly what this curious statement has to do with statistics or measurement eludes us" (p. 396). Rather, the problem with the scenario involving freshmen with lower football jersey numbers than seniors and the subsequent outrage by the comparably less value of the freshmen lies in the flawed interpretation drawn from the statistical comparison, rather than the statistical characters and analysis.

It is the representational paradigm in which the issue of scale-level correspondence with statistical procedures is most applicable. Importantly, this paradigm is most commonly practiced in psychological measurement. In representational theory, numbers represent an empirical relational system and, thus, these number values constitute an existing, objective structure. Thus, scientists argue that measurement is "the assessment of quantity" (Rozeboom, 1966, p. 224). So, nominal scale level is not included as a legitimate scale of measurement. Rather, the data must be quantitative and scaled as interval or ratio (Campbell, 1920).

According to a more lenient view, it is argued that the meaningfulness of the inferences that are made from a measure is the most important criterion in determining the adequacy of the scaling (Michell, 1990; Townsend & Ashby, 1984). That is, a measurement can produce meaningless statements or a statement's truth can be an artifact of the measurement scale chosen. According to Suppes and Zinnes (1963), "A numerical statement is meaningful if and only if its truth (or falsity) is constant under admissible scale transformations of any of its numerical assignments; that is, any of its numerical functions expressing the results of measurement" (p. 66). Moreover, as stated by Michell (1986), "The

question never was one of permissible statistics or of meaningfulness. It was always only one of legitimate inference" (p. 402). Thus, in this view, representational theory does not entail prescriptions about the matching of statistical procedures with scale levels (as Stevens thought), nor does it imply anything about the meaningfulness of measurement statements. Theories about measurement paradigms and their implications do not necessarily lead to an unambiguous endorsement of prohibitions about the statistical treatment of data. The differences among the various viewpoints may be responsible for most psychological researchers ignoring the implications of measurement scale for statistical inference.

Impact of Scale Level on Statistical Inferences in Latent Trait Measurement

On the basis of the previous discussion, it can be inferred that scale levels do not necessarily correspond with a particular statistical technique. Indeed, analysis often is considered most crucial because the scaling of data can take on so many forms that overlap with previously mentioned taxonomies. For example, rank and count data can be treated as interval level data. Moreover, if interval or ratio data exhibit a normal distribution, then most inferential statistics tests that rely on the latter as an assumption (e.g., t tests, ANOVA, general linear models) can be used for both (McDonald, 1999). Nevertheless, in some situations, the distinction between ordinal and interval is important—particularly when measuring latent traits for which operational definitions are insufficient and the nature of the scale values must be inferred.

Several studies have demonstrated the impact of nonlinear relationships between observed and latent scores on inferences about observed score means (Davison & Sharma, 1988; Townsend & Ashby, 1984). Other researchers have stressed the nonlinear relationships between observed and latent scores on the outcome of statistical tests (Davison & Sharma, 1990; Maxwell & Delaney, 1985). Maxwell and Delaney (1985) demonstrated that when the relationship between observed and latent trait scores is logistic, the results of a t test on the basis of observed scores can be inferred for latent variables as well if and only if observed score variances are equal between groups or the test difficulty level matches the respondents' trait level. Similarly, Davison and Sharma (1988) showed results of *t* tests involving observed test scores can be extended to the latent scores as long as statistical assumptions such as normality in score distributions and homogeneity of variance among scores are met. The importance of this requirement, however, often is not sufficiently emphasized in statistics textbooks. Moreover, the relationship between observed and latent scores must be monotonic. In other words, the exact form of the relationship between observed and latent scores need not be known to conduct analyses. These conditions are insufficient, however, for a factorial ANOVA with interaction terms (Davison & Sharma, 1990). Specifically, it can be shown that factorial ANOVA's may yield significant differences in observed score means for groups of respondents who, in actuality, have the same true, latent trait score. Thus, meeting statistical assumptions is insufficient, and the probability density functions (PDFs) of dependent variables must be thoroughly examined, post hoc, to determine the appropriateness of extending results for observed scores to latent scores (Davison & Sharma, 1990). Namely, the PDFs for multiple groups or conditions being compared must be the same, or at least overlap if the means are different. Similar results have been found for analyses such as multiple regression (Davison & Sharma, 1990).

More recently, studies have compared inferences under CTT versus IRT scaling of variables. The advantage of this approach is that for some IRT models interval-level scaling is supported, as noted. In CTT, the distributions of scores can be controlled by selecting items according to their difficulty and intercorrelations. Historically this process has entailed selecting items that yield normal distributions of scores, assuming that optimal scale properties are achieved when measures are distributed normally. The justification for this approach can be traced to Galton (1883), who found that performance on a broad array of tasks was distributed normally. Thus, for norm-referenced tests, means and standard deviations of tests scores are computed as if the scores had an interval scale level. Then, total

scores can be linearly transformed to standard scores that have meaning with respect to percentile ranks and relative frequencies on the normal distribution. According to Michell, this procedure of "inferring the existence of quantity from that of mere order is aptly designated the *psychometricians' fallacy*," and it is "central to the paradigm of modern psychometrics" (2009, p. 46). That is, achieving normally distributed scores does not in justify interval scale properties.

In contrast, estimating latent traits scores with an IRT model (particularly the Rasch, 1960, model) leads to scores with interval scale and some ratio scale properties. As shown, the relationship between task total scores and latent trait scores is nonlinear. The test characteristics curves in Figure 10.5 show that although the mapping of total scores to latent trait estimates is nearly linear near the center of the distribution, the relationship becomes nonlinear at the extremes. That is, changes in total score have greater meaning for the latent trait at the extremes.

The impact of using IRT latent trait scores versus CTT total test scores on inferences have been compared in several studies (Embretson, 1994, 1996, 2007; Kang & Waller, 2005). In these studies, simulations are used so that the true relationships are known. Embretson (1996) found that interaction effects in an analysis of variance procedure were unreliable. Using the total score scale resulted in (a) failing to find significant interactions that existed in the latent trait scale and (b) finding significant interactions when none existed in the latent trait scale. Similarly, Kang and Waller (2005) found that for moderated regression analysis, Type 1 error rates were significantly higher than expected when the total score scale was used. The IRT latent trait estimates, in contrast, yielded the expected error rate.

Other studies show that results from the test score scale are particularly misleading when the degree of nonlinearity is increased by test inappropriateness for one or more groups that are studied. When the test is either too easy or too hard, the degree of nonlinearity between latent trait scores and test scores increases. Embretson (1994, 2007) found that measuring change and trend for groups of individuals who differ initially on the latent trait is affected by test difficulty. That is, when using the total score scale, the greatest change across time or conditions will be shown for the group for which the measure was most appropriate. If the groups have different initial levels on the trait, a measure may be selected to show the most change for one of these groups, even if the change on the latent trait scale is the same. These empirical studies strongly indicate that the measurement scale level has a strong impact on inferences depending on the nature of the statistical analysis used to make the inference.

CONCLUSION

Although scaling is rich in measurement theory and application, the measurement paradigm on which the scaling is interpreted can result in limitations on the statistical inferences that can be made. Classical and operational measurement paradigms do not allow inferences to domains beyond a set of observed numerical values and the scale they form, whereas the representational paradigm does. Many psychologists have adopted this latter point of view because it is conducive to supporting empirically based general theories. That is, the variables that are of interest are not directly observable and must be inferred from responses to limited sets of tasks.

Scientists who adhere to the representational paradigm must be wary, however, of the statistical techniques used and the extent to which they are appropriate for a set of data, given the scale of measurement achieved by the data. For example, ideally nonparametric test procedures (chi-square; Spearman's rank correlation) should be used with nominal and ordinal (categorical) data because the order and intervals among values in a scale are indeterminable. Interval or ratio (continuous or quantitative) data can use parametric techniques (e.g., t tests; regression) to test hypotheses because the intervals and ratios among variable values are known. If the scaling level of variable is not appropriately matched with an analysis, important information in the variable values are ignored or misrepresented. Subsequently, the results of the tests and the inferences made from the results are questionable.

When latent variables, such as cognitive ability or personality, are of primary interest, CTT or latent trait theory (i.e., IRT) can be effective at testing whether the observed data approximate the latent variable. In CTT applications, the scaling of the data has a respondent-centered focus, and the relationship between test score and ability (or level of endorsement) changes depending on the region of the latent trait continuum in which the item is located, relative to the respondent. In IRT applications, interval properties can be supported because both the respondents and items are scaled along the same continuum and share measurement properties. As demonstrated in this chapter, the latter case is most clear with the Rasch (1960) IRT models.

References

Bock, R. D., & Jones, L. V. (1968). *The measurement and prediction of judgment and choice.* San Francisco, CA: Holden-Day.

Campbell, N. R. (1920). *Physics, the elements.* London, England: Cambridge University Press.

Cohen, J., Cohen, P., West, S. G., & Aiken, L. S. (1983). *Applied multiple regression/correlation analysis for the behavioral sciences* (2nd ed.). London, England: Erlbaum.

Coombs, C. H. (1950). Psychological scaling without a unit of measurement. *Psychological Review, 57,* 145–158. doi:10.1037/h0060984

Crocker, L., & Algina, J. (1986). *Introduction to classical and modern test theory.* Belmont, CA: Wadsworth.

Davison, M. L., & Sharma, A. R. (1988). Parametric statistics and levels of measurement. *Psychological Bulletin, 104,* 137–144. doi:10.1037/0033-2909.104.1.137

Davison, M. L., & Sharma, A. R. (1990). Parametric statistics and levels of measurement: Factorial designs and multiple regression. *Psychological Bulletin, 107,* 394–400. doi:10.1037/0033-2909.107.3.394

Embretson, S. E. (1994). Comparing changes between groups: Some perplexities arising from psychometrics. In D. Laveault, B. D. Zumbo, M. E. Gessaroli, & M. W. Boss (Eds.), *Modern theories of measurement: Problems and issues* (pp. 133–145). Ottawa, Ontario, Canada: Edumetric Research Group, University of Ottawa.

Embretson, S. E. (1996). Item response theory models and inferential bias in multiple group comparisons. *Applied Psychological Measurement, 20,* 201–212. doi:10.1177/014662169602000302

Embretson, S. E. (2007). Impact of measurement scale in modeling development processes and ecological factors. In T. D. Little, J. Bovaird, & N. A. Card (Eds.), *Modeling contextual effects in longitudinal studies* (pp. 63–87). Mahwah, NJ: Erlbaum.

Embretson, S. E., & Reise, S. P. (2000). *Item response theory for psychologists*. Mahwah, NJ: Erlbaum.

Fechner, G. T. (1948). Elements of psychophysics. In W. Dennis (Ed.), *Readings in the history of psychology* (pp. 206–213). New York, NY: Appleton-Century-Crofts. (Original work published 1860)

Gaito, J. (1980). Measurement scales and statistics: Resurgence of an old misconception. *Psychological Bulletin, 87*, 564–567. doi:10.1037/0033-2909.87.3.564

Galton, F. (1883). *Inquiry into human faculty and its development*. London, England: Macmillan.

Gulliksen, H. (1950). *Theory of mental tests*. New York, NY: Wiley.

Guttman, L. A. (1950). The basis for scalogram analysis. In S. A. Stouffer, L. Guttman, E. A. Suchman, P. F. Lazarsfeld, S. A. Star, & J. A. Clausen (Eds.), *Studies in social psychology in World War II: Vol. 4. Measurement and prediction*. Princeton, NJ: Princeton University Press.

Hölder, O. (1901). Die Axiome der Quantität und die Lehre vom Mass. Berichte über die Verhandlungen der Königlich Sächsischen Gesellschaft der Wissenschaften zu Leipzig [The axioms of quantity and the theory of measure. Reports on the final negotiation of the Royal Saxon Society of Sciences in Leipzig]. *Mathematisch-Physische Klasse, 53*, 1–46.

Kang, S.-M., & Waller, N. G. (2005). Moderated multiple regression, spurious interaction effects, and IRT. *Applied Psychological Measurement, 29*, 87–105. doi:10.1177/0146621604272737

Lord, F. M. (1952). *A theory of test scores* (Psychometric Monograph No. 7). Richmond, VA: Psychometric Corporation.

Lord, F. M. (1953). On the statistical treatment of football numbers. *American Psychologist, 8*, 750–751. doi:10.1037/h0063675

Lord, F. M., & Novick, M. R. (1968). *Statistical theories of mental test scores*. Reading, MA: Addison-Welsley.

Luce, R. D., & Tukey, J. W. (1964). Simultaneous conjoint measurement: A new type of fundamental measurement. *Journal of Mathematical Psychology, 1*, 1–27. doi:10.1016/0022-2496(64)90015-X

Maxwell, S. E., & Delaney, H. D. (1985). *Designing experiments and analyzing data: A model comparison perspective*. Belmont, CA: Wadsworth.

McDonald, R. P. (1999). *Test theory: A unified treatment*. Mahwah, NJ: Erlbaum.

Michell, J. (1986). Measurement scales and statistics: A clash of paradigms. *Psychological Bulletin, 100*, 398–407. doi:10.1037/0033-2909.100.3.398

Michell, J. (1990). *An introduction to the logic of psychological measurement*. Hillsdale, NJ: Erlbaum.

Michell, J. (1997). Quantitative science and the definition of measurement in psychology. *The British Journal of Psychology, 88*, 355–383. doi:10.1111/j.2044-8295.1997.tb02641.x

Michell, J. (2009). The psychometricians' fallacy: Too clever by half? *British Journal of Mathematical and Statistical Psychology, 62*, 41–55. doi:10.1348/000711007X243582

Mokken, R. J. (1971). *A theory and procedure of scale analysis with applications in political research*. New York, NY: De Gruyter.

Rasch, G. (1960). *Studies in mathematical psychology: I. Probabilistic models for some intelligence and attainment tests*. Oxford, England: Nielsen & Lydiche.

Roberts, J. S., & Laughlin, J. E. (1996). A unidimensional item response model for unfolding responses form a graded disagree-agree response scale. *Applied Psychological Measurement, 20*, 231–255. doi:10.1177/014662169602000305

Rozeboom, W. W. (1966). Scaling theory and the nature of measurement. *Synthese, 16*, 170–233. doi:10.1007/BF00485356

Russell, B. (1903). *Principles of mathematics*. Cambridge, England: Cambridge University Press.

Sijtsma, K., & Junker, B. W. (2006). Item response theory: Past performance, present developments, and future expectations. *Behaviormetrika, 33*, 75–102. doi:10.2333/bhmk.33.75

Stevens, S. S. (1946). On the theory of scales of measurement. *Science, 103*, 677–680. doi:10.1126/science.103.2684.677

Stevens, S. S. (1951). Mathematics, measurement, and psychophysics. In S. S. Stevens (Ed.), *Handbook of experimental psychology* (pp. 1–49). New York, NY: Wiley.

Suppes, P., & Zinnes, J. L. (1963). Basic measurement theory. In R. D. Luce, R. R. Bush, & E. Galanter (Eds.), *Handbook of mathematical psychology* (Vol. 1, pp. 3–76). New York, NY: Wiley.

Thurstone, L. L. (1927). A law of comparative judgment. *Psychological Review, 34*, 273–286. doi:10.1037/h0070288

Torgerson, W. S. (1958). *Theory and methods of scaling*. New York, NY: Wiley.

Townsend, J. T., & Ashby, F. G. (1984). Measurement scales and statistics: The misconception misconceived. *Psychological Bulletin, 96*, 394–401. doi:10.1037/0033-2909.96.2.394

van Schuur, W. H. (2003). Mokken scale analysis: Between the Guttman scale and parametric item response theory. *Political Analysis, 11*, 139–163. doi:10.1093/pan/mpg002

Weber, E. H. (1948). The sense of touch and common feeling. In W. Dennis (Ed.), *Readings in the history of psychology* (pp. 194–196). East Norwalk, CT: Appleton-Century-Crofts. (Original work published 1834)

CHAPTER 11

SAMPLE SIZE PLANNING

Ken Kelley and Scott E. Maxwell

The sample size necessary to address a research question depends on the goals of the researcher. Do researchers want to know *whether* a particular effect exists or do researchers want to know the *magnitude of the effect*? We begin this chapter with two illustrations. In one, knowledge of the existence of an effect is of interest and, in the second, the size of an effect is of interest. We use these illustrations to show the types of research questions that can be addressed using the statistical frameworks commonly employed by psychologists in the 21st century. Ultimately, we argue that the particular research question is what drives how it should be addressed statistically, either to infer an effect exists or to make inferences about the magnitude of an effect.

First, consider a team sporting competition. In general, the most important outcome is which team wins the game or if the game ends in a tie, rather than the score. If the score is known, then the winner can be determined by deduction, but of primary interest is simply knowing who won. Second, consider a retirement portfolio. In general, the outcome of interest is the amount the portfolio's value changed over some time period, either in raw dollars or as a percentage of the initial investments, not simply whether the portfolio increased or decreased in value over some time period. If the amount of change is known, it also is known whether the portfolio increased or decreased in value. Of primary interest, however, is how much the value of the portfolio changed.

We use the team sport and retirement portfolio examples as analogies for the types of questions that are generally of interest to psychologists and how

statistical methods can help answer a particular question. In some situations, the dichotomous decision of a *null hypothesis significance test* (NHST; specifically to reject or fail to reject the null hypothesis) answers the question of interest and in some situations with an additional benefit of finding the direction of an effect. Examples of dichotomous research questions are (a) does the proposed model explain variance in the outcome variable, (b) is there a relationship between a predictor and the criterion variable after other predictors have been controlled, (c) do the treatment and control groups have different means, and (d) is there a correlation between the two variables? For the latter three questions, the direction of the effect is immediately known if the effect can be deemed statistically significant. The first question does not have a directional component. All of these and many other questions that fit into the reject or fail-to-reject NHST framework can be useful for evaluating theories and learning from data. Such questions, however, are not the only type of scientific questions of interest.

In some situations, rather than answering a research question with "the results were statistically significant," the question concerns estimating the magnitude of an effect. For example, the four research questions can be reframed in the magnitude estimation context as follows: (a) How much of the variance in the outcome variable is explained by the proposed model? (b) How strong is the relationship between a predictor and the criterion variable after other predictors have been controlled? (c) How large is the mean difference between the treatment

DOI: 10.1037/13619-012
APA Handbook of Research Methods in Psychology: Vol. 1. Foundations, Planning, Measures, and Psychometrics, H. Cooper (Editor-in-Chief)

group and the control group? (d) How strong is the correlation between the two variables? Each of these questions attempts to quantify the magnitude of an effect with an effect size and corresponding confidence interval, where a confidence interval is an interval that will bracket the population value with some specified degree of confidence. The confidence intervals may contain the null value but still be narrow, which from a magnitude-estimation framework is considered a success, even though it would not be considered a success if the null hypothesis is false but not rejected. Thus, the magnitude-estimation framework, like the NHST framework, can be used to evaluate theories and learn from data, but it does so in a different way.

The various types of questions that researchers may pose have different implications for the methodological techniques required to address the question of interest. Correspondingly, the way in which a study is designed with regard to sample size planning is very much dependent on the type of research question. In this chapter, we discuss both approaches and the implications that choosing one approach over the other have for sample size planning. We discuss sample size planning, including (a) when the existence of an effect or the direction of an effect is of primary interest (from the power analytic perspective) and (b) when the magnitude of an effect is of primary importance (from the accuracy in parameter estimation [AIPE] perspective).

The power analytic approach and the AIPE approach are two fundamentally different ways to plan sample size. For now, however, it is necessary only to understand that the power analytic approach helps to plan sample size when research questions concern *whether an effect exists* and in some cases *the direction of the effect*, whereas the AIPE approach helps to plan sample size when research questions concern *the magnitude of an effect*, which in some but not all cases can also be concerned with *the direction of the effect*. Because the two approaches to sample size planning are fundamentally different, the sample sizes necessary for the approaches may

differ substantially. We do not claim that one approach is better than the other. Rather, we contend that the appropriate approach, and thus the appropriate sample size, is wedded to the research question(s) and the goal(s) of the study.[1]

Kelley and Maxwell (2008) provided a scheme for sample size planning. Their scheme consists of a two-by-two table. One dimension of the table concerns whether the approach to planning sample size is statistical power or AIPE. The other dimension concerns whether the effect of interest is omnibus (relates to the overall model; e.g., the proportion of variance accounted for by group membership) or targeted (relates to a specific well-defined part of the model; e.g., the contrast between a treatment group and control group). Figure 11.1 provides a modified version of the conceptualization presented in Kelley and Maxwell.

It is important to realize that the same research project can pursue questions that fall into more than one of the cells in Figure 11.1. Thus, a researcher could have a goal of obtaining an accurate parameter estimate for a targeted effect, whereupon AIPE for the targeted effect should be used, and also an additional goal of achieving statistical significance for the omnibus effect, whereupon statistical power for the omnibus effect should be used. Even when multiple goals exist, the researcher has to choose a single sample size for the study. We recommend that the largest needed sample sizes be used so that the multiple goals will each *individually* have at least an appropriate sample size. Jiroutek, Muller, Kupper, and Stewart (2003) discussed methods where multiple goals can be satisfied simultaneously with a specified probability.

We begin this chapter with a discussion of effect sizes and their role in research. We then discuss the interpretation of results from the NHST and the magnitude-estimation frameworks. Sample size planning to determine the existence of an effect and sample size planning to estimate the magnitude of the size of the effect are discussed. We then consider appropriate ways to specify the parameter(s)

---

[1]Of course, in research there are many other things to consider when designing a study besides sample size, such as the available resources. Nevertheless, because of the direct impact that sample size has on statistical power and accuracy in parameter estimation, sample size consideration is a necessary, but not sufficient, component of good study design.

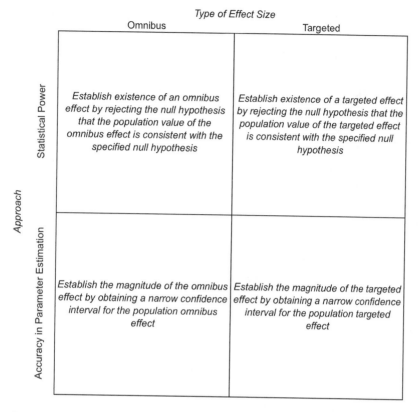

FIGURE 11.1.   Goals of statistical inference for a two-by-two conceptualization of possible scenarios when the approach (statistical power or accuracy in parameter estimation) is crossed with the type of effect size (omnibus or targeted). From "Power and Accuracy for Omnibus and Targeted Effects: Issues of Sample Size Planning With Applications to Multiple Regression," by K. Kelly and S. E. Maxwell, in *The Sage Handbook of Social Research Methods* (p. 168), edited by P. Alasuuta, L. Bickman, and J. Brannen, 2008, Newbury Park, CA: Sage. Copyright 2008 by K. Kelley and E. Maxwell. Adapted with permission of the authors.

necessary to begin a formal process of sample size planning.

EFFECT SIZES AND THEIR ROLE IN RESEARCH

Effect sizes come in many forms with many purposes. Preacher and Kelley (2011) give a general definition of effect size as "any measure that reflects a quantity of interest, either in an absolute sense or compared with some specified value" (p. 95; for more information, see Volume 3, Chapter 6, this handbook). As they note, the quantity of interest might refer to such measures as variability, association, difference, odds, rate, duration, discrepancy, proportionality, superiority, and degree of fit or misfit, among other measures that reflect quantities

of interest. Effect size estimation is the process of estimating the value of an effect size in the population (even if the population value is zero).

Omnibus and Focused Effect Sizes

An effect size of interest can be one that is omnibus or targeted. Consider multiple regression, a commonly used statistical method in psychology and related disciplines. A basic application of multiple regression considers both (a) the overall effectiveness of the model (i.e., an omnibus effect) via the squared multiple correlation coefficient and (b) the specific relationships linking each regressor (e.g., predictor, explanatory variable, independent variable) to the outcome or criterion variable (i.e., a targeted effect), while controlling for the other regressor(s) in the model, via the estimated regression coefficients. An example of other omnibus and targeted effect sizes are the root-mean-square error of approximation (RMSEA) in structural equation modeling, an omnibus effect size that quantifies the overall goodness of fit of the model, whereas path coefficients are targeted effect sizes that quantify the strength of the relationship between two variables. As another example, in fixed-effect one-way analysis of variance, eta-squared is an omnibus effect size that quantifies the proportion of the total variance accounted for by group status, whereas contrasts are targeted effects that quantify the difference between some specified linear combination of means. Similarly, Cramér's V is an omnibus effect size that quantifies the overall association among the rows and columns in a contingency table, whereas the odds ratio is a targeted effect size that quantifies the odds for a certain segment of the table to the odds for another segment of the table for the two-by-two subtable of interest. These examples of omnibus and targeted effect sizes are not exhaustive, but rather illustrate how some effect size measures quantify omnibus effects whereas other effect sizes quantify targeted effects and show how both types of effect sizes can be considered within the same study.[2]

Unstandardized and Standardized Effect Sizes

Effect sizes can be unstandardized or standardized. An unstandardized effect size is one in which a linear transformation of the scaling of the variable(s) changes the value of the effect size. For a standardized effect sizes linear transformations of the scaling of the variable(s) do not affect the value of the calculated effect size. For example, suppose there are five regressors in a multiple regression model. The squared multiple correlation coefficient remains exactly the same regardless of whether the variables in the model are based on the original units or standardized variables (i.e., z-scores). The value of the regression coefficients, however, generally will differ depending on whether variables are standardized or unstandardized.

A two-by-two scheme for types of effect sizes can be constructed by considering whether effect sizes are unstandardized or standardized on one dimension and omnibus or targeted on another dimension. Often, multiple effect sizes are of interest in a single study. Nevertheless, what is important is explicitly linking the type of effect size(s) to the research question(s). Without a clear linkage of the type of effect size to the research question, planning sample size is an ill-defined task; appropriate sample size depends heavily on the particular effect size and the goal(s) of the study. To design a study appropriately, the primary effect size that will be used to answer the research question needs to be identified and clearly articulated.

INTERPRETATION OF RESULTS

As discussed, there are two overarching ways to make inferences about population quantities on the basis of sample data. The first way is NHST, which attempts to reject a specified null value. The second way is magnitude estimation, which attempts to learn the size of the effect in the population on the basis of an estimated effect size and its corresponding confidence interval. We review these two approaches to inference before discussing how sample size planning can be based on one of the two approaches to inference, or possibly a combination of the two.

Null Hypothesis Significance Testing

The rationale of null hypothesis significance testing is to specify a null hypothesis, often that the value of the population effect size of interest is zero, and then to test whether the data obtained are plausible given that the null hypothesis is true. If the results obtained are sufficiently unlikely under the null hypothesis, then the null hypothesis is rejected. "Sufficiently unlikely" is operationalized as the p value from the test of the null hypothesis being less than the specified Type I error rate (e.g., .05).[3] The value of the null hypothesis depends on the situation and the test may concern an omnibus or

[2]To complicate matters somewhat, effect sizes can be partially omnibus or partially targeted. For example, Cramér's V can be applied to a subtable larger than a two-by-two table from a larger contingency table. In such a situation, the effect size represents a semitargeted (or semiomnibus) effect size. We do not consider such semitargeted effect sizes here, as they are not used often and are rarely of primary interest for the outcome of a study.

[3]Recall that the technical meaning of a p-value calculated in the context of an NHST is the probability, given that the null hypothesis is true, of obtaining results as or more extreme than those obtained.

targeted effect size that is either unstandardized or standardized. Regardless of the specific circumstance, the logic of a NHST is exactly the same.

The null hypothesis significance testing framework has been criticized on many occasions (e.g., Bakan, 1966; Cohen, 1994; Meehl, 1967; Rozeboom, 1960; for reviews, see also Harlow, Mulaik, & Steiger, 1997; Morrison & Henkel, 1970; Nickerson, 2000). It is not our intent to criticize or defend this framework. Nevertheless, by requiring statistical significance to infer *that there is an effect* and in certain cases to be able to infer *the direction of an effect* requires that a null hypothesis be specified and tested, generally in the formal NHST framework. Such a framework is a useful guide for evaluating research results so that there is assurance that what was observed in the sample is consistent with what is true in the population.[4]

In some cases, the basic research question involves directionality. For example, the questions might be as follows: (a) Is the population correlation coefficient positive or negative? (b) Does the treatment group have a larger population mean than the control group? (c) Is the population effect of a particular variable positive or negative after controlling for a set of variables? Inference for directionality usually is meaningful only for clearly defined targeted research questions. For example, consider a fixed-effects one-way analysis of variance with more than two groups. Knowledge that there is a statistically significant *F*-test for the null hypothesis that all group means are equal does not signify how the groups are different from one another. This phenomenon is true for many types of situations in which an NHST is used for an omnibus effect size: Rejection of an omnibus null hypothesis does not convey which one or which combination of the multiple target comparisons is responsible for the null hypothesis rejection. One group might have a different mean from the remaining groups with equal means, or, all of the groups might have group means that differ from one another. For a targeted test, however, such as the difference between two group means, rejection of the null hypothesis clearly indicates the direction of the difference.

Effect Sizes and Confidence Intervals

The rationale of confidence interval formation for population parameters comes from the realization that a point estimate almost certainly differs from its corresponding population value. Assuming that the correct model is used, observations are randomly sampled, and the appropriate assumptions are met, $(1 - \alpha)$ is the probability that any given confidence interval from a collection of confidence intervals calculated under the same circumstances will contain the population parameter of interest. The meaning of a $(1 - \alpha)100\%$ confidence interval for some unknown parameter was summarized by Hahn and Meeker (1991) as follows: "if one repeatedly calculates such intervals from many independent random samples, $(1 - \alpha)100\%$ of the intervals would, in the long run, correctly bracket the true value of [the parameter of interest]" (p. 31). Because the values contained within the $(1 - \alpha)100\%$ confidence interval limits are those that cannot be rejected with the corresponding NHST at a Type I error rate of α, they often are regarded as being plausible values of the parameter. The values outside of the $(1 - \alpha)100\%$ confidence limits can be rejected with the corresponding significance test at a Type I error rate of α and often are regarded as implausible values of the parameter.

When a confidence interval is wide, which is a relative statement made on the basis of a particular context, there is much uncertainty about the size of the population value. As Krantz (1999) stated, "a wide confidence interval reveals ignorance [about the population effect size] and thus helps dampen optimism about replicability" (p. 1374). All other things being equal, a narrower confidence interval is preferred to a wider confidence interval when interest concerns the magnitude of the population effect size. As the confidence interval width decreases, such as when sample size increases or when sampling variability decreases, more values are excluded from the confidence interval.

In some situations the confidence interval need not be exceedingly narrow for the confidence interval to be useful. A confidence interval width can be

---

[4]Confidence intervals can be used to evaluate NHST, too, in the sense that a reject or fail-to-reject conclusion is drawn on the basis of whether a specified null hypothesis is contained within the confidence interval. We believe the real strength of using confidence intervals is when estimating the magnitude of an effect size. We momentarily discuss confidence intervals but want to point out that confidence intervals generally can be used as a substitute for NHST.

relatively wide but still exclude parameter values that would support an alternative theory or demonstrate practical significance. For example, if the goal is only to reject a false null hypothesis but not necessarily to bracket the population value with a narrow confidence interval, the confidence interval can be wide but still exclude the specified null value.

The Relationship Between Hypothesis Testing and Confidence Intervals

There is a well-defined relationship between the rejection of a particular NHST and the corresponding upper and lower limits of the confidence interval. If the value corresponding to the null hypothesis falls within the $(1 - \alpha)100\%$ confidence interval limits, that particular null hypothesis value would not be rejected by the corresponding NHST at a Type I error rate of α. The converse is also true: All values outside of the $(1 - \alpha)100\%$ confidence interval limits would be rejected using a Type I error rate of α if any of those values were used as the value of the null hypothesis. Thus, there is a one-to-one relationship between NHST framework using a Type I error rate of α and inference based on the corresponding $(1 - \alpha)100\%$ confidence interval. For example, a confidence interval for an estimated standardized mean difference of 0.25 with equal sample sizes across two groups of 100 participants each has a 95% confidence interval of [−.03, .53]. Zero, a common value of the null hypothesis for the difference between two groups, is contained within the 95% confidence interval, which implies that the null hypothesis of a population standardized mean difference of zero cannot be rejected.

The existence of this relationship between hypothesis testing and confidence intervals has led some authors to suggest that confidence intervals can supplant NHSTs because the confidence interval immediately reveals whether any specific hypothesized

value can be rejected. Other authors have maintained that the NHST provides information not available in a confidence interval, such as a *p*-value.

Regardless of how one views this debate, we will show that both the NHST and AIPE approaches are necessary for sample size planning. The AIPE approach focuses solely on ensuring that an interval will be sufficiently narrow and gives secondary attention to where the center of the interval is likely to be. This is perfectly appropriate when the goal is to obtain an accurate estimate of the parameter. Conversely, power analysis for NHST requires specifying a hypothesized parameter value corresponding to the alternative hypothesis. This generally can be thought of as specifying the expected value of the center of the confidence interval. Sample size planning from the NHST perspective ensures that the confidence interval will not contain the value specified by the null hypothesis with the specified probability. This is fundamentally different from AIPE for estimating the magnitude of an effect with a narrow confidence intervals.

Although a relationship exists between confidence intervals and NHST, each offers its own advantages and each approach dictates its own sample size–planning procedures. Effect size estimates and their accompanying confidence intervals are good at placing boundaries on the magnitude of the corresponding population effect sizes. NHSTs are good at detecting whether effects exist and in certain cases the direction of such effects.[5] Depending on the question of interest, one framework may be more useful than the other, but both should often be used in the same study.

METHODS OF SAMPLE SIZE PLANNING

We have discussed NHST, effect sizes, types of effect sizes, confidence interval formation, and the relationship between NHST and confidence interval

---

[5]We say NHST is useful in some cases for detecting direction because some statistical tests allow directionality to be determined, whereas other types of statistical tests only test if an effect exists. For example, when *t* tests are used to test whether a difference between two group means exists, because the *t*-distribution has only a single degree of freedom parameter, it is known in the sample which group has the larger mean and thus the directionality in the population (e.g., $\mu_1 > \mu_2$) is probabilistically established. If the *F*-distribution is used to assess whether three or more means are all equal in the population, a statistically significant *F*-statistic identifies only that a difference among the means exists, but says nothing about where the difference(s) exists. The *F*-distribution has two degrees of freedom parameters and tests an omnibus hypothesis (except in the special case in which the numerator degrees of freedom equal one, such as when only two groups are involved). A twist on this can be found in Jones and Tukey (2000), in which they discussed a three-outcome framework for an NHST: (a) Reject the null hypothesis in favor of a negative effect, (b) reject the null hypothesis in favor of a positive effect, or (c) fail to reject the null hypothesis. The real twist is that the direction of an alternative hypothesis is not prespecified but is dictated from the sample data. This approach makes the presumption that the null hypothesis cannot literally be true, which in and of itself can be considered a controversial statement.

formation. We have discussed these topics extensively because designing a study with an appropriate sample size depends on these considerations, in addition to other issues. In particular, the approach taken to sample size planning and the planned sample size depends on how these factors come together to answer the research question(s). Without careful consideration of these issues, answering one of the most important questions in planning research, namely, "What sample size do I need?" cannot adequately be answered.

This brings us to two methods of sample size planning. Simply put, when interest concerns the existence or the direction of an effect, a power analysis should be performed to plan an appropriate sample size. If interest is in estimating the magnitude of an effect size, the AIPE approach should be used to plan an appropriate sample size. Recall Figure 11.1, which makes clear the distinction between the goal of establishing the existence of an effect and establishing the magnitude of an effect.

Determining Existence or Direction: Statistical Power and Power Analysis

Statistical power is the probability of correctly rejecting the null hypothesis. Statistical power is based on four quantities: (a) the size of the effect, (b) the model error variance, (c) the Type I error rate (i.e., α), and (d) the sample size. Often, the size of the effect and the model error variance are combined into a standardized effect size.[6] The Type I error rate is a design factor known a priori. In many cases $\alpha = .05$, which is essentially the standard value used in psychology and related disciplines, unless there are justified reasons for some other value to be used.[7] After the Type I error rate is specified and a particular value is chosen for the hypothesized value of the standardized effect size in the population (or effect size and the error variance), statistical power depends only on sample size. Sample size can be planned to obtain a desired level of statistical power on the basis of the specified conditions.

When testing a null hypothesis, the sampling distribution of the effect size of interest is transformed to a test statistic, which is a random variable that, provided the null hypothesis is true, follows a particular statistical distribution (e.g., a central t, χ^2, F). When the null hypothesis is false, however, the test statistic follows a different distribution, namely, the noncentral version of the statistical distribution (e.g., a noncentral t, χ^2, F). The noncentral version of a statistical distribution has a different mean, skewness, and variance, among other properties, as compared with its central distribution analog. Whereas $\alpha100\%$ of the sampling distribution under the null hypothesis is beyond the critical value(s), the noncentral distribution has a larger proportion of its distribution beyond the critical value(s) from the central distribution. If the effect size actually came from a distribution in which case the null hypothesis is false, then the probability will be higher of rejecting the null hypothesis than the specified value of α.

It is advantageous to have a sufficiently large area, which translates into a high probability, of the noncentral distribution beyond a critical value under the null distribution. The area of the noncentral distribution beyond a critical value of the central distribution can be quantified and is termed statistical power. Holding everything else constant, increases in sample size will lead to a larger area (i.e., higher probability) of the noncentral distribution being beyond the critical value from the central distribution. This happens for two reasons, specifically because (a) a larger sample size decreases variability of the null and alternative distributions and (b) larger sample sizes leads to a larger noncentrallity parameter, both of which magnify the difference between the null and alternative distributions.

Figure 11.2 shows the null (central) and alternative (noncentral) distributions in the situation in which there are four groups in a fixed effects analysis of variance design, where the null hypothesis is that the four groups have equal population means. In this situation the supposed population means

---

[6]In cases in which directionality is sensible, such as for a *t* test of the difference between means, in addition to specifying only the Type I error rate, the type of alternative hypothesis (e.g., directional or nondirectional) also must be specified. In other situations for tests that are inherently one tailed, such as for an analysis of variance, such a distinction is unnecessary.

[7]One place in which a Type I error rate other than .05 might be used is in the multiple comparison context, where, for example, a Bonferroni correction is used (e.g., .05/4 = .0125 if there were four contrasts to be performed).

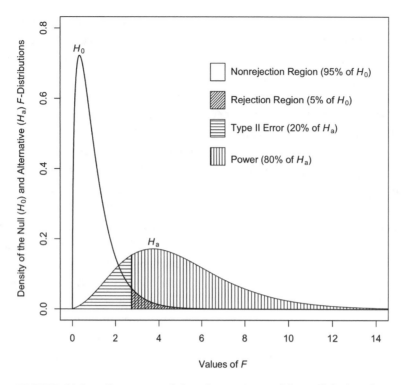

FIGURE 11.2.   Illustration of the relevant areas of the null (H_0) and alternative (H_a) distributions for statistical power of .80 in a four-group fixed effects analysis of variance when the population group means are specified as –0.50, 0.0, 0.0, 0.5 for the first through fourth groups, respectively, and where the within group standard deviation for each of the groups is 1.0, which requires 23 participants per group (92 total).

are [–.5, 0, 0, .5] for a common within group standard deviation of 1. The effect size, f, is then .35 (see Cohen, 1988, section 8.2, for information on f). To have power of .80, it is necessary to have a sample size of 23 per group (92 total). Figure 11.2 displays this situation, where the alternative distribution has a noncentrality parameter of 11.5. As can be seen in Figure 11.2, the mean of the noncentral F distribution (i.e., H_a) is much greater than it is for the central F distribution (i.e., H_0). The larger the noncentral parameter, the larger the mean of the alternative distribution, implying that, holding everything else constant, increases in the noncentral parameter will increase statistical power. The effect of this is that as the noncentral parameter becomes larger and larger (e.g., from increasing sample size), the bulk of the alternative distribution is shifted farther and farther to the right. At the same time, the null distribution is unchanged, which implies that a smaller area of the alternative distribution is less than the critical value from the

null distribution (i.e., the probability of a Type II error is decreased, where a Type II error is the failure to reject a null hypothesis when the null hypothesis is false).

It is often recommended that statistical power should be .80, that is, there should be an 80% chance that a false null hypothesis will be rejected. Although we do not think anything is wrong with a power of .80, we want to make it clear that when α is set to the de facto standard value of .05 and power is set at .80, the probability of a Type II error (1 – .80 = .20) is four times larger than the probability of a Type I error. Whether this is good is determined on the basis of a trade-off between false positives (Type I errors) and false negatives (Type II errors). The most appropriate way to proceed in such a situation is to consider the consequences of a Type I versus a Type II error. If an effect exists and it is not found (i.e., a Type II error has been committed), what are the implications? In some research settings, there may be little if any consequences. If finding the effect would have been used to advance a major initiative that would greatly benefit society or a specific population, a Type II error could have major implications. In such situations, the Type II error can be regarded as more important than a Type I error, and consistent with the importance, setting the probability of a Type II error to be more like, or even less than, the probability of a Type I error would be desirable.

Determining the Magnitude of an Effect: Accuracy in Parameter Estimation

In general, when an effect size is of interest, the corresponding confidence interval for that effect should be of interest as well. The estimated effect size from a sample almost certainly differs from its corresponding population value. The ultimate interest in research usually is the population value of an effect, rather than an estimate from some particular sample that necessarily contains sampling error. Thus, in addition to reporting the estimated effect size (i.e., the best single point estimate of the population parameter), researchers should report the confidence interval limits for the population value.

Confidence intervals are important in part because of a belief in the "law of small numbers," which states that people often employ the flawed intuition that there is a lack of variability of estimates from samples (Tversky & Kahneman, 1971). Tversky and Kahneman suggested that confidence intervals be reported because they provide "a useful index of sampling variability, and it is precisely this variability that we tend to underestimate" (1971, p. 110). Kelley (2005) has noted that reporting any point estimate "in the absence of a confidence interval arguably does a disservice to those otherwise interested in the phenomenon under study" (p. 52). Similarly, Bonett (2008) has argued that "the current practice of reporting only a point estimate of an effect size is actually a step backwards from the goal of improving the quality of psychological research" (p. 99; see also Thompson, 2002). The American Psychological Association (APA; 2010) *Publication Manual* clearly states the importance of effect sizes and confidence intervals: "It is almost always necessary to include some measure of effect size in the Results section," and "whenever possible, provide a

confidence interval for each effect size reported to indicate the precision of estimation of the effect size" (p. 34). Psychology and related disciplines have emphasized including effect sizes and their confidence intervals as an alternative to or in addition to NHSTs (e.g., see Grissom & Kim, 2005; Harlow, Mulaik, & Steiger, 1997; Hunter & Schmidt, 2004; Schmidt, 1996; Thompson, 2002; Wilkinson & the APA Task Force on Statistical Inference, 1999).

A wide confidence interval reflects the uncertainty with which a parameter has been estimated. Historically, confidence intervals were seldom reported in psychology and related disciplines. Although not routinely reported now, their use seems to have increased in at least some journals. Cumming et al. (2007) have shown that for 10 leading international psychology journals, the use of confidence intervals increased from 3.7% in 1989 to 10.6% in 2005–2006. This is not ideal, but it is a start. Cohen (1994) once suggested that the reason more researchers did not report confidence intervals was that their widths were often "embarrassingly large" (p. 1002). Wide confidence intervals often can be avoided with proper sample size planning from an AIPE approach, which differs from traditional methods of sample size planning whose goal is to obtain adequate statistical power. It may seem that because there is a one-to-one relationship with regards to rejecting the null hypothesis and the null value being outside of the confidence interval, there might be a one-to-one relationship between sample size planning for statistical power and sample size planning for AIPE. This is not the case, however. In particular, the goals of AIPE are satisfied even if the null value is contained within the confidence interval as long as the interval width is sufficiently narrow. The goals of power analysis can be satisfied even with a wide confidence interval as long as the hypothesized value is not contained within the interval. Although for any confidence interval it is known whether the null hypothesis value can be rejected, for sample size–planning purposes, the goals are fundamentally different and approached in an entirely different way. When magnitude is of interest, the computed confidence interval should be narrow, as that signifies less uncertainty about the value of the population parameter. So, the question confronting a researcher interested in magnitude estimation is how to choose a sample size that will provide a sufficiently narrow confidence interval.

The approach to sample size planning when the goal is to obtain narrow confidence intervals has been termed AIPE. The goal of the AIPE approach is to plan sample size so that the confidence interval for the parameter of interest will be sufficiently narrow, where *sufficiently narrow* is necessarily context specific. The AIPE approach to sample size planning has taken on an important role in the research design literature, as it is known that researchers (a) tend to overestimate how precise an estimate is, (b) prefer not to have wide confidence intervals, and (c) are expected to report effect sizes and their corresponding confidence intervals. This push in psychology (e.g., Journal Article Reporting Standards [JARS]; APA, 2010) and education (e.g., American Educational Research Association, 2006) to report effect sizes and confidence intervals is consistent with medical research, where the Consolidated Standard of Reporting Trials (CONSORT; Moher et al., 2010) and the Transparent Reporting of Evaluations with Nonrandomized Designs (TREND; Des Jarlais, Lyles, Crepaz, & the TREND Group, 2004) both state that effect sizes and confidence intervals should be reported for primary and secondary outcomes (see item 17 in both checklists). Because of the need for confidence intervals that are not "embarrassingly wide" (Cohen, 1994, p. 1002), we believe that the AIPE approach to sample size planning will play an integral role in research in the coming years.

Confidence interval width is in part a function of sample size. To understand why sample size planning for a narrow confidence interval is termed *accuracy in parameter estimation*, it is helpful to consider the definition of accuracy. In statistics, accuracy is defined as the square root of the mean square error (RMSE) for estimating some parameter θ of interest, which is formally defined as follows:

$$\text{RMSE} = \sqrt{\text{E}[(\hat{\theta} - \theta)^2]} \tag{1a}$$

$$= \sqrt{\text{E}[(\hat{\theta} - \text{E}[\hat{\theta}])^2] + (\text{E}[\hat{\theta}] - \theta])^2} \tag{1b}$$

$$= \sqrt{\sigma_{\hat{\theta}}^2 + B_{\hat{\theta}}^2}, \tag{1c}$$

where $\sigma_{\hat{\theta}}^2$ is the variance of the estimated parameter, which is inversely proportional to the precision of the estimator and $B_{\hat{\theta}}^2$ is the squared bias of the estimator. From Equation 1c, it can readily be seen for a fixed $\sigma_{\hat{\theta}}^2$, an increase in $B_{\hat{\theta}}^2$ yields a less accurate estimate (i.e., larger RMSE), with the converse also being true. Because we seek to obtain an accurate estimate, we must consider precision and bias simultaneously. In general, the AIPE approach uses estimates that are unbiased, or at least consistent (i.e., that converge to their population value as sample size increases). It would be entirely possible to have a precise estimate that was biased. For example, regardless of the data, a researcher could estimate a parameter on the basis of a theory-implied value. Doing so would not be statistically optimal, in general, because the theory-implied value is unlikely to be correct, but the estimate would be highly precise (e.g., its variance could be zero). Because AIPE simultaneously considers precision and bias when estimating sample size, the approach is most appropriately referred to as accuracy in parameter estimation.

Just as the Type I error rate usually is fixed at .05, as previously discussed for statistical power, the confidence level is essentially a fixed design factor, which almost always is set to .95. With the level of confidence fixed and with estimates for the model error variance and in some situations the size of the effect considered fixed, sample size is a factor that can be planned so that the expected confidence interval width is sufficiently narrow. Because the confidence interval width is itself a random variable, even if the expected confidence interval width is sufficiently narrow, any particular realization almost certainly will be either narrower or wider than desired. An optional specification allows a researcher to have some specified degree of assurance (e.g., 99%) that the obtained confidence interval will be sufficiently narrow. That is, a modification to the standard procedure, where only the expected width is sufficiently narrow, answers the question, "What size sample is necessary so that there is 99% assurance that the 95% confidence interval is sufficiently narrow?" What is "sufficiently narrow" necessarily depends on the particular context. Most important, the confidence interval will bracket the population value with the specified level of confidence, which implies that the estimated effect size on which the confidence interval was based, or its unbiased or more unbiased version, will be contained within a smaller range of plausible parameter values.[8] Because of the narrow range of plausible parameter values and the estimate of choice being within that narrow range, the estimate is one that is more accurate than one with a confidence interval wider than that observed, all other things being equal.

Parameter Specification When Planning Sample Size

One or more nondesign factors must be specified in all of the sample size planning procedures commonly used. The valuess that must be specified to plan the sample size depend on the statistics of interest and the type of sample size planning procedure. For example, planning sample size for statistical power for an unstandardized mean difference between two groups requires that a mean difference and the standard deviation must be separately specified. Alternatively, a standardized mean difference can be specified. For an unstandardized mean difference, from the AIPE approach, only the error variance (or standard deviation) must be specified, as the confidence interval width is independent of the size of the mean difference. Choosing relevant values to use for the approaches is often difficult because the many times the values are unknown. The values used, however, can have a sizable impact on the resulting sample size calculation. For this reason, the difficulty in estimating an effect size to use for purposes of sample size planning has been labeled the "problematic parameter" (Lipsey, 1990, p. 47).

The existing literature generally should be the guiding sources of information for choosing parameter values when planning sample size. Some areas have an ample body of literature that exists

and perhaps meta-analyses that estimate the effect size of interest. When such information is available, it should be used. When such information is not readily available, planning sample size often is difficult. Guidelines that seem to make the process easier generally have been shown to be inappropriate (e.g., Green, 1991; MacCallum, Widaman, Zhang, & Hong, 1999; Maxwell, 2004), largely because they tend to ignore one or more of the following: (a) the question of interest, (b) the effect size, (c) characteristics of the model to be used, (d) characteristics of the population of interest, (e) the research design, (f) the measurement procedure(s), (g) the failure to distinguish between targeted and omnibus effects, and (h) the desired level of statistical power or the width of the desired confidence interval. In the remainder of this section, we discuss the specification of parameters for power analysis and accuracy in parameter estimation.

For power analysis, there are two common approaches for choosing parameter values. The first approach uses the best estimates available for the necessary population parameter(s), which usually is made on the basis of a review of the literature (e.g., via meta-analytic methods) or data from a pilot study. The second approach uses the minimum parameter value of interest (MPVI) by linking the size of an effect to its meaningfulness for a theory or application. In using the MPVI, there will be sufficient power if the magnitude of the effect size is as large as specified and even more power if the effect size is larger in the population.[9]

Both the literature review and MPVI approaches are potentially useful when planning sample size, but the appropriate choice will depend on the information available and the research goals. If the goal is to plan sample size for what is believed true in the population, then the literature review approach generally should be used. If the goal is to plan sample size on the basis of the minimum value of the effect

---

[8]To better understand how sample size influences the width of a confidence interval, consider the case of normally distributed data when the population standard deviation, σ, is known and a 95% two-sided confidence interval is of interest. Such a confidence interval can be expressed as $\bar{x} \pm 1.96\, \sigma/\sqrt{n}$, where $\bar{x}$ is the sample mean and n is the sample size. The estimated mean, $\bar{x}$, is necessarily contained within the confidence interval limits. As the sample size increases, the margin of error (i.e., $1.96\, \sigma/\sqrt{n}$) decreases. For example, suppose $\sigma = 15$. For a sample size of $n = 10$, the margin of error is 9.30, whereas the margin of error is 2.94 when $n = 100$. Because the range of plausible parameter values is 5.88 for the later case, it is preferred, holding everything else constant, to the former case with a confidence interval width of 18.60. A similar relationship holds for confidence intervals for other quantities.

[9]We use standardized effect size here so that both the unstandardized effect size and the model error variance are considered simultaneously.

size that is of scientific or practical importance and interest, then the MPVI approach generally should be used.

As an example of using the MPVI, suppose that only a standardized mean difference of 0.20 in magnitude or larger would be of interest in a particular setting. Choosing this value for the MPVI essentially implies that any value of the population standardized mean difference less than 0.20 in magnitude is of little to no value in the particular research context. If this is the case, then the parameter value used for the sample size planning procedure need not be literally the true but unknown population effect size. Instead, it can be the minimum parameter value that is of theoretical or practical interest. If the population value of the effect size is larger than the chosen MPVI, then statistical power will be greater than the nominal level specified. Senn (2002) addressed this idea by saying,

> The difference you are seeking is not the same as the difference you expect to find, and again you do not have to know what the treatment will do to find a figure. This is common to all science. An astronomer does not know the magnitude of new stars until he [or she] has found them, but the magnitude of star he [or she] is looking for determines how much he [or she] has to spend on a telescope. (p. 1304)

Although using the MPVI to plan sample size can be useful in some situations, O'Brien and Castelloe (2007) illustrated that such a method potentially can be misguided, specifically in the power analytic approach. But, the issue is also relevant to some applications of the AIPE approach. O'Brien and Castelloe highlighted this potential problem with the MPVI approach using a hypothetical example in the context of lowering the mortality rate of children with malaria, which is estimated to be 15% for "usual care." They noted that reasonable people would tend to agree that a reduction in the rate of mortality by 5% of the usual care (which would

lower the mortality rate of 15% by 5% to 14.25%) would be "clinically relevant" (2007, pp. 244–245). In their scenario, however, the necessary sample size increases from 2,700 patients to detect a 33% reduction in mortality rate (which would lower the mortality rate of 15% by 33% to 10%;) to 104,700 patients to detect a 5% reduction. This is too large of a study to conduct in their specific context. With such a large number of patients required to detect the MPVI value, the study might not be conducted because resources may not be available for 104,700 patients. So, although a 5% reduction in mortality rate may be the MPVI, the sample size is such that the study might never be conducted. If a 33% reduction is a reasonable value for the size of the effect in the population, it almost certainly would be preferable to carry out the study with only 2,700 patients. In so doing, the study actually may be conducted because resources may be available for only 2,700 patients. O'Brien and Castelloe (2007) argued that their hypothetical scenario "exemplifies why confirmatory trials are usually designed to detect plausible outcome differences that are considerably larger than 'clinically relevant'" (p. 248). Thus, although the MPVI approach can be useful in certain situations, it is not necessarily universally preferred as a way to plan sample size from the power analytic perspective.

For power analysis, holding everything else constant, the larger the magnitude of the effect size, the more statistical power a study has to detect the effect. This is not necessarily the case with the AIPE approach, however. For example, Kelley and Rausch (2006) have showed that, holding everything else constant, confidence intervals for a sufficiently narrow expected width will require a larger sample size for larger population standardized mean differences than for smaller differences. That is, for a given expected confidence interval width (e.g., say 0.25 units), the sample size required for a population standardized mean of 0.05 requires a smaller sample size (347 per group) than does a population standardized mean difference of 1.00 (390 per group).[10]

---

[10]For fixed sample sizes, the larger the population standardized mean difference, the larger the noncentrality parameter, which implies a larger variance for the sampling distribution of observed standardized mean differences when the population standardized mean difference is larger (see Hedges & Olkin, 1985, for more details). Thus, the larger the population standardized mean difference, the larger the sample size will need to be for the same confidence interval width.

The relationship between necessary sample size for a particular expected confidence interval width and the size of the population standardized mean difference is monotonic in the AIPE approach—the larger the population standardized mean difference the larger the necessary sample size, holding everything else constant.[11] For narrow confidence intervals, however, for the population squared multiple correlation coefficient, the relationship between the size of the population multiple correlation coefficient and the necessary sample size for a specified width is nonmonotonic—necessary sample size for an expected confidence interval width is maximized around a population squared multiple correlation value of around .333 (Kelley, 2008). In other situations, the size of the effect is unrelated to the confidence interval width. Kelley, Maxwell, and Rausch (2003) showed that for an unstandardized mean difference, desired confidence interval width is independent of the population difference between means. Correspondingly, sample size from the AIPE approach does not consider the size of the unstandardized mean difference, and thus it is not necessary to specify the mean difference when planning sample size from the accuracy in parameter estimation approach, unlike the power analytic approach where it is necessary. The point is that the relationship between the size of the effect and the necessary sample size from the AIPE approach, holding everything else constant, depends on the particular effect size measure.

To summarize, for power analysis, the larger the magnitude of an effect size, the smaller the necessary sample size for a particular level of statistical power, holding all other factors constant. For AIPE, however, such a universal statement cannot be made. This is the case because the way in which the value of an effect size is used in the confidence interval procedure depends on the particular effect size measure. There are two broad categories of effect sizes as they relate to their corresponding confidence intervals: (a) those whose confidence intervals depend on the value of the effect size and (b) those whose confidence intervals are independent of

the value of the effect size. The literature on confidence intervals is a guide for the way in which confidence intervals are formed for the population value of an effect size (e.g., Grissom & Kim, 2005; Smithson, 2003). In the next section, we implement some of the ideas discussed in the context of multiple regression. In particular, we provide an example in which sample size is planned using the MBESS (Kelley, 2007b; Kelley & Lai, 2011) package in the program R (R Development Core Team, 2011) for a targeted (regression coefficient) and an omnibus (the squared multiple correlation coefficient) effect size from both the power analytic and AIPE perspectives.

Sample Size Planning for Multiple Regression: An Organizational Behavior Example

Core self-evaluations can be described as fundamental, subconscious conclusions that individuals reach about themselves, their relationships to others, and the world around them (e.g., Judge & Bono, 2001; Judge, Locke, & Durham, 1997; Judge, Locke, Durham, & Kluger, 1998). Judge et al. (1997) argued from a theoretical perspective that individuals' appraisals of objects are affected by their assumptions about themselves in addition to the attributes of the objects and their desires with respect to the objects. Judge et al. (1998) found empirical support for core self-evaluations having a consistent effect on job satisfaction, with core self-evaluations largely being unrelated to the attributes of the job.

Grant and Wrzesniewski (2010) noted that "little research has considered how core self-evaluations may interact with other kinds of individual differences to moderate the relationship between core self-evaluations and job performance" (p. 117). Grant and Wrzesniewski tested a model in which a measure of Performance (financial productivity over a 3-week period) was modeled as a linear function of Core Self-Evaluations, Duty, Anticipated Guilt, Anticipated Gratitude, and the three two-way interactions of Core Self-Evaluations with the remaining three regressors.

[11]Interestingly, in the power analytic approach, the relationship between necessary sample size and the size of the population standardized mean difference is also monotonic, but in the other direction—the larger the population standardized mean difference the smaller the necessary sample size for a particular level of statistical power (e.g., .90), holding everything else constant.

TABLE 11.1

Summary Statistics Taken (Means and Correlations) or Derived (Variances and Covariances)

Variable	Mean	1	2	3	4	5	6	7	8
1. Performance	3153.70	*11923209.000*	0.00	0.14	0.03	0.13	0.27	0.31	0.34
2. Core self-evaluation (CSE)	5.00	0.000	*0.608*	0.23	0.00	0.15	−0.10	−0.10	0.02
3. Duty	5.11	430.360	0.160	*0.792*	0.48	0.40	−0.05	−0.01	0.10
4. Guilt	3.97	152.318	0.000	0.628	*2.160*	0.33	−0.01	0.09	0.24
5. Gratitude	4.29	507.382	0.132	0.402	0.548	*1.277*	0.10	0.25	0.29
6. CSE x Duty	0.23	923.236	−0.077	−0.044	−0.015	0.112	*0.980*	0.38	0.38
7. CSE x Guilt	0.00	1017.182	−0.074	−0.008	0.126	0.268	0.357	*0.903*	0.26
8. CSE x Gratitude	0.15	1139.11	0.151	0.086	0.342	0.318	0.461	0.240	*0.941*

Note. Variances are in the principle diagonal and are italicized, covariances are in the lower diagonal, and correlation coefficients are in the upper diagonal. Sample size is 86. Adapted from "I Won't Let You Down . . . or Will I? Core Self-Evaluations, Other-Orientation, Anticipated Guilt and Gratitude, and Job Performance," by A. M. Grant and A. Wrzesniewski, 2010, *Journal of Applied Psychology, 95*, p. 115. Copyright 2010 by the American Psychological Association.

A primary focus of the research was an "other-orientation," which Grant and Wrzesniewski (2010) described as the "extent to which employees value and experience concern for the well-being of other people" (p. 109; see also De Dreu & Nauta, 2009). The Duty regressor, which quantifies the "tendency toward dependability and feelings of responsibility for others" (p. 111), is an other-oriented attribute and thus a driving force of the research, especially on how it is moderated by Core Self-Evaluation.

To test the model, data were collected from 86 call center employees engaged in an outbound calling campaign raising money for job creation at a university. Descriptive statistics obtained (means, standard deviations, and correlations) or derived (variances and covariances) from Grant and Wrzesniewski (2010) are contained in Table 11.1, with the results from a standardized regression model (i.e., a regression model applied to standardized scores) given in Table 11.2.[12] The results of the regression model show that two regression coefficients are statistically significant, namely, the interaction of Core Self-Evaluation with Duty and the interaction of Core Self-Evaluation with Gratitude. Although Duty was found to have an interaction with Core Self-evaluation on Performance, the conditional effect of Duty when Core Self-Evaluation equals zero (i.e., at the mean) has a 95% confidence interval for the population value that ranges from −0.038 to 0.456. Notice that zero is contained in the confidence interval for the conditional Duty regression coefficient, which is necessarily the case because the corresponding NHST failed to reach statistical significance (the *p* value for Duty is .097). Additionally, the interaction of Anticipated Gratitude and Core Self-Evaluation was also statistically significant. The squared multiple correlation coefficient for the entire model was .201 (*p* value is .01) with 95% confidence interval limits for the population value of [.01, .31]; the adjusted squared multiple correlation coefficient was .132.

Although the overall model was statistically significant and there were two statistically significant interactions, none of the four conditional effects

[12]Grant and Wrzesniewski (2010) fit the unstandardized model given in Table 11.2. Confidence intervals for regression coefficients and the squared multiple correlation coefficient were not given in Grant and Wrzesniewski but are provided here. The standardized solution is used here because the standardized regression coefficients quantify the expected change in the dependent variable in standard deviation units for a one standard deviation change in the particular regressor. For example, a standardized regression coefficient of .20 means that a 1 unit (corresponding to 1 standard deviation) change in the regressor will have a .20 unit (corresponding to .20 standard deviation) change on the dependent variable. Standardized regression coefficients have a straightforward interpretation and interest is in relative performance, not literally modeling the total 3-week productivity of employees.

TABLE 11.2

Results of Standardized Regression Model of Interest

Regressors	Coefficient	95% confidence interval limits
1. Core self-evaluation (CSE)	−0.016	[−.224, .192]
2. Duty	0.210	[−.038, .456]
3. Guilt	−0.142	[−.380, .098]
4. Gratitude	−0.052	[−.285, .182]
5. CSE x Duty	0.057	[−.185, .299]
6. CSE x Guilt	0.242*	[.016, .467]
7. CSE x Gratitude	0.278*	[.032, .521]
R^2	.203*	[.01, .31]
Adjusted R^2	.132	

Note. Values in brackets represent the lower and upper 95% confidence interval limits. All confidence intervals are based on noncentral methods because the effect sizes are standardized and are calculated with the MBESS R package. Data from Grant and Wrzesniewski (2010).
* $p < .05$.

(Duty, Anticipated Gratitude, Core Self-Evaluation, and Gratitude) reached statistical significance. Because of the importance of understanding how other-oriented attributes are associated with Performance as well as understanding how much Performance can be explained by such a model, suppose that a follow-up study based on Grant and Wrzesniewski (2010) needs to be planned. How might sample size be planned in such a context? We briefly review multiple regression so that notation can be defined and used in the sample size planning procedure. All sample sizes are planned with the MBESS (Kelley, 2007b; Kelley & Lai, 2011) R package (R Development Core Team, 2011). We will provide the necessary code to plan sample size, but because of space restrictions, we are unable to provide a detailed explanation of the MBESS functions used for sample size planning. Kelley (2007a), however, has reviewed methods of estimating effect sizes and forming confidence intervals for the corresponding population value, and Kelley and Maxwell (2008) have provided a more thorough treatment of using the MBESS R package for sample size planning in a regression context.

The Multiple Regression Model

The multiple regression model in the population is

$$Y_i = \beta_0 + X_{i1}\beta_1 + X_{i2}\beta_2 + \ldots + X_{iK}\beta_K + \varepsilon_i, \quad (2)$$

where Y_i is the dependent variable of interest for the ith individual ($i = 1, \ldots, N$), β_0 is the intercept, X_{ik} is the value of the kth ($k = 1, \ldots, K$) regressor variable for the ith individual, and ε_i is the error for the ith individual (i.e., $\varepsilon_i = Y_i - \hat{Y}_i$, where $\hat{Y}_i$ is the model implied value of the dependent variable for the ith individual). The K length vector of regression coefficients is obtained from the following expression:

$$\beta = \Sigma_{XX}^{-1}\sigma_{XY}, \quad (3)$$

where β is the K length vector of regression coefficients, Σ_{XX} is the population $K \times K$ covariance matrix of the regressor variables, with a "−1" exponent denoting the inverse of the matrix, and σ_{XY} is a K length column vector of the population covariances of the dependent variable with each of the regressors. The population intercept is obtained from

$$\beta_0 = \mu_Y - \mu_X'\beta, \quad (4)$$

where μ_Y is the population mean of the dependent variable and μ_x is the K length vector of population means for the regressors with the prime superscript denoting matrix–vector transposition (where columns are interchanged with rows).

The population squared multiple correlation coefficient is obtained as follows:

$$P_{Y\cdot X}^2 = \frac{\sigma_{XY}'\Sigma_{XX}^{-1}\sigma_{XY}}{\sigma_Y^2}, \quad (5)$$

where P is the uppercase Greek letter rho, with the subscript representing Y being regressed on (the centered dot) the set of regressors of interest.

Equation 5 has assumed population values for an unstandardized regression model. Sample values of the means, variances, and covariances can be substituted for the population values to obtain the usual ordinary least squares regression estimates. Should a standardized regression model be of interest, the means of the outcome variable and the regressors are all zero, thus eliminating the intercept from the model because of its value being zero, and the $K \times K$

correlation matrix of the regressor variables is then substituted for Σ_{XX} and the vector of correlations between the K regressors and Y is substituted for σ_{XY}. Because a correlation matrix is simply a standardized covariance matrix, Equations 2 through 5 hold for the point estimates from the multiple regression model in standardized form.[13] Using this notation, we will move forward with the examples of how sample size can be planned in the context of multiple regression from both the statistical power and AIPE perspectives, for targeted (the Duty regression coefficient) and omnibus (the squared multiple correlation coefficient) effect sizes.

THE POWER ANALYTIC APPROACH TO SAMPLE SIZE PLANNING

When interest concerns the existence of an effect, the power analytic approach to sample size planning should be used. The following two subsections illustrate power analysis for a regression coefficient and for the squared multiple correlation coefficient using the MBESS R package.

Statistical Power for a Targeted Effect (β_k)

Although the regression coefficient for the conditional effect of Duty was not statistically significant in the Grant and Wrzesniewski (2010) study, theory suggests that it is a nonzero positive value. It is possible that the Grant and Wrzesniewski (2010) study did not have sufficient power to detect this specific effect. Evidence that the conditional Duty regression coefficient in the population is a positive value would come from a statistically significant positive regression coefficient, signifying that when the other predictors are at their mean (i.e., zero), Duty has a linear impact on Performance. Using a Type I error rate of .05 and a two-sided NHST, we seek to answer the question, "What size sample is necessary in order to have statistical power of .95 to reject the null hypothesis that the conditional Duty regression coefficient equals zero?" Note that we plan sample size

for statistical power of .95 to weight the probability of a Type I and Type II error the same, implying that neither type of error has differential preference.

As is almost always the case with sample size planning, input parameters are necessary to define the alternative distribution. For lack of better information, we will use the sample values from Grant and Wrzesniewski (2010). Planning sample size in this context involves three parameters, which can be obtained from Σ_{XX} and σ_{XY}. In particular, the three necessary values are β_k, the value of the population regression coefficient of interest, $\mathrm{P}^2_{Y \cdot X}$, the value of the population squared multiple correlation coefficient, and $\mathrm{P}^2_{X_k \cdot X_{-k}}$, which is the value of the population squared multiple correlation coefficient when the regressor of interest is regressed on the remaining $K-1$ regressors. That is, $\mathrm{P}^2_{X_k \cdot X_{-k}}$ is the squared multiple correlation coefficient for a model where X_k is the outcome variable and the other $K-1$ regressors continue to be used as regressors. $\mathrm{P}^2_{X_k \cdot X_{-k}}$ can be obtained using the equations given above (if X_k is substituted for Y and regressed on the remaining $K-1$ regressors) or via the following expression:

$$\mathrm{P}^2_{X_k \cdot X_{-k}} = 1 - \left(\sigma_k^2 c_{kk} \right)^{-1}, \tag{6}$$

where c_{kk} is the kth diagonal element of Σ_{XX}^{-1} (Harris, 2001). In the Grant and Wrzesniewski (2010) study, the estimated $\mathrm{P}^2_{X_k \cdot X_{-k}} = .34$.

Given the preceding, the sample size needed so that the conditional Duty regression coefficient will have statistical power of .95 can be planned using the `ss.power.rc()` MBESS function is as follows:

```
ss.power.rc(β_k = .21, P²_Y·X = .20, P²_Y·X
    =.34, K = 7, desired.power =.95,
    α.level = 0.05, σ_Y = 1, σ_Y = 1)
```

where β_k is the hypothesized population value of the regression coefficient (standardized here), $\mathrm{P}^2_{Y \cdot X}$ is the hypothesized population value of the squared multiple correlation coefficient, $\mathrm{P}^2_{Y \cdot X}$ is the hypothesized

---

[13]Although multiple regression model in a standardized form can offer interpretational ease, exact confidence intervals for standardized regression coefficients are more difficult than their unstandardized counterparts. A discussion of this is provided in Kelley (2007b). We used software to compute the confidence intervals, which are based on noncentral t-distributions, and not delve into the details of computation here. Additionally, computing confidence intervals for the squared multiple correlation coefficient is also difficult, and we do not discuss the details. Kelley (2008) has reviewed methods of confidence interval formation for the squared multiple correlation coefficient, which is unchanged regardless of an unstandardized or standardized model that is fitted. In practice, the confidence intervals in these situations can be obtained easily with the MBESS software.

population value of the squared multiple correlation coefficient when the regressor of interest is regressed on the remaining K-1 regressors, `K` is the number of regressors, `desired.power` is the desired level of statistical power, `alpha.level` is the Type I error rate, and `sigma.X` and `sigma.Y` are the population standard deviations of the regressor of interest and the dependent variable. Implementation of the function as shown in Equation 7 returns a necessary sample size of 380. Thus, if a researcher wanted to have statistical power of .95 for the test of the conditional Duty regression coefficient, given our assumptions, a sample size of 380 would be necessary.

Statistical Power for the Omnibus Effect ($P^2_{Y \cdot X}$)

In some applications of multiple regression, no single regressor is of primary importance. Correspondingly, it is sometimes of interest only to have a model that, overall, accounts for a statistically significant portion of the variance of the outcome variable. In particular, of interest is obtaining a statically significant test of the squared multiple correlation coefficient. To plan sample size for statistical power of the squared multiple correlation coefficient, the only population value that must be known or estimated is $P^2_{Y \cdot X}$.

The `ss.power.R2()` MBESS function can be used to plan sample size for a specified value of power for the test of the squared multiple correlation coefficient. The way in which the function is used is as follows:

```
ss.power.R2(Population.R2=.20,
alpha.level = 0.05, desired.
power = 0.95, K = 7)
```

where `Population.R2` is the hypothesized population value of the squared multiple correlation coefficient, with the other parameters of the function as defined previously. Implementation of the above function returns a necessary sample size of 95. Thus, to have statistical power of .95 that some of the variability in the dependent variable (here

Performance) is being accounted for in the population by the set of regressors, where the presumed squared multiple correlation coefficient is .20 with seven regressors and a Type I error rate of .05, a sample size of 95 is necessary.

THE AIPE APPROACH TO SAMPLE SIZE PLANNING

When interest concerns the magnitude of an effect size, the AIPE approach to sample size planning should be used.

AIPE for a Targeted Effect (β_k)

The 95% confidence interval from the Grant and Wrzesniewski (2010) study for the standardized conditional Duty regression coefficient is [−.038, .456]. This confidence interval is so wide that it illustrates the lack of knowledge about the population value of the standardized conditional Duty regression coefficient. Correspondingly, it really is not clear how much of an impact, if any, the conditional effect of Duty has on Performance when the other regressors are zero. Although theory suggests that the conditional Duty should have a positive impact on Performance, the magnitude of that impact is important. Suppose there is a desire to have a 95% confidence interval for the conditional Duty regression coefficient that is .20 units wide. The population parameters that must be known or estimated for an application of AIPE to a standardized regression coefficient are $P^2_{Y \cdot X}$, $P^2_{X_k \cdot X_{-k}}$, and β_k, as in the context of statistical power.[14]

The function ss.aipe.src() from the MBESS R package can be used as follows:

```
ss.aipe.src(Rho2.Y_X=.20,
Rho2.k_X.without.k=.34, K = 7,
beta.k=.21, width=.20, conf.
level=.95, assurance = NULL)
```

where width is the desired confidence interval with and the other function parameters are as defined in the `ss.power.rc()` function. Implementation of the above function returns a necessary sample size of 482.

[14]The value of the regression coefficient is necessary in this case because we are working with a standardized solution. In the case of an unstandardized solution, however, the confidence interval for the (unstandardized) regression coefficient is independent of the confidence interval. Correspondingly, it is unnecessary to know or estimate an unstandardized regression coefficient in the context of AIPE. See Kelley (2007b) and Kelley and Maxwell (2008) for more details. The power analytic approach, for both unstandardized and standardized regression coefficients, requires the known or estimated population value of the regression coefficient.

Notice that `assurance = NULL` is specified above, which implies that an assurance parameter is not incorporated into this sample size planning procedure. Thus, approximately half of the time the confidence interval will be wider than the desired value of .20. By specifying some assurance value (a value greater than .50 but less than 1), however, the modified sample size can be obtained. For example, if the desired assurance is .99, the above code can be modified as follows

```
ss.aipe.src(Rho2.Y_X=.20,
Rho2.k_X.without.k=.34, K = 7,
beta.k=.21, width=.20, conf.
level=.95, assurance=.99)
```

where assurance is the desired level of assurance and conf.level is the confidence level of interest. Implementation of this function returns a necessary sample size of 528, which then ensure that 99% of confidence intervals formed using this procedure will be no wider than the desired value of .20.

AIPE for the Omnibus Effect ($P_{Y \cdot X}^2$)

The 95% confidence interval from the Grant and Wrzesniewski (2010) study for the population squared multiple correlation coefficient was [.01, .31]. Such a wide range for the plausible values of the population squared multiple correlation coefficient is undesirable, as the proportion of variance that is accounted for the model may be close to 0 or close to 0.33, correspondingly, with very different interpretations of how well the seven regressors are able to account for the variance of Performance in the population.

Suppose one desires a width of .15 for the confidence interval for the population squared multiple correlation coefficient. The only population parameter that must be presumed or estimated for an application of AIPE to the squared multiple correlation coefficient is $P_{Y \cdot X}^2$, like in the context of statistical power. The function `ss.aipe.R2()` from the MBESS R package can be used as follows:

```
ss.aipe.R2(Population.R2=.20,
width=.15, conf.level = 0.95,
K = 7, assurance = NULL)
```

where the parameters are the same as noted previously. Implementation of the above yields a necessary sample size of 361. This code does not incorporate an assurance parameter. Modifying the code to incorporate an assurance parameter of .99 leads to

```
ss.aipe.R2(Population.R2=.20,
width=.15, conf.level = 0.95,
K = 7, assurance=.99)
```

which returns a necessary sample size of 403.

It is important to remember here that the appropriate sample size depends on the research question. For illustrative purposes, we planned sample size for four different goals, which would ordinarily not be the case. If, however, multiple goals are of interest, then we recommend using the largest of the planned sample sizes.

SOFTWARE FOR SAMPLE SIZE PLANNING

We used the MBESS R package in our example of sample size planning. Many sample size planning software packages are available for a wide variety of research designs, effect sizes, and goals. Kelley (in press) has provided a table of such programs. Sample size planning for the majority of the most widely used statistical methods in psychology can be implemented with the programs listed in Table 11.3. We are not able to provide a review of exactly what each of the programs is capable of doing, as doing so is beyond the scope of this chapter.

DISCUSSION

Sample size planning has been discussed in numerous book length treatments (e.g., Aberson, 2010; Bausell & Li, 2002; Chow, Shao, & Wang, 2003; Cohen, 1988; Dattalo, 2008; Davey & Savla, 2010; Kraemer & Thiemann, 1987; Lipsey, 1990; Machin, Campbell, Tan, & Tan, 2009; Murphy, Myors, & Wolach, 2008). Despite the push for the use of effect sizes and confidence intervals, these works do not contain as much emphasis on the AIPE approach as they do on power analysis. Because a single chapter cannot compete with book-length treatments for depth (e.g., the how-tos) or breadth (e.g., the number of designs), we hope our chapter provides a *big picture* view of the overarching principles that should be considered when designing a study and planning an appropriate sample size.

TABLE 11.3

Software Titles Useful for Planning Sample Size

Software title*	Author(s)/publisher	Operating system(s)	Free?	Web resource
G*Power	E. Erdfelder, F. Faul, & A. Buchner	Windows/Mac	Yes	http://www.psycho.uni-duesseldorf.de/aap/projects/gpower
nQuery Advisor	Statistical Solutions	Windows	No	http://www.statistical-solutions-software.com/ products-page/nquery-advisor-sample-size-software
Optimal Design	J. Spybrook, S. W. Raudenbush, R. Congdon, & A. Martinez	Windows	Yes	http://www.wtgrantfoundation.org/resources/overview/research_tools
PASS	NCSS	Windows	No	http://www.ncss.com/pass.html
PinT	T. Snijders, R. Bosker, & H. Guldemond	Windows	Yes	http://stat.gamma.rug.nl/multilevel.htm#progPINT
Power and Precision	Biostat	Windows	No	http://www.power-analysis.com
R Package: asypow	B. W. Brown, J. Lovato, K. Russel, & K. Halvorsen	Windows/Mac/Unix	Yes	http://cran.r-project.org/web/packages/asypow/index.html
Package: MBESS	K. Kelley & K. Lai			http://cran.r-project.org/web/packages/MBESS/index.html
Package: pamm	J. Martin			http://cran.r-project.org/web/packages/pamm/index.html
Package: pwr	S. Champely			http://cran.r-project.org/web/packages/pwr/index.html
SAS PROC POWER	SAS Institute	Windows/Unix	No	http://support.sas.com/documentation/cdl/en/statug/63033/HTML/default/power_toc.htm
PROC GLMPOWER				http://support.sas.com/documentation/cdl/en/statug/63033/HTML/default/glmpower_toc.htm
SIZ	Cytel	Windows	No	http://www.cytel.com/Software/SiZ.aspx
SPSS (SamplePower)	SPSS	Windows	No	http://www.spss.com/software/statistics/samplepower
Statistica (Power Analysis and Interval Estimation)	StatSoft	Windows	No	http://www.statsoft.com/products/statistica-power-analysis
STPLAN	B. Brown, C. Brauner, A. Chan, D. Gutierrez, J. Herson, J. Lovato, K. Russel, & J. Venier	Windows/Unix	Yes	https://biostatistics.mdanderson.org/SoftwareDownload

Note. Software titles are listed in alphabetical order. The failure to list a sample size planning software does not imply that it should not be considered. Purposely not included, for example, are narrowly focused sample size planning software titles. Also not included are web resources (e.g., online calculators), some of which can be helpful. Additionally, general software titles that could be made to plan sample size with the appropriate programming are not included, as the listed software titles are those that were developed specifically to plan sample size or contain specialized functions or procedures for planning sample size. From *Oxford Handbook of Quantitative Methods* by T. Little (Ed.), in press, New York, NY: Oxford University Press. Reprinted with permission of Oxford University Press, Inc.

Altman and Gardner (1988) encouraged medical studies to move away from NHST and to focus on confidence intervals. They also cautioned, however, that "confidence intervals convey only the effects of sampling variation on the precision of the estimated statistics and cannot control for non-sampling errors such as biases in design, conduct, or analysis" (p. 747). Correspondingly, if biases creep into a research design, not only can the population value be estimated in a biased fashion, but also the wrong quantity can be estimated precisely. That is to say, a narrow confidence interval could be obtained that brackets the wrong population quantity. The importance of considering the various types of validity when planning a study needs to be taken seriously (e.g., Shadish, Cook, & Campbell, 2002).

Without careful consideration of the issues we have discussed, answering one of the most common questions asked when planning research, namely, "What sample size do I need?" cannot adequately be addressed. Having a solid grasp of the foundational issues and appropriately linking the question of interest to the most appropriate type of sample size planning will facilitate the process of sample size planning. Once these issues are addressed, a software program can be used to plan the appropriate sample size, if available. A critical evaluation of the process of sample size planning will lead to better designed studies that we believe will facilitate a more cumulative and productive research literature.

References

Aberson, C. L. (2010). *Applied power analysis for the behavioral sciences.* New York, NY: Psychology Press.

Altman, D. G., & Gardner, M. J. (1988). Calculating confidence intervals for regressions and correlation. *British Medical Journal, 296,* 1238–1242.

American Educational Research Association. (2006). *Standards for reporting on empirical social science research in AERA publications.* Washington, DC: Author.

American Psychological Association. (2010). *Publication manual of the American Psychological Association* (6th ed.). Washington, DC: Author.

Bakan, D. (1966). The test of significance in psychological research. *Psychological Bulletin, 66,* 423–437. doi:10.1037/h0020412

Bausell, R. B., & Li, Y-F. (2002). *Power analysis in experimental research: A practical guide for the biological, medical, and social sciences.* New York, NY: Cambridge University Press.

Bonett, D. G. (2008). Confidence intervals for standardized linear contrasts of means. *Psychological Methods, 13,* 99–109. doi:10.1037/1082-989X.13.2.99

Chow, S-C., Shao, J., & Wang, H. (2003). *Sample size calculations in clinical research.* New York, NY: Taylor & Francis.

Cohen, J. (1988). *Statistical power analysis for the behavioral sciences* (2nd ed.). Hillsdale, NJ: Erlbaum.

Cohen, J. (1994). The world is round ($p < .05$). *American Psychologist, 49,* 997–1003. doi:10.1037/0003-066-X.49.12.997

Cumming, G., Fidler, F., Leonard, M., Kalinowski, P., Christiansen, A., Lo, J., & Wilson, S. (2007). Statistical reform in psychology: Is anything changing? *Psychological Science, 18,* 230–232. doi:10.1111/j.1467-9280.2007.01881.x

Dattalo, P. (2008). *Determining sample size: Balancing power, precision, and practicality.* New York, NY: Oxford University Press.

Davey, A., & Savla, J. (2010). *Statistical power analysis with missing data: A structural equation modeling approach.* New York, NY: Routledge.

De Dreu, C. K. W., & Nauta, A. (2009). Self-interest and other-orientation in organizational behavior: Implications for job performance, prosocial behavior, and personal initiative. *Journal of Applied Psychology, 94,* 913–926. doi:10.1037/a0014494

Des Jarlais, D. C., Lyles, C. M., Crepaz, N., & the TREND Group. (2004). Improving the reporting quality of nonrandomized evaluations of behavioral and public health interventions: The TREND statement. *American Journal of Public Health, 94,* 361–366. doi:10.2105/AJPH.94.3.361

Grant, A. M., & Wrzesniewski, A. (2010). I won't let you down . . . or will I? Core self-evaluations, other-orientation, anticipated guilt and gratitude, and job performance. *Journal of Applied Psychology, 95,* 108–121. doi:10.1037/a0017974

Green, S. B. (1991). How many subjects does it take to do a regression analysis? *Multivariate Behavioral Research, 26,* 499–510. doi:10.1207/s15327906mbr2603_7

Grissom, R. J., & Kim, J. J. (2005). *Effect sizes for research: A broad practical approach.* Mahwah, NJ: Erlbaum.

Hahn, G. J., & Meeker, W. Q. (1991). *Statistical intervals: A guide for practitioners.* New York, NY: Wiley.

Harlow, L. L., Mulaik, S. A., & Steiger, J. H. (1997). *What if there were no significance tests?* Mahwah, NJ: Erlbaum.

Harris, R. (2001). *A primer of multivariate statistics* (3rd ed.). Mahwah, NJ: Erlbaum.

Hedges, L., & Olkin, I. (1985). *Statistical methods for meta-analysis*. Orlando, FL: Academic Press.

Hunter, J. E., & Schmidt, F. L. (2004). *Methods of meta-analysis: Correcting error and bias in research findings* (2nd ed.). Thousand Oaks, CA: Sage.

Jiroutek, M. R., Muller, K. E., Kupper, L. L., & Stewart, P. W. (2003). A new method for choosing sample size for confidence interval-based inferences. *Biometrics, 59*, 580–590. doi:10.1111/1541-0420.00068

Jones, L. V., & Tukey, J. W. (2000). A sensible formulation of the significance test. *Psychological Methods, 5*, 411–414. doi:10.1037/1082-989X.5.4.411

Judge, T. A., & Bono, J. E. (2001). Relationship of core self-evaluations traits—self-esteem, generalized self-efficacy, locus of control, and emotional stability—with job satisfaction and job performance: A meta-analysis. *Journal of Applied Psychology, 86*, 80–92. doi:10.1037/0021-9010.86.1.80

Judge, T. A., Locke, E. A., & Durham, C. C. (1997). The dispositional causes of job satisfaction: A core evaluations approach. *Research in Organizational Behavior, 19*, 151–188.

Judge, T. A., Locke, E. A., Durham, C. C., & Kluger, A. N. (1998). Dispositional effects on job and life satisfaction: The role of core evaluations. *Journal of Applied Psychology, 83*, 17–34. doi:10.1037/0021-9010.83.1.17

Kelley, K. (2005). The effects of nonnormal distributions on confidence intervals around the standardized mean difference: Bootstrap and parametric confidence intervals. *Educational and Psychological Measurement, 65*, 51–69. doi:10.1177/0013164404264850

Kelley, K. (2007a). Confidence intervals for standardized effect sizes: Theory, application, and implementation. *Journal of Statistical Software, 20*(8), 1–24.

Kelley, K. (2007b). Methods for the behavioral, educational, and social science: An RPackage. *Behavior Research Methods, 39*, 979–984. doi:10.3758/BF03192993

Kelley, K. (2008). Sample size planning for the squared multiple correlation coefficient: Accuracy in parameter estimation via narrow confidence intervals. *Multivariate Behavioral Research, 43*, 524–555. doi:10.1080/00273170802490632

Kelley, K. (in press). Effect size and sample size planning. In T. Little (Ed.), *Oxford handbook of quantitative methods*. New York, NY: Oxford University Press.

Kelley, K., & Lai, K. (2011). MBESS (Version 3.0.0) [computer software and manual]. Retrieved from http://cran.r-project.org

Kelley, K., & Maxwell, S. E. (2008). Power and accuracy for omnibus and targeted effects: Issues of sample size planning with applications to multiple regression. In P. Alasuuta, L. Bickman, & J. Brannen (Eds.), *The Sage handbook of social research methods* (pp. 166–192). Newbury Park, CA: Sage.

Kelley, K., Maxwell, S. E., & Rausch, J. R. (2003). Obtaining power or obtaining precision: Delineating methods of sample-size planning. *Evaluation and the Health Professions, 26*, 258–287. doi:10.1177/0163278703255242

Kelley, K., & Rausch, J. R. (2006). Sample size planning for the standardized mean difference: Accuracy in parameter estimation via narrow confidence intervals. *Psychological Methods, 11*, 363–385. doi:10.1037/1082-989X.11.4.363

Kraemer, H. C., & Thiemann, S. (1987). *How many subjects? Statistical power analysis in research*. Newbury Park, CA: Sage.

Krantz, D. H. (1999). The null hypothesis testing controversy in psychology. *Journal of the American Statistical Association, 94*, 1372–1381. doi:10.2307/2669949

Lipsey, M. W. (1990). *Design sensitivity: Statistical power for experimental research*. Newbury Park, CA: Sage.

MacCallum, R. C., Widaman, K. F., Zhang, S., & Hong, S. (1999). Sample size in factor analysis. *Psychological Methods, 4*, 84–99. doi:10.1037/1082-989X.4.1.84

Machin, D., Campbell, M. J., Tan, S. B., & Tan, S. H. (2009). *Sample size tables for clinical studies* (3rd ed.). Hoboken, NJ: Wiley-Blackwell.

Maxwell, S. E. (2004). The persistence of underpowered studies in psychological research: Causes, consequences, and remedies. *Psychological Methods, 9*, 147–163. doi:10.1037/1082-989X.9.2.147

Meehl, P. E. (1967). Theory-testing in psychology and physics: A methodological paradox. *Philosophy of Science, 34*, 103–115. doi:10.1086/288135

Moher, D., Hopewell, S., Schulz, K., Montori, V., Gøtzsche, P. C., Devereaux, P. J., & Altman, M. G. (2010). Consort 2010 explanation and elaboration: Updated guidelines for reporting parallel group randomized trials. *British Medical Journal, 340*, c869. doi:10.1136/bmj.c869

Morrison, D. E., & Henkel, R. E. (Eds.). (1970). *The significance test controversy: A reader*. Chicago, IL: Aldine.

Murphy, K. R., Myors, B., & Wolach, A. (2008). *Statistical power analysis: A simple and general model for traditional and modern hypothesis tests* (3rd ed.). Mahwah, NJ: Erlbaum.

Nickerson, R. S. (2000). Null hypothesis statistical testing: A review of an old and continuing controversy. *Psychological Methods, 5*, 241–301. doi:10.1037/1082-989X.5.2.241

O'Brien, R. G., & Castelloe, J. (2007). Sample-size analysis for traditional hypothesis testing: Concepts and issues. In A. Dmitrienko, C. Chuang-Stein, & R. D'Agostino (Eds.), *Pharmaceutical statistics using SAS: A practical guide* (pp. 237–272). Cary, NC: SAS Institute.

Preacher, K. J., & Kelley, K. (2011). Effect size measures for mediation models: Quantitative strategies for communicating indirect effects. *Psychological Methods, 16*, 93–115. doi:10.1037/a0022658

R Development Core Team. (2011). R: A language and environment for statistical computing [Computer software]. Vienna, Austria: R Foundation for Statistical Computing.

Rozeboom, W. W. (1960). The fallacy of the null-hypothesis significance test. *Psychological Bulletin, 57*, 416–428. doi:10.1037/h0042040

Schmidt, F. L. (1996). Statistical significance testing and cumulative knowledge in psychology: Implications for training of researchers. *Psychological Methods, 1*, 115–129. doi:10.1037/1082-989X.1.2.115

Senn, S. J. (2002). Power is indeed irrelevant in interpreting completed studies. *British Medical Journal, 325*, 1304. doi:10.1136/bmj.325.7375.1304

Shadish, W. R., Cook, T. D., & Campbell, D. T. (2002). *Experimental and quasi-experimental designs for generalized causal inference.* Boston, MA: Houghton-Mifflin.

Smithson, M. (2003). *Confidence intervals.* Thousand Oaks, CA: Sage.

Thompson, B. (2002). What future quantitative social science research could look like: Confidence intervals for effect sizes. *Educational Researcher, 31*, 25–32. doi:10.3102/0013189X031003025

Tversky, A., & Kahneman, D. (1971). Belief in the law of small numbers. *Psychological Bulletin, 76*, 105–110. doi:10.1037/h0031322

Wilkinson, L., & the Task Force on Statistical Inference. (1999). Statistical methods in psychology journals: Guidelines and explanations. *American Psychologist, 54*, 594–604. doi:10.1037/0003-066X.54.8.594

PART III

MEASUREMENT METHODS

SECTION 1

Behavior Observation

CHAPTER 12

BEHAVIORAL OBSERVATION

Roger Bakeman and Vicenç Quera

PRELIMINARIES

Like the 18th-century historian William Douglass who wrote, "As an historian, every thing is in my province" (1760, p. 230), the present-day behavioral scientist could say, "Every thing I know and do begins with observing behavior." More conventionally, however, behavioral observation is simply and primarily about measurement, which is why you find the present chapter in Measurement Methods, Part III of this volume.

Behavioral Observation Is Measurement

Measurement, as you have learned from other chapters in Part III, is understood as the act of assigning numbers to things: persons, events, time intervals, and so forth. Measurement is inherently quantitative, which means that most chapters in this handbook are potentially relevant to users of observational measurement. For example, studies often are categorized either as correlational or experimental (contrast Sampling Across People and Time with Designs Involving Experimental Manipulations, Volume 2, Parts II and IV, this handbook). True, many experimental studies are performed in laboratories, and behavioral observations often are employed in field settings not involving manipulation. As a result, sometimes nonexperimental studies are referred to as "observational," as though observational were a synonym for correlational, and are assumed to occur outside laboratories. In fact, correlational studies can be performed in laboratories and experimental ones in the field—and

behavioral observations can be employed for either type of study in either setting.

No matter the type of measurement, a key feature of any quantitative investigation is its design. As we plan an investigation and think forward to later data analysis, it is important at the outset to specify two key components: our basic *analytic units* and our *research factors*. Research factors usually are described as *between-subjects* (e.g., gender with two levels, male and female) or *within-subjects* (e.g., age with repeated observations at 18, 24, and 30 months). Between-subjects analytic units are, for example, the individual participants, parent–child dyads, families, or other groups (often called *cases* in standard statistical packages, *subjects* in older literature, or simply basic *sampling units*), whose scores are organized by our between-subjects research factors. When repeated measures exist, additional analytic units, each identified with a level of a repeated measure, are nested within cases.

Observational Sessions Are Analytic Units

An *observational session* is a sequence of coded events for which continuity generally can be assumed (although either planned or unplanned breaks might occur during an observational session). For behavioral observation, sessions are equated with analytic units. Statistics and indexes derived from the coded data for an observational session constitute scores; scores from the various subjects and sessions are then organized by any between- and within-subjects factors and are analyzed subsequently

DOI: 10.1037/13619-013
APA Handbook of Research Methods in Psychology: Vol. 1. Foundations, Planning, Measures, and Psychometrics, H. Cooper (Editor-in-Chief)

using conventional statistical techniques as guided by the design of the study.

Speaking broadly, designs are of two types: single-subject (as described in Volume 2, Chapter 31, this handbook) and group. As noted in the previous paragraph, the factors of group designs may be between-subjects, within-subjects, or both. For more information about the analysis of group designs, see Volume 3, Chapters 1 to 25, this handbook (especially Chapters 8 to 11); for information about issues relevant for quantitative analysis generally, also see Chapters 32 to 37 of this volume. No matter the design and no matter whether scores are derived from behavioral observation or other measurement techniques, the basic psychometric properties of validity and reliability need to be established (see Chapters 32 and 33 of this volume; reliability issues unique to behavioral observation, particularly observer agreement, are discussed later in this chapter).

Many measurement methods are simple and efficient. What is a person's weight? Step on a scale. What is a person's age? Ask him or her. What is a person's self-esteem? Have the person rate several items on a 1-to-5 scale and then compute the average rating. In contrast, behavioral observation is often time-consuming. Observational sessions can vary from a few minutes to several hours during which human observers need be present. Better (or worse), sessions can be recorded, which in spite of its advantages can take even more time as observers spend hours coding a few minutes of behavior. The data collected can be voluminous and their analysis seemingly intractable. Why bother with such a time-consuming method?

Reasons for Using Observational Measurement

Several sorts of circumstances can lead an investigator to observational measurement, but three stand out. First, behavioral observation is useful when nonverbal organisms such as human infants, nonhuman primates, or other animals are being studied. We cannot ask them whether they strongly disagree or agree somewhat with a particular statement nor can we ask them to fill out a daily diary saying how much they ate or drank or how much time they spent playing with their infant each day—only observational methods will work. And even when they are verbal, we may nonetheless use observational methods when studying nonverbal behavior specifically. Not surprisingly, many early examples of behavioral observation are found in studies of animal behavior and infant development.

Second, investigators often choose behavioral observation because they want to assess naturally occurring behavior. The behavior could be observed in field or laboratory settings but presumably is "natural," reflecting the participant's proclivities and untutored repertoire and not something elicited, for example, by an experimenter's task. From this point of view, filling out a questionnaire is "unnatural" behavior; it only occurs in contrived, directed settings and is never spontaneous. Still, you might ask, how natural is observed behavior? Like observer effects in physics, doesn't behavior change when it is observed? Does awareness of being observed alter our behavior? The answer seems to be that we habituate rapidly to observation, perhaps more so than in earlier years now that security cameras are everywhere. For example, for Bakeman's dissertation research (Bakeman & Helmreich, 1975), marine scientists living in a space-station-like habitat 50 feet below the surface of Coral Bay in the Virgin Islands were on camera continuously, yet as they went about their work awareness of the cameras seemingly disappeared within the first several minutes of their 2- to 3-week stay in the habitat.

Third, when investigators are interested in process—how things work and not just outcomes—observations capture behavior unfolding in time, which is essential to understanding process. A good example is Gottman's work on marital interaction (1979), which predicted whether relationships would dissolve on the basis of characterizations of moment-to-moment interaction sequences. One frequently asked process question concerns contingency. For example, when nurses reassure children undergoing a painful procedure, is children's distress lessened? Or, when children are distressed, do nurses reassure them more? Contingency analyses designed to answer questions like these may be one of the more common and useful applications of observational methods, and is a topic we return to later.

In sum, compared with other measurement methods (e.g., direct physical measurement or deriving a summary score from a set of rated items), observational measurement is often labor-intensive and time-consuming. Nonetheless, observational measurement is often the method of choice when nonverbal organisms are studied (or nonverbal behavior generally); when more natural, spontaneous, real-world behavior is of interest; and when processes and not outcomes are the focus (e.g., questions of contingency). As detailed in subsequent sections of this chapter, behavioral observation requires some unique techniques, but in common with other measurement methods, it produces scores attached to analytic units (i.e., sessions) that are organized by the within- and between-subjects factors of a group design or the within-subjects factors of a single-subject design. Consequently, if this chapter interests you, it is only a beginning; you should find at least some chapters in almost all parts of this three-volume handbook relevant to your interests and worth your attention. Longer treatments are also available: Bakeman and Gottman (1997) provided a thorough overview, Martin and Bateson (2007) emphasized animal and ethological studies, Yoder and Symons (2010) may be especially appealing to those concerned with typical and atypical development of infants and children, and Bakeman and Quera (2011) emphasized data analysis.

CODING SCHEMES: MEASURING INSTRUMENTS FOR OBSERVATION

Measurement requires a measuring instrument. Such instruments are often physical; clocks, thermometers, and rulers are just a few of many common examples. In contrast, a coding scheme—which consists of a list of codes (i.e., names, labels, or categories) for the behaviors of interest—is primarily conceptual. As rulers are to carpentry—a basic and essential measuring tool—coding schemes are to behavioral observation (although as we discuss, trained human observers are an integral part of the measuring apparatus).

As a conceptual matter, a coding scheme cannot escape its theoretical underpinnings—even if the investigator does not address these explicitly. Rulers say only that length is important. Coding schemes say these specific behaviors and particularly these distinctions are worth capturing; necessarily coding schemes reflect a theory about what is important and why. Bakeman and Gottman (1986, 1997) wrote that using someone else's coding scheme was like wearing someone else's underwear. In other words, the coding schemes you use should reflect your theories and not someone else's—and when you make the connections between your theories and codes explicit, you clarify how the data you collect can provide clear answers to the research questions that motivated your work in the first place.

Where then do coding schemes come from? Many investigators begin with coding schemes that others with similar interests and theories have used and then adapt them to their specific research questions. In any case, developing coding schemes is almost always an iterative process, a matter of successive refinement, and is greatly aided by working with video recordings. Pilot testing may reveal that codes that seemed important simply do not occur, or distinctions that seemed important cannot be reliably made (the solution is to lump the codes), or that the codes seem to miss important distinctions (the solution is to split original codes or define new ones). In its earlier stages especially, developing and refining coding schemes is qualitative research (see Volume 2, Chapters 1 to 13, this handbook).

Mutually Exclusive and Exhaustive Sets of Codes

In addition to content (e.g., the fit with your research questions), the structure of coding schemes can also contribute to their usefulness. Consider the three simple examples given in Figure 12.1. The first categorizes activity on the basis of Bakeman's dissertation research (Bakeman & Helmreich, 1975; as noted earlier, studying marine scientists living in a space-station-like habitat underwater); it is typical of coding schemes that seek to describe how individuals spend their day (time-budget information). The second categorizes infant states (Wolff, 1966), and the third categorizes children's play states (Parten, 1932). Each of these coding schemes consists of a set of mutually exclusive and exhaustive (ME&E) codes. This is a desirable and easily achieved property of

Activity	Infant state	Play state
1. doing scientific work	1. quiet alert	1. unoccupied
2. at leisure	2. crying	2. onlooker
3. eating	3. fussy	3. solitary play
4. habitat-maintenance	4. REM sleep	4. parallel play
5. self-maintenance	5. deep sleep	5. associative play
6. asleep		6. cooperative play

FIGURE 12.1.   Three examples of coding schemes; each consists of a set of mutually exclusive and exhaustive codes.

coding schemes, one that often helps clarify our codes when under development and that usually simplifies subsequent recording and analysis. Still, when first developing lists of potential codes, we may note codes that logically can and probably will co-occur. This is hardly a problem and, in fact, is desired when research questions concern co-occurrence. Perhaps the best solution is to assign the initial codes on our list to different sets of codes, each of which is ME&E in itself; this has a number of advantages we note shortly.

Of course, the codes within any single set can be made mutually exclusive by defining combinations, and any set of codes can be made exhaustive simply by adding a final code: none of the above. For example, if a set consisted of two codes, infant gazes at mother and mother gazes at infant, adding a third combination code, mutual gaze, would result in a mutually exclusive set, and adding a fourth nil code would make the set exhaustive. Alternatively, two sets each with two codes could be defined: mother gazes at infant or not, and infant gazes at mother or not. In this case, mutual gaze, instead of being an explicit code, could be determined later analytically. Which is preferable, two sets with two codes each or one set with four codes—or more generally, more sets with few if any combination codes, or fewer sets but some combination codes? This is primarily a matter of taste or personal preference—similar information can be derived form the data in either case—but especially when working with video records, there may be advantages to more versus fewer sets. Coders can make several passes, attending just to the codes in one set on each pass (e.g., first mother then infant), which allows them to focus on just one aspect of behavior at a time. More-

over, different coders can be assigned different sets, which gives greater credibility to any patterns we detect later between codes in different sets.

We do not want to minimize the effort and hard work usually required to develop effective coding schemes—many hours of looking, thinking, defining, arguing, modifying, and refining can be involved—but if the result is well-structured (i.e., consists of several sets of ME&E codes each of which characterizes a coherent dimension of interest), then subsequent recording, representing, and analysis of the observational data is almost always greatly facilitated. To every rule, there is an exception. Imagine that we list five codes of interest, any of which might co-occur. Should we define five sets each with two codes: the behavior of interest and its absence? Or should we simply list the five codes and ask observers to note the onset and offset times for each (assuming duration is wanted)? Either strategy offers the same analytic options, and thus it is a matter of taste. As with the fewer versus more combination codes question in the previous paragraph, a good rule is, whatever your observers find easiest to work with (and are reliable doing) is right.

Codes, which after all are just convenient labels, do not stand alone. The coding manual—which gives definitions for each code along with examples—is an important part of any observational research project and deserves careful attention. It will be drafted as coding schemes are being defined and thereafter stands as a reference when training coders; moreover, it documents your procedure and can be shared with other researchers.

Granularity: Micro to Macro Codes

One dimension worth considering when developing coding schemes is granularity. Codes can vary from micro to macro (or molecular to molar)—from detailed and fine-grained to relatively broad and coarse-grained. As always, the appropriate level of granularity is one that articulates well with your research concerns. For example, if you are more interested in moment-to-moment changes in expressed emotion than in global emotional state, you might opt to use the fine-grained facial action coding scheme developed by Paul

Ekman (Ekman & Friesen, 1978), which relates different facial movements to their underlying muscles. A useful guideline is, if in doubt, define codes at a somewhat finer level of granularity than your research questions require (i.e., when in doubt split, don't lump). You can always analytically lump later but, to state the obvious, you cannot recover distinctions never made.

Concreteness: Physically to Socially Based Codes

Another dimension, not the same as granularity, is concreteness. Bakeman and Gottman (1986, 1997) suggested that coding schemes could be placed on an ordered continuum with one end anchored by physically based schemes and the other by socially based ones. More physically based codes reflect attributes that are easily seen, whereas more socially based codes rely on abstractions and require some inference (our apologies if any professional metaphysicians find this too simple). An example of a physically based code might be infant crying, whereas an example of a more socially based code might be a child engaged in cooperative play. Some ethologists and behaviorists might regard the former as objective and the latter subjective (and so less scientific), but—again eliding matters that concern professional philosophers—we would say that the physically–socially based distinction may matter most when selecting and training observers. Do we regard them as detectors of things *really* there? Or more as cultural informants, able through experience to "see" the distinctions embodied in our coding schemes? To our mind, a more important question about coding schemes is whether we can train observers to be reliable, a matter to which we return later.

Examples often clarify. Figure 12.2 presents two additional coding schemes. The first categorizes the vocalizations of very young infants (simplified and adapted from Gros-Louis, West, Goldstein, & King, 2006; see Oller, 2000). It is a good example of a physically based coding scheme, so much so that it is possible to automate its coding using sound spectrograph information. Computer coding—dispensing with human observers—has tantalized investigators for some time, but remains mainly out

Infant vocalization	Maternal response
1. vowels	1. naming
2. syllables (i.e., consonant–vowel transitions)	2. questions
3. babbling (a sequence of repeated syllables)	3. acknowledgments
4. other (e.g., cry, laugh, vegetative sounds)	4. imitations
	5. attributions
	6. directives
	7. play vocalizations

FIGURE 12.2. Two additional examples of coding schemes; the first is more physically based and the second more socially based.

of reach. True, computer scientists are attempting to automate the process, and some limited success has been achieved with automatic computer detection of Ekman-like facial action patterns (Cohn & Kanade, 2007), but the more socially based codes become, the more elusive any kind of computer automation seems. Consider the second coding scheme for maternal vocalizations (also adapted from Gros-Lewis et al., 2006). It is difficult to see how this could be automated. For the foreseeable future at least, a human coder—a perceiver—likely will remain an essential part of behavioral observation.

Finally, consider the well-known coding scheme defined by S. S. Stevens (1946), which we reference subsequently. The scheme categorizes measurement scales as (a) nominal or categorical—requires no more than assigning names to entities of interest where the names have no natural order, (b) ordinal—requires ordering or ranking those entities, and (c) interval—involves assigning numbers such that an additional number at any point on the scale involves the same amount of whatever is measured, and (d) ratio—distinguishing between interval scales for which zero is arbitrary like degrees Celsius and for which zero indicates truly none of the quantity measured like kilograms. This last distinction is less consequential statistically than the first three.

In sum, for behavioral observation to succeed, the investigator's toolbox should include well-designed, conceptually coherent, and piloted-tested coding schemes—these are the primary measuring instruments for behavioral observation. Often, but not always, each scheme reflects a dimension of interest and consists of a set of mutually exclusive and exhaustive codes.

RECORDING CODED DATA: FROM PENCIL AND PAPER TO DIGITAL

In the previous section, we argued that coding schemes are a conceptual matter, necessarily reflect your theoretical orientation, and work best when they mesh well with your research questions. In contrast, recording the data that result from applying those coding schemes (i.e., initial data collection) is a practical matter requiring physical materials ranging from simple pencil and paper to sophisticated electronic systems.

Live Observation Versus Recorded Behavior

Perhaps the first question to ask is, are coders observing live or are they working with recordings (video–audio or just audio, on tape or in digital files)? Whenever feasible, we think recordings are preferable. First and most important, recorded material can be played and replayed—literally re-viewed—and at various speeds, which greatly facilitates the observer's task. Second, only with recorded materials can we ask our observers to code different aspects in different passes, for example, coding a mother's behavior in one pass and her infant's in another. Third, recorded materials facilitate checks on observers' reliability, both between observers who can be kept blind to the reliability check, and within observers when asked to code the same session later. Fourth, contemporary computer systems for capturing coded data work best with recorded material (especially digital files). Finally, video–audio recording devices are relatively inexpensive; cost is not the factor it was in past decades.

Nonetheless, live observation may still be preferred in certain circumstances. In some settings (e.g., school classrooms), video–audio recording devices may be regarded as too intrusive, or for ethical or political reasons, permanent recordings may be unwelcome. And in some circumstances (e.g., observing animal behavior in the field) trained human observers may be able to detect behaviors that are unclear on recordings. Moreover, live observation is simpler; there is no need to purchase, learn about, or maintain video–audio recording devices.

Events and Intervals Are Primary Recording Units

Earlier we defined measurement as assigning numbers to things. Given Stevens's (1946) coding scheme for scales, we can now see that "numbers" should be expanded to include categories (i.e., codes) and ranks (i.e., numbers representing ordinal position). Thus, behavioral observation almost always begins with categorical measurement: Codes are assigned to things (although ordinal measurement using ratings is another but less frequently used possibility). But to what "things" are codes assigned? The answer is this: events (which may vary in duration) or intervals (whose duration is fixed). These are the two primary recording units used for observational data.

Corresponding to the two primary recording units are two primary strategies for recording coded data: continuous and interval recording. As noted, the primary analytic unit for behavioral observation is a session. *Continuous recording* implies continuously alert observers, ready to code events when they do occur. In contrast, *interval recording* (also referred to as *time-sampling*; Altmann, 1974) requires that the session be segmented into fixed-length intervals and that observers assign a code or codes to each successive interval. The length of the interval may vary from study to study but relatively brief intervals are fairly common (e.g., 10–15 seconds). In subsequent paragraphs, we discuss interval and continuous recording in greater detail and note advantages and disadvantages of each.

Interval Recording

Arguably, interval recording is a limited technique, more used in the past than currently. Its merits are primarily practical: It can be easy and inexpensive to implement, but as a trade-off, data derived from interval recording may be less precise than data derived from other methods. Interval recording lends itself to pencil and paper. All that is needed is a timing device so that interval boundaries can be identified, a lined tablet with columns added (rows represent successive intervals and columns are labeled with codes), and a recording rule. A common recording rule is to check the interval if a behavior occurs once or more within it; this is called *partial-interval* or *zero-one* sampling. Another possibility is *momentary* sampling—check only if the behavior is occurring at a defined instant, such as the beginning of the interval (although in practice this often is interpreted as check the behavior that predominated during the interval). Another less used possibility is *whole-interval* sampling—check only if the behavior occurs throughout the interval (see Altmann, 1974; Suen & Ary, 1989). An example using infant state codes is shown in Figure 12.3; because each line is checked for one and only one of these ME&E codes, we can assume that momentary sampling was used.

As noted, with interval recording, summary statistics may be estimated only approximately. For example, with zero-one sampling, frequencies likely are underestimated (a check can indicate more than one occurrence in an interval), proportions are likely overestimated (a check does not mean the event occupied the entire interval), and sequences can be muddled (if more than one code is checked for an interval, which occurred first?)—and momentary and whole-interval sampling have other problems. There are possible fixes to these problems, but none seem completely satisfactory. As a result, unless approximate estimates are sufficient to answer your research questions and the practical advantages seem decisive, we usually recommend event and not interval recording whenever feasible.

interval	Infant code				
	alert	cry	fussy	REM	sleep
1				√	
2				√	
3			√		
4	√				
5	√				
6	√				
7		√			
8		√			
9		√			
10				√	
…					

FIGURE 12.3.   An example of interval recorded data for infant state.

Nonetheless, we recognize that interval recording has its partisans. Certainly interval recording seemed a good choice for Mel Konner studying mother–infant interaction among the !Kung in Botswana in the late 1960s and early 1970s (Bakeman, Adamson, Konner, & Barr, 1990; Konner, 1976). An electronic device delivered a click every 15 seconds to the observer's ear. Observers then noted which of several mother, infant, adult, and child behaviors had occurred since the last click. The remote location and the need for live observation in this era before inexpensive and reliable video made interval recording the method of choice.

A variant of interval recording could be termed *interrupted interval recording*, which is sometimes used in education and other settings. Coders observe for a fixed interval (e.g., 20 seconds) and then record for another fixed interval (e.g., 10 seconds). Such data are even less suitable for any sort of sequential analysis than ordinary interval recording, but as with standard interval recording, when approximate estimates are sufficient, simplicity of implementation may argue for even interrupted interval recording.

Continuous Untimed Event Recording

Imagine that we ask observers simply to note whenever an event of interest occurs and record its code. What could be simpler? Like interval recording, simple event recording is limited but nonetheless sufficient to answer some research questions. The sequence of events is preserved but no information concerning their duration is recorded. Thus, we can report how often different types of events occurred and in what sequence, but we cannot report the average time different types of events lasted or how much of the session was devoted to different types of events.

Again, like interval recording, untimed event recording lends itself to pencil and paper. Using a lined paper tablet, information identifying the session can be written at the top and then codes for each event noted on successive lines. Two refinements are possible. First, even though event durations remain unrecorded, the start and stop times for the session can be recorded. Then rates for the various events can be computed for each session and will be comparable across sessions that vary in length. Second, each event can be coded on more than one dimension using more than one set of ME&E codes, in effect cross-classifying the event and producing data appropriate for multidimensional contingency tables. Such multievent data are formally identical with interval recorded data and could be collected using forms similar to the one shown in Figure 12.3, adding columns for additional ME&E sets. The only difference is, lines are associated with successive intervals for interval recording and with successive events for multievent (but untimed) recording.

Recording simply the sequence of events, or sequences of cross-classified events, but ignoring the duration of those events, limits the information that can be derived from the coded data. If your research questions require nothing more than information about frequency (or rate), sequence, and possibly cross-classification, then the simplicity and low cost of untimed event recording could cause you to adopt this approach.

Continuous Timed-Event Recording

More useful and less limited data—data that offer more analytic options—result when not just events but their durations are recorded (i.e., their onset and offset times). In general, this is the approach we recommend. Of course, there is a price. Recording event onset and offset times is inevitably more complicated than either interval or untimed event recording. The good news is, advances in technology in the past few decades have made timed-event recording simpler and more affordable than in the past. Continuous timed-event recording does not absolutely require computer technology, but nonetheless works best with it.

Let us begin by describing what is possible with current computer technology. Users can play one or more (synchronized) digital video–audio files using on-screen controls. The image (or images) can be paused and then played forward or backward at various speeds, displaying the current time (rounded to a fraction of a second or accurate to the video frame—there are 29.97 per second per the National Television System Committee [NTSC] standard used in North America, much of South America, and

Japan and 25 per second per the Phase Alternating Line [PAL] standard used in most of Europe, the Near East, South Asia, and China). Typically, codes, their characteristics, and the recording method are defined initially. Then when a key is pressed on subsequent playback (or a code displayed on-screen is selected, i.e., clicked), a record of that code and the current time are shown on-screen and stored in an internal data file. With such systems, the human observers do not need to worry about clerical details or keep track of time; the computer system attends to these tasks. If you make a mistake and want to add or delete a code or change a time, typically edits can be accomplished on-screen with minimal effort. The result is a file containing codes along with their onset and (optionally) offset times. Programs vary in their conventions and capabilities, but when sets of ME&E codes are defined, most systems automatically supply the offset time for a code when the onset time of another code in that set is selected; and when some codes are defined as *momentary*, meaning that only their frequency and not their duration is of concern, offset times are not required.

Some systems permit what we call *post hoc coding*—first you detect an event and only afterward code it. For example, when you think an event is beginning, hold down the space bar, and when it ends, release, which pauses play. You can then decide what the code should be, enter it, and restart play. Another advanced feature allows subsequent choices for an event to be determined by prior ones (one term for this is lexical chaining). For example, if you select *mother* for an event, a list of mother behavior codes would be displayed (e.g., talk, rock), whereas if you had selected *infant,* a list of infant codes would be displayed (e.g., cry, sleep). The next list thereafter, if any, could be determined by the particular mother or infant behavior selected, and so on, until the end of the lexical chain.

Although capabilities vary, computer systems of the sort just described free coders to concentrate on making judgments; clerical tasks are handled automatically and thus the possibility of clerical error is greatly reduced. Such systems can work with live observation or videotapes, but they are at their best with digital files. With digital files, you can jump instantly to any point in the file, whereas with videotapes, you would wait while the tape winds; you can also ask that a particular episode be replayed repeatedly, and you can assemble lists of particular episodes that then can be played sequentially, ignoring other material. Such capabilities are useful for coding and training and for education purposes generally. (Two examples of such systems are Mangold International's INTERACT [see http://www.mangold-international.com] and Noldus Information Technology's The Observer [see http://www.noldus.com]; an Internet search will quickly reveal others.)

Still, there is no need for investigators who require continuous timed-event recording to despair when budgets are limited. Digital files can be played with standard and free software on standard computers, or videotapes can be played on the usual tape playback devices. Codes and times then can be manually entered into, for example, a spreadsheet program running on its own computer or simply written on a paper tablet. Times can even be written when coding live; only pencil, paper, and a clock are needed. Such low-tech approaches can be tedious and error-prone—and affordable. When used well, they can produce timed-event data that are indistinguishable from that collected with systems costing far more. Still, as our rich city cousin might say, it won't be as much fun.

Pencil-and-Paper Versus Electronic Methods

To summarize, once coding schemes are defined, refined, and piloted, and once observers are trained, you are ready to begin recording data. Derivation of summary measures and other data reduction comes later, but initial data collection (i.e., observational measurement) consists of observers assigning codes to either fixed time intervals or events. When codes are assigned to events, the events may be untimed, or onset and offsets times may be recorded (or in some cases inferred). No matter whether the behavior is observed live or first recorded, any of these strategies (interval, untimed, or timed-event recording) could be used with anything from pencil, paper, and perhaps a timing device to a high-end, bells-and-whistles computerized coding system. Pencil-and-paper methods have their advantages. As noted in Bakeman and Gottman (1986, 1997), pencil and

paper feel good in the hand, possess a satisfying physicality, rarely malfunction, and do not need batteries.

Interval and untimed event recording produce more limited, less rich, less precise data—data with fewer analytic options—than timed-event recording. At the same time, they can work satisfactorily with simple and inexpensive equipment, including pencil and paper observing either recorded material or live. In contrast, timed-event recording works best when video–audio recordings are used along with some electronic assistance. It is the usual trade-off: richer data, more analytic options, less tedious coding, fewer clerical errors, more tasks automated—as well as greater expense, longer learning times, and more resources devoted to maintenance. As always, the *right* recording system is the one that matches resources with needs, and when simpler, less precise data are sufficient to answer key research questions, simple and inexpensive may be best.

REPRESENTING OBSERVATIONAL DATA: THE CODE-UNIT GRID

Too often investigators take their data as collected and move directly to analysis, bypassing what can be an important step. This intervening step involves representing—literally, re-presenting—your data, by which we mean transforming the data-as-collected into a form more useful for subsequent analysis. As described in the previous section, when recording observational data initially, observer ease and accuracy are of primary importance. Therefore, it makes sense to design data collection procedures that work well for our observers; but analysis can be facilitated by how those data are represented subsequently, especially for timed-event recording.

When both preparing data for subsequent analysis and thinking about what those analyses should be, we have found it extremely helpful to organize observational data in one common underlying format (Bakeman, 2010). That underlying format is a grid, which is an ancient and useful organizing device. For observational data rows represent codes and columns represent units (which are either intervals for interval recorded data, or events for untimed event recorded data, or time units for timed-event recorded data). Thus, for interval and untimed event data, recording and representational units are the same, whereas for timed-event data, recording and representational units differ: events for recording and time units for representing.

The time units for timed-event data are defined by the precision with which time was recorded. If seconds, each column of the grid represents a second; if tenths of a second, each column represents a tenth of a second; and so forth (see Figure 12.4). Computer programs may display multiple digits after the decimal point but, unless specialized equipment is used, claiming hundredth-of-a-second accuracy is dubious. Video recording is limited by the number of frames per second (a frame is 0.033 seconds for NTSC and 0.040 seconds for PAL), which allows claims of tenth of a second or somewhat greater but not hundredth-of-a-second accuracy. Moreover, for most behavioral research questions, accuracy to the nearest second is almost always sufficient.

Understanding that investigators use different recording methods, as detailed in the previous section, yet also recognizing the advantages of representational standards, some years ago we defined conventions for observational data, which we called the Sequential Data Interchange Standard (SDIS) format (Bakeman & Quera, 1992). We defined five basic data types. As you might guess from the previous section, the two simplest were *event sequential data* and *interval sequential data*, which result from simple event and interval recording, respectively. *Multievent sequential data* result when events are cross-classified, as described earlier, and *timed-event sequential data* result from timed-event recording. A

fifth type, *state sequential data*, is simply a variant of timed-event sequential data for which data entry is simplified if all codes can be assigned to ME&E sets. For simple examples, see Bakeman, Deckner, and Quera (2005) and Bakeman and Quera (2011).

Once data are formatted per SDIS conventions, they can be analyzed with any general-purpose computer program that uses this standard, such as the Generalized Sequential Querier (GSEQ; Bakeman & Quera, 1995, 2009, 2011), a program we designed, not for initial data collection, but specifically for data analysis. Much of the power and usefulness of this program depends on representing observational data in terms of a universal code–unit grid, as just described. Three advantages are noteworthy. First, representing observational data as a grid in which rows represent codes and columns represent successive events, intervals, or time units makes the application of standard frequency or contingency table statistics easy (the column is the tallying unit). Second, the grid representation makes data modification easy and easy to understand. New codes (i.e., rows in the grid) can be defined and formed from existing codes using standard logical operations (Bakeman et al., 2005; Bakeman & Quera, 1995, 2011). Third, the discrete time-unit view (i.e., segmenting time into successive discrete time units defined by precision) of timed-event sequential data solves some, but not all, problems in gauging observer agreement, which is the topic of the next section.

OBSERVER AGREEMENT: EVENT BASED, TIME BASED, OR BOTH?

Observer agreement is often regarded as the sine qua non of observational measurement. Without it, we are left with individual narratives of the sort used in qualitative research (see Volume 2, Chapters 1 to 13, this handbook). Even so, a suitable level of agreement between two independent observers does not guarantee accuracy—two observers could share similar deviant views of the world—but it is widely regarded as an index of acceptable measurement. If test probes reveal that the records of two observers recorded independently do not agree (or an observer does not agree with a presumably accurate standard),

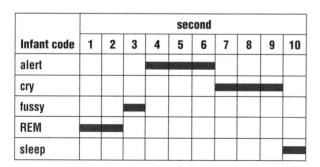

FIGURE 12.4. An example of a code-unit grid for timed-event recorded data with one-second precision (i.e., times recorded to nearest second).

the accuracy of any scores derived from data coded by those observers is uncertain: Further observer training, modification of the coding scheme, or both are needed. On the other hand, when test probes reveal that observers' records substantially agree (or an observer agrees with a presumably accurate standard), we infer that our observers are adequately trained and regard the data they produce as trustworthy and reliable.

Classic Cohen's Kappa and Interval Recorded Data

Probably the most commonly used statistic of observer agreement is Cohen's kappa (1960), although as we explain shortly it is most suited for interval recorded data. The classic Cohen's kappa characterizes agreement with respect to a set of ME&E codes while correcting for chance agreement. It assumes that things—demarcated units—are presented to a pair of observers, each of whom independently assigns a code to each unit. Each pair of observer decisions is tallied in a $K \times K$ table (also called an *agreement* or *confusion* matrix) where K is the number of codes in the ME&E set. For example, if 100 intervals were coded using the five infant state codes defined earlier, the agreement matrix might look like the one shown in Figure 12.5. In this case, the two observers generally agreed (i.e., most tallies were on the diagonal); the most frequent confusion—when Observer 1 coded *alert* but Observer 2 coded *fussy*—occurred just three times. Kappa is computed by dividing chance-corrected observed agreement (i.e., the probability of observed

agreement minus the probability of agreement expected by chance) by the maximum agreement not due to chance (i.e., 1 minus the probability of agreement expected by chance; see Bakeman & Gottman, 1997): $\kappa = (P_{obs} - P_{exp})/(1 - P_{exp})$. For this example, the value of kappa was .76 (Fleiss, 1981, characterized kappas more than .75 as excellent, .40 to .75 as fair to good, and below .40 as poor, p. 218).

Now here is the problem. Cohen's kappa assumes that pairs of coders make decisions when presented with discrete units and that the number of decisions is the same as the number of units. This decision-making model fits interval-recorded data well but fits event-recorded data only when events are presented to coders as previously demarcated units, for example, as turns of talk in a transcript. Usually events are not prepackaged. Instead, with event recording, observers are asked to first segment the stream of behavior into events (i.e., detect the seams between events) and then code those segments. Because of errors of omission and commission—one observer detects events the other misses—usually the two observer's records will contain different numbers of events and exactly how the records align is not always obvious. And when alignment is uncertain, how events should be paired and tallied in the agreement matrix is unclear.

Aligning Untimed Events When Observers Disagree

Aligning two observers' sequences of untimed events is problematic. Bakeman and Gottman (1997) wrote that especially when agreement is not high, alignment is difficult and cannot be accomplished without subjective judgment. Recently, however, Quera, Bakeman, and Gnisci (2007) developed an algorithm that determines the *optimal global alignment* between two event sequences. The algorithm is adopted from sequence alignment and comparison techniques that are routinely used by molecular biologists (Needleman & Wunsch, 1970). The task is to find an optimal alignment. The Needleman–Wunsch algorithm belongs to a broad class of methods known as *dynamic programming*, in which the solution for a specific subproblem can be derived from the solution for another, immediately preceding subproblem. It can be demonstrated that

Obs 1's codes	Obs 2's codes					TOTAL
	alert	cry	fussy	REM	sleep	
alert	26	2	3	0	0	31
cry	2	27	1	0	0	30
fussy	1	2	4	2	1	10
REM	0	0	1	17	1	19
sleep	0	0	0	2	8	10
TOTAL	29	31	9	21	10	100

FIGURE 12.5. Agreement matrix for two observers who independently coded 100 fixed-time intervals using the infant state coding scheme. For this example, Cohen's kappa = .76. Obs = observer.

the method guarantees an optimal solution, that is, it finds the alignment with the highest possible number of agreements between sequences (Sankoff & Kruskal, 1983/1999, p. 48) without being exhaustive, that is, it does not need to explore the almost astronomical number of all possible alignments (Galisson, 2000).

The way the algorithm works is relatively complex, but a simple example can at least show what results. Assume that two observers using the infant vocalization scheme described earlier recorded the two event sequences (S_1 and S_2) shown in Figure 12.6. The first observer coded 15 events and the second 14, but because of omission–commission errors, the optimal alignment shows 16. The 11 agreements are indicated with vertical bars and the two actual disagreements with two dots (i.e., a colon), but there were three additional errors: The algorithm estimated that Observer 1 missed one event that Observer 2 coded (indicated with a hyphen in the top alignment line) and Observer 2 missed two events that Observer 1 coded (indicated with hyphens in the bottom alignment line). The alignment then lets us tally paired observer decisions (using nil to indicate a missed event) and compute

kappa, with two qualifications. First, because observers cannot both code nil, the resulting agreement matrix contains a logical (or structural) zero; as a consequence, the expected frequencies required by the kappa computation cannot be estimated with the usual formula for kappa but instead require an iterative proportional fitting (IPF) algorithm (see Bakeman & Robinson, 1994). Second, because Cohen's assumptions are not met we should not call this a Cohen's kappa; it might better be alignment kappa instead (specifically, an event-based dynamic programming alignment kappa). For this example, we used our GSEQ program to determine the alignment and compute alignment kappa.

Time-Unit and Event-Based Kappas for Timed-Event Data

The alignment algorithm solves the problem for untimed event data but what of timed-event data? We have proposed two solutions. The first solution, which is the one presented by Bakeman and Gottman (1997), depends on the discrete view of time reflected in the code-time-unit grid described earlier. Assuming a discrete view of time and a code-time-unit grid like the one shown in Figure 12.4, agreement between successive pairs of time units can be tallied and kappa computed. As a variant, agreement could be tallied when codes for time units matched if not exactly at least within a stated tolerance (e.g., 2 seconds). Because time units are tallied, the summary statistic should be called time-unit kappa, or time-unit kappa with tolerance, to distinguish it from the classic Cohen's kappa.

One aspect of time-unit kappa seems troublesome. With the classic Cohen model, the number of tallies represents the number of decisions coders make, whereas with time-unit kappa, the number of tallies represents the length of the session (e.g., when time units are seconds, a 5-minute session generates 300 tallies). With timed-event recording, observers are continuously looking for the seams between events, but how often they are making decisions is arguable, probably unknowable. One decision per seam seems too few—the observers are continuously alert—but one per time unit seems too many. Moreover, the number of tallies increases with the precision of the time unit

Obs 1's codes	Obs 2's codes					TOTAL
	nil	vowel	syllable	babble	other	
nil	–	0	1	0	0	1
vowel	1	3	0	0	0	4
syllable	1	0	4	0	0	5
babble	0	0	0	3	0	3
other	0	1	1	0	1	3
TOTAL	2	4	6	3	1	16

```
Sequences:
  S1 = vvsbosbosvosbvs
  S2 = vsbssbsvsvobvs
Alignment:
  vvsbosb-osvosbvs
  |||:|| :||| |||
  -vsbssbsvsvo-bvs
```

FIGURE 12.6.   Alignment of two event sequences per our dynamic programming algorithm, and the resulting agreement matrix. For alignment, vertical bars indicate exact agreement, two dots (colon) disagreements, and hyphens events coded by one observer but not the other. For this example, alignment kappa = .60. Obs = observer.

(although multiplying all cells in an agreement matrix by the same factor does not change the value of kappa; see Bakeman & Gottman, 1997).

Thus the second solution is to align the events in the two observers' timed-event sequential data and compute an event-based kappa. Compared with tallying time units, tallying agreements and disagreements between aligned events probably underestimates the number of decisions observers actually make, but at least the number of tallies is closer to the number of events coded. Consequently, we modified our untimed event alignment algorithm to work with timed-event sequential data and compared this algorithm with ones available in The Observer and INTERACT (Bakeman, Quera, & Gnisci, 2009). Kappas with the different event-matching algorithms were not dramatically different; time-based and event-based kappas varied more.

In sum, we recommend as follows: When assessing observer agreement for interval-recorded data, use the classic Cohen's kappa. For untimed event recorded data, use our event-matching algorithm, which allows for omission–commission errors, and report the event-based kappa. For timed-event data, compute and report both an event-based and a time-based kappa (with or without tolerance); their range likely captures the *true* value of kappa (both are computed by GSEQ). Moreover, examining individual cells of the kappa table provides observers with useful feedback. In the case of timed-event data, observers should examine agreement matrixes for both event-based and time-unit-based kappas. Each provides somewhat different but valuable information about disagreements, which can be useful as observers strive to improve their agreement.

ANALYZING OBSERVATIONAL DATA: SIMPLE STATISTICS

Perhaps more with behavioral observation than other measurement methods, the data collected initially are not analyzed directly. Intervening steps may be required with other methods—for example, producing a summary score from the items of a self-esteem questionnaire—but with observational data, producing summary scores and data reduction generally are almost always required. In the process, the usual categorical measurements reflected in the data collected are transformed into scores for which, typically, interval- or ratio-scale measurement can be assumed. As with scores generally, so too with summary scores derived from behavioral observation, the first analytic step involves description, the results of which may limit subsequent analyses (as, e.g., when inappropriate distributions argue against analyses of variance). But what summary scores should be derived and described first?

It is useful to distinguish between simple statistics that do not take sequencing or contingency into account (described in this section) and contingency statistics that do take contingency into account (described in the section Analyzing Observational Data: Contingency Indexes). It makes sense to describe simple statistics first because, if their values are not appropriate, computation of some contingency statistics may be precluded or at best questionable. Simple statistics based on behavioral observation are relatively few in number but, as you might expect, their interpretation depends on the data recording and representation methods used. In the following paragraphs, we describe seven basic statistics, note how data type affects their interpretation, and recommend which statistics are most useful for each data type.

Frequency, Rate, and Relative Frequency

1. *Frequency* indicates how often. For event or timed-event data, it is the number of times an event occurred (i.e., was coded). For interval or multievent data, it is the number of bouts coded, that is, the number of times a code was checked without being checked for the previous interval or multievent; that is, if the same code occurred in successive intervals or multievents, one is added to its frequency count. As noted shortly, for interval and multievent data, duration gives the number of units checked.

2. *Rate*, which is the frequency per a specified amount of time, likewise indicates how often. Rate is preferable to frequency when sessions vary in length because it is comparable across sessions. Rates may be expressed per minute, per hour, or per any other time unit that makes sense. The session durations required to compute rate can be derived from the data for timed-event

and interval data but to compute rates for event or multievent data requires that session start and stop times be recorded explicitly.

3. *Relative frequency* indicates proportionate use of codes. For all data types it is a code's frequency, as just defined, divided by the sum of frequencies for all codes in a specified set, hence relative frequencies necessarily sum to 1. Alternatively, relative frequencies can be expressed as percentages summing to 100%. For example, if we only coded mother vocalization, we might discover that 22% of a mother's vocalizations were coded *naming*. As discussed shortly, depending on your specific research questions relative frequency may or may not be a statistic you choose to analyze.

Duration, Probability, and Relative and Mean Bout Duration

4. *Duration* indicates how long or how many. For timed-event data, duration indicates how much time during the session a particular code occurred. For simple event data, duration is the same as frequency. For interval or multievent data, duration indicates the number of intervals or multievents checked for a particular code, thus duration may be a more useful summary statistic for these data types than frequency, which as just noted indicates the number of bouts.

5. *Probability* indicates likelihood. It can be expressed as either a proportion or a percentage. For timed-event data, it is duration divided by total session time, leading to statements like, the baby was asleep for 46% of the session. For simple event data, it is the same as relative frequency. For interval or multievent data, it is duration divided by the total number of intervals or multievents, leading to statements like, solitary play was coded for 18% of the intervals.

6. *Relative duration* indicates proportionate use of time for timed-event data and of intervals or multievents for interval and multievent data. For all data types it is a code's duration, as just defined, divided by the sum of durations for all codes, thus it only makes sense when the codes specified form a single ME&E set. As with relative frequency, relative durations necessarily

sum to 1 and can also be expressed as percentages summing to 100%. For example, when coding mother vocalizations, we might discover that 37% of the time when mother's vocalizations were occurring they were coded *naming*. As with relative frequency, depending on your specific research questions, relative duration may or may not be a statistic you choose to analyze.

7. *Mean bout duration* indicates how long events last, on average, and makes sense primarily for timed-event data. It is duration divided by frequency, as just defined. When computed for interval or multievent data, it indicates the mean number of successive intervals or multievents checked for a particular code.

Recommended Statistics by Data Type

No matter whether your sessions are organized by a group or a single-subject design, we assume you will compute summary statistics for individual sessions (i.e., analytic units) and then subject those scores to further analyses. In the next few paragraphs, we discuss the simple summary statistics we think are most useful for each data type and, reversing our usual order, begin with timed-event data, which offers the most options.

For timed-event data, we think the most useful summary statistics indicate how often, how likely, and how long. Rate and probability are comparable across sessions (i.e., control for differences in session length) and therefore usually are preferable to frequency and duration. Mean bout duration provides useful description as well, but here you have a choice. These three statistics are not independent (mean bout length is duration divided by frequency), thus present just two of them, or if you describe all three, be aware that any analyses are not independent. Finally, use relative frequency or duration only if clearly required by your research questions.

With timed-event data a key question is, should you use rate, probability, or both? These two statistics provide different, independent information about your codes; they may or may not be correlated. The answer is, it depends on your research question. For example, do you think that how often a mother corrects her child is important? Then use rate. Or, do you think that the amount of time (expressed as a proportion or percentage of the session) a mother corrects her child (or a child experiences being corrected) is important? Then use probability. Whichever you use (or both), always provide your readers with an explicit rationale for your choice; otherwise, they may think your decision was thoughtless.

For other data types, matters are simpler. For simple event data, we think the most useful summary statistics indicate how often and how likely—that is, frequency (or rate when sessions vary in length and start and stop times were recorded) and probability. Finally, for interval and multievent data, we think the most useful summary statistic indicates how likely—that is, how many intervals or multievents were checked for a particular code. With these data types, use other statistics only if clearly required by your research questions.

ANALYZING OBSERVATIONAL DATA: CONTINGENCY INDEXES

The summary statistics described in the previous section were called simple, but they could also be called one-dimensional because each statistic is computed for a single code. In contrast, the summary statistics described in this section could be called two-dimensional because they combine information about two codes, arranged in two-dimensional contingency tables. Still, the overall strategy is the same; summary statistics are computed for individual sessions followed by appropriate statistical analyses.

Statistics derived from two-dimensional tables are of three kinds. First are statistics for individual cells; these are primarily descriptive. Second are summary statistics for 2×2 tables; these indexes of contingency often turn out to be the most useful analytically. And third are summary indexes of independence and association for tables of varying dimensions such as Pearson chi-square and Cohen's kappa; because these are well-known or already discussed, we will not discuss them further here but instead focus on individual cell and 2×2 table statistics.

Statistics for Individual Cells

Statistics for the individual cells of a contingency table can be computed for tables of varying dimension but for illustrative purposes we give examples for the 2×2 table shown in Figure 12.7. The rows represent infant cry, columns represent mother soothe, and the total number of tallies is 100. This could be 100 events, or 100 intervals, or 100 time units, depending on data type. Usually for timed-event and often for interval or multievent data, rows and columns are unlagged, that is, they represent concurrent time units, intervals, or events (i.e., Lag 0). For simple event data, columns usually are lagged (because all co-occurrences are zero); thus rows might represent Lag 0 and columns Lag 1, in which case the number of tallies would be one less than the number of simple events coded.

In the following paragraphs, we give definitions for the five most common cell statistics and provide numeric examples derived from the data in Figure 12.7. In these definitions, r specifies a row, c a column, f_{rc} the frequency count for a given cell, f_{r+} a row sum, f_{+c} a column sum, f_{++} the total number of tallies for the table, and p_i the simple probability for a row or column (e.g., $p_r = f_{r+} \div f_{++}$).

1. The *observed joint frequency* is f_{rc}. The joint frequency for cry and soothe is 13.
2. The *conditional probability* is the probability for the column (or target) behavior given the row (or given) behavior: $p(c|r) = f_{rc} \div f_{r+}$. The conditional

given	target			
	soothe	no soothe	TOTAL	
cry	13	11	24	
no cry	21	55	76	
TOTAL	34	66	100	

p(cry) = 24/200 = .24
p(soothe) = 34/100 = .34
p(cry|soothe) = 13/24 = .54

Odds ratio = (13/11)/(21/55) = 1.18/0.38 = 3.10
Log odds = 1.13
Yule's Q = .51

FIGURE 12.7. Determining the association between infant cry and maternal soothe: An example of a 2×2 table tallying 1-second time units and its associated statistics.

probabilities in a row necessarily sum to 1. The probability of a mother soothe given an infant cry is .54 and of no soothe given infant cry is .46.

3. The *expected frequency* is the frequency expected by chance given the simple probability for the column behavior and the frequency for the row behavior: $exp_{rc} = p_c \times f_{r+} = (f_{+c} \div f_{++}) \times f_{r+}$. The expected frequency for cry and soothe is 8.16, which is less than the observed value of 13.

4. The *raw residual* is the difference between observed and expected: $res_{rc} = f_{rc} - exp_{rc}$. The observed joint frequency for cry and soothe exceeds the expected value by 4.84 (13 – 8.16).

5. The *adjusted residual* is the raw residual divided by its estimated standard error: $z_{rc} = (f_{rc} - exp_{rc}) \div SE_{rc}$ where SE_{rc} = square root of $exp_{rc} \times (1 - p_c) \times (1 - p_r)$. The standard error is the square root of $8.16 \times .76 \times .66 = 2.02$, thus $z_{rc} = 4.84 \div 2.02 = 2.39$. If adjusted residuals were distributed normally we could say that the probability of a result this extreme by chance is less than .05 because 2.39 exceeds 1.96.

Of these statistics, perhaps the adjusted residual is the most useful. Values that are large and positive, or large and negative, indicate co-occurrences (or lagged associations) greater, or less, than expected by chance; a useful guideline is to pay attention to values greater than 3 absolute. Of the others, the conditional probability is useful descriptively but not analytically because its values are contaminated by its simple probabilities. For example, if cry occurs frequently, then values of soothe given cry are likely to be higher than if cry was not as frequent. In other words, the more frequently a code occurs, the more likely another code is to co-occur. The adjusted residual is a better candidate for subsequent analyses, but 2 × 2 contingency indexes as described in the next paragraph may be even better.

Contingency Indexes for 2 × 2 Tables

When research questions involve the contingency between two behaviors, one presumed antecedent and the other consequent (i.e., before and after, given and target, or row and column), tables of any dimensions can be reduced to a 2 × 2 table like the

one shown in Figure 12.7. In this table, rows are labeled given behavior, yes or no, and columns are labeled target behavior, yes or no. This is advantageous because then the contingency between the presumed given and target behavior can be assessed with standard summary statistics for 2 × 2 tables. In the next few paragraphs, we provide definitions for the four summary statistics typically defined but probably only one or two are needed. As is conventional, we label the cells of the 2 × 2 table as follows: $f_{11} = a, f_{12} = b, f_{21} = c, f_{22} = d$. Again, numeric examples are derived from the data in Figure 12.7.

1. The *odds ratio* is a measure of effect size whose interpretation is straightforward and concrete: $OR = (a/b)/(c/d)$. It is useful descriptively and deserves to be used more by behavioral scientists (it is already widely used by epidemiologists). As the name implies, it is the ratio of two odds, derived from the top and bottom rows of a 2 × 2 table. For example, the odds of soothe to no soothe when crying are 13 to 11 or 1.18 to 1 and when not crying are 21 to 55 or 0.38 to 1, thus $OR = 1.18/0.38 = 3.10$. Concretely, this means that the likelihood (odds) of the mother soothing her infant are more than three times greater when her infant is crying than when not.

   The odds ratio varies from 0 to infinity with 1 indicating no effect. Values greater than 1 indicate that the target behavior (in column 1) is more likely in the presence of the given behavior (row 1) than its absence (row 2), whereas values less than 1 indicate that the target behavior (in column 1) is more likely in the absence of the given behavior (row 2) than its presence (row 1). Because the odds ratio varies form 0 to infinity, its distributions often are skewed. Consequently, the odds ratio, although useful descriptively, is not so useful analytically.

2. The *log odds* is the natural logarithm of the odds ratio: $LnOR = log_e OR$. For example, $log_e 3.10 = 1.13$ (i.e., $2.718...^{1.13} = 3.10$). It varies from negative to positive infinity with zero indicating no effect, and compared with the odds ratio, its distributions are less likely to be skewed. However, it is expressed in difficult-to-interpret logarithmic

units. As a result, it is useful analytically but not descriptively.

3. *Yule's Q* is an index of effect size that is a straight-forward algebraic transform of the odds ratio: $Q = (ad - bc)/(ad + bc)$ (Bakeman et al., 2005). It is like the familiar correlation coefficient in two ways: it varies from –1 to + 1 with 0 indicating no effect, and its units have no natural meaning. Thus, its interpretation is not as concrete as the odds ratio.

4. The *phi coefficient* is a Pearson product-moment correlation coefficient computed for binary data. Like Yule's Q it can vary form –1 to + 1, but can only achieve its maximum value when $p_r = p_c = .5$, thus Yule's Q almost always seems preferable.

Which contingency index should you use, the odds ratio descriptively and the log odds analytically, or Yule's Q for both? It is probably a matter of taste. We think the odds ratio is more concretely descriptive, but Yule's Q may seem more natural to some, especially those schooled in correlation coefficients. Another consideration is computational vulnerability to zero cells. A large positive effect (column 1 behavior more likely given row 1 behavior) occurs as *b* (or *c*) tends toward zero and a large negative effect (column 1 behavior less likely given row 1 behavior) occurs as *a* (or *d*) tends toward zero. If only one cell is zero a large negative and a large positive effect is computed as –1 and + 1, 0 and infinity, and undefined (log of 0) and undefined (divide by 0), for Yule's Q, the odds ratio, and the logs odds, respectively. Thus Yule's Q is not vulnerable to zero cells, the odds ratio is vulnerable only if *b* or *c* are zero (using the computational formula, *ad/bc*, for the odds ratio), and the log odds is vulnerable if any cell is zero—which leads many to advocate adding a small constant, typically ½, to each cell before computing a log odds (e.g., Wickens, 1989).

One circumstance is always fatal. If two or more cells are zero—which means that one or more row or column sums are zero—no contingency index can be computed and subsequent analyses would treat its value as missing. After all, if one of the behaviors does not occur, no contingency can be observed. Even when row or column sums are not zero but simply small, it may be wise to treat the value as missing. With few observations, there is little reason to have confidence in its value even when computation is technically possible. Our guideline is, if any row or column sum is less than 5, regard the value of the contingency index as missing, but some investigators may prefer a more stringent guideline.

Lag Sequential Analysis for Simple Event Data

Given simple event data and lagged contingency tables, either the adjusted residuals or the contingency indexes just described could be used for a lag sequential analysis. For example, if Figure 12.7 represented Lag 1 event data (given labeled Lag 0, target Lag 1, and tallying events and not time units), we could say that the probability of a soothe event following a cry event was .54, which is greater than the simple probability of soothe (.34). Moreover, the adjusted residual was 2.39 and the Yule's Q was .51, both positive. (For a more detailed description of event-based lag sequential analysis see Bakeman & Gottman, 1997, pp. 111–116.)

Time-Window Sequential Analysis for Timed-Event Data

Given timed-event data, traditional lag sequential analysis (using time units to indicate lags) does not work very well. Time-window sequential analysis (Bakeman, 2004; Bakeman et al., 2005; Yoder & Tapp, 2004) works better, allows more flexibility, and, incidentally, demonstrates the usefulness of the contingency indexes just described (e.g., see Chorney, Garcia, Berlin, Bakeman, & Kain, 2010). The generic question is, is the target behavior contingent on the given behavior. First, we define a window of opportunity or *time window* for the given behavior. For example, we might say for a behavior to be contingent we need to see a response within 3 seconds; thus, we would code the onset second of the given behavior and the following 2 seconds as a given window (assuming 1-second precision). Second, we code any second in which the target behavior starts as a target onset. Third, we tally time units for the session into a 2 × 2 table, and fourth we compute a contingency index for the table (this can all be done with GSEQ).

For example, assume the tallies in Figure 12.7 represent 1-second time units, that *soothe* refers to the onset of verbal reassurance (it is probably better to imagine a behavior more quick and frequent than soothe for this example), and that *cry* refers to a cry window (e.g., within 3 seconds of a cry onset). Thus in 100 seconds there were 34 reassure episodes (onsets or bouts) and probably 8 episodes of infant cry (assuming the 24 seconds total divide into eight 3-second windows). For this example, reassure and cry appear associated. The likelihood that reassure would begin within 3 seconds of a cry starting was 3 times greater than at other times (and Yule's Q was .51). Descriptively, 38% (13 of 34) of reassure episodes began during cry windows although the windows accounted for 24% of the time. It only remains to compute such indexes for other sessions and use those scores in whatever analyses make sense given your design.

CONCLUSION

Behavioral observation is one of several measurement approaches available to investigators engaged in quantitative behavioral research. It is often the method of choice when nonverbal organisms are studied (or nonverbal behavior generally); when more natural, spontaneous, real-world behavior is of interest; and when processes and not outcomes are the focus (e.g., questions of contingency). Compared with other approaches, it is often labor-intensive and time-consuming. Coding schemes—the basic measuring instrument of behavioral observation—need to be developed and observers trained in their reliable use, and the often-voluminous data initially collected need to be reduced to simple rates and probabilities or contingency indexes for later analyses. Behavior can be observed live or recorded for later viewing (and re-viewing). Observers either assign codes to predetermined time intervals (interval recording) or detect and code events in the stream of behavior (event recording), using instruments that vary from simple pencil and paper to sophisticated computer systems. Coded data can be represented in a code-unit grid as interval, untimed event or multievent, or timed-event data; the latter offers the most options but works best with electronic equipment. Behavioral observation can be used for experimental or nonexperimental studies, in laboratory or field settings, and with single-subject or group designs using between- or within-subjects variables. Summary scores derived from observational sessions can be subjected to any appropriate statistical approach from null-hypothesis testing to mathematical modeling (Rodgers, 2010).

References

Altmann, J. (1974). Observational study of behaviour: Sampling methods. *Behaviour, 49,* 227–267. doi:10.1163/156853974X00534

Bakeman, R. (2004). Sequential analysis. In M. Lewis-Beck, A. E. Bryman, & T. F. Liao (Eds.), *The Sage encyclopedia of social science research methods* (Vol. 3, pp. 1024–1026). Thousand Oaks, CA: Sage.

Bakeman, R. (2010). Reflections on measuring behavior: Time and the grid. In G. Walford, E. Tucker, & M. Viswanathan (Eds.), *The Sage handbook of measurement* (pp. 221–237). Thousand Oaks, CA: Sage.

Bakeman, R., Adamson, L. B., Konner, M., & Barr, R. (1990). Kung infancy: The social context of object exploration. *Child Development, 61,* 794–809. doi:10.2307/1130964

Bakeman, R., Deckner, D. F., & Quera, V. (2005). Analysis of behavioral streams. In D. M. Teti (Ed.), *Handbook of research methods in developmental science* (pp. 394–420). Oxford, England: Blackwell. doi:10.1002/9780470756676.ch20

Bakeman, R., & Gottman, J. M. (1986). *Observing interaction: An introduction to sequential analysis.* Cambridge, England: Cambridge University Press.

Bakeman, R., & Gottman, J. M. (1997). *Observing interaction: An introduction to sequential analysis* (2nd ed.). Cambridge, England: Cambridge University Press. doi:10.1017/CBO9780511527685

Bakeman, R., & Helmreich, R. (1975). Cohesiveness and performance: Covariation and causality in an undersea environment. *Journal of Experimental Social Psychology, 11,* 478–489. doi:10.1016/0022-1031-(75)90050-5

Bakeman, R., & Quera, V. (1992). SDIS: A sequential data interchange standard. *Behavior Research Methods, Instruments, and Computers, 24,* 554–559. doi:10.3758/BF03203604

Bakeman, R., & Quera, V. (1995). *Analyzing interaction: Sequential analysis with SDIS and GSEQ.* Cambridge, England: Cambridge University Press.

Bakeman, R., & Quera, V. (2009). GSEQ 5 [Computer software and manual]. Retrieved from http://www.gsu.edu/~psyrab/gseq/gseq.html

Bakeman, R., & Quera, V. (2011). *Sequential analysis and observational methods for the behavioral sciences.* Cambridge, England: Cambridge University Press.

Bakeman, R., Quera, V., & Gnisci, A. (2009). Observer agreement for timed-event sequential data: A comparison of time-based and event-based algorithms. *Behavior Research Methods, 41*, 137–147. doi:10.3758/BRM.41.1.137

Bakeman, R., & Robinson, B. F. (1994). *Understanding log-linear analysis with ILOG: An interactive approach.* Hillsdale, NJ: Erlbaum.

Chorney, J. M., Garcia, A. M., Berlin, K. S., Bakeman, R., & Kain, Z. N. (2010). Time-window sequential analysis: An introduction for pediatric psychologists. *Journal of Pediatric Psychology, 35*, 1061–1070. doi:10.1093/jpepsy/jsq022

Cohen, J. A. (1960). A coefficient of agreement for nominal scales. *Educational and Psychological Measurement, 20*, 37–46. doi:10.1177/001316446002000104

Cohn, J. F., & Kanade, T. (2007). Use of automated facial image analysis for measurement of emotion expression. In J. A. Coan & J. J. B. Allen (Eds.), *Oxford University Press Series in Affective Science: The handbook of emotion elicitation and assessment* (pp. 222–238). New York, NY: Oxford University Press.

Douglass, W. (1760). *A summary, historical and political, of the first planting, progressive improvements, and present state of the British settlements in North-America* (Vol. 1). London, England: R. & J. Dodsley.

Ekman, P. W., & Friesen, W. (1978). *Facial Action Coding System: A technique for the measurement of facial movement.* Palo Alto, CA: Consulting Psychologist Press.

Fleiss, J. L. (1981). *Statistical methods for rates and proportions* (2nd ed.). New York, NY: Wiley.

Galisson, F. (2000, August). *Introduction to computational sequence analysis.* Tutorial presented at the Eighth International Conference on Intelligent Systems for Molecular Biology, San Diego, CA. Retrieved from http://www.iscb.org/ismb2000/tutorial_pdf/galisson4.pdf

Gottman, J. M. (1979). *Marital interaction: Experimental investigations.* New York, NY: Academic Press.

Gros-Louis, J., West, M. J., Goldstein, M. H., & King, A. P. (2006). Mothers provide differential feedback to infants' prelinguistic sounds. *International Journal of Behavioral Development, 30*, 509–516. doi:10.1177/0165025406071914

Konner, M. J. (1976). Maternal care, infant behavior, and development among the !Kung. In R. B. DeVore (Ed.), *Kalahari hunter-gathers* (pp. 218–245). Cambridge, MA: Harvard University Press.

Martin, P., & Bateson, P. (2007). *Measuring behaviour: An introductory guide* (3rd ed.). Cambridge, England: Cambridge University Press.

Needleman, S. B., & Wunsch, C. D. (1970). A general method applicable to the search for similarities in the amino acid sequence of two proteins. *Journal of Molecular Biology, 48*, 443–453. doi:10.1016/0022-2836(70)90057-4

Oller, D. K. (2000). *The emergence of the speech capacity.* Mahwah, NJ: Erlbaum.

Parten, M. B. (1932). Social participation among pre-school children. *The Journal of Abnormal and Social Psychology, 27*, 243–269. doi:10.1037/h0074524

Quera, V., Bakeman, R., & Gnisci, A. (2007). Observer agreement for event sequences: Methods and software for sequence alignment and reliability estimates. *Behavior Research Methods, 39*, 39–49. doi:10.3758/BF03192842

Rodgers, J. L. (2010). The epistemology of mathematical and statistical modeling: A quiet methodological revolution. *American Psychologist, 65*, 1–12. doi:10.1037/a0018326

Sankoff, D., & Kruskal, J. (Eds.). (1999). *Time warps, string edits, and macromolecules: The theory and practice of sequence comparison.* Stanford, CA: CSLI. (Original work published 1983)

Stevens, S. S. (1946). On the theory of scales of measurement. *Science, 103*, 677–680. doi:10.1126/science.103.2684.677

Suen, H. K., & Ary, D. (1989). *Analyzing quantitative behavioral data.* Hillsdale, NJ: Erlbaum.

Wickens, T. D. (1989). *Multiway contingency tables analysis for the social sciences.* Hillsdale, NJ: Erlbaum.

Wolff, P. H. (1966). The causes, controls, and organization of behavior in the neonate. *Psychological Issues, 5*, 1–105.

Yoder, P., & Symons, F. (2010). *Observational measurement of behavior.* New York, NY: Springer.

Yoder, P. J., & Tapp, J. (2004). Empirical guidance for time-window sequential analysis of single cases. *Journal of Behavioral Education, 13*, 227–246. doi:10.1023/B:JOBE.0000044733.03220.a9

Self-Reports

CHAPTER 13

QUESTION ORDER EFFECTS

Kenneth A. Rasinski, Lisa Lee, and Parvati Krishnamurty

In this chapter, we examine the research literature on question order effects. A question order effect occurs when responses to a prior question on a questionnaire affect responses to a subsequent one. Because questionnaire designers have to settle on some ordering of questions, question order effects are always a possibility. This chapter reviews the literature on empirical studies of survey question order effects, their mechanisms, and their moderators. In addition, we provide guidance for questionnaire construction on the basis of the results of these studies. Question order effects are sometimes categorized more generally as context effects because the prior question is thought to provide a context in which to view the subsequent question. Strictly speaking, survey context is broader than question order and can involve instructions, extra materials presented as part of the survey that are not questions (such as pictures or videos), or even the setting in which a survey is administered. A question order effect is a special type of context effect.

Three basic kinds of question order effects have been identified (Schuman & Presser, 1981): (a) Answers to the subsequent question are affected by having responded to the prior question but not necessarily affected by which response was given on the prior question (an *unconditional* question order effect), (b) answers to the subsequent question depend on the response given to the prior question (a *conditional* question order effect), and (c) the correlation between the prior question and the subsequent question changes depending on which is asked first (an *associational* question order effect).

Question order effects can present serious problems when measuring change over time, whether in longitudinal surveys or in repeated cross-sectional surveys, or even when comparing the results of different cross-sectional surveys. Unless the question order is the same for each data collection, it is difficult to know whether change (or its absence) is due to real respondent change or to question order.

Schuman and Presser (1981) presented the first extensive review of question order effects primarily in the area of public opinion. They conducted their own studies to replicate and see the extent of question order effects but did not systematically capture the behavioral or psychological dynamics underlying the effects. In general, among survey methodologists before the early to mid-1980s no general framework for understanding and predicting question order effects was widely accepted. The emphasis on psychology and surveys beginning in the early 1980s changed that. For the first time, the cognitive task of the respondent, rather than just the substance of the question, was given serious consideration. Once that breakthrough had been made researchers could develop theories about the types of judgment required by a question and experiments could be designed to manipulate the task demands of the respondent in theoretically derived ways to test hypotheses about the psychology of the survey response process. This information could be fed back to survey practitioners and, through pretesting, could improve the way questions are asked by taking into account the cognitive processes respondents brought to bear on the questions and the way that

DOI: 10.1037/13619-014
APA Handbook of Research Methods in Psychology: Vol. 1. Foundations, Planning, Measures, and Psychometrics, H. Cooper (Editor-in-Chief)
Copyright © 2012 by the American Psychological Association. All rights reserved.

the questions challenged respondent cognitive limitations.

An example of the attempt to extend psychological theory and research to survey responding in general and to question order effects in particular is the work by Tourangeau and his colleagues (Tourangeau, 1984; Tourangeau, Rips, & Rasinski, 2000). They presented a model of psychological mechanisms likely to underlie survey responding. The hope was to help focus research such that explanations for question order effects could be formed on the basis of tests of hypotheses generated from theories about how respondents approach questions, rather than on the basis of post hoc explanations of observed phenomena. Their model emphasizes the cognitive tasks of the survey respondent interpreting a question, retrieving relevant information from memory, forming a response, and reporting the response. For question order effects, all of these tasks may come into play.

For example, a prior question such as, "How many times have you been to the dentist in the past 12 months?" might cause some respondents to *interpret* the subsequent question "Does your employer provide health insurance?" to suggest that health insurance includes dental health insurance. A prior question such as "On a typical day, how long is your commute to work?" might affect responses to a subsequent question "Should your city invest more in public transportation, or is the current system adequate?" because the respondent may have *retrieved* the memory of standing on a crowded bus or train or of being stuck in traffic while answering the prior question.

The context that precedes a question may affect how respondents *form* their answer to the question. For example, responses to a question about likelihood of eating five servings of fresh fruits and vegetables each day may be influenced by whether the respondent is first asked a question about food prices. Those who are asked about food prices may consider the higher cost of fresh produce and subsequently report lower likelihood of eating fresh fruits and vegetables compared with respondents who did not consider food prices in advance. Even something as straightforward as asking about one's marital status might be affected by a prior question that asked how many sex partners the respondent had in the past year. Those reporting more than one may be reluctant to admit that they are married because of the social stigma associated with adultery. Or, if the marital status question is asked first, those reporting that they are married may deliberately suppress reporting of multiple sex partners, if this is in fact the case. This type of question order effect would arise at the *reporting* or "editing" stage of the survey response process, where answers depend not on respondents' cognitive limitations but on how they want to present themselves.

The most common methodology for studying question order effects is the randomized experiment conducted within a population-based survey. Typically, the experiments are embedded in longer questionnaires. Most of the time, the experiments have two conditions that study the effects of one question on another, although the effect of a set of prior questions on one or more subsequent questions may also be studied. For example, to study question order effects on responses to questions about abortion, two versions of the questionnaire may be created. Form A might contain the following order of two questions: (a) a question about a woman's right to an abortion if the baby was likely to have a genetic defect followed by (b) a question about a woman's right to an abortion simply because she does not want to have a child at this time. Form B would contain the reverse ordering (i.e., Question 2 preceding Question 1). Forms A and B would be distributed randomly across survey respondents. After data collection is completed, researchers would test for differences in the responses to the two questions across conditions. They might examine whether differences to the second question depend on responses to the first question and might also examine differences in the correlation (or some other measure of association) between the two questions across conditions. Conditional question order effects and associational effects are two different ways of looking at the same phenomenon. Most often, conditional effects are expressed as differences in association. Smith (1991) argued that it might be useful to examine conditional effects in more detail than they typically are examined.

We have mentioned that the first systematic review of question order effects was conducted by

Schuman and Presser (1981), who provided a thorough review of the existing literature and reported on their own experimental findings. Question order effects have been studied in other areas, most notably marketing and health research. This chapter updates Schuman and Presser's review in the area of public opinion, drawing on more recent literature across a broad range of topics. Furthermore, we extend the discussion of psychological mechanisms. Looking across different disciplines will enable us to compare mechanisms proposed for question order effects to see where there is convergence, where there are differences, and where one discipline may inform another.

In addition to documenting, comparing, and contrasting mechanisms we will discuss what the literature says about whether individual differences moderate context effects. Schuman and Presser (1981) addressed this topic, but since their review more studies have been conducted and more results are available. Just as understanding the mechanisms that underlie question order effects may provide insight about how to construct questionnaires that will diminish these effects, knowing which groups of individuals are more susceptible to them under some conditions may be useful in questionnaire construction. The more we can understand why question order effects occur, and for whom, the clearer it will be how best to ask questions in surveys and to interpret the potential effects of question order on the responses.

SOCIAL AND POLITICAL TOPICS

Social and political topics frequently have been examined for question order effects because questions are often of a broad nature (e.g., "Do you favor or oppose the privatization of Social Security?") potentially tapping into many different aspects of a particular respondent's attitudes, and attitudes themselves may fluctuate, especially on topics that the respondent has not thought much about.

Abortion

One of the major topics studied with regard to question order effects is abortion. A series of papers has examined discrepancies and possible explanations in the level of support that respondents express for a woman's right to an abortion. For example, the following two abortion questions have been the subject of intense scrutiny: (a) Do you think that it should be possible for a pregnant woman to obtain a legal abortion if she is married and does not want any more children? (b) Do you think it should be possible for a pregnant woman to obtain a legal abortion if there is a strong chance of serious defect in the baby? The first question is also referred as the *general* or *whole* question and the second question is referred to as the *specific* or *part* question.

The 1978 General Social Survey (GSS), conducted by NORC, found 40.3% of respondents said "yes" to the general question.[1] Schuman, Presser, and Ludwig (1981), using the general question on abortion from the GSS, found significantly greater support for abortion, 58.4%, than the NORC survey demonstrated. A key methodological difference between the studies was that in the 1978 GSS, the general abortion question was immediately preceded by the specific question on abortion in the case of a defect in the unborn child. The Schuman et al. survey (Survey Research Center [SRC]) asked only the general question.

Another factor may have contributed to the differences between the 1978 GSS and the Schuman et al. (1981) study. Two questions on children appeared before the GSS abortion questions. People were asked to rank the desirability of 17 values for children, such as having good manners, being honest, obeying parents, and so on. After answering this question, respondents were asked what they thought was the ideal number of children to have. For some respondents, these questions on children appeared before the abortion items. Smith (1983) found that support for abortion in the general case of not wanting any more children was lower when it followed the questions on children. He posited that a heightened focus on children reduced support for abortion.

To explore the differences between the 1978 GSS and the SRC findings, Schuman et al. (1981) conducted a split-ballot experiment in which both

[1]The 1978 GSS actually had a seven-part question on approval of legal abortions, of which the questions on a defect in the baby and not wanting any more children were the first two questions.

abortion questions were presented but with the order switched between ballots. They found that answers to the specific question did not differ significantly on the basis of that order. Support for abortion in the general question exhibited a *contrast* effect; support was lower when it followed the specific question. These questions are described as having a *part–whole* relationship (Schuman & Presser, 1981) because the specific question on the child with a defect is considered to be contained within the general question on a woman's right in the case of not wanting more children. The respondent's answer to the part question is considered predictable on the basis of their answer to the whole question. That is, someone who supports a woman's right in general to an abortion is likely to support that right in a specific case, such as when the child has a defect. The opposite may not be true, however; support for abortion in the specific case does not predict support in the general case. In their explanation for the contrast effect, Schuman et al. suggested that it is possible that when asked about the specific case first, respondents take that scenario out of consideration (hence, they *subtract* it) when considering their level of support for abortion more generally. Thus, the specific–general question order yields less general support for abortion than the general–specific order.

Bishop, Oldendick, and Tuchfarber (1985) conducted experiments to attempt to replicate the Schuman et al. (1981) findings. In a split-ballot experiment, one version of the questionnaire included the two abortion questions presented by Schuman et al. and Smith (1978) in specific–general order. Another version asked these questions in general–specific order.[2] Consistent with the SRC findings, responses to the specific question did not vary significantly across conditions. Responses to the general question showed an effect in the same direction as prior studies. However, although Bishop et al. (1985) reported higher agreement with the general abortion question when it was asked before the specific question as compared with after it, the difference between the two conditions

was not significant. Furthermore, a much larger order effect was observed in the SRC than in the Bishop et al. experiment. That is, Bishop et al.'s experiment did not replicate findings of a question order effect with the general and specific abortion questions. Bishop et al. speculated, however, that one contextual aspect of the experiment may have influenced the findings. The experimental manipulation of the order of the abortion questions was preceded by two questions, one on welfare and one on the respondent's identification as a liberal, moderate, or conservative (Bishop et al., 1985, p. 109). In contrast, Schuman et al. preceded the abortion questions with questions about labor unions in one study and about the Soviet Union in another study. Thus, Bishop et al. suggested that the preceding context could have influenced responses to the abortion items by prompting respondents to approach the abortion items as questions on whether they have a liberal versus conservative viewpoint.

To examine this possibility, Bishop et al. (1985) conducted a second experiment. In addition to varying the order of the abortion questions, they also varied whether those questions immediately preceded or followed the questions on welfare and political self-identification. Furthermore, they included an open-ended question after the general abortion question asking respondents why they felt a pregnant woman should or should not be able to obtain a legal abortion if she is married and does not want any more children. The order effect with the abortion questions was larger (but not significantly larger) when they appeared before the welfare and political self-identification questions as compared with after. To test the subtraction hypothesis, they examined reasons that respondents gave to the open-ended question following the general question. Results cast some doubt on a subtraction hypothesis and suggest instead an explanation on the basis of *implicit contrast*. That is, when the general abortion question comes first, a woman's right to an abortion seems reasonable to support on the basis of freedom of choice. When the general abortion question

---

[2]In a third questionnaire version, the questions were asked in specific–general order, but the questions were separated by about 40 questions on topics not related to abortion. No other questions before the split-ballot items dealt with abortion. The results in this condition were the same as for the first condition, that is, no effect of the buffer was found.

comes second, after the birth defect question, the freedom of choice argument is no longer viewed as favorably.

The U.S. and Communist Reporter Questions

The question order effects discussed above concern questions that have a part–whole relationship. A different phenomenon has been noted in questions that involve two competing parties. In these types of questions, an advantage, disadvantage, or standard of judgment applied to one party might be considered to apply to the other party as well. A well-known example involves the following questions on what U.S. and Communist reporters should be allowed to do: (a) Do you think a Communist country like Russia should let U.S. newspaper reporters come in and send back to the United States the news as they see it? (b) Do you think the United States should let Communist newspaper reporters from other countries come in here and send back to their papers the news as they see it?

Hyman and Sheatsley (1950) found that people overwhelmingly supported allowing U.S. reporters into Russia when this question was asked first (90%); support declined when this question was asked after the question on allowing Communist reporters into the United States (66%). When asked about Communist reporters first, support was low (36%); but after being asked about U.S. reporters in Russia, support for letting in Communist reporters increased dramatically (73%). In their own replication, Schuman and Presser (1981) found similar results. They termed this a *part–part* effect because of the equal level of specificity of both questions and denoted it as a *consistency* effect because the response to the subsequent question moves in the direction of being consistent with the response to the prior question. This effect may occur because respondents tend to answer the first question in a way that favors the United States (whether in favor of U.S. reporters or against Communist reporters), but they subsequently apply the norm of reciprocity in evaluating the second question in a way that is more consistent with their first answer (also called a *norm of evenhandedness* by Schuman & Ludwig, 1983).

In a further replication of this finding, Schuman, Kalton, and Ludwig (1983) introduced a third condition in which they presented the U.S. reporter question first and the Communist reporter question second, with 17 neutral items intervening. Consistent with prior findings, question order effects were found for the items when asked consecutively. When 17 other items separate the two questions, the effect was still observed. The persistence of the effect despite the interceding buffer suggests that question order effect may not simply be an artifact of asking the questions consecutively. Schuman et al. did not provide an explanation as to the mechanisms that may cause a question order effect to persist with the addition of buffer questions. It is possible, however, that the buffer was not sufficient for respondents to forget their response to the prior question when formulating their answer to the subsequent one.

An additional example of how question order can affect the context in which a question is answered, calling into play a norm of reciprocity, concerns questions on affirmative action (AA). In a 2003 Gallup survey, Wilson, Moore, McKay, and Avery (2008) conducted a question order experiment for the following questions: (a) Do you generally favor or oppose AA programs for racial minorities? (b) Do you generally favor or oppose AA programs for women? The findings revealed a significant order effect attributed to respondent consistency and the relative popularity of gender-based AA compared with race-based AA. When the women AA question was asked first, 63% favored AA programs for women and 29% were opposed, a 34% difference. When the women AA question appeared second, however, 57% favored and 37% were opposed, a 20% difference. When the minority AA question was asked first, 50% favored and 50% were opposed or unsure. In comparison, when the minority AA question was second, 57% favored and 43% were opposed or unsure. The results demonstrate a consistency effect. Respondents appear to answer the first question presented in a noncomparative context (Moore, 2002), that is, independently of the following question. The following question is presented in a comparative context, that is, in the context of the preceding question. The comparative context may invoke a *norm of reciprocity* or evenhandedness (Schuman & Presser, 1981, p. 28); support for one type of AA program will be affected by whether respondents consider that AA program alone or in the context of another one.

Political Identification

McAllister and Wattenberg (1995) demonstrated the absence of a question order effect on political party identification. They examined the effects of question order on party identification in a British election survey and a U.S. election survey. Respondents were asked for whom they were voting and their party affiliation, with these questions varying in order. The results show no question order effects on party identification in either the British or U.S. surveys. Asking respondents whom they voted for did not have a subsequent effect on their answers to a question on their political party affiliation.

These results stand in contrast to other findings that suggest that political identification is more malleable. Bishop, Tuchfarber, and Smith (1994) found question order effects for political party identification and presidential vote questions. They examined two versions of political party identification, the Gallup question (In politics, as of today, do you consider yourself a Republican, a Democrat, or an Independent?) and the SRC question (Generally speaking, do you usually think of yourself as a Republican a Democrat, an Independent, or what?). The SRC question may emphasize long-term party loyalty through reference to what the respondent "generally" or "usually" identifies with. The Gallup question may emphasize the effects of short-term events on feelings of partisanship by asking "as of today." This experiment included these two partisanship questions and a question on whom the respondent voted for in the 1992 presidential election (Bush, Clinton, or Perot). The 1992 election was notable because of the candidacy of a prominent independent candidate (Perot). Bishop et al. found that both the Gallup and SRC questions, when asked after the vote question, showed question order effects. When party identification was asked after the vote question, more respondents indicated themselves to be Independents and fewer identified

as Democrats, compared with when the party identification question was asked first, regardless of which version of the partisanship question was used (however, see Abramson & Ostrom, 1991, for an opposing view on the differences between the Gallup and SRC questions).

Happiness

Some of the early research on question order effects concerned responses to questions on happiness. This research focused on two questions: a general question and a specific question on marital happiness. The questions were as follows:

1. Taken altogether, how would you say things are these days? Would you say you are very happy, pretty happy, or not too happy? (*general question*)
2. Taking things all together, how would you describe your marriage? Would you say that your marriage is very happy, pretty happy or not too happy? (*specific question*)

Schuman and Presser (1981) found evidence for a contrast effect. When the general question followed the specific question, respondents were significantly less likely to report that they were very happy compared with when the question order was reversed. Specifically, 52.4% of respondents reported being generally very happy when the general question appeared first, whereas only 38.1% reported being very happy when the marital happiness question came first. Only the general question, and not the specific question, was subject to question order effects. Sudman and Bradburn (1982) suggested the subtraction hypothesis as a mechanism to explain the contrast effect. According to this hypothesis, when the general question follows the specific question on marital happiness, respondents interpret the general question as asking about other aspects of the respondent's life and not their marriage. Another explanation is that when the general question on happiness follows the marital happiness question, respondents consider other domains in their life while answering the general question to avoid redundancy.

Smith (1982) reported experimental results for the 1980 GSS in which he used the same questions on happiness but found an assimilation effect rather than a contrast effect. When the specific question on marital happiness preceded the general question, respondents were more likely to say that they generally were very happy. These results were similar to nonexperimental results reported in his earlier research (Smith, 1979). The assimilation effect seen here was fairly easy to explain. Because most people were happy in their marriages, the specific question primed them and made the information on their marital happiness cognitively accessible. Therefore, they included marital happiness in their assessment of general happiness.

Subsequent research (McClendon & O'Brien 1988; Strack, Martin, & Schwartz, 1988; Turner, 1984) has tried to replicate and reconcile the findings of these two early papers and find evidence to support various explanations for why the contrast effect or assimilation effect occurs. One reason for the apparently conflicting findings in these papers could be differences in the number of specific questions that preceded the general questions (Tourangeau & Rasinski, 1988). In Smith (1982), the happiness items were part of a series of five questions about satisfaction in different domains, whereas Schuman and Presser (1981) did not include other questions on life satisfaction. When a series of specific questions preceded the general question, respondents may have thought they were expected to provide a summary judgment of their overall happiness when responding to the general question. This would have led to assimilation effects. On the other hand, when there was only one specific question, respondents may have excluded the specific domain in their judgment of overall happiness, which produced a contrast effect (Tourangeau & Rasinski, 1988).

McClendon and O'Brien (1988b) conducted an experiment to examine the role of cognitive accessibility in question order effects in an experiment with a general question on well-being and multiple specific questions. The questions were part of a split-ballot experiment included in a telephone survey on living in the greater Akron area; the specific domains included marriage, health, employment, neighborhood, and standard of living. The general question on well-being was placed either fourth or

at the end of 11 questions on different domains. Analyses indicated that there were positive question order effects for domains such as marriage and health, which were closer to the general question, and negative effects for employment, which was further away from the general question. The authors concluded that putting the specific questions before the general question increased the cognitive accessibility of those domains. The domains, which were closer to the general question, were accessed more recently and therefore showed stronger question order effects.

Another experiment conducted by Strack et al. (1988) investigated the effect of including an introduction to the happiness questions to provide a common conversational context. The introduction stated that they were looking at two areas (a) happiness with dating and (b) happiness with life in general. The authors found that when the general question followed the specific question without the introduction, the correlation coefficient between the responses to the specific and general questions was significantly higher than with the introduction. They concluded that when the general and specific questions were presented in the same context, respondents excluded the information on dating while answering the general question. This is despite the fact that they had just accessed the information on dating to answer the prior question. Clearly, respondents thought they were expected to provide new information in the general question.

Schwartz, Strack, and Mai (1991) further explored the role of conversational context as a determinant of whether contrast or assimilation effects predominate. Their hypothesis was that when a specific question appeared before a general question in the same conversational context, then conversational norms applied and respondents tried to avoid the redundancy that would lead to a contrast effect. On the other hand, when the context appeared to be different, the placement of the specific marriage question before the general question increased the cognitive accessibility of the marriage domain, which would lead to an assimilation effect. When there were multiple preceding specific questions, the general question was also interpreted to be a summary judgment and an assimilation effect would be observed. Results generally supported their hypotheses. The expected contrast effect was observed only for unhappy respondents, however. Because this experiment used questions about satisfaction rather than happiness, it was not a direct replication of the earlier studies.

Tourangeau, Rasinski, and Bradburn (1991) used happiness questions to test for the subtraction hypothesis. Their experiment had four conditions: (a) a general happiness question that asked the respondent to include their marriage in their consideration, (b) the standard general happiness/marital happiness sequence, (c) the standard marital happiness/general happiness sequence, and (d) a general happiness question that asked respondents to exclude their marriage from their considerations. They expected to see an assimilation effect in the general first (b) and the explicit inclusion conditions (d) and a contrast effect in the marital first (c) and explicit exclusion (a) conditions.

The condition in which the general question came before the marital question showed a high correlation between the two questions and the condition in which the marital question appeared before the general question had a significantly lower correlation, giving some evidence of assimilation and contrast. The percentages of respondents who reported they were very happy, however, were similar across the four conditions. Thus, they did not find the directional evidence that could lend support to the subtraction hypothesis.

MARKET RESEARCH

Even before the seminal work of Schuman and Presser (1981), cited earlier, Bradburn and Mason (1964) discussed the implications of question order effects for those engaged in market research. They were both pessimistic and optimistic, having said, "From the fragmentary data available it appears that under some conditions the order of presentation of questions can have important effects on responses, but that under other conditions it makes little difference" (p. 58). They continued by saying that research up until then had not shown where question order mattered and where it did not and urged market researchers to conduct more question order experiments to build a body of data from which generalizations about the circumstances under which questions order effects could be made.

As our review shows, since that time, much has been learned about the conditions and mechanisms underlying question order effects. Market researchers, having heard Bradburn and Mason's (1964) call, have contributed to that understanding from their unique perspective. Their research makes a unique contribution to this area because compared with the survey research studies, which generally concern attitudes toward abstract notions (e.g., personal happiness, potential government policies), they are interested in evaluations of tangible objects such as products and services.

One example of such research was done by Bickart (1993), who studied whether assimilation and contrast effects (called *carryover* and *backfire* effects in her article) for question order that varied specific attribute and general product ratings would differ depending on the type of information received about a product and the respondent's self-rated product knowledge. Pretesting was used to determine which information was perceived to be diagnostic of (i.e., related to) the product quality and which information was not. When a diagnostic attribute was presented, the attribute rating for the product affected the general product rating as a carryover (assimilation) effect. A contrast- (backfire-) type question order effect favoring the specific–general question sequence occurred when a nondiagnostic attribute was given, but only for those in the high knowledge group. Bickart (1993) suggested that market researchers use assessments of product knowledge (which generally are collected in marketing research) to determine question order. Bickart stated that general evaluations of highly knowledgeable respondents may be more reactive to specific evaluations, whereas respondents with low to moderate levels of product knowledge may need to see diagnostic attributes to make an informed general evaluation.

An important topic of interest among marketing researchers is the evaluation of service quality. Areas that have been studied include banking, dentists, doctors, hair salons, customer service in utility companies, and computer support services. Surveys of service quality typically use a measure called

SERVQUAL (Parasuraman, Zeithami, & Berry, 1988), which assesses five dimensions of service. Several studies examine question order and other context effects in these surveys. We discuss two papers that specifically manipulate question order in their experiments.

DeMoranville and Bienstock (2003) studied how question order affected evaluation of service quality in banking, dental services, and hair salons. The respondents were undergraduate students and the questionnaire consisted of the 44-item SERVQUAL battery (22 performance questions and 22 expectation questions) either followed or preceded by a general item on overall service quality. The researchers hypothesized (a) that service quality would be rated more highly on the general question when the general question was asked after the specific questions (an assimilation effect), (b) that ratings on specific questions would be lower when the specific question was asked after the general question (a contrast effect), and (c) that the contrast effect predicted in the hypothesis stated in (b) would be present for performance ratings but not expectation ratings. Support for each hypothesis was found. The authors argued that because performance ratings are often used as a standard of quality, evaluators of a service need to be aware of the effects of question order, making sure to keep order constant when evaluating the same service across time.

Another study conducted by the same researchers (DeMoranville, Bienstock, & Judson, 2008) assessed the effect of question order on the predictive validity of the SERVQUAL battery. Three orderings were randomly distributed to users of banking, dental, and hair services. Order 1 consisted of 6 global quality items and the 44 SERVQUAL items (general–specific), Order 2 was the reverse of order 1 (specific–general), and Order 3 randomly mixed the SERVQUAL and global quality items. Each order was followed by three questions asking about the likelihood of future use of the service. The later questions formed the criterion measure. The results showed that the correlations between SERVQUAL and the three assessments of the likelihood of future interaction were highest when the SERVQUAL questions were asked just before the future interaction items (Order 2). The correlations among global

quality items and future interaction items were highest in the randomly mixed condition (Order 3). The researchers caution evaluators to pay careful attention to question order when general and specific questions are used to evaluate services—and, in particular, when using the SERVQUAL measure—because question order can enhance or degrade the apparent predictive validity of the measure.

HEALTH STUDIES

Although many health-related surveys have been conducted, our search of the health literature turned up only a handful of question order experiments, and these were, for the most part, conducted fairly recently. Using a telephone survey, Rimal and Real (2005) examined whether question order affected judgments about the perceived importance of skin cancer. They hypothesized that respondents who were more involved with the issue would be less likely to be influenced by prior health-related questions, including questions about other forms of cancer, than those who were involved with the issue. On the basis of the elaboration-likelihood model of Petty and Cacioppo (1981), they hypothesized that involvement would result in central processing, which would be immune from question order effects. Those less involved would engage in peripheral processing in which question order played a greater role in responding.

All respondents were asked to judge how important the issue of skin cancer was in their life. In the first condition, involvement questions were asked after the importance question; in the second condition, the involvement questions were asked before the importance question. Consistent with their hypothesis, when cognitive involvement (how much the respondent thought about skin cancer) was low, importance of skin cancer was rated as significantly greater when the question came first than when it came later. When cognitive involvement was high, there was no difference between question order conditions in importance ratings. Presumably, those respondents who had not thought much about skin cancer were engaging in a comparison of skin cancer with other health-related questions on the survey.

In contrast to findings that respondents who are highly involved or judge an issue to be of high importance are less subject to question order effects, a study of perceptions of neighborhood safety suggests a contrary relationship between the salience of an issue and context effects (McClendon & O'Brien, 1988a). The authors predicted that perceptions of neighborhood safety would have a greater effect on neighborhood satisfaction when the safety question preceded rather than followed the neighborhood evaluation question. The authors found that this was the case, but only for Black respondents for whom safety was a more salient issue.

Question order does not always affect responses. Bolman, Lechner, and van Dijke (2007) also structured their study of the assessment of physical activity on the idea from the elaboration likelihood model that involvement would moderate question order effects. In a national mail survey conducted in the Netherlands, respondents were asked to give a subjective assessment of the amount of physical activity in which they engage. Half of the respondents were asked the subjective question before they were asked a battery of questions about actual activities in which they engaged, the number of days in which they did them, and the intensity level. The other half of respondents were given the actual activities question first followed by the subjective assessment. Question order did not have a statistically significant impact on subjective or actual physical activity by itself or in interaction with involvement.

Bowling and Windsor (2008) examined question order effects on two versions of a single self-rated health question (a) "How is your health in general? Would you say it was very good, good, fair, bad or very bad?" and (b) "Would you say your health is excellent, very good, good, fair or poor?" This study used data from the English Longitudinal Study of Ageing, a national survey of the population of Great Britain age 50 and older. The survey was conducted by an interviewer in person in the respondent's household.

Two versions of the questionnaire were assigned at random to respondents. One version asked question (a) first followed by a series of specific health questions and then asked question (b). The second version asked question (b) first followed by a series

of specific health questions and then asked question (a). In addition, to test the impact of including an extreme positive response category, half of the versions used "excellent" as the first choice and half used "very good." Regardless of the question ordering or the extremity of response options, respondents rated their health as slightly but significantly more positively when the question came at the end of the specific health questions than when it came at the beginning. This effect held even among patients who reported a longstanding illness. The authors suggest that respondents were excluding information about their specific health conditions when they made the overall judgment last.

In a contingent valuation study Kartman, Stålhammar, and Johannesson (1996) used a telephone survey in Sweden to test question order effects on willingness to pay judgments of patients with reflex esophagitis. They found that a bid decision (i.e., a "yes, definitely"; "yes, probably"; "no, definitely not"; "no, probably not"; "don't know" decision) to pay an incremental amount to receive a superior hypothetical medication was not affected by the order in which scenarios explaining the superior compared with the inferior medication's properties were presented. Darker, French, Longdon, Morris, and Eves (2007) also found no question order effects in belief elicitation to open-ended questions used in a theory of planned behavior study of walking as exercise.

Gold and Barclay (2006) found significant differences resulting from question order in correlations between judgments of one's own risk and of an adverse event occurring (e.g., "What is the chance that you will get into a car accident in the next year?") and judgments of the risk of others (e.g., "What is the chance the average person will get into a car accident in the next year?"). The correlations were lower when the own risk question came first, largely because respondents give answers that were idiosyncratic to their own experience, ignoring the larger context of events. When the "average person" question came first, however, respondents were forced to take into account the larger context, which drove up correlations between judgments of their own risk and that of the average person.

Finally, Lee and Grant (2009) found question order effects on the self-rated general health question for female respondents interviewed with a Spanish language questionnaire compared with male respondents interviewed in Spanish and non-Latinos interviewed in English. The female respondents interviewed in Spanish reported poorer overall health when they were given the general health question before the specific questions.

Similar to the idea that specific health questions may help frame or anchor a more general health question for some respondents, a study by Rasinski, Visser, Zagatsky, and Rickett (2005) showed that prior questions designed to prime motivations to report honesty increased reporting of high-risk behaviors (in this case, excessive alcohol intake) among a group of college students. Students were given a self-administered questionnaire consisting of a set of health behavior questions about binge drinking and associated behaviors, such as driving under the influence of alcohol or missing class because of hangovers. Half of the students at random were primed to report honestly using a nonconscious priming task. This task, a word-matching exercise, preceded the health questionnaire and was in the same packet of materials, but it was formatted to look like a separate task. Results showed that students primed with honesty-related words reported more alcohol-related behaviors than students in the neutral priming condition.

SELF-ADMINISTERED SURVEYS

Many surveys incorporating question order experiments are administered by interviewers, either in person or by telephone. Surveys are often self-administered, however, as in mail or Internet surveys. It seems reasonable to argue that question order should have limited effects in self-administered surveys, especially if they are of the paper-and-pencil variety because respondents need not move sequentially through the questionnaire. In interviewer-administered surveys, the questions are presented sequentially. The respondent cannot look forward and back to preview later questions before answering the previous ones. In a self-administered format, respondents are free to read later questions before answering earlier ones. Context effects that have been noted to occur with specific question

orders in telephone mode therefore may not be observed in the mail mode.

Schwarz, Strack, Hippler, and Bishop (1991) found that in the telephone mode respondents were more likely to agree that Japanese imports to Germany should be limited than to agree that German imports to Japan should be limited when each of these questions was presented first. Furthermore, as would be expected under a norm of reciprocity or evenhandedness, support for limiting German imports to Japan increased when this question was asked after the question on limiting Japanese exports to Germany. In the self-administered mode, however, they found that the question order effect was no longer present.

Schwarz and Hippler (1995) reported on a related study they conducted in Germany. Respondents were randomly assigned to a mail or telephone condition and were asked how much money they would be willing to donate to help suffering people in Russia (a prominent issue at the time of the survey). Two questions on taxes were also asked. The tax questions came either before or after the question about helping Russia. In the telephone condition, respondents were willing to donate less money to Russia if asked after the tax question. In comparison, in the mail survey, donation amounts were low (comparably low to the lower donation in the telephone condition) in both question order conditions. Schwarz and Hippler argued that the subsequent questions may have influenced answers to a preceding question because of the ability of respondents to skip ahead.

The work by Ayidiya and McClendon (1990) examined question order effects for the reporter questions, but in the mail mode. Ayidiya and McClendon expanded on prior work by Bishop, Hippler, Schwarz, and Strack (1988), who found that question order effects apparent in their telephone surveys were eliminated in their self-administered surveys. A number of mode differences between mail and interview surveys may lead to differences in order effects. In the mail mode, effects such as acquiescence and social desirability biases may be less apparent because of the absence of an interviewer. Furthermore, respondents have the ability to view the questions in any order. The reduction of serial-order constraints may lead to reduced effects of question order.

To test for question order effects in the mail mode, Ayidiya and McClendon (1990) conducted a split-ballot mail survey with the Communist–U.S. reporter questions and the defect-in-child and woman's right abortion questions. Unlike the Bishop et al. (1988) findings, the results showed significant order effects for the Communist reporter item and near significant effects for the U.S. reporter item; these effects were in the same direction of consistency as in prior studies. That is, support for Communist reporters in the United States was higher when asked after the question on U.S. reporters in Russia; support for U.S. reporters in Russia was lower when asked after the question about Communist reporters in the United States. In accord with Bishop et al., with the abortion questions, no significant question order effects were found. The absence of an interviewer-administered mode in this study prevents conclusions about effects of mode. The authors speculated, however, that it is not an external source, the presence of an interviewer, which prompts respondents to apply a norm of reciprocity or evenhandedness with the reporter questions. Rather, respondents seem to have an internalized sense of evenhandedness. Further work would be necessary, however, to understand why the reporter and abortion questions yielded different patterns of results.

Although consistency effects continued to be observed with the Communist–U.S. reporter items in the mail mode, with the abortion items, the contrast effect that is often found with these items was not observed. The mail mode of the survey appears to have attenuated the question order effect only for the abortion items.

A mail survey of quality of life in rural areas presents an additional example of a self-administered survey that did not show attenuation of question order effects. Willits and Ke (1995) asked respondents 19 specific questions regarding the quality of rural life and one general question. They varied the order of the general question, presenting it either before or after the series of specific questions. Presenting the general question last yielded more positive assessments of the quality of rural life. Even

when respondents were instructed to read all the specific questions and the general question before responding, the same question order effect remained. The authors speculated that even though respondents had the opportunity to review all the questions, and were explicitly asked to do so, they may not have done so. Furthermore, they suggest that interpretation of the questions may be affected by the placement order of the general question, even in a self-administered mode that allows review of prior and subsequent questions.

INDIVIDUAL DIFFERENCES AND THEIR IMPACT ON QUESTION ORDER EFFECTS

Question order effects may vary among subgroups. The studies described in this section examine how individual differences in age, education, strength of respondent attitudes, or knowledge about the survey topic can moderate question order effects.

Age and Working Memory

The strength of question order effects may vary as a function of age because of declines in working memory capacity and speed of cognitive processing. As described, support for the woman's right question is higher when it is presented before, as compared with after, the defect-in-child question. However, analysis of the data by respondent age showed a difference of 19.5% for younger respondents, but no question order effect for respondents age 65 and above (Schwarz, 2003). If older respondents are less able to remember the preceding question, that question will have less effect on responses to the subsequent question (Knauper, Schwarz, Park, & Fritsch, 2007). To test the memory hypothesis Knauper et al. (2007) studied older adults with low and high working memory capacities and younger adults. An explanation based on working memory capacity would predict that older adults with high working memory should perform similarly to younger adults. As predicted, both younger respondents and older respondents with high working memory capacity showed a significant question order effect in the expected direction. The older adults with low working memory capacity showed no significant effects of question order.

Education and Cognitive Sophistication

In research on survey context or response effects, education level is often used as a proxy for cognitive sophistication and has been shown to interact with question order (e.g., Schuman & Ludwig, 1983). The evidence for education effects is mixed, however. In examining their findings with the Communist–U.S. reporter questions, Schuman and Presser (1981) noted that the question order effect is seen primarily in respondents with lower levels of education. They speculated that the college-educated respondents were already inclined to agree that Communist reporters should be allowed in the United States, so asking this question second does not invoke a norm of reciprocity and question order does little to affect response. Presumably, more educated respondents would have favored allowing Communist reporters in the United States regardless of whether the question was asked first or second; thus, question order would do little to change their responses. In a follow-up study that included an item on how the respondent perceived Communism, Schuman and Presser found that the question order effect was greatest among those with the greatest antipathy toward Communism. Schuman and Presser also looked for effects of education level on order effects with the abortion questions and found no interactions between education and question order (1981, p. 39).

In other research, Schuman and Ludwig (1983) found effects of education level on question order, but they varied by question. In questions on trade restrictions between Japan and the United States, greater effects of question order were seen for respondents with lower levels of education. Respondents with lower levels of education were more likely than those with higher education levels to favor restrictions by the United States on Japan when that question came first and were more likely to favor trade restrictions by Japan when that question came second. An order effect by education level interaction was not seen for questions on political contributions by corporations and by labor unions. Schuman and Ludwig noted that such differing results suggest that explanations other than cognitive sophistication may also underlie the question order effect. For example, nationalistic tendencies may encourage order effects in some contexts (e.g.,

the United States vs. Japan) but not in others (e.g., corporations vs. labor unions).

Narayan and Krosnick (1996) conducted a meta-analysis of the question order experiments described in Schuman and Presser (1981). Among the items examined were those that were explained in terms of a norm of reciprocity, such as the U.S. and Communist reporter questions. Narayan and Krosnick found that respondents with lower or medium levels of education showed greater question order effects. They proposed a different explanation, however. Respondents who *satisfice* (i.e., apply minimal effort to the task at hand; see Krosnick, 1991) would not be likely to consider reciprocity when answering the first question compared with respondents who optimize their response behavior. For satisficing respondents, the norm of reciprocity may not come to mind until presented with the second question, yielding a question order effect. In comparison, respondents who optimize are more likely to consider the norm of reciprocity when presented with the first question and to apply this norm to both questions regardless of order. Narayan and Krosnick showed that satisficing is more prevalent among respondents with lower education because they are less able to meet the cognitive demands of a long or complicated survey.

Respondents with lower education may be more greatly influenced by the context that precedes a question because that context highlights information that is relevant to answering the later question. In a split-ballot telephone survey, Sigelman (1981) presented a question on presidential approval either before or after a series of questions on social and energy problems, energy costs, pollution, drugs, and political corruption. Although he found no differences in presidential approval ratings by question order, a significant order effect was found for *opinionation*, defined as the willingness to give an opinion about the president. Fewer respondents who received the presidential approval question early in the questionnaire ventured to give an evaluative response when compared with those who received the question after the series of questions on social topics. This tendency was pronounced for less educated respondents.

In surveys that assessed evaluations of city government services, respondents who received a general evaluative question were more negative or neutral than those who were asked to evaluate whether specific services should be increased, be decreased, or stay the same (Benton & Daly, 1991, 1993). The effect was greater for respondents who had received less education, were currently employed (compared with those who were retired), and had made less contact with the city government. Benton and Daly (1991) did not attempt to disentangle the latter two effects, which may encompass some overlap of respondents.

Attitude Crystallization and Ambivalence

Schuman and Presser described a crystallized attitude as one that existed before measurement and that is stable across time (1981, p. 251). It would seem that question order effects may be less pronounced in respondents with more crystallized attitudes. Although the results of some studies suggest that question order effects are greatest in those with the weakest attitudes (e.g., Schuman et al., 1981; Wilson et al., 2008), a large-scale study found overall no evidence for a relationship between attitude strength and question order effects (Krosnick & Schuman, 1988).

Schuman et al. (1981, p. 220) speculated whether the order effect may be influenced by ambivalence about the topic. In their August 1979 SRC survey, they included the general and specific abortion items, separated by more than 50 items on other topics and added a question about the respondent's ambivalence on abortion. The order effect was larger among those expressing ambivalence about abortion. In support of this result, Wilson et al. (2008) noted that question order does not affect the reported attitudes toward AA among some groups whose views on AA are likely to be less ambivalent. Both Blacks and liberals were found not to be subject to question order effects in the amount of support they showed for AA programs for both racial minorities and women.

Krosnick and Schuman (1988) reported on experiments on question order effects with the defect-in-child and woman's right abortion questions and an experiment with questions on U.S. and Japanese import restrictions and assessed respondents' levels of attitude certainty about these topics.

In one of the four abortion question experiments, they found that respondents with greater uncertainty about abortion were more likely to show the effect. In the other three experiments, however, respondents who were high and low in certainty about abortion showed similar question order effects. Furthermore, the import restrictions questions also showed no relationship between attitude certainty and magnitude of context effects. Krosnick and Schuman concluded that attitude certainty does not distinguish respondents who demonstrate question order effects and respondents who do not.

Knowledge About Survey Topic

Some evidence suggests that the level of the respondent's knowledge about a topic influences their susceptibility to question order effects. One study showed that question order effects about political topics are dependent on political knowledge. The *third-person effect* is a phenomenon that has received much attention in communications research. This concept, first described by Davison (1983), is the common perception that media messages have a greater impact on others than on oneself. The effect, usually demonstrated by asking two questions, one about media effects on self and one about media effects on others, has been shown to be robust to question order (e.g. Gunther, 1995; Gunther & Hwa, 1996; Salwen & Driscoll, 1997). Price and Tewksbury (1996) examined question order under different levels of political knowledge. Respondents either received a single question about media effects on one's self, a single question about media effects on others, or both questions in either order. The authors found a question order effect, but only when the data were examined within the context of the respondent's political knowledge. Higher political knowledge resulted in lower estimates of the media's effect on oneself, but only when the self question followed the other question. There was no effect of knowledge on ratings of self-impact when the self question preceded the other question. Unfortunately, the researchers made no attempt to explain the joint effect of political knowledge and question order on third-person effects. They merely noted that although third-person effects are strong and usually robust to question order, there may be some respondents for whom question order does influence the judgments involved.

A study comparing consistency and framing explanations for context effects found that expressed interest in science could be moderated by the difficulty of science knowledge questions that preceded the interest question. Gaskell, Wright, and O'Muircheartaigh (1995) tested whether it is the respondents' perception of their knowledge about science or their perception of what interest in science entails that influences context effects. They reasoned that a consistency effect would be demonstrated by an interaction between knowledge and question order such that respondents who answered questions correctly before they received the interest question (and regardless of whether they received the easy or difficult knowledge questions) would show a greater interest than those who answered the questions correctly after being asked about interest. A framing effect would be demonstrated by a main effect of test difficulty in the condition when the knowledge questions preceded the interest question, independent of test performance. According to this argument, a difficult test would frame "interest in science" as something more than just enjoying a casual exposure to stories about science from the media. Results supported the framing hypothesis. That is, it is the respondents' interpretation of what it means to be interested in science rather than their perception of how knowledgeable they are about science that dictates question order effects.

IMPLICATIONS OF THE STUDY OF QUESTION ORDER EFFECTS FOR QUESTIONNAIRE DESIGN

Our review of the literature gives a strong indication that question order effects do occur. Although not every study had a positive result, most of the research indicated that respondents do not approach each new question independently, clearing their minds of what came before. The questionnaire designer is well advised to keep this in mind. But when should a researcher worry about question order effects? And what can be done to minimize them? We propose several answers to these two questions, noting that none of the answers are

perfect, and each must be evaluated from the point of view of the researcher's resources and information needs. It is our position that there is no one perfect way to construct a questionnaire or even to write a question, but some ways are, in most cases, better than others. We focus on those ways that are informed by methodological research.

We organize this discussion by the types of question order effects described by Schuman and Presser (1981). The first type, the unconditional context effect, occurs when answers to a subsequent question are affected not by the answer given to a prior question but by the question's topical material. Our general advice is to be on the lookout for question combinations in which the prior question is likely to affect the way in which the respondent thinks about the subsequent one—limiting or directing the way the respondent interprets the subsequent topic.

Research on context effects, a topic closely related to question order effects, has found that prior topic framing can have a substantial influence on responses to subsequent questions (Tourangeau & Rasinski, 1988; Tourangeau, Rasinski, Bradburn, & D'Andrade, 1989a, 1989b). For example, in a public opinion survey, a question asking about support for the war in Afghanistan is more likely to be thought of from an expense point of view when a prior question is about the national deficit than when a prior question is about the threat of terrorist attacks on U.S. soil. Many public policy issues, such as legalized abortion, stem cell research, AA programs, aid to foreign countries, aid to the poor, and tax increases or decreases (to name a few) are complex and multidimensional by nature and can be viewed from many positions and may fall prey to these framing effects imposed by prior questions.

Therefore, when designing a questionnaire, if the juxtaposition of two items is likely to result in a situation in which the topic of the first question affects the interpretation of the second question, it is advisable to separate the two questions in some way. Studies discussed in the literature review indicated that just separating two potentially reactive questions with other question may not solve the problem. We propose that explicit instructions designed to separate the topics in the respondent's mind may do the job (Schwarz, Strack, & Mai, 1991). Take the preceding example. If a question asking about support for the war in Afghanistan came after a prior question is about the national deficit, one way to cleanse the respondent's mental palate would be to phrase the Afghanistan question as follows: "Ignoring for a moment the financial cost, do you favor or oppose the war in Afghanistan?"

Here is a somewhat more elaborate example of this technique. Imagine that the following two questions were of interest: (a) "Do you think that the Illinois state income tax is too high, too low, or about right?" and (b) "Should Illinois provide more programs for developmentally disabled youth?" The first question may limit the respondent's perspective by inadvertently and incorrectly linking the provision of more programs to an income tax increase when other methods might be used to fund the programs. Asking a single question that makes the link explicit (if this is the researcher's intention) might seem to be the solution but can pose another problem. For example, the question "Should Illinois fund more programs for developmentally disabled children by raising the state income tax?" seems straightforward, but is double-barreled (i.e., has two foci), making it difficult for some respondents to answer and for researchers to interpret results. A better solution would be to ask the two questions separately in the following way: (a) "Should Illinois provide more programs for developmentally disabled children?" followed by (b) "Should these additional programs be funded by an increase in the state income tax or through some other means?" Depending on the depth of information needed, these questions could be followed by other questions on what other means might be used if the respondent rejects an income tax increase (e.g., increasing some other tax, trying to raise private philanthropic funds, creating charter schools that are a hybrid of public and private funding and can be run at a profit).

But how, then, does one ask about the state income tax? A suggestion is to use a technique borrowed from researchers who conduct contingent evaluation studies (Cameron & Carson, 1989) and pose the question in the following way: "Now, taking into account the services you and others receive from the state and the impact the state income tax

has on your personal or family budget, do you think that the state income tax is too high, too low or about right?" Admittedly, this is not a perfect solution. It may be better than simply juxtaposing the two questions, as in the first example, because it is explicit in its instruction to the respondent about what to consider when answering the question.

In this review, we have seen many examples of the second and third types of question order effects, conditional effects and correlational effects. Both of these effects occur when answers to the subsequent question depend on the response given to the prior question. As we have pointed out, under most circumstances, the two effects are really an indication of the same kind of reactivity of respondents to questions. Different studies have given these effects different names, such as part–whole effects, part–part effects, invoking a norm of evenhandedness or of reciprocity, violating conversational norms, assimilation or carryover effects, contrast or backfire effects, and subtraction effects. The different names are attempts by researchers to give a psychological explanation for the effect. From a practical consideration, the questionnaire designer must keep on the lookout for situations in which the juxtaposition of two questions is likely to set up a judgmental dependency.

There are different ways to avoid this. One is to omit one of the questions. In the case of part–whole effects, investigators must ask themselves whether it is necessary to have a global evaluation along with evaluation of parts. For example, if we were to design a questionnaire that evaluated satisfaction with an after-school tutoring program, we could ask a general evaluative question only ("How satisfied are you with the tutoring program?"), a general evaluation question and some specific questions evaluating specific aspects of the program ("How satisfied are you about the (a) orderliness of the tutoring environment, (b) resources available, (c) methods used, (d) attention to your child's learning style?"), or only the specific questions. The consensus from the literature is that if a general satisfaction question is included, it should be asked before the specific questions. If it were asked after the specific questions, the general evaluation likely would be heavily weighted by the content mentioned in the specific questions and would no longer reflect an overall evaluation. More useful information is obtained by asking carefully chosen specific questions and leaving out the general question entirely; however, others may be interested in only a general evaluation or may be interested in how the evaluation of specific components affects a general evaluation. In the latter case, we argue, it is essential to ask the general question first.

To push our recommendation further, we suggest that reliance on the subjectivity of satisfaction ratings can be reduced by asking about specific behaviors ("Was the room orderly, were the children unruly, was enough attention given to your child's style of learning, were teachers responsive to your concerns?"). The questionnaire developer should be aware, however, that if questions about specific behavior are used and a general evaluation question is desired as well, then the general question should come before the questions about the specific behaviors for the same reason.

Randomization of items is another way to minimize the effect of question order. If a researcher was interested in, for example, evaluating the acceptability of a list of political figures as the next president of the United States or mayor of their city or township, to avoid reactivity, the researcher could make sure that each respondent received the list of names in a random order. If this were impossible, then the researcher should consider putting the list in alphabetical order and pointing out to the respondent that it is simply the place in the alphabet of the first letter of the candidate's last name that determined the position on the list and reminding them to consider each candidate independent of the others. One might use the same strategies (randomization or alphabetization) with evaluation of products or services. If it is not possible to use a unique randomization for each person, product, or service in a list, then constructing different versions of the questionnaire such that each name, product, or service appears first for an equal number of respondents might be sufficient. It would be important that the different versions were administered to random subsamples of respondents for this technique to be effective.

We turn next to implications of the interaction of individual differences with question order for questionnaire design. As our review indicates, many studies have observed that question order effects may be more prevalent for social groups with different concerns, for older or more poorly educated respondents, and for those with less expertise in a content area compared with those who have more expertise. It is difficult to give specific advice about questionnaire construction for each of these particular types of respondents and for individual and social difference groups that have yet to be tested for new and emerging topics to be addressed in surveys. We have two suggestions for dealing with the issue of individual differences. The first is to consider whether topics might interact with group sensitivities or limitations. If that group is the sole focus of the survey—for example, a survey of Tea Party members (who oppose big government and high taxes)—then efforts to disconnect questions about state deficits and programs to aid disabled children certainly must be made. If the survey is of a general population, and Tea Party members are judged to be only a small proportion of the population, then the effort to disconnect the two questions might not be as necessary to avoid biased estimates on the basis of question order. If a long survey is planned for elderly respondents or for those with lower levels of education and two questions are thought to affect one another, ensure that the questions appear early in the survey rather than later, when limited memory effects are likely to be exaggerated because of fatigue (Holbrook, Green, & Krosnick, 2003). Perhaps the best advice is to keep in mind that whatever one does to limit the effect of question order effects, in general, will limit them for specific subgroups.

In this chapter we have reviewed the literature on question order effects in surveys and given specific advice to researchers constructing questionnaires. Whether the questionnaire is for a population-based probability survey, an evaluation of products and services using a convenience sample of those who happened to be available at a particular day or in a particular location, or for research performed at a university using a student or Internet sample, we hope that our survey of the literature and our recommendations are useful to help researchers collect the best data possible for their research purpose.

References

Abramson, P. R., & Ostrom, C. W. (1991). Response to question form and context effects in the measurement of partisanship: Experimental tests of the artifact hypothesis. *The American Political Science Review, 88,* 945–958.

Ayidiya, S. A., & McClendon, M. J. (1990). Response effects in mail surveys. *Public Opinion Quarterly, 54,* 229–247. doi:10.1086/269200

Benton, J. E., & Daly, J. L. (1991). A question order effect in a local government survey. *Public Opinion Quarterly, 55,* 640–642. doi:10.1086/269285

Benton, J. E., & Daly, J. L. (1993, Winter). Measuring citizen evaluations: The question of question order effects. *Public Administration Quarterly, 16,* 493–508.

Bickart, B. A. (1993). Carryover and backfire effects in marketing research. *Journal of Marketing Research, 30(1),* 52–62. doi:10.2307/3172513

Bishop, G., Hippler, H-J., Schwarz, N., & Strack, F. (1988). A comparison of response effects in self-administered and telephone surveys. In R. M. Groves, P. Biemer, L. Lyberg, J. T. Massey, W. L. Nicholls, & J. Waksberg (Eds.), *Telephone survey methodology* (pp. 321–340). New York, NY: Wiley.

Bishop, G. F., Oldendick, R. W., & Tuchfarber, A. J. (1985). The importance of replicating a failure to replicate: Order effects on abortion items. *Public Opinion Quarterly, 49,* 105–114. doi:10.1086/268904

Bishop, G. F., Tuchfarber, A. J., & Smith, A. E. (1994). Question form and context effects in the measurement of partisanship: Experimental tests of the artifact hypothesis. *The American Political Science Review, 88,* 945–958. doi:10.2307/2082718

Bolman, C., Lechner, L., & van Dijke, M. (2007). Question order in the assessment of misperception of physical activity. *The International Journal of Behavioral Nutrition and Physical Activity, 4,* 42. doi:10.1186/1479-5868-4-42

Bowling, A., & Windsor, J. (2008). The effects of question order and response-choice on self-rated health status in the English Longitudinal Study of Ageing (ELSA). *Journal of Epidemiology and Community Health, 62,* 81–85. doi:10.1136/jech.2006.058214

Bradburn, N. M., & Mason, W. M. (1964). The effect of question order on responses. *JMR, Journal of Marketing Research, 1(4),* 57–61. doi:10.2307/3150380

Cameron, R. M., & Carson, R. T. (1989). *Using surveys to value public goods: The contingent valuation method.* Washington, DC: Resources for the Future.

Darker, C. D., French, D. P., Longdon, S., Morris, K., & Eves, F. F. (2007). Are beliefs elicited biased by question order? A theory of planned behaviour belief elicitation study about walking in the UK general population. *British Journal of Health Psychology, 12(Pt. 1),* 93–110. doi:10.1348/135910706X100458

Davison, W. P. (1983). The third person effect in communication. *Public Opinion Quarterly, 47,* 1–15. doi:10.1086/268763

DeMoranville, C. W., & Bienstock, C. C. (2003). Question order effects in measuring service quality. *International Journal of Research in Marketing, 20,* 217–231. doi:10.1016/S0167-8116(03)00034-X

DeMoranville, C. W., Bienstock, C. C., & Judson, K. (2008). Using question order for predictive service quality measures. *Journal of Services Marketing, 22,* 255–262. doi:10.1108/08876040810871200

Gaskell, G. D., Wright, D. B., & O'Muircheartaigh, C. (1995). Context effects in the measurement of attitudes: A comparison of the consistency and framing explanations. *British Journal of Social Psychology, 34,* 383–393.

Gold, R. S., & Barclay, A. (2006). Order of question presentation and correlation between judgments of comparative and own risk. *Psychological Reports, 99,* 794–798. doi:10.2466/PR0.99.3.794-798

Gunther, A. C. (1995). Overrating the X rating: The third person perception and support for censorship of pornography. *The Journal of Communication, 45,* 27–38. doi:10.1111/j.1460-2466.1995.tb00712.x

Gunther, A. C., & Hwa, A. P. (1996). Public perceptions of television influence and opinions about censorship in Singapore. *International Journal of Public Opinion Research, 8,* 248–265.

Holbrook, A. L., Green, M. C., & Krosnick, J. A. (2003). Telephone versus face-to-face interviewing of national probability samples with long questionnaires: Comparisons of respondent satisficing and social desirability response bias. *Public Opinion Quarterly, 67,* 79–125. doi:10.1086/346010

Hyman, H. H., & Sheatsley, P. B. (1950). The current status of American public opinion. In J. C. Payne (Ed.), *The teaching of contemporary affairs: Twenty-first yearbook of the National Council of Social Studies* (pp. 11–34). Washington, DC: National Council of Social Studies.

Kartman, B., Stålhammar, N-O., & Johannesson, M. (1996). Valuation of health changes with the contingent valuation method: A test of scope and question order effects. *Health Economics, 5,* 531–541. doi:10.1002/(SICI)1099-1050(199611)5:6<531::AID-HEC235>3.0.CO;2-J

Knauper, B., Schwarz, N., Park, D., & Fritsch, A. (2007). The perils of interpreting age differences in attitude reports: Question order effects decrease with age. *Journal of Official Statistics, 23,* 515–528.

Krosnick, J. A. (1991). Response strategies for coping with the cognitive demands of attitude measures in surveys. *Applied Cognitive Psychology, 5*, 213–236. doi:10.1002/acp.2350050305

Krosnick, J. A., & Schuman, H. (1988). Attitude intensity, importance, and certainty and susceptibility to response effects. *Journal of Personality and Social Psychology, 54*, 940–952. doi:10.1037/0022-3514-.54.6.940

Lee, S., & Grant, D. (2009). The effect of question order on self-rated general health status in a multilingual survey context. *American Journal of Epidemiology, 169*, 1525–1530. doi:10.1093/aje/kwp070

McAllister, I., & Wattenberg, M. P. (1995). Measuring levels of party identification: Does question order matter? *Public Opinion Quarterly, 59*, 259–268. doi:10.1086/269472

McClendon, M. J., & O'Brien, D. J. (1988a). Explaining question order effects on the relationship between safety and neighborhood satisfaction. *Social Science Quarterly, 69*, 764–771.

McClendon, M. J., & O'Brien, D. J. (1988b). Question-order effects on the determinants of subjective well-being. *Public Opinion Quarterly, 52*, 351–364. doi:10.1086/269112

Moore, D. W. (2002). Measuring new types of question-order effects: Additive and subtractive. *Public Opinion Quarterly, 66*, 80–91. doi:10.1086/338631

Narayan, S., & Krosnick, J. A. (1996). Education moderates some response effects in attitude measurement. *Public Opinion Quarterly, 60*, 58–88. doi:10.1086/297739

Parasuraman, A., Zeithami, V., & Berry, L. L. (1988). SERVQUAL: A multiple item scale for measuring consumer perceptions of service quality. *Journal of Retailing, 64*, 12–40.

Petty, R. E., & Cacioppo, J. T. (1981). *Attitudes and persuasion: Classic and contemporary approaches.* Dubuque, IA: William C. Brown.

Price, V., & Tewksbury, D. (1996). Measuring the third person effect of news: The impact of question order, contrast and knowledge. *International Journal of Public Opinion Research, 8*, 120–141.

Rasinski, K. A., Visser, P. S., Zagatsky, M., & Rickett, E. (2005). Using non-conscious goal priming to improve the quality of self-report data. *Journal of Experimental Social Psychology, 41*, 321–327. doi:10.1016/j.jesp.2004.07.001

Rimal, R. N., & Real, K. (2005). Assessing the perceived importance of skin cancer: How question-order effects are influenced by issue involvement. *Health Education and Behavior, 32*, 398–412. doi:10.1177/1090198104272341

Salwen, M. B., & Driscoll, P. D. (1997). Consequences of the third person perception in support of press restrictions in the O. J. Simpson trial. *The Journal of Communication, 47*, 60–78. doi:10.1111/j.1460-2466.1997.tb02706.x

Schuman, H., Kalton, G., & Ludwig, J. (1983). Context and contiguity in survey questionnaires. *Public Opinion Quarterly, 47*, 112–115. doi:10.1086/268771

Schuman, H., & Ludwig, J. (1983). The norm of even-handedness in surveys as in life. *American Sociological Review, 48*, 112–120. doi:10.2307/2095149

Schuman, H., & Presser, S. (1981). *Questions and answers in attitude surveys.* New York, NY: Wiley.

Schuman, H., Presser, S., & Ludwig, J. (1981). Context effects on survey responses to questions about abortion. *Public Opinion Quarterly, 45*, 216–223. doi:10.1086/268652

Schwarz, N. (2003). Self-reports in consumer research: The challenge of comparing cohorts and cultures. *Journal of Consumer Research, 29*, 588–594. doi:10.1086/346253

Schwarz, N., & Hippler, H.-J. (1995). Subsequent questions may influence answers to preceding questions in mail surveys. *Public Opinion Quarterly, 59*, 93–97. doi:10.1086/269460

Schwarz, N., Strack, F., Hippler, H.-J., & Bishop, G. (1991). The impact of administration mode on response effects in survey measurement. *Applied Cognitive Psychology, 5*, 193–212. doi:10.1002/acp.2350050304

Schwarz, N., Strack, F., & Mai, H.-P. (1991). Assimilation and contrast effects in part-whole question sequences: A conversational logic analysis. *Public Opinion Quarterly, 55*, 3–23.

Sigelman, L. (1981). Question-order effects on presidential popularity. *Public Opinion Quarterly, 45*, 199–207. doi:10.1086/268650

Smith, T. W. (1978). In search of house effects: A comparison of responses to various questions by different survey organizations. *Public Opinion Quarterly, 42*, 443–463. doi:10.1086/268473

Smith, T. W. (1979). Happiness: Time trends, seasonal variations, intersurvey differences, and other mysteries. *Social Psychology Quarterly, 42*, 18–30. doi:10.2307/3033870

Smith, T. W. (1982). *Conditional order effects* (General Social Survey Tech. Rep. No. 33). Chicago, IL: NORC.

Smith, T. W. (1983). *Children and abortions: An experiment in question order* (General Social Survey Tech. Rep. No. 42). Chicago, IL: NORC.

Smith, T. W. (1991). Thoughts on the nature of context effects. In N. Schwarz & S. Sudman (Eds.), *Context effects in social and psychological research* (pp. 163–184). New York, NY: Springer-Verlag.

Strack, F., Martin, L. L., & Schwarz, N. (1988). Priming and communication: The social determinants of information use in judgments of life-satisfaction. *European Journal of Social Psychology, 18,* 429–442. doi:10.1002/ejsp.2420180505

Sudman, S., & Bradburn, N. M. (1982). *Asking questions: A practical guide to questionnaire construction.* San Francisco, CA: Jossey-Bass.

Tourangeau, R. (1984). Cognitive science and survey methods. In T. Jabine, M. Straf, J. Tanur, & R. Tourangeau (Eds.), *Cognitive aspects of survey design: Building a bridge between disciplines* (pp. 73–100). Washington, DC: National Academies Press.

Tourangeau, R., & Rasinski, K. A. (1988). Cognitive processes underlying context effects in attitude measurement. *Psychological Bulletin, 103,* 299–314. doi:10.1037/0033-2909.103.3.299

Tourangeau, R., Rasinski, K. A., & Bradburn, N. (1991). Measuring happiness in surveys: A test of the subtraction hypothesis. *Public Opinion Quarterly, 55,* 255–266. doi:10.1086/269256

Tourangeau, R., Rasinski, K. A., Bradburn, N., & D'Andrade, R. (1989a). Belief accessibility and context effects in attitude measurement. *Journal of Experimental Social Psychology, 25,* 401–421. doi:10.1016/0022-1031(89)90030-9

Tourangeau, R., Rasinski, K. A., Bradburn, N., & D'Andrade, R. (1989b). Carryover effects in attitude surveys. *Public Opinion Quarterly, 53,* 495–524. doi:10.1086/269169

Tourangeau, R., Rips, L. J., & Rasinski, K. (2000). *The psychology of survey response.* Cambridge, England: Cambridge University Press.

Turner, C. F. (1984). Why do surveys disagree? Some preliminary hypotheses and some disagreeable examples. In C. F. Turner & E. Martin (Eds.), *Surveying subjective phenomena* (Vol. 1, pp. 159–214). New York, NY: Russell Sage Foundation.

Willits, F. K., & Ke, B. (1995). Part-whole question order effects: Views of rurality. *Public Opinion Quarterly, 59,* 392–403. doi:10.1086/269483

Wilson, D. C., Moore, D. W., McKay, P. F., & Avery, D. R. (2008). Affirmative action programs for women and minorities: Expressed support affected by question order. *Public Opinion Quarterly, 72,* 514–522. doi:10.1093/poq/nfn031

CHAPTER 14

INTERVIEWS AND INTERVIEWING TECHNIQUES

Anna Madill

Interviews are the most popular method of generating data in the social sciences (Atkinson & Silverman, 1997). Interview data lend themselves to qualitative analysis but may be quantified, in some respects, if research questions can be addressed in terms of frequency of content or if the interview is conducted in a highly structured form that can be coded and scored much like a questionnaire.

A longstanding and useful definition of an interview is that it is a conversation with a purpose (Bingham & Moore, 1924). As this definition implies, interviewers and interviewees will draw on their everyday interactional competencies to do interviewing (Hester & Francis, 1994; Houtkoop-Steemstra, 1997). Even so, the limited empirical analyses available on interviews indicate that they involve a distinct *kind* of interaction. Interviews tend to be scheduled and conducted at a prearranged location, and the interviewee is usually offered some form of orientation to the task that prepares him or her for the potential strangeness of the interaction (Lee & Roth, 2004) and, sometimes, a financial incentive is offered. This strangeness allies interviews more with forms of institution talk than with ordinary conversation, in particular the interview's question–answer format (Potter & Hepburn, 2005), tendency to favor interviewer neutrality (Antaki, Houtkoop-Steemstra, & Rapley, 2000), and asymmetrical outcome agenda (Silverman,

1973). It may be that the most popular form—the semistructured interview—has greater similarity to ordinary conversation than most (Wooffitt & Widdicombe, 2006).

TYPES OF INTERVIEW

There is a large variety of interviewing types. Differences are evident in terms of interviewing style; however, procedural differences are rooted more fundamentally in methodological approach. This encompasses different epistemologies (ways in which knowledge is conceptualized), ontologies (which includes different understandings of subjectivity), and axiologies (values and ethos). Some interviewing methods offer a well-worked-out methodological framework in relation to such issues (e.g., Hollway & Jefferson, 2000), whereas for most, these remain implicit or vary according to the method of analysis the interviews serve. What is important, however, is that some consideration be given to the coherence between research questions, interview type, and method(s) of analysis.

Interviews seem designed to tap lived experience and, particularly in the semistructured format, are the most popular method of qualitative data collection and generation in psychology (Madill, 2007). A schedule is prepared that contains open-ended questions and prompts that, prima facie, appear relevant

I thank the participants on whose interviews I have drawn in this chapter. I extend my thanks also to the interviewers who contributed to these data sets and to the researchers who allowed me to comment on the discussions we have had about their interviewing experiences. I am extremely grateful to Siobhan Hugh-Jones, University of Leeds, United Kingdom, for her insightful comments on an early draft of this chapter. Paragraphs describing interviewing types are adapted from "Qualitative Research and Its Place in Psychological Science," by A. Madill and B. Gough, 2008, *Psychological Methods, 13*, 254–271. Copyright 2008 by the American Psychological Association.

DOI: 10.1037/13619-015
APA Handbook of Research Methods in Psychology: Vol. 1. Foundations, Planning, Measures, and Psychometrics, H. Cooper (Editor-in-Chief)

to the research topic, although the interview is conducted with flexibility in the ordering of questions and the follow-up of unanticipated avenues that the participant raises (Smith, 1995). There are, however, national differences in preferred technique with, for example, face-to-face interviewing being the norm in the United Kingdom and telephone interviewing predominating in Scandinavia (Bardsley, Wiles, & Powell, 2006).

The unstructured interview uses a free-flowing conversational style in contrast to the structured interview, in which specific, preprepared questions are asked in a determined order. Both appear rare in the qualitative literature because qualitative researchers typically prefer to strike a balance between retaining interviewer control and approximating normal conversation (see Houtkoop-Steemstra, 2000, for research on the conduct of the structured, standardized, or survey interview).

Although the semistructured and narrative formats both use nonleading, open questions, the narrative style prioritizes elicitation of personal stories with minimal researcher prompting (see Hollway & Jefferson, 2000, for a critique of the semistructured interview from a narrative perspective). Biographical interviews, by definition, focus on life history and may involve a narrative style. Moreover, inspired by the narrative style, the free-association narrative interview links the tradition of biographical interviewing with psychoanalytical theory. A central premise here is that participants will, unconsciously, provide important information about themselves that is then open to analytic interpretation by tracking the participant's chain of associations.

Interpersonal process recall involves asking participants to make explicit their internal experiences during review of prior (usually video recorded) therapy sessions in which he or she took part, although this technique can be extended to other forms of recorded interactions. In the ethnographic interview, it is the participant's tacit and explicit knowledge as a member that is tapped.

In theory, most of these interview styles may be used with more than one participant at a time, although the norm seems to be one to one. Defined purely in terms of there being more than one interviewee present, group interviewing can therefore be viewed as a distinct form of data collection (Morgan, 1997). Another reason for distinguishing the group interview is to contrast it to the focus group because these terms often are used interchangeably. The focus group might be considered a particular kind of group interview designed to elicit opinion about a product or topic, using particular terminology (e.g., moderator as opposed to interviewer), and originally was developed within in the field of market research (see Puchta & Potter, 2004, for research on the conduct of focus groups; see also the section Number of Interviewees per Interview and Their Characteristics).

One of the more radical approaches to interviewing is the reflexive mode proposed by Denzin (2001), who deconstructs established conventions and advocates using a variety of genres, for example, a game or a drama, to produce evocative data. This has resonances with the dramatological interview, in which the interviewer is encouraged to elicit effective communication through conceptualizing his or her own role as a conscious and reflective social performance: actor, director, choreographer.

INTERVIEWING DEVELOPMENT AND TECHNIQUES

The semistructured interview is the most popular interview format in psychological research and many of the techniques used in semistructured interviewing are transferable to other interview formats. I therefore focus on the semistructured interview in discussing interviewing techniques and illustrate each identified technique with examples from my own corpus of transcribed semistructure interviews.[1] But first, I consider how one might go about developing a schedule for a semistructured interview.

[1]Each extract is identified first with the corpus from which it is drawn and second with the gender of the participant. The author (Anna Madill) is the interviewer unless otherwise stated. The three data corpora are as follows: quarry (interviews with residents living near an active stone quarry in rural England, research funded by the Minerals Industries Research Organisation), medic (interviews with medical students undertaking a year of study intercalating in psychology in a university in the North of England, research funded by the Higher Education Funding Council of England), and boundaries (interviews with counselors and psychotherapists in the United Kingdom on managing sexual boundaries in their professional practice, research funded by the British Association for Counselling and Psychotherapy).

Developing an Interview Schedule

Virtually all research interviewing will require preparation of an interview schedule that acts as a prompt for the interviewer. At the most basic, this may take the form of a topic guide that merely lists the themes or subjects about which the interviewee will be asked to comment. If a more detailed schedule is required, this will include fully worked out and carefully worded questions and prompts in, what appears to be, an appropriate order. The level of detail and flexibility of the question order will depend on the type of interview conducted. It is also worth considering whether the interview should start with the collection of structured demographic or other factual information that is necessary for describing the study participants and for contextualizing the findings (e.g., see situating the sample in Elliott, Fischer, & Rennie, 1999).

A good approach to developing a schedule is to start by listing the kind of themes or content that should be covered in the interview to address the study research questions. This list then can be placed in an order that makes sense, although this order is likely to change if one is being appropriately responsive to the interviewee. Depending on the research, the interviews may have a fairly straightforward temporal structure, for example, if they follow the timeline in the interviewee's life. In general, potentially more sensitive themes should, if possible, be placed later in the interview because the interviewee has then had time to settle into the interview and, hopefully, rapport has been developed. If required and suitable for the interview format, these content themes can be developed into actual questions and prompts added. Finally, the interview schedule should be piloted to check both its acceptability and understandability to participants and its ability to generate relevant material for analysis. Many types of interviewing and approaches to research expect that the schedule will be revised continually throughout a study as data collection reveals the more and the less productive lines of questioning (Hollway & Jefferson, 2000).

This process does not necessarily make earlier interviews redundant if they still contribute some useful information to the study.

Discussion now turns to interviewing techniques. As I show, although guidance can be offered to help generate a productive semistructured interview, no specific technique guarantees success. What catalyses a rich and enlightening response with one interviewee at a certain juncture may misfire with another. The interviewer needs to be responsive to the ongoing interaction and, with experience, a good interviewer learns to draw on a range of strategies in flexible and contextually appropriate ways. I discuss and illustrate using extracts from my own corpus of transcribed semistructured interviews (see Footnote 1 for details) the following important considerations: nonleading questions, open questions, short questions, grounding in examples, prompts and follow-ups, silence, the not-knowing interviewer, formulations, interviewer self-disclosure, and challenging the interviewee.

Nonleading Questions

A principal technique in semistructured interviewing is the asking of nonleading questions. *Nonleading questions* are interrogatives that avoid steering the interviewee toward a specific answer. The rationale for using nonleading questions is that the aim of the research interview is to solicit the interviewee's experiences and point of view and, conversely, to avoid merely reproducing the interviewer's assumptions and preconceptions. A common mistake is to ask a question that is leading in that it contains within it an either–or candidate answer as I do, unfortunately, in the following extract (note that boldface is used to indicate the section of particular interest in each extract, I indicates *interviewer* and P indicates *participant*):

Extract 1 (quarry, female participant)[2]
I: I'm with you. So he's been there since February and are you expecting

---

[2]Transcription is light. Verbatim content is recorded with attention to general features of the talk that may impact the interpretation of that content: laughter ((laughs)); particular tone of voice ((smiley voice)); inaudible speech ((inaudible)); unclear content in double brackets with question mark, for example, ((To that end?)) yeah um; short untimed pauses (.); pauses timed in seconds (4); ? is upwards intonation indicating an interrogative; omitted names [town]; overlapping speech that does not constitute a new turn (I: Yes); speaker breaks off, for example, "Well so—but obviously"; the use of an ellipsis . . . at beginning or end of turn and (. . .) in the middle of a turn indicates truncated content.

it for a certain length of time or are you just going to see how it goes?

P: He is hoping that he can get it set up with other—he's already employed someone else. There's other staff out there and then he will just oversee it sort of fifty-fifty and then come home again.

Either–or questions are leading in that they delimit the scope of the interviewee's answer to a binary option, even if, as above, the interviewee refuses to be held to this. An appropriate nonleading question here would have been something like "How do you see this situation panning out?"

Leading questions can take the form of a statement with tone of voice indicating that they are to be taken as interrogatives. In the following extract from the same interview, I produced two of this kind of leading question in a row:

Extract 2 (quarry, female participant)
I: Yes it must be quite difficult him being away for three weeks out of four?
P: Well two years ago it was two weeks out of four in Russia so.
I: Oh right so you're reasonably used to it?
P: Yes my dad was the same. He was an engineer and ended up six months in India, Kuwait, South Africa, Canada, and so on.

My first question is leading in that I offer an answer within the question itself: that "it is quite difficult." The interviewee responds by offering further contextualizing information to which I again ask a question that itself contains an answer: that she is "reasonably used to it." This time she agrees explicitly and offers some further information. The contextualizing information is possibly useful but the status as data of the "difficulty" and of being "used to it" is unclear because it came from the interviewer. Another problem with leading items is that immediate agreement in response to the interviewer must be treated with caution. The preference in conversation is for agreement because agreement contributes to interactional ease (Pomerantz, 1984). A consensual first response may be followed by detail that suggests

more ambivalence or even disagreement. In Extract 2, an appropriate, nonleading question would have been something like "How do you feel about him being away for three weeks out of four?"

These are two passages in which my interviewing technique could have been better. Thankfully, most of the sequences offered in this chapter contain nonleading questions as shown in Questions 1, 2, 3, and 5 in Extract 8 below.

Open—and Closed—Questions

An open question is an interrogative produced in a form that requires more than a simple "yes–no–don't know" answer. For example, open questions might start in any of the following ways: "Tell me about," "To what extent," "In what ways." Open questions are arguably the central technique of semi-istructured interviewing. Their purpose is to invite interviewees to provide an extended, on-topic answer unconstrained as far as possible by the interviewer's assumptions, although this does not mean that open questions are not at times potentially leading (e.g., see Extracts 7 and 8). In Extract 3, the open question in the "tell me about" form catalyses a rich narrative as intended:

Extract 3 (medic, female participant)
I: So can you tell me um about how you came to be doing a medical degree then ((laughs))?
P: Yeah it's a bit (.) of a strange story ((laughs)).
I: Okay.
P: I actually wanted to be a vet in the beginning (I: Hm mm) and I applied to um vet (.) to do veterinary medicine at university and I didn't get a place so I kind of had to re-think about what I wanted to do . . .

Open questions deliberately offer little guidance on the specific content or structure of the response. One drawback is that interviewees may be flummoxed by this and seek clarification on how to answer. So, although the participant in Extract 3 understands that my question invites a story, she still checks out whether a (probably extended) narrative is acceptable. As you will see in Extract 4, virtually the same question appears to wrong-foot another participant more dramatically. The participant's response indicates an interactional difficulty or misalignment, which may disrupt rapport and possibly tempt the interviewer to be more leading than desired:

Extract 4 (medic, female participant)
I: Okay ((laughs)) so can you tell me how you come to be doing a degree in medicine then?
P: Um why did I choose it?
I: Yes.
P: Um it's a long time ago ((laughs)) (.) um I think my strongest subjects are in sciences so and that's what my interest was . . .

The interviewer needs to judge when a participant is ready and able to provide an extended account on a particular topic. Extracts 3 and 4 are taken from early in the respective interviews and were preceded by a series of closed, demographic-style questions of fact that provided information I needed, were simple to answer, and were designed to ease participants into the interview situation. Even so, this open question was often responded to with a request for clarification and the transcripts show that, actually, I often used a *why* question in the way suggested by the participant in Extract 4. There are, however, good reasons to avoid why questions in general, as I discuss in the section Grounding in Examples. An advantage of the "can you tell me" format is that it often provides better material for analysis as participants structure their answers in terms of what is important to them.

Another potential problem with open questions is that they can feel clumsy to say out loud and can seem overly formalized. With experience, I feel more comfortable using the open wording in my interview schedule, but this does take practice and confidence. A common effect of inexperienced interviewing is the production of a short, shallow interview. In the anxiety of the moment, interviewers transform the interview schedule into a series of easy-to-articulate closed questions, sticking to the sequence of the questions in the schedule too rigidly and not following up novel aspects of the interviewee's contribution. This is shown in Extract 5,

which is taken from a semistructured research interview conducted as part of an undergraduate project:

Extract 5 (quarry, female interviewer, male participant)
I: And has there been any physical damage to your property or any of your possessions that you're aware of?
P: No no.
I: Do you think the quarry being so close by has affected house prices in the village?
P: (.) Erm no I don't think so. I don't think so. Well I suppose it might a little bit just where it is anyway cause it's a cold and bleak place anyway. It's foggy a lot (I: Mm). It isn't everybody's cup of tea like and we used to get really hard winters ((inaudible)) so cold and you just get snowed in for weeks on end sometimes.
I: Yeah so you think you think in comparison it's it's not so bad?
P: No no.
I: So you've never considered moving?
P: No no.

Although the participant was not experienced by the interviewer as hostile, he was reticent to speak and this series of closed questions probably contributed to the production of short answers structured to a high degree by the interviewer. Even so, Extract 5 illustrates how a closed question, the second in this extract, can be responded to with more than a yes–no–don't know answer. Although closed questions tend to be considered bad practice in semistructure interviewing, I think they do actually have their place. They can feel less awkward to ask than some kinds of open questions, which is why inexperienced interviewers may fall back on them. More important, however, closed questions are often responded to in research interviews with the desirable, extended narrative without, for some participants, the anxiety of having to answer what might feel like a too open question:

Extract 6 (medic, female participant)
I: Have you ever been present when (.) a consultant or nurse or doctor has had to give any bad news to anybody?

P: Yeah yeah I have actually. Um, there was a man who had liver cancer and the doctor had to tell them um and that was also very surreal because (.) you can't you just can't believe that I'm there hearing (.) someone break this bad news to somebody and there wasn't much treatment that the patient could have so . . .

The participant in Extract 6 typically produces a yes (no–don't know) response to the closed question but goes on to provide a rich description of a relevant situation. Although I used a closed-question format, in not immediately coming in after "yeah, I have actually," I conveyed the impression of expecting additional material, which then was provided (see the section The Power of Silence).

As shown in Extract 7, a useful question to include toward the end of an interview is "Is there anything you'd like to add?" This is a closed question but illustrates a further reason why, I believe, some kinds of closed question are appropriate in research interviews. Changing this into an open question would produce something like "What more would you like to add?" Ironically, to me, this sounds too directive and, like open questions in general, presents the assumption that there is indeed something further to add. I prefer the interactional delicacy of the closed format here and find that it does not stop participants producing rich material—even if at first the response is "no":

Extract 7 (quarry, participant 1 is female, participant 2 is male)
I: Is there anything that I haven't covered that you'd like to add?
P1: I don't think so.
P2: No I'd say it's got no impact on us at all.
P1: Yes I mean I think the in-fill is a really good point and something that to think about.
P2: Yes I think the in-fill and showing the artifacts that they've found down at the pub would would bring it out the closet a little bit I think. I think they've been and I've been in this industry so I know . . .

Extract 8 is discussed more fully in the section Short Questions—and One Question at a Time, but it is worth pointing out here that it offers a good example of how the wording of open questions has to be considered carefully to avoid being leading. In Extract 8 my question, "How did you work with it?" is a less leading open question than, for example, "Do you work with it therapeutically?", which is closed. Rephrasing simply as an open question, "How do you work with it therapeutically?" is possibly leading in assuming that the participant does in fact do this.

Short Questions—and One Question at a Time

As I have become more experienced in research interviewing, I have become more comfortable asking shorter questions and, in general, saying less—and listening harder. Short questions can feel impolite, and rather direct, and a series of them can seem overly inquisitorial. Research interviewing is not an ordinary conversation, however, and, as long as there is good rapport, I think participants can find short questions helpful. In fact, in one pilot interview I conducted, my interviewee commented spontaneously to this effect. The following passage is from a research interview in which I deliberately practiced the short question technique [note that where content has been truncated midturn, this is indicated by (. . .)]:

Extract 8 (boundaries, male participant)
P: . . . I don't know what was in her mind or even half in her mind was was an unconscious sexual invitation. It might have been I don't know.
I: How did you work with it?
P: I think I just let it register (. . .) maybe if I think about it then maybe I was just afraid of my own reactions and wanted to put some kind of a ((inaudible word)).
I: How would you have dealt with it now?
P: Well in a dark street in downtown [name of town] I'm not sure I would stop (. . .) I'm not sure I would have done

what I—I don't know I'd hope I ((inaudible phrase)).

I: And in what kind of way do you think?

P: Well you can't—if it happens in a session you can actually do it within the framework of the therapy (. . .) swung their legs and I just I tend to mostly dampen that out by not reinforcing it.

I: Okay. Do you work with it therapeutically?

P: I can do yes I can do (. . .) I allow enough of my own responses and my relationship without crossing the boundary where it might become abusive.

I: How do you manage that?

P: I don't know ((laughing)) sometimes it's very—well I'll ask her if she's feeling uncomfortable (. . .) I might ask about her relationships and about her sexual needs you know. If it feels okay she will answer it.

A benefit of asking relatively brief questions is that it keeps the interview on task and avoids including possibly distracting or leading information (e.g., see the section Interviewer Self-Disclosure). Moreover, asking brief questions disciplines the interviewer to formulate one clearly worded question at a time. Asking long-winded questions that include several parts can overload the interviewee and often it is only the final part of the question that is answered. Some of this kind of muddle is illustrated in Extract 9:

Extract 9 (boundaries, male participant)
I: There's actually now two things I want to follow up with you ((laughs)) (P: Go on yeah). **Your own use of supervision** (P: Yeah sure) **um and I want to follow up about intimacy of that** (P: Yeah sure). **I want to go back one step also about when um to continue a little bit more on the um counselors themselves** (P: Yes) **and where they are sexually. When you were um interviewing** (P: Yes) **potential counselors can you tell me how did you judge where that person was ((inaudible over-speaking))?**

P: ((Laughs)) It's appalling I mean it's like all interviewing procedures are very imperfect aren't they (. . .) but again it does suggest.

I: Having affairs?

P: With other—with other counselors.

I: With the counselors?

P: Yeah marriages breaking up and things (. . .) makes one wonder about you know how far people's boundaries are intact um yeah.

I: How do you work with this in supervision (P: Yeah) **because it's still ((inaudible over-speaking)).**

P: Yeah as a supervisee or a supervisor?

This passage was preceded by a series of fairly extended responses from the interviewee. To retain the flow of his answers I avoided interrupting and made a mental note of issues I wanted to follow-up (see also the section Prompts and Follow-Up Questions). At the beginning of the extract, I list the issues, possibly as an aid to myself, in a rather muddled way and finally formulate a relevant question. I then have to remember to ask a question about the other issue I wanted to follow up—supervision—a bit later in the interview as indicated.

Grounding in Examples

The purpose of a research interview is to generate material for analysis. A common mistake is to treat the interviewee as a kind of protosocial scientist by asking questions that require answers at a high level of conceptualization, particularly on issues that participants probably have not before thought about in this way (Potter & Hepburn, 2005). Such answers are of questionable value as they will too often consist of spontaneously produced lay theorizations and generalizations—unless, for good reasons, this is what is sought. A better strategy is to ask interviewees questions about their actual experiences and to request specific examples with detailed description. This is more likely to produce rich material that the researcher then analyses within a relevant, rigorous framework:

Extract 10 (boundaries, male participant)
P: . . . I think you know these three examples may be you know the extremes

and extremes of how therapy was not managed very well. But these are the very same thing that went wrong in those relationships—go wrong or go well to various degrees in all relationships.

I: Okay can you give me an example then of maybe a process a similar kind of process in another therapy where you feel is very relevant to this management of the sexual boundary?

P: Well let's see. When patients have been referred and they attend for sexual dysfunction (. . .) for instance in my whole career I would occasionally be asked to assess women who were raped had been raped and I—they they never came back. And I think that that was which to do with with a a gender issue was also something about my particular approach to assessment . . .

Asking for specific examples from the interviewee's own experience has the benefit also of (almost always) ensuring that one is asking questions that the participant can actually answer. Had I followed this procedure, I would have avoided asking the participant in the following extract to speculate on things about which she could not know:

Extract 11 (boundaries, female participant)

I: Mm (2) do you think it might have been a difference in time that things have been more problematic for you in your personal life—that this particular client—that that the process with the client might have been difficult for you than it might?

P: Um (1) I think it might have been momentarily more difficult (. . .) I s—suspect in some ways it's a protection working with [client group] because it's a constant reminder that they they aren't there as partners.

I: And and I'm kind of struck that the kind of strength of that statement for you that your clients can't support your needs (P: Mm) that—if that's a right

interpretation of that—(P: Mm) and I'm wondering I'm wondering whether it might that might not be felt quite so strongly for some therapists in some situations do you think that's . . . ?

P: I think that's possibly and certainly I've a colleague who fell in love with a—(1) and I think she'd admit it fell in love with a male patient (. . .) and that it was a good ending and not see him again was very therapeutic.

I: Mm (1) f—for both of them do you think? ((laughs)) (P: Um) I'm wondering about it's was sometimes more two ways?

P: Possibly possibly I'm not so sure about (I: No) obviously.

I: Well yes you're talking a third third party here (P: Mm) . . .

In this extract, the participant provides a speculative answer to my question about how things might have been for her had circumstances been different—indeed, how would she know? She then does very well to provide a response to my question about other therapists by describing the experience of a colleague. However, she politely declines to speculate further when I ask about the client's perspective and I, at last, realize the inappropriateness of my line of questioning.

Perhaps surprisingly, it is usually good advice to avoid asking *why* questions. Interactionally, *why* questions may feel confrontational. Most important, however, people often have little knowledge about, or insight into, the reason for things or into what motivates them, and *why* questions too easily produce ad hoc rationalizations of questionable validity (see Hollway & Jefferson, 2000):

Extract 12 (medic, female participant)

P: Um well I did do a lot more work. [Person's name] did psychology as well and like I did a lot more work compared to him. He was really like I'll study the day before and.

I: ((Inaudible)) as you as well the same exams as you?

P: Yeah.

I: Right.

P: And he would like study maybe the next four and so like they almost feel better so.

I: Why do you think that was?

P: I dunno like he just (.) like he just probably (.) thought like you're not disciplined you know. Some people can do the work and some people don't.

I: Do you think it was to do with the subject matter because it was his first choice of degree and he'd already had a whole year of it before you came in and.

P: I suppose that's part of it . . .

In Extract 12, the participant indicates that she does not know the answer to my *why* question but, being helpful, goes on to offer a *probably* account. I go on to make the mistake of offering her a candidate answer, which she agrees is a possibility. The material produced, as in Extract 11, is therefore highly speculative and, because of this, probably difficult to analyze. I would have been much better asking her to describe her own study habits and, in relation to this, how her friend's strategy compared and how it made her feel about how she, herself, worked.

There are, of course, exceptions to the generally good advice of not asking why questions. Examples include research in which interviewees have been selected for their theoretical or professional knowledge and the study research questions require the tapping of this expertise. Another example is research that is interested in understanding the sense that people make of their experience when pushed to fall back on their stock of cultural commonsense. For example, I helped design an interview schedule for a study exploring cultural differences in the understanding of somatic symptoms in pregnancy. The interview schedule contained questions in which participants were asked to ground their experiences in actual examples, but we considered it appropriate also to include some why questions to force a rationalization from, or at least an articulation of, the women's stock of cultural assumptions. Responses to "why" questions were not taken at face value but rather were analyzed for what they revealed about differences in the underlying assumptions of the two cultural groups studied.

Prompts and Follow-Up Questions

A common mistake is sticking too rigidly to the interview schedule. This can produce a rather short, shallow interview. Good research interviewing requires active listening: monitoring constantly the links between what the interviewee is saying and the research schedule, noting which questions no longer need to be asked but also avenues needing to be explored in more detail through the use of prompts and follow-up questions. Prompts can be included in the interview schedule as they identify areas of prima facie interest, which, it is hoped, will be covered spontaneously by interviewees. If they are not covered by the interviewee, then the interviewer has a reminder in the schedule to ask.

Follow-up questions are developed during the interview by the interviewer to explore in more depth relevant, but unanticipated, information or direction in the talk. Follow-ups along the lines of "can you tell me more about" are usually productive and simple to use. Extract 13 offers an example of this format and also the technique of asking the interviewee to explain further their use of a specific word:

Extract 13 (boundaries, male participant)

P: . . . I mean look at the [name] guidelines for most of this can be savage and draconian in the sense of not just no relationships while you're working with somebody which is you know obvious but some will end up saying never and some say four years. Some of the guidelines say four years as you know and I mean that may be considered unduly prescriptive but.

I: Can I ask about (P: Yes) um you use the word draconian (P: Yes). Can you explain a little more to me?

P: Yeah yeah I suppose that seems to me to be unreasonably inhuman in terms of the kind of relationships . . .

In the following example, I start the interview by asking the first question in my interview schedule and then follow up with a question asking for more information about a novel aspect of the answer that is of research interest:

> Extract 14 (medics, female participant)
>
> I: You've had the whole cycle of a psychology degree. Can you tell me what your impression is about how this year has compared to what you've been used to in medicine?
>
> P: Okay it's been quite different (. . .) it sounds silly but like seeing how normal students ((laughs)) kind of go about and like we're—like there's no lectures to go to what do we do and yeah. So I've found I've had a lot of time to myself.
>
> **I: How did you fill that time?**
>
> P: ((Laughs)) Well so—but obviously you're meant to study in that time but like I got a job . . .

Identifying aspects of the participant's answer that are relevant to the study but not on the interview schedule and formulating good follow-up questions to explore these areas in more depth is vital to a productive semistructured interview. It is almost inevitable that some novel areas are not explored fully during the interview, but it very frustrating to analyze an interview when tantalizing comments are passed by without further discussion. Good follow-up questions—and at the right time—are, however, probably one of the most difficult aspects of research interviewing. Practice in phrasing short, open, non-leading questions is extremely helpful as is familiarity with a few stock follow-up questions: "Can you tell me more about that?" "Can you give me an example of that?" "How did that make you feel?"

The Power of Silence

One important way in which the research interview tends to be different from ordinary conversation is that the deliberate aim of one interactant (the interviewer) is to facilitate the other's (the interviewee's) contribution. Ordinary conversation is usually more democratic in the sharing of the floor. Conversation analysis demonstrates that conversational turns can be considered usefully as consisting of turn construction units (TCUs; Liddicoat, 2007). Unless in storytelling mode

or in certain institutional contexts, a speaker has the right to one TCU only before another speaker can take a turn, although of course there are strategies that can be employed to hold the floor such as rushing on past the end of a TCU. Identification of a TCU is context specific, but they do have three central characteristics: TCUs complete an action (*do* something in talk, such as make a question); are grammatically complete (if not always grammatically correct); and, although of less import, the speaker's prosody makes them *sound* finished (Liddicoat, 2007).

Semistructured interviews are designed to encourage storytelling sequences from interviewees as this usually provides a rich source of material for analysis. For example, the "can you tell me about" format prompts just this. Another important technique for encouraging an extended contribution from the participant is for the interviewer to resist taking the floor at the end of an interviewee's TCU, even if the interviewee offers to hand this over through stopping and the use of body language, such as making eye contact. Not taking the floor at this point will leave a gap in the conversation, and this tends to feel awkward. Leaving a silence and using encouraging body language, such as a smile and a nod, or a simple acknowledging backchannel such as "hm mm," will encourage the interviewee to fill this silence with further material and in a way that has not been lead by the interviewer. This simple technique is particularly useful but does mean resisting the social pressure to speak, and this can take confidence and practice. In the following extract, I managed to leave a rather extreme 24 seconds of silence after the interviewee's TCU—an obvious handover point:

> Extract 15 (boundaries, female participant)
>
> I: Because this is something as a you know as a lay person ((smiley voice)) um you—could confla—possibly in my mind I had a conflation between um supervision and personal therapy which was very nicely kind of untangled a bit in in discussion with my colleagues so we thought it would be a thing to particularly ask about and.

P: Well some people do run supervision like that and I think I'm not sure I think it's a very good idea personally um (24) I suppose there's a lot of themes on different levels aren't there about intrusion . . .

Working productively with silence can also take the form of avoiding rushing in to amend, re-ask, or add to a question but, instead, leaving time for the interviewee to think:

Extract 16 (boundaries, male participant)
I: Is there anything that we've not discussed that you think would be helpful to add?
P: (16) I I suppose the the an aspect of this is um is to do with you know we we talked about this in in terms of therapy that's that's okay but of course you know there are there are these very same points apply within professional relationships . . .

Working with silence needs careful judgment, though, to avoid spoiling rapport because silence is awkward socially. The following example occurred very early in an interview in which I was avoiding coming in too soon having asked my first question. However, even though the silence was shorter than that tolerated much later in the interview (see Extract 15), the interviewee's response, in which she checks out the reason for my delay in speaking, suggests that I had left it too long and caused some misalignment:

Extract 17 (boundaries, female participant)
P: . . . sometimes people have got into a predicament and have had nowhere to go but I like the tone of your advert and thinking because I think it addressed an area that is quite important really (1) um (3) is that enough um yeah?
I: And what is definition of sexual boundary can you work with.

Leaving silence, or responding to turn-completing TCUs with bland but encouraging backchannels

(such as "hm mm"), can also help to avoid interrupting the interviewee. Interruptions can spoil rapport and lose the flow of the participant's associations, which may be useful for analysis (Hollway & Jefferson, 2000). With experience one can make a mental note to return to a point later with a follow-up question (done, if badly, in Extract 9). Potentially worse than interruptions to ask a question are interruptions in which the interviewer attempts to finish the interviewee's turn—a type of exchange that is commonplace in ordinary conversation. In a research interview, finishing the interviewee's turn produces poor material for analysis because it is not clear whether it is the interviewee's perspective that is being captured, even if they subsequently agree with the statement:

Extract 18 (quarry, female participant)
P: . . . lets just say we've never been back for a meal cos we like to be leisurely and er.
I: And you've got other places that you can go.
P: Yes, that's right (I: Yes). You're quite right.

In this example, the interviewee hesitates in ending her statement but, rather than rushing in to finish it, I would have been much better leaving a silence and seeing where she went with this because the status of the material would then have been clear. Not all interviewee's will agree with how the interviewer completes their turn, however, as in the following example from an interview conducted for an undergraduate project:

Extract 19 (quarry, female interviewer, participant 1 is male, participant 2 is female)
P1: And the wind generally blows from west to east (I: Mm) which is fine but now that they've built this great big bund what does the wind do because at one time it used to whistle across the village and carry on. Now it whistles across the village and hits the bund so.
I: And whistles all the way back.
P1: But no.

P2: **Well no it it.**
P1: On the other side of the bund.
P2: On the other s—somebody who
used to live down [place name] er a farm
down there they used to say . . .

A possible benefit of getting it wrong is that the interviewer can, as here, catalyze an extended, corrective narrative. Getting it wrong, however, demonstrates misunderstanding on the part of the interviewer and in both Extract 18 and 19 mere silence would have been a better strategy.

The Not-Knowing Interviewer

The title of this section is derived from the therapeutic stance of the not-knowing therapist in which the client is seen as the principal author of the therapy dialogue (Anderson & Goolishian, 1988). In a very real sense, when generating interview data for analysis, the interviewer does not know in advance the content of the material that will be obtained. He or she may have a general idea of how it might go but good interviewing requires that the interviewer avoids influencing the material toward their own expectations, and the techniques discussed in this chapter can contribute to this general aim. It is therefore a good principle to approach a research interview with an extreme modesty as to one's understanding of the topic of investigation.

Taking a not-knowing stance does not take away the obligation to demonstrate expertise in the practice of interviewing. It does, however, if taken seriously as an approach to interviewing, predispose the interviewer to formulate good, probing questions that generate excellent material for analysis. So, for example, although I know what the word *draconian* (Extract 13) means, in taking a not-knowing approach, I did not take for granted that my understanding in that context was the same as that of my interviewee. In asking him to expand on his use of the word, I therefore generated more detailed information for analysis, which was central to my research interests.

Sometimes my use of a not-knowing stance is, possibly, a little less ingenious. In a series of interviews with counselors and psychotherapists about their professional practice, I found myself stressing

my lay status. In one sense, I was using this in a genuine manner to catalyze detailed explanation of sophisticated professional knowledge. On the other hand, I have a doctorate in psychotherapy research, have supervised and examined many doctorates in clinical psychology, and have taught abnormal psychology at the undergraduate level for 15 years. Something else was probably going on here:

Extract 20 (boundaries, female participant)
I: **Okay can I ask—as somebody who isn't a trained clinician or counselor or anything um what I I kinda have a query about which is the way that as s—taking a psychodynamic approach y—you do re—what it sounds like you do reinterpret the sexual feelings of of you may not—for this client in a similar way attraction in general um does does that mitigate against the the feeling of meeting the client as another person and just I'm slightly (1) can I have that clarified?**
P: ((To that end?)) yeah um (1).
I: **If if the the feelings of attraction are I mean kind of partly that kind of felt with meeting with for you the the the benefits of meeting with client also as a person that I don't know whether I'm interpreting er getting your meaning right and then I mean stepping back and reinterpreting that.**
P: So you're thinking about as transference . . .

Aside from the fact that my question(s) are extremely inarticulate and far too long (even though the interviewee in this pilot commented that eventually the question was good at prompting her into a useful clarification), there was no need to preface this with a statement as to my lay status. My take on this type of sequence is that it demonstrates some of the power issues that are probably endemic to research interviewing. In drawing attention to a way in which I may have been considered to have lower status in this interaction, I was probably trying to throw off any implication that I was taking a dominant position as interviewer. Hence, I was being, possibly, overdeferential to my interviewee, to some extent communicating my feeling of vulnerability, and intimating to the interviewee to go gently on me. With growing experience, I used this self-depreciating strategy less as I conducted the interviews in this series. That is not to say that this particular technique is always to be avoided. It is useful, however, to reflect on what one might be doing in such situations in order to draw on strategies knowingly rather than defensively. Moreover, reflecting on why one was interacting in a particular way during an interview allows assessment of its impact on the data, potentially modifying one's approach in subsequent interviews, and provides possibly useful material for the analysis.

With certain participants, taking a fully not-knowing stance may be in some ways counterproductive. One of my doctoral students conducted interviews with male ex-prisoners about their use of illegal drugs in prison and the interviewees used drug slang in their descriptions. Discussing this in a supervision meeting, we wondered if this told us something about how the interviewer, herself, was being positioned to some extent as an *insider* in these interviews because she was expected to understand these terms. Although she was familiar with most of the slang, she wondered if there was an element of testing out her expertise as well, and that her *knowing* response was important in terms of rapport, trust, and her credibility. So, although she did check out what was meant by some of the terms during the interviews, it seemed important to not appear overly naïve with these participants. It is important to be sensitive to such issues and there will be contexts, such as this, in which it might be appropriate to ask interviews to clarify or expand on some things specifically "for the tape" (see also the section Power and Vulnerability).

Interviewer Formulations
In conversation analytic research, a formulation is a summary of what has gone before in a discussion and, as such, exhibits an understanding of what has been talked about (Heritage & Watson, 1979). Formulations are common in ordinary conversation and interviewers may find themselves using formations spontaneously to summarize what the interviewee

has just said. A potential benefit of a within-interview formulation is that it can allow the interviewer to check out their understanding as I do in the following extract:

> Extract 21 (boundaries, male participant)
> P: . . . so just ask that how do you think things have been going recently you know and see what emerges from that.
> **I: It seems to be if I can check this understanding out with you that the therapist or a counselor probably uses quite a lot of self knowledge about possibly what their boundaries vulnerab— particular boundary vulnerabilities are. Isn't there a role for personal therapy? A contribution?**
> P: Yeah I think there probably is but the troubling thing is . . .

In this extract, I produce a formulation by way of a summarized gloss of the interviewee's seeming meaning and state explicitly that I am doing so to check out my understanding. However, I leave no time for the interviewee to comment on this candidate understanding or, at least, he does not attempt to take the floor at the relevant point, and I immediately ask a further question. This is problematic for analysis in that I do not have confirmation of, or commentary on, this formulation. Even if the participant agreed with me, however, the status of this agreement would have been questionable because we know that agreements are preferred overwhelmingly to disagreements in interaction. My advice would be to avoid the habit of providing formulations when conducting a research interviews and, instead, use the other techniques discussed in this chapter to draw the interviewee out on points that could do with further exploration. Leave the analysis to a later stage at which point one can consider the material generated in the context of the other research interviews and one's specific research questions.

Interviewer Self-Disclosure
Interviewing style can be usefully placed on a continuum from formal to informal (Schaeffer, 1991).

A more informal interviewing style may deliberately mirror aspects of ordinary conversation and, in so doing, include elements of interviewer self-disclosure. In self-disclosing, the interviewer comments as an individual, takes a personalized stance, and possibly reveals information about him- or herself. This can be contrasted to remaining in a more neutral, professionalized interviewing role. An informal interviewing style can increase the rapport between interviewer and interviewee and, hence, the potential openness of the participant (Babbie, 1995; Houtkoop-Steemstra, 1997; Koole, 2003). The evidence suggests, however, that informal interviewing is also likely to increase the chance of interviewees responding in the way they think the interviewer wants (Antaki, Young, & Finlay, 2002; Hyman, 1954). This converging of opinion does not have to be sought actively by the interviewer. The odd, inadvertent leading question or encouraging body language at points in the interview can provide the context for the production of an agreeable, shared account. On the other hand, a certain professional formality on the part of the interviewer, and avoiding taking a stance, may limit the chance of collusion. This is not to pretend, however, that total interviewer neutrally is possible, or probably always desirable (see the section Critique of Interviews as Data). Using the suggestions offered in this chapter, reflecting on the interactional impact of one's demeanor and questioning, and acknowledging that a research interview is different in many important respects to an ordinary conversation is probably a good general approach—not in terms of ensuring objectivity but in terms of facilitating the interviewee's account.

In the series of quarry interviews I conducted, I deliberately set out to undertake relatively informal, semistructured interviewing and, in so doing, to be open to self-disclosure. In the following extract, my self-disclosure may have contributed to rapport development, but otherwise it probably adds little to generating useful information for analysis. The extract illustrates the possibility that overly informal interviewing can produce interviewer–interviewee consensus accounts:

Extract 22 (quarry, female participant)
P: . . . that's not just this village and
I mean I've lived in a few and that's just

the way it is. They just don't take kindly to change of any type.

I: I don't live in a village but I can kind of—in my little street there's a bit over the way that they are trying to develop and we've had petitions and you know ((laughs)) not in your backyard. They don't want the extra cars and the extra parking and.

P: No you don't you just want to keep exactly what you've got . . .

In another interview in this series, my informal style appears to set the context for a subtle change of role and the interviewee asks me a question. A bit later on, although my first self-disclosure in the sequence achieves a response, my second appears to derail the conversation and is responded to minimally by the interviewee. I attempt to salvage the situation, badly, and go on to ask two questions at the one time, appearing to realize rather late that my disclosure could be seen as irrelevant and possibly intrusive:

Extract 23 (quarry, female participant)
P: Did you come up the hill or along the flat?
I: I came in this direction ((pointing)).
P: Right well they come that way and then they turn left towards [village name] the bulk of them.
I: Right so the majority of them go towards [village name].
P: Twice as many go that way as come this way but you do get them coming up the dales from [other village name] and through.
I: You know I live in [city name] although I'd heard about you know bikers being a problem in [region name] I hadn't really connected it cos I think it's so rural isn't it and then you know big bikes going fast I mean it's not quite what you associate.
P: And a lot of them now are mature men in their 40s and 50s who I think are having second childhood.

I: Yes I actually was introduced—a colleague of mine had a 50th birthday and introduced me to a friend of her's and erm a couple of weeks later she told me he'd been killed on his motorbike—again (I: Yes) yes ((laughs)). Oh mm erm okay so if you go back to—that that is relevant (P: Yes) ((laughter)). Thank you for the details of that. It gives me a little bit more about what you know what isn't a concern and what actually is and it's not not related to the quarry ((laughs)). So yeah erm can you tell me a little bit more about your quarry visit then and then how that visit made you think about you know coming and living out here.

My opinion now is that the safest strategy is to avoid interviewer self-disclosure. If remaining open to the possibility of interviewing toward the informal end of the spectrum and the likelihood of this including self-disclosures, disclosures need careful consideration and a lot of interviewing experience. For example, my self-disclosures in Extract 23 occurred in the context of a sensitive topic (violent and untimely deaths), which might, itself, have invited increased intimacy. With greater skill, I would have been more aware of this dynamic during the interview and avoided straying from role. Interviewing as a practice is pretty familiar in Western Hemisphere culture (Atkinson & Silverman, 1997), and I have not had the experience of being asked a personal question or for my own opinion during a research interviewer. However, these are always possibilities. A good strategy is to be clear with participants about the interview format before starting and, if asked for one's point of view, to say that you would rather leave that discussion until after the interview has ended.

Disagreeing With or Challenging the Interviewee

The interviewer's role is viewed, most often, as a professionally neutral one and, as my discussion of self-disclosure above reinforces, attempted neutrality is usually the safest option. Complete neutrality is probably impossible, however, as interviewers imply a stance, or may be construed as inhabiting certain positions from the questions asked, the institutions interviewers appear to represent, and the research practices on which interviewers draw. Engaging reflexively with interviewing as a means of generating data and considering the impact of the research context on the data obtained is key to working productively with such issues (see the section Critique of Interviews as Data). However, there may be times when the interviewer wishes, or is placed in the dilemma of needing, to disagree with or challenge the interviewee: that is, to take up explicitly a counter position.

In most interviews, it will be strictly outside the interviewer's remit to correct interviewees on presumed matters of fact even if the interviewer's opinion is sought as a perceived expert on the topic of the interview. A useful way of sidestepping such a request is to reiterate that it is the interviewee's opinion which is sought. Research on topics that may cover disturbing material (e.g., experiences in prison) or touch on the participant's known vulnerabilities (e.g., interviews about surviving cancer) make it essential ethically to provide interviewee's with information about appropriate sources of support. Providing such information is essential because it is not appropriate for the interviewer to take on a dual role as quasi-counselor, even if he or she has the appropriate training (see the section Ethical Considerations). Situations that are potentially more problematic include points in an interview when the interviewer finds it difficult not to provide information pertinent to the discussion that appears to be at odds with what the participant is saying. The following extract, for example, illustrates how an, otherwise appropriate, not-knowing stance brought the interviewer into an awkward situation in that she asked a question to which she knew the interviewee's response was incorrect (unfortunately, the recording is poor, hence the inaudibles):

Extract 24 (quarry, female interviewer, female participant)
I: Hmm how much information have you received from the people at the

quarry ((inaudible)) general areas ((inaudible)).

    P: None ((laughs)).

    I: Um cos there's been some weekly ((inaudible)) newsletter there about all ((inaudible)) you know like cos there's a liaison committee and they meet sometimes. We've been told the—you had the biggest quarterly newsletter that people in the village get.

    P: Oh wait a minute this this is to do with [village name] parish council and um ((laughter)). Yeah yeah it's it's we've we've got um a quarry liaison officer . . .

The undergraduate student interviewer makes a good job of recovering this situation. The participant had been pretty vehement in her criticism of the quarry throughout the interview and it would have been easy for the interviewer to have let this go for the sake of retaining rapport. However, bravely, she offers a gentle challenge to the interviewee's blanket statement "none," using the strategy of "we've been told" (two students were present during the interview), which allows the possibility that they have been incorrectly informed. Luckily, the interviewee, good humouredly, construes the problem as her own misunderstanding.

Challenges may be more deliberate and strategic. As part of my boundaries sequence of interviews, I took a calculated risk in questioning the position that appeared to be taken by one of the therapist participants. The highly mitigated way in which my challenge is made deliberately softens its force, but that it is indeed a challenge is, of course, not lost on my interviewee:

Extract 25 (boundaries, male participant)

    I: As a lay person ((smiley voice)) (P: Yes) which hopefully this might by enlightening me help dig a little deeper—is there—to me it feels appropriate to engage on a kind of human level as well as a therapeutic level but um so that the communication of being affected by what the client has gone through may be appropriate. I'd just like you to expand a bit on that for me

that by looking affected is that always inappropriate (P: No!) or is it.

    P: No (I: Yeah) no of course not! (I: No). It is that's that's about a degree of kind of empathy (I: Yeah) and of understanding (I: Mm) and a kind of genuineness around with a warmth with the material that's being presented that I mean that should be part you know of a good working alliance (I: Right). But but er and and um there are kind of like the way like with the second patient . . .

This sequence occurred quite late in the interview, and I would not have attempted such a question if I was not certain that a good level of rapport had been developed and that both I and the interviewee could tolerate and work productively with potential misalignment. The interviewee does not spare me but neither does he abandon the interview, and the matter is clarified as being one of "degree." I too, avoid taking this personally or being overly intimidated, although notice that I do work hard in my backchannels to demonstrate my realignment. I would certainly use the same technique again but it is probably to be avoided until one has quite a lot of interviewing experience.

I am in the fortunate position of having interviewed rather pleasant and helpful individuals on topics on which, in the main, I have had little stake or have been on the whole sympathetic to the interviewee's point of view. This will not be case for all interviewing experiences. It is very likely that in some interviews, or in some interviewing studies, the interviewer meets with people who have, to them, repugnant opinions. An example might be the interviews that formed the basis of Wetherell and Potter's (1992) book *Mapping the Language of Racism*. The reader is directed to this book and to van den Berg, Wetherell, and Houtkoop-Steemstra (2003) to see how the research interviews were undertaken, analyzed, and commented on.

INTERVIEWS: ADDITIONAL CONSIDERATIONS

There are many things to consider when preparing for and conducting research interviews over and above the techniques of interviewing. I will discuss four important kinds of additional considerations in this section: design choice, ethics, recording and transcription, and being informed by the critique of interviews as data.

Design Choice

There are several decisions to be made about the design of an interview study. Type of interview was discussed in the introductory section. I have been involved in interview studies that have differed in terms of the number and the characteristics of the interviewers, number of interviewees per interview and their characteristics, interview location, and use of follow-up interviews. Each of these is an important design consideration with practical implications and potential impact on the data collected.

Number and characteristics of the interviewers.

There may be good practical reasons to have more than one interviewer employed in a study. The workload can be shared and the project can be completed faster, and less interviewing chances are lost because of interviewer unavailability. These are important considerations when working to deadlines and when there are competing work obligations.

Four interviewers were involved in generating the quarry interviews: myself and three undergraduate students who joined the study for their final-year research project and who received expenses to thank them for their contribution (Hugh-Jones & Madill, 2009; Madill, in press). One of the students and I conducted interviews alone, whereas the other two students interviewed together, with one taking the lead in any particular interview. Although it is not the norm, benefits of the students interviewing together were that they were able to share transport out to a fairly isolated location and it increased their safety collecting data off campus. (The other student and I let a responsible other person know where we had gone and when we were due back, which is a department stipulation for interview research.) I have done some analysis of interviewing style in this corpus that shows the interviews I (with the most research experience) conducted tended to be longer, to be less formal, and to include more follow-up questions and flexible use of the interview schedule.

The impact on the interviews of having two interviewers present is, however, unclear. Transcripts show that usually only the lead interviewer spoke during an interview but, at times, the other did ask a follow-up question or make a comment and sometimes all who were present laughed together.

Five interviewers were involved in the boundaries project: three psychotherapy–counseling practitioners, one male and two female (all of whom also have academic posts); and two academic researchers, both female (one a sociologist and, myself, a psychologist; Martin, Godfrey, Meekums, & Madill, 2010). Each of us interviewed alone. As a team we have discussed the possible impact of our lay and professional status in relation to the interviewees, who were all psychotherapy–counseling practitioners. Our impression is that the participants may have spared the academic researchers some of the more difficult and intense material around their work with sexual boundaries with clients, possibly sensitive to our unfamiliarity working with such material. There was possibly more of a shared sense of struggle, use of a shared technical vocabulary, and trust that the more difficult material would be managed well emotionally during the interviews with another practitioner. On the other hand, in not assuming a shared experience or shared language, the academic interviewers may have asked the interviewees to explain in more detail their assumptions and frameworks for understanding. This is an extremely important point as having, on the face of it, facets of shared experience and shared identity with interviewees—particularly if this coincides with the topic of the research—is not always helpful. These may facilitate access and the chance of initial rapport, but the interviewer must guard against assuming that they do indeed share understandings with their participants and ensure that important information is fully articulated and explored.

A project with multiple interviewers can generate rich data, particularly if the interviewers have relevantly variable characteristics that facilitate interviewees in engaging with different aspects of the research topic. This is interesting to consider when analyzing the material. There may also be good ethical reasons for providing a range of interviewers. For example, in the boundaries project, although the four main researchers were female, we gave our interviewees the choice of having a male interviewer. Sexual boundaries are a sensitive topic and, because gender is implicated, it was appropriate to orient to this in our interviewing strategy. In fact, one male participant did opt for a male interviewer, and one of our male colleagues conducted this interview.

Number of interviewees per interview and their characteristics. As noted, focus groups are a well-known type of interviewing format that, by definition, includes more than one interviewee per interview. I like to distinguish focus groups from a more generic kind of group interview that does not hold to the specific format and aims of the focus group but, nevertheless, contains more than one interviewee (Madill & Gough, 2008). Interviews with more than one participant tend to be more difficult to organize because it means finding a time and location suitable for a number of different people. Participants also need to feel comfortable discussing the research topic with others so attention needs to be paid to the group's makeup. For example, group interviews would have been inappropriate for the boundaries study because interviewee anonymity was exceptionally important for participants to feel safe describing, what were at times, painful struggles in their work.

Single gender groups might be appropriate for some topics and cultural issues may need to be taken into account. For example, in a study on organ donation, I and my masters student, Clare Hayward, arranged for Pakistani men and women living in the north of England to be interviewed in single-gender groups to avoid potential barriers to discussing body parts and medical issues in the presence of the opposite sex (and extended this strategy to our White indigenous participants for methodological consistency; Hayward & Madill, 2003). In general, five to eight participants are ideal for a group research interview. This means recruiting more than eight people per group, however, with the expectation that fewer than those who confirm actually will attend.

In the quarry study, couples sometimes were interviewed together, and their children sometimes were present, although in this project none of the children contributed to the data. Interviewing couples together was productive in that passages of the interview became on-topic discussions between the couple. This has the benefit of minimizing at these points contribution from the interviewer while obtaining positions, arguments, and debates of interest. One of my doctoral students, Victoria O'Key, arranged family interviews on the topic of food choice in which she hoped that the children would join the discussion (O'Key, Hugh-Jones, & Madill, 2009). Many did so and added interesting material, often challenging their parents' presentation of the family's eating habits.

The decision as to how many interviewees to include in an interview, who they should be, and what relationship they should have to one another should be guided by the study research questions and sensitivity to the topic and cultural traditions of participants. Having more than one participant in an interview can be helpful if participants are not likely to be inhibited from discussing the topic with others and in cases in which group debate might open up productively different points of view.

Interview location. The location of a research interview can influence the way in which interviewer and interviewee relate and may exaggerate a power dynamic in one direction or another (see the section Power and Vulnerability). It is usual to offer interviewees a choice of location as part of facilitating their comfort and encouraging participation. However, the safety of the interviewer is an overriding consideration and, as mentioned, a minimal requirement should be that a responsible person knows where the interviewer has gone and when he or she is due back.

The quarry interviews all were conducted in interviewee's homes in a small village in the north of England. The role of interviewer in some respects was conflated with that of guest. Analysis of the overarching style of the interviewee contribution in this corpus of material suggests that, in general and as a group, interviewees responded to the interviewers as they would friends (as opposed to strangers or intimates such as a spouse), although none of the interviewers were known to participants before the study (Madill, in press). It is possible that some of this friendliness reflected hospitality obligations. Victoria O'Key was not always made to feel welcome when interviewing in family homes, however, so it cannot be assumed that one will be treated like a guest in such situations.

In contrast, the medics interviews were all conducted in my office at the university, and none of the participants took up my offer of the interview taking place elsewhere. I was also in a dual role to these students in that I taught one of their compulsory lecture courses, supervised some in their practical assignment, and marked (blind) subsequent exam scripts and reports. Because the interviews covered the experience of a year intercalating in psychology, there are sequences during which the students and I allude to our pedagogic relationship. This arose most clearly when some students mentioned, favorably, the course I taught them. At these points I tended to show embarrassed awareness that I might be perceived as having a degree of leverage over my participants by saying something like "you don't have to say that." I am aware that I was quite persistent in my e-mail invitations to attend interviews, and some students may have felt obliged to come given that I was one of their lecturers and assignment markers. (I also provided a small payment of £20 per interview.) There is some reassuring evidence, however, that the students felt they could act autonomously. In the first cohort, I had planned to conduct three interviews with each student, however, despite several e-mails, one did not reply to my invitation, or attend, the third interview. Moreover, the students were not reticent to use the interview as an opportunity to describe some of their disappointments with the psychology course.

The incipient power dynamic was in the opposite direction for me in the boundaries study. Here, I conducted one interview in a therapist's university office, two in consulting rooms at the interviewees' places of work, and one in the consulting room at the therapist's own home. These locations provided a strong cue for my lay status and bolstered my sense of the interviewees as high-status professionals (see the section The Not-Knowing Interviewer). Moreover, conducting three of these interviews in the interviewees' consulting rooms made for a rather strange dynamic. From my perspective, it probably contributed to a sense of vulnerability as the setting was suggestive, that on one level, I was there to receive therapy. On the other hand, as the interviewer it was my job to facilitate, listen, and ask questions on the intimate and charged topic of the therapists' experience of managing sexual boundaries in their work. I might surmise that the participants sensed a reversal of role in being invited to self-reveal within a setting in which this would be, otherwise, inappropriate. Added to this, the topic of the research was about boundaries and the research team has discussed the possible parallel processes occurring as we, as interviewers, attempted to manage intimacy boundaries with our participants—which was entwined, for me, in complex ways with interview location.

Thus, some thought needs to be given to the location of the research interview in light of safety, comfort, appropriateness to the research topic, and acceptability to interviewees and impact on the data generated. Interview location, however, is never fully neutral. Keeping a research interviewing diary and reflecting on the possible impact on the data of interview location, for example, through awareness of how one felt interviewing in particular locations, which will include the impact of the kind of relationship catalyzed with participants, might inform the analysis of that data.

Use of follow-up interviews. Longitudinal qualitative research is an important focus of methodological innovation in the United Kingdom (Timescapes, 2007). Single research interviews with participants are valuable and may be enough to furnish a study with appropriate and relevant information on a research topic. Some research designs and research questions, however, require at least one follow-up interview. The free association, narrative, and interview method (Hollway & Jefferson, 2000) makes use of a double interview: two interviews about 1 week apart. The psychoanalytic framework of this method posits interviewer and interviewee as anxious defended subjects and, hence, that the data generated will be shaped by such processes as transference and countertransference. The first interview allows the researcher to identify analytically interesting indicators of unconscious seepage: contradictions, avoidances, inconsistencies, and the way in which the interactants have been drawn together into a particular kind of relationship that has helped to cocreate the data, such as a mother–daughter dynamic. The second interview then allows the researcher to explore hunches about what this might mean in relation to the topic of research through a personalized interview with each participant, seeking further relevant information although, again, not taking responses at face value.

This kind of double interview is similar in some ways to the processes of member checking or participant validation. A central purpose of member checking is to test the researcher's insights with participants. This lends itself to a follow-up interview with participants, even if the original research was not interview based. Member checking can be used throughout a study in which findings are developed in an iterative cycle between researcher and participants, interviewer and interviewees. In cases in which the explicit purpose of a follow-up interview is a check on the validity of pretty much final results, the process is probably better captured by the term "participant validation" (Lincoln & Guba, 1985). Participant validation, although applauded by many is, I think, highly problematic because good research, from the perspective of the research community, may not always be acceptable to participants. (Exceptions might be projects conducted with and for participants themselves such as in the various forms of action research.) Participant validation therefore requires a sophisticated sensitivity to social and interactional context integrated with an appreciation of researcher and participant stake and investment in the results (see Ashworth, 1993; Bloor, 1978, 1983, 1997a, 1997b; Briggs, 1998; Lomax & Casey, 1998; Mays & Pope, 2000; McKeganey & Bloor, 1981; Sharpe, 1997). Follow-up contact with interviewees in these three contexts—the free association, narrative, and interview method; member checking; and participant validation—have

different aims and can be positioned within different approaches to knowledge generation (epistemologies) and models of subjectivity (ontologies). These complex issues are beyond the scope of this chapter. It is important to be aware of such design choices, however, and the interested reader can follow up the references cited in this section.

Follow-up interviews may be more straightforwardly connected to the topic of the research if it has a longitudinal facet. For example, I interviewed each of the intercalating medical students near the beginning of their psychology year and again toward the end. In the first interview, I was interested in their experience of medical training so far and, within this context, to learn about their decision to take a year of psychology. In the second interview, I tapped their actual experience of the year and any links they had made between psychology and their ongoing medical training.

Interviews may continue as an ongoing process. I had hoped to keep interviewing some of the intercalating medical students as they continued their medical training. I did not have enough resources and, although some of the students might have been interested in continuing, this kind of longitudinal study needs a lot of persistence and motivation on each side. One way to maintain such motivation is to engage in research such as memory work (e.g., Haug, 1987) in which research interviews, or at least recorded discussions, are conducted as a continual longitudinal process within a small dedicated research group, each member of whom has a stake in the result and where tasks, effort, and credit can be negotiated on a democratic and fair basis.

Ethical Considerations

There are many ethical considerations pertinent to interviewing research, many of which I have commented on in the previous section. Here, I will cover some further issues that may be particularly relevant to interviewing studies although, of course, the research must conform to the ethical guidelines of the professional organization or institutions to which the researchers are accountable. The issues covered here relate to informed consent, power and vulnerability, discredited participants, and interviewer experience.

Informed consent. The participant information sheet must give potential interviewees a good idea of what is involved if taking part in the research. This will include the general topics covered in the interview, where the interview might take place, how long it is expected to last, how it will be recorded, the ways in which participants' anonymity will be managed, and incentives offered. Some of these specifications already create problems for much interview research.

Although certain topics will be specified in an interview protocol, it is impossible to predict exactly what will be covered in anything but a highly structured interview. Moreover, although research questions can be stated, it is often difficult to know what will end up being the focus of analysis. The more exploratory forms of analysis, such as grounded theory (Strauss & Corbin, 1990/1998), will be led as far as possible by the data and thus open to revising the original research questions. To complicate matters, qualitative analysis is likely not to take, at some points at least, what the interviewee has said at face value but offer, for example, a psychoanalytically informed interpretation (e.g., Hollway & Jefferson, 2000) or an account on the basis of a functional approach to language (e.g., Edwards & Potter, 1992).

Consent forms can become complicated if seeking consent for the use of material over and above anonymized quotes in reports of the research. Anonymization can be complex, too, with different media and, even with a transcript of the audio recording, it requires sensitivity to contextualizing details that might, when taken together, identify a participant to others in their profession (see, e.g., Extract 11 in which I omitted the type of client group with which this interviewee worked). It might be considered good practice to consider true informed consent in interview research to require two distinguishable stages: (a) consent to undertake and record the interview and (b) consent to use the material in research after the interview has been conducted and the content known, or even after the interviewee has seen a copy of the transcript and has had a chance to remove sections, if desired. It is also worth considering whether the topic of study makes relevant a statement demarking the limits of confidentiality.

For example, we used the following statement in the boundaries study:

> The researchers are aware that sexual boundary violations with clients contravene the codes of ethics and practice to which practitioners adhere, and that for some of the team, their codes of ethics require that a serious breach of boundaries, particularly if there is potential future or actual harm to others, is reported. However, the focus of this study is on successful management of therapeutic boundaries; the interviewer will not ask you to provide information on actual breaches of sexual boundaries. Further, if the interviewer feels that the interview may be going that way, they will let you know, so that you have the opportunity to avoid disclosing details of sexual boundary violations that might require reporting to a professional body.

Whatever legitimate ethical position one takes on informed consent, an important stipulation is that participants know they can, and are able to, withdraw their material from the study. Beyond this, the extent to which the researcher facilitates participant control of their material is controversial, loaded with potentially vying interests (although I have never had a participant withdraw data), and not at all well worked out.

Power and vulnerability. Control over material raises the issue of power and vulnerability in interview studies. Early feminist work highlighted such issues but was possibly naive in assuming that techniques and (researcher) sensitivity could equalize power differences between researcher and participant, particularly when both are women (e.g., Oakley, 1981). My own, certainly not unique, point of view is that interviewer and interviewee likely inhabit different epistemic communities, meaning that each can claim different kinds of knowledge, the most relevant contrast possibly being professional learning versus lived experience relevant to the topic of research. There will likely be differences also in the social positionings and identifications of interviewer and interviewee in terms of such categories as gender, race, class, age, educational background, sexual orientation, marital and parental status and so on, which may give some indication of incipient structural power differences. Given this, however, no specific form or direction of power should be assumed in any particular research interaction, and the operation of power is likely to fluctuate over the course of an interview and to be experienced in different ways by the interactants (see also Cotterill, 1992). My experience is that interviewees have a lot of power in the research process. The researcher is reliant on their participation, and interviewees can decide not to attend an interview, can withdraw their data, and can use subtle strategies to make data collection an uncomfortable experience, for example, by being, often subtly, patronizing to the interviewer or derogatory about the value of research (e.g., see O'Key et al., 2009).

On the other hand, some kinds of interviewees may be considered particularly vulnerable if recruited specifically for relevant traumatic experiences (e.g., physical or mental health issues, problematic life experiences, and so on), although many different kinds of research topic will touch on sensitive issues for certain participants. When the research topic covers a personally sensitive area, the research interview may be experienced as a kind of protocounseling by some interviewees and the attention, rapport, and active listening of the interviewer may promote more intimate self-revelation than the interviewee had expected to give. This might generate good material for analysis but leave the interviewee feeling exposed. The interviewer needs to be aware that the research interview is not counseling and not to stray into this (dual) role, even if he or she has relevant training. It is good practice to provide, as a matter of course, a list of appropriate support services for interviewees to contact if they wish after the interview. This should be given to all participants before interviewing commences to avoid the possibility of any one feeling shamed that he or she had been perceived as particularly vulnerable or needy.

Discredited participants.   Another kind of interviewee worth discussing in terms of ethical

practice is those who could be considered in some way discredited. By *discredited*, I mean individuals whose accounts and perspectives are, at the outset, vulnerable to being undermined or treated with particular skepticism for a variety of reasons. This might include those with mental health problems, those who might be considered to have repulsive or antisocial opinions, and those who are known to engage in criminal activities. Such interviewees are discredited to the extent that the researcher and research audience are prima facie willing to question the content of, or motivation behind, the participant's account or to be unsympathetic to their point of view. This may create a particular tension for the qualitative researcher as many, but certainly not all, qualitative approaches have a humanistic, participant-centered, or emancipatory ethos.

As mentioned, one of my doctoral students has interviewed male ex-prisoners about their use of illegal drugs in prison. In a supervision meeting, I raised the issue of not taking what was said always at face value and asking, for instance, what might be achieved for the participants in offering one kind of description instead of another at a certain points in the interview. My student queried whether I was suggesting this strategy in particular because of the nature of her interviewees. I had meant this as a generally good approach to analyzing qualitative data, but this led to an interesting discussion about the ways in which her participants may be vulnerable to discreditation. In subsequent meetings we discussed markers in the data that might be used to speculate on possibly untold aspects of her participants' experience, for example the men's use of distancing pronouns such as "they." Although our overall impression of the interviews was of the men's candor, we also discussed ways in which some of their descriptions may be open to less self-serving interpretations than offered or implied during interview. This is not to suggest that any objectively true version was to be found, but to understand what might be being avoided in the men's accounts and to speculate on what this might mean.

Interviewer experience.   The previous discussions revealed how my student felt accountable and loyal to her interviewees, and I have had similar feelings toward participants in my work. The experience of the interviewer is important to consider in terms of ethics: both the interviewer's *expertise* and his or her *reaction* to the research. In particular, it is important to consider the relative sensitivity of the research topic and vulnerability of participants in relation to the expertise of the interviewer, frequency and intensity of research supervision, and opportunities for debriefing. For example, I consider it inappropriate for undergraduate students to interview participants who are under treatment for a psychological disorder or who are otherwise particularly vulnerable. Supervision should consider how the interviewer might be affected by the research and reflection might be facilitated by keeping a research diary. Debriefing meetings after interviewing can help the researcher to work productively with his or her reaction as possibly revealing something about the topic of research. For example, we recorded our debriefing meetings as part of the boundaries project and view this material as a further layer of data collection. As alluded to earlier, these debriefs raised our awareness, among other things, of a possible parallel process in relation to boundaries operating in our interviewing experiences, which might be considered reflexively in our analysis as telling us something more about the phenomenon we were researching.

Recording and Transcription

As discussed in the section Ethical Considerations, permission must be granted by the interviewee for the mode of recording, with it being usual to audio-record research interviews. One participant in the boundaries project refused to be audio recorded but agreed to the interviewer making written notes. This is not ideal because a lot of detail is lost and the notes are already a glossed, preinterpreted version of the discussion. The research team decided that useful information could still be obtained from notes, however, particularly given that we had also several audio-recorded interviews in our corpus.

The state of the art in conversation analytic research is to work with video-recorded naturalistic interactions, which may include interviews conducted as a matter of course in institutional settings, for example, between doctor and patient. Video

recording provides visual information about the setting, physically positioning, body language, actions, and movement of the participants. Such information may be important for many kinds of research, which might extend to some kinds of interviewing studies. For example, I am seeking to video record follow-up interviews between researchers and their participants to understand in detail how these interactions get done and with what result. However, particularly in relation to sensitive research topics, participants may be reticent to be video recorded, even though it is possible to obscure personal identity in video recordings. A graded consent form can be useful, which allows participants, if they wish, to consent to the use of video recordings for data analysis by the research team but for no other purpose.

To make recorded materials widely available, as increasingly expected, digital audio or video recording is necessary. Digital audio recorders are small and recordings are downloaded easily onto a computer using the accompanying software. I would advise investing in an additional plug-in microphone for some dictation-style recorders. Even if they have a conference facility, the sound quality can be much improved, and this means many less inaudibles in the transcripts. I would also advise buying a digital recorder with a visual display of audio frequency because this is a good check that one is actually recording. Free downloads are available from the Internet that allow short clips of material to be made for analysis and, with participant consent, presentation at conferences and workshops.

There is a convention that it is best to do one's own transcription. This may be a practical necessity if one has no research funding, usefully focuses the researcher on the detail of the text, and can be viewed as a stage of the analysis, particularly if ideas are noted down during the transcription process. My own opinion is that outsourcing at least some of the transcription can save valuable time for the analysis and take some of the stress out of the research process. Digital recording facilitates sending files for professional transcription. Many of these companies have an easy-to-use e-mail drop-box to transfer the files. It is good practice to select a professional company that offers to sign a confidentiality statement that includes deleting all the material once transcription is complete. If not using a professional service, check out the experience of any individual who might be doing the transcription and discuss confidentiality issues with them. Inexperienced transcribers can misunderstand the task and tidy up or otherwise summarize the talk. I know of one who edited out the odd swear word that was used and other content to which she objected.

If transcription has been outsourced, it is always necessary to check each transcript carefully against the recording. This can take a long time, even with a relatively good transcript. Mark where the speech is inaudible and indicate the sections you are not quite sure that the transcript is right but is as close as you can get. Verbatim, word-for-word, transcription of the interview is probably necessary for most research projects and forms of analysis. After this, the level of detail depends on the kind of analysis undertaken. Conversation analysis requires some of the most detailed transcription and has developed excellent standardized transcription conventions (see http://www.sscnet.ucla.edu/soc/faculty/schegloff/). Less detailed "Jefferson-lite" conventions may be quite appropriate for other forms of analysis (e.g., as here, but see Hugh-Jones & Madill, 2009). However, transcription is never a substitute for the actual recording, and I would recommend always referring back to the audio recording throughout an analysis.

Interestingly, I had the experience recently of doing quite of bit of initial analysis of an interview purely from the audio recording while I was waiting for the transcript. When I continued the analysis from the transcript, I found my attention drawn to different aspects of the interaction. The audio version had impressed on me the affability of the interaction through, most likely, the interactants' tone of voice and smoothness of communication. The transcript made more obvious differences of opinion between the interactants because the actual words used at points were, in and of themselves, much more hostile in implication than I had picked up in the audio recording. Neither analytic impression is more *true*. It was just interesting for me to experience so clearly the impact of working with the two media, and I have now an increased respect for the aspects of interaction possibly seen more clearly in transcript.

Critique of Interviews as Data

Conducting research using any form of interviewing should be informed by the growing critique in the social sciences of interviews as data. The essence of this critique is that interview data are contaminated by the research agenda. The researcher decides on the topic of the research, targets participants, designs the interview schedule, and coconstructs the interview discussion. A remedial approach is to use many of the techniques outlined in this chapter to limit the impact of the researcher on the material: open questions, nonleading questions, follow-up questions, and so on. Refining interviewing technique, however, does not tackle the more extended critique of interviews: that data coconstruction is endemic to research interviewing (and yet is often treated in analysis as if it were not) and that the interviewer's influence cannot be neutralized (and yet is often treated in analysis as if it were). Potter and Hepburn (2005) offered analysis of extracts from research interviews to substantiate this point of view. Their critique is based on a functional view of language as developed in discursive psychology (e.g., Edwards & Potter, 1992) in which the discussion generated in the interview is considered inseparable from the interview context in any meaningful way.

The strong critique of interviews as data, as illustrated by Potter and Hepburn (2005), argues for the use of naturally occurring data. These are interactions that would have occurred as they did whether or not the research had been undertaken. However, relevant interactions may be extremely difficult to obtain. Moreover, research questions often focus on understanding the meaning of experiences that need to be explored actively in a research interview, and many sophisticated methodologies have little issue with the validity of interview material per se (e.g., see Hollway, 2005; Smith, 2005). Hence, interview data are not completely undermined. The critique, however, challenges researchers to consider interview data in more complex ways and to work more reflectively and reflexively with interview material—to the benefit of interview research I am persuaded.

A middle ground might be to take critique seriously but to conceptualize interview data as still able to tell us something about the interviewee's life beyond the interview context. Analysis I conducted on the quarry corpus suggested that the interviewees interacted with the interviewers in a pattern similar to that typical between friends (but not strangers or intimates; Madill, in press). This might be the beginning of evidencing that, in general, material generated in research interviews may be transferable to other kinds of identifiable contexts. A way of working that I think is productive is to always interrogate, in a reflexive manner, the possible impact of the interview context on the data generated. This should include consideration of why people agreed to be interviewed, how the research was presented to them, and how the interview might have triggered dilemmas for participants' self-presentation. For example, Siobhan Hugh-Jones and I forefronted in our analysis of the quarry data how the act of interviewing raised implicit challenges to the interviewees' place-identity, and we examined the ways in which participants managed this discursively during interview (Hugh-Jones & Madill, 2009). We also argued that our analysis had currency beyond the interview situation because a similar tacit challenge to participants' place-identity might also occur in other kinds of interaction.

CONCLUSION

In this chapter, I have described different types of interviewing; identified and illustrated in more detail the central techniques of research interviewing (particularly with regard to the semistructured format); and discussed in depth several additional considerations such as design, ethics, recording, and transcription. I hope to have shown that interviewing research can be a rewarding endeavor. Good interviewing, however, is not easy and, in examining the central techniques, I have offered examples of where my own research interviewing could have been better. My technique has improved with practice, though, and my reminder to myself and to my students is that there is never the *perfect* interview, although there are definitely better and worse instances. I hope also to have shown that interviewing research is at an exciting methodological juncture in that we can no longer be unsophisticated

about the status of interviews as data. Creative developments are required that allow interviews to be conducted and analyzed in ways that recognize their situated and coconstructed nature and at the same time are informative on the topic of the research.

References

Anderson, H., & Goolishian, H. (1988). Human systems as linguistic systems: Preliminary and evolving ideas about the implications for clinical theory. *Family Process, 27,* 371–393. doi:10.1111/j.1545-5300.1988.00371.x

Antaki, C., Houtkoop-Steemstra, H., & Rapley, M. (2000). "Brilliant. Next question.": High-grade assessment sequences in the completion of interactional units. *Research on Language and Social Interaction, 33,* 235–262. doi:10.1207/S15327973RLSI3303_1

Antaki, C., Young, N., & Finlay, M. (2002). Shaping client's answers: Departures from neutrality in care-staff interviews with people with a learning disability. *Disability and Society, 17,* 435–455. doi:10.1080/09687590220140368

Ashworth, P. (1993). Participant agreement in the justification of qualitative findings. *Journal of Phenomenological Psychology, 24,* 3–16. doi:10.1163/156916293X00017

Atkinson, P., & Silverman, D. (1997). Kundera's *Immortality*: The interview society and the invention of the self. *Qualitative Inquiry, 3,* 304–325. doi:10.1177/107780049700300304

Babbie, E. (1995). *The practice of social research.* Belmont, CA: Wadsworth.

Bardsley, N., Wiles, R., & Powell, J. (2006). *Economic and Social Research Council National Centre for Research Methods report on a consultation exercise to identify the research needs in research methods in the UK social sciences. Stage 1 report.* Southampton, England: University of Southampton.

Bingham, W., & Moore, B. (1924). *How to interview.* New York, NY: Harper & Row.

Bloor, M. (1978). On the analysis of observational data: A discussion of the worth and uses of inductive techniques and respondent validation. *Sociology, 12,* 545–552. doi:10.1177/003803857801200307

Bloor, M. (1983). Notes on member validation. In R. M. Emerson (Ed.), *Contemporary field research: A collection of readings* (pp. 156–172). Boston, MA: Little, Brown.

Bloor, M. (1997a). On the analysis of observational data: A discussion of the worth and uses of inductive techniques and respondent validation. In M. Bloor (Ed.),

Selected writings in medical sociological research (pp. 33–44). Brookfield, VT: Ashgate.

Bloor, M. (1997b). Techniques of validation in qualitative research: A critical commentary. In G. Miller & R. Dingwall (Eds.), *Context and method in qualitative research* (pp. 37–50). London, England: Sage.

Briggs, C. L. (1998). *Learning how to ask: A sociological appraisal of the role of the interview in social science research.* Cambridge, England: Cambridge University Press.

Cotterill, P. (1992). Interviewing women: Issues of friendship, vulnerability, and power. *Women's Studies International Forum, 15,* 593–606. doi:10.1016/0277-5395(92)90061-Y

Denzin, N. K. (2001). The reflexive interview and a performative social science. *Qualitative Research, 1,* 23–46. doi:10.1177/146879410100100102

Edwards, D., & Potter, J. (1992). *Discursive psychology.* London, England: Sage.

Elliott, R., Fischer, C. T., & Rennie, D. L. (1999). Evolving guidelines for publication of qualitative research studies in psychology and related fields. *British Journal of Clinical Psychology, 38,* 215–229. doi:10.1348/014466599162782

Haug, F. (1987). *Female sexualisation: A collective work of memory.* London, England: Verso.

Hayward, C., & Madill, A. (2003). The meanings of organ donation: Muslims of Pakistani origin and white English nationals living in North England. *Social Science and Medicine, 57,* 389–401. doi:10.1016/S0277-9536(02)00364-7

Heritage, J. C., & Watson, D. R. (1979). Formulations as conversational objects. In G. Psathas (Ed.), *Everyday language: Studies in ethnomethodology* (pp. 123–162). New York, NY: Irvington.

Hester, S., & Francis, D. (1994). Doing data: The local organization of a sociological interview. *British Journal of Sociology, 45,* 675–695. doi:10.2307/591889

Hollway, W. (2005). Commentaries on Potter and Hepburn, "Qualitative interviews in psychology: Problems and possibilities." *Qualitative Research in Psychology, 2,* 312–314. doi:10.1191/1478088705qp046cm

Hollway, W., & Jefferson, A. (2000). *Doing qualitative research differently.* London, England: Sage.

Houtkoop-Steemstra, H. (1997). Being friendly in survey interviews. *Journal of Pragmatics, 28,* 591–623. doi:10.1016/S0378-2166(97)00018-0

Houtkoop-Steemstra, H. (2000). *Interaction and the standardized survey interview: The living questionnaire.*

New York, NY: Cambridge University Press. doi:10.1017/CBO9780511489457

Hugh-Jones, S., & Madill, A. (2009). "The air's got to be far cleaner here": A discursive analysis of place-identity threat. *British Journal of Social Psychology, 48,* 601–624. doi:10.1348/014466608X390256

Hyman, H. H. (1954). *Interviewing in social research.* Chicago, IL: University of Chicago Press.

Koole, T. (2003). Affiliation and detachment in interviewer answer receipts. In H. van den Berg, M. Wetherell, & H. Houtkoop-Steemstra (Eds.), *Analyzing race talk: Multidisciplinary perspectives on the research interview* (pp. 178–199). Cambridge, England: Cambridge University Press.

Lee, Y.-J., & Roth, W.-M. (2004, January). Making a scientist: Discursive "doing" of identity and self-presentation during research interviews. *Forum: Qualitative Social Research* [On-line journal], *5,* Art. 12. Retrieved from http://www.qualitative–research.net/fqs-texte/1–04/1-04leeroth-e.htm

Liddicoat, A. J. (2007). *An introduction to conversation analysis.* London, England: Continuum.

Lincoln, Y. S., & Guba, E. G. (1985). *Naturalistic inquiry.* Newbury Park, CA: Sage.

Lomax, H., & Casey, N. (1998). Recording social life: Reflexivity and video methodology. *Sociological Research Online, 3.* doi:10.5153/sro.1372

Madill, A. (2007). Survey of British Psychological Society Qualitative Methods in Psychology Section Members 2006. *British Psychological Society Qualitative Methods in Psychology Section Newsletter, 3,* 9–14.

Madill, A. (in press). Interaction in the semi-structured interview: A comparative analysis of the use and response to indirect complaints. *Qualitative Research in Psychology.*

Madill, A., & Gough, B. (2008). Qualitative research and its place in psychological science. *Psychological Methods, 13,* 254–271. doi:10.1037/a0013220

Martin, C., Godfrey, M., Meekums, B., & Madill, A. (2010). Staying on the straight and narrow. *Therapy Today, 21,* 11–14.

Mays, N., & Pope, C. (2000). Assessing quality in qualitative research. *British Medical Journal, 320,* 50–52. doi:10.1136/bmj.320.7226.50

McKeganey, N. P., & Bloor, M. J. (1981). On the retrieval of sociological descriptions: Respondent validation and the critical case of ethnomethodology. *The International Journal of Sociology and Social Policy, 1,* 58–69. doi:10.1108/eb012936

Morgan, D. L. (1997). *Focus groups as qualitative research.* London, England: Sage.

Oakley, A. (1981). Interviewing women: A contradiction in terms. In H. Roberts (Ed.), *Doing feminist research* (pp. 30–61). London, England: Routledge & Keegan Paul.

O'Key, V., Hugh-Jones, S., & Madill, A. (2009). Recruiting and engaging with people in deprived locales: Interviewing families about their eating patterns. *Social Psychological Review, 11,* 30–35.

Pomerantz, A. M. (1984). Agreeing and disagreeing with assessment: Some features of preferred/dispreferred turn shapes. In J. M. Atkinson & J. Heritage (Eds.), *Structures of social action: Studies in conversation analysis* (pp. 57–101). Cambridge, England: Cambridge University Press.

Potter, J., & Hepburn, A. (2005). Qualitative interviews in psychology: Problems and possibilities. *Qualitative Research in Psychology, 2,* 281–307. doi:10.1191/1478088705qp045oa

Puchta, C., & Potter, J. (2004). *Focus group practice.* London, England: Sage.

Schaeffer, N. C. (1991). Conversation with a purpose—or conversation? Interaction in the standardized interview. In P. P. Biemer, R. M. Groves, L. E. Lyberg, & N. A. Mathiowetz (Eds.), *Measurement errors in surveys* (pp. 367–391). New York, NY: Wiley.

Sharpe, L. (1997). Participant verification. In J. P. Keeves (Ed.), *Educational research, methodology, and measurement: An international handbook* (pp. 314–315). Oxford, England: Pergamon.

Silverman, D. (1973). Interview talk: Bringing off a research instrument. *Sociology, 7,* 31–48. doi:10.1177/003803857300700103

Smith, J. A. (1995). Semi-structured interviewing and qualitative analysis. In J. A. Smith, R. Harré, & L. Van Langenhove (Eds.), *Rethinking methods in psychology* (pp. 9–26). London, England: Sage.

Smith, J. A. (2005). Commentaries on Potter and Hepburn, "Qualitative interviews in psychology: Problems and possibilities." *Qualitative Research in Psychology, 2,* 309–311. doi:10.1191/1478088705qp046cm

Strauss, A., & Corbin, J. (1990/1998). *Basics of qualitative research.* London, England: Sage.

Timescapes. (2007). *Timescapes: An ESRC longitudinal qualitative study.* Retrieved from http://www.timescapes.leeds.ac.uk

van den Berg, H., Wetherell, M., & Houtkoop-Steemstra, H. (Eds.). (2003). *Analyzing race talk: Multidisciplinary perspectives on the research interview.* New York, NY: Cambridge University Press.

Wetherell, M., & Potter, J. (1992). *Mapping the language of racism.* London, England: Sage.

Wooffitt, R., & Widdicombe, S. (2006). Interaction in interviews. In P. Drew, G. Raymond, & D. Weinberg (Eds.), *Talk and interaction in social research methods* (pp. 28–49). London, England: Sage.

CHAPTER 15

USING DIARY METHODS IN PSYCHOLOGICAL RESEARCH

Masumi Iida, Patrick E. Shrout, Jean-Philippe Laurenceau, and Niall Bolger

Diary methods involve intensive, repeated self-reports that aim to capture events, reflections, moods, pains, or interactions near the time they occur. Although modern diary methods and designs are systematic and often highly structured, they are named after the venerable tradition among literate people of making repeated, casual, and usually private notes about their own experiences, observations, attitudes, and true feelings. One of the earliest diaries of this sort is *The Pillow Book* completed in 1002 by a Japanese court lady, Sei Shonagon. In the past century, Anne Franks's diary gave the public a first-hand account of a Jewish girl's life during World War II. Historians and literary scholars have noted that diaries provide a unique perspective on eras and events, and they often use diaries as primary sources of historical record. Two of the earliest examples of diary research date back to early 1900s. *How Working Men Spend Their Time* (Bevans, 1913) tracked how individuals used their time with repeated survey design, and *Round About Pound a Week* (Pember-Reeves, 1913) examined how poor middle-class families in London used their money through repeated interview visits.

Diary methods in psychological research build on the tradition of daily written accounts and the willingness of some persons to provide exquisite detail about their experiences on a daily basis for a specified period of time. The earliest diary study in psychological research that we know of is by Csikszentmihalyi, Larson, and Prescott (1977), who examined interpersonal contacts and interaction quality among adolescents. They structured reporting forms and response intervals to make the information more systematic than free-form diaries of the literary tradition. Larson and Csikszentimihalyi (1983) called this methodology *experience sampling methods* (also called *ecological momentary assessment* [EMA]), and their method revolutionized modern psychological research by allowing investigators to capture daily experiences in participants' own, natural environment.

In the 3 decades since this first study, diary methods have been refined in many ways, notably by embracing new technology for recording events. Diary studies have become increasingly common in a variety of fields of psychology, including social (e.g., Iida, Seidman, Shrout, Fujita, & Bolger, 2008), personality (e.g., Mroczek & Almeida, 2004), clinical (e.g., Cranford, Tennen, & Zucker, 2010), developmental (e.g., Kiang, Yip, Gonzales-Backen, Witkow, & Fuligni, 2006), organizational (e.g., Butler, Grzywacz, Bass, & Linney, 2005) and health (e.g., Skaff et al., 2009) psychology. In fact, in the past 3 years, more than 250 journal articles per year have reported diary results. In addition, texts now focus explicitly on diary methods (Bolger & Laurenceau, in press; Mehl & Conner, in press).

This work was partially supported by National Institute of Mental Health Grant R01-MH60366. We thank Lesa Hoffman for sharing details of her analyses, which allowed us to generate simulation data used in the Example 3 analysis.

DOI: 10.1037/13619-016
APA Handbook of Research Methods in Psychology: Vol. 1. Foundations, Planning, Measures, and Psychometrics, H. Cooper (Editor-in-Chief)

RESEARCH QUESTIONS USING DIARY METHODS

Proponents of diary methods point to the increased ecological validity of the data, which allow a bottom-up examination of psychological processes in the participants' daily environment. Because the reports are temporally close to the experience, they also greatly reduce retrospection bias that is associated with usual survey design. In addition to these methodological advantages, diary methods allow researchers to examine questions that are not amenable in traditional study designs. These research questions can be sorted broadly sorted into three major categories: (a) What are the average experiences of an individual, and how much do the experiences vary over time? (b) Is there systematic (e.g., linear, exponential) change in experiences across days, and do such trajectories differ across persons? (c) What processes underlie a person's changes, and how do people differ in this process?

The first question often involves between-person comparisons of quantities that are summarized over time. The second and third questions have to do with descriptions and explanations of change within person. They also allow a consideration of the sequencing of different behaviors. For example, an individual might seek social support when she or he experiences a stressor, but not when life is going smoothly. To study the structural relation of support to distress, a diary researcher might compare distress levels following support receipt to levels on days when support was not available, adjusting for the severity of the stressor.

This within-persons approach is in stark contrast to cross-sectional survey designs that involve only between-persons comparisons. For example, coping researchers who use cross-sectional data might ask whether the people who use particular coping strategy also have lower levels of distress. The problem with this approach is that the within-individual associations of coping and distress are often not the same as between-individuals associations. Tennen, Affleck, Armeli, and Carney (2000) illustrated this problem with an example of the association between drinking behaviors and anxiety. Using diary methods, they show that at the between-persons level,

people who drink alcohol to cope with a stressor tend to exhibit higher level of anxiety. Drinking is associated with decreased anxiety (within-person association is negative), which reinforces the behavior.

What Are the Average Experiences of an Individual, and How Much Do the Experiences Vary From Day to Day?

Many psychological phenomena are thought to operate as traits or relatively steady states. For example, attitudes, health experiences, or distress are often stable over days, if not longer. It is not uncommon for psychological measures to ask the respondent to summarize recent experience and attitudes into a single score when giving their reports. A typical example is the Dyadic Adjustment Scale (DAS) measure of relationship satisfaction symptoms (Spanier, 1976), which asks respondents to consider a statement such as, "Describe the degree of happiness . . . of your relationship," with responses that range from 0 (*extremely unhappy*) to 6 (*perfect*). Respondents are given no advice on how to weigh degree of the satisfaction or how to overcome recency biases.

With diary methods, it is easy not only to consider how happy you are from *extremely unhappy* to *perfect*, but also to consider variability in relationship satisfaction. These questions are addressed by aggregating the daily observation for each individual and calculating the means and variance over the multiple observations. This has several advantages over a retrospective assessment at one point in time. In particular, the responses obtained by diary methods, for example, daily questionnaires completed for a week, will minimize retrospective bias. Furthermore, because this approach allows for aggregation of responses, it will lead to a more valid and reliable measure.

The question on day-to-day variability often is overlooked by psychologists who are initially interested in stable traits of individuals. For example, many researchers are interested in ethnic identity as an individual difference that predicts cultural behavior, but Yip and Fuligni (2002) showed that the strength of ethnic identity varies in adolescents from day to day, depending on where they are and who they are with. For those who become interested in within-person variability, a descriptive analysis of day-to-day variation is a necessary step to see whether further analysis is warranted. Later in this chapter we review methods that can be used to determine if observed variation can be interpreted as reliable change, or if it is simply consistent with random measurement error.

What Is the Individual's Trajectory of Experiences Across Days, and How Do Trajectories Differ From Person to Person?

These questions are what Baltes and Nesselroade (1979) have referred to as examinations of "intraindividual change and interindividual patterns . . . of intraindividual change" (p. 3). The first part of the question concerns the temporal structure of the diary data. If there is a within-person variability of the outcome of interest, how much does the passage of time explain the variability? Simple descriptions of trends over time are often called trajectories. The simplest trajectory form to consider is a linear model, which summarizes a whole series of data points with an initial level and linear change. For example, in a study of college students preparing for the Medical College Admission Test (MCAT), Bolger (1990) observed a linear increase in anxiety leading up to the examination. Although it is beyond the scope of this chapter, it is also possible to assume nonlinear change across days. For example, Boker and Laurenceau (2007) showed that relationship intimacy followed a cyclical pattern across diary period and could be fit with a sinusoidal dynamic model that required only a few parameters for each person.

The question on interindividual differences captures whether there are between-person differences in trajectories. This is often the second step of a two-step process: (a) summarize each person's trajectory with a few parameters, and (b) study the variation of those parameters across persons. For example, in the example of the MCAT study by Bolger (1990), it is possible that some participants showed sharp increases (i.e., slopes) in anxiety as they approached

the exam day, whereas other participants showed very little increase in anxiety. The researchers can, then, try to explain what accounts for the differences in trajectories across days.

What Process Underlies a Person's Changes, and How Do People Differ in This Process?

The final research question is the most challenging, but it is also the most interesting question that can be asked when using diary designs. Diary designs can determine the antecedents, correlates, predictors, and consequences of daily experiences. Most of the diary studies are concerned with this question. For example, Gleason, Iida, Shrout, and Bolger (2008) examined the consequences of social support receipt on mood and relationship intimacy.

Furthermore, diary design allows for the examination of between-person differences in these processes, such that some people may show stronger within-person processes than others. Lastly, we can examine what contributes to the between-person differences. For example, Bolger and Zuckerman (1995) found that people who are high on neuroticism experienced more anxiety and depressed mood after interpersonal conflicts. The kinds of questions that can be asked of diary data continue to grow as new methodology develops. For example, Bollen and Curran (2004) described a class of statistical models called autoregressive latent trajectory (ALT) models that allow researchers to consider questions about trajectories while also considering how a process one day is especially affected by a process the day before.

TYPES OF DIARY DESIGNS

Traditional diary designs can be classified into two broad categories: time-based and event-based protocols (e.g., Bolger, Davis, & Rafaeli, 2003). In the first, data collection is scheduled or sampled according to the passage of time, and in the second, data collection is triggered by some focal experience of the participant. In addition to the traditional designs, there are innovative new designs such as device-contingent protocols. Recent developments in technology allow for design in which participants are prompted by an electronic device on the basis of their physiological condition or surroundings.

Time-Based Design

Time-based design serves the purpose of investigating experiences as they unfold over time. These designs include *fixed-interval* schedules, where participants report on their experiences or events at predetermined intervals, and *variable-interval* schedules, where signals prompt participants to report at either random intervals or some more complicated temporal-based pattern. In both schedules, time-based designs allow researchers to examine ongoing processes that occur over a certain period.

The most common diary design is a protocol in which participants answer a series of questions about their experiences and feelings at the same time each day, but researchers increasingly consider other time-based designs that involve several reports over the course of the day. The length of the interval between assessments should be informed by the nature of the research questions. In one of the diary studies, for example, adults with anxiety disorders and their spouses were asked to report on their relationship quality at the end of the day (Zaider, Heimberg, & Iida, 2010). In another diary study, participants reported on their mood at much shorter intervals (i.e., every 3 waking hours) because investigators were interested in within-day fluctuations of positive and negative affect (Rafaeli & Revelle, 2006; Rafaeli, Rogers, & Revelle, 2007).

One of the greatest challenges of fixed time-based design is deciding the suitable spacing between the assessments. We have already that intervals depend on the research questions, but there are other important considerations. Some processes (e.g., self-perceptions of personality traits) may not change as quickly as other processes (e.g., mood); the interval can be longer for slower processes, whereas shorter intervals may be more appropriate for processes that change quickly. Another issue is that the size of the effect can vary as a function of the length of time lag between predictor and outcome of interest (Cole & Maxwell, 2003; Gollob & Reichardt, 1987). For example, in coping research, if an outcome (e.g., anxiety) is assessed a week or a month after the coping takes place, researchers may fail to capture the coping effectiveness. Even after a general spacing of observations is chosen, investigators must consider the details of implementation. For example, a research might choose to obtain assessments at a specific time of the day (e.g., 8:00 a.m., noon, 4:00 p.m.), at a specific interval (every 3 waking hours, every evening), or in a time window when it is convenient for participants.

When considering the timing of fixed interval measurements, it is important to consider the prototypic pattern of change over time and to identify which components of change are of most interest. For example, if the investigators assess cortisol every 4 waking hours, morning rise of the cortisol (Cohen et al., 2006) will not be captured. It is also possible that an important event that occurs between assessments could be missed with longer intervals. In addition, accurate recall of events or experiences becomes challenging as the interval becomes longer, and the responses might be more susceptible to biases resulting from retrospective recall and current psychological state (Shiffman, Stone, & Hufford, 2008). On the other hand, shorter intervals introduce another set of problems. Investigators may miss some effects that take longer to manifest if assessments are collected at much shorter interval (e.g., daily) than what the process or phenomenon in question unfolds (e.g., week-to-week changes). Shorter intervals also increase participant burden, therefore, investigators may need to shorten the diary period (e.g., from 4 weeks to 1 week).

The important message here is that the intervals should complement the processes that are being investigated. For example, retrospective bias may be less of a concern if investigators are interested in examining concrete, objective events (e.g., minutes exercised) rather than subjective, transient states (e.g., Redelmeier & Kahneman, 1996). Even with the increased uses of diary methodology in psychological studies, the precise timings and dynamic processes of many phenomena are largely unknown. Investigators who choose to use fixed-interval designs, however, must pick an interval before collecting any data. When the theory cannot inform how the processes or phenomenon unfold over time, Collins (2006) has suggested choosing shorter intervals.

In the variable-interval schedule, participants are asked to report their experiences at different times, and typically the participants do not anticipate when they will be asked for the next report. The investigator might use a beeper, pocket electronic organizer, cell phone, or smartphone to indicate when reports should be given, and the timing of these probes might be genuinely random or based on a pattern that appears random to the participant. In some cases, designs might be a combination of the fixed- and variable-interval designs. For example, some assessments may be collected with random beeps throughout the day, and in addition an assessment might be scheduled at the end of each day. Signaling devices for variable-interval designs have changed with emerging technology. For example, one of the earliest diary studies used an electronic paging device to transmit random beeps five to seven times per day, at which point adolescents would fill out a paper questionnaire about current activities (Csikszentmihalyi et al., 1977).

In recent years, researchers who use a variable-interval schedule tend to be interested in online assessment (e.g., how are you feeling right now?), and this type of design could minimize the retrospective recall bias. It potentially allows for random sampling of events, experiences, and behavior throughout the day. Many studies of the EMA also fall in this category, where participants report whenever they are signaled (Shiffman et al., 2008). Variable-interval schedule may be suitable for processes that are sensitive to participant expectations in which case participants automatically answer in a particular way because of the circumstances or locations (e.g., evening diary may be filled out in the bedroom right before going to bed).

One of the disadvantages of this type of design is its reliance on a signaling device, which means that the device needs to be programmed to signal at certain times. It also requires participants to carry the signaling device. Some of the issues associated with this type of design are discussed in the section Diary Format and Technology, but the main shortcoming is that it could be disruptive to the participants' daily routines, which may lead to participants avoiding to carry the device. Because participants are sig-

naled at an interval undisclosed to them, it may also increase participant burden.

A final consideration regarding time-based diary designs is whether the time points will be considered to be distinguishable in the analysis. When all participants are surveyed at equal intervals over a fixed survey period (such as the 2 weeks before an election), then time points can be considered to be *crossed* with person. If different people are measured at different times, however, perhaps because of an event-contingent design, then the time points will be *nested* within person. Nested designs do not allow interactions of time points with other predictors to be studied as each person has a unique collection of time points. When interactions are of interest, investigators should consider using a crossed design.

Event-Based Design

When researchers are interested in rare events, such as conflicts in couples who usually are intimate and satisfied, or seizures among epileptic patients who generally are controlled, event-based designs (also known as *event-contingent* designs) are worth considering. Participants in this type of design will report every time an event meets the investigators' preestablished criterion. The most prototypical study of this kind is the Rochester Interaction Record (RIR; Reis & Wheeler, 1991). In one of their studies using RIR, Wheeler, Reis, and Nezlek (1983) asked college students to provide information on every social interaction longer than 10 minutes or more. Event-based design requires investigators to give a clear definition of the event in which they are interested. The events may go unreported or missed if the participants have ambiguous understanding of the event. One way to reduce confusion and participant burden is to choose one class of event (e.g., Laurenceau, Barrett, & Pietromonaco, 1998). Another disadvantage of this design is that there is no way to assess the compliance because it relies heavily on participants' ability to judge their situation.

Although we have presented time- and event-based designs as two separate categories, some recent studies have combined these two designs. For example, adolescents were asked to report about their environment (e.g., who they were with) whenever they experienced self-destructive thoughts or behavior and when their handheld computer beeped randomly twice a day (Nock, Prinstein, & Sterba, 2009). Combination design can markedly improve the study design, especially if the event is extremely rare, because researchers can collect daily data even if the event does not occur or goes unnoticed by the participants.

Device-Contingent Design

In addition to traditional diary entries that require participants to stop and report on their behaviors and feelings, there are now ways to collect time-intensive data that bypass explicit participant self-report. Device-contingent design has been made possible with ubiquitous adaptations of cell phones and other electronic devices running Windows and Mac operating systems. These devices often come with a set of inputs and outputs of sensory information, such as camera devices on cell phones, microphones, Bluetooth (for wireless networking of devices over short distance), accelerometer, and global positioning system (GPS). These capabilities allow researchers to collect collateral information, such as the location where the diaries are being filled out using GPS. It is also possible to have participants wear a heart-rate monitor that is synced with a diary collection device via Bluetooth.

Potential uses and combinations are limitless, but we review one possible application of this kind of design. Suppose one is interested in coping and feelings during times of stress. With a heart-rate monitor linked to the diary device, it is possible to prompt participants to report on their experiences and situations whenever their heart rate goes beyond 100 beats per minute for a sustained period of time and to collect additional information, such as a sound recording and visual record of the participant's environment. This design has a couple of advantages. The participants do not have to detect particular instances or events (especially in event-based design) because these devices trigger when sensors detect certain situations, which, to reduce participant burden, typically can be programmed to constrain the number of times a device can trigger. More important, this allows for the continuous monitoring of physiological data with little or no

awareness on the part of the participant. The designs are increasingly becoming feasible. Intille, Rondoni, Kukla, Anacona, and Bao (2003) developed a program called *context-aware experience sampling* (CAES) that allows researchers to acquire feedback from participants only in particular situations detected by sensors attached to the mobile devices.

Diary Method Design Issues

Although diary methods have important advantages over the traditional survey designs, there are some notable disadvantages as well. Some of these limitations can be minimized whereas some limitations are unavoidable. One practical concern is that most of the diary studies require a detailed training session with the participants to ensure that they understand the protocol (Reis & Gable, 2000). It is important that the participants are committed and dedicated to the participation to obtain reliable and valid data.

Diary methods often are used to capture the contexts and internal experiences of individuals as they unfold over time, so researchers ideally ask participants many questions as frequently as possible. A major obstacle of diary research is participant burden. There are three main aspects of burden: (a) length of the diary entry (e.g., 30-minute questionnaire), (b) frequency of diary responses (e.g., every 2 waking hours), and (c) length of the diary period (e.g., 9 weeks). Any one of these sources of burden can lead to subject noncompliance and attrition, and the three can have a cumulative effect on perceived burden. The challenge for any investigator is to balance the information yield with burden management. With a longer diary entry, researchers can include more questions or in-depth questions; however, less frequent responses may be more desirable to reduce participant burden. Similarly, if the participants are instructed to respond frequently (e.g., every 2 waking hours, or every time a physiological change triggers a diary entry request), researchers can closely monitor participants; however, longer diary periods may not be feasible. Broderick, Schwartz, Shiffman, Hufford, and Stone (2003) reported that using their EMA design, in which participants had to report at 10:00 a.m., 4:00 p.m., and 8:00 p.m., participant compliance significantly dropped after the 1st week. With a longer diary period design, researchers can follow participants over a longer period and capture some slow affecting processes, but frequent reports or a longer questionnaire may lead to participant burnout. In most diary studies, lengths of the diary entry are shorter than cross-sectional surveys and this presumably allows for the collection of more frequent responses or a longer diary period. Shortening protocols requires that researchers be selective about which questions to include. Shrout and Lane (in press) warned that protocols should not be shortened by relying on only one or two items per construct because this makes it difficult to distinguish reliable change from measurement error.

Like overall sample size, the length and number of assessments in a diary design involve expenditure of resources, whether money or effort. Thus, a fundamental question is how to balance the number of subjects versus the number and length of assessments. Part of the answer to the question will come from issues of feasibility—whether subjects are available and willing to submit to the diary protocol. The other part of the answer will come from considerations of the precision of statistical estimates from the study. If the diary study is being used to obtain reliable and valid measures of between-person differences, then subject sample size will dominate the design. If the study is being used to estimate the association of events that occur within person, then the number of assessments will have to be large. We comment further about the statistical issues in the section Analysis of Diary Data.

Another important issue is the degree to which the diary reporting process changes the subject experience and behavior. Diary methods are relatively new, and there is no general theory that explains when diary completion has an impact and when it does not. Several studies show changes in participants' responses over time: For example, Iida et al. (2008, Study 1) reported that the reports of support provision increased over the 28-diary period. Several effects, such as reactance and habituation, are possible, especially if the behavior is more socially reactive. On the other hand, there is evidence that reactance does not pose a threat to validity of diary questionnaires. For example, Litt,

Cooney, and Morse (1998) found that participants were more aware of the monitored behavior, but the behavior itself was not reactive. Gleason, Bolger, and Shrout (2003) also reported elevated levels of negative mood in the initial days, but the rise dissipated over 2 or 3 days. These authors argued that diaries may lead to habituation, which in turn would lead to less reactivity than other forms of survey research.

Another possibility is that participants' understanding of a particular construct becomes more complex or reliable. The repeated exposure to a diary questionnaire may enhance encoding or retrieval of relevant information. For example, in the study that observed increase in support provision (Iida et al., 2008), it is possible that participants included more behaviors that fell into the category of "social support," and it is also possible that these behaviors were more accessible at the time of diary entry. No study has directly examined this effect; however, a study by Thomas and Diener (1990) gave indirect evidence against increased complexity, at least with mood. They reported that the recall of mood did not differ following an intensive diary period. Another potential effect is that completing the diary may constrain participants' conceptualization of the domain to fit with those measured in the diary. For example, a study of social support that asks about two kinds of support (e.g., emotional and instrumental) will make participants more aware of these kinds of supportive behaviors, but they might become less sensitive to other kinds of support. Lastly, there is some evidence that a certain kind of self-reflective process has therapeutic effect (e.g., Pennebaker, 1997). This effect has not been observed with quantitative ratings, however.

A final limitation often listed for diary designs is that they produce only correlational data, and such data cannot be used to establish causal mechanisms. This limitation needs to be considered in the context of the research literature. Relative to a cross-sectional survey, diary studies allow effects to be ordered in time, and this structured data often can be used to test and reject various causal explanations. However, the same data cannot be used to establish definitively other causal explanations unless assurance can be made that the analytic model is an exact representation of the causal process, including the time lags of causal effects. As Cole and Maxwell (2003) have shown, an incorrect specification of the timing of the causal effect (e.g., how long it takes the aspirin to reduce headache pain and keep it reduced) will lead to biased and misleading causal estimates. Thus, we conclude that relative to randomized experiments, diary studies are limited, but relative to cross-sectional studies, diary studies are a giant leap forward for causal thinking. In the future, we hope that researchers will consider supplementing diary studies with experimental designs, if that is possible, to test causes and effects more definitively.

DIARY FORMAT AND TECHNOLOGY

Once investigators decide the design of the diary study that is optimal for their research questions, they must make decisions about how to collect the data. Recent technological developments have changed the way participants report, and it is also possible to collect additional information, such as the location in which the participants make a diary entry, or to integrate these reports with physiological measures. In this section, we will review the three most commonly used diary formats: paper and pencil, brief telephone interviews, and electronic (e.g., Internet-based diary, handheld computer) diary formats.

Paper-and-Pencil Format

Early diary studies tended to use paper-and-pencil format, and this format is still one of the most widely used. It remains a good option, especially when it is coupled with a device to check the compliance (e.g., Maisel & Gable, 2009). In paper-and-pencil diary studies, participants are given packets, folders, or booklets of questionnaires, one for each diary entry, and they are instructed when to fill out and return the diary. In some studies, investigators instruct participants to return the diary every week (e.g., Bolger, Zuckerman, & Kessler, 2000), whereas in other studies, they instruct participants to return the diary within 2 to 3 days (e.g., Impett, Strachman, Finkel, & Gable, 2008, Study 2). Diary entries are similar to usual survey questionnaires, but they tend to be shorter to reduce participant burden. In general, there is little effort needed to adapt survey

questions to a paper-and-pencil diary format. Another advantage of paper-and-pencil formats is that participants are familiar with the format, so it will be easier for them to fill it out. Paper-and-pencil diaries do not require complicated maintenance schedules, which is the case for some of the formats we will describe.

More and more researchers are moving away from the pencil-and-paper format because of its associated disadvantages. The main problem is participant forgetfulness with regard to compliance and diary completion. This could happen when participants fail to remember the time when they are supposed to fill out a diary entry (time-based study), or it could happen if they forget to bring the packet with them (both time- and event-based study). In either case, missed entries could lead to participants reconstructing their responses at later times, or fabricating responses. Either occurrence could undermine the advantages of the diary study. To avoid these incidences, investigators can emphasize the importance of filling out entries at specified times and that participants will not be penalized for missed entries. Asking the participants whether they filled out the entry on time may be helpful as the question suggests that some entries may not be filled out on time. It also may be useful to train the participants to use implementation intentions (Gollwitzer, 1999), which involve if–then scripts such as, "If I go to brush my teeth at bedtime, then I will complete my diary."

The bigger issue with this format is that investigators cannot track the compliance of participants without further technology. In a diary study, compliance needs to be considered both in terms of number of entries and the validity. The first one is easy to assess, but the latter is impossible to evaluate without another kind of device that tracks the compliance. For example, Rafaeli et al. (2007) asked participants to report on the time of the diary entry, and they compared their response with the information obtained from a separate computerized task. In another study, Maisel and Gable (2009) asked participants to put the entry in the envelope, seal the envelope, and stamp the date and time across the seal using an electronic stamp with a security-coded lock. Although these extra steps allow researchers to judge participant compliance, they do not ensure that participants follow the instructions. More certainty comes from using surreptitious time-stamp devices that record the time a paper diary is opened (e.g., Stone, Shiffman, Schwartz, Broderick, & Hufford, 2002), but such devices can increase the cost of a diary study considerably.

Another limitation of paper-and-pencil format is the burden of data entry. Although this is a problem with any survey study, the problem can be pronounced because of the volume of data that are collected by the participants. For example, some of us were involved in a diary study with bar examinees and their partners (Iida et al., 2008, Study 2) that collected 44 days of diary from 303 couples. This means there were total of 26,664 (303 × 2 × 44) entries over the course of the study. During the data entry process, researchers must interpret ambiguous responses (e.g., overlapping circles on Likert-type scale responses). There may be an error during data entry process even if the responses are not ambiguous. With paper-and-pencil data records, we recommend that all of the data be entered twice by independent people, but we acknowledge that this can be costly and time consuming.

Another shortcoming is that participants might make mistakes in responses. This could happen when participants do not understand the questions or when participants miss a section of the questionnaire. This limitation is, again, not limited to diary research, but it could lead to a larger problem because of the amount of data that are collected from one individual. This can be avoided if the researchers have participants come in on the 1st day of the study.

The final shortcoming of paper-and-pencil diaries is the potential breach of confidentiality. Because the previous responses may be viewed by others in their environment, participants may hesitate to be truthful in their responses. This problem could be avoided if the participants return the diary entries more frequently (e.g., Impett et al., 2008) or are asked to seal the envelope immediately after the completion (e.g., Maisel & Gable, 2009).

Since the first structured diary study, researchers have sought to overcome the limitations of paper-and-pencil formats by using pager signaling devices, (Csikszentmihalyi et al., 1977), preprogrammed

wristwatches (e.g., Litt et al., 1998), or phone calls (e.g., Morrison, Leigh, & Gillmore, 1999). Modern devices can be programmed to signal at certain times (fixed-interval schedule) or at random times (variable-interval schedule). These augmentations offer a remedy to one of the problems of paper-and-pencil format, which is participant forgetfulness. They also reduce the participant burden because they do not have to keep track of time or appropriate occasions to respond. On the other hand, these methods cannot be used for event-based sampling, and they involve additional expense.

The augmentation approach retains advantages of paper-and-pencil formats, but adds the advantage of reminding people when to fill out the questionnaires. On the other hand, participant compliance cannot be estimated by this device alone, and the cumbersome data entry remains a challenge. In addition, augmentation approaches are intrusive at times. If they are preprogrammed to signal randomly, they could go off during important meetings. This can discourage participants from carrying the signaling device, and this would defeat the purpose of the diary approach.

Brief Telephone Interviews

Another common diary data collection method is to simply call the participant using a telephone (e.g., Almeida, 2005; Waldinger & Schulz, 2010). As we discuss later in the chapter, automatic telephone systems, such as interactive voice response (IVR), also can be used to collect data. In personal telephone diary designs, trained interviewers make brief calls to the participants; the timing of the calls is determined by fixed or variable interval schedules that are set by the investigator. This data collection modality is suitable for both open-ended questions (in which participants can freely respond to a question in their own words) and questionnaires with fixed responses. The conversations can be audiotaped, or the interviewer might simply be asked to take notes and complete forms.

Brief telephone interviews have a number of advantages over paper-and-pencil dairies. One is that they can be used with persons who are not literate or who have impairments, such as visual impairments, so long as they have access to a telephone.

A second major advantage is that researchers can directly record compliance with the protocol. By actively engaging the participant, telephone interviews may help overcome participant forgetfulness and avoid any confusion about the diary protocols. In addition, researchers can allow for branching of questions (certain questions are asked depending on their previous responses), and presentation of items can be randomized to avoid habituation and boredom. If the participants provide invalid responses (out of range) or seem not to understand the questions, interviewers can correct and explain the questions. This feature of a telephone diary makes it suitable for older participants who may have trouble seeing the fonts on the diary. A key advantage of this procedure is that it involves personal interactions with the research team, and this can lead to more consistent participation and more engagement in any given interview.

Brief telephone designs also have a number of limitations. They are expensive to implement because they require hiring and training interviewers who are flexible when making calls, and who are professional in their demeanor. Almeida (2005) used a survey research center, which has professional telephone interviewers, but this can be especially costly. Participants often are not available when the interviewer makes the call, and so repeated callbacks are needed. Unless interviewers enter data directly into a computer, the same data entry costs as paper-and-pencil methods will accrue. Confidentiality may be limited especially if participants take calls at home when other family members are around, and participants may not provide honest responses to sensitive questions. Response biases may operate, and may be moderated by variables, such as ethnicity, gender of the interviewer, or other people being in the vicinity when the call is taken. The convention for most studies is to use female interviewers (ideally matched for ethnic background) because they are thought to elicit better data, and this convention is used on the basis of studies of interviewer effects in face-to-face surveys (e.g., Kane & Macaulay, 1993).

Electronic Response Formats

Electronic formats began to be used in the late 1990s (e.g., Stone et al., 1998) and have grown to be the most common design in the past decade. Uses of Internet and computer devices increased in the past decade, which also increased the comfort of participants using these formats. There are many different kinds of electronic diary data collection, but we will focus on two broad formats: fixed schedule format and variable–ambulatory assessment.

Fixed schedule formats are often implemented in diary studies that ask participants to log into a secure website and access an online questionnaire (e.g., Impett et al., 2008, Study 3). In most studies, participants are given the access code (or user name) and password to identify their data and to ensure that only one set of responses is provided. Investigators can remind the participants of the scheduled times using e-mail or phone-text messages. Some investigators provide participants with handheld devices, such as electronic personal organizers or pocket computer, which can be programmed with questions without connection to the Internet. This approach was made feasible by Barrett and Feldman-Barrett (2001), who developed a freeware diary program called ESP (Experience Sampling Program) with funding from the National Science Foundation. A third way to implement fixed schedule surveys is to ask participants to use their own phones to call a number that is associated with automatic telephone systems. These might be IVR systems that ask questions and accept verbal responses, or they might require participants to answer a few questions using their touchtone telephone pad (see Cranford et al., 2010).

Electronic response formats share many of the advantages of personal telephone interviews, and they have additional advantages. For example, they provide time stamps (and date stamps) for responses, and these give direct measures of participant compliance. By examining when responses were entered, researchers can easily identify which entries were made on time and which were not. In addition, they often allow investigators to record how long participants took to respond, and this information may be relevant to data quality and respondent burden. For example, if the participants take 3 hours to complete a diary entry that should only take 10 minutes to complete, researchers can take note.

One benefit of electronic response formats over many telephone interviews is that the responses can be easily uploaded onto the computer. This is especially true for some of the web-based questionnaires, which will put participant responses in some accessible format, such as an Excel spreadsheet or SPSS data file. This feature of electronic formats eliminates errors associated with hand entry, and it allows researchers to ensure data accuracy. Electronic formats also avoid out-of-range responses because participants are constrained to choosing a response that is available. Finally, electronic data entry avoids the contamination of the data collection by response biases and interviewer effects.

Limitations of electronic diaries are similar to those of paper-and-pencil diaries; participants must understand the diary protocol, and formatting of the web-based questionnaires must be clear. Special care must be taken to ensure that participants do not fall into a response set in which they click on responses that happen to be in the same column. Nonresponse can be a problem, but devices can be programmed to ask the respondent to check data for completeness.[1] Moreover, IVR can be scheduled to call the participant if the responses are not made within the given time frame, and researchers can contact the participants if they do not make an entry on the diary website.

Variable schedule electronic formats differ from fixed schedule formats in that participants may be asked at any time to provide information about their experience. This design requires that participants always have near them a data-entry device, such as handheld computers (i.e., palmtop computers, personal digital assistance) or a cell or smartphone. Handheld devices must be equipped with a program that allows for longitudinal data collection, such as Barrett and Feldman-Barrett's (2001) ESP software. This type of format is often coupled with variable-interval schedule designs because these devices allow for random and preprogrammed signaling. Device-contingent designs also often use this format to collect data as well. Recent technological advances, such as CAES (Intille et al., 2003), also allow for other kind of data collection, such as

physiological assessment combined with typical diary questionnaires, which assesses experiences and attitudes. For researchers who are interested in assessments of fluid and transient processes, combination signaling and time-stamp responses reduce the likelihood of participant forgetfulness or retrospective recall bias.

Final Comments on Diary Format

Whichever diary format researchers choose, it is essential that careful pilot studies be carried out with participants who are drawn from the same population that will be the target of the full study. In our experience, these pilot studies almost always lead to a refinement (and improvement) of the protocol or procedure, and they help ensure that the methods are feasible with the specific population. For example, conducting a handheld computer diary study may not be ideal for older participants who have difficulty reading small text on the screen or who may lack dexterity to properly respond.

ANALYSIS OF DIARY DATA

We consider data analysis issues related to the three questions that we posed previously: (a) What are the average experiences of an individual and how much do the experiences vary from day to day? (b) What is the individual's trajectory of experiences across days, and how do trajectories differ by person? (c) What process underlies a person's changes, and how do people differ in this process? Before addressing these substantive questions, we consider the important issue of measurement quality, particularly reliability and validity. To make these statistical considerations more concrete, we focus on two substantive examples, which we describe in the following sections.

Stress and Coping During Preparation for a Professional Licensing Exam (Bar Exam Data Set)

Several of us have been involved in a large survey of support and coping in intimate couples where one partner is a recent law school graduate who is

---

[1]Some web-based protocols can be programmed to require a response before the participant moves on, but this option often will be in violation of informed consent assurances that say that each response is voluntary.

preparing for the bar exam. As described in various places (Iida et al., 2008, Study 2; Shrout et al., 2010), we asked both examinees and partners to complete daily paper-and-pencil questionnaires for 5 weeks before the bar exam days, 2 days during the exam, and 1 week after the examination, for a total of 44 days. We asked them to report about their general mood, relationship feelings, support transactions, troublesome events, and coping strategies each evening.

Daily Affect and Blood Glucose Levels in Diabetic Patients (Diabetes Data Set)

Skaff et al. (2009) reported results from a daily diary study of 206 diabetic patients who completed diaries for 21 days and who provided blood samples so that blood glucose could be measured. We did not have access to the original data, but we simulated artificial data that show the same pattern of results as the published paper. Not only do we use these simulated data to illustrate methods of analysis, we also describe how simulation studies such as these can be useful when planning new studies.

Psychometric Analyses of Diary Data

When reporting results from experiments or cross-sectional studies, it is considered standard good practice to report the reliability of measures and to present some evidence that they are valid. Reliability is typically defined as the tendency for measures to be able to be replicated, whereas validity is defined as evidence that a measured quantity corresponds to the theoretical construct that is the focus of the research. Shrout and Lane give details about reliability theory in Chapter 33 of this volume, and Grimm and Widaman give details about validity theory in Chapter 32 of this volume.

Standard reliability designs focus on the reliability of between-person distinctions. The reliability coefficient is interpreted to be the proportion of observed measurement variation that can be attributed to true individual difference variation. The two most common approaches to estimating reliability in psychology are test–retest designs and internal consistency designs. Test–retest designs require the investigator to arrange to have second (retest) measurements taken on persons at another occasion but

before the construct of interest has changed. Under classical test theory assumptions (Crocker & Algina, 1986), a simple Pearson correlation between the test and retest provides an estimate of the reliability coefficient. Internal consistency designs allow the investigator to estimate reliability at one measurement occasion assuming that the measure is composed of two or more items. Instead of replicating the whole measurement process, the internal consistency approach asks whether different items can be considered to be replications. The most common estimate of internal consistency reliability is Cronbach's alpha. Like test–retest reliability, it measures the quality of between-person differences.

Cranford et al. (2006) showed how the internal consistency approach can be extended to the analysis of the reliability of diary data using generalizability theory (GT; Cronbach, Gleser, Nanda, & Rajaratnam, 1972). They pointed out that diary studies typically need separate reliability analyses to describe between-person differences and within-person change. The former is an extension of the usual approach of Cronbach's alpha, but it combines information from all diary days and all scale items into a summary score for each person. The reliability of change can be separately estimated whenever there are two or more items related to a concept included in each diary. For example, it will work if participants report in separate parts of the diary how (a) angry, (b) annoyed, and (c) resentful they feel. These replicate measures allow the investigator to determine whether a participant really does have a high anger day or if some apparent daily variation might be caused by sloppy reporting.

To calculate the between-person reliability and the change reliability, the investigator uses variance decomposition software that is available in most commercial systems used by psychological researchers. Variation at the item level is broken into pieces attributable to persons, time, items, Person × Item, Time × Item, and Person × Time. Shrout and Lane (in press) provided examples of syntax for calculating these effects and for combining them into the GT reliability coefficients of Cranford et al. (2006). These methods are illustrated in the next section.

Just as two versions of measurement reliability must be considered in diary studies, so too must we consider two versions of measurement validity. Self-report measures of fairly stable processes such as attachment style may show excellent patterns of validity in that they correlate highly with current relationship status and previous relationship difficulties, but such measures will not necessarily show validity when adapted to a daily diary research design. As Shrout and Lane (Chapter 33 of this volume) argue, a separate set of validity analyses are needed to describe how measures relate to other measures over time (rather than over people). Validity questions include face validity issues about whether participants agree that they can reflect on daily feelings related to stable self-constructs, convergent validity issues about whether daily variation in attachment feelings correlate with related constructs such as rejection sensitivity, and discriminant validity questions about whether the daily attachment measure can be shown to be distinct from (nonredundant with) related measures such as rejection sensitivity.

Multilevel Approaches to Diary Data

Many psychological measures are designed to represent *usual* levels of attitudes, behavior, affect, motivation, and so on. Some versions of measures specify a time window to consider (e.g., in the past month), whereas others make no mention of time. For example, the DAS (Spanier, 1976), a commonly used measure for relationship satisfaction, asks participants to report on various aspects of their relationships. To be specific, one of the items from the DAS asks the participants to "circle the dot which best describes the degree of happiness, all things considered, of your relationship." The response options are 0 (*extremely unhappy*) to 6 (*perfect*), with 3 (*happy*) as the midpoint. When responding, participants must mentally calculate and summarize their relationship over unspecified amount of time, and this summary may be biased by the participant's current state or situation. In a diary study, we can avoid these mental calculations by asking participants to report on their relationship satisfaction every day. We can then compute an estimate of usual satisfaction by taking the average of the daily relationship satisfaction reports by each person. These averages can be kept separate for members of the couple, or they can be

further averaged to represent a couple-level satisfaction value. In addition to the mean, the within-person variability can be derived by calculating the variance of the daily relationship satisfaction reports over days by each person. Calculating these descriptive statistics can be illuminating, and can inform one about both degree and volatility of relationship satisfaction. These calculations eliminate the dependent time observations through the creation of between-person summaries of the diary experience.

More formal analysis of between and within person variation can be done using multilevel modeling (also known as hierarchical linear model, random regression modeling, and general mixed models), which is described in detail by Nezlek (see Volume 3, Chapter 11, this handbook). These methods retain the dependent data in the analysis (e.g., daily reports within person), but they explicitly model the structure of the dependent data. A number of textbooks have been written about these methods (e.g., Raudenbush & Bryk, 2002; Singer & Willett, 2003), but the approach of Raudenbush and Bryk (2002) is particularly intuitive for analysis of diary data. In their language, the analysis of the repeated observations of each person is organized around a Level 1 equation, whereas the analysis of between-person differences is organized around Level 2 equations. The beauty of these models is that they both recognize some common structure to individual life experiences and allow the investigator to consider important individual differences in manifestations of this structure.

ANALYSIS EXAMPLE 1. WHAT ARE THE AVERAGE EXPERIENCES OF AN INDIVIDUAL, AND HOW MUCH DO THE EXPERIENCES VARY FROM DAY TO DAY?

The multilevel approach is well suited to address complicated questions such as we posed in the beginning of the chapter: "What are the average experiences of an individual and how much do the experiences vary from day to day?" As we illustrate in the example that follows, the question about the average experiences can be addressed by writing a simple Level 1 (within-person) model that essentially specifies a mean across diary days and nothing more. Level 2 (between-person) models allow the examination of individual differences such as gender and personality as well as dyadic variables such as time spent in the relationship. When we turn to questions about how the experiences vary from day to day, we build more complicated Level 1 models that describe how the participant's average experience is affected by such variables as time in the study, weekends, and even time-varying events such as conflicts or transient stressors. The participant-level experiences can then be summarized and analyzed using Level 2 models that compare time effects for males and females and so on. We illustrate the strengths of these methods in examples to follow.

Example Analysis Using Bar Exam Data Set

Our first example uses the bar exam data set described in the previous section. In this example,

we explore daily relationship satisfaction reported by the examinees and partners. The relationship satisfaction was measured with two items, "content" and "satisfied," and ratings were on a 5-point scale, ranging from 0 (*not at all*) to 4 (*extremely*). The form explicitly encouraged respondents to use midpoints, and thus 11 discrete rating values are possible. We first discuss how to structure diary data. Then, we provide a description of the patterns of data, and next carry out a GT analysis of between person reliability and reliability of change in satisfaction. Finally, we apply multilevel models to describe between-person differences in the context of the diary experience.

Preliminary steps. The first step of data analysis is restructuring the data set, and this step is particularly important to diary data set. In a cross-sectional study, data set is structured such that each participant's responses are entered in a single row. Figure 15.1a

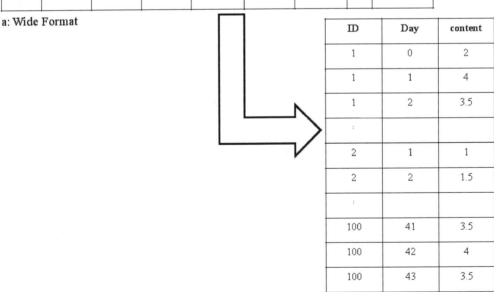

FIGURE 15.1.   Data restructuring.

shows an example such data structure (wide format), in which each row represents the means of relationship satisfaction across days (content 0–content 43). So the first person's average relationship satisfaction for the first day is 2, and this person's average satisfaction for the last day is 4. When conducting a diary analysis, it is easier to structure the data where each row represents each person's daily responses (long format); therefore, each person is going to have as many row as the diary days (see Figure 15.1b). In our current example, each participant has 44 rows of data, which means our data set consists of 4,400 rows (44 days × 100 participants).

Figure 15.2 shows a graph of four participants' trajectories of the item "content" across days. To illustrate within-person variability, we picked individuals whose average for relationship satisfaction during the diary period is 2 (*moderately*). One can see that all these participants reported higher satisfaction initially and then experienced some loss of satisfaction between Day 14 and Day 24. These are important examples of within-person change.

It is clear from Figure 15.2 that participants can differ both in level and in variability. The average score provides an efficient summary of the level and

the sample variance provides a useful index of the stability of reports. When diary data are stacked (with person-time as the unit of analysis), one can use special software features such as AGGREGATE in SPSS or PROC MEANS in SAS to calculate subject-level summaries of the diary reports. The distribution of these subject mean and variance estimates can then be studied, by calculating the mean-of-means, mean variance, and the variability of these subject-level summaries in terms of standard deviations and confidence bounds. When we do this using the examinees, we get a mean of 2.72 and a standard deviation of 0.84 with 5th and 95th percentiles of 1.28 and 3.99. For partners we find a mean of 2.73 and a standard deviation of 0.78 with 5th and 95th percentiles of 1.42 and 3.88. Within-person variance can be calculated in a similar manner. In this case, we find similar amounts of within-person variability for the members of the couple; the mean variances are 0.37 for both examinees and partners.

Once these summaries are computed, we can ask questions about their mutual associations. Is there evidence that variance of satisfaction is related to the level of satisfaction in the examinee and in the partner? Do examinees with high or low average

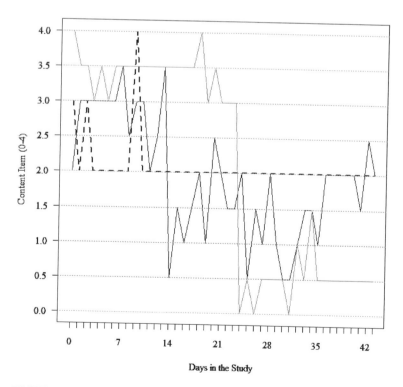

FIGURE 15.2. Trajectories of item content.

satisfaction levels have partners with similar averages? Do members of the couple tend to have similar levels of volatility of daily satisfaction during the bar exam period? These questions can be approached with simple Pearson correlations of the within person summaries. We find that there is a moderate relation between mean and variances ($r = -.29$ for examinees, and $r = -.35$ for partners). We do find substantial correlation between the mean satisfaction ratings of examinees and partners ($r = .60$), and we also find some evidence of correlation of volatility ($r = .30$).

Although these calculations are informative and easy to carry out, statisticians have suggested ways that they can be refined. The individual scores are a combination of signal and measurement error, but the above analysis treats the numbers as pure signal. Also, the simple procedure that we implemented would make use of all data, but some persons might miss a number of diary entries whereas others will make them all. This procedure does not take into account the number of days that are combined to create the summaries. Before we illustrate the multilevel statistical methods that address these issues, we first consider the question of how much error is apparent in the measurements. This requires applying the GT reliability methods of Cranford et al. (2006).

Reliability analyses using GT approach. Unlike the analyses presented so far, and the multilevel analyses that follow, the GT analysis uses variation in the item scores rather than the scale scores. Although Shrout and Lane (Chapter 33 of this volume) recommend that three or more items be used to measure important constructs, the bar exam study included only two daily items that addressed relationship satisfaction, "satisfied" and "content." On good days, both should get high scores, whereas on disappointing days both should get low scores. If the two items are discordant, the psychometric analysis concludes that error may be present.

The GT analysis states that the variability of the item scores across days and persons can be decomposed into the effects shown in Table 15.1: Person, Day, Item, Person × Day, Person × Item, Day × Item, and error. A special version of the data set was

TABLE 15.1

Results of G-Study—Examinee's Relationship Satisfaction From Bar Exam Data Set

Sources of variance	Symbol	Variance estimates	Percentage
Person	σ	0.689	58.7
Day	σ	0.007	0.6
Item	σ	0.013	1.1
Person X Day	σ	0.281	23.9
Person X Item	σ	0.020	1.7
Day X Item	σ	0.000	0.1
Error	σ	0.166	14.1
TOTAL		1.176	100.0

constructed in which each subject had two lines of data for each day, one with the response to "satisfied" and the other with the response to "content." These data were analyzed using the VARCOMP procedure of SAS, which uses as a default the MIVQUE method, which allows us to use the data with missing observations.[2] Table 15.1 shows the results of the variance composition analysis for partner's relationship satisfaction.

In this example, three components explained most of the data. The first component is the variance due to person, the second component is the variance due to Person × Day, and third component is error variation. Variance due to person tells us that there were individual differences in the amount of relationship satisfaction the examinees reported, and it explained more than half of the variation (58.7%). Variance due to Person × Day captures individual differences on change across the study period, meaning partners had different trajectories of relationship feelings across the study, and it explained slightly less than a quarter (23.9%) of the total variance. The third component is the variance due to error, which combines the random component and the variance due to Person × Day × Item, and it explained 14% of the variance.

Cranford et al. (2006) described how the estimates of the variance components can be compared to produce a number of different reliability coefficients. These make use of different variance

---

[2]A similar procedure, VARCOMP, exists in SPSS. Examples of the syntax for both SAS and SPSS can be found in Chapter 33 of this volume.

components and consider the number of days (indexed by k) and the number of items (indexed by m). In this example, we focus on only two versions of reliability, the reliability of the overall mean of item responses across days (what Cranford et al., 2006, called R_{KF}),[3] and the reliability of day-to-day changes in scale scores (R_{change}). Both of these involve calculations of variance ratios, for which the numerator contains the variance of the presumed signal, either variance due to person and person by item or variance due to person by day, and the denominator contains the variance of signal plus variance due to error. According to classical test theory, the noise variation is reduced by the number of responses (m) that are averaged. This is where the impact of including additional items is most apparent.

The reliability of the average of m item scores across k days is excellent, as can be seen from the following calculation that uses Equation 4 of Cranford et al. (2006) with results in our Table 15.1:

$$R_{KF} = \frac{\sigma^2_{PERSON} + \left(\left[\sigma^2_{PERSON*ITEM}\right]/m\right)}{\left[\sigma^2_{PERSON} + \left(\left[\sigma^2_{PERSON*ITEM}\right]/m\right) + \left(\sigma^2_{ERROR}/km\right)\right]}$$
$$= \frac{0.69 + (0.02/2)}{0.69 + (0.02/2) + [0.17/(44*2)]} = 0.99. \quad (1)$$

The reliability of daily change is estimated using Equation 5 of Cranford et al. (2006) along with the numerical values in our Table 15.1:

$$R_{Change} = \frac{\sigma^2_{PERSON*DAY}}{\left[\sigma^2_{PERSON*DAY} + \left(\sigma^2_{ERROR}/m\right)\right]}$$
$$= \frac{0.28}{0.28 + (0.17/2)} = 0.77. \quad (2)$$

This calculation suggests that about 77% of the variance of daily change is reliable variance. Although this level of reliability is often considered to be acceptable, we can note that if we had increased the number of items to, for example, $m = 4$ items, the reliability estimate (all other things being equal) would have been 0.87. In future studies, we

should take note of the possibility of improving measurement.

Multilevel analyses of diary data. Assuming the psychometric analysis suggests that there is a reliable signal in the short diary forms of measures, it is appropriate to move to substantive analyses, which are best approached using the multilevel framework introduced earlier. In a typical diary design, Level 1 units are time or event-based observations within-persons, and Level 2 units are between-persons units. Thus we say the Level 1 model is the within-person level and Level 2 is between-person level. In this chapter, we follow the notation used by Raudenbush and Bryk (2002), which distinguished the different levels rather than combining them into a reduced form equation (for alternative approach, see Fitzmaurice, Laird, & Ware, 2004).

The simplest of the multilevel equations is called a *fully unconditional* model or an intercept-only model. For the current example with examinees, the relationship satisfaction of the ith examinee at the jth time (Y_{ij}) can be represented by two equations:

$$\text{Level 1: } Y_{ij} = \beta_{0i} + \varepsilon_{ij}; \quad (3)$$
$$\text{Level 2: } \beta_{0j} = \gamma_{00} + u_{0i}. \quad (4)$$

In the Level 1 equation, Y_{ij}, relationship satisfaction of examinee i on day j, is represented as a function of the average over time points for each person, β_{0i}, and ε_{ij}, the deviation of relationship satisfaction on day j from the examinee's intercept. The parameter ε_{ij} can also be understood as the within-person residual, and its variance captures the within-person variance. The Level 2 equation models β_{0i}, the intercept for examinee i, as a function of grand mean, γ_{00}, and u_{0i}, the deviation of the examinee i from the grand mean. Thus, variance of u_{0i} captures the between-person variability of the average of relationship satisfaction across examinees in our data set. In multilevel modeling terms, γ_{00} is also known as a *fixed effect*, and u_{0i} is called a *random effect*. For partners, an identical model will be estimated with partners' data replacing the examinees' data.

---

[3]R_{KF} is named as such because it is the reliability of averages across K days for a set of fixed items. *Fixed items* mean that all participants answer the same set of items, as is the case in this example.

We can estimate this model using the MIXED procedure in SAS (syntax and partial output for examinees are available in Appendix 15.1) or other programs such as SPSS or HLM. When we do so, we get fixed effects of 2.72 for intercept for examinees and 2.73 for partners, which are identical to the estimates derived by taking the average of the averages. The variance of ε_{ij} is estimated to be 0.37 for examinees and 0.37 for partners, and the random effect of intercept is estimated to be 0.70 for examinees and 0.60 for partners. Note that the variance of the random effects from the unconditional model (0.70) is consistent with the between-person variability represented in the numerator of the formula for R_{KF} shown above. The value 0.70 is composed of the sum of overall person variance (0.689) plus one half of the person by item interaction (0.020).[4]

Assuming that the intercept estimates are normally distributed, we can estimate confidence intervals by computing a standard deviation (the square root of the variance) for each group and using the usual symmetric interval of mean $\pm (1.96*SD)$. In our study the standard deviations are 0.84 for examinees and 0.77 for partners. Using these estimates, we can calculate intervals that includes 95% of estimates ($2.72 \pm 1.96 \times 0.84$ for examinees; $2.73 \pm 1.96 \times 0.773$ for partners), which is 4.36 and 1.08 for examinees and 4.24 and 1.21 for partners. The assumption of normality is not quite correct, as is evident by the fact that the upper bounds of the confidence intervals are out of range; however, they are an approximate representation of the *spread* of intercepts in this sample.

We can build on this to look at simple between-person differences. In relationship research, we are often interested in gender differences, so we will examine how daily level of intimacy varies by the gender of the participants. To examine the gender differences, we will need to add gender as a predictor in the Level 2 question; thus the model looks as follows:

$$\text{Level 2: } \beta_{0i} = \gamma_{00} + \gamma_{01}(GENDER) + u_{0i}. \quad (5)$$

GENDER is a dummy variable that takes the value 0 for males and 1 for females. We do not find gender differences on the level of intimacy for either examinees or partners; γ_{01}(examinees) = -0.16, $SE = 0.17$; γ_{01}(partners) = 0.11, $SE = 0.16$. We can calculate 95% confidence bounds on these estimates, which are $[-0.49, 0.17]$ for examinees and $[-0.42, 0.20]$ for partners.

ANALYSIS EXAMPLE 2. EXAMINING CHANGES ACROSS TIME: WHAT IS THE INDIVIDUAL'S TRAJECTORY OF EXPERIENCES ACROSS DAYS, AND HOW DO TRAJECTORIES DIFFER FROM PERSON TO PERSON?

Once we know that there is sufficient within-person variance as evidenced by the variance of ε_{ij} in the previous model, the next simplest model is to examine whether passage of time explains the variance in outcome of interest, which in the current example is relationship satisfaction. Because these observations are ordered in time, this ordering may be relevant to one's analyses even if researchers have no direct interest in time. In most cases, responses from adjacent diary reports are more similar than reports farther apart. This idea is also known as the autoregressive effect. This could result if there is a change due to time. For example, marital satisfaction tends to decline after the birth of the first child (e.g., Hackel & Ruble, 1992). Autoregressive effect is also possible due to the factors not related to time. For example, fatigue could be driven by extra demands at work due to upcoming deadline.

Because we were able to examine the between-person variances of the intercept in the first research question, we can also estimate the between-person variances of trajectories. It is possible that some people show greater change compared with other people. If such between-person differences are observed, it is also possible to explain the differences. For example, people who are high in neuroticism may experience greater decline in marital satisfaction after the birth of the first child.

---

[4] Some programs, such as HLM, report an intraclass correlation from the multilevel model, and this is identical to R_{KF} for the fully unconditional model.

Example Analysis Using Bar Exam Data Set

We will continue to use the daily relationship satisfaction scale for this example analysis, but we will focus on partners' report for this example. Figure 15.3 shows the average of relationship satisfaction across participants for 44 days of the study, where day 35 is the first day of the examination. On average, the marital satisfaction reported by partner steadily decreases as the examinees approach the examination and starts to increase right before the examination. Formal conclusion must be withheld until we estimate a statistical model, however, because the figure is a representation of mean anxiety across participants for each day of the diary period, which ignores the within-person differences.

Modeling a linear trajectory. To formally test the within-person change in satisfaction, we must represent the multilevel model of individual change over time. We will first start with the simplest model of trajectory. Equations 6 through 8 are often referred to as *individual growth models* (Singer & Willett, 2003, pp. 49–51):

$$\text{Level 1: } Y_{ij} = \beta_{0i} + \beta_{1i} (DAY0)_j + \varepsilon_{ij}; \qquad (6)$$

$$\text{Level 2: } \beta_{0i} = \gamma_{00} + u_{0i}; \qquad (7)$$

$$\text{Level 2: } \beta_{1i} = \gamma_{10} + u_{1i}. \qquad (8)$$

In the Level 1 equation, Y_{ij}, represents satisfaction of partner i on Day j, and $DAY0$ is an indicator of the sequence of days, with the first day coded as 0. In the equation, satisfaction is modeled as a function of intercept, β_{0i}, which is the average satisfaction for partner i on Day 0, β_{1i}, which represents the linear change of anxiety for each successive day, and ε_{ij}, the deviation of satisfaction on day j from the partner's intercept after accounting for the linear effect of $DAY0$. The effects of day, in the current data set, is also a proxy variable for increased stressor because elapsed time also means approaching examination. The first Level 2 equation represents β_{0i}, the intercept for partner i on Day 0, as a function of γ_{00}, the mean of satisfaction on Day 0 after adjusting for linear change (a fixed effect), and u_{0i}, the deviation of the partner i from the mean (a random effect). The second Level 2 equation models β_{1i}, time slope for partner i, as a function of γ_{10}, fixed effect of the time slope, and u_{1i}, the deviation of the partner i from the average time slope (random effect of $DAY0$). In this model, because there are two random

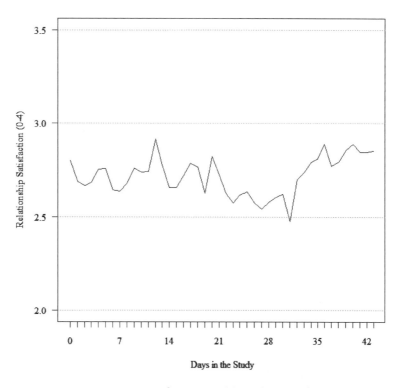

FIGURE 15.3.   Trajectory of average relationship satisfaction for partners.

effects, we can ask whether they are correlated. When random effects are positively correlated, it implies that as initial level increases, the slope also increases (e.g., partners who have high initial level of satisfaction also increases more with each passage of day); negative correlation means that as the initial level increases, the slope decreases (e.g., people who have high initial level of satisfaction show a decline in satisfaction across days).

Another important detail when modeling time is the specification of residual error structures (ε_{ij},), also known as the residual variance covariance matrix, because there is a statistical consequence for not specifying a proper structure (Greene & Hensher, 2007). In diary data, *residual error* refers to the unexplained variance associated with the particular day, and we expect errors to be correlated over time *within* people. There are several ways to structure the residual variance covariance matrix; however, we focus only on autoregressive structure. In an autoregressive model, the errors are structured as follows:

$$\begin{bmatrix} \sigma^2 & \sigma^2\rho & \sigma^2\rho^2 & \sigma^2\rho^3 & \cdots \\ \sigma^2\rho & \sigma^2 & \sigma^2\rho & \sigma^2\rho^2 & \cdots \\ \sigma^2\rho^2 & \sigma^2\rho & \sigma^2 & \sigma^2\rho & \cdots \\ \sigma^2\rho^3 & \sigma^2\rho^2 & \sigma^2\rho & \sigma^2 & \cdots \\ \vdots & \vdots & \vdots & \vdots & \ddots \end{bmatrix}. \quad (9)$$

The autoregressive model is relatively efficient because it estimates only two parameters, σ and ρ. For those who are interested in other types of residual structures, please see Singer (1998).

In the example at hand, the fixed effects of the intercept is 2.76, which implies that the average relationship satisfaction on Day 0 (see Appendix 15.2). The fixed effect of Day is –0.001, which means that satisfaction decreases over the entire study period by approximately 0.001 unit each day, but in this case, the effect is not significant. The random effect of intercept is estimated to be 0.52, so if we take the square root of the estimate ($\sqrt{0.52} = 0.72$), it will give us the standard deviation of intercepts in our sample. Again, we can calculate the 95% confidence interval of intercepts, and we get 1.35 and 4.17. Similarly, the random effect of day is estimated

to be 0.0001, which corresponds to a standard deviation of 0.01, and the 95% confidence interval of linear change is –0.02 and 0.02.

Thus far, we have not paid attention to the significance test of either fixed effects or random effects. The significance tests of fixed effects are tested by *t* test with degree of freedom approximated by Satterthwaite estimates, which recognize that several different variances are being estimated from the same data (Raudenbush & Bryk, 2002). The significance tests of random effects are slightly more complex. The Wald *z* test used to test random effects are known to be conservative, and methodologists recommend that differences in the deviance (–2 log likelihood, or –2LL) be used instead (Singer & Willett, 2003, pp. 116–117). In our example, the –2LL of full model is 7876.3, and the –2LL of the model without the random intercept is 8211.6. Therefore, the likelihood ratio difference is 335.3, and this value is significant at *p* = .001 level using the chi-square test with degree of freedom of 1. Similarly, the random effect of *DAY* is significant at *p* = .001 level, but remember that the fixed effect of *DAY* is not significant. In other words, there is no linear change in the relationship satisfaction *on average*, but there is significant variation around this effect, such that some people show a slight decline (–0.02 calculated in the preceding paragraph) yet other people show a slight increase (0.02) across the study period. The covariance between the random effects of intercept and effect of *DAY* are not significant. Because the random effects of intercept and *DAY* are significant, we know that there is systematic variation in these effects, which will be explored later.

Modeling a quadratic trajectory. The pattern in Figure 15.3 suggests a curvilinear trajectory of relationship satisfaction across days, so we will now test the quadratic effect of within-person change in satisfaction. The following equations capture the quadratic trajectory of satisfaction:

$$\text{Level 1: } Y_{ij} = \beta_{0i} + \beta_{1i}(DAYc)_j + \beta_{2i}(DAYc^2)_j + \varepsilon_{ij}, \quad (10)$$

$$\text{Level 2: } \beta_{0i} = \gamma_{00} + u_{0i}, \quad (11)$$

$$\text{Level 2: } \beta_{1i} = \gamma_{10} + u_{1i}, \text{ and} \quad (12)$$

$$\text{Level 2: } \beta_{2i} = \gamma_{20} + u_{2i}. \quad (13)$$

This model is similar to the prior set of equations, but with an inclusion of the squared day effect in Level 1 equation and additional equation in Level 2. Another difference from the prior equation is that *DAYc* is now centered on 15th day, which means that the 15th day is coded as 0, whereas *DAY0* was centered on the first day of the study in the linear trajectory model. The 15th day corresponds to 2 weeks before the examination. β_{2i} is the estimate for quadratic effect, and it is modeled as a function of γ_{20}, fixed effect of the quadratic effect and u_{1i}, the deviation of the examinee *i* from the average quadratic effect (random effect of *DAYc²*).

Table 15.2 summarizes the results of this quadratic trajectory analysis. The interpretation of intercept changes from the previous model. Instead of representing the adjusted value on the first day, and it is now the adjusted average level of satisfaction on Day 15, which is 2.69. The estimate of day also changes from previous model, and this is the linear change of satisfaction on Day 15. Therefore, marital satisfaction is decreasing by 0.009 unit on Day 15.

TABLE 15.2

Results of Analysis Examining Quadratic Change of Relationship Satisfaction

Effects		
Fixed effects	γ^a	*SE*
Intercept (level on Day 10)	2.688**	0.081
DAYc (linear change)	−0.009**	0.003
DAYc² (quadratic change)	0.001**	0.0001
Random effects[b]	τ	**LR**
Level 2 (between-person)		
Intercept	0.627***	762.9
DAY (linear change)	0.001***	45.1
DAYc² (quadratic change)	0.000	1.0
Level 1 (within-person)		
Autocorrelation	0.297***	438.7
Residual	0.333[a]	NA

Note. LR = likelihood ratio; NA = not applicable.
[a]The model without Level 1 residual variance is implausible; therefore, the deviance difference cannot be calculated. [b]Because the model that had covariances of random effects was unstable, we only estimated the random effects.
**$p < .01$. ***$p < .001$.

We also find that *DAYc²* is significant, which suggests that the satisfaction follows a quadratic pattern.

Moderation effect. We can explore how individuals vary in the linear and quadratic effects. This is especially useful when we have a theory about how to explain systematic individual differences. In our example, we chose relationship closeness as measured by Inclusion of Others (IOS) scale (Aron, Aron, & Smollan, 1992) as a potential source of the individual difference (e.g., moderator). IOS is a single-item, pictorial measure of relationship closeness that ranges from 1 (*two circles are barely touching*) to 7 (*two circles are highly overlapped*). We thought that persons who included their partner as part of their self-concept would be more influenced by the partner's stressful bar exam experience. To examine the moderating effect of IOS, we ran a cross-level interaction model, where centered IOS (IOSc) was included as predictors in Level 2 equations. The Level 1 equation remained the same as prior model, and the Level 2 equations were as follows:

$$\text{Level 2: } \beta_{0i} = \gamma_{00} + \gamma_{01}(IOSc) + u_{0i}, \qquad (14)$$

$$\text{Level 2: } \beta_{1i} = \gamma_{10} + \gamma_{11}(IOSc) + u_{1i}, \text{ and} \qquad (15)$$

$$\text{Level 2: } \beta_{2i} = \gamma_{20} + \gamma_{21}(IOSc) + u_{2i}. \qquad (16)$$

The first Level 2 equation models β_{0i}, the intercept for partner *i* on Day 0, as a function of γ_{00}, fixed effect of intercept; γ_{01}, fixed main effect of IOSc; and u_{0i}, the deviation of the partner *i* from the grand mean. In all of these models, IOSc was centered around 5.19, the mean in the sample. The second Level 2 equation models β_{1i}, the time slope for partner *i*, as a function of γ_{10}, fixed effect of the time slope; γ_{11}, fixed moderating effects of IOS of time on relationship satisfaction; and u_{1i}, the deviation of the partner *i* from the average time slope (random effect of DAYc). The third Level 2 equation models β_{2i}, the quadratic effect for partner *i*, as a function of γ_{20}, fixed effect of the quadratic effect; γ_{11}, fixed moderating effects of IOS of quadratic effect on relationship satisfaction; and u_{1i}, the deviation of the partner *i* from the average time quadratic effect (random effect of *DAYc²*).

We find that IOS is a significant between-person predictor of marital satisfaction such that people who are high on IOS tend to have higher levels of anxiety on the 15th day of the study by 0.33 units (γ_{01} = 0.33, SE = 0.05). Therefore, this gives some evidence that IOS explains the variability (random effects) across participants in our sample. IOS was also a marginally significant moderator of the quadratic effect (γ_{03} = –0.0002, SE = 0.0001), such that partners who were higher on IOS tended to show a smaller quadratic effect (see Figure 15.4), which suggests that their daily marital satisfaction is less affected by the impact of the bar examination. As for the day effect, IOS does not moderate the effect (γ_{02} = 0.002, SE = 0.002). In other words, IOS does not explain the variation in the effects of day across partners.

ANALYSIS EXAMPLE 3. PREDICTING CHANGE AND DAILY PROCESS: WHAT PROCESS UNDERLIES A PERSON'S CHANGES, AND HOW DO PEOPLE DIFFER IN THIS PROCESS?

Examining changes across time is interesting, but psychological researchers may be more interested in the predictors of the changes. Diary methods are a great way to model the proposed causal relationship as a temporal within-person process if the temporal measurement corresponds to when causes and effect change. Diary design does not permit inferences as strong as that of experimental designs, however, because experimental conditions are experienced in temporal order, which leaves open the possibility of (a) carryover effect from the previous experiences; (b) order effects, in which the particular order of experiences moderates the effects of interest; or (c) expectancy effects, in which previous experience changes the meaning of subsequent experience.

There are four ways in which diary methods can strengthen causal inferences. One is that diary studies differentiate between-person and within-person associations. Many within-person variables collected in diary data, such as mood, vary both within and between persons. Within-person associations often are referred to as using the person as his or her own control, and it allows us to treat results as pertaining to the relationship between within-person changes in X and Y. In practical terms, we can differentiate

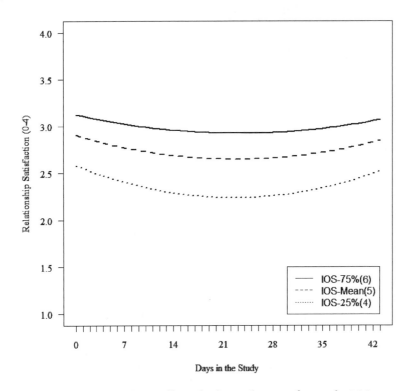

FIGURE 15.4. Quadratic effect of relationship satisfaction by IOS showing that higher IOS scores are associated with larger quadratic effects than lower IOS scores.

two sources of variation by including each person's mean value of X. Second is by including elapsed time because there could be an effect of time even if that is not the main research questions. For example, if the diary period is longer, participant boredom or habituation may affect the levels and interrelationships among variables. Third, analysis should accurately reflect the temporal structure of cause–effect relationship, which also includes having measurements at accurate times. Last, additional confounding within-person variables need to be taken into account. These could include lagged variables of Y that could be acting as an alternative explanation of the relationships that one is examining.

Example Analysis Using Health Psychology Data

To illustrate how we can examine the process underlying how a person changes, we use the simulated health psychology data on the basis of the study by Skaff et al. (2009). In this data set, we have negative affect (*NA*) and waking blood glucose from 207 Type 2 diabetic patients for 21 days. As in the previous two examples, we use multilevel modeling to examine the association between prior day affects and waking blood glucose measure. Before we run any analysis, it is important to calculate means of negative and positive affect for each person, and they will be used to derive the within-person centered variable of negative affect, which in turn allows us to estimate the within-person effect. As described, this approach allows us to differentiate the within- and between-person associations. The within-person effects can be understood as the effects of the negative affect that is greater than the person's average.

The model is represented in the following equations:

$$\text{Level 1: } Y_{ij} = \beta_{0i} + \beta_{1i}(NA_{j-1} - MeanNA_i) + \varepsilon_{ij}, \quad (17)$$

$$\text{Level 2: } \beta_{0i} = \gamma_{00} + \gamma_{01}(MeanNA)_i + u_{0i}, \text{ and} \quad (18)$$

$$\text{Level 2: } \beta_{1i} = \gamma_{10} + u_{1i}. \quad (19)$$

In the Level 1 equation, Y_{ij}, blood glucose of person i on day j, is modeled as a function of intercept, β_{0i} (the average blood glucose for person i), β_{1i} (within-person effect of *NA* from previous day), and

ε_{ij} (the deviation of negative mood on Day j). The lagged effects of *NA*, β_{1i}, addresses the main research questions in this example—the within-person associations of previous day negative affect and waking blood glucose. In other words, when the participants experience negative affect more than they usually do, how much the blood glucose changes the following morning.

The Level 2 equation models β_{0i}, the intercept for person i on Day 0, as a function of γ_{00}, fixed effects of intercept (grand mean of blood glucose on Day 0); γ_{01}, between-person effect of mean negative affect (*MeanNA*) for person i; and u_{0i}, the deviation of the person i from the grand mean. The second Level 2 equation models β_{1i}, effect of *NA* for person i, as a function of γ_{10}, average effect of *NA* for all participants in this sample (fixed effect of *NA*), and u_{1i}, the deviation of the person i from the average effect of *NA* (random effect of *NA*).

Table 15.3 summarizes the results of the analyses examining affect and blood glucose. The fixed effect of the intercept is 4.900, which is the estimate of the average blood glucose on the first day of the study (Day 0). The fixed within-person effect of NA is 0.022, which means that when participants

TABLE 15.3

Results of Analysis Predicting Blood Glucose

Effects		
Fixed effects	γ^a	*SE*
Intercept (level on Day 0)	4.900**	0.018
Negative affect (previous day)	0.022**	0.004
Mean negative affect (between-person)	0.085**	0.030
Random effects	τ	**LR**
Level 2 (between-person)		
Intercept	0.064***	26.8
Negative affect (previous day)	0.001	0.0
Intercept—negative affect covariance	−0.001***	20.2
Level 1 (within-person)		
Residual	0.030[a]	NA

Note. LR = likelihood ratio; NA = not applicable.
[a]The model without Level 1 residual variance is implausible; therefore, the deviance difference cannot be calculated.
**$p < .01$. ***$p < .001$.

experience more negative affect than usual, their glucose increases by approximately 0.02 unit the following day. The between-person effect of mean negative affect is 0.085, which means that individuals who, on average, have high negative affect across the diary period tend to have higher waking blood glucose.

DIARY EXTENSIONS

Diary methods provide us with rich data on psychological processes as they unfold. The statistical analyses we have reviewed so far are only a starting point. More advanced methods are available in Bolger and Laurenceau (in press) and Mehl and Conner (in press) as well in the current literature. In the next section, we mention some recent developments and speculations about future directions.

Dynamic Systems Model

One of the ways diary data can be examined is by using dynamic systems models, also known as dynamical systems models (see Volume 3, Chapter 16, this handbook). Dynamic systems, generally defined, are self-contained sets of elements that interact in complex, often nonlinear ways to form coherent patterns, with an underlying assumption that these systems regulate themselves over time. One of the key concepts is the idea of stationary attractor points (or equilibrium state), a set of points that regulates the system. The idea of stationary attractor points translates well into psychological terms; it can be thought of as the norm or the average state. When the oscillation can be described by a sine or cosine function, a mathematical property states that the rate of acceleration of the function (second derivative) is a linear combination of the rate of change (first derivative) and level of the function (see Boker, 2001, for a detailed explanation). Gottman, Murray, Swanson, Tyson, and Swanson (2002) applied more complicated dynamic models to investigate marital interaction in their book *The Mathematics of Marriage: Dynamic Linear Models*. Dynamic models can be appealing analytic techniques especially for researchers who collect physiological data because these data tend to exhibit cyclical patterns and abundant data are collected

from the individual. Applications dynamical systems modeling (second-order linear oscillator modeling) to dyadic diary data can be found in Boker and Laurenceau (2006, 2007).

Categorical Variables

In this chapter, we have focused on analysis for continuous outcomes; however, many of the variables that psychologists are interested in may be categorical or counts (e.g., whether support was received, whether a conflict occurred, number of alcoholic beverages consumed). For these types of outcomes, the analytic strategy described in this chapter will lead to misspecified models. Fortunately, however, a number of appropriate alternative methods can be considered, including nonlinear multilevel models. These are readily available in statistical packages like HLM and SAS (GLIMMIX and NLMIXED procedures). For details on these types of multilevel analyses, please see Bolger and Laurenceau (in press) and Hox (2010).

Multivariate Multilevel Analysis

Diary researchers typically ask participants to report on a variety of behaviors, feelings, and attitudes over time and are interested in how these processes operate in a multivariate system. For example, Gleason et al. (2008) wondered how the costs of daily support on anxiety could be reconciled with the benefits of daily support on relationship closeness. In the context of multilevel analyses, they used a multivariate approach that has been described in detail by Raudenbush and Bryk (2002). This approach involves a treating the different outcomes as if they were repeated measures, and the data on the different outcomes are stacked together. A special provision is needed, however, to recognize that each outcome has its own set of fixed and random effects. Multivariate systems can also be considered in the context of structural equation methods. Bollen and Curran (2004) described a class of models called ALT models that will be of special interest to researchers who have relatively few diary measurements.

Diaries in Dyads, Families, and Groups

One of the most growing types of diary is the diary in which more than one person from a dyad (e.g., married couples), families (e.g., parents and eldest children), and groups (e.g., students in classrooms) participate in the study. In these types of data, there are two different sources of nonindependence: Observations are repeated within persons, and persons are nested within dyads, families, or groups. To account for both types of nonindependence, it is sometimes useful to use three-level multilevel models for groups greater than three people. For the smaller groups (dyads and three-member family groups with prespecified roles), a two-level multilevel model is sufficient in which the lowest level represents the multivariate repeated measures mentioned in the previous section (Bolger & Laurenceau, in press; Bolger & Shrout, 2007; Laurenceau & Bolger, 2005). Other books have been dedicated to analyses of nonindependent data (e.g., Kenny, Kashy, & Cook, 2006).

Simulation as a Tool for Diary Researchers

When planning a diary study, how can one determine the sample size of persons and time points, and what is the trade-off between increasing either kind of *n*? Many diary researchers first carry out a statistical simulation study, using software such as SAS or Mplus (Muthén & Muthén, 2010). These simulations create data that are like what you hypothesize the process to be, and analyses of these artificial data give the researcher some idea of how small the standard errors get as the number of participants or time points increase. To carry out a simulation, one needs to go through six steps: (a) Write down a Level 1 statistical model for the within-subject responses, (b) write down a series of Level 2 statistical models that describe how the subjects differ in their within-subject process, (c) consult the literature to identify plausible effect sizes for the fixed effects, (d) consult the literature to identify plausible values to represent variability of within- and between-subject processes, (e) write a program to simulate data according to the model from Steps a through d, and (f) analyze the simulated data to determine how precise the results are. We have provided an example of simulated health data. Although we had access to an interesting published study (Skaff et al., 2009), we did not have access to the original data. From the published results and some personal communication with one of the authors, we were able to generate data that resembled daily glucose and mood patterns. We provide this simulation syntax as an example online (see https://sites.google.com/a/asu.edu/using-diary-methods-in-psychological-research).

If one hopes to carry out diary studies with participants who have some rare condition, it may be difficult to recruit more than a dozen or so subjects. Not only will statistical power be challenging in this case, but also the usual inferential methods of multilevel models may be misleading. Much of the statistical theory for multilevel models assumes large samples. In cases such as this, simulation studies can be used to study the impact of sample size on both power and the usual control of Type I error. If small sample data are available, one could use simulation methods to carry out resampling studies of those data. For an example of a simulation-based power analysis for diary data, please see Bolger, Laurenceau, and Stadler (in press).

CONCLUSION

Although relatively new to psychology, diary study designs are changing the way psychologists think about psychological process. They help survey workers determine when retrospective memory is problematic, and when it can be counted on. When spaced over months, they can provide invaluable information about development in youth and adolescents. Diary accounts provide new sources of compelling data for health psychologists, and they allow stable individual differences to be distinguished from meaningful change. We predict that the number of diary studies will continue to accelerate in the literature.

Nonetheless, there are many ways that diary designs will continue to be refined. Technological advances, particularly in microrecording devices, will open new doors for noninvasive measurement. Statistical methods will continue to be developed to deal with the complicated temporal patterns in nonstationary data. New methods for small samples and for complicated dependent data will be proposed. For those interested in making an impact on research methodology, the area of diary studies is fruitful ground.

Appendix 15.1
Syntax for SAS

```
PROC MIXED covtest noclprint;
CLASS couple;
MODEL content = /s;
RANDOM int / SUBJECT = couple TYPE = vc;
RUN;
```

PARTIAL OUTPUT

Covariance Parameter Estimates

Cov Parm	Subject	Estimate	Standard Error	Z Value	Pr > Z
Intercept	couple	0.6986	0.1005	6.95	< .0001
Residual		0.3706	0.007	993	46.37	< .0001

Solution for Fixed Effects

Effect	Estimate	Standard Error	DF	t value	PR > |t|
Intercept	2.7189	0.08409	99	32.33	< .0001

Appendix 15.2
Syntax for SAS

```
PROC MIXED covtest noclprint DATA = dchap4;
CLASS couple day;
MODEL pcontent = day0 /s;
RANDOM int day0 / SUBJECT = couple TYPE = UN
REPEATED day/SUBJECT = couple TYPE = ar(1);
TITLE "Linear Trajectory Analysis - Partners";
RUN;
```

PARTIAL OUTPUT

Covariance Parameter Estimates

Cov Parm	Subject	Estimate	Standard Error	Z Value	Pr > Z
UN(1,1)	couple	0.5177	0.08232	6.29	< .0001
UN(2,1)	couple	0.000153	0.001163	0.13	0.8950
UN(2,2)	couple	0.000126	0.000032	3.94	< .0001
AR(1)	couple	0.3442	0.01592	21.63	< .0001
Residual		0.3581	0.009352	38.29	< .0001

Fit Statistics
-2 Res Log Likelihood 7876.3
AIC (smaller is better) 7886.3
AICC (smaller is better) 7886.3
BIC (smaller is better) 7899.3
Solution for Fixed Effects

Effect	Estimate	Standard Error	DF	t Value	Pr > |t|
Intercept	2.7588	0.07606	99	36.27	< .0001
day0	-0.00116	0.001492	99	-0.78	0.4402

References

Almeida, D. M. (2005). Resilience and vulnerability to daily stressors assessed via diary methods. *Current Directions in Psychological Science, 14*(2), 64–68. doi:10.1111/j.0963-7214.2005.00336.x

Aron, A., Aron, E. N., & Smollan, D. (1992). Inclusion of other in the self scale and the structure of interpersonal closeness. *Journal of Personality and Social Psychology, 63*, 596–612. doi:10.1037/0022-3514.63.4.596

Baltes, P. B., & Nesselroade, J. R. (1979). History and rationale of longitudinal research. In J. R. Nesselroade & P. B. Baltes (Eds.), *Longitudinal research in the study of behavior and development* (pp. 1–39). New York, NY: Academic Press.

Barrett, L. F., & Feldman-Barrett, D. J. (2001). An introduction to computerized experience sampling in psychology. *Social Science Computer Review, 19*, 175–185. doi:10.1177/089443930101900204

Bevans, G. E. (1913). *How workingmen spend their time* (Unpublished doctoral thesis). Columbia University, New York, NY.

Boker, S. M. (2001). Differential models and "differential structural equation modeling of intraindividual variability." In L. M. Collins & A. G. Sayer (Eds.), *New methods for the analysis of change* (pp. 5–27). New York, NY: Oxford University Press. doi:10.1037/10409-001

Boker, S. M., & Laurenceau, J.-P. (2006). Dynamical systems modeling: An application to the regulation of intimacy and disclosure in marriage. In T. A. Walls & J. L. Schafer (Eds.), *Models for intensive longitudinal data* (pp. 195–218). New York, NY: Oxford University Press.

Boker, S. M., & Laurenceau, J.-P. (2007). Coupled dynamics and mutually adaptive context. In T. D. Little, J. A. Bovaird, & N. A. Card (Eds.), *Modeling contextual effects in longitudinal studies* (pp. 299–324). Mahwah, NJ: Erlbaum.

Bolger, N. (1990). Coping as a personality process: A prospective study. *Journal of Personality and Social Psychology, 59*, 525–537. doi:10.1037/0022-3514.59.3.525

Bolger, N., Davis, A., & Rafaeli, E. (2003). Diary methods: Capturing life as it is lived. *Annual Review of Psychology, 54*, 579–616. doi:10.1146/annurev.psych.54.101601.145030

Bolger, N., & Laurenceau, J.-P. (in press). *Diary methods.* New York, NY: Guilford Press.

Bolger, N., Laurenceau, J.-P., & Stadler, G. (in press). Power analysis for intensive longitudinal measurement designs. In M. R. Mehl & T. Conner (Eds.), *Handbook of research methods for studying daily life.* New York, NY: Guilford Press.

Bolger, N., & Shrout, P. E. (2007). Accounting for statistical dependency in longitudinal data on dyads. In T. D. Little, J. A. Bovaird, & N. A. Card (Eds.), *Modeling contextual effects in longitudinal studies* (pp. 285–298). Mahwah, NJ: Erlbaum.

Bolger, N., & Zuckerman, A. (1995). A framework for studying personality in the stress process. *Journal of Personality and Social Psychology, 69*, 890–902. doi:10.1037/0022-3514.69.5.890

Bolger, N., Zuckerman, A., & Kessler, R. C. (2000). Invisible support and adjustment to stress. *Journal of Personality and Social Psychology, 79*, 953–961. doi:10.1037/0022-3514.79.6.953

Bollen, K. A., & Curran, P. J. (2004). Autoregressive Latent Trajectory (ALT) models: A synthesis of two traditions. *Sociological Methods and Research, 32*, 336–383. doi:10.1177/0049124103260222

Broderick, J. E., Schwartz, J. E., Shiffman, S., Hufford, M. R., & Stone, A. A. (2003). Signaling does not adequately improve diary compliance. *Annals of Behavioral Medicine, 26*, 139–148. doi:10.1207/S15324796ABM2602_06

Butler, A. B., Grzywacz, J. G., Bass, B. L., & Linney, K. D. (2005). Extending the demands-control model: A daily diary study of job characteristics, work-family conflict and work-family facilitation. *Journal of Occupational and Organizational Psychology, 78*, 155–169. doi:10.1348/096317905X40097

Cohen, S., Schwartz, J. E., Epel, E., Kirschbaum, C., Sidney, S., & Seeman, T. (2006). Socioeconomic status, race, and diurnal cortisol decline in the coronary artery risk development in young adults (CARDIA) Study. *Psychosomatic Medicine, 68*, 41–50. doi:10.1097/01.psy.0000195967.51768.ea

Cole, D. A., & Maxwell, S. E. (2003). Testing mediational models with longitudinal data: Questions and tips in the use of structural equation modeling. *Journal of Abnormal Psychology, 112*, 558–577. doi:10.1037/0021-843X.112.4.558

Collins, L. M. (2006). Analysis of longitudinal data: The integration of theoretical model, temporal design, and statistical model. *Annual Review of Psychology, 57*, 505–528. doi:10.1146/annurev.psych.57.102904.190146

Cranford, J. A., Shrout, P. E., Iida, M., Rafaeli, E., Yip, T., & Bolger, N. (2006). A procedure for evaluating sensitivity to within-person change: Can mood measures in diary studies detect change reliably? *Personality and Social Psychology Bulletin, 32*, 917–929. doi:10.1177/0146167206287721

Cranford, J. A., Tennen, H., & Zucker, R. A. (2010). Feasibility of using interactive voice response to monitor daily drinking, moods, and relationship processes on a daily basis in alcoholic couples. *Alcoholism: Clinical and Experimental*

Research, 34, 499–508. doi:10.1111/j.1530-0277-.2009.01115.x

Crocker, L. M., & Algina, J. (1986). *Introduction to classical and modern test theory.* New York, NY: Holt, Rinehart, and Winston.

Cronbach, L. J., Gleser, G. C., Nanda, H., & Rajaratnam, N. (1972). *The dependability of behavioral measurements: Theory of generalizability for scores and profiles.* New York, NY: Wiley.

Csikszentmihalyi, M., Larson, R., & Prescott, S. (1977). Ecology of Adolescent Activity and Experience. *Journal of Youth and Adolescence, 6*, 281–294. doi:10.1007/BF02138940

Fitzmaurice, G. M., Laird, N. M., & Ware, J. H. (2004). *Applied longitudinal analysis.* Hoboken, NJ: Wiley-Interscience.

Gleason, M. E. J., Bolger, N. P., & Shrout, P. E. (2003, February). *The effects of study design on reports of mood: Understanding differences between cross-sectional, panel, and diary designs.* Poster presented at the annual meeting of the Society for Personality and Social Psychology, Los Angeles, CA.

Gleason, M. E. J., Iida, M., Shrout, P. E., & Bolger, N. P. (2008). Receiving support as a mixed blessing: Evidence for dual effects of support on psychological outcomes. *Journal of Personality and Social Psychology, 94*, 824–838. doi:10.1037/0022-3514-.94.5.824

Gollob, H. F., & Reichardt, C. S. (1987). Taking account of time lags in causal models. *Child Development, 58*, 80–92. doi:10.2307/1130293

Gollwitzer, P. M. (1999). Implementation intentions—Strong effects of simple plans. *American Psychologist, 54*, 493–503. doi:10.1037/0003-066X.54.7.493

Gottman, J. M., Murray, J. D., Swanson, C. C., Tyson, R., & Swanson, K. R. (2002). *The mathematics of marriage: Dynamic nonlinear models.* Cambridge, MA: MIT Press.

Greene, W. H., & Hensher, D. A. (2007). Heteroscedastic control for random coefficients and error components in mixed logit. *Transportation Research Part E: Logistics and Transportation Review, 43*, 610–623.

Hackel, L. S., & Ruble, D. N. (1992). Changes in the marital relationship after the first baby is born: Predicting the impact of expectancy disconfirmation. *Journal of Personality and Social Psychology, 62*, 944–957. doi:10.1037/0022-3514.62.6.944

Hox, J. J. (2010). *Multilevel analysis: Techniques and applications* (2nd ed.). Mahwah, NJ: Erlbaum.

Iida, M., Seidman, G., Shrout, P. E., Fujita, K., & Bolger, N. (2008). Modeling support provision in intimate relationships. *Journal of Personality and Social Psychology, 94*, 460–478. doi:10.1037/0022-3514.94.3.460

Impett, E. A., Strachman, A., Finkel, E. J., & Gable, S. L. (2008). Maintaining sexual desire in intimate relationships: The importance of approach goals. *Journal of Personality and Social Psychology, 94*, 808–823. doi:10.1037/0022-3514.94.5.808

Intille, S. S., Rondoni, J., Kukla, C., Anacona, I., & Bao, L. (2003, April). *A context-aware experience sampling tool.* Paper presented at the CHI '03 Extended Abstracts on Human Factors in Computing Systems, Fort Lauderdale, FL.

Kane, E. W., & Macaulay, L. J. (1993). Interviewer gender and gender attitudes. *Public Opinion Quarterly, 57*(1), 1–28. doi:10.1086/269352

Kenny, D. A., Kashy, D. A., & Cook, W. L. (2006). *Dyadic data analysis.* New York, NY: Guilford Press.

Kiang, L., Yip, T., Gonzales-Backen, M., Witkow, M., & Fuligni, A. J. (2006). Ethnic identity and the daily psychological well-being of adolescents from Mexican and Chinese backgrounds. *Child Development, 77*, 1338–1350. doi:10.1111/j.1467-8624.2006.00938.x

Larson, R., & Csikszentmihalyi, M. (1983). The experience sampling method. *New Directions for Methodology of Social and Behavioral Science, 15*, 41–56.

Laurenceau, J.-P., Barrett, L. F., & Pietromonaco, P. R. (1998). Intimacy as an interpersonal process: The importance of self-disclosure, partner disclosure, and perceived partner responsiveness in interpersonal exchanges. *Journal of Personality and Social Psychology, 74*, 1238–1251. doi:10.1037/0022-3514.74.5.1238

Laurenceau, J.-P., & Bolger, N. (2005). Using diary methods to study marital and family processes. *Journal of Family Psychology, 19*, 86–97. doi:10.1037/0893-3200.19.1.86

Litt, M. D., Cooney, N. L., & Morse, P. (1998). Ecological Momentary Assessment (EMA) with treated alcoholics: Methodological problems and potential solutions. *Health Psychology, 17*, 48–52. doi:10.1037/0278-6133.17.1.48

Maisel, N. C., & Gable, S. L. (2009). The paradox of received social support: The importance of responsiveness. *Psychological Science, 20*, 928–932. doi:10.1111/j.1467-9280.2009.02388.x

Mehl, M. R., & Conner, T. S. (Eds.). (in press). *Handbook of research methods for studying daily life.* New York, NY: Guilford Press.

Morrison, D. M., Leigh, B. C., & Gillmore, M. R. (1999). Daily data collection: A comparison of three methods. *Journal of Sex Research, 36*, 76–81. doi:10.1080/00224499909551970

Mroczek, D. K., & Almeida, D. M. (2004). The effect of daily stress, personality, and age on daily negative affect. *Journal of Personality, 72*, 355–378. doi:10.1111/j.0022-3506.2004.00265.x

Muthén, L. K., & Muthén, B. O. (2010). *Mplus user's guide* (6th ed.). Los Angeles, CA: Authors.

Nock, M. K., Prinstein, M. J., & Sterba, S. K. (2009). Revealing the form and function of self-injurious thoughts and behaviors: A real-time ecological assessment study among adolescents and young adults. *Journal of Abnormal Psychology, 118,* 816–827. doi:10.1037/a0016948

Pember-Reeves, M. (1913). *Round about a pound a week.* London, England: Bell.

Pennebaker, J. W. (1997). Writing about emotional experiences as a therapeutic process. *Psychological Science, 8,* 162–166. doi:10.1111/j.1467-9280.1997.tb00403.x

Rafaeli, E., & Revelle, W. (2006). A premature consensus: Are happiness and sadness truly opposite affects? *Motivation and Emotion, 30,* 1–12. doi:10.1007/s11031-006-9004-2

Rafaeli, E., Rogers, G. M., & Revelle, W. (2007). Affective synchrony: Individual differences in mixed emotions. *Personality and Social Psychology Bulletin, 33,* 915–932. doi:10.1177/0146167207301009

Raudenbush, S. W., & Bryk, A. S. (2002). *Hierarchical linear models: Applications and data analysis methods* (2nd ed.). Thousand Oaks, CA: Sage.

Redelmeier, D. A., & Kahneman, D. (1996). Patients' memories of painful medical treatments: Real-time and retrospective evaluations of two minimally invasive procedures. *Pain, 66,* 3–8. doi:10.1016/0304-3959(96)02994-6

Reis, H. T., & Gable, S. L. (2000). Event-sampling and other methods for studying everyday experience. In H. T. Reis & C. M. Judd (Eds.), *Handbook of research methods in social and personality psychology* (pp. 190–222). New York, NY: Cambridge University Press.

Reis, H. T., & Wheeler, L. (1991). Studying social-interaction with the Rochester Interaction Record. *Advances in Experimental Social Psychology, 24,* 269–318. doi:10.1016/S0065-2601(08)60332-9

Shiffman, S., Stone, A. A., & Hufford, M. R. (2008). Ecological momentary assessment. *Annual Review of Clinical Psychology, 4,* 1–32. doi:10.1146/annurev.clinpsy.3.022806.091415

Shrout, P. E., Bolger, N., Iida, M., Burke, C. T., Gleason, M. E. J., & Lane, S. P. (2010). The effects of daily support transactions during acute stress: Results from a diary study of bar exam preparation. In K. T. Sullivan & J. Davila (Eds.), *Support processes in intimate relationships* (pp. 175–200). New York, NY: Oxford University Press. doi:10.1093/acprof:oso/9780195380170.003.0007

Shrout, P. E., & Lane, S. P. (in press). Psychometrics. In M. R. Mehl & T. S. Conner (Eds.), *Handbook of*

research methods for studying daily life. New York, NY: Guilford Press.

Singer, J. D. (1998). Using SAS PROC MIXED to fit multilevel models, hierarchical models, and individual growth models. *Journal of Educational and Behavioral Statistics, 23,* 323–355. doi:10.3102/10769986023004323

Singer, J. D., & Willett, J. B. (2003). *Applied longitudinal data analysis: Modeling change and event occurrence.* New York, NY: Oxford University Press.

Skaff, M. M., Mullan, J. T., Almeida, D. M., Hoffman, L., Masharani, U., Mohr, D., & Fisher, L. (2009). Daily negative mood affects fasting glucose in Type 2 diabetes. *Health Psychology, 28,* 265–272. doi:10.1037/a0014429

Spanier, G. B. (1976). Measuring dyadic adjustment: New scales for assessing the quality of marriage and similar dyads. *Journal of Marriage and the Family, 38,* 15–28. doi:10.2307/350547

Stone, A. A., Schwartz, J. E., Neale, J. M., Shiffman, S., Marco, C. A., Hickcox, M., . . . Cruise, L. J. (1998). A comparison of coping assessed by ecological momentary assessment and retrospective recall. *Journal of Personality and Social Psychology, 74,* 1670–1680. doi:10.1037/0022-3514.74.6.1670

Stone, A. A., Shiffman, S., Schwartz, J. E., Broderick, J. E., & Hufford, M. R. (2002). Patient noncompliance with paper diaries. *British Medical Journal, 324,* 1193–1194. doi:10.1136/bmj.324.7347.1193

Tennen, H., Affleck, G., Armeli, S., & Carney, M. A. (2000). A daily process approach to coping: Linking theory, research, and practice. *American Psychologist, 55,* 626–636. doi:10.1037/0003-066X.55.6.626

Thomas, D. L., & Diener, E. (1990). Memory accuracy in the recall of emotions. *Journal of Personality and Social Psychology, 59,* 291–297. doi:10.1037/0022-3514.59.2.291

Waldinger, R. J., & Schulz, M. S. (2010). What's love got to do with it? Social functioning, perceived health, and daily happiness in married octogenarians. *Psychology and Aging, 25,* 422–431. doi:10.1037/a0019087

Wheeler, L., Reis, H., & Nezlek, J. (1983). Loneliness, social-interaction, and sex-roles. *Journal of Personality and Social Psychology, 45,* 943–953. doi:10.1037/0022-3514.45.4.943

Yip, T., & Fuligni, A. J. (2002). Daily variation in ethnic identity, ethnic behaviors, and psychological well-being among American adolescents of Chinese descent. *Child Development, 73,* 1557–1572. doi:10.1111/1467-8624.00490

Zaider, T. I., Heimberg, R. G., & Iida, M. (2010). Anxiety disorders and intimate relationships: A study of daily processes in couples. *Journal of Abnormal Psychology, 119,* 163–173. doi:10.1037/a0018473

CHAPTER 16

AUTOMATED ANALYSIS OF ESSAYS AND OPEN-ENDED VERBAL RESPONSES

Arthur C. Graesser and Danielle S. McNamara

One approach to analyzing psychological mechanisms is to perform qualitative and quantitative assessments of verbal content. Interviews, essays, and answers to open-ended questions are sometimes the best window to understanding psychological processes. These verbal protocols are routinely collected in many psychological fields, notably education, discourse processes, cognitive science, social and personality psychology, survey methods, forensics, and clinical psychology. In the past, human experts have often been recruited to annotate and score these verbal protocols. During the past decade, however, researchers have made ample progress in automated computer analyses of the verbal content. This chapter reviews methods for computer analyses of open-ended verbal responses.

This is a unique point in history because of the widespread access to hundreds of computer tools that quickly analyze texts and large text corpora. This increase in automated text analyses can be attributed to landmark advances in computational linguistics (Deane, Sheehan, Sabatini, Futagi, & Kostin, 2006; Jurafsky & Martin, 2008; Shermis & Burstein, 2003), discourse processes (Graesser, Gernsbacher, & Goldman, 2003; Kintsch, 1998; McNamara & Magliano, 2009), statistical representations of world knowledge (Landauer, McNamara, Dennis, & Kintsch, 2007; McNamara, 2011), corpus analyses (Biber, Conrad, & Reppen, 1998), word dictionaries with psychological attributes (Miller

et al., 1990; Pennebaker, Booth, & Francis, 2007), and automated analyses of discourse cohesion (Graesser & McNamara, 2011; Graesser, McNamara, Louwerse, & Cai, 2004). Thousands of texts can be quickly accessed and analyzed on thousands of measures in a short amount of time. Some levels of language and discourse cannot be automated reliability, such as complex novel metaphors, humor, and conversations with cryptic provincial slang. In such cases, human experts need to annotate the texts systematically. Essays on academic topics, however, can be analyzed by computers as reliably as by expert human graders (Shermis, Burstein, Higgins, & Zechner, 2010), as we discuss in this chapter.

Some readers will be skeptical of the notion that computers can analyze language and discourse because they believe that only humans have sufficient intelligence and depth of knowledge. Errors in computer assessment open the door to litigation when there are high stakes tests or psychological diagnoses of individuals or groups. People complain about computer errors even when the assessments of trained human experts are no better, if not worse, than computer assessments. It is worthwhile to take stock of the advantages of computer assessments of verbal responses when compared with humans. Computers can provide instantaneous feedback, do not get fatigued, are consistent, are unbiased in assigning scores to particular individuals,

This research was supported by National Science Foundation (NSF) Grants ITR 0325428, BCS 0904909, ALT-0834847, ALT-0834847, and DRK-12-0918409 and by Institute of Education Sciences (IES) Grants R305H050169, R305B070349, R305A080589, R305A080594. Any opinions, findings, conclusions, or recommendations expressed in this chapter are those of the authors and do not necessarily reflect the views of NSF or IES.

DOI: 10.1037/13619-017
APA Handbook of Research Methods in Psychology: Vol. 1. Foundations, Planning, Measures, and Psychometrics, H. Cooper (Editor-in-Chief)

provide greater detail on many dimensions, and can apply sophisticated algorithms that humans could never understand and apply (Shermis & Burstein, 2003; Shermis et al., 2010; Streeter, Psotka, Laham, & MacCuish, 2002). After the up-front costs of developing the computer systems, the application of computer assessments to thousands or millions of people is quite economical compared with human assessments. Human grading and annotation is an expensive, time-consuming enterprise that few humans enjoy. Moreover, the argument can be made that an objective analysis of language and discourse should not rely entirely on human intuitions for scoring and annotation.

The remainder of this chapter is divided into three parts. The first section discusses automated grading of essays of 150 words or longer. This work has enormous implications for high-stakes tests and writing portfolios assessed in kindergarten through 12th grade, college, and the workforce. The second section concentrates on shorter verbal responses that range from a few words to two or three sentences. Short verbal responses occur in short-answer test questions, conversational interactions, and computerized learning environments with natural language interaction. The third section briefly describes some recently developed systems that induce psychological attributes from verbal responses, such as emotions, status, and personality characteristics.

AUTOMATED ESSAY SCORING

Automated essay scoring (AES) has now reached a high enough level of accuracy that the scoring of many classes of written essays is as accurate as the scoring of expert human raters (Attali & Burstein, 2006; Burstein, 2003; Elliot, 2003; Landauer, Laham, & Foltz, 2003; Rudner, Garcia, & Welch, 2006; Shermis et al., 2010; Streeter et al., 2002; Valenti, Neri, & Cucchiarelli, 2003). This is indeed a remarkable achievement. How do these developers of an AES defend such a claim? The methodological approach to establishing this claim is straightforward. Two or three expert human raters grade a large sample of essays after they receive training on a scoring rubric. The grading scale typically has five

to seven levels on an ordinal scale. The essays are divided into a training set and a validation set. The computer program has a set of computational algorithms that are tuned to optimally fit the essays in the training set. The quantitative solution to the training set is typically a linear multiple regression formula or a set of Bayesian conditional probabilities between text characteristics and grade level. The quantitative solution is then applied to the essays in the validation set and these scores are compared with the scores of the human raters. An AES is considered successful if the scores between the computer and humans are about the same as the scores between humans.

Performance of Automated Essay Scoring

A Pearson correlation coefficient (r) is a simple way to assess the performance of an AES. Success of the AES is confirmed if two human raters show correlations of some value r, and the computer scores correlate with the raters with the value of either r, higher than r, or nearly the same value as r. Another scoring index is the percentage of exact agreements in the scores. An adjacent agreement index is the percentage of scores that are within one value of each other on the ordinal grading scale. Shermis et al. (2010) reviewed the performance of the three most successful AES systems: the e-rater system developed at Educational Testing Service (Attali & Burstein, 2006; Burstein, 2003), the Intelligent Essay Assessor developed at Pearson Knowledge Technologies (Landauer et al., 2003; Streeter et al., 2002), and the IntelliMetric Essay Scoring System developed by Vantage Learning (Elliot, 2003; Rudner et al., 2006). These systems have had exact agreements with humans as high as the mid-80s, adjacent agreements in the high to mid-90s, and correlations as high as the mid-80s. Just as impressive, these performance measures are slightly higher than agreement between trained human raters.

The performance of these AES systems has been sufficiently impressive to scale them for use in education applications. They are used in a scoring process for high-stakes tests, such as the Analytic Writing Assessment of the Graduate Management Admission Test (GMAT). In this test, there are two 30-minute writing tasks to measure the test taker's ability to think critically and to communicate ideas. One task involves an analysis of an issue; test takers receive an issue or opinion and are instructed to explain their point of view by citing relevant reasons or evidence. A second task is an analysis of an argument; the test taker reads a brief argument, analyzes the reasoning behind it, and writes a critique of the argument. The AES systems are also used in electronic portfolio systems to help students improve writing by giving them feedback on many features of their essays, as in the case of *Criterion* (Attali & Burstein, 2006) and *MY Access* (Elliot, 2003).

Although the practical use of AES is undeniable, critics do raise questions that challenge the ubiquitous use of these systems without some human expertise. The critics voice concerns about the aspects of writing that the AES systems fail to capture, the ethics of using computers rather than teachers to teach writing, and differences in the criteria that humans versus the computers use to grade the essays (Calfee, 2000; Ericsson & Haswell, 2006). Additionally, a persistent third variable robustly predicts essay scores, namely, the number of words in the essay. Although these AES systems do have predictive validity beyond word count, the incremental gain from the advanced computational algorithms is either not reported or is unspectacular in some evaluations that have controlled for number of words.

How Do the AES Systems Grade Essays?

It is beyond the scope of this chapter to give a precise specification of the computational algorithms in these AES systems, particularly because some are proprietary or the published reports do not reflect the current systems. An edited volume by Shermis and Burstein (2003) has provided detailed descriptions of these systems to the extent that the corporations are comfortable in sharing the information. The e-rater AES (Attali & Burstein, 2006) scores essays on six areas of analysis (12 features) which are aligned with human scoring criteria: errors in grammar, errors in word usage, errors in mechanics, style, inclusion of organizational segments (e.g., inclusion of a thesis statement or some evidence), and vocabulary content. The IntelliMetric AES (Elliot, 2003) matches the words to a vocabulary of more than 500,000 unique words, identifies more

than 500 linguistic and grammatical features that may occur in the text, and analyzes this content through a word concept net. These text characteristics are then associated with essays at each level of scoring rubric for the training corpus to discover which essay characteristics are diagnostic at each level.

The Intelligent Essay Assessor AES (Landauer et al., 2003) analyzes the words in the essay with latent semantic analysis (LSA; Landauer et al., 2007) and also sequences of words with an *n*-gram analysis (e.g., word pairs, word triplets). The algorithm computes the similarity of the words and word sequences between the incoming essay and the essays associated with each level of the scoring rubric. LSA is an important method of computing the conceptual similarity between words, sentences, paragraphs, or essays because it considers implicit knowledge. LSA is a mathematical, statistical technique for representing knowledge about words and the world on the basis of a large corpus of texts that attempts to capture the knowledge of a typical test taker. LSA captures knowledge in an encyclopedia rather than a dictionary. The central intuition of LSA is that the meaning of a word W is reflected in the company of other words that surround word W in naturalistic documents (imagine 40,000 texts or 11 million words). Two words are similar in meaning to the extent that they share similar surrounding words. For example, the word *glass* will be highly associated with words of the same functional context, such as *cup, liquid, pour, shatter,* and *transparent.* These are not synonyms or antonyms that would occur in a dictionary or thesaurus. LSA uses a statistical technique called *singular value decomposition* to condense a large corpus of texts to 100 to 500 statistical dimensions (Landauer et al., 2007). The conceptual similarity between any two text excerpts (e.g., word, clause, sentence, entire essay) is computed as the geometric cosine between the values and weighted dimensions of the two text excerpts. The value of the cosine typically varies from approximately 0 to 1.

A reader might object that these analyses of language are merely word crunchers and do not construct deep, structured, meanings. This observation is correct. There are, however, two counter arguments to this objection. First, a large proportion of the essays are written under extreme time pressure so a high density of content is ungrammatical, semantically ill formed, and lacking in cohesion. More sophisticated computational analyses of language and discourse is appropriate for text that has been edited and has passed publication standards. Second, an important distinction is made between a trin and a prox (Page & Petersen, 1995). A *trin* is an intrinsic characteristic of writing, such as content, creativity, style, mechanics, and organization. A *prox* (short for proxy) is a superficial observable countable feature of text that is diagnostic of a trin. One or more prox may be adequate to estimate a trin. Therefore, it is entirely an empirical question whether the prox landscape in an AES is adequate for recovering the essential intrinsic characteristics of writing.

Characteristics of Writing

A holistic grade for an essay has some value to the writer as an overall index of writing quality. Specific feedback on different characteristics of writing, however, provides more useful information to the student and instructor. Is there a problem with spelling, vocabulary, syntax, cohesion of the message, missing content, elements of style, and so on? The e-rater AES gives this feedback on 12 features in support of Criterion, an electronic portfolio of the students' writing. The portfolio of writing samples can be collected over time for students or instructors to track progress. Similarly, the LSA modules in the Intelligent Essay Assessor have been used in a system called Summary Street (Franzke, Kintsch, Caccamise, Johnson, & Dooley, 2005), which gives feedback to the student on the quality of their summaries of a text. Summary Street identifies sentences that have low LSA relevance scores with other sentences in the text and low scores with expected information in different content categories of an underlying content rubric. An ideal summary would cover the expected content and also have sentences that relate to one another conceptually.

Burstein, Marcu, and Knight (2003) developed an automated scoring technology for the Criterion system at ETS that identifies the extent to which an essay contains particular components of an ideal essay. The targeted categories of the essay include the title, the introductory material, a thesis statement, main ideas with respect to the thesis, supporting ideas, conclusions, and irrelevant segments. Trained human judges can identify these sections with kappa agreement scores of approximately 0.80 (between 0.86 and 0.95 on three different essay prompts). Kappa scores correct for guessing, adjust for the distribution of decisions, and vary between 0 (chance) and 1 (perfect agreement). Kappa scores have an advantage over correlations, but in practice the performance metrics lead to identical conclusions in this line of research. The kappa scores between the computer algorithms and human raters are respectable, typically above .70.

In addition to kappa and correlations, researchers in computational linguistics routinely collect recall, precision, and F-measure scores between the computer decision and the decision of a human judge (and also between one judge and another). A recall score for a computer system is the proportion of human decisions that receive the same decision as the computer. The precision score is the proportion of computer decisions that agree with a human. The F-measure is 2*recall*precision/(recall + precision), essentially an average between recall and precision scores. Burstein et al. (2003) reported that the scores between computer and human were approximately the same for these three metrics and averaged .76, depending on various parameters and criteria. Agreement between pairs of human judges averaged .91. Although not perfect, these automated systems are clearly making significant progress in identifying components of essays. These categories are important to identify in order to give informative guidance on how students can improve writing.

Coh-Metrix, developed in the Institute for Intelligent Systems at the University of Memphis (Graesser & McNamara, 2011; Graesser, McNamara, et al., 2004; McNamara, Louwerse, McCarthy, & Graesser, 2010), is another promising tool for analyzing writing. Coh-Metrix was originally developed to provide rapid automated analyses of printed text on a wide array of linguistic and discourse features, including word information (e.g., frequency, concreteness, multiple senses), syntactic complexity, semantic relations, cohesion, lexical diversity, and genre.

Coh-Metrix is available in both a public version for free on the web (http://cohmetrix.memphis.edu, Version 2.1) and an internal version. The public version provides 63 measures of language and discourse, whereas the internal research version has nearly a thousand measures that are at various stages of testing. According to a principal components analysis conducted on a large corpus of 37,351 texts (Graesser & McNamara, in press), the multiple measures provided by Coh-Metrix funnel into the following five major dimensions:

1. **Narrativity.** Narrative text tells a story, with characters, events, places, and things that are familiar to the reader. Narrative is closely affiliated with everyday oral conversation.
2. **Situation model cohesion.** Causal, intentional, and temporal connectives help the reader to form a more coherent and deeper understanding of the text.
3. **Referential cohesion.** High cohesion texts contain words and ideas that overlap across sentences and the entire text, forming threads that connect the explicit text together for the reader.
4. **Syntactic simplicity.** Sentences with few words and simple, familiar syntactic structures are easier to process and understand. Complex sentences have structurally embedded syntax.
5. **Word concreteness.** Concrete words evoke mental images and are more meaningful to the reader than abstract words.

One of the central purposes of Coh-Metrix is to examine the role of cohesion in distinguishing text types and in predicting text difficulty (Graesser & McNamara, 2011; McNamara, Louwerse, et al., 2010). Indeed, one underlying assumption of Coh-Metrix is that cohesion is an important component in facilitating comprehension. Cohesion arises from a variety of sources, including explicit referential overlap and causal relationships (Graesser, McNamara, & Louwerse, 2003; Halliday & Hasan, 1976; McNamara, 2001). For example, referential cohesion refers to the degree to which there is overlap or repetition of words or concepts across sentences, paragraphs, or the entire text. Causal cohesion refers to the degree to which causal relationships are expressed explicitly, often using connectives (e.g., *because, so,* and *therefore*) as linguistic cues.

The importance of cohesion to text comprehension begs the question of the relationship between the presence of cohesion cues and essay quality. Current studies are under way that use Coh-Metrix and other computer analyses of text complexity to analyze essays and other writing samples. A recent project by McNamara, Crossley, and McCarthy (2010) used Coh-Metrix to examine the role of cohesion in essays written by undergraduate college students. They found that linguistic features related to language sophistication characterized the essays that were rated as higher quality. The better essays featured less familiar words, more complex syntax, and greater diversity of ideas. By contrast, cohesion cues such as word overlap, conceptual overlap through LSA, causal cohesion, and the use of various types of connectives were not predictive of essay quality. The finding that the wording and syntax increased in complexity with higher quality essays is quite intuitive. Indeed, these results are compatible with the culture of English teachers who encourage more erudite language. It is surprising, however, that cohesion played such a small role in explaining essay quality. The role of cohesion and coherence in writing merit greater attention in future studies.

Challenges in Assessing Writing Instruction

A number of methodological challenges require attention for those who develop instructional systems that are designed to track and improve writing over time. One problem is the limited number of standardized tests of writing achievement with norms that allow gauging of progress over time. A second problem is that the available norm-referenced standardized tests, such as the Woodcock–Johnson or the Wechsler Individual Achievement Test, cover few writing skills and genres. A third problem is that the writing process is influenced by a number of factors associated with the pragmatic writing context, intended audience, writing prompts, time allotted for writing, mode of writing (handwriting vs. keyboard), choice of topics to write about, and characteristics of the writer (Graham & Perin, 2007).

The time-intensive nature of scoring written essays has traditionally limited teachers from giving a large number of writing assignments.

This limitation can be circumvented by AES systems. Teachers also have other methods than the use of computers. They can have students assess their own writing performance and progress as writers, a process that improves writing (Andrade & du Boulay, 2003; Graham & Perin, 2007; Ross, Rolheiser, & Hogaboam-Gray, 1999). Teachers can have students assess each other's writing. When learners are taught how to assess and provide feedback to their peers, their writing and the writing of their peers improves (Cho, Schunn, & Wilson, 2006; Graham & Perin, 2007). Future research needs to compare the computerized AES systems with self-assessment and peer assessment of writing over time.

SCORING OF SHORT VERBAL RESPONSES

Short verbal responses by students can vary from one word to two or three sentences. Currently, technologies, such as C-Rater developed at ETS (Leacock & Chodorow, 2003) or the AutoTutor system described in the section Scoring of Student Responses in Intelligent Tutoring Systems and Trainers, can score answers to short-answer questions that extend beyond single words. The verbal responses may be answers to open-ended questions or they may be contributions in dialogues or multiparty conversations. The computer is expected to score the students' answers or conversational turns on a variety of dimensions: accuracy compared with an expected answer, relevance, completeness, verbosity, style, and so on. Compared with the scoring of essays, the scoring of short verbal responses is easier in some ways but more difficult in others. It is easier because the computer has less information to process and a deeper analysis of the language can be accomplished. It is more difficult because less information implies some degradation in the reliability of statistical approximations of relevant parameters. In essence, there are trade-offs between the depth of processing and the reliability of parameter estimates.

The scoring of single-word answers is not a significant challenge when there are one or a few expected answers to a question. The computer can score exact matches, synonyms, semantic associates, and words that have a close match via LSA and other statistical algorithms (Landauer et al., 2007). This

is not a difficult technology for typed input but presents more of a challenge with spoken input (Mostow, 2008). This chapter does not address the scoring of single-word answers because this is a mature technology, and our goal is to address more challenging questions about the processing of human verbal responses beyond the word.

This chapter also does not cover spoken verbal responses even though the utility of such systems would be widespread. Unfortunately, the quality of these speech-to-text systems is still evolving and has not reached the level of accuracy for other than experimental use. There are limitations in the accuracy of speech-to-text technologies that have word error rates for conversational speech ranging from 14% to 50%, depending on the system, domain, and testing environment (D'Mello, Graesser, & King, 2010; Hagen, Pellom, & Cole, 2007; Litman et al., 2006; Zechner, Higgins, Xi, & Williamson, 2009; Zolnay, Kocharov, Schluter, & Ney, 2007). The SpeechRater system developed at ETS is promising (Zechner et al., 2009), but it still has a high error rate and has operational use only for students who volunteer to use the system for online practice.

Scoring of Student Responses in Intelligent Tutoring Systems and Trainers

Intelligent tutoring systems (ITS) are computerized learning environments with computational models that track the subject matter knowledge, strategies, and other psychological states of learners, a process called *student modeling* (Sleeman & Brown, 1982; Woolf, 2009). An ITS adaptively responds with activities that are both sensitive to these states and that advance the instructional agenda. The interaction between student and computer follows a large, if not an infinite, number of alternative trajectories that attempt to fit constraints of both the student and the instructional agenda. This is quite different from learning from a book or a lecture, which unfolds in a rigid linear order and is not tailored to individual students.

Assessment of student contributions in this turn-by-turn tutorial interaction is absolutely essential in any ITS. Such assessments are straightforward when the students' responses are selections among a fixed set of alternatives, as in the case of multiple-choice questions, true–false questions, ratings, or toggled decisions on a long list of possibilities. Challenges arise, however, when the student input is verbal responses in natural language, which is the focus of this subsection.

A number of ITSs and trainers have been developed that hold conversations in natural language. Two of these systems are described in some detail in this section because they have been systematically tested on the extent to which the computer accurately scores the students' verbal responses. These two systems are AutoTutor (Graesser, Chipman, Haynes, & Olney, 2005; Graesser, Jeon, & Dufty, 2008; Graesser, Lu, et al., 2004) and iSTART (Levinstein, Boonthum, Pillarisetti, Bell, & McNamara, 2007; McNamara, Levinstein, & Boonthum, 2004). A number of other systems have been developed with similar goals, such as ITSPOKE (Litman et al., 2006), Spoken Conversational Computer (Pon-Barry, Clark, Schultz, Bratt, & Peters, 2004), Tactical Language and Culture Training System (Johnson & Valente, 2008), and Why-Atlas (VanLehn et al., 2007). This section also includes a system called R-SAT that collects think-aloud protocols while students comprehend text and scores the extent to which these verbal protocols reflect particular comprehension processes (Millis et al., 2004; Millis & Magliano, in press).

AutoTutor.   AutoTutor is an ITS that helps students learn about computer literacy, physics, critical thinking skills, and other technical topics by holding conversations in natural language (Graesser et al., 2005, 2008; Graesser, Lu, et al., 2004). AutoTutor shows learning gains of approximately 0.80 sigma (standard deviation units) compared with pretests or with a condition that has students read a textbook for an equivalent amount of time (Graesser, Lu, et al., 2004; VanLehn et al., 2007). The tutorial dialogues are organized around difficult questions and problems that require reasoning and explanations in the answers. The following are examples of challenging questions on the topics of Newtonian physics and computer literacy:

PHYSICS QUESTION: If a lightweight car and a massive truck have a head-on collision, upon which vehicle is the impact force greater? Which vehicle undergoes the greater change in its motion, and why?

COMPUTER LITERACY QUESTION: When you turn on the computer, how is the operating system first activated and loaded into RAM?

These questions require the learner to construct approximately three to seven sentences in an ideal answer and to exhibit reasoning in natural language. When asked one of these questions, the students' answers are short during the first conversational turn, typically ranging from a couple of words to a couple of sentences. It takes a conversation to draw out more of what the student knows even when the student has reasonable subject matter knowledge. The dialogue for one of these challenging questions typically lasts 50 to 100 conversational turns between AutoTutor and the student. AutoTutor provides *feedback* to the student on what the student types in (positive or neutral, vs. negative feedback), *pumps* the student for more information ("What else?"), *prompts* the student to fill in missing words, gives the student *hints*, fills in missing information with *assertions*, *corrects* erroneous ideas and misconceptions, *answers* the student's questions, and *summarizes* answers. These acts of feedback—pumps, prompts, hints, assertions, corrections, answers, and summaries—are important *dialogue moves* of AutoTutor. A full answer to the question is eventually constructed during this dialogue.

There are many different ways to score the performance of AutoTutor (Graesser, Penumatsa, Ventura, Cai, & Hu, 2007; Jackson & Graesser, 2006; VanLehn et al., 2007). One method is to score the extent to which the students' verbal contributions match good answers to the question (called *expectations*) versus bad answers (called *misconceptions*). For example, listed below are some of the expectations and misconceptions in the example physics question.

(Expectation E1) The magnitudes of the forces exerted by the two objects on each other are equal.

(Expectation E2) If one object exerts a force on a second object, then the second

313

object exerts a force on the first object in the opposite direction.

(Expectation E3) The same force will produce a larger acceleration in a less massive object than a more massive object.

(Misconception M1) A lighter/smaller object exerts no force on a heavier/larger object.

(Misconception M2) A lighter/smaller object exerts less force on other objects than a heavier/larger object.

Students receive higher scores to the extent that they express more of the expectations and fewer of the misconceptions in the tutorial dialogue. Such expectation coverage scores and misconception scores can be computed during the first student turn or, alternatively, after they have finished the conversational dialogue. AutoTutor cannot interpret student contributions that have no matches to the anticipated expectations and misconceptions; it can only make comparisons between the student input and these anticipated ideas through pattern-matching algorithms.

Students rarely articulate the expectations perfectly because natural language is much too imprecise, fragmentary, vague, ungrammatical, and elliptical. AutoTutor has used a number of semantic match algorithms to evaluate the extent to the students' verbal responses match any given expectation E (Graesser et al., 2007). These semantic match algorithms have included keyword overlap scores, word overlap scores that place higher weight on words that have lower frequency in the English language, word overlap scores that consider the order in which words are expressed, LSA cosine values, and symbolic procedures that compute logical entailment (Rus & Graesser, 2006; Rus, McCarthy, McNamara, & Graesser, 2008). These computer match scores have shown correlations with human expert ratings of $r = .29$ to $.42$ (Graesser et al., 2007), depending on the automated algorithm tested. Expectation E is considered covered by the student if the verbal responses meet or exceed a threshold value T of a semantic match. Such assessments can be performed on individual student turns,

combinations of turns, or the cumulative sequence of turns that led up to any point of measurement in the dialogue. One metric of performance is a coverage score that compares (a) the proportion of expectations that are covered by the student according to the semantic match scores at an optimal threshold T and (b) the proportion of expectations covered according to expert human judges (Graesser et al., 2007; P. Wiemer-Hastings, K. Wiemer-Hastings, & Graesser, 1999). These correlations have varied between $r = .35$ and $.50$, with most estimates leaning toward $.50$. Other metrics of agreement, such as kappa scores, recall, precision, and F-measures, also reflect intermediate levels of agreement between computer scores and human experts.

Another method of assessing student performance in AutoTutor is to analyze the number and type of dialogue moves by AutoTutor that were selected to extract information from the student during the evolution of the answer. The system periodically identifies a missing expectation during the course of the dialogue and posts the goal of covering the expectation. When expectation E is posted, AutoTutor attempts to induce the student to articulate it by generating hints and prompts that encourage the student to fill in missing words and propositions. Learners often leave out a content word, phrase, or entire clause within E. Specific prompts and hints are generated that maximize the learner's filling in this content and boosting the match score above threshold. For example, suppose that expectation E1 needs to be articulated in the answer. The following family of candidate prompts is available for selection by AutoTutor to encourage the student to articulate particular content words in expectation E1 (*The magnitudes of the forces exerted by two objects on each other are equal*).

(a) The magnitudes of the forces exerted by two objects on each other are _____.

(b) The magnitudes of forces are equal for the two _____.

(c) The two vehicles exert on each other an equal magnitude of _____.

(d) The force of the two vehicles on each other are equal in _____.

If the student has failed to articulate one of the four content words (*equal, objects, force, magnitude*), then AutoTutor selects the corresponding prompt (a, b, c, and d, respectively).

Performance of a student in AutoTutor can be measured by computing the number of hints and prompts it takes for the student to generate an answer to a question. This was assessed in an analysis of four dialogue move categories that attempt to cover the content of particular expectations: pumps, hints, prompts, and assertions (Graesser et al., 2007; Jackson & Graesser, 2006). The proportion of dialogue moves in these categories should be sensitive to student knowledge of physics (as measured by a pretest of physics with multiple-choice questions similar to the Force Concept Inventory; Hestenes, Wells, & Swackhamer, 1992). There is a continuum from the student supplying information to the tutor supplying information as we move from pumps, to hints, to prompts, to assertions. The correlations with student knowledge reflected this continuum perfectly, with correlations of .49, .24, –.19, and –.40. For students with more knowledge of physics, AutoTutor can get by with pumps and hints, thereby encouraging the student to articulate the expectations. For students with less knowledge of physics, AutoTutor needs to generate prompts that elicit specific words or to assert the correct information, thereby extracting knowledge piecemeal or merely telling the student the correct information.

These analyses of student verbal responses through AutoTutor support a number of claims. First, several automated algorithms can score whether particular sentences are covered in verbal responses that evolve in conversational turns over the course of a conversation. Second, the computer scores for sentential content matches have a moderate, but unspectacular level of accuracy, at least compared with the scoring of lengthy essays. There is less content in a sentence than a lengthy essay, so this second conclusion is quite expected. On the other hand, the scoring of verbal responses is extremely high when the expectation unit is a single word, intermediate when it is a sentence, and high when it is an essay. Third, the scoring of verbal responses with AutoTutor requires an analysis of expected content and an assessment of the extent to which verbal responses match the expected content. It is

beyond the scope of AutoTutor to analyze content that is not on the radar of these expectations.

iSTART (Interactive Strategy Trainer for Automated Reading and Thinking). iSTART (Levinstein et al., 2007; McNamara, Levinstein, & Boonthum, 2004) is an interactive tutoring system that helps high school and college students learn and practice strategies to improve comprehension of challenging expository text. Studies evaluating iSTART's impact indicate that it enhances both strategy use and science comprehension (Magliano et al., 2005; McNamara, O'Reilly, Rowe, Boonthum, & Levinstein, 2007). iSTART is particularly effective in helping low knowledge and less skilled comprehenders better understand challenging text.

iSTART contrasts with AutoTutor because it focuses on the detection and training of strategy use rather than the accuracy of content understanding. iSTART has several modules. The students are first provided with information about strategies and examples of the use of reading strategies (i.e., bridging inferences and elaborations) in the context of generating self-explanations of text. The student moves on to tutoring modules in which they are asked to type self-explanations of science or history texts. A crucial aspect of iSTART's effectiveness is the feedback provided to students by a pedagogical agent as they type in self-explanations of text using the comprehension strategies. The automated algorithm detects the quality of the self-explanation so that directive feedback can be provided to the student.

Several versions of the iSTART evaluation algorithm have been developed and assessed (McNamara, Boonthum, Levinstein, & Millis, 2007). The ultimate goal was to develop an algorithm that was completely automated and did not rely on any human or hand-coded computations. The resulting algorithm uses a combination of both word-based approaches and LSA (Landauer et al., 2007). Word-based approaches include a length criterion in which the student's explanation must exceed a specified number of content words that are in the text. The LSA-based approach relies on a set of benchmarks from the target text, including the title of the passage, the words in the target sentence, and the words in the previous two sentences. The word-based algorithms provide feedback on shallow explanations (i.e., ones that are irrelevant or that simply repeat the target sentence). LSA augments the word-based algorithms by providing a deeper, qualitative assessment. More positive feedback is given for longer, more relevant explanations, whereas increased interactions and support are provided for shorter, less relevant explanations. For example, if the self-explanation appears irrelevant, an animated agent asks the student to add more information that is related to the sentence. Satisfactory explanations might receive feedback, such as "That's really great!" or "That's pretty good."

The accuracy of the iSTART evaluation algorithms has been assessed by computing linear equations on the basis of a discriminate analysis of one data set and calculating its ability to predict human ratings for a variety of data sets (Boonthum, Levinstein, & McNamara, 2007; Jackson, Guess, & McNamara, 2010; McNamara, Boonthum, et al., 2007; Millis et al., 2004). Across a number of evaluations, the iSTART algorithms have corresponded well to human ratings. McNamara, Boonthum, et al. (2007) reported that algorithms corresponded highly with human evaluations of the self-explanations on two texts in the initial iSTART practice module; there was a 62% to 64% agreement between the algorithm and the human judgments ($r = .64–.71$; $d' = 1.54–1.79$). The algorithms also successfully transferred to texts that were on a variety of science topics used in a classroom study that included 549 high school students who engaged in extended practice using iSTART across an academic year (Jackson et al., 2010). This study showed an $r = .66$ correlation between the human evaluations and iSTART's algorithms. This is remarkable given the variety of texts self-explained by the students in this study. Although, this performance appears to be higher than that of AutoTutor, it is important to consider that the two systems target quite different information. iSTART assesses the quality of the student's self-explanation strategies, whereas AutoTutor assesses the quality, depth, and accuracy of expected substantive content.

One computational challenge for the iSTART system is to provide the students with rapid and accurate feedback on the quality of their self-explanations. This evaluation challenge is achieved in several steps. First, the response is screened for meta-cognitive and frozen expressions (such as "I don't understand what they are saying here" or "I'm bored"). If the explanation is dominated by the frozen expressions and contains little other content, then the pedagogical agent responds directly to those statements using a pool of responses that are randomly chosen, "Please try to make a guess about what this means" or "Can you try to use one of the reading strategies? Maybe that will help your understanding."

After the frozen statements are removed from the explanation, then the remainder of the explanation is analyzed using both word-based and LSA-based methods (McNamara, Boonthum, et al., 2007). If the length of the explanation does not reach a particular threshold T relative to the length of the target text, then the student is asked to add more to the explanation. The agent might then say, "Could you add to your explanation? Try to explain how it relates to something you already know." If the explanation does not have sufficient overlap in words or semantically meaning to the target and surrounding text, then it is assessed as irrelevant. The two examples below show a target sentence (TS) and a self-explanation (SE). The SEs were categorized as irrelevant. The first is completely off topic, whereas the second is on topic but would not help the student to understand the target text.

> TS: Survival depends on the cell's ability to maintain the proper conditions within itself.
> SE: no i will not you crazy magic man haha.
> TS: What kinds of environmental changes do you notice?
> SE: trash on the ground

In both cases, the explanation would receive feedback such as "Please try to add information that is related to the sentence. Explain what the sentence means and how it relates to what you already know." The agent does not usually give feedback that may frustrate the student.

The explanation is further assessed in terms of its similarity to the target text. If it is too close to the target text in terms of the total number of words and the number of overlapping content words, as in the following example, then it is categorized as a repetition.

> TS: Inherited behavior of animals is called innate behavior.
> SE: the inherited behavior of animals is called innate behavior

A repetition might receive feedback such as "Try adding some more information that explains what the sentence means." The goal is to induce the student to go beyond the sentence.

The explanation might also be assessed as being beyond a repetition and into the realm of paraphrase, as in the next example.

> TS: The goldfish may depend on other living things for food, or it may be food for other life.
> SE: The goldfish is either predator or prey.

Paraphrasing is an excellent and optimal way to start an explanation, but the goal is usually to induce the student to go beyond paraphrasing by bringing in prior text or outside knowledge to the explanation. In that case, the student would receive feedback, such as "It looks like you've reworded the sentence. Now can you explain it by thinking about what else you know?"

Once the explanation passes the thresholds for length, relevance, and similarity, then feedback is provided on the quality of the explanation. Lower quality explanations are just at the threshold and have little content that goes beyond the target text.

> TS: Energy-storing molecules are produced on the inner folds.
> SE: Energy for the plant is produced within the inner folds of the mitochondrion
> TS: Inherited behavior of animals is called innate behavior.
> SE: if the behavior is inherited the animal has innate behavior

Both of the examples are closer to paraphrases and only slightly go beyond the meaning of the text,

if at all. In these cases, either cursory feedback such as okay is provided, or the student is provided with advice on how to do better on the next sentence, "For the next sentence, explain more about how it is related to other sentences or ideas."

For medium- and high-quality explanations, the student is provided with qualitative feedback only, such as "That's pretty good." for a medium-quality explanation, and "You're doing a great job!" for a high-quality explanation. Following are examples of medium- and high-quality explanations. It is evident from these explanations that the student is processing the text more deeply by either bringing information in from prior text or from prior knowledge, which is the objective of iSTART.

> Medium-Quality Self-Explanations
> TS: Energy-storing molecules are produced on the inner folds.
> SE: The kind of molecules that keep energy are made by the cilia on the inside.

> High-Quality Self-Explanations
> TS: They obtain nutrients by eating other organisms.
> SE: the consumer called the heterotroph eats the producers such as the grass or when an owl eats a rat
> TS: Survival depends on the cell's ability to maintain the proper conditions within itself.
> SE: Every cell that's alive keeps a steady balance, no matter what's going on inside or outside the cell. Doing this is what keeps the cell alive.

The current version of iSTART provides only verbal feedback. A new version (iSTART–Motivationally Enhanced or iSTART-ME) is more game based with points that are contingent on student performance (McNamara, Jackson, & Graesser, in press). This version attempts to enhance student motivation and to provide extended practice of strategies over longer periods of time.

RSAT (Reading Strategy Assessment Tool). RSAT was developed to identify the comprehension strategies that are manifested in think-aloud protocols that students type in (or say aloud) while reading texts (Gilliam, Magliano, Millis, Levinstein, & Boonthum, 2007; Millis & Magliano, in press; Millis, Magliano, & Todaro, 2006). The RSAT team has worked closely with the iSTART team in automated analyses of different types of self-explanations.

One important comprehension strategy measured by RSAT is to identify content that reflects causal connections or *bridges* between clauses in the text. Whereas iSTART only assesses the quality of self-explanations, RSAT distinguishes between local and distal bridges. Local bridges occur between the target sentence and the immediately prior sentence. Distal bridges occur between the target sentences and sentences located two or more sentences back. Skilled readers are more likely to make distal bridges whereas less-skilled readers tend to focus more on the immediate context surrounding each sentence (Coté, & Goldman, & Saul, 1998). A second type of strategy is *elaboration*. Elaborative inferences are constructed in a fashion that caters to the constraints of the text but also recruits relevant world knowledge (Graesser, Millis, & Zwaan, 1997; Long, Golding, & Graesser, 1992; McNamara & Magliano, 2009). Unlike bridges, elaborations do not connect sentences. A third strategy is *paraphrasing*. The student articulates explicit text information but in slightly different words. Some evidence indicates that the amount of paraphrasing in verbal protocols is negatively correlated with comprehension, whereas bridging and elaborating is positively correlated (Magliano & Millis, 2003).

RSAT uses a semantic benchmark rubric in identifying the strategies. There are expected responses when a target sentence S in the text is probed with the think-aloud protocol. The expectations refer to explicit sentences in the text, whereas other content constitutes inferences. The system counts the number of content words in the think-aloud response R for sentence S that matches a benchmark. A local bridging score computes a match to sentence S-1, the sentence immediately before sentence S, whereas a distal bridging score is the match to sentences that are two or more two sentences back from the sentence S. A paraphrasing score is the match to the target sentence S. An elaboration score is the number of content words in the answer that do not appear in the text. The scores from several target sentences in the text are averaged, thereby computing an overall score for comprehension as well as mean scores for the strategies of local and distal bridging, elaboration, and paraphrasing.

Assessments of RSAT report that RSAT does a reasonable job predicting overall comprehension and also discriminating comprehension strategies. In Millis and Magliano (in press), college students took one of three forms of RSAT and the Gates-MacGinitie test of comprehension as well as other open-ended experimenter-generated tests of comprehension that served as a gold standard. The correlation between the open-ended test and RSAT was $r = .45$, slightly lower than the $r = .52$ correlation with Gates-MacGinitie. Millis and Magliano also reported that the strategy scores predicted a significant 21% of the variance on the open-ended test with positive significant slopes for bridges and elaborations, but with a significant negative slope for paraphrases. Correlations between the automated strategy scores and expert human raters for those strategies varied between $r = .46$ and .70.

Summary. The analyses in this section support the claim that automated computer analyses are moderately successful in evaluating the quality of short verbal responses. The algorithms generally compare the short responses to a rubric of expected content. A variety of algorithms have been used to compute semantic matches between student verbal responses and sentence expectations. Most of these algorithms are based on the overlap of content words and inferential content through LSA, but a few consider the order in which words are expressed and occasionally deep symbolic analyses of the natural language. The performance of these computational analyses is moderately successful, but it is not as impressive as the automatic scoring of lengthier essays. We anticipate that future efforts will perform deeper analyses of the content with more sophisticated natural language processing (Olney, Graesser, & Person, 2010; Rus & Graesser, 2006; Rus, McCarthy, McNamara, & Graesser, 2008).

INDUCING PSYCHOLOGICAL ATTRIBUTES FROM VERBAL RESPONSES

The previous sections have discussed research that assesses how accurately computers can score the quality of information expressed by humans when their verbal responses are compared with a scoring rubric. The focus has been on the accuracy or quality of the content in the verbal protocols. This section takes a different angle. To what extent can computers infer psychological characteristics of people from the verbal responses? For example, can emotions, leadership, personality, status, familiarity, deception, and other psychological characteristics be accurately induced from verbal responses? This angle is aligned with a new research framework called *social language processing* (SLP), which marries social and psychological theory with computational techniques to understand relations between discourse and social dynamics (Hancock et al., 2010). For example, what are the keywords, language, and discourse patterns that identify the leader in a group? What verbal cues are diagnostic of deception, emotions, or familiarity between group members? Are there characteristics of language and discourse that predict whether groups are meeting their goals?

It is beyond the scope of this section to review the large and emerging literature that is relevant to social language processing. Instead, we focus on two topics. First, we discuss the Linguistic Inquiry and Word Count (LIWC) system that was developed by Pennebaker et al. (2007). The LIWC system has been used to analyze a wide range of phenomena in social language processing, far more than any other effort with automated systems. Second, we discuss research that infers emotions during learning on the basis of language and discourse.

Linguistic Inquiry and Word Count

LIWC is an automated word analysis tool that has received considerable attention in the social sciences (Pennebaker et al., 2007). LIWC reports the percentage of words in a given text devoted to grammatical (e.g., articles, pronouns, prepositions), psychological (e.g., emotions, cognitive mechanisms, social), or content categories (e.g., home, occupation, religion). For example, *crying* and *grief* are words in the "sad" category, whereas *love* and *nice* are words that are assigned the "positive emotion" category. The mapping between words and word categories is not mutually exclusive because a word can map onto several categories. The 2007 version of LIWC provides roughly 80 word categories and also groups these word categories into broader dimensions. Examples of the broader dimensions are linguistic words (e.g., pronouns, past tense), psychological constructs (e.g., causations, sadness), personal constructs (e.g., work, religion), paralinguistic dimensions (e.g., speech disfluencies), and punctuations (e.g., comma, period). A general descriptor category measures word count, number of words per sentence, and so on. LIWC operates by analyzing a transcript of naturalistic discourse and counting the number of words that belong to each word category. A proportion score for each word category is then computed by dividing the number of words in the verbal response that belong to that category by the total number of words in the text.

LIWC categories have been shown to be valid and reliable markers of a variety of psychologically meaningful constructs (Chung & Pennebaker, 2007; Pennebaker, Mehl, & Niederhoffer, 2003). The relative frequency of psychological words would obviously map onto relevant psychological constructs and these references review such trends. However, the more counterintuitive finding that Pennebaker et al. (2007) have documented is the role of the linguistic features of words. LIWC provides 28 linguistic features that include function words, various types of pronouns, common and auxiliary verbs, different tenses, adverbs, conjunctions, negations, quantifiers, numbers, and swear words. It is the function words rather than the content words that surprisingly are diagnostic of many social psychological states. Function words are difficult for people to deliberately control so examining their use in natural language samples provides a nonreactive way to explore social and personality processes.

Some of the basic findings of the work on function words have revealed demographic and individual differences in function word production.

Function word use has sex, age, and social class differences (Newman, Groom, Handleman, & Pennebaker, 2007; Pennebaker & Stone, 2003). For example, first-person singular pronouns (e.g., *I, me, my*) have higher usage among women, young people, and people of lower social classes. Pronouns have been linked to psychological states such as depression and suicide across written text, in natural conversations, and in published literature (Rude, Gortner, & Pennebaker, 2004; Stirman & Pennebaker, 2001). In an analysis of natural language from personal blogs, language exhibited a social coping model following the September 11 terrorist attacks (Cohn, Mehl, & Pennebaker, 2004). That is, talk about the terrorist attacks increased immediately, with a sharp increase in negative emotion words, and a sharp decrease in positive emotion words. Ironically, positive emotion words remained at an elevated rate of use for weeks after the attacks, whereas negative emotion words returned to baseline levels (i.e., pre–September 11 rates) within a few days after the attacks. In the days after the attacks, *I* use decreased and *we* use increased. These results suggest that after a terrorist attack, people felt more positive and psychologically connected with others.

Inferring Emotions

There are a number of different approaches to analyzing the affective content of text samples. One straightforward approach is to identify a small number of dimensions that underlie expressions of affect (Samsonovich & Ascoli, 2006). This research was pioneered decades ago by Osgood, May, and Miron (1975) who analyzed how people in different cultures rated the similarity of various emotional words. Their analyses converged on *evaluation* (i.e., good or bad), *potency* (i.e., strong or weak), and *activity* (i.e., active or passive) as the critical dimensions. These dimensions are very similar to valence and arousal, which today are considered to be the fundamental dimensions of affective experience (Barrett, Mesquita, Ochsner, & Gross, 2007; Russell, 2003). One could imagine using LIWC categories to map onto these fundamental dimensions as a plausible first-cut computational model.

The second approach is to conduct a more detailed lexical analysis of the text to identify words

that are predictive of specific affective states of writers or speakers (Cohn, Mehl, & Pennebaker, 2004; Kahn, Tobin, Massey, & Anderson, 2007; Pennebaker et al., 2003). Once again, the LIWC program provides a straightforward approach to conducting such analyses. Other researchers have developed lexical databases that provide affective information for common words. For example, WordNet-Affect (Strapparava & Valitutti, 2004) is an extension of WordNet for affective content.

The third approach to affect-detection systems goes beyond the words and into a semantic analysis of the text. For example, Gill, French, Gergle, and Oberlander (2008) analyzed 200 blogs and reported that texts judged by humans as expressing fear and joy were semantically similar to emotional concept words (e.g., phobia and terror for fear, but delight and bliss for joy). Gill et al. (2008) used LSA (Landauer et al., 2007) and the Hyperspace Analogue to Language (Burgess, Livesay, & Lund, 1998) to automatically compute the semantic similarity between the texts and emotion keywords (e.g., fear, joy, anger). Although this method of semantically aligning text to emotional concept words showed some promise for fear and joy texts, it failed for texts conveying six other emotions, such as anger, disgust, and sadness. D'Mello, Craig, Witherspoon, McDaniel, and Graesser (2008) analyzed whether student emotions could be induced from the language and discourse in tutorial dialogues with Auto-Tutor. Feedback, speech act categories (such as indirect hints), cohesion, negations, and other linguistic features could predict student affect states that are frequent during tutoring, such as boredom, frustration, confusion, and engagement.

The fourth and most sophisticated approach to text-based affect sensing involves systems that construct affective models from large corpora of world knowledge and that apply these models to identify the affective tone in texts (Breck, Choi, & Cardie, 2007; Pang & Lee, 2008; Wiebe, Wilson, & Cardie, 2005). For example, the word *accident* is typically associated with an undesirable event so the presence of *accident* will increase the assigned negative valence of the sentence "I was held up from an accident on the freeway." This approach is sometimes called *sentiment analysis*, *opinion extraction*, or *subjectivity analysis* because it focuses on valence of a textual sample (i.e., positive or negative; bad or good), rather than assigning the text to a particular emotion category (e.g., angry, sad). Sentiment and opinion analysis is gaining traction in the computational linguistics community (Pang & Lee, 2008).

CONCLUSION

Over the past few decades, enormous progress has been made in our ability to provide automated assessments of natural language and discourse. This progress has been fueled by advances in computational power, statistical techniques, linguistic databases, and theoretical understanding of discourse processes. These developments have undergirded techniques for scoring essays; analyzing characteristics of different types of writing and texts; assessing text difficulty; assessing the accuracy, quality, and type of student contributions in tutoring systems; inferring psychological characteristics of speakers and writers; and detecting affective dimensions in discourse.

Automated analyses of text and discourse are expected to flourish in the next decade and beyond. Indeed, this chapter has not covered all of the advances that are at the intersection of computational modeling and psychology. Some colleagues will continue to have a healthy skepticism of the automated analyses of language and discourse. At the other extreme are those who will continue to discover new algorithms that capture aspects of psychological mechanisms that can be automatically computed from text. Both of these mind-sets are needed to converge on automated assessments that are both reliable and valid.

References

Andrade, H. G., & du Boulay, B. A. (2003). Role of rubric-referenced self-assessment in learning to write. *Journal of Educational Research, 97*, 21–30. doi:10.1080/00220670309596625

Attali, Y., & Burstein, J. (2006). Automated essay scoring with e-rater R V. 2. *Journal of Technology, Learning, and Assessment, 4*, 1–30.

Barrett, L. F., Mesquita, B., Ochsner, K., & Gross, J. (2007). The experience of emotion. *Annual Review of Psychology, 58*, 373–403. doi:10.1146/annurev.psych.58.110405.085709

Biber, D., Conrad, S., & Reppen, R. (1998). *Corpus linguistics: Investigating language structure and use.* Cambridge, England: Cambridge University Press.

Boonthum, C., Levinstein, I., & McNamara, D. S. (2007). Evaluating self-explanations in iSTART: Word matching, latent semantic analysis, and topic models. In A. Kao & S. Poteet (Eds.), *Natural language processing and text mining* (pp. 91–106). London, England: Springer-Verlag. doi:10.1007/978-1-84628-754-1_6

Breck, E., Choi, Y., & Cardie, C. (2007). Identifying expressions of opinion in context. In M. M. Veloso (Ed.), *Proceedings of the 20th International Joint Conference on Artificial Intelligence* (pp. 2683–2688). New York, NY: Elsevier.

Burgess, C., Livesay, K., & Lund, K. (1998). Explorations in context space: Words, sentences, and discourse. *Discourse Processes, 25*, 211–257. doi:10.1080/01638539809545027

Burstein, J. (2003). The E-rater scoring engine: Automated essay scoring with natural language processing. In M. D. Shermis & J. C. Burstein (Eds.), *Automated essay scoring: A cross-disciplinary perspective* (pp. 113–122). Mahwah, NJ: Erlbaum.

Burstein, J., Marcu, D., & Knight, K. (2003). Finding the WRITE stuff: Automatic identification of discourse structure in student essays. *IEEE Intelligent Systems, 18*, 32–39. doi:10.1109/MIS.2003.1179191

Calfee, R. (2000). To grade or not to grade. *IEEE Intelligent Systems, 15*, 35–37.

Cho, K., Schunn, C. D., & Wilson, R. W. (2006). Validity and reliability of scaffolded peer assessment of writing from instructor and student perspectives. *Journal of Educational Psychology, 98*, 891–901. doi:10.1037/0022-0663.98.4.891

Chung, C., & Pennebaker, J. (2007). The psychological functions of function words. In K. Fielder (Ed.), *Social communication* (pp. 343–359). New York, NY: Psychology Press.

Cohn, M. A., Mehl, M. R., & Pennebaker, J. W. (2004). Linguistic markers of psychological change surrounding September 11, 2001. *Psychological Science, 15*, 687–693. doi:10.1111/j.0956-7976.2004.00741.x

Coté, N., Goldman, S. R., & Saul, E. U. (1998). Students making sense of informational text: Relations between processing and representation. *Discourse Processes, 25*, 1–53. doi:10.1080/01638539809545019

Deane, P., Sheehan, K., Sabatini, J., Futagi, Y., & Kostin, I. (2006). Differences in text structure and its implications for assessment of struggling readers. *Scientific Studies of Reading, 10*, 257–275. doi:10.1207/s1532799xssr1003_4

D'Mello, S. K., Craig, S. D., Witherspoon, A. W., McDaniel, B. T., & Graesser, A. C. (2008). Automatic detection of learner's affect from conversational cues. *User Modeling and User-Adapted Interaction, 18,* 45–80. doi:10.1007/s11257-007-9037-6

D'Mello, S., Graesser, A. C., & King, B. (2010). Toward spoken human–computer tutorial dialogues. *Human–Computer Interaction, 25,* 289–323.

Elliot, S. (2003). IntelliMetric: From here to validity. In M. D. Shermis & J. Burstein (Eds.), *Automated essay scoring: A cross-disciplinary perspective* (pp. 71–86). Hillsdale, NJ: Erlbaum.

Ericsson, P. F., & Haswell, R. (Eds.). (2006). *Machine scoring of student essays: Truth and consequences.* Logan: Utah State University Press.

Franzke, M., Kintsch, E., Caccamise, D., Johnson, N., & Dooley, S. (2005). Summary Street: Computer support for comprehension and writing. *Journal of Educational Computing Research, 33,* 53–80. doi:10.2190/DH8F-QJWM-J457-FQVB

Gill, A., French, R., Gergle, D., & Oberlander, J. (2008). Identifying emotional characteristics from short blog texts. In B. C. Love, K. McRae, & V. M. Sloutsky (Eds.), *30th Annual Conference of the Cognitive Science Society* (pp. 2237–2242). Washington, DC: Cognitive Science Society.

Gilliam, S., Magliano, J. P., Millis, K. K., Levinstein, I., & Boonthum, C. (2007). Assessing the format of the presentation of text in developing a Reading Strategy Assessment Tool (RSAT). *Behavior Research Methods, 39,* 199–204. doi:10.3758/BF03193148

Graesser, A. C., Chipman, P., Haynes, B., & Olney, A. (2005). AutoTutor: An intelligent tutoring system with mixed-initiative dialogue. *IEEE Transactions on Education, 48,* 612–618. doi:10.1109/TE.2005.856149

Graesser, A. C., Gernsbacher, M. A., & Goldman, S. (Eds.). (2003). *Handbook of discourse processes.* Mahwah, NJ: Erlbaum.

Graesser, A. C., Jeon, M., & Dufty, D. (2008). Agent technologies designed to facilitate interactive knowledge construction. *Discourse Processes, 45,* 298–322. doi:10.1080/01638530802145395

Graesser, A. C., Lu, S., Jackson, G. T., Mitchell, H., Ventura, M., Olney, A., & Louwerse, M. M. (2004). AutoTutor: A tutor with dialogue in natural language. *Behavior Research Methods, Instruments, and Computers, 36,* 180–192. doi:10.3758/BF03195563

Graesser, A. C., & McNamara, D. S. (2011). Computational analyses of multilevel discourse comprehension. *Topics in Cognitive Science, 3,* 371–398.

Graesser, A. C., & McNamara, D. S. (in press). Technologies that support reading comprehension. In C. Dede & J. Richards (Eds.), *Digital teaching platforms.* New York, NY: Teachers College Press.

Graesser, A. C., McNamara, D. S., & Louwerse, M. M. (2003). What do readers need to learn in order to process coherence relations in narrative and expository text? In A. P. Sweet & C. E. Snow (Eds.), *Rethinking reading comprehension* (pp. 82–98). New York, NY: Guilford Press.

Graesser, A. C., McNamara, D. S., Louwerse, M. M., & Cai, Z. (2004). Coh-Metrix: Analysis of text on cohesion and language. *Behavior Research Methods, Instruments, and Computers, 36,* 193–202. doi:10.3758/BF03195564

Graesser, A. C., Millis, K. K., & Zwaan, R. A. (1997). Discourse comprehension. *Annual Review of Psychology, 48,* 163–189. doi:10.1146/annurev.psych.48.1.163

Graesser, A. C., Penumatsa, P., Ventura, M., Cai, Z., & Hu, X. (2007). Using LSA in AutoTutor: Learning through mixed initiative dialogue in natural language. In T. Landauer, D. McNamara, S. Dennis, & W. Kintsch (Eds.), *Handbook of latent semantic analysis* (pp. 243–262). Mahwah, NJ: Erlbaum.

Graham, S., & Perin, D. (2007). A meta-analysis of writing instruction for adolescent students. *Journal of Educational Psychology, 99,* 445–476. doi:10.1037/0022-0663.99.3.445

Hagen, A., Pellom, B., & Cole, R. (2007). Highly accurate children's speech recognition for interactive reading tutors using subword units. *Speech Communication, 49,* 861–873. doi:10.1016/j.specom.2007.05.004

Halliday, M., & Hasan, R. (1976). *Cohesion in English.* London, England: Longman.

Hancock, J. T., Beaver, D. I., Chung, C. K., Frazee, J., Pennebaker, J. W., Graesser, A. C., & Cai, Z. (2010). Social language processing: A framework for analyzing the communication of terrorists and authoritarian regimes. *Behavioral Sciences of Terrorism and Political Aggression, 2,* 108–132.

Hestenes, D., Wells, M., & Swackhamer, G. (1992). Force concept inventory. *Physics Teacher, 30,* 141–158. doi:10.1119/1.2343497

Jackson, G. T., & Graesser, A. C. (2006). Applications of human tutorial dialog in AutoTutor: An intelligent tutoring system. *Revista Signos, 39,* 31–48.

Jackson, G. T., Guess, R. H., & McNamara, D. S. (2010). Assessing cognitively complex strategy use in an untrained domain. *Topics in Cognitive Science, 2,* 127–137. doi:10.1111/j.1756-8765.2009.01068.x

Johnson, L. W., & Valente, A. (2008). Tactical language and culture training systems: Using artificial intelligence to teach foreign languages and cultures. In M. Goker and K. Haigh (Eds.), *Proceedings of the Twentieth Conference on Innovative Applications of Artificial Intelligence* (pp. 1632–1639). Menlo Park, CA: AAAI Press.

Jurafsky, D., & Martin, J. H. (2008). *Speech and language processing: An introduction to natural language processing, computational linguistics, and speech recognition.* Upper Saddle River, NJ: Prentice-Hall.

Kahn, J. H., Tobin, R., Massey, A., & Anderson, J. (2007). Measuring emotional expression with the linguistic inquiry and word count. *American Journal of Psychology, 120,* 263–286.

Kintsch, W. (1998). *Comprehension: A paradigm for cognition.* Cambridge, England: Cambridge University Press.

Landauer, T., McNamara, D. S., Dennis, S., & Kintsch, W. (Eds.). (2007). *Handbook of latent semantic analysis.* Mahwah, NJ: Erlbaum.

Landauer, T. K., Laham, D., & Foltz, P. W. (2003). Automatic essay assessment. *Assessment in Education: Principles, Policy, and Practice, 10,* 295–308.

Leacock, C., & Chodorow, M. (2003). C-rater: Automated scoring of short-answer questions. *Computers and the Humanities, 37,* 389–405. doi:10.1023/A:1025779619903

Levinstein, I. B., Boonthum, C., Pillarisetti, S. P., Bell, C., & McNamara, D. S. (2007). iSTART 2: Improvements for efficiency and effectiveness. *Behavior Research Methods, 39,* 224–232. doi:10.3758/BF03193151

Litman, D. J., Rose, C. P., Forbes-Riley, K., VanLehn, K., Bhembe, D., & Silliman, S. (2006). Spoken versus typed human and computer dialogue tutoring. *International Journal of Artificial Intelligence in Education, 16,* 145–170.

Long, D. L., Golding, J. M., & Graesser, A. C. (1992). A test of the on-line status of goal-related inferences. *Journal of Memory and Language, 31,* 634–647. doi:10.1016/0749-596X(92)90032-S

Magliano, J. P., & Millis, K. K. (2003). Assessing reading skill with a think-aloud procedure. *Cognition and Instruction, 21,* 251–283. doi:10.1207/S1532690XCI2103_02

Magliano, J. P., Todaro, S., Millis, K. K., Wiemer-Hastings, K., Kim, H. J., & McNamara, D. S. (2005). Changes in reading strategies as a function of reading training: A comparison of live and computerized training. *Journal of Educational Computing Research, 32,* 185–208. doi:10.2190/1LN8-7BQE-8TN0-M91L

McNamara, D. S. (2001). Reading both high and low coherence texts: Effects of text sequence and prior knowledge. *Canadian Journal of Experimental Psychology, 55,* 51–62. doi:10.1037/h0087352

McNamara, D. S. (2011). Computational methods to extract meaning from text and advance theories of human cognition. *Topics in Cognitive Science, 3,* 3–17.

McNamara, D. S., Boonthum, C., Levinstein, I. B., & Millis, K. (2007). Evaluating self-explanations in iSTART: Comparing word-based and LSA

algorithms. In T. Landauer, D. S. McNamara, S. Dennis, & W. Kintsch (Eds.), *Handbook of latent semantic analysis* (pp. 227–241). Mahwah, NJ: Erlbaum.

McNamara, D. S., Crossley, S. A., & McCarthy, P. M. (2010). The linguistic features of quality writing. *Written Communication, 27,* 57–86. doi:10.1177/0741088309351547

McNamara, D. S., Jackson, G. T., & Graesser, A. C. (in press). Intelligent tutoring and games (ITaG). In Y. K. Baek (Ed.), *Gaming for classroom-based learning: Digital role-playing as a motivator of study* (pp. 44–65). Hershey, PA: IGI Global.

McNamara, D. S., Levinstein, I. B., & Boonthum, C. (2004). iSTART: Interactive strategy training for active reading and thinking. *Behavior Research Methods, Instruments, and Computers, 36,* 222–233. doi:10.3758/BF03195567

McNamara, D. S., Louwerse, M. M., McCarthy, P. M., & Graesser, A. C. (2010). Coh-Metrix: Capturing linguistic features of cohesion. *Discourse Processes, 47,* 292–330. doi:10.1080/01638530902959943

McNamara, D. S., & Magliano, J. P. (2009). Toward a comprehensive model of comprehension. In B. Ross (Ed.), *The psychology of learning and motivation* (Vol. 51, pp. 297–384). New York, NY: Elsevier. doi:10.1016/S0079-7421(09)51009-2

McNamara, D. S., O'Reilly, T., Rowe, M., Boonthum, C., & Levinstein, I. B. (2007). iSTART: A web-based tutor that teaches self-explanation and metacognitive reading strategies. In D. S. McNamara (Ed.), *Reading comprehension strategies: Theories, interventions, and technologies* (pp. 397–420). Mahwah, NJ: Erlbaum.

Miller, G. A., Beckwith, R., Fellbaum, C. D., Gross, D., & Miller, K. (1990). WordNet: An online lexical database. *International Journal of Lexicography, 3,* 235–244. doi:10.1093/ijl/3.4.235

Millis, K., Kim, H. J., Todaro, S., Magliano, J. P., Wiemer-Hastings, K., & McNamara, D. S. (2004). Identifying reading strategies using latent semantic analysis: Comparing semantic benchmarks. *Behavior Research Methods, Instruments, and Computers, 36,* 213–221. doi:10.3758/BF03195566

Millis, K. K., & Magliano, J. (in press). Assessing comprehension processes during reading. In J. P. Sabatini & E. Albro (Eds.), *Assessing reading in the 21st century: Aligning and applying advances in the reading and measurement sciences.* Lanham, MD: R&L Education.

Millis, K. K., Magliano, J., & Todaro, S. (2006). Measuring discourse-level processes with verbal protocols and latent semantic analysis. *Scientific Studies of Reading, 10,* 225–240. doi:10.1207/s1532799xssr1003_2

Mostow, J. (2008). Experience from a reading tutor that listens: Evaluation purposes, excuses, and methods.

In C. K. Kinzer & L. Verhoeven (Eds.), *Interactive literacy education: Facilitating literacy environments through technology* (pp. 117–148). Mahwah, NJ: Erlbaum.

Newman, M. L., Groom, C. J., Handleman, L. D., & Pennebaker, J. W. (2007). Gender differences in language use: An analysis of 14,000 text samples. *Discourse Processes, 45*, 211–236.

Olney, A. M., Graesser, A. C., & Person, N. K. (2010). Tutorial dialogue in natural language. In R. Nkambou, J. Bourdeau, & R. Mizoguchi (Eds.), *Advances in intelligent tutoring systems: Studies in computational intelligence* (pp. 181–206). Berlin, Germany: Springer-Verlag.

Osgood, C. E., May, W. H., & Miron, M. (1975). *Cross-cultural universals of affective meaning.* Urbana: University of Illinois Press.

Page, E. B., & Petersen, N. S. (1995). The computer moves into essay grading: Updating the ancient test. *Phi Delta Kappan, 76*, 561–565.

Pang, B., & Lee, L. (2008). Opinion mining and sentiment analysis. *Foundations and Trends in Information Retrieval, 2*, 1–135. doi:10.1561/1500000011

Pennebaker, J. W., Booth, R. J., & Francis, M. E. (2007). *Linguistic Inquiry and Word Count: LIWC 2007.* Austin, TX: LIWC.net.

Pennebaker, J. W., Mehl, M., & Niederhoffer, K. (2003). Psychological aspects of natural language use: Our words, our selves. *Annual Review of Psychology, 54*, 547–577. doi:10.1146/annurev.psych.54.101601.145041

Pennebaker, J. W., & Stone, L. D. (2003). Words of wisdom: Language use over the life span. *Journal of Personality and Social Psychology, 85*, 291–301. doi:10.1037/0022-3514.85.2.291

Pon-Barry, H., Clark, B., Schultz, K., Bratt, E. O., & Peters, S. (2004). Advantages of spoken language interaction in tutorial dialogue systems. In J. C. Lester, R. M. Vicari, & F. Paraguacu (Eds.), *Proceedings of the 7th International Conference on Intelligent Tutoring Systems* (pp. 390–400). Berlin, Germany: Springer-Verlag.

Ross, J. A., Rolheiser, C., & Hogaboam-Gray, A. (1999). Effects of self-evaluation training on narrative writing. *Assessing Writing, 6*, 107–132. doi:10.1016/S1075-2935(99)00003-3

Rude, S. S., Gortner, E. M., & Pennebaker, J. W. (2004). Language use of depressed and depression-vulnerable college students. *Cognition and Emotion, 18*, 1121–1133. doi:10.1080/02699930441000030

Rudner, L. M., Garcia, V., & Welch, C. (2006). An evaluation of the IntelliMetric essay scoring system. *Journal of Technology, Learning, and Assessment, 4*, 1–22.

Rus, V., & Graesser, A. C. (2006). Deeper natural language processing for evaluating student answers in intelligent tutoring systems. In Y. Gil & R. J. Mooney (Eds.), *Proceedings of the American Association of Artificial Intelligence* (pp. 1495–1500). Menlo Park, CA: AAAI Press.

Rus, V., McCarthy, P. M., McNamara, D. S., & Graesser, A. C. (2008). A study of textual entailment. *International Journal of Artificial Intelligence Tools, 17*, 659–685. doi:10.1142/S0218213008004096

Russell, J. A. (2003). Core affect and the psychological construction of emotion. *Psychological Review, 110*, 145–172. doi:10.1037/0033-295X.110.1.145

Samsonovich, A., & Ascoli, G. (2006). Cognitive map dimensions of the human value system extracted from natural language. In B. Goertzel & P. Wang (Eds.), *Advances in artificial general intelligence: Concepts, architectures, and algorithms* (pp. 111–124). Amsterdam, the Netherlands: IOS Press.

Shermis, M. D., & Burstein, J. (Eds.). (2003). *Automated essay scoring: A cross-disciplinary perspective.* Hillsdale, NJ: Erlbaum.

Shermis, M. D., Burstein, J., Higgins, D., & Zechner, K. (2010). Automated essay scoring: Writing assessment and instruction. In E. Baker, B. McGaw, & N. S. Petersen (Eds.), *International encyclopedia of education* (3rd ed., pp. 75–80). Oxford, England: Elsevier. doi:10.1016/B978-0-08-044894-7.00233-5

Sleeman, D., & Brown, J. S. (Eds.). (1982). *Intelligent tutoring systems.* Orlando, FL: Academic Press.

Stirman, S. W., & Pennebaker, J. W. (2001). Word use in the poetry of suicidal and non-suicidal poets. *Psychosomatic Medicine, 63*, 517–522.

Strapparava, C., & Valitutti, A. (2004). WordNet-Affect: An affective extension of WordNet. In M. T. Lino, M. F. Xavier, F. Ferreira, R. Costa, & R. Silva (Eds.), *Proceedings of 4th International Conference on Language Resources and Evaluation* (pp. 1083–1086). Lisbon, Portugal: LREC.

Streeter, L., Psotka, J., Laham, D., & MacCuish, D. (2002, December). *The credible grading machine: Essay scoring in the DOD.* Paper presented at the Interservice/Industry Training, Simulation, and Education Conference (I/ITSEC), Orlando, FL.

Valenti, S., Neri, F., & Cucchiarelli, A. (2003). An overview of current research on automated essay grading. *Journal of Information Technology Education, 2*, 319–330.

VanLehn, K., Graesser, A. C., Jackson, G. T., Jordan, P., Olney, A., & Rose, C. P. (2007). When are tutorial dialogues more effective than reading? *Cognitive Science, 31*, 1–60. doi:10.1080/03640210709336984

Wiebe, J., Wilson, T., & Cardie, C. (2005). Annotating expressions of opinions and emotions in language. *Language Resources and Evaluation, 39*, 165–210. doi:10.1007/s10579-005-7880-9

Wiemer-Hastings, P., Wiemer-Hastings, K., & Graesser, A. (1999). Improving an intelligent tutor's comprehension of students with latent semantic analysis. In S. P. Lajoie & M. Vivet (Eds.), *Proceedings of the 9th International Conference on Artificial Intelligence: Artificial intelligence in education* (pp. 535–542). Amsterdam, the Netherlands: IOS Press.

Woolf, B. P. (2009). *Building intelligent interactive tutors.* Burlington, MA: Morgan Kaufmann.

Zechner, K., Higgins, D., Xi, X., & Williamson, D. M. (2009). Automatic scoring of non-native spontaneous speech in tests of spoken English. *Speech Communication, 51,* 883–895. doi:10.1016/j.specom.2009.04.009

Zolnay, A., Kocharov, D., Schluter, R., & Ney, H. (2007). Using multiple acoustic feature sets for speech recognition. *Speech Communication, 49,* 514–525. doi:10.1016/j.specom.2007.04.005

Psychological Tests

CHAPTER 17

THE CURRENT STATUS OF "PROJECTIVE" "TESTS"

Robert E. McGrath and Elizabeth J. Carroll

The term *projective tests* is often used to encompass a variety of procedures that allow the target individual to provide free-form responses to ambiguous stimuli. The participant's responses are thought to be sensitive to implicit processes, and consequently they may be somewhat resistant to efforts at misrepresentation.

This class of instruments has had a particularly checkered past. Because of concerns about honesty in responding to self-report measures, and the psychoanalytic belief that much of mental activity is resistant to self-observation, psychologists became enamored with the potential of projective instruments. The development of the Rorschach Inkblot Method (Rorschach, 1921/1942) preceded formal discussions of projective psychological tests, but its popularity in the United States is largely attributable to its presumed projective qualities. The Rorschach was soon joined by other instruments, including the Thematic Apperception Test (TAT; Morgan & Murray, 1935; Murray, 1943), the Rosenzweig (1978) Picture–Frustration Study, and the Szondi Test (Deri, 1949). Even tests developed for other purposes came to be used as projectives, particularly the Bender Visual Motor Gestalt Test (Hutt, 1985). A 1959 survey found the three most commonly used psychological tests in clinical practice were projective tests (Sundberg, 1961).

By the 1960s, though, the allure was fading for two reasons. One was the general critique of traditional personality assessment that emerged out of behaviorism. Mischel (1968) questioned whether

the criterion-related validity of personality measures was sufficient to justify their use, whereas Goldfried and Kent (1972) criticized the practice of using latent constructs to account for associations between test behavior and behavioral outcomes. The second factor was a psychometric critique of projective methods (e.g., Cronbach, 1949; Entwisle, 1972; Swensen, 1957, 1968).

This second literature has engendered an enduring negative perception of projective instruments in the scientific community. Although surveys in the 1980s and 1990s found more than 75% of clinical doctoral programs required training in projective testing (Piotrowski & Keller, 1984; Piotrowski & Zalewski, 1993), a more recent update saw that rate drop to 59%, with more than half of program directors reporting reduced training in projectives (Belter & Piotrowski, 2001). A recent attempt to generate a list of discredited psychological tests was largely dominated by projective instruments (Norcross, Koocher, & Garofalo, 2006). Only a few instruments, primarily the TAT and Rorschach, continue to appear with regularity in the assessment research literature. The continuing popularity of the former can be traced at least in part to its successful use in motivational research (e.g., McAdams, 1982); that of the latter is directly attributable to the success of Exner's (2003) Comprehensive System, which brought uniformity in administration and scoring, normative data, and interpretation to the Rorschach.

In contrast, although clinicians are administering fewer tests, largely because of managed care

We are grateful to Luke Mason for our list of commonly used anachronistic labels.

DOI: 10.1037/13619-018
APA Handbook of Research Methods in Psychology: Vol. 1. Foundations, Planning, Measures, and Psychometrics, H. Cooper (Editor-in-Chief)

(Piotrowski, 1999), the popularity of the Rorschach, the TAT, and figure drawings relative to other instruments has remained consistent over a period of decades (Archer & Newsom, 2000; Lubin, Larsen, & Matarazzo, 1984; Musewicz, Marczyk, Knauss, & York, 2009). The disparity between clinical and academic attitudes underlies the discussion of broadband measurement in the section Implications.

The remainder of this chapter summarizes the current status of projective instruments as scientific instruments. The first section offers a conceptual analysis of the nature of projective assessment. Drawing on recent discussions of projective assessment and comparisons with other psychological measurement methods, it is suggested that applying both the word *projective* and the word *test* to these instruments is problematic and probably should be discontinued.

Current evidence on each of three projective instruments—the Rorschach, TAT, and figure drawings—is reviewed. Although other projective instruments are used in clinical assessment, particularly various forms of Incomplete Sentences Blank (Rotter, Lah, & Rafferty, 1992), these three techniques are the most extensively researched and effectively reflect the current status of projective instruments.

WHAT WE TALK ABOUT WHEN WE TALK ABOUT "PROJECTIVE" "TESTS"

Murray (1938) and L. K. Frank (1939) provided the seminal works on what is called the *projective hypothesis*. They hypothesized that free-format responding to ambiguous or "culture-free" (L. K. Frank, 1939, p. 389) stimuli would encourage the emergence of personal meanings and feelings. The labeling of certain instruments as projective also provided a clever phonetic contrast to "objective" measures, such as rating scales that restrict the set of acceptable response alternatives. The prototypical projective instrument demonstrates the following features:

1. Test stimuli are ambiguous in some important way. For example, the Rorschach Inkblot Method presents the respondent with a fixed series of inkblots and the question, "What might

this be?" The TAT requires the respondent to create a story on the basis of a picture in which people are engaged in uncertain behavior.

2. Although some responses are incompatible with the instructions, for example, refusing to respond to a Rorschach card (in some instructional sets) or saying it is an inkblot, the number of acceptable responses to the stimuli is infinite. Traditional Rorschach practice even allows the individual to decide how many responses to make to each inkblot.

3. The use of ambiguous stimuli is intended to elicit idiosyncratic patterns of responding, such as unusual percepts or justification for those percepts on the Rorschach, or unusual story content or story structure on the TAT.

4. Because of their free-response format, projective instruments often require individual administration and specialized training in administration and scoring.

The Problem With Projection

The use of the term *projective* carries with it certain implications about the cognitive process that determines important test behavior, implications that have been questioned in recent years by individuals closely associated with the study of the Rorschach (e.g., Exner, 1989; Meyer & Kurtz, 2006). To understand why this shift has occurred, it is important to recognize at least three problems associated with calling these instruments "projective."

The ambiguity of the word *projective*. A substantial literature now exists demonstrating that nonconscious activity molds our conscious thoughts, feelings, and intentions. As a result, advocates of psychoanalysis have asserted that modern cognitive science has corroborated the Freudian model of the unconscious (e.g., Westen, 1998). Kihlstrom (2008) has argued persuasively against this conclusion. Freud may have popularized the importance of unconscious activity, but it was already a widely respected hypothesis. What Freud added was the suggestion that adult mental activity is largely determined by primitive, selfish, and repressed wishes and feelings. Cognitive research has little to say about this more specific hypothesis.

Similar issues arise surrounding the concept of projection in connection with psychological instruments. Freud (1896/1962) used the term first to refer to a specific defense mechanism characterized by the unconscious attribution of one's unacceptable feelings and wishes to some external object or individual. Later he used the term in a more general sense to encompass any idiosyncratic construction of environmental stimuli (Freud, 1913/1990). It was this latter use of the term Murray (1938) referenced when he drew the connection between responding to psychological tests and psychoanalytic theory. Meehl's (1945) classic proposal that even objective tests have a dynamic aspect reflects the same understanding (see also L. K. Frank, 1948; Rapaport, 1946), although he was wise enough to put the word *projection* in quotes to reflect its ambiguity.

As in the case of the unconscious, there is nothing uniquely Freudian about the general proposition that different people construe stimuli differently, that ambiguity in the stimulus field can contribute to individual differences in stimulus responding, and that those differences can reveal something important about the individual. Once that proposition is couched in terms of projection, however, it takes on an ambiguous Freudian connotation.

The characterization of respondent behavior. If the concept of projection is unnecessary for understanding instruments such as the Rorschach, it is also clearly not sufficient. On the basis of prior attempts to define the scope of potentially interesting respondent behaviors to projective instruments

(e.g., Bellak, 1944; Exner, 1989; McGrath, 2008; Weiner, 1977) as well as personal experience with these instruments, we would suggest that at least six sources of information can be observed using a projective instrument (see Table 17.1), although these tend to be of varying importance across projective instruments and respondents.

Thematic material refers to the degree to which responses contain language or phrasing that reflects certain attitudes or emotional states. This is the information source that comes closest to the concept of projection, in that respondents may use words reflecting issues of particular concern for them, but these concerns need not be unavailable to consciousness.

Exner (1989, 2003) has argued that Rorschach (1921/1942) was particularly interested in his instrument as a method for detecting *perceptual idiosyncrasies.* This bias is evident in Rorschach's original instructional set, "What might this be?" It is also evident in his creation of the inquiry phase, an important and distinctive element of Rorschach administration in which the respondent is asked to explain how each response was formulated. Although perceptual idiosyncrasies play a particularly central in the Rorschach, they can be important for any projective instrument in which the respondent is expected to respond to stimulus materials, for example, when the respondent clearly ignores or distorts a central element of a TAT picture. Although such distortions can reflect a disordered perceptual style, perhaps suggestive of thought disorder, it is hypothesized they can also suggest issues discomforting the respondent.

TABLE 17.1

Information Sources Available Through Projective Tests

Source	Examples
Thematic material	Morbid themes (*R* and *T*); stories that focus on achievement (*T*)
Perceptual idiosyncrasies	Poor form quality (*T*); preoccupation with small details (*R* and *T*); omission of critical stimulus elements (*R* and *T*)
Extratest behavior	Card rotation (*R*); attempts to reject stimuli (*R* and *T*)
Self-descriptive statements	Indications of task-related discomfort or enjoyment (*R* and *T*)
Quality of thought	Illogical justification of percepts (*R*); tangentiality (*R* and *T*)
Quality of speech	Vocabulary, rhyming, or use of clang associations (*R* and *T*)

Note. R = Rorschach Inkblot Method variable; *T* = Thematic Apperception Test variable.

Extratest behavior encompasses anything distinct from responses on the basis of the instructional set, including the manner in which the person handles the physical stimuli or behaviors, such as odd mannerisms and expressions of resistance. Of these, expressly *self-descriptive statements* are significant enough to mention as a distinct source of information. Because of its free-response format, the Rorschach or TAT gives the respondent license to make statements providing clues about cardinal traits or distinctive ways of understanding themselves. This provides a complementary perspective to the standardized approach to trait description offered by objective instruments. In practice, however, self-descriptive statements during administration of projective instruments are often restricted to the respondent's reactions to the instrument.

Quality of thought refers to the logic or reasonableness of the thought processes evidenced during the administration. Finally, *quality of speech* encompasses various factors associated with effectiveness of communication, including the length of responses, complexity and precision of the language used, and so forth.

The role of ambiguity. It is worth speculating whether the emphasis on projection has led to misleading conclusions about the relationship between ambiguity and clinical usefulness, although the empirical basis for this point is thin. One of the corollaries of L. K. Frank's (1939) projective hypothesis was that greater ambiguity is associated with greater potential for projection. Perhaps the most extreme product of this proposition is Card 16 of the TAT, which is a white card for which the respondent is instructed to both imagine a picture and tell a story about that picture.

In fact, although some evidence indicates that responding to Card 16 is related to creativity (Wakefield, 1986), clinicians find the stories are often less interesting than those provided to other cards (Groth-Marnat, 2009). Similarly, recent evidence indicates Rorschach (1921/1942), who was something of an artist, touched up his original inkblots in a manner that made them more evocative of certain percepts (Exner, 2003)—that is, he made them less ambiguous and more culture-bound than they were

originally. It may well be the case that the evocative elements introduced by Rorschach's modifications of the blots engages the respondent more than would a completely amorphous blot and that this feature has contributed to the continuing preference for the Rorschach inkblots over more psychometrically defensible alternatives, such as the Holtzman Inkblot Test (Holtzman, Thorpe, Swartz, & Herron, 1961).

Implications

Taking these three arguments together, the conclusion has started to emerge within the community of clinical researchers interested in projective instruments that projection is not a necessary or even a particularly important contributor to the clinical value of such instruments. To state the overall conclusion simply, these measures seem to be interesting not because they are *projective* but because they are *provocative*.

McGrath (2008) discussed alternative conceptualizations for instruments traditionally considered projective. They can be distinguished from self-report measures in that they are performance-based or behavioral measures (McDowell & Acklin, 1996) in which the style of responding to the stimuli represents the behavior of interest.

They can be distinguished from performance-based measures of ability, such as intelligence tests, in that they are relevant to a person's characteristic manner of interpreting environmental stimuli, a concept thought to have relevance to understanding personality or interpersonal style. Although some variables may suggest the possible presence of a specific mental disorder—for example, certain perceptual or thinking irregularities can reflect a psychotic disorder—projective instruments are generally intended to reveal something about the respondent's characteristic style of interacting in the world.

Finally, they can generally be distinguished from other performance-based measures of characteristic style in that they are broadband in emphasis. A *broadband* measure is one that is sensitive to multiple latent constructs (Cronbach & Gleser, 1957). For example, one Rorschach variable described by Exner (2003) is Personalized Answers, which is the justification or clarification of a percept by reference to personal knowledge. Personalization can occur for various reasons, including discomfort with the Rorschach or with the testing in general, insecurity about one's abilities, an attempt to assert superiority over the tester through demonstration of personal knowledge, or narcissistic tendencies (Weiner, 2003).[1]

A number of more narrowband behavioral measures of characteristic style have become popular in recent years. These include behavioral measures such as the Strange Situation (Ainsworth, Blehar, Waters, & Wall, 1978) and the implicit measures that have emerged out of cognitive and social psychology, such as the Implicit Association Test (IAT; Greenwald, McGhee, & Schwartz, 1998) or the Stroop color word test (Phaf & Kan, 2007). The IAT is a more narrowband instrument because any one administration is intended to investigate speed of association between only two constructs. In contrast, as Table 17.1 attests, the less structured format of the Rorschach permits a much broader array of issues to emerge.

The broadband nature of projective instruments has several important implications. First, Weiner (1994) criticized the common practice of referring to the Rorschach as a test, which implies a fixed scoring protocol for purposes of detecting a specific latent variable. Instead, results of a Rorschach administration are more akin to the transcript of a therapy session. That is, the Rorschach is a technique or method of data collection that can be explored from multiple perspectives. For this reason, Weiner recommended referring to the Rorschach Inkblot Method. The dominance of the Comprehensive System has muddied this distinction between the Rorschach as a test and technique, but keep in mind that the Comprehensive System does not represent the only approach possible to deriving quantitative data from the Rorschach. This analysis suggests the TAT is not a test despite its name.

Second, when Cronbach and Gleser (1957) applied the concept of bandwidth to psychological testing, they introduced a second concept intended to raise cautions about broadband instruments. A broadband instrument is efficient as a screening device for a variety of personal attributes, and for

this reason can be a potentially valuable tool when the goal of testing is to generate a description of the respondent. However, they also noted that broadband measures tend to be low in fidelity, the degree to which a firm inference can be generated about a respondent on the basis of an outcome. Where relatively narrow bandwidth measures such as self-report tests with a high level of internal consistency tend to be higher in fidelity, and are therefore more easily interpreted, a score on a broadband variable can be ambiguous. It is the popularity of such relatively broadband, relatively low-fidelity instruments in clinical practice that account for references to clinical assessment as an art.

So what are we to call this set of sorely misunderstood instruments? A generally accurate term would be *broadband performance-based measures of characteristic style*, but this is quite a mouthful and unlikely to catch on. A second option would be to retain the simple term *projective*, because traditions often die hard, but with the recognition that—as in the case of starfish and the Pennsylvania Dutch—the term's use reflects precedent rather than precision. This approach still implies a necessary connection with psychodynamic theory, however.

We recommend discontinuing references to "projective" "tests" and using instead the terminology *broadband implicit techniques* (BITs; see also Fowler & Groat, 2008). This terminology is compact yet captures several key features of BITs: They are intended to access multiple information channels, they potentially access automatic or poorly self-observed mental activities that contribute to social identity, and they are primarily data-gathering techniques rather than standardized tests.

If it is true that broad bandwidth implies low fidelity, it has important implications for the empirical status of BITs. To the extent that BITs are useful in clinical screening, there is a strong rationale for research evaluating their reliability and validity. To the extent that BITs are ambiguous in meaning, however, the rationale is poor for using them as primary indicators of respondent status on a specific latent variable. One challenge facing proponents of BITs is to identify which latent variables these

---

[1] Broadband measures, where a single variable can reflect multiple latent constructs, should not be confused with multidimensional measures such as inventories that consist of multiple scales, each of which taps a single latent construct. The Rorschach is both multidimensional and broadband.

instruments reflect with sufficient fidelity to justify their use as operationalizations in research contexts, for example. This challenge will be addressed in the context of a general psychometric evaluation of the three most popular BITs.

THE PSYCHOMETRIC STATUS OF THE RORSCHACH

Reliability

Different authors have reached different conclusions about the reliability of the Rorschach, primarily because of different standards for adequate reliability. Some authors contend that reliability values of less than .85 are unacceptable, particularly when an instrument is used for clinical purposes (Nunnally & Bernstein, 1994; Wood, Nezworski, Lilienfeld, & Garb, 2003). In support of this argument, it has been noted that many intelligence test scores meet this standard. However, a much more common recommendation suggests reliability values of .60 or greater are acceptable and values of .80 or higher are considered exceptional (Cicchetti & Sparrow, 1981; Fleiss, 1981; Landis & Koch, 1977; Shrout, 1998). It is noteworthy that the manual for the Minnesota Multiphasic Personality Inventory (MMPI; Butcher, Dahlstrom, Graham, Tellegen, & Kaemmer, 1989) reports 26 internal reliability statistics for the 13 original broadband scales, some of the most extensively used scales in all of clinical assessment. Of those, 38% were less than .60, and another 35% were in the range .60 to .80, suggesting broadband instruments can be clinically valuable even when they do not meet desirable standards for reliability.

Interrater reliability. In the case of a behavioral observation technique such as the Rorschach, achieving consistency across settings requires consistency in administration and generating variables. For the Rorschach, the latter activity can be further subdivided into two phases. The first has to do with the assignment of a series of codes to individual responses, the second with the aggregation of code results into variables (although this second part is increasingly accomplished via software). The first phase can be referred to as *response coding*; the second as *protocol scoring*.

Before the emergence of the Comprehensive System, psychoanalytic assumptions about the inevitable emission of conflictual material in response to ambiguous stimuli and competing perspectives on what comprises optimal administration led to a crazy quilt of Rorschach practices. For example, Exner and Exner (1972) found that more than 20% of surveyed clinicians did not score the Rorschach at all, and another 59% had personalized scoring by choosing elements from different instructional sets. The Comprehensive System, which began as an attempt to integrate elements from five different approaches to the Rorschach, successfully brought uniformity to the technique.

Even within the Comprehensive System, however, interadministrator reliability may still be an important issue. Lis, Parolin, Calvo, Zennaro, and Meyer (2007) found more experienced administrators tended to produce richer, more complex protocols. This finding is likely reflective of differences in the inquiry phase of the testing.[2] Accordingly, this relationship between experience and *richness* may be unique to the Rorschach among commonly used assessment instruments.

Consistent with tradition, most of the literature on interrater reliability has focused on coding and scoring. Critical evaluations of the Comprehensive System have raised two key issues concerning its reliability. First, the original reliability data for the system was analyzed using percent agreement, which is not a true reliability statistic (McDowell & Acklin, 1996; Wood, Nezworski, & Stejskal, 1996). Second, many reliability studies are conducted in laboratory settings in which raters know their ratings will be evaluated, an awareness that would presumably contribute to scrupulousness. *Field reliability* refers to rating consistency in applied settings in which the rater is unaware the results will be evaluated. This is a potential problem for any

---

[2]In some ways the inquiry phase is more like the *testing of limits* often discussed in connection with the clinical use of performance-based psychological instruments rather than a standardized element of administration, because administrators decide on the number and focus of questions they ask about each response. Although clinically interesting, results from testing of limits generally do not contribute to quantitative outcomes on other tests. The inquiry phase in contrast is an integral contributor to Rorschach coding.

clinical instrument (e.g., see Vatnaland, Vatnaland, Friis, & Opjordsmoen, 2007), but Hunsley and Bailey (1999) suggested several reasons why the field reliability of the Comprehensive System could be particularly poor. In response, McGrath (2003) offered several reasons why the field reliability of the Comprehensive System might be no worse than typical.

These concerns inspired three large-scale studies of Comprehensive System interrater reliability using kappa coefficients for categorical response codes and intraclass correlation coefficients (ICCs) for dimensional protocol scores (Acklin, McDowell, Verschell, & Chan, 2000; McGrath et al., 2005; Meyer et al., 2002). In all three cases, the mean and median values for both kappa and the ICC were well within the acceptable range. However, the results merit more detailed analysis.

First, given the focus in the Rorschach on idiosyncratic responding, it is not surprising to find that some codes were extremely skewed. For example, less than 1% of responses involve an X-ray (McGrath et al., 2005; Meyer et al., 2002). McGrath et al. (2005) demonstrated that codes with very low base rates were associated with both poorer reliability and greater variability on average. In some studies, the authors chose to omit skewed codes or scores on the basis of skewed codes from their presentation of the results; in other cases, these codes were included.[3]

It is clear that codes of low reliability should be interpreted with caution. It is unclear, however, to what extent this factor undermines the Comprehensive System in practice. Some low-reliability codes are only interpreted after aggregation with other codes (see McGrath et al., 2005). Similarly, the Comprehensive System sometimes draws distinctions that do not enter into either the scoring or interpretation of the protocol, for example, whether a response was determined more by considerations of form or texture. Finally, the mean and median values for all four samples used in the three large-scale reliability studies were more than adequate,

and consistent with results for other scales commonly used in clinical practice.

Two of the large studies of Comprehensive System reliability provided data relevant to the issue of field reliability. The first rater in the McGrath et al. (2005) study believed the results would be used only for clinical purposes. Meyer et al.'s (2002) Sample 4 was collected under similar circumstances. The results from these samples were consistent with those collected under laboratory conditions, suggesting poor field reliability at least is not inevitable in the Comprehensive System.

One final point of concern was that mean reliability values for the Acklin et al. (2000) study (.73–.80) were somewhat lower than those in the other two studies (.79–.91). This difference raises the important issue that, as with any test, interrater reliability is setting specific. Despite this caution, the overall pattern of results indicates that adequate reliability is at least possible for Comprehensive System variables, even in field settings.

Although the Comprehensive System is the dominant approach to the Rorschach, many Rorschach scales were created outside the context of the system. Several reviews have now demonstrated good reliability for nonsystem variables thought to measure aggression (Gacono, Bannatyne-Gacono, Meloy, & Baity, 2005; Katko, Meyer, Mihura, & Bombel, 2009), individuation in relationships (Bombel, Mihura, & Meyer, 2009), therapy prognosis (Handler & Clemence, 2005), and dependency (Bornstein & Masling, 2005), among others.

Internal reliability. The concept of internal reliability has not generally been applied to the Rorschach. It is possible to compute coefficient alpha for Rorschach codes if each card is treated as an observation and the presence–absence or frequency of each code on each card is treated as the outcome. An example of this approach is provided by Bornstein and Masling (2005), who found reliabilities of .61 to .62 for a measure of dependency.

[3]Another option involves grouping codes into logical subsets called segments and basing kappa on agreement within the segment (Hilsenroth, Charnas, Zodan, & Streiner, 2007; McDowell & Acklin, 1996; Meyer, 1997a). Although segmenting the codes produces less skewed variables, scoring and interpretation is based on individual codes rather than segments. Segmenting codes may avoid skew but produces reliability estimates without relevance to applied practice. It may also be noted that the issue of skew is generally recognized as a problem in reliability estimation, resulting in the development of various statistics for evaluating consistency that are less sensitive to skew. Such statistics have been criticized as inconsistent with the psychometric definition of reliability (see Shrout, Spitzer, & Fleiss, 1987).

Internal reliability is likely to be poor for many Rorschach variables, however, given that the number and content of responses are allowed to vary freely.

It would also be possible to evaluate the internal reliability of Exner's (2003) global indexes. For example, his Perceptual Thinking Index aggregates information on the basis of several indicators of illogic or perceptual inaccuracy. To our knowledge such analyses have never been conducted. As in the case of the original MMPI scales, these indexes are explicitly formative measures (Edwards & Bagozzi, 2000) that were developed on the basis of correlations with an external criterion rather than internal consistency, so it may be argued the concept of internal reliability is not particularly relevant.

Test–retest reliability.   The evaluation of test–retest reliability is particularly problematic in the context of the Comprehensive System. It requires setting the interval between administrations so there is a reasonable likelihood that the latent construct underlying the scale remains consistent. The interpretation of many Comprehensive System variables was derived actuarially, a technique that often leaves the latent construct poorly specified (McGrath, 2008). In some cases, Exner (2003) even developed his hypothesis about the meaning of a scale in part using evidence of the variable's test–retest stability, an approach that reverses the usual pattern of test meaning determining the expected period of stability.

With these caveats in mind, the most extensive analysis of temporal stability in Rorschach variables was a meta-analysis conducted by Grønnerød (2003, 2006). As was the case for interrater reliability, mean correlations within variables over time were negatively skewed, with a small number falling below the value of .60. Within the Comprehensive System, many of the variables demonstrating poor test–retest reliability are interpreted largely in combination with other variables. For example, the Color-Form code (indicating a response mainly determined by color and secondarily by inkblot shape) was associated with a mean test–retest correlation of only .53, and the Color code (indicating a response determined purely by color with no

reference to form) was associated with a mean correlation of .57. Interpretation is based on the sum of these two codes, which was associated with a mean correlation of .76. Other variables such as Inanimate Movement (indicating a response involving movement by a nonliving object) and Diffuse Shading (indicating a response based on light–dark variation in the blot) are considered indicators of state latent variables. Despite these exceptions, Grønnerød estimated that the mean 6-month correlation for Rorschach variables was more than .70.

Validity

Several approaches to evaluating the validity of the Rorschach are flawed and will be dispensed with quickly. The first examines convergence between the Rorschach and a self-report indicator, such as the MMPI. Results of these efforts have been disappointing, with little evidence of correlation between variables that seem to be measuring similar variables (Archer & Krishnamurthy, 1993; Lindgren, Carlsson, & Lundbäck, 2007). Several hypotheses have been suggested to explain this failure to converge (e.g., Meyer, Riethmiller, Brooks, Benoit, & Handler, 2000), the most compelling of which suggests that psychologists tend to expect greater convergence across modes of functioning (McGrath, 2005) or methods of measurement (Bornstein, 2009) than tends to be the case. Research supporting this objection to using cross-method convergence as validity evidence has demonstrated the problem is endemic to implicit measures (Gawronski, LeBel, & Peters, 2007). In fact, good evidence indicates that implicit measures do not even converge among themselves, suggesting that each may tap a relatively discrete element of the construct (Nosek, Greenwald, & Banaji, 2007; Ziegler, Schmukle, Egloff, & Bühner, 2010). The failure to converge with self-report even suggests that BITs could demonstrate good incremental validity over self-report, a possibility that will be considered in the section Clinical Utility.

A second problematic approach involves meta-analyses generating a global estimate of validity across Rorschach variables and criteria (L. Atkinson, 1986; L. Atkinson, Quarrington, Alp, & Cyr, 1986; Hiller, Rosenthal, Bornstein, Berry, & Brunell-Neuleib, 1999; Parker, 1983; Parker, Hanson, &

Hunsley, 1988). These studies as a group support the conclusion that the Rorschach is an instrument of adequate validity and that it is on a par with the MMPI. Garb and his associates (Garb, Florio, & Grove, 1998, 1999; Garb, Wood, Nezworski, Grove, & Stejskal, 2001) have raised a number of methodological concerns about these studies. Some of their concerns are clearly justified, such as the omission of effect sizes from aggregates on the basis of the statistic used; others are more questionable, such as the omission of effect sizes on the basis of judgments of whether convergence would be expected (for responses from the meta-analysis authors, see Parker, Hunsley, & Hanson, 1999; Rosenthal, Hiller, Bornstein, Berry, & Brunell-Neuleib, 2001). The most problematic aspect of this line of research, however, is its global conclusions. It is universally accepted, for example, that the Rorschach is a valid indicator of thought disorder (e.g., Wood, Nezworski, & Garb, 2003). If 80% of published Rorschach studies focus on the prediction of thought disorder, a global meta-analysis could easily conclude the instrument as a whole is acceptably valid—even if only the variables related to thought disorder are valid. A more useful approach involves focused reviews targeting individual Rorschach variables. Such an analysis is in progress (Mihura, Meyer, Bombel, & Dumitrascu, 2010).

The substantial literature dedicated to the validity of Rorschach variables provides strong and consistent evidence that the Rorschach can validly predict at least five aspects of characteristic style: disordered thinking, intelligence, effort or engagement in the task (although it is unclear to what extent this reflects a characteristic level of engagement versus a Rorschach-specific response), therapy prognosis, and dependence (see Table 17.2). The evidence for several other variables is suggestive of validity but insufficient for a firm conclusion.

Clinical Utility

Recent discussions of the clinical utility of the Rorschach have focused largely on two issues. First, the technique's incremental validity over other commonly used evaluation techniques, particularly the clinical interview and the MMPI, has not been firmly established (Hunsley & Bailey, 1999). Insufficient evidence of incremental validity is particularly problematic in the case of the Rorschach since it is a costly instrument to use. Second, concerns have been raised concerning the normative data used to classify individuals for clinical purposes (Wood, Nezworski, Garb, & Lilienfeld, 2001).

Incremental validity. The information sources listed in Table 17.1 can be used to frame the debate over incremental validity. It is unclear to what extent a technique such as the Rorschach will improve over the clinical interview with regard to behavioral

---

TABLE 17.2

Valid Uses for the Rorschach

Target	Example variables
Clearly valid	
Disordered Thinking	Form Quality[a] (G. Frank, 1990), Thought Disorder Index (Holzman, Levy, & Johnston, 2005)
Intelligence	Response Complexity (Wood, Krishnamurthy, & Archer, 2003)
Effort/Engagement	Number of Responses[a] (Meyer, 1997b)
Therapy Prognosis	Prognostic Rating Scale (Handler & Clemence, 2005)
Dependency	Oral Dependency Scale (Bornstein & Masling, 2005)
Probably valid	
Quality of Relationships	Concept of the Object (Levy, Meehan, Auerbach, & Blatt, 2005); Mutuality of Autonomy (Bombel et al., 2009)
Body Boundaries	Barrier and Penetration (O'Neill, 2005)
Ego Functioning	Ego Impairment Index (Stokes et al., 2003); Primary Process Scoring (Holt, 2005)
Distress	Morbid Responses[a] (Mihura et al., 2010)
Organic Impairment	Piotrowski Signs (Minassian & Perry, 2004)

[a]Comprehensive System variables.

sampling, self-description, and the quality of thought and speech. It is a reasonable hypothesis that the emotional consequences of attempting to respond effectively to ambiguous stimuli can result in a different perspective than is provided by the interview, but this is an untested hypothesis.

In contrast, the Rorschach elicits thematic material and perceptual idiosyncrasies in a manner quite distinct from that offered by a clinical interview or a self-report measure. However, one of the important implications of a shift toward a cognitive rather than psychoanalytic perspective on implicit activity is the recognition that the activity may be easily self-observed (Gawronski et al., 2007; Kihlstrom, 2008). It is therefore important to evaluate whether implicit measures can enhance prediction over less expensive self-report measures.

Concerns about the incremental validity of the Rorschach have spurred several investigations in recent years. Dao, Prevatt, and Horne (2008) provided evidence that the Rorschach is a better predictor of psychosis than the MMPI. Although Dawes (1999) had earlier raised concerns about whether popular but complex Rorschach scores offer any incremental validity over simpler Rorschach scores for the evaluation of problems in thinking, this objection speaks not to the value of the Rorschach but of particular scores computed using the Rorschach. The Rorschach has also shown superiority to the MMPI as a predictor of therapy outcome (Meyer, 2000). Though encouraging, this small literature is an insufficient basis for concluding the relatively demanding Rorschach provides incremental validity over other methods. As one might expect, studies focusing on variables not listed in Table 17.2 have failed to support the Rorschach's incremental validity (see Archer & Krishnamurthy, 1997; Garb, 1984). More research is needed on this topic before evidence of the Rorschach's clinical utility is sufficient.

Normative data. Another issue of some concern in the literature on the clinical use of the Rorschach has to do with the accuracy of the normative data used to classify outcomes. Even if a Rorschach variable proves to be a valid predictor of reasonable criteria, the clinical results for that variable can be inaccurate if the normative standards used to classify the case are incorrect. Wood et al. (2001) presented evidence suggesting that the standard Comprehensive System norms were too liberal, resulting in an excessive false positive rate for detecting psychopathology. This led to some debate about whether the original normative sample was unrepresentative of the general population (Wood, Nezworski, Lilienfeld, & Garb, 2003) or whether the population had shifted in the intervening years (Meyer, 2001). A related question was whether the original normative data gathered in the United States was sufficiently general to apply to residents of other nations (Mattlar, 2004).

General Conclusions

Evidence is sufficient, at least for the key variables used in interpretation of the Comprehensive System, to indicate interrater reliability can be adequate. The evidence suggests there is a small set of constructs for which the Rorschach is a clearly valid indicator, and an additional set for which there is decent evidence of validity. It is troubling how many of the variables listed in Table 17.2 are not included in the Comprehensive System. This state of affairs reflects Exner's (2003) primary reliance on a select portion of the Rorschach literature as the inspiration for variables in the system.

Evidence also suggests that for thought disorder and therapy prognosis the Rorschach offers incremental validity over the MMPI. Additional research on incremental validity is warranted, particularly in comparison with other common instruments in addition to the MMPI.

The Rorschach continues to evolve, and substantial changes in recommended Rorschach practice are in process. Since John Exner's death in 2006, a group of his colleagues has been developing a modified system intended to address many of the criticisms leveled against his work, to be called the Rorschach Performance Assessment System (RPAS; Meyer, Viglione, Mihura, Erard, & Erdberg, 2010). A fair amount of information about RPAS has already been released. It will include a revised set of administration instructions intended to reduce variability in the number of responses per protocol (Dean, Viglione, Perry, & Meyer, 2007), a revised normative database using an international sample (Meyer, Erdberg, & Shaffer, 2007), modified scoring criteria for certain codes on the basis of psychometric considerations, and elimination of certain scores that seem to be invalid. Ideally, future validation of the RPAS will increase the basis for empirically informed Rorschach interpretation.

THE PSYCHOMETRIC STATUS OF THE TAT

Reliability

Concerns raised earlier about the importance of consistency in administration and scoring are particularly relevant in the case of the TAT. Murray (1943) identified a prescribed order for administering 20 cards to each respondent over two 50-minute sessions. Cost–benefit considerations led psychologists to reject that recommendation, but no standard alternative has emerged in its place. Clinicians and researchers have varied the number, content, and order of cards. Few clinicians engage in any formal scoring at all (Keiser & Prather, 1990; Pinkerman, Haynes, & Keiser, 1993), instead opting for a qualitative interpretation of uncertain validity. There are also alternative apperceptive pictures developed for special populations, such as children or African Americans as well as more narrowband picture sets intended to detect specific motivations (e.g., Bellak & Bellak, 1949, 1996; McClelland, Atkinson, Clark, & Lowell, 1953; Roberts & Gruber, 2005; Thompson, 1949). There are even differences in whether the respondent delivers the story verbally or in writing, which should have significant effects on productivity. The circumstances for the TAT are similar to the chaos described by Exner and Exner (1972) for the Rorschach before the emergence of the Comprehensive System. Any efforts to discuss *the* reliability or validity of the apperception technique are therefore problematic.

Although based on different scoring systems and different sets of drawings, some general conclusions can be drawn about the reliability of the TAT and apperceptive techniques in general (e.g., Entwisle, 1972; Lundy, 1985; Meyer, 2004). First, interrater reliability for scoring has consistently been found to be acceptable, although demonstrations of field

reliability are unavailable. Second, test–retest reliability is often quite poor, often failing to reach the .60 level. Finally, internal reliability is also usually unacceptable.

This last issue has received particular attention, as advocates of apperceptive techniques have argued that internal reliability should not be expected. J. W. Atkinson (1981) argued that themes should emerge in a saw-toothed pattern, where the response to one card *satiates* a need, but the failure to satiate on one card will then stimulate it on the next. This approach rests on several troubling assumptions, among them that needs must be regularly satiated, and that storytelling produces a labile pattern of satiation and activation. A more defensible alternative was offered by Schultheiss, Liening, and Schad (2008), who concluded that internal reliability analysis is irrelevant to the TAT because it is predicated on the assumption that the cards represent interchangeable observations. Instead, it is the person–situation interaction that accounts for most of the variance in productivity. Although this explanation sounds reasonable, it fails to explain why test–retest reliability is also poor.

As one would expect given the nature of reliability statistics, an important consideration in achieving adequate internal reliability on the TAT is the number of cards administered. Hibbard, Mitchell, and Porcerelli (2001) found that reliability coefficients on average were less than desirable for individuals administered four cards and did not consistently achieve acceptable levels except in their 10-card administration. The safest policy would therefore call for administering at least 10 cards, with five cards considered a bare minimum.

Validity

A number of different relatively narrowband scoring systems exist for the TAT (see Jenkins, 2008). This review focuses on four systems that have been particularly well researched.

Defense Mechanisms Manual. The Defense Mechanisms Manual (DMM; Cramer, 1991) was constructed to assess three defense mechanisms: denial, representing the most primitive of the three; projection; and identification, representing the most mature. Cramer (e.g., 1999, 2009) has presented a great deal of evidence to support the validity of the DMM. In some cases, however, the justification for this evidence seems strained or counterintuitive (e.g., that level of defense should not be related to intelligence among preadolescents, or that patients with *gender-incongruent* forms of depression used identification more because of its relationship to identity formation). Conclusions about the validity of the DMM await independent corroboration of reasonable hypotheses about the functioning of the defenses underlying the three scales.

Social Cognition and Object Relations Scale.
Westen (1991, 1995) developed the Social Cognition and Object Relations Scale (SCORS) to tap dimensions of psychological functioning derived from object relations theory. The most recent version is composed of eight scales (Complexity, Affect, Relationships, Morals, Causality, Aggression, Self-Esteem, and Identity), each of which is scored on a 1 to 7 global rating indicating level of maturity, although many studies use an earlier version involving 1 to 5 ratings of only four dimensions. The ratings for each SCORS variable are averaged across the TAT responses. A substantial body of literature from multiple laboratories supports the overall validity of the SCORS (e.g., Ackerman, Clemence, Weatherill, & Hilsenroth, 1999; Eurelings-Bontekoe, Luyten, & Snellen, 2009; Fowler et al., 2004; Niec & Russ, 2002). Although concerns were raised earlier about the lack of convergence among implicit measures, there is evidence of convergent validity between the SCORS and Rorschach, and in some cases even between the SCORS and self-report measures.

Motivational themes.
Murray (1943) originally intended the TAT as an indicator of the various motivations he referred to as needs, and evidence consistently supports the validity of the instrument for this purpose. An article by McClelland, Koestner, and Weinberger (1989) on the measurement of achievement motivation has sparked much of current interest in the TAT as a motivational measure, especially after a meta-analytic review by Spangler (1992) concluded the TAT was a better predictor of achievement motivation than self-report measures. However, Entwisle (1972) questioned whether

intelligence could account for the relationship, and this issue remains unresolved. Research into the TAT as a predictor of the motivation for power, affiliation, and intimacy (McAdams, 1982; McClelland, 1965, 1975) has produced similar evidence of validity, although studies of incremental validity are almost nonexistent (Winch & More, 1956).

Problem solving.
The TAT has been extensively studied as an indicator of ability to problem-solve effectively using the Personal Problem-Solving System—Revised (Ronan, Gibbs, Dreer, & Lombardo, 2008). The system has been validated in a number of studies, some of which have controlled for intelligence as a possible confound.

General Conclusions
The TAT cannot be considered a single technique at this time. A unified approach to the TAT would require a standardized, practical set of stimuli and instructions. It would also require the adoption of an empirically founded scoring system that respects the instrument's broadband nature, addresses issues relevant to clinicians, and can be scored in a cost-effective manner. Fulfilling this set of conditions in the near future seems unlikely.

THE PSYCHOMETRIC STATUS OF FIGURE DRAWINGS

General Comments
Figure drawings differ from most other projective techniques in that they call for a physical rather than verbal response. The information sources listed in Table 17.1 are still relevant, although some modifications are in order. Elements of drawing style such as the use of heavily elaborated lines can be conceptualized as consistent with thematic materials as implicit indicators of emotional issues, whereas unusual details such as omitting windows from a house are similar to the perceptual idiosyncrasies found in TAT and Rorschach responding. The observation of extratest behavior and self-descriptive statements remains potentially useful, and the quality of thought and speech can be evaluated if the administrator tests limits by asking questions about the drawings.

Several figure-drawing techniques have been particularly popular. The House–Tree–Person (H-T-P; Buck, 1948) calls for drawings of the three objects listed, each on a separate piece of paper. The Draw A Person (DAP; Machover, 1949) requires drawing a person, then a person of the opposite sex. A more recent alternative is the Kinetic Family Drawing (KFD; Burns & Kaufman, 1972), which involves drawing a picture of one's family doing something.

Figure drawings remain popular clinical instruments. They are easily administered to almost any individual. They also involve a familiar task that helps reduce anxiety about the testing, particularly in children. At the same time, they have suffered the most radical decline in respectability of the three BITs discussed in this chapter. Early work relied heavily on a sign approach, in which unusual drawing details were individually taken as evidence of a latent construct in a manner that relied heavily on psychoanalytic assumptions about the projection of unconscious conflicts onto ambiguous stimuli. This approach has been largely rejected (Joiner, Schmidt, & Barnett, 1996; Swensen, 1957, 1968), even by proponents of figure drawings as a clinical tool (e.g., Riethmiller & Handler, 1997).

Several scoring systems have since emerged for combining unusual drawing details and stylistic elements, usually with the goal of evaluating overall level of emotional distress. The best known of these methods were created by Koppitz (1968) and Naglieri, McNeish, and Bardos (1991), both of which are applied to the DAP. Accordingly, this review will focus on research evaluating these scoring systems, although it is uncertain whether the aggregative approach has superseded the sign or qualitative approach in the clinical use of figure drawings.

Reliability and Validity

Kinetic Family Drawings. Burns and Kaufman (1972) offered guidelines for scoring the KFD, but these were ambiguous and unsupported by research. Various scoring systems were suggested in subsequent years, but none has been subjected to more than a handful of empirical tests. Although these systems demonstrate adequate interrater reliability, evidence that they can identify children with emotional difficulties is weak (Cummings, 1986; Knoff & Prout, 1985). Tharinger and Stark (1990) found a holistic evaluation on the basis of four characteristics of the KFD drawing was a better predictor of criteria than a 37-item scoring system.

Koppitz scoring. Koppitz (1968) selected 30 DAP signs she thought were indicative of emotional distress on the basis of her clinical experience. Although this technique was for many years the best-known approach to the scoring of emotional distress, research results have not been encouraging (e.g., Pihl & Nimrod, 1976). Tharinger and Stark (1990) found a holistic evaluation system on the basis of four characteristics of the DAP drawing was again a better predictor of emotional distress.

Draw A Person: Screening Procedure for Emotional Disturbance. The Draw A Person: Screening Procedure for Emotional Disturbance (DAP:SPED; Naglieri et al., 1991) consists of 55 criteria expected to distinguish between normal children and children with emotional difficulties on the basis of a review of the DAP research literature. The authors reported interrater reliability statistics for the DAP:SPED greater than .90, and internal reliability coefficients that varied between .71 and .77. They also found 1-week test–retest reliability statistics that exceeded .90. Wrightson and Saklofske (2000) reported a test–retest correlation of only .48 over 23 to 27 weeks. They noted that some of the children in their sample were in treatment during the intervening period, but their results raise concerns about the stability of scores on the DAP:SPED over longer intervals.

The DAP:SPED correlated mildly (.20–.30) with self-report scales of emotional difficulties (e.g., Wrightson & Saklofske, 2000). Scores on the DAP:SPED also differentiated between children with and without emotional problems. The accuracy of classification was less than would be desirable (Matto, Naglieri, & Claussen, 2005; McNeish & Naglieri, 1993; Naglieri & Pfeiffer, 1992; Wrightson & Saklofske, 2000). Given that the DAP:SPED involves even more judgments than the Koppitz criteria, a direct comparison of the DAP:SPED to the Tharinger and Stark (1990) holistic evaluation of the DAP would seem to be a useful topic for research.

General Conclusions

The use of individual signs from figure drawings as indicators of specific personality descriptors has been largely invalidated, but the scoring systems that were subsequently developed have their own problems. It is unclear whether an extensive scoring dedicated solely to evaluating emotional distress represents a reasonable cost–benefit ratio. If drawings will be gathered anyway, to reduce anxiety or establish rapport with a child, the holistic coding described by Tharinger and Stark (1990) offers an intriguing alternative requiring simple judgments by the clinician. Future research might also look into whether increasing the number of pictures offers any increment in validity.

CONCLUSION

It is likely that BITs will continue to play an important role in clinical assessment. At least some BITs are useful for reducing anxiety or deflecting focus from the respondent. As Table 17.1 indicates, their broad bandwidth allows the clinician to observe the respondent from multiple perspectives. Clinicians' faith in the incremental validity of implicit measures over self-report measures has been used to justify their greater cost. Finally, gifted clinicians have described the use of their ambiguous qualities in a flexible way to test hypotheses about the respondent (e.g., Finn, 2003). One may expect continuing research to appear on BITs, and the Rorschach in particular, as clinical tools.

Their fate as research tools is more dubious. Complicating matters is the traditional association between BITs and psychoanalysis, an association that potentially interferes with a fair evaluation of their potential use in research. A more accurate and useful parallel may be drawn with narrowband implicit measures such as the IAT. This association allows one to draw several valuable conclusions about how best to understand BITs.

First, there is room yet for building a better mousetrap. The optimal BIT would consistently use stimuli that are obscure enough to encourage individual responding but evocative enough to engage the respondent. Second, popular narrowband techniques demonstrate an intuitive connection with the implicit process they attempt to gauge. A review of the constructs for which the BITs seem to demonstrate adequate fidelity would suggest they are all intuitively linked to the process or perceptual tendency they are intended to measure. The purely actuarial approach has largely failed as a means to identify BIT variables (McGrath, 2008).

Analytic theory suggests the drive to express conflicts and wishes will inevitably emerge in ambiguous situations. This assumption trivializes consistency in administration when there is consistent evidence that neutral instructions contribute to BIT validity (e.g., Lundy, 1988) and that variability in administration compromises reliability. It also exaggerates the likelihood that results will generalize. Research with implicit measures provides little evidence of convergence with self-report, and with each other, even as evidence is growing that narrowband implicit techniques can demonstrate incremental validity over self-report (Greenwald, Poehlman, Uhlmann, & Banaji, 2009). There is reasonable evidence that the three BITs reviewed demonstrate fidelity for some constructs; however, for figure drawings, this statement applies only to emotional disturbance. The widespread abandonment of BITs as research operationalizations may exceed the justification for doing so, although the administration costs may continue to suppress their use as research tools. These findings hardly represent a blanket endorsement of the use of BITs for research and clinical work, but they do suggest the right technique used in the right circumstances can potentially provide a useful method of measurement.

References

Ackerman, S. J., Clemence, A. J., Weatherill, R., & Hilsenroth, M. J. (1999). Use of the TAT in the assessment of *DSM–IV* Cluster B personality disorders. *Journal of Personality Assessment, 73*, 422–448. doi:10.1207/S15327752JPA7303_9

Acklin, M. W., McDowell, C. J., Verschell, M. S., & Chan, D. (2000). Interobserver agreement, intraobserver reliability, and the Rorschach Comprehensive System. *Journal of Personality Assessment, 74*, 15–47. doi:10.1207/S15327752JPA740103

Ainsworth, M. D. S., Blehar, M. C., Waters, E., & Wall, S. (1978). *Patterns of attachment: A psychological study of the strange situation.* Hillsdale, NJ: Erlbaum.

Archer, R. P., & Krishnamurthy, R. (1993). A review of MMPI and Rorschach interrelationships in adult samples. *Journal of Personality Assessment, 61,* 277–293. doi:10.1207/s15327752jpa6102_9

Archer, R. P., & Krishnamurthy, R. (1997). MMPI–A and Rorschach indices related to depression and conduct disorder: An evaluation of the incremental validity hypothesis. *Journal of Personality Assessment, 69,* 517–533. doi:10.1207/s15327752jpa6903_7

Archer, R. P., & Newsom, C. (2000). Psychological test usage with adolescent clients: Survey update. *Assessment, 7,* 227–235. doi:10.1177/1073191 10000700303

Atkinson, J. W. (1981). Studying personality in the context of an advanced motivational psychology. *American Psychologist, 36,* 117–128. doi:10.1037/0003-066X.36.2.117

Atkinson, L. (1986). The comparative validities of the Rorschach and MMPI: A meta-analysis. *Canadian Psychology/Psychologie canadienne, 27,* 238–247. doi:10.1037/h0084337

Atkinson, L., Quarrington, B., Alp, I., & Cyr, J. (1986). Rorschach validity: An empirical approach to the literature. *Journal of Clinical Psychology, 42,* 360–362. doi:10.1002/1097-4679(198603)42:2<360::AID-JCLP2270420225>3.0.CO;2-R

Bellak, L. (1944). The concept of projection: An experimental investigation and study of the concept. *Psychiatry: Journal for the Study of Interpersonal Processes, 7,* 353–370.

Bellak, L., & Bellak, S. (1949). *The Children's Apperception Test.* Larchmont, NY: CPS.

Bellak, L., & Bellak, S. (1996). *The Senior Apperception Technique.* Larchmont, NY: CPS.

Belter, R. W., & Piotrowski, C. (2001). Current status of doctoral-level training in psychological testing. *Journal of Clinical Psychology, 57,* 717–726. doi:10.1002/jclp.1044

Bombel, G., Mihura, J., & Meyer, G. (2009). An examination of the construct validity of the Rorschach Mutuality of Autonomy (MOA) Scale. *Journal of Personality Assessment, 91,* 227–237. doi:10.1080/00223890902794267

Bornstein, R. F. (2009). Heisenberg, Kandinsky, and the heteromethod convergence problem: Lessons from within and beyond psychology. *Journal of Personality Assessment, 91,* 1–8. doi:10.1080/0022389080 2483235

Bornstein, R. F., & Masling, J. M. (2005). The Rorschach Oral Dependency Scale. In R. F. Bornstein & J. M. Masling (Eds.), *Scoring the Rorschach: Seven validated systems* (pp. 135–157). Mahwah, NJ: Erlbaum.

Buck, J. N. (1948). The H-T-P technique: A qualitative and quantitative scoring manual. *Journal of Clinical Psychology, 4,* 317–396. doi:10.1002/1097-4679 (194810)4:4<317::AID-JCLP2270040402> 3.0.CO;2-6

Burns, R. C., & Kaufman, S. H. (1972). *Actions, styles and symbols in Kinetic Family Drawings (K-F-D): An interpretive manual.* New York, NY: Brunner-Routledge.

Butcher, J. N., Dahlstrom, W. G., Graham, J. R., Tellegen, A., & Kaemmer, B. (1989). *Minnesota Multiphasic Personality Inventory—2 (MMPI–2): Manual for administration and scoring.* Minneapolis: University of Minnesota Press.

Cicchetti, D. V., & Sparrow, S. S. (1981). Developing criteria for establishing the interrater reliability of specific items in a given inventory. *American Journal of Mental Deficiency, 86,* 127–137.

Cramer, P. (1991). *The development of defense mechanisms: Theory, research and assessment.* New York, NY: Springer-Verlag.

Cramer, P. (1999). Future directions for the Thematic Apperception Test. *Journal of Personality Assessment, 72,* 74–92. doi:10.1207/s15327752jpa7201_5

Cramer, P. (2009). The development of defense mechanisms from pre-adolescence to early adulthood: Do IQ and social class matter? A longitudinal study. *Journal of Research in Personality, 43,* 464–471. doi:10.1016/j.jrp.2009.01.021

Cronbach, L. J. (1949). Statistical methods applied to Rorschach scores: A review. *Psychological Bulletin, 46,* 393–429. doi:10.1037/h0059467

Cronbach, L. J., & Gleser, G. C. (1957). *Psychological tests and personnel decisions.* Urbana: University of Illinois Press.

Cummings, J. A. (1986). Projective drawings. In H. Knoff (Ed.), *The assessment of child and adolescent personality* (pp. 199–244). New York, NY: Guilford Press.

Dao, T. K., Prevatt, F., & Horne, H. L. (2008). Differentiating psychotic patients from nonpsychotic patients with the MMPI–2 and Rorschach. *Journal of Personality Assessment, 90,* 93–101.

Dawes, R. M. (1999). Two methods for studying the incremental validity of a Rorschach variable. *Psychological Assessment, 11,* 297–302. doi:10.1037/ 1040-3590.11.3.297

Dean, K. L., Viglione, D., Perry, W., & Meyer, G. (2007). A method to optimize the response range while maintaining Rorschach comprehensive system validity. *Journal of Personality Assessment, 89,* 149–161.

Deri, S. (1949). *Introduction to the Szondi test.* New York, NY: Grune & Stratton.

Edwards, J. R., & Bagozzi, R. P. (2000). On the nature and direction of relationships between constructs and measures. *Psychological Methods, 5,* 155–174. doi:10.1037/1082-989X.5.2.155

Entwisle, D. R. (1972). To dispel fantasies about fantasy-based measures of achievement motivation. *Psychological Bulletin, 77,* 377–391. doi:10.1037/h0020021

Eurelings-Bontekoe, E. H. M., Luyten, P., & Snellen, W. (2009). Validation of a theory-driven profile interpretation of the Dutch Short Form of the MMPI using the TAT Social Cognitions and Object Relations Scale (SCORS). *Journal of Personality Assessment, 91,* 155–165. doi:10.1080/00223890802634274

Exner, J. E., Jr. (1989). Searching for projection in the Rorschach. *Journal of Personality Assessment, 53,* 520–536. doi:10.1207/s15327752jpa5303_9

Exner, J. E., Jr. (2003). *The Rorschach: A comprehensive system: I. Basic foundations and principles of interpretation* (4th ed.). New York, NY: Wiley.

Exner, J. E., Jr., & Exner, D. E. (1972). How clinicians use the Rorschach. *Journal of Personality Assessment, 36,* 403–408. doi:10.1080/00223891.1972.10119784

Finn, S. E. (2003). Therapeutic assessment of a man with "ADD." *Journal of Personality Assessment, 80,* 115–129. doi:10.1207/S15327752JPA8002_01

Fleiss, J. L. (1981). *Statistical methods for rates and proportions.* New York, NY: Wiley.

Fowler, J. C., Ackerman, S. J., Speanburg, S., Bailey, A., Blagys, M., & Conklin, A. C. (2004). Personality and symptom change in treatment-refractory inpatients: Evaluation of the phase model of change using Rorschach, TAT, and *DSM–IV* Axis V. *Journal of Personality Assessment, 83,* 306–322. doi:10.1207/s15327752jpa8303_12

Fowler, J. C., & Groat, M. (2008). Personality assessment using implicit (projective) methods. In M. Hersen & A. Gross (Eds.), *Handbook of clinical psychology: Vol. 1. Adults* (pp. 475–494). Hoboken, NJ: Wiley.

Frank, G. (1990). Research on the clinical usefulness of the Rorschach: I. The diagnosis of schizophrenia. *Perceptual and Motor Skills, 71,* 573–578.

Frank, L. K. (1939). Projective methods for the study of personality. *Journal of Psychology: Interdisciplinary and Applied, 8,* 389–413. doi:10.1080/00223980.1939.9917671

Frank, L. K. (1948). *Projective methods.* Springfield, IL: Charles C Thomas.

Freud, S. (1962). Further remarks on the neuropsychoses of defence. In J. Strachey (Ed. & Trans.), *The standard edition of the complete psychological works of Sigmund Freud* (Vol. 3, pp. 159–188). London, England: Hogarth. (Original work published 1896)

Freud, S. (1990). *Totem and taboo: The standard edition.* New York, NY: Norton. (Original work published 1913)

Gacono, C. B., Bannatyne-Gacono, L., Meloy, J. R., & Baity, M. R. (2005). The Rorschach extended aggression scores. *Rorschachiana, 27,* 164–190. doi:10.1027/1192-5604.27.1.164

Garb, H. N. (1984). The incremental validity of information used in personality assessment. *Clinical Psychology Review, 4,* 641–655. doi:10.1016/0272-7358(84)90010-2

Garb, H. N., Florio, C. M., & Grove, W. M. (1998). The validity of the Rorschach and the Minnesota Multiphasic Personality Inventory: Results from meta-analyses. *Psychological Science, 9,* 402–404. doi:10.1111/1467-9280.00075

Garb, H. N., Florio, C. M., & Grove, W. M. (1999). The Rorschach controversy: Reply to Parker, Hunsley, and Hanson. *Psychological Science, 10,* 293–294. doi:10.1111/1467-9280.00154

Garb, H. N., Wood, J. M., Nezworski, M. T., Grove, W. M., & Stejskal, W. J. (2001). Toward a resolution of the Rorschach controversy. *Psychological Assessment, 13,* 433–448. doi:10.1037/1040-3590.13.4.433

Gawronski, B., LeBel, E. P., & Peters, K. R. (2007). What do implicit measures tell us? Scrutinizing the validity of three commonplace assumptions. *Perspectives on Psychological Science, 2,* 181–193. doi:10.1111/j.1745-6916.2007.00036.x

Goldfried, M. R., & Kent, R. N. (1972). Traditional versus behavioral personality assessment: A comparison of methodological and theoretical assumptions. *Psychological Bulletin, 77,* 409–420. doi:10.1037/h0032714

Greenwald, A. G., McGhee, D., & Schwartz, J. (1998). Measuring individual differences in implicit cognition: The Implicit Association Test. *Journal of Personality and Social Psychology, 74,* 1464–1480. doi:10.1037/0022-3514.74.6.1464

Greenwald, A. G., Poehlman, T., Uhlmann, E., & Banaji, M. (2009). Understanding and using the Implicit Association Test: III. Meta-analysis of predictive validity. *Journal of Personality and Social Psychology, 97,* 17–41. doi:10.1037/a0015575

Grønnerød, C. (2003). Temporal stability in the Rorschach method: A meta-analytic review. *Journal of Personality Assessment, 80,* 272–293. doi:10.1207/S15327752JPA8003_06

Grønnerød, C. (2006). Reanalysis of the Grønnerød (2003). Rorschach temporal stability meta-analysis data set. *Journal of Personality Assessment, 86,* 222–225. doi:10.1207/s15327752jpa8602_12

Groth-Marnat, G. (2009). *Handbook of psychological assessment* (5th ed.). Hoboken, NJ: Wiley.

Handler, L., & Clemence, A. J. (2005). The Rorschach Prognostic Rating Scale. In R. F. Bornstein & J. M. Masling (Eds.), *Scoring the Rorschach: Seven validated systems* (pp. 25–54). Mahwah, NJ: Erlbaum.

Hibbard, S., Mitchell, D., & Porcerelli, J. (2001). Internal consistency of the Object Relations and Social Cognition scales for the Thematic Apperception Test. *Journal of Personality Assessment, 77*, 408–419. doi:10.1207/S15327752JPA7703_03

Hiller, J. B., Rosenthal, R., Bornstein, R. F., Berry, D. T. R., & Brunell-Neuleib, S. (1999). A comparative meta-analysis of Rorschach and MMPI validity. *Psychological Assessment, 11*, 278–296. doi:10.1037/1040-3590.11.3.278

Hilsenroth, M., Charnas, J., Zodan, J., & Streiner, D. (2007). Criterion-based training for Rorschach scoring. *Training and Education in Professional Psychology, 1*, 125–134. doi:10.1037/1931-3918-.1.2.125

Holt, R. R. (2005). The Pripro scoring system. In R. F. Bornstein & J. M. Masling (Eds.), *Scoring the Rorschach: Seven validated systems* (pp. 191–235). Mahwah, NJ: Erlbaum.

Holtzman, W. H., Thorpe, J. S., Swartz, J. D., & Herron, E. W. (1961). *Inkblot perception and personality*. Austin, TX: University of Texas Press.

Holzman, P. S., Levy, D., & Johnston, M. H. (2005). The use of the Rorschach technique for assessing formal thought disorder. In R. F. Bornstein & J. M. Masling (Eds.), *Scoring the Rorschach: Seven validated systems* (pp. 55–95). Mahwah, NJ: Erlbaum.

Hunsley, J., & Bailey, J. M. (1999). The clinical utility of the Rorschach: Unfulfilled promises and an uncertain future. *Psychological Assessment, 11*, 266–277. doi:10.1037/1040-3590.11.3.266

Hutt, M. L. (1985). *The Hutt adaptation of the Bender-Gestalt Test: Rapid screening and intensive diagnosis* (4th ed.). New York, NY: Grune & Stratton.

Jenkins, S. R. (2008). *A handbook of clinical scoring systems for thematic apperceptive techniques*. Mahwah, NJ: Erlbaum.

Joiner, T., Schmidt, K., & Barnett, J. (1996). Size, detail, and line heaviness in children's drawings as correlates of emotional distress: (More) negative evidence. *Journal of Personality Assessment, 67*, 127–141.

Katko, N., Meyer, G., Mihura, J., & Bombel, G. (2009). The interrater reliability of Elizur's hostility systems and Holt's aggression variables: A meta-analytical review. *Journal of Personality Assessment, 91*, 357–364.

Keiser, R. E., & Prather, E. (1990). What is the TAT? A review of ten years of research. *Journal of Personality Assessment, 55*, 800–803. doi:10.1207/s15327752jpa5503&4_36

Kihlstrom, J. F. (2008). The psychological unconscious. In O. P. John, R. W. Robins, & L. A. Pervin (Eds.), *Handbook of personality: Theory and research* (3rd ed., pp. 583–602). New York, NY: Guilford Press.

Knoff, H. M., & Prout, H. T. (1985). *The kinetic drawing system: Family and school*. Los Angeles, CA: Western Psychological Services.

Koppitz, E. M. (1968). *Psychological evaluation of children's human figure drawings*. New York, NY: Grune & Stratton.

Landis, J. R., & Koch, G. G. (1977). The measurement of observer agreement for categorical data. *Biometrics, 33*, 159–174. doi:10.2307/2529310

Levy, K. N., Meehan, K. B., Auerbach, J. S., & Blatt, S. J. (2005). Concept of the Object on the Rorschach Scale. In R. F. Bornstein & J. M. Masling (Eds.), *Scoring the Rorschach: Seven validated systems* (pp. 97–133). Mahwah, NJ: Erlbaum.

Lindgren, T., Carlsson, A., & Lundbäck, E. (2007). No agreement between the Rorschach and self-assessed personality traits derived from the Comprehensive System. *Scandinavian Journal of Psychology, 48*, 399–408. doi:10.1111/j.1467-9450.2007.00590.x

Lis, A., Parolin, L., Calvo, V., Zennaro, A., & Meyer, G. (2007). The impact of administration and inquiry on Rorschach Comprehensive System protocols in a national reference sample. *Journal of Personality Assessment, 89*(Suppl. 1), S193–S200.

Lubin, B., Larsen, R., & Matarazzo, J. (1984). Patterns of psychological test usage in the United States: 1935–1982. *American Psychologist, 39*, 451–454. doi:10.1037/0003-066X.39.4.451

Lundy, A. (1985). The reliability of the Thematic Apperception Test. *Journal of Personality Assessment, 49*, 141–145. doi:10.1207/s15327752jpa4902_6

Lundy, A. (1988). Instructional set and Thematic Apperception Test validity. *Journal of Personality Assessment, 52*, 309–320. doi:10.1207/s15327752jpa5202_12

Machover, K. (1949). *Personality projection in the drawing of the human figure*. Springfield, IL: Thomas. doi:10.1037/11147-000

Mattlar, C.-E. (2004). Are we entitled to use Rorschach Workshop's norms when interpreting the Comprehensive System in Finland? *Rorschachiana, 26*, 85–109. doi:10.1027/1192-5604.26.1.85

Matto, H. C., Naglieri, J. A., & Claussen, C. (2005). Validity of the Draw-A-Person: Screening Procedure for Emotional Disturbance (DAP:SPED) in strength-based assessment. *Research on Social Work Practice, 15*, 41–46. doi:10.1177/1049731504269553

McAdams, D. P. (1982). Experiences of intimacy and power: Relationships between social motives and autobiographical memory. *Journal of Personality and Social Psychology, 42*, 292–302. doi:10.1037/0022-3514.42.2.292

McClelland, D. C. (1965). *N* achievement and entrepreneurship: A longitudinal study. *Journal of Personality and Social Psychology, 95,* 389–392. doi:10.1037/h0021956

McClelland, D. C. (1975). *Power: The inner experience.* New York, NY: Irvington.

McClelland, D. C., Atkinson, J. W., Clark, R. A., & Lowell, E. L. (1953). *The achievement motive.* New York, NY: Irvington. doi:10.1037/11144-000

McClelland, D. C., Koestner, R., & Weinberger, J. (1989). How do self-attributed and implicit motives differ? *Psychological Review, 96,* 690–702. doi:10.1037/0033-295X.96.4.690

McDowell, C., & Acklin, M. W. (1996). Standardizing procedures for calculating Rorschach interrater reliability: Conceptual and empirical foundations. *Journal of Personality Assessment, 66,* 308–320. doi:10.1207/s15327752jpa6602_9

McGrath, R. E. (2003). Achieving accuracy in testing procedures: The Comprehensive System as a case example. *Journal of Personality Assessment, 81,* 104–110. doi:10.1207/S15327752JPA8102_02

McGrath, R. E. (2005). Conceptual complexity and construct validity. *Journal of Personality Assessment, 85,* 112–124. doi:10.1207/s15327752jpa8502_02

McGrath, R. E. (2008). The Rorschach in the context of performance-based personality assessment. *Journal of Personality Assessment, 90,* 465–475. doi:10.1080/00223890802248760

McGrath, R. E., Pogge, D. L., Stokes, J. M., Cragnolino, A., Zaccario, M., Hayman, J., . . . Wayland-Smith, D. (2005). Comprehensive System scoring reliability in an adolescent inpatient sample. *Assessment, 12,* 199–209. doi:10.1177/1073191104273384

McNeish, T. J., & Naglieri, J. A. (1993). Identification of individuals with serious emotional disturbance using the Draw A Person: Screening Procedure for Emotional Disturbance. *The Journal of Special Education, 27,* 115–121. doi:10.1177/002246699302700108

Meehl, P. E. (1945). The dynamics of "structured" personality tests. *Journal of Clinical Psychology, 1,* 296–303.

Meyer, G. J. (1997a). Assessing reliability: Critical corrections for a critical examination of the Rorschach Comprehensive System. *Psychological Assessment, 9,* 480–489. doi:10.1037/1040-3590.9.4.480

Meyer, G. J. (1997b). On the integration of personality assessment methods: The Rorschach and MMPI–2. *Journal of Personality Assessment, 68,* 297–330. doi:10.1207/s15327752jpa6802_5

Meyer, G. J. (2000). Incremental validity of the Rorschach Prognostic Rating scale over the MMPI Ego Strength Scale and IQ. *Journal of Personality Assessment, 74,* 356–370. doi:10.1207/S15327752JPA7403_2

Meyer, G. J. (2001). Evidence to correct misperceptions about Rorschach norms. *Clinical Psychology: Science and Practice, 8,* 389–396. doi:10.1093/clipsy.8.3.389

Meyer, G. J. (2004). The reliability and validity of the Rorschach and Thematic Apperception Test (TAT) compared to other psychological and medical procedures: An analysis of systematically gathered evidence. In M. J. Hilsenroth & D. L. Segal (Eds.), *Comprehensive handbook of psychological assessment: Vol. 2. Personality assessment* (pp. 315–342). Hoboken, NJ: Wiley.

Meyer, G. J., Erdberg, P., & Shaffer, T. (2007). Toward international normative reference data for the Comprehensive System. *Journal of Personality Assessment, 89*(Suppl. 1), S201–S216.

Meyer, G. J., Hilsenroth, M., Baxter, D., Exner, J., Fowler, J., Piers, C., & Resnick, J. (2002). An examination of interrater reliability for scoring the Rorschach comprehensive system in eight data sets. *Journal of Personality Assessment, 78,* 219–274. doi:10.1207/S15327752JPA7802_03

Meyer, G. J., & Kurtz, J. (2006). Advancing personality assessment terminology: Time to retire "objective" and "projective" as personality test descriptors. *Journal of Personality Assessment, 87,* 223–225. doi:10.1207/s15327752jpa8703_01

Meyer, G. J., Riethmiller, R., Brooks, R., Benoit, W., & Handler, L. (2000). A replication of Rorschach and MMPI–2 convergent validity. *Journal of Personality Assessment, 74,* 175–215. doi:10.1207/S15327752JPA7402_3

Meyer, G. J., Viglione, D. J., Mihura, J. L., Erard, R. E., & Erdberg, P. (2010, March). *Introducing key features of the Rorschach Performance Assessment System (RPAS).* Symposium presented at the Midwinter Meeting of the Society for Personality Assessment, San Jose, CA.

Mihura, J., Meyer, G., Bombel, G., & Dumitrascu, N. (2010, March). *A review of the validity research as a basis for variable selection.* Presented at the Midwinter Meeting of the Society for Personality Assessment, San Jose, CA.

Minassian, A., & Perry, W. (2004). The use of projective tests in assessing neurologically impaired populations. In M. J. Hilsenroth & D. L. Segal (Eds.), *Comprehensive handbook of psychological assessment: Vol. 2. Personality assessment* (pp. 539–552). Hoboken, NJ: Wiley.

Mischel, W. (1968). *Personality and assessment.* New York, NY: Wiley.

Morgan, C., & Murray, H. A. (1935). A method for investigating fantasies: The Thematic Apperception Test. *Archives of Neurology and Psychiatry (Chicago), 34,* 289–306.

Murray, H. A. (1938). *Explorations in personality.* New York, NY: Oxford University Press.

Murray, H. A. (1943). *Manual for the Thematic Apperception Test.* Cambridge, MA: Harvard University Press.

Musewicz, J., Marczyk, G., Knauss, L., & York, D. (2009). Current assessment practice, personality measurement, and Rorschach usage by psychologists. *Journal of Personality Assessment, 91,* 453–461. doi:10.1080/00223890903087976

Naglieri, J. A., McNeish, T. J., & Bardos, A. N. (1991). *Draw A Person: Screening Procedure for Emotional Disturbance: Examiner's manual.* Austin, TX: Pro-Ed.

Naglieri, J. A., & Pfeiffer, S. I. (1992). Performance of disruptive behavior disordered and normal samples on the Draw-A-Person: Screening Procedure for Emotional Disturbance. *Psychological Assessment, 4,* 156–159. doi:10.1037/1040-3590.4.2.156

Niec, L. N., & Russ, S. (2002). Children's internal representations, empathy and fantasy play: A validity study of the SCORS-Q. *Psychological Assessment, 14,* 331–338. doi:10.1037/1040-3590.14.3.331

Norcross, J., Koocher, G., & Garofalo, A. (2006). Discredited psychological treatments and tests: A Delphi poll. *Professional Psychology: Research and Practice, 37,* 515–522. doi:10.1037/0735-7028-.37.5.515

Nosek, B. A., Greenwald, A. G., & Banaji, M. R. (2007). The Implicit Association Test at age 7: A methodological and conceptual review. In J. A. Bargh (Ed.), *Automatic processes in social thinking and behavior* (pp. 265–292). New York, NY: Psychology Press.

Nunnally, J. C., & Bernstein, I. H. (1994). *Psychometric theory* (3rd ed.). New York, NY: McGraw-Hill.

O'Neill, R. M. (2005). Body image, body boundary, and the Barrier and Penetration Rorschach scoring system. In R. F. Bornstein & J. M. Masling (Eds.), *Scoring the Rorschach: Seven validated systems* (pp. 159–189). Mahwah, NJ: Erlbaum.

Parker, K. (1983). A meta-analysis of the reliability and validity of the Rorschach. *Journal of Personality Assessment, 47,* 227–231. doi:10.1207/s15327752jpa4703_1

Parker, K. C. H., Hanson, R. K., & Hunsley, J. (1988). MMPI, Rorschach, and WAIS: A meta-analytic comparison of reliability, stability, and validity. *Psychological Bulletin, 103,* 367–373. doi:10.1037/0033-2909.103.3.367

Parker, K. C. H., Hunsley, J., & Hanson, R. K. (1999). Old wine from old skins sometimes tastes like vinegar: A response to Garb, Florio, and Grove. *Psychological Science, 10,* 291–292. doi:10.1111/1467-9280.00153

Phaf, R. H., & Kan, K. (2007). The automaticity of emotional Stroop: A meta-analysis. *Journal of Behavior Therapy and Experimental Psychiatry, 38,* 184–199. doi:10.1016/j.jbtep.2006.10.008

Pihl, R., & Nimrod, G. (1976). The reliability and validity of the Draw-A-Person Test in IQ and personality assessment. *Journal of Clinical Psychology, 32,* 470–472. doi:10.1002/1097-4679(197604)32:2<470::AID-JCLP2270320257>3.0.CO;2-I

Pinkerman, J. E., Haynes, J. P., & Keiser, T. (1993). Characteristics of psychological practice in juvenile court clinics. *American Journal of Forensic Psychology, 11,* 3–12.

Piotrowski, C. (1999). Assessment practices in the era of managed care: Current status and future directions. *Journal of Clinical Psychology, 55,* 787–796. doi:10.1002/(SICI)1097-4679(199907)55:7<787::AID-JCLP2>3.0.CO;2-U

Piotrowski, C., & Keller, J. W. (1984). Psychodiagnostic testing in APA-approved clinical psychology programs. *Professional Psychology: Research and Practice, 15,* 450–456. doi:10.1037/0735-7028.15.3.450

Piotrowski, C., & Zalewski, C. (1993). Training in psychodiagnostic testing in APA-approved Psy.D. and Ph.D. clinical psychology programs. *Journal of Personality Assessment, 61,* 394–405. doi:10.1207/s15327752jpa6102_17

Rapaport, D. (1946). *Diagnostic psychological testing* (Vol. 1). Chicago, IL: Yearbook Publishers.

Riethmiller, R. J., & Handler, L. (1997). Problematic methods and unwarranted conclusions in DAP research: Suggestions for improved research procedures. *Journal of Personality Assessment, 69,* 459–475. doi:10.1207/s15327752jpa6903_1

Roberts, G. E., & Gruber, C. P. (2005). *Roberts-2 manual.* Los Angeles, CA: Western Psychological Services.

Ronan, G. F., Gibbs, M. S., Dreer, L. E., & Lombardo, J. A. (2008). Personal Problem-Solving System—Revised. In S. R. Jenkins (Ed.), *A handbook of clinical scoring systems for thematic apperceptive techniques* (pp. 181–207). Mahwah, NJ: Erlbaum.

Rorschach, H. (1942). *Psychodiagnostics: A diagnostic test based on perception.* Oxford, England: Hans Huber. (Original work published 1921)

Rosenthal, R., Hiller, J., Bornstein, R., Berry, D., & Brunell-Neuleib, S. (2001). Meta-analytic methods, the Rorschach, and the MMPI. *Psychological Assessment, 13,* 449–451. doi:10.1037/1040-3590.13.4.449

Rosenzweig, S. (1978). *Rosenzweig Picture–Frustration Study (P-F)* (rev. ed.). Lutz, FL: Psychological Assessment Resources.

Rotter, J. B., Lah, M. I., & Rafferty, J. E. (1992). *Manual: The Rotter Incomplete Sentences Blank: College form.* New York, NY: Psychological Corporation.

Schultheiss, O., Liening, S., & Schad, D. (2008). The reliability of a Picture Story Exercise measure of implicit motives: Estimates of internal consistency, retest reliability, and ipsative stability. *Journal of Research in Personality, 42,* 1560–1571. doi:10.1016/j.jrp.2008.07.008

Shrout, P. E. (1998). Measurement reliability and agreement in psychiatry. *Statistical Methods in Medical Research, 7,* 301–317. doi:10.1191/096228098672090967

Shrout, P. E., Spitzer, R. L., & Fleiss, J. L. (1987). Quantification of agreement in psychiatric diagnosis revisited. *Archives of General Psychiatry, 44,* 172–177.

Spangler, W. (1992). Validity of questionnaire and TAT measures of need for achievement: Two meta-analyses. *Psychological Bulletin, 112,* 140–154. doi:10.1037/0033-2909.112.1.140

Stokes, J. M., Pogge, D., Powell-Lunder, J., Ward, A., Bilginer, L., & DeLuca, V. (2003). The Rorschach Ego Impairment Index: Prediction of treatment outcome in a child psychiatric population. *Journal of Personality Assessment, 81,* 11–19. doi:10.1207/S15327752JPA8101_02

Sundberg, N. (1961). The practice of psychological testing in clinical services in the United States. *American Psychologist, 16,* 79–83. doi:10.1037/h0040647

Swenson, C. H. (1957). Empirical evaluations of human figure drawings. *Psychological Bulletin, 54,* 431–466. doi:10.1037/h0041404

Swensen, C. H. (1968). Empirical evaluations of human figure drawings: 1957–21. *Psychological Bulletin, 70,* 20–44. doi:10.1037/h0026011

Tharinger, D. J., & Stark, K. (1990). A qualitative versus quantitative approach to evaluating the Draw-A-Person and Kinetic Family Drawings: A study of mood- and anxiety-disordered children. *Psychological Assessment, 2,* 365–375. doi:10.1037/1040-3590-.2.4.365

Thompson, C. E. (1949). *Thematic Apperception Test: Thompson modification.* Cambridge, MA: Harvard University Press.

Vatnaland, T., Vatnaland, J., Friis, S., & Opjordsmoen, S. (2007). Are GAF scores reliable in routine clinical use? *Acta Psychiatrica Scandinavica, 115,* 326–330. doi:10.1111/j.1600-0447.2006.00925.x

Wakefield, J. (1986). Creativity and the TAT blank card. *The Journal of Creative Behavior, 20,* 127–133.

Weiner, I. B. (1977). Approaches to Rorschach validation. In M. A. Rickers-Ovsiankina (Ed.), *Rorschach psychology* (pp. 575–608). Huntington, NY: Krieger.

Weiner, I. B. (1994). The Rorschach Inkblot Method (RIM) is not a test: Implications for theory and practice. *Journal of Personality Assessment, 62,* 498–504. doi:10.1207/s15327752jpa6203_9

Weiner, I. B. (2003). *Principles of Rorschach interpretation* (2nd ed.). Mahwah, NJ: Erlbaum.

Westen, D. (1991). Social cognition and object relations. *Psychological Bulletin, 109,* 429–455. doi:10.1037/0033-2909.109.3.429

Westen, D. (1995). *Social Cognition and Object Relations Scale: Q-sort for projective stories (SCORS Q).* Unpublished manuscript, Department of Psychology, Emory University, Atlanta, GA.

Westen, D. (1998). The scientific legacy of Sigmund Freud: Toward a psychodynamically informed psychological science. *Psychological Bulletin, 124,* 333–371. doi:10.1037/0033-2909.124.3.333

Winch, R. F., & More, D. M. (1956). Does TAT add information to interviews? Statistical analysis of the increment. *Journal of Clinical Psychology, 12,* 316–321. doi:10.1002/1097-4679(195610)12:4<316::AID-JCLP2270120403>3.0.CO;2-P

Wood, J. M., Krishnamurthy, R., & Archer, R. (2003). Three factors of the Comprehensive System for the Rorschach and their relationship to Wechsler IQ Scores in an adolescent sample. *Assessment, 10,* 259–265. doi:10.1177/1073191103255493

Wood, J. M., Nezworski, M. T., & Garb, H. N. (2003). What's right with the Rorschach? *The Scientific Review of Mental Health Practice, 2,* 142–146.

Wood, J. M., Nezworski, M. T., Garb, H. N., & Lilienfeld, S. O. (2001). The misperception of psychopathology: Problems with the norms of the Comprehensive System for the Rorschach. *Clinical Psychology: Science and Practice, 8,* 350–373. doi:10.1093/clipsy.8.3.350

Wood, J. M., Nezworski, M. T., Lilienfeld, S. O., & Garb, H. N. (2003). *What's wrong with the Rorschach? Science confronts the controversial inkblot test.* San Francisco, CA: Jossey-Bass.

Wood, J. M., Nezworski, M. T., & Stejskal, W. J. (1996). The Comprehensive System for the Rorschach: A critical examination. *Psychological Science, 7,* 3–10. doi:10.1111/j.1467-9280.1996.tb00658.x

Wrightson, L., & Saklofske, D. (2000). Validity and reliability of the Draw A Person: Screening Procedure for Emotional Disturbance with adolescent students. *Canadian Journal of School Psychology, 16,* 95–102. doi:10.1177/082957350001600107

Ziegler, M., Schmukle, S., Egloff, B., & Bühner, M. (2010). Investigating measures of achievement motivation(s). *Journal of Individual Differences, 31,* 15–21. doi:10.1027/1614-0001/a000002

CHAPTER 18

OBJECTIVE TESTS AS INSTRUMENTS OF PSYCHOLOGICAL THEORY AND RESEARCH

David Watson

The goal of this chapter is to help researchers understand, create, and evaluate objective psychological tests. Its restricted focus therefore reflects the traditional psychometric differentiation between *objective* and *projective* tests (e.g., see Loevinger, 1957), a distinction that some have recently questioned (Meyer & Kurtz, 2006). According to Loevinger (1957), the distinction between these two types of tests primarily "rests on item structure. Projective tests involve free response, as do most interviews, whereas objective tests, in the sense that the term is used here, require in principle that every individual choose one of the stated alternatives for each item" (p. 648). Similarly, Meyer and Kurtz (2006) have stated that

> the term *objective* typically refers to instruments in which the stimulus is an adjective, proposition, or question that is presented to a person who is required to indicate how accurately it describes his or her personality using a limited set of externally provided response options (true vs. false, yes vs. no, Likert scale, etc.). What is *objective* about such a procedure is that the psychologist administering the test does not need to rely on judgment to classify or interpret the test-taker's response; the intended response is clearly indicated and scored according to a pre-existing key. (p. 233)

CLASSIFYING OBJECTIVE TESTS

Ability Versus Nonability Tests

Objective tests can be further subdivided on a number of dimensions. One classic distinction is between *ability* and *nonability* tests (e.g., Anastasi & Urbina, 1997; Kaplan & Saccuzzo, 2009). These two types of tests differ in terms of (a) how the target constructs typically are assessed and (b) their resultant susceptibility to faking.

For instance, it now is well established that work performance is significantly influenced by both ability and personality factors. More specifically, individuals who are smart and conscientious tend to be better employees (Roberts, Kuncel, Shiner, Caspi & Goldberg, 2007; Schmidt, Shaffer, & Oh, 2008). Psychologists typically assess intelligence by obtaining performance samples; for instance, respondents are asked to solve math problems, detect patterns, recall or complete sequences, and define the meaning of words. In the absence of cheating, this makes it virtually impossible to fake one's level of ability. In contrast, however, nonability tests assess thoughts, feelings, behaviors, and preferences. For instance, a typical conscientiousness scale asks respondents to indicate how reliable, dependable, and goal-oriented they are. It therefore is quite easy for respondents to misrepresent themselves as having attributes (such as dependability and achievement motivation) that they actually do not possess, which creates considerable problems when using these measures in applied high-stakes testing. This chapter will discuss issues related to both types of tests, although the primary focus will be on nonability tests.

Broad Versus Narrow Tests

Objective tests also can be classified according to their scope and breadth of coverage. In this regard,

DOI: 10.1037/13619-019
APA Handbook of Research Methods in Psychology: Vol. 1. Foundations, Planning, Measures, and Psychometrics, H. Cooper (Editor-in-Chief)

it now is clear that most important psychological domains (such as ability, personality, psychopathology, and motivation) are ordered hierarchically at multiple levels of abstraction or breadth (e.g., Markon, Krueger, & Watson, 2005; Watson, 2005).

For example, the broad higher order trait of conscientiousness can be decomposed into several distinct yet empirically correlated components, such as deliberation (i.e., conscientious individuals plan carefully before acting), dependability (i.e., conscientious individuals are reliable and responsible), and achievement striving (i.e., conscientious individuals are willing to work hard to achieve long-term goals; Markon et al., 2005; Watson, Clark, & Harkness, 1994). Similarly, in the domain of cognitive ability, the overarching dimension of *g* or general mental ability (Schmidt & Hunter, 2004; Spearman, 1904) can be decomposed into more specific abilities, such as verbal comprehension, perceptual reasoning, working memory and processing speed (Benson, Hulac, & Kranzler, 2010; Bowden, Weiss, Holdnack, & Lloyd, 2006). In a related vein, Watson (2005) and others have proposed complex, multilevel hierarchical models of psychopathology—classifying diagnoses, for example, into broad *superclasses* of disorders (e.g., emotional or internalizing disorders), narrower groups of more closely related syndromes (e.g., fear disorders such as panic disorder, social phobia, and specific phobia), individual disorders (e.g., specific phobia), and even subtypes within existing disorders (e.g., animal, blood-injection, and natural environment fears). Issues related to both general and more specific measures will be examined in this chapter.

PSYCHOMETRICS: A HISTORICAL OVERVIEW

To understand, create, and evaluate objective tests, it is necessary to examine basic concepts and principles of psychological measurement. This topic can seem intimidating at times, in part because of the large number of potentially relevant concepts. Within the broad domain of validity, for instance, one encounters a confusing array of terms, including concurrent validity, construct validity, content validity, criterion validity, discriminant validity, external validity, face validity, incremental validity, and predictive validity

(e.g., Anastasi & Urbina, 1997; Kaplan & Saccuzzo, 2009; Simms & Watson, 2007; Watson, 2006).

To place these concepts into a meaningful context, a brief outline of the evolution of psychometric thinking over the course of the 20th century will be presented. This thinking has revolved around the interplay of two core concepts—reliability and validity. *Reliability* can be defined as the consistency of scores that are obtained across repeated assessments (Anastasi & Urbina, 1997; Kaplan & Saccuzzo, 2009; Watson, 2006). Reliability was the dominant concern among psychometricians and test developers during the first half of the 20th century, largely because it appeared to be a more straightforward and scientifically rigorous concept than validity. As I demonstrate subsequently, however, this apparent straightforwardness was deceptive; in fact, classical reliability theory was formed on the basis of some questionable assumptions that are unlikely to be fully met in many important areas of psychological research. Moreover, it eventually was discovered that maximizing reliability (or, to put it more accurately, maximizing the value of conventional indicators of reliability) actually could be counterproductive and could lead to the creation of less interesting and informative measures (the "attenuation paradox"; see Loevinger, 1954, 1957); the nature of this paradox is explained in the section Reliability later in this chapter.

Consequently, reliability gradually lost its position of preeminence and was supplanted by validity as the conceptual centerpiece of measurement (although interest in reliability has resurged in the 21st century, as discussed in the section Reliability). In the current *Standards for Educational and Psychological Testing* (American Educational Research Association [AERA], American Psychological Association [APA], & National Council on Measurement in Education [NCME], 1999), *validity* is defined as "the degree to which evidence and theory support the interpretation of test scores entailed by proposed uses of tests. Validity is, therefore, the most fundamental consideration in developing and evaluating tests" (p. 9). Throughout most of the 20th century, psychometricians distinguished between several distinct types of validity, including content validity, criterion validity, and construct validity. For instance, the 1974 edition of the *Standards* stated, "The kinds of validity depend upon the kinds of inferences one might wish to draw from test scores. Four interdependent kinds of inferential interpretation are traditionally described to summarize most test use: the *criterion-related* validities (*predictive* and *concurrent*); *content* validity; and *construct* validity" (AERA, APA, & NCME, 1974, pp. 25–26).

A major breakthrough occurred in the 1990s, however, when it was recognized that all other types of validity simply represent specific aspects of the all-encompassing process of construct validity (AERA, APA, & NCME, 1999; Messick, 1995). Thus, according to the current *Standards,* "Validity is a unitary concept. It is the degree to which all the accumulated evidence supports the intended interpretation of test scores for the proposed purpose" (AERA, APA, & NCME, 1999, p. 11). It must be emphasized, moreover, that this expanded conceptualization of construct validity also subsumes all of the major types of reliability evidence, including both internal consistency and retest reliability. As Messick (1995) put it, "Construct validity is based on an integration of any evidence that bears on the interpretation or meaning of the test scores" (p. 742). Consequently, construct validity—a concept that originally was articulated by Cronbach and Meehl (1955)—has emerged as the central unifying principle in contemporary psychometrics.

Another crucial insight was the recognition that construct validity is not simply a process of evaluating the properties of an already developed test. Rather, it also serves as the basic principle for creating and refining new tests. Put differently, construct validity considerations should guide the entire process of scale creation. This view originally was articulated by Loevinger (1957), and it subsequently has been elaborated by many others (e.g., Clark & Watson, 1995; Messick, 1995; Simms & Watson, 2007; Watson, 2006). Loevinger divided the scale development and validation process into three basic phases: the *substantive,* the *structural,* and the *external.* This remains a useful way of organizing this topic, and the following discussion follows this framework.

SUBSTANTIVE VALIDITY: DEVELOPMENT OF THE INITIAL ITEM POOL

Literature Review

The substantive phase primarily addresses issues related to the traditional psychometric concept of content validity. It begins with a thorough review of the relevant literature to discover how others have attempted to conceptualize and measure the target construct under consideration. Initially, this review should include previous attempts to assess both the same construct and any closely related concepts. Subsequently, the review should be broadened to encompass more tangentially related concepts to help define the conceptual boundaries of the target construct. Suppose, for instance, that one is interested in creating a new measure of guilt. One initially might focus on prior attempts to assess guilt and closely related affective states, such as shame and embarrassment. Eventually, however, a thorough review of the literature would reveal that a broad array of negative mood states (including guilt, shame, embarrassment, anxiety, depression and hostility) are strongly intercorrelated (Watson, 2005; Watson & Clark, 1984, 1992), so that it is important to clarify the hypothesized relation between guilt and these other negative affects as well. In this way, a test developer can begin to create a predicted pattern of convergent and discriminant relations at the earliest stages of scale development (see Clark & Watson, 1995; Watson, 2006).

A comprehensive review of the literature is important for several reasons. First, it will explicate the nature and range of the content subsumed within the target construct. Second, it often can help to identify a range of possible problems in existing measures (such as confusing instructions, suboptimal response formats, and poorly functioning item content) that then can be avoided. Finally—and most important—a thorough review will indicate whether the proposed new instrument is actually needed. If a good measure of the target construct already exists, why create another? The burden of proof is on the prospective test developer to articulate clearly how this new instrument represents a theoretical or empirical advance over existing measures; in the absence of such proof, there is no real justification for adding to the needless proliferation of assessment instruments.

Construct Conceptualization

Assuming that the test developer concludes that the new instrument actually is needed, the critical next step is to develop a precise and detailed conception of the target construct that will be the focus of assessment. Of course, test developers always have at least a sketchy understanding of what it is they are trying to measure. By itself, however, a vague conceptualization is insufficient and may create enormous (and often unsolvable) problems that reveal themselves in subsequent stages of the validation process. Unfortunately, many investigators fail to take the important next step of fleshing out the nature and scope of the target construct more precisely. Clark and Watson (1995) have recommended writing out a brief, formal description of the target construct, which can be useful in crystallizing one's conceptual model. An even better strategy would be to articulate a detailed *measurement model* that specifies both (a) the nature and scope of the overall construct and (b) all of the major hypothesized facets or subcomponents within it.

Suppose, for example, that a researcher is interested in developing a new measure of specific phobia. What is the appropriate range of content that should be included in this measure (for a discussion of this issue, see Cutshall & Watson, 2004; Watson, 2005, 2009b)? Moreover, what specific symptom dimensions might meaningfully emerge as subcomponents within this domain? In this regard, the *Diagnostic and Statistical Manual of Mental Disorders* (4th ed., text revision; *DSM–IV–TR*; American Psychiatric Association, 2000) formally recognizes four subtypes of specific phobia: animal, natural environment (e.g., storms, heights, water), blood–injection–injury, and situational (e.g., tunnels, bridges, elevators, enclosed spaces) fears. Does a review of the relevant literature support the value of this quadripartite scheme, or should an alternative measurement model be created? These types of issues all should be clearly addressed before creating the initial item pool.

Creation of the Initial Item Pool

Comprehensiveness and overinclusiveness. Once the nature and scope of the content domain have been clarified, one can begin the actual task of item writing (see Clark & Watson, 1995, for a discussion of basic principles of good item writing). No data analytic technique can remedy significant deficiencies in the initial item pool; consequently, the creation of this pool is an absolutely critical stage in test development.

The basic goal is to sample systematically all content that potentially is relevant to the target construct. As Loevinger (1957) put it, "*The items of the pool should be chosen so as to sample all possible contents which might comprise the putative trait according to all known alternative theories of the trait*" (p. 659). Two key implications of this *principle of overinclusiveness* are that the initial item pool should (a) be broader and more inclusive than one's own theoretical view of the target construct and (b) include content that ultimately will be shown to be unrelated to this construct. The logic underlying this principle is simple: Subsequent psychometric–structural analyses can identify weak, unrelated items that should be dropped, but they are powerless to detect relevant content that should have been included but was not. Thus, this principle of overinclusiveness ultimately serves the fundamental goal of *comprehensiveness*, which is a key consideration in establishing the content validity of a test (see Haynes, Richard, & Kubany, 1995; Messick, 1995).

Representativeness. Another important consideration is *representativeness*, that is, the degree to which the item pool provides an adequate sample of each of the major content areas within the domain subsumed by the target construct (Clark & Watson, 1995; Haynes et al., 1995). To ensure that each important aspect of the construct is assessed adequately, some psychometricians recommend that formal, rational item groups be created to tap each major content area within a domain (see Simms & Watson, 2007; Watson, 2006). Hogan (1983; see also Hogan & Hogan, 1992) has called these rational groupings "homogeneous item composites" (HICs).

For instance, Watson and colleagues recently created the Inventory of Depression and Anxiety Symptoms (IDAS; Watson et al., 2007, 2008); as its name suggests, the IDAS was designed to yield a multidimensional measure of mood and anxiety disorder symptoms. To assess symptoms of depression, the first step was the creation of an overinclusive pool of 117 items. In creating this item pool, the basic strategy was to include multiple markers to define all of the symptom dimensions that potentially could emerge in subsequent structural analyses. To ensure that sufficient markers were included for each potential dimension, the candidate items were rationally organized into 13 HICs, each of which contained eight to 14 items. Nine HICs corresponded to the basic symptom criteria for a major depressive episode in *DSM–IV–TR* (e.g., depressed mood, anhedonia or loss of interest, appetite disturbance). Four additional HICs tapped symptoms potentially relevant to the hopelessness subtype of depression (Abramson, Metalsky, & Alloy, 1989), the specific symptom features of melancholic depression (see Joiner, Walker, Pettit, Perez, & Cukrowicz, 2005), angry and irritable mood (which can be an alternative expression of depressed mood in children and adolescents; see American Psychiatric Association, 2000, p. 327), and markers of high energy and positive affect (which have been shown to be specifically related to depression; see Watson, 2009a; Watson & Naragon-Gainey, 2010). Finally, to help define the boundaries of this domain, seven additional HICs assessed various symptoms of anxiety (e.g., worry, panic, social anxiety).

It must be emphasized that the creation of rational HICs does not force a particular structure onto the items; rather, it simply ensures that hypothesized dimensions and scales have a reasonable opportunity to emerge in subsequent structural analyses. To illustrate this important point, Table 18.1 presents the items from two of the final, factor analytically derived IDAS scales—Dysphoria and Lassitude—along with their initial HIC placements. As can be seen, each factor-based scale includes items from three or more of the original HICs; indeed, it is particularly noteworthy that both scales contain items related to two or more *DSM–IV–TR* symptom criteria for a major depressive episode (e.g., Lassitude contains items related to both sleep disturbance and fatigue or anergia). Clearly, organizing items into rational, content-based groups does not force them to define a single common scale.

Relevance. A final substantive consideration is *relevance* (Haynes et al., 1995; Messick, 1995), which is the requirement that all of the item content in the finished instrument should fall within the boundaries

TABLE 18.1

Final Scale Assignments and Initial HIC Placements of Selected IDAS Items

Final scale/item	Initial HIC placement
Dysphoria	
I felt depressed	Depressed mood (C1)
I had little interest in my usual hobbies or activities	Anhedonia (C2)
I felt fidgety, restless	Motor problems (C5)
I talked more slowly than usual	Motor problems (C5)
I felt inadequate	Worthlessness/guilt (C7)
I blamed myself for things	Worthlessness/guilt (C7)
I had trouble concentrating	Cognitive problems (C8)
I had trouble making up my mind	Cognitive problems (C8)
I felt discouraged about things	Hopelessness
I found myself worrying all the time	Worry
Lassitude	
I had trouble waking up in the morning	Sleep disturbance (C4)
I slept more than usual	Sleep disturbance (C4)
I felt exhausted	Fatigue/anergia (C6)
I felt drowsy, sleepy	Fatigue/anergia (C6)
It took a lot of effort to get me going	Fatigue/anergia (C6)
I felt much worse in the morning than later in the day	Melancholic depression

Note. Numbers in parentheses indicate corresponding *Diagnostic and Statistical Manual of Mental Disorders* (4th ed., text revision; American Psychiatric Association, 2000) symptom criteria for a major depressive episode. HIC = Homogeneous Item Composite. IDAS = Inventory of Depression and Anxiety Symptoms.

of the target construct. This requirement may seem incompatible with the earlier principle of overinclusiveness, but it is not. The principle of overinclusiveness simply stipulates that some marginally relevant content should be included in the initial item pool to clarify the boundaries of the construct domain. Subsequent psychometric analyses then can determine these limits and identify construct-irrelevant content that ultimately should be discarded. Relevance-related concerns arise when this inappropriate content is not discarded for one reason or another.

Although this property of content relevance may sound easy to attain in principle, it often is more difficult to achieve in practice. A key problem is the dynamic nature of content validity (Haynes et al., 1995; Watson, 2006). As our understanding of the target construct evolves, content that previously was placed within the domain may now fall beyond its boundaries. An excellent example of this dynamic process can be seen in the assessment of anxiety and depression symptoms. Before the 1980s, most test developers failed to distinguish clearly between these constructs. Because of this, many older depression measures contain significant anxiety-related content, and vice versa (Clark & Watson, 1991; Gotlib & Cane, 1989). This irrelevant content now is judged to highly problematic, given that it necessarily lessens the discriminant validity of these instruments.

STRUCTURAL VALIDITY

Structural Fidelity

Structural fidelity is the basic principle underlying the structural phase of construct validation (Loevinger, 1957; see also Messick, 1995; Watson, 2006). This is the idea that the internal structure of the scale (i.e., the correlations among its component items) should be fully consistent with what is known about the internal organization of the underlying construct. In light of the fact that most constructs are posited to be homogeneous and internally consistent, this principle typically requires that the items in a test also should be homogeneous and internally consistent (although exceptions to this general rule are discussed in the section Reliability). Because of this, the structural phase also subsumes traditional forms of reliability evidence. Accordingly, the discussion of this stage will begin with an examination of the basic principles and methods of item selection and then turn to a consideration of major forms of reliability.

Methods of Item Selection

Classical test methods. After collecting data on the items in the initial pool, the next crucial step in the test construction process is to decide which of the items should be retained in the final scale(s). Several basic strategies can guide item selection. One strategy, criterion keying, is the focus of Chapter 19 in this volume. Consequently, the following discussion is limited to methods based on some form of internal consistency analysis.

Currently, the most widely used item selection method is based on classical test theory and involves the use of factor analysis to identify groups of interrelated items (see Clark & Watson, 1995; Floyd & Widaman, 1995). A detailed discussion of the factor analytic method is beyond the scope of this chapter, but a general outline is presented here. In the early stages of test construction, exploratory factor analysis (EFA) should be used to identify the underlying latent dimensions, which then can serve as a basis for creating the final scales (see also Clark & Watson, 1995; Simms & Watson, 2007); the resulting scales then can be refined using confirmatory factor analysis (CFA), where needed. Consistent with general guidelines in the broader factor analytic literature (see Fabrigar, Wegener, MacCallum, & Strahan, 1999; Floyd & Widaman, 1995; D. W. Russell, 2002), principal factor analysis is recommended over principal components analysis as the initial extraction method in EFA.

Othogonal (typically varimax) and oblique (usually promax) rotations both offer unique advantages that are invaluable in identifying the optimal set of items, and it therefore is recommended that both be used in the item selection process (for discussions of different factor rotation methods, see Fabrigar et al., 1999; D. W. Russell, 2002). The chief advantage of oblique rotations (which allow the factors to be correlated) is that they model the associations among the factors; this, in turn, helps to identify potential discriminant validity problems in the resulting scales (i.e., strongly correlated factors may translate into strongly correlated scales). The primary advantage of orthogonal rotations (which constrain the factors to be uncorrelated) is that they are better at identifying "splitter" items, that is, items that have significant cross-loadings on two or more factors. Splitters tend to create discriminant validity problems (by increasing correlations among scales) and are prime candidates for deletion.

This recommendation to use both oblique and orthogonal rotations may be surprising to some, particularly in light of the common misconception that orthogonal rotations should not be used when one is interested in assessing moderately to strongly correlated constructs (e.g., different subtypes of specific phobia; different facets of conscientiousness).

Although this misconception seems intuitively compelling (how can uncorrelated factors validly capture correlated constructs?), the fact is that orthogonal rotations can be used to construct scales that are moderately to strongly correlated once simple unit weighting is employed. For instance, Watson and Clark (1999) used orthogonal varimax rotations to create the scales included in the Expanded Form of the Positive and Negative Affect Schedule (PANAS-X). Despite this strict reliance on orthogonal rotation, several of the resulting scales consistently show correlations of .50 and greater with one another (Watson, 2005; Watson & Clark, 1999).

In an EFA-based approach, the basic idea is to select items that load moderately to strongly on the target factor (typically, at least |.35| or greater when conducting a principal factor analysis) and have much lower loadings on all other factors (Clark & Watson, 1995; Simms & Watson, 2007). Regardless of the specific strategy that is used, the goal is to select items that are moderately correlated with one another. Clark and Watson (1995) have recommended that the average interitem correlation generally should fall in the .15 to .50 range. This wide range is provided because the optimal value necessarily will vary with the generality versus specificity of the target construct. If one is measuring a relatively broad higher order construct such as conscientiousness, a lower mean interitem correlation (e.g., a value in the .15 to .30 range) likely will be optimal. In contrast, to measure a narrower construct such as deliberation, a higher mean correlation (e.g., in the .35 to .50 range) likely will be needed. Again, the key principle is structural fidelity: The magnitude of the item intercorrelations should faithfully reflect the internal organization of the underlying construct, an issue discussed further in the section Structural Fidelity.

Item response theory. Scales created using item response theory (IRT; Embretson, 1996; Reise, Ainsworth, & Haviland, 2005; Reise & Waller, 2009; Simms & Watson, 2007) still are relatively uncommon, but they are likely to become much more prevalent in the future with the increasing availability of sophisticated computer software. IRT is based on the assumption that test responses reflect levels of an underlying trait and, moreover, that the relation between the response and the trait can be described for each item by a monotonically increasing function called an *item characteristic curve* (ICC). Individuals with higher levels of the trait have greater expected probabilities for answering the item in the keyed direction (e.g., quantitatively gifted individuals are more likely to get a math problem correct), and the ICC provides the precise values of these probabilities at each level of the trait.

In IRT, the emphasis is on identifying those items that are likely to be most informative for each individual respondent, given his or her level of the underlying trait. For instance, a challenging problem in calculus may provide useful information for an individual with a high level of quantitative ability (who may or may not be able to get it correct), but it will be useless if given to an individual with little facility in mathematics (because one knows in advance that he or she will get it wrong). From an IRT perspective, the optimal item to be administered next is one that the individual has a 50% probability of endorsing in the keyed direction—given what is known about that individual's trait level on the basis of his or her responses to previous items—because this conveys the maximum amount of new trait-relevant information for that person.

Within the IRT literature, a variety of one-, two-, and three-parameter models have been proposed to model the data (e.g., Reise & Waller, 2003). Of these, a two-parameter model—more specifically, one with parameters for *item difficulty* and *item discrimination*—has been applied most consistently in the recent literature (Simms & Watson, 2007). Item difficulty refers to the point along the trait continuum at which a given item has a 50% probability of being endorsed in the keyed direction. High difficulty values are associated with items that have low endorsement probabilities (i.e., that reflect higher levels of the trait). Discrimination reflects the degree of psychometric precision, or information, that an item provides at its difficulty level.

In comparison to other item selection approaches, IRT offers two important advantages. First, it enables the test developer to specify the trait level at which a given item is maximally informative.

This information, in turn, can be used to identify a set of items that yield precise, reliable assessment across the entire range of the trait. Put differently, IRT-based scales offer an improved ability to discriminate among individuals at the extreme ends of the trait distribution (e.g., among those both very high and very low in quantitative ability). Second, IRT methods allow one to estimate an individual's trait level without having to rely on a fixed, standard set of items. This property permits the development of *computer-adaptive tests* in which assessment is focused primarily on the subset of items that are maximally informative for each individual respondent (e.g., difficult items for quantitatively gifted individuals, easier items for those low in mathematical ability). Because of this, computer adaptive tests are extremely efficient and can yield the same amount of trait-relevant information using far fewer items than conventional measures (typically providing item savings of 50% or more; see Embretson, 1996; Reise & Waller, 2009).

IRT can be an extremely useful adjunct to other scale development methods, such as EFA. As a scale development technique, its main limitation is that it requires a good working knowledge of the basic underlying traits that need to be modeled. Put differently, it requires that one's measurement model already be reasonably well established. Consequently, IRT methods are most useful in those domains in which the basic constructs already are well known; conversely, it is less helpful in areas in which these constructs still need to be identified. Thus, EFA remains the basic method of choice for the early stages of assessment within a domain. Once the basic factors, scales, and constructs within the domain have been identified, they can be further refined using approaches such as CFA and IRT.

Reliability

Overview.   As noted earlier, reliability evidence now is subsumed within the all-encompassing concept of construct validity. There are two common methods for estimating reliability: internal consistency and test–retest reliability. Both of these methods—at least as they typically are employed—are better viewed as indicators of the consistency of measurement across various conditions rather than

reliability per se. Indeed, they may either overestimate or underestimate the true level of reliability (as it is strictly defined) under various conditions.

To understand the material that follows, it will be helpful to summarize the central assumptions of classical reliability theory (see Anastasi & Urbina, 1997; Kaplan & Saccuzzo, 2009; Rushton, Brainerd, & Pressley, 1983; Watson, 2006). According to the logic that originally was articulated by Spearman (1910), any observed score can be decomposed into two independent components: the *true score* and *measurement error*. The true score (e.g., the individual's true level of intelligence or conscientiousness) is assumed to be invariant and perfectly correlated across different assessment conditions. Conversely, measurement error is assumed to be entirely random; consequently, this component should fluctuate chaotically and be entirely uncorrelated across different assessment conditions. Within this framework, reliability can be defined as the ratio of true score variance to total (i.e., observed score) variance.

These assumptions further explain two important features of classical reliability theory. First, as noted, reliability and error were equated with consistency (i.e., the extent to which indicators of the construct are correlated across different assessments) and inconsistency (i.e., a lack of correlation across assessments), respectively. Accordingly, regardless of the specific method that is used, reliability estimates will increase in magnitude as the assessed indicators of the construct (e.g., different items within a scale; different administrations of the same test over time; parallel forms of a test) become more highly interrelated. Second, reliability generally should increase as more and more indicators are aggregated together. Because random errors are, by definition, uncorrelated across assessments, they should increasingly cancel each other out as more observations are averaged. Rushton et al. (1983), for instance, stated, "There is always error associated with measurement. When several measurements are combined, these errors tend to average out, thereby providing a more accurate picture of relationships in the population" (p. 19).

Internal consistency.   Structural fidelity is the guiding consideration in evaluating the internal consistency of an objective test: The correlations among the items should faithfully parallel the internal organization of the underlying construct. Given that most constructs are posited to be homogeneous and internally consistent, the application of this principle typically means that the selected items also should be homogeneous and internally consistent. There are exceptions, however. These exceptions involve cases in which the items are designed to be *causal indicators* (i.e., causal contributors to some cumulative index) rather than *effect indicators* (i.e., parallel manifestations of a latent underlying construct; see Smith & McCarthy, 1995; Watson, 2006). This commonly is the case in the measurement of stress and trauma. For example, Simms, Watson, and Doebbeling (2002) created a Severe Exposures Index (SEI) to assess combat-related trauma in deployed veterans of the 1991 Gulf War. The SEI consisted of three items: "come under small arms fire," "exposure to nerve gas," and "exposure to mustard gas or other blistering agents." In this case, there is no expectation or requirement that these items should be significantly intercorrelated—for instance, that individuals who came under small arms fire also were more likely to be exposed to nerve gas. Rather, these items simply are seen as causal contributors that jointly create a cumulative index of combat-related trauma. It sometimes is unclear whether a given variable is a cause or an effect indicator. In such cases, statistical tests have been developed to help researchers make the appropriate decision (e.g., Bollen & Ting, 2000).

In most cases, however, the goal of assessment is to measure one thing (i.e., the target construct)—and only one thing—as precisely as possible. Unfortunately, an inspection of the contemporary literature makes it clear that this goal remains poorly understood by both test developers and users. The most obvious problem is the belief that item homogeneity can be established simply by demonstrating that a scale shows an acceptable level of internal consistency, as estimated by traditional indexes, such as K–R 20 (Kuder & Richardson, 1937) and coefficient alpha (Cronbach, 1951). However, psychometricians long have discouraged the practice of relying on these conventional reliability indexes to establish the homogeneity of a scale

(Clark & Watson, 1995; Cortina, 1993; Schmitt, 1996; Simms & Watson, 2007; Watson, 2006).

To understand this point, it is necessary to distinguish between internal consistency on the one hand versus homogeneity or unidimensionality on the other. *Internal consistency* refers to the overall degree to which the items that make up the scale are interrelated, whereas *homogeneity* and *unidimensionality* indicate whether the items assess a single underlying factor or construct (Clark & Watson, 1995; Cortina, 1993; Schmitt, 1996; Simms & Watson, 2007; Watson, 2006). Thus, internal consistency is a necessary but not sufficient condition for homogeneity. Put differently, a scale cannot be homogeneous unless all of its items are related, but a scale can contain many interrelated items and still not be unidimensional. Because the goal of assessment typically is to measure a single construct systematically, the test developer ultimately should be interested in homogeneity, rather than internal consistency.

Unfortunately, K–R 20 and coefficient alpha are measures of internal consistency rather than homogeneity and so are of limited use in establishing the unidimensionality of a scale. Moreover, they are imperfect indicators of internal consistency because they actually are a function of two different parameters: (a) the number of scale items and (b) the average correlation among these items (Clark & Watson, 1995; Cortina, 1993; Schmitt, 1996). That is, one can achieve a high coefficient alpha by having (a) many items, (b) highly correlated items, (c) some combination of the two. This complicates things because the number of items is irrelevant to the issue of internal consistency. In practical terms, this means that as the number of items becomes quite large, it is exceedingly easy to achieve a high coefficient alpha. In fact, Cortina (1993) has suggested that coefficient alpha is virtually useless as an index of internal consistency for scales containing 40 or more items.

To complicate things further, a scale can have an acceptable mean interitem correlation and still not be homogeneous. This can occur when many high item correlations are averaged with many low ones (Cortina, 1993; Schmitt, 1996). Cortina (1993), for instance, constructed an 18-item scale composed of two independent nine-item clusters. The items within each group were highly homogeneous and had an average interitem correlation of .50. These groups were created to be statistically independent of one another, such that items in different clusters were completely uncorrelated with each another. This scale was not unidimensional, but instead it reflected two uncorrelated factors. Nevertheless, it had a coefficient alpha of .85 and an average inter-item correlation of .24.

Thus, one cannot ensure unidimensionality simply by focusing on the mean interitem correlation; it also is necessary to examine the distribution and range of these correlations. Consequently, the earlier guideline that the average interitem correlations should fall in the .15 to .50 range needs to be further explicated to state that virtually all of the individual interitem correlations should fall somewhere in the range of .15 to .50. Put differently, unidimensionality is achieved when almost all of the interitem correlations are moderate in magnitude and cluster around the mean level.

In practical terms, the easiest way to establish the homogeneity of a scale is to show that all of its items have a significant loading (i.e., a value of |.35| or higher; see Clark & Watson, 1995) on the first unrotated factor. This establishes that all of the items are indicators of the same underlying construct, that is, that they assess the same thing. Schmitt (1996) advocated a somewhat different approach, recommending that test developers use CFA to test the fit of a single factor model. The focus here is somewhat different in that this CFA-based approach tests whether the items assess only one thing (i.e., that one can model the item correlations using only one latent dimension). Both approaches are informative, but it is important to realize that they provide somewhat different information about a test.

The difference between these two approaches can be illustrated using a simple hierarchical example. Watson, Clark, and Tellegen (1988) created the higher order Negative Affect scale of the PANAS by selecting negative mood terms from different content groups. This scale includes four different indicators of fear (e.g., scared, afraid), two items assessing guilt (guilty, ashamed), and two indicators of anger (irritable, hostile). The PANAS Negative

Affect items all assess the same thing, given that they are moderately to strongly intercorrelated and all load significantly on the same general factor. They do not measure only one thing, however, in that they also assess specific content variance (i.e., fear, guilt, anger) beyond this overarching general factor. Thus, for example, a simple one-factor model cannot account for the strong observed correlation between afraid and scared; additional factors need to be specified to model this overlapping item content. More generally, measures of higher order constructs often contain at least some quasi-redundant item content and, therefore, do not neatly fit a simple one-factor model. Nevertheless, these scales are homogeneous in the sense that their items all measure the same thing (i.e., the target higher order construct) to a significant extent.

The attenuation paradox. This discussion consistently has emphasized that the interitem correlations should be moderate in magnitude. This may seem puzzling to some readers, given that estimates of internal consistency will increase as the average interitem correlation becomes higher. Obviously, therefore, one can maximize coefficient alpha by retaining items that are highly correlated with others in the pool. Is it not desirable, therefore, to maximize reliability by retaining highly intercorrelated items in the final scale?

No, it is not. This is the crux of the classic *attenuation paradox* in psychometrics: Increasing item correlations beyond a certain point actually will lessen the construct validity of a scale (see Boyle, 1991; Clark & Watson, 1995; Loevinger, 1954, 1957). This paradox occurs for two related reasons. First, strongly correlated items also are highly redundant with one another. Once one of them is included in a scale, the others contribute virtually no incremental information. For example, an individual who endorses the item "I often feel uncomfortable at parties" almost certainly will also endorse the item "I usually feel uneasy at large social gatherings." Once one has asked the first item, there is no point in asking the second because the answer is evident. More generally, a scale will yield far more information—and, hence, be a more interesting and valid measure of a construct—if it contains clearly differentiated items that are only moderately correlated. Second, attempts to maximize internal consistency almost invariably produce scales that are quite narrow in content; if this content is narrower than the target construct, then the validity of the scale is compromised. To return to the earlier example, a scale that simply contained a series of items assessing the level of discomfort at parties would lack comprehensiveness as a measure of social anxiety and, therefore, would not be a valid measure of this construct.

This discussion of the attenuation paradox should make it clear that the goal of assessment is to maximize validity, not coefficient alpha. It was this realization, in fact, that eventually led psychometricians to embrace validity as the conceptual centerpiece of psychological measurement.

Alpha as an index of reliability. Conventional indexes such as coefficient alpha are best viewed as indicators of the consistency of measurement across various conditions, rather than reliability per se. Indeed, it is well established that alpha actually can either overestimate or underestimate the true level of reliability under different assessment conditions (see Becker, 2000; Green, 2003; McCrae, Kurtz, Yamagata, & Terracciano, 2011; Osburn, 2000; Schmidt, Le, & Ilies, 2003; Schmitt, 1996). Alpha will overestimate reliability when there are systematic errors of measurement. Unlike random errors, systematic measurement errors are significantly correlated across different assessments. Consequently, they are misclassified as *true score* variance in classical reliability theory (which, as noted, equates true scores with consistency in measurement).

Two kinds of systematic errors are worth noting. The first are response biases such as acquiescence and social desirability (see Watson & Tellegen, 2002; Watson & Vaidya, 2003). *Social desirability* refers to a tendency for respondents to distort their responses (either consciously or unconsciously) to make them more congruent with prevailing cultural norms (Paulhus & Reid, 1991; Watson & Vaidya, 2003). *Acquiescence* can be defined as "an individual-difference variable to agree or disagree with an item regardless of its content" (J. A. Russell, 1979, p. 346); in other words, acquiescence causes individuals to respond similarly to a wide range of item content. Both of these response biases can be expected to increase the magnitude of the inter-item correlations, thereby spuriously raising coefficient alpha.

Transient error represents another potentially important type of systematic error that can be a problem when assessment is confined to a single occasion (Becker, 2000; Chmielewski & Watson, 2009; Green, 2003; Osburn, 2000; Schmidt et al., 2003). Transient error reflects the influence of time-limited processes, such as the current mood of the respondent. As Green (2003) put it, "Respondents have moods, feelings, and mental states that affect their scores on a measure at a particular time, and these transient influences are likely to vary from week to week or even day to day and thus produce changes in the measure's scores when readministered" (p. 88). Generally speaking, transient errors can be expected to produce (a) inconsistency across different occasions but (b) consistent responses within the same assessment. For example, suppose that a respondent rates her job satisfaction on two different occasions. At the first assessment, her mood is happy and optimistic; however, at the time of the second testing, she is feeling down and discouraged. It is reasonable to expect that her current mood will distort her satisfaction ratings at least slightly, such that she reports being more satisfied with her job at Time 1 than at Time 2. Note, however, that these same mood effects should produce consistent within-occasion responses; that is, her Time 1 item ratings consistently should reflect greater satisfaction than her Time 2 responses. Consequently, transient errors will inflate values of coefficient alpha that are based on a single occasion.

Conversely, alpha will underestimate the true reliability of a measure that is heterogeneous and multidimensional (Cronbach, 1951; Osburn, 2000; Schmitt, 1996). As noted, classical reliability theory equates inconsistency with measurement error. Sometimes, however, inconsistency reflects the heterogeneity of item content, rather than error per se. This is a widespread problem that has long been recognized by psychometricians, but it remains poorly understood by test developers and users.

The potential magnitude of this underestimation problem can be illustrated using a concrete example.

For the purposes of this example, consider the fictitious construct of *anxious joy*, which can be defined as a state of nervous exhilaration. Two parallel forms of this imaginary concept were constructed using mood descriptors from the Fear and Joviality scales of the PANAS-X (Watson & Clark, 1999). Each form includes two Fear and two Joviality terms. Specifically, Form A consists of *afraid, shaky, joyful,* and *delighted,* whereas Form B contains *scared, nervous, happy,* and *cheerful.*

Table 18.2 presents item intercorrelation data for these two measures of anxious joy; these responses were obtained from large samples of undergraduate students at Southern Methodist University who rated their emotional experiences using one of six different time frames: Moment (i.e., how they felt "right now"), Today, Past Week, Past Few Weeks, Past Month, and General (i.e., how they felt "on average"). Table 18.2 clearly demonstrates that these measures are heterogeneous. Each scale consists of two item pairs that are slightly negatively correlated with one another. Thus, each scale taps two underlying dimensions (i.e., anxiety and joy), not one. Consistent with this observation, the average interitem correlations are predictably low, ranging from only .11 to .19 across the various samples.

Given that these are short scales with low average interitem correlations, one would expect the alpha reliabilities to be quite poor. Table 18.3 confirms that this is the case; across the various data sets, the coefficient alphas range from only .31 to .48. If the assumptions of classical reliability are true—and if alpha is an accurate estimate of reliability—then these low alpha coefficients would place serious limits on the ability of these scales to correlate with other measures (i.e., given that unreliability reflects pure randomness, scale correlations cannot exceed their reliabilities). Clearly, however, this is not the case; indeed, Table 18.3 also shows that these two parallel forms are highly correlated with one another, with coefficients ranging from .66 to .73 across the various data sets. Moreover, Table 18.3 further demonstrates that if one uses the traditional formula to "correct" these correlations for attenuation because of unreliability (Nunnally, 1978, Chapter 6)—with alpha as the estimate of reliability—the results are absurd, as the coefficients greatly exceed 1.00 in every sample. In this example, coefficient alpha obviously misspecifies

TABLE 18.2

Item Intercorrelations for Two Parallel Measures of "Anxious Joy" Across Different Time Instructions

Item intercorrelations	Moment	Today	Past Week	Past Few Weeks	Past Month	General
Form A						
Afraid—shaky	.39	.40	.51	.45	.44	.37
Afraid—joyful	−.08	−.06	−.11	−.14	−.10	−.01
Afraid—delighted	−.01	−.01	−.09	−.06	−.02	.04
Shaky—joyful	−.13	−.12	−.13	−.08	−.09	−.05
Shaky—delighted	−.05	−.03	−.10	−.05	−.06	−.01
Joyful—delighted	.69	.67	.67	.64	.64	.64
Average interitem *r*	.14	.14	.13	.13	.14	.16
Form B						
Scared—nervous	.58	.59	.60	.52	.49	.47
Scared—happy	−.17	−.08	−.13	−.17	−.18	−.07
Scared—cheerful	−.15	−.06	−.12	−.18	−.12	−.02
Nervous—happy	−.10	−.03	−.09	−.11	−.11	−.07
Nervous—cheerful	−.07	−.01	−.08	−.09	−.09	−.04
Happy—cheerful	.68	.75	.72	.67	.66	.67
Average interitem *r*	.13	.19	.15	.11	.11	.16

Note. N = 1,027 (Moment); 1,007 (Today); 1,278 (Past Week); 678 (Past Few Weeks); 1,006 (Past Month); 1,657 (General).

TABLE 18.3

Coefficient Alphas and Scale Correlations for Two Parallel Measures of "Anxious Joy" Across Different Time Instructions

Scale/statistic	Moment	Today	Past Week	Past Few Weeks	Past Month	General
Coefficient alphas						
Form A	.41	.41	.37	.37	.38	.45
Form B	.37	.48	.41	.31	.32	.41
Scale correlations						
Uncorrected	.73	.72	.73	.70	.68	.66
"Corrected"	1.88	1.61	1.88	2.06	1.94	1.54

Note. N = 1,027 (Moment); 1,007 (Today); 1,278 (Past Week); 678 (Past Few Weeks); 1,006 (Past Month); 1,657 (General). The *corrected* correlations were computed using the scale coefficient alphas to estimate the attenuating effects of unreliability.

measurement error and substantially underestimates the true level of reliability.

This discussion should not be taken to suggest that these anxious joy scales are good measures or that heterogeneity is desirable in a test. The point, rather, is that although heterogeneity is problematic and highly undesirable, it is not the same thing as random measurement error. Because of this, coefficient alpha can substantially underestimate the reliability of multidimensional scales.

Test–retest reliability. Classical reliability theory arose out of work on intelligence and related cognitive abilities (Spearman, 1910). Accordingly, it was assumed that basic dimensions of individual differences essentially are invariant over time, such that (a) the true score components were perfectly stable and (b) any observed change could be attributed to measurement error (Anastasi & Urbina, 1997; Kaplan & Saccuzzo, 2009; Watson, 2004). This assumption was incorporated into the concept of test–retest reliability, which is computed by correlating scores on the same test across two assessments separated by a specified time interval. Correlations that increasingly approach 1.00+ indicate greater and greater reliability.

Temporal stability data can provide interesting and useful information about virtually any measure, regardless of the construct that is being assessed. Nevertheless, similar to internal consistency indexes, test–retest coefficients can either underestimate or overestimate reliability depending

on the circumstances. For example, memory effects can inflate retest correlations on ability tests (thereby overestimating reliability), whereas practice effects potentially can reduce them, leading to an underestimation of reliability (Anastasi & Urbina, 1997).

The more general problem, however, is that retest correlations only represent clear, unambiguous indexes of reliability when it is reasonable to assume that there has been no actual change on the assessed variable, such that the underlying true score remains perfectly invariant (they also will model reliability accurately in the highly unlikely event that all participants change equally). For many areas of psychological research, this assumption is unreasonable for one of two reasons. First, many important psychological constructs—for example, moods and emotions—are inherently unstable and are expected to fluctuate substantially over time. For instance, a broad range of evidence has established that the PANAS-X scales are sensitive to multiple influences. Scores on several of the negative mood scales are elevated during episodes of stress and show significant decreases during exercise; conversely, positive mood scores increase following exercise and in response to a broad range of social activities (see Watson, 2000; Watson & Clark, 1999). The temporal instability of these scales obviously is not problematic, and it is not reflective of measurement error. Indeed, these theoretically meaningful effects have helped to establish the construct validity of these scales.

Second, even stable constructs may still show some true change that is not attributable to measurement error, particularly when the retest interval is quite lengthy. The personality literature provides an excellent illustration of this point. Various lines of evidence have established that personality traits are not static constructs; rather, they show meaningful change over time. Perhaps the most compelling evidence is that retest correlations for personality systematically decline as the elapsed time interval increases (e.g., Cattell, 1964a, 1964b; Roberts & DelVecchio, 2000). This finding is difficult to explain using the assumptions of classical reliability theory: If the underlying true scores are perfectly stable, and if errors are randomly distributed across assessments, then reliability estimates should be unaffected by the length of the retest interval (Watson, 2004). This finding makes perfect sense, however, if one assumes that true change is possible, because change is increasingly likely to occur with increasing retest intervals (Anastasi & Urbina, 1997; Kaplan & Saccuzzo, 2009).

Cattell (1964a, 1964b) emphasized this point several decades ago, arguing for the importance of distinguishing between dependability and stability. Cattell, Eber, and Tatsuoka (1970) defined *dependability* as "the correlation between two administrations of the same test *when the lapse of time is insufficient for people themselves to change* with respect to what is being measured" (p. 30). In contrast, they defined *stability* as the correlation between two administrations of a test across a retest interval that is lengthy enough for true change to occur. This distinction is crucial: It makes it quite clear that dependability correlations provide an unambiguous index of reliability, whereas stability coefficients do not.

Dependability data can—and should—play a crucial role in the validation of trait measures. Unfortunately, researchers have not taken proper advantage of this important evidence in recent decades (see Chmielewski & Watson, 2009; Watson, 2004). My laboratory has conducted a number of dependability studies over the past several years, examining data from a wide range of measures. These studies have yielded three important conclusions. First, there are no systematic differences between 2-week and 2-month retest coefficients, suggesting that both intervals can be used to establish the dependability of trait measures. Second, dependability is a consistent property of scales, such that some measures simply are more dependable than others. Third, even strongly correlated measures of the same basic construct can vary significantly in their dependability; for instance, some measures of neuroticism and negative affectivity consistently yield higher dependability coefficients than others (Chmielewski & Watson, 2009; Watson, 2004). These data demonstrate the importance of collecting dependability data as early as possible in the process of creating and validating trait measures.

EXTERNAL VALIDITY

Convergent Validity

In the final stage of construct validation, one moves beyond the test to examine how it relates to other variables. This external phase subsumes three basic considerations: convergent validity, discriminant validity, and criterion validity. First, the concept of *convergent validity* was formally introduced into psychometrics by Campbell and Fiske (1959). Convergent validity is assessed by examining the relations among different purported measures of the same construct (Anastasi & Urbina, 1997; Campbell & Fiske, 1959; Kaplan & Saccuzzo, 2009). This type of evidence obviously is crucial in the establishment of construct validity. If it can be shown that different indicators converge substantially, this significantly strengthens one's confidence that they actually do assess the target construct.

According to Campbell and Fiske (1959), these convergent correlations "should be significantly different from zero and sufficiently large to encourage further examination of validity" (p. 82). What does "sufficiently large" mean in this context? Campbell and Fiske were quite vague on this point, and their vagueness was entirely appropriate. In contrast to other types of construct validity evidence, one cannot offer simple guidelines for evaluating when convergent correlations are high enough to support the validity of a measure. This is because the expected magnitude of these correlations will vary dramatically as a function of various design features. The single most important factor is the nature of the different measures that are used to examine convergent validity. In their original formulation, Campbell and Fiske largely assumed that investigators would examine convergence across fundamentally different methods. In one analysis, for example, they examined the associations between trait scores assessed using (a) peer ratings versus (b) a word association task (see Campbell & Fiske, 1959, Table 2). In another analysis, they investigated the convergence among free behavior, role-playing, and projective test scores (see Campbell & Fiske, 1959, Table 8).

Over time, however, investigators began to interpret the concept of *method* much more loosely (indeed, some have even used retest correlations to assess convergent validity; e.g., see Longley, Watson, & Noyes, 2005; Watson et al., 2007). For instance, it is commonplace for contemporary researchers to establish convergent validity by reporting correlations among different self-report measures of the same target construct. This practice is not problematic. Clearly, however, it creates a situation that is very different from the one originally envisioned by Campbell and Fiske (1959). Most notably, convergent correlations will be—and should be—substantially higher when they are computed within the same basic method (e.g., between different self-report measures of conscientiousness) than when they are calculated across very different methods (e.g., between self-rated vs. teacher-rated conscientiousness). This, in turn, means that the same level of convergence might support construct validity in one context, but challenge it in another. Suppose, for instance, that a researcher obtains a .40 correlation between two self-report measures of self-esteem. Given this moderate level of association, it would be difficult to argue that both of these instruments actually assess the same construct. In contrast, a .40 correlation between self and parent ratings of self-esteem would be far more encouraging and likely would enhance the construct validity of these measures.

Discriminant Validity

Discriminant validity is assessed by examining how a measure relates to purported indicators of other constructs (e.g., Anastasi & Urbina, 1997; Kaplan & Saccuzzo, 2009). Campbell and Fiske (1959) formally introduced this concept in the context of a multitrait–multimethod (MTMM) matrix. This type of matrix can be created whenever one assesses two or more constructs in at least two different ways. For interpretative purposes, the MTMM matrix can be decomposed into two basic subcomponents: (a) the monomethod triangles and (b) the heteromethod block. For instance, Watson, Suls, and Haig (2002) assessed six different traits (self-esteem, neuroticism, extraversion, openness, agreeableness, and conscientiousness) using two different methods (self-ratings and peer-ratings; see Watson et al., 2002, Table 2). One monomethod triangle contained all of the correlations among the self-ratings; the second included all of the associations among the peer-ratings. Finally, the heteromethod block contained all of the correlations between the self and peer ratings.

According to Campbell and Fiske (1959), an MTMM matrix yields three basic types of discriminant validity evidence (pp. 82–83). First, each of the convergent correlations should be higher than any of the other values in its row or column of the heteromethod block. For instance, self-rated self-esteem should correlate more strongly with peer-rated self-esteem than with peer-rated extraversion or peer-rated neuroticism. This type of evidence is particularly important in establishing that highly correlated constructs within multilevel hierarchical models are, in fact, empirically distinguishable from one another (e.g., see Longley et al., 2005; Watson & Clark, 1992; Watson & Wu, 2005). Failure to achieve discriminant validity at this level signals a serious problem with either (a) one or more of the measures or (b) the construct itself.

One complication here is that the meaning of the word *higher* is ambiguous in this context. Many researchers interpret it rather loosely to mean simply that the convergent correlation must be descriptively higher than all of the other values in its row or column of the heteromethod block. For instance, if the convergent correlation is .50, and the highest relevant discriminant correlation is only .45, then it is assumed that this requirement is met.

It is better, however, to use the more stringent requirement that the convergent correlation must be significantly higher than all of the other values in its row or column of the heteromethod block. This requirement obviously is much more difficult to meet; it also requires relatively large sample sizes to have sufficient statistical power to conduct these tests in a meaningful way. Nevertheless, the payoff is well worth it in terms of the resulting precision in the validity analyses. For instance, Watson et al. (2008) examined the convergent and discriminant validity of the 11 nonoverlapping IDAS scales in a sample of 605 outpatients. The convergent correlations ranged from .52 to .71, with a mean value of .62. Significance tests further revealed that these convergent correlations exceeded all of the other values in their row or column of the heteromethod block in 219 of 220 comparisons (99.5%). These results thereby provide substantial evidence of discriminant validity.

The second type of discriminant validity evidence is that the convergent correlations should exceed all of the corresponding values in the monomethod triangles. As Campbell and Fiske (1959) put it, a test should "correlate higher with an independent effort to measure the same trait than with measures designed to get at different traits which happen to employ the same method" (p. 83). For instance, self-rated self-esteem should correlate more strongly with peer-rated self-esteem that with self-rated extraversion or self-rated neuroticism.

This much stronger test of discriminant validity is far more difficult to pass than the first. However, failure to achieve discriminant validity at this level is not necessarily catastrophic. A key consideration here is the true level of correlation among the underlying latent constructs. In this regard, it must be emphasized that—particularly within the context of hierarchical models—the most interesting tests of discriminant validity involve constructs that are known to be strongly related. For example, Watson and Clark (1992) reported several MTMM matrixes to examine relations among measures of fear, sadness, guilt, and hostility. It is well established that these negative affects are strongly related, so it is hardly surprising that the monomethod triangles in these analyses included a number of substantial correlations. Of course, the presence of these strong monomethod correlations makes it difficult to pass

this second test of discriminant validity, particularly when one uses very different methods (e.g., self vs. peer ratings) that can be expected to yield relatively modest convergent correlations.

The third and final consideration in discriminant validity is whether "the same pattern of trait interrelationship be shown in all of the heterotrait triangles" (Campbell & Fiske, 1959, p. 83). The key issue here is the extent to which these heterotrait coefficients reflect (a) true trait interrelations versus (b) the complicating influence of method variance. If the pattern of associations remains relatively consistent across all of the heterotrait triangles (e.g., fear and sadness are strongly related in every case), then it is reasonable to conclude that these coefficients are accurate reflections of the true relations among the underlying constructs. Conversely, if the patterns show substantial differences across the triangles, then method variance likely is implicated. This type of evidence is best examined using CFA, which allows one to model simultaneously both construct-based and method-based factors (Byrne, 1994; Watson et al., 2002).

Criterion Validity

Criterion validity is assessed by relating a measure to important nontest variables. This type of evidence traditionally is further subdivided into *concurrent validity* (which involves relations with nontest criteria that are assessed at the same time as the measure) and *predictive validity* (which examines associations with criteria assessed at some point in the future; Anastasi & Urbina, 1997; Kaplan & Saccuzzo, 2009). Criterion validity evidence is important for two reasons. The first is purely pragmatic: Measures that have no established links to nontest variables likely will be of little interest to most researchers.

Second, criterion validity evidence is critically important in clarifying the inferences that can be drawn from test scores; it therefore plays a crucial role in establishing the construct validity of a measure. As an example, Watson and Clark (1993) described the development and validation of a personality scale. As part of this process, they provide a range of criterion validity evidence. Among other things, they found that high scores on this scale were associated with (a) heavier and more problematic use of alcohol, marijuana, and other drugs; (b) more casual sexual activity, including a greater number of different sex partners and more one-night stands; (c) lower levels of self-reported spirituality and religiosity; and (d) poorer grades in both high school and college (see also Clark & Watson, 1999). Without knowing anything else about this instrument, one already can make a reasonably good guess about the trait it measures. In this case, the assessed trait is disinhibition, which "reflects broad individual differences in the tendency to behave in an undercontrolled versus overcontrolled manner" (Watson & Clark, 1993, p. 506). These behavioral correlates are quite consistent with this conceptualization and, therefore, enhance the construct validity of the test. In other instances, criterion data may be inconsistent with the current conceptualization of the construct (either because a predicted association was not found, or because an unexpected correlate has emerged); such inconsistencies indicate a significant problem that must be addressed.

CONCLUSION

This chapter has reviewed a large number of psychometric concepts. As was emphasized at the beginning, however, all of these different types of evidence now are viewed as aspects of the more general process of construct validation. In other words, they all simply are pieces in the larger puzzle that is construct validity. This focus on construct validity has fundamentally changed our understanding of these concepts. Most notably, it now is clear that they need to be applied flexibly to match the theoretical specifications of the target construct. Put differently, the same set of psychometric data may enhance the validity of one measure but challenge the validity of another, depending on the nature of the target construct.

For instance, retest reliability is a crucial consideration if the goal of assessment is to assess a stable dimension, such as conscientiousness or intelligence. In this regard, recent studies of dependability have established that even strongly correlated measures of the same basic trait can contain substantially different levels of measurement error. Note,

however, that change is to be expected—and instability is not inherently problematic—when one is assessing transient constructs, such as mood states. Similarly, although evidence of homogeneity is essential in establishing the construct validity of many measures, it is irrelevant when the goal of assessment is to create a cumulative index of traumatic experiences; here, there is no necessary expectation or requirement that different manifestations of trauma be interrelated. As a final example, a particular level of convergent validity may be encouraging in one context (e.g., between self-reported and supervisor-rated conscientiousness) but indicate significant problems in another (e.g., between two self-report measures of conscientiousness).

This emphasis on construct validity also underscores the need to develop clear, precise definitions of the key constructs in the target domain. This statement should not be misunderstood to mean that all of the important theoretical issues and disputes must be resolved before the start of scale development and data collection. Indeed, the scale development process offers a powerful mechanism for sorting through these disputes and resolving them. As originally articulated by Loevinger (1957), the key point is to incorporate all of these different theoretical schemes into the initial item tool, so that they can be subjected to empirical scrutiny. Thus, psychological measurement involves a constant interplay between theoretical expectations and empirical data.

Objective psychological tests compare favorably with those created in other areas of science and medicine (e.g., see Meyer et al., 2001) and represent a major success story within psychology. By adhering more closely to the principles articulated in this chapter, test developers can build on this tradition of success and create even better assessment instruments in the future.

References

Abramson, L. Y., Metalsky, G. L., & Alloy, L. B. (1989). Hopelessness depression: A theory based subtype of depression. *Psychological Review, 96,* 358–372. doi:10.1037/0033-295X.96.2.358

American Educational Research Association, American Psychological Association, & National Council on Measurement in Education. (1974). *Standards for educational and psychological testing*. Washington, DC: American Psychological Association.

American Educational Research Association, American Psychological Association, & National Council on Measurement in Education. (1999). *Standards for educational and psychological testing*. Washington, DC: American Educational Research Association.

American Psychiatric Association. (2000). *Diagnostic and statistical manual of mental disorders* (4th ed., text revision). Washington, DC: Author.

Anastasi, A., & Urbina, S. (1997). *Psychological testing* (7th ed.). New York, NY: Macmillan.

Becker, G. (2000). How important is transient error in estimating reliability? Going beyond simulation studies. *Psychological Methods, 5*, 370–379. doi:10.1037/1082-989X.5.3.370

Benson, N., Hulac, D. M., & Kranzler, J. H. (2010). Independent examination of the Wechsler Adult Intelligence Scale—Fourth Edition (WAIS–IV): What does the WAIS–IV measure? *Psychological Assessment, 22*, 121–130. doi:10.1037/a0017767

Bollen, K. A., & Ting, K. (2000). A tetrad test for causal indicators. *Psychological Methods, 5*, 3–22. doi:10.1037/1082-989X.5.1.3

Bowden, S. C., Weiss, L. G., Holdnack, J. A., & Lloyd, D. (2006). Age-related invariance of abilities measured with the Wechsler Adult Intelligence Scale—III. *Psychological Assessment, 18*, 334–339. doi:10.1037/1040-3590.18.3.334

Boyle, G. J. (1991). Does item homogeneity indicate internal consistency or item redundancy in psychometric scales? *Personality and Individual Differences, 12*, 291–294. doi:10.1016/0191-8869(91)90115-R

Byrne, B. M. (1994). *Structural equation modeling with EQS and EQS/Windows*. Thousand Oaks, CA: Sage.

Campbell, D. T., & Fiske, D. W. (1959). Convergent and discriminant validation by the multitrait-multimethod matrix. *Psychological Bulletin, 56*, 81–105. doi:10.1037/h0046016

Cattell, R. B. (1964a). Beyond validity and reliability: Some further concepts and coefficients for evaluating tests. *Journal of Experimental Education, 33*, 133–143.

Cattell, R. B. (1964b). Validity and reliability: A proposed more basic set of concepts. *Journal of Educational Psychology, 55*, 1–22. doi:10.1037/h0046462

Cattell, R. B., Eber, H. W., & Tatsuoka, M. M. (1970). *Handbook for the Sixteen Personality Factor Questionnaire (16PF)*. Champaign, IL: Institute for Personality and Ability Testing.

Chmielewski, M., & Watson, D. (2009). What is being assessed and why it matters: The impact of transient error on trait research. *Journal of Personality and Social Psychology, 97*, 186–202. doi:10.1037/a0015618

Clark, L. A., & Watson, D. (1991). Tripartite model of anxiety and depression: Psychometric evidence and taxonomic implications. *Journal of Abnormal Psychology, 100*, 316–336. doi:10.1037/0021-843X.100.3.316

Clark, L. A., & Watson, D. (1995). Constructing validity: Basic issues in objective scale development. *Psychological Assessment, 7*, 309–319. doi:10.1037/1040-3590.7.3.309

Clark, L. A., & Watson, D. (1999). Temperament: A new paradigm for personality. In L. Pervin & O. John (Eds.), *Handbook of personality* (2nd ed., pp. 399–423). New York, NY: Guilford Press.

Cortina, J. M. (1993). What is coefficient alpha? An examination of theory and applications. *Journal of Applied Psychology, 78*, 98–104. doi:10.1037/0021-9010.78.1.98

Cronbach, L. J. (1951). Coefficient alpha and the internal structure of tests. *Psychometrika, 16*, 297–334. doi:10.1007/BF02310555

Cronbach, L. J., & Meehl, P. E. (1955). Construct validity in psychological tests. *Psychological Bulletin, 52*, 281–302. doi:10.1037/h0040957

Cutshall, C., & Watson, D. (2004). The Phobic Stimuli Response Scales: A new self-report measure of fear. *Behaviour Research and Therapy, 42*, 1193–1201. doi:10.1016/j.brat.2003.08.003

Embretson, S. E. (1996). The new rules of measurement. *Psychological Assessment, 8*, 341–349. doi:10.1037/1040-3590.8.4.341

Fabrigar, L. R., Wegener, D. T., MacCallum, R. C., & Strahan, E. J. (1999). Evaluating the use of exploratory factor analysis in psychological research. *Psychological Methods, 4*, 272–299. doi:10.1037/1082-989X.4.3.272

Floyd, F. J., & Widaman, K. F. (1995). Factor analysis in the development and refinement of clinical assessment instruments. *Psychological Assessment, 7*, 286–299. doi:10.1037/1040-3590.7.3.286

Gotlib, I. H., & Cane, D. B. (1989). Self-report assessment of depression and anxiety. In P. C. Kendall & D. Watson (Eds.), *Anxiety and depression: Distinctive and overlapping features* (pp. 131–169). San Diego, CA: Academic Press.

Green, S. B. (2003). A coefficient alpha for test–retest data. *Psychological Methods, 8*, 88–101. doi:10.1037/1082-989X.8.1.88

Haynes, S. N., Richard, D. C. S., & Kubany, E. S. (1995). Content validity in psychological assessment: A functional approach to concepts and methods. *Psychological Assessment, 7*, 238–247. doi:10.1037/1040-3590.7.3.238

Hogan, R. T. (1983). A socioanalytic theory of personality. In M. Page (Ed.), *Nebraska Symposium on*

Motivation (Vol. 30, pp. 55–89). Lincoln: University of Nebraska Press.

Hogan, R. T., & Hogan, J. (1992). *Hogan Personality Inventory manual.* Tulsa, OK: Hogan Assessment Systems.

Joiner, T. E., Jr., Walker, R. L., Pettit, J. W., Perez, M., & Cukrowicz, K. C. (2005). Evidence-based assessment of depression in adults. *Psychological Assessment, 17,* 267–277. doi:10.1037/1040-3590 .17.3.267

Kaplan, R. M., & Saccuzzo, D. P. (2009). *Psychological testing: Principles, applications, and issues* (7th ed.). Belmont, CA: Wadsworth.

Kuder, G. F., & Richardson, M. W. (1937). The theory of the estimation of test reliability. *Psychometrika, 2,* 151–160. doi:10.1007/BF02288391

Loevinger, J. (1954). The attenuation paradox in test theory. *Psychological Bulletin, 51,* 493–504. doi:10.1037/ h0058543

Loevinger, J. (1957). Objective tests as instruments of psychological theory. *Psychological Reports, 3,* 635–694. doi:10.2466/PR0.3.7.635-694

Longley, S. L., Watson, D., & Noyes, R., Jr. (2005). Assessment of the hypochondriasis domain: The Multidimensional Inventory of Hypochondriacal Traits (MIHT). *Psychological Assessment, 17,* 3–14. doi:10.1037/1040-3590.17.1.3

Markon, K. E., Krueger, R. F., & Watson, D. (2005). Delineating the structure of normal and abnormal personality: An integrative hierarchical approach. *Journal of Personality and Social Psychology, 88,* 139–157. doi:10.1037/0022-3514.88.1.139

McCrae, R. R., Kurtz, J. E., Yamagata, S., & Terracciano, A. (2011). Internal consistency, retest reliability, and their implications for personality scale validity. *Personality and Social Psychology Review, 15,* 28–50. doi:10.1177/1088868310366253

Messick, S. (1995). Validity of psychological assessment: Validation of inferences from persons' responses and performances as scientific inquiry into score meaning. *American Psychologist, 50,* 741–749. doi:10.1037/0003-066X.50.9.741

Meyer, G. J., Finn, S. E., Eyde, L. D., Kay, G. G., Moreland, K. L., Dies, R. R., . . .Reed, G. M. (2001). Psychological testing and psychological assessment: A review of evidence and issues. *American Psychologist, 56,* 128–165. doi:10.1037/0003-066X.56.2.128

Meyer, G. J., & Kurtz, J. E. (2006). Advancing personality assessment terminology: Time to retire "objective" and "projective" as personality test descriptors. *Journal of Personality Assessment, 87,* 223–225. doi:10.1207/s15327752jpa8703_01

Nunnally, J. C. (1978). *Psychometric theory* (2nd ed.). New York, NY: McGraw-Hill.

Osburn, H. G. (2000). Coefficient alpha and related internal consistency coefficients. *Psychological Methods, 5,* 343–355. doi:10.1037/1082-989X.5.3.343

Paulhus, D. L., & Reid, D. B. (1991). Enhancement and denial in socially desirable responding. *Journal of Personality and Social Psychology, 60,* 307–317. doi:10.1037/0022-3514.60.2.307

Reise, S. P., Ainsworth, A. T., & Haviland, M. G. (2005). Item response theory: Fundamentals, applications, and promise in psychological research. *Current Directions in Psychological Science, 14,* 95–101. doi:10.1111/j.0963-7214.2005.00342.x

Reise, S. P., & Waller, N. G. (2003). How many IRT parameters does it take to model psychopathology items? *Psychological Methods, 8,* 164–184. doi:10.1037/1082-989X.8.2.164

Reise, S. P., & Waller, N. G. (2009). Item response theory in clinical measurement. *Annual Review of Clinical Psychology, 5,* 27–48. doi:10.1146/annurev. clinpsy.032408.153553

Roberts, B. W., & DelVecchio, W. F. (2000). The rank-order consistency of personality traits from childhood to old age: A quantitative review of longitudinal studies. *Psychological Bulletin, 126,* 3–25. doi:10.1037/0033-2909.126.1.3

Roberts, B. W., Kuncel, N. R., Shiner, R., Caspi, A., & Goldberg, L. R. (2007). The power of personality: The comparative validity of personality traits, socioeconomic status, and cognitive ability for predicting important life outcomes. *Perspectives on Psychological Science, 2,* 313–345. doi:10.1111/j.1745-6916.2007.00047.x

Rushton, J. P., Brainerd, C. J., & Pressley, M. (1983). Behavioral development and construct validity: The principle of aggregation. *Psychological Bulletin, 94,* 18–38. doi:10.1037/0033-2909.94.1.18

Russell, D. W. (2002). In search of underlying dimensions: The use (and abuse) of factor analysis in *Personality and Social Psychology Bulletin. Personality and Social Psychology Bulletin, 28,* 1629–1646. doi:10.1177/014616702237645

Russell, J. A. (1979). Affective space is bipolar. *Journal of Personality and Social Psychology, 37,* 345–356. doi:10.1037/0022-3514.37.3.345

Schmidt, F. L., & Hunter, J. (2004). General mental ability in the world of work: Occupational attainment and job performance. *Journal of Personality and Social Psychology, 86,* 162–173. doi:10.1037/0022-3514 .86.1.162

Schmidt, F. L., Le, H., & Ilies, R. (2003). Beyond alpha: An empirical examination of the effects of different sources of measurement error on reliability estimates for measures of individual differences constructs. *Psychological Methods, 8,* 206–224. doi:10.1037/1082-989X.8.2.206

Schmidt, F. L., Shaffer, J. A., & Oh, I.-S. (2008). Increased accuracy for range restriction corrections: Implications for the role of personality and general mental ability in job and training performance. *Personnel Psychology, 61*, 827–868. doi:10.1111/j.1744-6570.2008.00132.x

Schmitt, N. (1996). Uses and abuses of coefficient alpha. *Psychological Assessment, 8*, 350–353. doi:10.1037/1040-3590.8.4.350

Simms, L. J., & Watson, D. (2007). The construct validation approach to personality scale construction. In R. W. Robins, R. C. Fraley, & R. F. Krueger (Eds.), *Handbook of research methods in personality psychology* (pp. 240–258). New York, NY: Guilford Press.

Simms, L. J., Watson, D., & Doebbeling, B. N. (2002). Confirmatory factor analyses of posttraumatic stress symptoms in deployed and non-deployed veterans of the Gulf War. *Journal of Abnormal Psychology, 111*, 637–647. doi:10.1037/0021-843X.111.4.637

Smith, G. T., & McCarthy, D. M. (1995). Methodological considerations in the refinement of clinical assessment instruments. *Psychological Assessment, 7*, 300–308. doi:10.1037/1040-3590.7.3.300

Spearman, C. (1904). "General intelligence," objectively determined and measured. *The American Journal of Psychology, 15*, 201–293. doi:10.2307/1412107

Spearman, C. (1910). Correlation calculated from faulty data. *British Journal of Psychology, 3*, 271–295.

Watson, D. (2000). *Mood and temperament.* New York, NY: Guilford Press.

Watson, D. (2004). Stability versus change, dependability versus error: Issues in the assessment of personality over time. *Journal of Research in Personality, 38*, 319–350. doi:10.1016/j.jrp.2004.03.001

Watson, D. (2005). Rethinking the mood and anxiety disorders: A quantitative hierarchical model for *DSM–V. Journal of Abnormal Psychology, 114*, 522–536. doi:10.1037/0021-843X.114.4.522

Watson, D. (2006). In search of construct validity: Using basic concepts and principles of psychological measurement to define child maltreatment. In M. Feerick, J. Knutson, P. Trickett, & S. Flanzer (Eds.), *Defining and classifying child abuse and neglect for research purposes* (pp. 199–230). Baltimore, MD: Brookes.

Watson, D. (2009a). Differentiating the mood and anxiety disorders: A quadripartite model. *Annual Review of Clinical Psychology, 5*, 221–247. doi:10.1146/annurev.clinpsy.032408.153510

Watson, D. (2009b). Rethinking the anxiety disorders in *DSM-V* and beyond: Quantitative dimensional models of anxiety and related psychopathology. In J. Abramowitz, D. McKay, S. Taylor, & G. Asmundson (Eds.), *Current perspectives on the anxiety disorders: Implications for DSM–V and beyond* (pp. 275–302). New York, NY: Springer Press.

Watson, D., & Clark, L. A. (1984). Negative affectivity: The disposition to experience aversive emotional states. *Psychological Bulletin, 96*, 465–490. doi:10.1037/0033-2909.96.3.465

Watson, D., & Clark, L. A. (1992). Affects separable and inseparable: On the hierarchical arrangement of the negative affects. *Journal of Personality and Social Psychology, 62*, 489–505. doi:10.1037/0022-3514.62.3.489

Watson, D., & Clark, L. A. (1993). Behavioral disinhibition versus constraint: A dispositional perspective. In D. M. Wegner & J. W. Pennebaker (Eds.), *Handbook of mental control* (pp. 506–527). New York, NY: Prentice-Hall.

Watson, D., & Clark, L. A. (1999). *The PANAS-X: Manual for the Positive and Negative Affect Schedule—Expanded Form.* Unpublished manuscript, University of Iowa, Iowa City.

Watson, D., Clark, L. A., & Harkness, A. R. (1994). Structures of personality and their relevance to psychopathology. *Journal of Abnormal Psychology, 103*, 18–31. doi:10.1037/0021-843X.103.1.18

Watson, D., Clark, L. A., & Tellegen, A. (1988). Development and validation of brief measures of Positive and Negative Affect: The PANAS scales. *Journal of Personality and Social Psychology, 54*, 1063–1070. doi:10.1037/0022-3514.54.6.1063

Watson, D., & Naragon-Gainey, K. (2010). On the specificity of positive emotional dysfunction in psychopathology: Evidence from the mood and anxiety disorders and schizophrenia/schizotypy. *Clinical Psychology Review, 30*, 839–848. doi:10.1016/j.cpr.2009.11.002

Watson, D., O'Hara, M. W., Chmielewski, M., McDade-Montez, E. A., Koffel, E., Naragon, K., & Stuart, S. (2008). Further validation of the IDAS: Evidence of convergent, discriminant, criterion, and incremental validity. *Psychological Assessment, 20*, 248–259. doi:10.1037/a0012570

Watson, D., O'Hara, M. W., Simms, L. J., Kotov, R., Chmielewski, M., McDade-Montez, E., . . .Stuart, S. (2007). Development and validation of the Inventory of Depression and Anxiety Symptoms (IDAS). *Psychological Assessment, 19*, 253–268. doi:10.1037/1040-3590.19.3.253

Watson, D., Suls, J., & Haig, J. (2002). Global self-esteem in relation to structural models of personality and affectivity. *Journal of Personality and Social Psychology, 83*, 185–197. doi:10.1037/0022-3514.83.1.185

Watson, D., & Tellegen, A. (2002). Aggregation, acquiescence, and trait affectivity. *Journal of Research in Personality, 36,* 589–597. doi:10.1016/S0092-6566(02)00509-3

Watson, D., & Vaidya, J. (2003). Mood measurement: Current status and future directions. In J. A. Schinka & W. Velicer (Eds.), *Comprehensive handbook of psychology: Vol. 2. Research methods* (pp. 351–375). New York, NY: Wiley.

Watson, D., & Wu, K. D. (2005). Development and validation of the Schedule of Compulsions, Obsessions, and Pathological Impulses (SCOPI). *Assessment, 12,* 50–65. doi:10.1177/107319110 4271483

CHAPTER 19

NORM- AND CRITERION-REFERENCED TESTING

Kurt F. Geisinger

This chapter focuses on norm- and criterion-referenced testing. The distinction between norm- and criterion-referenced testing exists primarily within the realm of educational testing and, perhaps to a lesser extent, in industrial training. To understand this distinction, however, one must know something about the early days of psychological testing because it was the influence of psychological testing that shaped the early growth of educational testing. Of course, educational and psychological testing share much in common, as is evidenced by the fact that associations representing these professions have jointly collaborated for more than 50 years to develop professional standards in the fields of educational and psychological testing (American Educational Research Association, American Psychological Association, & National Council on Measurement in Education, 1999).

This chapter begins with a brief history of psychological testing. This historical introduction is brief and has been summarized by DuBois (1970) and with respect to ability testing, by Thorndike (1990). These references should be consulted for more information about the history of educational and psychological testing, the treatment of which is beyond the scope of this chapter. We begin the discussion of the history of psychological testing with a consideration of intelligence and then move to educational testing, which is the primary realm in which the norm- versus criterion-referenced testing distinction is made. Much of this history happened during the decades surrounding 1900. We then discuss the logic and methods (primarily basic psychometrics)

of norm-referenced testing. A special focus during that section is on validity of measurement (for more information on this topic, see Chapter 32 in this volume). The procedures often used in developing norm-referenced measures are also discussed. That section concludes with some concerns about norm-referenced testing when assessing student learning in education in the 21st century.

Criterion-referenced testing is described next. A brief historical overview details the beginning of this type of testing in the 1960s. The logic of criterion-referenced testing is addressed before the basic psychometrics for criterion-referenced testing are discussed. The setting of standards is particularly critical for criterion-referenced testing and these procedures are mentioned as well. The use of criterion-referenced testing in the assessment of student achievement concludes this section. The chapter concludes with a look at the similarities and differences between norm- and criterion-referenced testing.

THE EARLY DAYS OF MODERN PSYCHOLOGICAL TESTING

At the beginning of the 20th century, a number of highly interrelated and similar trends were occurring in education. This time period may be thought of as the birth of modern testing in psychology and education. In France, in reaction to students who were not succeeding in the earliest public education in the modern world, Binet had developed an approach to evaluate the intellectual ability of school children. This approach was related to the

DOI: 10.1037/13619-020
APA Handbook of Research Methods in Psychology: Vol. 1. Foundations, Planning, Measures, and Psychometrics, H. Cooper (Editor-in-Chief)

ability to solve problems both verbally and using what was called *performance measures*. This approach largely flew in the face of the work of others (e.g., James McKeen Cattell) who at that time had been attempting to measure physical attributes as well as the ability to perceive and feel sensations, and other relatively pure psychological attributes. It was thought that by measuring such pure measures, they could be combined to estimate one's ability to succeed in school, at work, and the like. Cattell, an American, studied under the famed Wilhelm Wundt in Leipzig, earning his doctoral degree, and then worked as an assistant in Galton's Anthropometric Laboratory in England for 3 years. Cattell argued that the advancement of psychology depended on a solid foundation of the measurement of human characteristics. A professor first at the University of Pennsylvania and later Columbia University, he developed batteries of tests, including measures of dynamometer pressure (i.e., strength), rate of movement, sensation areas, pressure-causing pain, least noticeable differences in weight, reaction time to sound, time for naming colors, bisection of a 50-centimeter line, judgment of 10 seconds of time, and the number of letters able to be repeated after hearing them once (DuBois, 1970). His more "elaborate measurements" (using his words) involved sight, hearing, taste and smell, touch and temperature, sense of effort and movement, mental time, mental intensity (mostly dealing with sensations), and mental extensity (involving memory and perception). These measures, created during the 1890s and early 1900s, represented what some have considered the state of the art in mental measurements around the turn of that century (DuBois, 1970).

On the other side of the Atlantic Ocean, Binet's publications (e.g., Binet & Simon, 1905b, 1905c) provided a basic description of his approach to understanding intellectual behavior, to measuring this behavior, and to diagnosing what was then called *mental retardation*. His measures were so successful that the number of research studies using his measures had approached 800 within 20 years after he had begun this work (Thorndike, 1990).

Binet and Simon's third paper (1905a) provided a description of the techniques used to score and norm the measures that they had described in their

previous paper (Thorndike, 1990). Some elements of the procedures that they used to build their measures were also provided in this later publication. Their 1908 paper expanded and reorganized the individually administered measure written about 1905. Questions or test items were organized by the chronological age at which successful responding to the question might be expected, much as they are today on a number of measures.

To call Binet's work a major breakthrough in the assessment of intelligence would be a gross understatement. Translations of his work into English in America happened quickly and by a number of individuals: Goddard (1908); Terman (1916); and Yerkes, Bridges, and Hardwick (1915), among others. Terman, who received his doctoral degree in the United States at about the time of Binet's work on intelligence and had performed a dissertation using his own test of intelligence, worked on this translation of the Binet measure after receiving a faculty appointment at Stanford University. Although a number of measures already existed at that time, "the scale with the widest acceptance . . . turned out to be the Stanford Revision of the Binet-Simon Scale, published originally in 1916 by L. M. Terman and revised by Terman and Merrill in 1937 and again in 1960" (DuBois, 1970, p. 49). The Stanford-Binet test was thought of as the standard against which many other tests of intelligence were compared. It was (and is) an individually administered test, typically with which a psychologist assesses a child using a variety of verbal and performance tasks. In developing the test, Terman administered the test to large numbers of children at all ages and collected and analyzed the data so that the median performance on the tests for all individuals at a given age was set to be an intelligence quotient of 100. These methods (described in the section The Psychometrics of Norm-Referenced Testing) represent an attempt to build a norm-referenced test, one in which the scores are associated with one's performance relative to the group as a whole.

After his success with the Stanford-Binet, Terman helped to develop the Stanford Achievement Tests (Kelley, Ruch, & Terman, 1922), measures of student learning still in use today. The Stanford Achievement Tests use essentially the same techniques that Terman used in setting scores for the Stanford-Binet intelligence tests, with one notable assessment. Rather than norming the tests on each chronological age, as does the Stanford-Binet, the Stanford Achievement Tests were normed on academic grade levels. That is, students in each grade could determine how they compared with their classmates across the country. The test has continued to be used since it was first developed by Terman in 1922. The Stanford Achievement Tests measure developed academic skills such as reading comprehension, mathematical skills, and science knowledge across the 13 grade levels, from kindergarten to 12th grade. The Stanford Achievement Tests currently are published by Pearson Assessments, Inc. and are a group-administered, norm-referenced test of academic achievement. As such, these tests are similar to a number of other major published measures that have been used for widespread assessment of student achievement in a norm-referenced fashion: the California Achievement Tests (CTB/McGraw-Hill, 2003), the Comprehensive Test of Basic Skills, Fifth Edition (CTBS/5; CTB/McGraw-Hill, 1997), the Iowa Tests (of Basic Skills and of Educational Development; Hoover, Dunbar, & Frisbie, 2007), and the Metropolitan Achievement Tests, Eighth Edition (MAT 8; Pearson Assessments, 2000).

Cattell's work was followed closely by that of one of his doctoral students, E. L. Thorndike, who earned his doctoral degree under Cattell in 1898 and who taught at Teacher's College, Columbia University, for decades. Thorndike's dissertation used mazes to measure the intelligence of cats; Cattell urged Thorndike to apply the same principles to the assessment of schoolchildren and, approximately 20 years later, Thorndike developed one of the first group-administered tests of intelligence in 1919. At the same time he was developing measures of intelligence, he was also concerned with the assessment of school achievement. Thorndike developed or worked with students to construct a great number of what we now consider tests of educational achievement. For example, in 1910 he developed a measure of handwriting for use with students in Grades 5 to 8. He differentiated examples of handwriting into different levels or score points and had several examples of handwriting for each score point.

To evaluate an individual student, a teacher had only to compare that student's writing to these examples. The exemplars each had scale values and the one closest to the student's handwriting became that student's handwriting score. Thorndike's student Hillegas (1912) used similar methodology to develop a scale for evaluating English compositions, a method largely similar to what is used in the 21st century, where student responses are compared with anchor papers so that a proper score along an operational scale can be assigned. Thorndike also published "measures of reading words and sentences in 1914" (DuBois, 1970, p. 73).

The early measurement of aptitudes, primarily intelligence, was seen as following a normal curve, or at least that the distribution of these abilities were well represented by the normal curve. It appears that this assumption carried forward to early achievement and other tests and the psychometric and statistical procedures that guided the development of student achievement tests were the same ones as used in the development of ability tests. These procedures are classified as *classical psychometrics* or *item-response theory* (Hambleton & Jones, 1993), although this chapter focuses primarily on the former. A standard normal ability distribution is commonly expected. That is, it was commonly held that "in the absence of any strong a priori beliefs, a normal distribution is a good approximation to the usually encountered distributions of ability measures" (Hulin, Lissak, & Drasgow, 1982, p. 254). (See the discussion of criterion-referenced testing later in this chapter.) Readers interested in a more detailed history of ability and testing are referred to DuBois (1970) and Thorndike (1990).

THE PSYCHOMETRICS OF NORM-REFERENCED TESTING

The Normal Curve

The normal curve is a statistical concept that has gained substantial acceptance in use in psychology and, in particular, in psychological and educational testing. A normal curve has a number of primary characteristics. It is ultimately a theoretical distribution, one that exists mathematically rather than as a law of nature. In mathematical usage, it is completely symmetrical. It is asymptotic, meaning that the end points of the curve never touch the axis; that is, it is always possible to have a small number of extreme values, although the vast majority of scores are in the middle of the distribution and follows the formula

$$f(x) = \frac{1}{\sqrt{2\pi\sigma^2}} e^{-\frac{(x-\mu)^2}{2\sigma^2}}, \qquad (1)$$

where *x* is the variable in question, σ represents the population standard deviation, and μ represents the population mean. This curve is sometimes known as the *Gaussian distribution* after the brilliant German mathematician, Carl Friedrich Gauss, who introduced it in 1809. Shortly thereafter, a French mathematician, Laplace, proved the central limit theorem. That is, he demonstrated that the normal curve serves as the distribution of arithmetic means of independent, random variables ultimately following the same distribution. Hence, the normal distribution is sometimes called *Laplacian* in French-speaking countries.

Quite important for psychologists, the normal curve has fixed proportions falling underneath specific sections of the curve. For example, there is always 34.13% of the curve (or in psychology, of the people in a distribution) falling between the mean of the distribution and one standard deviation above the mean. And because the curve is symmetrical, there are always at least that number between the mean and one standard deviation below the mean as well. Knowing that a set of test scores follows a normal curve permits knowledgeable psychologists to interpret where a person falls in a given distribution of scores just by looking at the score that the person has achieved. Of course, it is rare if ever that a distribution of actual test scores fits a normal curve exactly. Rather, if a frequency distribution or graph of actual test scores does not deviate from the theoretical normal distribution in a manner than exceeds chance, then we consider the curve to be essentially a normal distribution.

Magnusson (1967), in a commonly used textbook on classical test theory, described the assumption made in testing that scores follow a normal curve regularly. He stated,

> It was noticed long ago that, when human attributes are measured with objective measuring instruments which give the data on interval or ratio scales, the results are distributed approximately in accordance with the normal distribution. Such distributions are obtained for physical characteristics such as height, physiological characteristics such as temperature of human beings at rest, and performance variables such as hand strength, measured by means of a hand dynamometer. . . .
>
> In view of such facts a fundamental assumption has been proposed for practical test construction, namely that if we could measure differences between individuals on an interval scale, we would obtain a normal distribution of individual scores. (Magnusson, 1967, p. 11)

Thus, many of those in the testing profession were brought up to believe that the normal curve was essentially a given for the measurement of many human traits, including the learning of students in the schools. Therefore, a great number of tests were developed in ways that lead to distributions that approximated the normal curve. In other cases, transformations were made to the raw scores earned on a test that took any distribution of scores and reconstituted it as a normal curve using a monotonic, nonlinear transformation. The study of differential psychology accentuated this perception. Anastasi (1958), for example, demonstrated how a large number of human characteristics followed this distribution: height, lung capacity, autonomic balance, perceptual speed and accuracy, and intelligence test scores.

The Fundamental Unit of Assessment: The Test Item

Much of test theory and practice emerges from the use of individual test items. Given the limitations of testing time in virtually all contexts, one must be extremely selective in terms of which items should be used to compose a given measure. Especially for what is often called *cognitive measurement* (tests of ability, achievement, performance, and competency), where answers have right and wrong answers, the test item is the fundamental unit of analysis. By far the most common type of test item since about the 1930s has been the multiple-choice test item, but there are many other types of objective and subjectively scored items. In addition to the multiple-choice test item, other objective test items include true–false items, matching items, and the like. Early in the history of testing, such items could be manually scored using a template placed over the test response booklet or answer form. Now they are scored either by a scanning machine that reads filled-in bubbles on an answer sheet or by computer, in which case the test taker completes the test on computer and it is scored using the proper key by the computer. Subjectively scored items include essays, short answer essays, problems in mathematics where students must supply their own answer and sometimes their work and computations, performance assessments that were popular in education in the 1980s, and other exercises in which those with expertise must use their judgment to assign a score to the response. So-called fill-in-the-blank questions bridge the gap, especially when scoring is virtually objective. Increasingly, essays and other written answers are being scored by computers using techniques of artificial intelligence, but such programs are almost always built to model human raters, weighting those aspects of the essay that human raters value (Page, 1994; Williamson, Mislevy, & Bejar, 2006).

Items such as multiple-choice items are most typically scored as 0 (for an incorrect answer) or 1 (for a correct answer). This scoring pattern is a principle upon which classical psychometrics is essentially based. The proportion of the population that answers a question correctly is considered to be the variable p, and the proportion that does not answer the item correctly is q. (For this example, those who have not responded to the item or have not answered it correctly are both considered to be members of q.) In this instance, p and q together sum to 1, the total proportion of all the test takers. One can consider a single item as a minitest whereby scores 0 and 1 constitute a distribution. Those earning a 1 are at the top of this distribution and those scoring a 0, at the bottom. It might be noted that p is also the mean of the distribution; if one sums all the

1s and the 0s and divides by the number of persons taking the test, one has calculated the mean, which also is p, the proportion of individuals answering the question correctly. The term p is also called the *item difficulty* of a question. It has sometimes been suggested that this term should be called *item easiness*, not *item difficulty*, because the higher the value the easier the question. Nevertheless, it is almost certainly the most common index of item difficulty among item analysis procedures.

Many test construction texts suggested at one time that test developers select items with item difficulty values near .50, to maximize item variances (e.g., Nunnally, 1978; Wright & Panchapakesan, 1969). Because tests were mostly composed of multiple-choice test items, others (e.g., Plumlee, 1952) suggested that guessing be factored into the ideal item difficulty value. To clarify this point, consider the following example. Assume we have a multiple-choice item with four options, one correct and three incorrect. Assume further that the item difficulty without guessing is .50, the ideal value as stated. Now assume that those test takers who do not know the correct answer guess randomly. Thus, of the four options, each would be selected by a fourth of the remaining 50% of the test takers. It would hence be expected that the ideal item difficulty becomes .625, on the basis of the original .50 plus one fourth of the remaining .50 or .125. In practice, however, most test takers do not like taking tests where they only know about 50% of the items, and this approach to item selection is not commonly used in educational testing in the 21st century. Nevertheless, unless the test has a specialized use, the developers of norm-referenced tests rarely accept items shown to have very high or very low item difficulties (Wright & Panchapakesan, 1969). Such an examination is most reliable and makes the best differentiations in the middle of the distribution. If one wishes discrimination throughout the distribution, a mix of item difficulties is often sought. Finally, if the only critical decisions made by the test are at a particular point, item difficulties around that point are recommended (Nunnally, 1978).

Because the role of a norm-referenced test is to differentiate test takers in meaningful ways, the variance of an item is important, as variances are used to demonstrate the degree to which individuals differ in their scores. In the case of proportions, the mean and the variance are integrally related to one another. The variance of a proportion is the proportion of those passing the items (or p) multiplied by the proportion of those failing the item (q). Thus, the variance of an item scored 1 (correct) or 0 (incorrect) is $p \times q$. This value is maximized when the passing proportion equals that of the failing proportion at .50 each. Similarly, there is no variance for an item when either everyone gets the item correct or incorrect. Items that are very difficult or very easy have minimal variance. For this and other reasons, such items are not typically placed on norm-referenced tests. Thus, the item variance of an item with a p value of .50 is .25; the item variance of an easy item with a p value of .90 is .09. Thus, given that the role of a norm-referenced test is to differentiate people, then items of relatively larger variance are needed. Moreover, as discussed later, items need to correlate with other items for a test to be reliable using traditional definitions, and it is "easier" for an item to correlate with another item (or a variable) if the variance is relatively larger.

A second general class of techniques in which items are evaluated relates to the degree to which the different items composing a test correlate with each other, or presumably measure aspects of the same or highly related aspects of the same construct. Therefore, a fundamental manner in which items are individually evaluated is the degree to which they correlate with one another. The typical manner in which such relationships are computed is by correlating the responses to an item with total test scores. Thus, for each test taker, they have either a 0 or a 1 for each individual item and then they have a continuous score (from 0 to the maximum that equals the total number of items scored 0 or 1). Two such correlations are most common: the point–biserial and the biserial (Glass & Hopkins, 1995). These indexes are known as item discrimination indexes. Item discrimination is perhaps the most valuable aspect of an item in a norm-referenced test because it tells us the extent to which the item appears to validly differentiate people in a population according to the underlying or a related construct.

The point–biserial is a standard Pearson product–moment correlation coefficient between a dichotomous variable (in this case, the test item) and a continuous variable (in this case, the total test score). It can be computed using normal correlation coefficient calculations or using specialized formulae that were developed before computers. Essentially, both the point–biserial and the biserial indexes are based on the notion that one expects the mean on a test to be higher for those answering a question correctly (and thus demonstrating knowledge of the underlying construct) relative to those failing the item. If such a difference is not found, then it seems that the item provides little information about the underlying construct.

The biserial correlation coefficient differs from the point–biserial correlation in that it is not a Pearsonian correlation coefficient and instead is essentially an adaptation of it on the basis of certain assumptions. This index is based on the noted assumption that there is a normal distribution underlying most characteristics, including psychological characteristics. Although most students who have taken even a single course in statistics know that the maximum value of a Pearson correlation coefficient is 1 (or –1), not all recognize that correlations cannot reach those values unless the shapes of their distributions are identical (or mirror images in the case of –1). The fact that an item has only a dichotomous distribution and test scores typically have a more normal distribution greatly limits the maximum value of point–biserial correlations. The biserial index is essentially an adjustment of the point–biserial correlation that inflates the value from the perspective that the dichotomous distribution generated by a test item has an underlying normal distribution. A common caution regarding the biserial correlation is that one must believe that the distribution underlying construct assessed by the individual item is in fact normal or close to normal.

Both of the item discrimination indexes, the point–biserial and the biserial, suffer from one negative aspect. These correlations are inevitably somewhat spuriously high. They are somewhat high because the item itself is part of the total test score; it contributes to the total test score. This is equivalent to measuring the length of your left leg and measuring your height overall. If we correlated these to variables, one would expect a high correlation coefficient, but one that is less than the perfect 1. For this reason, a correction formula was devised in which the effect of the item is removed from the test (Henrysson, 1963). In effect, this means that the correlation is between one item and all the rest of the items composing the test or scale. Most software packages that perform item analysis provide this latter index rather than the point–biserial, but it is important to determine whether the package uses the correction or not. The spuriousness of the correlation coefficient is especially problematic when the number of items is relatively low. As the number of items increases, the effect of an individual item becomes minimized.

Internal Consistency Reliability

Reliability is more formally described elsewhere (see Chapter 33 in this volume). However, one of the primary effects of selecting test items that correlate highly with total test score is that the internal consistency reliability of the test is increased. One does not wish to have a variable composed of a number of restatements of the same question; such a variable, although likely to generate high internal consistency, is also likely to have a limited meaning from the perspective of validity. We believe that the internal consistency reliability of a test is important generally for most tests, whether norm-referenced or criterion-referenced, but it is more critically important for norm-referenced tests. Reliability as traditionally defined is consistency of measurement. In the case of internal consistency, most typically and generically defined as coefficient alpha, we have, for each test taker, multiple measures, one for each test item (Cronbach, 1951). Coefficient alpha provides an index of the degree to which these items provide similar assessments. Essentially, the coefficient is an index of the degree to which within-person variability (seen as $MS_{\text{within persons}}$) is small relative to between-person variability (seen as $MS_{\text{between persons}}$). As another way of perceiving this relationship, between-person variability should be large relative to total variability, which includes both between- and within-persons variability. In fact, this is the basis for a formula that is mathematically equivalent to coefficient alpha (Hoyt, 1941). To the extent that between-persons variability is large relative to within-persons variability, we can differentiate people easily and dependably and, hopefully, validly. And that is indeed the nature and purpose of norm-referenced assessments. Thus, these coefficients are critical when one is evaluating the value of norm-referenced tests. It is incumbent upon any test developer to pretest the questions expected to supply a form of a norm-referenced tests minimally to see whether they correlate highly with each other and hence foster high internal consistency reliability.

This situation may not be the case for criterion-referenced tests. Popham and Husek (1969) demonstrated the case of an extremely successful criterion-referenced test. In this instance, before instruction, the students all scored very low, near 0. At the conclusion of instruction, the students had all learned the material on the test and therefore scored very well, at or near 100%. Moreover, the consistency of students relative to each other was no longer in strict rank-ordered fashion; those who had scored well on the pretest did not necessarily score as well on the posttest. In such a case, both test–retest and internal consistency reliability are poor. The former is low because of the change in rank ordering of the students. The latter is due to little or no between-subject variability—that is, all students score at or near the same score point. How often such situations occur is an empirical matter.

Norms and Norm Groups

One of the absolutely critical elements in norm-referenced testing, which will be seen to be indirectly relevant to criterion-referenced testing, relates to the norms. Norms indicate the nature of the distribution of test scores. The key element in a norm-referenced test is that a person knows where they fall in a distribution of other, hopefully comparable, test takers. Therefore, much work has been done in psychometrics, test development, and related disciplines to develop score scales that provide relevant information to the users of test scores. Much of this work relates to ways of assigning scores given various raw scores that individuals achieve on tests. From the perspective of test developers, it is critical to amass a large and representative norm group—with representative meaning that it needs to be representative of the group for which the test will ultimately be used. Typically, regarding development of a norm group, the larger that the norm group is the better, but there is no easy solution if the norm group is not representative. From the perspective of a test user, it is critical to evaluate the membership of the group taking the test. When a potential test user is deciding whether to use a particular test, it is critical to decide the extent to which the group on which the norms were established compares with the group for which the test is given. For this reason, the test standards (American Educational Research Association, American Psychological Association, & National Council on Measurement in Education, 1999) have stressed that test publishers need to portray their norm group accurately in the representative publications, such as the test user manuals. Norms can be international (uncommon), national, statewide, or local. All of these norms have their own uses; the determination of the level of norms should depend on their use.

Judging the appropriateness of a norm group is one of the most critical questions a potential test user can make about a test that he or she is considering using. One must make certain that the population on which the norms are based is comparable to the population that will be assessed, particularly if one wishes the score interpretations to be valid and appropriate. This point is especially critical when the test is being used with special populations, including racial and ethnic minority groups, individuals with disabilities, and English language learners, which are among the groups most critical to review.

Some of the worst abuses of testing have occurred when tests are used with populations on which the tests have not been proportionately represented, especially for high-stakes uses (see Geisinger, 1998, 2005). For example, when Head Start—a program aimed at the initial educational experiences of underserved children before beginning their formal education—was initially evaluated, the Peabody Picture Vocabulary Test was used as part of the evaluation. This measure had been normed and validated using almost exclusively White children whose parents were college professors in one city in the United States. Although the following statement is probably a bit of an overstatement, scores of the young children who took the test as part of the evaluation program were largely members of minority groups from relatively poor sections of a number of inner cities. In such a situation, one must question the appropriateness of test use. A more appropriate sample would be one that is nationally representative of the people with whom the test is intended to be used. Another test, the Hiskey-Nebraska Test of Learning Aptitude (Hiskey, 1966) was developed as a measure to be used with children who were hearing impaired. It was initially normed on a group of children who were hearing but who were told to feign being deaf. The test was subsequently normed on a more appropriate group. This first norming occurrence for the Hiskey-Nebraska occurred some 60 years ago and, hopefully, a study like this one would not be performed in the 21st century. Nevertheless, the significance of these issues is such that they remain examples of what not to do. (These scenarios are also described in Geisinger, 2005.)

Achieving a representative norm sample is not always an easy task, especially if this sample must be acquired before the test being given in an operational form. Some testing programs collect normative data before a test is published; some intelligence tests for example compensate a large number of psychologists to assess children using a test that is being readied for publication. In such cases, the psychologists assessing children and adults are given prescriptions of the number of individuals of different types (by age, gender, racial and ethnic groups, and geographic residence), which ensure an overall apparent representativeness of the final sample. In many cases, tests attempt to replicate the population as identified in the U.S. Census. In other cases, publishers collect preliminary norms test data before a test is formally published and then enhance the data collection with the operational use. Reading and mathematics achievement tests given as part of statewide assessments under either No Child Left Behind (NCLB) Act of 2001 or the Elementary and Secondary Education Act (ESEA) of 1965 are often normed in this fashion, even though their primary purpose is not for use as a norm-referenced test.

The same test can utilize numerous norms groups, norms data, and resultant norms tables to be employed by test users. Some tests have used different norms for males and females; these measures probably tend to be personality measures and the like. Age-specific norms are used for most intelligence tests. In cases in which state or regional differences exist, in which scores differ largely for groups such as immigrants or English-language learners or in which disabilities are involved, it may make sense to use specialized norms.

The two key principles used in the evaluation of any normative data collection project are simple: We want samples to be as large as possible and to be representative.

> Cornell (1960) has pointed out that sample statistics lack precision when: (a) the errors of random sampling are large, i.e., when there is a wide dispersion of the distribution of the sample about the population parameter, (b) where there is a bias, e.g., when the mean for all such sample statistics and the parameter are not the same, and (c) when the observations themselves are inaccurate or incomplete. (Angoff, 1971, p. 549)

The larger the random sample, the smaller the errors of random sampling. That part of sampling is clear. It is difficult to ever find a sample that has truly been assembled through random sampling, however, if the population is large and national, or even statewide, in focus. Representative sampling sometimes is achieved when testing a population by *spiraling* test forms. Spiraling means that every *n*th test would contain specific common questions or the common test form in question. Stratified random sampling may be attempted to secure a representative sample that is somewhat smaller than it might be if it were collected solely through random sampling. With random sampling, errors of sampling can be known or estimated.

Often convenience, cluster, and quota samples are selected, and these samples may come with biases, known and unknown. Angoff (1971) provided perhaps the most comprehensive review of these methods, the biases that accompany them, and

other related issues, including ways to estimate standard errors (for more information, see Volume 2, Chapter 14, this handbook). For example, it is often the case that schools are invited to participate in the preoperational testing so that norms can be computed, and some of these schools decline to participate. Such decisions, although understandable from the perspective of instructional time, may nevertheless lead to biased norms. Angoff therefore suggested that when plans for norm samples are developed, they should include two to three times as many schools as are needed in the final sample.

Among the most important considerations in defining the norm sample for any test norming project is a careful and explicit definition of the population in question. Subsequently, the sample must be drawn with complete adherence to the rules drawn up for it, using random sampling whenever possible. When biases are present in drawing the sample, the norms may nevertheless be useful. "They may, in spite of their bias, represent a close enough approximation to the ideal for most purposes" (Angoff, 1971, p. 560). It is through the use of these norms that score interpretation within the group is made. Of course, the validity of the instrument must also always be considered, a statement that is omitted in discussions of norms.

Score Distributions

It is a given in psychometrics that raw scores (i.e., the number of correctly answered questions on a test) on a measure are essentially meaningless. There are several reasons for this statement. For one reason, the raw scores on different tests all follow a different distribution depending on the number of questions, the manner in which different questions are scored (e.g., dichotomous, polytomous), the difficulty of the test questions, and the relationships (correlations) among those questions. For this reason, testing development professionals typically transform raw score distributions to those that are commonly known among psychologists and other test users.

One of the most common interpretive aids of any test score distribution is the percentile rank. This value tells the test taker and other users the percentage of the norm group that falls below that score. Thus, if a person receives a percentile rank score of 73, it denotes that he or she scored more highly than 73% of the people in the norm group. This fact is an elementary but critical component of any test score, especially of a norm-referenced test score. In fact, in part, this single index is perhaps among the most critical interpretative factors basic to a norm-referenced score and is in some ways the essence of such scores. Such scores may carry this information whether or not there is a normal distribution underlying the score distribution.[1] Few test reporting systems rely simply on percentile ranks as their scoring system. Rather, they use scales that carry meaning to informed users, that is, scales that can be developed through the use of score transformations.

There are two kinds of transformations, linear and nonlinear. Furthermore, in almost all cases, the transformations are done in a manner that leaves the ordering of scores as they are in the raw score distribution. Most commonly, the transformation is linear, and this is described in the following paragraphs. A linear transformation is simply one that changes the numbering of the distribution, but the shape of the raw score distribution is unchanged. The basis for any linear transformation is that a slope and an intercept are used to transform the original distribution from raw scores to a commonly used scale. Numerous common scales can be achieved through transformations.

The formula for linear transformations is simply

$$Y = [(X - Mean_x) \times (S_y/S_x)] + Mean_y, \qquad (2)$$

where X is the raw score for a score in question on the raw score distribution, Y is the transformed score, S_y is the standard deviation of the resultant transformed score distribution, S_x is the standard deviation of the raw score distribution, $Mean_x$ is the mean of the scores on the raw score distribution, and $Mean_y$ is the mean of the scores on the resultant distribution. X, Y, $Mean_x$, and S_x are random variables and S_x and $Mean_y$ are fixed variables and constants. That is, we are defining a targeting distribution by its intended mean and standard deviation.

TABLE 19.1

Common Transformed Scales

Name of the distribution	M	SD
z score	0.00	1.00
College Board scale[a]	500	100
t scores	50	10
IQ	100	15[b]
Stanine	9	2

[a]Historically used for SAT and GRE test scores, among others. [b]For older Stanford-Binet test scores, the standard deviation was 16 rather than 15.

A number of distributions are commonly used, and these may be found in Table 19.1.

The advantage of using a score that is commonly understood is that professionals seeing the score know something about how a person has done relative to the group of people for whom the test is intended and from whom a representative sample was presumably drawn to develop the norms tables. For example, a college admissions counselor at a selective institution would know the range of SAT scores that are likely to be acceptable under normal circumstances, and even the lowest scores that might be accepted by a sought-after football recruit. Similarly, a school psychologist knows the scores on intelligence and educational tests that are likely to lead to special education placements, whether for gifted educational programs or those for needing other kinds of assistance. Of course, such scores also connote a sense of predictive validity—a sense of how well the student is likely to do in the proposed educational program. Such information can be ascertained only by validity studies, which are beyond the scope of this chapter (but see Chapter 18 in this volume).

The transformations that have been described thus far are all linear transformations. It is also possible to change the shape of the distribution. A common technique is called a *normalization transformation*. This transformation changes the shape of the distribution in a manner that permits a test

---

[1]Percentiles (sometimes known as *percentile ranks*) are uniform density (what is known as a *rectangular distribution*) and are thus, by definition, not normally distributed. Although percentiles are useful for their ability to provide interpretation, their distribution can provide problems for certain statistical analyses. Many statistical techniques are based on the notion that the underlying score distribution is normally distributed.

score user to apply normal curve tables to the scores. How such a transformation is calculated is beyond the scope of this chapter, but they can be found in Angoff (1971, pp. 515–521) or Magnusson (1967, pp. 235–238). The bottom line is that some transformations take scores that do not conform to a normal distribution and create new scores that approximate a normal distribution. The primary advantage of conducting a normalization transformation is that users may interpret test scores using a normal distribution, but there are other advantages as well. One additional advantage is that correlation coefficients representing the linear relationship between two variables are limited when the shapes of the distributions are not the same. By normalizing a distribution, one optimizes one's chance of maximizing the correlation between test scores that result from the test and other variables that tend to conform to a normal or, at least, symmetric distribution, such as criteria utilized in criterion-related validity studies.

Two other nonlinear transformations are often used, especially in school settings or with young children. These include age-equivalent and grade-equivalent score scales. Both were mentioned in regard to the Stanford tests of ability and achievement and each is described briefly in the following paragraphs.

Age-equivalent scores differ from all of the scales previously presented. Measurement specialists and psychometricians employ scales on the basis of standard deviation units to make the case that the measurement is at the interval level of measurement rather than the ordinal. Age-equivalent scores do not use standard deviation units in this way. Instead, these scales, which are most often used in conjunction with the ability testing of children, convey a sense of the age for which such results might be expected. Psychometricians, however, are not positive about this approach, which has been used in the schools and for communication with parents and other similar groups. The technique can perhaps be best understood by considering how age-equivalent scores are computed. First, a range of children across the age span with whom the test is intended to be used is assessed with the testing instrument. Second, children are grouped by their closest year of

chronological age. (Sometimes finer demarcations are used, such as half-year or quarter-year gradations.) Then the median score for each age becomes that age. (Sometimes the mean is also used.) Imagine a 20-question test. If the children who are all grouped at age 7 achieve a median raw score of 14, then a raw score of 14 is seen as 7 years, 0 months of age on this scale. This procedure is followed for every age of interest in the population and a smooth curve is drawn through the distribution using interpolation. Thus, the midpoint on the graph between age 7 and age 8 would be seen as the value representing 7 years, 6 months. Scores for each month can be interpolated from the graph (or table) in the same fashion. Although age-equivalent scores were utilized early in the history of psychological testing (Angoff, 1971), there are too many disadvantages of this type of scale to continue their use, except perhaps in rare circumstances. Angoff (1971) presented these disadvantages in some depth. A few example concerns should help the reader to decide to avoid these scores, however. First, the variation of performance around the line that is drawn may well vary throughout the age span of interest. In some cases, differences from the line may be rather extreme and yet the same difference from the line may be rather common at another age. A second and perhaps more problematic concern emerges from scores of children who score much higher than or more poorly than their peers at a given age. Imagine an advanced 7-year-old child who scores on the test equivalent to how 10-year-old children score. Such a finding does necessarily not mean that the child can think in the same manner as a child at the age of 10. Moreover, age-equivalent scores are only appropriate for children; it does not make sense to say that an individual who is 25 years old can answer questions equivalent to that of a 28-year-old. For these reasons, the use of age-equivalent scores has justifiably been reduced in recent years.

Grade-equivalent scores are similar to age-equivalent scores, except that rather than using the chronological age of children, their year in school is employed. Such scores continue to be used, and psychometricians are only slightly less favorable to these scores than age-equivalent scores for similar reasons. Scores are provided for the year and month of schooling. A score of 6.4 would indicate that the student had scored equivalent to that of a sixth grader in his or her 4th month of the school year. These scores too are much subject to misinterpretation. Imagine a fourth grader who earns a score on a mathematics test of 6.7. This score implies that the student has scored similarly to that of a sixth grader in his or her 7th month. However, there is much mathematics content that is covered during the students fourth, fifth, and sixth grades. It does not mean that the student has learned that material; it simply means that the child is much more advanced than a typical fourth grader.

Scales such as the age-equivalent and grade-equivalent scales must be seen as purely ordinal scales. Their use under normal circumstances should be avoided. Although modern statistical programs may permit the modeling of ordered data in appropriate ways, the interpretation of two identical tests scores, one earned on a fourth-grade test and the other earned on a sixth-grade test, is often problematic.

THE USES OF NORM-REFERENCED TESTS

Norm-referenced tests have many uses in psychology, education, and industry and continue to be widely used to this day. Their use in achievement testing has waned, however, in the assessment of student learning. During the 1980s, in virtually all states in the United States, the schools administered norm-referenced achievement tests such as the California Achievement Tests (CTB/McGraw-Hill, 2003), the Iowa Tests of Basic Skills (Hoover et al., 2007), the Metropolitan Achievement Tests (Harcourt Educational Measurement) or the Stanford Achievement Tests (Pearson Assessments, 2000). All of these tests were carefully developed so that they did indeed measure content relevant to the grades in question across the United States, or at least across the states where these measures were used. These measures were provided by test publishers who developed the tests to ensure that what was then called content validity and is now seen as content-related evidence of validity. The test developers provided information on how students compared with each other at each grade in terms of their achievement. They could also provide some information in terms of what students had learned. The use of these tests, although still prevalent and available, declined substantially during the 1990s when standards-based testing became the norm.

Norm-referenced tests are especially useful in situations in which comparative decisions must be made about individuals. Indeed, the meaning of the scores becomes evident when comparing scores to those from the fixed reference group. These situations generally involve the sorting of individuals into groups or a rank ordering and the selection of individuals for specific purposes or programs. Selection situations are perhaps the single instance of most positive use for norm-referenced tests. During World War I and World War II, a variety of mental and physical ability tests were able to be used effectively to select and sort individuals for positions in the military that enabled the armed forces to work efficiently (e.g., Chapman, 1988). Choosing students for highly selective and selective colleges is another example of an effective use of psychological tests (Camara & Kimmel, 2005; Zwick, 2002). Personnel selection in industry has a long history of finding individuals with the skills to perform specific jobs.

Chapter 18 in this volume includes much critical information about the use of tests in predictive situations. This information is only abstracted here. In any predictive situation, one of the chief sources of information is related to the quality of the test to predict future performance, whether future college success, success on a job, or the like. These relationships are most commonly indexed as correlation coefficients between the predictive performance and some criterion of school or job performance. One can also imagine the use of the college admissions test as a 2 × 2 table, in which case the test is used to accept or reject candidates for admission. Similarly, students at the college can either succeed or fail. Therefore, those individuals who are selected and who succeed may be seen as the valid acceptances, and those who are selected and fail out are false acceptances. We must then imagine how those who fail to be accepted would have done in college.

Those who indeed would not have succeeded may be considered as valid rejections. Those who would have succeeded in spite of their lower test performance may be thought of as false rejections. Most colleges (and employers) wish to maximize the numbers of valid decisions. They are especially concerned about false acceptances, but false rejections are also costly. The seat filled by a student who is a false acceptance could well have been occupied by a false rejection.

Two factors help institutions maximize their percentage of valid decisions and the effects of these factors, test validity and selection ratio, may be seen in the famous Taylor–Russell (Taylor & Russell, 1939) tables. Test validity is characterized by a correlation coefficient; the higher the correlation coefficient, the better able we are to make valid decisions. Selection ratio is the proportion of candidates to be selected. The lower the selection ratio, the more candidates there are for the positions to be filled. When there are many candidates for every position, even a test of moderate validity can help make a great number of valid decisions. Likewise, if one needs to accept every candidate, the test can have only limited or no value. A third factor is also involved in the Taylor–Russell tables: the base rate of successful performance, that is, the proportion of candidates who would be successful even if no test were used. Clearly, the higher this percentage, the easier it is to fill one's class or employment positions with successful individuals. It is for reasons of selection ratio and base rate that colleges and employers work hard to recruit many applications.

Selection tests such as the SAT and ACT provide useful information to colleges and universities making difficult admissions decisions, although it is always strongly recommended that such test scores not be used in isolation, or even with a single fixed cutoff for admission. Similarly, a number of well-known measures have been effectively used as part of admissions decisions for graduate and professional schools: the Graduate Record Examination (GRE) provided by the Educational Testing Service for admissions to many graduate school programs, the Law School Admission Test administered by the Law School Admission Council for admissions to

law schools, the Medical College Admissions Test by the Association of American Medical Colleges for medical colleges, and the Graduate Management Admission Test provided by the Graduate Management Admission Council for admission to masters of business administration programs at business schools. These measures typically have a number of scales measuring verbal skills (primarily reading comprehension), mathematical skills and reasoning, and writing. In some of the more specialized tests, they also include subtests of science knowledge or reasoning and the like as well. All of these tests can perhaps best be thought of as measures of both ability and achievement; they are really measures of developed abilities, skills taught over years of schooling and not just through a quick training program intended to achieve success purely on the test. Much debate has occurred over their possible usefulness of short-term training programs to "coach" students to achieve success (e.g., Bond, 1989). Bond (1989) rightly identified the debate over the effects of coaching as both a scientific and a political debate. A number of his conclusions have provided some information regarding this controversy. First, the more time one spends in a specialized training program, the more likely it is to have a positive effect. Second, the effects of most so-called coaching programs tend to be relatively minor, upwardly influencing scores by 0.10 to 0.20 standard deviations. Third, most of the largest gains that have been identified were found in studies that lacked a control group. Finally, in cases in which students have learned mathematical concepts but not used them for a considerable period of time, the coaching may serve as something of a refresher and yield some positive effects. Nevertheless, Bond concluded that students would have to sift through information on their own to make decisions relative to their taking such courses or even purchasing a preparation book.

Norm-referenced tests are just as useful in personnel selection in industry as in college admissions, if not more so. This topic is largely beyond the scope of this chapter, however, because the debate about norm-referenced versus criterion-referenced testing has largely occurred within the context of educational testing and, more specifically, the testing of student achievement. Nevertheless, tests do help in the selection of employees for a wide variety of positions. Just as in admissions testing, however, the biggest controversy in personnel selection relates to the fairness of tests in the personnel selection process. Specifically, in the United States, questions arise frequently to the effect that tests have negative effects on racial minorities, language minorities, women, and other underserved groups. Within industrial psychology, the controversy has arisen just as frequently, and it continues to raise its head in both the popular press as well as professional journals.

ITEM RESPONSE THEORY APPROACHES

This chapter has been written primarily from the perspective of classical psychometrics. Indexes such as p values, point–biserial correlations, and internal consistency reliability coefficients such as coefficient alpha are important in classical psychometrics. In the 21st century, many educational tests are built on the basis of item response theory (IRT; for an in-depth discussion of these models, see Chapter 36 of this volume). Many large-scale educational and licensure tests such as statewide achievement tests use IRT rather than classical psychometrics to analyze test data and achieve scores for test takers; nevertheless, all the principles provided thus far are valid and appropriate.

There are a variety of IRT models, most often utilizing one, two, or three parameters. If a one-parameter model is used, the parameter is b, item difficulty. If a two-parameter model is used, the parameters are b, item difficulty, and a, item discrimination. Both of these values are analogous to the p-value (i.e., proportion of correct responses to a test item) and point–biserial index. A common third parameter for large-scale tests is the c parameter, which is sometimes known as the *guessing parameter* because this value provides an index of the likelihood that test takers can answer an item correctly when they do not have sufficient knowledge to answer it from their knowledge base. I argue in this chapter that IRT procedures are appropriate for norm-referenced tests; however, in regard to criterion-reference tests, although some IRT procedures, such as the one-parameter model, are clearly appropriate, others,

such as those involving the a or discrimination index, may be somewhat more questionable.

Figure 19.1 provides two examples of the item characteristic curves that are representative of test-taker performance in IRT. The x-axis provides a scaling of ability, the trait that underlies the tested characteristic. These values typically range from about –3.00 to about +3.00 in z-score terms. The y-axis provides the probability of test takers getting an item correct. At the lowest level of ability, where the item characteristic curve approaches the graph line representing the probability of achieving a correct response, we can identify the proportion of examinees getting the item correct without appropriate knowledge, or hence, the c parameter. The point at which the midpoint of the curve falls relative to the x-axis represents the difficulty of an item; the further to the right the curve falls, the more difficult it is because the test taker needs a greater amount of ability to answer the questions correctly. The steepness of the curve represents the ability of the item to differentiate weaker test takers from stronger ones. It can be seen that the steepness may occur in specific portions of the curve where the discrimination of those who know the answer from those who do not is most intense.

THE ADVENT AND USES OF CRITERION-REFERENCED TESTING

In the early 1960s, a small group of psychologists and educational psychologists began to advocate for a different kind of testing (e.g., Glaser, 1963; Glaser & Klaus, 1962; Hammock, 1960). These individuals called for the construction and use of measures that did something different than norm-referenced, selection-type measures. Glaser (1963), in an article often seen as the birth of criterion-referenced testing, called for a kind of measurement that we might now refer to as *authentic assessment*. The nature of this new kind of measurement was a concept that had not yet been developed. In Glaser's words, "Achievement measurement can be defined as the assessment of criterion behavior; this involves the determination of the characteristics of student performance with respect to specific standards" (p. 519). He added, "Measures which assess student

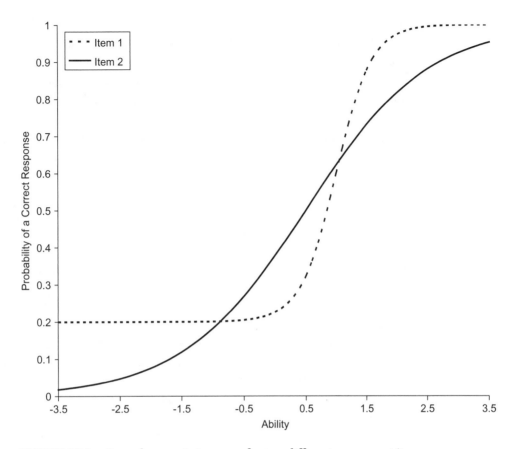

FIGURE 19.1. Item characteristic curves for two different assessment items.

achievement in terms of a criterion standard . . . provide information as to the degree of competence attained by a particular student which is independent of reference to the performance of others" (p. 520).

Millman (1974) defined the measures as tests that "provide information about the specific knowledge and skills of examinees and yield scores interpretable in terms of tasks or performances" (pp. 311–312). Millman also pointed out that the term *criterion* in *criterion-referenced testing* was confusing because it implied there was a criterion, as in a criterion-related validation study. Rather, the test is a criterion itself.

Perhaps because of that confusion, a number of different names were utilized to refer to criterion-referenced tests over the years, although the implications for these different names ascribe some differences in meaning and interpretation as well. Ebel (1962) used the phrase *content-standard test scores*. Others later used such terms as *objectives-based testing*; *domain-referenced testing*; *mastery tests*; *edumetric tests*; and the 21st century's name of

choice, *standards-based assessments*, but this listing is not complete. The basic distinction between norm-referenced tests and criterion-referenced tests can perhaps be best seen with the following two examples.

- **A norm-referenced interpretation**. On a 25-item multiple-choice grammar test, Janet scored 16 of the items correctly. This score placed her performance at the 75th percentile of all fourth graders who took the examination in a nationally representative norming sample.

- **A criterion-referenced interpretation**. On a 25-item multiple-choice grammar test, Janet scored 16 of the items correctly. This score identified her performance as proficient. Her performance was substantially higher than the cut score for that category, and we are 92% confident that she belongs in this grouping. Had she answered three more items correctly, her score would have moved her to the advanced proficient category.

These examples demonstrate Linn's (1994) characterization of criterion-referenced testing as "the essential idea that test results be interpreted in terms of a continuum of criterion performance that indicates what an individual can do" (p. 12). Essentially, the goal of criterion-referenced test use is to provide information that can be readily used by those guiding the instruction of students. A true criterion-referenced test would be one that provided elaborate direction to teachers and instructional supervisors and would permit such individuals to decide exactly what instruction a student needed next.

To accomplish such tasks, however, a test needs to be built differently than a norm-referenced test. Rather than selecting test questions using p values and item discrimination indexes so that individual differences in scores are maximized, the test developer needs to write items closely aligned to the curriculum in place and, to be sure, to the instruction that has been provided to students. The items need to assess whether students have learned the critical concepts in any instructional lesson or experience. So that such items can be developed, carefully written instructional and test specifications are needed. In fact, one of the leading proponents of criterion-referenced testing, James Popham (1994) stated that "the increased clarity attributed to criterion-referenced tests was derived from the test-item specifications that were generated in order to guide item writers. These specifications, in a very literal sense, operationalized what the test was intended to measure" (p. 16). Popham also identified a constant concern for developers of criterion-referenced tests, that one must find the correct and appropriate level of granularity. If one writes standards that are too narrow, then teachers are likely to teach to these narrow foci so that their students will succeed on the test; however, these foci will not generalize to the broader skill clusters that we hope to teach our students. If, on the other hand, test developers write objectives that are too general, it becomes very difficult to decide what we need to measure. Popham described this situation as a dilemma that must be faced by test developers of criterion-referenced tests.

Test items must be written carefully to address the standards and objectives of instruction. Numerous treatises have been written describing how test questions should be written for these tests (e.g., Davis & Diamond, 1974; Millman, 1980; Popham, 1980; Roid, 1984). This writer believes that the level of scrutiny required in terms of content validation is much more intense for a criterion-referenced educational achievement test than for a norm-referenced test.

During the 1980s, criterion-referenced testing became exceedingly popular with a large number of states requiring minimum competency tests. These tests were devised on the basis of the minimal expectations that those states held for all of their students and were therefore used, in some states, as graduation requirements, a matter that led to the Debra P. case in Florida (*Debra P. v. Turlington*). Briefly, the State of Florida was concerned about the quality of its public education system and enacted laws requiring the administration and use of a minimum competency examination covering certain basic academic skills. This test was to be used as a requirement for high school graduation, that is, receipt of a diploma. Although many students across the state passed the examination, a significant number failed, and the failing group included a disparate number or proportion of African American students. (During one administration of the test, 25% of White students failed to pass one or more sections of the test; during that same administration, 78% of African Americans failed to pass at least one section of the test.) A class action, brought on the behalf of these African American students, challenged the right of the state to impose the passing of the examination as a requirement for the receipt of a high school diploma. From the perspective of the courts, the overriding legal issue for this case was whether the State of Florida could deprive public school students of the high school diplomas that they expected to receive on the basis of an examination that may cover subject matter not taught through the curriculum. The Court of Appeals in this case held that the state was not permitted constitutionally to deprive its students of diplomas unless it submitted proof of the curricular validity and instructional validity of the test. Curricular validity was determined on the basis of whether the curriculum required instruction to all students on the material covered by the examination. Instructional validity was determined on the basis of whether all students actually received the instruction on the content to be covered by the test. (For more details on this landmark case, see the volume on this topic by Madaus, 1983.)

One of the distinctions made by Linn (1994) about criterion-referenced testing is that it is possible to develop norms for a test developed to be a criterion-referenced test; he believed, however, that it would rarely be possible to take a test built as a norm-referenced test and use it as a criterion-referenced test. Essentially, the manner in which a norm-referenced test is built simply would not permit such interpretations.

Linn (1994), one of the paragons of educational testing, wrote that he considered Glaser's (1963) idea for criterion-referenced testing to be one of the truly seminal ideas in educational testing. Perhaps it is not clear that criterion-referenced testing has achieved the goals Glaser and others originally desired. Criterion-referenced testing, especially in the current form of standards-based assessments, is now the primary way in which the educational achievement of students in the United States is measured. Moreover, techniques to ensure content validity such as alignment studies have helped close the gap between curriculum and testing, between instruction and assessment, and between state-mandated standards and the tests developed to assess whether the standards are being successfully taught and learned. Criterion-referenced testing in the early years of the 21st century is characterized by (a) the careful delineation of the content to be covered on an achievement test through its test specifications—for which a considerable attention is focused; (b) equally careful test construction procedures to meet those test specifications; (c) formal and informal checks that the test questions are measuring what they are supposed to on the basis of careful reviews by those not directly involved in the testing construction, including formal alignment studies; and (d) the test-related procedures that affect the quality of the test (e.g., standard setting).

PSYCHOMETRIC ISSUES IN CRITERION-REFERENCED TESTING

Item difficulty indexes have considerably less impact in true criterion-referenced testing. After all, should not the vast majority of students who have been exposed to effective instruction be able to answer questions that are written to represent that instruction (rather than to spread out the performance of students)? According to Harris (1974),

> It is important to distinguish between the difficulty of an item for a given student, which presumably is strictly a function of his (*sic*) experiences and his previous instruction (both formal and informal), and the normative concept of validity, which depends as well on who makes up the group of students whose responses provide the estimate of difficulty." (p. 101)

Thus, item difficulty, a key index in norm-referenced testing, typically has far less impact for criterion-referenced testing. Sometimes test constructors compare item difficulties before and after instruction. If the *p* value of an item does not change over this period, something would appear to be wrong with either the item or the instruction.

Variances of items are entirely dependent on item difficulty and, thus, also have much less impact in regard to criterion-referenced testing than they do in norm-referenced testing. Variances of test scores are of somewhat less criticality; rather, the key is the mastery status of test takers. In the early days of criterion-referenced testing, such states were mostly mastery and nonmastery. In 21st-century standards-based examinations, especially under the No Child Left Behind Act, there are likely to be three to five ordinally arranged status levels. After describing how one must construct test items to represent a domain of content carefully, Harris (1974) actually made a remarkable statement for a psychometrician: "I conclude that the construction of the particular test should proceed without attention to response data" (p. 104). In particular, he argued that item response data (e.g., item difficulty and discrimination) should not be used to decide whether an item is placed on a test. He perceived the really critical question as being how well a test can be used to sort students into meaningful groups, with each group qualitatively different in terms of their learning. He rightly argued that this question is really the validity argument. That is, if a test is able to identify those students who have learned the material in an instructional event and those who have not, it is a valid test. Clearly, the key question then is whether the test as a whole represents the content required by the standards, the curriculum, and the instruction in sequence; this question is an extreme one of content validity. Popham and Husek (1969) made some of these same points.

Berk (1980) provided a basic introduction to some item analysis techniques specifically for criterion-referenced tests. The techniques that Berk provided may be divided into (a) item–objective congruence, (b) item statistics, (c) item selection, and (d) item revision.

In general, the item–objective congruence approaches involve judgment on the part of those knowledgeable about both objectives or standards on the one hand and the test items on the other. These general techniques include the alignment studies now frequently used by states to assess the degree to which the high-stakes No Child Left Behind Act (the Elementary and Secondary Education Act) examinations match the standards that the state has selected to assess. Such indexes have pre-eminent value in the construction of most criterion-referenced tests.

The item statistics (the second category of techniques from Berk, 1980) involve the comparisons of item performance, typically comparing those who have received instruction on the content covered by the test with those who have not. Such analyses can either be pre- or posttest comparisons of a single group or a contrast of two preexisting groups that differ in their instructional background. Essentially, such comparisons contrast those who are expected to have knowledge with those who are not. A number of item analysis procedures analogous to those used in classical norm-referenced testing may also be provided. In fact, one possible analysis of items, for example, would perform traditional item analysis procedures using both students who have received instruction and those who have not. Such analyses should identify those items that are most sensitive to instruction. Berk (1980) also suggested that test constructors elicit informal student feedback about the questions.

Berk (1980) suggested that certain item analysis procedures be used to decide whether to include

items. These include item–objective congruence, item difficulty, and discrimination. Congruence between an item and the objective it is measuring is of paramount importance. Item difficulty and discrimination indexes are primarily to be used to identify the extent to which the item helps the test differentiate masters from nonmasters.

A final set of procedures described by Berk (1980) include those that help a test constructor to decide whether to revise an item. He provided the following general rules for identifying such items (and distractors within those items):

1. Each distractor should be selected by more students in the uninstructed group than in the instructed group.
2. At least a few uninstructed students should select each distractor.
3. No distractor should receive as many responses by the instructed group as the correct answer. (p. 70)

The reliability of criterion-referenced tests has been, at least in the early days of criterion-referenced testing, a somewhat controversial topic. Whereas norm-referenced tests are developed so that they differentiate test takers in terms of their level of achievement, criterion-referenced tests have a different purpose, and it is not clear that such indexes are as relevant. Ultimately, it is not essential that a criterion-referenced test has variability. Thus, at least according to Popham and Husek (1969), traditional indexes of internal consistency are not appropriate. Berk (1984) classified the attempts to assess the reliability of criterion-referenced tests into three general approaches, two of which are relevant to this discussion: (a) the reliability or consistency of classification decisions and (b) the more traditional reliability of test scores on criterion-referenced tests. Berk also stated, however, that "the use of the term reliability coefficient to characterize the indices recommended for criterion-referenced tests is inappropriate" (1984, p. 232). Classification accuracy is clearly the critical element of criterion-referenced examinations, which have as their primary purpose the sorting of test takers into the proper categories. Just as certainly, the closer the critical cutscores are to the median of the distribution, the more likely the decision consistency will be lower. Other reliability estimates use squared errors (e.g., Livingston, 1972), as they are used in variance estimates, but rather than computing these values by subtracting a score from the mean and squaring it, they are subtracted from the relevant cutscore and squared. One can imagine an analogue of the test–retest reliability coefficient in which rather than using the difference between a score and the mean of the distribution in the formula, one uses the difference between that same score and the cutscore. It might be noted, however, that these approaches have been criticized (e.g., Hambleton & Novick, 1973).

The separation of students into groups on the basis of their performance has been one of the most studied topics in criterion-referenced tests. Because of the large variety of methods, they have been grouped into logical categories of these methods. Several excellent books review these procedures (e.g., Cizek, 2001; Cizek & Bunch, 2007; Zieky, Perie, & Livingston, 2008). A few general principles are true of all methods, however. Some of these generalizations include the fact that all methods for setting *cutscores* (i.e., passing scores or scores for which one moves from one category of test taker to another) are ultimately made on the basis of judgment (Glass, 1978; Zieky et al., 2008). The nature of these judgments differs by class of method. Moreover, there is no true passing (or perfect) score for a test. Rather, different cutscores might be used for a test depending on the population of students taking the test, depending on the use to which the test scores are put, and so on. Finally, after any testing, students will have been misclassified into the incorrect groups. It is as hard to imagine a test that correctly classifies all students who take it (a criterion-referenced perspective) as it is to imagine a test in which every student receives a test score that perfectly and accurately estimates where they fall in the distribution of test takers (a norm-referenced perspective).

All techniques for setting passing scores involve judgment. The number of specific techniques or strategies for setting passing scores has easily reached 50 or more. The vast majority of these techniques can be broken into two categories: techniques

involving the judgments of test questions (composing the test) and techniques involving judgments about people. In the former, those knowledgeable about the nature of the content covered on the test review the test questions in a structured manner and use their knowledge and experience as well as their perceptions of the test to formulate judgments that permit those using the test operationally to set proper cutscores. One common method is the so-called Angoff method, a method that many people have modified to some extent. In this technique, judges define what a person who has just minimally reached a particular status (e.g., just passing) would be like. After some consensus is reached, the judges independently decide, item by item, what proportion of these minimally passing students would get each item correct. Once each judge has reviewed all the items and assigned each a proportion, then discussion among the judges ensues, often followed by a second or subsequent round of ratings. After a particular round has been concluded, the average proportion of test items is selected as the passing score. The description of this approach is overly simplified, and it represents just one of the many techniques that involve judgments of the test items composing a test.

The importance of judges should be clear. Scholars have described how judges should be selected and trained to engage in these processes (e.g., Raymond & Reid, 2001). A difficult aspect of these procedure is that the judges, typically teachers, are often not used to thinking about individual test items and the proportion of students at a particular level of achievement who would answer an item correctly. In short, they may not have accurate estimates of the proportion of minimally competent examinees answering a question correctly. For this reason, in some cases, test items are arranged in terms of difficulty (as determined by the collection of data) and judges then place bookmarks in the place where they believe cuts should be made. These values are translated into the ability level of the examinees who would get that last item correct. This technique is actually known as the bookmark technique. Both of these techniques have been mentioned to illustrate techniques judges use to consider test items.

Fewer techniques consider the test takers rather than test items. Two are the *borderline* (Impara & Plake, 1997) and the *contrasted group* (Livingston & Zieky, 1989) approaches. In the former, knowledgeable judges such as teachers identify those students (without access to their performance on the test) whom they believe should just barely pass the test or perhaps would have only a 50% chance of passing the test. Then, when the test performance of these students has been gathered, the average can be made the passing score. Similarly, in the contrasted group approach, teacher judges identify those students who are clearly passers and those who are not. A passing score is selected that maximally differentiates these two groups. Although teacher judgments about students are clearly within their normal practice, in too many cases, such as in the case of licensure and certification tests, such judgments are simply not practicable.

Some standard-setting techniques do not fit either of these categories, that is, they do not rely explicitly on judgments about individual test items or students. For example, there are techniques in which judges combine information from different subtests on a single test to identify a profile pattern that is needed to reach a (passing) status. There are also compromise techniques in which information from a variety of sources can be combined to set a passing score. Cizek (2001), Cizek and Bunch (2007), and Zieky et al. (2008) detailed these procedures well.

Two aspects of test validity must be considered in regard to criterion-referenced tests. First, it should be clear that the level of test content coverage on a well-made criterion-referenced test must be at least as high as that on a well-made norm-referenced test, and in most instances, it will need to be much higher. The detail that is needed in developing test specifications and in writing test questions to assess these specifications is reinforced by explicit procedures to check whether the items do measure those specifications independently. The second aspect that relates to the validity of the passing score is that of the standard that has been set (Kane, 2001). Simply put, if the standard is too high or too low, decisions will be incorrect and, therefore, the use of the test scores will be less valid than optimal.

One last comment about current practices in criterion-referenced testing is needed. In the 21st century, many states utilize tests that they identify as criterion-referenced tests in their documentation. These same states (and their contractors) use a three-parameter IRT model to analyze their test performance, select items, and otherwise maintain the tests. The second parameter in the three-parameter model is item discrimination, and as noted, many criterion-referenced theorists argue that item discrimination should not be a consideration in final item selection. The use of the three-parameter models does have other advantages, however, such as permitting test constructors to equate different forms of the test (e.g., from year to year) effectively so that test scores are meaningful regardless of the form utilized. Perhaps it might be best to consider such examinations to be hybrids of norm- and criterion-referenced approaches.

CONCLUSION

Norm-referenced testing has a long and successful history in regard to its usefulness in a wide variety of settings, especially those in which selection decisions are made. Testing professionals, following the lead of those who first built intelligence tests, know how to build tests that differentiate individuals in meaningful ways. To do so in terms of students' academic achievement in a manner comparable to how intelligence tests are constructed does not require that the content domain that is assessed be covered in a representative way; it does require that the test materials that are used on such tests be employed after considerable pretesting. Items must be selected that differentiate student examinees and that correlate highly with each other. We can do this validly and in ways that enable colleges making acceptance decisions and companies that are hiring to make better decisions. The tests of subject-matter achievement that are associated with such tests as the SAT and the GRE actually predict the future success of students quite well, as do the norm-referenced tests of ability or aptitude.

Criterion-referenced testing has a much shorter history. In one sense, criterion-referenced tests are simply tests whereby the tested domain is carefully mapped using test specifications and items built to meet those test specifications. The test questions that are used should be sensitive to instruction; they should reflect student learning rather than differences among students. The item review procedures, rather than being dominated by empirical procedures in the manner of norm-referenced testing, are often based on the judgment of educational professionals. As such, for measuring achievement in most contexts, these tests have taken on the preeminent role. Nevertheless, the interplay of the two types of tests is constant and is more present than many in education may believe. Hybrids of the two approaches seem to be a common type of testing in the 21st century.

A serious issue in using criterion-referenced tests is the setting of passing scores and cutscores. Norms tend to have real value in this case. Few states would wish to set passing scores on their academic tests so that every student failed or even that a disproportionately small number of students passed the examination. It is common practice in many cutscore studies to inform the panel of judges, after they have recommended an initial passing score, of the percentage of students who would pass the test were that initial passing score used. These judges typically have the opportunity to modify their recommended cutscore on the basis of this information.

Regardless of whether a test is a norm-referenced or a criterion-referenced one, the validity of the examination is the key issue. The techniques used to establish validity, however, may differ given the very different purposes of the tests.

References

American Educational Research Association, American Psychological Association, & National Council on Measurement in Education. (1999). *Standards for educational and psychological testing.* Washington, DC: American Educational Research Association.

Anastasi, A. (1958). *Differential psychology* (3rd ed.). New York, NY: Macmillan.

Angoff, W. H. (1971). Scales, norms, and equivalent scores. In R. L. Thorndike (Ed.), *Educational measurement* (2nd ed., pp. 508–600). Washington, DC: American Council on Education.

Berk, R. A. (1980). Item analysis. In R. A. Berk (Ed.), *Criterion-referenced measurement: The state of the art* (pp. 49–79). Baltimore, MD: Johns Hopkins University Press.

Berk, R. A. (1984). Selecting the index of reliability. In R. A. Berk (Ed.), *A guide to criterion-referenced test construction* (pp. 231–266). Baltimore, MD: Johns Hopkins University Press.

Binet, A., & Simon, T. (1905a). Application of new methods of the diagnosis of the intellectual level among normal and subnormal children n institutions and in the primary schools. *L'Année Psychologique, 11,* 245–336. doi:10.3406/psy.1904.3676

Binet, A., & Simon, T. (1905b). New methods for the diagnosis of the intellectual level of subnormals. *L'Année Psychologique, 11,* 191–244. doi:10.3406/psy.1904.3675

Binet, A., & Simon, T. (1905c). Upon the necessity of establishing a scientific diagnosis of inferior states of intelligence. *L'Année Psychologique, 11,* 163–190. doi:10.3406/psy.1904.3674

Bond, L. (1989). The effects of special preparation programs on measures of scholastic ability. In R. L. Linn (Ed.), *Educational measurement* (3rd ed., pp. 429–444). New York, NY: American Council on Education/Macmillan.

Camara, W. G., & Kimmel, E. W. (Eds.). (2005). *Choosing students: Higher education admissions tools for the 21st century.* Mahwah, NJ: Erlbaum.

Chapman, P. D. (1988). *Schools as sorters: Lewis M. Terman, applied psychology, and the intelligence testing movement, 1890–1930.* New York, NY: New York University Press.

Cizek, G. J. (Ed.). (2001). *Setting performance standards: Concepts, methods and perspectives.* Mahwah, NJ: Erlbaum.

Cizek, G. J., & Bunch, M. B. (2007). *Standard setting: A guide to establishing and evaluating performance standards on tests.* Thousand Oaks, CA: Sage.

Cornell, F. G. (1960). Sampling methods. In C. W. Harris (Ed.), *Encyclopedia of educational research* (3rd ed., pp. 1181–1183). New York, NY: Macmillan.

Cronbach, L. J. (1951). Coefficient alpha and the internal structure of tests. *Psychometrika, 16,* 297–334. doi:10.1007/BF02310555

CTB/McGraw-Hill. (1997). *Comprehensive Tests of Basic Skills* (5th ed.). Monterey, CA: Author.

CTB/McGraw-Hill. (2003). *California Achievement Tests* (6th ed.). Monterey, CA: Author.

Davis, F. B., & Diamond, J. J. (1974). The preparation of criterion-referenced tests. In C. W. Harris, M. C. Alkin, & W. J. Popham (Eds.), *Problems in criterion-referenced measurement* (pp. 116–138). Los Angeles: Center for the Study of Evaluation, University of California, Los Angeles.

Debra P. v. Turlington, 644 F.2d 397, 5th Cir. 1981, Unit B (1981).

DuBois, P. H. (1970). *A history of psychological testing.* Boston, MA: Allyn & Bacon.

Ebel, R. L. (1962). Content standard test scores. *Educational and Psychological Measurement, 22,* 15–25.

Elementary and Secondary Education Act of 1965, 20 U.S.C. § 241 (1965).

Geisinger, K. F. (1998). Psychometric issues in test interpretation. In J. Sandoval, C. L. Frisby, K. F. Geisinger, J. D. Scheuneman, & J. R. Grenier (Eds.), *Test interpretation and diversity: Achieving equity in assessment* (pp. 17–30). Washington, DC: American Psychological Association.

Geisinger, K. F. (2005). The testing industry, ethnic minorities, and individuals with disabilities. In R. P. Phelps (Ed.), *Defending standardized testing* (pp. 187–203). Mahwah, NJ: Erlbaum.

Glaser, R. (1963). Instructional technology and the measurement of learning outcomes: Some questions. *American Psychologist, 18,* 519–521. doi:10.1037/h0049294

Glaser, R., & Klaus, D. J. (1962). Proficiency measurement: Assessing human performance. In R. Gagné (Ed.), *Psychological principles in system development* (pp. 421–427). New York, NY: Holt, Rinehart & Winston.

Glass, G. V. (1978). Standards and criteria. *Journal of Educational Measurement, 15,* 237–261. doi:10.1111/j.1745-3984.1978.tb00072.x

Glass, G. V., & Hopkins, K. D. (1995). *Statistical methods in education and psychology* (3rd ed.). Boston, MA: Allyn & Bacon.

Goddard, H. H. (1908). The Binet and Simon tests of intellectual capacity. *The Training School, 5,* 3–9.

Hambleton, R. K., & Jones, R. W. (1993). Comparison of classical test theory and item response theory and their applications to test development. *Educational Measurement: Issues and Practice, 12*(3), 38–47. doi:10.1111/j.1745-3992.1993.tb00543.x

Hambleton, R. K., & Novick, M. R. (1973). Toward an integration of theory and method for criterion-referenced tests. *Journal of Educational Measurement, 10,* 159–170. doi:10.1111/j.1745-3984.1973.tb00793.x

Hammock, J. (1960). Criterion measures: Instruction vs. selection research. [Abstract]. *American Psychologist, 15,* 435.

Harris, C. W. (1974). Some technical characteristics of mastery tests. In C. W. Harris, M. C. Alkin, & W. J. Popham (Eds.), *Problems in criterion-referenced measurement* (pp. 98–115). Los Angeles: Center for the Study of Evaluation, University of California, Los Angeles.

Henrysson, S. (1963). Correction of item-total correlations in item analysis. *Psychometrika, 28,* 211–218. doi:10.1007/BF02289618

Hillegas, M. R. (1912). A scale for the measurement of quality of English composition by young people. *Teachers College Record, 12,* 331–384.

Hiskey, M. S. (1966). *Hiskey-Nebraska Test of Learning Aptitude.* Lincoln, NE: Union College Press.

Hoover, H. D., Dunbar, S. B., & Frisbie, D. A. (2007). *Iowa Tests of Basic Skills, Form C.* Chicago, IL: Riverside.

Hoyt, C. (1941). Test reliability estimated by analysis of variance. *Psychometrika, 6,* 153–160. doi:10.1007/BF02289270

Hulin, C. L., Lissak, R. I., & Drasgow, F. (1982). Recovery of two- and three-parameter logistic item characteristic curves: A Monte Carlo study. *Applied Psychological Measurement, 6,* 249–260. doi:10.1177/014662168200600301

Impara, J. C., & Plake, B. S. (1997). Standard setting: An alternative approach. *Journal of Educational Measurement, 34,* 353–366. doi:10.1111/j.1745-3984.1997.tb00523.x

Kane, M. T. (2001). So much remains the same: Conception and status of validation in setting standards. In G. J. Cizek (Ed.), *Setting performance standards: Concepts, methods and perspectives* (pp. 53–88). Mahwah, NJ: Erlbaum.

Kelley, T. L., Ruch, G. M., & Terman, L. M. (1922). *Stanford Achievement Test.* Yonkers, NY: World Book.

Linn, R. L. (1994). Criterion-referenced measurement: A valuable perspective clouded by surplus meaning. *Educational Measurement: Issues and Practice, 13*(4), 12–14. doi:10.1111/j.1745-3992.1994.tb00564.x

Livingston, S. A. (1972). Criterion-referenced applications of classical test theory. *Journal of Educational Measurement, 9,* 13–26. doi:10.1111/j.1745-3984.1972.tb00756.x

Livingston, S. A., & Zieky, M. J. (1989). A comparative study of standard-setting methods. *Applied Measurement in Education, 2,* 121–141. doi:10.1207/s15324818ame0202_3

Madaus, G. F. (Ed.). (1983). *The courts, validity, and minimum competency testing.* Boston, MA: Kluwer-Nijhoff.

Magnusson, D. (1967). *Test theory.* Reading, MA: Addison-Wesley.

Millman, J. (1974). Criterion-referenced testing. In W. J. Popham (Ed.), *Evaluation in education: Current applications* (pp. 309–397). Berkeley, CA: McCutchan.

Millman, J. (1980). Computer-based item generation. In R. A. Berk (Ed.), *Criterion-referenced measurement: The state of the art* (pp. 80–96). Baltimore, MD: Johns Hopkins University Press.

No Child Left Behind Act of 2001, Pub. L. 107-110, 20 U.S.C. § 6319 (2002).

Nunnally, J. C. (1978). *Psychometric theory* (2nd ed.). New York, NY: McGraw-Hill.

Page, E. B. (1994). Computer grading of student prose, using modern concepts and software. *Journal of Experimental Education, 62,* 127–142. doi:10.1080/00 220973.1994.9943835

Pearson Assessments. (2000). *Metropolitan Achievement Tests, Eighth Edition (MAT 8).* San Antonio, TX: Pearson Education.

Plumlee, L. G. (1952). The effect of difficulty and chance success on item-test correlation and on test reliability. *Psychometrika, 17,* 69–86. doi:10.1007/BF02288796

Popham, W. J. (1980). Domain specification strategies. In R. A. Berk (Ed.), *Criterion-referenced measurement: The state of the art* (pp. 15–31). Baltimore, MD: Johns Hopkins University Press.

Popham, W. J. (1994). The instructional consequences of criterion-referenced clarity. *Educational Measurement: Issues and Practice, 13(4),* 15–18, 30. doi:10.1111/j.1745-3992.1994.tb00565.x

Popham, W. J., & Husek, T. R. (1969). Implications of criterion-referenced measurement. *Journal of Educational Measurement, 6,* 1–9. doi:10.1111/j.1745-3984.1969.tb00654.x

Raymond, M. R., & Reid, J. B. (2001). Who made thee a judge? Selecting and training participants for standard setting. In G. J. Cizek (Ed.), *Setting performance standards: Concepts, methods and perspectives* (pp. 119–157). Mahwah, NJ: Erlbaum.

Roid, G. H. (1984). Generating the test items. In R. A. Berk (Ed.), *A guide to criterion-referenced test construction* (pp. 49–77). Baltimore, MD: Johns Hopkins University Press.

Taylor, H. C., & Russell, J. T. (1939). The relationship of validity coefficients to the practical effectiveness of tests in selection: Discussion and tables. *Journal of Applied Psychology, 23,* 565–578. doi:10.1037/ h0057079

Terman, L. M. (1916). *The measurement of intelligence.* Boston, MA: Houghton Mifflin. doi:10.1037/ 10014-000

Thorndike, R. M. (with Lohman, D. F.). (1990). *A century of ability testing.* Chicago, IL: Riverside.

Williamson, D. M., Mislevy, R. J., & Bejar, I. I. (Eds.). (2006). *Automated scoring of complex tasks in computer-based testing.* Mahwah, NJ: Erlbaum.

Wright, B. D., & Panchapakesan, N. A. (1969). A procedure for sample-free item analysis. *Educational and Psychological Measurement, 29,* 23–48. doi:10.1177/001316446902900102

Yerkes, R. M., Bridges, J. W., & Hardwick, R. S. (1915). *A point scale for measuring ability.* Baltimore, MD: Warwick & York.

Zieky, M. J., Perie, M., & Livingston, S. A. (2008). *Cutscores: A manual for setting standards of performance on educational and occupational tests.* Princeton, NJ: Educational Testing Service.

Zwick, R. (2002). *Fair game? The use of standardized admissions tests in higher education.* New York, NY: RoutledgeFalmer.

CHAPTER 20

BRIEF INSTRUMENTS AND SHORT FORMS

Gregory T. Smith, Jessica L. Combs, and Carolyn M. Pearson

In this chapter, we consider brief psychological instruments to be those measures that are developed with the goal of brevity; some brief instruments are short forms of previously validated measures. The specific meaning of *brief* varies according to the needs and context of the assessment. In some cases, measures of three items may be desired and appropriate.[1] In other cases, researchers may seek to develop a 30-min assessment to replace an existing, 2-hour evaluation process. As we describe in the following sections, reasons for brevity include the need to measure multiple constructs in a single assessment, the need to save time, the need to save resources, or other practical considerations. The theme of our chapter is this: Although most researchers have learned that longer measures tend to be more reliable and valid, that is not always true. Under the right conditions, brief measures can be as valid, or more valid, than longer measures of the same construct. We describe the (frequent) conditions under which this is likely to be true and provide guidance to researchers in the valid development of brief instruments. We also discuss procedures for developing reliable and valid shorter versions of existing measures.

The outline of the chapter is as follows. First, we review the standard psychometric argument in favor of longer measures. We then observe that as a result of this standard argument, many researchers'

choices to use brief instruments or short forms are made grudgingly: Researchers tend to do so for practical reasons, even though they view themselves as potentially sacrificing important content coverage. We then make an argument for the opposite: Brief instruments that are developed with careful consideration of the need to include content prototypic of the construct can, in fact, be more valid than longer instruments. We thus observe that the pursuit of the practical is not inconsistent with the pursuit of validity; put differently, construction of brief tests can enhance both validity and practicality. We address important issues in the construction of brief measures and limitations to the utility of brief measures. After providing examples of brief instruments for which there is good evidence of validity, we provide an overview for how to construct valid short forms of existing, longer measures. We then briefly consider item response theory (IRT) as an important vehicle for brief test construction.

PSYCHOMETRICS AND LONGER MEASURES

Psychological researchers are typically well aware of the test construction concept represented by the Spearman–Brown prophecy formula (SBPF; Spearman, 1910): Increasing the length of a test, by adding parallel items, will improve its reliability and

Portions of this work were supported by the National Institute on Alcohol Abuse and Alcoholism Grant R01 AA 016166 to Gregory T. Smith.

[1]In this chapter, we primarily use the term *item* to refer to an element of an assessment instrument. We do so for convenience of presentation; we do not intend to limit our discussion to questionnaires and questionnaire items. The principles we describe apply to any form of psychological assessment, including questionnaires, interviews, peer observations, behavioral observations, physiological assessments, and the like.

DOI: 10.1037/13619-021
APA Handbook of Research Methods in Psychology: Vol. 1. Foundations, Planning, Measures, and Psychometrics, H. Cooper (Editor-in-Chief)

thus its validity. The concept behind the SBPF is that there is an identified content domain of interest, and the items on a measure of that content domain are a random sample of all possible items. Under that assumption, if one were to add a certain number of parallel items (i.e., items also sampled randomly from the content domain), the SBPF predicts the reliability of the new, longer measure. One version of the formula is as follows (Spearman, 1910):

$$r_{ff} = \frac{k(r_{ss})}{1 + (k-1)r_{ss}}, \tag{1}$$

where r_{ss} refers to the reliability of the original (short) version of the measure, r_{ff} refers to the predicted reliability of the longer measure, and k is the factor by which the length of the measure is increased. Thus, if one had a measure with a reliability estimate of .75 and one doubled the measure length (using parallel items; $k = 2$), the formula would predict a reliability estimate for the new, longer measure of .86. Such a change would mean a drop in the proportion of estimated error variance from .25 to .14. Subsequent advances in the form of generalizability theory (Cronbach, Gleser, Nanda, & Rajaratnam, 1972) led to a removal of the requirement that items be strictly parallel; instead, items viewed simply as alternative indicators of the same construct (but without fully overlapping psychometric properties) could be included. One result of this advance is that it became even easier to add new items to measures.

In large part because of this seminal contribution by Spearman (1910), psychological researchers have placed a strong emphasis on lengthy tests. It is important to develop measures that are as reliable as possible (i.e., that have the least possible error variance), and one way to approach that goal is to lengthen tests by adding additional items. Accordingly, when researchers use very brief measures, such as those with two, three, or four items, it is often the case that they do so with a sense that they are probably not representing the full content domain sufficiently and thus are sacrificing reliability.

Nevertheless, researchers often do decide to use brief measures, typically for practical reasons. Many psychological theories are multivariate. For example,

risk researchers often propose models that involve the simultaneous operation of several risk factors, mediation of some risk factors by other risk factors, moderation effects, and the like. It is perhaps often the case that, as a practical matter, one cannot study such models by using lengthy tests for each construct in the model. In some cases, time constraints are paramount (participants are available only for a specified period of time, such as when children are studied during the course of the school day); in other cases, avoiding fatigue is important; and in others, financial limitations preclude lengthy assessments. As researchers face the competing demands of reliable assessment and valid representation of complex models, they often make the choice to represent individual constructs with brief measures. At times, comprehensive coverage of a construct gives way to the need to represent multiple constructs in a single study. Many researchers view this choice as a regrettable necessity.

ON THE VALIDITY OF BRIEF INSTRUMENTS

In contrast to this perspective, we now argue that researchers' devotion to lengthy tests is often not necessary and may actually lead to less valid assessment of target constructs. To introduce this argument, we note the relevance of the concepts of content validity (Cronbach & Meehl, 1955), construct representation (Embretson, 1998), and construct homogeneity (McGrath, 2005; Smith, McCarthy, & Zapolski, 2009).

Content Validity

Haynes, Richard, and Kubany (1995) present a useful discussion of content validity and methods of content validation. We would like to emphasize two aspects of the content validation procedure that they described. The first concerns construct definition. It is well known that when a researcher develops a measure of a construct, it is important to define the construct in precise terms. As Haynes et al. (1995) noted, precise definitions include specifying both what content is included in the target construct and what content is excluded. Perhaps in the past, in part because of the SBPF-based pressure to develop lengthier measures, researchers may have emphasized what to include more than they have emphasized what to exclude. We argue that consideration of what to exclude is every bit as important. There is a distinction between content that is prototypic of a target construct and content that is related to the target construct but actually representative of a different construct. Exclusion of related nonprototypic content is an essential part of constructing a content valid instrument.

One possible example of inclusion of related nonprototypic content was observed by Smith, Fischer, and Fister (2003), who contrasted two items from the Novelty Seeking scale of the Temperament and Character Inventory (Cloninger, Przybeck, & Svrakic, 1991). One item appears to be prototypic of novelty seeking (the item refers to doing new things for fun or for the thrill), but the other item, which refers to the ability to convince others to believe something you know is untrue, does not. Instead, the latter item may reflect a different construct that is correlated with novelty seeking. If the Smith et al. conjecture is correct, the inclusion of both items may increase estimates of internal consistency reliability but may lead to a test that includes content representing constructs related to, but separate from, novelty seeking.

This consideration is relevant to test length because (a) many lengthier tests include correlated but not prototypic content, and (b) evidence indicates that a construct's content domain can be represented with relatively few items. Ulrich (1985) showed that test validity does not increase with test length if the new items have even slightly different factor structures (or represent slightly different constructs). More recently, Burisch (1997) demonstrated empirically that shortened scales can have improved convergent validity over longer scales when the shortened scales included only items that had been prescreened for content validity. A small set of items that has been judged to validly represent the target construct (i.e., be prototypic of the target construct) can be combined to produce a more valid scale than a large set of items, in which not all items are prototypic of the target construct. In fact, Burisch (1997) found that scales of two to four items had estimates of convergent validity that were

at least as high, and often higher, than those of much lengthier scales. Lengthy attempts to reflect content domains may often not be necessary. (Of course, to conduct structural equation modeling or confirmatory factor analysis on a scale, it is advisable to have at least three items per scale for the purpose of factor identification.)

The second contribution by Haynes et al. (1995) that we would like to emphasize is the need for independent quantitative evaluation of content validity. When trained experts conduct independent reviews of whether instrument content represents the target construct, and the content does not represent related constructs, researchers can have increased confidence in the fidelity of their measures. It is often advisable to have multiple independent raters evaluate prospective content on the basis of inclusionary and exclusionary criteria: One can then retain items that meet both sets of criteria, and one can report the rate of agreement among the experts. The combined focus on inclusionary and exclusionary criteria is likely to result in a smaller item pool composed of items that are more prototypical of the target construct.

Construct Representation

Construct representation refers to the degree to which the tasks (items, observations, etc.) on an instrument validly represent the target construct (Embretson, 1998). This concept has often been used with respect to laboratory tasks, but the concept has a more general application. To consider construct representation in a measure, one might think in terms of what percentage of the variance in response to an item reflects variance in the target construct, and what percentage reflects other factors instead. For example, in our Eating Expectancy Inventory (a measure of a risk factor for eating disorders; Hohlstein, Smith, & Atlas, 1998), there is a scale understood to measure the tendency to eat to alleviate negative affect. The item "eating seems to decrease my level of anxiety if I am feeling tense or stressed" may have good construct representation: Perhaps the bulk of the variance in responses to that item is related to variance in the target construct. In contrast, the item "eating makes me feel loved," which is on the same scale, may not have as strong construct representation. It may well be that part of the variance in responses to that item does reflect variance in the target construct, whereas other sources of variance in response to that item are not reflective of eating to alleviate negative affect. By including only items for which variance in item response is likely to be highly related to variance in the target construct, test developers can trim away unnecessary items and create scales that are both more brief and more valid.

The allure of ever more reliable tests has perhaps led researchers to write new items, and add new items, at the expense of careful consideration of (a) whether each new item is truly prototypic of the target construct or (b) the degree to which variance in responses to the item represents variance in the target construct. It is true that when one adds items that are correlated to an existing item set, coefficient alpha estimates of reliability do go up. But this can occur even if the new items do not truly represent the target construct domain. The findings of Burisch (1997) and Ulrich (1985) have suggested that the promise of increased reliability estimates is not necessarily realized as increased validity. Brief instruments can be more valid than lengthier instruments.

Construct Homogeneity

Another concept that may prove helpful for researchers as they seek to develop content-valid brief measures is that of construct homogeneity. Several researchers have argued that scores on psychological measures should reflect variation along a single dimension, that is, variation on a definable, coherent, homogeneous psychological construct (Edwards, 2000; McGrath, 2005; Smith, McCarthy, & Zapolski, 2009; Strauss & Smith, 2009). McGrath (2005) and Smith et al. (2009) provided several examples of scientific and measurement uncertainty that occur when a single score is used to reflect variation on several dimensions simultaneously.

Consider a single score on posttraumatic stress disorder (PTSD). Several researchers have identified four different dimensions within that diagnosis: Simms, Watson, and Doebbling (2002) labeled them intrusions, avoidance, dysphoria, and hyperarousal. These four dimensions are only modestly correlated with each other, and they do appear to refer to dif-

ferent experiences. The same score on PTSD could be obtained by one person high on hyperarousal and low on the other three dimensions and by another person high on avoidance and low on the other three dimensions. Obviously, these two individuals are having different psychological experiences, even though they would get the same score on the composite measure. Thus, a single score risks obscuring important differences in symptom profiles for different individuals (this is true even though there may be some purposes for which a single score is useful).

The pursuit of construct homogeneity can facilitate the development of brief psychological instruments. To the degree it is possible, researchers should seek to define constructs that are homogeneous. The process of refining construct definitions toward homogeneity is likely to result in exclusion of some prospective content from the measure to be developed. An initial attempt to define unidimensional or homogeneous constructs, together with careful consideration of content validity and construct representation, can help researchers develop measures that are both valid and brief.

THE CREATION OF BRIEF INSTRUMENTS

First, and perhaps most important, nothing about the size of a scale alters the need to undergo careful and thorough scale construction and construct validation procedures. There is no basis for concluding that a brief measure needs less care in construction or less comprehensive validation. Other chapters in this handbook provide valuable guidance for many aspects of scale construction and validation (see Chapters 10, 14, 18, and 19 of this volume) as do other published articles (Clark & Watson, 1995; Smith et al., 2003; Smith & McCarthy, 1995) and books (Nunnally & Bernstein, 1994). Therefore, we will not review basic aspects of test construction here; instead, we will focus on considerations specific to the construction of valid, brief instruments.

It is important that the construction of a brief instrument use both theoretical and empirical approaches. When focusing on a particular construct to be measured, one must determine with precision which theoretical domain one wishes to access with the measure. It may be necessary to specify one domain of many, or one facet of many (as has been done so effectively in the field of personality). As researchers approach this task, we recommend that they review the concepts of content validity, construct representation, and construct homogeneity. Reexamination of each prospective item with respect to how likely it is that variance in response to the item reflects variance in the target construct, and with respect to whether each prospective item does represent the same carefully defined construct, can facilitate the identification of a reduced number of items for a brief instrument.

One of the challenges in developing a brief measure is to include content that is homogeneous, but that is not simply a slight rephrasing of exactly the same content (Burisch, 1997; Loevinger, 1957). The degree to which two items are parallel measures of the same content domain, or instead (a) are substantively identical or (b) actually represent two different but correlated content domains, can be evaluated only by careful judgment. Mistakes are likely, and an iterative process involving repeated reexamination of item content and construct definition may prove useful. It is crucial that the nature of the judgment process be specified, the judgments evaluated empirically, and then empirical content validation procedures be applied on the item pool independently by experts (Haynes et al., 1995).

It may often be the case that researchers do not need to develop new items from scratch. The essence of relevant item content is frequently available in existing, well-validated lengthier measures or in existing definitions of target constructs—such as when one wants to briefly assess a diagnosis described by the *Diagnostic and Statistical Manual of Mental Disorders* (4th ed., text revision; *DSM–IV–TR*; American Psychiatric Association, 2000). Researchers should avoid simply appropriating copyrighted items, while also drawing on previous researchers' efforts to assess the same content domain (Bischof et al., 2007; Lang & Stein, 2005; Lincoln, Liebschutz, Chernoff, Nguyen, & Amaro, 2006). A review of existing construct definitions and measure content may help one clarify the nature of the content domain one wants to assess.

Following item selection and empirical content validity procedures, corrected item-total correlations can be used to further prune the measure. We should note that there is no agreed-on rule for the optimal magnitude of item intercorrelations: Recommendations vary from .15 to .50, and even higher (Briggs & Cheek, 1986; Clark & Watson, 1995; Morey, 2003; Smith et al., 2003). These values reflect a balance between the concerns that items not be fully redundant and that they represent the same content domain. Of course, the optimal magnitude of interitem correlations is in part a function of the true breadth of the target construct. Moderately or very high item-total correlations do not prove construct homogeneity: An item can be correlated with the total while not reflecting the same construct, or two items can be substantively identical and so correlate very highly. On the other hand, if the item-total correlation is low, it is likely that the item does not reflect the target domain and should be excluded.

Item-total correlations are indeed helpful for building confidence that a judgment that an item represents the content domain was valid, but neither item-total correlations nor estimates of internal consistency (such as coefficient alpha) speak to the important goal of unidimensionality (Clark & Watson, 1995). There is an important difference between achieving strong internal consistency, which is reflected in coefficient alpha and interitem correlations, and construct homogeneity, which occurs when all items reflect a single underlying construct. One important tool for achieving the latter goal is factor analysis.

Factor analysis can be used to test hypotheses about the dimensional structure of an item set (Clark & Watson, 1995). For this analytic approach to be feasible, it is necessary to have a few items representing each possible dimension. For example, to test the competing hypotheses that an item set has one, two, or three underlying dimensions, one should have at least three items representing each of the three possible dimensions. There are two reasons for this recommendation. The first is statistical: A factor cannot be identified in confirmatory factor analysis, typically, without at least three items or indicators. The second is practical: If a putative dimension is represented by only a single item, that dimension cannot emerge in a factor analysis; it will simply not be noticed in a factor analysis.

If a researcher suspects a single item represents a different dimension from the intended construct, the researcher can consider deleting the item. If, instead, the researcher wants to test the dimensionality hypothesis, it may prove necessary to write two or more additional items parallel to the item in question, so that a comparative factor analysis can be conducted. Thus, the process of determining the dimensionality of an item set is likely to be an iterative one, consisting of content validity judgments, item deletion, item generation, and comparative factor analysis.

LIMITATIONS ON THE USE OF BRIEF INSTRUMENTS

Although we have argued for the potential value of brief instruments and described both conceptual and test construction procedures designed to produce valid brief measures, there are also limitations as to when brief instruments should be used. We consider two categories of limitations. First, some target constructs simply require a large number of items, or a large number of behavioral observations, or a lengthy interview for valid assessment. Second, when one seeks to assess a multidimensional construct, it is important to measure each dimension reliably and validly (Smith et al., 2003); as a result, multidimensional measures often require greater length.

The Need for Lengthier Measures

In a number of assessment circumstances, brevity may not be appropriate. We provide a few examples. First, if a psychologist wants to observe a certain target behavior and determine the degree to which emission of the behavior is a function of external circumstances, it may well be necessary to construct a lengthy observation protocol. Second, constructs that involve a skill, and thus require items of graduated difficulty, may require lengthier assessments than other constructs. For example, the Wechsler Adult Intelligence Scale (4th ed.; Wechsler, 2009), relies on 30 vocabulary items to facilitate discriminations at different levels of vocabulary skill. In fact, there may be many psychological constructs that are best assessed with a variety of items, each measuring a different intensity level of the construct: When that is true, it is necessary to begin with a larger item pool. In the section Item Response Theory and Tailored Testing and in Chapter 10 of this volume, IRT models and tailored testing are presented as tools that facilitate relatively brief assessment using items measuring differing intensity levels of target constructs. Third, researchers might well conclude that a small number of items (such as three to five) simply would not permit an adequate sampling of the content domain of a target construct, and thus they choose to construct a lengthier instrument.

The fourth circumstance under which lengthier measures may be necessary is when the goal is to assess a multidimensional construct. In some areas of psychological inquiry, such as the study of personality or the study of psychopathology, multidimensionality is the norm, not the exception. Concerning psychopathology, recall our earlier example of PTSD. It is now clear that to validly assess this disorder, one must validly assess each of the four dimensions of dysfunction. As reviewed in Smith and Combs (2010), numerous disorders described in the *DSM–IV–TR* have been demonstrated to be multidimensional. Examples include schizophrenia, depression, obsessive–compulsive disorder, and psychopathy, along with PTSD and many others. Concerning personality, virtually all comprehensive models of personality are hierarchical in nature. For example, the Revised NEO Personality Inventory (NEO-PI-R) version of the five-factor model (Costa & McCrae, 1992) includes five broad personality domains (Neuroticism, Extraversion, Agreeableness, Openness to Experience, and Conscientiousness) and six specific homogeneous traits within each domain. Thus, comprehensive measures of personality are multidimensional.

For many, if not most, purposes, valid assessment requires the separate assessment of each separate construct. In the case of PTSD, a single score simply averages across different constructs and, as noted, may reflect different psychological experiences for different individuals. There are validated and distinct treatments for the four PTSD dimensions of dysphoria and anhedonia, avoidance of stressful stimuli, excessively heightened arousal system, and intrusive, unwanted thoughts. For assessment to guide treatment effectively, it must validly assess each of the four dimensions. Similar concerns apply to the assessment of personality (Gosling, Rentfrow, & Swann, 2003). For example, two traits within the Neuroticism domain on the NEO-PI-R are depression and angry hostility. Measures of the two traits are only modestly correlated: One can be high on one trait and unremarkable on the other. A single Neuroticism score essentially averages the scores on the two traits. Two people could have exactly the same Neuroticism score and the first person could be angry and hostile, but the second person could be depressed. A single score can thus lack a clear, specific psychological referent (McGrath, 2005; Smith & Combs, 2010).

Accordingly, assessment of multidimensional construct domains requires enough items, interview questions, or observations to represent each individual construct reliably and validly. The assessment of each individual construct could be done briefly, but the combination of several brief measures may not itself be brief. The use of brief measures to collapse across constructs within a construct domain is not usually advisable because doing so can produce scores of unclear meaning. Gosling et al. (2003) offered five-item and 10-item versions of the five-factor model of personality. By measuring an entire trait domain, such as neuroticism, with one or two items, one cannot distinguish between one individual whose high score is based only on angry hostility and another whose high score is based only on depression. Thus, the meaning of the high score is unclear.

Examples of Brief Instruments With Good Validity Evidence

Although there are limitations to the utility of brief instruments, there are numerous examples of successful brief assessment. We briefly consider two. Spitzer, Kroenke, Williams, and Lowe (2006) created a brief measure for assessing generalized anxiety disorder, which they called GAD-7. The scale was created by selecting items from the *DSM–IV–TR* symptom set for generalized anxiety disorder and adding items that reflected the history and duration of the anxiety disorder. The authors began with 13 items thought to reflect the content domain of

generalized anxiety. Participants completed a questionnaire, including the original 13 items as well as demographic information, a general health survey, several measures of anxiety and depression, and the Structured Clinical Interview for Diagnosis–GAD. Spitzer et al. rank ordered the items with respect to their correlations with the 13-item composite scale, and found the same seven items had the highest item-total correlations in each of three samples (rs ranged from .75 to .85: higher than many current guidelines). The resulting seven-item scale had good internal consistency (α = .92) and test–retest reliability (r = .83), and the area under the receiver operating characteristic curve (.91) was as large as was obtained with the full 13-item set. Evidence of convergent validity with other anxiety measures was quite strong (rs ranged from .72 to .74), and factor analysis confirmed that the seven-item anxiety measure fell on a different factor from an eight-item depression measure, thus supporting the discriminant validity of the GAD-7. The authors reported good additional evidence for the construct validity of the measure by showing that the GAD-7 related to several external correlates, like functional status, disability days, and physician visits, as predicted by theory. In addition, sensitivity, specificity, predictive values, and likelihood ratios with respect to diagnosis through interview also supported the criterion validity of the measure. This is an example of a strong brief instrument created through dedication to the preservation of the construct and a focus on extensive testing for reliability and validity.

Mullins-Sweatt, Jamerson, Samuel, Olson, and Widiger (2006) developed a brief measure of the five-factor model of personality (the Five Factor Model Rating Form, or FFMRF). This effort is noteworthy, in that the authors' brief assessment included separate measures of each of the 30 traits represented within the five domains of personality. The FFMRF is a one-page measure that includes a single identifying term for each of the 30 traits, together with two to four adjectives to describe both poles of the trait. For example, the order facet of conscientiousness was assessed with the descriptors "ordered, methodical, organized versus haphazard, disorganized, sloppy"; in this way, a single item reflects each trait (Mullins-Sweatt et al., 2006).

In a series of five studies, Mullins-Sweatt et al. showed that (a) for the most part and consistent with past results using longer measures, each trait (measured by a single item) correlated significantly with FFMRF measures of traits from the same personality domain and not with FFMRF measures of traits from other personality domains; (b) FFMRF scores had good convergent validity with full NEO-PI-R scores and with other measures of the 30 traits; (c) FFMRF scores had good discriminant validity, in that FFMRF trait measures' correlations with NEO-PI-R scales from other domains approached zero; and (d) the FFMRF traits correlated with personality disorder descriptions largely as predicted by theory.

An interesting feature of this approach to brief assessment is that the authors used a format that enabled them to provide multiple descriptive adjectives for each single-item trait assessment. Doing so likely mitigates the degree to which idiosyncratic responses to terms compromises the validity of single items. We anticipate that future successful efforts to construct brief instruments will also use new, creative ways to provide sufficient content in a brief assessment format. At the same time, we are not advocating for the use of single-item measures. It may well be that two- or three-item scales for each of the 30 traits might improve the stability of response patterns.

SHORT FORMS

Next, we discuss *short forms* (i.e., abbreviated versions of existing measures). We discuss two different types of short forms. The first type involves abbreviating an instrument to improve its validity by removing items that are not prototypic of the target construct; much of the preceding content of this chapter is relevant to this situation. The second type involves abbreviating a valid instrument strictly for practical reasons. In this latter case, researchers remove content-valid prototypic items for the sake of efficiency. This latter situation is different from what we have discussed so far in this chapter; we therefore review procedures for shortening instruments that maintain reliability and validity as much as possible. In either case, reliable and valid short

forms can be developed provided that researchers take care to follow sound test construction and validation procedures.

Shortened measures have been a controversial topic since the early 20th century when Doll (1917) created a short form of the Binet–Simon Scale. Many original test developers have been highly critical of the development and use of short form measurements (Levy, 1968; Wechsler, 1967). In fact, Wechsler (1967) advised those who felt there was not sufficient time for a full assessment to simply "find the time" (p. 37). Critics argued that the use of short forms is never or rarely justified and that their development often fails to resolve the trade-off between time saved and psychometric strength lost (Levy, 1968; Smith, McCarthy, & Anderson, 2000).

Nonetheless, researchers continue to develop short forms. Some of the reasons for their development include the following: to use for screening purposes, to fit a measure into a large multivariate study, to apply for use with children, or to reduce behavioral–observation time to save costs (Smith et al., 2000). In clinical settings in the 21st century, there is pressure from health care providers to reduce assessment time and costs, and hence to find quicker ways to measure constructs than was necessary in the past.

A short-form developer is attempting to measure a construct or answer a question that the original test developer concluded required a more lengthy assessment (Smith et al., 2000). As a result, it is important for researchers to follow a set of methodological standards that lead to rigorous development and validation of useful short forms. This section provides guidance as to how to do so effectively. The guidelines mentioned here are most relevant for either classic, true-score theory approaches or behavioral-assessment approaches. To begin, one can think of a short form as a new alternative form of a measure; its reduced length and content coverage make it an alternative assessment to the original scale. It is therefore essential, as with any other measure, to independently establish validity and reliability of the new alternative measure. The short form must undergo the same validation process as did the original scale and meet the same standards of validity as required for any other test.

We first briefly discuss the circumstance in which one shortens a measure with the goal of improving its homogeneity and construct representation, typically by removing nonprototypic item content. We then discuss the classic conceptualization of short forms, which involves shortening valid scales and thus sacrificing validity for the benefit of time or cost savings.

Short Forms to Improve Validity

As we have discussed throughout this chapter, SBPF-based pressure to improve estimates of reliability can sometimes lead researchers to include items that measure content that is correlated with, but not prototypic of, the construct one intends to measure. This approach violates the assumption that all items are drawn from the same content domain, and so can result in scales with compromised validity and even unclear meaning. When researchers judge this to be the case, they may choose to improve the content validity of the measure by removing nonprototypic content.

When researchers do make this judgment, we suggest they proceed in the following way. First, they should define carefully the nature of the target construct, with a particular emphasis on what content is not included in that construct. We recommend that the researchers approach the task with an eye toward construct homogeneity and construct representation: Each item should be evaluated in terms of whether it reflects the target construct, and researchers should consider how likely it is that variation in response to each item represents variation in the target construct.

Second, they should make formal empirical judgments concerning the prototypicality of each item or each observation in the measure. If there is more than one researcher, they should make these judgments independently and evaluate their rate of agreement statistically. If their agreement is good, they should resolve differences by discussion and thus arrive at a candidate set of items to be removed from the measure. If their agreement is not good, they should review their definitions, review their training, and train colleagues to make the new judgments. Once there are two sets of items (those to be maintained as prototypic and thus to be excluded),

the researchers should train independent experts on the conceptual task (i.e., by reviewing the concepts of construct homogeneity and construct representation) and on the substantive task (i.e., the actual distinctions between prototypic and correlated content in this case). They should then have those experts provide quantitative content validity ratings for all items. Assuming agreement between the raters is good, and assuming the raters agree with the judgments of the researchers, the presumably few differences can be resolved by the researchers and items can be removed. At this point, the researchers have a draft of a new, shorter, and presumably more valid measure.

We suggest that researchers view this draft as a new measure that requires investigation into its reliability and construct validity. Researchers should not rely on validity evidence for the original measure because they found that measure wanting. Instead, they should follow standard validation procedures as described numerous times in the literature (Cronbach & Meehl, 1955; Landy, 1986; Loevinger, 1957; Messick, 1995; Smith, 2005; Strauss & Smith, 2009; for more information, see Chapter 32 of this volume). We do not review the validation process in this chapter.

Short Forms That Involve the Removal of Valid Content

Before one can develop a short form that involves removing valid content, one must have a good basis for believing that the original form does in fact have valid content (i.e., adequate reliability and validity). It should have an established history of construct validation (Marsh, Ellis, Parada, Richards, & Heubeck, 2005; Smith et al., 2000). One should not attempt to abbreviate an instrument that has not been shown to measure what it purports to measure. If an original measure is not sufficiently validated, there is little reason to believe that a short form of that measure will fare better.

Among the findings researchers must demonstrate upon developing a short form of a valid measure are (a) that the short form preserves the content domain of the target construct; (b) that the short form preserves the factor structure if the construct domain was multidimensional; (c) that the shortened scale is reliable (or each scale or facet of a multidimensional measure is reliable); (d) that evidence is good for the validity of the shortened scale on an independent sample and when the shortened scale is administered without the full original scale; (e) that the shortened scale and the original scale have a high degree of agreement; (f) where appropriate, whether the short form provides acceptable classification rates; and (g) that the time savings justifies the loss of content. For additional considerations, the reader may wish to consult Smith et al. (2000). We consider each of these points in turn.

When choosing items to reduce the size of an instrument, it is important that items are chosen to adequately cover the content domain of the target behavior or construct (Smith et al., 2000). This process begins with a clear statement of the content domain measured by the original measure and then is followed by a content validity analysis of the original scale's items. The content validity analysis might fruitfully address whether each item represents the target construct and whether any pair of items is fully redundant (e.g., asks the same question with very slightly different wording). To remove one of two redundant items does not sacrifice representation of the construct's content domain.

The choices the researcher faces are more difficult after removal of redundant content. For example, researchers may seek to maintain representation of nonredundant items that are judged to represent the content domain. Retaining all nonredundant content may not often be possible; when it is not, researchers should be aware of which aspects of the content domain they have sacrificed. A related concern is that if one part of the content domain is removed, a remaining part of the domain may have greater influence on measure scores than it did in the original measure. Should this occur, there is a risk that the shortened measure has a slightly different meaning from the original measure.

Content validity analysis is fruitfully supplemented by examination of interitem correlations: If two items are both judged to represent the target content domain, responses to them should correlate moderately highly. If they do not, researchers should revisit their content validity analysis. Within

whatever range of interitem and item-total correlations the researcher decides is optimal, and following consideration of content representation, researchers may retain items with the highest item-total correlations. Retaining these items can facilitate removal of the weakest items without unduly sacrificing content coverage (Smith et al., 2000).

It is important to appreciate that if investigators fail at maintaining content coverage, then the new short form represents a different, perhaps more narrow, construct domain. Researchers and consumers of research should not assume, just because a short form has the same name as the original form, that the short form measures the same construct. As we discuss further, it is necessary to demonstrate construct validity on the short form separately from what has been demonstrated on the original form.

If the original measure is multidimensional, such as is the case when there are separate facets of a larger construct, the same content validity analyses should be completed at the unidimensional or facet level. Optimally, each separate content domain in the original measure will be represented by a short form of that domain. If, instead, it is necessary to abbreviate a measure so severely that one cannot represent each dimension of the original measure, it is important that researchers state directly that the shortened measure does not provide the information available from the original measure and is not a substitute for the original measure. Assuming that each dimension is represented briefly in the short form, researchers should demonstrate that the short form has the same factor structure as the original measure. We think it is prudent not to assume that a factor structure is preserved after measure abbreviation and instead to test the factor structure empirically.

Shortening a measure does not lessen the need for reliable assessment. The SBPF predicts that a shorter measure will be less internally consistent, and indeed, researchers are often choosing to sacrifice reliability for brevity. But it is still true that low reliability means high error variance and a reduced probability of detecting relationships among variables that actually exist in the population. One guideline is to seek to maintain internal consistency reliability estimates of at least .70 for short forms (Smith et al., 2000). Anything less than .70 results in significant measurement problems because of random chance or error (Nunnally & Bernstein, 1994). Interestingly, researchers can use the SBPF in reverse to estimate the likely reliability of a shorter measure. Another possibility, for dichotomous items, is to experiment with use of Likert-type items that capture more variability per item (Smith & McCarthy, 1995). The idea behind this last suggestion is that if each item taps more variance in the target construct, fewer items may be necessary to measure the desired level of variability (Smith & McCarthy, 1995). Reliability analyses should be conducted using administration of the short form, separate from the longer original form: It is important to establish the reliability of the short form as it will be used (Smith et al., 2000).

Construct validation procedures should be applied to the short form, again separately from what has been done with the original measure. Neither researchers nor readers should assume that the body of validity evidence that exists for the long form necessarily applies to the short form. Instead, validation tests need to be conducted anew. Often, researchers extract a short form from a longer measure and then use data sets in which they had previously administered the longer measure to examine the validity of the short form. The economy of this approach is important, and it is likely true that validation evidence obtained in this way is informative; nevertheless, it is also important to demonstrate validity of the short form in new samples, when it is administered without the rest of the original measure. Readers need to know the performance of the measure when it is administered as it will be used in the future.

Most important, researchers and readers should not assume that the validity evidence of the original measure transfers automatically to the short form. The construct validation process is an ongoing one, and each new study provides evidence that pertains to the validity of the measures used in the study (Smith, 2005): Validity cannot be assumed. It is incumbent on researchers to demonstrate that a new short form has, for example, convergent and discriminant relationships with other external measures as predicted by theory (Smith et al., 2000).

It is true that an important part of demonstrating the construct validity of a short form is to show that scores on the short form covary highly with scores on the original measure (Silverstein, 1990; Smith et al., 2000). This correlation can be spuriously inflated, however, when investigators calculate the correlation between the two forms on the basis of one test administration; that is, they extract a short form score from the same set of responses as provided by the original measure score (Silverstein, 1990; Smith et al., 2000). When this is done, error variance in the responses to any of the short form items is completely reproduced in the long form and thus contributes to the correlation between the two (Smith et al., 2000). Also, systematic error effects on item responses, from neighboring items, will be present in both forms, thereby influencing the correlation between the two. The neighboring items will be different when the short form is administered separately, and that difference is not represented in such analyses.

The optimal method of controlling for these problems is to administer both the short form and the full-length form separately to the same participants (Smith et al., 2000). By giving both versions to participants, researchers reduce the likelihood of reporting biased estimates of correlations between the short and long forms and instead provide the best estimate of the overlap between the two forms. This often can be done during a single testing session, perhaps with filler questionnaires between the two forms. Alternatively, the two versions can be administered on separate occasions; when this is done, lack of perfect stability of what is measured over time introduces another source of disagreement between the two versions. In such a case, the correlation between the two forms can be compared with the test–retest correlation of the long form (Smith et al., 2000).

If one goal of a short form is to classify individuals accurately, investigators must assess classification using the short form on an independent sample. Of course, just as it is true that one should begin with a valid original measure, when classification is a goal, one should only develop short forms from longer measures that did classify with acceptable accuracy. To address classification accuracy, Smith et al. (2000) described one set of tools available to researchers. One can use the SBPF to estimate the loss of reliability for given possible short forms, apply a related formula to estimate loss of validity, and then use procedures described by Cliff (1987, p. 406) and Cohen and Cohen (1983, p. 39) to estimate classification accuracy given a certain validity level. If a certain necessary classification accuracy is to be achieved, researchers can use this procedure to decide whether more items should be retained or whether a short form is likely to perform adequately (Smith et al., 2000). This is an a priori estimation procedure and is not a substitute for an independent empirical test of a short form's accuracy.

The main purpose of developing a short form is to save valuable time or important resources. As Doppelt (1956) said, "a compromise must be made between economy of time and effort and accuracy of prediction" (p. 63). It is important for short-form authors to directly address this trade-off between assessment time and validity. Levy (1968) noted that "an equation must be found which defines a utility or cost function for the relationship between validity lost and time saved" (p. 415). Perhaps this goal can be approximated by applying the SBPF to estimate the likely loss of reliability, and then, as noted in Smith et al. (2000), the likely loss in validity, for different length short forms. One can then consider the trade-offs between the advantage of certain time or resource savings and the cost of reduced validity. In short, the net value of short-form development can be estimated quantitatively (Smith et al., 2000).

Researchers can take a series of steps that will greatly enhance faith in the validity of short forms that they develop. These steps include careful consideration of content coverage, full dimensional representation, independent demonstration of reliability and validity, high covariation with the original scale, classification accuracy where appropriate, and demonstration of time or resource savings. If these steps are taken, researchers will be in a strong position to argue that their short form is a reliable and valid alternative to a more comprehensive assessment (Smith et al., 2000).

ITEM RESPONSE THEORY AND TAILORED TESTING

So far in this chapter, we have assumed a classic true score theory approach to measurement. IRT is a very different approach that does not use true score theory: It focuses assessment on the item level, in terms of discriminating among individuals at different intensity levels of the target construct. Applications of the technique prove quite useful when the goal is brief assessment. IRT is becoming increasingly well known across fields within psychology, and there are good resources describing it (Hambleton, Swaminathan, & Rogers, 1991; Mellenbergh, 1996; for more information, see Chapter 10 of this volume). In this last section of the chapter, we briefly describe the IRT procedure and point to its advantages.

For each item in a measure, a curve that describes the ability or intensity level at which the item maximally discriminates can be defined. These item characteristic curves (ICCs) are often S-shaped: The item maximally discriminates where the slope is the steepest (with ability or intensity level on the *x*-axis and item endorsement on the *y*-axis). Items differ with respect to the attribute intensity level at which they discriminate. Although IRT has historically been used most often in achievement assessment, its function is not limited to the assessment of such constructs. Imagine a scale measuring romantic jealousy. Positive endorsement of the item "I feel jealous when my significant other kisses a member of the opposite sex romantically" would probably be quite common; presumably, only people with very little jealousy would fail to endorse it. Thus, differential endorsement would probably differentiate among people at very low levels of jealousy. In contrast, the item, "I feel jealous when my significant other talks to a member of the opposite sex" probably differentiates among individuals at much higher levels of jealousy. For every item, curves can be developed that describe the ability or intensity range at which the item will be maximally useful.

ICCs can then be used in a tailored testing approach. One begins with some estimate of intensity of an attribute (perhaps a sample's average intensity level) and administers an item that maximally discriminates at that level. If the examinee endorses or passes the item, then an item that discriminates at a higher intensity level is administered. If the examinee does not endorse or fails the first item, then an item that discriminates at a lower intensity level is administered instead. With the examinee's response to each new item, more information is available to estimate the examinee's intensity level of the attribute. Responses to each new item modify the estimate of attribute intensity, and the procedure continues until changes in the estimates from one item to the next become trivially small. When that occurs, one has a reliable estimate of attribute intensity for that examinee. Reliable estimates can be obtained with many fewer items than are typically used in traditional testing. Detailed discussion of the procedures involved is beyond our scope, but we do want to call attention to the technique as relevant to brief assessment.

CONCLUSION

Our intent in writing this chapter was to provide a perspective counter to the common emphasis on test length as a virtue for reliability and validity. The SBPF has perhaps been applied without sufficient consideration to a key assumption underlying the formula: That all items are parallel, or at least alternative, reflections of the same content domain. To the degree that researchers either include the same item reworded slightly, or items reflecting different though related constructs, longer tests do not necessarily bring increased validity. In fact, there is considerable evidence that carefully defined content domains can be assessed with relatively few items. We have drawn on existing psychometric theory to make this argument. In particular, we encourage researchers to give as much attention to exclusionary rules as to inclusionary rules as they select items, interview questions, or observational protocols. Attention to the concepts of content validity, construct representation, and construct homogeneity may facilitate researchers' efforts to develop brief yet valid measures.

As a ready extension of this set of concerns, we have addressed procedures for the valid development of short forms of existing instruments. We do not argue against the development of short forms; rather, we emphasize the need to develop and independently validate short forms with the same rigor as is applied to any test. We also briefly discuss IRT. It is perhaps most often true that different items within an instrument assess the target construct

at different levels of intensity (perhaps often as indicated by item endorsement rates in classic, true score theory approaches). IRT takes full advantage of this reality by developing curves that characterize the level of attribute intensity at which each item maximally discriminates. The information provided by ICCs leads readily to brief and accurate assessment.

In conclusion, the goal of any psychological assessment is to produce valid and accurate results. Lengthy tests are useful only insofar as they advance that goal, and test length is not as accurate an indicator of measure validity as has been presumed in the past. It is often quite possible to develop brief instruments that produce valid results.

References

American Psychiatric Association. (2000). *Diagnostic and statistical manual of mental disorders* (4th ed., text revision). Washington, DC: Author.

Bischof, G., Reinhardt, S., Grothues, J., Meyer, C., John, U., & Rumpf, H. (2007). Development and evaluation of a screening instrument for alcohol-use disorders and at-risk drinking: The Brief Alcohol Screening Instrument for Medical Care (BASIC). *Journal of Studies on Alcohol and Drugs, 68,* 607–614.

Briggs, S. R., & Cheek, J. M. (1986). The role of factor analysis in the development and evaluation of personality scales. *Journal of Personality, 54,* 106–148. doi:10.1111/j.1467-6494.1986.tb00391.x

Burisch, M. (1997). Test length and validity revisited. *European Journal of Personality, 11,* 303–315. doi:10.1002/(SICI)1099-0984(199711)11:4<303::AID-PER292>3.0.CO;2-#

Clark, L. A., & Watson, D. (1995). Constructing validity: Basic issues in objective scale development. *Psychological Assessment, 7,* 309–319. doi:10.1037/1040-3590.7.3.309

Cliff, N. (1987). *Analyzing multivariate data.* New York, NY: Harcourt Brace Jovanovich.

Cloninger, C. R., Przybeck, T. R., & Svrakic, D. M. (1991). The Tridimensional Personality Questionnaire: U.S. normative data. *Psychological Reports, 69,* 1047–1057. doi:10.2466/PR0.69.7.1047-1057

Cohen, J., & Cohen, P. (1983). *Applied multiple regression/correlation analysis for the behavior sciences* (2nd ed.). Hillsdale, NJ: Erlbaum.

Costa, P. T., Jr., & McCrae, R. R. (1992). *Revised NEO Personality Inventory (NEO-PI-R) and NEO Five-Factor Inventory (NEO-FFI) professional manual.* Odessa, FL: Psychological Assessment Resources.

Cronbach, L. J., Gleser, G. C., Nanda, H., & Rajaratnam, N. (1972). *The dependability of behavioral measurements: Theory of generalizability of scores and profiles.* New York, NY: Wiley.

Cronbach, L. J., & Meehl, P. E. (1955). Construct validity in psychological tests. *Psychological Bulletin, 52,* 281–302. doi:10.1037/h0040957

Doll, E. A. (1917). A brief Binet–Simon scale. *Psychological Clinic, 11,* 197–211.

Doppelt, J. E. (1956). Estimating the full scale score on the Wechsler Adult Intelligence Scale from scores on four subtests. *Journal of Consulting Psychology, 20,* 63–66. doi:10.1037/h0044293

Edwards, J. R. (2000). Multidimensional constructs in organizational behavior research: An integrative analytical framework. *Organizational Research Methods, 4,* 144–192. doi:10.1177/109442810142004

Embretson, S. E. (1998). A cognitive design system approach for generating valid tests: Approaches to abstract reasoning. *Psychological Methods, 3,* 380–396. doi:10.1037/1082-989X.3.3.380

Gosling, S. D., Rentfrow, P. J., & Swann, W. B., Jr. (2003). A very brief measure of the Big Five personality domains. *Journal of Research in Personality, 37,* 504–528. doi:10.1016/S0092-6566(03)00046-1

Hambleton, R. K., Swaminathan, H., & Rogers, H. J. (1991). *Fundamentals of item response theory* (Vol. 2). Newbury Park, CA: Sage.

Haynes, S. N., Richard, D. C. S., & Kubany, E. S. (1995). Content validity in psychological assessment: A functional approach to concepts and methods. *Psychological Assessment, 7,* 238–247. doi:10.1037/1040-3590.7.3.238

Hohlstein, L. A., Smith, G. T., & Atlas, J. G. (1998). An application of expectancy theory to eating disorders: Development and validation of measures of eating and dieting expectancies. *Psychological Assessment, 10,* 49–58. doi:10.1037/1040-3590.10.1.49

Landy, F. J. (1986). Stamp collecting versus science: Validation as hypothesis testing. *American Psychologist, 41,* 1183–1192. doi:10.1037/0003-066X.41.11.1183

Lang, A. J., & Stein, M. B. (2005). An abbreviated PTSD checklist for use as a screening instrument in primary care. *Behaviour Research and Therapy, 43,* 585–594. doi:10.1016/j.brat.2004.04.005

Levy, P. (1968). Short-form tests: A methodological review. *Psychological Bulletin, 69,* 410–416. doi:10.1037/h0025736

Lincoln, A. K., Liebschutz, J. M., Chernoff, M., Nguyen, D., & Amaro, H. (2006). Brief screening for co-occurring disorders among women entering substance abuse treatment. *Substance Abuse Treatment, Prevention, and Policy, 1,* 26. doi:10.1186/1747-597X-1-26

Loevinger, J. (1957). Objective tests as instruments of psychological theory. *Psychological Reports, 3(Supplement),* 635–694. doi:10.2466/PR0.3.7.635-694

Marsh, H. W., Ellis, L. A., Parada, R. H., Richards, G., & Heubeck, B. G. (2005). Short version of the Self Description Questionnaire II: Operational criteria for short-form evaluation with new applications of confirmatory factor analyses. *Psychological Assessment, 17,* 81–102. doi:10.1037/1040-3590.17.1.81

McGrath, R. E. (2005). Conceptual complexity and construct validity. *Journal of Personality Assessment, 85,* 112–124. doi:10.1207/s15327752jpa8502_02

Mellenbergh, G. J. (1996). Measurement precision in test score and item response models. *Psychological Methods, 1,* 293–299. doi:10.1037/1082-989-X.1.3.293

Messick, S. (1995). Validity of psychological assessment: Validation of inferences from persons' responses and performances as scientific inquiry into score meaning. *American Psychologist, 50,* 741–749. doi:10.1037/0003-066X.50.9.741

Morey, L. C. (2003). Measuring personality and psychopathology. In J. A. Schinka, W. F. Velicer, & I. B. Weiner (Eds.), *Handbook of psychology: Vol. 2. Research methods in psychology* (pp. 377–405). Hoboken, NJ: Wiley.

Mullins-Sweatt, S. N., Jamerson, J. E., Samuel, D. B., Olson, D. R., & Widiger, T. A. (2006). Psychometric properties of an abbreviated instrument of the five-factor model. *Assessment, 13,* 119–137. doi:10.1177/1073191106286748

Nunnally, J. C., & Bernstein, I. H. (1994). *Psychometric theory.* New York, NY: McGraw-Hill.

Silverstein, A. B. (1990). Short forms of individual intelligence tests. *Psychological Assessment, 2,* 3–11. doi:10.1037/1040-3590.2.1.3

Simms, L. J., Watson, D., & Doebbling, B. (2002). Confirmatiory factor analyses of posttraumatic stress symptoms in deployed and nondeployed veterans of the Gulf War. *Journal of Abnormal Psychology, 111,* 637–647. doi:10.1037/0021-843X.111.4.637

Smith, G. T. (2005). On construct validity: Issues of method and measurement. *Psychological Assessment, 17,* 396–408. doi:10.1037/1040-3590.17.4.396

Smith, G. T., & Combs, J. (2010). Issues of construct validity in psychological diagnoses. In T. Millon, R. F. Krueger, & E. Simonsen (Eds.), *Contemporary directions in psychopathology: Toward the* DSM–V *and* ICD-11 (pp. 205–222). New York, NY: Guilford Press.

Smith, G. T., Fischer, S., & Fister, S. M. (2003). Incremental validity principles in test construction.

Psychological Assessment, 15, 467–477. doi:10.1037/1040-3590.15.4.467

Smith, G. T., & McCarthy, D. M. (1995). Methodological considerations in the refinement of clinical assessment instruments. *Psychological Assessment, 7,* 300–308. doi:10.1037/1040-3590.7.3.300

Smith, G. T., McCarthy, D. M., & Anderson, K. G. (2000). On the sins of short-form development. *Psychological Assessment, 12,* 102–111. doi:10.1037/1040-3590.12.1.102

Smith, G. T., McCarthy, D. M., & Zapolski, T. C. B. (2009). On the value of homogeneous constructs for construct validation, theory testing, and the description of psychopathology. *Psychological Assessment, 21,* 272–284. doi:10.1037/a0016699

Spearman, C. (1910). Correlation calculated from faulty data. *British Journal of Psychology, 3,* 271–295.

Spitzer, R. L., Kroenke, K., Williams, J. B. W., & Lowe, B. (2006). A brief measure for assessing generalized anxiety disorder: GAD-7. *Archives of Internal Medicine, 166,* 1092–1097. doi:10.1001/archinte.166.10.1092

Strauss, M. E., & Smith, G. T. (2009). Construct validity: Advances in theory and methodology. *Annual Review of Clinical Psychology, 5,* 1–25. doi:10.1146/annurev.clinpsy.032408.153639

Ulrich, R. (1985). Die Beziehung zwischen Testlange und Validitat fur nicht-parallele Aufgaben: Verschiedene Methoden der Validitatsmaximierung [The relationship of test length and validity for non-parallel items: Various methods of validity maximization]. *Zeitschrift für Differentielle und Diagnostische Psychologie, 6,* 32–45.

Wechsler, D. (1967). *Manual for the Wechsler Preschool and Primary Scale of Intelligence.* New York, NY: Psychological Corporation.

Wechsler, D. (2009). *WAIS–IV administration and scoring manual.* San Antonio, TX: Psychological Corporation.

Chronometric and Psychophysical Measures

CHAPTER 21

EYE MOVEMENTS AND COGNITIVE PROCESSES

Keith Rayner and Reinhold Kliegl

Moving our eyes is one of the most frequent behavioral activities that we engage in during our waking hours. Indeed, we typically move our eyes three to four times per second throughout much of our day. We even move our eyes while we sleep (although a discussion of this topic is beyond the scope of this chapter), and on occasion we keep moving our eyes during cognitive processing tasks even if the mind wanders somewhere else. Because of the tight connection between the eyes and the brain, where we look and how long we look are pretty good online measures of the various cognitive activities in which we engage. In this chapter, we review the basic properties of eye movements and how they relate to on-going cognitive processing. In particular, we focus on eye movements during reading, scene perception, and visual search. In all three of these tasks, we continually make eye movements called *saccades*. Between the saccades, our eyes are relatively still in what are called *fixations*. It is during the fixations that we input new information from the visual stimulus that we are processing. During saccades, cognitive processing continues in some tasks (lexical processing), whereas in others (such as mental rotation) lack of reliable evidence suggests suspension of processing (Irwin, 1998).

BACKGROUND INFORMATION ON EYE MOVEMENTS AND COGNITIVE PROCESSES

Before reviewing eye movements in reading, scene perception, and search, we first provide some background information. Our general strategy is to discuss important issues, but we do not provide detailed citations to relevant work. Rather, most of the points we make in the various sections are discussed in articles by Rayner (1998, 2009b) and Kliegl, Nuthmann, and Engbert (2006). Citations throughout the chapter generally are to either these overview articles (where appropriate citations can be found) or to recent articles.

Saccades

Saccades are rapid movements of the eyes with velocities as high as 500° per second. Sensitivity to visual input is markedly reduced during eye movements,[1] and we are functionally blind during saccades. This phenomenon, *saccadic suppression*, historically was the topic of much debate, with some arguing for some type of central anesthesia in which the neurons in the retina turn off during a saccade and others arguing that visual masking causes suppression. It now appears that we do not obtain new information during saccades because our eyes are

Preparation of this chapter was made possible by an Alexander von Humboldt Award, enabling Keith Rayner to be a visiting Humboldt Professor at the University of Potsdam, Potsdam, Germany.

[1]There is also some visual suppression just before and after a saccade.

DOI: 10.1037/13619-022
APA Handbook of Research Methods in Psychology: Vol. 1. Foundations, Planning, Measures, and Psychometrics, H. Cooper (Editor-in-Chief)

moving so quickly across a relatively stable visual stimulus that only blur is perceived. Masking due to the information before and after the saccade results in our failing to perceive any blurring effect. Some suppression is found even when masking is eliminated, however, suggesting that there is also a central inhibitory contribution.

Plots of log peak velocity over log movement amplitude reveal a strikingly linear relationship, reflective of the ballistic nature of saccades. Thus, the velocity of a saccade is a monotonic function of how far the eyes move: a 2° saccade typical in reading takes about 30 ms whereas a 5° saccade, more typical of scene perception, takes about 40 ms to 50 ms and a 10° saccade takes about 60 ms to 80 ms. The velocity rises during the saccade to a maximum that occurs slightly before the midpoint of the movement and then drops at a slower rate until the target location is reached. Saccades are motor movements that take time to plan and execute. *Saccade latency* refers to the amount of time needed to decide to make an eye movement to a new stimulus. Average saccade latency is on the order of 200 ms to 250 ms, and even under situations in which uncertainty is eliminated about where to move, it is at least 150 ms to 175 ms. Thus, the time involved in perceiving the new target location and actually getting the eyes moving is due to the need to send a command to the oculomotor system for the actual movement. There is a point of no return at which if the program to execute a saccade has reached a certain point, the saccade cannot be canceled and is executed. During the time between when the command is given to the oculomotor system to execute the saccade and the actual movement, however, a second saccade can be programmed in parallel with the first.

Fixations and fixational movements. Fixations are the period of time during which the eyes are relatively still and new information is obtained. The eyes are never really still, however, as there are three physiological categories of fixational movements: tremor, drift, and microsaccades. *Tremor* is characterized as 30 Hz to 100 Hz oscillatory behavior superimposed on other fixational movements; it is quite small and its exact nature is somewhat unclear, although it is believed to be related to perceptual activity and helps the nerve cells in the retina to keep firing. During fixation the eyes usually *drift* (i.e., make small, slow movements) with a peak velocity smaller than 30-min arc per second. *Microsaccades* are rapid movements with amplitudes shorter than 1° or 1.5°, usually occurring at a rate of 1 to 2 per second. For many years their functional role was in doubt mostly because they can be voluntarily suppressed (although they are not under voluntary control). Recent research, however, established their relevance both at the perceptual level and the level of spatial attention (for reviews, see Engbert, 2006; Rolfs, 2009). Somewhat paradoxically these fixational movements are a prerequisite of perception of letter, words, or other objects because stabilizing the visual input on the retina bleaches receptors and causes a loss of objects, leaving only the homogeneous background as percept. In most cognitive research, fixational movements are usually treated as *noise*, and various algorithms are used to lump them together into larger fixations.

Binocular coordination of eye movements. The coordination of horizontal and vertical saccades is quite good, and it was long assumed that the two eyes move conjugately. It is now clear, however, that the movements of the *abducting* (temporally moving) eye are somewhat larger than the corresponding movements of the *adducting* (nasally moving) eye in simple scanning tasks. Recent reading research (for reviews, see Kirkby, Webster, Blythe, & Liversedge, 2008; Nuthmann & Kliegl, 2009) has demonstrated that up to 40% to 50% of the time the eyes are on different letters and sometimes more crossed than uncrossed. Interestingly, the amount of disparity tends to be greater in beginning readers than skilled readers.[2]

Eye movements and visual acuity. We make saccades so frequently because of acuity limitations. When we look straight ahead, the visual field can be divided into three areas: foveal, parafoveal, and

---

[2]Word frequency and case alternation affect fixation duration in reading (which we discuss in more detail in the following sections) but are not affected by fixation disparity. Thus, although researchers may need to worry about those rare situations in which the eyes are on different words, when both eyes are fixated within the same word robust effects like the frequency effect still emerge.

periphery. Although acuity is very good in the fovea (the central 2° of vision), it is not nearly as good in the parafovea (which extends 5° around fixation), and it is even poorer in the periphery (the area beyond the parafovea). Thus, we move our eyes to place the fovea on the part of the stimulus we want to see clearly. Properties of the stimulus in eccentric vision influence whether a saccade needs to be made to identify it. Words in normal-size print can be identified more quickly and accurately when a saccade is made. On the other hand, objects can often be identified in eccentric vision without a saccade.

Eye movements and attention.   Although we often need to move our eyes to identify objects in the scene before us, we can move attention without moving our eyes (Posner, 1980). There is considerable evidence suggesting that attention precedes a saccade to a given location in space and that attention and saccades are obligatorily coupled. Although we can easily decouple the locus of attention and eye location in simple tasks, in more complex tasks, the link between the two is probably quite tight.

Measuring eye movements.   Eye movements can be monitored in many ways including (a) surface electrodes (which can be used to determine when the eyes move, but not where they moved to), (b) infrared corneal reflections, (c) video-based pupil monitoring, (d) infrared Purkinje image tracking, and (e) search coils attached to the surface of the eyes. There has been much discussion concerning the measurement, evaluation, and reporting of eye-movement data, but no measurement standards have been adopted and many methodological issues remain unaddressed or unresolved. This may not necessarily be a bad thing, as most important findings have been replicated across different labs.

Eye Movements in Reading
Fixations and saccades.   The average fixation duration in reading is on the order of 200 ms to 225 ms, and the average saccade length is seven to nine letter spaces[3] for skilled readers of English and other alphabetic writing systems. However, these values are averages and there is considerable variability in both.

Thus, fixation durations can be as short as 50 ms to 75 ms and as long as 500 ms to 600 ms (or more). Saccade length can be as short as one letter space and as long as 15 to 20 letter spaces (or more), although such long saccades tend to occur after a regression (as readers typically move forward in the text past the point from which they originally launched the regression). Regressions (saccades that move backward in the text) occur about 10% to 15% of the time in skilled readers. Most regressions are to the immediately preceding word, although when comprehension is not going well, more long regressions occur to earlier in the text. Regressions are not well understood because it is difficult to control them experimentally. They need to be distinguished from return sweeps (right-to-left saccades from the end of one line to the beginning of the next). The first and last fixations on a line are typically five to seven letter spaces from the end of the line because about 80% of the text typically falls between the extreme fixations.

These average values can be influenced by text difficulty, reading skill, and characteristics of the writing system. Specifically, difficult text leads to longer fixations, shorter saccades, and more regressions. Typographical variables like font difficulty influence eye movements; more difficult to encode fonts yield longer fixations, shorter saccades, and more regressions (Slattery & Rayner, 2010). Beginning, less-skilled, and dyslexic readers have longer fixations, shorter saccades, and more regressions than skilled readers. Chinese is the writing system most different from English, but Chinese readers have average fixations that are quite similar to readers of English, and their regression rate does not differ dramatically. Where they do differ is that their average saccade length is much shorter than that of readers of alphabetic writing systems because they typically move their eyes only two to three characters (which makes sense given that linguistic information in Chinese is more densely packed than in English).

Different measures of fixation time.   Eye-movement data provide a good moment-to-moment indication of cognitive processes during reading. Thus, variables such as word frequency and word

---

[3]Letter spaces are the appropriate indicator of how far the eyes move; regardless of the reading distance of the text (which modulates text size on the retina), eye movements extend the same number of letter spaces, not the same degree of visual angle.

predictability have strong influences on fixation times on a word. However, average fixation duration is not a particularly informative measure; it is a valuable global measure, but a number of local measures also provide more informative estimates of moment-to-moment processing time. The problem with average fixation duration is related to two components of reading. First, readers skip words during reading;[4] content words are fixated about 85% of the time, whereas function words are fixated about 35% of the time. Function words are skipped more because they tend to be short. As word length increases, the probability of fixating the word increases. Words that are two to three letters are only fixated around 25% of the time, whereas words that are eight letters or more are almost always fixated. Second, longer words are often fixated more than once; that is, they are *refixated*. The joint problem of skipping and refixations led to the development of alternative measures of fixation time. These measures are first-fixation duration (the duration of the first fixation on a word), single-fixation duration (when only one fixation is made on a word), and gaze duration (the sum of all fixations on a word before moving to another word). Recently, first fixation durations in multiple-fixation cases have been distinguished from the traditional definition to reduce the overlap with single-fixation durations for purposes of computational modeling. All of the measures are contingent on the word being fixated on a first-pass forward fixation.

If it were the case that readers fixated once and only once on each word, then average fixation duration on a word would be a useful measure. But given that many words are skipped and some words are refixated, the solution is to utilize the three measures just described, which provide a reasonable estimate of how long it takes to process each word. These measures are not perfect estimates as (a) preview information is obtained from a word before fixating it and (b) the processing of a given word can spill over to the next fixation. When regions of interest are larger than a single word, other measures like first-pass reading time, second-pass reading time, go-past time (the elapsed time from when a reader first enters a region until they move past it forward in the text), and total reading time are computed.

The perceptual span in reading. How much information are we able to process and use during a fixation? Most readers have the impression that they can clearly see the entire line of text, even the entire page of text. But, this is an illusion as research utilizing a gaze-contingent moving-window technique (McConkie & Rayner, 1975) has shown. The rationale with the moving-window technique is to vary how much information is available and then determine how large the window of normal text has to be before readers read normally. Conversely, how small can the window be before there is disruption to reading? Thus, within the window area, text is normally displayed, but outside of the window, letters are replaced (with other letters, Xs, or a homogenous masking pattern).[5] Research using this paradigm has demonstrated that skilled readers of English and other alphabetic writing systems obtain useful information from an asymmetric region extending three to four character spaces to the left of fixation to about 14 to 15 character spaces to the right of fixation. Indeed, if readers have the fixated word and the word to the right of fixation available on a fixation (and all other letters are replaced with visually similar letters), they are not aware that the words outside of the window are not normal, and their reading speed decreases by only about 10%. Information from below the currently fixated line is not used, although if the task is visual search rather than reading, then information can be obtained below the currently fixated line. Finally, in moving-mask experiments (Rayner & Bertera, 1979), a mask moves in synchrony with the eyes covering the letters in the center of vision, making reading virtually impossible. This paradigm creates an artificial foveal

---

[4]The fact that words are skipped obviously means that readers do not invariably move forward in the text fixating on each successive word in its canonical order. However, some type of inner speech code presumably aids the reader to maintain the correct word order.

[5]In the most extreme situation, the window would contain only the fixated letter, thereby creating a situation in which the reader is literally forced to read letter by letter. In such a situation, normal readers' eye-movement data are very much like the eye-movement data of brain-damaged pure alexic or letter-by-letter readers.

scotoma that mimics patients with brain damage and effectively eliminates their use of foveal vision.

Characteristics of the writing system influence the perceptual span. Thus, for readers of Chinese (which is typically read from left to right in mainland China), the perceptual span extends one character to the left of fixation to two to three to the right. For Hebrew readers, the span is asymmetric and larger to the left of fixation because they read from right to left. Also, reading skill influences the perceptual span because beginning readers and dyslexic readers have smaller spans than more skilled readers. Presumably, difficulty encoding the fixated word leads to smaller spans (Rayner, Slattery, & Bélanger, 2010). Older readers read more slowly than younger college-age readers, and their perceptual span is slightly smaller and less asymmetric than younger readers (Rayner, Castelhano, & Yang, 2009).

Preview benefit in reading. Research using another type of gaze-contingent display change technique, the boundary technique (Rayner, 1975), has revealed what kind of information is obtained to the right of fixation. An invisible boundary is located just to the left of a target word, and before the reader's eyes cross the boundary, there is typically a preview different from the target word. When the eyes cross the boundary, the preview is replaced by the target word. Readers are generally unaware of the identity of the preview and of the display change. Research using this technique has revealed that when readers have a valid preview of the word to the right of fixation, they spend less time fixating that word (following a saccade to it) than when they do not have a valid preview (i.e., another word or nonword or random string of letters initially occupied the target word location). The size of this *preview benefit* is typically on the order of 30 ms to 50 ms. Research has revealed that readers do not combine a literal visual representation of information across saccades, rather abstract codes are used.

Information about abstract letter codes, letter position, and orthographic phonological codes is integrated across saccades (and serves as the basis of the preview benefit effect). Thus far, however, no reliable evidence has been reported for semantic preview benefit for reading English. That is, words that typically produce priming in a standard naming or lexical decision task (e.g., the prime word *tune* primes the target word *song*) do not yield priming when the prime word is in parafoveal vision (with the target word presented as soon as the reader crosses the invisible boundary location). This result is probably because words in parafoveal vision are degraded sufficiently that readers cannot typically process their meaning. There is also no evidence that morphological information is integrated across saccades in English.

Conversely, readers of Hebrew do integrate morphological information across saccades. Morphological information is more central to processing Hebrew than English, and the difference in findings presumably reflects this fact. Also, semantic preview benefit has been found for readers of Chinese (Yang, Richter, Shu, & Kliegl, 2009; Yang, Wang, Tong, & Rayner, in press). Moreover, with a variant of the boundary paradigm (with experimentally controlled parafoveal preview durations) semantic preview benefit has also been reported for German (Hohenstein, Laubrock, & Kliegl, 2010). This study suggested that semantic preview effects may depend on preview time—that is, both too long and too short previews may interfere rather than facilitate subsequent processing of the word. It is also the case that the amount of preview benefit readers obtain varies as a function of the difficulty of the fixated word. If it is difficult to process, readers get little or no preview benefit from the word to the right of fixation. Conversely, if the fixated word is easy to process, readers get better preview benefit from the word to the right of fixation. Also, preview benefit is larger within words than across words. A final issue concerns the spatial extent of preview benefit: Do readers obtain preview benefit from word $n + 2$? Although it is clear that readers generally obtain preview benefit from word $n + 1$ (the word to the right of fixation), it appears that readers typically do not get preview benefit from word $n + 2$. It may be that when word $n + 1$ is a very short word (two to three letters) that readers obtain preview benefit from word $n + 2$. And, it is also the case that when readers target their next saccade to word $n + 2$ that preview benefit is obtained. Moreover, there is evidence for *n* + 2 preview benefit in Chinese when word *n* + 1 is a high-frequency word (Yan, Kliegl, Shu, Pan, & Zhou, 2010; Yang, Wang, Xu, & Rayner, 2009).

Parafoveal-on-foveal effects. Do the characteristics of the word to the right of fixation influence the duration of the fixation on the currently fixated word? Such effects are referred to as parafoveal-on-foveal effects. Some studies have found that orthographic properties of the word to the right of fixation influence the duration of the current fixation. Other recent studies have suggested that the meaning of the word to the right of fixation can produce parafoveal-on-foveal effects. Yet, other studies have shown inconsistent or no parafoveal-on-foveal effects because of word frequency and no evidence of lexical parafoveal-on-foveal effects in analyses on the basis of select target words. Are parafoveal-on-foveal effects real, or are there other reasons why such effects sometimes appear in the eye-movement record? It has been demonstrated that some fixations in reading are mislocated because saccades are not perfectly accurate and do not land on the intended target; thus, some parafoveal-on-foveal effects may arise because of inaccurately targeted saccades. That is, some saccades that are meant to land on a given target word fall short of the target and land on the end of the previous word. In this scenario, however, attention is still allocated to the originally intended saccade target word such that processing of the target word influences the fixation on the previous word. We also note that reliable evidence for parafoveal-on-foveal effects from analyses of large eye-movement corpora (Kliegl, 2007) has been reported. Taken together, at this time, there seems to be some converging agreement concerning the validity of orthographic parafoveal-on-foveal effects. However, there still is controversy concerning lexical parafoveal-on-foveal effects.

The control of eye movements. There are two components to eye-movement control: *when to move the eyes* and *where to move the eyes*. These two decisions may be made somewhat independently: The decision of where to move next is largely driven by low-level properties of the text. The decision of when to move is driven by lexical properties of the fixated word (although models of eye movements in reading differ in the weight they give to lexical factors).

Where to move the eyes. For English and other alphabetic languages, where to move the eyes next is strongly influenced by low-level cues provided by word length and space information. Thus, saccade length is influenced by the length of the fixated word and the word to the right of fixation. If the word to the right of fixation is either very long or very short, the next saccade will be longer than when a medium-length word is to the right of fixation. For example, if the 10 letter spaces to the right of the fixated word consist of a four- and a five-letter word (with a space between) or a single 10-letter word, the saccade will be longer in the latter case. If there is a short word (two to four letters) to the right of fixation, the next saccade will tend to be longer than when the next word is five to seven letters, largely because the short word would be skipped. The spaces between words (which demarcate how long words are) are thus used in targeting where the next saccade lands. When space information is removed, reading slows down considerably. Specifically, when spaces are removed or filled with irrelevant characters, reading slows down by as much as 30% to 50%. Of course, spaces between words are not present in all writing systems. Interestingly, some recent evidence with nonalphabetic writing systems suggests that even when interword spaces are orthographically illegal, they can be beneficial to reading (Bai, Yan, Liversedge, Zang, & Rayner, 2008; Winskel, Radach, & Luksaneeyanawin, 2009).

Landing position effects. The space information in parafoveal vision leads to systematic tendencies with respect to where the eyes typically land. Readers' eyes tend to land halfway between the middle of a word and the beginning of that word; this is called the *preferred viewing location* (Rayner, 1979). It is generally argued that readers attempt to target the center of words, but their saccades tend to fall short. When readers' eyes land at a nonoptimal position in a word, they are more likely to refixate that word. Where readers fixate in a word can be viewed not only as a landing site for that word but also as the launch site for the next saccade. Although the average landing position in a word lies between the beginning and the middle of a word, this position varies as a function of the prior launch site. Thus, if the launch site for a saccade landing on a target word is far from that word (say 8–10 letter spaces), the landing position will be shifted to the left. Likewise, if the distance is small (2–3 letter spaces), the landing position is shifted to the right. Thus, the landing site distribution on a word depends on its launch site. Recently, Engbert and Krügel (2010) showed that the systematic variation of fixation positions within words, the saccadic range error, can be derived from Bayesian decision theory, suggesting that readers use Bayesian estimation for saccade planning.

Skipping effects. As noted, some words are skipped during reading. Two factors have a big impact on skipping: word length and contextual constraint. First, the most important variable in skipping is word length: Short words are much more likely to be skipped than long words. When two to three short words occur in succession, there is a good chance that two of them will be skipped. And, short words (like *the*) preceding a content word are often skipped. In situations such as this, groups of words (e.g., three short words in succession and when an article precedes a content word) tend to be processed on a single fixation. Second, words that are highly constrained by the context are much more likely to be skipped than those that are not predictable. Word frequency has an effect on word skipping, but the effect is smaller than that of predictability. Although predictability influences how long readers look at a word and whether it is skipped, it does not influence where in the word the fixation lands.

It is a mistake to think that if a word is skipped it is not processed. Fisher and Shebilske (1985) demonstrated this by examining the eye movements of readers on a passage of text. They then deleted all words from the passage that these readers had skipped and asked a second group of readers to read it. This group of readers had a hard time understanding the text. So, skipped words do get processed. But when are they processed? Although a bit controversial, some evidence suggests that when a word is skipped, it is processed on the fixation before or after the skip. It is complicated, however, because Kliegl and Engbert (2005) found that fixation durations were inflated before skipping long and infrequent words, but these durations were reliably shorter before skipping short and frequent words.

When to move the eyes. It is clear that the ease or difficulty associated with processing the fixated word strongly influences when the eyes move. Thus, fixation time on a word is influenced by a host of lexical and linguistic variables including word frequency, word predictability, number of meanings, age of acquisition, phonological properties of words, semantic relations between the fixated word and prior words, and word familiarity. It is clear that variables assumed to have something to do with the ease or difficulty of processing a word can influence how long readers look at the word. Some variables have strong influences immediately when a word is fixated, whereas other variables seem to yield later occurring effects.

Perhaps the most compelling evidence that cognitive processing of the fixated word is driving the eyes through the text comes from experiments in which the fixated word either disappears or is masked after 50 ms to 60 ms (Rayner, Liversedge, White, & Vergilino-Perez, 2003). Basically, these studies show that if readers are allowed to see the fixated word for 50 ms to 60 ms before it disappears, they read quite normally. This does not mean that words are completely processed in 50 ms to 60 ms but rather that this amount of time is sufficient for the processing system to encode the word. Interestingly, if the word to the right of fixation also disappears or is masked, then reading is disrupted; this quite strongly demonstrates that the word to the right of fixation is very important in reading. More critically, when the fixated word disappears after 50 ms to 60 ms, how long the eyes remain in place is determined by the frequency of the word that disappeared: If it is a low-frequency word, the eyes remain in place longer. Thus, even though the word is no longer there, how long the eyes remain in place is determined by that words' frequency; this is compelling evidence for cognitive processing having a very strong influence on eye movements.

Lexical variables thus have strong and immediate effects on how long readers look at a word. Although other linguistic variables can have an influence on how soon readers move on in the text, it is generally the case that higher level linguistic variables have somewhat later effects, unless the variable "smacks you in the eye." So, for example, when readers fixate on a disambiguating word in a syntactic garden path sentence there is increased fixation time on the word or a regression from the disambiguating word to earlier parts of the sentence. When readers encounter an anomalous word, they fixate on it longer, and the effect is quite immediate; when a word indicates an implausible but not truly anomalous event, an effect will be registered in the eye-movement record, but it is typically delayed a bit, showing up in later processing measures. Readers also have longer fixations at the end of clauses and sentences.

Using eye movements to study sentence and discourse processing. In much of the foregoing discussion, the premise has largely been that lexical processing is the engine driving the eyes through the text. As we have also noted, however, there is good reason to believe that higher order comprehension processes influence eye movements primarily when something does not compute. In cases such as this, higher order comprehension processes can override the normal default situation in which lexical processing is driving the eyes, and result in longer fixations or regressions back to earlier parts of the text. It is quite interesting that eye-movement data have more or less become the gold standard in experiments dealing with sentence processing and syntactic ambiguity resolution. Because of its precise temporal properties, eye tracking is generally deemed to be the preferred way to study online sentence processing. In contrast, it is quite striking that there have not been nearly as many studies utilizing eye-movement data to examine online comprehension and discourse-processing effects. Although there are a few studies (for a review, see Rayner, Chace, Slattery, & Ashby, 2006) in which eye movements were monitored to assess immediate comprehension in discourse processing, the number of such studies pales in comparison with the number of studies that used more gross reading time measures. The time may be ripe for more comprehension studies to use eye-movement data to understand moment-to-moment discourse processing.

Models of eye movement control in reading. Given the vast amount of information about eye movements during reading that has accumulated in the past 25 to 30 years, it is not surprising that a number of models of eye movements in reading have recently appeared. The E–Z Reader model (Reichle, Pollatsek, Fisher, & Rayner, 1998) and SWIFT (Engbert, Nuthmann, Richter, & Kliegl, 2005) are typically regarded as the most influential of these models. Because of space limitations, other models are not discussed here (see Rayner, 2009a). The models are all fully implemented, but they differ on a number of dimensions. In some of the models, the eyes are driven by lexical processing, whereas in others eye movements are largely viewed as being primarily influenced by oculomotor constraints. Some models allow for parallel processing of words, whereas in others lexical processing is serial so that the meaning of word $n + 1$ is not accessed until the lexical processing is complete (or nearly complete) for word n. E–Z Reader and SWIFT both do a good job of predicting how long readers look at words, which words they skip, and which words will most likely be refixated. They account for global aspects of eye movements in reading as well as more local processing characteristics. With careful experimentation and with the implementation of computational models that simulate eye movements during reading, great advances have been made in understanding eye movements in reading (and inferring the mental processes associated with reading).

Eye Movements During Scene Perception

The average fixation duration in scene perception tends to be longer than reading (closer to 300 ms, although it varies as a function of the task and the characteristics of the scene). Average saccade size tends to be 4° to 5° (and varies as a function of task and the exact nature of the scene). Whereas there is a well-defined task for readers, exactly what subjects should do in a scene perception task is more variable. Sometimes they are asked to look at the scene in anticipation of a memory test; other times they are asked to indicate whether a certain object is present in the scene. Under the latter instructions, scene perception becomes very much a visual search task. An examination of the scan path of a viewer on a scene demonstrates that viewers do not fixate every part of the scene. Most fixations tend to fall on the informative parts of the scene. Thus, for example, we do not fixate on the sky or unimportant parts of the scene. Finally, the gist of a scene is understood so quickly that it is generally obtained even before the eyes begin to move. The gist is thought to be acquired during the first fixation to orient subsequent fixations to interesting regions in the scene.

The perceptual span in scene perception. How much information can be obtained during fixation on a scene? Information is acquired over a wider range of the visual field in scene perception than reading. The best way to address this issue is via gaze-contingent paradigms, but very few such studies have been reported. In studies that have used the moving-window paradigm, scene information was presented normally within the window area around a fixation point, but the information outside of the window was degraded in a systematic way.[6] Studies using the moving-window paradigm found that the functional field of view can consist of about half of the total scene regardless of the absolute size of the scene (at least for scenes up to 14.4° by 18.8°). There was also a serious deterioration in recognition of a scene when the window was limited to a small area (about 3.3° by 3.3°) on each fixation. Studies that used the moving-mask procedure found that the presence of a foveal mask influenced looking time, but it was not nearly as disruptive as in reading.

Other studies have examined how close to fixation an object had to be for it to be recognized as having been in the scene. Objects located within about 2.6° from fixation are generally recognized, but recognition depends to some extent on the characteristics of the object. Generally, the research suggests that the functional field of view only extends about 4° away from fixation and that qualitatively different information is acquired from the region within 1.5° around fixation than from regions further away. The answer to the question of how large the perceptual span in scene perception is has not

been answered as conclusively as it has in reading. It appears that viewers typically gain useful information from a fairly wide region of the scene, which probably varies as a function of the scene and the task. Thus, the ease with which an object is identified may be related to its orientation, frequency within a scene context, and how well camouflaged it is. It is also likely that the ease of identifying a fixated object has an effect on the extent of processing in eccentric vision.

Preview benefit in scenes. Viewers obtain preview benefit from objects that they have not yet fixated (with the benefit on the order of 100 ms). Interestingly, viewers are rather insensitive to changes in scenes. In a series of experiments, while observers viewed a scene, changes were made during a saccade (when vision is suppressed). Remarkably, even though they were told that there would be changes, subjects were unaware of most changes, which included the appearance and disappearance of large objects and the changing of colors (McConkie & Currie, 1996). Apparently low-level sensory information is not preserved from one fixation to the next. The lack of awareness of changes during saccades does not mean that there is no recollection of any visual details, but rather that the likelihood of remembering visual information is highly dependent on the processing of that information.

Early theories of transsaccadic memory proposed that information is integrated across saccades in an integrative visual buffer (with properties like iconic memory). The experiments described thus far in the context of reading as well as nonreading experiments using relatively simply arrays demonstrated that this view is incorrect and that viewers do not integrate sensory information presented on separate fixations in a visual buffer. More recent work with more naturalistic scenes has arrived at the same conclusion, and evidence suggests that visual short-term memory, which is thought to be at a higher level than a visual buffer, serves a primary role in integrating information across saccades. Thus, memory across saccades during scene perception appears

---

[6]A promising variation on gaze-contingent moving windows and moving-masks paradigms, discussed in the context of visual search, that has not yet been fully exploited is to use multiresolution displays (Reingold & Loschky, 2002; Reingold, Loschky, McConkie, & Stampe, 2003). With these types of displays, for example, a clear view of the scene can be provided around the fixation point with increasing degradation of the scene outside of the window.

to be due to higher level visual codes, which are abstracted from precise sensory representations, with visual short-term memory as the basis for integration.

Where do viewers look in scenes? It has long been known that viewers' eyes are drawn to important aspects of the visual scene and that their goals in looking at the scene very much influence their eye movements. Quite a bit of early research demonstrated that the eyes are quickly drawn to informative areas in a scene. It is also clear that the saliency of different parts of the scene influence what part of the scene is fixated. A large amount of empirical and computational research has recently been devoted to understanding the factors that govern fixation position in scenes, and much of this work revolves around how saliency (which is typically defined in terms of low-level components of the scene, such as contrast, color, intensity, brightness, spatial frequency, etc.) influences where viewers look. Although saliency is clearly a factor, it is not the only factor involved in determining where to look. Indeed, it is also becoming increasingly clear that there are strong cognitive influences on where viewers look.

Are the eyes drawn to informative, unusual, or emotional parts of a scene? The evidence is somewhat uneven as some research indicates that the eyes are drawn to unusual parts of a scene, whereas other research suggests they are not. Early experiments found that the eyes move quickly to an object that is out of place in a scene. Unfortunately, these studies did not control physical distinctiveness well and, when it was controlled, the semantically inconsistent objects were not fixated earlier than consistent objects. However, recent experiments (Rayner, Castelhano, & Yang, 2009) with appropriate controls have found that the eyes are drawn to unusual parts of a scene earlier than when the weird aspect was missing (although the eyes moving to the unusual part of the scene is not instantaneous).

When do viewers move their eyes? Given that attention precedes an eye movement to a new location within a scene, it follows that the eyes will move once information at the center of vision has been processed and a new fixation location has been chosen. Research suggests that the extraction of

information at the fovea occurs fairly rapidly, and attention is then directed to the periphery to choose a viable saccade target almost immediately following the extraction of foveal information. Henderson and Pierce (2008) presented a visual mask at the beginning of eye fixations as viewers examined a scene. The duration of the mask was varied (with scene onset delays as short as 40 ms and as long as 1,200 ms), and the scene did not appear until the designated mask duration was exceeded. Then the scene appeared and remained visible until the viewer made a saccade. Scene onset delays took place on every 10th fixation. There was one population of fixations under direct control of the current scene, increasing in duration as the delay increased. However, a second population of fixations was relatively constant across delay. Rayner, Smith, Malcolm, and Henderson (2009) masked the scene at certain points after the onset of each new fixation. Interestingly, it was found that viewers needed 150 ms to view the scene before the mask was not disruptive. This is much longer than the 50 ms to 60 ms needed in reading for the mask to not cause disruption and longer than one might predict given that the gist of a scene can be gleaned on the first fixation.

Models of eye movement control in scene perception. A number of models of eye-movement control in scene perception have recently appeared. These models (Baddeley & Tatler, 2006; Itti & Koch, 2000, 2001; Parkhurst, Law, & Niebur, 2002) use the concept of a saliency map (following from Findlay & Walker, 1999) to model eye fixation locations in scenes. In this approach, bottom-up properties in a scene make explicit the locations of the most visually prominent regions of the scene. The models are basically used to derive predictions about the distribution of fixations on a given scene. Although these models can account for some of the variability in where viewers fixate in a scene, they are limited in that the assumption is that fixation locations are driven primarily by bottom-up factors; it is clear that higher level factors also come into play in determining where to look next in a scene (see Torralba, Oliva, Castelhano, & Henderson, 2006). More recently, the CRISP model (Nuthmann, Smith, Engbert, & Henderson, 2010) has been presented to deal with *when* the eyes move in scene perception.

Eye Movements and Visual Search

The majority of research on search has been done without measuring eye movements because it has often been assumed that they are not particularly important in understanding search. However, this attitude seems to be largely changing as many recent experiments have utilized eye movements to understand the process. Many of these studies deal with very low-level aspects of search and often focus on using the search task to uncover properties of the saccadic eye-movement system. It is becoming clear that eye-movement studies of visual search, like reading and scene perception, can provide important information on moment-to-moment processing in search. Here the focus will primarily be on research using eye movements to examine how viewers search through arrays to find specific targets. Fixation durations in search tend to be highly variable. Some studies report average fixation times as short as 180 ms, whereas others report averages on the order of 275–300 ms. This wide variability is probably due to the fact that the difficulty of the search array (or how dense or cluttered it is) and the nature of the search task strongly influence how long viewers pause on average.

The search array matters. Perhaps the most obvious thing about visual search is that the search array makes a big difference in how easy it is to find a target. When the array is cluttered or dense (with many objects or distractors), search is more costly than when the array is simple (or less dense), and eye movements typically reflect this fact. The number of fixations and fixation duration both increase as the array becomes more complicated, and the average saccade size decreases. Also, the configuration of the search array has an effect on the pattern of eye movements. In an array of objects arranged in an arc, fixations tend to fall between objects, progressively getting closer to the area where viewers think the target is located. On the other hand, in randomly arranged arrays, other factors such as color of the items and shape similarity to the target object influence the placement of fixations.

The perceptual span in search. Studies using the moving-window technique as viewers searched through horizontally arranged letter strings for a specified target letter found that the size of the perceptual span varied as a function of the difficulty of the distractor letters. When the distractor letters where visually similar to the target letter, the size of the perceptual span was smaller than when the distractor letters were distinctly different from the target letter. The research suggests that there are two qualitatively different regions within the span: a decision region (where information about the presence or absence of a target is available) and a preview region (where some letter information is available but where information on the absence of a target is not available). Studies using moving windows and moving masks as viewers searched through a randomly arranged array of letters and digits for the presence of a target letter have also been conducted. Not surprisingly, the moving mask had a deleterious effect on search time and accuracy, and the larger the mask, the longer the search time, the more fixations were made, and the longer the fixations. Saccade size was affected by array size, but mask size had little effect. In the moving-window condition, search performance reached asymptote when the window was 5° (all letters and digits falling within 2.5° from the fixation point were visible with such a window size, but all other letters were masked).

Finally, other recent studies investigated the perceptual span via gaze-contingent multiresolution moving windows. Within this paradigm, information outside the window is degraded in a manner that simulates resolution degradation (i.e., blurring) at various eccentricities from an observer's area of fixation. Eccentricity in degrees at which display resolution drops to one half of its value at the fixation point is termed ε_2. In a multiresolution display, the value of ε_2 controls the extent of blurring into the parafovea, such that the smaller the value of ε_2, the steeper the drop-off in resolution. Findings from these studies suggest that during any single fixation, when ε_2 is about 6°, the parafoveal blur imposed on a scene is not detectable. Thus, viewers do not notice that the scene has been artificially blurred. Consistent with other studies discussed here dealing with the use of information beyond the point of fixation, even when artificial blurring went undetected in eccentric vision, search performance was affected.

Preview benefit. It is undoubtedly the case that viewers obtain preview benefit during search. Typically, studies of preview benefit in search provide a viewer with a preview of the search array (or part of the array) for a set period of time (such as 500 ms), or no preview in a control condition. Then the array is presented in its entirety. Generally, it is found that there are fewer fixations on previewed stimuli (and if they are fixated, for shorter durations) than in the control condition in which no preview of the array is provided. Although studies of this type are interesting and suggestive of preview benefit, it is striking that little research directly uses the types of gaze-contingent boundary paradigms that have been used in reading to study preview benefit in visual search. Perhaps the time is ripe to develop boundary paradigms (as used in reading research) to study preview benefit in visual search.

Where and when to move the eyes. Although there have been considerable efforts to determine the factors involved in deciding where and when to move the eyes in visual search, a clear answer to the issue has not emerged. Some have concluded that fixation durations in search are the result of a combination of preprogrammed saccades and fixations that are influenced by the fixated information. Others have suggested that the completion of foveal analysis is not necessarily the trigger for an eye movement, whereas others have suggested that it is. Still others have demonstrated that fixation position is an important predictor of the next saccade and influences both the fixation duration and selection of the next saccade target. Rayner (1995) suggested that the trigger to move the eyes in a search task is something like this: Is the target present in the decision area of the perceptual span? If it is not, a new saccade is programmed to move the eyes to a location that has not been examined. As with reading and scene perception, attention would move to the region targeted for the next saccade.

The decision about where to fixate next and when to move the eyes is strongly influenced by the characteristics of the specific search task and the density of the visual array as well as viewer strategies. It seems that parallels between visual search and scene perception are greater than with reading,

in that visual saliency plays a greater role in directing fixations. Additionally, search for targets within visual search displays and scenes have different dimensions that are more variable than reading. For instance, with respect to search tasks, viewers may be asked to search for many different types of targets. Searching for a certain product in a grocery store shelf or searching for a person in a picture or for a word in a dictionary may yield very different strategies than skimming text for a word (and hence influence eye movements in different ways). Although the task is generally much better defined in visual search than in scene perception, it typically is not as well specified as in reading.

Models of eye movement control in search. The most well-known model of eye-movement control related to visual search is that of Findlay and Walker (1999). This model focuses on saccade generation on the basis of parallel processing and competitive inhibition, and like many of the models of scene perception, relies heavily on the notion of a saliency map. Although the model is unquestionably interesting and very much tied to neurophysiological properties of the oculomotor system, it is not a fully implemented model. One fully implemented model is the Target Acquisition Model (TAM) of Zelinsky (2008). This model accounts for eye movements in search contexts ranging from fully realistic scenes to objects arranged in circular arrays to search for Os embedded in Qs (and vice versa). It can also account for manipulations, such as set size, target eccentricity, and target-distractor similarity. It handles a number of important findings on eye movements and visual search. Comparisons of scan paths of the model to human viewers reveal that the model nicely mimics viewers' behavior, and it is difficult when presented with scan paths of the model and viewers to determine which is which. As impressive as TAM is with respect to simulating search behavior in terms of where the eyes go (and scan paths in finding targets), it does not provide an account of the determinants of when to move the eyes and, hence, it does not predict fixation durations in search. It also does not predict target absent trials (which is a difficult task for any search model). Hopefully, future instantiations of the model will lead to a better understanding of the mechanisms involved in accounting for how long the eyes pause in search.

Eye Movements and Visual Cognition

Although there are obviously many differences between reading, scene perception, and visual search, some important generalizations can be made. Here, we mention four. First, the perceptual span or functional field of view varies as a function of the task. The span is smaller in reading than in scene perception and visual search. As a result, fixations in scene perception tend to be longer and saccades are longer because more information is being processed on a fixation. Second, stimulus difficulty influences eye movements: (a) In reading, when the text becomes more difficult, eye fixations get longer and saccades get shorter; and (b) in scene perception and visual search, when the array is more difficult (crowded, cluttered, dense), fixations get longer and saccades get shorter. Third, the specific task (reading for comprehension vs. reading for gist, searching for a person in a scene vs. looking at the scene for a memory test) influences eye movements across the three tasks. Fourth, in all three tasks, it seems that viewers integrate visual information somewhat poorly across saccades and what is most critical is that there is efficient processing of information on each fixation.

We have focused on research on reading, scene perception, and visual search, and space limitations preclude discussion of eye movements during music perception, face perception, driving, problem solving and concept learning, sports, mental rotation, chess, and advertising. We have not covered the burgeoning research interests in real-world or natural tasks (like making a cup of coffee or a sandwich) or the visual world paradigm in which subjects hear some type of auditory input with a visual array in front of them. Eye movements show a systematic relationship between what is being listened to and where the eyes tend to go (and how quickly they go) in the visual array. The visual world paradigm as such combines aspects of scene perception, visual search, and language processing. These are active areas of research that utilize eye-movement data to elucidate underlying cognitive processes in the various tasks.

CONCLUSION

A great deal of knowledge has been gleaned from studies using eye movements to examine reading, scene perception, visual search, and other cognitive processing tasks. Research on eye movements during reading has advanced more rapidly and systematically than research on scene perception and visual search. This is probably due to the fact that stimulus characteristics (in reading, a limited set of letters make up words, whereas in scene perception the scene is not as constrained by stimulus properties) and the task (the task in reading and visual search is quite straightforward, but exactly what viewers do in scene perception is not as obvious) are more amenable to experimental manipulations in reading than scenes (especially) and search. Research on reading has significantly benefited from the use of the gaze-contingent paradigm. Although researchers in scene perception and visual search have been utilizing such paradigms recently, there are many issues in both domains where the paradigms could be effectively used. Another area where research on reading has been advanced over scene perception and visual search relates to the development of computational models to account for eye-movement data. Models of eye-movement control in reading tend to do a good job of accounting both for where readers look and how long they look at words. Models of eye-movement control in the domain of scene perception and visual search have largely focused on where viewers look to the exclusion of when they move their eyes, but the more recent CRISP model is a move in the right direction.[7]

Major advances have been made with respect to understanding eye movements in reading, scene perception, and visual search. More and more researchers are turning to eye-movement recording and data to examine important issues about how the brain

---

[7]There have been attempts to test the generalizability and limits of computational models developed for reading in the context of nonreading tasks like scene perception and search (Reichle, Pollatsek, & Rayner, in press; Trukenbrod & Engbert, 2007).

and mind handles information in various tasks. Many brain-imaging techniques now enable researchers to record eye movements (although rather crudely). Attempts to simultaneously record eye movements and event-related potentials in reading and other tasks look promising. Thus, the future looks bright with respect to the possibility of learning more about cognitive processing and how information is processed in the tasks described in this chapter via the use of eye movements.

References

Baddeley, R. J., & Tatler, B. W. (2006). High frequency edges (but not contrast) predict where we fixate: A Bayesian system identification analysis. *Vision Research, 46*, 2824–2833. doi:10.1016/j.visres.2006.02.024

Bai, X., Yan, G., Liversedge, S. P., Zang, X., & Rayner, K. (2008). Reading spaced and unspaced Chinese text: Evidence from eye movements. *Journal of Experimental Psychology: Human Perception and Performance, 34*, 1277–1287. doi:10.1037/0096-1523.34.5.1277

Engbert, R. (2006). Microsaccades: A microcosm for research on oculomotor control, attention, and visual perception. *Progress in Brain Research, 154*, 177–192.

Engbert, R., & Krügel, A. (2010). Readers use Bayesian estimation for eye movement control. *Psychological Science, 21*, 366–371. doi:10.1177/0956797610362060

Engbert, R., Nuthmann, A., Richter, E. M., & Kliegl, R. (2005). SWIFT: A dynamical model of saccade generation during reading. *Psychological Review, 112*, 777–813. doi:10.1037/0033-295X.112.4.777

Findlay, J. M., & Walker, R. (1999). A model of saccade generation based on parallel processing and competitive inhibition. *Behavioral and Brain Sciences, 22*, 661–721. doi:10.1017/S0140525X99002150

Fisher, D. F., & Shebilske, W. L. (1985). There is more that meets the eye than the eyemind assumption. In R. Groner, G. W. McConkie, & C. Menz (Eds.), *Eye movements and human information processing* (pp. 149–158). Amsterdam, the Netherlands: North Holland.

Henderson, J. M., & Pierce, G. L. (2008). Eye movements during scene viewing: Evidence for mixed control of fixation durations. *Psychonomic Bulletin and Review, 15*, 566–573. doi:10.3758/PBR.15.3.566

Hohenstein, S., Laubrock, J., & Kliegl, R. (2010). Semantic preview benefit in eye movements during reading: A parafoveal fast-priming study. *Journal of Experimental Psychology: Learning, Memory, and Cognition, 36*, 1150–1170.

Irwin, D. E. (1998). Lexical processing during saccadic eye movements. *Cognitive Psychology, 36*, 1–27. doi:10.1006/cogp.1998.0682

Itti, L., & Koch, C. (2000). A saliency-based search mechanism for overt and covert shifts of visual attention. *Vision Research, 40*, 1489–1506. doi:10.1016/S0042-6989(99)00163-7

Itti, L., & Koch, C. (2001). Computational modeling of visual attention. *Nature Reviews Neuroscience, 2*, 194–203. doi:10.1038/35058500

Kirkby, J. A., Webster, L. A. D., Blythe, H. I., & Liversedge, S. P. (2008). Binocular coordination during reading and non-reading tasks. *Psychological Bulletin, 134*, 742–763. doi:10.1037/a0012979

Kliegl, R. (2007). Towards a perceptual-span theory of distributed processing in reading: A reply to Rayner, Pollatsek, Drieghe, Slattery, and Reichle (2007). *Journal of Experimental Psychology: General, 136*, 530–537. doi:10.1037/0096-3445.136.3.530

Kliegl, R., & Engbert, R. (2005). Fixation durations before word skipping in reading. *Psychonomic Bulletin and Review, 12*, 132–138. doi:10.3758/BF03196358

Kliegl, R., Nuthmann, A., & Engbert, R. (2006). Tracking the mind during reading: The influence of past, present, and future words on fixation durations. *Journal of Experimental Psychology: General, 135*, 12–35. doi:10.1037/0096-3445.135.1.12

McConkie, G. W., & Currie, C. B. (1996). Visual stability across saccades while viewing complex pictures. *Journal of Experimental Psychology: Human Perception and Performance, 22*, 563–581.

McConkie, G. W., & Rayner, K. (1975). The span of the effective stimulus during a fixation in reading. *Perception and Psychophysics, 17*, 578–586. doi:10.3758/BF03203972

Nuthmann, A., & Kliegl, R. (2009). An examination of binocular reading fixations based on sentence corpus data. *Journal of Vision, 9*(5):31, 1–28.

Nuthmann, A., Smith, T. J., Engbert, R., & Henderson, J. M. (2010). CRISP: A computational model of fixation durations in scene viewing. *Psychological Review, 117*, 382–405.

Parkhurst, D., Law, K., & Niebur, E. (2002). Modeling the role of salience in the allocation of overt visual attention. *Vision Research, 42*, 107–123. doi:10.1016/S0042-6989(01)00250-4

Posner, M. I. (1980). Orienting of attention. *The Quarterly Journal of Experimental Psychology, 32*, 3–25. doi:10.1080/00335558008248231

Rayner, K. (1975). The perceptual span and peripheral cues during reading. *Cognitive Psychology, 7*, 65–81. doi:10.1016/0010-0285(75)90005-5

Rayner, K. (1979). Eye guidance in reading: Fixation locations within words. *Perception, 8,* 21–30.

Rayner, K. (1995). Eye movements and cognitive processes in reading, visual search, and scene perception. In J. M. Findlay, R. Walker, & R. W. Kentridge (Eds.), *Eye movement research: Mechanisms, processes and applications* (pp. 3–22). Amsterdam, the Netherlands: North Holland. doi:10.1016/S0926-907X(05)80003-0

Rayner, K. (1998). Eye movements in reading and information processing: 20 years of research. *Psychological Bulletin, 124,* 372–422. doi:10.1037/0033-2909.124.3.372

Rayner, K. (2009a). Eye movements in reading: Models and data. *Journal of Eye Movement Research, 2(5),* 1–10.

Rayner, K. (2009b). The 35th Sir Frederick Bartlett Lecture: Eye movements and attention in reading, scene perception, and visual search. *Quarterly Journal of Experimental Psychology, 62,* 1457–1506. doi:10.1080/17470210902816461

Rayner, K., & Bertera, J. H. (1979). Reading without a fovea. *Science, 206,* 468–469. doi:10.1126/science.504987

Rayner, K., Castelhano, M. S., & Yang, J. (2009). Eye movements and the perceptual span in older and younger readers. *Psychology and Aging, 24,* 755–760. doi:10.1037/a0014300

Rayner, K., Chace, K. H., Slattery, T. J., & Ashby, J. (2006). Eye movements as reflections of comprehension processes in reading. *Scientific Studies of Reading, 10,* 241–255. doi:10.1207/s1532799xssr1003_3

Rayner, K., Liversedge, S. P., White, S. J., & Vergilino-Perez, D. (2003). Reading disappearing text. *Psychological Science, 14,* 385–388.

Rayner, K., Slattery, T. J., & Bélanger, N. (2010). Eye movements, perceptual span, and reading speed. *Psychonomic Bulletin and Review, 17,* 834–839.

Rayner, K., Smith, T. J., Malcolm, G., & Henderson, J. M. (2009). Eye movements and encoding during scene perception. *Psychological Science, 20,* 6–10. doi:10.1111/j.1467-9280.2008.02243.x

Reichle, E. D., Pollatsek, A., Fisher, D. L., & Rayner, K. (1998). Toward a model of eye movement control in reading. *Psychological Review, 105,* 125–157. doi:10.1037/0033-295X.105.1.125

Reichle, E. D., Pollatsek, A., & Rayner, K. (in press). Using E-Z Reader to simulate eye movements in nonreading tasks: A unified framework for understanding the eye-mind link. *Psychological Review.*

Reingold, E. M., & Loschky, L. C. (2002). Saliency of peripheral targets in gaze-contingent multiresolutional displays. *Behavior Research Methods, Instruments, and Computers, 34,* 491–499. doi:10.3758/BF03195478

Reingold, E. M., Loschky, L. C., McConkie, G. W., & Stampe, D. M. (2003). Gaze-contingent multiresolutional displays: An integrative review. *Human Factors, 45,* 307–328. doi:10.1518/hfes.45.2.307.27235

Rolfs, M. (2009). Microsaccades: Small steps on a long way. *Vision Research, 49,* 2415–2441. doi:10.1016/j.visres.2009.08.010

Slattery, T. J., & Rayner, K. (2010). The influence of text legibility on eye movements during reading. *Applied Cognitive Psychology, 24,* 1129–1148.

Torralba, A., Oliva, A., Castelhano, M. S., & Henderson, J. M. (2006). Contextual guidance of eye movements and attention in real-world scenes: The role of global features in object search. *Psychological Review, 113,* 766–786. doi:10.1037/0033-295X.113.4.766

Trukenbrod, H. A., & Engbert, R. (2007). Oculomotor control in a sequential search task. *Vision Research, 47,* 2426–2443. doi:10.1016/j.visres.2007.05.010

Winskel, H., Radach, R., & Luksaneeyanawin, S. (2009). Eye movements when reading spaced and unspaced Thai and English: A comparison of Thai-English bilinguals and English monolinguals. *Journal of Memory and Language, 61,* 339–351. doi:10.1016/j.jml.2009.07.002

Yan, M., Kliegl, R., Shu, H., Pan, J., & Zhou, X. (2010). Parafoveal load of word N+1 modulates preprocessing effectiveness of word N+2 in Chinese reading. *Journal of Experimental Psychology: Human Perception and Performance, 36,* 1669–1676.

Yan, M., Richter, E., Shu, H., & Kliegl, R. (2009). Chinese readers extract semantic information from parafoveal words during reading. *Psychonomic Bulletin and Review, 16,* 561–566. doi:10.3758/PBR.16.3.561

Yang, J., Wang, S., Tong, X., & Rayner, K. (in press). Semantic and plausibility effects on preview benefit during eye fixations in Chinese reading. *Reading and Writing.* doi:10.1007/s11145-010-9281-8

Yang, J., Wang, S., Xu, Y., & Rayner, K. (2009). Do Chinese readers obtain preview benefit from word N+ 2? Evidence from eye movements. *Journal of Experimental Psychology: Human Perception and Performance, 35,* 1192–1204.

Zelinsky, G. J. (2008). A theory of eye movements during target acquisition. *Psychological Review, 115,* 787–835.

CHAPTER 22

RESPONSE TIME DISTRIBUTIONS

Roger Ratcliff

Response times (RTs) typically measure the time from presentation of a test stimulus to the response—for example, the time it takes to decide whether a test word was presented in a study list, or whether a stimulus was dark or light. In many domains of psychology, RTs are used to measure the duration of mental processes; in others, they are ignored and only accuracy measures are reported. In every task, however, responses take time and any serious account of the processes involved in a task should account for RT. RTs vary from trial to trial and produce a distribution skewed to the right. In one sense, the skew of this distribution is easily explained—responses cannot be too fast (they run up against some minimum time)—but there is no upper limit on how long they can take.

There are two main issues of concern when thinking about variability in distributions of RTs. The first is practical: How might one best characterize the data by reducing the impact of variability and outliers? The second is theoretical: How might one account for the shapes of RT distributions and how might the shapes help constrain and test models? These two issues interact in situations in which empirical models for the shapes of RT distributions are used as data summaries to examine which parts of the RT distribution change across experimental conditions.

One practical issue in using RT measures is how to handle outliers and contaminants. Usually, at least some outlier RTs can be found in the tail of a distribution. *Outliers* are responses outside of the normal spread of the RT distributions and can be random guesses (either fast or slow), or they can result from a delay in processing, for example, a delay because of a moment's inattention. These responses are *contaminants* in that they are spurious responses that can appear anywhere in the RT distribution; outliers are one kind of contaminant. Ratcliff and Tuerlinckx (2002) presented one theoretical approach to deal with contaminants within the framework of an explicit model of the decision process.

Long outliers, those that appear in the right tail of the RT distribution, are present in most data sets. These can affect estimates of mean RT moderately, sometimes enough to change significant effects into nonsignificant ones, and they also have serious effects on variance generally. A number of methods have been proposed to eliminate or reduce the impact of outliers. No one method is best under all situations. There are best options, however, if one knows how distribution shapes change across conditions.

The most important reason for examining variability in the duration of psychological processes is that it can help constrain models and hypotheses about processing. Usually in psychology, when RTs are considered, the main concern has been with their means. However, if a theory of processing is proposed, even in a relatively weak form, predictions about the distributions of processing times can

This article was supported by National Institute on Aging Grant R01-AG17083 and National Institute of Mental Health Grant R37-MH44640.

DOI: 10.1037/13619-023
APA Handbook of Research Methods in Psychology: Vol. 1. Foundations, Planning, Measures, and Psychometrics, H. Cooper (Editor-in-Chief)

sometimes be derived and used as tests of the theories. The even stronger claim is that even if a theory is consistent with data at the level of mean RT, it might be highly inconsistent with the behavior of RT distributions.

There are basic questions about what happens to the shapes of RT distributions when mean RT increases. Quite different conclusions are reached if the increase in mean RT is the result of the whole distribution of RTs slowing as opposed to the longer RTs slowing more than the shorter RTs. For example, if the whole distribution shifts from one condition to another, then one might conclude that a process has been added. If the distribution spreads, then one might examine diffusion or other sequential sampling models (that assume gradual accumulation of noisy information up to decision criteria, see Ratcliff & Smith, 2004, for a review of these models) in which the evidence-accumulation rate changes between conditions. There are a number of examples in which a model might be consistent with mean RT but inconsistent with the way distribution shape changes across conditions (see Hacker, 1980; Heathcote, Popiel, & Mewhort, 1991; Hockley, 1984; Ratcliff & Murdock, 1976).

In addition to RT distribution shape, it is important to realize that all behavioral cognitive tasks provide both accuracy and RT measures. Sometimes, examination of accuracy may suggest one effect, whereas examination of RT might suggest something different. For example, in several tasks in which the effects of aging on processing are examined, accuracy shows no decrement with age, whereas RT shows a large decrement (e.g., Ratcliff, Thapar, & McKoon, 2010). To understand processing, explicit decision process models can be fit to data and then parameters, which reflect components of processing, can be used to interpret the patterns of accuracy and RT.

In this chapter, I explain how to deal with outlier RTs and different ways of representing RT distribution shape. I describe fitting explicit RT distributions and then describe some remarkable invariances in RT distribution shape. Finally, I describe how processing models can account for distribution shape.

DENSITY, DISTRIBUTION, AND HAZARD RATE FUNCTIONS

There are three standard ways of representing distributions of responses: probability density functions, cumulative distribution functions, and hazard functions. The probability density function is the normalized version of the frequency distribution (Figure 22.1, top panels). A probability density function based on data involves dividing the RT scale into intervals, finding the number of observations in each interval (thus producing a histogram), and dividing these by the total number. The cumulative distribution provides the cumulative probability that a process has terminated as a function of time. A cumulative probability of 0.3 at some time means that 30% of responses have terminated by that time. The cumulative distribution function at some time t is the sum of the probabilities in the probability density function up to t. In the continuous case (for theoretical distributions), the sum is replaced by an integral: $F(t) = \int_0^t f(t')dt'$ where $f(t)$ is the probability density and $F(t)$ is the cumulative distribution.

A close relative of the density and distribution functions is the hazard function. The hazard function is defined as $h(t) = f(t)/(1-F(t))$. The hazard function represents the probability that a process will terminate in the next instant of time given that the process has not yet terminated. For example, the exponential function $f(t) = 1/\tau \, exp(-t/\tau)$, where τ is the time constant (the time by which two thirds of the processes have terminated), has a constant hazard function. This means that the probability of terminating at any time does not depend on how long the process has been running. Radioactive decay is an example of this: The probability of a particle decaying in the next instant of time is independent of how long the particle has been in existence. If the hazard function decreases over time, then the longer a process has been going, the more likely it is to terminate (e.g., old age in an animal population). If the hazard function increases over time, then the longer a process has been going, the longer it is likely to go on (e.g., an increasing survival rate of infants with age in high mortality situations).

The hazard function can serve as a signature to discriminate among models of different classes and

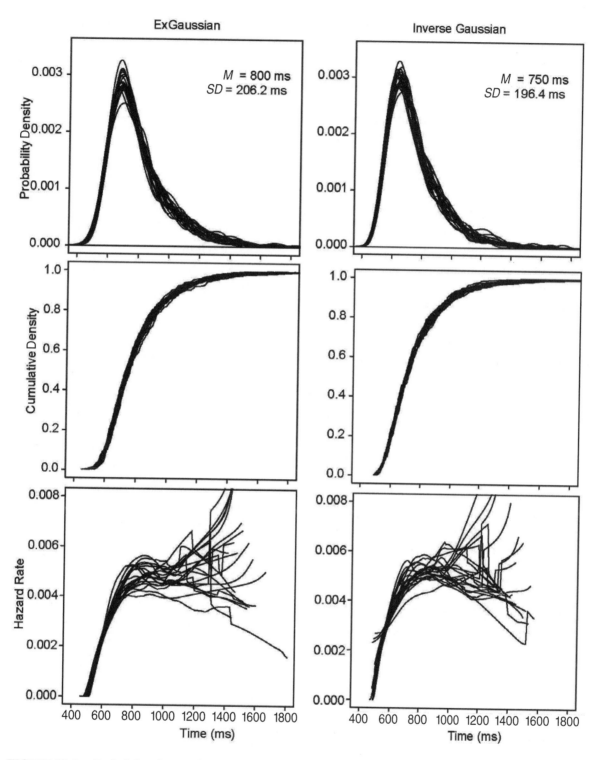

FIGURE 22.1. Probability density functions, cumulative density functions, and hazard functions for ex-Gaussian and inverse Gaussian distributions. The left-hand figures show 20 simulated ex-Gaussian distributions with 500 observations each with Gaussian mean $\mu = 600$ ms and standard deviation $\sigma = 50$ ms, and an exponential mean $\tau = 200$ ms. The right-hand figures show 20 simulated inverse Gaussian distributions with 500 observations per distribution with $\theta = 350$, $\lambda = 750$, and $T_{er} = 400$.

thus can be used to evaluate models that produce predictions for RT distributions (see Luce, 1986). The main limitation in using the hazard function to compare predictions to data is that often the part of the function that best discriminates between models is the part of the function in the right tail of the RT distribution corresponding to long RTs. The problem is that the tails of the distributions have few observations and so are less reliably estimated. Outliers can radically change the shape of the hazard function because they appear in the right tail. There has been little systematic examination of the effects of such outliers on the hazard function; therefore, serious use of it should include some examination of the effects of outliers.

RT distributions can provide strong evidence that a condition contains a mixture of processes. Two well-separated peaks in the RT distribution might indicate a mixture of two separate processes. It might be, for example, that observed increases in mean RT might be the result of one but not the other process slowing, or few responses in the faster process and more responses in the slower process.

Generally, when RTs are used as the dependent variable in testing a hypothesis, the way the RT distribution changes as a function of condition may lead to different conceptions of the processes under consideration. Thus, it is important to understand how RT distributions change as a function of condition when using RT measures.

THE EX-GAUSSIAN AND INVERSE GAUSSIAN DISTRIBUTION FUNCTIONS

To illustrate how distribution shape is evaluated, how outliers affect measures of shape, and how outliers affect applications of models to data, I use two simple explicit distributions that have shapes similar to empirically observed RT distributions, the ex-Gaussian and the inverse Gaussian. These distributions have been used in simulations that examine the power of statistical tests under a variety of conditions and methods of data analysis. The ex-Gaussian distribution (Hohle, 1965; Ratcliff, 1979; Ratcliff & Murdock, 1976) has also been widely used to summarize RT distribution shape; when the model fits experimental data reasonably well, then

the behavior of the model parameters can be used to interpret how the distribution changes across experimental conditions. The inverse Gaussian is the distribution that is produced by a one-boundary diffusion process (e.g., Burbeck & Luce, 1982; Ratcliff, 1978) and so has a more theoretical basis than the ex-Gaussian.

For the ex-Gaussian distribution, an RT from the distribution is the sum of a random value from a Gaussian (normal) distribution (mean μ and standard deviation σ) and a random value from an exponential distribution (with mean τ). The density function is as follows:

$$f(t) = \frac{e^{-[(t-\mu)/\tau - \sigma^2/(2\tau^2)]}}{\tau\sqrt{2\pi}} \int_{-\infty}^{([(t-\mu)/\sigma] - \sigma/\tau)} e^{-y^2/2} dy. \quad (1)$$

The mean of the distribution is $\mu + \tau$ and the standard deviation is $\sqrt{(\sigma^2 + \tau^2)}$.[1] When $\sigma = 0$, the distribution is shifted exponentially (starting at μ) and the mean is $\mu + \tau$, the standard deviation is τ, and the median is $\mu + \tau log_e(2)$. Thus Pearson's skewness, 3(mean − median)/*SD* (see later) is 0.912. For the ex-Gaussian, as σ increases, the skewness decreases.

The inverse Gaussian distribution is the distribution of finishing times in a one-boundary diffusion process. The density function (the mean is $\theta + T_{er}$ and the standard deviation is $\sqrt{(\theta^3/\lambda)}$) is as follows:

$$f(t) = \sqrt{\left(\frac{\lambda}{2\pi(t - T_{er})^3}\right)} e^{-\lambda(t - \theta - T_{er})^2/(2\theta^2(t - T_{er}))}. \quad (2)$$

This function can be rewritten with diffusion model parameters with the transformation between the forms: $\theta = a/v$ and $\lambda = a^2/s^2$, where a is boundary setting, v is drift rate, and s is within trial standard deviation.

For both the ex-Gaussian and inverse Gaussian functions, the probability density function rises quickly and then falls more slowly, like empirical RT distributions. Figure 22.1 illustrates the behavior of the probability density, the cumulative density, and the hazard function of the ex-Gaussian and inverse Gaussian distributions. The Gaussian mean is 600 ms, the Gaussian standard deviation is 50 ms, and the exponential mean is 200 ms. For the inverse Gaussian, the mean is 350 ms, T_{er} is 400 ms, and

$\lambda = 750$ (to give a standard deviation of 196.4 ms). In each panel, there are 20 distributions, each with 500 simulated observations per distribution. The cumulative density function is computed by sorting the data and producing cumulative counts at each RT. The probability density function and hazard functions use kernel estimation methods (Van Zandt, 2000). These essentially smooth the function at time t by averaging over data points around t.

Variability in the random samples of simulated data produces density functions and distribution functions (see the top two panels of Figure 22.1) that differ little across the different samples. However, most of the hazard functions show a rapid rise to a peak at around the mean RT, and then the function either rises, falls, or levels off. By 1,000 ms, it is difficult to see any regularity in the shape of the tail. The ex-Gaussian hazard function rises and then levels off with a flat tail. It is also interesting to note that there is no way to discriminate between the inverse Gaussian and ex-Gaussian by eye.

If either the ex-Gaussian or the inverse Gaussian distribution is fit to RTs, the parameter estimates can be used to summarize RT distribution shape, and comparisons of parameter values across conditions can be used to summarize the changes in distributions over conditions. Visual inspection of RT distributions at the most macroscopic level shows three main features: the location at which the front edge of the distribution begins to rise, the rate of rise in the front edge, and the rate of fall in the tail, that is, about 3 degrees of freedom. Both the ex-Gaussian and inverse Gaussian distributions have 3 parameters (3 degrees of freedom) with which to represent the whole distribution. The distribution that appears to be most useful is the ex-Gaussian. Its three parameters capture the aspects of empirical distributions as noted: the mean of the normal for the location of the fastest responses (and the mode), the standard deviation of the normal for the rise of the front edge of the distribution, and the exponential parameter for the spread of the right tail.

The model parameters describe the shape of RT distributions; it is dangerous, however, to assign meaning to them. In the ex-Gaussian, one might speculate that the Gaussian represents one process and the exponential another. Attempts to identify processes in this way have not been fruitful. The inverse Gaussian represents finishing times of a single boundary diffusion process. This has been considered to be a viable candidate for simple RT tasks (e.g., Burbeck & Luce, 1982; Luce, 1986; Smith, 1995), but it would not be appropriate for two-choice tasks.

Outlier RTs

Everyone who has used RT measures has realized that all the RTs that are collected do not come from the processes under consideration. One has only to observe subjects scratching themselves, adjusting a music player, or answering a phone during the response period to be aware that there is likely to be bad data mixed in with the good. Even if one tests oneself, it is apparent that a lapse of concentration sometimes produces a long RT. If outlier RTs were symmetric, so that a certain proportion of outlier RTs was long and another proportion was short (with the same spread on either side), then there would be no bias in detecting differences among conditions, except for a reduction in power. The mean would remain approximately constant, but the variance and other moments would increase. However, subjects in most cognitive paradigms (if they are attempting to comply with the experimenter) will mainly produce long outlier RTs. These will affect the mean, variance, and measures of distribution shape. Furthermore, just one very long reaction time can completely change the pattern of means in an experiment. For example, suppose that 100 observations per condition are collected in an experiment and the process means are as follows: Condition A, 600 ms and Condition B, 650 ms. Suppose in Condition A that there are two outliers at 2.5 s and 3.5 s. The observed mean in Condition A will then be 648 ms, thus masking the real 50-ms difference.

Fast guesses. One kind of outlier is a fast guess. It is possible to identify such guesses by setting an upper RT cutoff at say 150, 200, and 250 ms, and then examining accuracy. Fast guesses will produce chance or near-chance performance for the faster responses. As the upper cutoff is increased, the point at which accuracy starts to rise above chance will show the point at which RTs begin to come from the processes involved in the task. Specifically, accuracy might be examined within a series of RT windows, say 150 ms to 200 ms, then 200 ms to 250 ms, and so on.

We find that most subjects do not fast guess, but a few do when given the opportunity. Uncooperative subjects that fast guess would be able to leave the experiment earlier than if they tried to perform the experiment according to instructions. We have found that fast guessing can be almost completely eliminated by inserting a 1.5-s or 2-s delay (with a message saying "TOO FAST") after very fast responses, for example, responses less than 150 ms in a fast perceptual task or less than 300 ms in a recognition memory task. This long delay eliminates the motivation for fast guesses. However, sometimes fast guessing may be optimal (Bogacz, Brown, Moehlis, Holmes, & Cohen, 2006) or fast guesses may be a domain of study in their own right (Ollman, 1966). But usually in our work, they are a nuisance that can be eliminated with this simple modification.

Slow outliers. The following example will demonstrate the kind of results to be expected when long outliers are present. To demonstrate properties of the process for trimming long outlier RTs, 96 random numbers were generated from an ex-Gaussian distribution with parameters, $\mu = 500$ ms, $\sigma = 50$ ms, and $\tau = 200$ ms, values like those in observed recognition memory RT distributions. To these 96 RTs, 4 outlier RTs were added at 4, 3, 2, and 1 s. The mean and standard deviation in RT were calculated for all of the RTs at cutoffs of 3,100 ms; 2,100 ms; and 1,100 ms. The means were 786 ms, 754 ms, 716 ms, and 667 ms, and the standard deviations were 485 ms, 361 ms, 245 ms, and 154 ms. The theoretical mean for this ex-Gaussian distribution without outliers is 700 ms and the standard deviation is 206 ms.

With all of the RTs included, the mean is overestimated by 86 ms and the standard deviation is more than double the theoretical value (without the outliers). By the 1,100 ms cutoff, the mean is 33 ms less than the theoretical value and the standard deviation is 44 ms less than the theoretical value. These last two values at the 1,100 ms cutoff demonstrate an important problem with trimming—that is, in this case, seven RTs besides the outliers are trimmed out,

leading to a serious underestimation of both the mean and standard deviation.

The message is simple: In most sets of RT data, there are spurious long RTs. Trimming data will remove many spurious RTs, but it will also remove long RTs that come from the processes under study. The question is: Can we find a rule of thumb to maximize removal of the spurious RTs yet minimize removal of real data? Ratcliff (1993) examined this question and found that no rule of thumb did not fail in some situations. This study is reviewed in the following section.

Methods for reducing the impact of long outliers. The criterion that has been most often suggested involves trimming out data that falls some number of standard deviations outside the mean of that condition (e.g., 2 or 3 standard deviations). It is important to note that any trimming or otherwise removing of data should be done completely independently of the hypotheses being tested. In addition, it is also reassuring if the trimming procedure does not remove significantly more data points from one condition than other conditions.

A diagnostic signal that outliers may be present in a condition of an experiment is the standard deviation for the condition relative to those for other conditions. Suppose three conditions are expected to have an increasing RT from first to last (e.g., 500 ms, 600 ms, and 700 ms). Suppose that the means are 520 ms, 750 ms, and 680 ms. Then it may be thought that the results disconfirm the prediction. However, an examination standard deviation in each condition may show that the conclusion is premature: If the standard deviations are 250 ms, 500 ms, and 285 ms respectively, then it may be that outliers are responsible for the long mean RT in the middle condition. Trimming outliers may then produce the following set of results: 505 ms, 602 ms, and 678 ms respectively, with standard deviations, 220 ms, 249 ms, and 277 ms respectively. This pattern is more satisfactory because it shows monotonically increasing means and standard deviations.

Power of analysis of variance (ANOVA) and outliers. There are several alternative methods for dealing with long outlier RTs in common use (beside trimming). First, the data can be Winsorized:

Long RTs, instead of being trimmed out, can be replaced by RTs at some predetermined ceiling, for example, 3 standard deviations above the mean. This method makes the strong assumption that if there was no inattention (that produced the long outlier response), the process still would have produced a long RT. In general, I believe that this assumption is not justified in the RT domain. A second method involves use of medians. Typically, the median RT is computed for each subject in each condition and then these medians are used in an analysis of variance (for example). The advantage of medians is that they are insensitive to a few outliers. This raises the question: If medians avoid the problem of outliers, then why is the median not used routinely instead of mean RT? The reason is that medians have higher variability than means. Simulations using medians showed that they rarely produce as much power as other methods. A third method involves transforming the RT data, by a log or inverse transformation. Both of these transformations reduce the impact of long RTs on the means.

Ratcliff (1993) performed a number of simulations to mimic how these different methods influence the power of ANOVA to detect reliable differences. The methods differ in their ability to increase power as a function of how the RT distribution changes across conditions. Simulations were carried out with assumptions, first, that RT distributions spread with an increase in mean RT (as occurs with changes in memory strength or perceptual strength) or, second, that the distributions shifted with an increase in mean RT (as occurs with visual search when the order of search is controlled; Hockley, 1984). Simulations also examined the effects with and without outliers.

Results showed that no one method was optimal. If the difference in means between two conditions occurs because the RT distribution spreads with no change in the leading edge, and there are no outliers, then trimming reduces power as the cutoff is reduced. If there are outliers, then trimming increases power to a maximum as the cutoff is reduced, and then power decreases as more and more genuine RTs are eliminated (i.e., the data that are responsible for the difference in mean RTs). On the other hand, if the difference between two

conditions is caused by the distribution shifting with no change in the spread of the tail, then both with and without outliers, trimming increases power as more and more long RTs are eliminated (long RTs are more variable and so reduce power). Ratcliff (1993) reported results for log and inverse transformations, using medians, trimming the longest RT, trimming at some number of standard deviations above the mean, and Winsorizing. One method that seemed to give high power for studies with and without outliers and with distributions both spreading and shifting was the inverse transformation.

The prescription that we follow in dealing with outlier RTs in analyzing data is as follows: In a new experimental paradigm, we analyze the data in several different ways. We look at the results without trimming, we trim at several deadlines, and we calculate medians. If all of these measures tell us the same thing, then we proceed to other experiments with the measure derived from trimming at some reasonable point (if the mean is 700 ms and standard deviation is 300 ms, a cutoff of between 1,500 ms and 2,000 ms will probably work well) that is determined independently of the hypothesis being tested. What we want to see (if the means calculated from the raw data are noisy) is order coming out of variability as the RT cutoff is reduced. We also want to see that the median tells us the same thing as the trimmed mean. If the measures do not agree, then problems may result. It may be that there are no real trends in the data (statistical tests will usually confirm this by not producing significance at any cutoff or with medians). The results that are collected from the different cutoffs, transformations, and medians may then point the way toward a better design. But, in all of these analyses, one should not experiment with different methods on marginal data to try and find one that produces a significant effect. Such an effect may be spurious. The most important outcome is to have reported a result that replicates.

Fitting RT Distributions

This section describes two methods for fitting models of RT distributions to empirical data (Heathcote, Brown, & Mewhort, 2002; Ratcliff & Murdock, 1976; Ratcliff & Tuerlinckx, 2002; Van Zandt, 2000, 2002). The best is maximum likelihood; the estimates are best in the sense that variability in the estimates of the parameters is smaller than any other unbiased estimate. In this method, each RT is put into the expression for probability density to find the probability density for that RT (e.g., in the equation for the ex-Gaussian). Then, the densities for all the RTs are multiplied and this product is called the likelihood. If $f(t_i)$ is the density for the ith RT, then $L = \pi_i f(t_i)$ is the likelihood. The parameter values of the model are adjusted to find those that maximize the likelihood. In practice, because the product of many likelihoods can be small, the logarithm of each likelihood is taken and minus the sum of the log-likelihoods is minimized as a function of model parameters $(-log(ab) = -log(a)-log(b)$ so the log of products is the sum of logs). This works because the logarithm of a function is monotonically related to the function so the parameter values that maximize the function are those that minimize minus the log of the function. Minimization can be done by standard function minimization routines.

One problem with the maximum likelihood method for most distributions that are used to model RT is that a single short outlier RT can distort the whole fit. For example, the inverse Gaussian cannot produce an RT less than T_{er}. This means that if an RT is very short, T_{er} must be adjusted to be less than that RT to produce a probability density. Short RTs can be trimmed, but then the value of T_{er} will be partly determined by the value of the cutoff. This means that it will be the choice of the person fitting the model.

One way to mitigate this problem is to use quantile RTs instead of individual RTs. Quantile RTs are the times at which some quantile proportion of processes have terminated. The proportion of responses between the quantile RTs are used to compute either a chi-square or a G-square goodness-of-fit statistic (see Ratcliff & Smith, 2004). If we use the .05, .15, . . ., .95 quantile RTs, then .05 probability mass lies outside the .05 and .95 quantiles and .1 probability mass lies between the quantiles. These probability masses are multiplied by the number of observations to give the observed frequencies. The quantile RTs can be used with the theoretical cumulative density function to compute the probability mass between the quantile RTs, and these masses are multiplied by

the number of observations to give the expected values. Then, a chi-square or G-square goodness-of-fit measure can be computed, and model parameters can be adjusted to find its minimum. The observed probability masses (p_i) for the example above are .05, .1, .1, . . ., .05, and if the expected probability masses are πi, then the chi-square statistic is $\chi^2 = N\Sigma(p_i - \pi_i)^2/\pi_i$ (where N is the number of observations) and the G-square statistic is $G^2 = 2N\Sigma p_i ln(p_i/\pi_i)$. I have found that minimizing chi-square and minimizing G-square produces almost the same parameter estimates. This is not surprising because they are asymptotically equivalent (Jeffreys, 1961, pp. 196–197). A possible problem with the use of quantile RTs is that the quantiles are random variables and not fixed values, as likelihood theory would require (Speckman & Rouder, 2004). In the cases in which fixed nonrandom bins and quantile bins have been used, the results have been essentially the same (e.g., Fific, Little, & Nosofsky, 2010).

The use of quantiles has the major advantage that a few short RTs (e.g., less than 10% if the lowest quantile used is the .10 quantile) will not distort the fit. Along with some judicious trimming of short RTs (e.g., much shorter than a possible response given on the basis of processing the stimulus and not guessing), this avoids problems with short outliers. In addition, some trimming of long RTs (e.g., at say 2 s if the mean RT is 600 ms) along with the use of quantiles will reduce the effect of long outliers. Sometimes, especially within a process modeling framework, it is possible to model contaminant responses, either as delays in processing (Ratcliff & Tuerlinckx, 2002) or as random guesses (Ratcliff & Van Dongen, 2009; Vandekerckhove & Tuerlinckx, 2007), depending on the task and experimental manipulations.

Monte Carlo methods.   To see how well any fitting method recovers parameter values, we run Monte Carlo simulations. In these, we generate simulated data from the model and then fit the model to the simulated data. Then, we repeat this, say 100 times, that is, 100 Monte Carlo simulations, and compute the mean parameter values and the standard deviation in the parameter values. The values of the mean provide a way of looking at bias in the parameter estimates; that is, does the fitting method produce fits that systematically differ from the values that were used to generate the simulated data? The values of the standard deviations provide estimates of variability in the parameter estimates on the basis of the sample size, and these can be used to compare the efficiency of different estimation methods. In addition, the standard deviations provide estimates of variability for statistical tests on parameter values across conditions and also provide estimates that allow comparison with individual differences to see whether individual difference studies can be sensibly conducted. Finally, correlations between parameter values across the Monte Carlo trials can be used to examine trade-offs across parameters. The way to interpret such trade-offs is as follows: If one or more data points (e.g., quantile RTs) were extra high by chance, then the model may compensate for this by moving one parameter higher and another parameter (or more) may also move higher or lower to compensate. These correlations can be used to decide whether differences in parameter values might be the result of real differences or trade-offs. A detailed discussion is presented in Ratcliff and Tuerlinckx (2002, Figure 5), Ratcliff and Murdock (1976) provided theoretical estimates of standard deviations in ex-Gaussian parameter values, and Wagenmakers, Ratcliff, Gomez, and Iverson (2004) discussed such Monte Carlo methods in detail. Standard properties of estimators are presented in Ratcliff and Tuerlinckx (2002, Appendix A).

Representing Distribution Shape: RT Quantiles

In the prior section, we indicated that quantile RTs can be used in fitting a model to data; this section shows how they can be used to display distribution shape. The quantiles of an RT distribution are the times at which some proportion of the processes have terminated. In the middle panel of Figure 22.1, the .2 quantile RT is obtained by drawing a horizontal line from .2 on the y-axis to intersect the cumulative distribution function; the quantile RT is the RT on the x-axis where the two intersect. Quantiles of an RT distribution can be used as a summary of the distribution as is shown in the top panel of Figure 22.2. The circles connected with the jagged

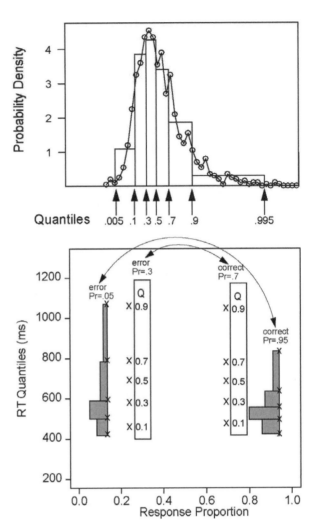

FIGURE 22.2.   The top panel shows a reaction time (RT) distribution as a frequency polygon, along with a quantile RT distribution with equal area rectangles drawn between the .1, .3, .5, .7, and .9 quantile RTs and rectangles with half the area outside the .1 and .9 quantile RTs. The bottom panel shows a quantile probability plot with the proportion of responses for that condition on the x-axis and quantile RTs plotted as xs on the y-axis. Equal areas rectangles are drawn between two of the sets of the quantiles to illustrate how to interpret RT distribution shape in the plot (these are comparable to the distribution in the top panel). Pr = proportion.

line show a frequency polygon, which is a histogram with the top of the bars replaced by the circles. On the x-axis, the arrows show RT quantiles. Because there is a probability mass of .2 between the .1, .3, .5, .7, and .9 quantiles, and .1 outside of each of two extreme values, rectangles with these areas can be constructed between and outside the quantiles. The further apart the quantiles are, the lower the height of the rectangle. The .005 and .995 quantiles are used to mark the extremes of the distribution because they provide relatively stable estimators of the fastest and slowest RTs. Because each of the rectangles has an area of .2 (with the remaining .2 shared between the two extremes), all of the information about distribution shape is carried by the spacing between the quantiles. As can be seen, the equal-area histogram captures the overall shape of the distribution, that is, its location, spread, and skewness, as does the frequency polygon. This correspondence works for RT distributions with as few as 5 quantiles because RT distributions are usually regular with a fast rise and a slower fall in the right tail.

Ratcliff (2001) presented plots of quantiles against accuracy as a way of showing how response proportion and RT distributions jointly change as a function of the independent variable. The bottom panel of Figure 22.2 shows a plot, termed a quantile probability plot. In this plot, the quantiles of the RT distribution for each condition are plotted vertically with response proportion for the condition providing the value on the x-axis. If the probability of a correct response for a particular stimulus discriminability is p, the quantiles of the distribution of correct responses are plotted in a vertical column against p on the x-axis and the quantiles of the distribution of errors are plotted against $1 - p$. In the figure, this correspondence is illustrated by the double-ended arrows connecting pairs of conditions. This means that correct responses appear (usually) on the right of the .5 point on the x-axis and errors appear on the left. In plots of this kind, the outermost pair of distributions in the figure are the errors and correct RTs for the easiest stimulus condition and the innermost pair are the errors and correct RTs for the most difficult stimulus condition. This example is for cases in which correct responses can be combined across the two choices of an experiment (e.g., bright responses to bright stimuli combined with dark responses to dark stimuli); in other cases, they cannot be combined in this way and separate plots are needed for the two response types (e.g., words and nonwords in lexical decision; see Ratcliff, Thapar, Gomez, & McKoon, 2004).

When one becomes familiar with the plot, one can see the way RT distributions change over conditions. For example, in the bottom panel of Figure 22.2, going from right to left, the leading edge (lower x, .1 quantile RT) increases a little, but the tail (top x, .9 quantile RT) increases from around 850 ms to 1,080 ms. This means that the RT distribution shifts only a little, but it spreads out a lot more. Comparing the extreme right and left quantiles (correct response proportion .95 and error proportion .05), error responses have a longer tail than correct responses, but the leading edges are about the same. These quantile probability plots can contain both the data and the predictions and hence provide a useful way of examining the joint fit of accuracy and correct and error RT distributions of a model to data (Ratcliff & Smith, 2004).

Averaging over subjects. In many situations in cognitive psychology, materials are difficult to construct or a limited number are available. With patient populations, relatively few observations may be possible to collect. For example, in text-processing research, it can be extremely difficult to construct paragraphs with the required structure while controlling potentially confounding variables; in clinical research, there may be relatively few words associated with, for example, anxiety, and in semantic memory research, there may be a limited number of typical members of a category or highly associated pairs of items. In these situations, it may be impossible to get more than 30 or 40 observations per subject per condition. Averaging quantiles over subjects provides a way of grouping data when the number of observations is small. Just combining the RTs from the different subjects does not work. For example, if RTs were combined from two subjects that had narrow distributions that were well separated (e.g., with means at 500 ms and 800 ms), then the resulting distribution would be bimodal and would not reflect the shape of either individual distribution.

A major advantage of using quantile RTs to represent distribution shape is that they can be averaged over subjects to give a reasonable representation of average quantiles and, hence, the distribution of the average subject. There are two methods of doing this. One is to simply average quantiles. The second is to produce "Vincentiles" (Ratcliff, 1979, after Vincent, 1912; see also Estes, 1956) in which mean RTs between quantiles are computed and then averaged over subjects. In fitting models to data over the past 10 years, I have used quantiles and not Vincentiles for the simple reason that quantiles can be computed from a model more easily than Vincentiles. Either the model is simulated to give a cumulative distribution function and then the quantile can be computed by interpolation (Ratcliff & Smith, 2004; Ratcliff & Starns, 2009; Usher & McClelland, 2001), or the data quantile RT can be entered into the computation for the cumulative distribution function and the predicted cumulative probability can be obtained (to be used in a chi-square or G-square fitting method, Ratcliff & Tuerlinckx, 2002). Visually, in the middle two panels of Figure 22.1, a straight line is projected up from the quantile RT on the *x*-axis, and the value on the *y*-axis where it intersects the cumulative density function is the cumulative probability. If Vincentiles were to be used, the model cumulative distribution function would have to be integrated between the quantile RTs, which would add a much larger computational load to the fitting program.

A number of exact results have been obtained for Vincent averaging (Thomas & Ross, 1980). Thomas and Ross (1980) described conditions under which the Vincent average distribution belongs to the same family as the individual distributions (this is true for the exponential, Weibull, and logistic distributions) and when the parameters from the Vincent average are averages of the parameters from the individual distributions. They showed that for the individual distributions to belong to the same family, a plot of quantiles for one subject versus quantiles for another subject (Q–Q plot) will be linear (Tukey, 1977).

In the process of fitting theoretical distribution functions to experimental data, it usually becomes necessary to obtain an average of the parameter values across subjects to make some statements about group trends. There are two main ways to do this: The first is to average the data across subjects in some way and then to fit the model and use those parameters as the summary. The second is to fit the model to each individual subject's data and then to

average the individual's parameters to provide the group parameters. In fitting the diffusion model to the data, we have performed this comparison a number of times. In almost all of the cases, the parameters of the fit of the model to group data are close (within 2 standard errors) to the average of the parameter values from fits to individual subjects (Ratcliff et al., 2010). To date, this is a practical result and not theoretically exact, and it applies for the diffusion model and not competing models.

Measures of Distribution Shape

The question that is of interest in this section is how to obtain information about distribution shape from real RT data. Distribution shape can be defined in several different ways. Probably the most reasonable and least theory-bound is given by Mosteller and Tukey (1977, Chapter 1). They define shape as what is left when location (position of the distribution) and scale (spread of the distribution) are eliminated, that is, the distribution is normalized. A probability density function is not sufficient to define shape as defined by Mosteller and Tukey, for example, their Figure 4 (1997, Chapter 1) shows that the family of beta-density functions has the same mathematical form but differs widely in shape. Because RT distributions have roughly the same shape (skewed to the right), and some probability density functions that have been proposed as models of the RT distribution fit reasonably well, the ways that the parameters in these models change across conditions provide a reasonable way of describing how shape changes over conditions (e.g., for the ex-Gaussian distribution).

Skewness.   Everyone who has taken an introductory statistics course is familiar with the mean, standard deviation, and variance of a set of scores. The mean represents the location of the distribution, and the standard deviation represents the spread or scale of the distribution. Introductory statistics books sometimes discuss skewness and kurtosis as measures of distribution shape. These measures are based on the moments of the distribution. For example, the *k*th moment can be written as follows:

$$\mu_k = \int_{-\infty}^{\infty} (t - \mu_1)^k f(t) dt. \tag{3}$$

Then skewness is defined as $Sk_\mu = \mu_3/s^3$ and kurtosis is defined as $\kappa = \mu_4/s^4$ (where $s^2 = \mu_2$ = variance and μ_1 is the mean). It can be demonstrated mathematically that if all the moments of the distribution are known, then the shape of the distribution is completely determined.

However, there are serious problems with using moments as measures of distribution shape (Ratcliff, 1979). First, the contributions to the third and fourth moments come from relatively far in the tail of the distribution (see Ratcliff, 1979, Figure 6, which was reprinted from Pearson, 1963). This means that these moments are sensitive to parts of the distribution that do not correspond to what we see as distribution shape by visual inspection. Second, the higher moments have very large standard errors associated with them. This means that many more observations are needed to obtain reasonable estimates (with low standard errors) than are usually collected in RT experiments. Third, outlier RTs can very severely affect the size of moments from the variance on up to the extent that if there are a few extreme reaction times, the higher moments essentially reflect these long RTs. The problem becomes critical if some of the outlier RTs are from processes other than the process under consideration (e.g., a second retrieval attempt or, even worse, a head scratch or a moment's distraction). Then, the higher moments are measuring outlier RTs, and these outliers are not of particular interest in determining distribution shape. Better measures of distribution shape are Pearson's second skewness measure and the quartile coefficient of skewness. Pearson's second skewness measure is $Sk_p = 3$ (mean – median)/s and quartile skewness is defined by $Sk_q = (Q_3 - 2Q_2 + Q_1)/(Q_3 - Q_1)$.

Ratcliff (1993) performed a set of simulation studies that compared the behavior of these different measures of skewness across different random samples of data from the same distribution. Results showed that Pearson's second skewness measure and quantile skewness correlated highly and neither correlated with skewness from the third moment. Practically, what one sees in visually examining a distribution corresponds to Pearson's second skewness measure and the quartile coefficient of skewness.

Diffusion models. Several different kinds of diffusion decision models account for distribution shape in two-choice tasks. These diffusion models (Ratcliff, 1978; Ratcliff & Smith, 2004; Usher & McClelland, 2001; also see reviews in Ratcliff & McKoon, 2008; Wagenmakers, 2009) provide an account of how accuracy and the shapes of RT distributions change across experimental conditions that manipulate difficulty and speed–accuracy criterion settings. The models assume accumulation of noisy evidence toward decision criteria for each alternative response. The models provide the following accounts of RT distributions for two-choice decisions. First, most empirical RT distributions have an approximately exponential tail, which leads to a flat hazard function in the extreme right tail. Diffusion models automatically produce this behavior. Second, RT distributions spread out to the right as mean RT increases with difficulty with only a small shift in the distribution. This is a strong prediction of diffusion models. Third, as speed–accuracy settings are altered (e.g., by instructions), RT distributions shift and spread. Again, this is a strong prediction of the models. Fourth, RT distribution shape is approximately invariant under all of these manipulations. Diffusion models also produce this kind of invariance. Fifth, diffusion models produce increasing hazard functions or functions that increase to a peak and then decrease a little (Ratcliff et al., 1999), and these are the patterns that are observed in most two-choice data. In sum, most observed behaviors of RT distributions are captured almost automatically by diffusion models of the decision process. Methods of fitting the model to data can be found in Ratcliff and Tuerlinckx (2002) and a computer package to fit the model is described in Vandekerckhove and Tuerlinckx (2007). These methods deal with outlier and contaminant RTs by explicitly modeling them and extracting estimates of the proportions of these responses.

Explicit distribution functions. Some of the earliest attempts to model the shape of RT distributions started with an assumed distribution and attempted to work back from fits of the distribution to empirical data, and then to the processes underlying the task. For example, McGill (1963) voiced the hope that the shape of the RT distribution would serve as a signature that would help identify the underlying processes. It seems that the strong version of this hope has not been realized; rather, RT distributions are critical in testing models, but they cannot be used to unambiguously identify processes (cf. the similar-shaped distributions in Figure 22.1).

There are several practical problems with working back from fits of the theoretical functions to the mechanisms: First, the theoretical distributions that are chosen for fitting have often been selected for mathematical tractability rather than for a description of theoretical mechanisms. Second, the method depends critically on comparison of different goodness-of-fit measures for the different distributions to be considered. These goodness-of-fit measures may interact with outlier problems that were discussed in the section Outlier RTs; that is, a particular distribution may fit data better than another distribution because it better fits the combination of regular RTs and outliers that may not come from the processes under consideration. Third, there is a major problem of mimicking, and it is certainly possible to produce distributions of much the same shape from many different processing assumptions. It is my opinion that the shape of RT distributions alone usually does not provide enough constraints to specify the underlying processing mechanisms. RT distribution shape provides the strongest constraints on process models that attempt to account for correct and error response times as well as accuracy.

In some cases, however, it may be possible to work back from distributions to processes. For example, if there was bimodality in the RT distribution, then this would strongly imply that there was a mixture of two component processes. However, the shapes of the two component distributions would not specify the components underlying those subprocesses.

The ex-Gaussian has been used in several applications to summarize the shape of RT distributions (e.g., Balota & Spieler, 1999; Hacker, 1980; Heathcote et al., 1991; Hockley, 1984; Ratcliff, 1979; Ratcliff & Murdock, 1976; Yap, Balota, Tse, & Besner, 2008). The advantage of using this distribution is that the parameter τ provides an estimate of the fall in the tail relative to the rise of the distribution (which is represented by σ). From a more

theoretical perspective, Matzke and Wagenmakers (2009) used the diffusion model to generate predictions and showed that if the diffusion model were correct, then the way diffusion model parameters change does not correspond to the way the ex-Gaussian parameters change, for example, a change in drift rate does not correspond to a change in one ex-Gaussian parameter.

CONCLUSION

This chapter discussed a number of issues, both practical and theoretical, that revolve around knowing the shape of RT distributions and how distributions change across conditions. From a theoretical perspective, I described methods of fitting distributions, methods of summarizing distributions with quantiles or explicit distributions, methods of averaging distributions over subjects, and covariances among model parameters. A practical consideration in most research using RT measures is how to identify and deal with outlier RTs. It is clear that methods are available to deal with outliers that can increase the power of an experiment substantially.

The most important empirical lesson that can be taken from the discussion presented here is that someone using RT measures needs to know how their RTs are distributed and how the RT distributions change over conditions. Knowing about RT distributions can lead to insights about processing that are not available from mean RT alone.

References

Balota, D. A., & Spieler, D. H. (1999). Word frequency, repetition, and lexicality effects in word recognition tasks: Beyond measures of central tendency. *Journal of Experimental Psychology: General, 128*, 32–55. doi:10.1037/0096-3445.128.1.32

Bogacz, R., Brown, E., Moehlis, J., Holmes, P., & Cohen, J. D. (2006). The physics of optimal decision making: A formal analysis of models of performance in two-alternative forced choice tasks. *Psychological Review, 113*, 700–765. doi:10.1037/0033-295X.113.4.700

Burbeck, S. L., & Luce, R. D. (1982). Evidence from auditory simple reaction times for both change and level detectors. *Perception and Psychophysics, 32*, 117–133. doi:10.3758/BF03204271

Estes, W. K. (1956). The problem of inference from curves based on group data. *Psychological Bulletin, 53*, 134–140. doi:10.1037/h0045156

Fific, M., Little, T. D., & Nosofsky, R. M. (2010). Logical-rule models of classification response times: A synthesis of mental-architecture, random-walk, and decision-bound approaches. *Psychological Review, 117*, 309–348.

Hacker, M. J. (1980). Speed and accuracy of recency judgments for events in short-term memory. *Journal of Experimental Psychology: Human Learning and Memory, 6*, 651–675.

Heathcote, A., Brown, S., & Mewhort, D. J. K. (2002). Quantile maximum likelihood estimation of response time distributions. *Psychonomic Bulletin and Review, 9*, 394–401.

Heathcote, A., Popiel, S. J., & Mewhort, D. J. K. (1991). Analysis of response time distributions: An example using the Stroop task. *Psychological Bulletin, 109*, 340–347. doi:10.1037/0033-2909.109.2.340

Hockley, W. E. (1984). Analysis of response time distributions in the study of cognitive processes. *Journal of Experimental Psychology: Learning, Memory, and Cognition, 10*, 598–615. doi:10.1037/0278-7393. 10.4.598

Hohle, R. H. (1965). Inferred components of reaction times as a function of foreperiod duration. *Journal of Experimental Psychology, 69*, 382–386. doi:10.1037/ h0021740

Jeffreys, H. (1961). *Theory of probability* (3rd ed.). Oxford, England: Oxford University Press.

Luce, R. D. (1986). *Response times*. New York, NY: Oxford University Press.

Matzke, D., & Wagenmakers, E-J. (2009). Psychological interpretation of ex-Gaussian and shifted Wald parameters: A diffusion model analysis. *Psychonomic Bulletin and Review, 16*, 798–817. doi:10.3758/ PBR.16.5.798

McGill, W. J. (1963). Stochastic latency mechanisms. In R. D. Luce, R. R. Bush, & E. Galanter (Eds.), *Handbook of mathematical psychology* (pp. 309–360). New York, NY: Wiley.

Mosteller, F., & Tukey, J. W. (1977). *Data analysis and regression*. Reading, MA: Addison- Wesley.

Ollman, R. T. (1966). Fast guesses in choice reaction time. *Psychonomic Science, 6*, 155–156.

Pearson, E. S. (1963). Some problems arising in approximating to probability distributions, using moments. *Biometrika, 50*, 95–112.

Ratcliff, R. (1978). A theory of memory retrieval. *Psychological Review, 85*, 59–108. doi:10.1037/0033-295X.85.2.59

Ratcliff, R. (1979). Group reaction time distributions and an analysis of distribution statistics. *Psychological Bulletin, 86*, 446–461. doi:10.1037/0033-2909. 86.3.446

Ratcliff, R. (1993). Methods for dealing with reaction time outliers. *Psychological Bulletin, 114*, 510–532. doi:10.1037/0033-2909.114.3.510

Ratcliff, R. (2001). Diffusion and random walk processes. In N. J. Smelser, J. Wright, & P. B. Baltes (Eds.), *International encyclopedia of the social and behavioral sciences* (Vol. 6, pp. 3668–3673). Oxford, England: Elsevier.

Ratcliff, R., & McKoon, G. (2008). The diffusion decision model: Theory and data for two-choice decision tasks. *Neural Computation, 20*, 873–922. doi:10.1162/ neco.2008.12-06-420

Ratcliff, R., & Murdock, B. B., Jr. (1976). Retrieval processes in recognition memory. *Psychological Review, 83*, 190–214. doi:10.1037/0033-295X.83.3.190

Ratcliff, R., & Smith, P. L. (2004). A comparison of sequential sampling models for two-choice reaction time. *Psychological Review, 111*, 333–367. doi:10.1037/0033-295X.111.2.333

Ratcliff, R., & Starns, J. J. (2009). Modeling confidence and response time in recognition memory. *Psychological Review, 116*, 59–83. doi:10.1037/ a0014086

Ratcliff, R., Thapar, A., Gomez, P., & McKoon, G. (2004). A diffusion model analysis of the effects of aging in the lexical-decision task. *Psychology and Aging, 19*, 278–289. doi:10.1037/0882-7974.19.2.278

Ratcliff, R., Thapar, A., & McKoon, G. (2010). Individual differences, aging, and IQ in two-choice tasks. *Cognitive Psychology, 60*, 127–157. doi:10.1016/j. cogpsych.2009.09.001

Ratcliff, R., & Tuerlinckx, F. (2002). Estimating the parameters of the diffusion model: Approaches to dealing with contaminant reaction times and parameter variability. *Psychonomic Bulletin and Review, 9*, 438–481. doi:10.3758/BF03196302

Ratcliff, R., & Van Dongen, H. P. A. (2009). Sleep deprivation affects multiple distinct cognitive processes. *Psychonomic Bulletin and Review, 16*, 742–751. doi:10.3758/PBR.16.4.742

Ratcliff, R., Van Zandt, T., & McKoon, G. (1999). Connectionist and diffusion models of reaction time. *Psychological Review, 106*, 261–300. doi:10.1037/ 0033-295X.106.2.261

Smith, P. L. (1995). Psychophysically principled models of visual simple reaction time. *Psychological Review, 102*, 567–593. doi:10.1037/0033-295X. 102.3.567

Speckman, P. L., & Rouder, J. N. (2004). A comment on Heathcote, Brown, and Mewhort's QMLE method for response time distributions. *Psychonomic Bulletin and Review, 11,* 574–576. doi:10.3758/BF03196613

Thomas, E. A. C., & Ross, B. H. (1980). On appropriate procedures for combining probability distributions within the same family. *Journal of Mathematical Psychology, 21,* 136–152. doi:10.1016/0022-2496(80)90003-6

Tukey, J. W. (1977). *Exploratory data analysis.* Reading, MA: Addison-Wesley.

Usher, M., & McClelland, J. L. (2001). The time course of perceptual choice: The leaky, competing accumulator model. *Psychological Review, 108,* 550–592. doi:10.1037/0033-295X.108.3.550

Vandekerckhove, J., & Tuerlinckx, F. (2007). Fitting the Ratcliff diffusion model to experimental data. *Psychonomic Bulletin and Review, 14,* 1011–1026. doi:10.3758/BF03193087

Van Zandt, T. (2000). ROC curves and confidence judgments in recognition memory. *Journal of Experimental Psychology: Learning, Memory, and Cognition, 26,* 582–600. doi:10.1037/0278-7393.26.3.582

Van Zandt, T. (2002). Analysis of response time distributions. In J. T. Wixted (Vol. Ed.) & H. Pashler (Series Ed.), *Stevens's Handbook of Experimental Psychology: Vol. 4. Methodology in experimental psychology* (3rd ed., pp. 461–516). New York, NY: Wiley.

Vincent, S. B. (1912). The function of the viborissae in the behavior of the white rat. *Behavioral Monographs, 1.*

Wagenmakers, E.-J. (2009). Methodological and empirical developments for the Ratcliff diffusion model of response times and accuracy. *European Journal of Cognitive Psychology, 21,* 641–671. doi:10.1080/09541440802205067

Wagenmakers, E.-J., Ratcliff, R., Gomez, P., & Iverson, G. J. (2004). Assessing model mimicry using the parametric bootstrap. *Journal of Mathematical Psychology, 48,* 28–50. doi:10.1016/j.jmp.2003.11.004

Yap, M. J., Balota, D. A., Tse, C.-S., & Besner, D. (2008). On the additive effects of stimulus quality and word frequency in lexical decision: Evidence for opposing interactive influences revealed by RT distributional analyses. *Journal of Experimental Psychology: Learning, Memory, and Cognition, 34,* 495–513. doi:10.1037/0278-7393.34.3.495

CHAPTER 23

PSYCHOPHYSICS

Paul T. Sowden

Imagine you are going to meet a friend and watch a movie. You are running late, the movie has started, and your friend sends you a message to say she has gone in. You walk into the movie theatre and search for your friend's face but have trouble finding her in the dark. Suddenly the screen lights up and you can see the seat numbers and faces of the people in the theater. You manage to spot your friend, she sees you and flashes you a smile—you are forgiven your lateness. You begin to squeeze your way along the row to her. The movie features characters speaking in unfamiliar accents to you and at times you find yourself struggling to understand what is being said. But at least your seats are near the front so you can clearly see everything that is going on.

This everyday situation contains multiple instances of a relation between physical stimuli and psychological responses. How do you tell the difference between your friend's face and other faces? How do you identify her emotional state? How much light do you need to be able to see and then read the seat numbers? How do you judge whether you can squeeze along the row to her? How loud does the volume on the movie need to be for you to discriminate the different words being spoken? How close do you need to sit to perceive different levels of detail in the visual images?

Psychophysics provides us with a theory and set of methods to answer these types of questions, essentially, methods that determine the relation between the intensity of a stimulus, the transformations it undergoes in the external and internal environment, and the sensation and subsequent response of an observer.[1]

CLASSICAL THRESHOLD THEORY

So what is a threshold? In many respects it is simply a boundary that defines a change in response. This might be detecting the presence of a stimulus versus not (a *detection* threshold), or detecting the difference between two different stimuli (a *discrimination* threshold). For example, how loud does the movie volume have to be for us to hear anything, and how loud does it need to be for us to discriminate the different words being spoken?

Thus, we can distinguish different varieties of threshold. *Absolute thresholds* refer to the minimum stimulus intensity that can be detected. *Difference thresholds* refer to the minimum difference between two stimuli that is noticed. This is often referred to as the *just noticeable difference* (JND). A flip side to the JND is the *point of subjective equality* (PSE), which is the point at which two stimuli cease to be distinguishable.

As described so far, a threshold might be seen as a simple step. That is, there is some range of stimulus intensities that are not detected, but once the threshold is crossed, performance changes abruptly so that any further intensity increase results in perfect detection. However, typical data are normally best fitted by a function like that shown in Figure 23.1.

I thank David Rose, who set me on the path to learning about psychophysics and taught me so much; Nigel Woodger for turning my scribbles into the artwork in this chapter; and Michelle Sowden for her always valuable comments on a draft of this chapter.

[1]Interested readers may find Gescheider (1997) and Macmillan and Creelman (2005) useful for furthering their knowledge of psychophysical theory and methods.

DOI: 10.1037/13619-024
APA Handbook of Research Methods in Psychology: Vol. 1. Foundations, Planning, Measures, and Psychometrics, H. Cooper (Editor-in-Chief)

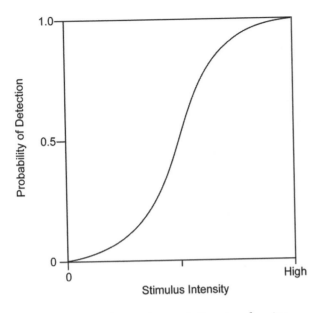

FIGURE 23.1. The psychometric function showing that as stimulus intensity increases so does the probability of detection. However, the relationship is nonlinear. At low intensities, noise dominates leading to a shallower slope, whereas at higher intensities, the response of the system saturates.

As stimulus intensity increases so does the probability of detection. At low intensities, the improvement in detection performance with increasing intensity is relatively slow, but becomes more rapid over a wide range of middle intensities until performance saturates at high intensities. This ogival-shaped *psychometric function* results because our detection of a given stimulus varies from moment to moment because of environmental factors and *noise* within the observer. The latter is assumed to reflect spontaneous random neural activity. At low intensities, the noise is simply greater than the stimulus, which is therefore not detected. As intensity grows, the stimulus may be detected some of the time depending on the noise level at any given point in time and with the probability of detection varying with intensity. As very high intensities are reached, the response of the sensory system ceases to increase. For instance, neurons hit a peak in the frequency of their action potentials. The slope of the psychometric function indicates the acuteness of the sense and the amount of noise in the system. A low noise system will have a very steep function because an increase in stimulus intensity is not swamped by noise.

Weber's Law

One might assume that the absolute size of the difference between two stimuli that can be detected remains constant regardless of the overall level of stimulus intensity. For instance, if we can tell the difference between a 10-gram weight and a 20-gram weight, a difference of 10 grams, we might also assume that we can tell the difference between a 110-gram weight and a 120-gram weight, which is again a 10-gram difference.

Working on the perception of weight, however, Ernst H. Weber (1834/1978) observed that this was not the case. Given a starting weight, Weber explored how much must be added to detect an increase. His observation was that the greater the starting weight the greater the increment in weight necessary to detect a change. He proposed that the ratio of the increment to the starting weight is a constant. Subsequent testing showed that this principle holds across many sensory modalities. As an everyday example of how sensory dimensions are compressed at large values, just think of how much brighter the headlights of a car appear at night than those same lights appear during the daytime. A much brighter headlight would be required during the daytime to have the same apparent brightness as a standard headlight does at night.

Weber's observations were formalized in what Gustav Fechner (1860/1966) called *Weber's Law*: $\Delta I / I = k$, in which I is the background stimulus intensity, ΔI is the change in intensity required to produce a just noticeable difference, and k is the resultant constant ratio. The value of k remains constant across most stimulus intensities but tends to increase at very low intensities and also deviates at very high intensities. Although Weber's Law is applicable across multiple modalities, the value of the Weber fraction varies widely (e.g., .016 for brightness, .033 for weight, .20 for taste intensity and .33 for loudness; see Woodworth & Schlosberg, 1954). A smaller Weber fraction indicates a *keener* sense because even a small change in stimulus intensity relative to the background intensity is noticed.

Fechner's Law

Building on Weber's work, Fechner (1860/1966) suggested that JNDs correspond to sensation (S).

In many respects, this can be understood most clearly when considering Fechner's *parallel law*, which states that "when the sensitivity of two stimuli changes in the same ratio, the perception of their difference will nevertheless remain the same" (p. 250). He rephrased this as "when two stimuli are both perceived as weaker or stronger than before, their difference appears unchanged, if both stimuli would have to be changed in the same ratio to restore them to their previous absolute sensation level" (p. 250). He went on to suggest that arithmetic increases in JND (1, 2, 3, 4 . . . etc.) are a logarithmic function of stimulus intensity scaled by a constant (k) that reflects the Weber fraction for a given sensory dimension. In simple form, Fechner's law can be written as $S = k \log I$. As is the case for Weber's law, Fechner's law compresses the dimension of stimulus intensity relative to increases in sensation such that ever-larger increases in intensity are required to yield the same change in sensation. Fechner went on to develop a set of methods for measuring changes in sensation that have become known as the classical psychophysical methods.

THE CLASSICAL PSYCHOPHYSICAL METHODS

Method of Adjustment

The *method of adjustment* is the simplest approach to measuring a threshold. For a detection threshold, the observer is given the means to adjust the intensity of the stimulus up and down (e.g., via a pair of buttons or a dial much like a volume control or heating thermostat) until he or she reports that it is just detectable and the setting is recorded at that point. For a difference threshold, the observer adjusts the intensity of a stimulus relative to some standard until it appears to be just different. The intensity of the stimulus as high or low at the start can be systematically varied so that sometimes the stimulus is not detectable (or different) to start with, requiring the observer to increase intensity, whereas other times it is clearly detectable (or different) to start with and the observer typically begins by reducing stimulus intensity. Method of adjustment is a very quick and easy way to get an estimate of a

threshold. However, it suffers from potential bias. The setting that is recorded by the observer will vary as a function of his or her own subjective criterion for reporting the stimulus. Some observers may not be confident in reporting their detection of a stimulus until it is beyond doubt, whereas others may be happy to report a much less obvious change in sensation as detection of the stimulus. Even a single observer's criterion may change over time, for instance, they may gain confidence as they become familiar with the procedure and so become more willing to classify very weak signals positively.

Response Mode

When considering the impact of the observer's criterion, it is useful to think about the mode of response. If a stimulus is presented on every trial and an observer is simply required to report whether they can detect it or not—a *yes–no* judgment—then an observer who is determined to be really good at the task can simply report that they detect the stimulus on every trial regardless of what they actually perceive. They may well convince themselves that they are always detecting the stimulus. One way to avoid this is to insert catch trials on which no stimulus is presented and keep track of how frequently the observer reports a stimulus even when none is presented. These data can be combined with correct detections using the *theory of signal detection* to yield further measures of performance, as discussed later in this chapter. An alternative to inserting catch trials is to require the observer to make forced-choice responses. In a *spatial-forced-choice* task, stimuli are presented at two or more different spatial locations and the observer is forced to report which location contains the target stimulus. In a *temporal-forced-choice* task, two or more stimuli are presented in successive intervals (signaled for instance by a concurrent noise) at the same spatial location and the observer is required to report which interval contained the target stimulus. The observer's performance can then be compared relative to chance, which varies as a function of the number of presentation locations or intervals (n) such that it will be 100%/n. Hence, chance performance will be 50% in a two-alternative-forced-choice (2AFC).

Forced-choice methods are generally preferred because they guard against the possible biasing effects of an observer's internal response criterion. They will often yield somewhat different estimates of threshold to yes–no methods. Indeed, observers are often surprised to find that their performance in a forced-choice task is above chance even though they perceive themselves to be guessing and report that they cannot detect the stimulus. If thresholds were instead measured using, say, method of adjustment, as described, many observers would require significantly more sensory evidence before they would be prepared to report detecting (or discriminating) a stimulus. This is one reason that method of adjustment often yields higher estimates of threshold relative to other methods that use forced-choice decisions. I will return to the application of forced-choice approaches in a variety of psychophysical methods after next describing the method of limits.

Method of Limits

The *method of limits* is similar to the method of adjustment except that the experimenter has control over stimulus intensity and adjusts the stimulus intensity in one direction only in a series. For instance, in an *ascending series*, to measure a detection threshold, the stimulus intensity is initially set to some low, undetectable, level and then increased in steps until the observer reports detecting the stimulus. In a *descending series*, the stimulus intensity is initially set very high and then is decreased in equal steps until the observer reports that the stimulus became undetectable. The experimenter typically runs a number of ascending and descending series, and the threshold is determined as the average of the points at which an observer's responses change from not detecting the stimulus to detection in an ascending series and from detection to nondetection in a descending series. To measure difference thresholds, the experimenter increases or decreases the intensity of the stimulus relative to the standard in ascending and descending series, respectively. The method of limits is generally a quick and easy-to-use procedure that yields quite reliable estimates of threshold, provided simple precautions are taken, such as varying the starting intensity in a series so that observers cannot simply keep track of how many step changes

have occurred before changing their response because they *expect* to have reached their threshold. It is also common to find that estimates of threshold are higher from ascending series than from descending series because of a tendency for observers to overshoot in the direction of the series because of their *habitually* responding no or yes, respectively. The other drawback of both method of adjustment and limits is that they do not provide much information about the relation between stimulus intensity and sensation other than in the region of the threshold. In other words, we cannot readily derive a psychometric function from these data, which, in turn, means that we cannot, for instance, determine the impact of noise on a given sensory continuum. However, the method of constant stimuli does provide this information.

Method of Constant Stimuli

In *method of constant stimuli*, typically, between five and 10 fixed stimulus intensities are chosen and presented in random order a large number of times (e.g., 50 presentations at each intensity). To some extent a trade-off can be made between the number of intensities and the number of stimulus presentations at each. The selection of the intensities to be tested can be guided by initial measurements using a technique such as the method of adjustment or limits to get in the right ballpark. Experience is also invaluable here. In a forced-choice task, the experimenter should aim to select a set of intensities that together span the range of percentage of correct responses above chance and below 100%. For a detection threshold, the observer reports the presentation location or interval at which they detect the stimulus on each trial. For a difference threshold, they report which of a standard stimulus and a test stimulus is greater (e.g., more blue, larger, louder, higher pitched). This method yields data that can be fit by a function like that shown in Figure 23.1, which is a cumulative Gaussian function. Once the function has been fit, the threshold can be estimated as the stimulus intensity (or difference) at which detection (or discrimination) performance reaches some criterion level, such as 75% correct detection. The influence of noise can be determined by measuring the slope of the psychometric function, as previously described. Note that separate estimates of the impact of external noise from the environment and internal noise from the observer are not available from the standard psychometric function. This problem has been tackled through the use of *external noise* methods, which are described later in this chapter. The method of constant stimuli provides a highly reliable estimate of threshold and noise. In particular, it is the large number of trials at different stimulus intensities that allows us to plot a full psychometric function and so estimate noise as described. Conversely, when we are only interested in estimating threshold the large number of trials renders the method of constant stimuli inefficient. To improve the reliability and efficiency of threshold measures, experimenters have derived a series of adaptive threshold estimation procedures.

ADAPTIVE METHODS

In many respects *adaptive methods* combine elements of the methods of adjustment and limits and can readily be used in forced-choice designs. The stimulus intensity is adjusted up and down much like the method of adjustment, but in fixed steps under the experimenter's control much like the method of limits. Importantly, the stimulus intensity is adjusted across trials as a function of the observer's previous response(s).

The Staircase Method

One of the simplest adaptive methods is known as the *staircase method* (Cornsweet, 1962). Usually, the initial stimulus intensity is set high so that the stimulus is clearly perceptible. For detection thresholds, on each trial, the observer reports which location or interval contains the stimulus. If he or she correctly detects the stimulus, then the intensity is lowered for the next trial. This procedure continues until the observer is no longer correct, whereupon, on the next trial, the stimulus intensity is increased. This continues until the observer correctly detects the stimulus; after this, on the next trial, intensity is lowered again. The intensity of the stimulus after each of these *turnarounds* is recorded, and after some number of turnarounds (typically 10–15), the

procedure is stopped and threshold is calculated as the average of the stimulus intensities at the turnaround points. For difference thresholds, the observer reports which of a standard stimulus and a test stimulus is greater (e.g., more blue, larger, louder, higher pitched), and depending on whether he or she is correct, the difference between the standard and test stimulus is decreased or increased respectively.

A critical issue in staircase methods is selection of the step size for changes in intensity. If the step size is too small, it will require many trials before a change in response occurs; therefore, completing sufficient turnarounds to estimate threshold can take a long time. Conversely, if the step size is too large, the observer's responses may swing from detection to nondetection, yielding an imprecise estimate of threshold. One trick is to begin the staircase with relatively large step sizes until the first few turnarounds have occurred and then to switch to smaller step sizes for the remainder of the run. Threshold can then be calculated on the basis of the turnarounds following the switch to smaller steps. This approach quickly gets the staircase into the threshold zone, improving efficiency, while basing threshold estimates on smaller stimulus changes, thereby improving reliability.

One problem with staircase methods is that the observer can predict the next stimulus on the basis of their most recent judgment. For instance, if they clearly detect the stimulus, they can anticipate a reduction in intensity on the next trial and this expectation may influence their performance. Interleaving two or more staircases, randomly, can prevent this anticipation.

Transformed Up–Down Rules

Sometimes a simple staircase used with a forced-choice task can yield significant underestimates of threshold. This is because a series of correct guesses can result in a stimulus intensity that is well below threshold. Thereafter, if the observer continues to guess correctly some of the time, a series of turnaround values will be recorded that are all well below threshold. Conversely, overestimates of threshold are unlikely because above threshold the stimulus will be obvious to the observer.

One way to avoid potential underestimates of threshold is through the use of *transformed up–down* rules (see Levitt, 1971). For instance, the one-up two-down rule increases the stimulus intensity after a single incorrect response, but it decreases the stimulus intensity only after two correct responses in a row. This rule has the effect of making it harder for the stimulus intensity to drift well below threshold. Increasing the number of alternatives in a forced-choice task can have similar benefits.

Different rules converge on threshold estimates for different values of percent correct responding. For instance, the one-up two-down rule estimates threshold at 70.7% correct responding, whereas a one-up three-down rule estimates threshold at 79.4% correct responding. Thus, transformed up–down rules allow for sampling detection or discrimination performance at a range of stimulus intensities, depending on the rule. In reality, the estimate of threshold often does not converge perfectly on the intended percent correct estimation point; it has been shown that the use of asymmetric step sizes for up and down intensity changes can improve convergence (García-Pérez, 1998).

Although not ideal, adaptive methods are sometimes used to estimate a psychometric function. The percentage of correct responses at a variety of stimulus intensities can be plotted because as the adaptive procedure tracks up and down, a range of stimulus intensities are presented. Because the number of observations at stimulus intensities farther away from threshold will be fewer, the estimated function is likely to be quite error prone.

Best PEST, QUEST, and ZEST

The adaptive methods described so far set the intensity of the stimulus on the current trial as a function of, at most, the last few responses. Best PEST, QUEST, and ZEST (King-Smith, Grigsby, Vingrys, Benes, & Supowit, 1994; Pentland, 1980; Watson & Pelli, 1983) are different in that they take account of all of the observer's responses up to the current trial to determine the intensity of the next stimulus. In these methods, the experimenter sets the form of the psychometric function (e.g., ogival, logistic, Weibull). In Best PEST and QUEST, following the presentation of each stimulus, a calculation estimates the most likely threshold stimulus intensity by determining the position along the signal intensity axis of the psychometric function that best accounts for the responses thus far. The slope of this function is fixed as a parameter value supplied by the experimenter. In addition, in QUEST, the experimenter provides an initial distribution of probabilities for the threshold at each of a range of stimulus intensities. Because the best fitting psychometric function is recalculated after every response using all the preceding responses, these procedures make use of all of the available data; this greatly improves their efficiency relative to other adaptive methods. Best PEST assumes that the psychometric function is logistic, whereas QUEST and ZEST use a Weibull function. Furthermore, whereas QUEST sets the current best estimate of threshold to be the mode of the distribution of probabilities of threshold stimulus intensity, ZEST uses the mean of this distribution.

Estimates of threshold made using these adaptive methods can be terminated after some fixed number of trials or, ideally, when the error associated with the estimate falls to within a predetermined acceptable level.

SIGNAL DETECTION THEORY

In the previous sections, we have considered various ways of estimating a threshold. We have also discussed the impact of noise on an observer's sensitivity and noted the desirability of using experimental designs that reduce the potential for an observer's response bias to influence the estimate of threshold. Signal detection theory (SDT) comes at these issues from a different standpoint. Rather than attempting to eliminate response bias, it provides measures that separately estimate an observer's sensitivity to a stimulus and his or her bias.

To think about the usefulness of SDT, let us return to the movie example that opened this chapter. When you enter the movie theater to find your friend, you might want to be very sure that you have correctly identified her before asking everyone to move out of the way as you shuffle along the row of seats to meet her. In SDT terms, correctly identifying your friend would be called a *hit* or *true positive*. A number of other possibilities could arise, however.

You might incorrectly identify someone as your friend (in SDT, a *false alarm* or *false positive*) only realizing your mistake when you get halfway along the row, causing you great embarrassment as you have to turn around and shuffle back past everyone. You might completely fail to recognize your friend in the dim lighting despite looking at her (in SDT, a *miss* or *false negative*). And, of course, through engaging in the process of searching for your friend, there will be many other faces that you correctly discount (in SDT, *correct rejections* or *true negatives*).

In an ideal world, each time you find yourself in this scenario, you would want to identify your friend and only your friend as being the person you have come to meet. In SDT, this type of performance would be characterized as showing high *sensitivity* (you always correctly identify your friend) and high *specificity* (you never mistakenly identify someone else as your friend). In reality, there are many reasons why this might not be the case. You might head for each empty seat in turn until eventually you find yourself in the one that happens to be next to your friend. Following this strategy, you would always find your friend (good sensitivity), but your specificity would be abysmal. You might be uncomfortable standing in the way of people trying to watch the movie while you search for your friend and make a dive for the first likely looking person, leading to errors in identification, or you might decide that it does not matter if you end up sitting with someone else; it could turn out to be fun. In other words, the relative *payoffs* of taking the time to find and sit with your friend as opposed to somewhere else may influence your decision. Furthermore, if there are very few people watching the movie, you might be more willing to take a chance and quickly head for someone that you think is your friend (the *probability* is higher) than if there are many people. These examples illustrate an important point of SDT. An observer's behavior is a function of both an observation and a decision about whether that observation matches the searched-for signal; the decision will be influenced by such factors as the payoff of different decisions and the probability of a signal. As well as being an important way of separately considering observer sensitivity and response bias, SDT is very useful when we want to analyze performance under conditions that reflect real-world situations better than a forced-choice psychophysical experiment can.

Let us now formalize the description somewhat. As noted, in a detection or discrimination task, the stimulation experienced will be a function of noise and potentially a signal (the target stimulus or difference). The noise is assumed to be random, giving rise to a Gaussian distribution. Thus, we can plot two distributions showing the probability that an observed stimulus is the signal given that either noise or a signal plus noise stimulus was presented, as a function of the sensory stimulation (see Figure 23.2).

The presence of a signal adds a constant value to the random noise distribution; hence, both distributions have the same shape. A strong signal will lead to a large separation between the two distributions (compare Figure 23.2c and 23.2d). The distance between the mean of the two distributions represents the sensitivity of the observer (d'). When the distributions overlap, it is difficult to distinguish whether a stimulus contains a signal or is pure noise. When they are widely separated, it becomes easier to determine when a stimulus includes the signal.

The position of the line marking the observer's decision criterion (β) indicates the strength of the *sensory evidence* required for a yes response. To the left of the line the observer will respond "no," and to the right they will respond "yes" (Figure 23.2). Depending on whether a signal was presented, this leads to four possible classifications of the observer's decision. Hits are equal to the proportion of the area under the signal plus noise distribution to the right of the criterion, whereas misses are the proportion to the left. Together they sum to 1. False alarms are equal to the proportion of the area under the noise distribution to the right of the criterion, whereas correct rejections are the proportion to the left. Again, together they sum to 1. Because *P(Hit)* and *P(Miss)* sum to 1, we need only consider one of these values, conventionally the hit rate. And likewise the same is true for *P(False Alarm)* and *P(Correct Rejection)*; conventionally, we consider just the false alarm rate. If the observer varies their criterion, the probability of hits and false alarms will vary. With a low value of β, the observer's hit rate will increase but so too will the false alarm rate,

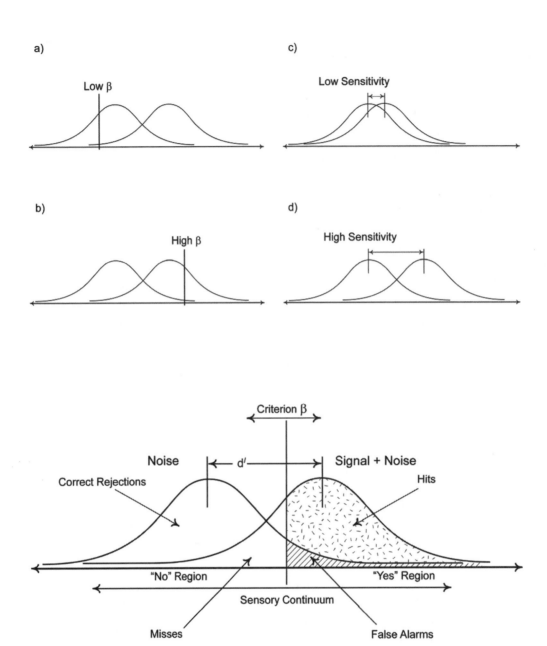

FIGURE 23.2. Noise and signal plus noise distributions in signal detection theory. Insets (a) and (b) show that moving the criterion varies both the proportion of hits and false alarms whereas insets (c) and (d) show that increasing the separation of the distributions at a given criterion increases only hits consistent with an increase in sensitivity.

whereas with a high value of β, the opposite will be true. On the other hand, an increase in sensitivity will shift the signal plus noise distribution to the right, increasing the hit rate but leaving the false alarm rate unchanged for a given criterion. As noted in our movie example, an observer's criterion will vary as a function of the payoff and signal probability; hence, we can obtain a series of paired *P*(*Hit*) and *P*(*False Alarm*) values by manipulating these

across conditions in an experiment. Plotting these pairs of values against each other yields a *receiver operating characteristic* (ROC) curve, such as the examples shown in Figure 23.3.

A more efficient way to get a series of paired *P*(*Hit*) and *P*(*False Alarm*) values than running multiple conditions, is to ask the observer to rate the confidence of their decisions on, say, a 5-point scale (cf. Macmillan & Creelman, 2005). Pairs of hit and

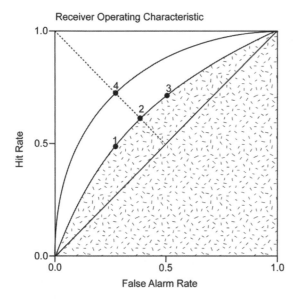

Receiver Operating Characteristic

Hit Rate

False Alarm Rate

FIGURE 23.3.   The receiver operating characteristic (ROC) curve. Points 1, 2, and 3 lie on the same ROC curve and indicate variation in criterion at a constant sensitivity. Point 4 lies on a second ROC curve that lies above the first curve indicating greater sensitivity. For instance, point 4 has the same false alarm rate as point 1 but a higher hit rate.

false alarm rate values can then be calculated by varying which ratings are scored as a hit. For instance, if a confidence rating of 1 is total confidence that a signal was presented and 5 is very unconfident, we can score hits as only correct responses to a signal when it was presented and confidence was 1. Then we can calculate another value of hits as correct responses to signal when it was presented and confidence was 1 or 2 and so on. We can do this similarly for the false alarm rate on noise-only trials. This procedure effectively simulates moving from a stringent (high β) to a lax (low β) criterion using the same set of data.

In Figure 23.3, we can see that a change in criterion will move along a given ROC curve (e.g., from point 1 to 2 or 3), such that both hits and false alarms will change. An increase in sensitivity will shift the whole ROC curve up and leftward, so it is possible to have an increase in hits with no change in false alarms. Thus, the difference between point 1 and point 4 represents an increase in sensitivity. The more the curve shifts toward the top left corner of the graph the higher the sensitivity, with perfect sensitivity corresponding to a hit rate of 1 and a false

alarm rate of 0. A useful measure of observer performance is the area under the ROC curve termed A_z, which is the shaded portion under the lower ROC curve in Figure 23.3.

Signal detection theory provides important information about observer detection and decision behavior, and like classical threshold theory, it assumes that performance will be a function of the strength of the signal and random noise. To characterize observer performance, however, it is useful to separate the extent to which it is limited by variance in the observer's detection and decision processes from variance in the stimulus itself. One method to achieve this is through the use of external noise methods.

External Noise Methods

A number of methods have been developed to distinguish the separate contributions of noise that is internal to the observer and external noise (cf. Lu & Dosher, 2008); I briefly summarize two methods here.

The *equivalent input noise method* adds fixed samples of external noise of increasing amplitude to the signal in order to estimate the amount of internal noise that has an impact on the observer's performance. Conducting an experiment such as this will yield a curve like that shown in Figure 23.4.

When the levels of external noise are lower than the level of internal noise, the external noise will have little impact on performance. However, as levels of external noise exceed internal noise levels, they will increasingly determine observer performance because they will mostly determine the signal-to-noise ratio. The point at which an elbow is apparent in the graph shown in Figure 23.4 is the point at which external noise is equivalent to internal noise. Thereafter, external noise exceeds internal noise and begins to have a significant impact on performance. Hence, the amount of added external noise at the elbow point provides an estimate of the observer's internal noise.

An alternative method to estimate internal noise is the *double-pass agreement* technique. In this method, a set of stimuli, each composed of a signal and an external noise sample, are presented twice. The stimuli are exactly the same on both presentations.

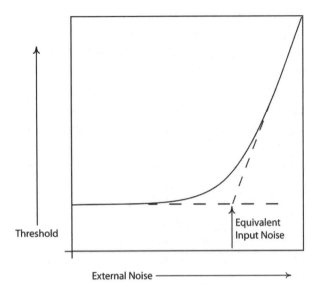

Threshold

External Noise ⟶

FIGURE 23.4. Estimating internal noise using the equivalent input noise technique. The elbow in the graph reflects the point at which external noise begins to have a significant impact on detection. At that point, external noise is equivalent to internal noise.

Because each external noise source is presented twice, any variation in observer performance across presentations will be due to the impact of internal noise; the greater the variation the greater the internal noise.

Ideal Observer Analysis

A further question concerns how effectively an observer makes use of all of the available information in a stimulus, known as *efficiency*. To do this, the performance of the observer is compared with that of an *ideal observer* that makes use of all the available information. An ideal observer is limited only by the properties of the stimulus, whereas a human observer may be limited by his or her task strategy and by internal noise. The closer the human observer's performance is to that of the ideal observer the less their performance is limited by these factors.

The nature of the ideal observer will vary depending on the task. To take one example, we can consider work that has compared the efficiency of human observers on face and letter identification tasks (Gold, Bennett, & Sekuler, 1999). Gold et al. (1999) presented face and letter stimuli that had

been spatial-frequency filtered in various bandwidths. Visual noise was added to the stimuli, and the ability of observers to identify the face and letter stimuli in the different bandwidths was measured as a function of the contrast energy of the signal. An ideal observer for this task calculates the cross-correlation between the face or letter template image and the signal plus noise stimulus and chooses the template with the highest correlation. Gold et al. found that the efficiency of the human observers was much better for the letter than face stimuli, which prompted them to explore the potential limitations of the mechanisms for face identification. The use of external noise methods and ideal observer analysis can make for a powerful combination to explore the various potential limitations on observer performance.

Reverse Correlation

As noted in our consideration of signal detection theory, sometimes an observer will report detecting a stimulus even when no stimulus is presented. One possible reason for this behavior is that the strength of the noise alone is sufficient to convince the observer that a signal is present. Starting with his doctoral thesis work in 1967, Ahumada (cf. Ahumada, 2002) explored the characteristics of an observer's filters that mediate detection or discrimination of a signal through the derivation of *noise classification images*. The essence of this technique can be distilled to an experiment in which observers are led to believe that on a proportion of trials they will be presented with a signal, say the image of a ghost, but they are actually presented with a noise sample alone on every trial. The experimenter keeps track of the noise samples that lead to the observer reporting a ghost and those that lead to a signal absent response. After a sufficient number of trials (in the thousands), average noise images can be computed for yes and no response trials, and the difference between these images can be calculated. This yields a classification image that reveals the observer's internal template of the searched-for signal, the virtual ghost in the machine (see Figure 23.5). This is informative because it provides information about the features of the signal to which the observer attends and those that he or she ignores in making his or her decision.

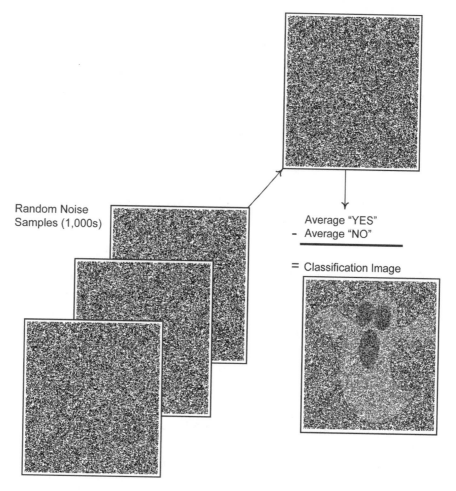

Random Noise
Samples (1,000s)

Average "YES"
- Average "NO"

= Classification Image

FIGURE 23.5. Schematic example of a classification image derived using reverse correlation. The observer classifies many random noise samples according to whether a signal (a ghost) is present. In this example, a signal is never actually presented. The difference between the average "yes" and "no" images yields a classification image revealing the observer's perceptual template, in this case, the virtual ghost in the machine.

DIRECT SCALING METHODS

I opened this chapter by considering the measurement of thresholds for the detection and discrimination of stimuli. However, much of human perceptual experience is not about threshold stimuli but instead is about making sense of stimuli that are well above threshold. Around threshold, observers' responses are probabilistic, whereas at suprathreshold values (above threshold), observers become more deterministic because of the diminishing effects of internal noise as stimulus intensity grows. The psychophysicist Stanley Stevens (1957) explored the relation between the intensity of a stimulus and the strength of sensation. He devised methods that

sought to *directly* measure the strength of sensation, and these methods have often been used with suprathreshold stimuli. These methods are direct in the sense that observers are simply asked to provide an estimate of the strength of the stimulus rather than asked to make some detection or discrimination responses that are used to infer sensitivity to the stimulus from the proportion of correct responses. Stevens suggested that there are two general classes of perceptual continua. The first he termed *prothetic*, which refers to continua that vary in quantity (e.g., loudness). The second he termed *metathetic*, which refers to stimuli that vary in quality (e.g., hue and spatial position), that is, the what and where of stimulation. Prothetic continua were hypothesized to reflect an additive physiological process such that greater stimulus intensity increases neural activity. Metathetic continua were hypothesized to reflect a substitutive process such that changes in a stimulus activate different neural populations.

Various methods have been applied to achieve direct estimates of stimulus strength, including ratio estimation, ratio production, magnitude estimation, and magnitude production. Probably the most widely used method has been *magnitude estimation*. In this method, observers are presented with a standard stimulus and are asked to assign a number to indicate its strength (a modulus), or they are given a preassigned value by the experimenter. They are then shown further stimuli and asked to rate their strength relative to the standard. Thus, a stimulus that seems half as strong should be assigned a number half that given to the standard, whereas a stimulus twice as strong as the standard should be given a value that is twice that given to the standard. By systematically varying the intensity (I) of the stimulus relative to the standard, it is possible to plot a function relating stimulus intensity to the strength of sensation (S). Averaged over observers, the data for prothetic continua are often fit well by a power function of the form $S = I^a$ such that strength of sensation varies with stimulus intensity raised to some power (a). The power–law relation between stimulus intensity and strength of sensation is similar to Weber and Fechner's laws in that stimulus intensity is considered in ratio terms. In addition, the power law means that strength of sensation is also considered in ratio terms such that equal ratios of stimulation correlate with equal ratios of sensation. The exponent observed for the power function varies widely across sensory dimensions with values, for example, of .33 for brightness, .67 for loudness, and 3.5 for electric shock (Stevens, 1975).

One query about standard magnitude estimation methods concerns whether observers are able to correctly assign numbers to stimuli of different magnitude. To address this issue, *cross-modality matching* methods were developed. In these methods, the observer is asked to adjust the strength of a stimulus from a second modality to that of a stimulus

presented in the first modality, for example, adjusting the intensity of light to match the loudness of a noise. By varying the stimulus intensity, a graph of the values from each modality plotted against each other can be compared with that found for each modality obtained from standard magnitude estimation methods, providing an indication of the validity of numerical estimates of magnitude.

Direct scaling methods have been widely applied both in psychophysics and other fields of psychology. For instance, the perceived seriousness of a theft is a power function of the amount of money stolen (Sellin & Wolfgang, 1964; but see Pease, Ireson & Thorpe, 1974).

Overall, these methods have proven useful for exploring the relation between stimulation and sensation at suprathreshold levels, but the validity of the power law has been questioned on a variety of grounds. Further, it has been suggested that neither Fechner's or Steven's laws may explain the psychophysical data in their current forms. Krueger (1989) has suggested that only by modifying the power law can we adequately explain the relation between stimulus intensity and strength of sensation.

PRACTICAL CONSIDERATIONS

In addition to knowledge about the theory and techniques of psychophysics, the experiments take patience and care. If we are to understand the relation between the intensity of the stimulus and the strength of sensation, it is essential that the properties of the stimulus are carefully controlled. Often, this will require the experimenter to devote considerable time to devising or selecting a method of stimulus generation and then carefully calibrating and measuring stimulus properties. In my experience, this is time well spent. Unintended variation in the stimulus will lead to unintended variation in the observer's sensations. At best, unintended variation is a source of external noise. At worst, it can lead to an unintended systematic bias in the observed responses that can invalidate the conclusions drawn from an experiment.

As well as the time taken to set up a psychophysical experiment, the time taken to participate in them can be significant. By their nature, many of these experiments require large numbers of repetitions of very simple tasks, such as the many forced-choice trials that might be necessary to measure a set of thresholds. Doing the same thing many times over is a recipe for boredom, so psychophysical experimenters should select their observers with care. Many psychophysicists have found that they can be reliable observers, and many papers have been published using data from the experimenter and a few other hardy volunteers (e.g., postdoctoral researchers in the lab). In fact, we have often thought that some work on the personality traits of the optimal psychophysical observer could pay dividends for the field at large. But often we need to collect data on larger groups of people who are blind to the expected findings. For such observers, simple tactics can make the task more palatable and help them to maintain concentration. For instance, we can appeal to their competitive instinct by providing various kinds of feedback (e.g., trial by trial and summary block feedback), we can offer them rewards for good performance (which might just be a reinforcing sound or some chocolate), and we can allow them to self-pace their trials so that they can rest whenever they need to. Furthermore, considering the comfort of your observer is essential when they are spending a long time sitting around doing a boring repetitive task. In such situations, it is very likely that they will begin to notice sources of discomfort, such as the room temperature or the chair they are sitting on, and these distractions will take their attention away from your task and add noise to your data.

CONCLUSION

Psychophysics, as a named subdiscipline, has been around for 150 years. During that time, it has given birth to much of modern experimental psychology and the methods and theories of psychophysics have influenced psychological science in general. In particular, psychophysics gives us a set of tools that provides exquisitely sensitive information about the nature and limits of human sensation and, at a fundamental level, gives us the means to begin understanding the relation between our physical and mental world. It is remarkable for the way that it has

revealed so much about our internal processes without ever directly observing them.

References

Ahumada, A. J. (2002). Classification image weights and internal noise level estimation. *Journal of Vision, 2*, 121–131. doi:10.1167/2.1.8

Cornsweet, T. N. (1962). The staircase method in psychophysics. *American Journal of Psychology, 75*, 485–491. doi:10.2307/1419876

Fechner, G. T. (1966). *Elements of psychophysics* (H. E. Adler, Trans.; D. H. Howes & E. G. Boring, Eds.). New York, NY: Holt, Rinehart & Winston. (Original work published 1860)

García-Pérez, M. A. (1998). Forced-choice staircases with fixed step sizes: Asymptotic and small sample sizes. *Vision Research, 38*, 1861–1881. doi:10.1016/S0042-6989(97)00340-4

Gescheider, G. A. (1997). *Psychophysics: The fundamentals* (3rd ed.). Mahwah, NJ: Erlbaum.

Gold, J., Bennett, P. J., & Sekuler, A. B. (1999). Identification of band-pass filtered faces and letters by human and ideal observers. *Vision Research, 39*, 3537–3560. doi:10.1016/S0042-6989(99)00080-2

King-Smith, P. E., Grigsby, S. S., Vingrys, A. J., Benes, S. C., & Supowit, A. (1994). Efficient and unbiased modifications of the QUEST threshold method: Theory, simulations, experimental evaluation and practical implementation. *Vision Research, 34*, 885–912. doi:10.1016/0042-6989(94)90039-6

Krueger, L. E. (1989). Reconciling Fechner and Stevens: Towards a unified psychophysical law. *Behavioral and Brain Sciences, 12*, 251–320. doi:10.1017/S0140525X0004855X

Levitt, H. L. (1971). Transformed up–down methods in psychophysics. *Journal of the Acoustical Society of America, 49*, 467–477. doi:10.1121/1.1912375

Lu, Z., & Dosher, B. A. (2008). Characterizing observers using external noise and observer models: Assessing internal representations with external noise. *Psychological Review, 115*, 44–82. doi:10.1037/0033-295X.115.1.44

Macmillan, N. A., & Creelman, C. D. (2005). *Detection theory: A user's guide* (2nd ed.). Mahwah, NJ: Erlbaum.

Pease, K., Ireson, J., & Thorpe, J. (1974). Additivity assumptions in the measurements of delinquency. *British Journal of Criminology, 14*, 256–263.

Pentland, A. (1980). Maximum likelihood estimation: The best PEST. *Perception and Psychophysics, 28*, 377–379. doi:10.3758/BF03204398

Sellin, T., & Wolfgang, M. E. (1964). *The measurement of delinquency*. New York, NY: Wiley.

Stevens, S. S. (1957). On the psychophysical law. *Psychological Review, 64,* 153–181. doi:10.1037/h0046162

Stevens, S. S. (1975). *Psychophysics: Introduction to its perceptual, neural, and social prospects.* New York, NY: Wiley.

Watson, A. B., & Pelli, D. G. (1983). QUEST: A Bayesian adaptive psychometric method. *Perception and Psychophysics, 33,* 113–120. doi:10.3758/BF03202828

Weber, E. H. (1978). *The sense of touch* (H. E. Ross & D. J. Murray, Trans.). London, England: Academic Press. (Original work published 1834)

Woodworth, R. S., & Schlosberg, H. (1954). *Experimental psychology* (3rd ed.). London, England: Methuen.

Measures in Psychophysiology

CHAPTER 24

PERIPHERAL PHYSIOLOGICAL MEASURES OF PSYCHOLOGICAL CONSTRUCTS

Louis G. Tassinary, Ursula Hess, and Luis M. Carcoba

For well over a century the noninvasive recording of peripheral physiological activity has enriched our understanding of embodied and embedded psychological processes. For the past 2 decades such measures have, in addition, afforded the necessary context for interpreting the significance of direct measures of neural activity. In this chapter, we review the state of the art on the psychophysiological measurement of activity in the skeletomotor, sudomotor, and cardiovascular systems.

The scientific roots of modern psychophysiology as well as cognitive, social, and affective neuroscience can be traced directly back to the second volume of Gustav Fechner's famous *Elemente der Psychophysik* (1860), with pre-echos earlier in the 19th century (see Tassinary, Geen, Cacioppo, & Swartzbaugh, 1989), and even as far back as the 18th and 17th centuries (see Geen & Tassinary, 2002). In this seminal volume, Fechner explored conceptually the functional relationship between the intensity of the sensation and the magnitude of brain activity, albeit limited by the paucity of empirical tools and methods. In seeking the elemental nature of consciousness, Wundt (1897) elaborated on these speculations, postulating that the contents of consciousness were divided into objective contents (sensations) and subjective contents (simple feelings). These simple feelings or affective elements differed significantly from sensations because they explicitly represented the psychological response to sensations, and they were characterized as forming a single interconnected manifold defined by the dimensions of unpleasantness–pleasantness,

strain–relaxation, and excitation–quiescence. There was intense debate throughout the early years of the 20th century regarding such formulations, ultimately ending in a theoretical cul-de-sac (see Gardiner, Metcalf, & Beebe-Center, 1937). Yet this framework, related but distinct from the one proposed independently by Carl Lange (1885) and William James (1884), fostered the use of peripheral physiological measures in psychological experiments because it explicitly linked specific changes in physiological function with each of the three dimensions of feeling. Wundt (1904) minimized such relationships, stating that observable processes "are merely indications and not in the slightest degree proofs. Where introspection does not show univocally the existence of a definite feeling, such a feeling can naturally not be deduced from objective events, no matter how numerous they may be" (p. 272). Nonetheless, the James–Lange theory spurred research on peripheral physiological measures of psychological states and processes, rationalized the search for lawful relationships between psychological constructs and physiological activity, and established the goal of finding invariant psychophysiological signatures. The methods, analyses, instruments, and theories have become vastly more sophisticated over the past century, yet the fundamental quest remains remarkably unchanged (see Cacioppo, Tassinary, & Berntson, 2007).

Despite the dizzying array of technological advances, the use of traditional peripheral psychophysiological measures continue to play a critical role in the interpretation of brain activity and

DOI: 10.1037/13619-025
APA Handbook of Research Methods in Psychology: Vol. 1. Foundations, Planning, Measures, and Psychometrics, H. Cooper (Editor-in-Chief)

overt behavior. To paraphrase the pioneering neuro-scientist Roger W. Sperry, the fundamental anatomical plan and working principles of the nervous system are understandable only by acknowledging that its principal function is the coordinated control of the body (Sperry, 1952).

INFERENTIAL CHALLENGES

Notably, our ability to measure and decipher a wide array of physiological events at multiple temporal and spatial scales expands almost daily and has afforded the routine measurement not only of brain activity but also of simultaneous activity throughout the entire nervous system, both within and between individuals (e.g., *hyperscanning*; see Montague et al., 2002). The search for unobtrusive ambulatory monitoring also continues unabated (Darrow, 1934; Poh, Swenson, & Picard, 2010). The interpretation of such measurements continues to spark controversy, however, regarding not only the simple reliability and validity of such measurements but also and more significantly their precise psychological significance.

Physiological changes are the product of an organism's ongoing adaptation to its environment, reflecting a large number of processes, only some of which are related to a given experimental manipulation. Put differently, observed changes in physiology, as with behavior, are routinely polysemous. For example, equivalent increases in heart rate (HR) may be due to sympathetic activation, parasympathetic withdrawal, or coactivation (Berntson, Cacioppo, & Quigley, 1993) each of which imply different psychological antecedents. In general, psychophysiological measures are multiply determined and psychological processes tend to be reflected in more than one measure.

Cacioppo and Tassinary (1990) distinguished four types of relations characterized as quadrants within the bivariate space defined by dimensions of specificity and generality. *Specificity* refers to the coupling between an empirical measurement and a theoretical process, the extent to which the presence or degree of a particular response unequivocally indicates the process in question (high specificity) or reflects the vagaries of many processes (low specificity). *Generality* refers to the extent to which such

relations are context bound, varying between context-dependent (low generality) to context-independent (high generality). Context-dependent multiply determined relations are referred to as *outcomes*. If it can be established that the measure has sufficient generality, the measure is a *concomitant*. If it can be shown that—at least within a particular measurement context—the measure is specific, it is a *marker*. And, if the measure is both specific and context independent, it is an *invariant*. The value of this taxonomy lies principally in its ability to simultaneously highlight inferential limitations and guide future research.

To illustrate, an outcome relation precludes the absence of a specific response being used to infer the absence of a specific psychological state. For example, it has been known for more than a decade that incipient brow furrowing detected via facial electromyography can be associated with anger (e.g., Dimberg & Öhman, 1996); however, the lack of such activity does not support the inference that the person is not angry. Similarly, the presence of increased muscle activity in the brow region does not unequivocally indicate anger. It may, for example, be due to increased mental effort (Pope & Smith, 1994) or even photophobia (Stringham, Fuld, & Wenzel, 2003). The primary means to avoid erroneous inferences is via experimental design; that is, honing our scientific understanding through creative experimental control coupled with careful multivariate measurement, building always upon the foundation of prior research.

GENERAL ISSUES

When attempting to infer psychological states or processes on the basis of observed physiological events, a small set of issues always demand explicit attention, issues that remain the bane of the psychophysiologist. They are baselines, ambient noise, and artifacts.

Baselines

Physiological data tend to be characterized by significant variability, both within and between individuals. Resting HR, for example, can vary between 40 beats per minute for a marathon runner to more than 100 beats per minute for an obese individual with a history of smoking. And the spontaneous recall of significant events (e.g., a forgotten appointment) may affect physiological responses across a series of trials. As a result, it is common in most research reports to find the analysis of responses "corrected" in some manner using baseline data. Such corrections range from quite sophisticated (e.g., longitudinal data analysis; see Singer & Willett, 2003) to deceptively simple (i.e., difference scores; see Edwards, 2001). In the latter case, measurements are taken during resting or pretrial periods (baselines), allowing subsequent measurements during experimental trials to be expressed as the difference between the data recorded in response to the stimulus or situation and that recorded during the baseline(s). This correction, however, presupposes that the participant is actually quiescent during the recorded baseline. In reality, participants are often somewhat stressed when first entering a psychophysiology laboratory. Unfamiliarity with the procedures and the environment also lead to increased vigilance. Over time these effects typically diminish. Yet, if resting baselines are taken before adaptation, the baseline measurements may actually be higher than trial levels late in the experiment. Alternatively, if the resting period lasts too long, participants may show relaxation levels that are considerably lower than during normal alertness, thereby inflating difference scores. And if the intertrial intervals are too brief to allow the aftermath of the prior stimulus to dissipate, the carryover effects undermine the presumed stability of the baseline. It is advisable, therefore, to allow sufficient time for participants both to become familiar with the laboratory environment and to recover between trials as well as to create an atmosphere that enables a relaxed attentive state. All of this can be achieved with comfortable, supportive furniture and a pleasant interior design (cf. Kweon, Ulrich, Walker, & Tassinary, 2007), combined with a protocol that respects both the psychological and physiological sequelae of repeated stimulus presentations.

A more sophisticated real-time procedure involves the use of a closed-loop procedure in which the onset of a trial is predicated on an immediately prior quiescent baseline (McHugo & Lanzetta,

1983). Tassinary and Cacioppo (2000) have pointed out that such a requirement may inadvertently shape the participants reactions in ways both undesirable and unknowable. When increased sensitivity is needed in a complex within-subjects design, however, such a procedure may be advisable (e.g., Cacioppo, Petty, & Morris, 1985).

In short, the choice of baseline depends on the specifics of the experimental procedure and the characteristics of the research participants. It is therefore critical to carefully consider the implications of this choice for the validity of the data-based inferences regarding psychological states and processes (see Fishel, Muth, & Hoover, 2007).

Ambient Noise

The ubiquitous bioamplifiers used in psychophysiological research nearly always involve bipolar sensor placements and employ differential amplification. The theory behind such measurement techniques is that any electrical activity common to both sensors is *noise* and any activity unique to a particular sensor is considered *signal*. Filters applied subsequent to the detection and preamplification stages are then used to more precisely restrict the activity passed on to the final amplification stage to the particular physiological signal of interest. Stray noise or unwanted signals can affect either of the two bipolar sensors differently, however, and hence would not be rejected as noise but rather allowed to pass as signal by the amplifier. Said differently, in certain situations, ambient noise or intruders can masquerade as signal. Common sources of noise are transformers; fluorescent lights; heaters; nearby electrical power lines; other physiological events; and, in rare cases, even local radio stations.

Best practices require minimizing noise to the extent possible by identifying and removing sources of interference. If the source can neither be removed nor shielded, it should simply be moved as far as possible from the participant and any cables connected to the participant. For example, unshielded extension or power cords should be replaced with well-shielded cables. Fluorescent lights or halogen lamps emit more noise than either incandescent light bulbs or light-emitting diode (LED) lights and, if problematic, may need to be replaced. Similarly, legacy cathode-ray tube (CRT) monitors emit far more noise than current generation LED monitors and, if possible, should also be replaced or moved a few feet away from the participant. The interference caused by endogenous sources (e.g., electrical potentials originating from the heart interfering with the recording of muscle activity) is typically addressed through sensor placement and filter selection.

Artifacts

Any movement, irrespective of its cause, may lead to observed activity. Forceful movements such as sneezing are usually readily discernible as large synchronized activity across multiple recording channels. Smaller yet stereotyped movements such as blinking and swallowing are similarly discernible. Yet, some movements, such as licking or scratching (i.e., adaptors; Ekman & Friesen, 1969), may generate activity that masquerades as signal. Because the appearance of these movements in the recording is likely fleeting and difficult to characterize or predict, a video record is an essential supplement, allowing the researcher to detect such interlopers and scrub the record accordingly. The ratio of the duration of the trial to the duration of the artifact is typically the primary determinant for whether the trial in question will need to be rejected entirely or the artifact can be excised from the data. Whatever the decision, it is critical to keep a record of the number of times such artifacts occur as their frequency may be coupled with particular experimental conditions or participant characteristics. As with ambient noise, best practices suggest redesigning the experimental protocol, when possible, to reduce the likelihood of artifacts. Unlike ambient noise, the likelihood of artifacts cannot be determined a priori and typically requires pilot testing.

Research Participant Considerations

In contrast to many experiments in psychology that focus exclusively on overt behavior, psychophysiological experiments nearly always require the physical attachment of sensors to a person's body. Such attachments routinely involve skin preparation (e.g., cleaning and mild abrasion) as well as the use of gels or pastes to bridge between the surface of the sensor and skin. Not surprisingly, some participants will be allergic to particular adhesives, particular soaps or astringents, or particular gels or pastes, all used when attaching sensors. Some participants will likely be uncomfortable with the degree of physical touching involved. And when recording from areas on the face, the presence of facial hair or makeup can be problematic. Finally, a few participants may feel uncomfortable in a situation in which they are literally connected to the recording equipment and unable to move freely. For these reasons and others it is very important for the experimenter to establish a good rapport with each participant as early as possible.

Overall, a participant must understand that they can freely communicate with the experimenter throughout the experiment, and the protocol should not unnecessarily undermine a participant's perceived sense of control. A simple way to achieve the goal of unfettered communication is via an intercom system coupled with video surveillance. This can be achieved by grouping the trial sequence into relatively short blocks, the initiation of which is controlled by the participant. Successful psychological experiments involving physiological monitoring require that each research participant be both well informed with respect to the recording environment they will encounter and allowed to maintain a modicum of perceived control.

In the following pages we briefly review and contextualize a highly selected set of traditional measures of cadiovascular, sudomotor, and skeletomotor activity, measures that have become part of the routine armamentarium of experimental psychology. Most of the issues touched on in this review are discussed in depth in recent handbooks (e.g., Cacioppo, Tassinary, & Berntson, 2007), textbooks (e.g., Andreassi, 2006), technical monographs (e.g., Stern, Ray, & Quigley, 2001), lab manuals (e.g., Stephens, Allen, & Thompson, 2009), and relevant committee reports (e.g., Fowles et al., 1981; Fridlund & Cacioppo, 1986).

CARDIOVASCULAR ACTIVITY

For well over two millennia the relationship between the mind and the blood has been discussed and debated. Recalling the allegory of *Cupid* and

Psyche, the great physicians of antiquity recognized the diagnostic value of the pulse. For example, a quickening pulse in the presence of a hidden and forbidden love object was believed to be diagnostic of lovesickness (Mesulam & Perry, 1972). An accurate understanding of the mechanism of circulation, however, was not arrived at until the early 17th century by English physician William Harvey, and it was not until the 18th century that a physical mechanism was proposed to explain the relationship between emotional states and cardiac reactivity (see Thayer & Lane, 2009).

Important technological advances at the turn of the 19th century greatly aided the measure of pulse rate; specifically, the invention of the electrocardiogram by the Dutch physiologist Willem Einthoven in 1901 (Fisch, 2000), which built upon earlier work demonstrating that the heart's electrical activity could be monitored noninvasively (Sykes, 1987). Such technological advances were exploited by early psychophysiologists to empirically explore the correspondences between psychological states and physiological activity and met with mixed success (cf. Ax, 1953; Darrow, 1929a, 1929b). More recent work has focused on sophisticated indexes of the neural control of the heart, with continuing special attention to reactivity (e.g., Obrist et al., 1978) and variability (e.g., Berntson et al., 1997).

Anatomy and Physiology

The cardiovascular system comprises a central pump (the heart) and an intricate system of vessels distributed through the body. Its primary function is to provide a continuous adequate supply of oxygen and nutrients and to eliminate carbon dioxide and waste products.

The heart is a cone-shaped organ located in the medial cavity of the thorax between the lungs. The myocardium or cardiac muscle performs the pumping function and has a thin inner tissue layer called the endocardium covering the wall of the cardiac chambers. There are four chambers in the heart, the right and left atria and the right and left ventricles. During a normal cardiac cycle, deoxygenated blood enters the right atria via the superior vena cava, the inferior vena cava, and the coronary sinus (transporting blood from the myocardium). Simultaneously,

oxygenated blood enters the left atrium from four pulmonary veins. Blood from the right atria enters the right ventricle through the right atrioventricular (tricuspid) valve, and is pumped through the pulmonary semilunar valve out to the lungs (pulmonary circuit). The left ventricle receives blood from the left atrium via the left atrioventricular (bicuspid or mitral) valve and is pumped through the aortic semilunar valve out to the rest of the body (systemic circuit). Put simply, the heart is essentially two hearts—a left heart in the systemic circuit and a right heart in the pulmonary circuit. With each heat beat, the systemic circuit supplies oxygenated blood to all the organs of the body via the systemic circuit, whereas the pulmonary circuit takes deoxygenated blood from the heart to the lungs.

The arterial system comprises three subgroups that vary by size and function. The elastic arteries are the biggest, conducting blood from the heart to medium-size muscular arteries responsible for supplying the major organs with oxygenated blood. The arterioles are the smallest, responsible for the intraorgan transfer of blood, and are the primary proximal mechanism involved in regulating both local blood flow and systemic blood pressure (BP). The capillaries, the smallest of all vessels, are primarily involved in the diffusion of gases and nutrient to and from surrounding tissues.

The venous system comprises distinct subgroups all of which, with one notable exception (i.e., the hepatic portal vein), conduct blood to the heart. Superficial veins course close to the skin and have no corresponding arteries, whereas deep veins course well below the surface and corresponding arteries. Systemic veins service the tissues of the body and deliver deoxygenated blood to the heart whereas pulmonary veins deliver oxygenated blood to the heart from the lungs. All of these vessels have the same three layers characteristic of all blood vessels, yet they are thinner and the lumens are significantly larger than in their corresponding arteries. Veins are very compliant and hold up to 65% of the blood supply, acting as blood reservoirs.

Neural Control

The heart has an intrinsic rhythm controlled by self-generated electrical impulses in the sinoatrial (SA) node. The brain, however, exerts a powerful modulatory influence on both the heart and vascular activity. Such control includes changes that originate at different levels of the central nervous system and that are affected primarily via either the sympathetic or parasympathetic branches of the autonomic nervous systems. Some of the main brain control centers are located in the medulla. For example, the cardioacceleratory center, when activated, produces a positive chronotropic effect (i.e., a decrease in heart period) and also increases the tone of the muscular tunica of the blood vessels. Information from this center is conducted via sympathetic pathways reaching the SA node where the release of norepinephrine causes a direct stimulation of the cells of the node. The medullary cardioinhibitory center has the opposite function—its activation produces negative chronotropic effects. This center is mediated primarily by parasympathetic fibers traveling via the vagus nerve. Other brain centers affecting autonomic control of heart and blood vessels are the limbic system and the cerebral cortex that, via efferent and afferent fibers, communicate with the amygdala. The amygdala, in turn, can modulate medullar centers resulting in both parasympathetic suppression and sympathetic activation generating a large positive chronotropic effect. The hypothalamus also plays an important role through its influence on autonomic and sensory responsiveness (Lumb & Lovick, 1993).

A different level of control exerted via the autonomic nervous system derives from a series of broadly distributed sensory receptors throughout the body (Secomb, 2008). The three main classes of receptors are chemical, pressure, and tension. *Chemoreceptors* are located in the medulla oblongata, in the carotid bodies and in the aortic arch. These receptors detect changes in blood pH, low oxygen pressure, and levels of carbon dioxide (CO_2). Stimulation of chemoreceptors activate compensatory changes at the respiratory and cardiovascular system levels. *Baroreceptors* are pressure sensors located in the internal carotid arteries and in the aorta. Their function is regulated by a special negative feedback circuit. These receptors have cells that under normal conditions are continually firing and sending inhibitory signals to the cardiac centers

in the medulla via the *nucleus tractus solitarius*. A detected decrease in blood presure triggers a reduction in their rate of firing, allowing the medullary cardiac centers to send excitatory signals to the heart, leading to a consequent decrease in heart period and a resulting increase in BP. Once BP is normalized, these receptors resume their normal activity. *Proprioceptors* are distributed in muscles and joints. They sense changes in movement and spatial orientation of the body and respond to length modification on muscle and tendons. In the heart, these receptors react to the changes in size of the cardiac chambers. During physical activity, a large number of these receptors are activated, resulting in the recruitment of sympathetic mechanisms (Mittelstaedt, 1998).

Measurement

Cardiovascular measures such as HR and BP have been employed since the early days of psychophysiology (Ax, 1953; Elliot, 1969, 1974; Graham & Clifton, 1966; McGinn, Harburg, Julius, & McLeod, 1964; Scott, 1930). A considerable number of indexes of different aspects of cardiovascular functioning can be derived and have been used in psychological research. Standard psychophysiological measurement procedures include the electrocardiogram for the assessment of HR or heart period, the finger pulse plethysmograph for the assessment of pulse volume as well as sometimes pulse rate, impedance cardiography for the assessment of cardiac output measures, and the measurement of BP. In what follows, we briefly discuss each of these procedures. Of the various measures of cardiovascular activity that can be derived, HR, HR variability (HRV), and BP are described in some detail and illustrated with research examples.

Electrocardiogram

The electrocardiogram (ECG) measures the electrical activity of the heart. During normal contractions the entire myocardium behaves as a single coherent system. As detailed, the heart cycle begins with a signal at the SA, the pacemaker tissue located in the right atrium of the heart, which generates the sinus rhythm. This impulse leads to a depolarization of the atria, which unfolds as the P-wave in the ECG. The depolarization of the ventricles unfolds as the QRS complex, and the T inflection indicates the repolarization of the ventricles. The total time from initiation of the impulse by the SA node to depolarization of the last ventricular muscle cell is about 0.3 to 0.4 s. The entire sequence of complete contraction and relaxation of the heart chambers is known as the cardiac cycle.

The time for one complete heart cycle, usually measured from one R-wave to the next and expressed in milliseconds, is the heart period or interbeat interval (IBI). HR is expressed in beats per second and is related to IBI as follows: HR = 60,000/IBI. Berntson et al. (1993) advocated the use of IBI because changes in heart period are linearly related to autonomic activity over a wide range of baseline values, whereas the relation between autonomic activity and HR is decidedly nonlinear.

Sensors. Usually disposable adhesive silver/silver chloride (Ag/AgCl) sensors are used. A number of different placements are possible. The standard placements are as follows: (a) Lead I: Left and right wrists on the inside of the arms, with the positive lead on the left arm; (b) Lead II: Right arm and left ankle, with the positive lead on the left ankle; and (c) Lead III: Left wrist and left ankle, with the positive lead on the ankle. The preparation of the skin surface typically requires at most a mild rub with an astringent and the sensors themselves are available in a wide variety of sizes and materials.

Because the arm and leg placements are quite sensitive to movement artifact, a modified Lead II placement is often used where the sensors are placed on the torso. In this case, the right sensor is placed under the right sternum and the left sensor under the left ribcage. When body hair makes the sternum placement impractical, the equivalent location on the back can also be used. When clothing hinders the attachment of a sensor to the lower ribcage, an ankle placement can be used, still leaving the arm free.

Traditional metrics. HR and IBI have been used routinely as dependent measures in the study of emotion (e.g., Ax, 1953; Lang, Davis, & Öhman, 2000), motivation (e.g., Elliot, 1969, 1974; Fowles, 1988), and attention (e.g., Cook & Turpin, 1997;

Graham & Clifton, 1966; Verschuere, Crombez, De Clercq, & Koster, 2004). Tonic HR has also been used as an individual difference measure—for example, as a correlate of antisocial behavior in children and adolescents (see, Ortiz & Raine, 2004). Because the heart is innervated by both sympathetic and parasympathetic branches of the autonomic nervous system, the interpretation of simple indexes such as HR can be challenging. As mentioned, quite distinct patterns of autonomic activation may lead to similar observed changes in HR and vice versa (Berntson et al., 1993). Hence, HR is often assessed in the context of other measures to improve its diagnostic utility. For example, when HR is used to assess task engagement and perceptions of ability, the additional use of BP measures has proven useful (Wright & Kirby, 2001).

An example: Attention or affect? The concealed information or Guilty Knowledge Test (GKT) was originally developed by Lykken (1959) and under laboratory conditions has been found to very accurate (Iacono, 2010). The test is based on the fact that an item of unique significance to the perpetrator (e.g., an iPhone that was used to break a window) but not to an innocent person will elicit a skin conductance response in the former but not the latter. Verschuere et al. (2004) addressed whether this response is due to an emotional defense reaction (Sokolov, 1963) or to an orientation reaction (see Lynn, 1966). Because HR has been found to decelerate during orientation but accelerate during defense (Cook & Turpin, 1997; Graham & Clifton, 1966), HR was recorded while each participant enacted only one of two mock crimes. Pictures related to both crimes were then presented, and HR and electrodermal activity (EDA) were measured concurrently. As expected, participants showed enhanced electrodermal response to pictures of the crime they had committed compared with pictures of the crime they had not. Importantly, this reaction was accompanied by HR deceleration, suggesting that the pictures linked to their specific crime elicited greater attention from the perpetrators in contradistinction to a negative emotional response.

HRV. In addition to HR and IBI, the ECG can also be used to derive measures of HRV. This measure is largely influenced by vagal tone and has been used as an individual difference measure of behavioral impulsivity (Lacey & Lacey, 1958) and self-regulation (Stephens, Harris, Brady, & Shaffer, 1975) as well as of emotional dispositions such as hostility (Sloan et al., 1994) and trait worry (Brosschot, Van Dijk, & Thayer, 2007). It has also been employed to assess states such as attention (Porges & Raskin, 1969), mental load (Kalsbeek & Ettema, 1963), and executive function (Hansen, Johnse, & Thayer, 2003).

The theoretical underpinnings of the psychophysiological utility of HRV, both evolutionary and neurophysiological, have been articulated in the polyvagal theory proposed by Steve Porges (1995). Polyvagal theory proposes that with respect to the heart, vagal egress supports the mobilization behaviors of fight and flight, whereas vagal ingress supports spontaneous social engagement behaviors. More specifically, the theory notes that in addition to the phylogenetically older unmyelinated branch involved primarily in visceral homeostasis (e.g., digestion), the mammalian vagus has a myelinated branch, which can rapidly regulate cardiac output (via modulated inhibition) to foster engagement and disengagement with the environment. The myelinated branch is further neuroanatomically linked to the brain regions that regulate social engagement via facial expression and vocalization and is thus characterized as the *smart* vagus. Generally, a high degree of vagal tone (i.e., the degree to which HRV is controlled by the smart vagus) has been shown to be positively associated with good psychological, physiological (e.g., Ruiz-Padial, Sollers, Vila, & Thayer, 2003), and sexual (e.g., Brody & Preut, 2003) functioning.

Quantification.   A number of different procedures can be used to derive HRV from both the temporal and the frequency domain (see Task Force of the European Society of Cardiology and the North American Society of Pacing and Electrophysiology [Task Force], 1996). For time domain measures, intervals between successive normal complexes are determined. Specifically, each QRS complex is first detected and an array of IBIs is created. Analysis in the frequency domain involves the decomposition of the ECG into its frequency components using techniques such as the Fast Fourier Transform (FFT) or autoregressive modeling. In addition, Porges and Bohrer (1990) developed a propriety hybrid method, the moving polynomial method.

A simple time domain measure, which provides accurate estimates under conditions of normal breathing (e.g., Hayano et al., 1991) and allows editing of spurious heart beats (Salo, Huikuri, & Seppänen, 2001) is the standard deviation of all IBIs in an epoch. Another common method is to calculate the square root of the mean-squared differences of successive IBIs. A common frequency domain measure is based on decomposing the time series using the FFT. The high frequency (HF) band from 0.15 to 0.4 Hz is used as an index of parasympathetic activity, whereas the low frequency (LF) band (.05–0.15 Hz) represents mixed influences. The choice of measure depends on a number of considerations. Even though the simple time domain measures have been shown to be adequate estimates of parasympathetic activity for typical experimental contexts, there are also good reasons to consider frequency-based measures if more detailed analyses are required (see Berntson et al., 1997).

Because HRV is derived from a time series, the length of the epoch is of importance. For frequency domain measures, the Task Force (1996) recommends a length 10 times the wavelength of the lowest frequency of interest. This translates into 1 min epochs for the HF and 2-min epochs for the LH band. Time domain measures should be based on at least 5-min epochs.

Artifact control.   As HRV is derived from the R–R interval of the ECG, the quality of the measure depends on the quality of the original ECG signal. One problem is that because most measures of HRV depend on an intact time series, artifacts cannot be simply deleted from the signal. The case of spurious R-wave detections (i.e., by mistaking a T-wave for an R-wave) can be addressed by summing the two short periods that were created by the spurious detection. Missing R-waves need to be replaced. This can be done by interpolating between the adjacent R–R intervals or by splitting the spuriously long interval in half.

The riddle of respiration. Respiratory sinus arrhythmia (RSA) refers to the observation that HR accelerates during inspiration and decelerates during expiration. This pattern was first observed by Hales (1733) in horses and Ludwig (1847) in dogs. On the basis of a wide variety of studies involving both chemical and surgical interventions, it is now well established that RSA is determined largely by vagal parasympathetic activity (see Berntson et al., 1997).

These measures, do not include controls for respiration. Yet the issue of control of respiration is a controversial one (for contrasting views, see Denver, Reed, & Porges, 2007; Grossman & Taylor, 2007). Denver at al. (2007) noted that the central issue is whether respiration is causal for HRV or whether HRV and respiratory frequency are parallel outputs of a common cardiopulmonary oscillator. In the latter case, control for respiration would not be necessary, possibly even counterproductive.

An example: Emotion regulation. As mentioned, HRV (specifically vagal tone) has been proposed as a global index of healthy functioning. On the basis of this hypothesis, Ruiz-Padial et al. (2003) predicted that individuals with high vagal tone would show a pattern of highly differentiated affect-modulated startle reflexes when viewing pleasant, neutral, and unpleasant images, whereas those with low vagal tone would show evidence of attenuated affective modulation.

Female participants were presented with affect-laden stimuli of varying durations, and their affective state was appraised by recording the amplitude of the startle blink response to a brief acoustic stimulus during viewing. In such paradigms, the eye-blink startle reflex, on average, is routinely observed to be potentiated when participants view negative images and reduced when participants view positive images compared with neutral images. As predicted, however, this pattern was clearly evident for participants with high vagal tone, yet it was conspicuously absent for those with low HRV.

Blood Pressure

Because of its relative ease of measurement, BP was a popular measure in the early days of psychophysiological research and was used to investigate a variety of constructs such as deception (Mager, 1931) and emotion (Landis, 1926; Scott, 1930) as well as to characterize individual differences (see McGinn et al., 1964). The difficulties associated with continuous noninvasive BP measurement and the relative obtrusiveness of the measure, however, pose challenges. BP measurement remains nonetheless a basic tool in the assessment of cardiovascular reactions. Typical domains in which BP is assessed include stress (e.g., Obrist et al., 1978; Taylor et al., 2010), perceived threat (e.g., Blascovich, Spencer, Quinn, & Steele, 2001; Manuck, Harvey, Lechleiter, & Neal, 1978), and mental effort (see Wright & Kirby, 2001).

Traditional methods. There are several ways to measure BP. The best known is the *auscultatory* method, which relies on the use of a sphygmomanometer. The procedure typically involves placing an inflatable cuff around the upper arm and a stethoscope is placed over the brachial artery. The cuff is inflated until the arterial blood flow is cut off and then the pressure is slowly released. When the blood first begins to flow again, an audible sound is generated by the ensuing turbulence. As more pressure is released, the sound intensity and quality changes, eventually disappearing. The pressure level at which the first sound is heard corresponds to the pressure in the arterial system during heart systole or contraction; the pressure level at which the sound disappears corresponds to the pressure in the arterial system during heart diastole or relaxation. Although the time-honored method is still valid and continues to have diagnostic clinical value, the intermittent nature and the obtrusiveness of the procedure limit its psychophysiological utility in the laboratory.

A number of automated BP measurement devices are available, however, that do not require continual human intervention. These devices are based either on the auscultatory method or on the oscillometric method. For the latter method, the cuff is first inflated to a pressure in excess of the systolic arterial pressure and then pressure is reduced to below diastolic pressure. At this point blood flows, but the blood flow is restricted. Under these conditions the cuff pressure oscillates in synchrony with the cyclic expansion and contraction of the brachial artery.

From these oscillations it is possible to compute both systolic BP (SP) and diastolic BP (DP).

The advantage of such automated measures is that they can be taken several times within the framework of an experiment without interrupting the procedure. The inflation and deflation of the cuff, however, is a salient stimulus, which may affect reactions. Continuous BP measurement is also possible with devices that use either tonometric or vascular unloading methods and may be designed for use on either the finger or wrist (see Stern et al., 2001). In all cases the BP measurement remains obtrusive to some degree and over time may become uncomfortable or otherwise disruptive.

Quantification. BP is typically expressed in millimeters of mercury pressure (mmHg) and reflects the amount of pressure on the blood vessel walls during the cardiac cycle. SP is the peak pressure in the arteries and occurs when the ventricles are contracting, near the end of the cardiac cycle. DP is the minimum pressure in the arteries and occurs near the beginning of the cardiac cycle when the ventricles are filling with blood. Pulse pressure is approximated by subtracting DP from SP. Mean arterial pressure is a weighted average of both DP and SP, approximated by adding DP to .33 pulse pressure. The simple unweighted arithmetic mean more closely approximates the true mean arterial pressure at very high HRs because of changes in the morphology of the actual pressure pulse.

An example: Evaluative threat. Performing a task in the presence of others often results in an improvement compared with performing it alone (Zajonc, 1965). This effect is moderated, however, by how well the task is learned. When task outcomes are uncertain, then the presence of an audience (e.g., evaluative threat) can interfere with performance (e.g., Kamarck, Manuck, & Jennings, 1990). Allen, Blascovich, Tomaka, and Kelsey (1991) tested this notion by asking women to perform a stressful task first in the laboratory with only the experimenter present and then 2 weeks later at home either again in the presence of just the experimenter or with the additional presence of either a female friend or a pet dog. The pet dog was chosen because a dog was considered to be a supportive other who—unlike the friend—would likely not pose an evaluative threat. Skin conductance reactions, pulse rate, and BP were assessed. In the home setting, the presence of a friend was associated with larger task-related skin conductance reactions and SP changes than in the neutral control conditions (i.e., neither friend nor pet present), whereas the presence of a pet was associated with smaller such changes. Task performance was also poorer in the friend present condition. This study illustrates that the perceived nature of the other in terms of evaluative threat can either exacerbate or ameliorate task-induced stress.

Other Cardiovascular Measures

Plethysmography. Blood volume, pulse volume, and pulse rate can be detected using plethysmography—a technique used to measure volumetric changes. Blood volume refers to slow or tonic changes of volume in a limb, whereas pulse volume refers to rapid or phasic changes and is usually assessed on the finger. The fingerclip photoplethysmograph is commonly used in psychophysiological research. This is a photometric technique that exploits the fact that when an infrared light shines through in vivo tissue, the amount of absorption of the light depends on the amount of blood in the blood vessels. In psychophysiological research the amplitude change from the lowest to the highest volume is usually measured, and the time between amplitude peaks can be used to estimate IBIs. The advantage of this measurement is that, unlike the recording of a traditional ECG, participants will not have to move clothing as the sensor is affixed to the finger. Research comparing ECG and photoplethysmograph-derived IBIs, however, suggest that although the two measures correlate well at rest, they can become uncoupled during task performance (e.g., Giardino, Lehrer, & Edelberg, 2002). In addition, it is difficult to compare absolute values both between and within participants because variation in skin characteristics influences the measure (Jennings, Tahmoush, & Redmond, 1980), and pulse volume estimates have been found to be unreliable when derived over multiple sessions (e.g., Speckenback & Gerber, 1999). The use of this convenient measure, therefore, must be carefully considered in each experimental context.

Impedance cardiography. The amount of blood in the aorta changes during the cardiac cycle, resulting in corresponding changes in electrical impedance measured across the chest, with lower impedance values indicating greater blood volume. Impedance cardiography allows the calculation of a variety of hemodynamic parameters, in particular an estimate of *stroke volume*—the volume of blood pumped by the heart with each beat. Because cardiac output equals HR times stroke volume, the combination of ECG and impedance cardiography permits the noninvasive estimate of this parameter as well. For additional measures derived from impedance cardiography and more detail on the technique, see Sherwood (1993) or Sherwood et al. (1990).

Measures derived from impedance cardiography have been used prominently in social psychophysiological investigations of threat and challenge responses to stressors (e.g., Blascovich, Mendes, Tomaka, Salomon, & Seery, 2003; Tomaka, Blascovich, Kelsey, & Leitten, 1993) and research on loneliness (e.g., Cacioppo & Hawkley, 2009; Cacioppo et al., 2002; Hawkley, Burleson, Berntson, & Cacioppo, 2003).

SUDOMOTOR ACTIVITY

The measurement of electrical changes in the human skin caused by sudomotor activity is a robust psychophysiological technique used routinely over the past century to track the intensive aspects of emotion and attention across a wide variety of situations (Dawson, Schell, & Filion, 1990; Knezevic & Bajada, 1985; Venables & Christie, 1980). It has been used as well in some controversial contexts, such as forensic lie detection and Dianetic auditing.

The initial development of techniques to measure the electrical conductivity of skin occurred in France during the last decades of the 19th century with the work of Romain Vigoroux (1879). Vigoroux's work was not the first to detect electrical surface activity, yet he appears to have been the first to recognize that the electrical activity observed in previous experiments and considered merely an "electric disturbance" was actually an expression of changes in the skin's electrical conductivity (Ho, Popp, & Warnke, 1994). Additional work by

Charles Féré and Ivan Romanovish Tarchanoff in the following decade further clarified the nature of this phenomenon. By passing a small electrical current between two sensors placed on the surface of the skin, Féré (1888) observed changes in skin resistance when an individual was presented with evocative stimuli. Tarchanoff (1890), however, measured endogenous changes in electrical potential between two sensors placed on the surface of the skin and attributed the observed variations to changes in the secretory activity of sweat glands (Neumann & Blanton, 1970).

The significance of these discoveries for psychophysiology was not generally recognized, however, until the renowned Swiss psychologist Carl Jung reported on the results of word association experiments using such techniques in *Studies in Word Association* (1906/1918). In the following year he expanded his examination on the topic in a seminal publication that explored the "value of the so-called 'psycho-physical galvanic reflex' as a recorder of psychical changes in connection with sensory and psychical stimuli . . . [and] . . . its normal and pathological variations" (Peterson & Jung, 1907, p. 154). Such explorations have profitably continued for more than a century, with implications for our embodied understanding of emotion and attention already acknowledged by the 1950s (see Woodworth & Schlosberg, 1954).

Anatomy and Physiology

The skin is composed of two layers: the epidermis and dermis. The uppermost layer, the epidermis, constitutes the cellular part of the skin and is a very thin structure (Forslind et al., 1997). Because of its peculiar organization, however, the structure of the epidermis provides the key to understanding the electrical properties of the skin. The epidermis comprises five sublayers of closely packed cells: the stratum corneum, lucidum, granulosum, spinosum, and germinativum, names that reflect either their function or their appearance. The *stratum corneum* or "horny layer" is the superficial layer composed of thin, flat, dead cells filled with protein keratin that are continually being sloughed off and replaced by new dead cells. This layer is an important barrier against heat, chemicals, light, and microorganisms but also provides a significant pathway for ion conductance, thus contributing significantly to the electrical properties of the skin (Edelberg, 1977). The other layers constitute essentially a "cell factory," with new cells originating in the deepest layer, the *stratum germinature*. The *dermis*, the second layer of the skin, is located below the epidermis and is formed principally of elastic and fibrous connective tissue. This layer contains loops of capillary blood vessels, terminal receptors of sensory nerves, coiled tubes of sweat glands, and sebaceous glands. Ducts from sweat glands pass through the dermis and epidermis as spiral canals and open onto the skin surface.

Two kinds of sweat glands exist in the human body, eccrine and apocrine. The phylogenetically newer eccrine sweat glands—found only in primates—occur in nearly all regions of the skin, yet they are most numerous in the soles, palms, and scalp. In contrast, the phylogenetically older apocrine sweat glands are far less numerous and are located primarily in the axilla and perianal areas. It is the eccrine system that forms the proximal basis for nearly all psychophysiological measurement. As mentioned, gland ducts traverse the dermis and the epidermis, opening onto the surface of the skin. When active, these ducts fill with sweat, with consequent variations in conductivity (Jacob & Francone, 1982). The resistance of a given gland duct to the passage of an applied current is inversely proportional to the amount of sweat in the duct. To understand observed changes in overall conductivity across thousands of gland ducts, it is useful to conceptualize the sweat glands as variable resistors wired in parallel. Overall conductance, therefore, is quite simply the sum of all the individual conductances.

Neural Control

Sweating is a normal physiological reaction, having both thermoregulatory and psychogenic antecedents. Psychogenic sweating tends to be more pronounced in areas like the palms and soles, whereas thermoregulatory sweating is a more generalized response (Darrow, 1933; Edelberg, 1972), and distinct mechanisms of neural control appear to be involved (Shibasaki, Wilson, & Crandall, 2006; Wang, 1964). Specifically, thermoregulatory sweating is a complex system controlled primarily by the

hypothalamus via sympathetic cholinergic pathways. Even though parasympathetic modulation is also mediated by acetylcholine, the general parasympathetic influence on sudomotor function is imperceptible (Illigens & Gibbons, 2009). Afferent pathways from the peripheral thermoreceptors in the skin connect to the central thermoregulatory center of the hypothalamus where the information is integrated with information arriving from other brain areas involved with fluid regulation (Boulant, 1981). Efferent pathways descend ipsilaterally via the brainstem, medulla, and mediolateral spinal cord, and then preganglionic sympathetic fibers relay to paravertebral sympathetic ganglia where unmyelinated postganglionic efferents fibers innervate the sweat glands (Boucsein, 1992; Nagai, Critchley, Featherstone, Trimble, & Dolan, 2004). Additional regulation exists at spinal level possibly via reflex circuits (Ogawa, 1981).

The brain systems involved in psychogenic sweating are those associated with emotional and cognitive processes. The most important areas are the premotor cortex and its connections with the basal ganglia, the sensorimotor cortex, and the anterior cingulate cortex (ACC; Neafsey, 1991), all of which are implicated in the control of emotional experience and the arousal mechanisms involved in attention (Vetrugno, Liguori, Crotelli, & Montagna, 2003). Other important structures that play a role in the psychogenic sweating are the hypothalamus, hippocampus, and amygdala via their role in motivation (Dawson et al., 1990) and the reticular formation via its role in vigilance (Roy, Sequeira, & Delerm, 1993).

On the basis of a recent functional magnetic resonance imaging study, Critchley, Elliott, Mathias, and Dolan (2000) concluded that the brain areas implicated in emotion and attention are differentially involved in the generation and representation of psychogenic sweating. Additional evidence has suggested that such sweating is related to fear-induced activation of the amygdala (Cheng, Knight, Smith, & Helmstetter, 2006; Phelps et al., 2001).

Measurement

Using the terminology discussed in this chapter, the recording of sudomotor activity via of the measurement of electrodermal changes is a prototypical example of an outcome relation. That is, EDA is influenced by a variety of factors and can originate from multiple regions of the brain, making it quite risky to impart particular psychological significance to any observed activity. Not unlike reaction time, however, its egalitarian sensitivity and relative ease of use make it an ideal dependent measure, whether alone or in combination with other measures, when carefully incorporated into a well-designed experiment. An excellent example of such a partnership is the GKT used for lie detection (Lykken, 1959). It has been observed repeatedly that phasic EDA is observed following the presentation of novel relevant (i.e., significant) stimuli (Öhman, 1979), yet such activity is mute with respect to the precise nature of the significance. The GKT is predicated on the presence of information that would be significant only for the perpetrator (i.e., a specific item used in a crime or some salient object at a crime scene). The goal is to properly construct a multiple-choice test, which embeds the significant item among other plausible items. The guilty person is expected to show consistent EDA to the significant items but not to the plausible alternatives, whereas none of the alternatives should be of significance to an innocent person. The exploitation of significance also undergirds the use of EDA in discrimination classical conditioning (Grings & Dawson, 1973).

Recording Technique

In the introduction to their proposal for the standardization of electrodermal measurement, Lykken and Venables (1971) famously noted the usefulness of EDA "in spite of being frequently abused by measurement techniques which range from the arbitrary to the positively weird" (p. 656). Lykken and Venables's insistence on standardized procedures did bear fruit, however, and standard procedures are now the norm and not the exception in psychophysiological laboratories. Although there remain a variety of valid options in particular contexts (i.e., skin potential, skin resistance, and skin impedance; see Boucsein, 1992), the use of skin conductance is ubiquitous.

Sensors.   Because of the need to accurately record slow changes in the conductivity of the skin,

nonpolarizing Ag/AgCl sensors are highly recommended. Because of the differential distribution of the eccrine sweat glands, sensors are nearly always placed on the palmar surfaces of either the hand or foot. The hands are preferred when working with adults (but see Carpenter, Andrykowski, Freedman, & Munn, 1999), but for small children and infants, the foot may be the better choice. Commonly used placements on the hand are either the thenar and hypothenar eminences, or the medial and distal phalanges of the index and ring finger. Because the conductive properties of the skin are being measured, best practices suggest that skin should not be abraded before sensor placement. The standard recommendation is simply to ask the participants to wash their hands with a neutral soap.

The guidelines published by the Society for Psychophysiological Research (Fowles et al., 1981) suggest a sensor surface area of 1 cm², but 10 mm diameter circular sensors are commercially available and are in most cases sufficient. It is not uncommon to find commercial ECG or electroencephalography (EEG) gels used as conducting media, yet because these media are designed explicitly to reduce resistance they will affect measurements, especially in longer duration experiments (see Boucsein, 1992). Hence, a neutral conducting medium is recommended. In the past, such media were not commercially available and had to be compounded in-house (see Dormire & Carpenter, 2002; Fowles et al., 1981). Although relatively easy, such compounding is sometimes unnecessary because neutral media are presently available in some markets (e.g., EC33; Grass Technologies, United States).

Traditional metrics.   Skin conductance can be either assessed tonically, as skin conductance level (SCL), or phasically, as skin conductance response (SCR). Event-related reactions occur in a window of 1 s to 4 s after event onset. They also occur spontaneously—so-called nonspecific skin conductance responses (NS-SCRs). A number of possible metrics can be derived from the recorded waveform (see Table 24.1). Of these, the frequency of NS-SCRs, the SCL, and the electronic response skin conductance responses (ER-SCR) amplitude are among the more commonly used.

TABLE 24.1

Electrodermal Measures, Definitions, and Typical Values

Measure	Definition	Typical Values
Skin conductance level (SCL)	Tonic level of electrical conductivity of skin	2–20 μS
Change in SCL	Gradual changes in SCL measured at two or more points in time	1–3 μS
Frequency of NS-SCRs	Number of SCRs in absence of an identifiable eliciting stimulus	1–3 per min
ER-SCR amplitude	Phasic increase in conductance shortly following stimulus onset	0.2–1.0 μS
ER-SCR latency	Temporal interval between stimulus onset and SCR initiation	1–3 s
ER-SCR rise time	Temporal interval between SCR initiation and SCR peak	1–3 s
ER-SCR half recovery time	Temporal interval between SCR peak and point of 50% recovery of SCR amplitude	2–10 s
ER-SCR habituation (trials to habituation)	Number of stimulus presentations before two or three trials with no response	2–8 stimulus presentations
ER-SCR habituation (slope)	Rate of change of ER-SCR amplitude	0.01–0.5 μS per trial

Note. ER-SCR = event-related skin conductance response; NS-SCR = nonspecific skin conductance response. From *Principles of Psychophysiology: Physical, Social, and Inferential Elements* (p. 304), by J. T. Cacioppo and L. G. Tassinary (Eds.), 1990, New York, NY: Cambridge University Press. Copyright 1990 by Cambridge University Press. Adapted with permission.

An example: Prejudice. Dotsch and Wigboldus (2008) hypothesized that prejudical behavior toward outgroup members in social interactions results from nonconscious automatic categorization processes. Specifically, the authors predicted that implicitly held negative attitudes toward, but not explicit stereotypes of, Moroccans would be related to the avoidance behavior shown by Dutch participants. SCL was used as a measure of basic affective responding on the basis of its association with amygdala activation. It was predicted that the relation between implicit prejudice and behavior would be mediated by SCL. Participants were placed into an immersive virtual environment in which they encountered European- and Moroccan-appearing avatars. Avoidance was operationalized as the distance that the participants kept from the avatars. Implicit prejudice was measured using a single target implicit association test (see Bluemke & Friese, 2008; de Liver, Wigboldus, & van der Pligt, 2007). Participants high in implicit prejudice kept a larger distance between themselves and the avatar and showed larger SCLs. Explicit stereotype did not predict distance and SCL. As predicted by the authors, the effect of implicit prejudice on distance was fully mediated by SCL. The authors concluded that this finding provided evidence for the automatic activation of a previously learned prejudice that is accompanied by a basic affective reaction—that is, an activation resulting in an aversive, uncontrolled behavioral reaction toward the target.

An example: Task engagement. Nonspecific skin conductance activity has been found to vary with task engagement or more generally the effortful allocation of resources to a task (see Dawson et al., 1990). Pecchinenda and Smith (1996) hypothesized that when coping potential—the perceived ability to deal with a task—is high, participants should stay engaged in a task but when coping potential is low, participants should disengage from the task. They gave participants a series of anagram tasks. Task difficulty was manipulated by varying both the difficulty of the anagrams and the available solution time. Participants reported that their coping potential was lower when the task was more difficult. Within trials, nonspecific skin conductance activity was initially high in all conditions. In the most difficult condition, however, it decreased significantly by the end of the trial, suggesting that participants gave up. In support of the initial hypothesis, NS-SCRs were positively correlated within subjects with self-reports of coping potential and with actual time to solution.

SKELETOMOTOR ACTIVITY

The history of muscle physiology can be traced back to the 4th century B.C.E., when Aristotle provided clear descriptions of coordinated motor acts (e.g., locomotion and the importance of the mechanism of flexion) in his books *De Motu Animalium* and *De Incessu Animalium*. It was not until the early 19th century, however, that a sensitive instrument for measuring small electric currents was invented (i.e., the galvanometer). In 1833, Carlo Matteucci used such a device to demonstrate an electrical potential between an excised frog's nerve and its damaged muscle. Du-Bois Reymond, a student of the renowned physiologist Johannes Müller, built on Matteucci's then-recent publication, eventually publishing the results of an extensive series of investigations on the electrical basis of muscular contraction as well as providing the first *in vivo* evidence of electrical activity in human muscles during voluntary contraction (see Basmajian & Deluca, 1985). The foundations of modern electromyography were finally laid in the 1930s with publications of Adrian and Bronk (1929), Jacobson (1927), and Lindsley (1935), and the introduction of the differential amplifier (Mathews, 1934).

Detecting myoelectric signals using surface sensors remained difficult throughout the 19th and early 20th centuries. Electrically stimulating a muscle cutaneously was considerably simpler, however. Perhaps best known for this work was Guillaume Duchenne de Boulogne, who used this technique in the mid-19th century to investigate the dynamics and function of the human facial muscles in vivo (Duchenne, 1862/1990). Not surprisingly, Charles Darwin corresponded with Duchenne to evaluate his own observations about facial expressions and emotion (Cuthbertson, 1990).

Darwin's interest in muscular action was based upon his belief that many behaviors were in part inherited. He focused his inquiry on the expression of emotions in man and animals to buttress this belief and presaged contemporary studies of the patterns of muscle contractions and facial actions that are undetectable to the naked eye with his conclusion that "whenever the same state of mind is induced, however feebly, there is a tendency through the force of habit and association for the same movements to be performed, though they may not be of the least use" (Darwin, 1872/1873, p. 281).

The somatic elements of William James's (1884) theory of emotions and the various motor theories of thinking prevalent at the turn of the century (e.g., Washburn, 1916) further fueled interest in objective measures of subtle or fleeting muscle contractions. Among the more creative procedures used to magnify tiny muscular contractions were sensitive pneumatic systems used to record finger movements during conflict situations (Luria, 1932) as well as elaborate lever-based systems to record subtle tongue movements during thinking (Thorson, 1925). Sensitive and specific noninvasive recordings, however, awaited the development of metal surface sensors, vacuum tube amplifiers, and the cathode-ray oscilloscope early in this century to enable the pioneering work of Edmund Jacobson (1927, 1932) on electrical measurements of muscle activity during imagery. The results of these studies and others (e.g., Davis, 1938) demonstrated that electromyographic (EMG) activity was evoked by psychologically relevant tasks (e.g., recall a poem), were minute and highly localized, and often occurred in the part of the body that one would use had the task called for an overt response.

Anatomy and Physiology

Fundamentally, muscle is a tissue that both generates and transmits force. Striated muscle, in particular, is a hierarchical material made up of a very large number of parallel fibers whose diameters are orders of magnitude smaller than a millimeter and yet may be up to several centimeters in length. The term "striated" comes from the fact these fibers are actually bundles of thinner structures, known as *fibrils*, which have repeating cross-striations throughout their length known as *Z-lines* or *Z-bands*. Each striated muscle is innervated by a single motor nerve whose cell bodies are located primarily in the anterior horn of the spinal cord or, in the case of the muscles of the head, in the cranial nerves of the brain stem. All behavior—that is, all actions of the striated muscles regardless of the brain processes involved—result from neural signals traveling along these motor nerves. For this reason, the set of lower motor nerves has been designated the final common pathway (Sherrington, 1906/1923). The most elementary functional unit within the final common pathway, referred to as the motor unit, comprises the motoneuron cell body, its axon, its axon fibrils, and the individual muscle fibers innervated by these axon fibrils.

The depolarization of a motoneuron results in the quantal release of acetylcholine at the motor end plates. The activating neurotransmitter acetylcholine is quickly metabolized by the enzyme acetylcholinesterase so that continuous efferent discharges are required for continued propagation of muscle action potentials (MAPs) and fiber contraction. Nonetheless, the transient excitatory potential within a motor end plate can lead to a brief (e.g., 1 ms) depolarization of the resting membrane potential of the muscle cell and a MAP that is propagated bidirectionally across the muscle fiber with constant velocity and undiminished amplitude. The MAP travels rapidly along the surface of the fiber and flows into the muscle fiber itself via a system of T-tubules, thus ensuring that the contraction (known as a *twitch*) involves the entire fiber. The physiochemical mechanism responsible for the twitch involves a complex yet well-characterized self-regulating calcium-dependent interaction between the actin and myosin molecules.

The initial force of contraction produced by a muscle is attributable to small motoneurons discharging intermittently and then discharging more frequently. Stronger muscle contractions are attributable to the depolarization of increasingly large motoneurons within the motoneuron pool concurrent with increases in the firing rates of the smaller motoneurons already active. As muscle contraction approaches maximal levels, further increases in force are attributable primarily to the entire pool of motoneurons firing more rapidly. This cascade of processes appears to be regulated by unidimensional increases in the aggregate neural input to the motoneuronal pool, a process referred to as "common drive" (Brown, 2000; Deluca & Erim, 1994).

A small portion of the changing electromagnetic field confederated with these processes passes through the extracellular fluids to the skin and it is these voltage fluctuations that constitute the major portion of the surface EMG signal. The voltage changes that are detected in surface EMG recording do not emanate from a single MAP but rather from MAPs traveling across many muscle fibers within a motor unit (i.e., motor unit action potential, or MUAP) and, more typically, from MAPs traveling across numerous motor fibers because of the activation of multiple motor units. Thus, the EMG does not provide a direct measure of tension, muscular contraction, or movement but rather the electrical activity associated with these events. More specifically, the surface EMG signal represents the ensemble electromagnetic field detectable at the surface of the skin at a given moment in time. Reliable, valid, and sensitive information about the aggregate actions (or inactions) of motoneuron pools across time, however, can nonetheless be obtained by careful attention to the elements of surface EMG recording and analysis (see Tassinary, Cacioppo, & Vanman, 2007).

Neural Control

Our understanding of the neural control of movement has undergone rapid development over the past two decades and although an even better understanding is still needed (Graziano, Taylor, & Moore, 2002), traditional notions remain useful. In simple classical terms, the initiation of a discrete voluntary movement begins in the motor association premotor area of the frontal lobes and continues on to the primary motor area located in the precentral gyrus and the anterior bank of the central sulcus. At this point, the upper motor neurons send signals to the brainstem and spinal cord via the corticobulbar and corticospinal pathways. Below these areas, the descending fibers from the upper motor neurons synapse with lower motor neurons, and the axons from these neurons innervate the striated musculature. The signals traversing this pathway are modulated via a wide variety of structures, including the cerebellum, reticular formation, and basal nuclei, structures that enable coordination, regulate muscle tone, and support the planning and execution of movements. The complexity of the reentrant circuits and corticocortical connections, combined with subcortical control structures involving both reflexes and central pattern generators, complicate the classical story considerably (see Solodkin, Hlustik, & Buccino, 2007).

Measurement

As discussed, EMG is a measure of the electric activity generated during muscle contraction. Specifically, striated muscles consist of groups of bundles composed of individual muscle fibers, and the electromyographic signal reflects the changes in electrical potential that result from the conduction of action potentials along these muscle fibers. In nearly all psychophysiological research, the EMG signal is recorded via sensors attached to the skin overlying the muscle region of interest. The frequency range of the EMG spans from a few Hz to about 500 Hz, with amplitudes ranging from fractions of microvolt to nearly a millivolt. These characteristics of the EMG overlap with the characteristics of most other electrical signals generated by the body (e.g., ECG, EEG) as well as with ambient noise emitted by AC-powered equipment.

Recording Technique

Electromyographic signals are small in two ways: They have low voltage and low current. An amplifier supplies both voltage gain (turning low into high voltages), which can be controlled by the investigator, and current gain, a function of the ratio of the input and output impedances of the amplifier. Electromyographic signals are amplified using differential amplifiers wherein the difference signal between two sensors (with respect to a third ground electrode) is amplified and carried through the signal processing chain. Any bioelectrical or extraneous electrical signal that is common to both electrodes (the common-mode signal) is therefore attenuated (see Marshall-Goodell, Tassinary, & Cacioppo, 1990). The most commonly used method of recording EMG signals is one in which sensor pairs are aligned parallel to the course of the muscle fibers and is referred to as bipolar. This alignment, coupled with the high common-mode rejection capability of modern differential amplifiers, produces a relatively sensitive and selective recording of the activity of the underlying muscle groups (Basmajian & Deluca, 1985; cf. Tassinary, Cacioppo, & Geen, 1989).

Sensors. Surface EMG electrodes can be attached to the skin in a variety of ways, but the most common is via double-sided adhesive collars. A highly conductive medium (paste or gel) is used routinely between skin and the detection surface. This medium stabilizes the interface between the skin and each detection surface by minimizing movement artifacts (by establishing an elastic connection between the detection surface and the skin), reducing interelectrode impedances (by forming a highly conductive pathway across the hornified layers of the skin), and stabilizing the hydration and conductivity of the skin surface.

Before the application of the conductive medium and electrodes, the designated site on the skin surface is usually cleaned to remove dirt and oil and typically abraded gently to lower intersensor impedances. The electrodes are then commonly affixed in a bipolar configuration. The proximity of the ground electrode to the EMG sites being monitored is less important than the impedance of the skin–ground contact to help minimize extraneous electrical noise in the EMG recording. Consequently, care and reflection can and should be used to ensure a stable and low-impedance connection to ground. Finally, to avoid obstructing movement resulting from the attachment of surface electrodes, thought should be given to the orientation of electrode collars and wires. Electrode wires, for instance, should be draped and secured to minimize distraction, annoyance, or obstruction of movement or vision.

Signal conditioning. Some filtering of the raw EMG signal is necessary to increase the signal-to-noise ratio, decrease 50/60 Hz or ECG/EEG artifact, and reduce cross-talk. The primary energy in the bipolar recorded surface EMG signal lies between approximately 10 Hz and 200 Hz (van Boxtel, Goudswaard, & Shomaker, 1984). Between 10 Hz and 30 Hz, this power is due primarily to the firing rates of motor units; beyond 30 Hz, it is due to the shapes of the aggregated motor unit action potentials (Basmajian & Deluca, 1985). Attenuating the high frequencies in the EMG signal (e.g., using 500-Hz low-pass filters) reduces amplifier noise but rounds peaks of the detected motor unit action potentials. Retaining sharp signal peaks may be important for waveform or spectral analysis but is less critical for obtaining overall estimates of muscle tension. Attenuating the low frequencies (e.g., using 90-Hz high-pass filters) reduces 50/60 Hz noise from AC power lines, EEG and ECG artifacts, and, to some extent, cross-talk (because of the intervening tissue's preferential transmission of low frequencies) and also eliminates a significant and sizable portion of the EMG signal. Use of an overly restricted EMG signal passband may result in inaccurate appraisal of the level and form of EMG activity or in a failure to detect small changes in the level of EMG activity. Hence, selection of an EMG detection passband must proceed on the basis of susceptibility to artifact, presence of extraneous electrical noise at the source and high frequency noise internal to the amplifier, consideration of the amplitude of the EMG signals to be detected, need to minimize cross-talk, and variations across conditions in muscular fatigue. A passband from 10 Hz to 500 Hz is satisfactory for most psychophysiological recording situations (van Boxtel, 2001); if low-frequency artifact and cross-talk are problematic, then a 20 Hz or 30 Hz high-pass filter may be used. The investigator should realize one consequence of this selection is that weak signals from the target muscle may also be attenuated.

The two most common signal conditioning techniques are integration and smoothing, terms that are often confused. True *integration* is the temporal summation or accumulation of EMG activity, whereas *smoothing* typically refers to performing integration with a built-in signal decay and is accomplished either by low-pass filtering or some type of signal averaging. Because the total energy in the EMG signal in any epoch of time is roughly equivalent to the rectified and smoothed EMG response, considerable economy in terms of data acquisition and signal processing can be achieved by rectification and smoothing before digitization when frequency components of the raw signal are not of interest.

Quantification and analysis. Many investigators have performed frequency analyses on surface EMG recordings to determine whether there are shifts in the EMG spectra (i.e., changes in magnitude or power across frequency) as a function of some psychological or physiological variable. A particularly robust finding is that shifts in the central tendency of the EMG spectra (e.g., median frequency) are associated with muscle fatigue (e.g., Merletti, 1994; Mulder & Hulstijn, 1984; van Boxtel, Goudswaard, & Janssen, 1983). The persistent lack of attention to spectral analyses of the surface EMG in psychophysiology, however, continues to be attributable primarily to the fact that sophisticated spectral analyses have proven no more sensitive to psychological processes than relatively inexpensive amplitude and time-based analyses (Dollins & McGuigan, 1989; McGuigan, Dollins, Pierce, Lusebrink, & Corus, 1982).

Signal representation. Electromyographic activity unfolds over time and, like many other psychophysiological responses, the complexity of the raw signal enjoins data reduction. Whether represented in the time, amplitude, or frequency domains, the first step involves the conversion of the digitized signal to a descriptive (e.g., physiological) unit of measurement.

Most psychophysiological research using EMG has focused on some variation of EMG signal amplitude as the dependent variable. Simple averaging of the raw EMG amplitudes is uninformative, however, because the nature of the signal ensures that the average expected value is zero. Counting or averaging the peaks in the EMG signal, or tallying its directional changes or zero crossings, are relatively easy methods to implement and are useful for gauging differences in EMG activity provided a sufficiently high sampling rate is used. As discussed, muscles consist of large numbers of homogeneous units, generating similarly sized action potentials recruited at similar levels of effort. Consequently, increments in the level of effort are generally found to be more accurately reflected in an integral-based measure rather than in a frequency-based measure. EMG signals consisting of low rates of widely varying spikes (e.g., those generated by small numbers of recruited motor units or closely spaced differential electrodes), however, generate poorly fused and noisy integrals, whereas the zero-crossing counts may reflect more accurately the level of effort (Loeb & Gans, 1986, Chapter 17).

The phrase "integrated EMG" has been used in this research to refer to the output of several different quantification techniques. Two of the most common parameters in contemporary research are the arithmetic average of the rectified and smoothed EMG signal and the root-mean-square of the raw EMG signal. Both processing techniques transform the EMG voltage-time function into a waveform that is nonnegative and bounded in time and amplitude. The moment-by-moment amplitude of this function represents an estimate of the total energy of the signal across time, the mean amplitude of this voltage-time function represents the average level of electrical energy emanating from the underlying muscle region(s) during a given recording epoch, and the integral of this function (e.g., the sum of the amplitudes) represents the total electrical activity (i.e., the size of the response) emanating from the underlying muscle region(s) during the recording epoch.

One unfortunate consequence of the traditional focus on the amplitude domain of the EMG signal is that the form of the response across time has been largely ignored (but see Cacioppo, Martzke, Petty, & Tassinary, 1988; Hess, Kappas, McHugo, & Kleck, 1988). A notable exception is Malmo's (1965) use of "EMG gradients" (Davis & Malmo, 1951), defined as an "electromyographic (EMG) voltage that rises continuously during motor performance or mental activity and falls precipitately at the end" (Malmo & Malmo, 2000, p. 145). Electromyographic gradients are still used successfully to assess variations across time in tonic muscle tension (e.g., Braathen & Svebak, 1994; Ritz, Dahme, & Claussen, 1999).

Facial EMG. The most common use of surface EMG measurement in psychophysiological settings is to record transient affective reactions linked to facial expressions. Such expressions, however, can also be assessed by naïve observer ratings as well as by objective coding systems. Observer ratings typically require a relatively large number of observers, and the interrater reliability can be quite variable depending on the specific rating task (Rosenthal, 2005). The systematic coding of facial expressions (i.e., Facial Action Coding System [FACS], Ekman & Friesen, 1978) requires highly trained observers or an automated system (e.g., Cohn, Zlochower, Lien, & Kanade, 1999; Zeng, Pantic, Roisman, &

Huang, 2009). FACS provides a complete assessment of observable facial movements but is restricted to the measurement of observable facial behavior. The specific advantages of facial EMG by contrast are its high spatial and temporal resolution combined with its ability to track incipient facial reactions too subtle or fleeting to be result in visible changes (Tassinary & Cacioppo, 1992).

Facial EMG has been used for the assessment of affective states in a large number of contexts and has become an accepted index of affective reactions to a variety of emotive visual (e.g., Davis, Rahman, Smith, & Burns, 1995; Larsen, Norris, & Cacioppo, 2003), auditory (e.g., Dimberg, 1990), gustatory (e.g., Hu et al., 1999), and olfactory (e.g., Jäncke & Kaufmann, 1994) stimuli; emotional faces (e.g., Dimberg, 1982; Dimberg & Öhman, 1996), real (e.g., Hess & Bourgeois, 2010) or virtual (e.g., Mojzisch et al., 2006); interaction partners; and nicotine (e.g., Robinson, Cinciripini, Carter, Lam, & Wetter, 2007) and other drugs (e.g., Newton, Khalsa-Denison, & Gawin, 1997). It has also become an accepted index of attitudes toward others (e.g., Brown, Bradley, & Lang, 2006; Dambrun, Després, & Guimond, 2003) and oneself (e.g., Buck, Hillman, Evans, & Janelle, 2004) in adults and in children (e.g., Armstrong, Hutchinson, Laing, & Jinks, 2007) using supra- as well as subliminal stimuli (e.g., Arndt, Allen, & Greenberg, 2001).

For certain questions, facial EMG measures of affect have been found to be more reliable and revealing than self-report measures, making this method specifically attractive (e.g., Hazlett & Hazlett, 1999; Vanman, Paul, Ito, & Miller, 1997; see also below). In addition, facial EMG has been used to assess attention (e.g., Cohen, Davidson, Senulis, & Saron, 1992) and fatigue (e.g., Veldhuizen, Gaillard, & de Vries, 2003).

An example: Prejudice. Vanman, Saltz, Nathan, and Warren (2004) employed facial EMG as a measure of prejudice. Specifically, they measured EMG at the *zygomaticus major* (smile) and *corrugator supercilii* (frown) sites to assess White university students' positive and negative affective reactions to pictures of Black and White individuals. In a separate task on a different day, the same university students were asked to choose the best of three applicants (two were White and one was Black) for a prestigious teaching fellowship. White individuals who showed less zygomaticus major activity when looking at photos of Black individuals were found to be more likely to show a bias against selecting a Black applicant. Interestingly, the implicit attitude task (Greenwald, McGhee, & Schwartz, 1998)—an implicit measure of racial bias—did not predict selection bias. Furthermore, motivation to control prejudice influenced the implicit attitude task but not the EMG measure, suggesting that facial EMG can be used as a sensitive measure of implicit prejudice related to overt discrimination.

Summary. Facial EMG is an ideal tool for the real-time measurement of emotional and cognitive processes. In particular, facial EMG has a high temporal and spatial resolution and thus allows the measurement of fleeting and subtle movements. Studies like those by Vanman et al. (2004) point to its use as an implicit measure that is not easily influenced by voluntary action—not because participants cannot produce expressions voluntarily but simply because they are not aware of their incipient expressions. The use of facial EMG does require, however, that the researcher can specify in advance which of a few muscles will be of interest in a given context.

Reflex probe. Another popular use of facial EMG is for the assessment of the potentiation of eyeblinks in reaction to a startling sound (see Blumenthal & Franklin, 2009). Ample research has demonstrated that the startle eyeblink reflex to a sudden acoustic probe is modulated by the individual's emotional state (e.g., Lang, 1995; Lang, Bradley, & Cuthbert, 1990; Vrana, Spence, & Lang, 1988). According to Lang (1995; Lang et al., 1990), when an individual is exposed to an unpleasant stimulus, the relevant subcortical aversive system circuitry is activated, leading to the augmentation of defensive reflexes such as the eyeblink reflex. Because appetitive and aversive–defensive states are opponent states, the opposite effect can be observed when the individual is exposed to pleasant stimuli. Lesion and blockade studies support a key mediational role of the central nucleus of the amygdala for startle potentiation.

More recently, Benning, Patrick, and Lang (2004) obtained a pattern opposite to that for the eyeblink reflex for the reflexive contraction of the postauricular muscle, which serves to pull the ear back and up (Bérzin & Fortinguerra, 1993). The postauricular reflex (PAR) can be observed in response to nonstartling sounds as well. This reflexive reaction to a sound is augmented when individuals are exposed to pleasant stimuli and a reduced one when exposed to unpleasant stimuli.

An example: Approach and avoid. Hess, Sabourin, and Kleck (2007) explored people's reaction to male and female anger and happiness expressions. Specifically, they tested a prediction on the basis of the functional equivalence hypothesis (Hess, Adams, & Kleck, 2007), which postulates that facial expressive behavior and morphological cues to dominance and affiliation are similar in their effects on emotional attributions. They noted that the cues linked to perceived dominance (e.g., square jaw, heavy eyebrows, high forehead) are more typical for men, and men are generally perceived as more dominant than are women. In contrast, baby-facedness, a facial aspect more closely linked to perceived affiliation, is more common in women. This leads to the hypothesis that anger in men should be seen as more threatening because of the double association with dominance of both anger and male features. Likewise, because of the double association of happiness and female features, smiling women should be perceived as more appetitive. Hess, Sabourin, and Kleck (2007) measured both eyeblink startle and the PAR while participants were viewing happy and angry expressions shown by men and women. Overall, the PAR was potentiated during happy expressions and inhibited during anger expressions and, as predicted, this pattern was more clearly found for female expressers. Also as predicted, eyeblink startle was potentiated during viewing of angry faces and inhibited during viewing of happy faces only for expressions shown by men.

CONCLUSION

It has become customary in the cognitive and social sciences to view peripheral physiological measures in the same way as reaction time—namely as an index, or an observable correlate of some aggregate property of a psychological process, and not as a response computed explicitly by a psychological processes. This assumption affords such measures their great potential to illuminate putative mechanisms (Pylyshyn, 1980). Psychophysiological measures thus play a major role in efforts to understand the mind–brain as both an embodied and embedded phenomenon. Their applied utility continues to expand, most recently making significant inroads into the burgeoning fields of game research (Kivikangas et al., 2010) and human computer interaction (Dirican & Gokturk, 2011). Coupled with advances in signal acquisition and analysis, we predict that these traditional measures will be increasingly incorporated into sophisticated theoretical frameworks on the basis of our evolving understanding of the myriad transactions between organisms and their environment.

References

Adrian, E. D., & Bronk, D. W. (1929). The discharge of impulses in motor nerve fibers. Part II. The frequency of discharge in reflex and voluntary contractions. *Journal of Physiology, 67*, 119–151.

Allen, K. M., Blascovich, J., Tomaka, J., & Kelsey, R. M. (1991). Presence of human friends and pet dogs as moderators of autonomic responses to stress in women. *Journal of Personality and Social Psychology, 61*, 582–589. doi:10.1037/0022-3514.61.4.582

Andreassi, J. L. (2006). *Psychophysiology: Human behavior and response* (4th ed.). Hillsdale, NJ: Erlbaum.

Armstrong, J. E., Hutchinson, I., Laing, D. G., & Jinks, A. L. (2007). Facial electromyography: Responses of children to odor and taste stimuli. *Chemical Senses, 32*, 611–621. doi:10.1093/chemse/bjm029

Arndt, J., Allen, J. J. B., & Greenberg, J. (2001). Traces of terror: Subliminal death primes and facial electromyographic indices of affect. *Motivation and Emotion, 25*, 253–277. doi:10.1023/A:1012276524327

Ax, A. F. (1953). The physiological differentiation between fear and anger in humans. *Psychosomatic Medicine, 15*, 433–442.

Basmajian, J. V., & Deluca, C. J. (1985). *Muscles alive: Their functions revealed by electromyography* (5th ed.). Baltimore, MD: Williams & Wilkins.

Benning, S. D., Patrick, C. J., & Lang, A. R. (2004). Emotional modulation of the post-auricular reflex. *Psychophysiology, 41*, 426–432. doi:10.1111/j.1469-8986.00160.x

Berntson, G. G., Bigger, J. T., Eckberg, D. L., Grossman, P., Kaufmann, P. G., Malik, M., . . . van der Molen, M. W. (1997). Heart rate variability: Origins, methods, and interpretive caveats. *Psychophysiology, 34*, 623–648. doi:10.1111/j.1469-8986.1997.tb02140.x

Berntson, G. G., Cacioppo, J. T., & Quigley, K. S. (1993). Cardiac psychophysiology and autonomic space in humans: Empirical perspectives and conceptual implications. *Psychological Bulletin, 114*, 296–322. doi:10.1037/0033-2909.114.2.296

Bérzin, F., & Fortinguerra, C. R. (1993). EMG study of the anterior, superior, and posterior auricular muscles in man. *Anatomischer Anzeiger, 175*, 195–197.

Blascovich, J., Mendes, W. B., Tomaka, J., Salomon, K., & Seery, M. (2003). The robust nature of the biopsychosocial model challenge and threat: A reply to Wright and Kirby. *Personality and Social Psychology Review, 7*, 234–243. doi:10.1207/S15327957PSPR0703_03

Blascovich, J., Spencer, S. J., Quinn, D., & Steele, C. (2001). African Americans and high blood pressure: The role of stereotype threat. *Psychological Science, 12*, 225–229. doi:10.1111/1467-9280.00340

Bluemke, M., & Friese, M. (2008). Reliability and validity of the Single-Target IAT (ST-IAT): Assessing automatic affect towards multiple attitude objects. *European Journal of Social Psychology, 38*, 977–997. doi:10.1002/ejsp.487

Blumenthal, T. D., & Franklin, J. C. (2009). The startle eyeblink response. In E. Harmon-Jones & J. S. Beer (Eds.), *Methods in social neuroscience* (pp. 92–117). New York, NY: Guilford Press.

Boucsein, W. (1992). *Electrodermal activity*. New York, NY: Plenum Press.

Boulant, J. A. (1981). Hypothalamic mechanisms in thermoregulation. *Federation Proceedings, 40*, 2843–2850.

Braathen, E. T., & Svebak, S. (1994). EMG response patterns and motivational styles as predictors of performance and discontinuation in explosive and endurance sports among talented teenage athletes. *Personality and Individual Differences, 17*, 545–556. doi:10.1016/0191-8869(94)90091-4

Brody, S., & Preut, R. (2003). Vaginal intercourse frequency and heart rate variability. *Journal of Sex and Marital Therapy, 29*, 371–380. doi:10.1080/0092 6230390224747

Brosschot, J. F., Van Dijk, E., & Thayer, J. F. (2007). Daily worry is related to low heart rate variability during waking and the subsequent nocturnal sleep period. *International Journal of Psychophysiology, 63*, 39–47. doi:10.1016/j.ijpsycho.2006.07.016

Brown, L. M., Bradley, M. M., & Lang, P. J. (2006). Affective reactions to pictures of ingroup and outgroup members. *Biological Psychology, 71*, 303–311. doi:10.1016/j.biopsycho.2005.06.003

Brown, P. (2000). Cortical drives to human muscles: The Piper and related rhythms. *Progress in Neurobiology, 60,* 97–108. doi:10.1016/S0301-0082(99)00029-5

Buck, S. M., Hillman, C. H., Evans, E. M., & Janelle, C. M. (2004). Emotional responses to pictures of oneself in healthy college age females. *Motivation and Emotion, 28,* 279–295. doi:10.1023/B:MOEM.0000040155.79452.23

Cacioppo, J. T., & Hawkley, L. C. (2009). Loneliness. In M. R. Leary & R. H. Hoyle (Eds.), *Handbook of individual differences in social behavior* (pp. 227–240). New York, NY: Guilford Press.

Cacioppo, J. T., Hawkley, L. C., Crawford, E., Ernst, J. M., Burleson, M. H., Kowalewski, R. B., . . . Berntson, G. G. (2002). Loneliness and health: Potential mechanisms. *Psychosomatic Medicine, 64,* 407–417.

Cacioppo, J. T., Martzke, J. S., Petty, R. E., & Tassinary, L. G. (1988). Specific forms of facial EMG response index emotions during an interview: From Darwin to the continuous flow hypothesis of affect-laden information processing. *Journal of Personality and Social Psychology, 54,* 592–604. doi:10.1037/0022-3514.54.4.592

Cacioppo, J. T., Petty, R. E., & Morris, K. (1985). Semantic, evaluative, and self-referent processing: Memory, cognitive effort, and somatovisceral activity. *Psychophysiology, 22,* 371–384. doi:10.1111/j.1469-8986.1985.tb01618.x

Cacioppo, J. T., & Tassinary, L. G. (Eds.). (1990). *Principles of psychophysiology: Physical, social, and inferential elements.* New York, NY: Cambridge University Press.

Cacioppo, J. T., Tassinary, L. G., & Berntson, G. G. (Eds.). (2007). *The handbook of psychophysiology* (3rd ed.). New York, NY: Cambridge University Press. doi:10.1017/CBO9780511546396

Carpenter, J. S., Andrykowski, M. A., Freedman, R. R., & Munn, R. (1999). Feasibility and psychometrics of an ambulatory hot flash monitoring device. *Menopause, 6,* 209–215.

Cheng, D. T., Knight, D. C., Smith, C. N., & Helmstetter, F. J. (2006). Human amygdala activity during the expression of fear responses. *Behavioral Neuroscience, 120,* 1187–1195. doi:10.1037/0735-7044.120.5.1187

Cohen, B. H., Davidson, R. J., Senulis, J. A., & Saron, C. D. (1992). Muscle tension patterns during auditory attention. *Biological Psychology, 33,* 133–156. doi:10.1016/0301-0511(92)90028-S

Cohn, J. F., Zlochower, A. J., Lien, J., & Kanade, T. (1999). Automated face analysis by feature point tracking has high concurrent validity with manual FACS coding. *Psychophysiology, 36,* 35–43. doi:10.1017/S0048577299971184

Cook, E. W., & Turpin, G. (1997). Differentiating orienting, startle and defense responses: The role of affect and its implications for psychopathology. In P. J. Lang, R. F. Simons, & M. T. Balaban (Eds.), *Attention and orienting: Sensory and motivational processes* (pp. 137–164). Hillsdale, NJ: Erlbaum.

Critchley, H. D., Elliott, R., Mathias, C. J., & Dolan, R. J. (2000). Neural activity relating to generation and representation of galvanic skin conductance responses: A functional magnetic resonance imaging study. *Journal of Neuroscience, 20,* 3033–3040.

Cuthbertson, R. A. (1990). The highly original Dr. Duchenne. In R. A. Cuthbertson (Ed.), *The mechanism of human facial expression* (pp. 225–241). New York, NY: Cambridge University Press. doi:10.1017/CBO9780511752841.024

Dambrun, M., Desprès, G., & Guimond, S. (2003). On the multifaceted nature of prejudice: Psychophysiology responses to ingroup and outgroup ethnic stimuli. *Current Research in Social Psychology, 8,* 200–204.

Darrow, C. W. (1929a). Electrical and circulatory responses to brief sensory and ideational stimuli. *Journal of Experimental Psychology, 12,* 267–300. doi:10.1037/h0064070

Darrow, C. W. (1929b). Differences in the physiological reactions to sensory and ideational stimuli. *Psychological Bulletin, 26,* 185–201. doi:10.1037/h0074053

Darrow, C. W. (1933). Functional significance of the galvanic skin reflex and perspiration on the back and palms of the hands. *Psychological Bulletin, 30,* 712.

Darrow, C. W. (1934). The refloxohmmeter (pocket type). *Journal of General Psychology, 10,* 238–239. doi:10.1080/00221309.1934.9917731

Darwin, C. (1873). *The expression of the emotions in man and animals.* New York, NY: Appleton. (Original work published 1872)

Davis, F. H., & Malmo, R. B. (1951). Electromyographic recording during interview. *American Journal of Psychiatry, 107,* 908–916.

Davis, R. C. (1938). The relation of muscle action potentials to difficulty and frustration. *Journal of Experimental Psychology, 23,* 141–158. doi:10.1037/h0059544

Davis, W. J., Rahman, M. A., Smith, L. J., & Burns, A. (1995). Properties of human affect induced by static color slides (IAPS): Dimensional, categorical, and electromyographic analysis. *Biological Psychology, 41,* 229–253. doi:10.1016/0301-0511(95)05141-4

Dawson, M. E., Schell, A. M., & Filion, D. L. (1990). The electrodermal system. In J. T. Cacioppo & L. G. Tassinary (Eds.), *Principles of psychophysiology: Physical, social, and inferential elements* (pp. 295–324). New York, NY: Cambridge University Press.

de Liver, Y., Wigboldus, D., & van der Pligt, J. (2007). Positive and negative associations underlying ambivalent attitudes: Evidence from implicit measures. *Journal of Experimental Social Psychology, 43,* 319–326.

Deluca, C. J., & Erim, Z. (1994). Common drive of motor units in regulation of muscle force. *Trends in Neurosciences, 17,* 299–305. doi:10.1016/0166-2236(94)90064-7

Denver, J. W., Reed, S. F., & Porges, S. W. (2007). Methodological issues in the quantification of respiratory sinus arrhythmia. *Biological Psychology, 74,* 286–294. doi:10.1016/j.biopsycho.2005.09.005

Dimberg, U. (1982). Facial reactions to facial expressions. *Psychophysiology, 19,* 643–647. doi:10.1111/j.1469-8986.1982.tb02516.x

Dimberg, U. (1990). Perceived unpleasantness and facial reactions to auditory stimuli. *Scandinavian Journal of Psychology, 31,* 70–75. doi:10.1111/j.1467-9450.1990.tb00804.x

Dimberg, U., & Öhman, A. (1996). Behold the wrath: Psychophysiological responses to facial stimuli. *Motivation and Emotion, 20,* 149–182. doi:10.1007/BF02253869

Dirican, A. C., & Gokturk, M. (2011). Psychophysiological measures of human cognitive states applied in human computer interaction. *Procedia Computer Science, 3,* 1361–1367. doi:10.1016/j.procs.2011.01.016

Dollins, A. B., & McGuigan, F. J. (1989). Frequency analysis of electromyographically measured covert speech behavior. *Pavlovian Journal of Biological Science, 24,* 27–30.

Dormire, S. L., & Carpenter, J. S. (2002). An alternative to unibase/glycol as an effective nonhydrating electrolyte medium for the measurement of electrodermal activity. *Psychophysiology, 39,* 423–426. doi:10.1111/1469-8986.3940423

Dotsch, R., & Wigboldus, D. H. R. (2008). Virtual prejudice. *Journal of Experimental Social Psychology, 44,* 1194–1198. doi:10.1016/j.jesp.2008.03.003

Duchenne, G. B. (1990). *The mechanism of human facial expression* (R. A. Cuthbertson, Ed. & Trans.). New York, NY: Cambridge University Press. (Original work published 1862) doi:10.1017/CBO9780511752841

Edelberg, R. (1972). Electrical activity of the skin: Its measurements and uses in psychophysiology. In N. S. Greenfield & R. A. Sternbach (Eds.), *Handbook of psychophysiology* (pp. 367–418). New York, NY: Holt.

Edelberg, R. (1977). Relation of electrical properties of skin to structure and physiologic state. *Journal of Investigative Dermatology, 69,* 324–327. doi:10.1111/1523-1747.ep12507771

Edwards, J. R. (2001). Ten difference score myths. *Organizational Research Methods, 4,* 265–287. doi:10.1177/109442810143005

Ekman, P., & Friesen, W. V. (1969). The repertoire of nonverbal behavior categories, origins, usage, and coding. *Semiotica, 1,* 49–98.

Ekman, P., & Friesen, W. V. (1978). *The Facial Action Coding System: A technique for the measurement of facial movement.* Palo Alto, CA: Consulting Psychologists Press.

Elliot, R. (1969). Tonic heart rate: Experiments on the effects of collative variables lead to a hypothesis about its motivational significance. *Journal of Personality and Social Psychology, 12,* 211–228. doi:10.1037/h0027630

Elliot, R. (1974). The motivational significance of heart rate. In P. A. Obrist, A. H. Black, J. Brener & L. V. DiCara (Eds.), *Cardiovascular psychophysiology* (pp. 505–537). Chicago, IL: Aldine.

Fechner, G. (1860). *Elemente der Psychophysik.* Leipzig, Germany: Breitkopf & Härtel.

Féré, C. (1888). Note sur les modifications de la résistance électrique sous l'influence des excitations sensorielles et des emotions [Note on the modification of electrical resistance under the effects of sensory stimulation and emotional excitement]. *Comptes Rendus des Seances de la Societe de Biologie, 5,* 217–219.

Fisch, C. (2000). Centennial of the string galvanometer and the electrocardiogram. *Journal of the American College of Cardiology, 36,* 1737–1745. doi:10.1016/S0735-1097(00)00976-1

Fishel, S. R., Muth, E. R., & Hoover, A. W. (2007). Establishing appropriate physiological baseline procedures for real-time physiological measurement. *Journal of Cognitive Engineering and Decision Making, 1,* 286–308. doi:10.1518/155534307X255636

Forslind, B., Lindberg, M., Roomans, G. M., Pallon, J., & Werner-Linde, Y. (1997). Aspects on the physiology of human skin: Studies using article probe analysis. *Microscopy Research and Technique, 38,* 373–386. doi:10.1002/(SICI)1097-0029(19970815)38:4<373::AID-JEMT5>3.0.CO;2-K

Fowles, D. C. (1988). Psychophysiology and psychopathology: A motivational approach. *Psychophysiology, 25,* 373–391. doi:10.1111/j.1469-8986.1988.tb01873.x

Fowles, D. C., Christie, M. J., Edelberg, R., Grings, W. W., Lykken, D. T., & Venables, P. H. (1981). Publication recommendation for electrodermal measurements. *Psychophysiology, 18,* 232–239. doi:10.1111/j.1469-8986.1981.tb03024.x

Fridlund, A. J., & Cacioppo, J. T. (1986). Guidelines for human electromyographic research. *Psychophysiology, 23,* 567–589.

Gardiner, H. M., Metcalf, R. C., & Beebe-Center, J. G. (1937). *Feeling and emotion: A history of theories.* New York, NY: American Book Company.

Geen, T. R., & Tassinary, L. G. (2002). The mechanization of expression in John Bulwar's Pathomyotonia.

American Journal of Psychology, 115, 275–299. doi:10.2307/1423439

Giardino, N. D., Lehrer, P. M., & Edelberg, R. (2002). Comparison of finger plethysmograph to ECG in the measurement of heart rate variability. *Psychophysiology, 39*, 246–253. doi:10.1111/1469-8986.3920246

Graham, F. K., & Clifton, R. K. (1966). Heart-rate change as a component of the orienting response. *Psychological Bulletin, 65*, 305–320. doi:10.1037/h0023258

Graziano, M. S. A., Taylor, C. S. R., & Moore, T. (2002). Complex movements evoked by microstimulation of precentral cortex. *Neuron, 34*, 841–851.

Greenwald, A. G., McGhee, D. E., & Schwartz, J. L. K. (1998). Measuring individual differences in implicit cognition: The implicit association test. *Journal of Personality and Social Psychology, 74*, 1464–1480. doi:10.1037/0022-3514.74.6.1464

Grings, W. W., & Dawson, M. E. (1973). Complex variables in conditioning. In W. F. Prokasy & D. C. Raskin (Eds.), *Electrodermal activity in psychological research* (pp. 203–254). New York, NY: Academic Press.

Grossman, P., & Taylor, E. W. (2007). Toward understanding respiratory sinus arrhythmia: Relations to cardiac vagal tone, evolution and biobehavioral functions. *Biological Psychology, 74*, 263–285. doi:10.1016/j.biopsycho.2005.11.014

Hales, S. (1733). *Statical essays: Haemastaticks.* Lausanne, Switzerland: Universität Lausanne.

Hansen, A. L., Johnse, B. H., & Thayer, J. F. (2003). Vagal influence on working memory and sustained attention. *International Journal of Psychophysiology, 48*, 263–274. doi:10.1016/S0167-8760(03)00073-4

Hawkley, L. C., Burleson, M. H., Berntson, G. G., & Cacioppo, J. T. (2003). Loneliness in everyday life: Cardiovascular activity, psychosocial context, and health behaviors. *Journal of Personality and Social Psychology, 85*, 105–120. doi:10.1037/0022-3514.85.1.105

Hayano, J., Sakakibara, Y., Yamada, A., Yamada, M., Mukai, S., Fujinami, T., . . . Takata, K. (1991). Accuracy of assessment of cardiac vagal tone by heart rate variability in normal subjects. *American Journal of Cardiology, 67*, 199–204. doi:10.1016/0002-9149(91)90445-Q

Hazlett, R. L., & Hazlett, S. Y. (1999). Emotional response to television commercials: Facial EMG vs. self-report. *Journal of Advertising Research, 39*, 7–23.

Hess, U., Adams, R. B., Jr., & Kleck, R. E. (2007). When two do the same it might not mean the same: The perception of emotional expressions shown by men and women. In U. Hess & P. Philippot (Eds.), *Group dynamics and emotional expression* (pp. 33–50). New York, NY: Cambridge University Press. doi:10.1017/CBO9780511499838.003

Hess, U., & Bourgeois, P. (2010). You smile—I smile: Emotion expression in social interaction. *Biological Psychology, 84*, 514–520. doi:10.1016/j.biopsycho.2009.11.001

Hess, U., Kappas, A., McHugo, G. J., & Kleck, R. E. (1988). An analysis of the encoding and decoding of spontaneous and posed smiles: The use of facial electromyography. *Journal of Nonverbal Behavior, 13*, 121–137. doi:10.1007/BF00990794

Hess, U., Sabourin, G., & Kleck, R. E. (2007). Postauricular and eye-blink startle responses to facial expressions. *Psychophysiology, 44*, 431–435. doi:10.1111/j.1469-8986.2007.00516.x

Ho, M. W., Popp, F. A., & Warnke, U. (Eds.). (1994). *Bioelectrodynamics and biocommunication.* London, England: World Scientific.

Hu, S., Player, K. A., Maschesney, K. A., Dalistan, M. D., Tyner, C. A., & Scozzafava, J. E. (1999). Facial EMG as an indicator of palatability in humans. *Physiology and Behavior, 68*, 31–35.

Iacono, W. G. (2010). Psychophysiological detection of deception and guilty knowledge. In J. L. Skeem, K. S. Douglas, & S. O. Lilienfeld (Eds.), *Psychological science in the courtroom: Controversies and consensus* (pp. 224–241). New York, NY: Guilford Press.

Illigens, B. M., & Gibbons, C. H. (2009). Sweat testing to evaluate autonomic function. *Clinical Autonomic Research, 19*, 79–87. doi:10.1007/s10286-008-0506-8

Jacob, S. W., & Francone, C. A. (Eds.). (1982). *Structure and function of man* (2nd ed.). Philadelphia, PA: Saunders.

Jacobson, E. (1927). Action currents from muscular contractions during conscious processes. *Science, 66*, 403. doi:10.1126/science.66.1713.403

Jacobson, E. (1932). Electrophysiology of mental activities. *American Journal of Psychology, 44*, 677–694. doi:10.2307/1414531

James, W. (1884). What is an emotion? *Mind, 9*, 188–205. doi:10.1093/mind/os-IX.34.188

Jäncke, L., & Kaufmann, N. (1994). Facial EMG responses to odors in solitude and with an audience. *Chemical Senses, 19*, 99–111. doi:10.1093/chemse/19.2.99

Jennings, J. R., Tahmoush, A. J., & Redmond, D. P. (1980). Non-invasive measurement of peripheral vascular activity. In I. Martin & P. H. Venables (Eds.), *Techniques in psychophysiology* (pp. 69–137). New York, NY: Wiley.

Jung, C. G. (1918). *Studies in word association* (M. D. Eder, Trans.). London, England: William Heinemann. (Original work published 1906)

Kalsbeek, J. W. H., & Ettema, J. H. (1963). Scored irregularity of the heart pattern and the measurement of perceptual or mental load. *Ergonomics, 6*, 306–307.

Kamarck, T. W., Manuck, S. B., & Jennings, J. R. (1990). Social support reduces cardiovascular reactivity to psychological challenge: A laboratory model. *Psychosomatic Medicine, 52*, 42–58.

Kivikangas, J. M., Ekman, I., Chanel, G., Jarvela, S., Cowley, B., Salminen, M., . . . Ravaja, N. (2010). *Review on psychophysiological methods in game research.* Retrieved from http://www.digra.org/dl/db/10343.06308.pdf

Knezevic, W., & Bajada, S. (1985). Peripheral autonomic surface potential. *Journal of the Neurological Sciences, 67*, 239–251.

Kweon, B., Ulrich, R. S., Walker, V., & Tassinary, L. G. (2007). Anger and stress: The role of art posters in an office setting. *Environment and Behavior, 40*, 355–381. doi:10.1177/0013916506298797

Lacey, J. I., & Lacey, B. C. (1958). Verification and extension of the principle of autonomic response stereotypy. *American Journal of Psychology, 71*, 50–73. doi:10.2307/1419197

Landis, C. (1926). Studies of emotional reactions. V. Severe emotional upset. *Journal of Comparative Psychology, 6*, 221–242. doi:10.1037/h0071773

Lang, P. J. (1995). The emotion probe: Studies of motivation and attention. *American Psychologist, 50*, 372–385. doi:10.1037/0003-066X.50.5.372

Lang, P. J., Bradley, M. M., & Cuthbert, B. N. (1990). Emotion, attention, and the startle reflex. *Psychological Review, 97*, 377–395. doi:10.1037/0033-295X.97.3.377

Lang, P. J., Davis, M., & Öhman, A. (2000). Fear and anxiety: Animal models and human cognitive psychophysiology. *Journal of Affective Disorders, 61*, 137–159. doi:10.1016/S0165-0327(00)00343-8

Lange, C. G. (1885). *Om Sindsbevagelser* [The mechanisms of the emotions: A psychophysiological study]. Copenhagen, Denmark: Kronar.

Larsen, J. T., Norris, C. J., & Cacioppo, J. T. (2003). Effects of positive and negative affect on electromyographic activity over zygomaticus major and corrugator supercilii. *Psychophysiology, 40*, 776–785. doi:10.1111/1469-8986.00078

Lindsley, D. B. (1935). Electrical activity of human motor units during voluntary contraction. *American Journal of Physiology, 114*, 90–99.

Loeb, G. E., & Gans, C. (1986). *Electromyography for experimentalists.* Chicago, IL: University of Chicago Press.

Ludwig, C. (1847). Beitrage zur Kenntnis des Einflusses der Respirations-bewegungen auf den Blutulauf im Aortensystem [Contribution to the knowledge of the influence of respiratory movements on the blood flow in the aortic system]. *Archiv für Anatomie, Physiologie und wissenschaftliche Medicin*, 242–257.

Lumb, B. M., & Lovick, T. A. (1993). The rostral hypothalamus: An area for the integration of autonomic and sensory responsiveness. *Journal of Neurophysiology, 70*, 1570–1577.

Luria, A. R. (1932). *The nature of human conflicts.* New York, NY: Liveright.

Lykken, D. T. (1959). The GSR in the detection of guilt. *Journal of Applied Psychology, 43*, 385–388. doi:10.1037/h0046060

Lykken, D. T., & Venables, P. H. (1971). Direct measurement of skin conductance: A proposal for standardization. *Psychophysiology, 8*, 656–672. doi:10.1111/j.1469-8986.1971.tb00501.x

Lynn, R. (1966). *Attention, arousal, and the orientation reaction.* Oxford, England: Pergamon.

Mager, H. (1931). Deception: A study in forensic psychology. *Journal of Abnormal and Social Psychology, 26*, 183–198. doi:10.1037/h0074408

Malmo, R. B. (1965). Physiological gradients and behavior. *Psychological Bulletin, 64*, 225–234. doi:10.1037/h0022288

Malmo, R. B., & Malmo, H. P. (2000). On electromyographic (EMG) gradients and movement-related brain activity: Significance for motor control, cognitive functions, and certain psychopathologies. *International Journal of Psychophysiology, 38*, 143–207. doi:10.1016/S0167-8760(00)00113-6

Manuck, S. B., Harvey, A. H., Lechleiter, S. L., & Neal, K. S. (1978). Effects of coping on blood pressure responses to threat of aversive stimulation. *Psychophysiology, 15*, 544–549. doi:10.1111/j.1469-8986.1978.tb03107.x

Marshall-Goodell, B., Tassinary, L. G., & Cacioppo, J. T. (1990). Principles of bioelectrical measurement. In J. T. Cacioppo & L. G. Tassinary (Eds.), *Principles of psychophysiology: Physical, social, and inferential elements* (pp. 113–148). New York, NY: Cambridge University Press.

Mathews, B. H. C. (1934). A special purpose amplifier. *Journal of Physiology, 81*, 28.

McGinn, N. F., Harburg, E., Julius, S., & McLeod, J. M. (1964). Psychological correlates of blood pressure. *Psychological Bulletin, 61*, 209–219. doi:10.1037/h0043509

McGuigan, F. J., Dollins, A., Pierce, W., Lusebrink, V., & Corus, C. (1982). Fourier analysis of covert speech behavior. *Pavlovian Journal of Biological Science, 17*, 49–52.

McHugo, G., & Lanzetta, J. T. (1983). Methodological decisions in social psychophysiology. In J. T. Cacioppo & R. E. Petty (Eds.), *Social psychophysiology: A sourcebook* (pp. 630–665). New York, NY: Guilford Press.

Merletti, R. (1994). Surface electromyography: Possibilities and limitations. *Journal of Rehabilitation Sciences, 7*, 24–34.

Mesulam, M. M., & Perry, J. (1972). The diagnosis of love-sickness: Experimental psychophysiology without the polygraph. *Psychophysiology, 9*, 546–551. doi:10.1111/j.1469-8986.1972.tb01810.x

Mittelstaedt, H. (1998). Origin and processing of postural information. *Neuroscience and Biobehavioral Reviews, 22*, 473–478. doi:10.1016/S0149-7634(97)00032-8

Mojzisch, A., Schilbach, L., Helmert, J. R., Pannasch, S., Velichkovsky, B. M., & Vogeley, K. (2006). The effects of self-involvement on attention, arousal, and facial expression during social interaction with virtual others: A psychophysiological study. *Social Neuroscience, 1*, 184–195.

Montague, P. R., Berns, G. S., Cohen, J. D., McClure, S. M., Pagnoni, G., Dhamala, M., & Fisher, R. E. (2002). Hyperscanning: Simultaneous fMRI during linked social interactions. *NeuroImage, 16*, 1159–1164. doi:10.1006/nimg.2002.1150

Mulder, T., & Hulstijn, W. (1984). The effect of fatigue and repetition of the task on the surface electromyographic signal. *Psychophysiology, 21*, 528–534. doi:10.1111/j.1469-8986.1984.tb00237.x

Nagai, Y., Critchley, H. D., Featherstone, E., Trimble, M. R., & Dolan, R. J. (2004). Activity in ventromedial prefrontal cortex covaries with sympathetic skin conductance level: A physiological account of a "default mode" of brain function. *NeuroImage, 22*, 243–251. doi:10.1016/j.neuroimage.2004.01.019

Neafsey, E. J. (1991). Prefrontal autonomic control in the rat: Anatomical and electrophysiological observations. *Progress in Brain Research, 85*, 147–165. doi:10.1016/S0079-6123(08)62679-5

Neumann, E., & Blanton, R. (1970). The early history of electrodermal research. *Psychophysiology, 6*, 453–475. doi:10.1111/j.1469-8986.1970.tb01755.x

Newton, T. F., Khalsa-Denison, M. E., & Gawin, F. H. (1997). The face of craving? facial muscle EMG and reported craving in abstinent and non-abstinent cocaine users. *Psychiatry Research, 73*, 115–118. doi:10.1016/S0165-1781(97)00115-7

Obrist, P. A., Gaebelein, C. J., Teller, E. S., Langer, A. W., Grignolo, A., Light, K., C., et al. (1978). The relationship among heart rate, carotid dP/dt, and blood pressure in humans as a function of the type of stress. *Psychophysiology, Psychophysiology*, 102–115.

Ogawa, T. (1981). Dermatomal inhibition of sweating by skin pressure. In Z. Szelenyi & M. Szekely (Eds.), *Advances in physiological sciences: Vol. 32. Contribution to thermal physiology* (pp. 413–415). Budapest, Hungary: Akademiai Kiado.

Öhman, A. (1979). The orientation response, attention, and learning: An information-processing perspective. In H. D. Kimmel, E. H. van Olst, & J. F. Orlebeke (Eds.), *The orienting reflex in humans* (pp. 443–471). Hillsdale, NJ: Erlbaum.

Ortiz, J., & Raine, A. (2004). Heart rate level and antisocial behavior in children and adolescents: A meta-analysis. *Journal of the American Academy of Child and Adolescent Psychiatry, 43*, 154–162. doi:10.1097/00004583-200402000-00010

Pecchinenda, A., & Smith, C. A. (1996). The affective significance of skin-conductance activity during a difficult problem-solving task. *Cognition and Emotion, 10*, 481–504. doi:10.1080/026999396380123

Peterson, F., & Jung, C. G. (1907). Psycho-physical investigations with the galvanometer and pneumograph in normal and insane individuals (from the Psychiatric Clinic of the University of Zürich). *Brain: A Journal of Neurology, 30*, 153–218. doi:10.1093/brain/30.2.153

Phelps, E. A., O'Connor, K. J., Gatenby, C., Gore, J. C., Grillon, C., & Davis, M. (2001). Activation of the left amygdala to a cognitive representation of fear. *Nature Neuroscience, 4*, 437–441. doi:10.1038/86110

Poh, M. Z., Swenson, N. C., & Picard, R. W. (2010). A wearable sensor for unobtrusive, long-term assessment of electrodermal activity. *IEEE Transactions on Bio-Medical Engineering, 57*, 1243–1252. doi:10.1109/TBME.2009.2038487

Pope, L. K., & Smith, C. A. (1994). On the distinct meanings of smiles and frowns. *Cognition and Emotion, 8*, 65–72. doi:10.1080/02699939408408929

Porges, S. W. (1995). Orienting in a defensive world: Mammalian modifications of our evolutionary heritage: A polyvagal theory. *Psychophysiology, 32*, 301–318. doi:10.1111/j.1469-8986.1995.tb01213.x

Porges, S. W., & Bohrer, R. E. (1990). The analysis of periodic processes in psychophysiological research. In J. T. Cacioppo & L. G. Tassinary (Eds.), *Principles of psychophysiology: Physical, social, and inferential elements* (pp. 708–753). New York, NY: Cambridge University Press.

Porges, S. W., & Raskin, D. C. (1969). Respiratory and heart rate components of attention. *Journal of Experimental Psychology, 81*, 497–503. doi:10.1037/h0027921

Pylyshyn, Z. (1980). Computation and cognition: Issues in the foundation of cognitive science. *Behavioral and Brain Sciences, 3*, 111–169. doi:10.1017/S0140525X00002053

Ritz, T., Dahme, B., & Claussen, C. (1999). Gradients of facial EMG and cardiac activity during emotional stimulation. *Journal of Psychophysiology, 13*, 3–17. doi:10.1027//0269-8803.13.1.3

Robinson, J. D., Cinciripini, P. M., Carter, B. L., Lam, C. Y., & Wetter, D. W. (2007). Facial EMG as an index of affective response to nicotine. *Experimental and Clinical Psychopharmacology, 15*, 390–399. doi:10.1037/1064-1297.15.4.390

Rosenthal, R. (2005). Conducting judgment studies: Some methodological issues. In J. A. Harrigan, R. Rosenthal, & K. R. Scherer (Eds.), *The new handbook of methods in nonverbal behavior research* (pp. 199–234). Oxford, England: Oxford University Press.

Roy, J. C., Sequeira, H., & Delerm, B. (1993). Neural Control of Neurodermal Activity: Spinal and Reticular Mechanisms. In J. C. Roy, W. Boucsein, D. C. Fowles, & J. H. Gruzelier (Eds.), *Progress in electrodermal research* (pp. 73–92). New York, NY: Plenum Press.

Ruiz-Padial, E., Sollers, J. J., III, Vila, J., & Thayer, J. F. (2003). The rhythm of the heart in the blink of an eye: Emotion-modulated startle magnitude covaries with heart rate variability. *Psychophysiology, 40,* 306–313. doi:10.1111/1469-8986.00032

Salo, M. A., Huikuri, H. V., & Seppänen, T. (2001). Ectopic beats in heart rate variability analysis: Effects of editing on time and frequency domain measures. *Annals of Noninvasive Electrocardiology, 6,* 5–17. doi:10.1111/j.1542-474X.2001.tb00080.x

Scott, J. C. (1930). Systolic blood-pressure fluctuations with sex, anger and fear. *Journal of Comparative Psychology, 10,* 97–114. doi:10.1037/h0073671

Secomb, T. W. (2008). Theoretical models for regulation of blood flow. *Microcirculation, 15,* 765–775. doi:10.1080/10739680802350112

Sherrington, C. S. (1923). *The integrative actions of the nervous system.* New Haven, CT: Yale University Press. (Original work published 1906)

Sherwood, A. (1993). Use of impedance cardiography in cardiovascular reactivity research. In J. J. Blascovich & E. S. Katkin (Eds.), *Cardiovascular reactivity to psychological stress and disease* (pp. 157–199). Washington, DC: American Psychological Association. doi:10.1037/10125-007

Sherwood, A., Allen, M. T., Fahrenberg, J., Kelsey, R. M., Lovallo, W. R., & van Doornen, L. J. (1990). Methodological guidelines for impedance cardiography. *Psychophysiology, 27,* 1–23. doi:10.1111/j.1469-8986.1990.tb02171.x

Shibasaki, M., Wilson, T. E., & Crandall, C. G. (2006). Neural control and mechanisms of eccrine sweating during heat stress and exercise. *Journal of Applied Physiology, 100,* 1692–1701. doi:10.1152/japplphysiol.01124.2005

Singer, J. D., & Willett, J. B. (2003). *Applied longitudinal data analysis: Modeling change and event occurrence.* New York, NY: Oxford University Press.

Sloan, R. P., Shapiro, P. A., Bigger, J. T., Bagiella, E., Steinman, R. C., & Gorman, J. M. (1994). Cardiac autonomic control and hostility in healthy subjects. *American Journal of Cardiology, 74,* 298–300. doi:10.1016/0002-9149(94)90382-4

Sokolov, E. N. (1963). *Perception and the conditioned reflex.* New York, NY: Macmillan.

Solodkin, A., Hlustik, P., & Buccino, G. (2007). The anatomy and physiology of the motor system in humans. In J. T. Cacioppo, L. G. Tassinary, & G. G. Berntson (Eds.), *Handbook of psychophysiology* (3rd ed., pp. 507–539). New York, NY: Cambridge University Press.

Speckenbach, U., & Gerber, W. D. (1999). Reliability of infrared plethysmography in BVP biofeedback therapy and the relevance for clinical application. *Applied Psychophysiology and Biofeedback, 24,* 261–265.

Sperry, R. (1952). Neurology and the mind-brain problem. *American Scientist, 40,* 291–312.

Stephens, C., Allen, B., & Thompson, N. (2009). *Psychophysiology/cognitive neuroscience.* Biopac Student Lab Manual. Dubuque, IA: Kendall Hunt.

Stephens, J. H., Harris, A. H., Brady, J. V., & Shaffer, J. W. (1975). Psychological and physiological variables associated with large magnitude voluntary heart rate changes. *Psychophysiology, 12,* 381–387. doi:10.1111/j.1469-8986.1975.tb00006.x

Stern, R. M., Ray, W. J., & Quigley, K. S. (2001). *Psychophysiological recording.* New York, NY: Oxford University Press.

Stringham, J. M., Fuld, K., & Wenzel, A. J. (2003). Action spectrum for photophobia. *Journal of the Optical Society of America, 20,* 1852–1858. doi:10.1364/JOSAA.20.001852

Sykes, A. H. (1987). A. D. Waller and the electrocardiogram. *British Medical Journal, 294,* 1396–1398. doi:10.1136/bmj.294.6584.1396

Tarchanoff, I. (1890). Über die galvanischen Erscheinungen an der Haut des Menschen bei Reizung der Sinnesorgane und bei verschiedenen Formen der psychischen Tätigkeit [On the galvanic aspect of the human skin in response to stimulation of sense organs and with different forms of psychological activity]. *Pflügers Archiv für die gesamte. Physiologie, 46,* 46–55.

Task Force of the European Society of Cardiology and the North American Society of Pacing and Electrophysiology. (1996). Heart rate variability: Standards of measurement, physiological interpretation, and clinical use. *Circulation, 93,* 1043–1065.

Tassinary, L. G., & Cacioppo, J. T. (1992). Unobservable facial actions and emotion. *Psychological Science, 3,* 28–33.

Tassinary, L. G., & Cacioppo, J. T. (2000). The skeletomotor system: Surface electromyography. In J. T. Cacioppo, L. G. Tassinary, & G. G. Berntson (Eds.), *Handbook of psychophysiology* (2nd ed., pp. 163–199). New York, NY: Cambridge University Press.

Tassinary, L. G., Cacioppo, J. T., & Geen, T. R. (1989). A psychometric study of surface electrode placements for facial electromyographic recording: I. The brow and cheek muscle regions. *Psychophysiology, 26,* 1–16. doi:10.1111/j.1469-8986.1989.tb03125.x

Tassinary, L. G., Cacioppo, J. T., & Vanman, E. J. (2007). The skeletomotor system: Surface electromyography. In J. T. Cacioppo, L. G. Tassinary, & G. G. Berntson (Eds.), *Handbook of psychophysiology* (3rd ed., pp. 267–299). New York, NY: Cambridge University Press.

Tassinary, L. G., Geen, T. R., Cacioppo, J. T., & Swartzbaugh, R. (1989). Born of animal magnetism: 150 years of psycho-physiology. *Psychophysiology, 26,* 713–715. doi:10.1111/j.1469-8986.1989. tb03178.x

Taylor, S. E., Seeman, T. E., Eisenberger, N. I., Kozanian, T. A., Moore, A. N., & Moons, W. G. (2010). Effects of a supportive or an unsupportive audience on biological and psychological responses to stress. *Journal of Personality and Social Psychology, 98,* 47–56. doi:10.1037/a0016563

Thayer, J. F., & Lane, R. D. (2009). Claude Bernard and the heart–brain connection: Further elaboration of a model of neurovisceral integration. *Neuroscience and Biobehavioral Reviews, 33,* 81–88. doi:10.1016/j. neubiorev.2008.08.004

Thorson, A. M. (1925). The relation of tongue movements to internal speech. *Journal of Experimental Psychology, 8,* 1. doi:10.1037/h0073795

Tomaka, J., Blascovich, J., Kelsey, R. M., & Leitten, C. L. (1993). Subjective, Physiological, and Behavioral Effects of Threat and Challenge Appraisal. *Journal of Personality and Social Psychology, 65,* 248–260. doi:10.1037/0022-3514.65.2.248

van Boxtel, A. (2001). Optimal signal bandwidth for the recording of surface EMG activity of facial, jaw, oral, and neck muscles. *Psychophysiology, 38,* 22–34. doi:10.1111/1469-8986.3810022

van Boxtel, A., Goudswaard, P., & Janssen, K. (1983). Changes in EMG power spectra of facial and jaw-elevator muscles during fatigue. *Journal of Applied Physiology, 54,* 51–58.

van Boxtel, A., Goudswaard, P., & Shomaker, L. R. B. (1984). Amplitude and bandwidth of the frontalis surface EMG: Effects of electrode parameters. *Psychophysiology, 21,* 699–707. doi:10.1111/j.1469-8986.1984.tb00260.x

Vanman, E. J., Paul, B. Y., Ito, T. A., & Miller, N. (1997). The modern face of prejudice and structural features that moderate the effect of cooperation on affect. *Journal of Personality and Social Psychology, 73,* 941–959. doi:10.1037/0022-3514.73.5.941

Vanman, E. J., Saltz, J. L., Nathan, L. R., & Warren, J. A. (2004). Racial discrimination by low-prejudiced Whites: Facial movements as implicit measures of attitudes related to behavior. *Psychological Science, 15,* 711–714. doi:10.1111/j.0956-7976.2004.00746.x

Veldhuizen, I. J. T., Gaillard, A. W. K., & de Vries, J. (2003). The influence of mental fatigue on facial EMG activity during a simulated workday. *Biological Psychology, 63,* 59–78. doi:10.1016/S0301-0511(03)00025-5

Venables, P. H., & Christie, M. J. (1980). Electrodermal activity. In I. Martin & P. H. Venables (Eds.), *Techniques in psychophysiology* (pp. 3–67). New York, NY: Wiley.

Verschuere, B., Crombez, G., De Clercq, A., & Koster, E. H. W. (2004). Autonomic and behavioral responding to concealed information: Differentiating orienting and defensive responses. *Psychophysiology, 41,* 461–466. doi:10.1111/j.1469-8986.00167.x

Vetrugno, R., Liguori, R., Cortelli, P., & Montagna, P. (2003). Sympathetic skin response: Basic mechanisms and clinical applications. *Clinical Autonomic Research, 13,* 256–270. doi:10.1007/s10286-003-0107-5

Vigoroux, R. (1879). Sur la rôle de la resistance electrique des tissus dans l'electrodiagnostique [On the role of the electrical resistance of tissues on electrodiagnostics]. *Comptes Rendus des Seances de la Societe de Biologie, 31,* 336–339.

Vrana, S. R., Spence, E. L., & Lang, P. J. (1988). The startle probe response: A new measure of emotion? *Journal of Abnormal Psychology, 97,* 487–491. doi:10.1037/0021-843X.97.4.487

Wang, G. H. (1964). *The neural control of sweating.* Madison: University of Wisconsin Press.

Washburn, M. F. (1916). *Movement and imagery: Outlines of a motor theory of the complexer mental processes.* Boston, MA: Houghton Mifflin. doi:10.1037/11575-000

Woodworth, R. S., & Schlosberg, H. (1954). *Experimental psychology* (Rev. ed.). New York, NY: Holt.

Wright, R. A., & Kirby, L. D. (2001). Effort determination of cardiovascular response: An integrative analysis with applications in social psychology. In M. P. Zanna (Ed.), *Advances in experimental social psychology* (Vol. 33, pp. 255–307). San Diego, CA: Academic Press.

Wundt, W. (1897). *Outlines of psychology.* Leipzig, Germany: Wilhelm Engelmann.

Wundt, W. (1904). *Principles of physiological psychology.* London, England: Swan Sonnenschein.

Zajonc, R. B. (1965). Social facilitation. *Science, 149,* 269–274. doi:10.1126/science.149.3681.269

Zeng, Z., Pantic, M., Roisman, G. I., & Huang, T. S. (2009). A survey of affect recognition methods: Audio, visual and spontaneous expressions. *IEEE Transactions on Pattern Analysis and Machine Intelligence, 31,* 39–58. doi:10.1109/TPAMI.2008.52

CHAPTER 25

HORMONE ASSAYS

Oliver C. Schultheiss, Anja Schiepe-Tiska, and Maika Rawolle

Hormones can be assayed from blood, urine, and saliva. Because measuring hormones in saliva samples is the easiest and least stressful method for research participants, it is often the method of choice for psychologists. In this chapter, we give an overview about the measurement of hormones in saliva samples. We first describe hormones that can be assessed in saliva and their general effects. In the next section, we discuss how hormones can be assessed and how to deal with saliva samples. In closing, we make suggestions about how to analyze data obtained with hormone assays and how to report hormone data in research journals.

A PRIMER ON CONCEPTS AND MEASUREMENT ISSUES IN BEHAVIORAL ENDOCRINOLOGY

Hormones are messenger molecules that are released by specialized neurons in the brain and by glands in the body into the blood stream or the interstitial fluid and that carry a signal to other parts of the brain or body. Which specific responses they trigger in target organs depends on the receptors involved and the function of the organ. Thus, one hormone can drive several different physiological and psychological functions through its effects on several target organs.

Generally, two broad classes of hormonal effects on physiology and behavior must be distinguished. *Organizational effects* are lasting influences that hormones exert on the organism, thus changing its shape and functional properties in various ways.

Organizational hormone effects often occur during development or when significant hormonal changes take place, such as puberty. For instance, the development of the female and male body morphology is largely under hormonal control during fetal development, and deviations from typical gendered body morphology are frequently the result of deviations in hormone production, enzymatic conversion, or receptor action. In contrast to organizational effects, *activational effects* are those that hormones exert temporarily, without producing lasting changes in the brain or the body. For instance, because of peaking estradiol levels around ovulation, women become more sensitive to sexual stimuli, as indicated by an enhanced pupillary response. This effect vanishes again after ovulation, when estradiol levels decrease (Laeng & Falkenberg, 2007).

The relationship between hormones and behavior is *bidirectional*. Hormones can have a facilitating effect on behavior, such as when high levels of testosterone increase aggressive responses in a game setting (Pope, Kouri, & Hudson, 2000). Such hormone → behavior effects can be most conclusively demonstrated through experimental manipulation of hormone levels, a method that uses hormone assays only to verify that circulating hormone levels were indeed affected by the experimental manipulation. Conversely, the situational outcome of a person's behavior as well as the stimuli and events impinging on the person can influence current hormone levels, such as when watching romantic movies leads to an increase in viewers' progesterone levels (Schultheiss, Wirth, & Stanton, 2004).

DOI: 10.1037/13619-026
APA Handbook of Research Methods in Psychology: Vol. 1. Foundations, Planning, Measures, and Psychometrics, H. Cooper (Editor-in-Chief)

Because hormones have far-reaching and broad effects on physiology and behavior, their release is tightly controlled and monitored, primarily through negative feedback loops. For instance, circulating levels of the steroid hormone cortisol are monitored by the brain. If levels fall below a critical threshold, the hypothalamus releases corticotropine-releasing hormone (CRH), which in turn triggers the release of the adrenocorticotrope hormone (ACTH). ACTH travels from the brain to the cortex of the adrenals, small glands that sit on top of the kidneys, where it stimulates the release of cortisol. If rising levels of cortisol exceed a certain threshold, CRH releases and thus the subsequent release of ACTH and cortisol is suppressed until cortisol levels fall below the critical threshold again because of metabolic clearance. As a consequence of this negative-feedback-loop mechanism, many hormones are released in repeated bursts occurring every 30 min to 120 min. Hormones can also influence the release of other hormones. The quick (i.e., within minutes) testosterone increase in response to dominance challenges observed in male mammals (Mazur, 1985) is a good example. These rapid changes are the result of the stimulating effects of epinephrine and norepinephrine (NE), which are released within seconds after the onset of a situational challenge, on the testes (which produce testosterone in males). This effect is independent of the hypothalamic–pituitary–gonadal feedback mechanism normally involved in testosterone release (Sapolsky, 1987).

Like other physiological measures, such as heart rate or blood pressure, hormone levels are *multiply determined*, and to tease out the effects of interests (i.e., relationships between hormones and behavior), it is almost always necessary to control for or hold constant other influences on hormone levels. Chief among those influences are the strong circadian variations observed in many endocrine systems (hormones like testosterone, estradiol, and cortisol start out high in the morning and then decline through the course of the day), menstrual cycle changes in hormone levels (e.g., progesterone is low in the first half of the cycle and rises in the second), age and reproductive status (e.g., many hormonal systems operate differently in prepubertal children than in adults in their reproductive years), and the use of medications that alter hormone levels or endocrine responses (e.g., oral contraceptives). The variance generated by these factors can easily drown out whatever between-subject differences one hopes to observe in an experiment if it is not taken into account through proper study design (e.g., test participants only in the afternoon) or measurement of potential confounds (e.g., recording of information related to cycle stage, age, time of day, or use of medications; see Schultheiss & Stanton, 2009, for a screening questionnaire covering the most important variables).

The second issue of concern to a behavioral scientist who wants to use endocrine measures is how easy or difficult it is to assess a particular hormone. This in turn depends primarily on the biochemical properties of the hormone. *Peptide hormones* (i.e., short protein molecules, composed of a small number of amino acids), such as insulin, arginine-vasopressin, ACTH, NE, or oxytocin, are by molecular standards large structures and therefore do not easily pass through cell membranes. As a consequence, they can be measured only in the medium or body compartment into which they have been released or actively transported. Also, peptide hormone concentrations measured in the body may not accurately reflect peptide hormone levels in the brain because they are released by different hypothalamic neuron populations. Moreover, peptide hormones break down easily, and special precautions are necessary to stabilize their molecular structure after sampling. The other major class of hormones besides peptides are *steroid hormones*, which are synthesized in the body from cholesterol. In contrast to peptide hormones, steroid hormones are highly stable, and in their free bioactive form (i.e., not bound to larger proteins) can pass through cell membranes, leading to roughly similar levels of the free fraction of a hormone across body compartments. This means that, for instance, cortisol levels measured in saliva are similar to (free) cortisol levels measured in blood or cortisol levels in the brain. For this reason, and because saliva sampling is much easier and free of stress for research participants than the collection of blood samples or spinal fluid samples (to get at hormone levels within the central nervous system) salivary hormone assessment has become the method of choice among behavioral endocrinologists and psychologists working with human populations (Dabbs, 1992; Hofman, 2001; Kirschbaum & Hellhammer, 1994). Table 25.1 provides an overview of hormones that can be assessed in saliva, their psychological correlates and effects, and references that discuss the validity of saliva assays for each hormone.

HOW CAN HORMONES BE ASSESSED?

Assays are procedures for determining the presence and amount of a substance in a biological sample. For the assessment of hormones, a variety of assays are available that utilize the capacity of antibodies produced by an organism's immune system to bind in a precise way to a specific substance—hence the term *immunoassay*. For instance, antibodies can be raised in animals against human cortisol, and these antibodies are then used in immunoassays for the quantification of cortisol. One of the oldest and still most precise immunoassays is the radioimmunoassay (RIA). In RIAs, *radio* signifies that a fixed quantity of hormone molecules with radioactive labels (typically radioiodine [125-I], also called *tracer*) is added to the assay, and these molecules compete with molecules from samples collected from research participants for antibody binding sites. After a fixed incubation time, all excess tracer and sample are discarded, and only the antibody-bound molecules (both with and without radioactive label) are retained. The more signal from the radioactive substance is detected in a test tube, the more tracer-labeled hormone and the less natural sample hormone is present in the tube. Conversely, the less signal is detected, the more natural hormone is present. Adding known amounts of unlabeled hormone to the RIA enables the researcher to construct a standard curve—essentially a regression formula that allows estimating the amount of hormone

TABLE 25.1

Hormones and Endocrine Markers That Can Be Assayed in Saliva

Hormone	Psychological functions	Reviews
Cortisol	Indicates activation of the hypothalamus–pituitary–adrenal axis during stress; affects cognitive processes (memory, executive functions)	Kirschbaum & Hellhammer (1994); Kudielka, Hellhammer, & Wüst (2009)
Alpha-amylase	Marker of sympathetic nervous system activation during stress, release is stimulated by norepinephrine	Nater & Rohleder (2009)
Dehydroepiandrosterone	Associated with high psychological and physical well-being, memory function	Wolkowitz & Reus (2003)
Testosterone	Facilitates aggressive and nonaggressive forms of social dominance; enhances libido in men and women; supports male sexual behavior; influences cognition (e.g., mental rotation)	Dabbs (1992)
Estradiol	Enhances libido; involved in social dominance and sexual behavior; has profound effects on cognitive processes (e.g., verbal ability, memory); potentiates sensitization to psychostimulants	Riad-Fahmy, Read, Walker, Walker, & Griffiths (1987)
Progesterone	Decreases libido (particularly in men); anxiolytic; associated with affiliation motivation	Riad-Fahmy, Read, Walker, Walker, & Griffiths (1987)
Oxytocin	Facilitates pair bonding and parental behavior; increases trust; counteracts the stress response	Carter et al. (2007)

present in a given sample from the strength of the signal detected in the tube (see Schultheiss & Stanton, 2009, for more details on this procedure).

Although RIAs are widely considered the most valid and direct way of assessing hormones, they are increasingly being replaced by enzymatic immunoassays (EIAs) because of the hassles of licensing and properly running a radioisotope laboratory. EIAs operate according to the same principles as RIAs, except that the tracer signal is not based on radioactive decays but rather on enzymatic reactions, leading, for instance, to differences in sample coloration or luminescence that can be quantified. Among the drawbacks of EIAs, in comparison to RIAs, are the complexity of the assay protocols and the relatively lower accuracy and sensitivity (cf. Raff, Homar, & Burns, 2002).

A hormone assay, regardless of whether it is a RIA or an EIA, has to meet a number of criteria to be deemed valid and reliable. Assay validity is assessed through specificity, sensitivity, and accuracy; assay reliability is assessed through the precision of the measurements. Because it is important to understand these concepts, regardless of whether one reads assay quality information in a published paper, receives this type of information along with the data from an assay service, or is conducting one's own assays, we will briefly discuss each of these concepts in the following sections (for a thorough discussion of hormone assay validation, see O'Fegan, 2000).

Specificity is defined as the ability of an assay to maximize measurement of the targeted analyte and minimize measurement of other analytes. Specificity is often established by measuring the degree to which an assay produces measurements different from zero for nontargeted analytes (e.g., in the case of a cortisol assay, measurements greater than zero for progesterone, aldosterone, pregnenolone, and other related steroid hormones). Cross-reactivity with such nontarget analytes is estimated by dividing the measured, apparent concentration of the analyte by the amount added (e.g., 1,000 ug/dL aldosterone added, 0.4 ug/dL measured: (0.4/1,000) * 100 = 0.04% cross-reactivity).

Sensitivity is defined as the lowest dose of an analyte that can be distinguished from a sample containing no analyte. It is often pragmatically derived by calculating the lower limit of detection (LLD), which is defined as signal obtained from a sample with zero analyte (B_0), minus three times the standard deviation of the signal at B_0. Values outside of the $B_0 - 3 \times SD$ range are considered valid nonzero measurements.

Accuracy is defined as the ability of the assay to measure the true concentrations of the analyte in the samples being tested. Accuracy is measured by including control samples with known amounts of analyte in the assay and then comparing the amount of analyte estimated by the assay (e.g., 46 pg/mL) with the actual amount added (e.g., 50 pg/mL testosterone). The result is expressed as the percentage of the actual amount that is recovered by the assay (e.g., accuracy = (46/50) * 100 = 92%). Recovery coefficients between 90% and 110% reflect good accuracy.

Precision is defined as the degree of agreement between test results repeatedly and independently obtained under stable conditions. Precision is typically estimated by the coefficient of variation ($CV\%$), which is calculated as the mean of replicate measurements of a given sample, divided by the standard deviation of the measurements, multiplied by 100. The *intraassay* $CV\%$ is calculated as the average of the $CV\%$s of all duplicate samples in a given assay or set of assays; the *interassay* $CV\%$ is calculated from the between-assay mean and SD of a control sample (e.g., a saliva pool) included in all assays. Intra- and interassays $CV\%$s less than 10% are considered good.

Information about sensitivity, accuracy, and precision should be routinely obtained in hormone assays and reported in published research. Omission of these measurement credentials of an assay makes it difficult to judge the validity and reliability of the assay method used and may call into question the results obtained with it. Measures of specificity are not routinely included in hormone assays or research reports in behavioral endocrinology, but specificity should at least be carefully examined when a new assay is adopted.

COLLECTING, PROCESSING, AND ASSAYING SALIVA SAMPLES

High-quality hormone assessment starts with the careful collection and processing of the samples that will later be assayed for hormone concentrations. In keeping with our focus on salivary hormone assessment, we restrict our review of the necessary steps to the collection, processing, and analysis of saliva samples.

The goal of the saliva-collection phase is to collect high-quality samples (i.e., samples free of contaminants) in an exactly identified sequence and with a sufficient amount of saliva to later allow the measurement of all targeted hormones. Because hormone release is influenced by distal factors (e.g., age, genes) and by more proximal factors such as circadian changes and pulsatile secretion patterns on the order of hours, timing of the sampling process is critical for making sense of the data and capturing the effects of interest.

If salivary hormones are assessed with the goal of using the hormone measurements as individual difference variables (e.g., to address a question such as "Is salivary testosterone correlated with having a committed relationship to a partner?"; cf. Burnham et al., 2003), samples should be collected at the same time of day from all participants. Participants need to indicate the number of hours since waking as a key control variable that can be used as a covariate in analyses. If a researcher is interested in using hormone levels as a dependent variable in a study (e.g., to address a question such as "Does arousal of affiliation motivation lead to increases in salivary progesterone?"; cf. Brown et al., 2009; Schultheiss et al., 2004), at least two samples are needed to address the research question meaningfully: one baseline sample taken before the critical intervention or experimental procedure and one sample taken after the procedure.

The baseline sample should be collected immediately before the intervention takes place to account in later statistical analyses for as much hormone-level variance as possible that is not attributable to the intervention. Placement of the postintervention sample depends on the dynamics of salivary hormone changes and the properties of the intervention. Hormones released from their glands take seconds to minutes to spread out via the blood stream through the body and reach their target organs. It takes another 5 min to 10 min for these hormones to then cross from the blood stream to the salivary glands (Riad-Fahmy, Read, Walker, Walker, & Griffiths, 1987). Thus, it can take as much as 15 min to 20 min from the onset of a critical event that changes the amount of hormone released from a gland to the effect of these changes to show up in saliva as a robust signal that makes it across the statistical threshold. A meta-analysis on the effects of social–evaluative threat on salivary cortisol release found that the highest effect sizes can be detected about 20 min to 30 min after the intervention (Dickerson & Kemeny, 2004). Similarly, research on the effects of winning or losing a dominance contest on testosterone changes in men found replicable evidence for a testosterone response maximum 15 min to 30 min after the end of the contest (for summaries, see Schultheiss, 2007; Stanton & Schultheiss, 2009). In comparison, samples taken immediately after the end of an intervention or more than 45 min later are less likely to yield detectable effects of an experimental manipulation (Dickerson & Kemeny, 2004; Schultheiss et al., 2005; Schultheiss & Rohde, 2002; Wirth & Schultheiss, 2006).

Thus, if only one postintervention sample can be assayed in addition to a baseline sample, it should be placed about 20 min to 30 min after the end of the experimental procedure (or, if the intervention has a long duration [> 10 min], after its presumably most impactful component). If more than one postintervention sample can be taken, they should cover this *sweet spot* of situationally induced changes in steroid hormone levels, but, because of the time it takes for the salivary glands to fill up again and for hormones to pass into saliva, with intervals no less than 10 min between individual samples (e.g., taking samples at 15–20 and 30–35 min postintervention). Collecting samples is not expensive: It usually costs only cents in terms of expenses for collection tubes and storage. Therefore, more than one postintervention sample can be collected without much additional cost and the decision to assay only one or several of them can be deferred to a later date.

Over the years, several methods for collecting saliva have been introduced and evaluated. Some methods have aimed at stimulating saliva flow and speeding up the collection process (e.g., through the use of chewing gum or citric acid); others have attempted to combine this with a reduction of the embarrassment of letting spit drool out of one's mouth (e.g., through collecting saliva with the use of dental rolls that participants chew on). However, many of these methods alter the levels of the measured hormones and can add unsystematic error to the assessment of salivary hormones (see Dabbs, 1991; Shirtcliff, Granger, Schwartz, & Curran, 2001). As the overview of saliva collection methods provided in Table 25.2 indicates, very few methods can be recommended across the board for the assessment of salivary hormones. The method that is least likely to produce interference through the collection process is having participants spit directly into 50 mL centrifugation tubes, perhaps with the aid of a plastic straw through which saliva can flow into the tube. The only drawback of this method is that it can take some participants a long time to collect a sufficient quantity of saliva. Perhaps the only viable alternative to this is the use of sugarless chewing gum (Dabbs, 1991, found Trident Original Flavor sugarless gum to produce no interference) to stimulate saliva flow. This method has been validated only for use with salivary testosterone assessment, however, and its validity for the assessment of other hormones remains to be tested.

The amount of saliva to be collected for each sample depends on the number and type of assays to be performed on them later. For instance, if only one hormone will be assessed, the net amount needed for an assay is < 1 mL; if more hormones will be measured, the amount collected needs to be increased accordingly. We recommend obtaining information about how much saliva will be needed for each hormone assessment, adding up the volumes and adding 1 mL to account for sample attrition during saliva processing to calculate the target sample volume. Thus, if testosterone and cortisol will be assessed via RIA, 2×400 uL will be needed for each hormone, and a total volume of 2.6 mL (4×400 uL + 1 mL) should be collected at each sampling point. In our experience, it is easy to collect as much as 5 mL within 5 min, which easily accommodates the assessment of three or four hormonal parameters per sample. To ensure that participants collect a sufficient amount of saliva, we routinely mark the collection tubes at the targeted volume and instruct participants to fill the tube to the mark (see Schultheiss & Stanton, 2009, for more details on sample collection instructions).

TABLE 25.2

Overview and Evaluation of Saliva Collection Methods

Collection method	Recommendation
Passive drooling into plastic collection tube (can be aided by plastic straw)	Recommended, produces no interference; potential drawback: some participants may take several minutes to collect a sample (Dabbs, 1991; Shirtcliff et al., 2001)
Sugarless chewing gum	Recommended, produces little interference and speeds up sample collection; potential drawback: slight transient rise (< 1 min after onset of chewing) in salivary testosterone levels, but this can be avoided by asking participants to start collecting saliva only 2 min after onset of chewing (Dabbs, 1991; Granger et al., 2004); effects on other salivary hormones are unknown
Sugared chewing gum	Not recommended, produces elevated salivary testosterone levels (Dabbs, 1991); effects on others salivary hormones are unknown
Cotton rolls (Salivette)	Not recommended, produces increased measurements (relative to passive drooling into tube) for dehydroepiandrosterone, estradiol, testosterone, and progesterone, although not for cortisol (Shirtcliff et al., 2001)
Polyester rolls	Not recommended, produces increased measurements (relative to passive drooling into tube) for testosterone (Granger et al., 2004); effects on others salivary hormones are unknown
Citric acid (crystals or powder)	Not recommended, alters pH value of samples, which may later interfere with pH-critical immunoassays, and produces increased measurements (relative to passive drooling into tube) for testosterone (Granger et al., 2004); effects on other salivary hormones are unknown

To avoid contaminants like blood or residues from a meal, participants should be instructed to refrain from eating and brushing their teeth for at least 1 hour before coming to the lab. Research indicates that even though teeth-brushing can lead to blood leaking into saliva and thus to altered salivary hormone levels, this effect is transitory and no longer detectable 1 hour after brushing for all hormones tested so far (cortisol, dehydroepiandrosterone, testosterone, progesterone, estradiol; see Kivlighan, Granger, & Schwartz, 2005; Kivlighan et al., 2004). On arrival, participants are asked to rinse their mouths with water. Collection of the first sample should start no earlier than 5 min after rinsing to avoid dilution of saliva samples with water.

More generally, because research participants may not always comply with instructions or fail to inform the experimenter beforehand of conditions and medications that may alter hormone levels and endocrine functions (see Granger, Hibel, Fortunato, & Kapelewski, 2009), we recommend including a screening questionnaire in behavioral endocrinology studies that covers the most important factors that can influence circulating hormone levels (including menstrual cycle stage and duration). Schultheiss and Stanton (2009) included such a questionnaire in their Appendix. We recommend adding two questions to this questionnaire, namely, "How many hours did you sleep last night?" and "At what time did you wake up this morning?" These questions will allow researchers to calculate the time that has elapsed between getting up and the start of the data-collection session for each participant and to control for the effect of sleep duration on the functional capacity of the endocrine system. Finally, date and start time of each session should routinely be noted for each participant.

After a data-collection session has ended, all samples should be sealed and frozen immediately. Salivary hormone levels can undergo significant changes if samples are not frozen for extended periods of time, presumably because of bacterial activity in the samples (Granger, Shirtcliff, Booth, Kivlighan, & Schwartz, 2004; Whembolua, Granger, Singer, Sivlighan, & Marguin, 2006). If samples are stored only for a couple of weeks before assaying, a regular –20 °C chest freezer will suffice to preserve salivary

steroid concentrations. If, however, other analytes (alpha amylase, oxytocin) are targeted or samples have to be stored for extended periods of time (> 6 months), a –80 °C freezer is necessary to keep salivary hormone levels stable (Dabbs, 1991; Granger et al., 2004).

The goal of the second phase—saliva processing—is to make the saliva samples amenable to precise pipetting in the actual assay. To achieve this goal, all samples are first thawed and frozen three times after all data collection has been completed for the study. This procedure helps break down the long molecule chains (e.g., mucins) that make saliva sticky and viscous and turn the chains into a more watery, and thus precisely pipettable, fluid. The breakdown of molecular chains can be enhanced by speeding up freezing and thawing through the use of dry ice and a warm water bath—the stronger shearing forces associated with the fast temperature differential induced by the use of these aids facilitates the degradation of the molecule chains. After the third thaw, samples are spun for 10 min at 1,000 g in a refrigerated centrifuge to push all coarse content to the bottom of the tube (this process is similar to the separation of serum and plasma in blood samples). After centrifugation, the supernatant (i.e., the watery part of the sample that stays on top after centrifugation) of each sample is transferred to aliquot tube(s) (e.g., 5-mL, 2-mL, or 1.5-mL tubes). Care must be taken to avoid stirring up and transferring the coarse, sticky contents of saliva from the bottom of the tube during transfer. For this reason, we recommend centrifuging and aspirating only small batches of tubes (≤ 12) at a time. Coarse and watery components of saliva tend to mingle again after long waits between centrifugation and sample transfer to aliquots, particularly if samples are not refrigerated during and after centrifugation. After aliquoting, samples can be assayed right away or refrozen for later assaying.

The goal of assaying the samples is to provide a specific, sensitive, accurate, and reliable measurement of their hormone content. There are several ways to get saliva samples assayed for hormone content. Ideally, a researcher's university has an endocrinology lab whose services can be used or that at least provides researchers with an opportunity to run their assays. Such a lab can be found in biochemistry or anthropology departments or in medical schools and university hospitals. For the novice, we recommend teaming up with another researcher who has experience with the assessment of hormones and who can provide help and know-how with (salivary) hormone assays.

For a researcher who plans to include salivary hormone measures in her or his research on a regular basis, setting up a dedicated salivary hormone laboratory may be another option. The bare bones of such a lab include sufficient bench space (approximately 8 m to 10 m) and storage space, a lab freezer (–20 °C: approximately $2,000; –80 °C: approximately $8,000), a refrigerator (approximately $500), a refrigerated centrifuge (approximately $7,000), a water bath (approximately $500), a vacuum pump for the aspiration of fluids (approximately $300), and an assortment of pipets ranging from 10 uL to 1 mL (approximately $1,000 for three pipets). Depending on whether the lab uses only enzymatic immunoassays or also works with radioimmunoassay, the purchase of a plate reader in the former case (approximately $5,000) and a gamma counter in the latter ($15,000 to $50,000, depending on whether it is used or new and how many samples can be counted simultaneously) will be required. Finally, another $1,000 should be dedicated to the purchase of lab glassware, tubing, stoppers, and so forth. Thus, the price tag for a salivary hormone lab can run anywhere between $17,000 and $70,000, depending on the type of equipment purchased and not factoring in the cost of providing room, bench space, water supply, and air conditioning.

A third option is to have saliva sample analysis conducted by commercial assay labs that specialize in salivary hormone measurement. We strongly recommend that researchers not simply trust the claims these labs are making, but actually test their validity before and after sending off the samples. A thorough understanding of the quality parameters of good endocrine measurement as outlined is essential for this testing. A simple way to pick a good assay service is to compare the claims of the assay provider with the published literature. Good assay services offer assays that cover the range of hormone concentrations typically observed in salivary hormones and also report validity data (i.e., specificity, sensitivity,

accuracy, and precision) for this range. We recommend including accuracy checks calibrated for the hormone concentrations expected in the study sample (e.g., cortisol accuracy checks at 1.5 and 3.5 ng/mL, corresponding to low and high salivary levels of this hormone). The investment in a set of commercially available calibrator samples (e.g., Lyphochek from BioRad, Hercules, CA), a pipet, and a couple of tubes and pipet tips is comparatively small (less than $700) and ensures independent verification of the quality of the outsourced assays. Finally, customers of commercial assay services should expect to receive a complete set of data that includes not only the mean hormone level and $CV\%$ for each sample but also the values for each individual measurement (for verification of the intra-assay $CV\%$), the values for standard pools used across assays (for verification of interassay $CV\%$s), and the complete data on the standard curve, including the zero-concentration calibrator, which can be used to verify the service's claims about the sensitivity (LLD) of the assay.

Hormone assays come at a cost in terms of collection and processing materials, reagents, and work hours invested, and researchers need to factor in this cost when planning their studies and applying for funding. In our experience, the following rule of thumb works reasonably well when calculating the cost of a hormone assay, regardless of whether the test is conduct in your own lab or in a colleague's lab or whether you send the samples to a commercial lab: For each sample and each hormone assessed in duplicate (i.e., when the same sample is assayed twice to get an estimate not only of the mean concentration but also the measurement error in $CV\%$), expect a cost of approximately $10. Thus, if a researcher wants to collect three samples each from 60 participants and would like to have them assayed for cortisol and testosterone, she should plan a budget of $3,600 for the hormone assays (3 samples × 60 participants × 2 hormones × $10). Shipping and handling fees for mailing samples to an external lab need to be added to this estimate.

DATA ANALYSIS AND RESEARCH REPORT WRITING

Once the raw data from the assays have been collected, they need to be processed to arrive at estimates of the actual sample hormone concentrations. Schultheiss and Stanton (2009) provided a guided tour through the steps of data processing, and Nix and Wild (2000) provided an excellent in-depth treatment of the ins and outs of assay data processing. We next concentrate on data analytic strategies and presentation of the findings.

In general, the same rules and best practices for analyzing and reporting other kinds of data also apply to hormone measures. Thus, hormone data distributions should be examined for skew and, if necessary, transformed to bring them closer to a normal distribution (this is frequently necessary for salivary cortisol data and may be required for other hormones); this should be reported. If outliers are present in the hormone data (e.g., elevated estradiol caused by ovulation, high progesterone levels sometimes observed in women in the luteal phase or in the early stages of pregnancy, or extreme levels of cortisol sometimes observed in individuals with undiagnosed endocrine disorders) and they cannot be accommodated through standard data transformations, analyses should be run and reported with and without the outliers. If the findings hold up to scrutiny either way, nothing is lost by pointing this out; if they emerge only in one or the other case, this needs to be considered before deciding on whether to report the results; and if the research is reported, the information should be included in the Discussion section of the paper.

As discussed previously, almost all hormone measures are influenced by factors such as gender, time of day, and menstrual cycle stage. The influence of such factors needs to be controlled for in data analyses, particularly when salivary hormone levels have been assessed only once, often as a marker of a personality or behavioral disposition (see Sellers, Mehl, & Josephs, 2007). In this case, an analysis of covariance (ANCOVA) approach, in which the effect of the hormone of interest on the criterion measure is tested after such outside influences have been held constant, is suitable. Keep in mind, however, that the ANCOVA approach is valid only if the controlled-for variables exert only main effects on the criterion and do not significantly interact with the hormone in question.

If more than one sample has been collected in pre-and postintervention designs, the effects of extraneous factors such as time of day, gender, and so forth are already represented in the baseline hormone measure. If the baseline is being held constant in a (repeated-measures) ANCOVA design while testing the effects of an experimental manipulation on subsequently assessed hormone levels, controlling for extraneous factors usually does not account for additional significant portions of variance in the postintervention hormone measure(s), because their effect is already represented in the variance of the baseline hormone measure (see Schultheiss et al., 2005, for an example). Here, too, the researcher needs to ensure that the effects of the extraneous factors contained in the baseline measure are strictly additive and that no interaction effects with the experimental manipulation are present. This should not be presumed a priori but needs to be verified empirically. For instance, Stanton and Schultheiss (2007) tested the effects of implicit power motivation and winning or losing a dominance contest on changes in women's salivary estradiol levels. Because estradiol release is suppressed by oral contraceptives, simply controlling for baseline salivary estradiol (or, in addition, for oral contraceptive use) and then testing for effects of the predictors of interest on estradiol changes would have obscured the fact that the predicted estradiol changes could be observed only in women who did not take oral contraceptives: In this group of participants, salivary estradiol increased in power-motivated winners and decreased in power-motivated losers. This effect did not emerge in women who were taking oral contraceptives, and simply controlling for oral contraceptive use (instead of running analyses separately for women on and off oral contraceptives) would have amounted to throwing apples and oranges into one data-analytical basket.

Although we use the term *ANCOVA design* in the preceding paragraphs, we have done this as a conceptual shorthand for regression–analytic designs in which hormone levels as predictor or baseline variables are entered as quantitative predictors. Median-splits of hormone measures to make the design conform to the *design-cells* approach of classical analysis of variance is not recommended because of the loss of associated test power (Cohen & Cohen, 1983).

Similar to the reporting of other findings, reporting the results of hormone assays involves two steps. First, the method of assessment and its quality should be reported in the methods section. Second, the actual findings are reported in the results section. Description of the method should include the exact type and make of the assay; a short summary of the sample processing and sample assay protocol; and a statement of the main quality control parameters of the assay, that is, measures of validity (accuracy, LLD, analytical range) and reliability (intra- and interassay *CV*). Assay quality parameters provided by the manufacturers of commercially available assays should *not* be reported because these typically represent best-case scenarios that are included with the assay to promote sales and that may have little to do with the quality of the conducted assays on which the data are based. Reporting of findings should include descriptive data on the hormone levels observed in the sample and their relationship to major influences on endocrine function, such as gender, menstrual cycle stage, use of oral contraceptives, and time of day when samples were collected. In behavioral endocrinology journals like *Hormones and Behavior* and *Psychoneuroendocrinology*, presentation of actual hormone data and their associations with the key variables of interest in a given study typically takes the form of line or bar graphs with error bars in the case of repeated-measures designs or scatter plots with fitted regression lines in the case of correlations. Researchers who want to publish their findings in psychology journals should follow these standards because they conform to the guidelines of the American Psychological Association Task Force on Statistical Inference (Wilkinson & American Psychological Association Task Force on Statistical Inference, 1999) and allow the reader to evaluate the suitability of the statistical procedures used and inferences made, given the shape of the data.

CONCLUSION

To summarize, hormones are messenger molecules that are released in the brain and by glands in the body to carry a signal to other parts of the brain or body and thereby exert broad effects on physiology and behavior. For this reason, exploring the role of hormones to identify endocrine indicators of specific psychological phenomena and processes (e.g., stress, motivational and emotional states) has become a fruitful field of inquiry for psychologists. Hormone measures bear the advantage that they simultaneously meet personality psychologists' need for rank-order stability and social psychologists' need for measures being sensitive to the social stimuli impinging on the person. Potential drawbacks of the use of hormone measures, however, might be that (a) a particular hormone does not map onto a particular psychological construct in a one-to-one fashion, and (b) there are numerous complex interactions of hormonal systems with each other, the immune system, various brain systems, and peripheral organs. We believe, however, that a good understanding of the basic endocrine literature and careful, open-minded analysis of the findings one obtains from research employing hormone assays helps to master this complexity and can suggest exciting new lines of inquiry and discovery. This is work well invested because linking psychology with endocrinology paves the way for more fruitful interdisciplinary work in the behavioral and brain sciences.

References

Brown, S. L., Fredrickson, B. L., Wirth, M. M., Poulin, M. J., Meier, E. A., Heaphy, E. D., . . . Schultheiss, O. C. (2009). Social closeness increases salivary progesterone in humans. *Hormones and Behavior, 56,* 108–111. doi:10.1016/j.yhbeh.2009.03.022

Burnham, T. C., Chapman, J. F., Gray, P. B., McIntyre, M. H., Lipson, S. F., & Ellison, P. T. (2003). Men in committed, romantic relationships have lower testosterone. *Hormones and Behavior, 44,* 119–122. doi:10.1016/S0018-506X(03)00125-9

Carter, C. S., Pournajafi-Nazarloo, H., Kramer, K. M., Ziegler, T. E., White-Traut, R., Bello, D., & Schwertz, D. (2007). Oxytocin: Behavioral associations and potential as a salivary biomarker. *Annals of the New York Academy of Sciences, 1098,* 312–322. doi:10.1196/annals.1384.006

Cohen, J., & Cohen, P. (1983). *Applied multiple regression/correlation analysis for the behavioral sciences* (2nd ed.). Hillsdale, NJ: Erlbaum.

Dabbs, J. M. (1991). Salivary testosterone measurements: Collecting, storing, and mailing saliva samples. *Physiology and Behavior, 49,* 815–817. doi:10.1016/0031-9384(91)90323-G

Dabbs, J. M. (1992). Testosterone measurements in social and clinical psychology. *Journal of Social and Clinical Psychology, 11*, 302–321. doi:10.1521/jscp.1992.11.3.302

Dickerson, S. S., & Kemeny, M. E. (2004). Acute stressors and cortisol responses: A theoretical integration and synthesis of laboratory research. *Psychological Bulletin, 130*, 355–391. doi:10.1037/0033-2909.130.3.355

Granger, D. A., Hibel, L. C., Fortunato, C. K., & Kapelewski, C. H. (2009). Medication effects on salivary cortisol: Tactics and strategy to minimize impact in behavioral and developmental science. *Psychoneuroendocrinology, 34*, 1437–1448. doi:10.1016/j.psyneuen.2009.06.017

Granger, D. A., Shirtcliff, E. A., Booth, A., Kivlighan, K. T., & Schwartz, E. B. (2004). The "trouble" with salivary testosterone. *Psychoneuroendocrinology, 29*, 1229–1240. doi:10.1016/j.psyneuen.2004.02.005

Hofman, L. F. (2001). Human saliva as a diagnostic specimen. *Journal of Nutrition, 131*, 1621S–1625S.

Kirschbaum, C., & Hellhammer, D. H. (1994). Salivary cortisol in psychoneuroendocrine research: Recent developments and applications. *Psychoneuroendocrinology, 19*, 313–333. doi:10.1016/0306-4530(94)90013-2

Kivlighan, K. T., Granger, D. A., & Schwartz, E. B. (2005). Blood contamination and the measurement of salivary progesterone and estradiol. *Hormones and Behavior, 47*, 367–370. doi:10.1016/j.yhbeh.2004.12.001

Kivlighan, K. T., Granger, D. A., Schwartz, E. B., Nelson, V., Curran, M., & Shirtcliff, E. A. (2004). Quantifying blood leakage into the oral mucosa and its effects on the measurement of cortisol, dehydroepiandrosterone, and testosterone in saliva. *Hormones and Behavior, 46*, 39–46. doi:10.1016/j.yhbeh.2004.01.006

Kudielka, B. M., Hellhammer, D. H., & Wüst, S. (2009). Why do we respond so differently? Reviewing determinants of human salivary cortisol responses to challenge. *Psychoneuroendocrinology, 34*, 2–18. doi:10.1016/j.psyneuen.2008.10.004

Laeng, B., & Falkenberg, L. (2007). Women's pupillary responses to sexually significant others during the hormonal cycle. *Hormones and Behavior, 52*, 520–530. doi:10.1016/j.yhbeh.2007.07.013

Mazur, A. (1985). A biosocial model of status in face-to-face primate groups. *Social Forces, 64*, 377–402. doi:10.2307/2578647

Nater, U. M., & Rohleder, N. (2009). Salivary alpha-amylase as a non-invasive biomarker for the sympathetic nervous system: Current state of research. *Psychoneuroendocrinology, 34*, 486–496. doi:10.1016/j.psyneuen.2009.01.014

Nix, B., & Wild, D. (2000). Data processing. In J. P. Gosling (Ed.), *Immunoassays: A practical approach* (pp. 239–261). Oxford, England: Oxford University Press.

O'Fegan, P. (2000). Validation. In J. P. Gosling (Ed.), *Immunoassays: A practical approach* (pp. 211–238). Oxford, England: Oxford University Press.

Pope, H. G., Jr., Kouri, E. M., & Hudson, J. I. (2000). Effects of supraphysiologic doses of testosterone on mood and aggression in normal men: A randomized controlled trial. *Archives of General Psychiatry, 57*, 133–140; discussion 155–136.

Raff, H., Homar, P. J., & Burns, E. A. (2002). Comparison of two methods for measuring salivary cortisol. *Clinical Chemistry, 48*, 207–208.

Riad-Fahmy, D., Read, G. F., Walker, R. F., Walker, S. M., & Griffiths, K. (1987). Determination of ovarian steroid hormone levels in saliva. An overview. *Journal of Reproductive Medicine, 32*, 254–272.

Sapolsky, R. M. (1987). Stress, social status, and reproductive physiology in free-living baboons. In D. Crews (Ed.), *Psychobiology and reproductive behavior: An evolutionary perspective* (pp. 291–322). Englewood Cliffs, NJ: Prentice-Hall.

Schultheiss, O. C. (2007). A biobehavioral model of implicit power motivation arousal, reward and frustration. In E. Harmon-Jones & P. Winkielman (Eds.), *Social neuroscience: Integrating biological and psychological explanations of social behavior* (pp. 176–196). New York, NY: Guilford Press.

Schultheiss, O. C., & Rohde, W. (2002). Implicit power motivation predicts men's testosterone changes and implicit learning in a contest situation. *Hormones and Behavior, 41*, 195–202. doi:10.1006/hbeh.2001.1745

Schultheiss, O. C., & Stanton, S. J. (2009). Assessment of salivary hormones. In E. Harmon-Jones & J. S. Beer (Eds.), *Methods in the neurobiology of social and personality psychology* (pp. 17–44). New York, NY: Guilford Press.

Schultheiss, O. C., Wirth, M. M., & Stanton, S. J. (2004). Effects of affiliation and power motivation arousal on salivary progesterone and testosterone. *Hormones and Behavior, 46*, 592–599. doi:10.1016/j.yhbeh.2004.07.005

Schultheiss, O. C., Wirth, M. M., Torges, C. M., Pang, J. S., Villacorta, M. A., & Welsh, K. M. (2005). Effects of implicit power motivation on men's and women's implicit learning and testosterone changes after social victory or defeat. *Journal of Personality and Social Psychology, 88*, 174–188. doi:10.1037/0022-3514.88.1.174

Sellers, J. G., Mehl, M. R., & Josephs, R. A. (2007). Hormones and personality: Testosterone as a marker of individual differences. *Journal of

Research in Personality, 41, 126–138. doi:10.1016/j.jrp.2006.02.004

Shirtcliff, E. A., Granger, D. A., Schwartz, E., & Curran, M. J. (2001). Use of salivary biomarkers in biobehavioral research: Cotton-based sample collection methods can interfere with salivary immunoassay results. *Psychoneuroendocrinology, 26*, 165–173. doi:10.1016/S0306-4530(00)00042-1

Stanton, S. J., & Schultheiss, O. C. (2007). Basal and dynamic relationships between implicit power motivation and estradiol in women. *Hormones and Behavior, 52*, 571–580. doi:10.1016/j.yhbeh.2007.07.002

Stanton, S. J., & Schultheiss, O. C. (2009). The hormonal correlates of implicit power motivation. *Journal of Research in Personality, 43*, 942–949. doi:10.1016/j.jrp.2009.04.001

Whembolua, G. L., Granger, D. A., Singer, S., Kivlighan, K. T., & Marguin, J. A. (2006). Bacteria in the oral mucosa and its effects on the measurement of

cortisol, dehydroepiandrosterone, and testosterone in saliva. *Hormones and Behavior, 49*, 478–483. doi:10.1016/j.yhbeh.2005.10.005

Wilkinson, L., & American Psychological Association Task Force on Statistical Inference. (1999). Statistical methods in psychology journals: Guidelines and explanations. *American Psychologist, 54*, 594–604. doi:10.1037/0003-066X.54.8.594

Wirth, M. M., & Schultheiss, O. C. (2006). Effects of affiliation arousal (hope of closeness) and affiliation stress (fear of rejection) on progesterone and cortisol. *Hormones and Behavior, 50*, 786–795. doi:10.1016/j.yhbeh.2006.08.003

Wolkowitz, O. M., & Reus, V. I. (2003). Dehydroepiandrosterone in psychoneuroendocrinology. In O. M. Wolkowitz & A. J. Rothschild (Eds.), *Psychoneuroendocrinology: The scientific basis of clinical practice* (pp. 205–242). Washington, DC: American Psychiatric Publishing.

Measures in Neuroscience

CHAPTER 26

ELECTROENCEPHALOGRAPHIC METHODS IN PSYCHOLOGY

Eddie Harmon-Jones and David M. Amodio

PHYSIOLOGY UNDERLYING ELECTROENCEPHALOGRAPHY

Electroencephalography (EEG) refers to the recording of electrical brain activity from the human scalp. This method of measurement was discovered by Hans Berger in the late 1920s in experiments in which two sponges were soaked in saline and were then connected to a differential amplifier (Berger, 1929). EEG measurement techniques have advanced considerably since that time, and they now represent one of the most common methods for measuring brain function in studies of basic psychological and motor processes and in studies of psychological and motor dysfunction.

The observed EEG at the human scalp is the result of electrical voltages generated inside the brain. Electrical activity that is associated with neurons comes from action potentials and postsynaptic potentials. Action potentials are composed of a rapid series of electrochemical changes that run from the beginning of the axon at the cell body to the axon terminals where neurotransmitters are released. Postsynaptic potentials occur when the neurotransmitters bind to receptors on the membrane of the postsynaptic cell. This binding causes ion channels to open or close and it leads to a graded change in the electrical potential across the cell membrane. In contrast to EEG measurements, when electrical activity is measured by placing an electrode in the intercellular space, action potentials are more easily measured than postsynaptic potentials because it is difficult to

isolate a single neuron's postsynaptic potentials in extracellular space. Thus, the recording of individual neurons (or single-unit recordings) assesses action potentials but not postsynaptic potentials.

EEG differs from *electrocorticography* (ECoG), in which electrodes are placed directly on the exposed surface of the cortex. In ECoG, electrodes may be placed outside of the outer cranial membrane or dura mater (epidural) or under the dura mater (subdural). This technique is typically performed in a medical operating room because a surgical incision into the skull is needed to implant the electrode grid onto the cortex. ECoG is often used to identify the origins of epileptic seizures in individuals whose epilepsy cannot be treated with nonsurgical methods. During such sessions, ECoG is also used for functional cortical mapping to ensure that important functions (e.g., language production) are not harmed during surgery. Once the regions that are responsible for epileptic seizures are identified, they are surgically removed from the cortex. During such surgeries, researchers have also been able to use ECoG to identify cortical regions that are involved in psychological and behavioral processes (e.g., Crone, Sinai, & Korzeniewska, 2006).

ECoG signals are composed of synchronized postsynaptic potentials. These potentials occur primarily in cortical pyramidal cells. Because the potentials are recorded from the surface of the cortex, they must be conducted through several layers of the cerebral cortex, cerebrospinal fluid, pia mater, and

The work presented herein was funded in part by National Science Foundation Grant 0921565, awarded to Eddie Harmon-Jones.

DOI: 10.1037/13619-027

arachnoid mater before reaching subdural recording electrodes that are placed just below the dura mater (outer cranial membrane). With EEG, electrical signals must also be conducted through the skull; thus, the electrical potentials are severely reduced because of the low conductivity of bone. Consequently, the spatial resolution of ECoG is much higher than EEG.

Scalp-recorded EEG reflects the summation of postsynaptic potentials rather than action potentials because of the timing of action potentials and the physical arrangement of axons. That is, unless the neurons fire within microseconds of each other, action potentials in different axons will typically cancel each other out. If one neuron fires shortly after another one, then the current at a given location will flow into one axon at the same time that it flows out of another one; thus, they cancel each other out and produce a much smaller signal at the electrode. Although the duration of an action potential is approximately 1 ms, the duration of postsynaptic potentials is much longer, often tens or hundreds of milliseconds. Postsynaptic potentials are also mostly confined to dendrites and cell bodies and occur instantaneously rather than traveling down the axon at a fixed rate. These factors allow postsynaptic potentials to summate rather than to cancel, which results in voltage changes that have larger amplitudes and can be recorded on the cortical surface or at the scalp. Hence, EEG signals are most likely the result of postsynaptic potentials, which have a slower time course and are more likely to be synchronous and summate than presynaptic potentials.

Scalp-recorded electrical activity is the result of the activity of populations of neurons. This activity can be recorded on the scalp surface because the tissue between the neurons and the scalp acts as a volume conductor. The activity generated by one neuron is small; thus, the activity that is recorded at the scalp is the integrated activity of numerous neurons that are active synchronously. Moreover, for activity to be recorded at the scalp, the electric fields that are generated by each neuron must be oriented in such a way that their effects accumulate. That is, the neurons must be arranged in an open as opposed to a closed field. In an open field, the neurons' dendrites are all oriented on one side of the structure, whereas their axons all depart from the other side.

Open fields are present where neurons are organized in layers, as in most of the cortex, parts of the thalamus, the cerebellum, and other structures.

The raw EEG signal is a complex waveform that can be analyzed in the temporal domain or frequency domain. Processing of the temporal aspect is typically done with event-related potential designs and analyses, and has been discussed by Bartholow and Amodio (2009). In this chapter, we focus on frequency analyses of EEG, in which frequency is specified in hertz or cycles per second.

EEG RECORDING

In contemporary psychological research, EEG is recorded from 32, 64, 128, or more electrodes that are often mounted in a stretch-lycra electrode cap. Caps are relatively easy to position on a participant's head, and they include electrodes positioned over the entire scalp surface. Electrodes are often made of tin or silver and silver chloride; the latter are nonpolarizable but are typically much more expensive. Most modern EEG amplifiers with high input impedance utilize very low electrode currents. Thus, polarizable electrodes (tin) can often be used to record the typical range of electrical frequencies that are of interest in psychology experiments without distortion. However, for frequencies less than 0.1 Hz, nonpolarizable electrodes are recommended (see Polich & Lawson, 1985).

The electrode placements are typically based on the 10–20 system (Jasper, 1958), which was subsequently extended to a 10% electrode system (Chatrian, Lettich, & Nelson, 1988) and beyond. The naming convention for electrode positions is as follows. The first letter of the name of the electrode refers to the brain region over which the electrode sits. Thus, Fp refers to frontal pole, F refers to frontal region, C to central region, P to parietal region, T to temporal region, and O to occipital region. Electrodes in between these regions are often designated by using two letters, such as FC for frontal-central. After the letter is a number, as in F3, or another letter, as in FZ. Odd numbers are used to designate sites on the left side of the head and even numbers are used to designate sites on the right side of the head. Numbers increase as distance from the middle of the head increases, so F7 is farther from the midline than F3. Z is used to designate the midline, which goes from the front to the back of the head. Figure 26.1 illustrates a modern multichannel system based on the 10–20 system. Caps often contain a ground electrode, which is connected to the isoground of the amplifier and assists in reducing electrical noise. Eye movements, recorded using an electro-oculogram (EOG), are also recorded to facilitate artifact scoring of the EEG. EOG can be recorded from the supra- and suborbits of the eyes, to assess vertical eye movements, and from the left and right outer canthus, to assess horizontal eye movements. Additional electrodes are often placed

on earlobes so that offline digitally derived references can be computed. See the section titled Referencing for a more complete discussion of reference electrodes.

Sites where electrodes will be placed must be abraded (i.e., exfoliated) and cleaned to reduce electrode impedances, typically to under 5,000 ohms. Mild skin abrasion removes dead skin cells and oils that impede electrical conductance. Conductive gel is used as a medium between the scalp and electrodes. EEG, EOG, and other signals are then amplified with bio-amplifiers. For EEG frequency analyses, the raw signals are often bandpass filtered online (e.g., 0.1 Hz to 100 Hz) because the

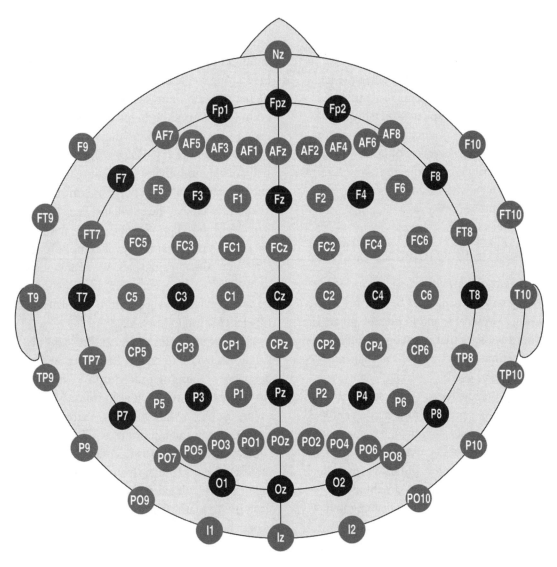

FIGURE 26.1. Electrode layout and labels commonly used in electroencephalography recording. The figure shows the top of the head, with the triangle at the top representing the nose. The electrodes displayed in black are the original 10–20 electrodes.

frequencies of interest fall within a relatively narrow frequency band (e.g., between 1 Hz and 40 Hz). Online 60 Hz notch filters (in the United States; 50 Hz in Europe) may also be used to further reduce electrical noise from alternating current (AC) sources, such as lamps and computers.

From the amplifiers, the raw signals are digitized onto a computer at a sampling rate greater than twice the highest frequency of interest. For example, if one is only interested in frequencies below 40 Hz, then 80 samples per second are sufficient. This sampling rate is necessary because of the Nyquist theorem, which states that reliable reconstruction of a continuous signal from its samples is possible if the signal is of limited bands and if it is sampled at a rate that is a least twice the actual signal bandwidth. If this sampling condition is not met, then frequencies will overlap; that is, frequencies above half the sampling rate will be reconstructed as frequencies below half the sampling rate. This distortion is called *aliasing* because the reconstructed signal is said to be an alias of the original signal. Given the power and large storage capacity of modern computers, however, sampling rates well above the Nyquist frequency are typically used, allowing for high-fidelity digital representations of analog signals.

PREPARING THE PARTICIPANT

Before running each participant, we recommend that the equipment be calibrated by running a sine wave of known amplitude and frequency through the amplifier to ensure that it is working appropriately. Many commercial systems have calibration routines that can be used.

Most EEG protocols require the researcher to spend almost an hour preparing the participant for EEG data collection; thus, we offer a few comments regarding the behavior of the researcher. When talking with the participants, we avoid using words such as *electricity*, *electrodes*, *needles*, or anything that sounds painful. Instead, we say, "I am going to be putting a cap on your head to measure brain activity." We also train our experimenters to adopt the mindset of a person who has done this *very routine procedure* many times. We work with them so that they appear confident and do not cause the participant to

worry about the procedure. For example, mistakes may be made during the attachment procedure, but we avoid announcing them to the participant because they can often be corrected easily. We also recommend that researchers avoid being too friendly because this can drastically alter the mood of the participants. In general, researchers working with participants should be encouraged to adopt a professional mind-set (and to wear lab coats).

Once the equipment is calibrated and all of the materials that are needed for the attachment of the EEG electrodes are ready (e.g., adhesive collars, conductive gel), the participant is brought into the experiment room. With many EEG systems, electrical impedance of the scalp will need to be brought under 5,000 ohms. To assist in reducing impedance, we ask participants to brush their hair vigorously for about 5 min with a stiff-bristled brush, which aids in exfoliating the scalp. For example, we tell participants, "Be sure to press the brush hard against your scalp as you brush. It helps with the attachment process. I will tell you when you can stop."

Once they are finished brushing their scalp, participants are told that we are going to use an exfoliant to clean some areas of their skin and use rubbing alcohol to remove the exfoliant. We clean their forehead, ear lobes, temples, and above and below the eyes with a mildly abrasive cleaning solution (e.g., Green Prep) and gauze pad. We follow the cleaning by wiping the areas with alcohol, which assists in removing the cleaning solution but also assists with further cleaning of the area.

Because most labs now use EEG caps instead of single electrodes to collect EEG data, we will describe the capping procedure. We first use a metric tape to measure the length from the *nasion* (a point just below the eyebrows where there is an indentation at the top of the nose) to the *inion* (bump on skull over the occipital region at the back of head). Then, 10% of this total distance (in centimeters) is calculated and measured up from the nasion. We mark this spot on the forehead with a wax pencil and explain this by saying, "I am going to make a mark on your forehead with a wax pencil. It will wipe right off." This mark will aid cap placement. Cap size is determined by measuring the distance around the participant's head, crossing the marks on the forehead and the inion. Caps often come in small, medium, and large sizes. When using some types of caps (e.g., from ElectroCap, Eaton, OH), two adhesive, cushioned collars are placed on cap sites Fp1 and Fp2 (if the cap has high-profile plastic housing enclosures around the electrodes). These collars are then adhered to the forehead in line with the wax pencil marks and centered over the nose. These adhesive-cushioned collars are not usable with some types of caps. When collars are not used, the experimenter aligns the Fp1 and Fp2 electrodes with the wax pencil marking. The cap is then stretched toward the back of the participant's head and down. Having the participant hold the cap in place on the forehead helps get the cap over the head. After the cap is straightened so that the midline electrodes align with the midline of the head, the distance from the nasion to the inion should be remeasured to ensure that Cz is halfway between these sites. If it is not, adjust the cap so that it is. Cz is centered horizontally by measuring from the preauricular indention in front of each ear; the indention can be found by having participants open their mouths and then feeling for the indention.

After attaching the cap's connectors to the preamplifier (e.g., the headbox), electrodes are often attached to each earlobe because one of these sites is often used as a reference site and the other is recorded as a separate channel so that off-line rereferencing of the average of the ears can be performed (online averaging of ears is not recommended; see the section Referencing). The electrodes are attached by placing an adhesive collar on the flat side and sticking it on the ear. Additional adhesive collars may be placed on top of the electrode to ensure that the electrode remains attached. Fill sensors with conductive gel but do not overfill; that is, avoid having gel run between two sensors or outside the adhesive collar because this will cause measurement problems or interfere with the adhesion of the collar. Next, abrade the ground electrode site with the blunt tip of a wooden cotton swab or the blunt tip of a large gauge needle, and apply gel with a syringe. We demonstrate to participants how we do this by making a motion with the syringe and blunt tip on their hands so that they know what to expect.

We then say, "I am going to put gel into each sensor." Impedances should be below 5,000 ohms. Some systems permit measuring EEG with higher impedances, but some researchers have questioned the reliability and validity of the data under certain recording conditions (Kappenman & Luck, 2010). Finally, a chinstrap for the cap is positioned comfortably under the participant's chin to ensure that the cap stays in place.

Eye movements are often measured in EEG research so that procedures can later be taken to remove eye movements from the EEG or to correct the EEG from these movements (see the section Eye Movement Artifacts). The eyeball is polarized, with a dipole running from the cornea to the retina, and the relatively large voltage changes from eye movements are recorded from scalp electrodes (especially toward the front of the scalp near the eyes). These measurements are referred to as *electro-oculograms* (EOG). Electrodes are affixed to the face using double-sided adhesive collars. For measuring vertical eye movements (e.g., caused by eye blinks), one electrode is placed 10% of the inion–nasion distance above the pupil and another is placed 10% of the inion–nasion distance below the pupil. These two electrodes are referenced to each other rather than to the EEG reference electrode. For measuring horizontal eye movements, one electrode is placed on the right temple and another is placed on the left temple. These electrodes are also referenced to each other. Because the EOG signal is relatively large, impedances up to 10,000 ohms are acceptable, and thus less face abrasion may be needed.

In addition to ensuring that the EEG equipment is properly attached, it is equally important to ensure that the participant is in a state of mind that is desired for the research question. For instance, if the study concerns personality characteristics or individual differences, it is important that characteristics of the situation not be so intense as to overwhelm potential individual differences of interest. Along these lines, we avoid making participants self-conscious by covering the computer monitor until it is ready to be used because as a black-screened computer monitor can act as a mirror. Similarly, video cameras are best hidden to avoid the arousal of excessive self-consciousness.

Artifacts

Artifacts, whether of biological or nonbiological origin, are best dealt with by taking preventative measures. When they do occur, procedures exist to reduce their effects on EEG measurements.

Muscle artifact. Muscle artifact (electromyography; EMG) typically comprises electrical signals that cycle at higher frequencies than EEG. Most EEG signals of interest are less than 40 Hz, whereas EMG is typically greater than 40 Hz. Some EMG, however, may blend in with the EEG frequencies, so it is advisable to limit muscle artifacts by instructing the participants to limit their muscle movements. If muscle artifacts do appear in studies in which muscle movements should not occur, the artifacts can be removed during the data-processing stage. Often, this is done manually, through visual inspection and exclusion by someone trained in EEG scoring.

In some experiments, particularly those that evoke emotion, muscle artifacts cannot be avoided. That is, if an intense amount of fear is evoked, the facial muscles of the participant will move and create muscle artifact in the EEG, particularly in frontal and temporal regions. Removing these muscle movements is not advisable because the removal process would also exclude signals of interest related to emotion. One way to handle the EMG that may contaminate the EEG is to measure facial EMG directly and then use the facial EMG responses (in EMG frequency ranges, such as 50–250 Hz) in covariance analyses. This analysis would indicate whether any observed effects for EEG were related to EMG responses or whether statistical adjustment may be needed to reveal effects. Similarly, one can obtain EMG frequencies from the scalp electrode sites, rather than facial muscle sites, and use these EMG frequencies in covariance analyses (see Coan, Allen, & Harmon-Jones, 2001, for examples). These issues have been investigated extensively in recent research (e.g., McMenamin, Shackman, Maxmell, Greischar, & Davidson, 2009).

Eye movement artifacts. Eye movement artifacts are also best dealt with in advance of EEG recording. That is, training participants to limit eye movements during EEG recording is recommended. Researchers must not encourage participants to control their blinking, because blinks and spontaneous eye movements are controlled by several brain systems in a highly automatic fashion (e.g., Brodal, 1992), and the instruction to suppress these systems may act as a secondary task, creating distraction and cognitive load (see Verleger, 1991, for a discussion).

Participants will inevitably blink, and these blinks will influence the EEG data, particularly in the frontal electrodes. Therefore, epochs containing blinks should be removed from the EEG or corrected via a computer algorithm (Gratton, Coles, & Donchin, 1983; Semlitsch, Anderer, Schuster, & Presslich, 1986). These algorithms often rely on regression techniques, but other techniques involving principal or independent component analyses have been recommended as well (e.g., Joyce, Gorodnitsky, & Kutas, 2004; Wallstrom, Kass, Miller, Cohn, & Fox, 2004). In the regression approaches to EOG correction, the actual EEG time-series is regressed on the EOG time-series, and the resulting residual time-series represents a new EEG from which the influence of the ocular activity is statistically removed. Then, eye-movement, artifact-corrected EEG data may be processed as would EEG data without EOG artifacts. This latter procedure has the advantage of not losing data; in contrast, the eye-movement rejection procedure can cause significant amounts of data loss. Some disadvantages of eye-movement artifact correction have been discussed (Hagemann & Naumann, 2001), but evidence suggests that it does not cause a distortion of frontal EEG asymmetry (Hagemann, 2004), a measure of interest in contemporary psychology that will be discussed in detail later.

Nonbiological artifacts. Nonbiological artifacts are those that typically involve external electrical noise coming from elevator motors, electric lights, computers, or almost anything running electricity nearby the subject. Again, prevention is the best defense against such artifacts. Although full electrical shielding is not usually necessarily with modern EEG amplifiers, it is important to remove or repair any poorly shielded electrical equipment. It is also helpful to limit the use of power outlets in the EEG recording chamber and to use direct current lamps if possible. High electrode impedances or a faulty ground connection can also increase AC noise (e.g., 60 Hz). Electrodes need to be carefully washed after each use to prevent corrosion and to assist in prevention of artifacts. When electrical noise is present, it can be dealt with through filtering of the signal; that is, 60-Hz activity can be removed with an online filter or after the data are collected.

OFF-LINE DATA PROCESSING

Referencing

EEG signals are often rereferenced. The issue of referencing is the subject of some debate (Allen, Coan, & Nazarian, 2004; Davidson, Jackson, & Larson, 2000; Hagemann, 2004; Nunez & Srinivasan, 2006). All bioelectrical measurements reflect the difference in activity between at least two sites. In EEG research, one site is typically placed on the scalp, whereas the other site may be on the scalp or on a nonscalp area, such as an earlobe or nose tip. Researchers strive to obtain measures that reflect activity in particular brain regions; thus, they often search for a relatively inactive reference, such as the earlobe. There are no "inactive sites," however; all sites near the scalp reflect some EEG activity because of volume conduction. To address this issue, some researchers suggest using an average reference composed of the average of activity at all recorded EEG sites. The average reference should approximate an inactive reference if a sufficiently large array of electrodes is placed in a spherical arrangement around the head. That is, activity generated from dipoles will be positive at one site and negative at a site 180 degrees opposite to this site. Thus, the sum across sites should approach zero with a representative sample of the sphere. Electrodes are not placed under the head; thus, this assumption is rarely met. Moreover, use of smaller montages of electrodes causes more residual activity in the average reference.

Other researchers have recommended the use of linked earlobes as a reference because of the relatively low EEG activity in the earlobes and because linking the earlobes should theoretically center the reference on the head, making the determination of lateralized activity more accurate. Linking the ears into one reference electrode has been questioned

(Katznelson, 1981), however, because it can produce a low-resistance shunt between the two sides of the head, reducing any asymmetries that are observed at the scalp. Research, however, has suggested that physically linking the ears does not alter the observed EEG asymmetries (Andino et al., 1990). Some EEG researchers have suggested that the original idea was ill conceived because electrode impedances will be higher than the internal resistance within the head. Hence, linked earlobes do not provide a shunt that is lower in resistance than what is present inside the head (Davidson et al., 2000). Physically linking the ears is inappropriate for another reason. When the ears are linked before input into the amplifier, variations in the impedances of the left and right electrodes will change the spatial location of the reference and potentially alter the magnitude and direction of any observed differences in left versus right EEG activity (Davidson et al., 2000). This does not happen when creating an averaged ears reference off-line, after the data have been collected, because most contemporary amplifiers have very high input impedances (around 100 kΩ) and variations in electrode impedances of several thousand ohms will have a tiny effect on the observed voltage. To create an off-line linked or averaged ears reference, the collected EEG data need to be actively referenced online to one of the ears or some other location (e.g., Cz). Then, electrical signals need to be collected from the other ear when the active reference is one ear, or both ears, in the case of a Cz reference. Off-line, the data are rereferenced to the average of the two ears.

Which reference should be used? From the perspective of psychological construct validity, use and comparison of different reference schemes in each study might be advisable (see Coan & Allen, 2003, for an example). A significant interaction involving reference factor would indicate that the EEG–psychological variable relation is moderated by the reference. If such research is conducted over several years, EEG researchers may establish good psychological construct validity of the particular EEG measure.

From the perspective of neurophysiological construct validity, selecting a particular reference in advance might be advisable, considering the advantages and disadvantages of each method for the EEG measurement construct. For example, in research on asymmetrical frontal cortical activity and emotion and motivation, Hagemann (2004) recommended against using the average reference if only limited head coverage was used, as in the 10–20 system. He indicated that the average reference may cause increased anterior alpha activity; averaging of the whole head can inflate anterior alpha because anterior regions have much lower alpha power than posterior regions. Thus, the off-line average of earlobes may be more appropriate. Although this reference shows some alpha activity and, thus, is not inactive, it may yield better signal-to-noise ratio for anterior sites than the average (whole head) reference.

Obtaining the Frequencies of the EEG Signal

Several steps are involved in transforming EEG signals into indices that are used in data analyses. First, a signal is collected in the time-domain and is then converted to a frequency-domain representation, usually in the form of a power spectrum. The spectrum, which collapses data across time, summarizes which frequencies are present. See Figure 26.2 for an illustration. Spectral analysis involves examining the frequency composition of short windows of time (epochs), often 1 or 2 s each. The spectra are averaged across many epochs. Epochs of 1 or 2 s are used to meet an assumption underlying the Fourier transform, which is the method used to derive power spectra. The Fourier transform assumes a periodic signal, or one that repeats and does so at a uniformly spaced interval. Any periodic signal can be decomposed into a series of sine and cosine functions of various frequencies, with the function for each frequency beginning at its own particular phase. EEG signals are not exactly periodic because the repetition of features is not precisely spaced at uniform intervals. The use of short epochs allows one to analyze small segments of data that will have features that repeat in a highly similar fashion at other points in the waveform.

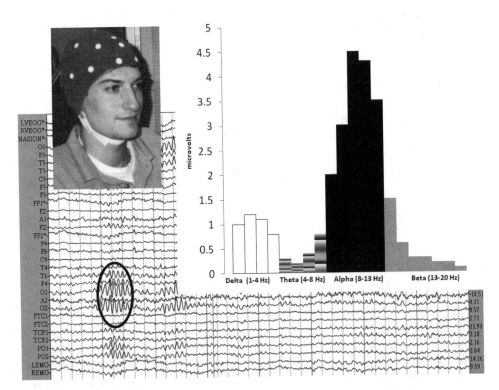

FIGURE 26.2. The background displays raw electroencephalograhy (EEG), and the circled portion is an example of a prominent alpha burst obtained over occipital region when a subject's eyes are closed. The picture in the upper right displays the results of a fast Fourier transform at one electrode. The picture in the upper left displays David Amodio wearing an EEG cap.

In EEG research, epochs are often overlapped. This is done to prevent a problem that occurs with *windowing*, a necessary part of the EEG data processing. Windowing, as with a Hamming window, is used to avoid creating artifactual frequencies in the resultant power spectra. Windowing tapers the power of signals in an epoch toward the endpoints of the epoch, reducing the endpoints to near-zero values so that discontinuities will not occur if copies of the epochs are placed immediately before or after the epoch. This assists in meeting the Fourier assumption that the epoch repeats infinitely both forward and backward in time. Fourier methods introduce spurious frequencies if windowing is not used to prevent discontinuities in the signal. Windowing prevents discontinuity, but also prevents data near the ends of the epoch from being fully represented in the power spectrum. Overlapping epochs provides a solution to this problem because data minimally weighted at the end of one epoch will be weighted more heavily in subsequent epochs.

Most signal processing programs use a fast Fourier transform (FFT). The FFT requires that the epochs to be analyzed have data points that are a power of 2 (e.g., 128, 256, 512, or 1,048 data points). The FFT produces two spectra, a power spectrum and a phase spectrum. The power spectrum reflects the power in the signal at each frequency from direct current (DC) to the Nyquist frequency, with a spectral value every $1/T$ points, where T is the length of the epoch analyzed. The phase spectrum presents the phase of the waveform at each interval $1/T$. Often, analyses focus only on the power spectrum. The FFT of each epoch produces a power spectrum, and the average of the obtained power values is used in analyses. Further reduction is accomplished by summarizing data within conventionally defined frequency bands.

Frequency Bands of Interest

Past discussions of EEG frequency bands have suggested that there are five bands with relationships to psychological and behavioral outcomes. These bands are delta (1–4 Hz), theta (4–8 Hz), alpha (8–13 Hz), beta (13–20 Hz), and gamma (> 20 Hz). Many of the psychological and behavioral correlates of these frequency bands that are mentioned in past

reviews were based on visual inspection of the frequency bands and not on mathematical derivations of the frequencies of interest, as is now commonly done with spectral analyses. Recent research with these more precise and accurate methods of measuring EEG frequencies has questioned some earlier conclusions, although much of the work is relatively recent and has not been incorporated into psychology as of yet. Moreover, the extent to which these bands are discrete from each other or differ as a function of scalp region has not been examined in a rigorous statistical fashion. Finally, research has suggested that the frequency bands below 20 Hz are highly and positively correlated (Davidson, Chapman, Chapman, & Henriques, 1990; Harmon-Jones & Allen, 1998). Consequently, we review research that has focused on alpha power, as it has attracted most of the attention of psychologists, perhaps in part because it accounts for a large percentage of the adult EEG.

RESEARCH EXAMPLES

Several psychological studies have examined differences in left and right frontal cortical activity in relationship to emotional and motivational processes (Coan & Allen, 2004; Harmon-Jones, Gable, & Peterson, 2010). In this research, alpha power has been used because it appears to be inversely related to cortical activity according to studies using a variety of methods, such as positron emission tomography (Cook et al., 1998) and functional magnetic resonance imaging (fMRI; Goldman, Stern, Engel, & Cohen, 2002). Moreover, behavioral tasks that are presumed to activate a particular brain region have been shown to cause alpha power suppression in that region (e.g., Davidson et al., 1990).

Power within the alpha frequency range is obtained using the methods described in the previous section. Alpha power values are often log transformed for all sites to normalize the distributions. Then, in the research that is reviewed in the section Research Examples, asymmetry indexes (natural log right minus natural log left alpha power) are computed for all homologous sites, such as F3 and F4 or P3 and P4. Because alpha power is inversely related to cortical activity, higher scores on the asymmetry indexes indicate greater relative left-hemispheric activity.

Frontal Alpha Power Asymmetry at the Trait Level

A large portion of the frontal EEG alpha-power asymmetry literature on individual differences has examined relations between personality and resting baseline asymmetry. In these studies, resting asymmetry is utilized as a stable index of an individual's dispositional style across situations. For example, resting EEG asymmetry appears to relate to social behavior. In one study, EEG data recorded from infants at 9 months old were used to predict social wariness at 4 years old (Henderson, Fox, & Rubin, 2001). Negative emotionality, as reported by the infants' mothers, predicted social wariness in infants who displayed relatively greater right-frontal activity. This relationship was not found in infants who displayed relatively greater left-frontal activity (Henderson et al., 2001). Another study found that socially anxious preschool children exhibited increased right frontal activity compared with their peers (Fox et al., 1995).

The largest body of literature examining relations with resting EEG asymmetry stems from the research on emotion. Greater relative left- and greater relative right-frontal activity have been found to relate to individual differences in dispositional positive and negative affect, respectively (Tomarken, Davidson, Wheeler, & Doss, 1992). Individuals with stable relative left-frontal activity report greater positive affect to positive films, whereas individuals with stable relative right-frontal activity report greater negative affect to negative films (Wheeler, Davidson, & Tomarken, 1993). The positive affect–left versus negative affect–right frontal asymmetry has been referred to as the *affective-valence* hypothesis of frontal asymmetry.

More recent research has suggested that affective valence does not explain the relation between emotive traits and asymmetric frontal activity and that approach–withdrawal motivational direction may provide a more accurate explanation of this relation (Harmon-Jones, 2003). For example, Harmon-Jones and Allen (1997) compared resting frontal asymmetry to behavioral withdrawal–approach sensitivities,

as measured by the Behavioral Inhibition System/Behavioral Activation System (BIS/BAS) scales (Carver & White, 1994). They found that higher left-frontal cortical activity during a resting baseline period related to higher trait-approach motivation scores. Sutton and Davidson (1997) replicated this effect and found that asymmetrical frontal activity was more strongly related to approach–withdrawal motivation than positive and negative affectivity (as measured with the Positive and Negative Affect Schedule; Watson, Clark, & Tellegen, 1988). Consistent with findings linking left-frontal asymmetry to BAS, Master et al. (2009) recently observed an association between greater left-sided baseline activity and individual differences in emotional approach coping, another form of self-regulatory tendencies that are linked to approach motivation.

Other research examining relations between resting frontal asymmetry and psychopathology has also supported the role of motivational direction. Depression, for example, has been characterized by a general lack of approach motivation and decreased positive affect. Research has shown that higher scores on the Beck Depression Inventory (Beck, Ward, Mendelson, Mock, & Erbaugh, 1961) relate to greater relative right-frontal cortical activity at resting baseline (Schaffer, Davidson, & Saron, 1983). Further studies support the relation, showing that depression relates to trait-level, increased right-frontal activity or reduced left-frontal activity (Allen, Iacono, Depue, & Arbisi, 1993; Henriques & Davidson, 1990, 1991). Other examples come from research on bipolar disorder: Increased relative right-frontal activity at resting baseline has been observed in bipolar depression (Allen et al., 1993), whereas increased relative left-frontal activity at resting baseline has been observed in mania (Kano, Nakamura, Matsuoka, Iida, & Nakajima, 1992).

The evidence that most strongly challenges the affective-valence hypothesis comes from research on anger. Most research examining relations between frontal asymmetry and emotion have confounded valence and motivational direction, for example, because most of the negative affects that have been examined are withdrawal oriented (e.g., fear, disgust). Anger, however, is an approach-oriented negative emotion (Carver & Harmon-Jones, 2009) that appears to relate to relatively greater left-frontal resting cortical activity rather than relatively greater right-frontal cortical activity (Harmon-Jones, 2004). For example, Harmon-Jones and Allen (1998) assessed dispositional anger using the Buss and Perry (1992) Aggression Questionnaire and then measured resting alpha power asymmetries over the whole head. Trait anger correlated positively with left-frontal activity and negatively with right-frontal activity (Harmon-Jones & Allen, 1998). These findings support the *motivational direction* model of frontal asymmetry, which proposes that approach motivation relates to relatively greater left- than right-frontal activity, whereas withdrawal motivation relates to relatively greater right- than left-frontal activity (Harmon-Jones, 2004).

Frontal Asymmetry and State Manipulations

Although resting baseline frontal asymmetries predict certain dispositional styles and psychopathologies, there have been failures to replicate some of the resting baseline asymmetry and affective trait relations (see Coan & Allen, 2004, for review). This may be because asymmetrical frontal cortical activity is also sensitive to state manipulations (e.g., Hagemann, Naumann, Becker, Maier, & Bartussek, 1998; Reid, Duke, & Allen, 1998). In fact, approximately half of the variance in baseline resting measurements is associated with state rather than trait variance (Hagemann, Naumann, Thayer, & Bartussek, 2002). Variance in resting EEG has even been found to be caused by time of day and time of year, such that relative right-frontal activity is greatest during fall mornings (Peterson & Harmon-Jones, 2009). This latter finding fits with other work suggesting that (a) seasonal variations influence mood such that the fall is associated with more depression than other seasons and (b) circadian variations influence the release of the stress hormone, cortisol, such

that mornings are associated with greater cortisol. These factors need to be considered in EEG asymmetry research.

Several studies have revealed asymmetric alpha power activations during the experience of emotive states. For instance, newborn infants evidenced greater relative left-hemispheric activation (suppression of alpha power) in response to a sucrose solution placed on the tongue, whereas they evidenced greater relative right-hemispheric activation in response to a water solution, which elicited a disgust facial expression (Fox & Davidson, 1986).

Other experiments have examined the effect of manipulated facial expressions of emotion on asymmetric frontal alpha power. In one experiment, participants made expressions of disgust, fear, anger, joy, and sadness while EEG was recorded. Relatively less left- than right-frontal activity was found during facial expressions of withdrawal-oriented emotions (disgust, fear) compared with approach-oriented emotions (joy, anger; Coan et al., 2001).

Experiments on asymmetric alpha power have also examined more complex emotions such as guilt. Manipulated feelings of guilt, as a result of feedback informing low-prejudice participants that they had responded with racial bias, were found to cause a reduction in relative left-frontal cortical activity, and greater reductions were correlated with greater self-reported guilt but not with other negative emotions (Amodio, Devine, & Harmon-Jones, 2007).

To further compare the affective-valence (positive–negative) model with the motivational direction (approach–withdrawal) model of asymmetric frontal cortical activity, experiments were conducted in which anger was manipulated. For example, Harmon-Jones and Sigelman (2001) manipulated state anger by leading participants to believe that another participant (ostensibly in the next room) had insulted them on the basis of an essay that they wrote on an important social issue. EEG activity recorded immediately following the insult revealed an increase in left-frontal activation compared with individuals in the no-insult condition (Harmon-Jones & Sigelman, 2001). This increase in left-frontal activation related to an increase in self-reported anger and aggressive behavior, which was not the case in the no-insult condition (Harmon-Jones & Sigelman, 2001). Subsequent studies have conceptually replicated these effects demonstrating that increases in state self-reported anger (and jealousy) relate to greater relative left-frontal activation after social rejection (Harmon-Jones, Peterson, & Harris, 2009; Peterson, Gravens, & Harmon-Jones, in press). Additional research has found that manipulating sympathy before an angering event reduces the left-frontal activation that is caused by anger (Harmon-Jones, Vaughn-Scott, Mohr, Sigelman, & Harmon-Jones, 2004). Other research has revealed that it is specifically the approach-motivational character of anger that increases relative left-frontal activation (Harmon-Jones, Lueck, Fearn, & Harmon-Jones, 2006; Harmon-Jones, Sigelman, Bohlig, & Harmon-Jones, 2003).

Motivation often involves body movements and postures, so it may come as no surprise that body postures antithetical to approach motivation would reduce patterns of neural activity that are associated with approach motivation. When individuals were in a supine body posture and angered, they did not respond with an increase in relative left-frontal cortical activity that is typically observed during anger (Harmon-Jones & Peterson, 2009). These results may have important implications for research using neuroimaging methods that require individuals to be in a supine position during experiments.

In the above studies, anger and approach motivation were manipulated and EEG was assessed. To more firmly establish the causal role of relative left-frontal activity in aggressive motivation, a study was conducted in which asymmetrical frontal cortical activity was manipulated, and the effects of this manipulation on aggression was measured (Peterson, Shackman, & Harmon-Jones, 2008). In this experiment, participants made either left-hand or right-hand contractions for four periods of 45 s. The contractions caused contralateral activation of the motor cortex and prefrontal cortex (i.e., right-hand contractions caused greater relative left activation and vice versa). Participants were then insulted by another ostensible participant. Following the insult, participants played a reaction-time game against the insulting participant. Participants were told that they would be able to administer a blast of white noise (and could decide the length and intensity of the noise blast) to the other participant if they responded faster to the stimulus than did the other participant. Individuals who made right-hand contractions were significantly more aggressive during the game than individuals who made left-hand contractions, and the degree of relative left-frontal

activation correlated with aggression in the right-hand contraction condition (Peterson et al., 2008).

The motivational direction model can also be compared with the affective-valence model by examining positive affects that differ in motivational intensity. Some positive affects are more strongly associated with approach motivation than others. According to the motivational direction model, positive affects that are higher in approach motivational intensity should evoke greater relative left-frontal activation than positive affects that are lower in approach motivational intensity. To test these ideas, participants were asked to recall and write about one of three things: (a) a neutral day; (b) a time when something positive happened to them that they did not cause, such as a surprise gift from a friend; or (c) a goal they were committed to achieving. The second condition was designed to manipulate positive affect that was low in approach motivation. The third condition was designed to manipulate positive affect that was higher in approach motivation. Past research suggested that this third condition increases positive affect (Harmon-Jones & Harmon-Jones, 2002; Taylor & Gollwitzer, 1995). Results from the experiment revealed greater self-reported positive affect in the two positive affect conditions relative to the neutral condition. More important, greater relative left-frontal cortical activity was found in the approach-oriented positive affect condition compared with the neutral condition and the low-approach positive affect condition (Harmon-Jones, Harmon-Jones, Fearn, Sigelman, & Johnson, 2008).

Individual Differences Predict Asymmetry During State Manipulations

Research has also examined the role of individual differences in responses to state manipulations. For example, the BAS dysregulation theory posits that individuals with bipolar disorder are extremely sensitive to reward and failure cues, so that they show "an excessive increase in BAS activity in response to BAS activation-relevant events (e.g., reward incentives, goal striving) and an excessive decrease in BAS activity in response to BAS deactivation-relevant events (e.g., definite failure)" (Nusslock, Abramson, Harmon-Jones, Alloy, & Hogan, 2007, p. 105).

Given that the left-frontal cortical region is associated with approach motivation, it was predicted and confirmed that individuals with bipolar disorder would show increased left-frontal activation in response to goal-striving (Harmon-Jones, Abramson, et al., 2008).

Another study examined how hypomanic and depressive traits affected frontal asymmetry in response to an anger-inducing event (Harmon-Jones et al., 2002). Research on hypomania has suggested the involvement of increased BAS activity, whereas depression may be associated with decreased BAS activity. In support of these ideas, proneness toward hypomania related to an increase in left-frontal activation and proneness toward depression related to a decrease in left-frontal activation in response to an anger-inducing event (Harmon-Jones et al., 2002).

Research has also been conducted on normal populations. Gable and Harmon-Jones (2008) examined individual differences in response to appetitive stimuli. They found that self-reported time since last eating and reported liking for dessert related to greater relative left-frontal activation during viewing of desirable food pictures (Gable & Harmon-Jones, 2008; see also Harmon-Jones & Gable, 2009).

The research on asymmetrical frontal cortical activity has shed light on a number of questions of interest to psychologists. Indeed, of the EEG frequency research to date within psychology, research on EEG asymmetry is the most prevalent. Other EEG frequency research is of interest to psychologists, and we briefly review some of this exciting work in the next section.

Other Analyses of Interest

Relations among frequency bands. Recent research has suggested that the ratio between resting-state frontal theta and beta activity might shed light on important psychological processes. For example, increased theta–beta ratio has been observed in children with attention-deficit/hyperactivity disorder (Barry, Clarke, & Johnstone, 2003). Other research has revealed that increased theta–beta ratios are associated with disadvantageous decision-making strategies on the Iowa gambling task (Schutter & van Honk, 2005). Scientists have suggested that slower frequency waves such as delta and theta are associated with subcortical brain regions involved in affective processes (Knyazev & Slobodskaya, 2003), whereas faster frequency waves such as beta are associated with thalamo-cortical- and cortico-cortical-level activations that may be involved in cognitive control processes (Pfurtscheller & Lopes da Silva, 1999).

Event-related desynchronization. Event-related desynchronization (ERD) is a measurement of the time-locked average power associated with the desynchronization of alpha rhythms. It is measured using event-related potential designs, which are described in Bartholow and Amodio (2009). That is, across multiple experimental events, an average is taken within the same stimulus condition. The time window is usually 1 s in length, and the amount of desynchronization is examined over 100-ms bins within the 1-s window. We have examined alpha ERD in an experiment in which participants viewed photographs of attractive desserts or neutral items. Results indicated that relatively greater left-frontal activity, as measured by ERD, occurred during the first second of viewing of the photograph (Gable & Harmon-Jones, 2008). Moreover, this effect appeared to peak at 400 ms.

Coherence. Coherence measures the degree to which EEG signals (within a given frequency band) that are measured at two distinct scalp locations are linearly related to one another. High coherence implies that amplitudes at a given frequency are correlated across EEG samples. Moreover, there tends to be a constant phase angle (or time lag) between the two signals. Research has suggested that high EEG coherence occurs between scalp regions that are connected by known white matter tracts (Thatcher, Krause, & Hrybyk, 1986). For instance, during right-hand contractions, individuals with greater trait-approach motivational tendencies show greater EEG alpha power coherence between the left motor cortex and left-frontal region than do individuals with lower trait-approach motivational tendencies (Peterson & Harmon-Jones, 2008). Perhaps the appetitive processes associated with trait approach motivation and activation of the left-frontal cortical region require close connectivity with the motor cortex.

Similarly, phase synchrony in gamma band (30–80 Hz) EEG has been used to investigate various cognitive phenomena, such as selective attention and working memory (e.g., Fell, Fernandez, Klaver, Elger, & Fries, 2003) and in understanding clinical problems such as schizophrenia (e.g., Lee, Williams, Breakspear, & Gordon, 2003).

Source localization. EEG frequency analyses do not provide direct information about the anatomical origins of the observed signals. With high-density EEG arrays, it is possible to conduct source localization techniques to estimate intracerebral electrical sources underlying EEG activity that is recorded at the scalp. These methods thus provide information regarding the neural generators of the observed signals. These techniques use mathematical models to represent the location, orientation, and strength of a hypothetical dipole current source.

A number of source localization methods have been proposed. One that has generated much interest is LORETA (Pascual-Marqui et al., 1999). It computes current density (i.e., the amount of electrical current flowing through a solid) without assuming any active sources. The LORETA solution space (i.e., the locations in which sources can be found) is composed of 2,394 cubic elements (voxels, $7 \times 7 \times 7$ mm) and is limited to cortical gray matter and hippocampi, as defined by a digitized MRI available from the Montreal Neurologic Institute (Montreal, Quebec, Canada).

LORETA solutions have been cross-modally validated with studies combining LORETA and fMRI (Mulert et al., 2004; Vitacco, Brandeis, Pascual-Marqui, & Martin, 2002), structural MRI (Worrell et al., 2000), positron emission tomography (PET; Pizzagalli et al., 2004), and intracranial recordings (Seeck et al., 1998). The core assumptions of LORETA, its mathematical implementation, and additional technical details, including relations between scalp-recorded EEG and LORETA data, are described in detail in Pascual-Marqui et al. (1999) and Pizzagalli et al. (2002, 2004).

ADVANTAGES AND DISADVANTAGES OF EEG METHODS

We hope that we have conveyed some advantages of using EEG methods in our brief review. In addition to these advantages, EEG methods are relatively inexpensive compared with other neuroimaging methods. For instance, time on an fMRI scanner averages $500 per hour (as of April 2010), and the scanner typically costs around $5 million to set up. The hourly rate that is charged to researchers assists in covering the maintenance contracts and salaries of the support personnel. In contrast, most EEG researchers have their own equipment, which costs less than $100,000. In this situation, no hourly fees are charged and maintenance contracts rarely exceed $3,000 per year. EEG caps need to be replaced approximately once per year (depending on use), and they cost between $300 and $2,000, depending on the number and type of electrodes. There are also other regular expenses for conducting gel, adhesive collars, and sterilizing solution, but these costs are relatively minimal.

In relation to PET and fMRI, EEG provides better temporal resolution but poorer spatial resolution. EEG measures electrical activations instantaneously, at sub-millisecond resolution. However, EEG is less able to give precise information regarding the anatomical origin of the electrical signals. In contrast, PET and fMRI have better spatial resolution but poorer temporal resolution. Ultimately, both PET and fMRI rely on metabolism and blood flow to brain areas that have been recently involved in neuronal activity, although other changes affect fMRI such as oxygen consumption and blood volume changes. Because both PET and fMRI measure blood flow rather than neuronal activity, the activations are not in real time with neuronal activations but rather are blood responses to neuronal responses. Thus, there is a biological limit on the time resolution of the response, such that even in the best measurement systems, the peak blood flow response occurs 6 s to 9 s after stimulus onset (Reiman, Lane, Van Petten, & Bandettini, 2000). However, there are suggestions that experimental methods can be designed to detect stimulus condition differences as early as 2 s (Bellgowan, Saad, & Bandettini, 2003). Finally, PET and EEG permit measurement of tonic (e.g., resting, baseline) activity as well as phasic (e.g., in response to a state manipulation) activity, whereas fMRI permits measurement of phasic but not tonic activity.

Spatial and temporal resolution comparisons are often made between EEG, fMRI, and PET, but rarely do researchers consider that EEG and PET or fMRI may provide different information about neural activity. For instance, correlations between EEG alpha power and fMRI or PET measures are only of moderate magnitude, suggesting that the two measures are not assessing exactly the same signals or activations. Moreover, EEG measures are selective measures of current source activity, often corresponding to small subsets of total synaptic action in tissue volumes and largely independent of action potentials, as discussed. By contrast, hemodynamic and metabolic measures are believed to increase with action potential firing rates (Nunez & Silberstein, 2000). Consider, for example, cortical stellate cells. They occupy roughly spherical volumes and, as such, their associated synaptic sources provide a closed field structure. Thus, these stellate cells are electrically invisible to EEG sensors. Although stellate cells constitute only about 15% of the neural population of neocortex (Braitenberg & Schuz, 1991; Wilson, Ó Scalaidhe, & Goldman-Rakic, 1994), they contribute disproportionately to cortical metabolic activity because of their higher firing frequencies of action potentials (Connors & Gutnick, 1990). Thus, they appear as large signals in fMRI and PET. On the other hand, strong EEG signals can appear while weak metabolic activity occurs. EEG can be large if only a few percent of neurons in each cortical column are synchronously active, provided a large-scale synchrony among different columns produces a large dipole in which individual columns tend to be phase locked in particular frequencies. Because, in this scenario, the majority of neurons in each intracolumn population are relatively inactive, minimal metabolic activity is produced. Consequential dissociations between electrical and metabolic measures have been found in studies of epilepsy (e.g., Olson, Chugani, Shewmon, Plelps, & Peacock, 1990). For example, in one study of children with lateralized epileptic spikes (measured with EEG), regional glucose metabolism that was measured with PET was not lateralized, suggesting that "metabolic changes associated with interictal spiking cannot be demonstrated with PET with 18F-flurodeoxyglucose" (Van Bogaert, Wikler, Damhaut, Szliwowski, & Goldman, 1998, p. 123).

Methodologically, fMRI and EEG differ in an important way, particularly for research on motivational processes. Typically, fMRI studies require participants to lie flat on their backs while brain images are collected. In contrast, EEG studies often have participants in upright, sitting positions. Given the connection between body posture and motivation (Riskind & Gotay, 1982), we should expect that lying in a supine position may decrease approach motivation, as this position is often antithetical to approaching goals. In line with these ideas, EEG research has suggested that these body postures influence regional brain activity, with a supine posture leading to relatively less left-frontal cortical activation in response to approach motivation manipulations (Harmon-Jones & Peterson, 2009). Moreover, simply leaning forward causes greater relative left-frontal activity (as measured by EEG) than lying in a supine position (Price & Harmon-Jones, 2011).

CONCLUSION

As we have described in this chapter, EEG measures of neural activity provide an important method for testing psychological theories and hypotheses. Among the most exciting new developments in EEG that are awaiting applications in psychological studies is the examination of distributed patterns of activation. Many psychological processes likely involve widely distributed networks of brain dynamics and most past work in EEG, fMRI, and PET has failed to examine the dynamics of brain activations as they unfold on the order of milliseconds. Given the exquisite temporal resolution of EEG, it will be the method of choice in addressing these questions. When brain operations are viewed as a "combination of quasi-local processes allowed by functional segregation and global processes facilitated by functional integration" (Nunez & Silberstein, 2000, p. 93), the importance of EEG methods, in conjunction with other neurobiological methods, at addressing important psychological questions will be obvious.

References

Allen, J. J., Iacono, W. G., Depue, R. A., & Arbisi, P. (1993). Regional electroencephalographic asymmetries in bipolar seasonal affective disorder before and after exposure to bright light. *Biological Psychiatry, 33*, 642–646. doi:10.1016/0006-3223(93)90104-L

Allen, J. J. B., Coan, J. A., & Nazarian, M. (2004). Issues and assumptions on the road from raw signals to metrics of frontal EEG asymmetry in emotion. *Biological Psychology, 67*, 183–218. doi:10.1016/j.biopsycho.2004.03.007

Amodio, D. M., Devine, P. G., & Harmon-Jones, E. (2007). A dynamic model of guilt—Implications for motivation and self-regulation in the context of prejudice. *Psychological Science, 18*, 524–530. doi:10.1111/j.1467-9280.2007.01933.x

Andino, S. L., Pascual Marqui, R. D., Valdes Sosa, P. A., Biscay Lirio, R., Machado, C., Diaz, G., . . . Castro Torrez, C. (1990). Brain electrical field measurements unaffected by linked earlobes reference. *Electroencephalography and Clinical Neurophysiology, 75*, 155–160. doi:10.1016/0013-4694(90)90169-K

Barry, R. J., Clarke, A. R., & Johnstone, S. J. (2003). A review of electrophysiology in attention-deficit/hyperactivity disorder: I. Qualitative and quantitative electroencephalography. *Clinical Neurophysiology, 114*, 171–183. doi:10.1016/S1388-2457(02)00362-0

Bartholow, B. D., & Amodio, D. M. (2009). Using event-related brain potentials in social psychological research: A brief review and tutorial. In E. Harmon-Jones & J. Beer (Eds.), *Methods in social neuroscience* (pp. 198–232). New York, NY: Guilford Press.

Beck, A. T., Ward, C. H., Mendelson, M., Mock, J., & Erbaugh, J. (1961). An inventory for measuring depression. *Archives of General Psychiatry, 4*, 561–571.

Bellgowan, P. S., Saad, Z. S., & Bandettini, P. A. (2003). Understanding neural system dynamics through task modulation and measurement of functional MRI amplitude, latency, and width. *Proceedings of the National Academy of Sciences of the United States of America, 100*, 1415–1419. doi:10.1073/pnas.0337747100

Berger, H. (1929). Electroencephalogram in humans. *Archiv für Psychiatrie und Nervenkrankheiten, 87*, 527–570. doi:10.1007/BF01797193

Braitenberg, V., & Schuz, A. (1991). *Anatomy of the cortex. Statistics and geometry.* New York, NY: Springer-Verlag.

Brodal, P. (1992). *The central nervous system.* New York, NY: Oxford University Press.

Buss, A. H., & Perry, M. (1992). The aggression questionnaire. *Journal of Personality and Social Psychology, 63*, 452–459. doi:10.1037/0022-3514.63.3.452

Carver, C. S., & Harmon-Jones, E. (2009). Anger is an approach-related affect: Evidence and implications. *Psychological Bulletin, 135*, 183–204. doi:10.1037/a0013965

Carver, C. S., & White, T. L. (1994). Behavioral inhibition, behavioral activation, and affective responses to impending reward and punishment: The BIS/BAS scales. *Journal of Personality and Social Psychology, 67*, 319–333. doi:10.1037/0022-3514.67.2.319

Chatrian, G. E., Lettich, E., & Nelson, P. L. (1988). Modified nomenclature for the 10-percent electrode system. *Journal of Clinical Neurophysiology, 5*, 183–186. doi:10.1097/00004691-198804000-00005

Coan, J. A., & Allen, J. J. B. (2003). Frontal EEG asymmetry and the behavioral activation and inhibition systems. *Psychophysiology, 40*, 106–114. doi:10.1111/1469-8986.00011

Coan, J. A., & Allen, J. J. B. (2004). Frontal EEG asymmetry as a moderator and mediator of emotion. *Biological Psychology, 67*, 7–50. doi:10.1016/j.biopsycho.2004.03.002

Coan, J. A., Allen, J. J. B., & Harmon-Jones, E. (2001). Voluntary facial expression and hemispheric asymmetry over the frontal cortex. *Psychophysiology, 38*, 912–925. doi:10.1111/1469-8986.3860912

Connors, B. W., & Gutnick, M. J. (1990). Intrinsic firing patterns of diverse neocortical neurons. *Trends in Neurosciences, 13*, 99–104. doi:10.1016/0166-2236(90)90185-D

Cook, I. A., O'Hara, R., Uijtdehaage, S. H. J., Mandelkern, M., & Leuchter, A. F.. (1998). Assessing the accuracy of topographic EEG mapping for determining local brain function. *Electroencephalography and Clinical Neurophysiology, 107*, 408–414. doi:10.1016/S0013-4694(98)00092-3

Crone, N. E., Sinai, A., & Korzeniewska, A. (2006). High-frequency gamma oscillations and human brain mapping with electrocorticography. *Progress in Brain Research, 159*, 275–295. doi:10.1016/S0079-6123(06)59019-3

Davidson, R. J., Chapman, J. P., Chapman, L. J., & Henriques, J. B. (1990). Asymmetrical brain electrical activity discriminates between psychometrically-matched verbal and spatial cognitive tasks. *Psychophysiology, 27*, 528–543. doi:10.1111/j.1469-8986.1990.tb01970.x

Davidson, R. J., Jackson, D. C., & Larson, C. L. (2000). Human electroencephalography. In J. T. Cacioppo, L. G. Tassinary, & G. G. Berntson (Eds.), *Handbook of psychophysiology* (2nd ed., pp. 27–52). New York, NY: Cambridge University Press.

Fell, J., Fernandez, G., Klaver, P., Elger, C. E., & Fries, P. (2003). Is synchronized neuronal gamma activity relevant for selective attention? *Brain Research Reviews, 42*, 265–272. doi:10.1016/S0165-0173(03)00178-4

Fox, N. A., & Davidson, R. J. (1986). Taste-elicited changes in facial signs of emotion and the asymmetry of brain electrical activity in human newborns.

Neuropsychologia, 24, 417–422. doi:10.1016/0028-3932(86)90028-X

Fox, N. A., Rubin, K. H., Calkins, S. D., Marshall, T. R., Coplain, R. J., Porges, S. W., . . . Stewart, S. (1995). Frontal activation asymmetry and social competence at four years of age. *Child Development, 66*, 1770–1784. doi:10.2307/1131909

Gable, P., & Harmon-Jones, E. (2008). Relative left frontal activation to appetitive stimuli: Considering the role of individual differences. *Psychophysiology, 45*, 275–278. doi:10.1111/j.1469-8986.2007.00627.x

Goldman, R. I., Stern, J. M., Engel, J., & Cohen, M. S. (2002). Simultaneous EEG and fMRI of the alpha rhythm. *Neuroreport, 13*, 2487–2492. doi:10.1097/00001756-200212200-00022

Gratton, G., Coles, M. G. H., & Donchin, E. (1983). A new method for off-line removal of ocular artifact. *Electroencephalography and Clinical Neurophysiology, 55*, 468–484. doi:10.1016/0013-4694(83)90135-9

Hagemann, D. (2004). Individual differences in anterior EEG asymmetry: Methodological problems and solutions. *Biological Psychology, 67*, 157–182. doi:10.1016/j.biopsycho.2004.03.006

Hagemann, D., & Naumann, E. (2001). The effects of ocular artifacts on (lateralized) broadband power in the EEG. *Clinical Neurophysiology, 112*, 215–231. doi:10.1016/S1388-2457(00)00541-1

Hagemann, D., Naumann, E., Becker, G., Maier, S., & Bartussek, D. (1998). Frontal brain asymmetry and affective style: A conceptual replication. *Psychophysiology, 35*, 372–388. doi:10.1111/1469-8986.3540372

Hagemann, D., Naumann, E., Thayer, J. F., & Bartussek, D. (2002). Does resting EEG asymmetry reflect a trait? An application of latent state–trait theory. *Journal of Personality and Social Psychology, 82*, 619–641. doi:10.1037/0022-3514.82.4.619

Harmon-Jones, E. (2003). Clarifying the emotive functions of asymmetrical frontal cortical activity. *Psychophysiology, 40*, 838–848. doi:10.1111/1469-8986.00121

Harmon-Jones, E. (2004). Contributions from research on anger and cognitive dissonance to understanding the motivational functions of asymmetrical frontal brain activity. *Biological Psychology, 67*, 51–76. doi:10.1016/j.biopsycho.2004.03.003

Harmon-Jones, E., Abramson, L. Y., Nusslock, R., Sigelman, J. D., Urosevic, S., Turonie, L. D., . . . Fearn, M. (2008). Effect of bipolar disorder on left frontal cortical responses to goals differing in valence and task difficulty. *Biological Psychiatry, 63*, 693–698.

Harmon-Jones, E., Abramson, L. Y., Sigelman, J., Bohlig, A., Hogan, M. E., & Harmon-Jones, C. (2002).

Proneness to hypomania/mania symptoms or depression symptoms and asymmetrical cortical responses to an anger-evoking event. *Journal of Personality and Social Psychology, 82*, 610–618. doi:10.1037/0022-3514.82.4.610

Harmon-Jones, E., & Allen, J. J. B. (1997). Behavioral activation sensitivity and resting frontal EEG asymmetry: Covariation of putative indicators related to risk for mood disorders. *Journal of Abnormal Psychology, 106*, 159–163. doi:10.1037/0021-843X.106.1.159

Harmon-Jones, E., & Allen, J. J. B. (1998). Anger and frontal brain activity: EEG asymmetry consistent with approach motivation despite negative affective valence. *Journal of Personality and Social Psychology, 74*, 1310–1316. doi:10.1037/0022-3514.74.5.1310

Harmon-Jones, E., & Gable, P. A. (2009). Neural activity underlying the effect of approach-motivated positive affect on narrowed attention. *Psychological Science, 20*, 406–409. doi:10.1111/j.1467-9280.2009.02302.x

Harmon-Jones, E., Gable, P. A., & Peterson, C. K. (2010). The role of asymmetric frontal cortical activity in emotion-related phenomena: A review and update. *Biological Psychology, 84*, 451–462. doi:10.1016/j.biopsycho.2009.08.010

Harmon-Jones, E., & Harmon-Jones, C. (2002). Testing the action-based model of cognitive dissonance: The effect of action-orientation on post-decisional attitudes. *Personality and Social Psychology Bulletin, 28*, 711–723. doi:10.1177/0146167202289001

Harmon-Jones, E., Harmon-Jones, C., Fearn, M., Sigelman, J. D., & Johnson, P. (2008). Action orientation, relative left frontal cortical activation, and spreading of alternatives: A test of the action-based model of dissonance. *Journal of Personality and Social Psychology, 94*, 1–15. doi:10.1037/0022-3514.94.1.1

Harmon-Jones, E., Lueck, L., Fearn, M., & Harmon-Jones, C. (2006). The effect of personal relevance and approach-related action expectation on relative left frontal cortical activity. *Psychological Science, 17*, 434–440. doi:10.1111/j.1467-9280.2006.01724.x

Harmon-Jones, E., & Peterson, C. K. (2009). Supine body position reduces neural response to anger evocation. *Psychological Science, 20*, 1209–1210. doi:10.1111/j.1467-9280.2009.02416.x

Harmon-Jones, E., Peterson, C. K., & Harris, C. R. (2009). Jealousy: Novel methods and neural correlates. *Emotion, 9*, 113–117. doi:10.1037/a0014117

Harmon-Jones, E., & Sigelman, J. (2001). State anger and prefrontal brain activity: Evidence that insult-related relative left prefrontal activation is associated with experienced anger and aggression. *Journal of Personality and Social Psychology, 80*, 797–803. doi:10.1037/0022-3514.80.5.797

Harmon-Jones, E., Sigelman, J. D., Bohlig, A., & Harmon-Jones, C. (2003). Anger, coping, and frontal cortical activity: The effect of coping potential on anger-induced left frontal activity. *Cognition and Emotion, 17*, 1–24. doi:10.1080/02699930302278

Harmon-Jones, E., Vaughn-Scott, K., Mohr, S., Sigelman, J., & Harmon-Jones, C. (2004). The effect of manipulated sympathy and anger on left and right frontal cortical activity. *Emotion, 4*, 95–101. doi:10.1037/1528-3542.4.1.95

Henderson, H. A., Fox, N. A., & Rubin, K. H. (2001). Temperamental contributions to social behavior: The moderating roles of frontal EEG asymmetry and gender. *Journal of the American Academy of Child and Adolescent Psychiatry, 40*, 68–74. doi:10.1097/00004583-200101000-00018

Henriques, J. B., & Davidson, R. J. (1990). Regional brain electrical asymmetries discriminate between previously depressed and healthy control subjects. *Journal of Abnormal Psychology, 99*, 22–31. doi:10.1037/0021-843X.99.1.22

Henriques, J. B., & Davidson, R. J. (1991). Left frontal hypoactivation in depression. *Journal of Abnormal Psychology, 100*, 535–545. doi:10.1037/0021-843-X.100.4.535

Jasper, H. H. (1958). The ten-twenty electrode system of the International Federation. *Electroencephalography and Clinical Neurophysiology, 10*, 371–375.

Joyce, C. A., Gorodnitsky, I. F., & Kutas, M. (2004). Automatic removal of eye movement and blink artifacts from EEG data using blind component separation. *Psychophysiology, 41*, 313–325. doi:10.1111/j.1469-8986.2003.00141.x

Kano, K., Nakamura, M., Matsuoka, T., Iida, H., & Nakajima, T. (1992). The topographical features of EEGs in patients with affective disorders. *Electroencephalography and Clinical Neurophysiology, 83*, 124–129. doi:10.1016/0013-4694(92)90025-D

Kappenman, E. S., & Luck, S. J. (2010). The effects of electrode impedance on data quality and statistical significance in ERP recordings. *Psychophysiology, 47*, 898–904. doi:10.1111/j.1496-8986.2010.01009.x

Katznelson, R. D. (1981). Increased accuracy of EEG scalp localization by measurement of current source density using a Laplacian derivation. *Electroencephalography and Clinical Neurophysiology, 51*, 45.

Knyazev, G. G., & Slobodskaya, H. R. (2003). Personality trait of behavioral inhibition is associated with oscillatory systems reciprocal relationships. *International Journal of Psychophysiology, 48*, 247–261. doi:10.1016/S0167-8760(03)00072-2

Lee, K. H., Williams, L. M., Breakspear, M., & Gordon, E. (2003). Synchronous Gamma activity: A review and contribution to an integrative neuroscience model of schizophrenia. *Brain Research Reviews, 41*, 57–78. doi:10.1016/S0165-0173(02)00220-5

Master, S. L., Amodio, D. M., Stanton, A. L., Yee, C. Y., Hilmert, C. J., & Taylor, S. E. (2009). Neurobiological correlates of coping through emotional approach. *Brain, Behavior, and Immunity, 23*, 27–35. doi:10.1016/j.bbi.2008.04.007

McMenamin, B. W., Shackman, A. J., Maxwell, J. S., Greischar, L. L., & Davidson, R. J. (2009). Validation of regression-based myogenic correction techniques for scalp and source-localized EEG. *Psychophysiology, 46*, 578–592. doi:10.1111/j.1469-8986.2009.00787.x

Mulert, C., Jager, L., Schmitt, R., Bussfeld, P., Pogarell, O., Moller, H. J., … Hegerl, U. (2004). Integration of fMRI and simultaneous EEG: Towards a comprehensive understanding of localization and time-course of brain activity in target detection. *NeuroImage, 22*, 83–94. doi:10.1016/j.neuroimage.2003.10.051

Nunez, P. L., & Silberstein, R. B. (2000). On the relationship of synaptic activity to macroscopic measurements: Does co-registration of EEG with fMRI make sense? *Brain Topography, 13*, 79–96. doi:10.1023/A:1026683200895

Nunez, P. L., & Srinivasan, R. (2006). *Electrical fields of the brain: The neurophysics of EEG* (2nd ed.). Oxford, England: Oxford University Press. doi:10.1093/acprof:oso/9780195050387.001.0001

Nusslock, R., Abramson, L. Y., Harmon-Jones, E., Alloy, L. B., & Hogan, M. (2007). A goal-striving life event and the onset of hypomanic and depressive episodes and symptoms: Perspective from the behavioral approach system (BAS) dysregulation theory. *Journal of Abnormal Psychology, 116*, 105–115. doi:10.1037/0021-843X.116.1.105

Olson, D. M., Chugani, H. T., Shewmon, D. A., Plelps, M. E., & Peacock, W. J. (1990). Electrocorticographic confirmation of focal positron emission tomography abnormalities in children with epilepsy. *Epilepsia, 31*, 731–739. doi:10.1111/j.1528-1157.1990.tb05514.x

Pascual-Marqui, R. D., Lehmann, D., Koenig, T., Kochi, K., Merlo, M. C., Hell, D., & Koukkou, M. (1999). Low resolution brain electromagnetic tomography (LORETA) functional imaging in acute, neuroleptic-naive, first-episode, productive schizophrenia. *Psychiatry Research, 90*, 169–179. doi:10.1016/S0925-4927(99)00013-X

Peterson, C. K., Gravens, L., & Harmon-Jones, E. (2011). Asymmetric frontal cortical activity and negative affective responses to ostracism. *Social Cognitive and Affective Neuroscience, 6*, 277–285. doi:10.1093/scan/nsq027

Peterson, C. K., & Harmon-Jones, E. (2008). Proneness to hypomania predicts EEG coherence between left motor cortex and left prefrontal cortex. *Biological Psychology, 78*, 216–219. doi:10.1016/j.biopsycho.2008.01.011

Peterson, C. K., & Harmon-Jones, E. (2009). Circadian and seasonal variability of resting frontal EEG asymmetry. *Biological Psychology, 80*, 315–320. doi:10.1016/j.biopsycho.2008.11.002

Peterson, C. K., Shackman, A. J., & Harmon-Jones, E. (2008). The role of asymmetrical frontal cortical activity in aggression. *Psychophysiology, 45*, 86–92.

Pfurtscheller, G., & Lopes da Silva, F. H. (1999). Event-related EEG/MEG synchronization and desynchronization: Basic principles. *Clinical Neurophysiology, 110*, 1842–1857. doi:10.1016/S1388-2457(99)00141-8

Pizzagalli, D. A., Nitschke, J. B., Oakes, T. R., Hendrick, A. M., Horras, K. A., Larson, C. L., . . . Davidson, R. J. (2002). Brain electrical tomography in depression: The importance of symptom severity, anxiety and melancholic features. *Biological Psychiatry, 52*, 73–85. doi:10.1016/S0006-3223(02)01313-6

Pizzagalli, D. A., Oakes, T. R., Fox, A. S., Chung, M. K., Larson, C. L., Abercrombie, H. C., . . . Davidson, R. J. (2004). Functional but not structural subgenual prefrontal cortex abnormalities in melancholia. *Molecular Psychiatry, 9*, 325–405. doi:10.1038/sj.mp.4001469

Polich, J., & Lawson, D. (1985). Event-related potential paradigms using tin electrodes. *The American Journal of EEG Technology, 26*, 187–192.

Price, T. F., & Harmon-Jones, E. (2011). Approach motivational body postures lean toward left frontal brain activity. *Psychophysiology, 48*, 718–722. doi:10.1111/j.1469-8986.2010.01127.x

Reid, S. A., Duke, L. M., & Allen, J. J. B. (1998). Resting frontal electroencephalographic asymmetry in depression: Inconsistencies suggest the need to identify mediating factors. *Psychophysiology, 35*, 389–404. doi:10.1111/1469-8986.3540389

Reiman, E. M., Lane, R. D., Van Petten, C., & Bandettini, P. A. (2000). Positron emission tomography and functional magnetic resonance imaging. In J. T. Cacioppo, L. G. Tassinary, & G. G. Berntson (Eds.), *Handbook of psychophysiology* (2nd ed., pp. 85–118). New York, NY: Cambridge University Press.

Riskind, J. H., & Gotay, C. C. (1982). Physical posture: Could it have regulatory or feedback effects on motivation and emotion? *Motivation and Emotion, 6*, 273–298. doi:10.1007/BF00992249

Schaffer, C. E., Davidson, R. J., & Saron, C. (1983). Frontal and parietal electroencephalogram asymmetry in depressed and nondepressed subjects. *Biological Psychiatry, 18*, 753–762.

Schutter, D. J. L. G., & van Honk, J. (2005). Electrophysiological ratio markers for the balance between reward and punishment. *Cognitive Brain Research, 24*, 685–690. doi:10.1016/j.cogbrainres.2005.04.002

Seeck, M., Lazeyrasb, F., Michela, C. M., Blankea, O., Gerickea, C. A., Ivesc, J., . . . Landisa, T. (1998). Non-invasive epileptic focus localization using EEG-triggered functional MRI and electromagnetic tomography. *Electroencephalography and Clinical Neurophysiology, 106*, 508–512. doi:10.1016/S0013-4694(98)00017-0

Semlitsch, H. V., Anderer, P., Schuster, P., & Presslich, O. (1986). A solution for reliable and valid reduction of ocular artifacts, applied to the P300 ERP. *Psychophysiology, 23*, 695–703. doi:10.1111/j.1469-8986.1986.tb00696.x

Sutton, S. K., & Davidson, R. J. (1997). Prefrontal brain asymmetry: A biological substrate of the behavioral approach and inhibition systems. *Psychological Science, 8*, 204–210. doi:10.1111/j.1467-9280.1997.tb00413.x

Taylor, S. E., & Gollwitzer, P. M. (1995). Effects of mindset on positive illusions. *Journal of Personality and Social Psychology, 69*, 213–226. doi:10.1037/0022-3514.69.2.213

Thatcher, R. W., Krause, P. J., & Hrybyk, M. (1986). Corticocortical associations and EEG coherence—A 2-compartmental model. *Electroencephalography and Clinical Neurophysiology, 64*, 123–143. doi:10.1016/0013-4694(86)90107-0

Tomarken, A. J., Davidson, R. J., Wheeler, R. E., & Doss, R. C. (1992). Individual differences in anterior brain asymmetry and fundamental dimensions of emotion. *Journal of Personality and Social Psychology, 62*, 676–687. doi:10.1037/0022-3514.62.4.676

Van Bogaert, P., Wikler, D., Damhaut, P., Szliwowski, H. B., & Goldman, S. (1998). Cerebral glucose metabolism and centrotemporal spikes. *Epilepsy Research, 29*, 123–127. doi:10.1016/S0920-1211(97)00072-7

Verleger, R. (1991). The instruction to refrain from blinking affects auditory P3 and N1 amplitudes. *Electroencephalography and Clinical Neurophysiology, 78*, 240–251. doi:10.1016/0013-4694(91)90039-7

Vitacco, D., Brandeis, D., Pascual-Marqui, R., & Martin, E. (2002). Correspondence of event-related potential tomography and functional magnetic resonance imaging during language processing. *Human Brain Mapping, 17*, 4–12. doi:10.1002/hbm.10038

Wallstrom, G. L., Kass, R. E., Miller, A., Cohn, J. F., & Fox, N. A. (2004). Automatic correction of ocular artifacts in the EEG: A comparison of regression-based and component-based methods. *International Journal of Psychophysiology, 53*, 105–119. doi:10.1016/j.ijpsycho.2004.03.007

Watson, D., Clark, L. A., & Tellegen, A. (1988). Development and validation of brief measures of positive and negative affect: The PANAS scales. *Journal of Personality and Social Psychology, 54,* 1063–1070. doi:10.1037/0022-3514.54.6.1063

Wheeler, R. E., Davidson, R. J., & Tomarken, A. J. (1993). Frontal brain asymmetry and emotional reactivity: A biological substrate of affective style. *Psychophysiology, 30,* 82–89. doi:10.1111/j.1469-8986.1993.tb03207.x

Wilson, F. A., Ó Scalaidhe, S. P., & Goldman-Rakic, P. S. (1994). Functional synergism between putative gamma-aminobutyrate containing neurons and pyramidal neurons in prefrontal cortex. *Proceedings of the National Academy of Sciences of the United States of America, 91,* 4009–4013. doi:10.1073/pnas.91.9.4009

Worrell, G. A., Lagerlund, T. D., Sharbrough, F. W., Brinkmann, B. H., Busacker, N. E., Cicora, K. M., & O'Brien, T. J. (2000). Localization of the epileptic focus by low-resolution electromagnetic tomography in patients with a lesion demonstrated by MRI. *Brain Topography, 12,* 273–282. doi:10.1023/A:1023407521772

CHAPTER 27

EVENT-RELATED POTENTIALS

Steven J. Luck

Event-related potentials (ERPs) are electrical *potentials* generated by the brain that are *related* to specific internal or external *events* (e.g., stimuli, responses, decisions). They can be recorded noninvasively from almost any group of research participants, and they can provide information about a broad range of cognitive and affective processes. Consequently, the ERP technique has become a common tool in almost all areas of psychological research, and students and researchers must be able to understand and evaluate ERP studies in the literature. These studies often involve a set of terms and concepts that are unfamiliar to many psychologists, however; several technical issues must be understood before a student or researcher can read and evaluate ERP studies. This chapter provides students and researchers with this background information so that they can be informed consumers of ERP studies in their area of interest. More detailed works are available for those who would like to learn more or who would like to conduct their own ERP experiments (Handy, 2005; Luck, 2005).

This chapter begins with an example of a particular ERP component—the N170 wave—and describes how it has been used to address issues ranging from perception and attention to development and neurodevelopmental disorders. This discussion will be followed by an overview of the major ERP components, which will provide both a vocabulary and a sense of the topics that are commonly explored with

ERPs. The next sections describe how ERPs are generated in the brain and how the neural generator site of a given ERP can be localized. This information is followed by a discussion of the basic technical issues involved in recording and analyzing ERPs, using a study of impaired cognition in schizophrenia patients as a concrete example. The chapter ends with a set of questions that should be asked when reading and evaluating an ERP study.

EXAMPLE 1: THE N170 COMPONENT AND FACE PROCESSING

Figure 27.1 shows the results of an experiment focusing on the N170 component, a negative-going wave over visual cortex that typically peaks around 170 ms after stimulus onset. In a typical N170 paradigm, photographs of faces and various types of nonface objects are briefly flashed on a computer monitor and the participants passively view the stimuli. In the ERP waveforms shown in Figure 27.1a, the *x*-axis represents time relative to stimulus onset (measured in milliseconds) and the *y*-axis represents the magnitude of the neural response (in microvolts [μV]). In the scalp map shown in Figure 27.1b, the shading indicates the voltage measured at each electrode site during the time period of the N170 (with interpolated values between the individual electrode sites).

In the early days of ERP research, waveforms were plotted with negative upward and positive

Preparation of this chapter was supported by National Institute of Mental Health Grants R01MH076226, R01MH065034, R01MH087450, and R25 MH080794.

DOI: 10.1037/13619-028

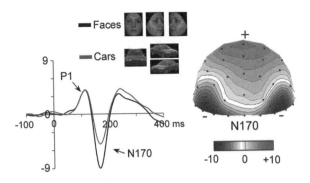

FIGURE 27.1. Example N170 experiment, including ERP waveforms from an occipito–temporal electrode site (a) and the scalp distribution of the voltage in the N170 latency range (b). From *Oxford Handbook of Event-Related Potential Components*, by S. J. Luck & E. S. Kappenman (Eds.), 2012, New York, NY: Oxford University Press. Copyright 2012 by Oxford University Press. Adapted with permission.

downward (largely because of historical accident). Many researchers now use the more common Cartesian convention of plotting positive upward, but this is not universal, so it is important to check which convention is used in a given ERP waveform plot. The waveforms in this chapter are all plotted with positive upward.

The N170 component is notable because it is larger when the eliciting stimulus is a face compared with when the stimulus is a nonface object such as an automobile (see review by Rossion & Jacques, 2012). The difference between faces and nonface objects begins approximately 150 ms after the onset of the stimulus; this simple fact allows us to conclude that the human brain is able to distinguish between faces and other objects within 150 ms. The scalp distribution helps us to know that this is the same component that is observed in similar studies of the N170, and it suggests that the N170 generator lies in visual cortex (but note that conclusions on the basis of scalp distributions are not usually definitive).

Many researchers have used the N170 to address interesting questions about how faces are processed in the brain. For example, some studies have asked whether face processing is automatic by testing whether the face-elicited N170 is smaller when the faces are ignored. The results of these experiments indicate that face processing is at least partially automatic (Carmel & Bentin, 2002) but can be

modulated by attention under some conditions (e.g., when the faces are somewhat difficult to perceive; Sreenivasan, Goldstein, Lustig, Rivas, & Jha, 2009). Other studies have used the N170 to ask whether faces are processed in a specialized face module or whether the same neural process is also used when people process other sorts of complex stimuli for which they have extensive expertise. Consistent with a key role for expertise, these studies have shown that bird experts exhibit an enhanced N170 in response to birds, dog experts exhibit an enhanced N170 in response to dogs, and fingerprint experts exhibit an enhanced N170 in response to fingerprints (Busey & Vanderkolk, 2005; Tanaka & Curran, 2001). Developmental studies have used N170 to track the development of face processing, showing that face-specific processing is present early in infancy but becomes faster and more sophisticated over development (Coch & Gullick, 2012). Studies of neurodevelopmental disorders have shown that the N170 is abnormal in children with autism spectrum disorder (Dawson et al., 2002).

This example makes several important points. First, it shows that ERPs can be used to address important questions across a wide range of basic science and clinical domains. Second, it illustrates the precise temporal resolution of the technique. ERPs reflect ongoing brain activity with no delay, and an ERP effect observed at 150 ms reflects neural processing that occurred at 150 ms. Consequently, ERPs are especially useful for answering questions about the timing of mental processes. Sometimes this timing information is used explicitly, by asking whether two conditions or groups differ in the timing of a given neural response (just as one might ask whether reaction time differs across conditions or groups). In other cases, the timing information is used to ask whether a given experimental manipulation influences sensory activity that occurs shortly after stimulus onset or higher level cognitive processes that occur hundreds of milliseconds later. For example, ERPs have been used to ask whether attentional manipulations influence early sensory processes or whether they instead influence postperceptual memory and decision processes (see, e.g., Luck & Hillyard, 2000). More broadly speaking, ERPs are commonly used to determine which specific cognitive process is influenced by a given experimental manipulation. For example, reaction times (RTs) are slowed when people perform two tasks at the same time compared with when they perform a single task, and ERPs have been used to show that this does not reflect a delay in discriminating the identity of the stimuli (Luck, 1998), but instead it reflects a slowing in determining which response is appropriate for the stimulus (Osman & Moore, 1993). ERPs can also be used to assess the anticipatory processes that occur before a stimulus (Brunia, van Boxtel, & Böcker, in press) and the performance monitoring processes that occur during and after a behavioral response (Gehring, Liu, Orr, & Carp, in press).

A third important point is that the high temporal resolution of the ERP technique is accompanied by relatively low spatial resolution. The topographic map of the N170 component shown in Figure 27.1b is very coarse compared with the maps of face-related brain activity provided by functional magnetic resonance imaging (fMRI). For reasons that will be detailed later in this chapter, it is difficult to localize ERPs purely on the basis of the observed scalp distribution, and converging evidence (e.g., lesion data) is usually necessary to know with certainty the neuroanatomical origins of a given ERP effect. For example, several converging sources of evidence indicate that the N170 is generated along the ventral surface of the brain near the border between the occipital and temporal lobes, but it is difficult to be certain that this is the source of the effect in most individual N170 experiments. Thus, ERPs are usually most appropriate for answering questions about timing rather than questions about specific brain regions (although there are some clear exceptions to this generalization).

A fourth key attribute of ERPs is that they can be used to "covertly" monitor mental activity in the absence of a behavioral response. For example, the N170 can be used to assess the ability of preverbal infants to discriminate between different types of faces (e.g., male vs. female faces). Similarly, dissociations between ERP activity and behavioral responses can sometimes be informative. For example, ERPs have been used to show that stimuli that cannot be reported (because of inattention or

subliminal presentation) have been processed to the point of activating semantic information (Luck, Vogel, & Shapiro, 1996) and premotor response codes (Dehaene et al., 1998).

In addition to knowing what kinds of issues can be readily explored with ERPs, it is also useful to know what kinds of issues are *not* easily studied with this technique. As will be discussed in detail later, ERPs are extracted from the electroencephalogram (EEG) by averaging together many trials, using a discrete event such as the onset of a stimulus as a time-locking point. ERPs are typically not useful in situations that make it difficult to perform this averaging process. For example, the averaging process cannot be performed if the mental process being studied is not reasonably well time-locked to a discrete, observable event (e.g., spontaneous emotional responses). In addition, tens or hundreds of trials must typically be averaged together for each condition, and some experimental paradigms do not permit this many repetitions of a given condition (e.g., certain paradigms that require deception). ERPs also tend to be most sensitive to processes that unfold over a period of 2 sec or less, and slower processes are difficult to see in ERPs (e.g., long-term memory consolidation). Finally, as mentioned, ERPs are not usually appropriate for answering neuroanatomical questions.

A final implication of the N170 example is that ERP studies usually focus on specific ERP components. To use ERPs, it is important to learn about the major components because the components are tools that can be used to address many interesting questions. Moreover, a component that reflects one type of process might be very useful for studying other processes. For example, deficits in executive control resulting from aging and from prefrontal lesions have been studied by examining how the impaired control leads to changes in sensory ERP activity (Chao & Knight, 1997). Similarly, language-related ERP components have been used to study how attention influences perception (Luck et al., 1996), and ERP components related to motor preparation have been used to study syntax (van Turennout, Hagoort, & Brown, 1998). Thus, it is important to acquire a basic vocabulary of the major ERP components across domains.

Before we get to these components, however, it is important to ask what is meant by the term *component* in the context of ERPs. An ERP component can be defined, at least approximately, as a voltage deflection that is produced when a specific neural process occurs in a specific brain region. Many components will be elicited by a stimulus in a given task, and the different components sum together to produce the observed ERP waveform. The observed waveform clearly consists of a set of positive and negative peaks that are related to the underlying components, but the relation is imperfect. For example, the voltage recorded at 170 ms does not reflect a single face-selective N170 component, but instead it reflects the sum of all of the components that are active at this time. A full discussion of the methods used to isolate ERP components is beyond the scope of this chapter, but this is an important issue in ERP research (for detailed discussions, see Kappenman & Luck, in press; Luck, 2005, Chapter 2).

A BRIEF OVERVIEW OF THE MAJOR ERP COMPONENTS

This section covers the major ERP components, providing both a vocabulary for understanding ERP research and an overview of the breadth of research areas in which ERPs have been used. ERP components can be divided into three main categories: (a) *exogenous* sensory components that are obligatorily triggered by the presence of a stimulus (but may be modulated to some degree by top-down processes), (b) *endogenous* components that reflect neural processes that are entirely task dependent, and (c) *motor* components that necessarily accompany the preparation and execution of a given motor responses. This section will cover these three classes of components. Given space limitations, the discussion of each component will necessarily be brief, and many minor components will not be discussed at all. For a comprehensive treatment of the broad range of ERP components, see Luck and Kappenman (in press).

Naming Conventions

Before discussing individual components, it is necessary to say a few words about the naming conventions for ERP components. Unfortunately, the naming is often inconsistent and sometimes ill conceived. The most common convention is to begin with a P or N to indicate that the component is positive-going or negative-going, respectively. This is then followed by a number indicating the peak latency of the waveform (e.g., N400 for a negative component peaking at 400 ms) or the ordinal position of the peak within the waveform (e.g., P2 for the second major positive peak). This seems like a purely descriptive, theory-free approach, but it is not usually used this way. For example, the term *P300* was coined because it was positive and peaked at 300 ms when it was first discovered (Sutton, Braren, Zubin, & John, 1965). In most studies, however, the same functional brain activity typically peaks between 350 and 600 ms, but this component is still often labeled P300. Many investigators therefore prefer to use a number that represents the ordinal position of the component in the waveform (e.g., P3 instead of P300). This can still be confusing. For example, the first major peak for a visual stimulus is the P1 wave, which is observed over posterior electrode sites with a peak latency of approximately 100 ms. This component is not typically visible at anterior scalp sites, where the first major positive peak occurs at approximately 200 ms. This anterior positive peak at 200 ms is typically labeled *P2* because it is the second major positive peak overall, even though it is the first positive peak in the waveform recorded at the anterior electrode sites.

Using the polarity to label the component is also problematic because any given component will produce a positive potential on one side of the head and a negative potential on the other side of the head. The polarity will also depend on which electrode serves as the active site and which electrode serves as the reference site (as discussed in more detail later in this chapter). Moreover, some components vary in polarity depending on the experimental conditions (e.g., the C1 component inverts in polarity for stimuli presented in the upper visual field compared with stimuli presented in the lower visual field).

Another problem is that a given label may refer to a completely different component when different sensory modalities are considered. For example, the auditory P1 wave bears no special relationship to the visual P1 wave. However, later components are largely modality independent, and the labels for these components refer to the same brain activity whether the stimuli are auditory or visual. For example, N400 refers to the same brain activity whether the eliciting stimulus is auditory or visual.

Although this convention for naming ERP components can be confusing to novices, experts usually have no trouble understanding exactly what is meant by these names. This is just like the problem of learning words in natural languages: two words that mean different things may sound exactly the same (*homophones*); two different words may have the same meaning (*synonyms*); and a given word may be used either literally or metaphorically. This is certainly an impediment to learning both natural languages and ERP terminology, but it is not an insurmountable problem, and in both cases, some work is needed to master the vocabulary.

ERP components are sometimes given more functional names, such as the *syntactic positive shift* (which is observed when the participant detects a syntactic error in a sentence) or the *error-related negativity* (which is observed when the participant makes an obviously incorrect behavioral response). These names are often easier to remember, but they can become problematic when subsequent research shows that the same component can be observed under other conditions. For example, some investigators have argued that the error-related negativity is not directly related to the commission of an error and is present (although smaller) even when the correct response is made (Yeung, Cohen, & Botvinick, 2004).

Exogenous Sensory ERP Components

Figure 27.2 shows the typical ERP components evoked by the presentation of an auditory stimulus (see review by Pratt, in press). If the stimulus has a sudden onset (such as a click), a distinctive set of peaks can be seen over the first 10 ms that reflect the flow of information from the cochlea through the brainstem and into the thalamus. These *auditory brainstem responses* (ABRs) are typically labeled with Roman numerals (Waves I–VI). They are highly automatic and can be used to assess the integrity of the auditory pathways. The ABRs are followed by

the *midlatency responses* (MLRs) between 10 and 60 ms, which reflect the flow of information through the thalamus and into auditory cortex. The MLRs are influenced both by sensory factors (e.g., age-related hearing decline) and cognitive factors (e.g., attention). The MLRs are followed by the *long-latency responses*, which typically begin with the P50 (P1), N100 (N1), and P160 (P2). The phrase *long-latency response* is a bit confusing because these are relative short latencies compared with high-level cognitive components, such as P300 and N400. However, the transmission of information along the auditory pathway is very fast, and 100 ms is a relatively late time from the perspective of auditory sensory processing. The long-latency auditory responses can be strongly influenced by high-level factors, such as attention and arousal.

The midlatency and long-latency auditory responses become much smaller when the interval between successive stimuli decreases, with refractory periods that may exceed 1,000 ms (this is true for sensory components in other modalities as well). Moreover, the ERP elicited by one stimulus may not be finished before the next stimulus begins when the interval between stimuli is short, which can also confound the results of an experiment. Thus, when evaluating an ERP study, it is important to assess whether a difference between groups or conditions might be confounded by differences in the inter-stimulus interval.

When visual stimuli are presented, the initial ERP response does not begin until approximately 50 ms poststimulus. This greater onset latency for visual relative to auditory stimuli is a result of the relatively long period of time required by the retina to accumulate enough photons to produce a reliable response. The typical scalp ERP waveform for a visual stimulus is shown in Figure 27.3. The waveforms are shown for the most common ERP paradigm, the *oddball paradigm*. In this paradigm (which is similar to the *continuous performance task*), two classes of stimuli are used, a frequently occurring *standard* stimulus and an infrequently occurring *oddball* stimulus. For example, 80% of the stimuli might be the letter X and 20% might be the letter O. Each stimulus is presented briefly (e.g., 100 ms–200 ms), and the interval between successive stimulus onsets is

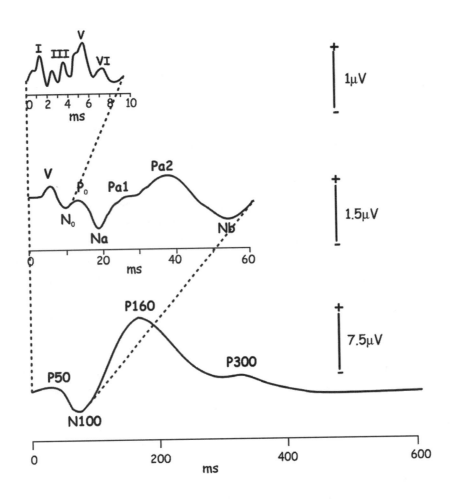

FIGURE 27.2. Typical sequence of auditory sensory components. The wave-form elicited by a click stimulus is shown over different time ranges with different filter settings to highlight the auditory brainstem responses (top), the midlatency responses (middle), and the long-latency responses (bottom). From *Oxford Handbook of Event-Related Potential Components*, by S. J. Luck & E. S. Kappenman (Eds.), 2012, New York, NY: Oxford University Press. Copyright 2012 by Oxford University Press. Adapted with permission.

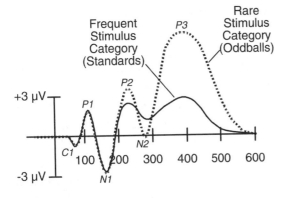

FIGURE 27.3. Typical event-related potential waveforms elicited by standards and oddballs at a posterior electrode site in a visual oddball paradigm.

typically 1,000 ms to 2,000 ms. Participants typically count or make a manual response to the oddball stimuli.

The initial sensory response is usually the same for the standards and the oddballs. It begins with the *C1* wave, which is generated in primary visual cortex and is negative for upper-field stimuli and positive for lower-field stimuli (Clark, Fan, & Hillyard, 1995). The C1 wave is strongly influenced by sensory factors but is not usually influenced by the task. The C1 wave is followed by the P1 wave, which is generated in extrastriate areas of visual cortex and is influenced by sensory factors, attention, and arousal

(Hillyard, Vogel, & Luck, 1998; Vogel & Luck, 2000). The P1 is followed by the N1 wave, which consists of several distinct subcomponents. That is, several different brain areas produce negative voltages in the same approximate time range, which sum together to produce the overall N1 voltage. The N1 complex includes the N170 component described earlier. It also includes a subcomponent that is present when the participant attempts to discriminate the identity of the stimulus rather than merely detecting the presence of a stimulus (Vogel & Luck, 2000). These N1 subcomponents are also influenced by attention (Hillyard et al., 1998). Distinct sensory responses are also produced by somatosensory, olfactory, and gustatory stimuli, as reviewed by Pratt (2012).

The P3 Family of Components

The most common endogenous ERP component is the P3 or P300 wave (see review by Polich, in press). As illustrated in Figure 27.3, the most distinctive property of the P3 wave is that it is much larger for infrequently occurring stimulus categories than for frequently occurring stimulus categories. It is most often observed in the oddball paradigm, in which the oddball stimuli elicit a larger P3 than the standard stimuli. Two distinctly different P3 components can be observed. The most common is called P3b, and it is sensitive to *task-defined* probability. That is, it is larger for improbable stimuli only when the task requires sorting the stimuli in a way that makes a given stimulus category improbable. Imagine, for example, an experiment in which the stimuli are the digits 0 through 9, with each digit occurring with equal likelihood. If the participant is asked to count occurrences of the number 4, then the task requires sorting the stimuli into the "4" category and the "non-4" category. The "4" category will have a probability of .1 and the "non-4" category will have a probability of .9, and the P3b component will be much larger for the "4" category than for the "non-4" category (even though the probability of a 4 is equal to the probability of any other individual digit). This dependence on the task-defined category means that task-irrelevant stimuli generate very little P3b activity, and probability along task-irrelevant dimensions does not influence P3b amplitude. For

example, if 10% of the stimuli are red and 90% are blue, red and blue stimuli will elicit equivalent P3 waves if color is not relevant for the task.

Because P3b amplitude depends on task-defined probability, the difference in amplitude between the oddball and standard stimuli cannot occur until the brain has begun to determine the category of a given stimulus. As a result, factors that influence the time required to perceive and categorize a stimulus strongly influence the onset and peak latency of the P3 wave, and P3 latency is often tightly tied to RT (for an example, see Luck & Hillyard, 1990). However, RT is often influenced by postcategorization factors, such as the complexity of the stimulus-response mapping, and P3 latency sometimes varies independently of RT (Kutas, McCarthy, & Donchin, 1977). Thus, P3 latency can be used to distinguish between pre- and postcategorization processes (but see Verleger, 1997, for a different perspective).

A different P3 subcomponent—called either *P3a* or the *novelty P3*—is elicited by highly distinctive improbable stimuli, even when the task does not require discrimination of these stimuli. For example, if participants are required to count the Xs in a stream of Xs and Os, and photographs of distinctive scenes are occasionally presented, the scenes will elicit a P3a component even if participants are not required to treat them any differently from the frequent O stimuli. The P3a component has a frontal scalp distribution and is reduced in individuals with lesions of prefrontal cortex, whereas the P3b component is largest over central and parietal electrodes and is reduced in individuals with lesions near the temporal-parietal junction.

The N2 Family of Components

Several anatomically and functionally distinct components contribute to the overall N2 wave (see review by Folstein & Van Petten, 2008). Like the P3b, the N2c subcomponent of the N2 complex is typically larger for infrequent stimulus categories This component appears to reflect the actual process of categorizing the stimulus (whereas the P3b reflects a process that follows stimulus categorization). The N2c is present for both auditory and visual stimuli, but with quite different scalp distributions.

When auditory stimuli are used, the oddballs also elicit a component that was originally called *N2a* but is now called the *mismatch negativity* or MMN (see review by Näätänen & Kreegipuu, in press). Unlike the N2c and P3b components, the MMN is enhanced for rare stimuli even if the stimuli are task irrelevant. In a typical MMN study, a sequence of low- and high-pitched tones is presented while the participant reads a book. If the pitch difference is discriminable, and one of the two pitches is less probable than the other, then the oddball pitch will elicit an enhanced negative voltage peaking around 200 ms at anterior electrode sites. This MMN is very useful for determining whether the auditory system can distinguish between different stimulus categories, especially in participants who cannot easily respond behaviorally to indicate the category of a stimulus. For example, the MMN can be used to determine whether infants of a given age can differentiate between two phonemic categories (Coch & Gullick, in press). The MMN is specific for auditory stimuli.

In the visual domain, the *N2pc* component can be used to track the allocation of spatial attention (Luck, in press). The pc in N2pc stands for "posterior contralateral," because the N2pc is observed over posterior scalp sites contralateral to the location of an object that is being attended. As participants shift attention from one side of the display to the other, the N2pc shifts from one hemisphere to the other. In addition, the timing of the N2pc can be used to track how long it takes an individual to find a task-relevant object and shift attention to it. When the attended item must be stored in working memory over a delay interval, a sustained voltage is observed over the delay interval (Perez & Vogel, in press). This *contralateral delay activity* is strongly correlated with individual differences in working memory capacity.

An *anterior N2* component also can be observed at frontal and central electrode sites. This component appears to be sensitive to the mismatch between an expectation and a stimulus, and it is often seen when participants are asked to compare sequentially presented stimuli and the two stimuli mismatch. It is also observed on incompatible trials in the Eriksen flankers task and in the Stroop task;

in these situations, the mismatch is between two elements of a single stimulus array (see review by Folstein & Van Petten, 2008). Yeung et al. (2004) proposed that this component reflects the operation of a conflict detection system and that this same system is also responsible for the error-related negativity (ERN; for a review, see Gehring et al., in press). That is, the ERN occurs when the conflict is so great that an incorrect response occurs. By this account, the anterior N2 and the ERN are actually the same component.

Language-Related ERP Components

Several ERP components have been discovered that are related to language comprehension (see review by Swaab, Ledoux, Camblin, & Boudewyn, in press). The most widely used language-related component is the N400, which is typically observed for words that are semantically, lexically, or associatively unrelated to preceding words, phrases, or sentences. For example, if sentences are presented one word at a time (in either the visual or auditory modality), the last word of a sentence will elicit a larger N400 if its meaning fits poorly with the sentence than if it fits well (as in "She sat down on the large, fluffy pencil"). The N400 can also be seen with simple word pairs that vary in their degree of relatedness. For example, the ERP elicited by the word *table* will be larger in the pair *bicycle–table* than in the pair *chair–table*. Physical and syntactic deviances do not produce a large change in N400 amplitude.

Syntactic anomalies typically produce a P600 component (sometimes called the *syntactic positive shift*). For example, a larger P600 would be elicited by the word *to* in the syntactically incorrect sentence "The broker persuaded to sell the stock" than in the syntactically correct sentence "The broker hoped to sell the stock." Syntactic anomalies may also produce a *left anterior negativity* (LAN) 300 ms to 500 ms after the anomalous word. For example, the LAN is observed when the participant is expecting a word in one syntactic category but instead sees or hears a word in a different category (as in the last word of the sentence "He went outside to take a walking"). The LAN is also larger for words that play a primarily syntactic role (e.g., articles, prepositions) than for words that have strong semantic content (e.g., nouns and verbs).

Memory-Related ERP Components

As with language, several ERP components have been identified that are related to memory. In working memory paradigms, sustained activity can be observed during the retention interval at frontal electrode sites and—when lateralized visual stimuli are used—over the posterior contralateral electrode sites (Perez & Vogel, in press). In long-term memory paradigms, separate ERPs components have been identified that operate during the encoding and retrieval phases of the task. Encoding-related ERPs are often studied by sorting ERPs that were recorded during the encoding phase according to whether a given item was later remembered. Any difference in the ERP between stimuli that were later remembered and stimuli that were later forgotten is called a *Dm effect* (difference because of memory) or a *subsequent memory effect*. In most cases, the Dm effect contains a broad positivity from approximately 400 ms to 800 ms over centroparietal electrode sites. It may also contain left anterior activity, however, and the details of the scalp distribution depend on whether the stimuli were words or pictures and on the instructions given to the participants. Thus, Dm is not a single component, but instead reflects many different processes that can influence whether a stimulus is later remembered.

Two main ERP components have been identified that operate at the time of a recognition judgment. These components are typically identified by comparing the waveforms for stimuli that had been presented during encoding (*old* stimuli) and stimuli that had not (*new* stimuli) or by comparing the waveforms elicited by old stimuli that were correctly judged to be old or incorrectly judged to be new. The two main ERP components that have been observed in such experiments correspond closely with two different mechanisms that have been hypothesized to underlie correct recognition performance. First, an item can be recognized as being from the studied set by a *recollection* process that involves a clear memory of the encoding episode, which may include other incidental information about that episode (e.g., the item that immediately

preceded the tested item). When participants recognize an item in this manner, the recognized items elicit a positive voltage that is largest over the left parietal lobe from approximately 400 ms to 800 ms (called the *left-parietal old-new effect*). It is also possible to correctly report that an item was previously studied because it creates a sense of familiarity, even if the details of the encoding episode cannot be retrieved. When participants recognize an item on the basis of familiarity, the item elicits a somewhat earlier and more anterior positive voltage from approximately 300 ms to 500 ms (called the *midfrontal old-new effect*).

Emotion-Related ERP Components

ERP studies of emotion have typically used emotion-inducing pictures as stimuli. The emotional content of the stimuli influences many of the components that have already been described. For example, the P1, N1/N170, N2, and P3 components may all be increased for emotion-inducing stimuli relative to neutral stimuli (see review by Hajcak, Weinberg, MacNamara, & Foti, in press). Two emotion-related components have been the focus of most research. First, the *early posterior negativity* is a negative potential over visual cortex in the N2 latency range that is enhanced for emotion-inducing stimuli, particularly those with a positive valence. This component is thought to reflect the recruitment of additional perceptual processing for emotion-inducing stimuli. Second, the *late positive potential* is a positive voltage that typically has the same onset time and scalp distribution as the P3 wave (i.e., onset around 300 ms and parietal maximum). It may extend for many hundreds of milliseconds and may become more centrally distributed over time. The initial portion may actually consist of an enlarged P3 component, reflecting an effect of the intrinsic task relevance of emotion-inducing stimuli. Interestingly, the amplitude of the late positive potential is correlated with subjective arousal ratings for the stimuli, suggesting that it may reflect subjective emotional experience.

Response-Related ERP Components

If one creates averaged ERP waveforms time-locked to a motor response rather than time-locked to a stimulus, it is possible to see ERP components reflecting the processes that lead up to the response. If a participant is asked to make self-paced responses every few seconds, a large negative voltage is observed over motor cortex that builds up gradually over a period of several hundred milliseconds. This is called the *Bereitschaftspotential* (BP) or *readiness potential* (RP; see Brunia et al., 2012). This component is also present when participants are presented with stimuli and asked to make speeded responses, but the components reflecting stimulus processing become intermixed with the RP in this situation, making it difficult to isolate the response-related brain activity. However, a portion of the RP is larger over the hemisphere contralateral to the response than over the ipsilateral hemisphere, and the difference in voltage between the two hemispheres can be used to isolate the response-specific activity. This difference is called the lateralized readiness potential (LRP), and it has been widely used to study the processes that are involved in selecting an appropriate response following an imperative stimulus (see Smulders & Miller, in press).

ERP Components in Special Populations

The discussion of ERP components up to this point has focused on studies of healthy young adults. However, ERPs have also been widely used to study typical development across infancy and childhood (Coch & Gullick, in press), to study healthy aging and dementia (Friedman, in press), and to study a variety of psychological disorders, including schizophrenia (O'Donnell, Salisbury, Brenner, Niznikiewicz, & Vohs, in press) and affective disorders (Bruder, Kayser, & Tenke, in press). In the context of infants and young children, ERPs are particularly useful because these individuals have relatively poor control over their behavior, and the ERPs can reveal mental processes that are difficult to assess behaviorally. ERPs are relatively well tolerated in infants and young children, for whom fMRI is not a realistic option. In the domain of aging, ERPs are useful for determining whether the overall slowing of responses reflects slowing in specific processes (e.g., perceptual vs. motor processes). In the context of mental health disorders, ERPs can be useful in determining exactly which processes are impaired

(by determining which components are changed). In addition, ERPs can potentially be used as biomarkers to define specific treatment targets and assess the effectiveness of new treatments (Javitt, Spencer, Thaker, Winterer, & Hajos, 2008; Luck et al., 2011). Moreover, many human ERP components have animal homologues, creating opportunities for translating between animal and human research.

Neural Origins of ERPs

In almost all cases, ERPs originate as postsynaptic potentials (PSPs), which occur during neurotransmission when the binding of neurotransmitters to receptors changes the flow of ions across the cell membrane. ERPs are not associated with action potentials except for a few of the very earliest, subcortical sensory responses. When PSPs occur at the same time in large numbers of similarly oriented neurons, they summate and are conducted at nearly the speed of light through the brain, meninges, skull, and scalp. Thus, ERPs provide a direct, instantaneous, millisecond-resolution measure of neurotransmission-mediated neural activity. This contrasts with the blood-oxygen-level-dependent (BOLD) signal in fMRI, which reflects a delayed secondary consequence of neural activity. Moreover, the close link to neurotransmission make ERPs potentially valuable as biomarkers in studies of pharmacological treatments.

When a PSP occurs within a single neuron, it creates a tiny electrical dipole (an oriented flow of current). Measureable ERPs can be recorded at the scalp only when the dipoles from many thousands of similarly oriented neurons sum together. If the orientations of the neurons in a given region are not similar to each other, the dipoles will cancel out and will be impossible to detect at a distant electrode. The main neurons that have this property are the pyramidal cells of the cerebral cortex, which are the main input-output cells of the cortex. That is, these cells are oriented perpendicular to the cortical surface, and their dipoles add together rather than canceling out. Consequently, scalp-recorded ERPs almost always reflect neurotransmission that occurs in these cortical pyramidal cells. Nonlaminar structures such as the basal ganglia do not typically generate ERPs that can be recorded from the scalp, nor do interneurons within the cortex. Thus, only a fraction of brain activity leads to detectable ERP activity on the scalp.

ERP components can be either positive or negative at a given electrode site. The polarity depends on a combination of at least four factors: (a) the orientation of the neurons with respect to the recording electrode, (b) the location of the reference electrode, (c) the part of the cell in which the neurotransmission is occurring (the apical dendrites or the basal dendrites), and (d) whether the neurotransmission is excitatory or inhibitory. If three of these factors were known, then the fourth could be inferred from the polarity of the ERP component. One almost never knows three of these factors, however, so it is usually impossible to draw strong conclusions from the polarity of an ERP component.

When the dipoles from many individual neurons sum together, they can be represented quite accurately with a single *equivalent current dipole* that is the vector sum of the individual dipoles. For the rest of this chapter, the term *dipole* will refer to these summed equivalent current dipoles.

The voltage recorded on the surface of the scalp will be positive on one side of the dipole and negative on the other, with a single line of zero voltage separating the positive and negative sides (see Figure 27.4a). The voltage field spreads out through the conductive medium of the brain, and the high resistance of the skull and the low resistance of the overlying scalp lead to further spatial blurring. Thus, the voltage for a single dipole will be fairly broadly distributed over the surface of the scalp, especially for ERPs that are generated in relatively deep cortical structures, such as the cingulate cortex. This can be seen in the more diffuse voltage distribution for the relatively deep dipole in Figure 27.4b compared with the relatively superficial dipole in Figure 27.4a.

Electrical dipoles are always accompanied by magnetic fields, but the skull is transparent to magnetism, leading to less blurring of the magnetic fields. Consequently, it is sometimes advantageous to record the magnetic signal (the magnetoencephalogram [MEG]) rather than—or in addition to—the electrical signal (the EEG). However, MEG recordings require extremely expensive equipment and are much less common than EEG recordings.

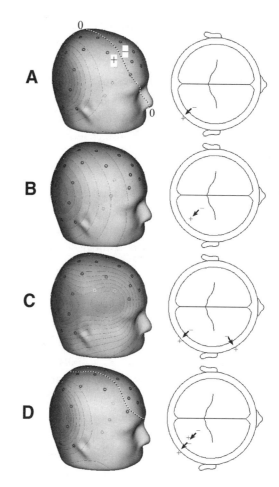

FIGURE 27.4. Scalp distributions (left) produced by different dipole configurations (right). Courtesy of Jesse Bengson.

ERP Localization

When a single dipole is present, one can use the observed scalp distribution to estimate the location and orientation of the dipole with good accuracy unless the dipole is relatively deep in the brain or the data are noisy (for an overview of ERP localization techniques, see Luck, 2005, Chapter 7). When multiple dipoles are simultaneously active, they simply sum together. That is, the voltage distribution for two dipoles will simply be the sum of the two individual distributions. For example, Figure 27.4c shows the same dipole as in Figure 27.4a plus another dipole, and clear voltage foci can be seen over each dipole. Some precision is lost in localizing two dipoles together, but localization can still be reasonably accurate as long as the dipoles are relatively far apart and the noise level is low. However, it can be difficult to separately localize two dipoles that are similar in orientation and fall within several centimeters of each other. For example, the scalp distribution for the two dipoles in Figure 27.4d is nearly identical to the distribution of the single dipole in Figure 27.4a. As more and more simultaneous dipoles are added, it becomes more and more difficult to determine how many dipoles are present and to localize them, especially when the data are noisy. Under these conditions, a set of estimated dipole locations that matches the observed scalp distribution can be quite far from the actual locations.

In many experiments, the number of dipoles could be very large, and localizing ERPs solely on the basis of the observed scalp distribution becomes impossible. Formally speaking, the number of internal generator configurations that could explain an observed voltage distribution is infinite (Helmholtz, 1853). In other words, there is no unique solution to the problem of determining the internal generators solely on the basis of the observed scalp distribution. The only way to localize ERPs in this case is to add external constraints, and this is how existing procedures for localizing ERPs solve the nonuniqueness problem. For example, some common procedures allow the user to simply specify the number of dipoles (Scherg, 1990). Other procedures use structural MRI scans and constrain the dipoles to be in the gray matter. This constraint is still not enough to produce a unique solution, however, so these procedures include additional constraints, such as choosing the solution that minimizes sudden changes from one patch of cortex to the next (Pascual-Marqui, Esslen, Kochi, & Lehmann, 2002). Although these constraints produce a unique solution, they do not necessarily produce the correct solution.

Generally speaking, the most significant shortcoming of mathematical procedures for localizing ERPs is that they do not typically provide a well-justified margin of error. That is, they do not indicate the probability that the solution is incorrect by more than some number of millimeters. Without a margin of error, it is difficult to judge the credibility of a given localization estimate. In most cases, the strongest claim that can be made is that the observed data are consistent with a given generator location. ERP papers often state that the ERPs were *localized* to a certain brain region, as if the localization procedure simply found with certainty the actual location of the generator. Indeed, some papers show the estimated waveforms from specific areas of the brain as if those waveforms were the actual data, without showing the actual observed waveforms from the electrodes. One should be cautious when evaluating studies in which the conclusions rely heavily on these approaches to localizing ERPs, especially when multiple generators are likely to be present.

Although it is usually impossible to definitively localize ERPs solely on the basis of the observed scalp distributions, this does not mean that ERPs can never be localized. Although mathematical localization procedures are usually insufficient, ERPs can be localized using the general hypothesis-testing approach that is used throughout psychology. That is, a hypothesis about the generator location for a given ERP effect leads to a set of predictions, which are then tested by means of experiments. One prediction, of course, is that the observed scalp distribution will be consistent with the hypothesized generator location. Confirming this prediction is not usually sufficient to have strong confidence that the hypothesis about the generator location is correct. Thus, it is important to test additional predictions. For example, one could test the prediction that damage to the hypothesized generator location eliminates the ERP component. Indeed, researchers initially hypothesized that the P3 component was generated in the hippocampus, and this hypothesis was rejected when experiments demonstrated that the P3 is largely intact in individuals with medial temporal lobe lesions (see review by Polich, in press). Similarly, one could predict that an fMRI experiment should show activation in the hypothesized generator location under the conditions that produce the ERP component (see, e.g., Hopf et al., 2006). It is also possible to record ERPs from the surface of the cortex in neurosurgery patients, and this can been used to test predictions about ERP generators (see, e.g., Allison, McCarthy, Nobre, Puce, & Belger, 1994). This hypothesis-testing approach has been quite successful in localizing ERP components.

EXAMPLE 2: IMPAIRED COGNITION IN SCHIZOPHRENIA

This section will provide a somewhat more detailed discussion of a specific experiment, in which ERPs were used to study impaired cognition in schizophrenia (Luck et al., 2009). This will both show how ERPs can be used to isolate specific cognitive processes and provide a concrete example that will be used in the following sections, which focus on the technical details that one must understand to read and evaluate published ERP studies.

The goal of this example experiment was to ask why RTs are typically slowed in schizophrenia patients when they perform simple sensorimotor tasks. That is, are RTs slowed because of an impairment in perceptual processes, in decision processes, or in response processes? ERPs are ideally suited for answering this question because they provide a direct means of measuring the timing of the processes that occur between a stimulus and a response. On the basis of prior research, we hypothesized that the slowing of RTs in schizophrenia in simple tasks does not result from slowed perception or decision, but instead results from an impairment in the process of determining which response is appropriate once the stimulus has been perceived and categorized (the *response selection* process).

To test this hypothesis, we recorded ERPs from 20 individuals with schizophrenia and 20 healthy control participants in a modified oddball task (Luck et al., 2009). In each 5-min block of trials, a sequence of letters and digits was presented at fixation. One stimulus was presented every 1,300 ms to 1,500 ms, and participants made a button-press response for each stimulus, pressing with one hand for letters and with the other hand for digits. One of these two categories was rare (20%) and the other was frequent (80%) in any given trial block. Both the category probabilities and the assignment of hands to categories was counterbalanced across trial blocks.

This design allowed us to isolate specific ERP components by means of *difference waves*, in which the ERP waveform elicited by one trial type is subtracted from the ERP waveform elicited by another trial type (much like difference images in fMRI studies).

Difference waves are valuable because they isolate neural processes that are differentially active for two trial types, separating these processes from the many concurrently active brain processes that do not differentiate between these trial types. In the current study, difference waves were used to isolate the P3 wave (subtracting frequent trials from rare trials) and the LRP (by subtracting ipsilateral electrode sites from contralateral electrode sites, relative to the responding hand). The P3 difference wave reflects the time course of stimulus categorization (e.g., determining whether the current stimulus falls into the rare or frequent category), whereas the LRP difference wave reflects the time course of response selection following stimulus categorization (e.g., determining whether the left button or right button is the appropriate response for the current stimulus). We found that RTs were slowed by approximately 60 ms in patients compared with control participants, and the question was whether this reflects a slowing of perception and categorization (which would be seen in the P3 difference wave) or whether it reflects a slowing of postcategorization response selection processes (which would be seen in the LRP difference wave).

Figure 27.5 shows the P3 difference waves (rare minus frequent) and the LRP difference waves (contralateral minus ipsilateral for the frequent stimulus category) overlaid for the patients and control participants. These are *grand average* waveforms, meaning that average waveforms were first computed across trials for each participant, and then these waveforms were averaged together to view the data. In the grand average waveforms, the P3 wave was virtually indistinguishable for patients versus controls (although the preceding N2 was diminished in the patients). In contrast, the LRP was delayed by 75 ms in onset time and diminished by 50% in amplitude for patients versus controls. Moreover, the degree of amplitude reduction across patients was significantly correlated with the degree of RT slowing. Thus, for a relatively simple perceptual task, the slowed RTs exhibited by the schizophrenia patients appear to result primarily from a slowing of response selection (as evidenced by the later and smaller LRP) rather than a slowing of perception or

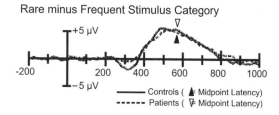

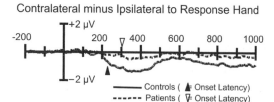

FIGURE 27.5. The P3 was isolated by constructing rare-minus-frequent difference waves at the Pz electrode site (top), and the lateralized readiness potential was isolated by constructing contralateral-minus-ipsilateral difference waves at the C3 and C4 electrode sites (bottom). Triangles show mean latency values. Figure created on the basis of data from the study of Luck et al. (2009).

categorization (as evidenced by no slowing or reduction of the P3).

Recording the Electroencephalogram

We will now turn to the technical details of how ERPs are recorded and analyzed, using the schizophrenia experiment as an example. ERPs are extracted from the EEG, so we will begin by discussing how the EEG is recorded. The EEG is a fluctuating electrical potential (pellets) on the scalp, with a conductive gel or liquid between the electrode and the skin to make a stable electrical connection. The electrical potential (voltage) can then be recorded from each electrode, resulting in a separate waveform from each electrode, with time on the x-axis and voltage on the y-axis (see Figure 27.6b). This waveform will be a mixture of actual brain activity, artifactual electrical potentials produced outside of the brain (by the skin, the eyes, the muscles, etc.), and induced electrical activity from external sources (e.g., video monitors) that are picked up by the head, electrodes, or electrode wires. If precautions are taken to minimize the nonneural potentials, the voltage produced by the brain (the EEG) will be relatively large compared with the nonneural potentials.

The necessary precautions are not always taken, however, and studies that fail to control these sources of noise may have poor statistical power. The impact of the noise on the data can be evaluated by examining the prestimulus baseline period in the waveforms. In a well-designed experiment, any differences between conditions before stimulus onset must be caused by noise. In Figure 27.5, for example, the waveforms include a 200-ms prestimulus baseline period, and although the waveforms are not perfectly flat during this prestimulus period, the differences between patients and controls during this period are much smaller than the P3 and LRP deflections. As a rule of thumb, one should be cautious if a paper reports significant differences between conditions or groups in some poststimulus interval when there are differences of comparable magnitude in the prestimulus interval.

The EEG is quite small (usually under 100 microvolts [μV]), so the signal from each electrode is usually amplified by 1,000 to 100,000 times (an amplifier *gain* of 5,000 was used in the experiment shown in Figure 27.5). The continuous voltage signal is then turned into a series of discrete digital values for storage in a computer. In most experiments, the voltage is sampled from each channel at a rate of between 200 and 1,000 evenly spaced samples per second (Hz; see Figure 27.6c). In the experiment shown in Figure 27.5, the EEG was sampled at 500 Hz (1 sample every 2 ms). In addition, filters are usually used to remove very slow voltage changes (< 0.01–0.1 Hz) and very fast voltage changes (>15–100 Hz), because scalp-recorded voltages in these frequency ranges are likely to be noise from nonneural sources. Frequencies below 0.1 Hz and above 18.5 Hz were filtered from the waveforms shown in Figure 27.5. Filters can dramatically distort the time course of an ERP waveform and can induce artifactual oscillations when the low cutoff is greater than approximately 0.5 Hz or when the low cutoff is less than approximately 10 Hz, so caution is necessary when extreme filters are used.

The EEG is typically recorded from multiple electrodes distributed across the scalp. The standard nomenclature for electrode sites is shown in Figure 27.6a. Each electrode name begins with one to two letters denoting a general brain region (Fp for frontal pole,

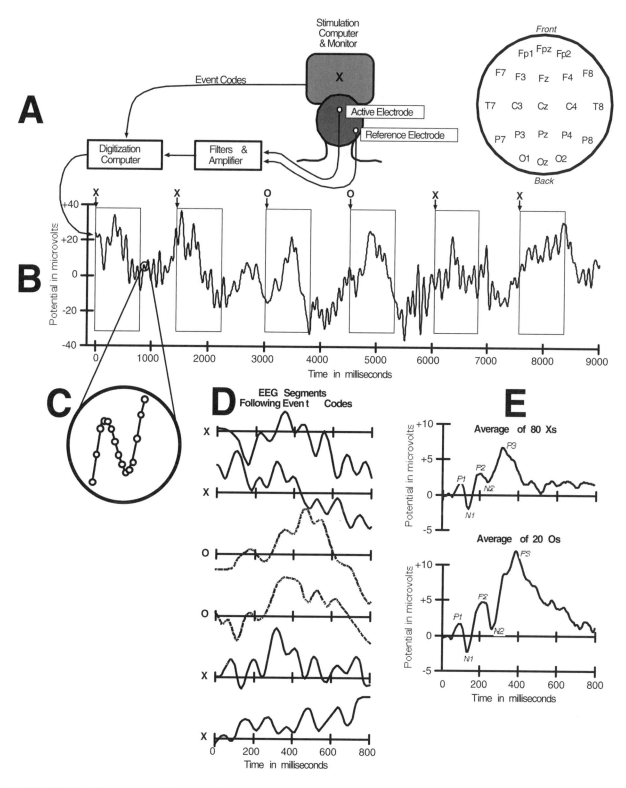

FIGURE 27.6.   Illustration of the procedures used to measure the electroencephalogram (EEG) and construct averaged event-related potential waveforms in a typical visual oddball paradigm.

F for frontal lobe, C for central sulcus, P for parietal lobe, O for occipital lobe, T for temporal lobe). The letters are followed by a number that reflects the distance from the midline (1 is close the midline; 5 is far from the midline). Odd numbers are used for the left hemisphere and even numbers are used for the right, with z for zero when the electrode is on the midline. Thus, F3 lies over frontal cortex to the left of midline, Fz lies over frontal cortex on the midline, and F4 lies over frontal cortex to the right of midline. Different studies use very different numbers of electrodes. For some studies, almost all of the relevant information can be obtained from five to six electrodes; for others, as many as 256 electrodes are needed. Although it might be tempting to assume that more is better, it is actually more difficult to ensure that high-quality data are being recorded when the number of electrodes becomes large, and methods for rapidly applying large numbers of electrodes may lead to poorer signal quality and lower statistical power (Kappenman & Luck, 2010). An intermediate number of electrodes (10–64) is best for most studies. Only 13 scalp sites were used in the study shown in Figure 27.5. Because ERPs are spatially blurred by the skull, it is very unlikely that an effect will be missed because of insufficient sampling of the scalp unless the number of electrodes is very small.

It is important to note that voltage is the potential for electrical charges to move between two locations, and the EEG is therefore measured as the voltage between two electrodes. One is called the *active* electrode and the other is called the *reference* electrode, and a single reference electrode is typically used for all of the scalp electrodes. The reference is often placed at a location such as the earlobe, the *mastoid process* (a bony protrusion behind the ear), or the tip of the nose. These sites are sometimes thought to be electrically neutral, with all of the brain activity originating from the active electrode. This is a misconception, however, and there is no electrically neutral location. Thus, it is important to realize that the voltage attributed to a given site is really the potential between two sites, and brain activity at both the active and reference sites contribute to the recorded signal. This problem can be partially solved by using the average across all electrodes as the reference, but the effectiveness of this depends on whether a sufficiently broad range of electrode sites is used (Dien, 1998). Thus, when reading the method section of a published ERP study, it is important to see what reference site was used. The average of the left and right earlobes was used in the study shown in Figure 27.5.

Artifact Rejection and Correction

Several common artifacts are picked up by EEG recordings and require special treatment. The most common of these arise from the eyes. Whenever the eyes blink, a large voltage deflection is observed over the front of the head. This artifact is usually much larger than the ERP signals. Moreover, eyeblinks are sometimes systematically triggered by tasks and may vary across groups or conditions, yielding a systematic distortion of the data. In addition, large potentials are produced by eye movements, and these potentials can confound experiments that use lateralized stimuli or focus on lateralized ERP responses. In most ERP experiments, the participants are instructed to maintain fixation on a central point and to minimize eyeblinks. Most participants cannot avoid blinking entirely, and they may be unable to avoid making eye movements toward lateralized stimuli. Thus, trials containing blinks, eye movements, or other artifacts are typically excluded from the averaged ERP waveforms. In the study shown in Figure 27.5, for example, three patients and two controls were excluded from the final analysis because more than 50% of trials were rejected (mainly because of blinks). In the remaining participants, an average of 23% of trials was rejected.

This approach has two shortcomings. First, a fairly large number of trials may need to be rejected, thus reducing number of trials remaining in the averaged ERP waveforms. Second, the mental effort involved in suppressing eyeblinks may impair task performance (Ochoa & Polich, 2000). These problems are especially acute in individuals with neurological or psychiatric disorders, who may blink on almost every trial or may perform the task poorly because of the effort devoted to blink suppression. Fortunately, methods have been developed to estimate the artifactual activity and subtract it out, leaving artifact-free EEG data that can be included in the averaged ERP waveforms. Some of these artifact correction techniques are known to make systematic errors in estimating and removing the artifactual activity (see, e.g., Lins, Picton, Berg, & Scherg, 1993), but many of these techniques work reasonably well.

These techniques correct the electrical artifact that is directly produced by an eyeblink or eye movement, but it is impossible to correct for the change in sensory input produced by these events. If an eyeblink causes the eyes to be closed when the stimulus is presented, then the ERPs will be radically changed by the absence or delay of sensory processing, and removing the electrical potential produced as the eyelid slides over the cornea cannot correct for this change in sensory processing. Thus, the best approach is to reject trials on which blinks or eye movements occurred at a time when they might change the sensory input, but to correct for the artifactual voltage when the timing of the blink or eye movement should not change task performance.

Extracting Averaged ERPs From the EEG

ERPs are typically small in comparison with the rest of the EEG activity, and ERPs are usually isolated from the ongoing EEG by a simple averaging procedure. To make this possible, it is necessary to include *event codes* in the EEG recordings that mark the events that happened at specific times, such as stimulus onsets (Figure 27.6a). These event codes are then used as a time-locking point to extract segments of the EEG surrounding each event.

To illustrate this, Figure 27.6 shows the EEG recorded over a 9-sec period in an oddball task with infrequent X stimuli (20%) and frequent O stimuli (80%). Each box highlights the 800-ms segment of EEG following one of these stimuli. Figure 27.6d shows these same segments of EEG, lined up in time. Stimulus onset is time zero. There is quite a bit of variability in the EEG waveforms from trial to trial, and this variability largely reflects the fact that the EEG reflects the sum of many different sources of electrical activity in the brain, many of which are not involved in processing the stimulus. To extract the activity that is related to stimulus processing

from the unrelated EEG, the EEG segments following each X are averaged together into one waveform, and the EEG segments following each O are averaged together into a different waveform (Figure 27.6e). Any brain activity that is not time-locked to the stimulus will be positive at a given latency on some trials and negative at that latency on other trials, and if many trials are averaged together, these voltages will cancel each other out and approach zero. However, any brain activity that is consistently elicited by the stimulus—with approximately the same voltage at a given latency from trial to trial—will remain in the average. Thus, by averaging together many trials of the same type, the brain activity that is consistently time-locked to the stimulus across trials can be extracted from other sources of voltage (including EEG activity that is unrelated to the stimulus and nonneural sources of electrical noise). Other types of events can be used as the time-locking point in the averaging process (e.g., button-press responses, vocalizations, saccadic eye movements, electromyographic activity).

How many trials must be averaged together? That depends on several factors, including the size of the ERP response of interest, the amplitude of the unrelated EEG activity, and the amplitude of nonneural activity. For large components, such as the P3 wave, very clear results can usually be obtained by averaging together 10 to 30 trials. For smaller components, such as the P1 wave, it is usually necessary to average together 100 to 500 trials for each trial type to see reliable differences between groups or conditions. Of course, the number of trials that is required to observe a significant difference will also depend on the number of participants and the magnitude of the difference between conditions. Also, as discussed, looking at the prestimulus baseline period in the ERP waveforms can be useful in evaluating whether enough trials were averaged together to minimize noise. In the experiment shown in Figure 27.5, each participant received 256 oddball stimuli and 1,024 standard stimuli. This is more trials than would be typical for a P3 study, but it was appropriate given that we were also looking at the much smaller LRP and that we anticipated rejecting a large percentage of trials because of eyeblinks.

Although the averaging procedure can be extremely useful in extracting consistent brain responses from the EEG, it is based on a key assumption that is not always valid. Specifically, averaging the EEG segments across trials will work well only if the timing of the neural response is the same across trials. Figure 27.7a shows an example of several single trials in which the latency varies substantially from trial to trial. The average across these trials begins at the onset time of the earliest single trials and ends at the offset time of the latest single trials, and the peak amplitude of the average is much smaller than the peak amplitude of the individual trials. Figure 27.7b shows an example with less variability in latency, resulting in an average that is less broad and has a greater peak amplitude. Thus, if the averaged ERPs are compared for two conditions in which the single-trial ERPs are of equivalent amplitude, but one condition has greater latency variability, the difference in the peak amplitudes of the averaged waveforms might lead to the incorrect conclusions that these conditions differ in the magnitude of the ERP response when in fact they differ in the timing of the response.

This can be a significant problem in practice, especially when a patient group is compared with a control group, because the patient group might appear to have a smaller amplitude as a result of greater variability in timing. There are several ways to address this problem (see Luck, 2005, Chapter 4). The simplest is to measure the amplitude of an ERP component as the mean voltage over a broad time range rather than as the peak voltage because the mean amplitude is not influenced by latency variability (with one exception, described in the next paragraph).

Figure 27.7c shows a situation that is even more problematic. In this example, each stimulus elicits a sequence of two sinusoidal oscillations. The first oscillation is phase-locked to the stimulus (e.g., the oscillation starts at the same part of the sine wave on each trial), and this oscillation is captured well in the averaged waveform. The second oscillation, however, varies in phase from trial to trial. Consequently, even though the oscillation occurs in the same general time range on each trial, the voltage at a given time point is positive on some trials and

negative on other trials, leading to nearly complete cancellation in the averaged waveform. Using mean amplitude to quantify the amplitude of the response in the averaged waveform does not work in this example because the single-trial waveform has both positive and negative parts; mean amplitude is effective in the face of latency or phase variability only for monophasic ERPs.

There is, however, a solution that works for oscillations such as those shown in Figure 27.7c. As shown in Figure 27.7d, it is possible to convert the data into a *time-frequency* representation on each trial, which quantifies the power present in different frequency bands at each point in time. The power of a frequency band is represented independently of its phase. Consequently, when the time-frequency representations are averaged across trials, the phase variation does not cause cancellation of the power. These time-frequency analyses have become quite popular because they can reveal brain activity that is lost by conventional averaging (for a review, see Bastiaansen, Mazaheri, & Jensen, in press). Although this approach is extremely useful, the results are often overinterpreted. The main problem is that nonoscillating brain activity also produces power in time-frequency analyses, and it can be quite difficult to distinguish between true oscillations and transient, nonoscillating activity. Thus, one should be cautious when a study makes claims about oscillations from time-frequency analyses. That is, these analyses reveal real neural activity that would be obscured by conventional averaging, but they do not usually prove that the neural activity consists of bona fide oscillations.

Quantification of Component Magnitude and Timing

The most common way to quantify the magnitude and timing of a given ERP component is to measure the amplitude and latency of the peak value within some time window. For example, to measure the peak of the P3 wave in the data shown in Figure 27.5, one would define a measurement window (e.g., 400 ms–700 ms) and find the most positive point in that window. Peak amplitude would be the voltage at this point, and peak latency would be defined as the time of this point (it is also possible to

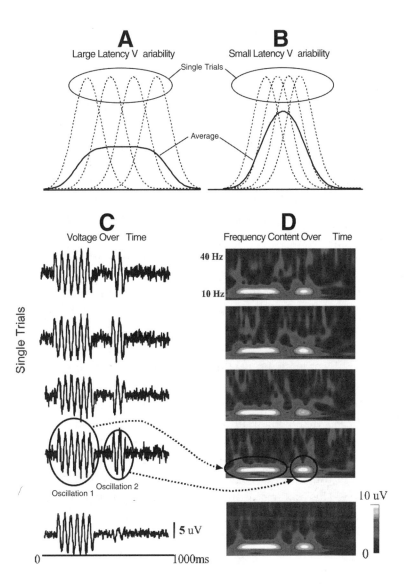

FIGURE 27.7. Illustration of the effects of latency and phase variability on averaged event-related potentials. With a monophasic component, like the P3 wave, a large amount of latency variability in the individual trials leads to a broad averaged waveform with a reduced peak amplitude (a), and reduced latency variability leads to a narrower averaged waveform with a larger peak amplitude (b). When an oscillation is elicited by the stimulus, it will remain in the average if the phase is constant from trial to trial but will virtually disappear from the average if the phase varies randomly (c). The problem of phase variability can be addressed by first converting each single trial into the frequency domain and then averaging across trials (d). The second oscillation remains in this time-frequency average, even though it was largely lost in the conventional average. From *Oxford Handbook of Event-Related Potential Components*, by S. J. Luck and E. S. Kappenman (Eds.), 2012, New York, NY: Oxford University Press. Copyright 2012 by Oxford University Press. Adapted with permission.

search for negative peaks). This was the simplest approach to measuring ERPs before the advent of inexpensive computers, when a ruler was the only available means of quantifying the waveform. This approach is still widely used, but it has several drawbacks. First, there is nothing special about the point at which the waveform reaches an extreme value, and the peak does not represent the magnitude or timing of the entire component. Second, because peak measures are based on extremes, they tend to be sensitive to noise. Third, peak measures are not linear, so the peak in an average waveform will not be the same as the average of the peaks from the individual trials. This makes peak amplitude highly sensitive to trial-to-trial latency variability, and it can also result in grand averages that are not representative of the waveforms from the individual participants. Fourth, peak measures can be greatly influenced by overlapping ERP components, making it difficult to know whether a given effect truly reflects the component of interest.

Because of these limitations, other methods for quantifying ERP amplitudes and latencies have been developed. For measuring the magnitude of a component, it is possible to simply measure the mean voltage over a given time window. This captures all or most of a component, not just the most extreme value, and it is less sensitive to noise than peak amplitude. In addition, mean amplitude is a linear measure, so the mean voltage measured from the waveforms on multiple single trials and then averaged together will be equal to the mean voltage measured from the averaged waveform, and trial-to-trial latency variability will have no effect on the measured amplitude (for monophasic components). Thus, mean amplitude is almost always superior to peak amplitude as a measure of the magnitude of a component.

A related measure can be used to quantify component latency. Specifically, it is possible to define the midpoint of a component as the point that divides the region under the waveform into two equal-area subregions. This is called the 50% area latency measure, and it was used to quantify the timing of the P3 wave in the data shown in Figure 27.5. Measuring the onset latency of a component is more difficult because the onset is the point at which the signal is infinitesimally greater than the noise. It is possible to use a 25% *area latency measure*, which finds the time point that divides the region under the waveform into the first 25% and second 75%. Another approach is to find the peak amplitude and then find the time of the first point that exceeds 50% of that amplitude. This is the approach that was used to measure LRP onset latency in Figure 27.5. These approaches tend to be both more accurate and more sensitive than other approaches for quantifying component timing (Kiesel, Miller, Jolicoeur, & Brisson, 2008).

Statistical Analysis

In most ERP experiments, an averaged ERP waveform is constructed at each electrode site for each subject in each condition. The amplitude or latency of a component of interest is then measured in each one of these waveforms, and these measured values are then entered into a statistical analysis just like any other variable. Thus, the statistical analysis of ERP data is not usually very different from the analysis of traditional behavioral measures.

One issue, however, is important to consider when reading published ERP studies. Specifically, ERP experiments provide extremely rich data sets, usually consisting of several gigabytes of data. This can lead to both the implicit and explicit use of many statistical comparisons per study, which can dramatically increase the probability of a Type I error (i.e., concluding that a difference is real when it was actually a result of sampling error or measurement error). The explicit use of multiple comparisons arises when, for example, separate statistical analyses are reported for several different components. The implicit use of multiple comparisons occurs when researchers conduct many different analyses and then report only a subset (mainly those that yielded significant results). A related problem occurs when researchers first look at the waveforms and then decide on the time windows to be used for quantifying component amplitudes and latencies. If a time window is chosen because the difference between conditions is greatest in that time window, then this biases the results in favor of statistical significance, even if the difference was caused by noise. An analogous problem arises in studies using a large number of electrode sites, when the sites with the largest differences between conditions are chosen for the statistical analyses. With enough electrode sites, it is almost always possible to find a statistically significant difference between two groups or two conditions at a few electrode sites simply because of random noise. Thus, one should be suspicious if unusual, idiosyncratic, and unjustified electrode sites or measurement windows are selected for the statistical analyses.

A second important statistical issue in the analysis of ERP data arises because nearby electrodes are almost always more correlated with each other than distant electrodes. When an electrode site is entered as a within-subjects factor in an analysis of variance (ANOVA), this produces heterogeneity of covariance, which increases the Type I error rate. That is, the actual probability of falsely rejecting the null hypothesis is higher than indicated by the p value. This problem can be addressed in several ways (see Luck, 2006, Chapter 6), but the most common approach is to use the Greenhouse-Geisser epsilon correction, which produces an adjusted p value that more closely reflects the actual probability of a Type I error. Other factors can also produce heterogeneity of covariance, so this adjustment is used even when electrode site is not entered into the ANOVA.

CONCLUSION

The ERP technique is extremely valuable for answering questions about the processes that lead up to and follow a behavioral response, providing information that cannot be obtained from any other noninvasive technique. In addition, ERPs are useful for evaluating cognitive and affective processes in individuals who cannot easily perform complex tasks, and they can be used to reveal processes that are not evident in overt behavior. Moreover, ERPs can be useful in evaluating pharmacological interventions because they reflect the PSPs generated during neurotransmission. Many technical factors, however, can prevent a given ERP study from reaching strong conclusions. The following is a summary of questions to consider when evaluating an ERP study:

1. Are there substantial voltage deflections during the prestimulus baseline period? If so, then the noise level may have been too high or the number of trials averaged together may have been too low, and the reported differences between groups or conditions may be spurious.

2. Could differences in interstimulus interval confound a comparison between conditions or groups, either because of changes in sensory responsiveness or overlapping activity from the previous trial?

3. What reference site was used? It is important to remember that the voltage at a given electrode reflects the potential between that site and the reference electrode

4. What were the filter settings? Extreme filter settings can cause large temporal distortions and artificial oscillations. Be especially cautious if the cutoff for low frequencies is greater than 0.1 Hz.

5. If artifact rejection was used, how many trials were rejected per participant? If artifact correction was used, might blinks or eye movements have changed the sensory input in a manner that confounded the experiment?

6. How many trials were averaged together for each condition? For large components such as P3 and N400, this should typically be 10 to 50. For small components such as P1 and N1, this should typically be 100 to 500.

7. Might differences in peak amplitudes in the averaged ERP waveforms be a result of differences in latency variability rather than true differences in the magnitude of the single-trial ERP responses?

8. Does the study imply that the generator source of a given effect is known with certainty? If so, is this well justified?

9. Does the study conclude that oscillations were present in a given frequency band simply because a time-frequency analysis indicated that significant power was present in that frequency band? Even transient, nonoscillating brain responses can produce such effects.

10. Could changes in the ERP waveform that are attributed to changes in a specific ERP component actually be a result of changes in some other component?

11. Were peak measures used to quantify the magnitude and timing of an ERP component? If so,

then this may have reduced the accuracy and statistical power of the study.

12. Were unusual, idiosyncratic, and unjustified measurement windows and electrode sites chosen for the statistical analysis? If so, the results may be spurious, and a replication may be necessary for the conclusions to be believable.

References

Allison, T., McCarthy, G., Nobre, A., Puce, A., & Belger, A. (1994). Human extrastriate visual cortex and the perception of faces, words, numbers, and colors. *Cerebral Cortex, 4*, 544–554. doi:10.1093/cei•or/4.5.544

Bastiaansen, M., Mazaheri, A., & Jensen, O. (2012). Beyond ERPs: Oscillatory neuronal dynamics. In S. J. Luck & E. S. Kappenman (Eds.), *Oxford handbook of event-related potential components*. New York, NY: Oxford University Press.

Bruder, G. E., Kayser, J., & Tenke, C. E. (2012). Event-related brain potentials in depression: Clinical, cognitive and neurophysiologic implications. In S. J. Luck & E. S. Kappenman (Eds.), *Oxford handbook of event-related potential components*. New York, NY: Oxford University Press.

Brunia, C. H. M., van Boxtel, G. J. M., & Böcker, K. B. E. (2012). Negative slow waves as indices of anticipation: The bereitschaftspotential, the contingent negative variation, and the stimulus preceding negativity. In S. J. Luck & E. S. Kappenman (Eds.), *Oxford handbook of event-related potential components*. New York, NY: Oxford University Press.

Busey, T. A., & Vanderkolk, J. R. (2005). Behavioral and electrophysiological evidence for configural processing in fingerprint experts. *Vision Research, 45*, 431–448. doi:10.1016/j.visres.2004.08.021

Carmel, D., & Bentin, S. (2002). Domain specificity versus expertise: Factors influencing distinct processing of faces. *Cognition, 83*, 1–29. doi:10.1016/S0010-0277(01)00162-7

Chao, L. L., & Knight, R. T. (1997). Prefrontal deficits in attention and inhibitory control with aging. *Cerebral Cortex, 7*, 63–69. doi:10.1093/cercor/7.1.63

Clark, V. P., Fan, S., & Hillyard, S. A. (1995). Identification of early visually evoked potential generators by retinotopic and topographic analyses. *Human Brain Mapping, 2*, 170–187. doi:10.1002/hbm.460020306

Coch, D., & Gullick, M. M. (2012). Event-related potentials and development. In S. J. Luck & E. S. Kappenman (Eds.), *Oxford handbook of event-related potential components*. New York, NY: Oxford University Press.

Dawson, G., Carver, L., Meltzoff, A. N., Panagiotides, H., McPartland, J., & Webb, S. J. (2002). Neural correlates of face and object recognition in young children with autism spectrum disorder, developmental delay, and typical development. *Child Development, 73*, 700–717. doi:10.1111/1467-8624.00433

Dehaene, S., Naccache, L., Le Clec'H, G., Koechlin, E., Mueller, M., Dehaene-Lambertz, G., . . . Le Bihan, D. (1998). Imaging unconscious semantic priming. *Nature, 395*, 597–600. doi:10.1038/26967

Dien, J. (1998). Issues in the application of the average reference: Review, critiques, and recommendations. *Behavior Research Methods, Instruments, and Computers, 30*, 34–43. doi:10.3758/BF03209414

Folstein, J. R., & Van Petten, C. (2008). Influence of cognitive control and mismatch on the N2 component of the ERP: A review. *Psychophysiology, 45*, 152–170.

Friedman, D. (2012). The components of aging. In S. J. Luck & E. S. Kappenman (Eds.), *Oxford handbook of event-related potential components*. New York, NY: Oxford University Press.

Gehring, W. J., Liu, Y., Orr, J. M., & Carp, J. (2012). The error-related negativity (ERN/Ne). In S. J. Luck & E. S. Kappenman (Eds.), *Oxford handbook of event-related potential components*. New York, NY: Oxford University Press.

Hajcak, G., Weinberg, A., MacNamara, A., & Foti, D. (2012). ERPs and the study of emotion. In S. J. Luck & E. S. Kappenman (Eds.), *Oxford handbook of event-related potential components*. New York, NY: Oxford University Press.

Handy, T. C. (Ed.). (2005). *Event-related potentials: A methods handbook*. Cambridge, MA: MIT Press.

Helmholtz, H. (1853). Ueber einige Gesetze der Vertheilung elektrischer Ströme in körperlichen Leitern mit Anwendung auf die thierisch-elektrischen Versuche [On laws of the distribution of electric currents in bodily conductors with application to electrical experiments in animals]. *Annalen der Physik und Chemie, 89*, 211–233, 354–377.

Hillyard, S. A., Vogel, E. K., & Luck, S. J. (1998). Sensory gain control (amplification) as a mechanism of selective attention: Electrophysiological and neuroimaging evidence. *Philosophical Transactions of the Royal Society B: Biological Sciences, 353*, 1257–1270. doi:10.1098/rstb.1998.0281

Hopf, J. M., Luck, S. J., Boelmans, K., Schoenfeld, M. A., Boehler, N., Rieger, J., & Heinze, H.-J. (2006). The neural site of attention matches the spatial scale of perception. *Journal of Neuroscience, 26*, 3532–3540. doi:10.1523/JNEUROSCI.4510-05.2006

Javitt, D. C., Spencer, K. M., Thaker, G. K., Winterer, G., & Hajos, M. (2008). Neurophysiological biomarkers for drug development in schizophrenia. *Nature*

Reviews Drug Discovery, 7, 68–83. doi:10.1038/nrd2463

Kappenman, E. S., & Luck, S. J. (2010). The effects of electrode impedance on data quality and statistical significance in ERP recordings. *Psychophysiology, 47,* 888–904. doi:10.1111/j.1469-8986.2010.01009.x

Kappenman, E. S., & Luck, S. J. (2012). ERP components: The ups and downs of brainwave recordings. In S. J. Luck & E. S. Kappenman (Eds.), *Oxford handbook of event-related potential components.* New York, NY: Oxford University Press.

Kiesel, A., Miller, J., Jolicoeur, P., & Brisson, B. (2008). Measurement of ERP latency differences: A comparison of single-participant and jackknife-based scoring methods. *Psychophysiology, 45,* 250–274. doi:10.1111/j.1469-8986.2007.00618.x

Kutas, M., McCarthy, G., & Donchin, E. (1977). Augmenting mental chronometry: The P300 as a measure of stimulus evaluation time. *Science, 197,* 792–795. doi:10.1126/science.887923

Lins, O. G., Picton, T. W., Berg, P., & Scherg, M. (1993). Ocular artifacts in recording EEGs and event-related potentials. II: Source dipoles and source components. *Brain Topography, 6,* 65–78. doi:10.1007/BF01234128

Luck, S. J. (1998). Sources of dual-task interference: Evidence from human electrophysiology. *Psychological Science, 9,* 223–227. doi:10.1111/1467-9280.00043

Luck, S. J. (2005). *An introduction to the event-related potential technique.* Cambridge, MA: MIT Press.

Luck, S. J. (2012). Electrophysiological correlates of the focusing of attention within complex visual scenes: N2pc and related ERP components. In S. J. Luck & E. S. Kappenman (Eds.), *Oxford handbook of event-related potential components.* New York, NY: Oxford University Press.

Luck, S. J., & Hillyard, S. A. (1990). Electrophysiological evidence for parallel and serial processing during visual search. *Perception and Psychophysics, 48,* 603–617. doi:10.3758/BF03211606

Luck, S. J., & Hillyard, S. A. (2000). The operation of selective attention at multiple stages of processing: Evidence from human and monkey electrophysiology. In M. S. Gazzaniga (Ed.), *The new cognitive neurosciences* (pp. 687–700). Cambridge, MA: MIT Press.

Luck, S. J., & Kappenman, E. S. (Eds.). (2012). *Oxford handbook of event-related potential components.* New York, NY: Oxford University Press.

Luck, S. J., Kappenman, E. S., Fuller, R. L., Robinson, B., Summerfelt, A., & Gold, J. M. (2009). Impaired response selection in schizophrenia: Evidence from the P3 wave and the lateralized readiness potential. *Psychophysiology, 46,* 776–786. doi:10.1111/j.1469-8986.2009.00817.x

Luck, S. J., Mathalon, D. H., O'Donnell, B. F., Spencer, K. M., Javitt, D. C., Ulhaaus, P. F., & Hämäläinen, M. S. (2011). A roadmap for the development and validation of ERP biomarkers in schizophrenia research. *Biological Psychiatry, 70,* 28–34.

Luck, S. J., Vogel, E. K., & Shapiro, K. L. (1996). Word meanings can be accessed but not reported during the attentional blink. *Nature, 383,* 616–618. doi:10.1038/383616a0

Näätänen, R., & Kreegipuu, K. (2012). The mismatch negativity (MMN). In S. J. Luck & E. S. Kappenman (Eds.), *Oxford handbook of event-related potential components.* New York, NY: Oxford University Press.

Ochoa, C. J., & Polich, J. (2000). P300 and blink instructions. *Clinical Neurophysiology, 111,* 93–98. doi:10.1016/S1388-2457(99)00209-6

O'Donnell, B. F., Salisbury, D. F., Brenner, C., Niznikiewicz, M., & Vohs, J. L. (2012). Abnormalities of event-related potential components in schizophrenia. In S. J. Luck & E. S. Kappenman (Eds.), *Oxford handbook of event-related potential components.* New York, NY: Oxford University Press.

Osman, A., & Moore, C. M. (1993). The locus of dual-task interference: Psychological refractory effects on movement-related brain potentials. *Journal of Experimental Psychology: Human Perception and Performance, 19,* 1292–1312. doi:10.1037/0096-1523.19.6.1292

Pascual-Marqui, R. D., Esslen, M., Kochi, K., & Lehmann, D. (2002). Functional imaging with low-resolution brain electromagnetic tomography (LORETA): A review. *Methods and Findings in Experimental and Clinical Pharmacology, 24*(Suppl. C), 91–95.

Perez, V. B., & Vogel, E. K. (2012). What ERPs can tell us about working memory. In S. J. Luck & E. S. Kappenman (Eds.), *Oxford handbook of event-related potential components.* New York, NY: Oxford University Press.

Polich, J. (2012). Neuropsychology of. In S. J. Luck & E. S. Kappenman (Eds.), *Oxford handbook of event-related potential components* (p. 300). New York, NY: Oxford University Press.

Pratt, H. (2012). Sensory ERP components. In S. J. Luck & E. S. Kappenman (Eds.), *Oxford handbook of event-related potential components.* New York, NY: Oxford University Press.

Rossion, B., & Jacques, C. (2012). The N170: Understanding the time course of face perception in the human brain. In S. J. Luck & E. S. Kappenman (Eds.), *Oxford handbook of event-related potential components.* New York, NY: Oxford University Press.

Scherg, M. (1990). Fundamentals of dipole source potential analysis. In F. Grandori, M. Hoke, & G. L. Romani (Eds.), *Auditory evoked magnetic fields* and potentials. *Advances in audiology VI* (pp. 40–69). Basel, Switzerland: Karger.

Smulders, F. T. Y., & Miller, J. O. (2012). Lateralized readiness potential. In S. J. Luck & E. S. Kappenman (Eds.), *Oxford handbook of event-related potential components*. New York, NY: Oxford University Press.

Sreenivasan, K. K., Goldstein, J. M., Lustig, A. G., Rivas, L. R., & Jha, A. P. (2009). Attention to faces modulates early face processing during low but not high face discriminability. *Attention, Perception, and Psychophysics, 71*, 837–846. doi:10.3758/APP.71.4.837

Sutton, S., Braren, M., Zubin, J., & John, E. R. (1965). Evoked potential correlates of stimulus uncertainty. *Science, 150*, 1187–1188. doi:10.1126/science.150.3700.1187

Swaab, T. Y., Ledoux, K., Camblin, C. C., & Boudewyn, M. (2012). Language-related ERP components. In S. J. Luck & E. S. Kappenman (Eds.), *Oxford handbook of event-related potential components*. New York, NY: Oxford University Press.

Tanaka, J. W., & Curran, T. (2001). A neural basis for expert object recognition. *Psychological Science, 12*, 43–47. doi:10.1111/1467-9280.00308

van Turennout, M., Hagoort, P., & Brown, C. M. (1998). Brain activity during speaking: From syntax to phonology in 40 milliseconds. *Science, 280*, 572–574. doi:10.1126/science.280.5363.572

Verleger, R. (1997). On the utility of P3 latency as an index of mental chronometry. *Psychophysiology, 34*, 131–156. doi:10.1111/j.1469-8986.1997.tb02125.x

Vogel, E. K., & Luck, S. J. (2000). The visual N1 component as an index of a discrimination process. *Psychophysiology, 37*, 190–203. doi:10.1111/1469-8986.3720190

Yeung, N., Cohen, J. D., & Botvinick, M. M. (2004). The neural basis of error detection: Conflict monitoring and the error-related negativity. *Psychological Review, 111*, 931–959. doi:10.1037/0033-295X.111.4.931

CHAPTER 28

FUNCTIONAL MAGNETIC RESONANCE IMAGING

Bianca C. Wittmann and Mark D'Esposito

Functional magnetic resonance imaging (fMRI) is a powerful technique for measuring the neural activity that underlies cognitive processes. It provides high spatial resolution compared with electroencephalography (EEG) and lesion studies and adequate temporal resolution on the order of seconds, and it accommodates a variety of cognitive tasks. fMRI relies on an indirect measurement of neural activity that is based on the link between local neuronal firing and cerebral blood flow. Because it is a noninvasive technique, it is an ideal tool for repeated measurements, such as longitudinal studies of brain function. These advantages as well as its widespread availability for research have made it a central tool for studies of brain–behavior relations.

MRI scanners create static magnetic fields that are about 30,000 to 80,000 times as strong as the Earth's magnetic field. The most common MRI scanners use field strengths of 1.5 T or 3 T, although the use of 7-T scanners for whole-brain functional studies is becoming possible (Poser, Koopmans, Witzel, Wald, & Barth, 2010). With increasing magnetic field, however, artifacts because of distortion and image loss near the boundary of brain tissue and sinuses become more difficult to control. These artifacts mostly affect the orbitofrontal cortex (OFC) and regions within the anterior and inferior temporal lobe. Improvements can be made using special shimming procedures (Balteau, Hutton, & Weiskopf, 2010), specialized pulse sequences for data acquisition (Weiskopf, Hutton, Josephs, & Deichmann, 2006; Weiskopf, Hutton, Josephs, Turner, & Deichmann, 2007), and distortion correction of functional images (Hutton et al., 2002; Hutton, Deichmann, Turner, & Andersson, 2004; Yung-Chin, Ching-Han, & Tseng, 2009).

Functional neuroimaging, as well as other functional methods such as EEG (see Chapters 26 and 27 of this volume) and magnetoencephalography (MEG; see Chapter 29 of this volume), relies on correlational analyses whose interpretations are limited and must be made cautiously. Inferences are made about the association between activity in certain brain areas with cognitive processes that are engaged by a predefined task. A statistical correlation of this type does not allow researchers to conclude that the observed activity is necessary for the cognitive operation targeted by the task design. It is possible to say, however, that the task manipulation was causal for the observed brain activity (Buchsbaum, 2009; Weber & Thompson-Schill, 2010). This difference is crucial when interpreting fMRI research findings. For example, we can report that stimulus A caused increased activity in a certain brain region compared with stimulus B, but we cannot claim that this increased activity is necessary for processing stimulus A, and we cannot claim that it caused behavioral differences observed between the two stimuli. In addition, the experimenter can often not fully control a participant's cognitive processes during an experiment—for example, a visual memory task or a navigational task may also engage language processes that may not be fully matched in a control condition. Even well-controlled tasks do not provide conclusive evidence that differential brain activity is related to the specific cognitive operation under study.

DOI: 10.1037/13619-029
APA Handbook of Research Methods in Psychology: Vol. 1. Foundations, Planning, Measures, and Psychometrics, H. Cooper (Editor-in-Chief)

Another limitation of fMRI studies is that some brain areas may be activated but not necessary for the cognitive process of interest. For example, the hippocampus is activated in many working memory studies, but hippocampal lesions cause impairments only on specific subtypes of working memory tasks (Cashdollar et al., 2009; Nichols, Kao, Verfaellie, & Gabrieli, 2006; Piekema, Kessels, Mars, Petersson, & Fernandez, 2006; Piekema, Kessels, Rijpkema, & Fernandez, 2009). This suggests that some brain areas may be involved in a process and may be part of task-relevant networks but may not perform necessary computations. fMRI can therefore provide information about regional involvement that cannot be easily obtained in lesion studies and provide information about human brain functions that complements the information from animal studies. Its results, however, cannot be taken alone without considering the wider context of the relevant literature from other modalities and populations. In particular, information from lesion studies can be effectively combined with fMRI data (e.g., Badre, Hoffman, Cooney, & D'Esposito, 2009; D'Esposito, Cooney, Gazzaley, Gibbs, & Postle, 2006; Kishiyama, Yonelinas, & Knight, 2009). If a region is activated in healthy subjects during a task and lesions of this region cause impaired performance, then researchers can be more confident that this region supports necessary cognitive processes.

These considerations imply that it is not valid to infer the cognitive operation performed by participants from the activation of brain areas (a practice known as *reverse inference*; D'Esposito, Ballard, Aguirre, & Zarahn, 1998; Poldrack, 2006; Van Horn & Poldrack, 2009). For example, activation of the amygdala in a task cannot be ascribed to negative emotions, such as fear, despite the common activation of the amygdala in aversive conditioning tasks (Sehlmeyer et al., 2009), because amygdalar activations have also been found for other types of tasks (Rademacher et al., 2010; Walter, Abler, Ciaramidaro, & Erk, 2005). This may seem an obvious logical error, but conclusions of this kind are unfortunately not uncommon (Poldrack, 2006).

When the limitations of fMRI are taken into account, it offers a range of excellent methods to help answer questions related to functional specialization and integration within the brain. For an excellent review on current developments in neuroimaging, see Bandettini (2009); for a summary of the neurophysiological basis of fMRI and the resulting limitations, see Logothetis (2008).

CHARACTERISTICS OF THE SIGNAL: TEMPORAL AND SPATIAL RESOLUTION

To understand the temporal limitations of the fMRI signal, it is necessary to look at its source (for an excellent introduction, see Huettel, Song, & McCarthy, 2008). fMRI measures brain activity indirectly by recording changes in blood flow that are linked to neural activity. The change in blood flow is called the *hemodynamic response*; it is based on increased metabolic demands of active neurons leading to increased blood flow in local capillaries. This leads to a change in blood oxygenation level, which can be detected because oxygenated and deoxygenated hemoglobin have different magnetic properties. The measured signal is called blood-oxygenation-level-dependent (BOLD) response. Cortical neurons can respond to stimuli as early as tens of milliseconds following a sensory stimulus, but the vascular response develops more slowly. It reaches its peak about 5 s to 6 s after a brief neuronal response and goes back to baseline within about 12 s to 16 s (Figure 28.1; Aguirre, Zarahn, & D'Esposito, 1998; Bandettini, Wong, Hinks, Tikofsky, & Hyde, 1992; Boynton, Engel, Glover, & Heeger, 1996). The delay between neural and vascular signals imposes constraints on the study design because events that are presented in close temporal succession cause a summation of the BOLD response, making it more difficult to ascribe activations to single events.

There are two main approaches to account for this hemodynamic delay when analyzing fMRI data (see Figure 28.2). The first solution is to use slow-task paradigms. Researchers use blocked designs with block durations of 20 s to 40 s, during which many stimuli of the same condition are presented in rapid succession. This approach leads to good signal-to-noise ratio, but many cognitive tasks cannot be adapted to long blocks. Researchers may want to examine brain responses to rare events, or they may want to classify trials a posteriori. For example, if we

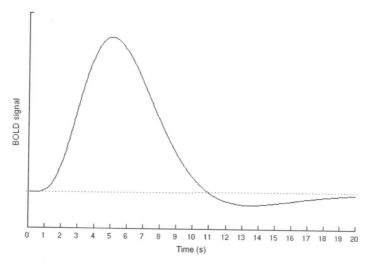

FIGURE 28.1.   Schematic representation of the hemodynamic blood-oxygen-level-dependent (BOLD) response. The signal peaks at about 5 s to 6 s after the sensory or behavioral event (at Time 0).

want to dissociate successful memory retrieval from retrieval failure, we need to be able to separate individual trials on the basis of participants' responses (Buckner et al., 1998; Wagner et al., 1998). Often, researchers want to separate short individual phases of a task (Courtney, Ungerleider, Keil, & Haxby, 1997; D'Esposito, Postle, Jonides, & Smith, 1999). Blocked designs do not give satisfactory results in these cases. In addition, estimation of the shape of the hemodynamic response in long blocks is poor. Some of the disadvantages of blocked designs can be avoided by using random stimulus presentation with long intertrial intervals (ITIs); this allows a full sampling of the hemodynamic response. Long ITIs, however, limit the number of stimuli that can be presented in a session of given length, thereby decreasing power (Dale, 1999), and make it more difficult for participants to sustain attention to the task. Researchers cannot exclude the possibility of subjects performing other cognitive operations in the period between stimulus presentations.

The second, currently most common, approach to dealing with the slow hemodynamic response uses random stimulus presentation at variable (*jittered*) ITIs (see Figure 28.2). This solution, called *event-related design*, allows the shape of the hemodynamic response to be estimated despite summation effects (Rosen, Buckner, & Dale, 1998). Its advantages lie in more flexible task presentation that

allows randomizing stimuli and trials, selecting specific time windows during a task (such as delay periods in a working memory task), and classifying trials on the basis of participants' responses. Depending on the experimental hypotheses, a mixed block and event-related design can also be used (Visscher et al., 2003). For a mixed design, trials are jittered and randomly presented within task blocks that alternate with control blocks. This approach can distinguish brain activity that is sustained during an ongoing task from activity elicited by single trials of the task. For example, two types of cognitive processes during memory retrieval are related to an ongoing *retrieval mode* and to successful retrieval of individual items (Donaldson, Petersen, Ollinger, & Buckner, 2001). For a more detailed comparison of available scanning designs, see Amaro and Barker (2006).

The sampling rate of the MRI signal also needs to be considered. The sampling unit for the timing of fMRI data is called *repetition time* (TR). Its duration is defined by the time that is necessary for the acquisition of one functional volume and ranges from a few hundred milliseconds to several seconds. Each functional volume consists of a number of sequentially acquired slices. As a result of sequential acquisition, each slice is measured only once per TR, and the signal has to be interpolated. Depending on the task design, it may be desirable to get an accurate estimate of the shape of the hemodynamic response,

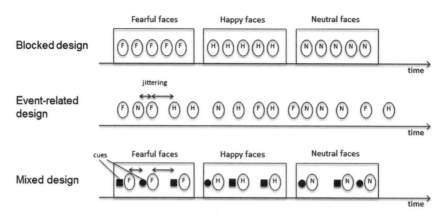

FIGURE 28.2.   Schematic representation of blocked, event-related and mixed designs.Top row: In a blocked design, the events of interest (here: presentation of fearful, happy and neutral faces; designated F, H, and N) are separated into blocks of trials. The hemodynamic response is estimated per block. Middle row: In an event-related design, the events of interest are presented in a random sequence. To separate the hemodynamic response between events, individual trials are presented with a temporal jitter. Bottom row: In a mixed design, there are blocks of separated conditions (here: fearful, happy, and neutral faces) within which there are separable, temporally jittered events of interest (here: two types of cues that indicate the task for subjects, e.g., rate faces based on emotion or attractiveness).

and the TR should be kept short to provide more time points for interpolation. This does not increase the temporal resolution of the experiment because the slow hemodynamic response remains unchanged. Short TRs will limit the extent of spatial coverage because the acquisition time for a single slice cannot be decreased beyond a certain limit. With task designs that use longer ITIs or blocks, however, the TR can be extended to several seconds while still providing a sufficient estimate of the hemodynamic response. In practice, most event-related experiments use TRs of 1.5 s to 3 s. If the shape of the hemodynamic response is taken into account in the task design, even brief stimuli of < 50-ms duration can be detected (Savoy et al., 1995).

The spatial resolution of fMRI data is specified as three-dimensional voxel sizes (e.g., $3 \times 3 \times 3$ mm³). The first two values specify the in-plane dimension of a slice, and the third value specifies the slice thickness. Choosing the spatial resolution for a study depends on the research question and on a trade-off between spatial-temporal resolution and coverage that results because slice acquisition times increase with increasing spatial resolution. In other words, if we want to maintain adequate temporal resolution, fewer

slices can be acquired per TR and spatial coverage decreases. This is acceptable if we are interested in a predefined region of cortex, such as the visual occipital cortex (such studies often use voxel sizes of $1.5 \times 1.5 \times 1.5$ mm³). For experiments that require whole-brain coverage, however, voxel sizes increase and a resolution of $3 \times 3 \times 3$ mm³ is widely used. An additional consideration is the change in signal-to-noise ratio with decreasing voxel size (Tabelow, Piěch, Polzehl, & Voss, 2009). The MRI signal depends on the changing amount of deoxygenized hemoglobin per voxel. Smaller voxels yield smaller changes and therefore lower signal-to-noise ratio. Whether this is acceptable may depend on assumptions about the brain region that is being studied. If we assume that a large number of neurons per millimeter will fire in response to our stimulus, the measured brain signal will be larger and a smaller voxel size may be sufficient. On the other hand, if we expect activity of a smaller number of specialized neurons, the measured change will be smaller and larger voxels may be required to dissociate the signal from noise.

Spatial resolution is further decreased during data analysis by common techniques such as smoothing and normalization. *Smoothing* refers to the use of a three-dimensional Gaussian filter (usually several voxels in width) to average adjacent voxels, resulting in a spread of activity across neighboring voxels. Its main advantage lies in improved signal-to-noise ratio by taking into account correlations in activity between adjacent voxels. Normalization techniques transform individual subjects' data to a common template to facilitate interindividual comparisons and statistical group tests. The difficulty of capturing individual anatomical differences in this step further reduces the final spatial resolution in our statistical tests.

To summarize, fMRI has the potential for both relatively high temporal (hundreds of milliseconds) and spatial (millimeter) resolution. There is a trade-off between high resolution in the spatial and temporal domains and spatial coverage; optimal settings need to be determined for each experiment on the basis of the research question and underlying assumptions about brain activity in the regions of interest.

Statistical Analysis of Regional Specialization

The most common type of fMRI study seeks to determine whether particular parts of the brain are functionally specialized. This is achieved by identifying which regions of the brain become active in response to certain stimuli or tasks. There are many analysis packages designed for MRI data, all of which rely on a statistical comparison of the condition of interest with a control condition. Generally, the raw data from the scanner are processed to some extent before being entered into the statistical analysis (this phase is often called *preprocessing*). These steps deal with common characteristics of data acquisition and analysis goals. Good practice requires that the quality of raw data be assessed before processing. Several automated scripts are available to check and possibly correct for instances of bad data, for example, caused by signal loss on single slices. After data quality has been established, common preprocessing techniques address the following issues: the difference in timing of slice acquisition in areas of the brain that are acquired at different times with respect to the volume acquisition (TR), correction for small head motions (realignment), correction for field inhomogeneities

(unwarp), transformation of each subject's data into a common anatomical space to enable group analysis (normalization), and spatial smoothing.

The statistical analysis of preprocessed data depends on the task design and the research questions. In most experiments, some type of group analysis is performed combining individuals' statistical brain maps, although for some research questions, individual subjects' data are used to obtain better functional localization. For example, research on the visual system often employs retinotopic mapping using functional localizers for each individual because retinotopic maps differ substantially across individuals (McFadzean, Condon, & Barr, 1999; Tootell et al., 1998). Functional localizers are used to identify the voxels that are activated by a predefined stimulus or task that is designed to engage the functional system under study. For group analyses, studies suggest that using more than the most commonly reported number of 12 to 16 subjects substantially increases reliability (Bennett & Miller, 2010; Thirion et al., 2007). Most analysis techniques test how well the measured signal fits the expected shape of the hemodynamic signal at a set of specified onsets for each condition, commonly using a general linear model (see Volume 3, Chapter 9, this handbook) and generating a statistical map for each subject. For a group analysis, these individual maps are then tested in a random-effects model for applicability of the findings to the population from which subjects were drawn. An important caveat for all group analyses, independent of the analysis method, is that participants for most studies are young, healthy students, and the results cannot be assumed to reflect other groups in the population. Activation results of group analyses are reported on the basis of normalization to a standard anatomical template. The most reliable way to identify the areas of activation is to compare activation maps to brain atlases, a technique that requires particular care on the part of the researcher (Devlin & Poldrack, 2007). Alternatively, researchers may be interested in predefined functional or anatomical regions. These can be analyzed using region-of-interest (ROI) analyses. The region is defined either anatomically, usually by manually tracing the borders of the region on anatomical images, or functionally by using functional localizers.

The regions that are identified using either of these approaches are then selectively analyzed for activity in the main task of interest.

Advantages of the ROI method are higher signal-to-noise ratio by summing over a number of voxels, and reduction of the problem of multiple comparisons (see the following paragraphs). Its disadvantage lies in the difficulty of ROI definition. Anatomical definition is labor intensive and may differ among researchers. Additionally, anatomical boundaries may not match the functional system that is being studied. Functional ROIs, on the other hand, increase the likelihood of evaluating the targeted functional system when the functional localizer task is chosen carefully. For example, a study in our laboratory used a functional localizer to define face- and scene-selective regions and then independently investigated reward-related top-down effects on these regions during working memory processing (Krawczyk, Gazzaley, & D'Esposito, 2007).

In addition to analyses based on contrasts of two or more conditions, it is possible to include parametric analyses that examine the effects of a trial-wise covariate on functional activity. The parametric regressor can be based directly on behavior such as reaction times on each trial, or it can test a computational model of functional activity (for an introduction to computational models, see Volume 2, Chapters 20 and 21, this handbook). The combination of computational modeling with fMRI experiments offers exciting possibilities for testing hypotheses about brain function (Deco, Jirsa, Robinson, Breakspear, & Friston, 2008; Horwitz & Smith, 2008). For example, many studies have demonstrated that the human striatum processes rewards in a manner consistent with findings from animal experiments that have identified brain substrates of prediction errors that are described in computational theories of value learning (e.g., O'Doherty, Dayan, Friston, Critchley, & Dolan, 2003; Palminteri, Boraud, Lafargue, Dubois, & Pessiglione, 2009; Valentin & O'Doherty, 2009). Computational models of learning can provide predictions of optimal choice behavior and theories of brain function that can integrate human and animal studies into a common framework and inform research on clinical disorders (Dayan, 2009; Dayan &

Daw, 2008; Gläscher & O'Doherty, 2010; Huys & Dayan, 2009). The computational approach can be further enhanced by combining it with genetic and pharmacological methods (Krugel, Biele, Mohr, Li, & Heekeren, 2009; Pessiglione, Seymour, Flandin, Dolan, & Frith, 2006). Moreover, computational models can also be used to inform studies of the functional integration across brain areas (den Ouden, Daunizeau, Roiser, Friston, & Stephan, 2010; Kahnt et al., 2009).

A fundamental trade-off exists in the analysis of fMRI data between accepting Type I and Type II statistical errors. Type I errors occur when the null hypothesis (that there is no difference in brain activity between two conditions) is falsely rejected, that is, we conclude that there is activity where there is none. Type II errors occur when the null hypothesis is accepted despite a real difference in activation between the conditions. fMRI studies mostly focus on avoiding Type I errors, although some researchers have pointed out the shortcomings of this strategy (Lieberman & Cunningham, 2009). The most common approach to reducing Type I errors is a correction for the multiple statistical comparisons that are performed when analyzing fMRI data. Because a whole-brain scan generates a large number of observations (>10,000) that are tested for statistical significance, the alpha values of the statistical test need to be adjusted. If researchers are interested in testing hypotheses using only a limited number of predefined brain regions, then an ROI analysis can be performed. Alpha value correction then only requires correcting for the number of observations within the ROI because a smaller number of independent statistical tests are conducted relative to a map-wise analysis. No inferences about activations in the rest of the brain can therefore be made. ROI analyses can, however, be combined with a stringent whole-brain correction to achieve the sensitivity of smaller volume approaches while permitting inference about brain regions outside the focus of the study.

There are several ways to adjust alpha values, for example, by using a family-wise error rate correction. There is currently no gold standard for error correction in the field. Note that a reduction of Type I errors means an increase of Type II errors. How stringent a correction is applied will depend on the type of question being addressed. Another approach to reducing Type I errors is cluster-size thresholding, which defines a minimum number of contiguous voxels that have to be activated for the cluster to be considered significant (Forman et al., 1995; Xiong, Gao, Lancaster, & Fox, 1995). Cluster-size thresholding is valid because the probability of activated clusters occurring because of random chance is low, much lower than the probability of a Type I error on single voxels.

Because there is a greater emphasis on avoiding Type I than Type II errors in most fMRI studies, researchers must be careful about overinterpreting negative findings (i.e., "null results") as evidence of inactivity in a brain region during performance of a task. If a brain region's inactivity is crucial for the hypothesis being evaluated, a power analysis can be used to estimate the required power to detect activity in that region (Hayasaka, Peiffer, Hugenschmidt, & Laurienti, 2007; Mumford & Nichols, 2008; Van Horn, Ellmore, Esposito, & Berman, 1998; Zarahn & Slifstein, 2001). Power can be increased, for instance, by increasing the number of trials per condition or scanning more subjects (Bennett & Miller, 2010; Desmond & Glover, 2002; Thirion et al., 2007).

Many fMRI studies test hypotheses about the relation between brain activity and behavior or psychological constructs such as personality and mood. A common method involves extracting a measure of average task activity in a region or in a representative voxel from an activation cluster (usually the voxel with the maximum response, *peak voxel*). This value can then be tested to examine correlations with interindividual behavioral measures of interest. For example, researchers have assessed whether amygdala activity in response to emotional faces correlates with an individual measure of anxiety (Stein, Simmons, Feinstein, & Paulus, 2007). Alternatively, the behavioral measure of interest can be included as a covariate in a statistical analysis of whole-brain data, without regional preselection. Both approaches are valid tools for investigating interindividual differences. Recently, however, criticism has arisen concerning invalid double-dipping methods (Baker, Hutchison, & Kanwisher, 2007; Kriegeskorte, Simmons, Bellgowan, & Baker, 2009;

Vul, Harris, Winkielman, & Pashler, 2009): circular analyses that use the same data to identify a set of voxels that show an effect and then to compute the magnitude of the effect on these pre-selected voxels. In statistics, this is known as a nonindependence error. These errors substantially overestimate statistical correlations because a correlation analysis relies on the inclusion of the full data set to produce meaningful values. If one excludes data (voxels) that do not show the correlation, the correlation analysis will be biased toward significance. Care must therefore be taken to avoid this type of error, either by using one of the approaches discussed thus far, in which the voxels of interest are determined from a different task contrast, or by using a cross-validation method. The latter method involves selecting brain regions from a correlation analysis on a subset of the data (e.g., half of the runs) and computing the magnitude and significance of the effect on another subset of the data (e.g., the other half of the runs), or by excluding a number of subjects from the region selection or analysis (Esterman, Tamber-Rosenau, Chiu, & Yantis, 2010). Confounds of this type can also occur in analyses that do not correlate brain activity with behavior or personality. For example, in ROI or pattern classifier analyses (see the section Multivariate Pattern Analysis), researchers also need to be vigilant to avoid these unintentional biases (Kriegeskorte et al., 2009).

Functional Connectivity Analyses

In contrast to univariate approaches toward analyzing fMRI data, which are designed to test functional regional specialization, multivariate approaches are designed to test functional integration in networks of connected brain regions. Unfortunately, the term "network" is often used to describe a group of brain regions that are coactive on a statistical map produced by univariate analysis. Coactivity does not indicate that these regions are connected and form a functional network. For example, two regions can both be activated by stimulation relative to rest, but we cannot conclude that there are direct pathways connecting the regions because both may be influenced by a third region. In addition, coactivation patterns provide no evidence for the direction of the effects. Region A could affect processing in region B or vice versa, or there may be no asymmetric influence of one region on another.

Researchers can choose from among a variety of techniques for identifying functional networks in fMRI data sets. All such analyses are motivated by the idea that complex cognitive operations do not rely on one brain area alone; rather, they rely on interactions among computations carried out in several areas (Friston, 2002; Mesulam, 1990). These methods are based on the covariance of activation levels in different brain regions, that is, on correlated temporal patterns of activation and deactivation. Two analytic approaches can be distinguished: functional and effective connectivity methods (for an introduction, see Friston, 1994). Effective connectivity analyses such as structural equation modeling, dynamic causal modeling, and Granger causality rely on a priori models of expected causal relations among activity in a set of selected regions (Friston, Harrison, & Penny, 2003; Penny, Stephan, Mechelli, & Friston, 2004; Stephan et al., 2010). Functional regions can be selected on the basis of previously published studies or on the results of activation analyses from the same experiment. The models are informed by prior knowledge about anatomical connections between the regions and can be combined with tractography measures such as diffusion tensor imaging (Rykhlevskaia, Gratton, & Fabiani, 2008). In general, the number of existing anatomical connections and possible causal models is very high, and a selection based on the assumed importance of each pathway is needed to simplify the model (Ramsey et al., 2010). These model-based methods are powerful but sensitive to the specifications of the a priori model. Functional connectivity analyses, on the other hand, are model-free approaches to identifying brain areas whose activity covaries over time, that is, they do not require a priori hypotheses about how brain regions interact. Therefore, they are well suited for exploratory analyses, such as identifying networks that are involved in specific cognitive processes. Analyses can be based on activation patterns (McIntosh, Chau, & Protzner, 2004; Roebroeck, Formisano, & Goebel, 2005) or coherence in periodic temporal fluctuations, that is, in the frequency domain (Havlicek,

Jan, Calhoun, & Brazdil, 2009; Kayser, Sun, & D'Esposito, 2009). Both model-free and model-based connectivity analyses are potentially vulnerable to confounds introduced by the indirectness of the fMRI measurement, such as variability in the shape and delay of the hemodynamic response between regions. Reliable analysis is still possible, however, and phase information (i.e., temporal periodicity) is not affected (David et al., 2008; Deshpande, Sathian, & Hu, in press). The interpretation of connectivity results should always be made cautiously because the method is indirect and, in the case of effective connectivity, because it depends on a correct a priori model. In combination with information about the influence of specific brain regions on processing in other areas as gained through lesion and transcranial magnetic stimulation (TMS) studies of human subjects and results from animal models, however, connectivity analyses of fMRI data can provide relevant evidence on the basis of noninvasive studies in healthy participants.

One of the main applications of model-free connectivity analyses is the investigation of the brain's resting state. Interest in intrinsic brain activity while an individual is not performing a task arose because researchers observed task-related activity decreases compared with resting control conditions (Gusnard & Raichle, 2001). This observation gave rise to the hypothesis that there is a baseline state or *default mode* with which all task-related activity can be compared and that this state is relevant to understanding the brain because of the large energy consumption associated with it (Gusnard & Raichle, 2001). Thus, several studies of the resting-state network have used a *reverse cognition subtraction* strategy in which rest is contrasted with cognitive tasks, but most current studies use functional connectivity approaches (Auer, 2008; Damoiseaux & Greicius, 2009; Rogers, Morgan, Newton, & Gore, 2007; Voss & Schiff, 2009). These studies found a consistent network of regions that are active at rest, including posterior cingulate, medial prefrontal, and parietal regions. The idea that the *default mode network* is of special interest in understanding brain function has been questioned (Morcom & Fletcher, 2007), and discussions of its functional significance are ongoing. However, it is of practical use for investigations of clinical populations (Broyd et al., 2009; Buckner & Vincent, 2007; Greicius, 2008) and can provide additional evidence for interpretation of functional task data (Wang et al., 2010). In addition to providing evidence on the default mode network, resting-state data can reveal other intrinsic networks that can reflect tasks performed before rest, such as working memory (Pyka et al., 2009), long-term memory (Albert, Robertson, Mehta, & Miall, 2009; Tambini, Ketz, & Davachi, 2010; van Kesteren, Fernández, Norris, & Hermans, 2010), and category viewing (Stevens, Buckner, & Schacter, 2010). Analyses of resting-state data can also be based on prior knowledge about task-related connectivity and enable further differentiation of known networks (Dosenbach et al., 2007).

Multivariate Pattern Analysis

Information is not only contained in the regional distribution of activation clusters and in connections among interacting brain regions but also in relatively small-scale patterns of activated and deactivated single voxels. Standard univariate analysis techniques do not reveal this information because each voxel is analyzed independently and because results are displayed as large regional activations; thus, differences between functional representations within a region can remain undetected (Haxby et al., 2001). In contrast, multivariate techniques utilize distributed patterns of small-scale activations to infer the differential representation of the processes being studied, for example, different stimulus categories. Because the brain codes information on many scales down to the level of individual neurons, pattern classification is limited by the spatial resolution of fMRI and benefits from high-resolution scanning techniques (e.g., Diana, Yonelinas, & Ranganath, 2008; Kriegeskorte, Formisano, Sorger, & Goebel, 2007), although the same resolution trade-offs that occur in activation studies need to be considered.

As with other fMRI analyses, there are several approaches to pattern analysis, generally based on training a decoder to classify the conditions on the basis of their (noisy) distributed activation patterns. To assess whether these patterns contain true information about the conditions, the classifier is then tested on its ability to predict each condition from the brain data. Because of the problem associated with nonindependent analyses, the data need to be split into a training set and a test set, for example, by using alternating runs for training and testing. To reduce the amount of data, it is advantageous to preselect a set of voxels that are responsive to the conditions of interest before training the classifier. This selection must be made independently of the test set (Kriegeskorte et al., 2009). The results obtained from evaluating the classifier on the test set are usually reported as percent accuracy, and statistical tests are conducted to assess whether the classification results are better than chance. (For an introduction to the most common classification methods, see Mur, Bandettini, & Kriegeskorte, 2009; Norman, Polyn, Detre, & Haxby, 2006; and Pereira, Mitchell, & Botvinick, 2009.)

Pattern recognition is a promising approach that can be used to investigate a large number of scientific questions. Researchers have addressed cognitive operations as diverse as covert intention (Haynes et al., 2007), economic valuation (Clithero, Carter, & Huettel, 2009; Grosenick, Greer, & Knutson, 2008), complex visual categorization (Walther, Caddigan, Fei-Fei, & Beck, 2009), primary and secondary sensory processing (Beauchamp, LaConte, & Yasar, 2009; Okada et al., 2010; Seymour, Clifford, Logothetis, & Bartels, 2010), conscious perception (Haynes & Rees, 2005), cognitive control (Esterman, Chiu, Tamber-Rosenau, & Yantis, 2009), emotional states (Fu et al., 2008), memory retrieval (Polyn, Natu, Cohen, & Norman, 2005), clinical impairments (Yoon et al., 2008), semantic categories (Mitchell et al., 2008), and spatial navigation (Rodriguez, 2010). Multivariate approaches allow the investigation of questions that cannot be answered by univariate analysis, such as detecting reactivation or maintenance of specific patterns over time and detecting the content of novel stimuli on the basis of features extracted from a training set of different stimuli (Kay, Naselaris, Prenger, & Gallant, 2008; Mitchell et al., 2008). The available analytic methods are continually developing (e.g., Jin et al., 2009; Kuncheva & Rodríguez, 2010) and will continue to gain importance in many research areas.

Real-Time fMRI Analysis

Because fMRI studies generate large data sets, standard experiments are analyzed after the scanning is completed (off-line). A particular fascination and challenge lies in recent developments toward enabling real-time (online) analysis of functional data while the participant or patient is being scanned. Real-time monitoring of brain states could be used for (a) subject- and time-specific stimulus presentation (e.g., present certain images only if region A shows high activity), (b) neurofeedback in healthy populations to help elucidate brain function (if participants increase or decrease activity in region A, do they make fewer or more errors on the task?), or (c) neurofeedback in clinical populations (e.g., teach patients to control pain processes; deCharms et al., 2005). In the past decade, there has been growing interest in this methodological approach, and several groups have demonstrated that participants can learn to control the level of activation in a specific region when they receive real-time feedback (for reviews, see deCharms, 2007; Weiskopf et al., 2004; Weiskopf, Sitaram, et al., 2007). Feedback is usually determined by the level of activity in an ROI and provided within seconds after the BOLD change, although more complex patterns can be used (Papageorgiou, Curtis, McHenry, & LaConte, 2009). Clinical interest is mostly focused on two applications: (a) enabling communications with patients unable to communicate in other ways and (b) helping patients to control emotion and attention processes (Birbaumer et al., 2009; Sorger et al., 2009).

Combining fMRI With Genetic and Pharmacological Approaches

fMRI provides measures of brain activity on several levels: small-scale patterns of local activity, large-scale regional specialization, and functional networks. It cannot distinguish neural systems on the basis of molecular properties such as transmitter and receptor expression. Combining fMRI with methods that are designed to investigate these systems holds enormous promise for understanding brain function underlying complex cognition. Two approaches have gained increasing importance in the past decade: imaging genetics and pharmacological imaging. As a noninvasive approach, imaging genetics relies on correlating interindividual genetic variation with measures of brain activity. Pharmacological imaging investigates the effect of central nervous system–active drugs on brain activity.

The primary interest in imaging genetics studies lies in the investigation of interindividual differences (Hariri, 2009). There is a large degree of variation between individuals on many cognitive and emotional measures, and the contribution of genetic variation to these behaviors and to stable personality traits has long been a matter of speculation and the object of indirect investigations such as twin studies. Developments in the field of molecular biology in the past 15 years have now made it possible to directly assess how participants differ in specified genes and how these differences affect brain functioning. In an imaging genetics study, participants are typically genotyped for one or two common genetic variants (polymorphisms) that are hypothesized to affect behavior or the neural processing that underlies the cognitive process of interest. Individuals can be genotyped beforehand and then be invited to participate in the study on the basis of their genotype, or they can be scanned first and genotyped afterward. The advantages of the first method are that the group size of each genotype can be chosen (results are possible with as few as 12 subjects per group) and that the groups can be matched on age and other variables. Its disadvantages lie in practical matters such as participants having to come to the research site twice, which increases the dropout rate.

The contribution of genetic approaches to the understanding of physiological variation in specific brain systems will increase with better understanding of the functional significance of identified polymorphisms (Green et al., 2008). The physiological changes caused by many known polymorphisms are still unclear. For example, even when there is evidence that a polymorphism causes increased expression of a presynaptic transporter that is involved in reuptake of a transmitter from the synaptic cleft, postsynaptic adaptations to this change in transmission (such as receptor up- or downregulation) can affect the system as a whole and may counteract the primary effect of the genetic variation. These possibilities have to be considered in the interpretation of any imaging genetics study. In spite of these limitations, however, genetic analysis has already made significant contributions to understanding some brain systems (e.g., prefrontal function; Egan et al., 2001) and will only gain in importance with increased understanding of the effects of individual genetic polymorphisms. It will also become increasingly important to include several polymorphisms that affect the same processes (e.g., Bertolino et al., 2008, 2009; Caldú et al., 2007; Passamonti et al., 2008; Smolka et al., 2007).

Pharmacological imaging directly investigates the contribution of a particular brain system to behavioral and neural processes. Participants either receive placebo or a drug that increases or decreases synaptic transmission in a specified way. They are usually scanned at the expected time of peak drug effect, although it is possible to test the effect of prior drug exposure on brain activity in the drug-free state depending on the experimental hypothesis. For example, researchers can test whether drug exposure during picture viewing affects emotions or memories during reexposure to these pictures. This approach avoids possible confounds arising from drug effects on local vasculature or general cardiovascular effects. Pharmacology can also be combined with genetics, behavioral, and other methods to achieve a more detailed understanding of a cognitive system (Honey & Bullmore, 2004). For example, dopaminergic drugs affect prefrontal function differentially depending on participants' baseline working memory capacity and genotype (Apud et al., 2007; Gibbs & D'Esposito, 2006; Kimberg & D'Esposito, 2003; Mattay et al., 2003).

Data Sharing and Publishing Standards

fMRI is a relatively young and dynamic method that is continually changing, refining the way studies are conducted and published. From the early days, debates on data sharing have been ongoing (Marshall, 2000; Van Horn et al., 2001). To date, it is still the exception, not the norm, although several public databases exist (https://ida.loni.ucla.edu/login.jsp; http://central.xnat.org/app/template/Index.vm; http://sumsdb.wustl.edu/sums/index.jsp; http://

www.rotman-baycrest.on.ca/index.php?section = 532#Overview; and http://www.fmridc.org/f/fmridc, which is not accepting any new data but retains a large number of data sets). In addition to databases of raw data, there are also efforts to create databases of functional activation coordinates, for example http://brainmap.org (for an overview and comparison, see Derrfuss & Mar, 2009). The applicability and usefulness of data sharing for functional studies of the human brain have been demonstrated (Biswal et al., 2010; Van Horn & Ishai, 2007). The advantages of data sharing lie in the possible combination of data collected at many institutions into large-scale analyses (Kober & Wager, 2010) and in the availability of existing data sets for reanalysis when new techniques become available. Maintaining a large database of raw data, however, requires substantial investments, such as dedicated public funding, and requires researchers' cooperation in uploading data and detailing data-collection procedures. There are also challenges arising from the number of analysis packages and from differences in data structuring and labeling across institutions (Hasson, Skipper, Wilde, Nusbaum, & Small, 2008; Small, Wilde, Kenny, Andric, & Hasson, 2009). The Biomedical Informatics Research Network maintains a database and also offers quality control information and tips on how to conduct multicenter studies (see http://www.birncommunity.org).

As in other fields of science, adequate description of the study and analysis protocol is necessary upon publication to ensure transparency of the methods and to enable replication by other researchers. In fMRI, there is special need for detailed methods sections because of the multitude of acquisition and analysis protocols used at different institutions. Some suggestions have been made concerning standards for reporting in the literature, both for methods sections (Poldrack et al., 2008) and for anatomical description of activation results (Devlin & Poldrack, 2007). Researchers should always be aware of these issues when designing, analyzing, and reporting their experiments.

ETHICAL CONSIDERATIONS

With the proliferation of fMRI experiments and the resulting increase in knowledge about the human brain, fMRI is having an impact on society that raises several ethical questions. The basis of almost all of these issues is the right to what has been called *mental privacy* or *brain privacy* (Alpert, 2007; Farah, Smith, Gawuga, Lindsell, & Foster, 2009). Advances in imaging techniques and analysis methods, such as pattern analysis, are raising the possibility that private thoughts and emotions are becoming accessible to others (Farah et al., 2009; Haynes & Rees, 2006). Even if the current state of the field does not yet support the extraction of reliable information about a single subject's' cognitive processes, there is reason to assume that the field will progress to a point at which these issues become problematic. As scientists, we are expected to participate in ethical debates and inform society about developments in our area of specialization (Illes et al., 2010). Several issues are being discussed: privacy issues arising from the use of fMRI for commercial purposes, legal issues relating to lie detection applications, and considerations of the implications of measuring brain activity in patients who are in a locked-in or vegetative state.

Businesses in the field of neuromarketing have become interested in the promise of fMRI for opening a window into the minds of consumers, revealing their hidden preferences and reactions to various forms of product presentation (Ariely & Berns, 2010; Lee, Broderick, & Chamberlain, 2007). Several ethical concerns need to be addressed with respect to these commercial enterprises (Murphy, Illes, & Reiner, 2008). First, participants in these studies are not protected in the same way as participants at research institutions, where experiments are monitored by institutional review boards. A second consideration is damage to the public's understanding of science that can arise from over-interpretation of research findings and overstatement of commercial claims (Murphy et al., 2008). There is considerable potential for influencing public opinion; a notorious example is an experiment on political preferences that was published in the *New York Times*, outside of the peer-review process (Iacoboni et al., 2007), and whose overinterpretation caused an outcry from the imaging community (Aron et al., 2007; "Mind Games," 2007).

There are also ethical and legal issues related to the use of fMRI (and other functional methods such

as event-related potentials) in lie detection. Two main points need to be considered: Are lie detection techniques sufficiently good to tell a lie from what the participant believes to be the truth (with low false positive and false negative rates), and should they be used in criminal trials if they are scientifically reliable? The first point is crucial if our societies want to avoid the consideration of random decisions as legal evidence. The scientific community should take an active part in the decision process on this point, although legal scholars may challenge their participation (Schauer, 2010). The current consensus holds that fMRI-based lie detection is not yet reliable enough (Greely & Illes, 2007; Miller, 2010; Monteleone, Phan, Nusbaum, Fitzgerald, & Irick, 2009; Moriarty, 2008), but the ethical and legal implications of potential future use are being discussed actively (Meegan, 2008, and comments on it; Simpson, 2008, and comments; Tovino, 2007). Scientists are responsible for pointing out the limitations of neuroimaging methods, especially because brain images and neuroscientific statements have been shown to be particularly convincing to laypeople (McCabe & Castel, 2008; Racine, Bar-Ilan, & Illes, 2005; Weisberg, Keil, Goodstein, Rawson, & Gray, 2008), which could have serious consequences in trials involving jury decisions.

A third area for ethical discussion concerns the use of fMRI to detect and decode brain activity in patients who are in a minimally conscious or vegetative state (Monti et al., 2010; Owen & Coleman, 2007, 2008; Sorger et al., 2009; Tshibanda et al., 2010). This application of fMRI holds great promise for improving the lives of these patients by enabling them to communicate. However, we also need to be aware of possible consequences that advancements in the field could have. What kind of treatment decisions will be made on the basis of fMRI results? What paradigms and tasks are suitable as clinical assessment? The relevant techniques will need to be evaluated and confirmed further before they can be used in clinical practice (Bernat, 2009; Farah, 2008; Fins & Shapiro, 2007).

The increase in discriminative power through the combination of neuroimaging and genetics is another area for ethical consideration (Tairyan & Illes, 2009). With the development of technologies and the advancement of understanding in brain research, researchers need to be aware of the implications for society and should take an active part in discussing these matters. On the most fundamental level, this can be done by carefully communicating one's own research to the public (Illes et al., 2010).

CONCLUSION

fMRI is a flexible tool for studying the human brain, allowing adjustment of the acquisition and analysis parameters to suit the experimental question and allowing investigations both of whole-brain networks and of strongly localized functions. New approaches in experimental design and analysis are constantly being developed and add to this flexibility. The integration of information gained from these different approaches with results from EEG, MEG, TMS, intracranial recordings, and lesion studies in humans will advance our understanding of functional processes in the brain. fMRI has opened a window onto cognitive functions in healthy humans that offers an exciting glimpse of future insights.

References

Aguirre, G. K., Zarahn, E., & D'Esposito, M. (1998). The variability of human, BOLD hemodynamic responses. *NeuroImage, 8*, 360–369. doi:10.1006/nimg.1998.0369

Albert, N. B., Robertson, E. M., Mehta, P., & Miall, R. C. (2009). Resting state networks and memory consolidation. *Communicative and Integrative Biology, 2*, 530–532. doi:10.4161/cib.2.6.9612

Alpert, S. (2007). Brain privacy: How can we protect it? *The American Journal of Bioethics, 7*, 70–73. doi:10.1080/15265160701518862

Amaro, E., & Barker, G. J. (2006). Study design in fMRI: Basic principles. *Brain and Cognition, 60*, 220–232. doi:10.1016/j.bandc.2005.11.009

Apud, J. A., Mattay, V., Chen, J., Kolachana, B. S., Callicott, J. H., Rasetti, R., . . . Weinberger, D. R. (2007). Tolcapone improves cognition and cortical information processing in normal human subjects. *Neuropsychopharmacology, 32*, 1011–1020. doi:10.1038/sj.npp.1301227

Ariely, D., & Berns, G. S. (2010). Neuromarketing: The hope and hype of neuroimaging in business. *Nature Reviews Neuroscience, 11*, 284–292. doi:10.1038/nrn2795

Aron, A., Badre, D., Brett, M., Cacioppo, J., Chambers, C., Cools, R., . . . Winkielman, P. (2007, November 14). Politics and the brain. *New York Times*. Retrieved from http://www.nytimes.com/2007/11/14/opinion/lweb14brain.htmlb

Auer, D. P. (2008). Spontaneous low-frequency blood oxygenation level-dependent fluctuations and functional connectivity analysis of the "resting" brain. *Magnetic Resonance Imaging, 26*, 1055–1064. doi:10.1016/j.mri.2008.05.008

Badre, D., Hoffman, J., Cooney, J. W., & D'Esposito, M. (2009). Hierarchical cognitive control deficits following damage to the human frontal lobe. *Nature Neuroscience, 12*, 515–522. doi:10.1038/nn.2277

Baker, C. I., Hutchison, T. L., & Kanwisher, N. (2007). Does the fusiform face area contain subregions highly selective for nonfaces? *Nature Neuroscience, 10*, 3–4. doi:10.1038/nn0107-3

Balteau, E., Hutton, C., & Weiskopf, N. (2010). Improved shimming for fMRI specifically optimizing the local BOLD sensitivity. *NeuroImage, 49*, 327–336. doi:10.1016/j.neuroimage.2009.08.010

Bandettini, P. A. (2009). What's new in neuroimaging methods? *Annals of the New York Academy of Sciences, 1156*, 260–293.

Bandettini, P. A., Wong, E. C., Hinks, R. S., Tikofsky, R. S., & Hyde, J. S. (1992). Time course EPI of human brain function during task activation. *Magnetic Resonance in Medicine, 25*, 390–397. doi:10.1002/mrm.1910250220

Beauchamp, M. S., LaConte, S., & Yasar, N. (2009). Distributed representation of single touches in somatosensory and visual cortex. *Human Brain Mapping, 30*, 3163–3171. doi:10.1002/hbm.20735

Bennett, C. M., & Miller, M. B. (2010). How reliable are the results from functional magnetic resonance imaging? *Annals of the New York Academy of Sciences, 1191*, 133–155.

Bernat, J. L. (2009). Ethical issues in the treatment of severe brain injury. *Annals of the New York Academy of Sciences, 1157*, 117–130.

Bertolino, A., Di Giorgio, A., Blasi, G., Sambataro, F., Caforio, G., Sinibaldi, L., . . . Dallapiccola, B. (2008). Epistasis between dopamine regulating genes identifies a nonlinear response of the human hippocampus during memory tasks. *Biological Psychiatry, 64*, 226–234. doi:10.1016/j.biopsych.2008.02.001

Bertolino, A., Fazio, L., Di Giorgio, A., Blasi, G., Romano, R., Taurisano, P., . . . Sadee, W. (2009). Genetically determined interaction between the dopamine transporter and the D2 receptor on prefronto-striatal activity and volume in humans. *The Journal of Neuroscience, 29*, 1224–1234. doi:10.1523/JNEUROSCI.4858-08.2009

Birbaumer, N., Ramos Murguialday, A., Weber, C., & Montoya, P. (2009). Neurofeedback and brain-computer interface: Clinical applications. *International Review of Neurobiology, 86,* 107–117. doi:10.1016/S0074-7742(09)86008-X

Biswal, B. B., Mennes, M., Zuo, X-N., Gohel, S., Kelly, C., Smith, S. M., . . . Milham, M. P. (2010). Toward discovery science of human brain function. *Proceedings of the National Academy of Sciences of the United States of America, 107,* 4734–4739. doi:10.1073/pnas.0911855107

Boynton, G. M., Engel, S. A., Glover, G. H., & Heeger, D. J. (1996). Linear systems analysis of functional magnetic resonance imaging in human V1. *The Journal of Neuroscience, 16,* 4207–4221.

Broyd, S. J., Demanuele, C., Debener, S., Helps, S. K., James, C. J., & Sonuga-Barke, E. J. S. (2009). Default-mode brain dysfunction in mental disorders: A systematic review. *Neuroscience and Biobehavioral Reviews, 33,* 279–296. doi:10.1016/j.neubiorev.2008.09.002

Buchsbaum, B. R. (2009, August 23). fMRI is not an inherently correlational method. [Web log post]. Retrieved from http://flowbrain.blogspot.com/

Buckner, R. L., Koutstaal, W., Schacter, D. L., Dale, A. M., Rotte, M., & Rosen, B. R. (1998). Functional-anatomic study of episodic retrieval: II. Selective averaging of event-related fMRI trials to test the retrieval success hypothesis. *NeuroImage, 7,* 163–175. doi:10.1006/nimg.1998.0328

Buckner, R. L., & Vincent, J. L. (2007). Unrest at rest: Default activity and spontaneous network correlations. *NeuroImage, 37,* 1091–1096. doi:10.1016/j.neuroimage.2007.01.010

Caldú, X., Vendrell, P., Bartrés-Faz, D., Clemente, I., Bargalló, N., Jurado, M. Á., . . . Junqué, C. (2007). Impact of the COMT Val108/158 Met and DAT genotypes on prefrontal function in healthy subjects. *NeuroImage, 37,* 1437–1444. doi:10.1016/j.neuroimage.2007.06.021

Cashdollar, N., Malecki, U., Rugg-Gunn, F. J., Duncan, J. S., Lavie, N., & Duzel, E. (2009). Hippocampus-dependent and -independent theta-networks of active maintenance. *Proceedings of the National Academy of Sciences of the United States of America, 106,* 20493–20498. doi:10.1073/pnas.0904823106

Clithero, J. A., Carter, R. M., & Huettel, S. A. (2009). Local pattern classification differentiates processes of economic valuation. *NeuroImage, 45,* 1329–1338. doi:10.1016/j.neuroimage.2008.12.074

Courtney, S. M., Ungerleider, L. G., Keil, K., & Haxby, J. V. (1997). Transient and sustained activity in a distributed neural system for human working memory. *Nature, 386,* 608–611. doi:10.1038/386608a0

Dale, A. M. (1999). Optimal experimental design for event-related fMRI. *Human Brain Mapping,* 8, 109–114. doi:10.1002/(SICI)1097-0193(1999)8:2/3<109::AID-HBM7>3.0.CO;2-W

Damoiseaux, J. S., & Greicius, M. D. (2009). Greater than the sum of its parts: A review of studies combining structural connectivity and resting-state functional connectivity. *Brain Structure and Function, 213,* 525–533. doi:10.1007/s00429-009-0208-6

David, O., Guillemain, I., Saillet, S., Reyt, S., Deransart, C., Segebarth, C., & Depaulis, A. (2008). Identifying neural drivers with functional MRI: An electrophysiological validation. *PLoS Biology, 6,* 2683–2697. doi:10.1371/journal.pbio.0060315

Dayan, P. (2009). Dopamine, reinforcement learning, and addiction. *Pharmacopsychiatry, 42(S 01),* S56–S65.

Dayan, P., & Daw, N. D. (2008). Decision theory, reinforcement learning, and the brain. *Cognitive, Affective and Behavioral Neuroscience, 8,* 429–453. doi:10.3758/CABN.8.4.429

deCharms, R. C. (2007). Reading and controlling human brain activation using real-time functional magnetic resonance imaging. *Trends in Cognitive Sciences, 11,* 473–481. doi:10.1016/j.tics.2007.08.014

deCharms, R. C., Maeda, F., Glover, G. H., Ludlow, D., Pauly, J. M., Soneji, D., . . . Mackey, S. C. (2005). Control over brain activation and pain learned by using real-time functional MRI. *Proceedings of the National Academy of Sciences of the United States of America, 102,* 18626–18631. doi:10.1073/pnas.0505210102

Deco, G., Jirsa, V. K., Robinson, P. A., Breakspear, M., & Friston, K. (2008). The dynamic brain: From spiking neurons to neural masses and cortical fields. *PLoS Computational Biology, 4,* e1000092. doi:10.1371/journal.pcbi.1000092

den Ouden, H. E. M., Daunizeau, J., Roiser, J., Friston, K. J., & Stephan, K. E. (2010). Striatal Prediction Error Modulates Cortical Coupling. *The Journal of Neuroscience, 30,* 3210–3219. doi:10.1523/JNEUROSCI.4458-09.2010

Derrfuss, J., & Mar, R. A. (2009). Lost in localization: The need for a universal coordinate database. *NeuroImage, 48,* 1–7. doi:10.1016/j.neuroimage.2009.01.053

Deshpande, G., Sathian, K., & Hu, X. (in press). Effect of hemodynamic variability on Granger causality analysis of fMRI. *NeuroImage.*

Desmond, J. E., & Glover, G. H. (2002). Estimating sample size in functional MRI (fMRI) neuroimaging studies: Statistical power analyses. *Journal of Neuroscience Methods, 118,* 115–128. doi:10.1016/S0165-0270(02)00121-8

D'Esposito, M., Ballard, D., Aguirre, G. K., & Zarahn, E. (1998). Human prefrontal cortex is not specific for working memory: A functional MRI study. *NeuroImage, 8,* 274–282. doi:10.1006/nimg.1998.0364

D'Esposito, M., Cooney, J. W., Gazzaley, A., Gibbs, S. E. B., & Postle, B. R. (2006). Is the prefrontal cortex necessary for delay task performance? Evidence from lesion and fMRI data. *Journal of the International Neuropsychological Society, 12,* 248–260. doi:10.1017/S1355617706060322

D'Esposito, M., Postle, B. R., Jonides, J., & Smith, E. E. (1999). The neural substrate and temporal dynamics of interference effects in working memory as revealed by event-related functional MRI. *Proceedings of the National Academy of Sciences of the United States of America, 96,* 7514–7519. doi:10.1073/pnas.96.13.7514

Devlin, J. T., & Poldrack, R. A. (2007). In praise of tedious anatomy. *NeuroImage, 37,* 1033–1041; discussion 1050–1038.

Diana, R. A., Yonelinas, A. P., & Ranganath, C. (2008). High-resolution multi-voxel pattern analysis of category selectivity in the medial temporal lobes. *Hippocampus, 18,* 536–541. doi:10.1002/hipo.20433

Donaldson, D. I., Petersen, S. E., Ollinger, J. M., & Buckner, R. L. (2001). Dissociating state and item components of recognition memory using fMRI. *NeuroImage, 13,* 129–142. doi:10.1006/nimg.2000.0664

Dosenbach, N. U. F., Fair, D. A., Miezin, F. M., Cohen, A. L., Wenger, K. K., Dosenbach, R. A. T., . . . Petersen, S. E. (2007). Distinct brain networks for adaptive and stable task control in humans. *Proceedings of the National Academy of Sciences of the United States of America, 104,* 11073–11078. doi:10.1073/pnas.0704320104

Egan, M. F., Goldberg, T. E., Kolachana, B. S., Callicott, J. H., Mazzanti, C. M., Straub, R. E., . . . Weinberger, D. R. (2001). Effect of COMT Val108/158 Met genotype on frontal lobe function and risk for schizophrenia. *Proceedings of the National Academy of Sciences of the United States of America, 98,* 6917–6922. doi:10.1073/pnas.111134598

Esterman, M., Chiu, Y-C., Tamber-Rosenau, B. J., & Yantis, S. (2009). Decoding cognitive control in human parietal cortex. *Proceedings of the National Academy of Sciences of the United States of America, 106,* 17974–17979. doi:10.1073/pnas.0903593106

Esterman, M., Tamber-Rosenau, B. J., Chiu, Y-C., & Yantis, S. (2010). Avoiding non-independence in fMRI data analysis: Leave one subject out. *NeuroImage, 50,* 572–576. doi:10.1016/j.neuroimage.2009.10.092

Farah, M. J. (2008). Neuroethics and the problem of other minds: Implications of neuroscience for the moral status of brain-damaged patients and nonhuman animals. *Neuroethics, 1,* 9–18. doi:10.1007/s12152-008-9006-8

Farah, M. J., Smith, M. E., Gawuga, C., Lindsell, D., & Foster, D. (2009). Brain imaging and brain privacy: A realistic concern? *Journal of Cognitive Neuroscience, 21,* 119–127. doi:10.1162/jocn.2009.21010

Fins, J. J., & Shapiro, Z. E. (2007). Neuroimaging and neuroethics: Clinical and policy considerations. *Current Opinion in Neurology, 20,* 650–654. doi:10.1097/WCO.0b013e3282f11f6d

Forman, S. D., Cohen, J. D., Fitzgerald, M., Eddy, W. F., Mintun, M. A., & Noll, D. C. (1995). Improved assessment of significant activation in functional magnetic resonance imaging (fMRI): Use of a cluster-size threshold. *Magnetic Resonance in Medicine, 33,* 636–647. doi:10.1002/mrm.1910330508

Friston, K. J. (1994). Functional and effective connectivity in neuroimaging: A synthesis. *Human Brain Mapping, 2,* 56–78. doi:10.1002/hbm.460020107

Friston, K. (2002). Beyond phrenology: What can neuroimaging tell us about distributed circuitry? *Annual Review of Neuroscience, 25,* 221–250. doi:10.1146/annurev.neuro.25.112701.142846

Friston, K. J., Harrison, L., & Penny, W. (2003). Dynamic causal modelling. *NeuroImage, 19,* 1273–1302. doi:10.1016/S1053-8119(03)00202-7

Fu, C. H. Y., Mourao-Miranda, J., Costafreda, S. G., Khanna, A., Marquand, A. F., Williams, S. C. R., & Brammer, M. J. (2008). Pattern classification of sad facial processing: Toward the development of neurobiological markers in depression. *Biological Psychiatry, 63,* 656–662. doi:10.1016/j.biopsych.2007.08.020

Gibbs, S. E. B., & D'Esposito, M. (2006). A functional magnetic resonance imaging study of the effects of pergolide, a dopamine receptor agonist, on component processes of working memory. *Neuroscience, 139,* 359–371. doi:10.1016/j.neuroscience.2005.11.055

Gläscher, J. P., & O'Doherty, J. P. (2010). Model-based approaches to neuroimaging: Combining reinforcement learning theory with fMRI data. *Wiley Interdisciplinary Reviews: Cognitive Science, 1,* 501–510.

Greely, H. T., & Illes, J. (2007). Neuroscience-based lie detection: The urgent need for regulation. *American Journal of Law and Medicine, 33,* 377–431.

Green, A. E., Munafo, M. R., DeYoung, C. G., Fossella, J. A., Fan, J., & Gray, J. R. (2008). Using genetic data in cognitive neuroscience: From growing pains to genuine insights. *Nature Reviews Neuroscience, 9,* 710–720. doi:10.1038/nrn2461

Greicius, M. (2008). Resting-state functional connectivity in neuropsychiatric disorders. *Current Opinion in Neurology, 21,* 424–430. doi:10.1097/WCO.0b013e328306f2c5

Grosenick, L., Greer, S., & Knutson, B. (2008). Interpretable classifiers for FMRI improve prediction of purchases. *IEEE Transactions on Neural Systems and Rehabilitation Engineering, 16*, 539–548. doi:10.1109/TNSRE.2008.926701

Gusnard, D. A., & Raichle, M. E. (2001). Searching for a baseline: Functional imaging and the resting human brain. *Nature Reviews Neuroscience, 2*, 685–694. doi:10.1038/35094500

Hariri, A. R. (2009). The neurobiology of individual differences in complex behavioral traits. *Annual Review of Neuroscience, 32*, 225–247. doi:10.1146/annurev.neuro.051508.135335

Hasson, U., Skipper, J. I., Wilde, M. J., Nusbaum, H. C., & Small, S. L. (2008). Improving the analysis, storage and sharing of neuroimaging data using relational databases and distributed computing. *NeuroImage, 39*, 693–706. doi:10.1016/j.neuroimage.2007.09.021

Havlicek, M., Jan, J., Calhoun, V. D., & Brazdil, M. (2009, September). *Extended time-frequency granger causality for evaluation of functional network connectivity in event-related FMRI data.* Paper presented at the 31st Annual International Conference of the IEEE Engineering in Medicine and Biology Society, Minneapolis, MN.

Haxby, J. V., Gobbini, M. I., Furey, M. L., Ishai, A., Schouten, J. L., & Pietrini, P. (2001). Distributed and overlapping representations of faces and objects in ventral temporal cortex. *Science, 293*, 2425–2430. doi:10.1126/science.1063736

Hayasaka, S., Peiffer, A. M., Hugenschmidt, C. E., & Laurienti, P. J. (2007). Power and sample size calculation for neuroimaging studies by non-central random field theory. *NeuroImage, 37*, 721–730. doi:10.1016/j.neuroimage.2007.06.009

Haynes, J.-D., & Rees, G. (2005). Predicting the stream of consciousness from activity in human visual cortex. *Current Biology, 15*, 1301–1307. doi:10.1016/j.cub.2005.06.026

Haynes, J.-D., & Rees, G. (2006). Decoding mental states from brain activity in humans. *Nature Reviews Neuroscience, 7*, 523–534. doi:10.1038/nrn1931

Haynes, J.-D., Sakai, K., Rees, G., Gilbert, S., Frith, C., & Passingham, R. E. (2007). Reading hidden intentions in the human brain. *Current Biology, 17*, 323–328. doi:10.1016/j.cub.2006.11.072

Honey, G., & Bullmore, E. (2004). Human pharmacological MRI. *Trends in Pharmacological Sciences, 25*, 366–374. doi:10.1016/j.tips.2004.05.009

Horwitz, B., & Smith, J. F. (2008). A link between neuroscience and informatics: Large-scale modeling of memory processes. *Methods, 44*, 338–347. doi:10.1016/j.ymeth.2007.02.007

Huettel, S. A., Song, A. W., & McCarthy, G. (2008). *Functional magnetic resonance imaging* (2nd ed.). Sunderland, MA: Sinauer.

Hutton, C., Bork, A., Josephs, O., Deichmann, R., Ashburner, J., & Turner, R. (2002). Image distortion correction in fMRI: A quantitative evaluation. *NeuroImage, 16*, 217–240. doi:10.1006/nimg.2001.1054

Hutton, C., Deichmann, R., Turner, R., & Andersson, J. L. R. (2004, May). *Combined correction for geometric distortion and its interaction with head motion in fMRI.* Paper presented at the 12th Scientific Meeting and Exhibition of the International Society for Magnetic Resonance in Medicine, Kyoto, Japan.

Huys, Q. J., & Dayan, P. (2009). A Bayesian formulation of behavioral control. *Cognition, 113*, 314–328.

Iacoboni, M., Freedman, J., Kaplan, J., Jamieson, K. H., Freedman, T., Knapp, B., & Fitzgerald, K. (2007, November 11). This is your brain on politics. *New York Times.* Retrieved from http://www.nytimes.com/2007/11/11/opinion/11freedman.html?_r=1&sq=marco%20iacoboni%202007&st=cse&oref=slogin&scp=1&pagewanted=all

Illes, J., Moser, M. A., McCormick, J. B., Racine, E., Blakeslee, S., Caplan, A., . . . Weiss, S. (2010). Neurotalk: Improving the communication of neuroscience research. *Nature Reviews Neuroscience, 11*, 61–69. doi:10.1038/nrn2773

Jin, B., Strasburger, A., Laken, S., Kozel, F. A., Johnson, K., George, M., & Lu, X. (2009). Feature selection for fMRI-based deception detection. *BMC Bioinformatics, 10*(Suppl 9), S15. doi:10.1186/1471-2105-10-S9-S15

Kahnt, T., Park, S. Q., Cohen, M. X., Beck, A., Heinz, A., & Wrase, J. (2009). Dorsal striatal-midbrain connectivity in humans predicts how reinforcements are used to guide decisions. *Journal of Cognitive Neuroscience, 21*, 1332–1345. doi:10.1162/jocn.2009.21092

Kay, K. N., Naselaris, T., Prenger, R. J., & Gallant, J. L. (2008). Identifying natural images from human brain activity. *Nature, 452*, 352–355. doi:10.1038/nature06713

Kayser, A. S., Sun, F. T., & D'Esposito, M. (2009). A comparison of Granger causality and coherency in fMRI-based analysis of the motor system. *Human Brain Mapping, 30*, 3475–3494. doi:10.1002/hbm.20771

Kimberg, D. Y., & D'Esposito, M. (2003). Cognitive effects of the dopamine receptor agonist pergolide. *Neuropsychologia, 41*, 1020–1027. doi:10.1016/S0028-3932(02)00317-2

Kishiyama, M. M., Yonelinas, A. P., & Knight, R. T. (2009). Novelty enhancements in memory are dependent on lateral prefrontal cortex. *The Journal of Neuroscience, 29*, 8114–8118. doi:10.1523/JNEUROSCI.5507-08.2009

Kober, H., & Wager, T. D. (2010). Meta-analysis of neuroimaging data. *Wiley Interdisciplinary Reviews: Cognitive Science, 1*, 293–300.

Krawczyk, D. C., Gazzaley, A., & D'Esposito, M. (2007). Reward modulation of prefrontal and visual association cortex during an incentive working memory task. *Brain Research, 1141*, 168–177. doi:10.1016/j.brainres.2007.01.052

Kriegeskorte, N., Formisano, E., Sorger, B., & Goebel, R. (2007). Individual faces elicit distinct response patterns in human anterior temporal cortex. *Proceedings of the National Academy of Sciences of the United States of America, 104*, 20600–20605. doi:10.1073/pnas.0705654104

Kriegeskorte, N., Simmons, W. K., Bellgowan, P. S. F., & Baker, C. I. (2009). Circular analysis in systems neuroscience: The dangers of double dipping. *Nature Neuroscience, 12*, 535–540. doi:10.1038/nn.2303

Krugel, L. K., Biele, G., Mohr, P. N., Li, S. C., & Heekeren, H. R. (2009). Genetic variation in dopaminergic neuromodulation influences the ability to rapidly and flexibly adapt decisions. *Proceedings of the National Academy of Sciences of the United States of America, 106*, 17951–17956.

Kuncheva, L. I., & Rodríguez, J. J. (2010). Classifier ensembles for fMRI data analysis: An experiment. *Magnetic Resonance Imaging, 28*, 583–593. doi:10.1016/j.mri.2009.12.021

Lee, N., Broderick, A. J., & Chamberlain, L. (2007). What is "neuromarketing"? A discussion and agenda for future research. *International Journal of Psychophysiology, 63*, 199–204. doi:10.1016/j.ijpsycho.2006.03.007

Lieberman, M. D., & Cunningham, W. A. (2009). Type I and Type II error concerns in fMRI research: Re-balancing the scale. *Social Cognitive and Affective Neuroscience, 4*, 423–428. doi:10.1093/scan/nsp052

Logothetis, N. K. (2008). What we can do and what we cannot do with fMRI. *Nature, 453*, 869–878. doi:10.1038/nature06976

Marshall, E. (2000). Neuroscience: A ruckus over releasing images of the human brain. *Science, 289*, 1458–1459. doi:10.1126/science.289.5484.1458

Mattay, V. S., Goldberg, T. E., Fera, F., Hariri, A. R., Tessitore, A., Egan, M. F., . . . Weinberger, D. R. (2003). Catechol O-methyltransferase val158-met genotype and individual variation in the brain response to amphetamine. *Proceedings of the National Academy of Sciences of the United States of America, 100*, 6186–6191. doi:10.1073/pnas.0931309100

McCabe, D. P., & Castel, A. D. (2008). Seeing is believing: The effect of brain images on judgments of scientific reasoning. *Cognition, 107*, 343–352. doi:10.1016/j.cognition.2007.07.017

McFadzean, R. M., Condon, B. C., & Barr, D. B. (1999). Functional magnetic resonance imaging in the visual system. *Journal of Neuro-Ophthalmology, 19*, 186–200. doi:10.1097/00041327-199909000-00008

McIntosh, A. R., Chau, W. K., & Protzner, A. B. (2004). Spatiotemporal analysis of event-related fMRI data using partial least squares. *NeuroImage, 23*, 764–775. doi:10.1016/j.neuroimage.2004.05.018

Meegan, D. V. (2008). Neuroimaging techniques for memory detection: Scientific, ethical, and legal issues. *The American Journal of Bioethics, 8*, 9–20. doi:10.1080/15265160701842007

Mesulam, M.-M. (1990). Large-scale neurocognitive networks and distributed processing for attention, language, and memory. *Annals of Neurology, 28*, 597–613. doi:10.1002/ana.410280502

Miller, G. (2010). fMRI Lie Detection Fails a Legal Test. *Science, 328*, 1336–1337. doi:10.1126/science.328.5984.1336-a

Mind games. (2007). *Nature, 450*, 457–457.

Mitchell, T. M., Shinkareva, S. V., Carlson, A., Chang, K-M., Malave, V. L., Mason, R. A., & Just, M. A. (2008). Predicting human brain activity associated with the meanings of nouns. *Science, 320*, 1191–1195. doi:10.1126/science.1152876

Monteleone, G. T., Phan, K. L., Nusbaum, H. C., Fitzgerald, D., & Irick, J. S. (2009). Detection of deception using fMRI: Better than chance, but well below perfection. *Social Neuroscience, 4*, 528–538. doi:10.1080/17470910801903530

Monti, M. M., Vanhaudenhuyse, A., Coleman, M. R., Boly, M., Pickard, J. D., Tshibanda, L., . . . Laureys, S. (2010). Willful modulation of brain activity in disorders of consciousness. *The New England Journal of Medicine, 362*, 579–589. doi:10.1056/NEJMoa0905370

Morcom, A. M., & Fletcher, P. C. (2007). Does the brain have a baseline? Why we should be resisting a rest. *NeuroImage, 37*, 1073–1082. doi:10.1016/j.neuroimage.2006.09.013

Moriarty, J. C. (2008). Flickering admissibility: Neuroimaging evidence in the U.S. courts. *Behavioral Sciences and the Law, 26*, 29–49. doi:10.1002/bsl.795

Mumford, J. A., & Nichols, T. E. (2008). Power calculation for group fMRI studies accounting for arbitrary design and temporal autocorrelation. *NeuroImage, 39*, 261–268. doi:10.1016/j.neuroimage.2007.07.061

Mur, M., Bandettini, P. A., & Kriegeskorte, N. (2009). Revealing representational content with pattern-information fMRI–an introductory guide. *Social Cognitive and Affective Neuroscience, 4*, 101–109. doi:10.1093/scan/nsn044

Murphy, E. R., Illes, J., & Reiner, P. B. (2008). Neuroethics of neuromarketing. *Journal of Consumer Behaviour, 7*, 293–302. doi:10.1002/cb.252

Nichols, E. A., Kao, Y.-C., Verfaellie, M., & Gabrieli, J. D. E. (2006). Working memory and long-term memory for faces: Evidence from fMRI and global amnesia for involvement of the medial temporal lobes. *Hippocampus, 16*, 604–616. doi:10.1002/hipo.20190

Norman, K. A., Polyn, S. M., Detre, G. J., & Haxby, J. V. (2006). Beyond mind-reading: Multi-voxel pattern analysis of fMRI data. *Trends in Cognitive Science, 10*, 424–430. doi:10.1016/j.tics.2006.07.005

O'Doherty, J. P., Dayan, P., Friston, K., Critchley, H., & Dolan, R. J. (2003). Temporal difference models and reward-related learning in the human brain. *Neuron, 38*, 329–337. doi:10.1016/S0896-6273(03)00169-7

Okada, K., Rong, F., Venezia, J., Matchin, W., Hsieh, I-H., Saberi, K., . . . Hickok, G. (2010). Hierarchical organization of human auditory cortex: Evidence from acoustic invariance in the response to intelligible speech. *Cerebral Cortex, 20*, 2486–2495.

Owen, A. M., & Coleman, M. R. (2007). Functional MRI in disorders of consciousness: Advantages and limitations. *Current Opinion in Neurology, 20*, 632–637. doi:10.1097/WCO.0b013e3282f15669

Owen, A. M., & Coleman, M. R. (2008). Detecting awareness in the vegetative state. *Annals of the New York Academy of Sciences, 1129*, 130–138. doi:10.1196/annals.1417.018

Palminteri, S., Boraud, T., Lafargue, G., Dubois, B., & Pessiglione, M. (2009). Brain hemispheres selectively track the expected value of contralateral options. *The Journal of Neuroscience, 29*, 13465–13472. doi:10.1523/JNEUROSCI.1500-09.2009

Papageorgiou, T. D., Curtis, W. A., McHenry, M., & LaConte, S. M. (2009). Neurofeedback of two motor functions using supervised learning-based real-time functional magnetic resonance imaging. *Conference Proceedings; Annual International Conference of the IEEE Engineering in Medicine and Biology Society, 2009*, 5377–5380.

Passamonti, L., Cerasa, A., Gioia, M. C., Magariello, A., Muglia, M., Quattrone, A., & Fera, F. (2008). Genetically dependent modulation of serotonergic inactivation in the human prefrontal cortex. *NeuroImage, 40*, 1264–1273. doi:10.1016/j.neuroimage.2007.12.028

Penny, W. D., Stephan, K. E., Mechelli, A., & Friston, K. J. (2004). Modelling functional integration: A comparison of structural equation and dynamic causal models. *NeuroImage, 23*(Suppl 1), S264–S274. doi:10.1016/j.neuroimage.2004.07.041

Pereira, F., Mitchell, T., & Botvinick, M. (2009). Machine learning classifiers and fMRI: A tutorial overview. *NeuroImage, 45*(Suppl 1), S199–S209. doi:10.1016/j.neuroimage.2008.11.007

Pessiglione, M., Seymour, B., Flandin, G., Dolan, R. J., & Frith, C. D. (2006). Dopamine-dependent prediction errors underpin reward-seeking behaviour in humans. *Nature, 442*, 1042–1045. doi:10.1038/nature05051

Piekema, C., Kessels, R. P., Mars, R. B., Petersson, K. M., & Fernandez, G. (2006). The right hippocampus participates in short-term memory maintenance of object-location associations. *NeuroImage, 33*, 374–382. doi:10.1016/j.neuroimage.2006.06.035

Piekema, C., Kessels, R. P., Rijpkema, M., & Fernandez, G. (2009). The hippocampus supports encoding of between-domain associations within working memory. *Learning and Memory, 16*, 231–234. doi:10.1101/lm.1283109

Poldrack, R. A. (2006). Can cognitive processes be inferred from neuroimaging data? *Trends in Cognitive Sciences, 10*, 59–63. doi:10.1016/j.tics.2005.12.004

Poldrack, R. A., Fletcher, P. C., Henson, R. N., Worsley, K. J., Brett, M., & Nichols, T. E. (2008). Guidelines for reporting an fMRI study. *NeuroImage, 40*, 409–414. doi:10.1016/j.neuroimage.2007.11.048

Polyn, S. M., Natu, V. S., Cohen, J. D., & Norman, K. A. (2005). Category-specific cortical activity precedes retrieval during memory search. *Science, 310*, 1963–1966. doi:10.1126/science.1117645

Poser, B. A., Koopmans, P. J., Witzel, T., Wald, L. L., & Barth, M. (2010). Three dimensional echo-planar imaging at 7 Tesla. *NeuroImage, 51*, 261–266. doi:10.1016/j.neuroimage.2010.01.108

Pyka, M., Beckmann, C. F., Schöning, S., Hauke, S., Heider, D., Kugel, H., . . . Konrad, C. (2009). Impact of working memory load on fMRI resting state pattern in subsequent resting phases. *PLoS ONE, 4*, e7198. doi:10.1371/journal.pone.0007198

Racine, E., Bar-Ilan, O., & Illes, J. (2005). fMRI in the public eye. *Nature Reviews Neuroscience, 6*, 159–164. doi:10.1038/nrn1609

Rademacher, L., Krach, S., Kohls, G., Irmak, A., Grunder, G., & Spreckelmeyer, K. N. (2010). Dissociation of neural networks for anticipation and consumption of monetary and social rewards. *NeuroImage, 49*, 3276–3285. doi:10.1016/j.neuroimage.2009.10.089

Ramsey, J. D., Hanson, S. J., Hanson, C., Halchenko, Y. O., Poldrack, R. A., & Glymour, C. (2010). Six problems for causal inference from fMRI. *NeuroImage, 49*, 1545–1558. doi:10.1016/j.neuroimage.2009.08.065

Rodriguez, P. F. (2010). Neural decoding of goal locations in spatial navigation in humans with fMRI. *Human Brain Mapping, 31*, 391–397.

Roebroeck, A., Formisano, E., & Goebel, R. (2005). Mapping directed influence over the brain using Granger causality and fMRI. *NeuroImage, 25*, 230–242. doi:10.1016/j.neuroimage.2004.11.017

Rogers, B. P., Morgan, V. L., Newton, A. T., & Gore, J. C. (2007). Assessing functional connectivity in the human brain by fMRI. *Magnetic Resonance Imaging, 25*, 1347–1357. doi:10.1016/j.mri.2007.03.007

Rosen, B. R., Buckner, R. L., & Dale, A. M. (1998). Event-related functional MRI: Past, present, and future. *Proceedings of the National Academy of Sciences of the United States of America, 95,* 773–780. doi:10.1073/pnas.95.3.773

Rykhlevskaia, E., Gratton, G., & Fabiani, M. (2008). Combining structural and functional neuroimaging data for studying brain connectivity: A review. *Psychophysiology, 45,* 173–187. doi:10.1111/j.1469-8986.2007.00621.x

Savoy, R. L., Bandettini, P. A., O'Craven, K. M., Kwong, K. K., Davis, T. L., Baker, J. R., . . . Rosen, B. R. (1995, August). *Pushing the temporal resolution of fMRI: Studies of very brief visual stimuli, onset variability and asynchrony, and stimulus-correlated changes in noise.* Paper presented at the Third Annual Meeting of the Society of Magnetic Resonance Imaging, New York, NY.

Schauer, F. (2010). Neuroscience, lie-detection, and the law: Contrary to the prevailing view, the suitability of brain-based lie-detection for courtroom or forensic use should be determined according to legal and not scientific standards. *Trends in Cognitive Sciences, 14,* 101–103. doi:10.1016/j.tics.2009.12.004

Sehlmeyer, C., Schöning, S., Zwitserlood, P., Pfleiderer, B., Kircher, T., Arolt, V., & Konrad, C. (2009). Human fear conditioning and extinction in neuroimaging: A systematic review. *PLoS ONE, 4,* e5865. doi:10.1371/journal.pone.0005865

Seymour, K., Clifford, C. W. G., Logothetis, N. K., & Bartels, A. (2010). Coding and binding of color and form in visual cortex. *Cerebral Cortex, 20,* 1946–1945.

Simpson, J. R. (2008). Functional MRI lie detection: Too good to be true? *Journal of the American Academy of Psychiatry and the Law, 36,* 491–498.

Small, S. L., Wilde, M., Kenny, S., Andric, M., & Hasson, U. (2009). Database-managed grid-enabled analysis of neuroimaging data: The CNARI framework. *International Journal of Psychophysiology, 73,* 62–72. doi:10.1016/j.ijpsycho.2009.01.010

Smolka, M. N., Buhler, M., Schumann, G., Klein, S., Hu, X. Z., Moayer, M., . . . Heinz, A. (2007). Gene–gene effects on central processing of aversive stimuli. *Molecular Psychiatry, 12,* 307–317.

Sorger, B., Dahmen, B., Reithler, J., Gosseries, O., Maudoux, A., Laureys, S., & Goebel, R. (2009). Another kind of "BOLD Response": Answering multiple-choice questions via online decoded single-trial brain signals. *Progress in Brain Research, 177,* 275–292.

Stein, M. B., Simmons, A. N., Feinstein, J. S., & Paulus, M. P. (2007). Increased amygdala and insula activation during emotion processing in anxiety-prone subjects. *The American Journal of Psychiatry, 164,* 318–327. doi:10.1176/appi.ajp.164.2.318

Stephan, K. E., Penny, W. D., Moran, R. J., den Ouden, H. E., Daunizeau, J., & Friston, K. J. (2010). Ten simple rules for dynamic causal modeling. *NeuroImage, 49,* 3099–3109. doi:10.1016/j.neuroimage.2009.11.015

Stevens, W. D., Buckner, R. L., & Schacter, D. L. (2010). Correlated low-frequency bold fluctuations in the resting human brain are modulated by recent experience in category-preferential visual regions. *Cerebral Cortex, 20,* 1997–2006.

Tabelow, K., Piëch, V., Polzehl, J., & Voss, H. U. (2009). High-resolution fMRI: Overcoming the signal-to-noise problem. *Journal of Neuroscience Methods, 178,* 357–365. doi:10.1016/j.jneumeth.2008.12.011

Tairyan, K., & Illes, J. (2009). Imaging genetics and the power of combined technologies: A perspective from neuroethics. *Neuroscience, 164,* 7–15. doi:10.1016/j.neuroscience.2009.01.052

Tambini, A., Ketz, N., & Davachi, L. (2010). Enhanced brain correlations during rest are related to memory for recent experiences. *Neuron, 65,* 280–290. doi:10.1016/j.neuron.2010.01.001

Thirion, B., Pinel, P., Mèriaux, S., Roche, A., Dehaene, S., & Poline, J-B. (2007). Analysis of a large fMRI cohort: Statistical and methodological issues for group analyses. *NeuroImage, 35,* 105–120. doi:10.1016/j.neuroimage.2006.11.054

Tootell, R. B., Hadjikhani, N. K., Vanduffel, W., Liu, A. K., Mendola, J. D., Sereno, M. I., & Dale, A. M. (1998). Functional analysis of primary visual cortex (V1) in humans. *Proceedings of the National Academy of Sciences of the United States of America, 95,* 811–817. doi:10.1073/pnas.95.3.811

Tovino, S. A. (2007). Functional neuroimaging and the law: Trends and directions for future scholarship. *The American Journal of Bioethics, 7,* 44–56. doi:10.1080/15265160701518714

Tshibanda, L., Vanhaudenhuyse, A., Boly, M., Soddu, A., Bruno, M-A., Moonen, G., . . . Noirhomme, Q. (2010). Neuroimaging after coma. *Neuroradiology, 52,* 15–24. doi:10.1007/s00234-009-0614-8

Valentin, V. V., & O'Doherty, J. P. (2009). Overlapping prediction errors in dorsal striatum during instrumental learning with juice and money reward in the human brain. *Journal of Neurophysiology, 102,* 3384–3394.

Van Horn, J. D., Ellmore, T. M., Esposito, G., & Berman, K. F. (1998). Mapping voxel-based statistical power on parametric images. *NeuroImage, 7,* 97–107. doi:10.1006/nimg.1997.0317

Van Horn, J. D., Grethe, J. S., Kostelec, P., Woodward, J. B., Aslam, J. A., Rus, D., . . . Gazzaniga, M. S. (2001). The Functional Magnetic Resonance Imaging Data Center (fMRIDC): The challenges and rewards of large-scale databasing of neuroimaging studies. *Philosophical Transactions of the Royal Society of London. Series B, Biological Sciences, 356*, 1323–1339. doi:10.1098/rstb.2001.0916

Van Horn, J. D., & Ishai, A. (2007). Mapping the human brain: New insights from fMRI data sharing. *Neuroinformatics, 5*, 146–153. doi:10.1007/s12021-007-0011-6

Van Horn, J. D., & Poldrack, R. A. (2009). Functional MRI at the crossroads. *International Journal of Psychophysiology, 73*, 3–9. doi:10.1016/j.ijpsycho.2008.11.003

van Kesteren, M. T. R., Fernández, G., Norris, D. G., & Hermans, E. J. (2010). Persistent schema-dependent hippocampal-neocortical connectivity during memory encoding and postencoding rest in humans. *Proceedings of the National Academy of Sciences of the United States of America, 107*, 7550–7555. doi:10.1073/pnas.0914892107

Visscher, K. M., Miezin, F. M., Kelly, J. E., Buckner, R. L., Donaldson, D. I., McAvoy, M. P., . . . Petersen, S. E. (2003). Mixed blocked/event-related designs separate transient and sustained activity in fMRI. *NeuroImage, 19*, 1694–1708. doi:10.1016/S1053-8119(03)00178-2

Voss, H. U., & Schiff, N. D. (2009). MRI of neuronal network structure, function, and plasticity. *Progress in Brain Research, 175*, 483–496.

Vul, E., Harris, C., Winkielman, P., & Pashler, H. (2009). Puzzlingly high correlations in fMRI studies of emotion, personality, and social cognition. *Perspectives on Psychological Science, 4*, 274–290. doi:10.1111/j.1745-6924.2009.01125.x

Wagner, A. D., Schacter, D. L., Rotte, M., Koutstaal, W., Maril, A., Dale, A. M., . . . Buckner, R. L. (1998). Building memories: Remembering and forgetting of verbal experiences as predicted by brain activity. *Science, 281*, 1188–1191. doi:10.1126/science.281.5380.1188

Walter, H., Abler, B., Ciaramidaro, A., & Erk, S. (2005). Motivating forces of human actions: Neuroimaging reward and social interaction. *Brain Research Bulletin, 67*, 368–381. doi:10.1016/j.brainresbull.2005.06.016

Walther, D. B., Caddigan, E., Fei-Fei, L., & Beck, D. M. (2009). Natural scene categories revealed in distributed patterns of activity in the human brain. *The Journal of Neuroscience, 29*, 10573–10581. doi:10.1523/JNEUROSCI.0559-09.2009

Wang, L., LaViolette, P., O'Keefe, K., Putcha, D., Bakkour, A., Van Dijk, K. R. A., . . . Sperling, R. A. (2010). Intrinsic connectivity between the hippocampus and posteromedial cortex predicts memory performance in cognitively intact older individuals. *NeuroImage, 51*, 910–917. doi:10.1016/j.neuroimage.2010.02.046

Weber, M. J., & Thompson-Schill, S. L. (2010). Functional neuroimaging can support causal claims about brain function. *Journal of Cognitive Neuroscience, 22*, 2415–2416. doi:10.1162/jocn.2010.21461

Weisberg, D. S., Keil, F. C., Goodstein, J., Rawson, E., & Gray, J. R. (2008). The seductive allure of neuroscience explanations. *Journal of Cognitive Neuroscience, 20*, 470–477. doi:10.1162/jocn.2008.20040

Weiskopf, N., Hutton, C., Josephs, O., & Deichmann, R. (2006). Optimal EPI parameters for reduction of susceptibility-induced BOLD sensitivity losses: A whole-brain analysis at 3 T and 1.5 T. *NeuroImage, 33*, 493–504. doi:10.1016/j.neuroimage.2006.07.029

Weiskopf, N., Hutton, C., Josephs, O., Turner, R., & Deichmann, R. (2007). Optimized EPI for fMRI studies of the orbitofrontal cortex: Compensation of susceptibility-induced gradients in the readout direction. *Magma, 20*, 39–49. doi:10.1007/s10334-006-0067-6

Weiskopf, N., Scharnowski, F., Veit, R., Goebel, R., Birbaumer, N., & Mathiak, K. (2004). Self-regulation of local brain activity using real-time functional magnetic resonance imaging (fMRI). *Journal of Physiology, Paris, 98*, 357–373. doi:10.1016/j.jphysparis.2005.09.019

Weiskopf, N., Sitaram, R., Josephs, O., Veit, R., Scharnowski, F., Goebel, R., . . . Mathiak, K. (2007). Real-time functional magnetic resonance imaging: Methods and applications. *Magnetic Resonance Imaging, 25*, 989–1003. doi:10.1016/j.mri.2007.02.007

Xiong, J., Gao, J-H., Lancaster, J. L., & Fox, P. T. (1995). Clustered pixels analysis for functional MRI activation studies of the human brain. *Human Brain Mapping, 3*, 287–301. doi:10.1002/hbm.460030404

Yoon, J. H., Tamir, D., Minzenberg, M. J., Ragland, J. D., Ursu, S., & Carter, C. S. (2008). Multivariate pattern analysis of functional magnetic resonance imaging data reveals deficits in distributed representations in schizophrenia. *Biological Psychiatry, 64*, 1035–1041. doi:10.1016/j.biopsych.2008.07.025

Yung-Chin, H., Ching-Han, H., & Tseng, W. Y. I. (2009). Correction for susceptibility-induced distortion in echo-planar imaging using field maps and model-based point spread function. *IEEE Transactions on Medical Imaging, 28*, 1850–1857.

Zarahn, E., & Slifstein, M. (2001). A reference effect approach for power analysis in fMRI. *NeuroImage, 14*, 768–779. doi:10.1006/nimg.2001.0852

CHAPTER 29

BEYOND ERP AND fMRI: OTHER IMAGING TECHNIQUES FOR STUDYING HUMAN BRAIN FUNCTION

Gabriele Gratton and Monica Fabiani

The past few decades have seen an explosion of psychological research using noninvasive (or low-invasivity) measures of human brain function. This work is motivated by two main goals: Measures of brain function may (a) provide additional information, beyond that obtained from overt response variables, about intermediate states of the information processing system and (b) illuminate some of the physiological mechanisms that underlie the psychological phenomena of interest. The vast majority of this work has employed two measures: event-related brain potentials (ERPs; see Fabiani, Gratton, & Federmeier, 2007) and functional magnetic resonance imaging (fMRI; see Van Horn & Poldrack, 2009). Brain function, however, is a complex phenomenon, and several other measures are currently available that allow investigators to explore its various facets. These measures complement ERPs and fMRI, generating a more articulated view of this enormously complex organ's functions. In this chapter, we review some of these methods, their rationale, the types of data they provide, and their advantages and limitations. Specifically, we review the following techniques: magnetoencephalography (MEG); single-photon emission computerized tomography (SPECT) and its higher resolution counterpart, positron emission tomography (PET); fast (i.e., the event-related-optical signal [EROS]) and slow (i.e., near-infrared spectroscopy [NIRS]) optical methods; and transcranial magnetic stimulation (TMS). These techniques vary widely with

respect to the physical mechanisms involved, the types of data they can provide, and the subject populations to and environments in which they can be applied. They also do not exhaust all possible physiological techniques that can be used to study human brain function in a noninvasive manner, but they do represent the most used complementary approaches to ERPs and fMRI found in the literature in the past decade or 2.

REVIEW OF METHODS

Magnetoencephalography

MEG is a technique used to measure the tiny magnetic fields linked to the electrical currents associated with the depolarization and hyperpolarization of neurons (for reviews see Hari, 1996; Hari, Levänen, & Raij, 2000; Stufflebeam, Tanaka, & Ahlfors, 2009). To be measurable at the surface of the head, the magnetic fields generated by individual neurons must summate, which requires that individual fields be oriented in the same direction. This means that only certain structures and neuronal populations possessing a specific geometric organization may generate surface-recordable MEG (e.g., the cortex). Even so, the magnetic fields generated by the brain's electrical currents are extremely small (on the order of 10^1–10^3 fT), much smaller than the magnetic fields from various environmental sources, such as the Earth's magnetic field (10^8 fT). Therefore their recording requires special instruments

We acknowledge the support of National Institute of Mental Health Grant MH80182 to G. Gratton and of National Institute on Aging Grant 1RC1AG035927 to M. Fabiani.

DOI: 10.1037/13619-030

called *superconducting quantum interference devices* (SQUIDs). In current MEG systems, up to 300 different SQUID detectors are used to generate maps of the magnetic fields over the head. These devices need to be kept at extremely low temperatures (a few degrees Kelvin), which permit superconducting phenomena to occur. Thus, the recording instrument needs to be supercooled, making it bulky and costly (around $1.5–2 million). In addition, special methods are used to reduce the influence of environmental magnetic sources on the measurements. These include (a) shielding, which is expensive and adds significantly to the cost of the machine, and (b) special circuit design, which makes MEG particularly sensitive to locally generated compared with distantly generated fields, measuring field gradients rather than absolute magnitudes.

Although effective, these circuit designs restrict MEG measures to activity in fairly superficial areas of the brain. They also make MEG particularly sensitive to currents flowing in a direction tangential to the surface of the head compared with currents flowing in a radial direction. As a consequence, MEG measures are more sensitive to phenomena occurring in sulci (which tend to be orthogonal to the surface of the head, resulting in currents oriented tangentially) than to those occurring in gyri (which are parallel to the surface of the head, resulting in currents oriented orthogonally).

Notwithstanding its high cost, MEG is progressively gaining acceptance from researchers and clinicians. Its ability to describe rapid brain events (on the order of milliseconds) coupled with a spatial resolution on the order of a few centimeters make it useful for a number of research areas. In particular, MEG has been used extensively in studies of language processing (Frye, Rezaie, & Papanicolaou, 2009)[1] and to some degree also in studies of attention and memory (e.g., Hopf, Boehler, Schoenfeld, Heinze, & Tsotsos, 2010; Stephane et al., 2010). A particularly attractive feature of MEG is the absence of invasivity, as no substance or energy is introduced into the body for its measurement. Thus, MEG can be used with many types of populations, including children (e.g., Tesan, Johnson, Reid,

Thornton, & Crain, 2010) and even fetuses (e.g., Sheridan, Matuz, Draganova, Eswaran, & Preissl, 2010). Specialized instruments, however, are required for these populations. Furthermore, because of its high sensitivity to electromagnetic noise, MEG cannot be easily combined with other methods for studying brain function (such as magnetic resonance [MR] methods).

Single-Photon Emission Computerized Tomography and Positron Emission Tomography

SPECT and PET are two related techniques used in radiology and nuclear medicine. Both techniques introduce a radioactive substance (radiotracer or radioligand) into the body and obtain images of its diffusion in the body by mapping the radioactivity it generates. SPECT is based on *gamma decay*, a radioactive decay characterized by the production of a single gamma ray by a decaying isotope. The most common isotope used is ^{99m}Tc, which has a half-life of a couple of hours. PET instead is based on *beta decay*, in which a radioactive isotope emits a positron, which then reacts with electrons in the medium annihilating and producing a pair of high-energy gamma rays oriented 180 degrees from each other. Several types of isotopes are used for PET, depending on the application, including ^{11}C (half-life ≈ 20 min), ^{13}N (half-life ≈10 min), ^{15}O (half-life ≈ 2 min), and ^{18}F (half-life ≈ 110 min). Because two gamma ray photons traveling in opposite directions are produced, it is possible to determine a line where the annihilation occurred by determining whether they arrived almost simultaneously (within a few nanoseconds) to two among a circular array of detectors located around the head. As the annihilation occurs within 1 cm to 2 cm from where the radioactive decay happened, this provides a way of mapping the decay process in the body, or in its psychology applications, within the brain.

The great advantage of PET and SPECT is that they can be used for a wide variety of purposes. Radioligands can be incorporated in a number of different substances, each of which can provide interesting information about the physiology and

---

[1]This includes the use of MEG to assess the lateralization of language in preparation for surgery, as an alternative to more invasive methods such as the Wada test (e.g., Doss, Zhang, Risse, & Dickens, 2009).

metabolism of the body. Of specific interest for psychologists are two classes of applications: (a) analysis of blood flow and metabolism in different regions of the brain (e.g., Petersen, Fox, Posner, Mintun, & Raichle, 1989) and (b) mapping of neurotransmitter receptors or other biochemicals of interest within the brain (e.g., Tateno, Kobayashi, & Saito, 2009).

Analysis of blood flow and metabolism is typically carried out using PET. Two methods have been most extensively used: ^{15}O incorporated in water and ^{18}F incorporated in fluorodeoxyglucose. The first compound is used to study blood flow. Importantly for cognitive studies, ^{15}O has a very short half-life, allowing for multiple measurements to be taken within a session. This enables investigators to study the difference in the amount of blood flowing through a particular region during different task conditions, through digital subtraction of different maps obtained under each condition. This methodology, developed by the Washington University group in the 1980s, has had a significant role in the history of cognitive neuroscience (see Raichle, 1998). The spatial resolution of the images obtained with this approach is about 1 cm to 2 cm. The temporal resolution is of the order of minutes. Currently, however, this approach has been largely supplanted by fMRI, which provides images with a greater spatial and, importantly, temporal resolution. In addition, ^{15}O PET is expensive, requiring a cyclotron on site and rapid incorporation and delivery technology.

^{18}F deoxyglucose PET is used to monitor glucose consumption by tissue. Deoxyglucose is processed only through the initial stages of oxidative metabolism, and is then retained in the cells for an extended period of time: Thus, the greater the glucose consumption, the greater the accumulation of deoxyglucose. Because the half-life of ^{18}F is much longer than that of ^{15}O, only one measurement can be carried out within a session, limiting its use in human studies (a similar technique, autoradiography, has been used extensively in animal studies) because a control condition is not easy to implement. LaBerge and Buchsbaum (1990) used a contralateral control approach to provide a reference

for the measurement obtained on the stimulated side. Note that ^{15}O PET decay is so fast that the injection of the radioactive material and the psychological task of interest need to be conducted while the subject is in the scanner. This is not necessary with the ^{18}F deoxyglucose technique, which is based on the accumulation of the radiotracer over an extended period of time, allowing for the injection and the psychological task to be conducted before placing the subject in the scanner. This enables the use of a greater variety of tasks, although only a summary image of total deoxyglucose accumulation during the experiment can be obtained.

In the past decade or so, a number of new radiotracer molecules have been developed, and more are currently being tested. These molecules allow investigators to map a number of important chemicals in the brain. Specifically, radioisotopes are incorporated into selective agonists (or antagonists) of various neurotransmitters and neuromodulators (e.g., dopamine and acetylcholine), making it possible to visualize in vivo the distribution and quantity of the receptors for these substances.[2] This can be used to compare different subject groups, such as those who differ along some important physiological, psychological, or genetic dimension. For example, a recently developed tracer (the Pittsburgh compound B, or PiB), allows for the measurement of beta amyloid deposition, which can be used for in vivo diagnosis of Alzheimer's disease (e.g., Jagust, 2009; Nordberg, 2010). Also, by comparing images obtained at different times, it is possible to determine whether certain treatments (e.g., pharmacological or psychiatric therapies) lead to changes in the quantity and distribution of receptors for specific neurotransmitter within the brain.

From a practical standpoint, several factors have limited the diffusion of PET and SPECT. PET is very expensive, with costs of more than several million dollars. These costs are due to the price of the scanner and to the necessity for both a cyclotron to generate the radioisotopes of interest and the machinery (and expertise) required to incorporate the radioisotope into the molecule of interest in situ. Although costs are lower for SPECT, its inferior

---

[2]By appropriately selecting the pharmachological agent, it is possible to distinguish among different types of neurotransmitter receptors.

spatial resolution makes it a less than ideal alternative to PET. Finally, because both techniques involve ionizing radiation, there are limitations to their extensive use for experimental purposes. To guarantee the safety of subjects, the amount of radiation absorbed during a PET or SPECT experiment is strictly regulated, as is the number of times a subject can participate in studies involving these measures.

In summary, PET and SPECT remain important imaging tools for psychologists in the 21st century, although the types of questions that are now addressed with these techniques are different from those that were addressed 15 to 20 years ago. They are no longer the methods of choice to generate images of brain activity (measured as a change in blood flow) during a task (as they have been supplanted by fMRI for this particular application), but their great chemical flexibility provides an extremely useful approach for studying brain biochemistry in vivo.

Diffusive Optical Imaging

Diffusive optical imaging is a relatively new imaging modality, with the first human data obtained in the early 1990s (for reviews see E. Gratton, Fantini, Franceschini, G. Gratton, & Fabiani, 1997; G. Gratton & Fabiani, 2009; Villringer & Chance, 1997). It studies how light is transmitted and diffused through tissue (in this case the head) to determine properties of the tissue itself. Light in the red to near-infrared (NIR) wavelength range (650–900 nm) is used. At these wavelengths, there is relatively little light absorption by most tissues in the human head, permitting photons to travel several centimeters through the tissue. However, NIR light (unlike X-rays or gamma rays) is strongly scattered by head tissues, with mean free paths on the order of 5 mm or less. For this reason, photons do not travel straight through the tissue but tend to diffuse according to a random-walk process. Therefore, if a source of NIR light is located on the surface of the head, it will generate a *halo* into the tissue itself, with a maximum penetration of a few centimeters. If a detector is also located on the surface of the tissue, at a distance of a few centimeters from the source, it will pick up some of the photons produced by the source (see Figure 29.1 for an example of recording montage).

FIGURE 29.1. Typical setup for recording optical imaging data from a large set of sources and detectors.

Interestingly, the photons generated from the source and arriving to a detector located on the same surface will most likely have followed not a straight trajectory (as would occur in a nonscattering medium) but rather a curved trajectory reaching some depth in between the source and the detector. This occurs because the head tissue (a highly scattering medium) is surrounded by air (a nonscattering medium). Therefore, photons traveling close to the surface of the medium are likely, in their random motion, to reach the surface of the medium before reaching the detector. If this occurs, they will move out of the medium and never reach the detector. Because of this principle, diffusive optical imaging can provide data about changes in optical properties that occur inside the head, at depths up to 2 cm to 3 cm. This permits measurements from cortical areas relatively close to the surface of the head.

For this approach to be useful in functional brain imaging, changes in optical properties of the brain need to occur in association with neural activity. There are at least two phenomena causing changes in optical properties of the tissue. The first are changes in the coloration of tissue caused by variations in the concentration of oxy- and deoxy-hemoglobin, which have distinctive absorption spectra in the NIR range (see Frostig, Lieke, Ts'o, & Grinvald, 1990; Villringer & Chance, 1997). These effects are related to blood flow changes studied with fMRI and [15]O PET. The second are changes in the scattering properties of tissue associated with neuronal activity (G. Gratton, Corballis, Cho, Fabiani, & Hood, 1995; Rector, Carter, Volegov & George, 2005). These changes are related to the movement of ions across the neuronal membranes and are in some way related to ERP and MEG measures.

Both signals have been investigated using optical imaging, generating two types of imaging modalities: NIRS (related to hemodynamic signals; Kato, Kamei, Takashima, & Ozaki, 1993; see Villringer & Chance, 1997) and EROS (related to neuronal signals; G. Gratton, Corballis, et al., 1995; see G. Gratton & Fabiani, 2009). Two types of instruments have been most commonly used: continuous-wave (CW) instruments, in which light sources have a fixed intensity over time (or are modulated at low frequencies, < 10 kHz); and frequency-domain (FD) instruments, in which light sources are modulated at high frequencies (typically > 100 MHz). Although CW instruments are simpler and less expensive, FD instruments measure both the amount of light moving between sources and detectors and the time taken by photon to cross this distance (on the order of nanoseconds). The time measurement can be useful in estimating the extent to which photons scatter through the tissue. Furthermore, it can be particularly sensitive to deep phenomena, increasing the penetration of the procedure and making it more specific for brain (vs. nonbrain) phenomena, thus providing higher spatial resolution.

Near-infrared spectroscopy. NIRS uses spectroscopy to estimate changes in the concentration of oxy- and deoxy-hemoglobin in tissue. This is done by comparing changes in light absorption occurring in different conditions at different wavelengths, exploiting the fact that oxy- and deoxy-hemoglobin have different absorption spectra within the NIR range. This can be accomplished through a system of linear equations on the basis of the modified Beer-Lambert Law (see Villringer & Chance, 1997), which states that the proportion of light absorbed by tissue is related to the concentration of the absorbers in the tissue (in this case oxy- and deoxy-hemoglobin), their coefficients of extinction (i.e., ability to absorb light of a particular wavelength), and the length of the photon path through the tissue (which in most cases is estimated on the basis of the source-detector distance and a correction factor derived from the literature to account for scattering).[3] For these computations, a minimum of two light wavelengths with distinct extinction coefficients needs to be used; some instruments use three or more. Because a number of source-detector pairs can be used within a study, maps of oxy- and deoxy-hemoglobin concentration changes can be obtained. Maps can be obtained very quickly, up to 100 or more times per second. Thus NIRS yields maps of brain activity with a spatial resolution of 1 cm to 2 cm and a temporal resolution limited only by the time required for hemodynamic phenomena to occur (a few seconds).

In the past few years, the use of NIRS has increased. Compared with fMRI (the most comparable imaging method), it has some disadvantages but also some advantages. Unlike MR technology, current optical methods do not provide anatomical images. Optical data can, however, be coregistered with MR data with relatively good accuracy (Whalen, Maclin, Fabiani, & Gratton, 2008). Optical methods have limited penetration through the head and therefore, unlike fMRI, cannot be used to image deep structures (i.e., located more than 3–4 cm from the head surface). The spatial resolution of NIRS data (1–2 cm) is more limited than that of fMRI (which in some cases can be as low as a few millimeters but most typically is in the 5–10 mm range). Optical data also have a number of advantages.

[3]The influence of scattering can be calculated using FD instruments, allowing in principle for the measurement of absolute concentrations of oxy- and deoxy-hemoglobin.

Their recording is flexible and does not require bulky or expensive equipment. This makes them usable in a variety of different environments and populations, such as with children and other patients who may be difficult to image with fMRI. Optical technology is completely compatible with MR (e.g., Toronov, Zhang, Fabiani, Gratton, & Webb, 2005; Zhang, Toronov, Fabiani, Gratton, & Webb, 2005), electrophysiological methods (including electroencephalogram [EEG], ERPs, and MEG), and TMS, allowing for the simultaneous recording of different modalities. It is also possible to obtain NIRS and EROS data (see the next section) simultaneously with the same instrument, providing concurrent neuronal and hemodynamic measures. NIRS can provide separate measurements of oxy- and deoxy-hemoglobin concentrations, which is not normally possible with fMRI. In fact, if FD technology is used, absolute concentrations of these substances can be obtained, again something not possible with fMRI. Finally, optical technology is less expensive than MR technology, with costs between $200,000 and $400,000.

In summary, NIRS is a useful developing technique that has some specific practical advantages (but also limitations) with respect to fMRI. Its use, especially in the applied field, is likely to grow significantly in the next few years.

Event-related optical signal. EROS is another application of diffusive optical imaging. The main difference with respect to NIRS is the time scale: instead of looking at phenomena occurring several seconds after a particular area of the brain is activated, it focuses on phenomena that occur at the same time as electrophysiological (postsynaptic) events, on a millisecond time scale. These phenomena are likely due to the swelling or shrinking of dendritic trees, which have been demonstrated to occur with depolarization and hyperpolarization of neuronal membranes (Rector et al., 2005). EROS signals are smaller than NIRS signals, requiring more advanced methods for their recording. Although EROS has been obtained with intensity measures (e.g., Franceschini & Boas, 2004; G. Gratton, Fabiani, et al., 1995; Maclin, Low, Sable, Fabiani, & Gratton, 2004; Medvedev, Kainerstorfer,

Borisov, Barbour, & VanMeter, 2008; Wolf et al., 2002), most studies have used measures of photon time of flight (i.e., the time taken by photons to move between source and detector) obtained using FD instruments (e.g., G. Gratton, 1997; G. Gratton et al., 2006; G. Gratton, Corballis, et al., 1995; G. Gratton & Fabiani, 2003; G. Gratton, Fabiani, et al., 1995; G. Gratton, Fabiani, Goodman-Wood, & DeSoto, 1998; G. Gratton, Goodman-Wood, & Fabiani, 2001; G. Gratton, Sarno, Maclin, Corballis, & Fabiani, 2000; Tse, Tien, & Penney, 2006; Wolf et al., 2002; also see G. Gratton & Fabiani, 2009, for a review), which have greater localization and depth sensitivity. In addition, EROS measurement is facilitated by high-density recording systems (e.g., G. Gratton, Rykhlevskaia, Wee, Leaver, & Fabiani, 2009; Low, Leaver, Kramer, Fabiani, & Gratton, 2009), appropriate frequency filtering (Maclin, Gratton, & Fabiani, 2003), and extensive signal averaging (e.g., G. Gratton & Fabiani, 2003; G. Gratton et al., 2006). When all of these techniques are employed, data with spatial resolution of up to 5 mm and temporal resolution around 10 ms to 20 ms can be obtained (G. Gratton & Fabiani, 2003).

EROS has been used in a number of paradigms and conditions, including visual (e.g., G. Gratton, Corballis, et al., 1995), auditory (e.g., Rinne et al., 1999), somatosensory (e.g., Maclin et al., 2004), and motor modalities (e.g., DeSoto, Fabiani, Geary, & Gratton, 2001). In each modality, simultaneous electrophysiological recordings indicate that the latency of the EROS activity is similar to the latency of the main ERP components (e.g., DeSoto et al., 2001; E. Gratton et al., 1997; Maclin et al., 2004; Rinne et al., 1999). Furthermore, the locations of the responses correspond to those obtained with fMRI (e.g., E. Gratton et al., 1997; G. Gratton et al., 2000; Toronov et al., 2005).

In summary, the main advantages of EROS are good spatial (5–10 mm) and temporal (10–20 ms) resolution; the possibility of simultaneous recording with ERP, fMRI, and TMS (in addition to NIRS); its relatively low cost (between $200,000 and $400,000); and its adaptability to a number of experimental populations and paradigms. Its major disadvantages are low penetration and relatively low signal-to-noise ratio (compared with ERPs, fMRI, and NIRS).

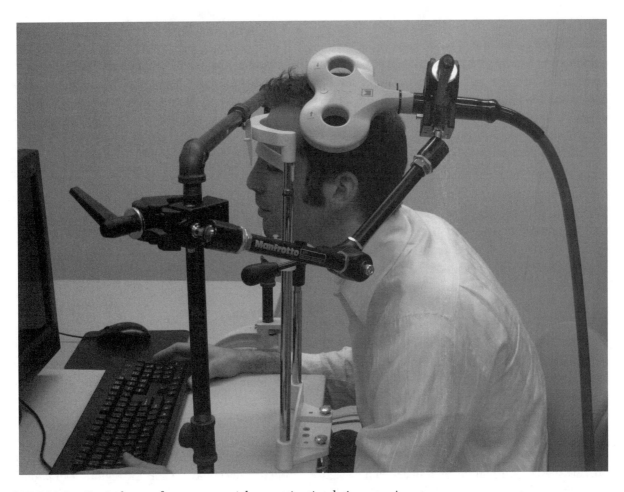

FIGURE 29.2.   Typical setup for a transcranial magnetic stimulation experiment.

Transcranial Magnetic Stimulation

TMS is a method for influencing the neural activity in selected areas of the brain (for reviews, see Pascual-Leone, Walsh, & Rothwell, 2000; Wagner, Valero-Cabre, & Pascual-Leone, 2007). TMS is based on the induction of weak electric currents in cortical regions through strong magnetic fields (of the order of 1 Tesla or more) produced by coils located just outside the head (see Figure 29.2). It is commonly thought that the weak electric currents induce brief depolarization of small cortical regions, whose extent depends on the type of coil and may vary between 5 mm and 10 mm or so, followed by prolonged periods of excitability or more often by inhibition, akin to long-term potentiation and long-term depression phenomena, respectively. In essence, TMS can be used to produce temporary lesions in specified cortical regions, which, because

of their limited duration, can be compared within the same subject with conditions in which the temporary lesion does not occur. This makes TMS a unique technique, in that it allows scientists to manipulate directly the brain from the outside, and therefore to make causal statements about the role that a particular brain structure may have in information processing or in a psychological task.

Two different TMS approaches are possible. The first, called *single- or double-pulse TMS* (sTMS) is based on the presentation of very short pulses of current (a few milliseconds in duration), which generate relatively rapid effects in the cortex that quickly wane when stimulation ceases. The advantages of this method are the possibility of testing the role of activity occurring at a particular time within a specific brain region in the performance of a task and its limited invasivity.[4] Its main limitations are

[4]There are a few side effects, for the most part limited to people with a history of epilepsy, which is therefore considered an exclusionary criterion for participation.

that the effects are weak, often only visible after averaging over a large number of trials. A possible confounding factor is that the sTMS pulse may generate stimulation not only through the induction of currents in the brain but also through the induction of muscle contractions in the scalp, and it may do so through auditory stimulation related to deformation of the TMS coil during the pulse. The latter confound can be controlled by running a control condition in which the magnetic field is redirected outside the head. The possible role of muscle artifacts is typically controlled for by using sham stimulation of other regions of the scalp, corresponding to cortical regions that are not considered relevant for the task.

The second method, called *repetitive TMS* (rTMS), is based on the presentation of very long (up to several minutes) low-frequency (up to 10 Hz) pulse sequences. These sequences induce sustained depression of the cortical regions involved, which may last 30 min or longer. The paradigm typically consists of comparing results obtained in two sessions: an experimental one in which rTMS is applied and a control one in which a sham rTMS is applied. Because of the long duration of the effects, rTMS can provide spatial information about whether a particular segment of the cortex is important for the performance of a task but does not provide specific information about the time at which this role is performed. rTMS is more invasive than sTMS: In some rare cases, seizures were reported even in subjects with no previous history of epilepsy (unlike sTMS), leading to the establishment of standards for its appropriate use (Rossi, Hallett, Rossini, Pascual-Leone, & the Safety of TMS Consensus Group, 2009). In addition, short duration headaches are often reported as aftereffects of rTMS.

Notwithstanding these potential issues, TMS has attracted the interest of many scientists because of its unique potential for allowing causal inferences about the role of different brain regions. That said, there are a few important limitations of the technique. Only regions that are close to the surface of the head can be subjected to the procedure. The extent of the cortical region manipulated is not well established, and it is also possible that other regions may be affected through the transmission of the signal by neural tracts. sTMS is difficult to combine with other brain imaging methods (but see Parks et al., in press, for concurrent EROS and sTIMS recordings; Thut & Pascual-Leone, 2010, for a review of combined TMS-EEG recordings). This is less of a problem for rTMS. Finally, the possible side effects associated with the procedure (especially for rTMS) may discourage some investigators from its adoption.

In summary, TMS is an intriguing technique for manipulating brain function nearly noninvasively. Its practical use is partly limited by safety and experimental issues. The possibility of making causal statements and the contained cost of the device (around $50,000), however, have made its popularity grow exponentially in the past few years.

COMPARISONS AMONG MEASURES OF NONINVASIVE HUMAN BRAIN FUNCTION

To understand the relative utility of current measures of human brain function, it is important to consider that they vary along a number of dimensions and provide different types of information. We can distinguish the following dimensions: (a) type of brain function measured; (b) spatial and temporal resolution; (c) selectivity for specific regions, cell populations, or brain systems; (d) extent to which the procedure is a measurement method versus a manipulation tool; and (e) practical factors such as degree of invasivity, flexibility, cost, availability, and population(s) to whom it can be most readily applied. Each of these dimensions plays a critical role in determining the suitability of a specific technique in investigating a particular psychological problem. In this section we briefly discuss each dimension and present a table (see Table 29.1) summarizing how different methods can be classified accordingly.

Type of Brain Function Measured

Although brain activity if often regarded as a well-defined concept, in reality it is composed of a complex and multifaceted set of phenomena, which can be summarized as follows:

1. *Membrane phenomena*: Depolarization and hyperpolarization of neurons, associated with ion exchanges across the neuronal membranes (important for integrating information coming

TABLE 29.1

Dimensions of Human Brain Function

Method	Type of function	Spatial/ temporal resolution (scales)	Selectivity	Measurement vs. manipulation	Population	Other factors
EEG ERPs	Membrane	cm ms	Postsynaptic activity Pyramidal neurons; open fields	Measurement	Infants to older adults; patient populations	Least expensive and most portable technique; very limited spatial resolution
fMRI	Metabolic/ hemodynamic	mm s	Postsynaptic activity Glutamergic cells?	Measurement	Older children to adults; some restrictions	Expensive; requires large footprint equipment and special environments
PET SPECT	Metabolic/ hemodynamic; synaptic	cm min	Very selective depending on tracer and method used	Measurement	Adults	Moderately invasive; very expensive
EROS	Membrane	sub-cm ms	Postsynaptic activity; superficial structures	Measurement	Infants to older adults; patient populations	Limited penetration and low signal-to-noise ratio
NIRS	Metabolic/ hemodynamic	cm s	Superficial structures Glutamergic cells?	Measurement	Infants to older adults; patient populations	Limited penetration
MEG	Membrane	sub-cm ms	Postsynaptic activity Pyramidal neurons; open fields; tangential orientation (i.e., sulci)	Measurement	Older children to adults	Expensive; requires large footprint equipment and insulated environment
TMS	Membrane?	cm sub-s	Largely unknown; superficial structures	Manipulation	Adults	Moderately invasive

Note. The methods with gray background (EEG/ERPs and fMRI) represent the gold standards with which other methods are compared. EEG = electroencephalogram; ERPs = event-related brain potentials; fMRI = functional magnetic resonance imaging; PET = positron emission tomography; SPECT = single-photon emission computerized tomography; EROS = event-related-optical signal; NIRS = near-infrared spectroscopy; MEG = magnetoencephalography; TMS = transcranial magnetic stimulation.

from different neurons and transmitting this information over long distances).

2. *Synaptic phenomena*: Various biochemical events that occur at the synapses between neurons (critical for interchanging information between neurons and for modulating neuronal function).

3. *Metabolic and hemodynamic phenomena*: A variety of corollary homeostatic and trophic phenomena, such as oxygen and glucose consumption,

vasodilation, increased blood flow, and so on, which often involve other cells (such as glial cells) in addition to neurons but intrinsically relate to neuronal function.

Each of these phenomena results in biophysical and biochemical changes, which can be monitored with different brain imaging techniques. EEG, ERPs, MEG, TMS, and EROS are sensitive to membrane phenomena; NIRS and fMRI are sensitive to hemodynamic effects; and PET and SPECT can be rendered sensitive to a number of different phenomena, both synaptic and metabolic or hemodynamic, depending on the type of tracer used. All of these phenomena are intrinsically related to each other, albeit in a complex and typically nonlinear fashion. Therefore results obtained with different techniques are likely associated with each other according to complex and sometimes not well-understood rules.

Temporal and Spatial Resolution

The different methods vary significantly in terms of the temporal and spatial resolution of the information they provide. In some cases, the temporal or spatial specificity of the information is limited by properties of the physiological phenomenon they probe. For example, changes in the receptors for particular neurotransmitters, which can be in some cases measured with PET and SPECT, may occur relatively slowly, over the course of hours, days, or even longer. The vasodilation response that follows neuronal activation (also called blood-oxygen-level-dependent [BOLD] response), measured by techniques such as fMRI, ^{15}O-PET, and NIRS, requires the relaxation of smooth muscle fibers surrounding the arterioles, which takes place over several seconds.

Other limitations come from properties of the measurement system. A basic limit for all noninvasive imaging methods is that the size, number, and extracranial location of the detectors used makes it impossible to target individual neurons (or individual synapses). Rather, all noninvasive human brain-imaging methods refer to the summation of signals from a large number (on the order of at least thousands) of cells and neurons. In this sense, these measures are logically different from the single- or multiple-unit electrophysiological recordings obtained intracranially in animals. The statistical properties of the imaging signals have further consequences: They bias the measurements toward those systems that are most likely to generate signals that summate over space or time. This is true even for procedures with relatively good spatial and or temporal resolution. For instance, ERPs are more

likely to be the result of (dendritic) postsynaptic activity (which extends over tenths to hundredths of milliseconds) than to presynaptic (axonal) action potentials (which only last for a few milliseconds) because the probability of temporal summation of the activity of different neurons is higher in the former than in the latter case. In addition, the larger size (diameter and number of arborizations) of dendritic trees compared with axons makes the import of the physical and chemical events associated with postsynaptic activity overwhelmingly greater (and therefore more likely to be detected at some distance) than that of the axons. Finally, different techniques employ methodologies that may further limit the spatial or temporal resolution of the results. For instance, the temporal resolution of methods relying on radioactive tracers, such as PET and SPECT, may partly depend on the time-decay function of the particular isotope used. Similarly, the spatial resolution of measures based on electrical potentials may be limited by the conductivity of the tissue, which spreads electrical signals over a large area.

Selectivity. Various techniques are more sensitive to certain forms of brain activities than to others. In some cases, this is intentional: SPECT and PET methods that are used to investigate the location and numerosity of specific receptors are intentionally selective for them. In other cases, however, the bias, or selectivity, is not necessarily intentional and may provide important limitations to the types of data that a technology can provide. For example, several techniques (such as ERPs, MEG, optical methods, and TMS) are more sensitive to superficial than to deep events. Finally, biases may depend on other factors, such as dependence on particular biochemical (as may be the case for hemodynamic-based measures) or geometric (as is the case for ERPs and MEG) factors.

Measurement versus manipulation. Most brain-imaging methods passively observe changes in brain activity; only TMS allows for its manipulation. Thus most techniques only provide correlational data, whereas TMS can be used in support of causal inferences, indicating the extent to which activity in a particular region is critical for the performance of a given task.

Practical considerations.   Several practical reasons often lead to the selection of which procedures to use to investigate a particular psychological phenomenon. Some techniques may be less acceptable than others because they may be more intrusive or even invasive. Similarly, some techniques may be unfeasible for some subject populations (e.g., infants and young children). Some, such as fMRI, involve large equipment and require participants to refrain from moving. This may be incompatible with certain environments (e.g., field- or bedside applications) or certain behavioral tasks (e.g., those requiring extensive motion). Finally, other practical factors may include cost and availability of a particular technique.[5]

COMBINING DIFFERENT IMAGING MODALITIES

Because different modalities offer data varying along a number of dimensions, many researchers have combined them with the intent of providing a more complete view of brain function (Barinaga, 1997). The approaches used can be classified into two major classes: (a) a combination based on the comparison of completely analyzed data from each modality (e.g., Logothetis, Pauls, Augath, Trinath, & Oeltermann, 2001) and (b) a combination of relatively unanalyzed data from each modality that is fused based on physical or statistical principles (e.g., Dale, 2000). Both of these approaches can be based on data that are recorded separately (e.g., Huettel et al., 2004; Logothetis et al., 2001) or simultaneously (e.g., Mackert et al., 2008; Toronov et al., 2005). In practice, the simultaneous recording of different modalities often creates compatibility issues. When this occurs, such as for the simultaneous recording of EEG or ERP and fMRI data, special methods need to be used to minimize artifacts that originate in each modality from their concurrent recordings. Because of the complexities

involved in this process, concurrent recording (although preferable in principle) is often limited to cases in which it is absolutely necessary. In many cases, superimposition of data collected at different times at the moment of data analysis is sufficient. Some imaging modalities (such as optical) generate a small amount of mutual interference with others modalities (such as EEG or ERPs, fMRI, and TMS) and therefore appear particularly suited for concurrent recording and for providing a bridge across techniques.

In fusing data from different imaging methods, it is critical that the differences among the modalities be taken into account. As such, the relative roles of the various measures need to be conceptualized in a theoretical model describing their mutual relationship. The best understood integration issues relate to the spatial and temporal superimposition between measures. Spatial superimposition requires two steps: (a) three-dimensional reconstruction of the data in each modality and (b) coregistration of the two data sets. Similarly, temporal superimposition requires (a) modeling the temporal relation between the two measures and (b) their relative time-locking. In other words, the two sets of measures need to be placed in the same space-time reference frame. Data fusion also requires understanding how differences in the underlying biophysical phenomena (as well as possible biases) affect fused data. For example, if one technique is particularly sensitive to cells placed in open-field configurations (such as EEG/ERPs or MEG) whereas the other is not (such as fMRI or optical measures), we need to consider whether the structures involved have open or closed configurations in evaluating the relationships between the two measures. Similarly, differential biases toward superficial versus deep structures need to be taken into account when comparing NIRS data with MRI data.

In summary, data fusion requires careful consideration of the various characteristics of the imaging modalities involved. This may require a series of studies comparing the measures. In the past 15 years, a number of studies of this type have been conducted (e.g., G. Gratton et al., 2001; Huettel

[5]This issue has lead to the adoption of a shared-instrumentation model (which involves access fees) for equipment that is too costly or difficult to maintain or operate to reside in a single lab. This is almost always the case for PET, SPECT, and fMRI, but it is more rarely the case for the other methods reviewed in this chapter.

et al., 2004; Logothetis et al., 2001), and presumably several more will be conducted in the future. Hopefully these studies will pave the way for a new approach describing brain activity as a complex, multifaceted phenomenon involving membrane, synaptic, and hemodynamic effects. The integration of anatomical information within this description may further enrich our knowledge of brain and psychological function.

References

Barinaga, M. (1997). New imaging methods provide a better view into the brain. *Science, 276,* 1974–1976. doi:10.1126/science.276.5321.1974

Dale, A. M., Liu, A. K., Fischl, B. R., Buckner, R. L., Belliveau, J. W., Lewine, J. D., & Halgren, E. (2000). Dynamic Statistical Parametric Mapping: Combining fMRI and MEG for high-resolution imaging of cortical activity. *Neuron, 26,* 55–67. doi:10.1016/S0896-6273(00)81138-1

DeSoto, M. C., Fabiani, M., Geary, D. L., & Gratton, G. (2001). When in doubt, do it both ways: Brain evidence of the simultaneous activation of conflicting responses in a spatial Stroop task. *Journal of Cognitive Neuroscience, 13,* 523–536. doi:10.1162/08989290152001934

Doss, R. C., Zhang, W., Risse, G. L., & Dickens, D. L. (2009). Lateralizing language with magnetic source imaging: Validation based on the Wada test. *Epilepsia, 50,* 2242–2248. doi:10.1111/j.1528-1167-.2009.02242.x

Fabiani, M., Gratton, G., & Federmeier, K. (2007). Event related brain potentials. In J. Cacioppo, L. Tassinary, & G. Berntson (Eds.), *Handbook of psychophysiology* (3rd ed., pp. 85–119). New York, NY: Cambridge University Press. doi:10.1017/CBO9780511546396.004

Franceschini, M. A., & Boas, D. A. (2004). Noninvasive measurement of neuronal activity with near-infrared optical imaging. *NeuroImage, 21,* 372–386. doi:10.1016/j.neuroimage.2003.09.040

Frostig, R. D., Lieke, E., Ts'o, D. Y., & Grinvald, A. (1990). Cortical functional architecture and local coupling between neuronal activity and the microcirculation revealed by in-vivo high resolution optical imaging of intrinsic signals. *Proceedings of the National Academy of Sciences of the United States of America, 87,* 6082–6086. doi:10.1073/pnas.87.16.6082

Frye, R. E., Rezaie, R., & Papanicolaou, A. C. (2009). Functional neuroimaging of language using magnetoencephalography. *Physics of Life Reviews, 6,* 1–10. doi:10.1016/j.plrev.2008.08.001

Gratton, E., Fantini, S., Franceschini, M. A., Gratton, G., & Fabiani, M. (1997). Measurements of scattering and absorption changes in muscle and brain. *Philosophical Transactions of the Royal Society of London: Series B, Biological Sciences, 352,* 727–735. doi:10.1098/rstb.1997.0055

Gratton, G. (1997). Attention and probability effects in the human occipital cortex: An optical imaging study. *Neuroreport, 8,* 1749–1753. doi:10.1097/00001756-199705060-00036

Gratton, G., Brumback, C. R., Gordon, B. A., Pearson, M. A., Low, K. A., & Fabiani, M. (2006). Effects of measurement method, wavelength, and source-detector distance on the fast optical signal. *NeuroImage, 32,* 1576–1590. doi:10.1016/j.neuroimage.2006.05.030

Gratton, G., Corballis, P. M., Cho, E., Fabiani, M., & Hood, D. (1995). Shades of gray matter: Noninvasive optical images of human brain responses during visual stimulation. *Psychophysiology, 32,* 505–509. doi:10.1111/j.1469-8986.1995.tb02102.x

Gratton, G., & Fabiani, M. (2003). The event related optical signal (EROS) in visual cortex: Replicability, consistency, localization and resolution. *Psychophysiology, 40,* 561–571. doi:10.1111/1469-8986.00058

Gratton, G., & Fabiani, M. (2009). Fast optical signals: Principles, methods, and experimental results. In R. Frostig (Ed.), *In vivo optical imaging of brain* (2nd ed., pp. 435–460). Boca Raton, FL: CRC Press. doi:10.1201/9781420076851.ch15

Gratton, G., Fabiani, M., Friedman, D., Franceschini, M. A., Fantini, S., Corballis, P. M., & Gratton, E. (1995). Rapid changes of optical parameters in the human brain during a tapping task. *Journal of Cognitive Neuroscience, 7,* 446–456. doi:10.1162/jocn.1995.7.4.446

Gratton, G., Fabiani, M., Goodman-Wood, M. R., & DeSoto, M. C. (1998). Memory-driven processing in human medial occipital cortex: An event-related optical signal (EROS) study. *Psychophysiology, 35,* 348–351. doi:10.1017/S0048577298001292

Gratton, G., Goodman-Wood, M. R., & Fabiani, M. (2001). Comparison of neuronal and hemodynamic measure of the brain response to visual stimulation: An optical imaging study. *Human Brain Mapping, 13,* 13–25. doi:10.1002/hbm.1021

Gratton, G., Rykhlevskaia, E., Wee, E., Leaver, E., & Fabiani, M. (2009). Does white matter matter? Spatiotemporal dynamics of task switching in aging. *Journal of Cognitive Neuroscience, 21,* 1380–1395.

Gratton, G., Sarno, A. J., Maclin, E., Corballis, P. M., & Fabiani, M. (2000). Toward non-invasive 3-D imaging of the time course of cortical activity: Investigation of the depth of the event-related optical signal (EROS). *NeuroImage, 11*, 491–504. doi:10.1006/nimg.2000.0565

Hari, R. (1996). MEG in the study of human cortical functions. *Electroencephalography and Clinical Neurophysiology Supplement, 47*, 47–54.

Hari, R., Levänen, S., & Raij, T. (2000). Timing of human cortical functions during cognition: Role of MEG. *Trends in Cognitive Sciences, 4*, 455–462. doi:10.1016/S1364-6613(00)01549-7

Hopf, J. M., Boehler, C. N., Schoenfeld, M. A., Heinze, H. J., & Tsotsos, J. K. (2010). The spatial profile of the focus of attention in visual search: Insights from MEG recordings. *Vision Research, 50*, 1312–1320.

Huettel, S. A., McKeown, M. J., Song, A. W., Hart, S., Spencer, D. D., Allison, T., & McCarthy, G. (2004). Linking hemodynamic and electrophysiological measures of brain activity: Evidence from functional MRI and intracranial field potentials. *Cerebral Cortex, 14*, 165–173. doi:10.1093/cercor/bhg115

Jagust, W. (2009). Mapping brain beta-amyloid. *Current Opinion in Neurology, 22*, 356–361. doi:10.1097/WCO.0b013e32832d93c7

Kato, T., Kamei, A., Takashima, S., & Ozaki, T. (1993). Human visual cortical function during photic stimulation monitoring by means of near-infrared spectroscopy. *Journal of Cerebral Blood Flow and Metabolism, 13*, 516–520.

LaBerge, D., & Buchsbaum, M. S. (1990). Positron emission tomographic measurements of pulvinar activity during an attention task. *Journal of Neuroscience, 10*, 613–619.

Logothetis, N. K., Pauls, J., Augath, M., Trinath, T., & Oeltermann, A. (2001). Neurophysiological investigation of the basis of the fMRI signal. *Nature, 412*, 150–157. doi:10.1038/35084005

Low, K. A., Leaver, E. E., Kramer, A. F., Fabiani, M., & Gratton, G. (2009). Share or compete? Load-dependent recruitment of prefrontal cortex during dual-task performance. *Psychophysiology, 46*, 1–11.

Mackert, B-M., Leistnera, S., Sander, T., Liebert, A., Wabnitz, H., Burghoff, M., . . . Curio, G. (2008). Dynamics of cortical neurovascular coupling analyzed by simultaneous DC-magnetoencephalography and time-resolved near-infrared spectroscopy. *NeuroImage, 39*, 979–986. doi:10.1016/j.neuroimage.2007.09.037

Maclin, E. L., Gratton, G., & Fabiani, M. (2003). Optimum Filtering for EROS Measurements. *Psychophysiology, 40*, 542–547. doi:10.1111/1469-8986.00056

Maclin, E. L., Low, K. A., Sable, J. J., Fabiani, M., & Gratton, G. (2004). The Event Related Optical Signal (EROS) to electrical stimulation of the median nerve. *NeuroImage, 21*, 1798–1804. doi:10.1016/j.neuroimage.2003.11.019

Medvedev, A. V., Kainerstorfer, J., Borisov, S. V., Barbour, R. L., & VanMeter, J. (2008). Event-related fast optical signal in a rapid object recognition task: Improving detection by the independent component analysis. *Brain Research, 1236*, 145–158. doi:10.1016/j.brainres.2008.07.122

Nordberg, A. (2010). Amyloid imaging in early detection of Alzheimer's disease. *Neuro-Degenerative Diseases, 7*(1–3), 136–138. doi:10.1159/000289223

Parks, N. A., Maclin, E. L., Low, K. A., Beck, D. M., Fabiani, M., & Gratton, G. (in press). Examining cortical dynamics and connectivity with concurrent simultaneous single-pulse transcranial magnetic stimulation and fast optical imaging. *NeuroImage*.

Pascual-Leone, A., Walsh, V., & Rothwell, J. (2000). Transcranial magnetic stimulation in cognitive neuroscience–virtual lesion, chronometry, and functional connectivity. *Current Opinion in Neurobiology, 10*, 232–237. doi:10.1016/S0959-4388(00)00081-7

Petersen, S. E., Fox, P. T., Posner, M. I., Mintun, M., & Raichle, M. E. (1989). Positron emission tomography studies of the processing of single words. *Journal of Cognitive Neuroscience, 1*, 153–170. doi:10.1162/jocn.1989.1.2.153

Raichle, M. E. (1998). Imaging the mind. *Seminars in Nuclear Medicine, 28*, 278–289. doi:10.1016/S0001-2998(98)80033-0

Rector, D. M., Carter, K. M., Volegov, P. L., & George, J. S. (2005). Spatio-temporal mapping of rat whisker barrels with fast scattered light signals. *NeuroImage, 26*, 619–627. doi:10.1016/j.neuroimage.2005.02.030

Rinne, T., Gratton, G., Fabiani, M., Cowan, N., Maclin, E., Stinard, A., . . . Näätänen, R. (1999). Scalp-recorded optical signals make sound processing from the auditory cortex visible. *NeuroImage, 10*, 620–624. doi:10.1006/nimg.1999.0495

Rossi, S., Hallett, M., Rossini, P. M., & Pascual-Leone, A., & the Safety of TMS Consensus Group. (2009). Safety, ethical considerations, and application guidelines for the use of transcranial magnetic stimulation in clinical practice and research. *Clinical Neurophysiology, 120*, 2008–2039. doi:10.1016/j.clinph.2009.08.016

Sheridan, C. J., Matuz, T., Draganova, R., Eswaran, H., & Preissl, H. (2010). Fetal magnetoencephalography—Achievements and challenges in the study of prenatal and early postnatal brain responses: A review. *Infant and Child Development, 19*, 80–93. doi:10.1002/icd.657

Stephane, M., Ince, N. F., Kuskowski, M., Leuthold, A., Tewfik, A. H., Nelson, K., . . . Tadipatri, V. A. (2010). Neural oscillations associated with the primacy and recency effects of verbal working memory. *Neuroscience Letters, 473*, 172–177.

Stufflebeam, S. M., Tanaka, N., & Ahlfors, S. P. (2009). Clinical applications of magnetoencephalography. *Human Brain Mapping, 30,* 1813–1823. doi:10.1002/hbm.20792

Tateno, M., Kobayashi, S., & Saito, T. (2009). Imaging improves diagnosis of dementia with lewy bodies. *Psychiatry Investigation, 6,* 233–240. doi:10.4306/pi.2009.6.4.233

Tesan, G., Johnson, B. W., Reid, M., Thornton, R., & Crain, S. (2010). Measurement of neuromagnetic brain function in pre-school children with custom sized MEG. *Journal of Visualized Experiments, 36,* 1693. doi:10.3791/1693

Thut, G., & Pascual-Leone, A. (2010). A review of combined TMS-EEG studies to characterize lasting effects of repetitive TMS and assess their usefulness in cognitive and clinical neuroscience. *Brain Topography, 22,* 219–232. doi:10.1007/s10548-009-0115-4

Toronov, V. Y., Zhang, X., Fabiani, M., Gratton, G., & Webb, A. G. (2005). Signal and image processing techniques for functional near-infrared imaging of the human brain. *Proceedings of the Society of Photo Optics Instrumentation and Engineering, 5696,* 117–124.

Tse, C. Y., Tien, K. R., & Penney, T. B. (2006). Event-related optical imaging reveals the temporal dynamics of right temporal and frontal cortex activation in pre-attentive change detection. *Neuroimage, 29,* 314–320.

Van Horn, J. D., & Poldrack, R. A. (2009). Functional MRI at the crossroads. *International Journal of Psychophysiology, 73,* 3–9. doi:10.1016/j.ijpsycho.2008.11.003

Villringer, A., & Chance, B. (1997). Non-invasive optical spectroscopy and imaging of human brain function. *Trends in Neurosciences, 20,* 435–442. doi:10.1016/S0166-2236(97)01132-6

Wagner, T., Valero-Cabre, A., & Pascual-Leone, A. (2007). Noninvasive human brain stimulation. *Annual Review of Biomedical Engineering, 9,* 527–565. doi:10.1146/annurev.bioeng.9.061206.133100

Whalen, C., Maclin, E. L., Fabiani, M., & Gratton, G. (2008). Validation of a method for coregistering scalp recording locations with 3D structural MR images. *Human Brain Mapping, 29,* 1288–1301. doi:10.1002/hbm.20465

Wolf, M., Wolf, U., Choi, J. H., Gupta, R., Safonova, L. P., Paunescu, L. A., . . . Gratton, E. (2002). Functional frequency-domain near-infrared spectroscopy detects fast neuronal signal in the motor cortex. *NeuroImage, 17,* 1868–1875. doi:10.1006/nimg.2002.1261

Zhang, X., Toronov, V. Y., Fabiani, M., Gratton, G., & Webb, A. G. (2005). The study of cerebral hemodynamic and neuronal response to visual stimulation using simultaneous NIR optical tomography and BOLD fMRI in humans. *Proceedings of the Society of Photo Optics Instrumentation and Engineering, 5686,* 566–572.

CHAPTER 30

COMBINED NEUROIMAGING METHODS

Christian C. Ruff

The scientific study of cognition and emotion has been fundamentally transformed in the past decades by the advent of techniques for functional neuroimaging and neuromodulation. The methods that have gained the most popularity among psychologists are functional magnetic resonance imaging (fMRI), electroencephalography (EEG), magnetoencephalograpy (MEG), and transcranial magnetic stimulation (TMS). Development of these techniques has made it possible to study cognitive processes and emotional states via their effect on behavior as well as by inspecting or manipulating intervening brain activity. Numerous psychological constructs—such as perception, attention, memory, language, action control, emotional states, and so on—have now been investigated in terms of underlying brain activity, and the novelty and worth of this work has been acknowledged by high public interest. The perceived increase in explanatory power that comes with the use of these techniques has led to the foundation of specialized learned societies for cognitive neuroscience, affective neuroscience, and social neuroscience. Moreover, other sciences that study human behavior (e.g., economics) have started to take note and have introduced neuroimaging into their field.

As exciting and promising as findings of brain-behavior relations are, their ultimate worth depends crucially on properties of the research methods with which they are derived. As described in several preceding chapters (see Chapters 26 through 29 of this volume), each neuroimaging or neuromodulation method can only capture, or influence, specific aspects of brain activity. Thus, it remains difficult to give one overarching explanation of how, for example, the act of reading this printed word is instantiated in our brains. Few would doubt that this mental act should depend on a well-defined set of neural processes, but researchers using either MEG or fMRI might give somewhat different accounts of what this set includes, simply because these techniques focus on different aspects of brain function (e.g., event-related potential [ERP] components, fMRI activations, and so on). This raises the question as to what common true brain state may underlie these method-specific observations.

This chapter gives an overview of methodological developments that attempt to deal with this fundamental problem. All of these developments focus on combinations of existing methods from the present armory of cognitive neuroscientists, an approach often referred to as *multimodal imaging*. Three such combinations are described and discussed: fMRI–EEG/MEG, TMS–EEG, and TMS–fMRI. These approaches allow researchers to capitalize on complementary strengths of two methods, thereby gaining a more complete picture of neural processing and reducing uncertainties associated with the use of each method in isolation. Of course, this does not come for free; multimodal imaging techniques are technically and conceptually more complicated than the use of each single method and currently are used by only a few groups worldwide. But it may only be a matter of time until standardized solutions are established and these methods are employed by the community at large.

DOI: 10.1037/13619-031
APA Handbook of Research Methods in Psychology: Vol. 1. Foundations, Planning, Measures, and Psychometrics, H. Cooper (Editor-in-Chief)

The chapter begins with a brief description of the basic mechanisms of action for EEG/MEG, fMRI, and TMS. Because detailed accounts of these methods are given in the preceding chapters (see Chapters 26 through 29 of this volume), this section outlines only the strengths and shortcomings of these techniques, hence motivating their multimodal combination. I then describe the three possible multimodal combinations in detail in separate sections. The sections start with the general rationale of each approach, give a brief outline of technical considerations, and discuss the unique insights that can be gained with the particular methodical combination by means of illustrative studies.

USES AND LIMITATIONS OF SINGLE NEUROIMAGING METHODS

EEG/MEG

EEG and MEG are somewhat related methods in that both measure electrical activity in the brain noninvasively, via signals recorded outside the head. Both methods rely on the fact that neuronal activity is associated with weak electric currents inside the nerve cells and in the extracellular tissue (for detailed mechanisms, see Chapters 26 and 27 of this volume). EEG can detect these currents as weak electric potentials at the scalp, via a set of electrodes mounted on the skin. MEG, in contrast, measures changes in magnetic fields associated with these currents.

Although the signals measured by MEG and EEG index somewhat different types of neural activity, both techniques occupy a largely similar niche in research on brain-behavior relations. Both methods measure neural activity directly via associated electric signals and can index neural activity with millisecond precision. Averaging EEG signal epochs following repetitions of one type of experimental event can yield an ERP. This technique is mirrored in MEG research by the averaging of event-related magnetic field changes to produce an event-related field (ERF). ERPs and ERFs visualize the typical time course of neural processing associated with a mental event, thus providing information about neural changes during different temporal stages of processing (for examples, see Chapters 26, 27, and 29 of this volume).

A further strength of EEG and MEG is that the acquired data are highly multidimensional and can reveal many different aspects of neural dynamics. For instance, both methods allow researchers to study changes in neural oscillations in different frequency bands (such as delta: 1–4 Hz, theta: 4–7 Hz, alpha: 8–13 Hz, beta: 14–30 Hz, and gamma: > 30 Hz). Changes in the power spectral density of each frequency band can be averaged for comparable experimental episodes to reveal systematic changes in oscillatory activity that are time-locked to experimentally induced mental events (for details, see Chapter 26 of this volume).

The strengths of EEG and MEG for brain-behavior research are complemented by equally salient weaknesses. For instance, the underlying biophysics result in EEG being most sensitive to neural activity in the neocortex, as firing of subcortical cell assemblies is not usually associated with clearly detectable electric potentials at the scalp (this problem is somewhat less severe for magnetic field changes measured by MEG; see Chapters 26 and 29 of this volume). Perhaps even more critically, it is usually difficult to determine the anatomical location of a cortical source for a particular ERP or ERF or for a change in oscillatory power, as infinite theoretical solutions exist that may result in a particular arrangement of electric scalp potentials or magnetic fields. Solutions to this *inverse problem* (of determining what precise intracranial sources produce observed signals outside the head) can be provided by mathematical approaches (e.g., see Horwitz & Poeppel, 2002; Laufs, Daunizeau, Carmichael, & Kleinschmidt, 2008). Nevertheless, there always remains a degree of uncertainty about the neuroanatomical origin of observed EEG/MEG signals. Finally, it may be critical that both methods are sensitive to the firing of only specific cell types and thus may index different types of neural activity: EEG signals are thought to mainly reflect activity of pyramidal cells that are perpendicular to the scalp, on the crown of cortical gyri, whereas MEG signals may be most sensitive to pyramidal cells located in the sulci, tangential to the scalp (Nunez & Srinivasan, 2006).

In sum, EEG and MEG offer psychologists good ways to study the precise temporal aspects of cortical processing associated with experimental tasks.

The data are multidimensional and provide several different approaches to cortical dynamics that are associated with mental states. These methods do not allow strong inferences about the neuroanatomical structures that show changes in neural activity. They also cannot reliably measure activity in many brain areas that are of interest to psychologists (for instance, various subcortical areas relevant for emotion processing and memory).

fMRI

fMRI measures neural activity only indirectly, via associated changes in blood oxygenation (a detailed account of the relevant physics and physiology is given in Chapter 28 of this volume). In short, oxygenated hemoglobin has different magnetic properties than deoxygenated hemoglobin, so that the ratio of oxygenated to deoxygenated hemoglobin (the so-called blood-oxygen-level-dependent [BOLD] contrast) can be readily detected by means of specific magnetic resonance (MR) image sequences. Neural activity leads to an inflow of oxygenated blood to the active tissue and hence to a local increase of oxygenated relative to deoxygenated hemoglobin. This so-called hemodynamic response to neural events is the signal measured by fMRI studies (for detailed descriptions, see Chapter 28 of this volume).

The major strength of fMRI is that it can visualize neural activity (indirectly via its metabolic consequences) throughout the whole brain with good spatial resolution (around 2–3 mm^3 at present, but less than 1 mm^3 may be possible on high-field scanners; see Chapter 28 of this volume). The high spatial resolution and the ability to measure BOLD activity for all regions of the brain with equal sensitivity make fMRI arguably the current gold standard for testing hypotheses about brain-behavior relations in humans (Logothetis, 2008).

The strengths of fMRI are fully complementary to those of EEG/MEG and the same can be said of its weaknesses. For instance, the temporal resolution of fMRI is relatively modest. The hemodynamic response to a discrete neural event is temporally sluggish, peaking at around 4 s to 7 s after the relevant neural activity and returning to baseline several seconds later. Further complicating matters, standard fMRI sequences covering the full cortex can only sample this hemodynamic response with a temporal resolution of seconds. Although standardized deconvolution procedures can nevertheless resolve neural events that are spaced within approximately 2 sec of one another (for details, see Chapter 28 of this volume), it is very difficult to use fMRI to make inferences about different temporal stages of processing during a trial. fMRI data thus normally only present a temporally averaged snapshot of neural activity associated with a mental event rather than a detailed account of associated neural dynamics (but see, e.g., Valdés-Sosa, Kötter, & Friston, 2005, for an overview of mathematical modeling procedures to infer neural dynamics underlying BOLD time series).

Use of the hemodynamic response to infer neural processing is not only complicated with respect to temporal resolution but also regarding the question of which aspect of neural activity is causing the measured signals. The relation between BOLD increases and neural activity is intensely debated. Issues that appear most relevant for researchers of brain-behavior relations include whether BOLD increases reflect mostly spiking output of neural populations or synaptic input and local processing within an area, whether BOLD increases reflect only activity of neurons or also of glial cells, whether neural inhibition of an area produces BOLD signal increases or decreases, and whether BOLD signal increases linearly with neural activity (for detailed discussion, see Logothetis, 2008). Answers to all of these questions will be important for the interpretation of fMRI results and for establishing links between the fMRI and the EEG/MEG literatures.

TMS

Both EEG/MEG and fMRI are purely correlative methods, revealing which electrical or blood flow changes in the brain are associated with experimental manipulations of psychological processes. Such correlative data have greatly advanced our understanding of brain-behavior relations, but they nevertheless leave doubt as to whether the observed brain activity is causally necessary for the observed behavior. Moreover, many neuroimaging findings leave open questions as to which aspect of the experimental situation may have triggered electrical or hemodynamic activity. In principle, only some of the observed brain activations may relate to performance of the experimental task, whereas others may reflect changes in task-correlated psychological or physiological context factors (e.g., arousal).

These shortcomings have triggered great interest in the use of noninvasive *neuromodulation* techniques, allowing tests of whether and how focal manipulation of neural activity in specific regions of the brain can affect behavior in experimental situations. The most popular of these techniques—TMS—works by electromagnetic induction (for details, see Chapter 29 of this volume). An encased copper coil (often consisting of two loops put together in a figure-eight form) is connected to a set of capacitors that store a large electrical charge. For each TMS pulse, this charge is released via an electric switch that shorts the charged elements through the TMS coil, leading to a strong current (several thousand amperes) passing rapidly (in less than 1 ms) through the coil. The current is associated with a magnetic field that falls off exponentially with increasing distance from the coil, but it can permeate head tissue without attenuation. If the coil is placed tangentially on the scalp overlying a cortical region of interest, the magnetic flux (rate of change of the magnetic field) associated with each pulse electromagnetically induces a current in the underlying conductive neural tissue. This current will elicit action potentials in neurons with appropriate orientations relative to the electric current (for a more detailed description of the biophysics of TMS and necessary apparatus, see Chapter 29 of this volume and Wassermann, Epstein, & Ziemann, 2008).

The neural activity induced by TMS can be used to mask or disrupt the neural processing necessary for an experimental task, if pulses are applied in an online fashion, during task execution. Alternatively, repetitive TMS (rTMS) can be used off-line, applying a long-lasting train of low-frequency pulses before task performance. This leads to changes in the excitability of the stimulated region that persist for a limited time beyond the stimulation period. Both approaches have been referred to as the *virtual lesion method* (e.g., Walsh & Pascual-Leone, 2003), as such reversible changes in focal brain excitability may provide a model for the behavioral effects of lesions to the affected brain structure.

A unique strength of TMS is that it allows truly causal evidence for the necessity of neural processing in the stimulated brain region for task performance. In this respect, TMS appears closely related to neuropsychological studies of deficits in patients with brain lesions; however, TMS can overcome many of the shortcomings of the lesion approach. It can be used to target focal regions in the brains of healthy people, who unlike patients do not suffer from possible side effects of clinical states, such as neural reorganization, medication, and so on. Moreover, all effects of TMS are fully reversible and can be studied on a within-subject basis, by comparing each participant during and after TMS with him- or herself during a matched control condition. Last but not least, TMS has excellent temporal resolution: Pulses applied in an online manner, during different temporal stages of task performance, can reveal the involvement of the stimulated region for each specific phase (see Walsh & Pascual-Leone, 2003).

Like all other neuroimaging methods, TMS has shortcomings. At present, it can only be used to target brain areas on the outer cortical convexity. Many subcortical and medial brain regions are located too far from the scalp to be reached by magnetic fields produced by conventional TMS coils. Another critical point is that the mechanism of action of TMS is still not fully understood. It is currently debated as to which types of neurons are most prone to be stimulated by the currents associated with TMS pulses, how exactly the artificial activity induced by TMS interferes with ongoing cortical activity that is relevant for behavior, and how the effects of TMS may depend on the current functional state of the tissue (see Chapter 29 of this volume and Wassermann et al., 2008). Finally, TMS studies, by themselves, provide no information as to whether observed behavioral changes are due only to disruption of neural processing in the region directly underneath the TMS coil or whether effects on remote brain areas interconnected with the TMS site may also contribute.

In sum, any researcher who uses EEG/MEG, fMRI, and TMS to study brain-behavior relations will only be able to focus on specific aspects of neural function (such as timing, neurophysiology, anatomical origin, cortical versus subcortical regions, or causality), while being partially blind to other aspects. Luckily it appears that the weaknesses of one method are usually the strength of another, motivating the combination of neuroimaging techniques to overcome many of these limitations. In the next sections, three such combinations will be discussed in detail, touching on both the conceptual and technical considerations associated with each.

EEG/MEG–fMRI

fMRI can provide detailed information about where in the brain neural processing increases during task performance, whereas EEG/MEG can reveal the timing and cortical dynamics of these effects. Hence, recording both types of signals during performance of the same task and combining their information may give a spatio-temporal perspective on cortical processes associated with the task. This very logic has been successfully used in several studies, as described in the section Sequential Combination of EEG/MEG and fMRI. But there are also more subtle methodological reasons for why EEG/MEG–fMRI combinations may be informative.

The biophysics and neurophysiology of electrical neural activity (as measured with MEG/EEG) and the BOLD response (as measured with fMRI) suggest that neural activations detected with either of these methods may not always correspond to those found in the other (Nunez & Srinivasan, 2006). Parts of the observed signals may be truly specific to either method because of each technique's unique sensitivity for certain types of neural activity, insensitivity for others, and method-specific artifacts (Debener, Ullsperger, Siegel, & Engel, 2006). Measuring both EEG/MEG and fMRI during performance of the same task may thus "separate the wheat from the chaff," identifying the types of neural activity that leave a trace in both modalities concurrently. Such shared neural markers can refine our understanding of the signals detected by both methods, resolve uncertainties about the spatial origin and temporal characteristics of the constituting neural processes, and provide strong evidence for a distinct brain state associated with behavior. Thus, now that many reliable effects have been documented with each method used in isolation, establishing correspondences between neural signatures

of cognitive processes in MEG/EEG and fMRI may be a crucial next step for cognitive neuroscience. Such data fusion requires either sequential, off-line combinations of the two methods, or online parallel acquisition of data in both modalities. Both of these approaches have advantages and disadvantages, as described in the following.

Sequential combination of EEG/MEG and fMRI.
From a technical perspective, sequential combinations of EEG/MEG and fMRI are straightforward. No special apparatus is needed other than the devices used for either method alone. The same participants take part in the same experiment twice, once in the MR scanner and once in the EEG/MEG setup. This allows individual combination of fMRI data and the corresponding ERP/ERF scalp maps and hence information on both timing and spatial localization of neural activity associated with the behavioral task.

The biggest challenge for off-line combinations of EEG/MEG and fMRI may be the experimental design, as it is crucial that the experiment be exactly replicated in the two different contexts. This is often difficult, as there are obvious differences between the two settings that may influence results. For instance, MR scanners are usually noisy and vibrate, and participants lie in a supine position, whereas EEG/MEG setups usually require complete silence and that participants sit upright. Moreover, differences in psychological state between experiments may affect results; such differences may include learning effects, effects of different session or condition ordering, different levels or fluctuations of fatigue across sessions, or different levels of task performance. Careful counterbalancing and close matching of all relevant context factors across sessions may thus be essential.

Off-line combinations of EEG/MEG and fMRI have traditionally been used for modeling cortical sources of the observed ERPs. Peak fMRI activations are taken to indicate likely candidates for cortical generators of electrophysiological activity, and these regions are used as informed guesses when trying to localize observed ERPs by means of fMRI-informed mathematical algorithms (see e.g., Dale et al., 2000; Horwitz & Poeppel, 2002). One of the first studies to use this approach was conducted by Heinze et al.

(1994), who used positron emission tomography (PET; see Chapter 29 of this volume) rather than fMRI to identify brain regions in visual cortex that showed higher metabolic activity during attention to one hemifield of a display versus the other. Such attention-responsive regions were found in contralateral extrastriate cortex in the fusiform gyri. ERPs recorded in the same participants revealed significant modulations at the scalp contralateral to the side of attention, at 80 ms to 130 ms after stimulus onset. A dipole-fit model suggested that the extrastriate regions identified with PET were indeed likely generators of the ERPs identified with EEG. Fusing PET and EEG data thus demonstrated that effects of spatial attention in extrastriate visual cortex presumably arise at an early stage of stimulus processing (80 ms–130 ms after stimulus onset). Following this initial study, subsequent fMRI–EEG (Martínez et al., 1999) and fMRI–EEG–MEG (Noesselt et al., 2002) studies further demonstrated that BOLD activity increases in striate visual cortex during spatial attention reflect delayed (emerging 140 ms after stimulus onset) and hence presumably reentrant neural activity. All of these combined multimodal neuroimaging studies reveal a spatio-temporal profile of neural activity that could not have been derived with any method alone.

A second interesting way in which off-line EEG/MEG and fMRI data can be combined is based on parametric stimulus variations to elicit changes in both ERPs and fMRI data. The parametric manipulation is used to elicit a neural process that can be identified in parallel for both the ERP and fMRI data, via its association with the same experimental variable. For example, Horovitz, Skudlarski, and Gore (2002) varied the probability with which an auditory oddball stimulus would occur in a sequence of tones. Separately recorded ERP and fMRI data showed that some ERP components, and BOLD increases in some cortical regions, covaried with oddball probability. The regions exhibiting such parametric BOLD changes to oddballs were thus unlikely to reflect method-specific variance (e.g., because of differences between the testing sessions) and could be interpreted as a likely neural origin for the parametrically increasing ERPs.

Concurrent combination of EEG and fMRI. A unique strength of EEG/MEG is that both methods can visualize dynamic and spontaneous aspects of neural activity with millisecond temporal resolution. These signal properties are lost in cases in which EEG/MEG is combined with fMRI in an off-line fashion, as corresponding stimulus-locked episodes have to be averaged to yield typical responses to events (e.g., ERPs/ERFs and average BOLD responses, respectively). For this reason, increasing effort is directed at recording EEG signals inside the scanner bore during fMRI. Such online EEG–fMRI allows researchers to relate those aspects of electrical brain activity that are hard to control experimentally and that are variable over time with information on metabolic changes throughout the brain.

Online combination with fMRI is not possible for MEG because it relies on recording weak magnetic field changes (in the range of femtoTesla [fT]). This is incompatible with the strong static magnetic fields (at present 1.5 to 7 Tesla in human scanners), switching gradients, and radio-frequency (RF) pulses inside an MR scanner. By contrast, EEG electrodes and cables can be introduced in the MR environment, but this combination is quite complicated and requires considerable methodical expertise. A comprehensive discussion of technical problems arising in this context is beyond the scope of this chapter, but interested readers can consult several reviews (e.g., Herrmann & Debener, 2008; Laufs et al., 2008; Mulert & Lemieux, 2010; Ritter & Villringer, 2006). The following paragraphs give a brief overview of dedicated EEG-recording hardware and procedures required to prevent equipment damage, ensure participant safety, and acquire artifact-free MR images and EEG signals.

All equipment used inside the scanner room (e.g., electrodes, cables, amplifier/digitizer) must be nonferromagnetic and must not emit RF noise at frequencies relevant for fMRI. MR-compatible EEG electrodes and conductive pastes must be chosen to prevent MR-image distortion. Such static effects of EEG equipment on MR images, however, are usually much less problematic than dynamic interactions of the MR scanner with the EEG equipment. That is, rapid changes in magnetic field gradients, because of the fMRI sequence or subject and equipment movement inside the field, can induce currents in the EEG electrodes and leads. These currents can pose a severe risk to the participant because they may lead to electrical stimulation and even tissue damage. The RF pulses used for the fMRI sequence can also lead to dangerous heating of the EEG electrodes and cables if these are resonant at the corresponding frequencies. It is thus essential that the electrode and wire arrangement be carefully tested before conducting any EEG–fMRI experiment, using the very scanner and sequence employed for the subsequent testing sessions with human participants. Moreover, several standardized procedures have been established to minimize participant risks associated with dynamic interactions of fMRI and EEG equipment (e.g., for details, see Laufs et al., 2008; Mulert & Lemieux, 2010).

Interactions of magnetic field changes and RF pulses with EEG equipment affect recorded EEG signals. The currents induced in the electrodes and leads by the fMRI sequence are much stronger than the signals generated by neuronal activity, and thus they overshadow the typical EEG signals. This so-called *scanner artifact* can be avoided if the acquisition of EEG and fMRI data is interleaved in temporal gaps between adjacent MR image volumes (e.g., Bonmassar et al., 2001). If measurements are spaced apart appropriately, the temporal delay of the BOLD response then allows matching of episodes in both signals that correspond to the same neural events. However, this approach cannot provide EEG signal types that need to be identified in longer periods of continuous data acquisition (e.g., oscillatory activity).

Most current studies hence record EEG concurrently with fMRI and attempt to exclude the scanner artifact by using filtering and correction routines that rely on knowledge about its shape. A prerequisite for this approach is an amplifier with sufficient bandwidth to capture the full range of the scanner artifact without being driven into saturation but still with enough sensitivity for small signal fluctuations in all frequency bands represented in the EEG. Moreover, unbiased sampling or even minimization of the artifact can be achieved by synchronizing EEG acquisition with gradient switching in the fMRI sequence. Using such special hardware and data acquisition routines in conjunction with filtering

and correction algorithms usually allows successful removal of the scanner artifact from concurrent EEG–fMRI data sets (e.g., Ritter & Villringer, 2006).

More problematic to remove is a second artifact that is usually present in combined EEG–fMRI data. The *ballistocardiac artifact* results from the participant's heartbeat, which triggers small head movements, movements of electrodes overlying superficial blood vessels, and pulsatile blood flow in large body vessels. In contrast to the scanner gradients, this artifact is largely unpredictable a priori because it is less periodic and stable, and less distinct from the electric activity measured by EEG (see e.g., Herrmann & Debener, 2008). Finally, movements of the head and equipment unrelated to blood flow can also produce artifacts that are even harder to remove from the data (and may pose a safety risk, as described previously). It is therefore advisable that the participant's head and all equipment be fixated inside the bore with cushions or sandbags and that scanner sequences are tested so as not to induce too much vibration inside the bore (Laufs et al., 2008).

A final technical consideration concerns data analysis. The previous section on off-line EEG–fMRI introduced the strategy of using BOLD changes to inform the analysis of EEG data, in particular source modeling for ERP components. A similar strategy can be employed for concurrently acquired EEG–fMRI data but now with the knowledge that both data sets were recorded under exactly the same circumstances. Conversely, effects in the EEG data (ERPs, oscillations, and so on) can be used to analyze fMRI data for corresponding BOLD changes. Both of these strategies are often referred to as asymmetrical because they constrain analysis of signals recorded in one modality by detailed information on effects in the other modality. Such analyses can be biased because not all neural processes that generate one type of signal may also induce responses detected by the other method (Debener et al., 2006). Hence asymmetrical analyses may be partially blind to effects that are only expressed in one modality. This deficit may be overcome using analysis strategies that explicitly attempt to model how neural activity translates into the effects measured by both methods. Several such symmetrical analysis approaches—that give equal weight to both modalities—have been developed (e.g., see Daunizeau, Laufs, & Friston, 2010).

From a conceptual perspective, the major advantage of acquiring EEG concurrently with fMRI lies in the ability to study spontaneous neural events that are not under direct experimental control but that can be defined via their EEG signatures. This strategy has been a major motivation driving development of concurrent EEG–fMRI because of clinical interest in the neuroanatomical basis of ictal and interictal epileptic activity (for an overview, see Mulert & Lemieux, 2010). Such pathological abnormalities in electrical brain activity occur spontaneously and are of very brief duration, so that concurrent recording of fMRI may be essential for determining the individual cortical sites where these effects originate. Although tremendous progress has been made in this respect, it has also become clear that BOLD increases are detected not only at the cortical loci where discharges are triggered but also at remote brain sites affected by spreading neural activity. This is due to the temporally sluggish nature of the BOLD signal, leading to integration of neural activity over much longer time frames than EEG signals. Hence concurrent EEG–fMRI does not measure brain activity with the same temporal resolution as EEG alone. Rather, the method enables researchers to use temporal profiles and dynamics of EEG effects to define different brain states and to investigate with fMRI which brain regions show correlated changes in metabolic activity (Ritter & Villringer, 2006).

This very logic has also been employed in sleep research in which different stages of sleep are usually defined via characteristic waveforms in the EEG (e.g., delta waves, sleep spindles, and so on). Concurrent measurements with fMRI have focused on the cortical origins of these waveforms and have used the online EEG information to define different sleep states that are then further investigated with fMRI. For instance, Portas et al. (2000) used interleaved EEG–fMRI to study how different levels of consciousness (wakefulness vs. non–rapid eye movement [NREM] sleep) affect the processing of auditory stimuli. The EEG measurements were used to define whether participants were wakeful or in NREM sleep, allowing a comparison of the fMRI-recorded BOLD responses to similar auditory stimuli presented during both phases. Auditory responses were largely comparable during wakefulness and sleep, and activity in the amygdala and prefrontal regions still differentiated between neutral and meaningful affective stimuli during NREM sleep. Portas et al. (2000) concluded that during NREM sleep, the brain still analyzes and classifies auditory input for its behavioral relevance; this conclusion could hardly have been reached without simultaneous recording of EEG and fMRI.

Spontaneous brain activity is relevant for research on epilepsy and sleep, and it is increasingly being investigated in basic cognitive and affective neuroscience. For instance, a classic finding from the EEG literature is that the power of neuronal oscillations in particular frequency bands (e.g., alpha over occipital electrodes) can directly relate to the participant's vigilance state. Endogenous fluctuations of such neural activity can be behaviorally relevant. For instance, the degree of lateralized suppression of alpha activity over occipital electrodes, immediately before visual stimulus presentation, can predict whether the stimulus is detected (Thut, Nietzel, Brandt, & Pascual-Leone, 2006). Characterizing which cortical regions generate cortical oscillations may thus inform neural models of cognition and behavior. Such questions are best answered with concurrent EEG–fMRI, and several studies are beginning to address this issue (e.g., Scheeringa et al., 2009).

Spontaneous brain activity oscillations can also be observed in fMRI data but at different time scales than in the EEG. BOLD signals in several networks of interconnected areas can fluctuate at temporal frequencies of around 0.1 Hz (e.g., Fox, Snyder, Vincent, & Raichle, 2007), even when no experimental task is currently performed. The current state of such endogenous activity fluctuations may influence subsequent behavior. For instance, Hesselmann, Kell, Eger, and Kleinschmidt (2008) showed participants bistable pictures that could be perceived either as a face or a vase, providing long breaks between adjacent stimuli. Whether participants perceived a face stimulus on a given trial was significantly related to the prestimulus level of spontaneous BOLD activity in the fusiform face area, a cortical region specialized for face perception. To understand the neural origin of such effects, it may be helpful to relate the endogenous, slow fluctuations of BOLD signals with the fluctuations of electrical cortical rhythms, as observed with EEG. This is only possible with EEG and fMRI recorded concurrently, and some studies have begun to study this relation (e.g., Mantini, Perrucci, Del Gratta, Romani, & Corbetta, 2007).

A final advantage of combined EEG–fMRI recordings is that this combination allows researchers to use information contained in trial-to-trial variability in ERPs (Debener et al., 2005; Eichele et al., 2005) or cortical oscillations (Scheeringa et al., 2009). This approach also defines variation of a brain state by means of EEG data; however, now this state is time-locked to stimulus presentation on each experimental trial. Variability in EEG signatures across trials is assumed to relate to dynamic changes in functional contributions of cortical regions; these regions can be identified by analyzing the simultaneously recorded fMRI data for BOLD changes covarying with the EEG components across trials. For instance, Debener et al. (2005) used concurrent EEG–fMRI of a speeded flanker task to record the single-trial variability in the error-related negativity (ERN)—that is, an ERP component reflecting the participant's monitoring of her task performance. ERN magnitude on a given trial could be used to predict reaction time on the subsequent trial, underlining that the ERN allows successful tracking of performance monitoring. ERN variability across trials correlated with BOLD signal in a circumscribed region in posterior medial frontal cortex. Although this general cortical region had already been implicated in performance monitoring by previous fMRI studies, concurrent EEG–fMRI made it possible to identify the precise area in which BOLD signal changes reflected dynamic, trial-by-trial changes in this cognitive function.

In sum, combinations of EEG and fMRI allow researchers to characterize neural activity with the temporal precision of EEG and the spatial resolution of fMRI. It is crucial to keep in mind that both methods do not necessarily index the same types of neural activity; combined measurements are nevertheless able to reveal distinct brain states expressed jointly in both imaging modalities. Combining EEG and fMRI enhances our understanding of the origins of EEG and BOLD signals, and our understanding of the relation between brain activity and cognition, emotion, and behavior.

TMS–fMRI

TMS occupies a distinct niche among the tools available to cognitive neuroscientists. It is one of the few methods that can demonstrate the causal necessity of neural activity in a brain region for a given mental function. Nevertheless, the use of TMS can greatly benefit from combination with correlative neuroimaging methods such as fMRI. For instance, purely behavioral TMS studies usually do not provide information on the neural mechanisms that mediate stimulation-induced changes in behavior (but see Harris, Clifford, & Miniussi, 2008; Silvanto, Muggleton, & Walsh, 2008). Conversely, TMS can add an interesting causal dimension to neuroimaging studies of functional brain responses because it can be used to directly affect neural function in one area and visualize the effects of this intervention on activity throughout the brain (see the section Concurrent Combination of TMS and fMRI). As TMS can have immediate, short-term, and long-lasting effects on brain function, the method can be combined with fMRI either sequentially or concurrently.

Sequential combination of TMS and fMRI.
Sequential use of TMS and fMRI requires no special hardware other than a conventional TMS setup and an fMRI scanner. No major technical problems need to be addressed for this methodical combination. The only point to note is that the TMS setup should be located in the vicinity of the MR scanner, so that the time between TMS application and fMRI can be kept to a minimum. This may be essential for some studies, as the neural effects of off-line TMS protocols only last for a limited amount of time.

Many purely behavioral TMS studies have nevertheless combined this technique with fMRI to determine stimulation sites for TMS by means of individual fMRI activations or anatomical scans. Only few regions in the human brain can be identified with certainty on the basis of TMS effects alone.

One example of such a region is the hand area in the primary motor cortex, which produces measurable motor-evoked potentials (MEPs) in hand muscles when stimulated (Rothwell et al., 1987). Another example is retinotopic visual cortex, in which TMS can lead to the perception of brief, spatially circumscribed flashes of light (so-called "phosphenes"; Marg & Rudiak, 1994). For regions in the association cortex, however, finding the appropriate stimulation site can be more complicated. One popular strategy is to acquire anatomical MR images for each participant and define the cortical stimulation site in these images on the basis of neuroanatomical criteria (e.g., via the individual patterns of sulci and gyri). Many brain regions in the association cortex show large variability in their position, however, and can only be properly defined by patterns of neural responsiveness to specific stimuli. For such regions, fMRI can be used in each participant before TMS to determine the individual stimulation sites for the TMS experiment. The optimal scalp position for TMS coil placement over an anatomically or functionally defined region can then be determined with commercially available stereotactic procedures.

As an example for this approach, Pitcher, Charles, Devlin, Walsh, and Duchaine (2009) asked whether different regions in extrastriate visual cortex show functional specialization for the processing of faces, objects, and bodies; or whether discrimination for all of these stimuli depend on similarly distributed neural processing in visual cortex. The previous fMRI literature had shown specific activations in three distinct regions during the viewing of faces (in the occipital face area), objects (lateral occipital area), and bodies (occipital body area), respectively. Pitcher et al. (2009) used TMS to study whether neural processing in each of these regions was indeed causally necessary only for discrimination of the preferred class of stimuli. The three extrastriate regions were defined in each participant by means of fMRI, and subsequent TMS experiments revealed a triple dissociation of discrimination performance in the expected direction: TMS of each fMRI-defined visual area impaired visual performance only for the preferred stimulus class, but not for the other two. This result provides evidence that visual stimuli are discriminated by the

activity of specialized processing modules in extrastriate cortex, and it demonstrates that purely behavioral TMS studies can greatly benefit from off-line combination with fMRI.

A diametrically opposite way to combine both methods is to acquire fMRI immediately following application of rTMS, to better understand the cortical processes that bring about TMS effects on behavior. This multimodal combination relies crucially on the finding that specific types of rTMS protocols lead to changes in cortical excitability that outlast the duration of the stimulation by periods of minutes to hours (e.g., Huang, Edwards, Rounis, Bhatia, & Rothwell, 2005; Nyffeler, Cazzoli, Hess, & Müri, 2009). Such protocols are often used to study causal contributions of a stimulated region to behavior, with the advantage that behavioral measurements are conducted after the rTMS and hence in the absence of TMS pulses and their side effects (e.g., sounds and tactile sensations at the scalp). It is essential for such approaches to know—or to be able to estimate—how long the neural effects of stimulation persist. This has been most convincingly characterized for rTMS of motor cortex, using MEPs triggered by single TMS pulses as probes of excitability changes for different time points following the initial rTMS (e.g., Huang et al., 2005). For regions outside the motor cortex, however, combinations of TMS with off-line fMRI (or PET) can be essential for providing information on the nature and duration of TMS-elicited changes in neural activity, both in the stimulated region and for interconnected brain areas (Eisenegger, Treyer, Fehr, & Knoch, 2008; Pleger et al., 2006; Rounis et al., 2006; Siebner et al., 2001).

As an example for this approach, O'Shea, Johansen-Berg, Trief, Göbel, and Rushworth (2007) used offline rTMS and fMRI to investigate short-term reorganization in premotor cortex. rTMS was applied to a region in the left dorsal pre-motor cortex (PMd) usually found activated during action selection, and fMRI was acquired immediately afterward, during a motor task requiring either action selection or simple movement execution. BOLD signal increases were observed during action selection in right PMd, opposite to the stimulated hemisphere. These BOLD increases in the hemisphere opposite to rTMS resembled the contralesional hyperactivity commonly observed after a stroke; such hyperactivity is often assumed to reflect compensatory neural activity sustaining task performance. O'Shea et al. (2007) directly tested this hypothesis in a subsequent study; in the aftermath of the same left-PMd rTMS protocol as used for the preceding fMRI study, they applied TMS pulses to right PMd during task performance. A behavioral deficit caused by TMS was observed, demonstrating that right PMd shows functionally relevant activity increases following neuronal challenge (rTMS) of left PMd. Only the sequential combination of rTMS and fMRI made it possible to obtain this finding.

Concurrent combination of TMS and fMRI.

A cardinal strength of TMS is its good temporal resolution, allowing researchers to selectively interfere with neural processing during specific trials in an experiment or even during different temporal epochs of task performance on a given trial. Harnessing these features of TMS requires specific online protocols that apply one or several pulses during task performance. Such protocols are increasingly popular in studying the neural basis of perception and cognition, and they can provide unique information when combined with concurrent neuroimaging measures such as fMRI. Before discussing some applications of concurrent TMS–fMRI in detail, the technical requirements for this multimodal technique are briefly discussed (for a more detailed description, see Bestmann et al., 2008; Wassermann et al., 2008).

TMS and fMRI both use strong magnetic fields, considerably complicating online combination of these methods. Starting in the late 1990s, a few pioneering groups developed special apparatus and procedures for this combination (e.g., Baudewig, Paulus, & Frahm, 2000; Bohning et al., 1998). For instance, only special nonferromagnetic TMS coils can be used inside an MR scanner. The presence of such coils will introduce some static distortion in MR images, but fortunately these distortions are often present only within a few centimeters of the TMS coil and hence only affect MR image sections that correspond to the outer convexity of the skull (Baudewig et al., 2000). A further requirement for

MR-compatible TMS coils is that they should be solidly encased and mechanically strengthened to withstand the considerable Lorentz forces generated by interaction of the magnetic fields of the TMS-pulse and the scanner. The resulting coil vibrations can be further minimized by robust mechanical holding devices that keep the TMS coil in position, while still allowing flexible positioning over the specific stimulation site (see, e.g., Bohning, Denslow, Bohning, Walker, & George, 2003; Moisa, Pohmann, Ewald, & Thielscher, 2009). Moreover, MR-compatible TMS coils need a cable of appropriate length to connect with the stimulator, which has to be located outside the scanner room or in specifically shielded encasings. This is because the stimulator contains ferromagnetic material and generates radio-frequency noise that would produce artifacts in the MR images. Any connecting cables from stimulator to coil should be passed through specific RF filters to prevent transmission of RF noise from the stimulator and other devices nearby into the scanning environment. Moreover, it may be advisable to electronically prevent recharging and other processes in the stimulator circuitry to induce currents in the coil that can affect MR image quality (Weiskopf et al., 2009).

Besides dedicated hardware, concurrent TMS–fMRI requires specific procedures to coordinate the stimulation with fMRI measurements. Application of a TMS pulse generates a strong, varying magnetic field, which can interact in many ways with the RF pulses used for a typical fMRI sequence (for details of the physics underlying fMRI, see Chapter 28 of this volume). Hence, a TMS pulse applied at the same time as RF pulses used for fMRI can distort the image or introduce artificial signal changes in several image volumes recorded subsequently (Bestmann et al., 2008). It is thus crucial to coordinate the timing of TMS pulse application with that of the fMRI sequence.

One strategy for this coordination is to introduce small temporal gaps between acquisition of adjacent image volumes (or MR slices) in which sequences of TMS pulses can be introduced. Such temporal interleaving ensures that MR image acquisition is not affected by TMS, even if the exact timing, frequency, and duration of the TMS pulse sequence varies. A major disadvantage is that this method is not well suited for event-related fMRI designs because TMS pulses always need to be given at the same moment in time with respect to the MR sequence (i.e., in the gap). A fundamentally different approach is to apply TMS pulses specifically during periods in each MR slice during which no gradients or RF pulses are applied by the scanner (e.g., during signal readout). This will lead to complete loss of signal for the slices during which TMS pulses are applied, but slices with TMS-induced artifact can be replaced at the analysis stage by appropriate signal estimates. Because this approach is highly flexible with respect to when TMS is applied during acquisition of an MR image volume, it is ideal for event-related fMRI designs of TMS effects. The frequency of TMS pulses given on each trial is constrained by the repetition rate of MR slice acquisition, and slight timing errors in TMS pulse application can strongly interfere with subsequent MR image acquisition. The best strategy for applying TMS during fMRI will thus depend on constraints imposed by the required TMS procedure, the designated type of fMRI design, and details of the technical setup.

So why undergo the effort to apply TMS concurrently with fMRI? One basic motivation is to find out how TMS affects neural processing throughout the brain. Knowledge about this can be essential in developing and optimizing TMS protocols to influence brain activity whether it is clinical contexts or for neurophysiological research. The unique contribution of concurrent TMS–fMRI is that it can visualize the immediate, short-term impact of TMS pulses on brain activity, whereas sequential rTMS–fMRI can only reveal medium-term compensatory changes in neural processing in the aftermath of rTMS. The concurrent combination is thus essential for researchers who want to evaluate the effectiveness of TMS protocols to immediately stimulate the targeted brain area. Moreover, concurrent TMS–fMRI allows researchers to use TMS pulses as controlled experimental inputs into the stimulated brain regions to study context-dependent changes in neural excitability of the stimulated tissue. This strategy has been used, for instance, to evaluate the effects of anticonvulsant pharmacological agents on cortical excitability (e.g., Li et al., 2010).

Assessing the neurophysiological effects of TMS might arguably be of peripheral interest to most psychologists and cognitive neuroscientists. Studies of brain-behavior relations can also benefit from the use of concurrent TMS–fMRI, however, because this method allows direct study of causal functional interactions between different areas of interconnected brain networks. Inducing a brief change in activity of one node of a brain network, by means of TMS, should influence activity specifically in interconnected brain regions that are currently receptive for incoming neural signals from the stimulated region. Hence, using fMRI to measure neural activity throughout the brain during TMS can help us to identify interconnected brain regions that are influenced in their function by neural signals from a stimulated site. This approach thus increases the explanatory power of fMRI, by adding a causal approach to the study of functional networks in the human brain.

This general approach, sometimes referred to as *perturb-and-measure*, was first established with combinations of TMS and PET (see Paus, 2005, for review). Subsequent TMS–fMRI studies (e.g., Baudewig et al., 2001; Bohning et al., 1998) mostly applied TMS to the hand representation of the motor cortex, as the resulting MEPs in hand muscles provided some external validation—in addition to the measured BOLD changes—for the effectiveness of neural stimulation. To infer that BOLD changes in areas remote from the stimulation site really reflect neural transmission of TMS-induced signals, it is crucial for such studies to adequately control for neural processing of unspecific side effects of TMS (any elicited hand movements, sound and tactile sensation of TMS pulses, eyeblinks, and so on). This can be achieved by comparing TMS pulses of different intensities, or different TMS sites, or TMS during different tasks. Using such strategies, several studies have now generally confirmed the notion that TMS of one cortical site during fMRI can elicit specific patterns of BOLD changes in interconnected areas, reflecting neural interactions of the affected regions with the stimulated site (for reviews, see Bestmann et al., 2008; Ruff, Driver, & Bestmann, 2009).

For example, Ruff et al. (2006) used concurrent TMS–fMRI to test whether a region in the frontal cortex of the human brain (the frontal eye field [FEF]) has the capability to causally influence activity in early retinotopic visual cortex. This had often been proposed in the literature on the basis of repeated fMRI observations that the FEF jointly shows BOLD activity increases with visual cortex when visual activity is modulated in a top-down fashion (e.g., during attention or eye movement preparation). The new experiment involved applying TMS to this region during fMRI, varying the intensity of right-FEF TMS from trial to trial. A distinct pattern of BOLD activity changes in retintopic visual areas V1 to V4 was found to covary with TMS intensity, with stronger FEF–TMS leading to activity increases for cortical representations of the peripheral visual field but to activity decreases for the central visual field. This pattern of BOLD changes caused by FEF–TMS was reliably different from the (null) effects caused by TMS of a control site, confirming that the BOLD signal changes in visual cortex did not reflect unspecific side effects of TMS pulses. The study by Ruff et al. (2006) thus demonstrated that neural activity in the right human FEF can causally influence processing in remote but interconnected retinotopic visual cortex and illustrated how concurrent TMS–fMRI can be used to test hypotheses about such functional interactions in the human brain.

The use of concurrent TMS–fMRI in cognitive neuroscience is still new, and many important properties of the method are just being established. For instance, crucial recent findings showed that remote BOLD changes caused by TMS change with experimental manipulations of context, such as levels of visual stimulation, motor performance, or tactile stimulation (reviewed in Bestmann et al., 2008; Driver, Blankenburg, Bestmann, Vanduffel, & Ruff, 2009). Such findings provide evidence for flexible changes in the functional impact of stimulated areas on interconnected brain regions. Adaptive changes in effective connectivity may be a fundamental property of neural processing in brain networks, which has been suggested by neuroimaging studies employing sophisticated analyses of statistical dependencies between activity time courses in different brain areas (Valdés-Sosa et al., 2005). The recent concurrent TMS–fMRI findings now confirm this notion and add a directed and causal dimension to existing analysis methods for purely correlative neuroimaging data.

A final important set of findings concerns the functional significance of remote activity changes resulting from TMS. If TMS is used to interfere with behavior in a trial-by-trial fashion, then concurrent fMRI can be used to study which short-term neural effects across the brain, remote from the stimulation site, may underlie the observed behavioral impairments. For example, Sack et al. (2007) applied TMS over parietal cortex during fMRI while participants completed a visuospatial task or a nonspatial control task. Effects of right-parietal TMS on reaction times and BOLD signal were found specifically during the visuospatial task. Crucially, BOLD signal decreases resulting from TMS were observed in the (stimulated) right parietal cortex as well as in a portion of the right-medial frontal gyrus thought to be interconnected with the stimulation site. The BOLD signal changes in both regions (right parietal and frontal cortex) correlated with the behavioral effects of TMS. This suggests that concurrent TMS–fMRI can visualize the areas of distributed brain networks working together during performance of specific cognitive tasks.

TMS–EEG

Brain-behavior questions motivating the combination of TMS and EEG are similar to those driving combination of TMS and fMRI. The focus of both approaches is on somewhat different aspects of neural activity, however. For instance, TMS–EEG allows us to focus on the timing and the dynamics of TMS effects on neural function rather than on the detailed neuroanatomy of implicated brain networks (as for fMRI). In principle, EEG can be used in many different ways to further specify the effects of TMS on neural activity. Some of these approaches relate to different analysis methods for EEG data (e.g., in terms of ERPs, oscillations in different frequency bands, or synchronization and desynchronization, see Chapter 26 of this volume). Others relate to the principle that, as for fMRI, EEG can be combined with TMS either sequentially or simultaneously.

Sequential combination of TMS and EEG.

Applying TMS to influence cognition and behavior requires some prior knowledge, or assumptions, about the neural process that is to be influenced by

TMS pulses. As outlined in the previous section, the brain regions to be stimulated are often determined by means of fMRI data acquired before TMS. Following a similar logic, EEG signals recorded before TMS experiments can be a powerful tool to derive the number, frequency, and temporal pattern of TMS pulses that should be applied to manipulate task-related neural processing. TMS protocols can be tailored on the basis of several different aspects of EEG data, for example, timing of ERP components or changes in neural oscillations in different frequency bands.

For example, Sauseng, Griesmayr, Freunberger, and Klimesch (2010) found with EEG that working memory maintenance was associated with increased power of neural oscillations in the alpha band, measured at parietal electrodes ipsilateral to the remembered hemifield (participants always had to maintain target visual stimuli on one side of a bilateral visual array, while ignoring distractor stimuli presented in the opposite hemifield). The alpha-power increase correlated across trials with the number of contralateral distractor stimuli. On the basis of these EEG findings, Sauseng et al. (2010) reasoned that the alpha-power increase may reflect neural suppression of task-irrelevant distractor information and set out to test this hypothesis with TMS. During the working memory retention interval of the task, they applied a series of TMS pulses over left- or right-parietal cortex, at a temporal frequency (10 Hz) corresponding to the band in which they had found power increases in the prior EEG study. This form of stimulation is thought to entrain neural oscillations in the alpha band and hence may amplify neural processes related to distractor exclusion. The authors indeed found better short-term memory performance when alpha-frequency TMS was applied contralateral to the distractors (ipsilateral to the targets), whereas stimulation with another temporal frequency had no such effects. This shows that information derived from prior EEG sessions can be used to tailor the temporal dynamics of TMS protocols to optimally influence corresponding cognition and behavior.

TMS and EEG can be combined sequentially to investigate medium-term effects of off-line rTMS protocols. As discussed previously, such protocols apply repetitive TMS pulses over an extended time to produce neural (and behavioral) effects that outlast the stimulation period. Any effects of such rTMS on spontaneous neural oscillations or ERPs can then be studied with subsequently recorded EEG (in analogy to how fMRI can be used to identify regions showing BOLD changes following rTMS). Studies using such approaches have yielded somewhat divergent results, depending on the precise stimulation site and rTMS protocol (for a review, see Thut & Pascual-Leone, 2010). But most studies demonstrate that this strategy can be used to validate and optimize the capability of an rTMS protocol to influence brain function.

In terms of technical setup, application of TMS following EEG is straightforward and does not require any special hardware or software on top of that needed for use of either method alone. Measuring EEG following TMS is somewhat more complicated, as electrode setup and measurement preparation for an EEG session with standard equipment can often take longer than the aftereffects of conventional rTMS protocols. Those researchers interested in this specific combination thus often fully prepare EEG measurements before applying rTMS, using a special setup of EEG-compatible electrodes (see next section for details).

Simultaneous combination of TMS and EEG.
TMS and EEG operate on similar time scales, rendering concurrent combinations of these techniques well suited to investigate neural and behavioral effects of TMS with millisecond temporal resolution. Efforts to apply TMS during EEG were thus started in the late 1980s (Cracco, Amassian, Maccabee, & Cracco, 1989; Ilmoniemi et al., 1997), only a few years after the groundbreaking technical developments that enabled TMS in humans (Barker, Jalinous, & Freeston, 1985). The greatest problem in combining TMS and EEG online are the severe artifacts introduced in the EEG, resulting from the strong currents, mechanical vibration, and peripheral nerve stimulations associated with each TMS pulse. Many of these artifacts can be successfully prevented or corrected, however.

Conventional TMS stimulators and coils can be used for combinations with EEG. It is advisable to use small coils and hold these firmly in position during the experiment (e.g., by special mechanical devices) to ensure minimal contact between the coil and electrodes used for the EEG. Any movements of the EEG electrodes relative to the head due to vibrations or movements of the TMS coil can produce artifacts in the EEG data or can even ruin the measurement. Conventional disk electrodes should not be used for combination with TMS because each magnetic pulse will induce large currents in these electrodes. Such currents may strongly affect signal quality and can lead to heating of the electrodes, possibly resulting in skin burns. Special TMS-compatible electrodes are now available to minimize current and heat induction resulting from TMS; moreover, specific procedures have been proposed to optimize electrode contacts on the head so that TMS pulses can be applied safely and with minimum artifacts. (For details, see Ilmoniemi & Kičić, 2010.)

Concurrent TMS–EEG requires special amplifiers that can deal with the large currents induced by each TMS pulse in the circuit formed by the head, EEG leads, and amplifier. Conventional amplifiers may saturate at these currents, leading to complete data loss for several hundreds of milliseconds following each TMS pulse. Some TMS-compatible amplifiers try to prevent the strong currents from affecting the EEG signal by means of dedicated electronics that block or weaken the induced currents in the amplifier circuits during pulse application (e.g., sample-and-hold mechanisms or attenuation). Other types of amplifiers record the EEG signal continuously during the TMS pulses, but modify sensitivity of the amplifier so that it does not saturate and recovers quickly from the induced current. Use of such amplifiers requires artifact correction routines, for example, subtraction of a generic template of the position-specific TMS artifact as determined in a control condition. This strategy can also be used to account for any possible artifacts associated with recharging of the stimulator following each TMS pulse (for further details on apparatus and artifacts, see Ilmoniemi & Kičić, 2010; Veniero, Bortoletto, & Miniussi, 200).

Besides interactions of TMS-induced currents and amplifiers, other types of artifacts can affect concurrent EEG recordings. For instance, TMS pulses can lead to polarization of stimulated EEG electrodes, and the resulting potentials may persist for up to hundreds of milliseconds. Such effects can be removed by fitting exponential functions to the data after each pulse. Moreover, each TMS pulse produces a characteristic sound and tactile scalp sensation; neural processing of these sensations will evidently affect the EEG. Comparison with appropriate control conditions (e.g., the same TMS protocol during rest or a different task) can help to remove any such unspecific side effects of TMS. TMS pulses can also stimulate peripheral nerves on the scalp and thus trigger muscle movement, resulting in strong artifacts lasting up to about 30 ms. These effects may be counteracted by reorienting the coil and reducing TMS intensity. Finally, TMS can trigger eye movements and blinks, which typically produce strong characteristic artifacts in the EEG. It is hence advisable to monitor the participants' eyes by means of eye tracking devices or dedicated electrodes.

Researchers have used concurrent TMS–EEG since its inception to investigate dynamic neural effects triggered by application of single TMS pulses. It has become apparent that a TMS pulse applied over a cortical site elicits a typical ERP waveform (Ilmoniemi et al., 1997). In addition to such TMS-evoked potentials (TEPs), several studies have found that TMS pulses can trigger a temporary increase in oscillatory activity (e.g., Fuggetta, Fiaschi, & Manganotti, 2005; Paus, Sipila, & Strafella, 2001), which may be expressed in different frequency bands depending on which cortical site is stimulated (e.g., alpha for occipital cortex, beta for parietal cortex, and fast beta or gamma for frontal cortex; Rosanova et al., 2009). Such studies can elucidate the possible neurophysiological basis of TMS effects on cortical processing and behavior. They also demonstrate that concurrent TMS–EEG may provide a tool to directly probe and compare dynamic properties of neural processing for different cortical systems and to compare these properties between different contexts (e.g., within subject for different cognitive contexts or between subjects for different groups of participants). For example, Ferrarelli et al. (2008) used concurrent TMS–EEG to compare the functioning of thalamocortical circuits in the brains of schizophrenic patients and healthy controls without engaging the participants in a behavioral task. The same type of TMS was applied over prefrontal cortex for both groups, and EEG recorded concurrently. A decrease in gamma-band oscillations was found over fronto-central electrodes for schizophrenic patients. This suggests that the brains of schizophrenic patients may exhibit a distinct difference in the dynamic function of thalamo-cortical circuits, as revealed by concurrent TMS–EEG in the absence of any potential confound because of task-performance differences.

Concurrent TMS–EEG can also establish a potential functional role for neural oscillations. It is often assumed that the effects of TMS pulses on neural function and behavior depend on the functional state of the cortical tissue at the moment of pulse application (e.g., Bestmann et al., 2008; Silvanto et al., 2008). This issue can be addressed directly with concurrent TMS–EEG by using EEG to determine the strength of cortical oscillations in the period before each TMS pulse and relating this strength to the resulting behavioral effects. For instance, Romei et al. (2008) applied TMS pulses over occipital cortex of blindfolded participants at an intensity around the threshold for eliciting the perception of phosphenes. Concurrent EEG was used to measure the strength of oscillatory activity in the alpha band in the period before each pulse for electrodes close to the stimulated site. TMS pulses that elicited a phosphene were preceded by lower levels of alpha activity than those that were not, suggesting that oscillatory activity in the alpha band for occipital electrodes reflects the excitability of visual cortex.

The section on TMS–fMRI introduced the notion that TMS to one brain area can affect neural processing in interconnected areas and that such remote effects of TMS can be used to directly study effective connectivity in brain networks. A similar logic has been applied by TMS–EEG studies since the early days of this technique (e.g., Ilmoniemi et al., 1997; Komssi et al., 2002). Such studies focus on the spread of cortical activity from the stimulated site to other regions, with a particular interest in temporal properties of such network interactions. Several studies have now used this approach to demonstrate differences in effective connectivity of cortical

networks between different contexts, such as different sleep stages (Massimini et al., 2005) or different states of consciousness induced by pharmacological agents (Ferrarelli et al., 2010). All of these studies illustrate that concurrent TMS–EEG provides an interesting research tool to directly trigger and assess the dynamic spread of neural activity in cortical networks.

Concurrent TMS–EEG can also be used to examine how manipulations of processing in one region (via TMS) can change ERPs or oscillations originating in specific interconnected brain regions during task performance. Any such effects reflect dynamic functional interactions between both sets of brain areas during task performance, not unlike effects observed in corresponding TMS–fMRI studies (see the previous section). The unique strength of concurrent TMS–EEG in this context is the excellent temporal resolution with which such interactions can be assessed. A major weakness, however, is the uncertainty about the anatomical origin of signals observed in the EEG data (see also the section on EEG–fMRI). Concurrent TMS–EEG is thus perhaps best suited for investigating remote influences on those ERP components, or cortical oscillations, that are well understood with respect to their cortical origin.

For instance, Taylor, Nobre, and Rushworth (2007b) used concurrent TMS–EEG to study how the dorsal medial frontal cortex (dMFC) may functionally interact with motor cortex during action selection under high or low conflict. On every trial, participants were instructed to respond with their left or right hand, by means of an instructing arrow stimulus. This resulted in the well-known lateralized readiness potential (LRP) in the EEG data, reflecting preparatory neural activity in motor cortex. Response conflict was induced on half of the trials by means of response-incongruent arrow stimuli presented alongside the instructing stimulus. On such conflict trials, the LRP was deflected positively, indicating initial partial activation of the incorrect response. Crucially, this effect was more marked on trials in which rTMS was applied concurrent with the visual cue over the dFMC. Error rates were generally increased during incongruent versus congruent trials but particularly for incongruent trials with rTMS over the dMFC. Taylor et al. (2007b) con-cluded from these results that the dFMC can caus-ally influence processing in the motor cortex to resolve conflict during action selection.

Conceptually similar approaches have been used to investigate how TMS applied over frontal or pari-etal cortex during visual attention tasks may influ-ence neural processing in remote parieto-occipital areas, both with respect to ERPs (Fuggetta, Pavone, Walsh, Kiss, & Eimer, 2006; Morishima et al., 2009; Taylor, Nobre, & Rushworth, 2007a) and anticipa-tory alpha rhythms (Capotosto, Babiloni, Romani, & Corbetta, 2009). All of these studies illustrate how concurrent TMS–EEG can reveal the cortical dynamics of functional interactions among remote but interconnected brain areas underlying task performance.

CONCLUSION

Over the past few decades, there has been rapid growth in the use of neuroimaging methods to study the brain basis of human perception, cognition, emotion, and behavior. The most popular methods (EEG/MEG, fMRI, and TMS) differ strongly in their sensitivity for different aspects of neural activity. Moreover, each method has its unique profile of strengths and weaknesses for making inferences about brain-behavior relations. No single method presently available represents the ideal tool for investigating, for all brain regions, whether specific temporal patterns of neural activity are causally nec-essary for a mental state of interest. For this reason, different neuroimaging methods are increasingly being combined in a single study to obtain optimal results in terms of explanatory power and hence a more complete picture of the neural processes underlying behavior.

The three combinations most frequently employed at present are EEG–fMRI, TMS–fMRI, and TMS-EEG. Studies using any of these combinations have the potential to elucidate the relative sensitivity of EEG, fMRI, and TMS to different types of neural activity. Even more important for psychologists, these methodological combinations can reveal dis-tinct brain states relating to behavior, which could not be assessed with either neuroimaging method

alone. For example, EEG combined with fMRI can characterize spatio-temporal neural processes (brain regions that generate specific patterns of ERPs or neural oscillations), whereas TMS combined with fMRI or EEG can demonstrate causal functional interactions among remote but interconnected brain regions. Such largely unexplored aspects of neural function may play a central role during the next few decades of research on brain-behavior relations. Sequential combinations of two neuroimaging meth-ods are technically straightforward and possible to implement with standard setup and procedures for both techniques. Simultaneous combinations, by contrast, require special hardware and software for safe and reliable combination and are used by only a few laboratories at present. But the history of tech-nological developments in neuroimaging suggests that the community at large may soon employ mul-timodal methods to enhance our understanding of how brain activity enables perception, cognition, emotion, and behavior.

References

Barker, A. T., Jalinous, R., & Freeston, I. L. (1985). Non-invasive magnetic stimulation of human motor cortex. *Lancet, 325,* 1106–1107. doi:10.1016/S0140-6736(85)92413-4

Baudewig, J., Paulus, W., & Frahm, J. (2000). Artifacts caused by transcranial magnetic stimulation coils and EEG electrodes in T(2)*-weighted echo-planar imaging. *Magnetic Resonance Imaging, 18,* 479–484. doi:10.1016/S0730-725X(00)00122-3

Baudewig, J., Siebner, H. R., Bestmann, S., Tergau, F., Tings, T., Paulus, W., & Frahm, J. (2001). Functional MRI of cortical activations induced by transcranial magnetic stimulation (TMS). *Neuroreport, 12,* 3543–3548. doi:10.1097/00001756-200111160-00034

Bestmann, S., Ruff, C. C., Blankenburg, F., Weiskopf, N., Driver, J., & Rothwell, J. C. (2008). Mapping causal interregional influences with concurrent TMS–fMRI. *Experimental Brain Research, 191,* 383–402.

Bohning, D. E., Denslow, S., Bohning, P. A., Walker, J. A., & George, M. S. (2003). A TMS coil positioning/holding system for MR image-guided TMS inter-leaved with fMRI. *Clinical Neurophysiology, 114,* 2210–2219.

Bohning, D. E., Shastri, A., Nahas, Z., Lorberbaum, J. P., Andersen, S. W., Dannels, W. R., . . . George, M. S. (1998). Echoplanar BOLD fMRI of brain activa-tion induced by concurrent transcranial magnetic stimulation. *Investigative Radiology, 33,* 336–340. doi:10.1097/00004424-199806000-00004

Bonmassar, G., Schwartz, D. P., Liu, A. K., Kwong, K. K., Dale, A. M., & Belliveau, J. W. (2001). Spatiotemporal brain imaging of visual-evoked activity using interleaved EEG and fMRI recordings. *NeuroImage, 13,* 1035–1043. doi:10.1006/nimg.2001.0754

Capotosto, P., Babiloni, C., Romani, G. L., & Corbetta, M. (2009). Frontoparietal cortex controls spatial attention through modulation of anticipatory alpha rhythms. *Journal of Neuroscience, 29,* 5863–5872.

Cracco, R. Q., Amassian, V. E., Maccabee, P. J., & Cracco, J. B. (1989). Comparison of human transcallosal responses evoked by magnetic coil and electrical stimulation. *Electroencephalography and Clinical Neurophysiology, 74,* 417–424. doi:10.1016/0168-5597(89)90030-0

Dale, A. M., Liu, A. K., Fischl, B. R., Buckner, R. L., Belliveau, J. W., Lewine, J. D., & Halgren, E. (2000). Dynamic statistical parametric mapping: Combining fMRI and MEG for high-resolution imaging of cortical activity. *Neuron, 26,* 55–67. doi:10.1016/S0896-6273(00)81138-1

Daunizeau, J., Laufs, H., & Friston, K. J. (2010). EEG–fMRI information fusion: Biophysics and data analysis. In C. Mulert & L. Lemieux (Eds.), *EEG–fMRI: Physiological basis, technique, and applications* (pp. 511–526). Heidelberg, Germany: Springer.

Debener, S., Ullsperger, M., Siegel, M., & Engel, A. K. (2006). Single-trial EEG–fMRI reveals the dynamics of cognitive function. *Trends in Cognitive Sciences, 10,* 558–563. doi:10.1016/j.tics.2006.09.010

Debener, S., Ullsperger, M., Siegel, M., Fiehler, K., von Cramon, D. Y., & Engel, A. K. (2005). Trial-by-trial coupling of concurrent electroencephalogram and functional magnetic resonance imaging identifies the dynamics of performance monitoring. *Journal of Neuroscience, 25,* 11730–11737. doi:10.1523/JNEUROSCI.3286-05.2005

Driver, J., Blankenburg, F., Bestmann, S., Vanduffel, W., & Ruff, C. C. (2009). Concurrent brain-stimulation and neuroimaging for studies of cognition. *Trends in Cognitive Sciences, 13,* 319–327. doi:10.1016/j.tics.2009.04.007

Eichele, T., Specht, K., Moosmann, M., Jongsma, M. L. A., Quiroga, R. Q., Nordby, H., & Hugdahl, K. (2005). Assessing the spatiotemporal evolution of neuronal activation with single-trial event-related potentials and functional MRI. *Proceedings of the National Academy of Sciences of the United States of America, 102,* 17798–17803. doi:10.1073/pnas.0505508102

Eisenegger, C., Treyer, V., Fehr, E., & Knoch, D. (2008). Time-course of "off-line" prefrontal rTMS effects–a PET study. *NeuroImage, 42,* 379–384. doi:10.1016/j.neuroimage.2008.04.172

Ferrarelli, F., Massimini, M., Peterson, M. J., Riedner, B. A., Lazar, M., Murphy, M. J., . . . Tononi, G. (2008). Reduced evoked gamma oscillations in the frontal cortex in schizophrenia patients: A TMS/EEG study. *American Journal of Psychiatry, 165,* 996–1005. doi:10.1176/appi.ajp.2008.07111733

Ferrarelli, F., Massimini, M., Sarasso, S., Casali, A., Riedner, B. A., Angelini, G., . . . Pearce, R. A. (2010). Breakdown in cortical effective connectivity during midazolam-induced loss of consciousness. *Proceedings of the National Academy of Sciences of the United States of America, 107,* 2681–2686.

Fox, M. D., Snyder, A. Z., Vincent, J. L., & Raichle, M. E. (2007). Intrinsic fluctuations within cortical systems account for intertrial variability in human behavior. *Neuron, 56,* 171–184. doi:10.1016/j.neuron.2007.08.023

Fuggetta, G., Fiaschi, A., & Manganotti, P. (2005). Modulation of cortical oscillatory activities induced by varying single-pulse transcranial magnetic stimulation intensity over the left primary motor area: A combined EEG and TMS study. *NeuroImage, 27,* 896–908. doi:10.1016/j.neuroimage.2005.05.013

Fuggetta, G., Pavone, E. F., Walsh, V., Kiss, M., & Eimer, M. (2006). Cortico-cortical interactions in spatial attention: A combined ERP/TMS study. *Journal of Neurophysiology, 95,* 3277–3280. doi:10.1152/jn.01273.2005

Harris, J. A., Clifford, C. W. G., & Miniussi, C. (2008). The functional effect of transcranial magnetic stimulation: Signal suppression or neural noise generation? *Journal of Cognitive Neuroscience, 20,* 734–740. doi:10.1162/jocn.2008.20048

Heinze, H. J., Mangun, G. R., Burchert, W., Hinrichs, H., Scholz, M., Münte, T. F., . . . Hillyard, S. A. (1994). Combined spatial and temporal imaging of brain activity during visual selective attention in humans. *Nature, 372,* 543–546. doi:10.1038/372543a0

Herrmann, C. S., & Debener, S. (2008). Simultaneous recording of EEG and BOLD responses: A historical perspective. *International Journal of Psychophysiology, 67,* 161–168. doi:10.1016/j.ijpsycho.2007.06.006

Hesselmann, G., Kell, C. A., Eger, E., & Kleinschmidt, A. (2008). Spontaneous local variations in ongoing neural activity bias perceptual decisions. *Proceedings of the National Academy of Sciences of the United States of America, 105,* 10984–10989. doi:10.1073/pnas.0712043105

Horovitz, S. G., Skudlarski, P., & Gore, J. C. (2002). Correlations and dissociations between BOLD signal and P300 amplitude in an auditory oddball task: A parametric approach to combining fMRI and ERP. *Magnetic Resonance Imaging, 20,* 319–325. doi:10.1016/S0730-725X(02)00496-4

Horwitz, B., & Poeppel, D. (2002). How can EEG/MEG and fMRI/PET data be combined? *Human Brain Mapping, 17*, 1–3. doi:10.1002/hbm.10057

Huang, Y. Z., Edwards, M. J., Rounis, E., Bhatia, K. P., & Rothwell, J. C. (2005). Theta burst stimulation of the human motor cortex. *Neuron, 45*, 201–206. doi:10.1016/j.neuron.2004.12.033

Ilmoniemi, R. J., & Kičić, D. (2010). Methodology for Combined TMS and EEG. *Brain Topography, 22*, 233–248. doi:10.1007/s10548-009-0123-4

Ilmoniemi, R. J., Virtanen, J., Ruohonen, J., Karhu, J., Aronen, H. J., Näätänen, R., & Katila, T. (1997). Neuronal responses to magnetic stimulation reveal cortical reactivity and connectivity. *NeuroReport, 8*, 3537–3540. doi:10.1097/00001756-199711100-00024

Komssi, S., Aronen, H. J., Huttunen, J., Kesäniemi, M., Soinne, L., Nikouline, V. V., . . . Ilmoniemi, R. J. (2002). Ipsi- and contralateral EEG reactions to transcranial magnetic stimulation. *Clinical Neurophysiology, 113*, 175–184.

Laufs, H., Daunizeau, J., Carmichael, D. W., & Kleinschmidt, A. (2008). Recent advances in recording electrophysiological data simultaneously with magnetic resonance imaging. *NeuroImage, 40*, 515–528. doi:10.1016/j.neuroimage.2007.11.039

Li, X., Ricci, R., Large, C. H., Anderson, B., Nahas, Z., Bohning, D. E., & George, M. S. (2010). Interleaved transcranial magnetic stimulation and fMRI suggests that lamotrigine and valproic acid have different effects on corticolimbic activity. *Psychopharmacology, 209*, 233–244.

Logothetis, N. K. (2008). What we can do and what we cannot do with fMRI. *Nature, 453*, 869–878. doi:10.1038/nature06976

Mantini, D., Perrucci, M. G., Del Gratta, C., Romani, G. L., & Corbetta, M. (2007). Electrophysiological signatures of resting state networks in the human brain. *Proceedings of the National Academy of Sciences of the United States of America, 104*, 13170–13175. doi:10.1073/pnas.0700668104

Marg, E., & Rudiak, D. (1994). Phosphenes induced by magnetic stimulation over the occipital brain: Description and probable site of stimulation. *Optometry and Vision Science, 71*, 301–311.

Martínez, A., Anllo-Vento, L., Sereno, M. I., Frank, L. R., Buxton, R. B., Dubowitz, D. J., . . . Hillyard, S. A. (1999). Involvement of striate and extrastriate visual cortical areas in spatial attention. *Nature Neuroscience, 2*, 364–369. doi:10.1038/7274

Massimini, M., Ferrarelli, F., Huber, R., Esser, S. K., Singh, H., & Tononi, G. (2005). Breakdown of cortical effective connectivity during sleep. *Science, 309*, 2228–2232. doi:10.1126/science.1117256

Moisa, M., Pohmann, R., Ewald, L., & Thielscher, A. (2009). New coil positioning method for interleaved transcranial magnetic stimulation (TMS)/functional MRI (fMRI) and its validation in a motor cortex study. *Journal of Magnetic Resonance Imaging, 29*, 189–197. doi:10.1002/jmri.21611

Morishima, Y., Akaishi, R., Yamada, Y., Okuda, J., Toma, K., & Sakai, K. (2009). Task-specific signal transmission from prefrontal cortex in visual selective attention. *Nature Neuroscience, 12*, 85–91. doi:10.1038/nn.2237

Mulert, C., & Lemieux, L. (Eds.) (2010). *EEG–fMRI*. Heidelberg: Springer. doi:10.1007/978-3-540-87919-0

Noesselt, T., Hillyard, S. A., Woldorff, M. G., Schoenfeld, A., Hagner, T., Jäncke, L., . . . Heinze, H.-J. (2002). Delayed striate cortical activation during spatial attention. *Neuron, 35*, 575–587. doi:10.1016/S0896-6273(02)00781-X

Nunez, P. L., & Srinivasan, R. (2006). *Electric fields of the brain: The neurophysics of EEG* (2nd ed.). New York, NY: Oxford University Press.

Nyffeler, T., Cazzoli, D., Hess, C. W., & Müri, R. M. (2009). One session of repeated parietal theta burst stimulation trains induces long-lasting improvement of visual neglect. *Stroke, 40*, 2791–2796. doi:10.1161/STROKEAHA.109.552323

O'Shea, J., Johansen-Berg, H., Trief, D., Göbel, S., & Rushworth, M. F. S. (2007). Functionally specific reorganization in human premotor cortex. *Neuron, 54*, 479–490. doi:10.1016/j.neuron.2007.04.021

Paus, T. (2005). Inferring causality in brain images: A perturbation approach. *Philosophical Transactions of the Royal Society of London: Series B, Biological Sciences, 360*, 1109–1114. doi:10.1098/rstb.2005.1652

Paus, T., Sipila, P. K., & Strafella, A. P. (2001). Synchronization of neuronal activity in the human primary motor cortex by transcranial magnetic stimulation: An EEG study. *Journal of Neurophysiology, 86*, 1983–1990.

Pitcher, D., Charles, L., Devlin, J. T., Walsh, V., & Duchaine, B. (2009). Triple dissociation of faces, bodies, and objects in extrastriate cortex. *Current Biology, 19*, 319–324. doi:10.1016/j.cub.2009.01.007

Pleger, B., Blankenburg, F., Bestmann, S., Ruff, C. C., Wiech, K., Stephan, K. E., . . . Dolan, R. J. (2006). Repetitive transcranial magnetic stimulation-induced changes in sensorimotor coupling parallel improvements of somatosensation in humans. *Journal of Neuroscience, 26*, 1945–1952.

Portas, C. M., Krakow, K., Allen, P., Josephs, O., Armony, J. L., & Frith, C. D. (2000). Auditory processing across the sleep-wake cycle: Simultaneous EEG and fMRI monitoring in humans. *Neuron, 28*, 991–999. doi:10.1016/S0896-6273(00)00169-0

Ritter, P., & Villringer, A. (2006). Simultaneous EEG–fMRI. *Neuroscience and Biobehavioral Reviews, 30,* 823–838. doi:10.1016/j.neubiorev.2006.06.008

Romei, V., Brodbeck, V., Michel, C., Amedi, A., Pascual-Leone, A., & Thut, G. (2008). Spontaneous fluctuations in posterior alpha-band EEG activity reflect variability in excitability of human visual areas. *Cerebral Cortex, 18,* 2010–2018.

Rosanova, M., Casali, A., Bellina, V., Resta, F., Mariotti, M., & Massimini, M. (2009). Natural frequencies of human corticothalamic circuits. *Journal of Neuroscience, 29,* 7679–7685. doi:10.1523/JNEUROSCI.0445-09.2009

Rothwell, J. C., Thompson, P. D., Day, B. L., Dick, J. P., Kachi, T., Cowan, J. M., & Marsden, C. D. (1987). Motor cortex stimulation in intact man. 1. General characteristics of EMG responses in different muscles. *Brain, 110,* 1173–1190. doi:10.1093/brain/110.5.1173

Rounis, E., Stephan, K. E., Lee, L., Siebner, H. R., Pesenti, A., Friston, K. J., . . . Frackowiak, R. S. (2006). Acute changes in frontoparietal activity after repetitive transcranial magnetic stimulation over the dorsolateral prefrontal cortex in a cued reaction time task. *Journal of Neuroscience, 26,* 9629–9638.

Ruff, C. C., Blankenburg, F., Bjoertomt, O., Bestmann, S., Freeman, E., Haynes, J. D., . . . Driver, J. (2006). Concurrent TMS–fMRI and psychophysics reveal frontal influences on human retinotopic visual cortex. *Current Biology, 16,* 1479–1488.

Ruff, C. C., Driver, J., & Bestmann, S. (2009). Combining TMS and fMRI: From "virtual lesions" to functional-network accounts of cognition. *Cortex, 45,* 1043–1049.

Sack, A. T., Kohler, A., Bestmann, S., Linden, D. E. J., Dechent, P., Goebel, R., & Baudewig, J. (2007). Imaging the brain activity changes underlying impaired visuospatial judgments: Simultaneous FMRI, TMS, and behavioral studies. *Cerebral Cortex, 17,* 2841–2852.

Sauseng, P., Klimesch, W., Gerloff, C., & Hummel, F. C. (2009). Spontaneous locally restricted EEG alpha activity determines cortical excitability in the motor cortex. *Neuropsychologia, 47,* 284–288. doi:10.1016/j.neuropsychologia.2008.07.021

Sauseng, P., Klimesch, W., Heise, K. F., Gruber, W. R., Holz, E., Karim, A. A., . . . Hummel, F. C. (2009). Brain oscillatory substrates of visual short-term memory capacity. *Current Biology, 19,* 1846–1852. doi:10.1016/j.cub.2009.08.062

Scheeringa, R., Petersson, K. M., Oostenveld, R., Norris, D. G., Hagoort, P., & Bastiaansen, M. C. M. (2009). Trial-by-trial coupling between EEG and BOLD identifies networks related to alpha and theta EEG power increases during working memory maintenance. *NeuroImage, 44,* 1224–1238. doi:10.1016/j.neuroimage.2008.08.041

Siebner, H. R., Takano, B., Peinemann, A., Schwaiger, M., Conrad, B., & Drzezga, A. (2001). Continuous transcranial magnetic stimulation during positron emission tomography: A suitable tool for imaging regional excitability of the human cortex. *NeuroImage, 14,* 883–890. doi:10.1006/nimg.2001.0889

Silvanto, J., Muggleton, N., & Walsh, V. (2008). State-dependency in brain stimulation studies of perception and cognition. *Trends in Cognitive Sciences, 12,* 447–454. doi:10.1016/j.tics.2008.09.004

Taylor, P. C., Nobre, A. C., & Rushworth, M. F. (2007a). FEF TMS affects visual cortical activity. *Cerebral Cortex, 17,* 391–399. doi:10.1093/cercor/bhj156

Taylor, P. C. J., Nobre, A. C., & Rushworth, M. F. S. (2007b). Subsecond changes in top down control exerted by human medial frontal cortex during conflict and action selection: A combined transcranial magnetic stimulation electroencephalography study. *Journal of Neuroscience, 27,* 11343–11353.

Thut, G., & Pascual-Leone, A. (2010). A review of combined TMS-EEG studies to characterize lasting effects of repetitive TMS and assess their usefulness in cognitive and clinical neuroscience. *Brain Topography, 22,* 219–232. doi:10.1007/s10548-009-0115-4

Valdés-Sosa, P. A., Kötter, R., & Friston, K. J. (2005). Introduction: Multimodal neuroimaging of brain connectivity. *Philosophical Transactions of the Royal Society of London: Series B, Biological Sciences, 360,* 865–867. doi:10.1098/rstb.2005.1655

Veniero, D., Bortoletto, M., & Miniussi, C. (2009). TMS-EEG co-registration: On TMS-induced artifact. *Clinical Neurophysiology, 120,* 1392–1399. doi:10.1016/j.clinph.2009.04.023

Walsh, V., & Pascual-Leone, A. (2003). *Neurochronometrics of mind: Transcranial magnetic stimulation in cognitive science.* Cambridge, MA: MIT Press.

Wassermann, E. M., Epstein, C. M., & Ziemann, U. (2008). *The Oxford handbook of transcranial stimulation.* Oxford, England: Oxford University Press.

Weiskopf, N., Josephs, O., Ruff, C. C., Blankenburg, F., Featherstone, E., Thomas, A., . . . Deichmann, R. (2009). Image artifacts in concurrent transcranial magnetic stimulation (TMS) and fMRI caused by leakage currents: Modeling and compensation. *Journal of Magnetic Resonance Imaging, 29,* 1211–1217. doi:10.1002/jmri.21749

CHAPTER 31

NONINVASIVE STIMULATION OF THE CEREBRAL CORTEX IN SOCIAL NEUROSCIENCE

Dennis J. L. G. Schutter

Transcranial magnetic and electric current stimulation are noninvasive brain stimulation (NBS) techniques that are used to study the relation between neurophysiology and behavior by influencing nerve cells with electric currents. This chapter provides an overview of brain stimulation techniques that are progressively finding their way into modern social and affective neuroscientific research. The main part of the chapter describes the basic principles, paradigms, and contributions of NBS to unraveling the neural mechanisms of motivation, emotion, and social cognition. In addition, critical analyses of safety, strengths, and weaknesses of NBS technology and current developments in the field are provided. The final part of this chapter gives a brief summary and some concluding remarks on the role of NBS in understanding the workings of the social brain.

TRANSCRANIAL MAGNETIC STIMULATION

Credited with the discovery of a physical phenomenon called *electromagnetic induction*, Michael Faraday (1791–1867) can be considered the founding father of modern transcranial magnetic stimulation (TMS). He was the first to show that when a conductor is placed inside a rapidly varying magnetic field, an electric current will be created in the conductor. In other words, time varying magnetic fields can be used to induce electric currents in

conductive materials such as nerve cells. Even though the main principle of TMS was discovered in 1820, it was not until 1985 that the human cerebral cortex was successfully stimulated by applying magnetic pulses in a noninvasive and painless manner (Barker, Jalinous, & Freeston, 1985). When the stored energy in the capacitors connected to the coil is released via an electronic switch (thyristor), an electric current starts to flow through the coil and a strong but short (~200 ms) magnetic pulse is generated (i.e., Ørsted's law). In accordance with Faraday's law of electromagnetic induction, the magnetic field will cause a secondary electric current in neurons. This secondary current gives rise to a transmembrane potential; when this potential is strong enough, neurons will depolarize and produce action potentials (Bohning, 2000). Figure 31.1 shows the basic circuitry underlying TMS. Figure 31.2 illustrates the principle of electromagnetic induction and current flows necessary for stimulating nerve cells (Hallett, 2007).

The magnetic field strength is highest directly under the coil and is usually on the order of 1 to 3 Tesla. However, the direct effects of TMS are confined to the superficial parts of the brain that face the cranium (i.e., cerebral and cerebellar cortex) because the strength of the magnetic field decays exponentially with distance (Hallett, 2007). The spatial resolution of the magnetic pulse for effective stimulation, which shares an inverse relation with magnetic field strength, can be in the order of several squared centimeters. The circular and eight-shaped coil types

Dennis J. L. G. Schutter was supported by an Innovational Research Grant (452-07-012) from the Netherlands Organization for Scientific Research. The author reports no conflict of interest.

DOI: 10.1037/13619-032

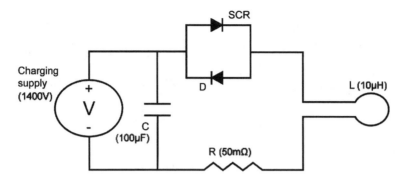

FIGURE 31.1.   Biphasic pulse circuit. C = capacitor, D = diode,
L = induction (coil), R = resistor, SCR = silicon-controlled rectifier.

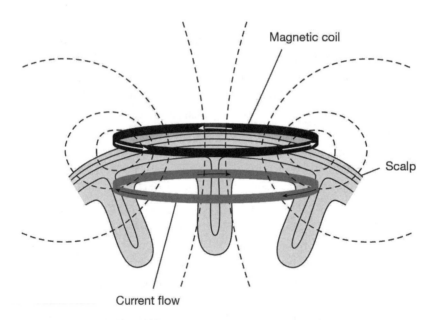

FIGURE 31.2.   Magnetic and electric current flows in the brain. From
"Transcranial Magnetic Stimulation and the Human Brain," by M. Hallett,
2000, *Nature, 406,* p. 147. Copyright 2000 by Macmillan Publishers Ltd.
Reprinted with permission.

are most commonly used in research and clinical applications. As can be seen from Figure 31.3, the distribution of the magnetic field depends on coil type. The highest focality can, however, be obtained by the iron core coil, which is a modified eight-shaped coil wired around soft iron (Wassermann et al., 2008).

Single-Pulse Magnetic Stimulation

The intensity of the magnetic pulse that is needed to excite nerve tissue depends on scalp-cortex distance and physiological properties of the stimulated tissue. When controlled for distance, the magnetic field strength that is required for activating neuronal

populations provides a direct index of cortical excitability of that particular population of cells, and it likely reflects excitability of axonal fibers of neurons and excitatory and inhibitory interneurons that act on these neurons (Moll et al., 1999). For example, in line with frontal lateralization theories of motivation, asymmetries in left- and right-cortical excitability have been associated with differences in approach and avoidance-related motivational tendencies (Schutter, de Weijer, Meuwese, Morgan, & van Honk, 2008). Interestingly, the opposite asymmetry has been found in nonmedicated patients suffering from major depressive disorder (Bajbouj et al., 2006).

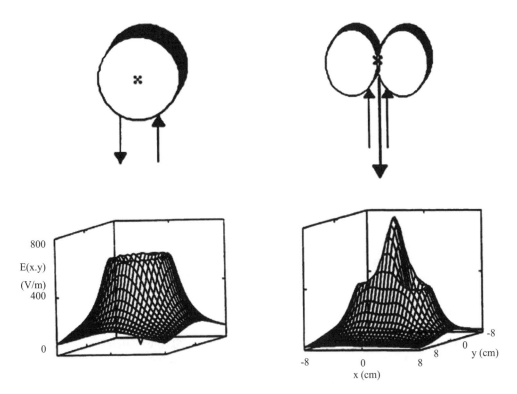

FIGURE 31.3.   Electric field distribution of a standard circular (left) and eight-shaped coil (right). The induced electric field of the circular coil (mean diameter: 66.5 mm) is at its maximum at the outer radius of the copper windings, whereas the induced electric field of the eight-shaped coil (mean diameter: 73 mm) is at its maximum (i.e., sum of both fields) at the intersection of the two smaller coils. From "Transcranial Magnetic Stimulation: A Primer," by M. Hallett, 2007, *Neuron, 55*, p. 188. Copyright 2007 by Elsevier. Modified from "Effects of Coil Design on Delivery of Focal Magnetic Stimulation: Technical Considerations," by L. G. Cohen, B. J. Roth, J. Nilsson, N. Dang, M. Panizza, S. Bandinelli, W. Friauf, and M. Hallett, 1990, *Electroencephalography and Clinical Neurophysiology, 75*, pp. 351 and 353. Copyright 1990 by Elsevier. Reprinted with permission.

On the macroscopic level, cortical excitability can be measured by studying the amplitude of the motor-evoked potential (MEP) recorded from different finger muscles following suprathreshold stimulation of the motor cortex (Figure 31.4a). Moreover, when a single suprathreshold TMS pulse targeting the primary motor cortex is preceded by voluntary contralateral muscle contraction, the MEP will be followed by a transient silencing of muscle activity, called the cortical silent period (CSP; Figure 31.4b). Pharmacological manipulation studies have shown that inhibitory gamma-aminobutyric acid (GABA) interneurons are responsible for the CSP (Cantello, Gianelli, Civardi, & Mutani, 1992).

Single-pulse TMS has been used to establish the role of emotional saliency on the interrelation between perception and action in a direct way. In a study by Hajcak et al. (2007), increased-baseline-controlled MEP amplitudes were found in response to the presentation of highly arousing scenes that were selected from the International Affective Picture System (IAPS). Evidence in further support of evolutionary views on the relation between threat signals and action readiness (Öhman, 1986) was obtained in another study that showed significant MEP amplitude increases in response to viewing fearful as compared with happy and neutral facial expressions (Schutter, Hofman, & van Honk, 2008). The latter finding provides direct evidence for motor cortex involvement in brain circuits that are devoted to threat and action preparation (Davis & Whalen, 2001). Furthermore, anticipatory anxiety has a facilitating effect on MEP amplitude, providing evidence for relations among worrying, anxiety, action preparedness, and frontal cortex excitability (Oathes, Bruce, & Nitschke, 2008).

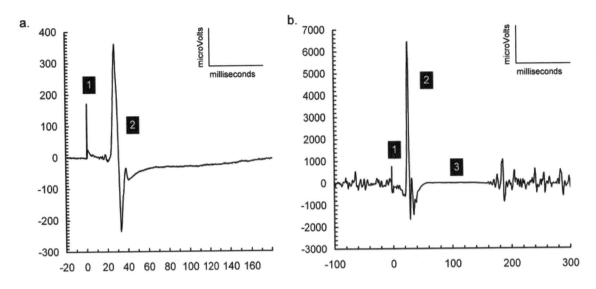

FIGURE 31.4. Motor evoked potential (MEP) recorded from abductor pollicis brevis (APB) to contralateral suprathreshold single-pulse transcranial magnetic stimulation (TMS) over the primary motor cortex (a). MEP followed by a cortical silent period (CSP) recorded from APB contralateral suprathreshold single pulse TMS over the primary motor cortex during voluntary muscle contraction (b). 1 = TMS pulse artifact; 2 = MEP amplitude; 3 = CSP.

In addition to the study of local excitability levels, single-pulse TMS can also be used to study interhemispheric connectivity between the cerebral hemispheres. Signal transfer between the hemispheres is based on a cortical mechanism of excitatory transcallosal fibers targeting inhibitory interneurons on the contralateral hemisphere and is known as transcallosal inhibition (TCI). TCI can be demonstrated by the suppression of voluntary muscle activity in the ipsilateral hand to a unilateral magnetic pulse, known as the *ipsilateral silent period* (iSP). This inhibitory process starts between 30 ms and 40 ms in response to a contralateral magnetic pulse over the primary motor cortex (Figure 31.5).

For example, abnormalities in TCI as evidenced by relatively long iSP have been observed in children with attention-deficit/hyperactivity disorder (ADHD; Buchmann et al., 2003; Garvey et al., 2005). Emotion dysregulation, impulsivity, and motor hyperactivity observed in ADHD may find its origins in suboptimal development of interhemispheric interactions and possible delayed brain maturation as shown by reduced transcallosal inhibition. The developmental aspect of TCI was further illustrated in a study by Garvey et al. (2005), who demonstrated that TCI increases with age.

In sum, single-pulse TMS can be used to study direct emotion, motivation in relation to cortical excitability levels, and functional interhemispheric connectivity.

Paired-Pulse Magnetic Stimulation

Cortical excitability is considered a general term for the responsivity of neurons to suprathreshold single-pulse TMS, whereas paired-pulse TMS provides additional physiological information on inhibitory and excitatory processes that underlie excitability levels in the cerebral cortex (Wassermann et al., 2008).

In a typical paired-pulse TMS paradigm, a low-intensity conditioning pulse is preceded by a suprathreshold test pulse to the primary motor cortex. When the interval between the two pulses is between 1 and 6 ms, the test pulse MEP will be smaller compared with the test MEP pulse without the preceding conditioning pulse. This phenomenon is known as *intracortical inhibition* (ICI) and reflects GABA-ergic activity of cortical interneurons (Ziemann, 2004).

If the low-intensity conditioning pulse is preceded 8 ms to 30 ms by the test pulse, then the test MEP amplitude will be larger than the test MEP

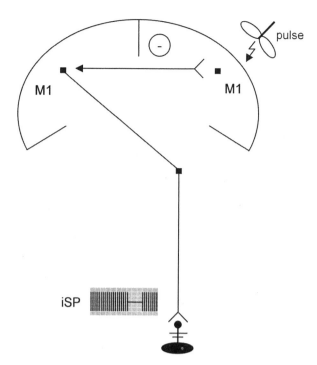

FIGURE 31.5. Single-pulse transcranial magnetic stimulation and transcallosal inhibition. − = inhibitory projections; iSP = ipsilateral silent period; M1 = primary motor cortex. From *Methods in Social Neuroscience* (p. 248), by E. Harmon-Jones and J. S. Beer (Eds.), 2009, New York, NY: Guilford Press. Copyright 2009 by Guilford Press. Adapted with permission.

amplitude without the conditioning pulse. This phenomenon is referred to as *intracortical facilitation* (ICF; Chen et al., 1998) and is associated with excitatory-related processes in the cortex (Ziemann, 2004). Typically, the degree of ICI and ICF are presented as the ratio between the unconditioned and conditioned test MEP amplitude. Figure 31.8 illustrates paired-pulse TMS associated with ICI and ICF, respectively.

As mentioned, paired-pulse TMS can provide indirect information on GABA-mediated inhibitory and glutamate-mediated excitatory processes in the cortex. Using paired pulse, TMS associations between reduced ICI of the frontal cortex and neuroticism as measured in the general population have been established (Wassermann, Greenberg, Nguyen, & Murphy, 2001). Reduced GABA-ergic inhibitory tone in the frontal cortex may provide a neurophysiological proxy for elevated vigilance and feelings of

anxiety. Notably, drug agents that act as GABA agonists have been effective in reducing feelings of anxiety (Breier & Paul, 1990), which suggests that the working mechanisms of anxiolytic drugs may involve changes in GABA-ergic function on the level of the cerebral cortex as evidenced by paired-pulse TMS (Wassermann et al., 2001).

Furthermore, deficits in GABA neurotransmission have recently been found in treatment-resistant major depressive disorder (MDD; Levinson et al., 2010). In this study, unmedicated MDD patients and medicated euthymic patients with a history of MDD were compared with healthy participants and tested on ICI with paired-pulse TMS. Patients with treatment-resistant MDD had lower ICI in the left primary motor cortex compared with medicated and healthy volunteers. Together with the significantly elevated motor threshold in the left primary motor cortex, these findings suggest that left-frontal cortex hypoexcitability is part of the pathophysiology associated with treatment-resistant MDD (Bajbouj et al., 2006). Interestingly, this observation concurs with assumed interrelations between underactivation of the left frontal cortex and the chronic absence of approach-related behavior seen in MDD patients.

Even though slightly different from single-pulse TMS, paired-pulse TMS can also be deployed to measure TCI (Ferbert et al., 1992). In the paired-pulse TMS variant, the MEP amplitude to a single unilateral pulse is compared with the MEP amplitude to a unilateral magnetic (test) pulse that is preceded by a contralateral magnetic (conditioning) pulse. When the test pulse is given ~10 ms after the conditioning stimulus, a significant reduction in MEP size of the test response can be observed as compared with when the test pulse is not preceded by the contralateral conditioning pulse. Figure 31.6 shows a schematic illustration of how TCI can be elicited in a paired-pulse TMS setup.

In a recent study, Hofman and Schutter (2009) found evidence for a link between an aggressive personality style and differences in interhemispheric connectivity between the left- and right-frontal cortex (Hofman & Schutter, 2009). Consistent with their proposal that an aggressive personality style is associated with asymmetry in the frontal cortex, higher levels of left-to-right TCI were correlated

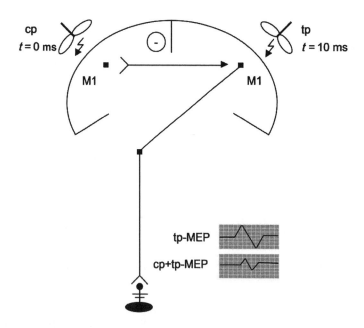

FIGURE 31.6.   Paired-pulse transcranial magnetic stimulation
and transcallosal inhibition. – = inhibitory projections;
M1 = primary motor cortex; cp = conditioning pulse (t = 0 ms);
tp = test pulse (t = ~10 ms); MEP = motor-evoked potential.
From *Methods in Social Neuroscience* (p. 247), by E. Harmon-
Jones and J. S. Beer (Eds.), 2009, New York, NY: Guilford Press.
Copyright 2009 by Guilford Press. Adapted with permission.

with a more aggressive personality style. In addition, increased left-to-right, together with reduced right-to-left, TCI was associated with an attentional bias for angry faces. These findings provide for the first time a neurophysiological mechanism for frontal asymmetry models of emotion and motivation.

In sum, paired-pulse TMS paradigms can be used to investigate unique aspects of cortical physiology in vivo and contribute to our understanding of how intracortical physiology and interhemispheric connectivity relate to emotion, motivation, and its disorders.

Repetitive Magnetic Stimulation

The effects of a single or short train of TMS pulses are transient in nature and the duration of the effects is usually very short. However, when single pulses are applied at a particular frequency for an extended period of time (e.g., ≥ 10 min), the effects can easily outlast the stimulation period. This repetitive TMS (rTMS) approach provides researchers with a time window for examining rTMS-related effects on the level of emotion and motivation. Intensity and frequency of stimulation determine whether rTMS

reduces or increases cortical excitability in the stimulated area. Repetitive stimulation between 0 Hz and 1 Hz, called *slow-frequency* rTMS, reduces cortical excitability, whereas repetitive stimulation at frequencies of ≥ 5 Hz, termed *fast-frequency* rTMS, increases cortical excitability (Wassermann & Lisanby, 2001). The physiological working mechanisms are still unclear, but slow-frequency rTMS may lower the resting state potential of neurons, producing a state of neuronal hyperpolarization, whereas fast-frequency rTMS may increase the resting state potential of neurons, causing a state of neuronal depolarization (Pascual-Leone et al., 1998). This is somewhat comparable to the long-term depression (LTD) and long-term potentiation (LTP) models involving electrical stimulation of the hippocampus in animals (Hoogendam, Ramakers, & Di Lazzaro, 2010). In addition, the effects of slow- and fast-frequency rTMS on cortical excitability may also depend on the modulation of GABA-ergic activity (Daskalakis et al., 2006; Khedr, Rothwell, Ahmed, Shawky, & Farouk, 2007). The effects of rTMS on behavior, however, are likely to depend on the current excitability state of the brain as well as the type of mental process that is being investigated (Silvanto, Muggleton, & Walsh, 2008).

Intensity of rTMS is another important parameter that contributes to its effects on the brain. Stimulation intensity is usually established by finding the lowest threshold for eliciting small finger movements by applying single-pulse TMS to the hand area of the motor cortex, the motor threshold (Wassermann, 1998). Studies have shown that that low-intensity (subthreshold) rTMS mainly affects underlying tissues, whereas high-intensity (suprathreshold) produces both local and distal effects (Ilmoniemi et al., 1997; Speer et al., 2003).

In social neuroscience, rTMS has been used to investigate frontal lateralization models in emotion, motivation, and decision making. From an evolutionary perspective, a fine-tuned balance between approach- and avoidance-related responses to rewards and punishments is crucial for survival and signifies psychobiological well-being (Davidson, 1984). This view argues against the affective-valence model, which is among the primary cortical-centered theories in the social neurosciences, and proposes that the left prefrontal cortex (PFC) subserves approach-related positive emotions, whereas the right PFC subserves avoidance-related negative emotions (Harmon-Jones, 2003). There is increasing debate on the positive-negative valence dimension in this model, however, because experimental findings from electroencephalography (EEG) research indicate that the left PFC is involved in the processing of anger and aggression (Harmon-Jones, 2003). This alternative model of motivational direction suggests that approach-related emotion (with its prototype, anger) is processed by the left PFC, whereas avoidance-related emotion (with its prototype, fear) is processed by the right PFC (van Honk & Schutter, 2006b, 2007). In an off-line slow-frequency (inhibitory) rTMS design employing an affective response task, vigilant and avoidant attentional responses to angry facial expressions were observed after right and left PFC slow-frequency rTMS, respectively (d'Alfonso, van Honk, Hermans, Postma, & de Haan, 2000). Slow-frequency rTMS to the left PFC resulted in (fearful) avoidance of angry faces because of a shift in dominant processing to

the right PFC (van Honk & Schutter, 2006b). Inhibitory rTMS to the right PFC, on the other hand, resulted in vigilant, approach-related responses to angry faces, pointing at dominant left PFC processing. In a follow-up study, reductions in vigilant attention to fearful faces were observed after slow frequency rTMS over the right PFC in a sham-controlled study (van Honk, Schutter, d'Alfonso, Kessels, & de Haan, 2002). Moreover, interleaved rTMS-EEG demonstrated that these reductions in fear responsivity were likely to be anxiolytically mediated and that the locally inhibitory effects of right PFC rTMS actually produce left PFC excitation (Schutter, van Honk, d'Alfonso, Postma, & de Haan, 2001). Finally, in an off-line sham-controlled slow-frequency subthreshold rTMS to the left and the right PFC of healthy volunteers, significant reductions in the processing of anger occurred exclusively after left PFC rTMS, whereas the processing of happiness remained unaffected (van Honk & Schutter, 2006a).

The field of neuroeconomics has recently tackled PFC laterality of risk-taking behaviors by way of sophisticated experimental paradigms using rTMS (Fehr & Camerer, 2007). Increased risky decision making was demonstrated in an experiment applying slow-frequency rTMS to study the right PFC (Knoch, Gianotti, et al., 2006). Twenty-seven healthy subjects received 15 min of 1-Hz rTMS (100% MT), after which participants played a risk task in which the probability of either getting a reward or punishment was determined by the ratio of pink-to-blue boxes displayed during each trial. Significant reductions were observed for the percentage choices of the low-risk prospect in right ($n = 9$) compared with left ($n = 9$) and sham ($n = 9$) rTMS. According to Knoch, Gianotti, et al. (2006), the right, and not the left, PFC are involved in actively inhibiting attractive options (i.e., high reward probability). Interestingly, the laterality findings are also in agreement with idea that the right PFC is associated with avoidance-related motivation and punishment sensitivity. Even though the authors propose that the effects were due to local disruption of right PFC function, providing causal evidence for right PFC involvement in the inhibitory cognitive regulation of risk taking, a shift in frontal cortical asymmetry to more approach-related motivation (reward) and reduced avoidance-related motivation (punishment) provides an explanation as well (Schutter, de Weijer, et al., 2008).

In another study, slow-frequency rTMS was used to examine the involvement of the right PFC in reciprocal fairness (Knoch, Pascual-Leone, Meyer, Treyer, & Fehr, 2006). Reciprocal fairness is linked to the moral standard that implies that, for instance, social behavior is reciprocated with kindness, whereas antisocial behavior is reciprocated with hostility (Rabin, 1993). Following right-PFC rTMS in comparison to both left PPC and sham rTMS, healthy volunteers accepted more unfair offers despite suffering personal financial loss (Knoch, Pascual-Leone, et al., 2006). The results suggest that the right PFC plays an important role in accepting unfair monetary offers. These findings build upon earlier rTMS findings that established a link between the right PFC and strategic decision making (van 't Wout, Kahn, Sanfey, & Aleman, 2005). In sum, the rTMS paradigm can be used to modulate the cerebral cortex and to address issues concerning the relation between cortical areas and their associated functions.

Safety

TMS is a noninvasive way to convey electric charges into the brain by way of a magnetic field that can elicit adverse events, of which the induction of an accidental seizure is considered to be the most serious one (Wassermann, 1998). Potential risk factors are a family history of epilepsy, certain types of medication that lower cortical excitability levels, brain trauma, metal inside the cranium, and exposure to fast-frequency rTMS at high intensities. General safety guidelines were introduced in 1998 and amended in 2009 by the International Federation of Clinical Neurophysiology (Rossi, Hallett, Rossini, & Pascual-Leone, 2009; Wassermann, 1998). TMS has been around for 25 years, and it is estimated that, around the world, tens of thousands of subjects have participated in research. Reports on accidental seizures have been extremely rare. In fact, slow frequency rTMS is increasingly being used to treat epilepsy by reducing cortical excitability in the epileptic foci (Santiago-Rodríguez et al., 2008). Some preliminary evidence suggests that rTMS exhibits neuroprotective properties and facilitates the growth of dendrites (Post, Müller, Engelmann, & Keck, 1999).

Sham Stimulation

A sham stimulation condition is routinely included in rTMS experiments for subject blinding purposes as well as to control for intrinsic procedural and time-related effects in the variables of interest that are with rTMS. An often-used method for sham stimulation is to tilt the stimulation coil 45 to 90 degrees, so presumably, the magnetic field does not reach the cortical target tissues. More recently, sham coils have been used that look identical to real coils but have an aluminum plate inside the housing of the coil that prevents the magnetic pulse from reaching the cortical surface. Even newer sham coils make use of additional electrodes that apply small electric pulses to the scalp that exactly mimic the scalp sensations, making it impossible to distinguish real from fake rTMS (Arana et al., 2008).[1]

Spatial Resolution and Localization

The surface area that is covered by TMS critically depends on the configuration of the coil (see Figure 31.5) and is usually in the order of several square centimeters. Furthermore, the exponential decay of the magnetic field does not allow stimulation of deep brain regions that are critically involved in emotion and motivation, such as the ventral striatum and amygdala. Even if the magnetic field was strong enough to reach deep brain regions, the large drop in focality that is associated with the large field would become a substantial problem in localizing functions at greater depths. Interestingly, local effects induced by suprathreshold TMS usually give rise to distal effects and are caused by signal propagation from the stimulated area to interconnected regions. Ilmoniemi et al. (1997) were among the first to successfully combine single-pulse TMS with EEG recordings. They showed increases in

---

[1]Even weak currents can have physiological effects on the brain (see also the section Transcranial Direct Current Stimulation later in this chapter), which could compromise the true sham concept.

electrophysiological activity over the right primary motor cortex starting approximately 20 ms after stimulation of the left primary motor cortex. The distal pattern of activation originates from nerve impulses that (via white matter fibers of the corpus callosum) activate the contralateral site. On the basis of paired-pulse TMS research, it has been suggested that the EEG activity is a correlate of transcallosal inhibition of the ipsilateral cortex. These transsynaptic effects provide a physiological basis for studying interconnected networks in the brain. Using this methodology, breakdown of cortico–cortical connectivity, for instance, has been demonstrated to correlate with the loss of consciousness (Ferrarelli et al., 2010). Other neuroimaging modalities including positron emission tomography have shown distributed effects in cortical and subcortical brain regions in response to rTMS over the frontal cortex (Speer et al., 2003).

The MEP recorded from hand muscles is the most common, although indirect, method for assessing cortical excitability. Even though epidural stimulation and recordings studies suggest that the effects of TMS have a cortical basis, subcortical and spinal contributions to the MEP cannot be excluded (Di Lazzaro et al., 2010). Furthermore, results found for the primary motor cortex cannot simply be generalized to other cortical areas that do not share the same underlying neural architectonics. Combined single-pulse TMS-EEG studies have found that TMS-evoked electric potentials over the primary motor cortex correlate to TMS-evoked electric potentials over the PFC (Kähkönen, Komssi, Wilenius, & Ilmoniemi, 2005). Additional paired-pulse TMS-EEG research on intracortical inhibition have yielded comparable electrophysiological results for the primary motor cortex and PFC (Fitzgerald, Maller, Hoy, Farzan, & Daskalakis, 2009). In addition, a positive relation has been observed between the motor threshold of the primary motor cortex and phosphene threshold of the primary visual cortex (Deblieck, Thompson, Iacoboni, & Wu, 2008).

In sum, the generalization of primary motor cortex to other cortical areas remains an outstanding issue, but increasing evidence indicates that the physiological workings of the primary motor cortex may nonetheless provide valuable information concerning the physiology of other cortical areas.

Developments in the Field

One way to overcome the generalization issue would be to develop a standard way of recording and interpreting online EEG responses to single-pulse TMS over a given area that represents a true marker for cortical excitability of that area. Interleaved TMS-EEG still faces technical challenges, however, which include how to deal with muscle, auditory, and somatosensory artefacts that contaminate the first 100 ms to 150 ms of the EEG trace. Fortunately, increasing numbers of research groups are starting to combine TMS and EEG technology and currently are working out ways to optimize the recordings and unravel the exact functional relations between EEG and cortical physiology (for a review, see Thut & Miniussi, 2009).

A recently developed TMS paradigm called *theta burst stimulation* (TBS) has proven highly effective in augmenting neuronal excitability by applying, in total, 600 pulse-trains of 50 Hz TMS to the cortex in a 5-Hz repetitive fashion (Huang, Edwards, Rounis, Bhatia, & Rothwell, 2005). According to Huang et al. (2005), TBS influences both excitatory and inhibitory intracortical processes, but the excitatory effects build up faster than the inhibitory effects, causing a net result of increased levels of cortical excitability. TBS is a rapid procedure that is capable of producing reliable and long-lasting (> 60 min) effects on cortical physiology and appears more effective than the traditional fast-frequency rTMS paradigms.

In addition to refining the stimulation paradigms, researchers focus on the development of the Hesed (H)-coil that can stimulate deep brain structures. Studies have shown that the H-coil is able to activate cortical tissue at a distance of 5 cm to 6 cm (Zangen, Roth, Voller, & Hallett, 2005). Despite holding great promise in targeting deep brain structures, optimizing the spatial resolution of the H-coil is currently the major challenge in targeting isolated areas.

Last, in addition to the traditional focus on the frontal cortex with respect to cognitive and emotive processes associated with social behavior, rTMS to the parietal cortex as well as the cerebellum has been used to investigate the contributions of these areas in the neural architecture of motivation and emotion (Schutter, Enter, & Hoppenbrouwers, 2009; van Honk, Schutter, Putman, de Haan, & d'Alfonso, 2003). In sum, despite the relatively short career of TMS in neurology and social neurosciences, its contributions have already been substantial in providing unique as well as novel insights into the workings of the social brain.

TRANSCRANIAL DIRECT CURRENT STIMULATION

A new wave of systematic research involving transcranial direct current stimulation (tDCS) has been sparked by a research group that has started to measure changes in cortical excitability following tDCS using single-pulse TMS. In a series of studies, Priori, Berardelli, Rona, Accornero, and Manfredi (1998) showed that weak electric currents (< 0.5 mA) that were applied via two scalp electrodes targeting cortical motor regions yielded changes in MEP amplitude in response to single-pulse TMS.

General Principles

In tDCS, a current generator is used to deliver a constant one-directional flow of electric current between two water-soaked sponge electrodes (Priori, 2003). The electrode size typically ranges from 20 cm² to 35 cm² and conductive gel is used to reduce the impendence between the electrode and scalp (Nitsche et al., 2008). The intensity of the administered current typically lies between 0.5 mA and 2.0 mA (Wagner, Valero-Cabre, & Pascual-Leone, 2007). Even though the scalp and skull act as a large shunt, studies have demonstrated that a small but significant part of the weak current underlying the electrodes actually reaches the cortical surface (Nitsche et al., 2008; Wagner, Valero-Cabre, & Pascual-Leone, 2007). The biophysical principle underlying tDCS involves the polarization of nerve tissue. Because of the low intensity and the fact that the injected current does not vary in time, tDCS, unlike TMS, cannot induce transmembrane potentials that are strong enough to cause action potentials in the underlying tissue. There is ample

evidence, however, that tDCS can influence spontaneous firing rates through the modulation of cortical excitability levels (Nitsche et al., 2008). Importantly, the direction of the current flow has differential effects on cortical excitability. The positively charged anode (+) electrode increases neuronal excitability, whereas the negatively charged cathode (−) electrode decreases neural excitability levels in the cortical tissue underneath the electrode (Priori, 2003). The modulation of firing probability of inhibitory interneurons in the superficial parts (layer 2) of the cerebral cortex is a possible mechanism for the changes in cortical excitability. In vitro studies suggest that tDCS sorts effects on ion channels that are in line with the up- (i.e., depolarization) or down regulation (i.e., hyperpolarization) of resting-state potentials (Nitsche et al., 2008). Even though the effects of tDCS are transient, studies of the time course of tDCS effects have shown that a session of 15 min of continuous tDCS can induce aftereffects that can last up to 1 hour (Priori, 2003). Finally, because of the shunting of scalp and skull and because of the relatively large electrode sizes, the stimulation focality of tDCS remains limited. Despite this limitation, tDCS is now generally accepted as an effective way of modulating cortical excitability by making use of weak electric currents (Figure 31.7).

The role of the right PFC in fairness behavior during simultaneous social interactions in a large experimental group (*n* = 64) was examined using cathodal tDCS (Knoch et al., 2008). The cathode electrode (35 cm²) was placed over right dorsolateral

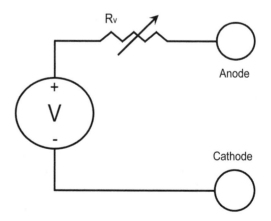

FIGURE 31.7. Electric current stimulation circuit. V = power supply, Rv = variable resistor.

PFC and the reference electrode (35 cm²) over the left orbit to reduce cortical excitability of the right PFC. A constant current of 1.5 mA intensity was started 4 min before the onset of the fairness game and lasted until termination of the game (~10 min). During sham tDCS, only 30 sec of real stimulation was applied at the onset of stimulation. Subjects who received cathodal (*n* = 30) tDCS to the right PFC were less likely to punish unfair behavior compared with sham tDCS (*n* = 34). In other words, during right PFC cathodal tDCS, subjects were more prone to accept smaller rewards during unfair offers rather than to reject the offer and receive no reward at all. In an additional study, the role of the left and right PFC in decision making was investigated by using a cathodal-anodal tDCS montage (electrode size: 35 cm², intensity: 2mA) in 36 healthy participants (Fecteau et al., 2007). Percentage of risky decision making was examined during anodal–right cathodal tDCS (*n* = 12), left cathodal–right anodal tDCS (*n* = 12), and sham tDCS (*n* = 12) over the PFC. During left cathodal–right anodal tDCS,

subjects displayed significant reductions in risky decision making as compared with left anodal–right cathodal tDCS and sham tDCS (Figure 31.8).

According to Knoch et al. (2008), these findings stress the importance of the interhemispheric balance across the PFC in decision making. Interestingly, the findings are also partially in line with the frontal lateralization model of motivation and emotion. The lateralization model predicts that the left cathodal–right anodal tDCS-induced shift in cortical asymmetry to the right PFC increases the sensitivity to punishment and risk aversion.

Finally, in a randomized sham-controlled experiment, the effects of tDCS to the PFC on reward processing and decision making in relation to food craving was investigated in 23 healthy participants (Fregni et al., 2008). Electrodes (35 cm²) were attached over the left and right PFC and a constant current was applied for 20 min at an intensity of 2mA. The experiment consisted of three different treatments: (a) anodal left–cathodal right, (b) cathodal left–anodal right, and (c) sham tDCS. The

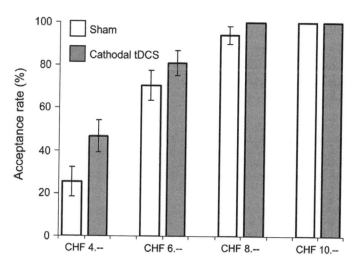

FIGURE 31.8. Responders' behavioral responses to all offers and fairness judgments. Acceptance rates (means ± standard error of the mean) across the two treatment groups. Subjects whose function of the right DLPFC is disrupted by cathodal tDCS exhibit a much higher acceptance rate than those who received placebo tDCS. CHF = Swiss franc. From "Studying the Neurobiology of Social Interaction With Transcranial Direct Current Stimulation: The Example of Punishing Unfairness," by D. Knoch, M. A. Nitsche, U. Fischbacher, C. Eisenegger, A. Pascual-Leone, and E. Fehr, 2008, *Cerebral Cortex, 18,* p. 1989. Copyright 2008 by Oxford University Press. Adapted with permission.

significant increase in food craving that was observed after sham tDCS was not present after right anodal–left cathodal tDCS. Furthermore, following right anodal–left cathodal tDCS, participants fixated less frequently on food-related pictures and participants consumed less food after receiving right anodal–left cathodal tDCS and left anodal–right cathodal tDCS as compared with sham tDCS. These findings provide evidence that tDCS applied over the frontal cortex can influence food craving and, arguably, the cortical structures that are involved in appetite control, reward sensitivity, and decision making. In sum, the first series of studies demonstrate the feasibility of applying weak electric currents to the scalp to address social neuroscientific issues by in vivo manipulation of the human brain in a transient fashion.

Safety

Transcranial electric stimulation has been associated with three potential sources of damage: (a) generation of electrochemical toxins, (b) tissue heating, and (c) excitotoxicity. Because the electrodes in tDCS do not make direct contact with the brain's surface, generation of electrochemical toxins are limited to the skin. Furthermore, chemical reactions at the electrode-skin interface can be minimized by using nonmetallic water-soaked sponge electrodes. Nonetheless, anecdotal reports of skin irritation following repeated daily tDCS strongly suggest that subjects with skin disease or a history of skin disease should not participate. Tissue heating as a result of dissipation may be an additional source of damage during electric stimulation. Several experiments have shown that tDCS (current density 0.029 mA/cm^2) that is applied for up to 13 min does not cause heating effects under the electrodes (Nitsche & Paulus, 2000). Finally, *excitotoxicity*, which is the phenomenon of calcium influx causing a disruption of the electrolytic balance in the nerve tissue that is due to overdriven neurons, is not considered a hazard for tDCS. Even though tDCS is able to increase spontaneous firing rates that remain within the physiological range, tDCS cannot induce action potentials in neurons that are not active (Nitsche et al., 2008). Thousands of participants have undergone tDCS worldwide and, except for itching under

the electrodes and a few reported cases of headache and nausea, no serious negative side effects have been observed.

Sham Stimulation

Similar to rTMS experiments, sham tDCS is routinely performed for subject blinding and to control for possible confounding effects of the procedure. Because tDCS uses weak electric currents and does not produce sound clicks as in TMS, participants in general are not able to distinguish real from fake tDCS. To mimic the itching sensation that is often reported during the first 30 sec following stimulation onset, researchers usually apply 30 sec of real stimulation in the sham condition as well. This procedure makes it very hard to discern real from fake stimulation.

Spatial Resolution and Localization

The low spatial resolution that is associated with tDCS resulting from the relative large electrode (20–35 cm^2) should be considered a limitation, particularly in cortical mapping studies. Reducing electrode size is one way to improve the focality of stimulation, but the noninvasive character and nature of stimulation (i.e., electricity) will limit the degree of spatial resolution that is attainable with the modification of electrode sizes. Additionally, similar to TMS, the direct effects of tDCS are limited to the superficial tissues that face the cranium. Indirect effects on distal interconnected structures can be expected when higher intensities are used. For example, unilateral anodal tDCS induces changes in cortical excitability of both ipsi- and contralateral motor cortex (Vines, Cerruti, & Schlaug, 2008).

In contrast to TMS, in which stimulation intensity is determined by individual thresholds to overcome individual differences in scalp-cortex distance and cortical excitability, participants in tDCS experiments usually get a fixed dose of electric stimulation. Without additional anatomical data, the exact amount of injected current that reaches the cortical surface and whether the amount is sufficient to elicit local and possibly distal effects can therefore not be known. Furthermore, individual differences in cortical physiology may yield different effects of tDCS in the brain using fixed parameters. The use of TMS in determining the intensity to excite cortical neurons may have some additional value in guiding the proper intensity needed for effective tDCS in forthcoming research. The use of neuroimaging techniques will become necessary to more fully capture the tDCS-related changes in distributed brain circuits.

An interesting feature of tDCS is the fact that the anode-cathode electrode montage allows for the simultaneous modulation of two cortical sites. Research questions involving the modulation of cortical asymmetries and hemispheric interactions may benefit from dual-site stimulation. The reference electrode is not inert. As discussed, tDCS involves an electric current that flows between two electrodes and, depending on its direction, the electrodes function as anodes or cathodes. In short, cephalic references may have an effect on cortical physiology as well. One way to overcome possible reference effects is by increasing the size of the electrode, thereby reducing the current density and its effects on physiology. Alternatively, noncephalic references (i.e., shoulder) are increasingly being used to minimize the possible confounding effects of the reference electrode. One should be careful in applying electrode montages (i.e., frontal electrode with reference attached to the leg) that can potentially cause stimulation of the brain stem or heart (Nitsche et al., 2008).

Developments in the Field

Rather than applying a constant unidirectional current as in tDCS, electric stimulation can also be applied in an alternating fashion according to a predefined frequency (Figure 31.9). Transcranial alternating current stimulation (tACS) has its roots in the idea that local and distal oscillations reflect the synchronization of large populations of neurons and constitute an important organizing principle of brain functions.

This opens new exciting possibilities in the field of noninvasive neuromodulation of the cortex by mimicking natural brain oscillations (Kanai, Chaieb,

Antal, Walsh, & Paulus, 2008).[2] Because current direction is constantly changing during tACS, polarization of cortical tissue is unlikely. Thus, one of the mechanisms by which tACS reaches its effects may be through the induction of a rhythm or by way of amplification of an existing dominant rhythm (Zaghi, Acar, Hultgren, Boggio, & Fregni, 2010). An increasing number of experiments have now replicated prior studies by showing that the application of low-intensity alternating currents to the scalp can manipulate cortical physiology and alter cognitive behavior in humans (Marshall, Helgadóttir, Mölle, & Born, 2006; Schroeder & Barr, 2001). For example, Marshall et al. (2006) applied 0.75 Hz tACS during non-rapid-eye-movement sleep, increasing slow wave sleep and declarative memory retention. In sum, even though electric current stimulation research in the field of social and affective neuroscience is in its infancy the noninvasive manipulation of the human brain using weak electric current in studying the neurological correlates of social behavior holds great potential.

CONCLUSION

NBS provides a unique window for studying the mind–brain relation in a relatively direct fashion by way of intervention and allows for a more causal approach in linking functions with the underlying neural representations in spatial as well as temporal domains of information processing (Schutter, van Honk, & Panksepp, 2004).

In addition to the modulation of cortical circuits and functionally connected networks, NBS is used to study inhibitory and excitatory properties of the cerebral cortex and functional connectivity in vivo. Moreover, results from basic social neuroscientific experiments expand our knowledge on the workings of the social brain and provide a rationale for modulating cortical excitability and subsequent affective processes to treat psychiatric disorders with NBS stimulation techniques.

On a final, critical note, the workings of complex affective behavior may not be unraveled on the basis of decomposition approaches, for the

---

[2]Repetitive TMS can also be viewed as a form of oscillatory stimulation of the cerebral cortex.

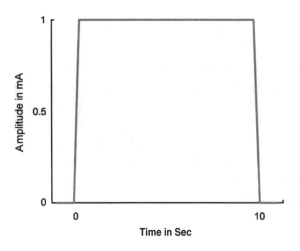

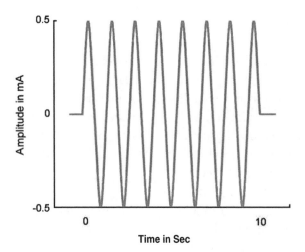

FIGURE 31.9.   Wave form of constant direct current and 0.8-Hz alternating current stimulation. Sec = seconds.

assumption of a one-to-one relation between the function and the localization of its underlying neural representations may be false. Although NBS stimulation cannot account for the explanatory gap between neurophysiological dynamics and how subjective experiences arise from such functions of the social brain, these new and innovative techniques can identify and locate certain psychoneural entities or at least key nodes within the greater whole by means of true causal analyses (Schutter et al., 2004).

References

Arana, A. B., Borckardt, J. J., Ricci, R., Anderson, B., Li, X., Linder, K. J., . . . George, M. S. (2008). Focal electrical stimulation as a sham control for repetitive transcranial magnetic stimulation: Does it truly mimic the cutaneous sensation and pain of active prefrontal repetitive transcranial magnetic stimulation? *Brain Stimulation, 1,* 44–51. doi:10.1016/j.brs.2007.08.006

Bajbouj, M., Lisanby, S. H., Lang, U. E., Danker-Hopfe, H., Heuser, I., & Neu, P. (2006). Evidence for impaired cortical inhibition in patients with unipolar major depression. *Biological Psychiatry, 59,* 395–400. doi:10.1016/j.biopsych.2005.07.036

Barker, A. T., Jalinous, R., & Freeston, I. L. (1985). Non-invasive magnetic stimulation of human motor cortex. *Lancet, 325,* 1106–1107. doi:10.1016/S0140-6736(85)92413-4

Bohning, D. E. (2000). Introduction and overview of TMS physics. In M. S. George & R. H. Belmaker (Eds.),

Transcranial magnetic stimulation in neuropsychiatry (pp. 3–44). Washington, DC: American Psychiatric Press.

Breier, A., & Paul, S. M. (1990). The GABA-A/benzodiazepine receptor: Implications for the molecular basis of anxiety. *Journal of Psychiatric Research, 24*(Suppl. 2), 91–104. doi:10.1016/0022-3956(90)90040-W

Buchmann, J., Wolters, A., Haessler, F., Bohne, S., Nordbeck, R., & Kunesch, E. (2003). Disturbed transcallosally mediated motor inhibition in children with attention deficit hyperactivity disorder (ADHD). *Clinical Neurophysiology, 114*, 2036–2042. doi:10.1016/S1388-2457(03)00208-6

Cantello, R., Gianelli, M., Civardi, C., & Mutani, R. (1992). Magnetic brain stimulation: The silent period after the motor evoked potential. *Neurology, 42*, 1951–1959.

Chen, R., Tam, A., Bütefisch, C., Corwell, B., Ziemann, U., Rothwell, J. C., & Cohen, L. G. (1998). Intracortical inhibition and facilitation in different representations of the human motor cortex. *Journal of Neurophysiology, 80*, 2870–2881.

d'Alfonso, A. A. L., van Honk, J., Hermans, E., Postma, A., & de Haan, E. H. F. (2000). Laterality effects in selective attention to threat after repetitive transcranial magnetic stimulation at the prefrontal cortex in female subjects. *Neuroscience Letters, 280*, 195–198. doi:10.1016/S0304-3940(00)00781-3

Daskalakis, Z. J., Möller, B., Christensen, B. K., Fitzgerald, P. B., Gunraj, C., & Chen, R. (2006). The effects of repetitive transcranial magnetic stimulation on cortical inhibition in healthy human subjects. *Experimental Brain Research, 174*, 403–412. doi:10.1007/s00221-006-0472-0

Davidson, R. J. (1984). Affect, cognition, and hemispheric specialization. In C. E. Izard, J. Kagan, & R. B. Zajonc (Eds.), *Emotion, cognition, and behavior* (pp. 320–365). New York, NY: Cambridge University Press.

Davis, M., & Whalen, P. J. (2001). The amygdala: Vigilance and emotion. *Molecular Psychiatry, 6*, 13–34. doi:10.1038/sj.mp.4000812

Deblieck, C., Thompson, B., Iacoboni, M., & Wu, A. D. (2008). Correlation between motor and phosphene thresholds: A transcranial magnetic stimulation study. *Human Brain Mapping, 29*, 662–670. doi:10.1002/hbm.20427

Di Lazzaro, V., Profice, P., Pilato, F., Dileone, M., Oliviero, A., & Ziemann, U. (2010). The effects of motor cortex rTMS on corticospinal descending activity. *Clinical Neurophysiology, 121*, 464–473. doi:10.1016/j.clinph.2009.11.007

Fecteau, S., Knoch, D., Fregni, F., Sultani, N., Boggio, P., & Pascual-Leone, A. (2007). Diminishing risk-taking behavior by modulating activity in the prefrontal cortex: A direct current stimulation study. *Journal*

of Neuroscience, 27, 12500–12505. doi:10.1523/JNEUROSCI.3283-07.2007

Fehr, E., & Camerer, C. F. (2007). Social neuroeconomics: The neural circuitry of social preferences. *Trends in Cognitive Sciences, 11*, 419–427. doi:10.1016/j.tics.2007.09.002

Ferbert, A., Priori, A., Rothwell, J. C., Day, B. L., Colebatch, J. G., & Marsden, C. D. (1992). Interhemispheric inhibition of the human motor cortex. *Journal of Physiology, 453*, 525–546.

Ferrarelli, F., Massimini, M., Sarasso, S., Casali, A., Riedner, B. A., Angelini, G., . . . Pearce, R. A. (2010). Breakdown in cortical effective connectivity during midazolam-induced loss of consciousness. *Proceedings of the National Academy of Sciences of the United States of America, 107*, 2681–2686. doi:10.1073/pnas.0913008107

Fitzgerald, P. B., Maller, J. J., Hoy, K., Farzan, F., & Daskalakis, Z. J. (2009). GABA and cortical inhibition in motor and non-motor regions using combined TMS-EEG: A time analysis. *Clinical Neurophysiology, 120*, 1706–1710. doi:10.1016/j.clinph.2009.06.019

Fregni, F., Orsati, F., Pedrosa, W., Fecteau, S., Tome, F. A., Nitsche, M. A., . . . Boggio, P. S. (2008). Transcranial direct current stimulation of the prefrontal cortex modulates the desire for specific foods. *Appetite, 51*, 34–41.

Garvey, M. A., Barker, C. A., Bartko, J. J., Denckla, M. B., Wassermann, E. M., Castellanos, F. X., & Dell, M. L. (2005). The ipsilateral silent period in boys with attention-deficit/hyperactivity disorder. *Clinical Neurophysiology, 116*, 1889–1896. doi:10.1016/j.clinph.2005.03.018

Hajcak, G., Molnar, C., George, M. S., Bolger, K., Koola, J., & Nahas, Z. (2007). Emotion facilitates action: A transcranial magnetic stimulation study of motor cortex excitability during picture viewing. *Psychophysiology, 44*, 91–97. doi:10.1111/j.1469-8986.2006.00487.x

Hallett, M. (2007). Transcranial magnetic stimulation: A primer. *Neuron, 55*, 187–199. doi:10.1016/j.neuron.2007.06.026

Harmon-Jones, E. (2003). Clarifying the emotive functions of asymmetrical frontal cortical activity. *Psychophysiology, 40*, 838–848. doi:10.1111/1469-8986.00121

Hofman, D., & Schutter, D. J. L. G. (2009). Inside the wire: Aggression and functional interhemispheric connectivity in the human brain. *Psychophysiology, 46*, 1054–1058. doi:10.1111/j.1469-8986.2009.00849.x

Hoogendam, J. M., Ramakers, G. M. J., & Di Lazzaro, V. (2010). Physiology of repetitive transcranial magnetic stimulation of the human brain. *Brain Stimulation, 3*, 95–118.

Huang, Y. Z., Edwards, M. J., Rounis, E., Bhatia, K. P., & Rothwell, J. C. (2005). Theta burst stimulation of the human motor cortex. *Neuron, 45*, 201–206. doi:10.1016/j.neuron.2004.12.033

Ilmoniemi, R. J., Virtanen, J., Ruohonen, J., Karhu, J., Aronen, H. J., Näätänen, R., & Katila, T. (1997). Neuronal responses to magnetic stimulation reveal cortical reactivity and connectivity. *NeuroReport, 8*, 3537–3540. doi:10.1097/00001756-199711100-00024

Kähkönen, S., Komssi, S., Wilenius, J., & Ilmoniemi, R. J. (2005). Prefrontal TMS produces smaller EEG responses than motor-cortex TMS: Implications for rTMS treatment in depression. *Psychopharmacology, 181*, 16–20. doi:10.1007/s00213-005-2197-3

Kanai, R., Chaieb, L., Antal, A., Walsh, V., & Paulus, W. (2008). Frequency-dependent electrical stimulation of the visual cortex. *Current Biology, 18*, 1839–1843. doi:10.1016/j.cub.2008.10.027

Khedr, E. M., Rothwell, J. C., Ahmed, M. A., Shawky, O. A., & Farouk, M. (2007). Modulation of motor cortical excitability following rapid-rate transcranial magnetic stimulation. *Clinical Neurophysiology, 118*, 140–145. doi:10.1016/j.clinph.2006.09.006

Knoch, D., Gianotti, L. R., Pascual-Leone, A., Treyer, V., Regard, M., Hohmann, M., & Brugger, P. (2006). Disruption of right prefrontal cortex by low-frequency repetitive transcranial magnetic stimulation induces risk-taking behavior. *Journal of Neuroscience, 26*, 6469–6472. doi:10.1523/JNEUROSCI.0804-06.2006

Knoch, D., Nitsche, M. A., Fischbacher, U., Eisenegger, C., Pascual-Leone, A., & Fehr, E. (2008). Studying the neurobiology of social interaction with transcranial direct current stimulation: The example of punishing unfairness. *Cerebral Cortex, 18*, 1987–1990. doi:10.1093/cercor/bhm237

Knoch, D., Pascual-Leone, A., Meyer, K., Treyer, V., & Fehr, E. (2006). Diminishing reciprocal fairness by disrupting the right prefrontal cortex. *Science, 314*, 829–832. doi:10.1126/science.1129156

Levinson, A. J., Fitzgerald, P. B., Favalli, G., Blumberger, D. M., Daigle, M., & Daskalakis, Z. J. (2010). Evidence of cortical inhibitory deficits in major depressive disorder. *Biological Psychiatry, 67*, 458–464. doi:10.1016/j.biopsych.2009.09.025

Marshall, L., Helgadóttir, H., Mölle, M., & Born, J. (2006). Boosting slow oscillations during sleep potentiates memory. *Nature, 444*, 610–613. doi:10.1038/nature05278

Moll, G. H., Heinrich, H., Wischer, S., Tergau, F., Paulus, W., & Rothenberger, A. (1999). Motor system excitability in healthy children: Developmental

aspects from transcranial magnetic stimulation. *Electroencephalography and Clinical Neurophysiology Supplement, 51*, 243–249.

Nitsche, M. A., Cohen, L. G., Wassermann, E. M., Priori, A., Lang, N., Antal, A. W., . . . Pascual-Leone, A. (2008). Transcranial direct current stimulation: State of the art. *Brain Stimulation, 1*, 206–223. doi:10.1016/j.brs.2008.06.004

Nitsche, M. A., & Paulus, W. (2000). Excitability changes induced in the human motor cortex by weak transcranial direct current stimulation. *Journal of Physiology, 527*, 633–639. doi:10.1111/j.1469-7793.2000.t01-1-00633.x

Oathes, D. J., Bruce, J. M., & Nitschke, J. B. (2008). Worry facilitates corticospinal motor response to transcranial magnetic stimulation. *Depression and Anxiety, 25*, 969–976. doi:10.1002/da.20445

Öhman, A. (1986). Face the beast and fear the face: Animal and social fears as prototypes for evolutionary analyses of emotion. *Psychophysiology, 23*, 123–145. doi:10.1111/j.1469-8986.1986.tb00608.x

Pascual-Leone, A., Tormos, J. M., Keenan, J., Tarazona, F., Cañete, C., & Catalá, M. D. (1998). Study and modulation of human cortical excitability with transcranial magnetic stimulation. *Journal of Clinical Neurophysiology, 15*, 333–343. doi:10.1097/00004691-199807000-00005

Post, A., Müller, M. B., Engelmann, M., & Keck, M. E. (1999). Repetitive transcranial magnetic stimulation in rats: Evidence for a neuroprotective effect in vitro and in vivo. *European Journal of Neuroscience, 11*, 3247–3254. doi:10.1046/j.1460-9568.1999.00747.x

Priori, A. (2003). Brain polarization in humans: A reappraisal of an old tool for prolonged non-invasive modulation of brain excitability. *Clinical Neurophysiology, 114*, 589–595. doi:10.1016/S1388-2457(02)00437-6

Priori, A., Berardelli, A., Rona, S., Accornero, N., & Manfredi, M. (1998). Polarization of the human motor cortex through the scalp. *NeuroReport, 9*, 2257–2260.

Rabin, M. (1993). Incorporating fairness into game theory and economics. *American Economic Review, 83*, 1281–1302.

Rossi, S., Hallett, M., Rossini, P. M., & Pascual-Leone, A. (2009). Safety of TMS Consensus Group. Safety, ethical considerations, and application guidelines for the use of transcranial magnetic stimulation in clinical practice and research. *Clinical Neurophysiology, 120*, 2008–2039. doi:10.1016/j.clinph.2009.08.016

Santiago-Rodríguez, E., Cárdenas-Morales, L., Harmony, T., Fernández-Bouzas, A., Porras-Kattz, E., & Hernández, A. (2008). Repetitive transcranial magnetic stimulation decreases the number of seizures in patients with focal neocortical epilepsy. *Seizure, 17,* 677–683. doi:10.1016/j.seizure.2008.04.005

Schroeder, M. J., & Barr, R. E. (2001). Quantitative analysis of the electroencephalogram during cranial electrotherapy stimulation. *Clinical Neurophysiology, 112,* 2075–2083. doi:10.1016/S1388-2457(01)00657-5

Schutter, D. J. L. G. (2009). Transcranial magnetic stimulation. In E. Harmon-Jones & J. S. Beer (Eds.), *Methods in social neuroscience* (pp. 233–258). New York, NY: Guilford Press.

Schutter, D. J. L. G., de Weijer, A. D., Meuwese, J. D., Morgan, B., & van Honk, J. (2008). Interrelations between motivational stance, cortical excitability, and the frontal electroencephalogram asymmetry of emotion: A transcranial magnetic stimulation study. *Human Brain Mapping, 29,* 574–580. doi:10.1002/hbm.20417

Schutter, D. J. L. G., Enter, D., & Hoppenbrouwers, S. S. (2009). High-frequency repetitive transcranial magnetic stimulation to the cerebellum and implicit processing of happy facial expressions. *Journal of Psychiatry and Neuroscience, 34,* 60–65.

Schutter, D. J. L. G., Hofman, D., & van Honk, J. (2008). Fearful faces selectively increase corticospinal motor tract excitability: A transcranial magnetic stimulation study. *Psychophysiology, 45,* 345–348. doi:10.1111/j.1469-8986.2007.00635.x

Schutter, D. J. L. G., van Honk, J., d'Alfonso, A. A. L., Postma, A., & de Haan, E. H. F. (2001). Effects of slow rTMS at the right dorsolateral prefrontal cortex on EEG asymmetry and mood. *NeuroReport, 12,* 445–447. doi:10.1097/00001756-200103050-00005

Schutter, D. J. L. G., van Honk, J., & Panksepp, J. (2004). Introducing transcranial magnetic stimulation (TMS) and its property of causal inference in investigating brain-function relationships. *Synthese, 141,* 155–173. doi:10.1023/B:SYNT.0000042951.25087.16

Silvanto, J., Muggleton, N., & Walsh, V. (2008). State-dependency in brain stimulation studies of perception and cognition. *Trends in Cognitive Sciences, 12,* 447–454. doi:10.1016/j.tics.2008.09.004

Speer, A. M., Willis, M. W., Herscovitch, P., Daube-Witherspoon, M., Shelton, J. R., Benson, B. E., . . . Wassermann, E. M. (2003). Intensity-dependent regional cerebral blood flow during 1-Hz repetitive transcranial magnetic stimulation (rTMS) in healthy volunteers studied with H215O positron emission tomography: II. Effects of prefrontal cortex rTMS. *Biological Psychiatry, 54,* 826–832. doi:10.1016/S0006-3223(03)00324-X

Thut, G., & Miniussi, C. (2009). New insights into rhythmic brain activity from TMS-EEG studies. *Trends in Cognitive Sciences, 13,* 182–189. doi:10.1016/j.tics.2009.01.004

van 't Wout, M., Kahn, R. S., Sanfey, A. G., & Aleman, A. (2005). Repetitive transcranial magnetic stimulation over the right dorsolateral prefrontal cortex affects strategic decision-making. *NeuroReport, 16,* 1849–1852. doi:10.1097/01.wnr.0000183907.08149.14

van Honk, J., & Schutter, D. J. L. G. (2006a). From affective valence to motivational direction: The frontal asymmetry of emotion revised. *Psychological Science, 17,* 963–965. doi:10.1111/j.1467-9280.2006.01813.x

van Honk, J., & Schutter, D. J. L. G. (2006b). Unmasking feigned sanity: A neurobiological model of emotion processing in primary psychopathy. *Cognitive Neuropsychiatry, 11,* 285–306. doi:10.1080/13546800500233728

van Honk, J., & Schutter, D. J. L. G. (2007). Vigilant and avoidant responses to angry facial expressions: Dominance and submission motives. In E. Harmon-Jones & P. Winkielman (Eds.), *Fundamentals in social neuroscience* (pp. 197–223). New York, NY: Guilford Press.

van Honk, J., Schutter, D. J. L. G., d'Alfonso, A. A. L., Kessels, R. P. C., & de Haan, E. H. F. (2002). 1 Hz rTMS over the right prefrontal cortex reduces vigilant attention to unmasked but not to masked fearful faces. *Biological Psychiatry, 52,* 312–317. doi:10.1016/S0006-3223(02)01346-X

van Honk, J., Schutter, D. J. L. G., Putman, P., de Haan, E. H. F., & d'Alfonso, A. A. L. (2003). Reductions in phenomenological, physiological, and attentional indices of depressive mood after 2 Hz rTMS over the right parietal cortex in healthy human subjects. *Psychiatry Research, 120,* 95–101.

Vines, B. W., Cerruti, C., & Schlaug, G. (2008). Dual-hemisphere tDCS facilitates greater improvements for healthy subjects' non-dominant hand compared to uni-hemisphere stimulation. *BMC Neuroscience, 9,* 103. doi:10.1186/1471-2202-9-103

Wagner, T., Valero-Cabre, A., & Pascual-Leone, A. (2007). Non-invasive human brain stimulation. *Annual Review of Biomedical Engineering, 9,* 527–565. doi:10.1146/annurev.bioeng.9.061206.133100

Wassermann, E. M. (1998). Risk and safety of repetitive transcranial magnetic stimulation: Report and suggested guidelines from the International Workshop on the Safety of Repetitive Transcranial Magnetic Stimulation, June 5–7, 1996. *Electroencephalography and Clinical Neurophysiology, 108,* 1–16.

Wassermann, E. M., Epstein, C. M., Ziemann, U., Walsh, V., Paus, T., & Lisanby, S. H. (2008). *Oxford handbook of transcranial magnetic stimulation.* New York, NY: Oxford University Press.

Wassermann, E. M., Greenberg, B. D., Nguyen, M. B., & Murphy, D. L. (2001). Motor cortex excitability correlates with an anxiety-related personality trait. *Biological Psychiatry, 50*, 377–382. doi:10.1016/S0006-3223(01)01210-0

Wassermann, E. M., & Lisanby, S. H. (2001). Therapeutic application of repetitive transcranial magnetic stimulation: A review. *Clinical Neurophysiology, 112*, 1367–1377. doi:10.1016/S1388-2457(01)00585-5

Zaghi, S., Acar, M., Hultgren, B., Boggio, P. S., & Fregni, F. (2010). Noninvasive brain stimulation with low-intensity electrical currents: Putative

mechanisms of action for direct and alternating current stimulation. *The Neuroscientist, 16*, 285–307. doi:10.1177/1073858409336227

Zangen, A., Roth, Y., Voller, B., & Hallett, M. (2005). Transcranial magnetic stimulation of deep brain regions: Evidence for efficacy of the H-coil. *Clinical Neurophysiology, 116*, 775–779. doi:10.1016/j.clinph.2004.11.008

Ziemann, U. (2004). TMS and drugs. *Clinical Neurophysiology, 115*, 1717–1729. doi:10.1016/j.clinph.2004.03.006

PART IV

PSYCHOMETRICS

CHAPTER 32

CONSTRUCT VALIDITY

Kevin J. Grimm and Keith F. Widaman

In this chapter, we consider construct validity as an overarching idea with two broad aspects—internal validity and external validity—each of which has more specific components. Various aspects of construct validation have been discussed in a number of key papers over the past half-century (e.g., Cronbach, 1980; Cronbach & Meehl, 1955; McArdle & Prescott, 1992; Messick, 1989, 1995; Shepard, 1993), and we draw from this collection of work in framing the current chapter. Construct validity, or validity in general, has been regarded as the most fundamental and important aspect of *psychometrics*, the study of psychological measures and measurement encompassing direct assessments (e.g., fluid reasoning test and depression inventory), surveys of attitudes (e.g., political views), observations (e.g., classroom observations), among others (Angoff, 1988). However, despite its centrality to the scientific enterprise, few, if any, clear standards regarding construct validation have been proposed. This situation contrasts distinctly with procedures related to reliability, for which several standard options for calculating reliability are routinely recommended, and reliabilities of .80 or higher are generally considered adequate to strong. One reason for the less structured approach to construct validity is due to the conception that construct validity is a multifaceted process; construct validity is often not considered to be a property of a test, but rather to be a property regarding the use of scores derived from a test or of inferences made from test scores. Because researchers and practitioners can and do devise new ways to use test scores, construct validation is a

lengthy process (Cronbach, 1989) that is never finished (Cronbach, 1988).

THE HISTORY OF CONSTRUCT VALIDITY

To introduce the concept of construct validity, a brief sketch of the history of the notion is in order. Constructs and the validity of constructs were core aspects of psychological research for well over a half century before the term *construct validity* made its way into the scientific lexicon in Cronbach and Meehl (1955). In this brief introduction, we identify three phases in the history of construct validity, phases that we identify as the preoperational, concrete operational, and formal operational phases, with apologies to Piaget.

The preoperational phase of research related to construct validity encompasses the period from the emergence of psychology as a distinct discipline, during the 1870s, until the early 1920s. During the preoperational phase, researchers pursued wide-ranging studies of many different constructs, but they displayed little serious reflection on the tie between manifest measurements and the constructs that were assessed. For example, sensory thresholds and relations between sensation and perception were topics of great research interest, and many enduring methods of establishing thresholds (e.g., the method of constant stimuli) were developed during this phase. But little methodological criticism was aimed at measurements, perhaps because the tie between manifest measures and the constructs they were to represent were very close in many domains

DOI: 10.1037/13619-033
APA Handbook of Research Methods in Psychology: Vol. 1. Foundations, Planning, Measures, and Psychometrics, H. Cooper (Editor-in-Chief)

of inquiry. This is not to say that research pursued during this period concerned only constructs subject to relatively direct measurement. Indeed, investigators were interested in initiating studies of rather nebulous concepts, such as the human soul and its relation to the mind–body problem. Still, arguments centered more on the experimental evidence produced for phenomena than on qualities of the measurements and their ties to the intended constructs.

The second phase, which we have termed the concrete operational phase, was occasioned by conflicting interpretations of results from the massive psychological testing enterprise undertaken by psychologists on behalf of the U.S. war effort during World War I (Yerkes, 1921). Early precursors of this phase can be seen in the behaviorist manifestos by Watson (1913), which emphasized a hard-nosed approach to measuring behavior and dispensing with measures of unseen, latent, mentalistic constructs. But the concrete operational phase was forced onto the field of psychology by a nonpsychologist, Walter Lippmann, in the early 1920s. In a series of short articles in the *New Republic*, Lippmann (e.g., 1922) lambasted interpretations of results from the World War I testing enterprise. On the basis of their testing of recruits, psychologists had claimed that the mental age of the average Army recruit was 14 years, a value listed in the Yerkes (1921) volume. A later book by Brigham (1923) argued that Army recruits from Northern European countries were clearly above the mean in intelligence and that recruits from Southern European countries, on average, had mean intelligence levels that were on the borderline of mental retardation. Lippmann argued that such conclusions could not be true; if they were true, the United States could not function as a modern society. If mean levels of performance by Army recruits were at the level of a 14-year-old, then perhaps intelligence was not what was being measured by the tests. Responses by psychologists were simple and direct. Perhaps the most well known came from Boring (1923), who stated that intelligence was what intelligence tests measure; if the tests indicate that the mean mental age of recruits was 14 years, then the emerging science of psychology would stand behind that claim.

This approach of emphasizing how a construct was operationalized—a given construct was what a measure of that construct measured—became central to the operational definition of constructs. This approach was propounded in notable contributions such as Bridgman (1932), who wrote about operational definitions in physics. The operational definition of constructs was carried over directly into this field, providing an objective way to measure constructs of importance to a scientific psychology. Moreover, this operational approach was consistent with the emerging logical positivist movement associated with the Vienna Circle. A core tenet of the Vienna Circle was the verificationist theory of truth—that is, the truth value of a statement is whether it is amenable to verification; statements that have no means of verification are not meaningful and therefore have no truth value. Translated into a scientific setting, the validity of a measurement is the way it is formulated or operationalized and the resulting experimental evidence associated with the resulting scores. Unfortunately, this emphasis on the operational definition of constructs led to a proliferation of constructs. Different ways of operationalizing a particular construct—whether it be rather abstract, like intelligence, or more concrete, such as hunger—resulted in different constructs, and different constructs might obey rather different psychological laws.

The third and most mature phase of work on construct validity—the formal operational phase—began officially with the publication of the seminal paper by Cronbach and Meehl (1955), which was an outgrowth of work by a committee of the American Psychological Association. Once again, however, this phase had a transition, with an earlier paper by MacCorquodale and Meehl (1948) on the distinction between hypothetical constructs and intervening variables being a clear precursor of the later, more celebrated, paper by Cronbach and Meehl. MacCorquodale and Meehl argued for a distinction between two types of concepts. Intervening variables are simply shorthand verbal labels for objective phenomena or results, and the meaning of an intervening variable is shown by the empirical relations exhibited by the measurements and is limited by these relations. In contrast, hypothetical constructs imply certain forms of empirical relations, but they imply something beyond those empirical relations—some unseen processes that underlie the empirical relations. This idea about hypothetical constructs propounded by MacCorquodale and Meehl is quite consistent with the modern view of constructs and their validity.

One outcome of the continuing concerns about intervening variables and hypothetical constructs was the formation of a working group by the American Psychological Association headed by Cronbach and Meehl. The most well-known product of this working group was the statement by Cronbach and Meehl (1955) of the nature of construct validity, outlining the nature of the idea of construct validity and various ways of investigating construct validity. With the publication of this paper, the field entered the modern era, and the stage was set for future developments such as validation using the multitrait–multimethod (MTMM) matrix (Campbell & Fiske, 1959) and reformulations of the nature of construct validity by Messick and others, to be described in the following sections.

COMPONENTS OF CONSTRUCT VALIDITY

Validity has been organized in several different ways, with *content validity*, *criterion-related validity*, and *construct validity* as the most prominent. More recently, Messick (1995) argued that all forms of validity fell under the umbrella of construct validity, and that construct validity had six facets: (a) content relevance and representation, (b) substantive theories underlying the sampling of domain tasks, (c) scoring models and their relation to domain structure, (d) generalizability and the boundaries of score meaning, (e) convergent and discriminant validity with external variables, and (f) consequences of validation evidence. The 1999 Standard for Educational and Psychological Testing organized validity evidence into five categories, including evidence based on (a) test content, (b) response processes, (c) internal structure, (d) relations with other variables, and (e) consequences of testing.

In this chapter, we consider construct validity as a multifaceted process revolving around two major axes. Following McArdle and Prescott (1992), the two major axes are *internal validity* and *external validity*. Similar to internal and external validity of a study, internal validity of a test is focused primarily on relationships internal to the test, whereas external validity is focused primarily on relationships external to the test. Specifically, the focus of internal validity is placed on relations among the items making up the test—how participant responses to items function as a whole or in groups. The focus of external validity, on the other hand, is placed on relations between test scores and external criteria.

Internal validity can be *part* of determining whether test items measure the intended construct. However, common statistical approaches to examining internal validity (e.g., classical notions of reliability) focus narrowly on whether test items measure a hypothetical construct, although not necessarily the construct the test is intended to measure. To circumnavigate this issue, theoretical expectations regarding dimensionality, strength of factor loadings, discrimination, difficulty, and so on are important parts of internal validity in helping to determine whether items represent the intended construct.

External validity, on the other hand, revolves around a test score's association with additional variables, including measures of the same construct, measures of different constructs, and clinical diagnoses. The focus of external validity is placed on the extent to which the test measures the construct it is intended to measure. In this chapter, we consider external validity as having several components—including criterion-related validity—composed of concurrent, predictive, and postdictive validity as well as convergent and discriminant validity, change validity, score interpretation, and consequences.

Construct validity has also been organized around a set of goals or objectives, which is practical when taking on such an endeavor. The broad goal of construct validity is determining the extent to which the test measures the construct it is intended to measure. However, recent treatments of validity (e.g., Messick, 1989) have focused on interpretations of test scores, and these can be considered two sides of construct validity. Examining internal and external validity is necessary for evaluating construct validity, and both contribute, in different ways, to the broad goal of construct validity. More-over, certain types of tests and test goals lend themselves to different evaluations of construct validity.

Internal validity is most applicable to the goal of determining the extent to which a test measures the construct it is intended to measure; however external validity equally contributes to this endeavor. This objective can be seen as a more academic or research-oriented objective. A second objective is to determine the extent to which the interpretations and uses of test scores are appropriate. This objective relates more to the applied aspects of a test outside of a research setting and is closely aligned with evaluations of external validity. These objectives are closely related to Whitely's (1983) *construct representation* and *nomothetic span* as well as to Cronbach's (1971) two uses of tests: (a) making decisions about the person tested and (b) describing the person tested. These objectives are distinct, and evidence for one does not, in any way, provide evidence for the other. Both objectives are important to understanding construct validity of a test; however, one of the two objectives can take priority depending on the test purposes. For example, a primary use of the SAT is to predict freshman-year grade point average, so this objective should take priority over making sure the test measures writing, critical reading, and mathematics achievement.

Internal Validity

Internal validity of a test places the focus on the items that make up the test and how they are theoretically derived, relate to each other, and relate to the underlying construct(s) and whether they have the same meaning and difficulty for people with different background characteristics. These aspects of internal validity and methods for studying them are in the following sections.

Content validity. Content validity begins in the design phase of a psychological test. The creation of a psychological test or any test designed to generalize to a larger set of behaviors, occasions, situations, and so on should begin with precise definitions of the construct the test is intended to measure; the test's objectives; proposed uses of the test scores; the range of abilities, attitudes, feelings, and attributes

the test is supposed to cover; and the population of individuals for whom the test will be administered. Once these questions are answered, items are written to capture the underlying construct. In a sense, test makers attempt to build validity into the test (Anastasi, 1986).

Take, for example, the development of a child behavior scale. In this development, we must first define the construct, whether it be general behavior, behavior problems, or positive behaviors. Furthermore, we need to specify how finely we want to define our construct—is it behavior problems, distinct aspects of behavior problems such as externalizing and internalizing behavior problems, or even more specific aspects of externalizing and internalizing behaviors such as aggressive behaviors and withdrawal? Once the underlying construct is specified, we need to consider the objectives or goals for the test. Is it to distinguish between children who have clinical (exceptionally high) levels of behavior problems and children with normative levels of behavior problems? Is it to accurately measure children along a continuum from little to no behavior problems up to high levels of behavior problems? These objectives may not be mutually exclusive; however, different objectives can change what items should be included in the scale. These objectives also lead to different uses of the scores obtained from the scale. Next, the population of children needs to be specified. The types of behavior problems that young children show are much different from the types of behavior problems that adolescents demonstrate. If the scale is designed to be appropriate for young children and adolescents, then the scale needs to contain items appropriate for each age level, which may be weighted differentially on the basis of age.

In the evaluation of content validity, there is not a falsifiable statistical model to use, which has led some researchers to suggest content validity should not be used to defend a scale (Messick, 1975) as evaluation is based on judgments, much like the scale development process (Shepard, 1993). A test developer must be able to defend whether the construct is appropriate, whether the items appropriately sample the construct, and whether the items are appropriate given the objectives and intended population. Usually, content validity is evaluated by a panel of expert judges. *Expert* is sometimes used loosely because it is reasonable that expert judges may strongly disagree on certain aspects of scale. Lawshe (1975) proposed a rater-agreement method to measure content validity in the job performance domain. In this method, each item was rated by a panel of expert judges on the degree to which the skill measured by the item was essential to job performance. Judges' ratings were made using a three-point scale that included the items "essential," "useful but not essential," and "not necessary." Lawshe suggested that if more than half of the judges indicate the item is essential, then the item has some degree of content validity, and when a higher percentage of judges rate the item as essential, higher levels of content validity exist. Lawshe developed the *content validity ratio (CVR)* for each item as follows

$$CVR = \frac{n_e - N/2}{N/2}, \tag{1}$$

where n_e is the number of judges indicating the item is essential, and N is the total number of judges. This formula yields values ranging from -1 to $+1$, where positive *CVRs* indicate at least half of the judges indicated the item is essential. The mean *CVR* across items can be used as a measure of the content validity of the scale. This method may be more difficult to implement with scales designed to measure psychological constructs because psychological constructs may not be closely tied to observable behaviors in narrowly defined situations, such as job performance.

Another potential issue for this approach with psychological scales is that the construct the test is measuring may become too narrowly defined, which may make the test, in the end, less representative of the range of behaviors the construct defines and thus less valid. The issue of item selection is important, and there are several ways to approach this issue (e.g., Little, Lindenberger, & Nesselroade, 1999).

Dimensionality. A first question once data are collected from a psychological test is the dimensional-

ity of the items. Often, the question is whether test items make up a unidimensional scale. The main question, however, is whether the theoretical dimensionality of the scale is supported. If so, a second step is checking whether items designed to measure each dimension do so in expected ways. If so, a third step is evaluating the degree of association between the various dimensions and whether the test dimensions relate in expected ways. If the theoretical dimensionality is not supported, the question turns to how many and what dimensions are assessed and how items relate to each dimension. Once dimensionality is determined, additional aspects of internal validity can be studied, which include deeper assessments of item performance using item response methods (e.g., Whitely, 1983) to understand reliability, determinants of item performance, and item bias.

The study of dimensionality of a set of items is best studied with item factor analysis (for reviews, see Chapter 35 of this volume; Wirth & Edwards, 2007). There are several types of item factor models, which are also referred to as *multidimensional item response models* depending on the context of the model's derivation. The various types of models depend on the response type (e.g., ordered polytomous responses, dichotomous responses, or unordered polytomous responses), whether guessing is modeled, and model properties. All models can be considered variants of the general item factor analytic framework (Thissen & Steinberg, 1986; Wirth & Edwards, 2007). Here, we describe two basic models often applied in psychological research. The first is appropriate for dichotomous responses, such as cognitive items scored correct or incorrect, and the second is appropriate for ordered polytomous responses, such as rating scale items scored 0, 1, and 2 for *never*, *sometimes*, and *often* and other scales that use Likert-type response formats. Furthermore, these models are described in two frameworks—structural-equation modeling and item response modeling; however, the two contexts can lead to functionally equivalent models.

In describing these models, we begin with dichotomous responses (e.g., incorrect or correct; disagree or agree) in a structural-modeling framework. The factor analysis model for dichotomous responses can be viewed as having two parts. The first part relates the dichotomous response to a latent response distribution, an underlying continuous and normally distributed response propensity for each item, and the second part relates latent response distributions to the common factors. In the first part of the model, individual *i*'s (dichotomous) response to item *j*, denoted x_{ij}, is considered a manifestation of individual *i*'s latent continuous response for item *j*, denoted x_{ij}^*. At the sample level, the proportion of individuals who endorse each response category provide information about the latent response distribution. This information is conveyed in terms of threshold parameters, τ, which are locations on the latent response distribution separating one response category from the next (e.g., from incorrect to correct, disagree to agree). Mathematically, this relationship can be represented by

$$x_{ij} = \begin{cases} 0 \ if \ x_{ij}^* < \tau \\ 1 \ if \ x_{ij}^* > \tau \,, \end{cases} \qquad (2)$$

such that the manifest response equals 0 or 1 depending on whether the score on the latent response distribution is less than or greater than τ, respectively. Graphically, x_{ij}^* is considered to have a standard normal distribution, and τ represents the location of the item on this distribution. This relationship is presented in Figure 32.1, where $\tau = .6$ suggesting that 27.43% of individuals endorsed the

item (scored 1) and 72.57% did not endorse the item (scored 0). The threshold, therefore, provides information regarding the location or how difficult the item was to endorse or answer correctly. The second part of the model relates latent response distributions to the common factor model, such that

$$x_{ij}^* = \lambda_{j1}\eta_{1i} + \lambda_{j2}\eta_{2i} + ... + \lambda_{jk}\eta_{ki} + u_{ij}\,, \qquad (3)$$

where λ_{jk} is the factor loading for the *j*th item on the *k*th factor, η_{ki} is the *k*th factor score for the *i*th person, and u_{ij} is a residual for person *i*'s response to item *j*. The population covariance matrix for the item factor analysis model can be written as

$$\Sigma_{xx}^* = \Lambda\Phi\Lambda' + U, \qquad (4)$$

where Σ_{xx}^* is a *j* × *j* matrix of population correlations between item response propensities (tetrachoric/polychoric correlations), Λ is a *j* × *k* matrix of factor loadings, Φ is a *k* × *k* matrix of common factor covariances, and U is a *j* × *j* matrix of unique factor variances and covariances, which is often specified to be diagonal. When U is diagonal, item covariances are entirely represented by the common factor(s). This is a common assumption in item response models and is termed local or conditional independence.

The main issues addressed by the item factor analysis model are (a) the number of dimensions needed to adequately represent item correlations,

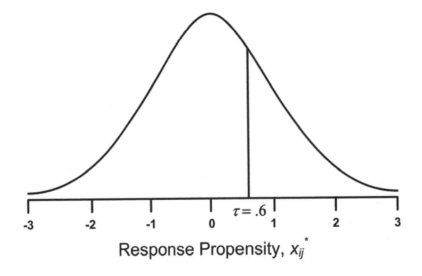

FIGURE 32.1.   Representation of the relation between the latent response propensity and the observed response for a dichotomous item with a single threshold, τ.

(b) which items represent each factor, (c) the strength of the associations between items and factors, and (d) the magnitude and direction of associations among factors. Often, a goal of test developers is to measure a single construct, and therefore they want to determine whether a single dimension underlies item responses. In certain situations, test developers may remove items that are more closely related to a secondary dimension, loosely related to the dominant factor, or multidimensional. This practice may limit the generalizabilty and validity of the construct by making the test's representation of the construct too narrowly defined. Little, Lindenberger, and Nesselroade (1999) discussed how some of these practices, while increasing estimates of reliability, decrease factor representation.

The item factor analysis model can be extended to model ordered polytomous responses (e.g., rating scales), often used in psychology, by means of invoking additional threshold parameters that relate multiple categorical responses to latent response distributions. For example, items with three response options (e.g., 1–3) would have two thresholds (τ_1–τ_2) to separate response categories. This relationship between the latent response distribution and a three-category item is depicted in Figure 32.2 and can be written as

$$x_{ij} = \begin{cases} 1 & if\ x_{ij}^{*} < \tau_1 \\ 2 & if\ \tau_1 < x_{ij}^{*} < \tau_2. \\ 3 & if\ x_{ij}^{*} > \tau_2 \end{cases} \quad (5)$$

This relationship is considered a *cumulative* response process whereby each threshold distinguishes between responding *at or below* a given category versus *above* a given category. This is opposed to an *adjacent* response process whereby the comparison is between two adjacent categories and is conditional on responding in one of those two response categories. In the cumulative model, all responses aid in the estimation of the threshold parameters.

The next series of models described were developed specifically to model item responses and come from the historical perspective of item response theory (IRT). More recently, these models have been shown to be quite similar to the models described thus far (Kamata & Bauer, 2008; Reise, Widaman, & Pugh, 1993) with a constraint on the number of dimensions (e.g., 1). Models described in this section, however, can and have been expanded to include multiple dimensions. Again, we begin with a model that is appropriate for modeling dichotomous item responses before presenting a model that can handle polytomous responses. The first item response model we describe is the two-parameter logistic model. This model directly models the probability of a specific response and is written as

$$P\left(x_{ij} = 1 \middle| \theta_i, \alpha_j, \beta_j\right) = \frac{\exp\left(\alpha_j\left(\theta_i - \beta_j\right)\right)}{1 + \exp\left(\alpha_j\left(\theta_i - \beta_j\right)\right)}, \quad (6)$$

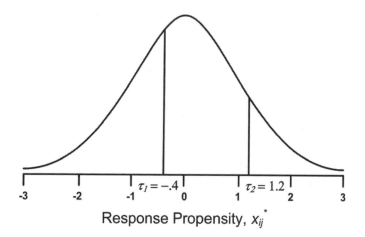

FIGURE 32.2.   Representation of the relation between the latent response propensity and the observed response for a three-category item with two thresholds, τ_1 and τ_2.

where $P\left(x_{ij}=1\middle|\theta_i,\alpha_j,\beta_j\right)$ is the probability of individual i responding in the higher of the two categories (e.g., agree or correct) for item j conditional on item and person parameters. Item parameters include α_j, the discrimination parameter, and β_j, the location parameter. The only person parameter is θ_i, person i's latent trait. The discrimination parameter indicates the strength of the association between the item and latent trait and the location parameter is the point on the latent trait at which there is a 50% chance of responding in the higher category. Figure 32.3 is a plot of three item characteristic curves that vary with respect to their discrimination ($\alpha_j = 0.8$, 1.3, and 1.7) and location ($\beta_j = -1.5, 0.2,$ and 1.6) parameters. The midpoint of items with higher location parameters appear further to the right, indicating a higher trait level is needed to have a 50% change of responding in the higher category. Items with stronger discrimination parameters show sharper differences in the likelihood of responding in the higher category (steeper slopes). When an equality constraint is placed on the discrimination parameters, the model reduces to the one-parameter logistic model or Rasch model (Rasch, 1960). Item parameters from Equation 6 map onto the factor loading and threshold parameters from the item factor analysis model and can be derived from one another (see Kamata & Bauer, 2008).

Several item response models are appropriate for polytomous response scales. Commonly used polytomous item response models for ordered responses include the partial credit model (PCM; Masters, 1982), generalized PCM (Muraki, 1992), and graded response model (GRM; Samejima, 1969). These models differ in the number of item parameters and constraints and in whether the response process is modeled as cumulative or adjacent. These differences cause the models to have different measurement properties, which can lead test developers to prefer one model over another. We present the GRM because it is one of the most general models for polytomous responses and is often used in psychological research. The graded response model can be written as

$$P^*\left(x_{ij}=c\middle|\theta_i,\alpha_j,\beta_{jc}\right)=\frac{\exp\left(\alpha_j\left(\theta_i-\beta_{jc}\right)\right)}{1+\exp\left(\alpha_j\left(\theta_i-\beta_{jc}\right)\right)},\quad(7)$$

where $P^*\left(x_{ij}=c\middle|\theta_i,\alpha_j,\beta_{jc}\right)$ is the probability of responding in or above category c conditional on person and item parameters. As with the 2PL, item parameters include α_j, a discrimination parameter, and β_{jc}, the location parameter separating category $c-1$ from c, and person parameters include θ_i, the latent trait. The probability of responding in a given category can be calculated by subtracting the

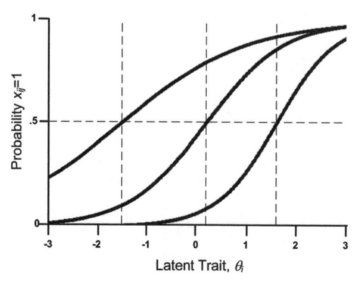

FIGURE 32.3. Item characteristic curve for a single item with $\alpha = 1$ and $\beta = 0$. Probability of endorsement is on the y-axis, and the latent trait is on the x-axis.

probability of responding in or above category $c + 1$ from the probability of responding in or above category c.

In addition to the use of these models in assessing dimensionality, researchers should pay close attention to the absolute and relative size of item parameters. For example, the Center for Epidemiologic Studies—Depression (CES–D) scale has an item that directly asks the respondent how depressed he or she has felt. In an item analysis of the CES–D, it is logical to expect this item to have a strong discrimination parameter and one that is greater than any other item. This would indicate the scale is appropriately centered on the construct. Furthermore, items related to the inability to shake off the blues or feeling sad would be expected to also have strong discrimination parameters but not as strong as the feeling depressed item. These items may represent a second tier in the magnitude of discrimination parameters as they are closely related to the construct. A collection of expectations regarding the size of discrimination and location parameters can be useful in establishing internal validity. Additionally, metrics, such as those proposed by Westen and Rosenthal (2003) and discussed later in the chapter, can be utilized to quantify how an expected pattern of discrimination and location parameters matches the observed patterns.

Reliability and test information.   Once the construct space is appropriately understood in terms of dimensionality, the next question is how reliably each dimension is measured. Often, researchers estimate Cronbach's alpha to assess reliability. This view of reliability only assesses internal consistency, however, and heavy reliance on Cronbach's alpha can lead to item homogeneity and a lack of construct representation. IRT offers another approach to reliability and recognizes that a test does not have a single reliability but rather that reliability is a function of (a) the strength of associations between items and construct (α_j, λ_j) and (b) the distance between item difficulty (location) and person's latent trait ($\theta_i - \beta_j$). If the test is not well targeted to the population, scores obtained from the test will not adequately represent the person's latent trait. In IRT, item and test information are used to determine the

standard error of measurement. For the 2*PL* model, item information is calculated as

$$I_j(\theta) = \alpha_j^2 P(\theta)\big(1 - P(\theta)\big), \tag{8}$$

where $I_j(\theta)$ is item information for item j at a trait level of θ, α_j is the item discrimination parameter, and $P(\theta)$ is the probability of endorsing (responding correctly, scoring 1 vs. 0) the item at a trait level of θ. Item information varies as a function of θ, which leads to reliability depending on θ. Test information is simply the sum of the item information curves (if local independence holds),

$$I(\theta) = \sum_{j=1}^{J} I_j(\theta). \tag{9}$$

Finally, the standard error is the square root of the reciprocal of test information at a specific trait level:

$$SE(\theta) = \frac{1}{\sqrt{I(\theta)}}. \tag{10}$$

In terms of validity, it is important to know how reliability varies as a function of trait level—for a test to be valid, it should demonstrate adequate reliability for the range of trait levels assessed.

Measurement invariance and differential item functioning.   Another important aspect of internal validity is whether items show any bias, whether it be related to gender, ethnicity, English language learner status, and so on. The examination of item, and thus test, bias is a question of whether item parameters are invariant for people of different groups, controlling for trait level. In the structural modeling framework, this is referred to as a question of measurement invariance (Meredith, 1964, 1965, 1993; Meredith & Horn, 2001), and in IRT, it is referred to as a question of differential item functioning (DIF; Thissen, Steinberg, & Gerrard, 1986). Both the structural equation model (SEM) and IRT frameworks are appropriate for examining item and test bias. However, SEM and IRT approaches to the study of measurement invariance often proceed in different ways. In either framework, there are a few different analytic techniques for studying measurement invariance (see Woods, 2009). We briefly describe the multiple group method here because of its common usage for studying measurement invariance and refer readers to Muthén (1985), Muthén and Lehman (1985), and Woods (2009) for a more in-depth discussions of the Multiple Indicator–Multiple Cause (MIMIC) Model approach.

A major analytic technique for studying measurement invariance is the multiple group approach in which the data are separated in two (or more) non-overlapping (mutually exclusive) groups, and the item factor analysis model or item response model is fit to the data for each group. Researchers familiar with SEM often take more of an entire test-based approach and begin with separately estimating all item parameters and identifying the model by fixing the mean and variance of the latent factor to 0 and 1, respectively. In the next model, factor loadings, λ, are constrained to be equal over groups, and the factor variance is estimated for all the groups except the first in the weak factorial invariance model. The fit weak model is compared with the baseline model. If the fit of the weak model is not significantly worse than the fit of the baseline model, then the process is continued. Next, item thresholds, τ, are constrained to be equal over groups, and the factor mean is estimated for all the groups except the first in the strong factorial invariance model. The fit of the strong model is compared with the weak model. If the strong model does not fit significantly worse than the weak model, then the items do not show bias with respect to the grouping variable. If the comparisons of the weak and baseline or strong and weak models lead to significant differences in model fit, then a more in-depth evaluation of the sources of the lack of invariance are studied and partial invariance models may be considered. Occasionally, strict invariance, the invariance of residual variances, is examined at the item level; however, at the item level, this investigation can lead to estimation issues and does not provide information regarding item or test bias.

Researchers familiar with IRT often take more of an item-by-item approach. The approach is initiated by fitting models for each group for which discrimination and location parameters are constrained to

be equal for all items, and the mean and variance of θ are separately estimated for each group. This is considered the invariance model because all item parameters are equated. Then, one by one the discrimination and location parameters for a single item, referred to as the target item, are separately estimated for each group. The fit of this alternate model is compared with the invariance model. If the fit of the alternate and invariance model are not significantly different, then the process is repeated until all items are examined. If the difference in model fit is significant, then this is noted because the item *may* show bias and the process is repeated. The goal of this procedure is to determine the anchor items—items whose parameters are invariant over groups. This process is iterative as all items are examined. If relaxing the equality constraint on item parameters for multiple items leads to an improvement in fit, then the item that led to the largest improvement is set aside and the process is repeated until the anchor set is determined. Once the anchor set is determined, item parameters for all potentially biased items are examined for a lack of invariance with respect to the anchor set. If the alternate model fits significantly better than the invariance model, then item parameters are examined separately to see whether the discrimination or location parameter(s) are the source of the change in model fit. If the location parameter is the only source of the difference in model fit, then the item shows *uniform* DIF. If the discrimination parameter is a source of the difference in model fit, then the item shows *nonuniform* DIF.

Uniform DIF indicates the item is universally easier (or harder depending on the direction of the group difference) for one of the groups. Figure 32.4a contains two item characteristic curves from a reference and focal group for an item that shows uniform DIF. As seen in this figure, a member of the focal group always needs a higher latent trait score (θ) to have the same probability of correctly responding (or agreeing) to the item as a member from the reference group. Nonuniform DIF indicates that the item is easier at certain levels of θ and harder for others. Figure 32.4b contains two item characteristic curves from an item that shows nonuniform DIF. As seen in this figure, for lower ability participants, the

(a)

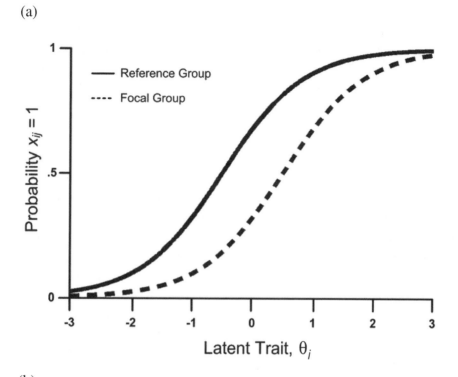

(b)

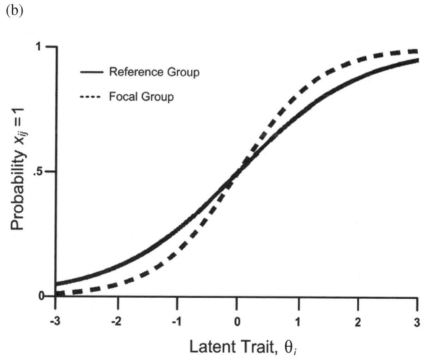

FIGURE 32.4. Item characteristic curves for an item with uniform differential item functioning (a) and nonuniform differential item functioning (b).

reference group is more likely to correctly respond controlling for θ; however, for higher ability participants, the focal group is more likely to correctly respond controlling for θ.

External Validity

External validity of a test places the focus on a test score's association with additional variables, including measures of the same construct, measures of different constructs, and clinical diagnoses. These associations provide information regarding whether the test measures the construct it is intended to measure and begins to examine the appropriateness of test score interpretations. For all external validity, strong theoretical notions regarding expected associations are necessary for external validity to be demonstrated. We consider external validity as having several components, including criterion-related validity (which is composed of concurrent, predictive, and postdictive validity), convergent and discriminant validity, and change validity as well as thorough examinations of the interpretations and consequences of test scores. We describe each of these components and how they can be studied.

Criterion-related validity. Criterion-related validity is the degree to which scores from the test under examination correlate in expected ways with a network of measures that have previously been validated. When examining criterion-related validity, it is important for the criteria to have been previously validated and for researchers to know the degree of validity the criteria have demonstrated.

Criterion-related validity is composed of concurrent validity, predictive validity, and postdictive validity. Differences between them simply relate to when the criteria measurements are taken. Correlations with criteria measured at the same time as the test under examination provide information regarding concurrent validity, correlations with criteria measured at some time in the future provide information regarding predictive validity, and correlations with criteria measured at some time in the past provide information regarding postdicitive validity. When examining criterion-related validity, researchers often correlate the test under examination with a variety of measures that are expected to show a range of correlations— strong positive, weak positive, zero, weak negative, and strong negative. If the test correlates in expected ways with criteria, then validity is demonstrated. It can be difficult to determine the degree of validity, however, because test developers and researchers are not often specific regarding the size of expected correlations. We propose some guidelines regarding the expected size of correlations and highlight Westen and Rosenthal's (2003) work on construct validity.

Theory often guides expected correlations with criteria, and we agree that this should be the driving force; however, at the same time, it is important to have certain universal standards. For example, measures of the same construct should correlate at least .6 with one another; measures designed to measure different but related constructs should have correlations that range from .3 to .5. When testing whether the test correlates with additional variables in expected ways, it is important to specifically test whether the obtained correlation is significantly different from the expected correlation (as opposed to 0), and if so, by how much. In these cases, distance measures may be useful (see Westen & Rosenthal, 2003).

Westen and Rosenthal (2003) proposed two measures, based on the pattern of expected and obtained correlations, to quantify construct validity. The first measure, termed $r_{alerting-CV}$, is calculated as the correlation between expected and obtained correlations. Westen and Rosenthal noted that more accurate results can be obtained by first transforming expected and observed correlations into their *Fisher Z* equivalents—for example, if we are examining the external validity of a new measure of externalizing behavior and collect six additional measures for validation purposes. We expect the externalizing behavior measure to correlate with our criteria as follows: (a) .6 with the Child Behavior Checklist (CBCL) Externalizing, (b) .3 with CBCL Internalizing, (c) .1 with depression, (d) –.2 with nonverbal intelligence, (e) –.3 with teacher-rated academic skills, and (f) –.5 with the Social Skills Rating System (SSRS) Cooperation. Data are then obtained and the following correlation pattern is found: (a) .4 with CBCL Externalizing, (b) .3 with CBCL Internalizing, (c) .3 with depression, (d) –.3 with nonverbal intelligence, (e) –.4 with teacher-rated academic skills, and (f) –.4 with SSRS Cooperation. These correlations are then transformed into their Fisher Z equivalents and correlated. The resultant is the $r_{alerting-CV}$ and is .92. This value suggests that there is a good match between expected and obtained correlations. As more criteria variables are collected, $r_{alerting-CV}$ becomes more stable and therefore a more reliable index of criteria-related validity. The focus of $r_{alerting-CV}$ is on relative and not absolute magnitudes of expected and observed correlations.

For example, if observed correlations in our example changed by $-.2$, then $r_{alerting-CV}$ would remain high even though the expected and observed correlations would be quite different. However, a distance measure would increase appropriately. This highlights why several measures should be used in conjunction to assess validity.

The second index Westen and Rosenthal (2003) proposed is termed $r_{contrast-CV}$ and, like $r_{alerting-CV}$, is based on the match between the expected and observed correlations but also includes information about the median intercorrelation among criteria variables and the absolute values of the correlations between the validating test and criteria measures. This measure is not described in detail here and we refer readers to Rosenthal, Rosnow, and Rubin (2000) and Westen and Rosenthal (2003).

Convergent and discriminant validity. Convergent and discriminant validity are aspects of external validity and criteria-based validity whereby the test under examination is expected to correlate highly with measures of the same construct and not correlate highly with measures of different constructs. Campbell and Fiske (1959) presented a method for examining convergent and discriminant validity via the MTMM design. An MTMM design is when multiple traits are assessed with multiple methods of data collection. This design can be very informative in psychology because many constructs can be assessed with a variety of assessment methods, and the various methods of assessment may influence scores. For example, when attempting to measure externalizing behaviors, it is useful to observe the child at home and at school as well as ask his or her parents, teacher, friend's parent, and caregiver to complete questionnaires. These various methods of assessing the child's level of externalizing behavior are likely to show a degree of similarity because they are measures of externalizing behavior, but they also show differences caused by the method of assessment or the context of assessment. Differences caused by the method or context of assessment can lead to biased correlations with additional variables depending on whether the additional variables share the method or context of assessment. When multiple traits are crossed with multiple methods of

assessment, variability associated with the method or context can be accounted for and removed when examining relations among the traits.

Campbell and Fiske (1959) discussed how a systematic exploration of a correlation matrix derived from MTMM data can provide information regarding convergent and discriminant validity and method effects. The correlation matrix from MTMM data can be decomposed into sections reflecting various combinations of traits and methods: monotrait–heteromethod, heterotrait–heteromethod, heterotrait–monomethod, and monotrait–monomethod. Monotrait–heteromethod correlations are obtained from measures of a given trait obtained from multiple methods; heterotrait–heteromethod correlations are obtained from different traits measured by different methods; heterotrait–monomethod correlations are obtained from different traits by a single method; and monotrait–monomethod correlations are reliability estimates. Comparisons between these configurations of correlations can be used to examine convergent and discriminant validity and to evaluate method-related variance in the observed scores. Specifically, convergent validity is shown by strong monotrait–heteromethod correlations; discriminant validity is shown by weak heterotrait–heteromethod correlations, and method effects are indicated by strong heterotrait–monomethod correlations.

Since Campbell and Fiske (1959) proposed the MTMM design, several statistical methods have been proposed to analyze MTMM data as opposed to Campbell and Fiske's correlation comparison approach, including analysis of variance, principal components analysis, and confirmatory factor models (CFM). Currently, CFMs are the most commonly utilized analytic technique and include various specifications, including the correlated uniqueness (CU) model (Marsh, Byrne, & Craven, 1992; Marsh & Grayson, 1995), correlated trait–correlated method (CT-CM) model (Kenny & Kashy, 1992; Marsh & Hocevar, 1983; Widaman, 1985), correlated trait–correlated method minus one (CT-C(M-1)) model (Eid, 2000), and direct product model (Browne, 1984; Cudeck, 1988; Wothke & Browne, 1990). Each of these models has benefits and drawbacks (Lance, Noble, & Scullen, 2002); however, we focus on the CT-CM model because of its more common use and intuitive appeal, and because traits and methods are directly modeled with latent factors (Grimm, Pianta, & Konold, 2009).

The CT-CM model is a CFM with trait, method, and unique factors. Trait factors are indicated by monotrait–heteromethod variables and method factors are indicated by heterotrait–monomethod variables. In a CT-CM model, trait factors covary with one another and method factors covary with one another, but trait factors are independent from method factors for identification purposes (Grayson & Marsh, 1994; Widaman, 1985). Unique factors account for variability that remains unexplained by trait and method factors. A CT-CM model with m methods and t traits can be written as

$$y_i = \Lambda_t \eta_{ti} + \Lambda_m \eta_{mi} + u_i , \qquad (11)$$

where y_i is an $mt \times 1$ vector of observed scores for individual i, Λ_t is an $mt \times t$ matrix of *trait* factor loadings, η_{ti} is a $t \times 1$ vector of latent *trait* factor scores for individual i, Λ_m is an $mt \times m$ matrix of *method* factor loadings, η_{mi} is an $m \times 1$ vector of latent *method* factor scores for individual i, and u_i is an $mt \times 1$ vector of residual scores for individual i.

The population and covariance structure (Σ) of the observed data can be written as

$$\Sigma = \Lambda_t \Phi_t \Lambda_t' + \Lambda_m \Phi_m \Lambda_m' + U , \qquad (12)$$

where Σ is an $mt \times mt$ population covariance matrix, Φ_t is a $t \times t$ latent variable covariance matrix for the *trait* factors, Φ_m is an $m \times m$ latent variable covariance matrix for the *method* factors, and U is an $mt \times mt$ matrix of unique factor covariances. Figure 32.5 is a path diagram of the CT-CM model with three traits (internalizing, externalizing, and attention problems) and three methods or informants (self, mother, and father). In the CT-CM model, convergent validity is shown by strong trait factor loadings, discriminant validity is shown by weak trait factor correlations, and strong method factor loadings indicate method effects are contaminating observed scores (Widaman, 1985).

CT-CM models have been fit to a variety of psychological measures, and many measures have shown considerable amounts of method variance,

especially measures that rely on self- and other-reports (e.g., Grimm et al., 2009; Konold & Pianta, 2007). Occasionally measures show more method variance than trait variance. For example, in a longitudinal study of behavior changes during elementary school, Grimm et al. (2009) analyzed data from the National Institute of Child Health and Human Development's Study of Early Child Care and Youth Development. These data included reports of child behavior by the child's mother, father, and teacher in first, third, fourth, and fifth grades. Grimm et al. (2009) fit a longitudinal CT-CM model and found that 4% to 74% of the observed variance in child behavior ratings was related to the informant who completed the form whereas 9% to 55% of the variance was associated with the trait being assessed.

The CT-CM factor model, along with other MTMM CFMs, can be embedded into analytic models to account for method variance and yield unbiased estimates of associations between traits and additional variables. For example, analyses conducted for Grimm et al. (2009), but not presented, included a series of child, mother, and father variables as predictors of the trait and method factors. Maternal depression, while predictive of children's behavior problems, also significantly predicted the mother method factor. Similarly, paternal depression was predictive of the father factor in addition to children's behavior problems. These results suggest that parental depression skewed their view of the child's level of behavior problems.

Change

Cronbach and Meehl (1955) discussed studying the change aspect of construct validity; however it appears to often be overlooked when examining construct validity. How observed test scores change should match theoretical notions regarding how the construct is expected to change (Grimm, Ram, & Hamagami, 2011). Studying change requires theoretical notions regarding specific aspects of change, such as timing, tempo, acceleration, transitions, and asymptotes as well as how these aspects are expected to vary over persons (Ram & Grimm, 2007). For example, many aspects of academic achievement follow elongated *S*-shaped developmental patterns that can be approximated by logistic, Gompertz, and

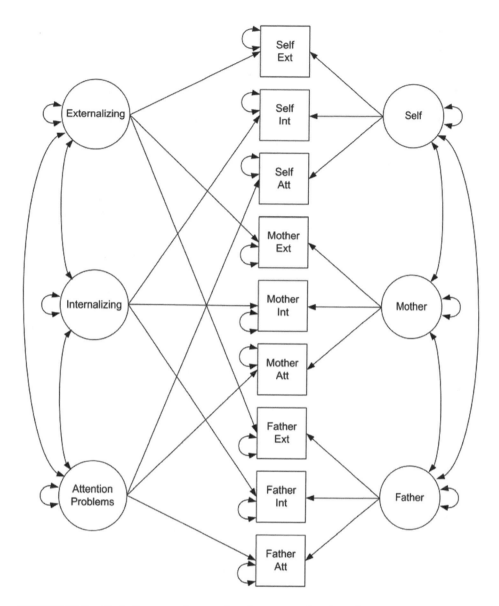

FIGURE 32.5. Path diagram of a correlated-trait correlated-method model with three traits and three methods or informants.

Richards' growth curves (Choi, Harring, & Hancock, 2009; Grimm & Ram, 2009). Measures of academic achievement that do not follow the predicted pattern of changes may lack construct validity related to change processes.

Change can be systematically examined using latent growth curves (McArdle & Epstein, 1987; Meredith & Tisak, 1990). Latent growth curves allow for modeling within-person change and between-person differences in change. Growth curves can be structured to take on many functional forms (e.g., linear and exponential), which describe specific patterns of change over time and, as such,

offer developmentalists a collection of models useful for testing specific hypotheses about change (Burchinal & Appelbaum, 1991). Growth curves can be fit in the structural modeling and multilevel modeling frameworks (Ferrer, Hamagami, & McArdle, 2004), each framework has its advantages and disadvantages (Ghisletta & Lindenberger, 2004), and mathematically identical models can be specified in each framework. As a structural model, the latent growth curve is specified as a restricted common factor model, which can be written as

$$y_i = \Lambda \eta_i + u_i, \qquad (13)$$

where y_i is a $p \times 1$ vector of repeated measurements of variable y for individual i, Λ is a $p \times q$ matrix of factor loadings, η_i is a $q \times 1$ vector of latent factor scores, and u_i is a $p \times 1$ vector of unique variances. Latent factor scores are composed of sample-level means and individual deviations written as

$$\eta_i = \alpha + \zeta_i, \qquad (14)$$

where α is a $q \times 1$ vector of latent factor means and ζ_i is a $q \times 1$ vector of latent factor mean deviations. Specific hypotheses are tested by placing constraints on the Λ matrix, where the pattern of changes are structured. For example, a linear change model is specified by placing 1s in the first column of Λ, to define the intercept, and linearly changing values in the second column, to define the linear slope. Various constraints on the Λ matrix allow researchers to test specific expectations regarding how the change process unfolds, which can be used to evaluate change validity.

Interpretations and implications. Much of the work on validity has focused on interpretations and implications of measurement. It is often said that one does not validate a test, rather the interpretations of test scores, which can have many interpretations. Test interpretations and the decisions made on the basis of those interpretations are the most far-reaching aspect of validity because of their effect on people's lives. Important decisions are made on the basis of psychological and other types of tests. Examples include the use of intelligence tests to help determine whether a defendant is able to stand trial, the use of SAT scores to help determine college admissions, and a self-report depression measure to help determine whether a person should be referred for clinical help. We used the term "help determine" because most decisions are multifaceted; however, it is important to note that several decisions are almost entirely made on the basis of a test score, such as state licensing (e.g., teaching) exams.

In many cases, a criterion measure is categorical, such as a decision to be referred for additional services or a clinical diagnosis. Categorical criteria can be included to evaluate validity in the ways discussed thus far. However, there are additional aspects of validity to examine when a test is used to make a yes or no decision (see Meehl & Rosen, 1955) because there is a cutoff score, a specific score on the test that determines what decision is made. For example, when validating a new measure of depression, it may be of interest to know what score best distinguishes between persons who are and are not diagnosed with depression.

Decision theory (Chernoff & Moses, 1959; Cronbach & Gleser, 1965; Meehl & Rosen, 1955) is a statistical framework for determining optimal cutoff scores that maximize prediction accuracy. To aid in this discussion, we provide simulated data partly based on empirical data on SAT scores and the likelihood of graduating from the University of California within 6 years, using archival data from university files. In the simulated data, we increased the strength of the association between SAT scores and the likelihood of graduation. This is not an ideal example because admission decisions were partially based on the SAT, so the sample is not a random sample of students who *applied* for admission and decided to attend the University of California but rather a sample of students who had been *accepted* for admission and decided to attend.

Decision theory is largely based on logistic regression because the outcome is often dichotomous (e.g., graduation status and referral for special services). However, logistic regression alone does not provide information regarding an optimal cutoff score. When decisions are made regarding an unobservable dichotomy (e.g., gold standard) on the basis of an observed test score, there are four possible outcomes—two correct decisions and two incorrect decisions. The two correct decisions are true positives and true negatives. In our SAT example, a true positive is when we decide to accept the student on the basis of their SAT score and the student graduates. A true negative is when we decide to reject the student on the basis of their SAT score and, if accepted, the student would not have graduated. The two incorrect decisions are false positives and false negatives. A false positive is when we decide to accept the student on the basis of their SAT score, but the student does not graduate. A false negative is when we decide to reject the student on the basis of their SAT score, but, if accepted, the student would have graduated. These decisions highlight why a random sample collected before any decision criteria were imposed is necessary for conducting decision theory.

In practice, we often want to maximize the likelihood of true positive and true negatives and minimize the likelihood of false positives and false negatives. However, there are situations in which false positives and false negatives are not created equal as certain mistakes are seen as more detrimental than others (often in terms of cost or opportunity). For example, denying a student admission to the University of California who would have graduated (false negative) may be seen as a greater mistake than admitting a student who would not have graduated (false positive). When conducting decision theory analyses, it is necessary to consider the relative weighting of false positive and false negatives because, as we will show, it can have a large impact on the cutoff score.

Going back to our example, we fit a logistic regression model predicting the likelihood of graduating from the students' high school SAT score. In these analyses, SAT scores were rescaled (divided by

100) to range from 0 to 16. Thus, a 1-point change in the rescaled variable represents a 100-point change in the SAT. High school SAT was a significant predictor of the graduation likelihood, $\chi^2(1) = 3,063$, accounting for a maximum rescaled R^2 of .30. The odds ratio for high school SAT was 2.17, suggesting that students were 2.17 times more likely to graduate for a 100-point change in their observed SAT score. Figure 32.6 is a plot of the predicted relationship between the high school SAT score and the probability of graduating. As seen in this figure, there is a strong positive relationship between high school SAT scores and the probability of graduating; however, this plot does not provide any information regarding an appropriate location for a cutoff score.

A classification table was then constructed for various levels of the predicted probability of graduating, estimated from the relationship between graduation status and SAT scores. The columns in this table include the number of correct and incorrect events (graduates) and nonevents (nongraduates) as well as several percentages, including (a) overall accuracy, (b) sensitivity, (c) specificity, (d) false positives, and

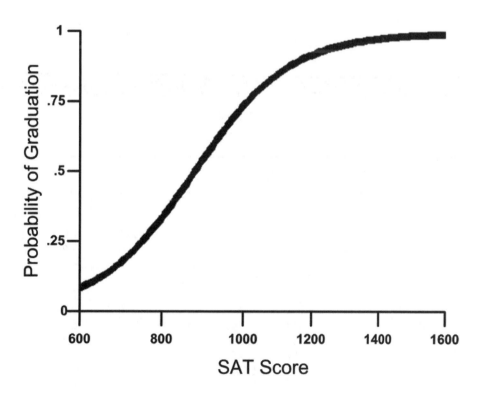

FIGURE 32.6. Predicted association between SAT score and probability of graduating within 5 years.

(e) false negatives. These values vary as a function of the cutoff score, and researchers may pay closer attention to certain classification indexes on the basis of the specific goals for test use. *Overall accuracy* is simply the percentage of correctly predicted events and nonevents divided by the total number of events and nonevents. Put another way, it is the percentage of true positives and true negatives. *Sensitivity* is the ratio of true positives to the number of actual positive events (true positives and false negatives) and is a measure of whether the cutoff score is sensitive to positive occurrences (graduation). For example, granting admission to everyone who applied to the University of California is 100% sensitive because everyone that would have graduated was admitted. *Specificity*, on the other hand, is the ratio of true negatives to the total number of actual negative events (true negatives and false negatives) and is a measure of how well the cutoff score only selects individuals who have positive outcomes. For example, granting admission to everyone who applied to the University of California is 0% specific because everyone that would not have graduated was admitted.

SAT is the only predictor variable in our logistic regression. Thus, we can calculate the SAT score that relates directly to the predicted probability. This classification table is presented in Table 32.1 for predicted probabilities between 0 and 1 in increments of .10. The table has four columns that contain information regarding correct and incorrect events (graduates) and nonevents (nongraduates). A *correct event* is an individual who was predicted to graduate, on the basis of the SAT cutoff, and did graduate. A *correct nonevent* is an individual who was predicted not to graduate and did not graduate. An *incorrect event* is an individual who was predicted to graduate and did not graduate. An *incorrect nonevent* is an individual who was predicted not to graduate but did graduate. As seen from the classification table, the highest overall accuracy is obtained with a predicted probability of .50 or a cutoff score on the SAT of 909. If this cutoff score were implemented on these data, the overall accuracy would be 80.7% compared with 77.0%, the baseline accuracy representing the likelihood of graduating if everyone was admitted. A cutoff score of 909 yields a sensitivity of 95.0% and a specificity of 32.7%. Thus, the score is very sensitive—accepting students who will graduate; however, the score is not very specific—high likelihood of rejecting students who would have graduated.

The cutoff score of 909 is the optimal cutoff score, if false positives and false negatives are considered to be equally poor outcomes. In applied work, however, it is common for the different types

---

TABLE 32.1

Decision Information for Various Cutscores on the Basis of the Association Between SAT Score and Probability of Graduation

Predicted probability	SAT score	Correct		Incorrect		Percentages				
		Event	Nonevent	Event	Nonevent	Accuracy	Sensitivity	Specificity	False positives	False negatives
.00	—	15,075	0	4,493	0	77.0	100.0	0.0	23.0	—
.10	626	15,070	84	4,409	5	77.4	100.0	1.9	22.6	5.6
.20	730	15,022	307	4,186	53	78.3	99.4	9.6	21.3	18.3
.30	799	14,910	576	3,917	165	79.1	98.9	12.8	20.8	22.3
.40	857	14,690	1,005	3,488	385	80.2	97.4	22.4	19.2	27.7
.50	909	14,319	1,467	3,026	756	80.7	95.0	32.7	17.4	34.0
.60	961	13,524	2,078	2,415	1,551	79.7	89.7	46.2	15.2	42.7
.70	1018	12,429	2,669	1,824	2,646	77.2	82.4	59.4	12.8	49.8
.80	1087	10,336	3,396	1,097	4,739	70.2	68.6	75.6	9.6	58.3
.90	1,192	6,008	4,177	316	9,067	52.0	39.9	93.0	5.0	68.5
1.00	>1,600	0	4,493	0	15,075	23.0	0.0	100.0	—	77.0

Note. Dashes indicate values are undefined.

of mistakes to not be considered equal. In our example, it is likely that denying a student admission who would graduate is thought of as a bigger mistake than granting admission to a student who would not graduate. The next question is "how much"? If the ratio is 2:1, with false negatives considered twice as bad of a mistake as false positives, then the cutoff score shifts to 830. At a 3:1 ratio, the cutoff score shifts to 750. If granting admission to a student who would not graduate is considered the bigger of the two mistakes and the ratio is 1:2, then the cutoff score shifts to 1,010. A 1:3 ratio pushes the cutoff score higher to a value of 1,040. Often the relative weights are derived from the costs associated with mistakes; however, in certain applications, costs are difficult to determine. This example is, of course, oversimplified as there are many criteria (e.g., high school grades, letters of recommendation, and so on) and constraints (e.g., class size, likelihood of attending if accepted) when making admissions decisions.

Consequences.   A recent addition to discussions of construct validity is the idea of the positive and negative as well as the intended and unintended consequences of assessment and score-based inferences at both the individual and societal levels (Messick, 1980, 1989; Shepard, 1993). For example, demographic (e.g., gender) differences in a score distribution may have unintended consequences if the test was used for selection. This is not to say there can never be any demographic-based differences in the score distributions; however, it is necessary to determine whether any differences are due to construct relevant or irrelevant test variance or criterion-relevant or -irrelevant test variance (Messick, 1989). A thorough examination of measurement invariance at the item and test level can help determine whether demographic-based differences are construct relevant or irrelevant. Additionally, a similarly thorough analysis of criterion-related validity can help determine whether demographic-based differences are criterion relevant or irrelevant.

Measurement, however, can bring about unintended consequences, which may be difficult or impossible to avoid. For example, through the No Child Left Behind Act, children in third through eighth grade are assessed annually in reading and mathematics. School-level scores from these tests are made public and important decisions are made on the basis of these results. One possible unintended consequence of this measurement program is having class time set aside to review for these tests, possibly taking time away from topics such as science, art, physical education, and social studies. Another consequence is having teachers teach to the test, which may artificially inflate scores, making them less valid. In the grand scheme of measurement, all of the possible consequences need to be considered before implementation.

DISCUSSION

In this chapter, construct validity is conceived as having two broad areas: internal and external validity representing two axes of construct validity. This representation was chosen specifically to denote that the various components of construct validity do not always neatly fall in line with either one of these broad areas of construct validity. For example, item analyses, such as those described in this chapter, primarily examine internal validity; however, examining item and test bias can be seen as part of evaluating consequences of testing, which is primarily an aspect of external validity.

Properly validating psychological measurement is the most important aspect of academic and applied psychological research because all inferences hinge on having scores with meaning that generalize to other situations and times. In this chapter, we highlighted several aspects of validity that should be considered when designing a new scale, creating a short form, revising an existing scale, or considering using an existing test for new purposes. Validation, like reliability, has a continuum—a test score is neither valid nor invalid for a specific purpose. However, it can be difficult to determine the degree of validity a test or scores from a test have. The most we can do is be explicit regarding how the validation process was conducted, including important study information, such as sample characteristics and test conditions. It is also important to be explicit regarding the outcomes of all validation studies, including estimates of item parameters and the size of all associations along with their standard errors.

In this chapter, we have focused on advanced quantitative methods that are useful for evaluating construct validity. These methods have long histories but have not always been specifically connected with studying validity. These advanced methods are able to highlight aspects of construct validity or invalidity that simple correlation and regression analyses cannot. It is our hope that advanced quantitative methods will be more commonly utilized when investigating construct validity.

References

Anastasi, A. (1986). Evolving concepts of test validation. *Annual Review of Psychology, 37*, 1–16. doi:10.1146/annurev.ps.37.020186.000245

Angoff, W. H. (1988). Validity: An evolving concept. In H. Wainer & H. I. Braum (Eds.), *Test validity* (pp. 19–32). Hillsdale, NJ: Erlbaum.

Boring, E. G. (1923). Intelligence as the tests test it. *New Republic, 35*, 35–37.

Bridgman, P. W. (1932). *The logic of modern physics.* New York, NY: Macmillan.

Brigham, C. C. (1923). *A study of American intelligence.* Princeton, NJ: Princeton University Press.

Browne, M. W. (1984). The decomposition of multitrait–multimethod matrices. *British Journal of Mathematical and Statistical Psychology, 37*, 1–21.

Burchinal, M., & Appelbaum, M. I. (1991). Estimating individual developmental functions: Methods and their assumptions. *Child Development, 62*, 23–43. doi:10.2307/1130702

Campbell, D. T., & Fiske, D. W. (1959). Convergent and discriminant validity by the multitrait–multimethod matrix. *Psychological Bulletin, 56*, 81–105. doi:10.1037/h0046016

Chernoff, H., & Moses, L. E. (1959). *Elementary decision theory.* Oxford, England: Wiley.

Choi, J., Harring, J. R., & Hancock, G. R. (2009). Latent growth modeling for logistic response functions. *Multivariate Behavioral Research, 44*, 620–645. doi:10.1080/00273170903187657

Cronbach, L. J. (1971). Test validation. In R. L. Thorndike (Ed.), *Educational measurement* (2nd ed., pp. 443–507). Washington, DC: American Council on Education.

Cronbach, L. J. (1980). Validity on parole: How can we go straight? New directions for testing and measurement: Measurement achievement over a decade. In *Proceedings of the 1979 ETS Invitational Conference* (pp. 99–108). San Francisco, CA: Jossey-Bass.

Cronbach, L. J. (1988). Five perspectives on the validity argument. In H. Wainer & H. I. Braum (Eds.), *Test validity* (pp. 3–17). Hillsdale, NJ: Erlbaum.

Cronbach, L. J. (1989). Construct validation after thirty years. In R. L. Linn (Ed.), *Intelligence: Measurement, theory, and public policy: Proceedings of a symposium in honor of Lloyd G. Humphreys* (pp. 147–171). Champaign: University of Illinois Press.

Cronbach, L. J., & Gleser, G. C. (1965). *Psychological tests and personnel decisions.* Urbana: University of Illinois Press.

Cronbach, L. J., & Meehl, P. E. (1955). Construct validity in psychological tests. *Psychological Bulletin, 52*, 281–302. doi:10.1037/h0040957

Cudeck, R. (1988). Multiplicative models and MTMM matrices. *Journal of Educational Statistics, 13*, 131–147. doi:10.2307/1164750

Eid, M. (2000). A multitrait–multimethod model with minimal assumptions. *Psychometrika, 65*, 241–261. doi:10.1007/BF02294377

Ferrer, E., Hamagami, F., & McArdle, J. J. (2004). Modeling latent growth curves with incomplete data using different types of structural equation modeling and multilevel software. *Structural Equation Modeling, 11*, 452–483. doi:10.1207/s15328007sem1103_8

Ghisletta, P., & Lindenberger, U. (2004). Static and dynamic longitudinal structural analyses of cognitive changes in old age. *Gerontology, 50*, 12–16. doi:10.1159/000074383

Grayson, D. A., & Marsh, H. W. (1994). Identification with deficient rank loading matrices in confirmatory factor analysis: Multitrait–multimethod models. *Psychometrika, 59*, 121–134. doi:10.1007/BF02294271

Grimm, K. J., Pianta, R. C., & Konold, T. (2009). Longitudinal multitrait–multimethod models for developmental research. *Multivariate Behavioral Research, 44*, 233–258. doi:10.1080/00273170902794230

Grimm, K. J., & Ram, N. (2009). Nonlinear growth models in Mplus and SAS. *Structural Equation Modeling, 16*, 676–701. doi:10.1080/10705510903206055

Grimm, K. J., Ram, N., & Hamagami, F. (2011). Nonlinear growth curves in developmental research. *Child Development, 82*, 1357–1371.

Kamata, A., & Bauer, D. J. (2008). A note on the relation between factor analytic and item response theory models. *Structural Equation Modeling, 15*, 136–153.

Kenny, D. A., & Kashy, D. A. (1992). Analysis of the multitrait–multimethod matrix by confirmatory factor analysis. *Psychological Bulletin, 112*, 165–172. doi:10.1037/0033-2909.112.1.165

Konold, T. R., & Pianta, R. C. (2007). The influence of informants' on ratings of children's behavioral functioning: A latent variable approach. *Journal of Psychoeducational Assessment, 25,* 222–236. doi:10.1177/0734282906297784

Lance, C. E., Noble, C. L., & Scullen, S. E. (2002). A critique of the correlated trait-correlated method and correlated uniquesness models for multitrait–multimethod data. *Psychological Methods, 7,* 228–244. doi:10.1037/1082-989X.7.2.228

Lawshe, C. H. (1975). A quantitative approach to content validity. *Personnel Psychology, 28,* 563–575. doi:10.1111/j.1744-6570.1975.tb01393.x

Lippmann, W. (1922). The mental age of Americans. *New Republic, 32,* 213–215.

Little, T. D., Lindenberger, U., & Nesselroade, J. R. (1999). On selecting indicators for multivariate measurement and modeling with latent variables: When "good" indicators are bad and "bad" indicators are good. *Psychological Methods, 4,* 192–211. doi:10.1037/1082-989X.4.2.192

MacCorquodale, K., & Meehl, P. E. (1948). On a distinction between hypothetical constructs and intervening variables. *Psychological Review, 55,* 95–107. doi:10.1037/h0056029

Marsh, H. W., Byrne, B. M., & Craven, R. (1992). Overcoming problems in confirmatory factor analyses of MTMM data: The correlated uniqueness model and factorial invariance. *Multivariate Behavioral Research, 27,* 489–507. doi:10.1207/s15327906mbr2704_1

Marsh, H. W., & Grayson, D. (1995). Latent variable models of multitrait–multimethod data. In R. H. Hoyle (Ed.), *Structural equation modeling: Concepts, issues, and applications* (pp. 177–198). Thousand Oaks, CA: Sage.

Marsh, H. W., & Hocevar, D. (1983). Confirmatory factor analysis of multitrait–multimethod matrices. *Journal of Educational Measurement, 20,* 231–248. doi:10.1111/j.1745-3984.1983.tb00202.x

Masters, G. N. (1982). A Rasch model for partial credit scoring. *Psychometrika, 47,* 149–174. doi:10.1007/BF02296272

McArdle, J. J., & Epstein, D. (1987). Latent growth curves within developmental structural equation models. *Child Development, 58,* 110–133. doi:10.2307/1130295

McArdle, J. J., & Prescott, C. A. (1992). Age-based construct validation using structural equation modeling. *Experimental Aging Research, 18,* 87–115.

Meehl, P. E., & Rosen, A. (1955). Antecedent probability and the efficiency of psychometric signs, patterns, or cutting scores. *Psychological Bulletin, 52,* 194–216. doi:10.1037/h0048070

Meredith, W. (1964). Notes on factorial invariance. *Psychometrika, 29,* 177–185. doi:10.1007/BF02289699

Meredith, W. (1965). A method for studying differences between groups. *Psychometrika, 30,* 15–29. doi:10.1007/BF02289744

Meredith, W. (1993). Measurement invariance, factor analysis and factorial invariance. *Psychometrika, 58,* 525–543. doi:10.1007/BF02294825

Meredith, W., & Horn, J. L. (2001). The role of factorial invariance in modeling growth and change. In L. M. Collins & A. Sayer (Eds.), *New methods for the analysis of change* (pp. 203–240). Washington, DC: American Psychological Association. doi:10.1037/10409-007

Meredith, W., & Tisak, J. (1990). Latent curve analysis. *Psychometrika, 55,* 107–122. doi:10.1007/BF02294746

Messick, S. (1975). The standard problem: Meaning and values in measurement and evaluation. *American Psychologist, 30,* 955–966. doi:10.1037/0003-066X.30.10.955

Messick, S. (1980). Test validity and the ethics of assessment. *American Psychologist, 35,* 1012–1027. doi:10.1037/0003-066X.35.11.1012

Messick, S. (1989). Validity. In R. L. Linn (Ed.), *Educational measurement* (pp. 13–103). New York, NY: Macmillan.

Messick, S. (1995). Validity of psychological assessment: Validation of inferences form persons' responses and performances as scientific inquiry into score meaning. *American Psychologist, 50,* 741–749. doi:10.1037/0003-066X.50.9.741

Muraki, E. (1992). A generalized partial credit model: Application of an EM algorithm. *Applied Psychological Measurement, 16,* 159–176. doi:10.1177/014662169201600206

Muthén, B. O. (1985). A method for studying the homogeneity of test items with respect to other relevant variables. *Journal of Educational Statistics, 10,* 121–132. doi:10.2307/1164839

Muthén, B. O., & Lehman, J. (1985). Multiple-group IRT modeling: Applications to item bias analysis. *Journal of Educational Statistics, 10,* 133–142. doi:10.2307/1164840

Ram, N., & Grimm, K. J. (2007). Using simple and complex growth models to articulate developmental change: Matching method to theory. *International Journal of Behavioral Development, 31,* 303–316. doi:10.1177/0165025407077751

Rasch, G. (1960). *Probabilistic models for some intelligence and attainment tests.* Copenhagen, Denmark: Danish Institute for Educational Research.

Reise, S. P., Widaman, K. F., & Pugh, R. H. (1993). Confirmatory factor analysis and item response theory: Two approaches for exploring measurement invariance. *Psychological Bulletin, 114*, 552–566. doi:10.1037/0033-2909.114.3.552

Rosenthal, R., Rosnow, R. L., & Rubin, D. B. (2000). *Contrasts and effect sizes in behavioral research: A correlational approach.* New York, NY: Cambridge University Press.

Samejima, F. (1969). *Estimation of latent ability using a response pattern of graded scores.* New York, NY: Psychometric Society.

Shepard, L. A. (1993). Evaluating test validity. *Review of Research in Education, 19*, 405–450.

Thissen, D., & Steinberg, L. (1986). A taxonomy of item response models. *Psychometrika, 51*, 567–577. doi:10.1007/BF02295596

Thissen, D., Steinberg, L., & Gerrard, M. (1986). Beyond group-mean differences: The concept of item bias. *Psychological Bulletin, 99*, 118–128. doi:10.1037/0033-2909.99.1.118

Watson, J. B. (1913). Psychology as the behaviorist views it. *Psychological Review, 20*, 158–177. doi:10.1037/h0074428

Westen, D., & Rosenthal, R. (2003). Quantifying construct validity: Two simple measures. *Journal of Personality and Social Psychology, 84*, 608–618. doi:10.1037/0022-3514.84.3.608

Whitely, S. E. (1983). Construct validity: Construct representation versus nomothetic span. *Psychological Bulletin, 93*, 179–197. doi:10.1037/0033-2909.93.1.179

Widaman, K. (1985). Hierarchically nested covariance structure models for multitrait–multimethod data. *Applied Psychological Measurement, 9*, 1–26. doi:10.1177/014662168500900101

Wirth, R. J., & Edwards, M. C. (2007). Item factor analysis: Current approaches and future directions. *Psychological Methods, 12*, 58–79. doi:10.1037/1082-989X.12.1.58

Wothke, W., & Browne, M. W. (1990). The direct product model for the MTMM matrix parameterized as a second order factor analysis model. *Psychometrika, 55*, 255–262. doi:10.1007/BF02295286

Woods, C. M. (2009). Evaluation of MIMIC-Model methods for DIF testing with comparison to two-group analysis. *Multivariate Behavioral Research, 44*, 1–27. doi:10.1080/00273170802620121

Yerkes, R. M. (Ed.). (1921). Psychological examining in the United States Army. *Memoirs of the National Academy of Sciences, 15*, 1–890.

CHAPTER 33

RELIABILITY

Patrick E. Shrout and Sean P. Lane

One of the first principles in research design is that measures should be selected that are reliable. *Reliability* is defined as the reproducibility of measurements, and this is the degree to which a measure produces the same values when applied repeatedly to a person or process that has not changed. This quality is observed when there are no or few random contaminations to the measure. If reliability is compromised, then the validity of the measure will also be compromised. Validity is defined as the degree to which a measure corresponds to the theoretical construct of interest. The more a measure is contaminated by measurement error, the less useful it is likely to be, and hence establishing reliability is usually considered to be the first step in ascertaining measurement quality.

In this chapter, we review the basics for reliability theory and show why it is important to quantify the degree of reliability of a measure. We provide a summary of ways to improve measurement reliability, with a special emphasis on statistical approaches. The bulk of the chapter is concerned with designs and procedures for estimating reliability of ratings and self-report measures constructed from items. We conclude with suggestions for steps to take to assess and report reliability in research studies.

RELIABILITY FROM THE PERSPECTIVE OF CLASSICAL TEST THEORY

To help make the theory of reliability concrete, we start with a few examples of ratings and self-report measurements. Suppose 10 nominations for an

award have been collected, and three judges are asked to independently rate the importance of the nominee's contributions using a 9-point scale. In addition, suppose they make binary judgments of whether participants should be considered for an award. Table 33.1 shows an example of data from such a design. We constructed this example to illustrate one judge that tends to use higher numbers (Judge 1) and another that tends to use lower numbers (Judge 3). How reliable is a randomly selected rating or judgment? How reliable is the average of the three ratings?

In a second scenario, suppose that 100 subjects are asked to report how much they agree with six different statements about gun control and gun rights. Endorsement of each item is collected on a 7-point ordinal scale. As illustrated with the hypothetical example in Table 33.2, the statements that define the attitude items might vary in extremity, and therefore the average endorsements might vary considerably from item to item. For example, on average, participants do not tend to endorse Item 3 very highly, whereas they do endorse Item 6 rather highly. How reliable is a measure based on a response to a single statement? How reliable is the average of all six responses? Can the attitude be reliably assessed with a smaller set of items than six?

Whatever the measurement procedure, we will represent the numerical score by a variable X. When an individual i has been measured by a procedure j, we write the measure as X_{ij}. X can represent quantitative values or binary (0, 1) values. Individuals are sampled from a specific population, and we will be

DOI: 10.1037/13619-034
APA Handbook of Research Methods in Psychology: Vol. 1. Foundations, Planning, Measures, and Psychometrics, H. Cooper (Editor-in-Chief)

TABLE 33.1

Example of Simulated Data for Three Judges Rating 10 Nominees for an Award

Nominee	Judge 1	Judge 2	Judge 3	**Mean for Nominee**	*SD* for Nominee
1	9 [1]	9 [1]	5 [0]	7.67 [.67]	2.31 [.47]
2	8 [0]	7 [1]	6 [1]	7.00 [.67]	1.00 [.47]
3	7 [0]	5 [0]	4 [0]	5.33 [.00]	1.53 [.00]
4	5 [0]	3 [0]	2 [0]	3.33 [.00]	1.53 [.00]
5	6 [0]	5 [0]	2 [0]	4.33 [.00]	2.08 [.00]
6	4 [0]	1 [0]	1 [0]	2.00 [.00]	1.73 [.00]
7	5 [0]	4 [0]	2 [0]	3.67 [.00]	1.53 [.00]
8	4 [0]	1 [0]	1 [0]	2.00 [.00]	1.73 [.00]
9	8 [1]	8 [1]	5 [1]	7.00 [1.0]	1.73 [.00]
10	6 [0]	5 [0]	3 [0]	4.67 [.00]	1.53 [.00]
Judge *M*	6.20 [.20]	4.80 [.30]	3.10 [.20]		
Judge *SD*	1.75 [.40]	2.70 [.46]	1.79 [.40]		

Note. The first value is a quantitative rating of the importance of the nominee's contribution on a 1-to-9 scale. In brackets is a binary indicator of whether the person is recommended for an award (1) or not recommended (0). Means and standard deviations correspond to importance scores and recommendations.

interested in both the mean and variance of X over various individuals.

According to *classical test theory* (e.g., Crocker & Algina, 1986; Lord & Novick, 1968), the overall variation in X might be influenced by error variation as well as true differences between persons. Returning to the example in Table 33.1, suppose 30 experts were available and each was asked to rate one of the 10 nominees. In this case, the ratings in the three judge columns would all be from different raters, and it is conceivable that the raters themselves might differ in how they use the rating scale. Some might tend to use somewhat lower scores and others might tend to use higher scores. If raters differ in how they use the rating scale across all nominees, then the variation of X in each column will be larger than if we use the same rater to make all the ratings in that column. In the former case, a nominee would benefit (randomly) from having a positive rater, whereas she would be penalized if assigned a tough-minded rater, and this random benefit or penalty would add variance to the ratings. In the latter case, the tendency of the rater to be impressed or skeptical would be applied to all the X values. The absolute values of the ratings would be affected by the choice of raters, but the relative ordering of nominees would not be affected by selecting a single rater. However, even a single rater might have lapses

in judgment or might be distracted for a given rating. If that rater provided replicate measures, he or she might not give the same ratings to the same nominee. In this example, the ratings could be affected by three different components: (a) the qualifications of the nominee, (b) the skepticism or rating style of the rater, and (c) random measurement error. We will initially collapse the latter two random components into a generic error variable.

The top portion of Figure 33.1 shows a path model for a measurement X (Model A). The model shows the true individual difference, T, and the random error, E, influencing a single measurement of X. Classical test theory envisions a possibly infinite number of replicate measurements, and the bottom portion of Figure 33.1 shows three such possible replications (Model B). In fact, the value of T_i is defined simply as the population average of replicate measurements for person i, which is sometimes written as $E(X_i) = T_i$. It is not observed, but it is well defined, and T_i is therefore called a *latent variable*.

The variance of X, σ_X^2, describes how much the observed measurements differ from person to person in the population being studied, whereas the variance of T, σ_T^2, describes how much the true features of persons vary in the population. In some populations σ_T^2 might be relatively small, whereas in other populations, the variance might be large. Small variance

TABLE 33.2

Example of Simulated Responses by 100 Participants Rating Agreement to Six Items About Gun Control on a 1-to-7 Scale

Participant	Item 1	Item 2	Item 3	Item 4	Item 5	Item 6	Mean for participant	SD[a] of participant responses
1	5	6	2	5	5	7	5.00	1.67
2	4	5	1	4	6	6	4.33	1.86
3	6	5	3	6	4	7	5.17	1.47
4	1	2	1	1	3	2	1.67	0.82
5	4	4	1	3	6	6	4.00	1.90
6	3	4	1	3	4	5	3.33	1.37
7	4	5	1	4	5	5	4.00	1.55
. . .[b]	. . .	. . .	. . .	. . .	. . .	. . .	. . .	. . .
99	5	3	3	6	5	7	4.83	1.60
100	4	3	1	4	5	5	3.67	1.51
Item Mean	3.94	3.77	1.34	3.74	4.78	5.75		
Item SD[a]	1.04	1.14	0.62	1.13	1.32	1.13		

[a] Sample standard deviations. [b] Lines 8 through 98 of the data are not shown here.

A

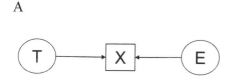

B

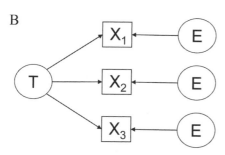

FIGURE 33.1.   Path model depicting the different components of a measured variable, *X*, as true score, *T*, and error, *E* (Model A). Path model depicting the true score, *T*, of an underlying latent variable, as measured by three replicate measures X_1, X_2, and X_3 (Model B). In classical test theory, each replicate measure is assumed to have equal error variance, although this assumption can be relaxed.

implies that the measurement distinction is subtle in the population, whereas large variation implies the opposite. In populations with small overall true score variation in *X*, any measurement error may be quite serious, leading to low values of reliability.

Classical test theory defines *error* to be the difference between X_1 and T_1, and therefore the errors are independent of the value of T_i. This allows us to decompose σ_X^2 into two components, $\sigma_X^2 = \sigma_T^2 + \sigma_E^2$, where σ_T^2 is variance resulting from systematic differences between persons and σ_E^2 is variance resulting from measurement noise. This equation shows that random measurement noise increases the total measurement variation. If measurement errors can be eliminated, then the error variance, σ_E^2, goes to zero and the total variance of *X* shrinks to σ_T^2. If errors dominate the measurement, then the majority of σ_X^2 may be attributable to σ_E^2, even if there is systematic variation between persons that is of interest. The reliability coefficient, R_X, is defined as the ratio of the population parameters, σ_T^2 and σ_X^2:

$$R_X = \frac{\sigma_T^2}{\sigma_X^2} = \frac{\sigma_T^2}{[\sigma_T^2 + \sigma_E^2]}. \quad (1)$$

R_X provides a quantitative measure of how reliable the measure *X* is. It varies from zero (*X* is due entirely to unsystematic random processes) to unity (*X* is due entirely to systematic individual differences). It can be thought of as the proportion of σ_X^2 that represents genuine, replicable differences in subjects.

From Equation 1, we can make three important points. First, because it is a function of population variances, the reliability of a specific measurement procedure can never be globally established. R_X needs to be estimated anew each time an investigator moves from one population (e.g., men, women, college students, community members, retired persons, workers from company A, workers from company B) to another. One should not claim that a measure is reliable on the basis of previous studies unless those studies were of the same subject population. Second, the reliability of a measure can be improved by either reducing error variation or by shifting to a population with more true score variation. In some cases, the population may have limited true variation because of the way it is defined (LeBreton, Burgess, Kaiser, Atchley, & James, 2003). Third, the classic definition of reliability assumes constant error variance across replicate measures. When we consider ways to obtain estimates of R_X, we will have to consider whether that assumption is reasonable.

Spearman (1910) showed that if one is interested in the correlation of *T* and another variable *Y*, but only has *X* to represent *T*, then the correlation will be too small by a factor of the square root of R_X. If both *X* and *Y* are measured with error, and one is interested in the correlation of T_X and T_Y, then ρ_{XY}, the correlation of *X* and *Y*, will equal

$$\rho_{XY} = \rho_{T_X T_Y} \sqrt{R_X R_Y} . \qquad (2)$$

For example, if both *X* and *Y* have reliabilities of .70, then a true correlation of .30, which Cohen (1988) called "medium" in size, would on average be estimated to be .21, which is by convention called "small." This is called the *attenuation effect of unreliability* (see Cochran, 1968).

The consequences of unreliable measurement are even more pernicious in multivariate analyses. For example, Hoyle and Kenny (1999) examined the impact of measurement error on inferences about

mediation processes. Suppose one believes that the effect of *X* on *Y* is completely explained by an intervening variable. Baron and Kenny (1986) have famously described how the mediation analysis involves two separate regression equations. The mediator variable, *M*, is regressed on *X*, and the outcome variable, *Y*, is simultaneously regressed on *X* and *M*. If *M* is measured with error, then the estimate of the path *M* → *Y* will be too small, and the indirect mediation path will also be too small. If *X* is measured with error, then the path *X* → *M* will be too small, but the effect of *M* → *Y* might be too large because of incomplete adjustment for *X*. In other words, the pattern of mediation results can be obscured in complicated ways by the measurement error. In some cases, complete mediation might be claimed when other important processes need to be considered, and in other cases, the researchers might fail to detect the mediated path even though the process is truly mediated.

How do we evaluate different values of R_X? If we know that a measure truly has a reliability of .50, then we know that only half its variance is systematic. That may not be what we hope for, but it might be good enough for some preliminary studies. For more definitive studies, we should aim to have reliability above .80. To provide some interpretive guidelines, Shrout (1998) has recommended the following characterizations of reliability values: .00 to .10, *virtually no reliability*; .11 to .40, *slight*; .41 to .60, *fair*; .61 to .80, *moderate*; .81 to 1.0, *substantial reliability*.

Statistical Remedies for Low Reliability

If an investigator discovers that a quantitative measure is not sufficiently reproducible, there are several remedies available that have been mentioned briefly. The measure itself can be changed, the training of those administering it can be improved, or perhaps some special instructions can be developed for the respondents that improve the purity of the measurement outcome. These are examples of procedural remedies that are often effective. There is also a statistical remedy: Obtain several independent replicate measurements and average their results. The idea is simple: Averages of replicate measures are by definition more systematic than the individual measures, so the reliability of the sum or average of items or ratings will be consistently higher than that of the components. The degree to which reliability is expected to improve in the composites has been described mathematically by Spearman (1910) and Brown (1910). Let the sum of k ratings or items $(X_1, X_2, X_3, \ldots, X_k)$ be called $W(k)$. Then the expected reliability of $W(k)$ can be written as a function of k and the reliability of the typical measurement, R_X, according to the Spearman–Brown formula:

$$R_{W(k)} = \frac{k R_X}{1 + (k-1) R_X}. \tag{3}$$

Equation 3 is based on assumptions about the comparability of the measurements that are averaged or summed into $W(k)$ and not on the form or distribution of the individual measurements. Because the result is not limited by the distribution of the X measures, the formula is even useful in calculating the expected reliability of a scale composed of k binary (0,1) items as well as scales composed of quantitative ratings or items. Averaging measures is a remedy for low reliability only if there is some evidence of replicability. It is clear that R_W will be zero if R_X is zero, regardless of the magnitude of k.

The relationship described in the Spearman–Brown formula can be used in studies of rater reliability to determine how many independent ratings need to be averaged to obtain an ideal level of reliability, say C_R. If the obtained level of reliability for a single rater is R_X, then the number of raters that are needed to produce an averaged-rater reliability of C_R is

$$k = \frac{C_R (1 - R_X)}{R_X (1 - C_R)}. \tag{4}$$

For example, if each rater only has a reliability of $R_X = .40$ and one wants a reliability of $C_R = .75$, then Equation 4 gives $k = 4.5$. This means that averages of four raters would be expected to have less than .75 reliability, whereas averages of five raters would exceed the target reliability of .75.

Special Considerations for Binary Measures

Reliability theory does not make strong assumptions about the kind of measurement embodied in X, and many of the results just described can be used when the measurement X is yes or no, such as choice of a negotiation strategy or selection of a candidate for a prize as in Table 33.1. Kraemer (1979) showed explicitly how the results work with binary judgments, such as $X = 1$ for selection and $X = 0$ for not selected. From her mathematical analysis of the problem, it can be seen that the systematic component of X that we have called $T = E(X)$ will end up as a proportion falling between the extremes of 0 and 1. If replicate measures are obtained from independent raters, T represents the expected proportion of raters who would give the award to the respondent being evaluated. If T is close to 1, then most raters would say that the respondent deserves the award, and if T is close to 0, then most would say that the respondent does not deserve the award. Although X is binary, T is quantitative in the range (0,1).

Because averages are quantitative (at least as n gets large), the psychometric results from the Spearman–Brown formula are applicable only when the composite of interest is quantitative. If the outcome of a panel of raters is a single binary selection, however, then the Spearman–Brown result does not apply. The single binary rule might depend on a consensus rule (award if all raters vote to give the award), or some similar arbitrary cutpoint. If the consensus rule is required, then the result might be *less reliable* than some of the individual raters (see Fleiss & Shrout, 1989). The total consensus rule is as weak as the least reliable rater because each has veto power regarding whether the consensual diagnosis is made.

Another special feature of binary measures is that the expected mean is related to the expected variance of that variable. For variables that are normally distributed, the mean contains no information about the variance of the variable; however, for variables that are binomial (a common distribution for binary variables), the variance is necessarily small for variables with means near 0 or 1. This fact has implications in the interpretation of Equation 1, the definition of the reliability coefficient. If the rate of endorsement of an item is low in a population, then σ_T^2 will be small. If the level of error variance is held constant, but σ_T^2 is made smaller, then R_X will be smaller. This is particularly important in clinical psychology in which certain disorders are rare in the population. One implication is that the level of error must be reduced to study disorders that have smaller base rates in the population. Any randomly false positive diagnosis makes the diagnostic system seem unreliable for rare disorders. The fact that reliability is empirically related to prevalence has caused some commentators to question the utility of reliability measures in binary variables (Grove, Andreason, McDonald-Scott, Keller, & Shapiro, 1981; Guggenmoos-Holzmann, 1993; Spitznagel & Helzer, 1985). Others have argued that dropping the statistic because of the challenge of measuring rare disorders is misguided (Shrout, 1998; Shrout, Spitzer, & Fleiss, 1987) because the reliability statistic is useful in describing the effects of measurement error on statistical analyses. Kraemer (1992) provided a clear description of the rationale of reliability studies and showed how the challenge of establishing reliability for categorical data is affected by various features of the measurement situation and the design of the reliability study.

Estimating Reliability in Practice

To estimate R_X, we need to distinguish systematic individual differences from measurement noise associated with sources of variation such as sampling a specific rater, random misunderstandings, or clerical errors. In practice, this is done by obtaining replicate measures of the latent variable T in Figure 33.1B. In these replications, T presumably stays the same but different E values occur. Classical psychometric theory defines the replication hypothetically. Suppose that a subject is selected and is measured over and over to produce the scores $X_1, X_2, X_3, \ldots, X_K$. These measures are taken independently without affecting the subject or involving recall of previous X_j values (where j indexes each replicate measure). If the measurement were height or weight, then it would be easy to take many repeated measurements of this sort, but for self-reported moods or attitudes or for taxing cognitive tasks, this ideal is difficult to achieve because the measurement process often affects the mood or attitude of interest.

Test–retest reliability.   There are a variety of measurement designs for obtaining replicate measures. The most common approach is the *test–retest* design,

which calls for making the X measurement at two points in time. Variation in the X values across replications and across respondents can be used to estimate σ_E^2, σ_T^2, and σ_X^2, and therefore R_X. The simplest estimate from this design is based on the Pearson product–moment correlation of the two measures, and Fisher's transformation can be readily applied to provide a confidence interval (e.g., Cohen, Cohen, West, & Aiken, 2003, pp. 45–46). This interval will be correct when the ratings are approximately normal in distribution. Sometimes only a sample of persons is selected for the retest phase of the reliability study (e.g., Jannarone, Macera, & Garrison, 1987). If the probability of selection is based on the scores from the first administration, then adjustment for the sampling design should be made when calculating the Pearson correlation (e.g., Shrout & Napier, 2011).

Although it is intuitively appealing, the test–retest design falls short of the ideal replication in at least two ways. On one hand, the second measurement is often affected by systematic psychological, biological, and social changes in the respondent. Insofar as one is interested in the quantity T at a given time (e.g., mood, baseline attitude, or memory at that instance), then legitimate change needs to be distinguished from measurement error. However, most test–retest studies confound legitimate change with error. In this case, the estimate of the error variance it too large and the estimate of the reliability of the first assessment will be too small. On the other hand, if the respondents remember their original responses, and then try to be *good* by reporting the same thing, then the reliability estimate may be too large. Methodologists who address these opposing biases recommend that the second assessments be carried out after a long enough period to reduce memory artifacts but promptly enough to reduce the probability of systematic changes. Recommendations of how long the period should be are more products of opinion than science, but 2 weeks often seems to work well.

Interrater reliability.   When measurements are ratings, then *interrater reliability* designs can be used. For example, if raters are evaluating the records of nominees for an award, then replicate measures are easily obtained by asking more than one rater to evaluate the same set of nominees. In this case each rater has exactly the same information about the nominee, and the differences in the ratings will reflect unreliability of the rating protocol. There are other instances when raters have different information. For example, employees who are asked to evaluate the management style of their supervisor would have possibly had different experiences. One might have felt supported and charmed by the supervisor, whereas another might have felt criticized and challenged. Although the test–retest reliability of each employee might be high, the interrater reliability of a randomly chosen employee could be low (see Murphy & Cleveland, 1995).

If the measurement design specifies that one or more raters evaluate all of the targets of study (such as nominees, film clips, or essays), and if the same set of raters is used for all summary ratings, then we say that the rater is a *fixed effect*. To estimate the reliability of fixed raters, the reliability design should specify that a sample of targets each be rated by the same set of judges. This is a crossed design with n targets crossed with k raters. A common example of a fixed-effect rater would be an investigator hiring one or two raters to do all the ratings in a given study. In this case one can estimate the reliability by having a subsample of targets rated by an additional set of fixed raters. Because the inclination of a rater to use higher or lower scores on the average is applied to all the targets, the reliability analysis focuses on the consistency of the ratings rather than absolute agreement.

If raters are randomly sampled and each target is evaluated by different raters, then we say raters are *random effects*. The reliability of raters as random effects can be estimated either using the same crossed design or a nested design in which replicate ratings are provided by different raters for each target. Because the tendency of the rater to use higher or lower scores will have important implications if different targets have different raters, the reliability analysis is influenced by the absolute agreement of ratings rather than simple consistency.

Shrout and Fleiss (1979) recommended that reliability estimates from interrater studies be calculated as *intraclass correlations* (ICC), and they

described six different ICC versions (see also McGraw & Wong, 1996). Which version is appropriate depends on whether raters are considered to be fixed or random, whether we are interested in the reliability of a single rater or the average of k raters, and whether the reliability study design is crossed or nested. Table 33.3 shows the six different ICC forms expressed as variance ratios. Shrout and Fleiss also showed how these six versions can be calculated using information from an analysis of variance (ANOVA) applied to the rating data. There are two alternate ANOVA designs, a one-way design in which ratings are nested within each of n targets, and a two-way design in which k raters are crossed with targets in an n by k design. The formulas presented by Shrout and Fleiss assume that each of the n targets is rated by the same number (k) of judges. The more general formulas in Table 33.3 can be applied to data for which there is not perfect balancing of ratings to targets, as we illustrate here.

The ICC equations in Table 33.3 essentially describe how variance component estimates can be combined to form reliability coefficients of the form described in Equation 1. ICC(1,1) is based on estimating variance components from a reliability design in which each target has his or her own raters. It refers to the expected reliability of a single rater. When k ratings are averaged, the reliability of the combined score is estimated using ICC(1,k). An example of this design would be admissions to graduate school for which each applicant submits three recommendations. The estimate of the between-target variance, σ_T^2, is based on the differences in the mean ratings of targets, after adjusting for the within-target error variance σ_W^2. This latter estimate is affected by both rater variation and error variation. A comparison of the expressions for ICC(1,1) and ICC(1,k) shows that the latter will always be equal to or larger than the former. This is because averaging the ratings reduces the size of the error term by a factor of ($1/k$).

We illustrate the calculation of ICC(1,1) and ICC(1,k=3) coefficients using the data shown in Table 33.1. We obtained the variance component estimates using standard statistical software (in this case, the VARCOMP procedure of IBM SPSS Inc., 2011; the syntax is shown in Appendix 33.1). In the

TABLE 33.3

Versions of Intraclass Correlation Statistics for Various Reliability Designs

Type of reliability study design	Raters fixed or random?	Version of intraclass correlation
Part A: Reliability of single rater		
Nested: *n* subjects rated by *k* different raters	Random	$ICR(1,1) = \dfrac{\hat{\sigma}_T^2}{\hat{\sigma}_T^2 + \hat{\sigma}_w^2}$
Subject by rater crossed design	Random	$ICR(2,1) = \dfrac{\hat{\sigma}_T^2}{\hat{\sigma}_T^2 + \hat{\sigma}_J^2 + \hat{\sigma}_e^2}$
Subject by rater crossed design	Fixed	$ICR(3,1) = \dfrac{\hat{\sigma}_T^2}{\hat{\sigma}_T^2 + \hat{\sigma}_e^2}$
Part B: Reliability of an average of *k* raters		
Nested: *n* subjects rated by *k* different raters	Random	$ICC(1,k) = \dfrac{\hat{\sigma}_T^2}{\hat{\sigma}_T^2 + \hat{\sigma}_w^2/k}$
Subject by rater crossed design	Random	$ICC(2,k) = \dfrac{\hat{\sigma}_T^2}{\hat{\sigma}_T^2 + \left(\hat{\sigma}_J^2 + \hat{\sigma}_e^2\right)/k}$
Subject by rater crossed design	Fixed	$ICC(3,k) = \dfrac{\hat{\sigma}_T^2}{\hat{\sigma}_T^2 + \hat{\sigma}_e^2/k}$

Note. ICC(1,1) and ICC(1,k) are appropriate for reliability designs in which *n* targets are rated by *k* different raters (raters nested within target). The statistical model for the *j*th rating of the *i*th target is $Y_{ij} = T_i + W_{ij}$, where W_{ij} represents the deviation of each rating from the true score of the target. ICC(2,1) and ICC(2,k) are appropriate for reliability designs in which *n* targets are rated by the same *k* raters (raters crossed target) but where raters are considered to be random and exchangeable. The statistical model for the *j*th rating of the *i*th target is $Y_{ij} = T_i + J_j + e_{ij}$, where J_j represents the average level of rating for the *j*th rater and e_{ij} represents the deviation of each rating from the true score of the target and the average rating level of the rater. ICC(3,1) and ICC(3,k) are also appropriate for reliability designs in which *n* targets are rated by the same *k* raters (raters crossed target) but where raters are considered to be fixed. The statistical model for the *j*th rating of the *i*th target is $Y_{ij} = T_i + J_j + e_{ij}$, where J_j represents the average level of rating for the *j*th rater and e_{ij} represents the deviation of each rating from the true score of the target and the average rating level of the rater.

example there is considerable variation between targets. Nominee 1 has an average rating of 7.67, whereas Nominee 6 has an average rating of 2.00. As we show in Table 33.4, the estimated variation in the nominee true scores, σ_T^2, is 3.19, and the variability of ratings within candidates is 2.90. If one hoped to use a measurement procedure that samples only one rater per target, one could only expect a reliability of ICC(1,1) = 0.52. When three ratings are averaged, the reliability goes up to ICC(1,3) = 0.77.

Even if the raters are considered to be random, an investigator might ask a set of *k* raters to make judgments on each of *n* targets in a preliminary reliability study. If the subsequent study samples one rater for each target, then we would use ICC(2,1), and if the subsequent study samples *k* raters, then we would use ICC(2,*k*). ICC(2,1) differs from ICC(1,1) in two important ways. First, the estimates of σ_T^2 and σ_E^2 are obtained from the Rater × Target crossed design, and second the denominator of the ICC explicitly takes into account the variation in judges, which we call σ_M^2 (variation of measures). The crossed design allows us to learn more about the raters than we could in the nested design. As noted previously, the ratings of Judge 1 are systematically higher than the ratings of Judge 3, and

TABLE 33.4

Variance Decompositions and Estimated Intraclass Correlations for the Table 33.1 Example Data

Variance Component	Nested		Crossed	
	Estimate	%	Estimate	%
σ^2_T	3.193	52.4	3.978	57.8
σ^2_W	2.900	47.6	–	–
σ^2_J	–	–	2.356	34.3
σ^2_E	–	–	0.544	7.9
Total	6.093	100	6.878	100
ICC(1,1)	0.52 (0.147, 0.831)		–	
ICC(1,3)	0.77 (0.341, 0.937)		–	
ICC(2,1)	–		0.58 (0.044, 0.877)	
ICC(2,3)	–		0.80 (0.121, 0.955)	
ICC(3,1)	–		0.88 (0.695, 0.965)	
ICC(3,3)	–		0.96 (0.873, 0.988)	

Note. Example has three judges evaluate 10 nominees on a 1-to-9 scale. The nested design treats each nominee as being rated by three unique judges. The crossed design treats nominees as being rated by the same three judges.

Judge 2 appears to be midway between the other two. This new information allows us to decompose the sources of error into rater variation and residual error variation. Table 33.4 shows how the estimates of the variance components (see SPSS syntax in Appendix 33.1) can be combined to estimate the reliability of a randomly selected rater (ICC(2,1) = 0.58) as well as the reliability of the average of three randomly selected raters (ICC(2,3) = 0.80).

The final ICC forms in Table 33.3 describe the reliability of ratings made by fixed raters. These forms use the same variance component estimates as ICC(2,1) and ICC(2,3), but they exclude the judge variance, σ^2_M, from the denominator of the reliability expression. Under this reliability model, any bias or tendency of a rater to be high or low applies equally to all the ratings, and therefore it does not affect the final ordering of the candidates. In this case ICC(3,1) is 0.88 and ICC(3,3) is 0.96. This indicates that after rater differences in scale usage are taken into account, the ratings in Table 33.1 are quite consistent. Therefore, a fixed rater might be reliable whereas a randomly selected rater might not.

In addition to the estimates of each ICC form, Table 33.4 shows 95% confidence intervals for the reliability results. These intervals are based on formulas reported in Shrout and Fleiss (1979), but they are easily obtained from standard software such as RELIABILITY procedure of SPSS or the psych library of the R language (Revelle, 2010). In most cases we are not interested in whether the reliability is significantly different from zero—very low reliability that is estimated in a large sample might well be significant. Instead, we should be interested in how precise the reliability estimates are, and confidence intervals tell us what range of population values are consistent with the data at hand. The Shrout and Fleiss intervals are appropriate for ratings that are approximately normally distributed.

In addition to the ANOVA-based ICC measures of rater reliability, there is an extensive literature on measuring interrater agreement when the number of targets may be limited. For example, if ratings are being made of a few executives or leaders, it might not be possible to apply the methods just reviewed. LeBreton and Senter (2008) provide an overview of interrater agreement methods and how they relate to ICC reliability estimates.

Internal consistency estimates of reliability. One of the most common ways that psychologists assess reliability is to use internal consistency estimates from measures that have multiple items. The best known version of this approach is Cronbach's alpha (Cronbach, 1951), but the approach was developed by other measurement experts in the 1930s and 1940s (Guttman, 1945; Kuder & Richardson, 1937; see also Sijtsma, 2009, for more history). The approach essentially treats different items in a scale to be replicate measures of the same construct, and these items become the analogue to raters in the section before. The justification for why different items should be considered replicate measures is part of the construct validity process (for more information on construct validity, see Chapter 32, this volume).

For many—if not most—self-report measurements in psychology, a scale is formed by summing or averaging a fixed set of items that are designed to relate to a single underlying psychological trait or symptom dimension. From the classical test theory perspective, the causal model in Figure 33.1B is usually assumed. For example, if a latent variable is degree of anxiety, then the responses to items about nervousness, tenseness, sleep disturbance, and upset stomach are all caused by high or low levels of the trait. If a person was able to reduce his level of anxiety, then presumably all of the items in the scale would be endorsed with lower scores.

If it is reasonable to assume that all the items in a scale have the same degree of association with the latent variable, and if the overall measure is an average or sum of k items, then the intraclass form ICC(3,k) shown in Table 33.3 is appropriate. In fact, this is mathematically identical to Cronbach's alpha, even though the latter traditionally is computed using correlations among the k items. There are several advantages of carrying out the computations using the more general ICC approach. One is that confidence intervals can be computed in the same way as described. Another is that investigators can consider variations of standard reliability questions. Suppose that a measurement protocol is too long—will it be possible to reduce the number of items from k to k' while still maintaining acceptable internal consistency? When the variance components for person, item (analogous to judge), and error have been estimated, it is simple to try different values of k in ICC(3,k).

We illustrate these calculations using the simulated data in Table 33.2. Using SPSS VARCOMP (see Appendix 33.1 for syntax), we estimated σ_T^2 to be .66, the variance of items σ_M^2 to be 2.15, and the residual variance σ_E^2 to be .53. Cronbach's alpha is computed by setting $k = 6$ for six fixed items in ICC(3,k) = .88. The 95% confidence interval is obtained by standard software as (.84, .92), indicating that the sample is consistent with a fairly narrow range of values of reliability (see Appendix 33.1 for syntax). If one wanted to shorten the measure to three items, how reliable would we expect the shortened scale to be? If we set $k = 3$, we obtain ICC(3,3) = [.659/(.659 + .525/3)] = 0.79. This is precisely the same result we would obtain by applying the Spearman–Brown formula (Equation 3).

Although Cronbach's alpha is the most widely used measure of reliability in the substantive literature in psychology, it is often criticized by measurement experts (e.g., Green & Yang, 2009a; Kraemer, Shrout, & Rubio-Stipec, 2007; Revelle & Zinbarg, 2009; Sijtsma, 2009) as being overly simplistic and

sometimes misleading. Authors, editors, and reviewers sometimes equate alpha with reliability rather than as an estimate with documented shortcomings. Alpha is known sometimes to underestimate actual reliability (Cortina, 1993; Sijtsma, 2009) and other times to provide estimates that are too large (Raykov, 1997). Often the bias is relatively small, but sometimes it can be striking.

The conditions that allow alpha to be considered an unbiased estimate of reliability are quite restrictive: (a) Items must be replicate indicators of the same underlying latent trait, (b) responses to the items must be independent after adjusting for the level of the latent trait, and (c) the magnitude of error associated with each item must be the same. These conditions can be represented by a variation of the path model in Figure 33.1B, which explicitly states that the path from the latent variable (the circle) to each item (the box) has the same weight and that the variance of each error term is identical across items. When these conditions hold, psychometricians say the items are *parallel* and acknowledge that in this case, alpha is an excellent way to estimate reliability.

Alpha will grossly underestimate reliability if it is applied to items for which the measurement model in Figure 33.1B does not hold. Bollen and Lennox (1991, p. 306) described Figure 33.1B as an *effects indicator model* (EIM) because the item responses are effects of the latent variable, and they distinguished it from an alternate model in which the direction of the arrows between items and latent variable are reversed. They call the alternate model a *causal indicator model* (CIM). An example of a CIM is a life-stress inventory in which some items are about stresses at home, others at work, and others in transition, such as transportation. Imagine a working mother who has a conflict with her adolescent daughter in the morning, then is delayed in arriving at work by a traffic jam caused by an accident, and finally arrives at her office to find that a deadline has been moved up by her boss. Responses to the life-stress measures of these events might be highly reliable, and the accumulation of these stressors into a single score might be valid, and yet alpha would not be high because the stressors are independent environmental events rather than something that is caused by a latent individual difference. When the

CIM is appropriate, alpha should not be computed or reported. A test–retest design or other–informant reliability design can be used to estimate reliability.

Alpha will also underestimate reliability if the items vary in the strength of their association with the latent variable, or if they are affected by more than one latent variable. For example, a scale of depression symptoms may contain some items on mood, others on psychophysiological complaints, and yet others on cognitive beliefs. Although these are all expected to be related to depression, they are not exact replications of each other. To the degree that the correlations among the items is due to the different item content rather than error, the overall reliability estimate will be smaller than it should be. Psychometricians have developed other estimators of reliability that overcome these limitations of alpha. For example, *McDonald's omega* (McDonald, 1999) takes into account the possibility that items differ in their relation to a common latent variable, and Raykov and Shrout (2002) extended omega to take into account more than one latent variable. These alternate methods can be easily implemented in the context of structural equation models (Green & Yang, 2009b) as well as in the psych package in the R language (Revelle, 2010).

Reliability can also be overestimated by Cronbach's alpha if the whole item set is affected by irrelevant global response patterns, such as mood or response biases. For instance, some computer-administered questionnaires make it easy for a participant to endorse the same response alternative (e.g., "agree somewhat") repeatedly, regardless of item content. Unless steps are taken to counteract these *response bias* patterns, they will lead to correlated errors and inflated internal consistency reliability estimates. Response biases are often addressed by mixing the items across many conceptual domains, editing the items so that half are keyed as a symptom when the respondent says "no" and half are keyed the opposite way. Scales of yea-saying and need-for-approval are sometimes constructed to identify those respondents who are susceptible to response biases. The validity of these scales, however, is a subject of discussion.

Proposed standards of evidence of reliability. Given that coefficient alpha is susceptible to

opposing biases, sometimes producing values that are too large and other times that are too small, how can we evaluate this commonly reported estimate of reliability? If the results appear to indicate high reliability, look for response artifacts that might have inflated the estimate. If provisions have been taken to address response biases, then the high level of reliability might be real. If the results indicate that there is low reliability, then look to see whether the items included within the internal consistency analysis are heterogeneous in content. It is possible that a set of items that are heterogeneous might have adequate test–retest reliability even though the internal consistency estimate is low.

Perhaps a more compelling piece of evidence is the track record of the measure being considered. If a measure has been widely used in various populations and investigators have reported high levels of test–retest and internal consistency reliability, then it might be adequate for a researcher to report an alpha coefficient or the results of a small reliability study, especially if the study design reduced the impact of response biases. Such evidence would satisfy our recommendation that reliability be studied in every new study population, and it would not impose a high burden on the investigator.

When a measure is being newly developed and proposed, the standards of evidence must be raised considerably. Suppose a measure is based on responses to *k* items, and the investigator hopes that an average response can be used as a scale score. In this case a simple report of coefficient alpha is inadequate. The EIM measurement should be justified, data collection should be structured to avoid response biases, and a factor analysis should be carried out. This analysis will indicate the number of latent variables needed to account for item correlations and the relation of each item to the loadings, and the structure should be evaluated from both reliability and validity perspectives. Unless the assumptions of coefficient alpha are met, the more flexible estimates of internal consistency reliability such as McDonald's omega should be used.

If the factor analysis step leads to selection of certain items and discarding of others, then a new sample should be drawn to assess internal consistency. Internal consistency measures, whether alpha or omega, will be upwardly biased if based on the same sample that was used to select the items.

When developing new measures, it is particularly useful to incorporate multiple designs into a reliability program. By systematically studying the kinds of replication, one can gain an insight into sources of measurement variation. This is what is recommended by Cronbach, Gleser, Nanda, and Rajaratnam (1972) in their comprehensive extension of classical test theory known as *generalizability theory* (GT). This theory encompasses both reliability and validity by asking about the extent to which a measurement procedure gives comparable results in different populations, at different times and in different contexts (for more information on generalizability theory, see Chapter 34, this volume). When raters are involved, their level of training and their demographics are also considered. Insofar as a latent variable is considered theoretically to be a trait, the generalizability program expects test–retest to yield strong stability and reliability, whereas a latent variable that is a state might be internally consistent at several times but not highly correlated over retests. Generalizability theory tends to blur the classic distinction of reliability and validity (see Brennan, 2001). How to interpret the blurred distinction has led to some controversy (Murphy & DeShon, 2000; Schmidt, Viswesvaran & Ones, 2000).

Reliability of binary and categorical measures. When binary data such as the nominations for awards in Table 33.1 is collected, reliability can be estimated directly using a special reliability statistic called *Cohen's kappa* (Cohen, 1960). Fleiss and Cohen (1973) showed that kappa is conceptually equivalent to ICR(2,1) in Table 33.3. It can be calculated simply using the entries of a 2 × 2 table showing the diagnostic agreement. In general, this agreement table is laid out as shown in the top of Figure 33.2, where the four cells are designated, *a* through *d*. Cohen (1960) pointed out that although cells *a* and *d* represent agreement, it is not sufficient to evaluate reliability by reporting the overall proportion of agreement, $P_o = (a + d)/n$. This statistic may be large even if raters assigned diagnoses by

flipping coins or rolling dice. His kappa statistic adjusts for simple chance mechanisms:

$$\text{kappa} = \frac{P_o - P_c}{1 - P_c}, \tag{5}$$

where P_o is the observed agreement, $[(a + d)/n]$, and P_c is the expected agreement because of chance:

$$P_c = [(a + c)(a + b) + (b + d)(c + d)]/n^2. \tag{6}$$

When computing kappa by hand, it is sometimes more convenient to use the following equivalent expression:

$$\text{kappa} = \frac{ad - bc}{ad - bc + n(b + c)/2}. \tag{7}$$

One advantage of calculating the reliability of binary judgments using kappa instead of intraclass correlation methods is that the expressions for kappa's standard error and confidence bounds are explicitly suited to binary data. Kappa can also be generalized to describe the overall reliability of classifications into multiple categories. Fleiss, Levin, and Paik (2003) provided an overview of many forms of kappa, and Donner and his colleagues (Donner, 1998; Donner & Eliasziw, 1992, 1994, 1997; Donner, Eliasziw, & Klar, 1996; Donner, Shoukri, Klar, & Bartfay, 2000) have done much to describe the sampling variation of kappa statistics.

The bottom section of Figure 33.2 illustrates the calculations with the binary ratings in the Table 33.1 example. Judges 1 and 3 each recommended that two persons be given an award, whereas Judge 2 recommended three persons. All three pairings of judges showed that they agreed that seven persons not be given the award, and overall agreement [calculated as $(a + d)/10$] was 90% for the pairing of Judge 1 with Judge 2 and with Judge 3, and 80% for the pairing of Judge 2 with Judge 3. Kappa, on the other hand, took the value 0.74 for the first two pairings and 0.38 for the last. These values represent estimates of how reliable a single randomly sampled rater would be in making judgments about the award. As shown in Figure 33.2, the 95% confidence bound computed using the method of Donner and Eliasziw (1992) was (0.09, 0.95) for the first two pairings and (–0.12, 0.82) for the last. The small sample does not give much closure about what the

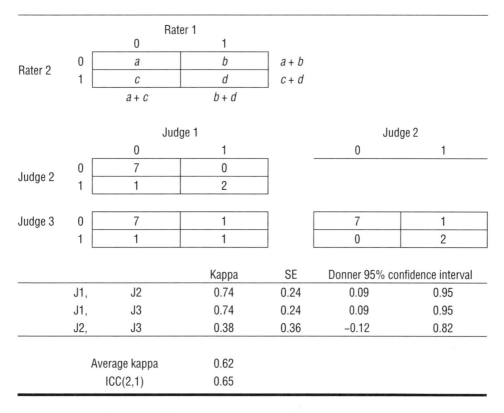

FIGURE 33.2. Illustration of prototype agreement table and numerical illustration based on binary outcomes in Table 33.1.

level of reliability is in this example. If a single summary measure of reliability were required, Fleiss et al. (2003) have recommended averaging the three pair-wise estimates or calculating the ICC(2,1) from Table 33.3. These approaches estimate the same quantity, although the unweighted average would be expected to be less efficient. The simple average in this case is 0.62, and the ICC(2,1) estimate is 0.65.

Extensions of reliability analysis. Although the estimation of reliability is an old topic in quantitative psychology, there continue to be new methodological developments in the psychometric and biostatistical literatures. One area of particular importance is the extension to longitudinal measures of change and development. For example, Laenen and her colleagues (Laenen, Alonso, & Molenberghs, 2007; Laenen, Alonso, Molenberghs, & Vangeneugden, 2009) introduced two reliability statistics that make use of longitudinal data when estimating the reliability of measures over time. One estimates the average

reliability of a measure that is administered multiple times (R_T) and the other estimates the global reliability of a measure across all time points (R_Λ).

Other procedures have been developed to estimate the reliability of change in longitudinal measurements, such as those collected in diary studies. Cranford et al. (2006) provided estimates of the reliability of change on the basis of a GT framework in which person-by-time variability is of particular interest. Wilhelm and Schoebi (2007) presented an alternate approach using multilevel modeling. These two approaches make strong assumptions about the equivalence of items in the diary scales, and so we (Lane & Shrout, 2011) have suggested a less restrictive framework for estimating the reliability of change from a factor-analytic perspective. We have proposed longitudinal analogs of McDonald's (1999) omega to take into account possible heterogeneity of items.

Other ways to quantify precision and measurement error. As a summary of measurement quality, the reliability coefficient represented by Equation 1 has many positive features. It is easy to interpret, is fairly easy to estimate, and is the relevant measure for understanding bias in statistical analysis cased by contamination with error. It has the disadvantage, however, of being a statistic that is relative to the population being studied. The amount of error in a measure is always considered in the context of the true score variation in the population. An alternate approach to studying precision and error is to focus on the relation of each item response pattern to the underlying dimension. When items are clearly phrased and related to the underlying (latent) dimension, the probability of endorsing an item category will be systematically related to the latent dimension (e.g., see Embretson & Reise, 2000). Of special interest are the slope and location of each item, indicating the relevance and severity of each item with regard to the latent dimension. Item response theory (IRT) methods are especially useful for comparing the measurement equivalence of items across different groups (e.g., Gregorich, 2006; for more information on IRT methods, see Chapter 36, this volume). These methods are related to factor analysis (McDonald, 1999; Raykov & Marcoulides, 2011), which also provides direct information about the quality of measures in relation to the latent variable of interest. Because the IRT models describe the probability of responding to an item conditional on (i.e., holding constant) the latent variable, the distribution of the latent variable in the population is considered to be less important. Some argue that IRT analyses should supplant traditional reliability analyses (e.g., Embretson & Reise, 2000).

CONCLUSION

Inadequate reliability is a measurement problem that can often be rectified by improving interview procedures or by using statistical sums or averages of replicate measures. Determining the extent to which unreliability is a problem, however, can be challenging. There are various designs for estimating reliability, but virtually all have some biases and shortcomings. Studies of sampling variability of reliability statistics (Cantor, 1996; Donner, 1998; Dunn, 1989; Walter, Eliasziw, & Donner, 1998)

suggest that sample sizes in pilot studies are often not adequate to give stable estimates about the reliability of key measurement procedures. Reliance on internal consistency measures of reliability, such as Cronbach's alpha, can give a false sense of security unless care is taken to evaluate sources of statistical bias.

When reliability is only modest, we know that validity studies and other empirical relationships will be biased. If properly specified, measurement models in structural equation methods can adjust for this bias, but often the adjustment comes at a price of less precise estimates of correlations and regression coefficients. Some researchers attempt to make ad hoc adjustments for unreliability by using Equation 2 to solve for the true correlation, corrected for attenuation. This can work if the reliability coefficient is known exactly, but as we have seen in this chapter, estimates of reliability are often subject to bias or imprecision. If one uses conservative estimates of reliability with Equation 2 such as described in Revelle and Zinbarg (2009), one would make an anticonservative adjustment of the correlation. We recommend that corrections for attenuation be used with caution.

Far better than adjusting for unreliability is attention to the improvement of measures themselves. In this quest, it is important to critically evaluate reliability studies. Specifically, if the reliability of a measure appears to be very good, ask whether there are features of the reliability design that might bias the results optimistically. Were the respondents sampled in the same way in the reliability study that they will be in the field study? Was the respondent given the chance to be inconsistent, or did the replication make use of archived information? If serious biases are not found, and the reliability study produced stable estimates, then one can put the issue of reliability behind you, at least for the population at hand.

If the reliability of a measure appears to be poor, one should also look for biases in the reliability design. How similar were the replications? Could the poor reliability results be an artifact of legitimate changes over time, heterogeneous items within a scale, or artificially different measurement conditions? Was the sample size large enough to ensure that reliability is in fact bad? Be especially suspicious if you have evidence of validity of a measure that is purported to be unreliable. Rather than dismissing a measure with apparently poor reliability, ask whether it can be improved to eliminate noise.

APPENDIX 33.1: SPSS SYNTAX FOR EXAMPLE 1 (SEE TABLE 33.1)

* Importance ratings (continuous ratings).
* (SPSS comments start with asterisk and end in period).
* Data file should have targets in rows and raters or items in columns.
* First we estimate ICC(1,1) & ICC(1,k) and their confidence intervals.

RELIABILITY
/VARIABLES = Judge1 Judge2 Judge3
/ICC = MODEL(ONEWAY).

* Next we estimate ICC(2,1) & ICC(2,k) and their **confidence intervals.**

RELIABILITY
/VARIABLES = Judge1 Judge2 Judge3
/ICC = MODEL(MIXED) TYPE(ABSOLUTE).

* Finally we estimate ICC(3,1) & ICC(3,k) and their confidence intervals.

RELIABILITY
/VARIABLES = Judge1 Judge2 Judge3
/ICC = MODEL(RANDOM) TYPE(CONSISTENCY).

* Next SPSS is asked to restructure the data file so that each rating is on a separate line.
* An index for target and for rater identifies the rating which is named Score.

VARSTOCASES
/MAKE Score FROM Judge1 Judge2 Judge3
/INDEX = Judge(3)
/KEEP = Nominee
/NULL = KEEP.

* First we decompose the variance as a nested design (one-way ANOVA).
* This would be appropriate if each nominee has different raters.

VARCOMP Score BY Nominee
/RANDOM = Nominee

/DESIGN.

* Next we decompose the variance for a crossed design.
* This would be appropriate if the same raters judged all nominees.

VARCOMP Score BY Nominee Judge
/RANDOM = Nominee Judge
/DESIGN = Nominee Judge.

* Nominations (binary ratings).
* The next syntax assumes that Table 33.1 has been opened with each nominee on a different line.
* Three binary rating variables are J1Nom, J2Nom & J3Nom.
* Estimate kappa for each of the three combinations of judges.

CROSSTABS
/TABLES = J1Nom BY J2Nom
/STATISTICS = KAPPA.
CROSSTABS
/TABLES = J1Nom BY J3Nom
/STATISTICS = KAPPA.
CROSSTABS
/TABLES = J3Nom BY J2Nom
/STATISTICS = KAPPA.

* Estimate ICC(2,1) for agreement across all 3 judges.

RELIABILITY
/VARIABLES = J1Nom J2Nom J3Nom
/ICC = MODEL(MIXED) TYPE(ABSOLUTE).

* End of SPSS syntax example.

R syntax for Example 1
Importance ratings (continuous ratings)
Comments in R follow a pound (cross hatch)
symbol
If not already loaded, get the psych package from
http://cran.r-project.org/ and load the library
before proceeding
Construct data matrix of 3 judges' importance
ratings of the 10 nominees
importance <- matrix(c(
9, 9, 5,
8, 7, 6,

```
7, 5, 4,
5, 3, 2,
6, 5, 2,
4, 1, 1,
5, 4, 2,
4, 1, 1,
8, 8, 5,
6, 5, 3),
ncol = 3,byrow = TRUE)
colnames(importance) <- paste("J",1:3,sep="")
#Names judges
rownames(importance) <- paste("N",1:10,sep="")
#Names nominees
importance #Confirms data were entered in correctly
ICC(importance) #ICC function
# Nominations (binary ratings)
nominate <- matrix(c(
1, 1, 0,
0, 1, 1,
0, 0, 0,
0, 0, 0,
0, 0, 0,
0, 0, 0,
0, 0, 0,
0, 0, 0,
1, 1, 1,
0, 0, 0),
ncol = 3,byrow = TRUE)
colnames(nominate) <- paste("J",1:3,sep="")
rownames(nominate) <- paste("N",1:10,sep="")
nominate #display nomination data
ICC(nominate)
# End of R syntax for Example 1
```

This syntax and the example data sets are available at htpp://www.psych.nyu.edu/couples/APA_reliability.

References

Baron, R. M., & Kenny, D. A. (1986). The moderator–mediator variable distinction in social psychological research: Conceptual, strategic, and statistical considerations. *Journal of Personality and Social Psychology, 51,* 1173–1182. doi:10.1037/0022-3514.51.6.1173

Bollen, K., & Lennox, R. (1991). Conventional wisdom on measurement: A structural equation perspective. *Psychological Bulletin, 110,* 305–314. doi:10.1037/0033-2909.110.2.305

Brennan, R. L. (2001). *Generalizability theory.* New York, NY: Springer.

Brown, W. (1910). Some experimental results in the correlation of mental abilities. *British Journal of Psychology, 3,* 296–322.

Cantor, A. B. (1996). Sample-size calculations for Cohen's kappa. *Psychological Methods, 1,* 150–153. doi:10.1037/1082-989X.1.2.150

Cochran, W. G. (1968). Errors in measurement in statistics. *Technometrics, 10,* 637–666. doi:10.2307/1267450

Cohen, J. (1960). A coefficient of agreement for nominal scales. *Educational and Psychological Measurement, 20,* 37–46. doi:10.1177/001316446002000104

Cohen, J. (1988). *Statistical power analysis for the behavioral sciences.* Hillside, NJ: Erlbaum.

Cohen, J., Cohen, P., West, S., & Aiken, L. (2003). *Applied multiple regression/correlation analysis* (3rd ed.). Mahwah, NJ: Erlbaum.

Cortina, J. M. (1993). What is coefficient alpha? An examination of theory and applications. *Journal of Applied Psychology, 78,* 98–104. doi:10.1037/0021-9010.78.1.98

Cranford, J. A., Shrout, P. E., Iida, M., Rafaeli, E., Yip, T., & Bolger, N. (2006). A procedure for evaluating sensitivity to within-person change: Can mood measures in diary studies detect change reliably? *Personality and Social Psychology Bulletin, 32,* 917–929. doi:10.1177/0146167206287721

Crocker, L., & Algina, J. (1986). *Introduction to classical and modern test theory.* Belmont, CA: Wadsworth.

Cronbach, L. J. (1951). Coefficient alpha and the internal structure of tests. *Psychometrika, 16,* 297–334. doi:10.1007/BF02310555

Cronbach, L. J., Gleser, G. C., Nanda, H., & Rajaratnam, N. (1972). *The dependability of behavioral measurements: Theory of generalizability for scores and profiles.* New York, NY: Wiley.

Donner, A. (1998). Sample size requirements for the comparison of two or more coefficients of inter-observer agreement. *Statistics in Medicine, 17,* 1157–1168. doi:10.1002/(SICI)1097-0258(19980530)17:10<1157::AID-SIM792>3.0.CO;2-W

Donner, A., & Eliasziw, M. (1992). A goodness-of-fit approach to inference procedures for the kappa statistic: Confidence interval construction, significance-testing and sample size estimation. *Statistics in Medicine, 11,* 1511–1519. doi:10.1002/sim.4780111109

Donner, A., & Eliasziw, M. (1994). Statistical implications of the choice between a dichotomous or continuous trait in studies of interobserver agreement. *Biometrics, 50,* 550–555. doi:10.2307/2533400

Donner, A., & Eliasziw, M. (1997). A hierarchical approach to inferences concerning interbserver agreement for multinomial data. *Statistics in Medicine, 16*, 1097–1106. doi:10.1002/(SICI)1097-0258(19970530)16:10<1097::AID-SIM523>3.0.CO;2-8

Donner, A., Eliasziw, M., & Klar, N. (1996). Testing the homogeneity of kappa statistics. *Biometrics, 52*, 176–183. doi:10.2307/2533154

Donner, A., Shoukri, M. M., Klar, N., & Bartfay, E. (2000). Testing the equality of two dependent kappa statistics. *Statistics in Medicine, 19*, 373–387. doi:10.1002/(SICI)1097-0258(20000215)19:3<373::AID-SIM337>3.0.CO;2-Y

Dunn, G. (1989). *Design and analysis of reliability studies.* New York, NY: Oxford University Press.

Embretson, S. E., & Reise, S. P. (2000). *Item response theory for psychologists.* Mahwah, NJ: Erlbaum.

Fleiss, J. L., & Cohen, J. (1973). The equivalence of weighted kappa and the intra-class coefficient as measures of reliability. *Educational and Psychological Measurement, 33*, 613–619. doi:10.1177/001316447303300309

Fleiss, J. L., Levin, B., & Paik, M. C. (2003). *Statistical methods for rates and proportions* (3rd ed.). Hoboken, NJ: Wiley. doi:10.1002/0471445428

Fleiss, J. L., & Shrout, P. E. (1989). Reliability considerations in planning diagnostic validity studies. In L. Robbins (Ed.), *The validity of psychiatric diagnoses* (pp. 279–291). New York, NY: Guilford Press.

Green, S. B., & Yang, Y. (2009a). Commentary on coefficient alpha: A cautionary tale. *Psychometrika, 74*, 121–135. doi:10.1007/s11336-008-9098-4

Green, S. B., & Yang, Y. (2009b). Reliability of summed item scores using structural equation modeling: An alternative to coefficient alpha. *Psychometrika, 74*, 155–167. doi:10.1007/s11336-008-9099-3

Gregorich, S. E. (2006). Do self-report instruments allow meaningful comparisons across diverse population groups? *Medical Care, 44*(11 Suppl 3), S78–S94. doi:10.1097/01.mlr.0000245454.12228.8f

Grove, W. M., Andreason, N. C., McDonald-Scott, P., Keller, M. B., & Shapiro, R. w. (1981). Reliability studies of psychiatric diagnosis: Theory and practice. *Archives of General Psychiatry, 38*, 408–413.

Guggenmoos-Holzmann, I. (1993). How reliable are chance-corrected measures of agreement? *Statistics in Medicine, 12*, 2191–2205. doi:10.1002/sim.4780122305

Guttman, L. (1945). A basis for analyzing test-retest reliability. *Psychometrika, 10*, 255–282. doi:10.1007/BF02288892

Hoyle, R. H., & Kenny, D. A. (1999). Sample size, reliability, and tests of statistical mediation. In R. H. Hoyle (Ed.), *Statistical strategies for small sample research* (pp. 195–222). Thousand Oaks, CA: Sage.

IBM SPSS Inc. (2011). *SPSS for Windows* (Version 20). Chicago, IL: SPSS Inc.

Jannarone, R. J., Macera, C. A., & Garrison, C. Z. (1987). Evaluating interrater agreement through "case-control" sampling. *Biometrics, 43*, 433–437. doi:10.2307/2531825

Kraemer, H. C. (1979). Ramifications of a population model for kappa as a coefficient of reliability. *Psychometrika, 44*, 461–472. doi:10.1007/BF02296208

Kraemer, H. C. (1992). Measurement of reliability for categorical data in medical research. *Statistical Methods in Medical Research, 1*, 183–199. doi:10.1177/096228029200100204

Kraemer, H. C., Shrout, P. E., & Rubio-Stipec, M. (2007). Developing the diagnostic and statistical manual V: What will "statistical" mean in *DSM–V*? *Social Psychiatry and Psychiatric Epidemiology, 42*, 259–267. doi:10.1007/s00127-007-0163-6

Kuder, G. F., & Richardson, M. W. (1937). The theory of estimation of test reliability. *Psychometrika, 2*, 151–160. doi:10.1007/BF02288391

LeBreton, J. M., Burgess, J. R. D., Kaiser, R. B., Atchley, E. K., & James, L. R. (2003). The restriction of variance hypothesis and interrater reliability and agreement: Are ratings from multiple sources really dissimilar? *Organizational Research Methods, 6*, 80–128. doi:10.1177/1094428102239427

LeBreton, J. M., & Senter, J. L. (2008). Answers to 20 questions about interrater reliability and interrater agreement. *Organizational Research Methods, 11*, 815–852. doi:10.1177/1094428106296642

Laenen, A., Alonso, A., & Molenberghs, G. (2007). A measure for the reliability of a rating scale based on longitudinal clinical trial data. *Psychometrika, 72*, 443–448. doi:10.1007/s11336-007-9002-7

Laenen, A., Alonso, A., Molenberghs, G., & Vangeneugden, T. (2009). Reliability of a longitudinal sequence of scale ratings. *Psychometrika, 74*, 49–64. doi:10.1007/s11336-008-9079-7

Lane, S. P., & Shrout, P. E. (2011). *Measuring the reliability of within-person change over time: A dynamic factor analysis approach* (Tech. Rep. No. 11.1). Available at http://www.psych.nyu.edu/couples/Reports/11.01_Lane&Shrout.pdf

Lord, F. M., & Novick, M. R. (1968). *Statistical theories of mental test scores.* Reading, MA: Addison-Wesley.

McDonald, R. P. (1999). *Test theory: A unified treatment.* Mahwah, NJ: Erlbaum.

McGraw, K. O., & Wong, S. P. (1996). Forming inferences about some intraclass correlation coefficients. *Psychological Methods, 1*, 30–46. doi:10.1037/1082-989X.1.1.30

Murphy, K. R., & Cleveland, J. N. (1995). *Understanding performance appraisal: Social, organizational, and goal based perspectives.* Thousand Oaks, CA: Sage.

Murphy, K. R., & DeShon, R. (2000). Progress in psychometrics: Can industrial and organizational psychology catch up? *Personnel Psychology, 53,* 913–924. doi:10.1111/j.1744-6570.2000.tb02423.x

Raykov, T. (1997). Scale reliability, Cronbach's coefficient alpha, and violations of essential tau-equivalence with fixed congeneric components. *Multivariate Behavioral Research, 32,* 329–353. doi:10.1207/s15327906mbr3204_2

Raykov, T., & Marcoulides, G. A. (2011). *Introduction to psychometric theory.* New York, NY: Routledge.

Raykov, T., & Shrout, P. E. (2002). Reliability of scales with general structure: Point and interval estimation using a structural equation modeling approach. *Structural Equation Modeling, 9,* 195–212. doi:10.1207/S15328007SEM0902_3

Revelle, W. (2010). *Psych: Procedures for psychological, psychometric, and personality research. R package version 1.0–88.* Retrieved from http://CRAN.R-project.org/package=psych

Revelle, W., & Zinbarg, R. E. (2009). Coefficients alpha, beta, omega, and the glb: Comments on Sijtsma. *Psychometrika, 74,* 145–154. doi:10.1007/s11336-008-9102-z

Schmidt, F. L., Viswesvaran, C., & Ones, D. S. (2000). Reliability is not validity and validity is not reliability. *Personnel Psychology, 53,* 901–912. doi:10.1111/j.1744-6570.2000.tb02422.x

Shrout, P. E. (1998). Measurement reliability and agreement in psychiatry. *Statistical Methods in Medical Research, 7,* 301–317. doi:10.1191/096228098672090967

Shrout, P. E., & Fleiss, J. L. (1979). Intraclass correlations: Uses in assessing rater reliability. *Psychological Bulletin, 86,* 420–428. doi:10.1037/0033-2909-.86.2.420

Shrout, P. E., & Napier, J. L. (2011). Analyzing survey data with complex sampling designs. In K. H. Trzesniewski, M. B. Donnellan, & R. E. Lucas (Eds.), *Secondary data analysis: An introduction for psychologists* (pp. 63–81) Washington, DC: American Psychological Association.

Shrout, P. E., Spitzer, R. L., & Fleiss, J. L. (1987). Quantification of agreement in psychiatric diagnosis revisited. *Archives of General Psychiatry, 44,* 172–177.

Sijtsma, K. (2009). On the use, the misuse, and the very limited usefulness of Cronbach's alpha. *Psychometrika, 74,* 107–120. doi:10.1007/s11336-008-9101-0

Spearman, C. (1910). Correlation calculated from faulty data. *British Journal of Psychology, 3,* 271–295.

Spitznagel, E. L., & Helzer, J. E. (1985). A proposed solution to the base rate problem in the kappa statistic. *Archives of General Psychiatry, 42,* 725–728.

Walter, S. D., Eliasziw, M., & Donner, A. (1998). Sample size and optimal designs for reliability studies. *Statistics in Medicine, 17,* 101–110. doi:10.1002/(SICI)1097-0258(19980115)17:1<101::AID-SIM727>3.0.CO;2-E

Wilhelm, P., & Schoebi, D. (2007). Assessing mood in daily life: Structural validity, sensitivity to change, and reliability of a short-scale to measure three basic dimensions of mood. *European Journal of Psychological Assessment, 23,* 258–267. doi:10.1027/1015-5759.23.4.258

CHAPTER 34

GENERALIZABILITY THEORY

Xiaohong Gao and Deborah J. Harris

Generalizability (G) theory is an extension of classical test theory for evaluating the dependability of measurement procedures (Cronbach, Gleser, Nanda, & Rajaratnam, 1972; see also Brennan, 2001a; Shavelson & Webb, 1991). It liberalizes classical test theory by providing a comprehensive conceptual framework and broad statistical procedures for addressing various measurement issues in behavioral, social, and health sciences. In particular, G theory broadens the conception and estimation of reliability in classical test theory. It enables people not only to identify and disentangle multiple sources of measurement error but also to understand the impact of measurement error on score interpretations. Furthermore, G theory, to some extent, presents a unified approach toward reliability and validity by both recommending careful construct explication and designing dependable measurement procedures.

The primary goals of this chapter are to enable readers (a) to understand the fundamental concepts in G theory and (b) to be familiar with basic models and designs under both univariate and multivariate G theory frameworks. In this chapter, we first present both single-facet and multifacet designs under univariate G theory and then briefly describe multivariate generalizability analysis. Both computational procedures and examples of generalizability analyses are presented. In addition, several computer programs and advanced issues are discussed to promote further exploration and applications of G theory.

Classical test theory has been the dominant measurement theory in evaluating reliability of behavioral measurement (for more information about the treatment of classical test theory, see Chapter 33 of this volume). The theory was developed in the early 20th century after scientists recognized error in scientific observations (Traub, 1997). The concept of *true score* is central in classical test theory, which is conceived as the average score that a person would get on an infinite number of independent and parallel measures (Feldt & Brennan, 1989; Haertel, 2006; Lord & Novick, 1968). A person's observed score (X), thus, consists of the person's true score (T) plus a random error (E), or $X = T + E$. Similarly, the total variance of observed scores is the sum of the true score variance and the error variance. In classical test theory, however, all error sources are indistinguishable. Reliability analyses are often conducted with a two-way table of data: persons (p) crossed by items (i) for internal consistency, raters (r) for interrater reliability, or occasions (o) for test–retest reliability. These indexes of reliability are used to demonstrate consistency in differentiating or rank ordering individuals in behavioral measurement.

In the early 1950s, Lord (1955) introduced the concept of randomly parallel tests. It led to the distinction between the reliability coefficient calculated from a single set of persons and items and the reliability estimate considered as the average over many random samples of items (Cronbach, 2004).

The first author thanks both Richard J. Shavelson and Robert L. Brennan for leading her into the field of generalizability theory and for helping her gain understanding of the richness and complexity it affords. The authors also acknowledge both Shavelson and Brennan for their insightful comments on an earlier version of this chapter.

DOI: 10.1037/13619-035
APA Handbook of Research Methods in Psychology: Vol. 1. Foundations, Planning, Measures, and Psychometrics, H. Cooper (Editor-in-Chief)
Copyright © 2012 by the American Psychological Association. All rights reserved.

Furthermore, the development of Fisher's analysis of variance (ANOVA) for experimental designs (Hoyt, 1941) and the need for handling more complex data structures than the two-way table motivated Cronbach and his colleagues to carry the approach in the direction of developing generalizability (G) theory (see Cronbach, 2004, with editorial assistance by Shavelson). Thus, G theory was born in the recognition of undifferentiable measurement error in classical test theory and the availability of analysis of variance (ANOVA) procedures to systematically estimate sources of error (for the history of G theory, see Brennan, 1997).

BASIC CONCEPTS IN GENERALIZABILITY THEORY

Generalizability Study

Random sampling is a fundamental assumption in interpreting behavioral measurement data and social science inquiries. It is also a central assumption in G theory. Under the G theory framework, any assessment outcome (e.g., a test score or behavioral rating) is a random sample from a *universe of admissible observations* (e.g., permissible items). The universe consists of many measurement *facets* with various conditions analogous to factors and levels in ANOVA. In G theory, the facets are considered as potential sources of error from which the measurement samples are drawn. To evaluate the dependability or consistency of the behavioral measurement, a *generalizability study* (G-study) is designed to disentangle and to estimate as many facets of measurement error in the universe of admissible observations as is reasonable and feasible. Although G theory uses experimental designs and applies ANOVA procedures, it focuses on the characterization and quantification of sources of variance associated with measurement facets rather than on traditional significance testing. Sampling variabilities or random effects associated with the *population* and the measurement facets are estimated in the form of *variance components* in G-studies. These estimates provide information about what sources contribute to performance variance and the importance of the effects.

Consider a research study in which a psychologist is interested in self-regulation behavior in preschool children. The population can be defined as all preschool-age children (*p*). The psychologist may consider the universe of admissible observations containing different observation conditions or measurement facets, such as a list of self-regulation behavior, measurement methods (e.g., direct observational checklists, indirect behavioral ratings), observers (e.g., caregivers, parents), session times (occasions), environmental settings (e.g., psychology laboratory, playground, home), and so forth. Thus, any measurement about a child's self-regulation behavior is only a sample from the universe of possible combinations of different items (*i*), measurement methods (*m*), raters (*r*), occasions (*o*), environmental settings (*s*), and so on. The measurement outcome can potentially be affected by all these sources of error because of random sampling.

In behavioral sciences, if a measurement model or a data collection design does not reflect or cannot capture the sources of variability that influence the observed responses, the resulting variance components will be incomplete and reliability estimates can be inappropriate. The goal of conducting a G-study, thus, is to anticipate the multiple uses of the measurement to provide as much information as possible about potentially important sources of variation. For example, behavioral ratings of self-regulation may be considered appropriate measures across different observers, occasions, and environmental settings. To investigate the magnitudes of the sampling error and pinpoint major sources of error, a comprehensive G-study would include all the facets that potentially contribute to measurement error. Because of practical constraints in implementation as well as difficulty in defining all facets, however, we cannot necessarily take account of all facets in a single G-study. The psychologist, in this case, may only be able to conduct a G-study with three random facets, treating other potential sources as hidden (see Cronbach, Linn, Brennan, & Haertel, 1997). For example, a Persons × Items × Raters × Occasions G-study design may be considered where items, raters, and occasions are randomly sampled from all permissible items, raters, and occasions in the universe (× often stands for "crossed" in G theory notation). Alternatively, a Person × Item × Rater × Setting G-study design can be used if the psychologist is more concerned about sampling error associated with different environmental settings than occasions. Moreover, the psychologist can conduct multiple G-studies to estimate *variance components* for the universe of admissible observations and then decide where to focus future research efforts by dropping some less influential facets.

In the G-study analysis, the magnitudes of the variance components pinpoint the major sources of measurement error and identify how more reliable and efficient measurement procedures can be developed using these building blocks. For the psychologist, a Persons × Items × Raters × Occasions G-study would provide information about which of the three facets, item, rater, or occasion, contributes most to observation variability and thus can help him or her use this information to design accurate and efficient measurement procedures.

Decision Study

In the same way a G-study is associated with the universe of admissible observations, a *decision study* (D-study) is related to the *universe of generalization,* which is either similar to or smaller than the universe of admissible observations. Under G theory, an investigator must define the universe of generalization to which he or she wishes to generalize the measurement outcomes about the *objects of measurement* before addressing the issues of measurement error and reliability. G theory's D-study permits the investigator to have different universes of generalization for different purposes. Thus, an individual may have different *universe scores* depending on how the investigator wants to interpret the measure within the universe of generalization. All measurement error and reliability estimates are also specific to and depend on the universe of generalization. There is no single number for *the* reliability applicable to all kinds of measurement procedures. For the psychologist, the universe of generalization under a Persons × Items × Raters × Occasions design (with the uppercase letters representing D-study facets) is different from the universe of generalization for a Persons × Items × Raters × Settings design: generalizing the measurement over the items, raters, and occasions versus over the items, raters, and settings. Consequently, the reliability-like coefficients can be different under these two universes.

A D-study often deals with practical applications of measurement procedures, such as numbers of raters and occasions needed in behavioral observations, and it provides estimates of universe-score variance, error variances, and reliability-like coefficients associated with a specified universe of generalization and a particular measurement decision. True score in classical test theory is conceived as the average score that a person would get on an infinite number of parallel and independent measures. The concept of *universe score* in G theory is analogous to that of true score. It is defined as an expected value of the mean score over randomly parallel replications of the measurement procedure in the universe of generalization. For the psychologist, the universe score could be the expected value of the mean score over replications of the measurement procedure with 10 items, two raters, and three observation occasions randomly sampled from all admissible items, raters, and occasions. The variance of universe scores over all objects of measurement (e.g., persons in the population) is called *universe-score variance* and is analogous to true score variance in classical test theory.

G- and D-Studies

In practice, the distinction between the G-study and D-study is often blurred. Usually, in a D-study, an investigator uses the estimates of variance components and information about their relative contributions to the total score variance obtained from a G-study to design a measurement procedure (D-study design and levels of conditions in the facets) that minimizes measurement error for a particular purpose. Strictly speaking, we may call it a *D-study consideration* because no additional data are collected. In our example, a D-study or D-study consideration may contain some or all of the facets (i.e., item, raters, occasions, and settings) and the same or different numbers of conditions within each facet as those in the G-study. Moreover, different D-study designs (e.g., nested) or models (e.g., mixed) can be considered to make the measurement more efficient or practical. For example, instead of a randomly crossed design, the psychologist may use a partially nested D-study design: Persons × Items × (Raters: Settings) where ":" usually stands for "nested within" in G theory notation. In other words, the children will be observed by different raters (e.g., parents vs. daycare staff) in different settings (home vs. daycare center) using the same list of items. Alternatively, the psychologist may only select home, playground, and daycare center as setting levels for score generalization and thus considers the setting facet as fixed.

Definition of Measurement Error and Types of Reliability Coefficients

When defining measurement precision, G theory also makes distinctions between two types of measurement decisions. The *relative decision*, as in classical test theory, concerns the differentiations or rank orders of the objects of measurement (e.g., norm-referenced interpretations of test scores for between-person comparisons). The *absolute decision* focuses on the interpretation of the response or performance levels, regardless of rank (e.g., within-person criterion- or domain-referenced interpretations). The amount of measurement error and reliability depend on not only the universe of generalization but also the type of measurement decision. Associated with these two types of decisions are two kinds of measurement error variances and reliability-like coefficients: *relative error variance* and *generalizability coefficient* for relative decisions and *absolute error variance* and *index of dependability* (or *dependability coefficient*) for absolute decisions, respectively. In our example, the psychologist may want to rank order a child's self-regulation behavior among other children (a relative decision) or decide whether the child's behavior is appropriate for his or her age (an absolute decision).

In classical test theory, each observation has a single true score belonging to one family of classical parallel observations (e.g., items, raters, or occasions), which yields a single reliability coefficient. In G theory, however, the universe score is associated with a complex and multifaceted universe and reliability-like coefficients are associated with the universe of generalization. Furthermore, in classical test theory, a general equation for reliability is the ratio of true score variance to the observed score variance, which is the sum of true score variance and undifferentiated error variance. In G theory, the

error variance is tied to the universe of generalization and decision type, and this variance is partitioned into different components associated with multiple sources of sampling error.

Reliability and Validity Coalesce

In behavioral sciences, assessments are designed for developing an understanding of what the observed responses mean and consequently deciding how the scores can or should be interpreted and used. In G theory, "the theory of 'reliability' and the theory of 'validity' coalesce; the analysis of generalizability indicates how validly one can interpret a measure as representative of a certain set of possible measures" (Cronbach, Rajaratnam, & Gleser, 1963, p. 157). The use of the terms *generalizability* and *dependability* instead of *reliability* in G theory reflects the interest in unifying reliability and validity. In fact, by acknowledging that the generalizability of the measurement depends on the universe about which the investigator intends to draw inferences or to make decisions, G theory, to a certain extent, overcomes the traditional distinction between reliability and validity.

In summary, the development of G theory has extended classical test theory to assess multiple sources of measurement error so that a reliable and cost-efficient measurement can be built for appropriate interpretations and decisions. The following sections present some basic G theory models and designs as well as examples. After presenting the essentials, we briefly discuss some advanced issues in G theory and its applications.

SINGLE-FACET DESIGN AND ANALYSIS

Although the power of using G theory to evaluate measurement precision can be achieved best by using multifaceted data collection designs, a single-facet design connects G theory directly to classical test theory. In a single-facet generalizability analysis, the universe of admissible observations consists of only one measurement facet such as items (i), raters (r), or occasions (o), instead of a combination of the multiple facets. The objects of measurement may be persons (p). Under classical test theory, a coefficient for internal consistency, interrater reliability, or test–retest reliability is estimated to differentiate or rank order the individuals. Within the G theory framework, we can estimate these reliability coefficients not only for rank ordering individuals (i.e., generalizability coefficient for a relative decision) but also for judging their response levels (i.e., *index of dependability* for an *absolute decision*) using a $p \times i$, $p \times r$, or $p \times o$ design. In addition, the investigator can conduct a D-study to examine the impact of using different levels of conditions such as the numbers of items or raters or employing a different design on measurement consistency.

Single-Facet G-Study

Consider a one-facet $p \times i$ design, or a two-way crossed design, in which each of n_p persons randomly sampled from the population responds to the same sample of n_i items in the universe of admissible observations. Similarly, for a $p \times r$ design, n_p persons are scored by the same sample of n_r raters, or in a $p \times o$ design, n_p persons take a test or are observed on the same sample of n_o occasions. Because these are single-facet designs, only a single potential source of error is the focus of interest and other potential sources of error are unidentified in the universe. A linear model for decomposing the observed score X_{pi} for person p on item i can be represented as

$$X_{pi} = \mu \text{ (grand mean)} \qquad (1)$$
$$+ \mu_p - \mu \text{ (person effect)}$$
$$+ \mu_i - \mu \text{ (item effect)}$$
$$+ X_{pi} - \mu_p - \mu_i + \mu \text{ (residual effect)}.$$

Under a single-facet design, all the above effects are considered random. In other words, it is conceptualized that persons are randomly sampled from the population, and items are randomly selected from the universe. Both the population and universe are often assumed to be essentially infinite.

Each score effect, except for the grand mean, is assumed to have a distribution with a mean of zero and a variance of $\sigma_p^2, \sigma_i^2,$ or σ_{pi}^2, respectively. More specifically,

$$\sigma_p^2 = E_p (\mu_p - \mu)^2, \qquad (2)$$
$$\sigma_i^2 = E_i (\mu_i - \mu)^2, \qquad (3)$$
$$\sigma_{pi}^2 = E_p E_i (X_{pi} - \mu_p - \mu_i + \mu)^2. \qquad (4)$$

Under G theory, these variances are also assumed to be uncorrelated. Therefore, the total variance for the observed scores can be decomposed into the *variance components*:

$$\sigma_{X_{pi}}^2 = \sigma_p^2 + \sigma_i^2 + \sigma_{pi}^2.$$

These variance components are estimated using ANOVA procedures that involve setting the expected mean squares (MS) equal to the observed mean squares to obtain estimated variance components:

$$\hat{\sigma}_p^2 = \frac{MS_p - MS_{pi}}{n_i}, \ \hat{\sigma}_i^2 = \frac{MS_i - MS_{pi}}{n_p}, \text{ and } \hat{\sigma}_{pi}^2 = MS_{pi}.$$

Strictly speaking, the purpose of conducting a G-study is to estimate the variance components associated with the universe of admissible observations and the population. After the variance components are estimated in the G-study, the investigator can identify the major source of the total variability by comparing the relative magnitudes of the variance components.

Single-Facet D-Study

After evaluating the G-study variance components, the investigator may ask what can be done to improve the measurement precision or to reduce the cost. Thus, the G-study variance components can be further used to design reliable and cost-effective measurement procedures. For example, short tests are becoming more popular in clinical and organizational psychology to reduce costs and increase administration flexibility. G theory can be used to examine the potential impact of reducing the test length on measurement precision. Similarly, the psychologist can predict the impact of increasing the numbers of observers or occasions on measurement error in the self-regulation study.

Because the variance components estimated in the G-study are based on a single observation (e.g., a single person on a single item), but measurement decisions are often based on the average or total scores over multiple observations (e.g., a set of items), G theory allows a decision maker to choose n items and to then estimate associated measurement error and reliability using the estimated G-study variance components. This is parallel with the Spearman–Brown formula (Brown, 1910;

Spearman, 1910) and indicates that you can do what-if simulations varying the levels of one or more facets. Thus, the n_i' items used in the D-study are not required to be the same n_i in the G-study, and different numbers of n_i' can be tested to evaluate their impact on measurement precision. By convention, G theory uses mean scores in a D-study rather than total scores, as is common in classical test theory, although total scores can be used (see Brennan, 2001a). The mean score over a sample of n_i' items is denoted as X_{pI} in the $p \times I$ D-study for the single-facet design where the uppercase letter I designates a D-study design to distinguish it from a lower case i for the G-study design. Accordingly, the total variance for the $p \times I$ D-study design can be presented as $\sigma^2_{X_{pI}} = \sigma^2_p + \sigma^2_I + \sigma^2_{pI}$, where $\sigma^2_I = \sigma^2_i / n_i'$ and $\sigma^2_{pI} = \sigma^2_{pi} / n_i'$, and the universe-score variance, σ^2_p, is unchanged. The variance component for persons (σ^2_p) indicates the variability of the expected person mean scores (i.e., universe scores) over different random samples of n_i' items. The variance component associated with items (σ^2_I) represents the variability among the means of randomly selected sets of n_i' items in the universe. And the variance component σ^2_{pI} shows the variability of rank ordering individuals on the basis of their mean scores across the random samples of n_i' items as well as unmeasured random sources of variation. Because the D-study variance components are divided by n_i' on the basis of the single-score G-study variance components, they are often smaller than the corresponding G-study variance components.

Depending on the universe of generalization and measurement decisions, the generalizability analysis provides different types of error variances (relative and absolute) and reliability-like coefficients (i.e., generalizability coefficient and index of dependability). If differentiating individuals is of concern (e.g., norm-referenced interpretations of test scores), then the relative error variance and generalizability coefficient can be used. If the focus is on the absolute level of individual performance (e.g., domain-referenced or criterion-referenced interpretations), then the absolute error variance and index of dependability should be computed.

Relative error variance is the expected variance of the discrepancies between observed deviation scores

and universe deviation scores: $\underset{p}{E}\underset{I}{E}\delta^2_{pI}$ where $\delta_{pI} \equiv (X_{pI} - \mu_I) - (\mu_p - \mu)$ in a $p \times I$ D-study. Because the main effect of items affects all persons and does not change the relative standing of individuals, σ^2_I is not a part of the relative error variance. For the $p \times I$ D-study, relative error variance can be defined as $\sigma^2_\delta = \sigma^2_{pI} = \sigma^2_{pi} / n_i'$. *Absolute error variance*, on the other hand, is the expected variance of the discrepancies between observed scores and universe scores: $\underset{p}{E}\underset{I}{E}\Delta^2_{pI}$ where $\Delta_{pI} \equiv X_{pI} - \mu_p$. The sampling variability of items, σ^2_I, affects the level of performance; the absolute error variance for the $p \times I$ D-study is thus defined as $\sigma^2_\Delta = \sigma^2_I + \sigma^2_{pI} = \sigma^2_i / n_i' + \sigma^2_{pi} / n_i'$. The square root of the error variance is considered to be the standard error of measurement (SEM) for a relative or absolute score interpretation, respectively.

The *generalizability coefficient* (G coefficient) for a relative decision is the ratio of universe-score variance (numerator) to the expected observed-score variance (denominator):

$$E\rho^2 = \frac{\sigma^2_p}{\sigma^2_p + \sigma^2_\delta}. \qquad (5)$$

Similarly, the *index of dependability* (Φ) for an absolute decision is the ratio of the universe-score variance to the total variance:

$$\Phi = \frac{\sigma^2_p}{\sigma^2_p + \sigma^2_\Delta}. \qquad (6)$$

Note that because σ^2_I contributes to the absolute error variance, usually $\sigma^2_\delta \leq \sigma^2_\Delta$ and $E\rho^2 \geq \Phi$.

In general, the estimates of error variances are more stable than the estimates of coefficients (see Gao & Brennan, 2001). Also, in test construction and use, the SEM has a clear meaning for score interpretation. Thus, an optimization procedure should also look into the impact of manipulating levels of a measurement facet on the SEM in addition to the coefficients.

Example

Consider an illustrative example of a generalizability analysis for a random-effects $p \times i$ design in which a 35-item mathematics test was administered to 100 examinees. Table 34.1 presents both the estimated G-study variance components $\hat{\sigma}^2(\alpha)$ where α

TABLE 34.1

Illustrative Example of Generalizability Analysis for a Random-Effects *P* x *I* Design

Effect (α)	MS	G-study $\hat{\sigma}^2(\alpha)$		D-study $\hat{\sigma}^2(\bar{\alpha})$			
				$n_i' = 20$		$n_i' = 35$	
P	1.13931	0.02688	(11.34%)	0.02688	(71.67%)	0.02688	(81.58%)
I	1.61114	0.01413	(5.90%)	0.00071	(1.88%)	0.00040	(1.22%)
pi	0.19836	0.19836	(82.87%)	0.00992	(26.44%)	0.00567	(17.20%)
$\hat{\sigma}_\delta^2$						0.00992	0.00567
$\hat{\sigma}_\Delta^2$						0.01062	0.00607
$E\hat{\rho}^2$						0.731	0.826
$\hat{\Phi}$						0.717	0.816

Note. Values in parentheses are the percentages of the total variance in the G-study and D-study. MS = mean square.

denotes a G-study single score effect and D-study variance components $\hat{\sigma}^2(\bar{\alpha})$ where $\bar{\alpha}$ represents the D-study average score effect. In the G-study, the variance component associated with items ($\hat{\sigma}_i^2$) is relatively small and accounts for about 6% of the total variance, indicating the mean of any one randomly selected mathematics item does not vary much from the mean of all items in the content domain. However, the variance component associated with the person-by-item interaction ($\hat{\sigma}_{pi}^2$) is large, suggesting that the relative ordering of persons differs by individual items. Thus, the results suggest that a large number of items should be used in the assessment to reduce item sampling variability.

The D-study variance components are for average scores over replications of the measurement procedures in which samples of n_i' items (e.g., 20 or 35) are randomly selected from the universe of generalization (e.g., content domain). The variance component associated with item samples ($\hat{\sigma}_I^2$) indicates the variability among the means of any random samples of n_i' items in the domain. The variance component $\hat{\sigma}_{pI}^2$ estimates the variability of rank ordering of individuals on the basis of their mean scores across the random samples. The percents of the total variance in the D-study show the relative contribution of each mean score effect. For example, when a random sample of 35 items from the universe is used, the estimated universe-score variance contributes about 82% to the total variance and the error variances contribute less than 20% to the total

variance. Thus, the D-study results indicate that increasing the number of items can reduce measurement error and increase reliability. The use of the randomly sampled 35 items would result in a generalizability coefficient greater than .80, which is considered sufficient in many practical situations.

Single-facet designs can take only one potential source of measurement error into account at a time. Here, only item sampling error is considered but other error sources such as raters or occasions are not specified. Therefore, single-facet designs will underestimate measurement error and overestimate reliability if the true universe of generalizability has more than one random facet.

MULTIFACET DESIGNS AND ANALYSES

Most behavioral assessments, such as the self-regulation example, contain multiple sources of error. G theory provides a powerful method for disentangling and quantifying measurement error and for developing appropriate measurement procedures under multifacet designs.

Multifacet G-Study

Some researchers consider six types of error variance or facets as particularly applicable in behavioral measurement: item, dimension or category, rater, time, setting, and instrument or method (Bergeron, Floyd, McCormack, & Farmer, 2008). A universe of admissible observations can consist of a combination of one or more of those measurement conditions (facets). For the self-regulation example, the behavior of a child (*p*) observed at one observation session, in one setting (e.g., playground), by one observer (e.g., caregiver), using one method (e.g., direct observation) would be considered only a sample of the child's self-regulation behavior from the multifaceted universe of admissible observations. We can view the *item* (*i*) facet to be representative of the self-regulation behavioral category. The time or *occasion* (*o*) facet includes all possible occasions on which the psychologist would be equally willing to accept an observation result. We can consider the *rater* (*r*) facet as including all possible individuals (e.g., laboratory assistants, parents, caregivers) who could be trained to assign scores appropriately. The instrument or *method* (*m*) facet can include all possible ways of measuring the behavior, and the *setting* (*s*) facet includes all possible environmental contexts of collecting responses. Among these facets, some may be considered as random and infinite (e.g., items, occasions) and others may be considered as fixed or finite (e.g., settings, methods). These facets can constitute various multifaceted universes of admissible observations with crossed (×) or nested (:) designs, such as $i \times r \times o$, $i \times (r{:}s)$, or $i \times r \times (o{:}s)$. Thus, any measure should be viewed as a random sample of responses drawn from a complex universe.

After defining the universe of admissible observations, an investigator can design a G-study by considering resources and other constraints. For example, a $p \times i \times r \times o$ G-study can be conducted in which a random sample of individuals are administered a random sample of items on randomly selected occasions and the responses are scored by a random sample of raters defined in the universe of admissible observations. The G-study can address such questions as what the major sources of measurement variability (items, rater, or occasion) are in assessing individual behavior. However, if administering the assessment across the three-facet $i \times r \times o$ is not feasible, a two-facet $p \times i \times r$, $p \times i \times o$, or $p \times r \times o$ G-study can be considered. In each of the two-facet G-studies, there can be a hidden facet: occasion facet in $p \times i \times r$, rater facet in $p \times i \times o$, or item facet in $p \times r \times o$.

To visually represent the relationship between objects of measurement and facets as well as the decomposed score effects (variance components), Venn diagrams can be used. Figure 34.1 represents a set of Venn diagrams for different two-facet designs. Under the $p \times i \times r$ G-study design, p is designated as the population, which can be the object of measurement in a subsequent D-study, and i and r can be any two random facets. For example, a group of preschool children (*p*) is observed by two raters (*r*) on five different occasions (*o*) on their self-regulation behavior, or a group of raters (*r*) fills out observer ratings (*i*) for a sample of parent–child dyads (*p*) in terms of parent–child interaction. The observed scores X_{pir} have a variance of $\sigma^2_{X_{pir}}$, which can be partitioned into seven variance components under the $p \times i \times r$ G-study design as indicated in the Venn diagram in Figure 34.1A:

$$\sigma^2_{X_{pir}} = \sigma^2_p + \sigma^2_i + \sigma^2_r + \sigma^2_{pi} + \sigma^2_{pr} + \sigma^2_{ir} + \sigma^2_{pir}. \qquad (7)$$

These variance components can be estimated by setting the expected MS equal to the observed MS and solving the equations shown similar to those for the $p \times i$ design (for details, see Brennan, 2001a, Appendix B).

Multifacet D-Study

Depending on the universe of generalization, the G-study variance components can be used to estimate universe-score variance and error variances of different measurement procedures and to examine the impact on generalizability of changing the number of levels in measurement facets. For the $p \times I \times R$ random-effects D-study design (e.g., a sample of individuals receive n'_i item scores or ratings from n'_r multiple raters), which is the same design as the $p \times i \times r$ G-study, error variance for relative decisions is

$$\sigma^2_\delta = \sigma^2_{pi} / n'_i + \sigma^2_{pr} / n'_r + \sigma^2_{pir} / n'_i n'_r. \qquad (8)$$

The number of levels (*n'*) in the D-study can be any number that a decision maker considers appropriate or suitable for the universe of generalization. For absolute decisions, the error variance is

$$\sigma^2_\Delta = \sigma^2_i / n'_i + \sigma^2_r / n'_r + \sigma^2_{pi} / n'_i + \sigma^2_{pr} / n'_i$$
$$+ \sigma^2_{ir} / n'_i n'_r + \sigma^2_{pir} / n'_i n'_r. \qquad (9)$$

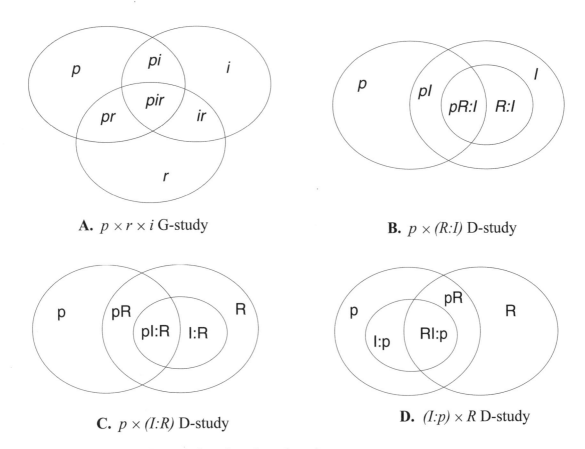

A. $p \times r \times i$ G-study

B. $p \times (R{:}I)$ D-study

C. $p \times (I{:}R)$ D-study

D. $(I{:}p) \times R$ D-study

FIGURE 34.1.   Venn diagrams for selected two-facet designs.

The *main effects* of items (the difficulty of items) and raters (the strictness of raters) as well as the Rater × Item interaction do not contribute to the relative error variance for rank ordering individuals because any difference in item difficulty, rater strictness, or rank order of item difficulty by raters equally affects all individuals. However, these main effects and interactions do influence absolute performance levels and enter into the absolute error variance. The square roots of the error variances are measurement errors for relative and absolute decisions. Similarly, both the generalizability coefficient ($E\hat{\rho}^2$) and index of dependability ($\hat{\Phi}$) can be computed using the general Equations 5 and 6.

One of the most important outcomes of a G-study is the quantification of the relative importance of sampling error in the universe of admissible observations. Whenever possible, a crossed design should be used because both main effects and interaction effects can be fully examined (see Figure 34.1 for two-facet crossed and nested G-study and

D-study designs). When interaction effects are small or negligible, in addition to changing the levels of a measurement facet (e.g., n_i'), we can also modify the D-study design by using a nested design for cost-efficiency considerations. A crossed G-study can have both crossed and nested D-studies, but a nested G-study can only have limited nested D-studies if all facets in the G-study need to be considered (see Webb, Shavelson, & Haertel, 2006, for a list of possible two-facet designs). Similarly, a random-effects G-study can have either random- or mixed-effects D-studies, but a fixed facet in a G-study cannot become a random facet in D-studies. For example, the psychologist can evaluate children's self-regulation behavior under different settings by conducting a random-effects $p \times r \times (o{:}s)$ G-study in which the universe for the setting facet may be conceptualized as various environmental conditions such as home, playground, classrooms, theme parks, movie theaters, and so forth. The psychologist can further modify the design to a mixed-effect $p \times R \times (O{:}S)$ D-study with S fixed in which he or she does not have any intention of generalizing the observations to the contexts other than home and playground.

In understanding and interpreting estimated variance components and other associated statistics, investigators should keep in mind that these estimates may be unstable and subject to sampling variability, especially when the number of levels of each facet and the sample size from the population in the G-study are small and a design is complicated in which more MS terms are involved in computing variance components (Webb et al., 2006). Sampling variability of an estimated variance component can be estimated with different procedures, such as jackknife and bootstrap resampling procedures (see Brennan, 2001a, for details).

In addition, sometimes a negative variance component estimate can occur even though, by definition, variance components are positive. Negative estimates tend to arise when sample sizes are small, when the design involves a large number of facets, or when there is a very small score effect. Possible solutions for dealing with negative estimates may include (a) substituting zero for the negative variance component estimate and carrying through the zero in other expected mean square equations (Cronbach, Gleser, Nanda, & Rajaratnam, 1972), or (b) setting all negative estimates of variance to zero (Brennan, 2001a). From a practical perspective, however, choosing among these procedures is seldom a critical issue because the results are not very different.

Example

Although a universe of admissible observations may contain many conditions, in behavioral measurement, often a two- or three-facet G-study design is used because of practical constraints. For example, a random-effects Persons × Items × Raters or Persons × Items × Occasions design is often used in education assessment and a random-effects Persons × Raters × Occasions or Persons × Items × Settings design may be common in behavior assessment. For illustration purposes, a Persons × Items × Raters writing assessment example is presented. The discussion can be easily conveyed to other two-facet random effects designs.

In a study to evaluate measurement properties of a six-item (prompt) writing assessment, a sample

($n = 239$) of examinees (p) was administered the test and their short essays (i) were scored independently by two trained raters (r) on a 0–5 scale. A random-effects $p \times i \times r$ G-study was conducted to assess the multiple sources of variability. In that study, persons were considered randomly sampled from a target population, items and raters were assumed to be randomly selected from the universe of admissible observations containing all admissible items and trained raters. The results are presented in Table 34.2.

The G-study results $\hat{\sigma}^2(\alpha)$ indicate that variability among the examinees ($\hat{\sigma}_p^2$) contributes most to the performance differences. The person-by-item interaction ($\hat{\sigma}_{pi}^2$) is the second-largest variance component followed by $\hat{\sigma}_{pri}^2$ and $\hat{\sigma}_i^2$, and the variance components associated with the rater effects are relatively small. Thus, increasing the number of items (n_i') in decision studies could greatly reduce measurement error and improve generalizability, whereas adding more raters (n_r') may not show a large impact. On the basis of the $p \times R \times I$ D-study results, about six items would be needed to reach a coefficient of .80 with one rater. Because the rater variability is small, the use of two raters should be sufficient. Nevertheless, decisions about how many raters and items are needed should be made on the basis of both technical and practical considerations.

Furthermore, alternative D-study designs may be considered in addition to the $p \times R \times I$ D-study for various practical considerations, such as rater training and scoring. Table 34.3 presents the error variances and coefficients under the crossed and three nested designs (see Figure 34.1 for the Venn diagrams). The results show the impact of using different combinations of raters and items on measurement precision under these designs. More specifically, under the $p \times R \times I$ D-study design, each individual writes four or six short essays (n_i'), which are all scored by the same two raters (n_r'). Although only two raters were used in the study, it may not be feasible for the same raters to score all responses in a large-scale testing program. Under the $p \times (R:I)$ D-study design, each individual writes four or six short essays, but two different raters score each of the essays ($n_{r:i}'$). Thus, a total of eight or 12 raters (n_{r+}') need to be trained, but each one

---

TABLE 34.2

Illustrative Example of Generalizability Analysis for a Random-Effects $p \times R \times I$ Design

G-study	$\hat{\sigma}^2(\alpha)$		D-study $\hat{\sigma}^2(\bar{\alpha})$			
		n'_r	1	1	2	2
		n'_i	4	6	4	6
$\hat{\sigma}^2(p)$	0.31057	$\hat{\sigma}^2(p)$	0.31057	0.31057	0.31057	0.31057
$\hat{\sigma}^2(i)$	0.04913	$\hat{\sigma}^2(I)$	0.01228	0.00819	0.01228	0.00819
$\hat{\sigma}^2(r)$	0.00279	$\hat{\sigma}^2(R)$	0.00279	0.00279	0.00140	0.00140
$\hat{\sigma}^2(pi)$	0.27165	$\hat{\sigma}^2(pI)$	0.06791	0.04527	0.06791	0.04527
$\hat{\sigma}^2(pr)$	0.00167	$\hat{\sigma}^2(pR)$	0.00167	0.00167	0.00084	0.00084
$\hat{\sigma}^2(ri)$	0.00022	$\hat{\sigma}^2(RI)$	0.00006	0.00004	0.00003	0.00002
$\hat{\sigma}^2(pri)$	0.07655	$\hat{\sigma}^2(pRI)$	0.01914	0.01276	0.00957	0.00638
		$\hat{\sigma}^2(\delta)$	0.08872	0.05971	0.07832	0.05249
		$\hat{\sigma}^2(\Delta)$	0.10385	0.07072	0.09202	0.06209
		$E\hat{\rho}^2$	0.778	0.839	0.799	0.855
		$\hat{\Phi}$	0.749	0.815	0.771	0.833

TABLE 34.3

Alternative D-Studies Based on the $p \times R \times I$ G-Study

Design	$p \times R \times I$				$p \times (R:I)$		$p \times (I:R)$		$(I:p) \times R$	
Total n'_r	2	2	8	12	2	2	2	2		
Total n'_i	4	6	4	6	4	6	4p	6p		
$\hat{\sigma}^2(\delta)$	0.07832	0.05249	0.07769	0.05179	0.08872	0.05971	0.09063	0.06070		
$\hat{\sigma}^2(\Delta)$	0.09202	0.06209	0.09035	0.06023	0.10385	0.07072	0.09202	0.06209		
$E\hat{\rho}^2$	0.799	0.855	0.800	0.857	0.778	0.839	0.774	0.837		
$\hat{\Phi}$	0.771	0.833	0.775	0.838	0.749	0.815	0.771	0.833		

Note. In the $p \times (R:I)$ design, $n'_{r:i} = 2$ for each item; in the $p \times (I:R)$ design, $n'_{i:r} = 2$ or 3 for each rater; and in the $(I:p) \times R$ design, $n'_{i:p} = 4$ or 6. 4p and 6p = four and six items per person, respectively.

of them needs to score only one essay from all individuals. This design requires more raters but less individual rating time. Under the $p \times (I:R)$ D-study design, each individual still writes four or six short essays and half of the essays (two or three) are scored by the first rater, but the other half of the essays are scored by the second rater ($n'_{i:r}$). Thus, each of the two raters scores only two or three essays across all individuals. Under the $(I:p) \times R$ D-study design, each individual still writes four or six short essays, and they are all scored by the two raters. Under this design, however, a large number

of items (n'_{i+}) needs to be developed, and because each individual has unique items, each rater would have to score all different essays. Therefore, under these designs, even though the testing time and number of items are the same for the individuals, the requirements for item writing, rater training, and scoring are very different, which can have important practical implications.

When the objects of measurement (p) are nested within a measurement facet that contributes to measurement error, such as a $(p:R) \times I$ D-study where R denotes a random sample of raters, the variance component, $\hat{\sigma}^2_p$, would contain both $\hat{\sigma}^2_p$ (universe-score variance) and $\hat{\sigma}^2_{pR}$ (a component of error variance). Consequently, both error variances and reliability-like coefficients cannot be appropriately estimated. However, persons can be nested within a group (e.g., class) where the objects of measurement are nested (*p:c*). In that case, both $\sigma^2_{p:c}$ and σ^2_c contribute to the universe-score variance (see Cardinet, Johnson, & Pini, 2010; Shavelson, Gao, & Baxter, 1996).

MIXED-MODEL G- AND D-STUDIES

G theory is perceived as essentially a random-effects theory in which objects of measurement are randomly sampled from an infinite population and measurement observations are randomly selected from an indefinitely large universe. In some practical situations, however, variations from both random and fixed sources are meaningful to measurement and can be incorporated in a generalizability analysis.

Generally speaking, in the following situations, a facet may be considered as fixed: (a) Measurement levels are from a finite universe, such as content domains in a mathematics achievement test and categories or dimensions in a behavioral inventory, and all conditions in the universe are included in the measurement design; and (b) an investigator does not intend to, or it is not reasonable to, generalize the measurement outcome beyond the sampled conditions in the facet. When a study consists of a fixed facet in addition to other random facet(s), it has a mixed-effects model.

When a facet is fixed in a D-study in univarite G theory, the universe score is based on an average score over the finite levels of the fixed facet. If persons are the objects of measurement, any person effects specific to the fixed facet, or the person-by-facet interaction, become part of the universe-score variance rather than the error variance. For example, in the self-regulation example, the psychologist could conduct a Persons × Raters × Settings D-study with *S* fixed. If he or she is only interested in generalizing behavioral ratings to the specific settings such as playground and home in the *S* facet, the scores for that facet can be averaged over the two

levels, and the Person × Setting interaction, or σ^2_{pS}, becomes part of the universe-score variance (σ^2_τ):

$$\sigma^2_\tau = \sigma^2_p + \sigma^2_{pS} = \sigma^2_p + \frac{\sigma^2_{ps}}{n'_s} . \qquad (10)$$

Note that σ^2_τ is the universe-score variance for a mixed-effects model when the same levels of the facet *s* are used in the G- and D-studies.

With the increase of the universe-score variance in the *p x I x S* D-study when *S* is fixed, both relative and absolute error variances are decreased: $\sigma^2_\delta = \sigma^2_{pI} + \sigma^2_{pIS}$ and $\sigma^2_\Delta = \sigma^2_I + \sigma^2_{pI} + \sigma^2_{IS} + \sigma^2_{pIS}$. Consequently, the generalizability coefficient ($E\rho^2$) and index of dependability (Φ) are increased. Therefore, generalizations to narrow universes (or fixing a facet) reduce measurement error as compared with generalizations to broad universes (or random effects). However, narrowing a universe can restrict the extent to which inferences can be made about the measurement outcome. In other words, there can be trade-offs between reliability and validity. Ultimately, an investigator should define the extent to which observations can or should be generalized.

Fixed facets are often treated by averaging over their condition levels. When it does not make conceptual sense to average over the levels of a fixed facet, a separate G-study can be conducted for each condition (Shavelson & Webb, 1991) or a multivariate generalizability analysis may be considered.

MULTIVARIATE GENERALIZABILITY ANALYSIS

For behavioral measurement involving multiple scores on levels of a fixed facet, multivariate G theory often provides a powerful and flexible approach. Cronbach et al. (1972) and Brennan (2001a) provided an extensive treatment of multivariate G theory (also see Webb, Shavelson, & Maddahian, 1983). Provided here is a brief introduction to some basic features. Notation is similar to that in Brennan (2001a).

The fundamental difference between multivariate G theory and univariate G theory is that multivariate G theory models two or more universe scores simultaneously. Under a multivariate generalizability model, each object of measurement has multiple universe scores, each of which is associated with one level of the fixed facet. For example, the psychologist may want to use two different instruments (or methods) such as a direct observational checklist and an indirect behavioral rating scale to obtain information in regard to children's self-regulation behavior. Each child would have two observed scores from each method. Multivariate G theory can be used to (a) estimate correlations between the universe scores and possibly correlated errors on the distinct levels (e.g., two methods), (b) estimate measurement precision of composite or difference scores, and (c) estimate consistency between observed profile scores and universe profile scores (see Brennan, Gao, & Colton, 1995; Clauser, Harik, & Margolis, 2006; Yin, 2005). In a multivariate G-study, both observed variances and covariances are decomposed into components for each score effect. An important feature in multivariate G theory is the distinction between *linked* and *unlinked* conditions, denoted as • and ∘, respectively. When the levels of conditions are linked or jointly sampled (e.g., the same behavior inventory is used across two observation settings), the expected values of covariance components are nonzero. However, when conditions for distinct levels are unlinked or selected independently (e.g., different items are used in the two instruments), the expected values of associated error covariance components are zero.

Many assessments are developed on the basis of a table of specifications in which a different set of items is nested within each category of a fixed facet, for example, a mathematics test with items nested within algebra and geometry, ratings of job analysis items in terms of frequency and importance, or behavioral ratings of externalizing and internalizing problems. For these assessments, a $p \times i$ random-effects design is associated with each level of the fixed facet (Jarjoura & Brennan, 1983). If each person (p) responds to items (i) in n_v categories, but the items in these categories are different or sampled independently, the multivariate G-study design is designated as $p^\bullet \times i^\circ$. However, in the study in which an investigator observes a sample of preschool children in different environmental settings using the same behavioral inventory, because the same items (i) were used, we can designate the G-study design as $p^\bullet \times i^\bullet$ to indicate the linked condition of the items.

The observed scores on two distinct levels (v and v') of the fixed facet can be modeled as $X_{piv} = \mu_v + v_p + v_i + v_{pi}$ and $X_{piv'} = \mu_{v'} + \xi_p + \xi_i + \xi_{pi}$, where v and ξ are score effects for variables v and v'. The observed scores for the population and universe of admissible observations in the $p^\bullet \times i^\bullet$ G-study can be decomposed into three symmetric matrixes:

$$\begin{bmatrix} \sigma_v^2(X_{pi}) & \sigma_{vv'}(X_{pi}) \\ \sigma_{vv'}(X_{pi}) & \sigma_{v'}^2(X_{pi}) \end{bmatrix}, \tag{11}$$

$$= \begin{bmatrix} \sigma_v^2(p) & \sigma_{vv'}(p) \\ \sigma_{vv'}(p) & \sigma_{v'}^2(p) \end{bmatrix} (\Sigma_p \text{ for person effect}),$$

$$+ \begin{bmatrix} \sigma_v^2(i) & \sigma_{vv'}(i) \\ \sigma_{vv'}(i) & \sigma_{v'}^2(i) \end{bmatrix} (\Sigma_i \text{ for item effect}), \text{ and}$$

$$+ \begin{bmatrix} \sigma_v^2(pi) & \sigma_{vv'}(pi) \\ \sigma_{vv'}(pi) & \sigma_{v'}^2(pi) \end{bmatrix} (\Sigma_{pi} \text{ for residual effect}).$$

In this equation, the variance components are on the main diagonals and covariance components are off the diagonals: $\sigma_{vv'}(p)$ is the covariance between universe scores for v and v'. Dividing this covariance by the product of the square roots of the corresponding universe-score variances $\sigma_v^2(p)$ and $\sigma_{v'}^2(p)$ produces the disattenuated correlation between the two measures. The rest of the covariance terms are error covariance components. Similarly, correlated error can be estimated from the error variance and covariance components. In a $p^\bullet \times i^\circ$ G-study design, the error covariance components for the item and residual effects are zero because of the independent sampling of items.

After estimating the variance and covariance components in the G-study, the investigator can estimate variance–covariance matrixes for a D-study. For any multivariate D-study, there are variance–covariance matrixes for universe scores (Σ_τ), relative errors (Σ_δ), and absolute errors (Σ_Δ). The variance components in Σ_δ and Σ_Δ are the same as those in the univarite D-studies and the covariance components are directly analogous to relative error and absolute error variance components, which are computed by dividing the G-study covariance components by the numbers of levels (n') in the D-studies.

In situations in which composite scores are of interest (e.g., an intelligence or achievement test with several subtests), a composite universe score can be defined as $\mu_{\tau C} = \sum_v w_v \mu_{\tau v}$, where the w_v are weights for the distinct levels (e.g., subtests) in the multivariate model and can be defined a priori by an investigator, usually such that $\sum_v w_v = 1$ and $w_v \geq 0$ for all v. In other cases, the weights are proportional to the number of items in each subtest. Sometimes the weights do not sum to 1; for example, $w_1 = 1$ and $w_1 = -1$ for difference scores. A composite universe-score variance is a weighted sum of the elements in the universe-score variance-covariance matrix Σ_τ:

$$\sigma_C^2(\tau) = \sum_v w_v^2 \sigma_v^2(\tau) + \sum_{v \neq v'} \sum w_v w_{v'} \sigma_{vv'}(\tau)$$
$$= \sum_v \sum_{v'} w_v w_{v'} \sigma_{vv'}(\tau), \qquad (12)$$

where $\sigma_{vv'}(\tau) = \sigma_v^2(\tau)$ when $v = v'$. Similarly, relative error variance for the composite is

$$\sigma_C^2(\delta) = \sum_v \sum_{v'} w_v w_{v'} \sigma_{vv'}(\delta), \qquad (13)$$

and absolute error variance for the composite is

$$\sigma_C^2(\Delta) = \sum_v \sum_{v'} w_v w_{v'} \sigma_{vv'}(\Delta). \qquad (14)$$

The multivariate generalizability coefficient and index of dependability can be defined as the ratio of composite universe-score variance to itself plus composite relative error variance or composite absolute error variance, respectively:

$$E\rho^2 = \frac{\sigma_C^2(\tau)}{\sigma_C^2(\tau) + \sigma_C^2(\delta)} \qquad (15)$$

and

$$\Phi = \frac{\sigma_C^2(\tau)}{\sigma_C^2(\tau) + \sigma_C^2(\Delta)}. \qquad (16)$$

Example. In a science achievement assessment, two different methods (hands-on experiment and computer simulation) with the same items were used (Gao, Shavelson, Brennan, & Baxter, 1996). The investigators were interested in how exchangeable the different methods are.

Table 34.4 presents the variance–covariance matrixes for this example for a $p^{\bullet} \times i^{\bullet}$ multivariate generalizability analysis with items linked across the assessment methods (v_1 and v_2). The estimated variance–covariance matrixes for the person (p) effect, the item (i) effect, and the residual (pi) effect are denoted by $\hat{\Sigma}p$, $\hat{\Sigma}i$, and $\hat{\Sigma}pi$, respectively. Under the G-study results, the values on the diagonals of the matrixes are variance component estimates, those below the diagonals are covariance component estimates, and those above the diagonals are correlation coefficients. The results indicate that the universe scores between the two measures are highly correlated (a .959 disattenuated or error-free correlation) and the errors associated with the item variability are also highly correlated (e.g., the rank orders of item difficulty are similar across the two assessment methods). However, the rank orders of individuals on the items may vary between the two measures (a correlation of .344). Table 34.4 also presents error variances and coefficients for composite scores when different numbers of items and weights are considered in the D-studies. The results suggest that five items may be needed for each measure to reach a .80 generalizability coefficient ($E\hat{\rho}^2$) for rank ordering examinees on the basis of their composite scores. However, more than five items should be used for making decisions about individual performance levels to reach a dependability coefficient ($\hat{\Phi}$) of .80. In addition, different weights could be given to v_1 and v_2 to potentially increase reliability. Again, choice of measurement procedures, including weights, should be made on the basis of both theoretical and practical considerations instead of just maximizing generalizability coefficients.

PROGRAMMING INFORMATION

Some general statistical packages, such as SAS or SPSS, provide G-study estimates of variance components. However, D-study variance components and associated statistics, such as error variances and coefficients, need to be computed afterward. Users should also understand what estimation assumptions are made in these programs. A few computer programs have been specifically developed for

TABLE 34.4

Illustrative Example of Multivariate Generalizability Analysis for a $p^\bullet \times i^\bullet$ Design

Source	V	G-study V_1	G-study V_2	D-study ($n_i = 2$) V_1	D-study ($n_i = 2$) V_2	D-study ($n_i = 5$) V_1	D-study ($n_i = 5$) V_2
$\hat{\Sigma}\, p$	1	0.80526	0.95901	0.80526		0.80526	
	2	0.68379	0.63134	0.68379	0.63134	0.68379	0.63134
$\hat{\Sigma}\, i$	1	1.82142	1.00000[a]	0.91071		0.36428	
	2	1.15987	0.73122	0.57994	0.36561	0.23197	0.14624
$\hat{\Sigma}\, pi$	1	2.51712	0.34396	1.25856		0.25171	
	2	0.67698	1.53902	0.33849	0.76951	0.06770	0.15390
Composite score weight (w_1, w_2)				**(0.5, 0.5)**	**(0.25, 0.75)**	**(0.5, 0.5)**	**(0.25, 0.75)**
$\hat{\sigma}_c^2(\tau)$				0.70105	0.66188	0.70105	0.66188
$\hat{\sigma}_c^2(\delta)$				0.67626	0.63844	0.13525	0.12769
$\hat{\sigma}_c^2(\tau)$				1.60439	1.11849	0.50650	0.31971
$E\hat{\rho}^2$				0.509	0.509	0.838	0.838
$\hat{\Phi}$				0.304	0.372	0.581	0.674
Composite score weight (w_1, w_2)				**(0.6, 0.4)**	**(0.75, 0.25)**	**(0.5, 0.5)**	**(0.75, 0.25)**
$\hat{\sigma}_c^2(\tau)$				0.70105	0.74884	0.70105	0.74884
$\hat{\sigma}_c^2(\delta)$				0.67626	0.88297	0.13525	0.17659
$\hat{\sigma}_c^2(\tau)$				1.60439	1.63557	0.50650	0.47763
$E\hat{\rho}^2$				0.509	0.459	0.838	0.809
$\hat{\Phi}$				0.304	0.314	0.581	0.611

[a] A correlation coefficient above 1.0 was set to the unity.

generalizability analyses (see Clauser, 2008, for a review). Two special programs are available for conducting univariate generalizability analysis under balanced designs with both random-effects and mixed-effects models: *GENOVA* (GENeralized analysis Of Variance) originally developed by Crick and Brennan (1983) and *EDUG* designed by Jean Cardinet and associates (Cardinet, Johnson, & Pini, 2010; available at http://www.irdp.ch/edumetrie/englishprogram.htm). The functionality of these programs is similar in terms of providing both G-study and D-study variance components, error variances, and coefficients. *EDUG* has a simple user interface and directly implements the notions of symmetry (i.e., the same behavioral measurement may be used for different purposes with alternative roles of objects of measurement and facets) and nested objects of measurement (e.g., children are nested within gender groups) in the program (see Cardinet et al., 2010). However, *GENOVA* is combined with two other programs—*urGENOVA*

(Brennan, 2001b) and *mGENOVA* (Brennan, 2001c)—into a *GENOVA* suit to conduct generalizability analysis under balanced and unbalanced designs on the basis of both univariate and multivariate G theory frameworks (available at http://www.education.uiowa.edu/casma).

For random-effects unbalanced designs mainly due to nesting, *urGENOVA* (Brennan, 2001b) provides univariate G-study variance components, but it has no D-study capabilities. A complementary program to *urGENOVA*, *G-STRING II*, written by Ralph Bloch and Geoff Norman (2011), can be downloaded from http://fhsperd.mcmaster.ca/g_string/download.html. *G-String II* calculates generalizability coefficients using specifications provided by the user. Furthermore, *mGENOVA* (Brennan, 2001c), a program to conduct multivariate generalizability analyses, can be viewed as an extension of *GENOVA* for univariate balanced designs and an extension of *urGENOVA* for unbalanced designs. *mGENOVA* performs both multivariate G- and

D-studies for a certain set of balanced or unbalanced designs. The programming command setups and input data conventions are similar across the three programs in the *GENOVA* suite.

The availability of computer programs for conducting generalizability analyses can surely give people easy access to the procedures and increase the applications of G theory in behavioral measurement. However, software cannot substitute for the conceptualization of measurement error, which is at the center of G theory.

SOME ADVANCED ISSUES

Since the publication of Cronbach et al.'s book, *The Dependability of Behavioral Measurements: Theory of Generalizability of Scores and Profiles* (1972), G theory has emerged as one of the modern test theories. Applications of G theory have extended into many scientific fields, including behavioral and social sciences (e.g., see Bergeron et al., 2008; Chafouleas, Christ, & Riley-Tillman, 2009; Hintze & Matthews, 2004; Lakes & Hoyt, 2008; Lei, Smith, & Suen, 2007; Murphy & DeShon, 2000; O'Brian, O'Brian, Packman, & Onslow, 2003; Shavelson, Baxter, & Gao, 1993). In this chapter, however, we have only scratched the surface of the theory and provided a taste of its uses. As challenges arise in behavioral measurement, some new concepts and procedures are being developed or explored. The following advanced topics deal with some important issues that have practical implications in using G theory.

Symmetry

G theory was developed from classical test theory, which focuses on differentiating individuals. Thus, its objects of measurement are often persons. In many practical situations, however, factors other than persons can be the focus of measurement (e.g., estimation of differences in performance tasks). In addition, there are not only nested facets of measurement (e.g., raters nested within occasions) but also nested objects of measurement (e.g., students nested within classes). During the 1970s and 1980s, Cardinet, Tourneur, and Allal (1976, 1981) introduced the concept of *symmetry,* which states that any factor in a measurement

design can be selected as an object of measurement. This principle flexibly extends the practical applicability of G theory to a wide range of measurement contexts. They divided the factors in a generalizability analysis into two categories: *differentiation facet* (i.e., object of measurement) and *instrumentation facet* (i.e., error facets in the universe). Cardinet et al. (1976, 1981) recognized that the same behavioral measurement might be used for more than one purpose: A factor can be a differentiation facet under one measurement context but an instrumentation facet under another. For example, an achievement test can be used to evaluate individual student performance in which persons are the differentiation facet. The same observations, however, can also be used to evaluate generalizability of the variation in the item difficulty in which persons become an instrumentation facet and the variation among persons contributes to error. The intention behind developing the symmetry concept was to encourage the application of G theory to objects of study other than individuals (Cardinet et al., 2010).

The principle of symmetry has also led to the extensions of G theory in several directions by Cardinet et al. (2010), including analysis of multifaceted populations. In large-scale assessments and survey research as well as some behavioral measurement, individuals are often nested within group variables (e.g., classes, schools). For different uses of the measurement outcomes, different factors in the multifaceted objects of measurement can be of interest. The allocation of the variance components for the estimation of measurement error and reliability-like coefficients will be different. At the individual-level measurement, person variability is considered as true-score variance. At the group-level assessment, however, person variability introduces uncertainty about the group scores and contributes to the error variances (Cronbach et al., 1997). The 1999 Standards for Educational and Psychological Testing state,

> When an instrument is used to make group judgments, reliability data must bear directly on interpretations specific to groups. Standard errors appropriate to individual scores are not appropriate

measures of the precision of group averages. A more appropriate statistic is the standard error of the observed score means. G theory can provide more refined indices when the sources of measurement are numerous and complex. (American Educational Research Association [AERA], American Psychological Association [APA], & National Council on Measurement in Education, 1999, p. 30)

Reliability–Validity Paradox

In classical test theory, reliability and validity are two distinct themes. However, as G theory liberalized classical test theory to broaden the conceptualization of reliability, certain aspects of the validity issues have been mingled into the G theory framework.

Validity theory has evolved from separate models (i.e., criterion, content, and construct) to a unified model (Kane, 2006). Construct validation has become the basis for the unified model, which includes all evidence for validity, including content, criterion, reliability, and theoretical argument (Messick, 1989). The 1999 Standards for Educational and Psychological Testing suggested that "validity logically begins with an explicit statement of the proposed interpretation of test scores along with a rational for the relevance of the interpretation to the proposed use" (AERA et al., 1999, p. 9). G theory requires an investigator to specify the measurement conditions (facets) over which generalization will be made, which explicitly defines the relevance of score interpretations.

Almost all score interpretations involve generalization. Evidence for the generalizability of scores can support validation in terms of expected performance over some universe of possible performances (Kane, 2006). Generalizability analyses give empirical checks on the degree of invariance from particular observations to a universe of possible observations (Kane, 1999). Furthermore, G theory provides a tool to evaluate the impact of random sampling on observed scores. If sampling errors are substantial, inferences from the observed scores to the universe scores are uncertain or unjustified. To reduce sampling error, we can either increase the sample sizes of the facet that contributes the most to the error or

modify the definition of the universe. In the later case, a trade-off between reliability and validity can occur. For example, narrowing the domain or making the domain more homogeneous could increase measurement precision, but this may restrict the universe of generalization and thus limit the use of the measurement.

Conversely, according to Kane (1999), the proposed interpretation also determines the appropriate estimates of measurement error variances and generalizability coefficients. For example, specifications of content domains can affect sampling variability. In other words, domain misspecifications can either underestimate or overestimate measurement error (Shavelson et al., 1996). Therefore, the accuracy of domain specification and representativeness of the items (content validity) can influence estimates of measurement errors and generalizability coefficients.

Furthermore, convergent validity evidence is provided on the basis of correlations between different measures of the same construct. Generalizability across different measures (e.g., assessment methods) refers to their exchangeability for measuring the same attribute and may be interpreted as an instance of convergent validity (Gao et al., 1996).

Generalizability Theory and Item Response Theory

In modern psychometric society, G theory and item response theory (IRT) provide two powerful measurement frameworks for modeling measurement error and scaling latent traits. Fundamentally, G theory can be viewed as a macromeasurement model that focuses on test scores and IRT can be considered principally as a scaling model that pays close attention to item scores (Brennan, 2001a). More specifically, G theory conceptualizes measurement precision on the basis of a sampling framework under the multifaceted universe. It assumes an additive linear model of independent score effects, and it focuses on disentangling and quantifying multiple sources of measurement error as well as designing optimized measurement procedures within a specified context (universe) of score inferences. IRT, on the other hand, emphasizes statistical properties of items and focuses on estimating a latent trait (e.g., a person's ability) under strong assumptions, such as unidimensionality and local independence. The test information function in IRT expresses the accuracy of the maximum likelihood estimate of the latent variable. Although the square root of the inverse of the test information function provides the standard error of the maximum likelihood estimate on the true value of the latent variable, IRT treats measurement error as undifferentiated and estimates both item and person parameters with other measurement conditions fixed. Consequently, standard errors of estimates in IRT are usually smaller than the SEM in G theory.

Because G theory and IRT view measurement from different perspectives, and have different assumptions in modeling responses, instead of simply considering one theory as superior to the other or rejecting one in favor of the other, we should recognize the merits and limits of each and utilize them jointly to tackle measurement issues. A few efforts have been made to bring together the sampling model of G theory with the scaling model of IRT (see Bock, Brennan, & Muraki, 2002; Briggs & Wilson, 2007; Kolen & Harris, 1987). Bock et al. (2002) acknowledged that the conditional standard error of estimates (SEEs) in IRT do not distinguish among multiple sources of error. They proposed an ad hoc solution to modify information functions on the basis of results from a generalizability analysis so that the SEEs can be adjusted to consider both item and rater sampling errors. Briggs and Wilson (2007) derived variance component estimates from estimates of item and person parameters obtained within the Rasch IRT framework. G theory and IRT have been used sequentially or simultaneously to exploit their relative strength in monitoring error variances and identifying specific incidences that contribute the most to the measurement variabilities to improve the quality of measurement (see Bachman, Lynch, & Mason, 1995; Kim & Wilson, 2009; Iramaneerat, Yudknowsky, Myford, & Downing, 2008; Jeon, Lee, Hwang, & Kang, 2009). Building a crosswalk between the two modern test theories, IRT and G theory, can be challenging because both theories have their strengths, but efforts to utilize them both should be continued.

CONCLUSION

G theory has introduced a change in the conceptualization of measurement error. It offers a powerful framework for understanding measurement error and the impact of measurement error on score interpretation in behavioral and social sciences as well as other fields in which measurements are not absolutely precise. Whether we are attempting to measure general ability or achievement, or to assess behavior or personality, our scores or observations are subject to measurement error. G theory provides a useful tool for quantifying multiple sources of error and offers building blocks to design reliable and efficient measurement procedures. Moreover, G theory not only regroups classical reliability indexes within a unified conceptual framework and procedures but also raises conceptual challenges to our thinking about validity.

Born from classical test theory, G theory has several distinctive features of classical test theory. G theory (a) focuses on conceptualization of potential multiple sources of error (universe of admissible observations), (b) provides detailed information about the relative importance of the different sources of measurement error by quantifying their variability (G-study and variance components), (c) casts measurement precision within a specific context (universe of generalization and relative vs. absolute decisions), (d) identifies how measurement procedures can be improved (D-study), (e) evaluates measurement precision beyond differentiations of individuals (symmetry), and (f) unifies some conceptualizations of traditional reliability and validity (generalizability and dependability coefficients).

In recent decades, the use of G theory has been extended beyond education assessments to experimental and survey research, naturalistic studies, and instrument development in areas of education, psychology, social sciences, and medicine. The 1999 Standards for Educational and Psychological Testing have pointed out the need to refer to G theory when establishing evidence for reliability and validity:

> Where feasible, the error variances arising from each source should be estimated. Generalizability studies and variance component analyses are

especially helpful in this regard. These analyses can provide separate error variance estimates for tasks within examinees, for judges and for occasions within the time period of trait stability. (AERA et al., 1999, p. 34)

Because of its diverse applications and the richness of the theory, G theory continues to play an important role in exploring and controlling sources of measurement error in behavioral and social sciences.

References

American Educational Research Association, American Psychological Association, & National Council on Measurement in Education. (1999). *Standards for educational and psychological testing.* Washington, DC: American Educational Research Association.

Bachman, L. F., Lynch, B. K., & Mason, M. (1995). Investigating variability in tasks and rater judgments in a performance test of foreign language speaking. *Language Testing, 12,* 238–257. doi:10.1177/026553229501200206

Bergeron, R., Floyd, R. G., McCormack, A. C., & Farmer, W. L. (2008). The generalizability of externalizing behavior composites and subscale scores across time, rater, and instrument. *School Psychology Review, 37,* 91–108.

Bloch, R., & Norman, G. (2011). *G_String: A Windows wrapper for urGENOVA.* Hamilton, Ontario, Canada: PERD. Retrieved from http://fhsperd.mcmaster.ca/g_string/download.html

Bock, R. D., Brennan, R. L., & Muraki, E. (2002). The information in multiple ratings. *Applied Psychological Measurement, 26,* 364–375. doi:10.1177/014662102237794

Brennan, R. L. (1997). A perspective on the history of generalizability theory. *Educational Measurement: Issues and Practice, 16,* 14–20. doi:10.1111/j.1745-3992.1997.tb00604.x

Brennan, R. L. (2001a). *Generalizability theory.* New York, NY: Springer-Verlag.

Brennan, R. L. (2001b). *Manual for mGENOVA.* Iowa City: Iowa Testing Programs, University of Iowa.

Brennan, R. L. (2001c). *Manual for urGENOVA.* Iowa City: Iowa Testing Programs, University of Iowa.

Brennan, R. L., Gao, X., & Colton, D. A. (1995). Generalizability analyses of Work Keys Listening and Writing tests. *Educational and Psychological Measurement, 55,* 157–176. doi:10.1177/0013164495055002001

Briggs, D. C., & Wilson, M. (2007). Generalizability in item response modeling. *Journal of Educational Measurement, 44,* 131–155. doi:10.1111/j.1745-3984.2007.00031.x

Brown, W. (1910). Some experimental results in the correlation of mental abilities. *The British Journal of Psychology, 3,* 296–322.

Cardinet, J., Johnson, S., & Pini, G. (2010). *Applying generalizability theory using EduG.* New York, NY: Routledge.

Cardinet, J., Tourneur, Y., & Allal, L. (1976). The symmetry of generalizability theory: Applications to educational measurement. *Journal of Educational Measurement, 13,* 119–135. doi:10.1111/j.1745-3984.1976.tb00003.x

Cardinet, J., Tourneur, Y., & Allal, L. (1981). Extension of generalizability theory and its applications in educational measurement. *Journal of Educational Measurement, 18,* 183–204. doi:10.1111/j.1745-3984.1981.tb00852.x

Chafouleas, S. M., Christ, T. J., & Riley-Tillman, T. C. (209). Generalizability of scaling gradients on direct behavior ratings. *Educational and Psychological Measurement, 69,* 157–173. doi:10.1177/0013164408322005

Clauser, B. E. (2008). A review of EDUG software for generalizability analysis. *International Journal of Testing, 8,* 296–301. doi:10.1080/15305050802262357

Clauser, B. E., Harik, P., & Margolis, M. J. (2006). A multivariate generalizability analysis of data from a performance assessment of physicians' clinical skills. *Journal of Educational Measurement, 43,* 173–191. doi:10.1111/j.1745-3984.2006.00012.x

Crick, J. E., & Brennan, R. L. (1983). *Manual for GENOVA: A generalizability analysis of variance system* (American College Testing Technical Bulletin No. 43). Iowa City, IA: ACT, Inc.

Cronbach, L. J. (2004). My current thoughts on coefficient alpha and successor procedures (editorial assistance by R. J. Shavelson). *Educational and Psychological Measurement, 64,* 391–418. doi:10.1177/0013164404266386

Cronbach, L. J., Gleser, G. C., Nanda, H., & Rajaratnam, N. (1972). *The dependability of behavioral measurements: Theory of generalizability of scores and profiles.* New York, NY: Wiley.

Cronbach, L. J., Linn, R. L., Brennan, R. L., & Haertel, E. H. (1997). Generalizability analysis for performance assessments of student achievement or school effectiveness. *Educational and Psychological Measurement, 57,* 373–399. doi:10.1177/0013164497057003001

Cronbach, L. J., Rajaratnam, N., & Gleser, G. C. (1963). Theory of generalizability: A liberalization of reliability theory. *British Journal of Statistical Psychology, 16,* 137–163.

Feldt, L. S., & Brennan, R. L. (1989). Reliability. In R. L. Linn (Ed.), *Educational measurement* (3rd ed., pp. 105–146). New York, NY: American Council on Education & Macmillan.

Gao, X., & Brennan, R. L. (2001). Variability of estimated variance components and related statistics in performance assessment. *Applied Measurement in Education, 14*, 191–203. doi:10.1207/S15324818 AME1402_5

Gao, X., Shavelson, R. J., Brennan, R. L., & Baxter, G. P. (1996, April). A multivariate generalizability theory approach to convergent validity of performance-based assessment. In G. Ensign (Chair), *Theory and practice in large-scale performance assessments.* Invited symposium conducted at the Annual Meeting of the National Council on Measurement in Education, New York, NY.

Haertel, E. H. (2006). Reliability. In R. L. Brennan (Ed.), *Educational measurement* (4th ed., pp. 65–110). Westport, CT: American Council on Education/ Praeger.

Hintze, J. M., & Matthews, W. J. (2004). The generalizability of systematic direct observations across time and setting: A preliminary investigation of the psychometrics of behavioral observation. *School Psychology Review, 33*, 258–270.

Hoyt, C. (1941). Test reliability estimated by analysis of variance. *Psychometrika, 6*, 153–160. doi:10.1007/ BF02289270

Iramaneerat, C., Yudknowsky, R., Myford, C. M., & Downing, S. M. (2008). Quality control of an OSCE using generalizability theory and many-facet Rasch measurement. *Advances in Health Sciences Education, 13*, 479–493. doi:10.1007/s10459-007-9060-8

Jarjoura, D., & Brennan, R. L. (1983). Multivariate generalizability models for tests developed from tables of specifications. In L. J. Fyans Jr. (Ed.), *Generalizability theory: Inferences and practical applications: New directions for testing and measurement* (pp. 83–101). San Francisco, CA: Jossey-Bass.

Jeon, M., Lee, G., Hwang, J., & Kang, S. (2009). Estimating reliability of school-level scores using multilevel and generalizability theory models. *Asia Pacific Education Review, 10*, 149–158. doi:10.1007/ s12564-009-9014-3

Kane, M. T. (1999, April). *The role of generalizability in validity.* Paper presented at the Annual Meeting of the National Council on Measurement in Education, Montreal, Quebec, Canada.

Kane, M. T. (2006). Validation. In R. L. Brennan (Ed.), *Educational measurement* (4th ed., pp. 65–110). Westport, CT: American Council on Education/ Praeger.

Kim, S. C., & Wilson, M. (2009). A comparative analysis of the ratings in performance assessment using generalizability theory and the many-facet Rasch model. *Journal of Applied Measurement, 10*, 408–423.

Kolen, M. J., & Harris, D. J. (1987, April). *A multivariate test theory model based on item response theory and generalizability theory.* Paper presented at the Annual Meeting of the American Educational Research Association, Washington, DC.

Lakes, K. D., & Hoyt, W. T. (2008). What sources contribute to variance in observer ratings? Using generalizability theory to assess construct validity of psychological measures. *Infant and Child Development, 17*, 269–284. doi:10.1002/icd.551

Lei, P., Smith, M., & Suen, H. K. (2007). The use of generalizability theory to estimate data reliability in single-subject observational research. *Psychology in the Schools, 44*, 433–439. doi:10.1002/pits.20235

Lord, F. M. (1955). Estimating test reliability. *Educational and Psychological Measurement, 15*, 325–336. doi:10.1177/001316445501500401

Lord, F. M., & Novick, M. R. (1968). *Statistical theories of mental test scores.* Reading, MA: Addison-Wesley.

Messick, S. (1989). Validity. In R. L. Linn (Ed.), *Educational measurement* (3rd ed., pp. 13–103). New York, NY: American Council on Education/ Macmillan.

Murphy, K. R., & DeShon, R. (2000). Progress in psychometrics: Can industrial and organizational psychology catch up? *Personnel Psychology, 53*, 913–924. doi:10.1111/j.1744-6570.2000.tb02423.x

O'Brian, N., O'Brian, S., Packman, A., & Onslow, M. (2003). Generalizability theory I: Assessing reliability of observational data in the communication sciences. *Journal of Speech, Language, and Hearing Research, 46*, 711–717. doi:10.1044/1092-4388(2003/056)

Shavelson, R. J., Baxter, G. P., & Gao, X. (1993). Sampling variability of performance assessments. *Journal of Educational Measurement, 30*, 215–232. doi:10.1111/j.1745-3984.1993.tb00424.x

Shavelson, R. J., Gao, X., & Baxter, G. P. (1996). On the content validity of performance assessments: Centrality of domain specification. In M. Birenbaum & F. J. R. C. Dochy (Eds.), *Alternative in assessment of achievements, learning processes and prior knowledge* (pp. 131–141). Boston, MA: Kluwer.

Shavelson, R. J., & Webb, N. M. (1991). *Generalizability theory: A primer.* Newbury Park, CA: Sage.

Spearman, C. (1910). Correlation calculated from faulty data. *The British Journal of Psychology, 3*, 271–295.

Traub, R. E. (1997). Classical test theory in historical perspective. *Educational Measurement: Issues and*

Practice, 16, 8–14. doi:10.1111/j.1745-3992.1997. tb00603.x

Webb, N. M., Shavelson, R. J., & Maddahian, (1983). Multivariate generalizability theory. In L. J. Fyans (Ed.), *Generalizability theory: New directions for testing and measurement* (pp. 67–82). San Francisco, CA: Jossey-Bass.

Webb, N. M., Shavelson, R. J., & Haertel, E. H. (2006). Reliability coefficients and generalizability theory. *Handbook of Statistics, 26*, 1–44.

Yin, P. (2005). A multivariate generalizability analysis of the multistate bar examination. *Educational and Psychological Measurement, 65*, 668–686. doi:10.1177/0013164404273940

CHAPTER 35

ITEM-LEVEL FACTOR ANALYSIS

Brian D. Stucky, Nisha C. Gottfredson, and A. T. Panter

Fundamental research questions in psychology center on establishing the factor structure of new measures and understanding how unobserved constructs assessed by these measures relate to other constructs. The standard factor analytic model assumes that response data are based on continuously measured indicators of constructs, yet the individual items used in social science research rarely meet this assumption. Items appearing in surveys (such as in attitude or knowledge scales), obtained through observation codes, or gathered in interview settings may be dichotomous, ordered categorical, censored counts or zero-inflated counts. They may also have a variety of other distribution forms. This chapter addresses the historical traditions and current data analytic recommendations for conducting data analysis using latent variable models with item-level indicators.

The general topic of how to describe the factor structure and item-level characteristics of a collection of items emerged from two main theoretical routes (social sciences: item-level factor analysis [IFA]; education: item response theory [IRT]); the connection between these routes has been elucidated formally in the past few decades. In considering analytic options for modeling item-level data, we first discuss issues related to item measurement, response distributions, and estimation methods. We then address appropriate modeling conditions for focusing on individual items versus composites that are formed by the researcher from item subsets, such as item parcels or testlets, and we review

methods for assessing measurement invariance across groups. Because most commercially available factor analysis and structural equation modeling (SEM) computer programs allow for estimation approaches and options for conducting item-level analyses, distinctions among computer programs are made when useful. Finally, specific recommendations are provided about appropriate research design conditions for modeling item-level data.

FACTOR ANALYSIS

Factor analyses of categorical and continuous measures have the same goal: to explain the relationships among the variables by a smaller set of underlying, or latent, variables. Traditionally, factor analysis emphasizes understanding the dimensionality of a set of variables (e.g., exploratory factor analysis [EFA] and confirmatory factor analysis [CFA], respectively) and modeling the causal relationships among those dimensions (e.g., SEM). Although these analytic procedures are applicable for categorical response data, the key difference between the approaches lies in where the investigator places emphasis and the nature of the research questions. In the historical treatment of factor analysis for continuously measured items, item-level characteristics were often seen as problematic (McDonald, 1967, 1999; McDonald & Ahlawat, 1974). For example, the very notion of item difficulty (the probability of endorsement) is conceptually challenging from a

The authors thank members of the PROMIS pediatric network (funded by Grant 5U01AR052181) and Deb Irwin, Michelle Langer, David Thissen, Esi DeWitt, Jim Varni, Karin Yeatts, and Darren DeWalt for use of these data.

DOI: 10.1037/13619-036
APA Handbook of Research Methods in Psychology: Vol. 1. Foundations, Planning, Measures, and Psychometrics, H. Cooper (Editor-in-Chief)

continuously distributed factor analytic perspective, and hence techniques such as data transformations and standardization are commonly used to mask item differences in response distributions and scales.

The IFA approach, on the other hand, appreciates item behavior and characteristics as intrinsically meaningful. Concepts such as item discrimination (the strength of the relationship between an item and its factor) and item difficulty are key tools that psychometricians use to analyze item response data. To further develop the importance of item characteristics, we provide some background on the traditional factor analysis model.

The common factor model (Jöreskog, 1969, 1970) is based on a set of assumptions that the observed variables y = (y_1, . . ., y_i) are continuous, normally distributed with mean σ and covariance Σ and that the relationship between observed and latent variables ξ = ($ξ_1$,. . ., $ξ p$) is best described by a linear model:

$$y = \alpha + \Lambda\xi + e, \tag{1}$$

where observed responses y are functions of factor loadings Λ, latent variables ξ, item means α, and measurement error (residuals). Incorporating the covariance matrix of ξ, called Φ, and the covariance matrix of (typically uncorrelated) residuals Ψ, the relationships among y are represented by the covariance matrix Σ:

$$\Sigma = \Lambda\Phi\Lambda' + \Psi. \tag{2}$$

Items appearing in research in psychology and the behavioral sciences typically have categorical response options that violate these assumptions (Krosnick, 1999). In these situations, an appropriate alternative to the linear common factor model is IFA (Mislevy, 1986; Muthén, 1978; Wirth & Edwards, 2007). Categorical confirmatory factor analysis (CCFA) assumes that a researcher is focused on the measurement features of responses to categorical items and that these items are "discrete representations of continuous latent responses" (Wirth & Edwards, 2007, p. 59). Items with these characteristics range from dichotomous responses common in education settings (i.e., correct or incorrect, true or false) to polytomous responses, or ordered categorical responses, now common in most psychological

disciplines (i.e., Likert-type scales such as agreement, self-description).

It is not statistically appropriate to ignore the categorical nature of items and apply the common factor model to such data; attempting to do so can result in a variety of problems. Perhaps most central, categorical response variables are bounded by the minimum and maximum response options (e.g., 0 for an item that is not endorsed and 1 for an item that is endorsed), and only through nonlinear functions (such as the normal ogive and logistic cumulative distribution functions) is one able to place discrete item responses on the scale of the unobserved continuous latent variable (McDonald & Ahlawat, 1974). If ignored, the model is misspecified, and the linear approximation of the nonlinear relationship will be heavily influenced by the observed variable's mean (McDonald, 1999; Mislevy, 1986). Second, fitting a factor analysis linear model to categorical data often leads to biased parameter estimates (DiStefano, 2002). In addition, factor loadings may be attenuated in cases of sparse response coverage (such as skewness), which is typical of scale items with response options that measure only extreme trait locations. The accumulation of these problems results in untrustworthy model fit statistics.

In parallel with emergent developments for the factor analysis of dichotomous and ordered categorical data in the mid-1980s, important advances in the IRT tradition also allowed for analyses of these types of items (Mislevy, 1986). Examples from early adopters of these two traditions in psychology and related fields include assessment of depression (Childs, Dahlstrom, Kemp, & Panter, 1992; Schaeffer, 1988), need for cognition (Tanaka, Panter, & Winborne, 1988), self-monitoring (Panter & Tanaka, 1987), and psychopathology and personality (e.g., Reise & Waller, 1990) as well as several studies focusing on general issues in item order, scale design, and administration (Panter, Tanaka, & Wellens, 1992; Steinberg, 1994; Waller & Reise, 1989). Review articles and early conference presentations were specifically targeted at communicating these developments in the analysis item response data to psychological researchers (e.g., Panter, Swygert, Dahlstrom, & Tanaka, 1997; Reise,

Widaman, & Pugh, 1993; Steinberg & Thissen, 1995; Thissen, 1992).

Thissen and Steinberg (1986) described a taxonomy of models in the psychometric literature to properly analyze categorical response data in a confirmatory analytic setting allowing items to be linked to underlying latent variables. Many of these models originated in the IRT tradition, including one-, two-, and three-parameter logistic models for binary data, the graded-response model (GRM; Samejima, 1969), the generalized partial credit model (Muraki, 1992) for ordered categorical response items, models for nominal response data (Bock, 1972), and many others. For simplicity of discussion, however, we review the binary–dichotomous item response case (e.g., *agree* or *disagree*) as well as a generalization to model polytomous item responses (e.g., Likert-type items).

For dichotomous items, a respondent's location on the continuous underlying trait (ξ in factor analysis notation and θ in IRT notation) is expressed through her choice of response option. In other words, one's location on the latent variable, y_i^*, is modeled through the common factor and item-specific residual:

$$y_i^* = \lambda_i \xi + e_i, \qquad (3)$$

where the continuous latent response y_i^* has a variance of 1.0. Assuming that higher scores reflect more of a given trait, the relationship between observed item responses y_i, location on the trait y_i^*, and the threshold parameters is

$$\begin{aligned} y_i = 1 \ &if \ y_i^* \geq o_i \\ 0 \ &if \ y_i^* \geq o_i \end{aligned} \qquad (4)$$

The answers that respondents provide to a given scale item can be arranged along the latent response distribution y_i^*, by thresholds, τ_i. Thus, a threshold represents the location on the latent continuum that separates discrete responses to a given item.

THE ITEM RESPONSE THEORY TRADITION

Chapter 36 of this volume reviews traditional IRT modeling and several new directions in the field. We discuss the more common set of IRT models, their

assumptions, and their uses to motivate our discussion of the close relation between IFA and IRT. When binary data are modeled in an IRT context, one often uses logistic functions. While capitalizing on the mathematical convenience of the model (Birnbaum, 1968, p. 400), the logistic function closely follows the cumulative normal distribution. The two-parameter logistic (2PL) model may be written as

$$T\left(u_i = 1 | \theta = \frac{1}{(1 + \exp[-Da_i(\theta - b_i)])}\right). \qquad (5)$$

In keeping with Lazarsfeld's (1950) classic notation, T traces the probability of a correct response, $u = 1$, to item i conditional on ability θ, whereas an incorrect response has the probability $T(0|\theta) = 1 - T(1|\theta)$, or $T_0 = 1 - T_1(\theta)$ in more compact notation. The logistic function describes each response probability on the basis of the slope or discrimination parameter (a_i), which indicates the strength of association between the item response and latent dimension, and a difficulty or threshold parameter (b_i), which indicates the location on the ability continuum for which individuals' probability of correct response is 50%. The constant D (approximately 1.7) is commonly used to place the model on the same scale as the normal ogive, the precursor to the logistic representation (Lord, 1952).

For polytomous (ordered categorical) response data, a generalization of the 2PL, Samejima's (1969) GRM, is often used. The GRM describes the probability of a response in category k or higher, where $k = 0, 1, \ldots, m - 1$:

$$T*\left(y_i = k | \theta = \frac{1}{(1 + \exp[-a_i(\theta - b_{ik})])}\right), \qquad (6)$$

noting that $T*(0|\theta) = 1$ and $T*(m|\theta) = 0$. Here the probability of responding in category k is the difference between the probabilities of responding in k or higher and the higher response:

$$T_i(k | \theta) = T_i^*(k | \theta) - T_i^*(k+1 | \theta). \qquad (7)$$

The model describes the response process by estimating one less threshold than the number of response alternatives. Each threshold or cutpoint marks the boundary between a response in category k from $k + 1$. Although such a model is useful for a variety of psychological scales with ordinal response category items, many other IRT models characterize item responses (for a review, see Embretson & Reise, 2000).

Relations Between the Two Traditions

The histories and notational differences between Jöreskog's (1969) common factor model and the IRT models popularized by Lord and Novick (1968) seem to indicate some inherent difference across the traditions. Actually, the relation between IRT and CCFA frameworks has been presented by Bartholomew (1983), Muthén (1983), and Muthén and Lehman (1985). Takane and de Leeuw (1987) have provided the mathematical equivalence between the common models. Indeed, under certain conditions, IFA can be conducted entirely in an IRT framework. Given item parameters in either IRT or IFA, one may translate and back-translate between parameterizations. IRT-equivalent slopes and thresholds may be obtained easily from factor analysis notation:

$$a_i = \left(\frac{a_i}{\sqrt{1+a_i}} \right) D \text{ and } b_i = \frac{a_i}{y_i^*}, \quad (8)$$

where a and b are as previously defined, and τ_i represents the location on the latent variable scale that distinguishes between responses. The square root of one minus the squared factor loading is the residual standard deviation of y_i^* (with y_i^* standardized to have a variance of 1.0, as is common in many IFA approaches). Additionally, if the IRT parameters are in the normal metric, the scaling factor D is not needed and drops out of the equation. With little algebra, one may translate the IRT parameters back into factor analysis notation loadings (Λ) and thresholds (τ):

$$\lambda_i = \left(\frac{a_i / D}{\sqrt{1+(a_i / D)^2}} \right) \text{ and } \tau_i = \left(\frac{(a_i / D)b_i}{\sqrt{1+(a_i / D)^2}} \right). \quad (9)$$

Actually, most software programs estimate the model in a slope-intercept parameterization. This parameterization utilizes the logit, $Da_i (\theta - b_i)$, and after multiplying the slope through, provides the intercept, $-a_i b_i$, which, when $D = 1$ is the log odds of a correct response at $\theta = 0$. In typical IRT applications, however, intercepts are converted into the common slope-threshold parameterization by dividing the intercept by the negative slope.

As Wirth and Edwards (2007) made clear, there is some practical utility in these conversions. In many instances these translations help identify unreasonable parameter estimates. Item-level data are virtually never perfectly related to the latent trait. More often, items contain some degree of error variance, so when this error variance becomes suspiciously low, one can anticipate when item parameters are untrustworthy. Wirth and Edwards (2007) suggested skepticism when interpreting factor loadings > .95 (and hence a parameters above about 3) and objection to loadings > .97 (and a parameters above about 4). In both instances, such values would be considered near-Heywood (1931) cases.

Estimating Models Within the Two Traditions

If one considers IFA to be the intersection of traditional factor analysis and IRT, then it may be helpful to consider why these closely related techniques evolved from largely separate literatures. In part, the distinction has less to do with differences in the hypothesized models for item responses and more to do with differences in estimation employed within each tradition (Mislevy, 1986). Estimation methods for CCFA traditionally made use of the sample tetrachoric (for binary–dichotomous data) and polychoric (for polytomous–ordered categorical data) correlation matrix (Christofferson, 1975; Muthén, 1978, 1984) in addition to a weight matrix that grew substantially with the number of items. Mixtures of item types, which often occur in research settings in psychology, also could be handled as well as models with many factors (e.g., SEM). Two widely used least squares estimators that make use of the sample tetrachoric–polychoric correlation matrix are (a) diagonally weighted least squares (Jöreskog & Sörbom, 2001) as used in LISREL (Jöreskog & Sörbom, 2001), and (b) mean- and variance-adjusted weighted least squares (WLSMV; Muthén, du Toit, & Spisic, 1997) as used in M*plus* (Muthén & Muthén, 1998–2007). Both estimators use only the diagonal elements of a weight matrix (see Jöreskog, 1990; Muthén, 1984), thereby greatly reducing the burdensome operation of inverting a weight matrix for models with many items (for some other estimators see Christofferson, 1975; Jöreskog & Sörbom, 2001).

An alternative to weighted least squares estimation is full-information maximum likelihood (FIML), traditionally used in IFA and SEM approaches. Rather than employing a polychoric correlation matrix, FIML takes *full* advantage of the entire data matrix. Here, the underlying data structure is reproduced by way of the matrix of factor loadings (Λy), covariance matrixes of latent variables (Φ_ξ), and measurement errors (Θ_δ). The FIML method produces unbiased standard errors for the model parameters (factor loadings, interrelations among latent variables, measurement errors) and model fit indexes, unlike adjusted weighted least squares approaches that require corrections for biased standard errors and fit indexes (see Satorra & Bentler, 1994). FIML introduces the problem of multiple dimensions, however. Specifically, integration—finding the area of a region defined by a function—must be approximated by a number of quadrature points (e.g., Gauss-Hermite) over the number of dimensions. So, for many reasonable-size models (and quadrature points), computing time is calculated in hours, a problem less often encountered when using least squares estimators.

Alternatively, estimation of IRT parameters is typically conducted using maximum likelihood. Birnbaum's (1968, p. 420) use of *joint-maximum likelihood* (JML) provided the first directly estimated IRT parameters.[1] With JML, the parameters describing how the item behaves and the score reflecting a person's level on the underlying trait dimension are simultaneously estimated. Currently, the popularity of JML has been surpassed by the use of *marginal maximum likelihood* (MML; Bock & Lieberman, 1970), which, rather than attempting to estimate item and person parameters simultaneously, considers person parameters as nuisance parameters (and integrates over them), leaving only the item

parameters to be estimated in the marginal distribution. Application of the expectation–maximization (EM) algorithm (Bock & Aitkin, 1981) alleviated much computational time for models with few factors and many items by iteratively estimating *trial* item parameters, then using these to find the expected number of responses and the proportions of individuals at given levels of the latent variable (E-step), and finally resubstituting these values back into the likelihood equation (M-step). MML/EM is used in widely available IRT software, such as *BILOG-MG* (Zimowski, Muraki, Mislevy, & Bock, 2003), *MULTILOG* (Thissen, 2003), and soon, *IRTPRO* (Cai, du Toit, & Thissen, 2011).

More recently, advances in parameter estimation have overcome the challenge of dimensionality posed by using MML/EM, and have made high-dimensional IRT and IFA models more tractable (e.g., multidimensional IRT [MIRT]; Reckase, 2009). That is, when researchers discretely measure items, they can now model a larger number of underlying factors than was previously possible in traditional unidimensional IRT models. Here, we briefly highlight three recent developments that, with time, may see more use from applied researchers in psychology and the behavioral sciences with high-dimensional data: (a) EM with adaptive quadrature (ADQ), (b) Markov chain Monte Carlo (MCMC), and (c) the Metropolis-Hastings Robbins-Monro (MH-RM) algorithm for maximum likelihood estimates (MLEs). For a moderate number of dimensions, ADQ is an attractive alternative to MML/EM. Instead of using fixed-point quadrature, ADQ adapts the number of points needed so that the estimation process becomes more efficient (Schilling & Bock, 2005). More recently, MH-RM (Cai, 2010a) uses a Metropolis-Hastings (Hastings, 1970) Robbins-Monro algorithm (Robbins & Monro, 1951), which has enabled efficient estimation of high-dimensional models that had previously been intractable. (MH-RM will be an estimation option in the software package *IRTPRO*; Cai et al., 2011). Finally, MCMC algorithms allow for the inspection of the quality of other maximum likelihood estimates by

---

[1]Rasch (1960) provided a substantially simpler estimation method, *conditional maximum likelihood* (CML), which capitalizes on the fact that summed item scores are sufficient statistics. CML estimates item difficulty (the only item parameter estimated; discrimination parameters are 1.0) conditional on summed scores.

constructing a Markov chain with a stationary distribution as its target, at which point samples (i.e., random draws) taken from the chain serve as posterior estimates. Although MCMC is an attractive solution to dimensionality problems in FIML contexts, the efficiency of current MCMC techniques (i.e., the computational burden; Edwards, 2010) makes its use, from an applied researcher's perspective, somewhat limited. Hopefully, however, these new estimation approaches will provide psychologists with the tools to test models whose complexity exceeded the boundaries of the past software.

The preceding discussion highlighted two analytic traditions that focus on understanding the underlying factor structure of item-level data with different measurement levels. The *less than* continuously measured items present more of an analytic challenge than do the continuously measured indicators. In the next section, we consider current research on a related approach that investigators have used to circumvent complexities associated with analyses conducted at the item level.

IF ITEMS ARE MORE COMPLICATED TO ANALYZE, WHY NOT PARCEL THEM?

Under certain circumstances, a researcher may decide to aggregate (i.e., create a sum score from) a collection of items to serve as factor indicators, rather than using individual items as indicators, before conducting their factor analysis. This practice is known as *parceling*.[2] Parceling involves splitting a relatively large number of items thought to represent a latent variable into a smaller set of sum scores. These sum scores are then used in place of the individual items to identify the latent variable.

Little, Cunningham, Shahar, and Widaman (2002) and Little, Lindenberger, and Nesselroade (1999) described a latent variable's domain as consisting of an infinite pool of potential items, each deviating to some degree from the centroid of the latent variable. Assuming that the expected value of these deviations is zero, and assuming that each

item's error is uncorrelated with every other item's error, then a parcel that is constructed of a randomly selected sample of items should be, on average, a less biased and more reliable indicator of the latent construct. If, however, items are not conditionally independent from one another after accounting for the common factor (i.e., item responses are related for a reason other than the underlying dimension such as when two or three items share similar word stems), then parcels of these correlated items will be biased away from the latent variable's centroid. If it makes sense to conceive of sampling from an infinite pool of independently distributed items in a given content domain, then using parcels will represent the latent construct in a more stable, replicable way than if the same number of items were used to represent the same latent construct. Indeed, a frequently cited benefit of parceling is improved indicator reliability (Cattell & Burdsal, 1975). The Spearman–Brown prophecy formula reveals that if each item representing a latent construct consists partially of true score variability and partially of error variance, then the sum of several such items will contain a higher proportion of true score variability than any individual item (Coffman & MacCallum, 2005).

Coffman and MacCallum (2005) advocated using parcels as latent variable indicators when such a large number of items are needed to achieve adequate representation of the latent variable domain and when it is implausible to use individual items as factor indicators. For example, if a researcher has a very large number of items to factor analyze, IFA estimation in both of the traditions is more difficult. In such situations, when there are too many items to estimate a latent variable using individual items, researchers are forced to choose between (a) creating parcels so that model estimation is possible (because estimation with many discrete items is computationally intensive) or (b) aggregating the items into a single measured variable (e.g., by summing the items or outputting an estimated factor score). Coffman and MacCallum demonstrated that the parceling method is superior to alternative

---

[2]In IRT, aggregated indicators of latent variables are called *testlets*. In this setting, testlets are formed to alleviate local dependence between correlated items that is irrelevant to the latent variable of interest, often resulting from related test sections or similar item stems (Wainer, Bradlow, & Wang, 2007).

analysis options, such as path analysis, that do not allow the explicit modeling of unreliability of measurement.

Especially relevant to IFA, many researchers who use parcels do so to meet normality assumptions of their estimation method. When items are Poisson-distributed counts, dichotomous, or ordinal with only a few response categories (e.g., a 4-point Likert-type scale), then individual item distributions will badly violate normality assumptions. If normality is assumed, parameters obtained by maximum likelihood (ML) or generalized least squares (GLS) estimation will be downwardly biased. In other words, using this approach will lead to serious consequences: Standard errors for factor loadings will be underestimated and chi-square tests of model fit will be too high (West, Finch, & Curran, 1995). West et al. (1995) suggested three potential solutions for handling nonnormal factor indicators. First, they suggest that researchers can use the Satorra–Bentler correction for nonnormal data in conjunction with the ML estimator for a better approximation of the model chi-square statistic, factor loadings, and associated standard errors (Satorra & Bentler, 1994). Second, it may be feasible to use an alternative estimator that does not require items to be normally distributed, such WLSMV. Flora and Curran (2004) found that WLSMV works well even if the latent distribution underlying the discretely distributed observed variable is not normally distributed. Finally, West et al. (1995) suggested that a researcher may create parcels so that factor indicators more closely approximate a normal distribution to use with ML or GLS.

Hau and Marsh (2004) evaluated the use of parcels as a technique for handling nonnormally distributed items when the WLSMV assumption of continuous latent underlying variables is not plausible. They compared this method to the technique of using nonnormally distributed items as indicators

with the Satorra–Bentler (1994) correction. The authors did not find support for the claim that factor loading estimates would be less biased when parcels are used, but they did find that estimates were less variable with this technique. The Satorra–Bentler correction resulted in less biased parameter estimates. Bandalos (2008) compared the parceling strategy to WLSMV estimation with nonnormal items and found that parameter estimates were biased when parcels were used, particularly when unidimensionality of parcels was violated. This result was obtained for both factor loadings and structural parameter estimates between latent factors. Furthermore, Bandalos showed that model fit was overestimated (i.e., thought to be better than it was) if parcels were used when unidimensionality was violated. In contrast, estimates obtained using WLSMV estimation were unbiased, particularly when sample size increased.

Several authors have shown that parceling leads to overly optimistic model fit indexes when multidimensionality is present (Bandalos, 2008; Little et al., 2002). When locally dependent items are combined into a parcel, the irrelevant item correlation is attributed to shared variance because of the common factor, thus masking multidimensionality and artificially inflating model fit. Bandalos pointed out that unplanned multidimensionality is common; method factors are one example of this. In addition to inflating model fit, the masking of a multidimensional factor structure leads to confounded and uninterpretable latent constructs (Hagtvet & Nasser, 2004). Given the potential pitfalls of parceling with locally dependent items, Coffman and MacCallum (2005) and Little et al. (2002) recommended testing the unidimensionality assumption and proceeding with parceling only if the assumption is reasonable.[3]

When researchers decide whether they should factor analyze individual items that are not continuously measured, the current research suggests that

---

[3]If violations of unidimensionality exist, the joint probability of item responses is no longer equal to the product of marginal probabilities, which leads to biased parameter estimates (Reckase, 1979) and overestimates of score precision (Thissen, Steinberg, & Mooney, 1989). Methods for detecting violations of unidimensionality may be broadly categorized as those stemming from unidimensional models that are diagnostic tests (e.g., Chen & Thissen, 1997; Yen, 1984), those that introduce additional model parameters and latent variables to account for local dependence (e.g., Bradlow, Wainer, & Wang, 1999; Hoskens & De Boeck, 1997), and those that test the assumption of conditional independence (e.g., Stout, 1987). Diagnostic methods are useful data analytic tools for researchers interested in identifying locally dependent pairs or subsets of items. Modeling the local dependence directly is useful in situations in which local dependence is expected and is a requirement of the test (e.g., the use of testlets in modeling passage-dependent items; Wainer & Kiely, 1987).

parcels are more reliable than individual items and may allow researchers to represent more fully the domains of their latent constructs. Parcels seem to be the best option when too many items are present to estimate a full measurement model. On the other hand, if the relation between items and factors is substantively meaningful, parcels may mask true relations that exist within the data, such as local dependence or a complex factor structure (Little et al., 2002). Furthermore, alternative methods of estimation exist that negate the necessity of parceling in most circumstances, and these alternatives have been empirically demonstrated to produce less biased estimates than those obtained with parceling. Given these contrasting arguments, Little et al. (2002) suggested using parcels when unidimensionality is ensured, when constructs have been well established and defined, and when the measurement model is not of primary interest. That is, parceling may be a reasonable technique to use when the structural relations among latent variables are more interesting than the measurement model. Alternative methods, such as analyses from the factor analytic tradition, should be considered before proceeding with a parceling strategy.

MEASUREMENT INVARIANCE COMPLEXITIES IN ITEM FACTOR ANALYSIS

Testing whether the factor structure of items is similar or invariant across independent groups is an important extension of the IFA problem.[4] Inferences about group differences are only accurate if the latent construct being measured is *invariant* across groups.

Types of Invariance
Configural invariance occurs when the same factor structure exists across groups (Thurstone, 1947). If factor loadings are equivalent across groups such that a one-unit increase in the latent variable mean is associated with an identical λ unit increase in the

expected value for all items, regardless of group membership, then *weak factorial invariance* exists (Horn & McArdle, 1992; Millsap, 1997; Millsap & Kwok, 2004; Millsap & Meredith, 2007; Thurstone, 1947; Widaman & Reise, 1997). If weak factorial invariance is met and item intercepts and thresholds are constant across groups, then there is *strong factorial invariance* (Meredith, 1993; Millsap & Kwok, 2004; Millsap & Meredith, 2007; Steenkamp & Baumgartner, 1998). Strong factorial invariance is desirable because it means that no systematic differences are present in the measurement models across groups. *Partial invariance* occurs when some, but not all, factor loadings, means, and thresholds are invariant (Millsap & Kwok, 2004). When strong invariance holds and unique factor variances are also equivalent across groups, then *strict factorial invariance* is present (Meredith, 1993; Millsap & Meredith, 2007). Strict factorial invariance implies that systematic group differences in item means and covariances are solely a function of group differences in factor means and covariances. According to McArdle (2007) and Meredith and Horn (2001), strong invariance should be expected to hold if two subgroups are equivalent with respect to the latent variable of interest; however, strict invariance is not necessarily expected to hold.

Partial Invariance and Other Complications
If measurement invariance is not met in studies involving predictive relations among latent variables, then regression parameter bias will be present (Humphreys, 1986; Millsap, 1998). If item intercepts vary across groups, but the noninvariance is ignored such that the noninvariant measurement model is used to test structural hypotheses, then not only will group differences in regression parameter estimates in the structural part of the model represent any true group differences in the relations between latent variables, but also the structural parameter estimates will be confounded with group differences in measurement. Thus, it is necessary to

---

[4] The factor analytic idea of measurement invariance parallels the concept of *differential item functioning* (DIF) within IRT. DIF exists when, controlling for individuals' true latent variable score, the conditional probability of answering an item correctly is not the same across groups of individuals (i.e., measurement noninvariance). This is a major concern for psychometricians who are responsible for creating bias-free standardized tests.

test for measurement invariance before proceeding to tests of predictive models and making inferences about true group differences. Millsap (1998) described a formal test of measurement invariance that is necessary to ensure that observed structural differences are due to differences in the population rather than to differences in measurement. Millsap and Tein (2004) extended this work to include simple factor models with ordered categorical or dichotomous response types.

Before providing an IFA application, it is important to note that there are a variety of ways in which item factor analytic methods can be conducted depending on the analyst's goals. In situations in which researchers have little a priori knowledge of the factor structure of a set of items, the data analytic process might begin by fitting unrestricted EFA models where items have as many loadings as factors (see Jöreskog, 1990; Jöreskog & Moustaki, 2001; Muthén, 1984). It is more common in the IFA tradition to begin the data analysis process by fitting models that are restrictions on the general EFA framework (i.e., constraining some or many factor loadings to be zero concurrent with the research hypothesis). Often these models are variations on hierarchical models, where all items receive a loading from a general factor that is assumed to underlie all the items, with subsets of the items receiving loadings that account for a shared association specific to the subset of items but that are above and beyond the relationship accounted for by the general factor.

As an alternative to bifactor or hierarchical models, and useful in situations in which multidimensionality may not be explicitly expected, there is often utility in beginning the data analytic process by fitting a single factor model and then considering local dependence (LD) statistics as evidence of nuisance or *extra* dimensionality. This approach may be preferred in situations in which the analyst does not begin with the expectation of multidimensionality. In less common situations, where the analyst has no prior beliefs about the structure of the items, EFA may still provide a satisfactory starting position. In the application that follows, we conduct EFA initially to show the strengths and weakness of such an approach and then move into more traditional IFA models.

AN APPLICATION OF IFA

In this final section we provide a brief example of IFAs, involving less than continuously measured items, that merges the two IFA traditions that we have discussed. The data are from the Patient Reported Outcomes Measurement Information System (PROMIS), a multisite project that aims to develop self-reported item banks for clinical research. Although content domains in many areas of health are included as part of this project, for the purposes of our example, we focus on the emotional distress domain.

Anxiety and depressive symptoms items were split between two test administration forms. For brevity, we report only the results of Form 1, which had 759 children respond to 10 anxiety items and 10 depressive symptom items (Irwin et al., 2010). All items had the same 5-point response scale with the options *never* (0), *almost never* (1), *sometimes* (2), *often* (3), and *almost always* (4).

Our first step was to examine the factor structure of the individual items to determine whether there was a single dimension underlying them (a precondition for unidimensional IRT). Initial EFA models were fit to the Form 1 data, as shown in Table 35.1. The factor structure generally revealed depressive symptoms and anxiety factors but not simple structure. A close inspection reveals many instances of items loading (in part) on the incorrect factor. Had commonly used techniques for deciding the number of factors been used (scree plot, fit indexes, magnitude of factor loadings, inspection of eigenvalues), two factors would have been extracted.

Taking an IFA approach to this problem would consider item-level characteristics (e.g., item content and the location of the item on the scale) in identifying subsets of locally dependent items while resolving dimensionality concerns. In such instances, a bifactor model, which estimates two loadings for all items, a nonzero general factor loading, and a group-specific loading (here, depressive symptoms and anxiety), serves as an excellent compromise between an EFA and traditional simple-structure CFA. In this case, a bifactor model is particularly relevant because the goal of the analysis is both to determine whether depressive symptoms

TABLE 35.1

Exploratory Factor Loadings for 20 PROMIS Anxiety (A) and Depression (D) Items

	Factor	
Item	**1**	**2**
A1. I got scared really easy.	.88	–.12
A2. I felt afraid.	.89	–.10
A3. I worried about what could happen to me.	.65	.14
A4. It was hard for me to stop worrying.	.59	.24
A5. I woke up at night scared.	.55	.25
A6. I worried when I was away from home.	.42	.27
A7. I was afraid that I would make mistakes.	.34	.37
A8. I felt nervous.	.40	.27
A9. It was hard for me to relax.	.30	.42
A10. I felt afraid or scared.	.64	.23
D1. I wanted to be by myself.	–.08	.47
D2. I felt that no one loved me.	.04	.76
D3. I cried more than usual.	.39	.44
D4. I felt alone.	.06	.75
D5. I felt like I couldn't do anything right.	.08	.75
D6. I felt so bad that I didn't want to do anything.	.12	.64
D7. I felt everything in my life went wrong.	.06	.78
D8. Being sad made it hard for me to do things with my friends.	.28	.58
D9. It was hard to do school work because I felt sad.	.25	.59
D10. I felt like crying.	.42	.43

Note. Model fit using Crawford-Ferguson varimax oblique rotation and mean- and variance-adjusted weighted least squares estimation. The correlation between factors is 0.55. $\chi^2(88) = 529$, comparative fit index = 0.91, Tucker-Lewis index = 0.97, root-mean-square error of approximation = 0.08.

and anxiety are best treated as separate dimensions, and hence scales, while also identifying sources of LD (i.e., violations of unidimensionality). Finally, detecting LD in this manner allows the researcher to control the dimensionality of the scale. If LD is detected in either pairs or subsets of items, selecting one item from each grouping, and setting aside the LD-inducing items, should result in a unidimensional set of items, as the residuals of the offending items will no longer covary with the selected item.

A modified bifactor model was then fit using M*plus* with WLSMV estimation. This model is considered a modified version of the traditional bifactor model because potential sources of LD identified in the expanded EFA were modeled as subfactors (i.e., three or more items receiving an additional factor loading) and correlated errors, which represent correlations between the residuals after accounting for the covariance occurring for the general and domain-specific factor (Table 35.2).[5] Goodness-of-fit indexes suggested that the augmented bifactor model fit the data well: $\chi^2(76, N = 621) = 247.83$, comparative fit index = .95, Tucker-Lewis index = 0.99, root-mean-square error of approximation = .06.

Used in this fashion, the bifactor model provides information regarding the intended dimensionality and the presence of nuisance multidimensionality. The PROMIS researchers were initially interested in determining whether these data provided evidence that emotional distress was a single dimension, or whether distinguishable individual variation occurred between the anxiety items and then again between the depressive symptoms items. The fact that substantial loadings differed significantly from zero on the group-specific factor for the depressive symptoms items in Table 35.2 indicated that the covariation among the item responses could not be adequately explained with the theory that a single emotional distress dimension of individual differences underlies responses to all of the items. It is a curiosity of the data that the general factor in Table 35.2 is anxiety-dominated negative affect, leaving little unique variance for the anxiety group-specific factor. This fact is noted by comparing the ratio of the general factor to the domain-specific factors and demonstrated in the large number of nonsignificant loadings on the anxiety factor.

The analysis also highlights the precision with which IFA can detect nuisance dimensionality. Researchers who rely on EFA to determine the dimensionality of the items may have settled on the set of depressive symptoms and anxiety items originally hypothesized; however, a closer inspection

---

[5]If using FIML estimation, the Gibbons and Hedeker (1992) method would apply. In this context, integration would occur over eight orthogonal dimensions (1 general, 2 domain specific, 1 subfactor, and 4 error correlations), which with four quadrature points per dimension amounts to 65,536 points. Cai (2010b) considered a similar analytic problem, and using a prototype of IRTPRO with the MH-RM algorithm, reached model convergence in under 3 minutes compared with an ML/EM solution with adaptive quadrature, which took more than 4 hours.

TABLE 35.2

Factor Loadings and Residual Correlations for an Augmented Bifactor Model Fitted to the Items on Form 1

| Item stem | General factor | Orthogonal group: Specific factors | | | Doublet residual correlations |
		Anxiety	Depressive symptoms	Afraid/ scared	
I felt afraid.	.68	*.11*		.67	
I got scared really easy.	.64	.30		.38	
I felt afraid or scared.	.76	.15		.20	
It was hard for me to stop worrying.	.73	*.11*			.32
I worried about what could happen to me.	.70	*.10*			
I woke up at night scared.	.72	.40			
I was afraid that I would make mistakes.	.70	-.39			
It was hard for me to relax.	.68	-.15			
I worried when I was away from home.	.64	*.10*			
I felt nervous.	.63	-.19			
I felt everything in my life went wrong.	.61		.56		
I felt like I couldn't do anything right.	.62		.55		
I felt so bad that I didn't want to do anything.	.57		.48		
I felt alone.	.59		.50		.27
I felt that no one loved me.	.60		.47		
Being sad made it hard for me to do things with my friends.	.72		.28		.26
It was hard to do school work because I felt sad.	.66		.31		
I felt like crying.	.66		.24		.49
I cried more than usual.	.64		.23		
I wanted to be by myself.	.27		.30		

Note. Italicized entries are less than 2 standard errors from 0. From "An Item Response Analysis of the Pediatric PROMIS Anxiety and Depressive Symptoms Scales," by D. E. Irwin, B. D. Stucky, M. M. Langer, D. Thissen, E. M. DeWitt, J. S. Lai, J. W. Varni, K. Yeatts, and D. A. DeWalt, 2010, *Quality of Life Research, 19*, p. 600. Copyright 2010 by Springer Science+Business Media. Reprinted with permission.

reveals that the general and group-specific factors are not (all) conditionally independent. In Table 35.2, note that a cluster of items involves being "scared or afraid" with responses that are more correlated than expected given the general factor and the anxiety-specific factor, and four more pairs of items have significant residual correlations. Beginning at the top of Table 35.2, the pairs of items modeled with residual correlations are about "worrying," "feelings of loneliness," "sadness," and "crying." Items in these pairs or triplets are (in part) like asking the same question twice. In each instance, including a single item on the scale is sufficient and providing both (or all three in the case of the triplet) would violate assumptions of unidimensionality.

Conducting IFA in this careful manner is useful for identifying and eliminating violations of local independence. However, this modeling approach is not without its own complexities. In the present application, knowledge of the factor structure served as a foundation for later unidimensional IRT parameter calibration (i.e., after setting aside locally dependent items, the factors anxiety and depressive symptoms were separately fit with unidimensional IRT models). If the modified bifactor model is considered in a MIRT framework, however, many difficult interpretation and scoring issues remain. If IRT-based scores are desired, then, including residual correlations, eight dimensions require integration, and hence, eight possible scores. The computation of scores for such models is underdeveloped. Although MIRT scoring is slowly gaining some use, uses typically do not involve cases with small subsets of locally dependent items. With current scoring techniques, the scores per factor must be interpreted as conditional on the model's other latent variables. Interpretation of such scores remains limited. When IFA is conducted to explore or identify multidimensionality that often occurs in psychological data, it serves as a useful alternative to traditional EFA models. Had our previous analyses concluded after the EFA, we would have missed a great deal of LD. The situation shown in this data example is not rare. In well-constructed, expert-reviewed scales, LD is often missed, and it may be too minor to be identified via an EFA but large enough to affect item calibration. With recent advances in both efficient algorithms and computational speed, we expect IFA to continue to grow as more researchers become aware of the benefits of considering both scale dimensionality and item effects.

References

Bandalos, D. L. (2008). Is parceling really necessary? A comparison of results from item parceling and categorical variable methodology. *Structural Equation Modeling, 15,* 211–240. doi:10.1080/10705510801922340

Bartholomew, D. J. (1983). Latent variable models for ordered categorical data. *Journal of Econometrics, 22,* 229–243. doi:10.1016/0304-4076(83)90101-X

Birnbaum, A. (1968). Some latent trait models and their use in inferring an examinee's ability. In F. M. Lord & M. R. Novick (Eds.), *Statistical theories of mental test scores* (pp. 395–479). Reading, MA: Addison-Wesley.

Bock, R. D. (1972). Estimating item parameters and latent ability when responses are scored in two or more nominal categories. *Psychometrika, 37,* 29–51. doi:10.1007/BF02291411

Bock, R. D., & Aitkin, M. (1981). Marginal maximum likelihood estimation of item parameters: An application of the EM algorithm. *Psychometrika, 46,* 443–459. doi:10.1007/BF02293801

Bock, R. D., & Lieberman, M. (1970). Fitting a response model for n dichotomously scored items. *Psychometrika, 35,* 179–197.

Bradlow, E. T., Wainer, H., & Wang, X. (1999). A Bayesian random effects model for testlets. *Psychometrika, 64,* 153–168. doi:10.1007/BF02294533

Cai, L. (2010a). High-dimensional exploratory item factor analysis by a Metropolis-Hastings Robbins-Monro algorithm. *Psychometrika, 75,* 33–57.

Cai, L. (2010b). Metropolis-Hastings Robbins-Monro algorithm for confirmatory item factor analysis. *Journal of Educational and Behavioral Statistics, 35,* 307–335.

Cai, L., du Toit, S. H. C., & Thissen, D. (2011). IRTPRO: Flexible, multidimensional, multiple categorical IRT modeling [Computer software]. Chicago, IL: Scientific Software International.

Cattell, R. B., & Burdsal, C. A. (1975). The radial parcel double factoring design: A solution to the item-vs.-parcel controversy. *Multivariate Behavioral Research, 10,* 165–179. doi:10.1207/s15327906mbr1002_3

Chen, W. H., & Thissen, D. (1997). Local dependence indices for item pairs using item response theory. *Journal of Educational and Behavioral Statistics, 22,* 265–289.

Childs, R. A., Dahlstrom, W. G., Kemp, S., & Panter, A. T. (1992). *Item response theory in personality assessment: The MMPI-2 Depression Scale* (Report 92-1). Chapel Hill: Thurstone Psychometric Laboratory, University of North Carolina at Chapel Hill.

Christofferson, A. (1975). Factor analysis of dichotomized variables. *Psychometrika, 40,* 5–32. doi:10.1007/BF02291477

Coffman, D. L., & MacCallum, R. C. (2005). Using parcels to convert path analysis models into latent variable models. *Multivariate Behavioral Research, 40,* 235–259. doi:10.1207/s15327906mbr4002_4

DiStefano, C. (2002). The impact of categorization with confirmatory factor analysis. *Structural Equation Modeling, 9,* 327–346. doi:10.1207/S15328007SEM0903_2

Edwards, M. C. (2010). A Markov chain Monte Carlo approach to confirmatory item factor analysis. *Psychometrika, 75,* 474–497.

Embretson, S. E., & Reise, S. P. (2000). *Item response theory for psychologists.* Mahwah, NJ: Erlbaum.

Flora, D. B., & Curran, P. J. (2004). An empirical evaluation of alternative methods of estimation for confirmatory factor analysis with ordinal data. *Psychological Methods, 9,* 466–491. doi:10.1037/1082-989X.9.4.466

Gibbons, R. D., & Hedeker, D. R. (1992). Full-information item bi-factor analysis. *Psychometrika, 57,* 423–436. doi:10.1007/BF02295430

Hagtvet, K. A., & Nasser, F. M. (2004). How well do item parcels represent conceptually-defined latent constructs? A two-facet approach. *Structural Equation Modeling, 11,* 168–193. doi:10.1207/s15328007sem1102_2

Hastings, W. K. (1970). Monte Carlo simulation methods using Markov chains and their applications. *Biometrika, 57,* 97–109. doi:10.1093/biomet/57.1.97

Hau, K. T., & Marsh, H. W. (2004). The use of item parcels in structural equation modeling: Non-normal data and small sample sizes. *British Journal of Mathematical and Statistical Psychology, 57,* 327–351. doi:10.1111/j.2044-8317.2004.tb00142.x

Heywood, H. B. (1931). On finite sequences of real numbers. *Proceedings of the Royal Society: Series A, 134*, 486–501. doi:10.1098/rspa.1931.0209

Horn, J. L., & McArdle, J. (1992). A practical and theoretical guide to measurement invariance in aging research. *Experimental Aging Research, 18*, 117–144.

Hoskens, M., & De Boeck, P. (1997). A parametric model for local dependence among test items. *Psychological Methods, 2*, 261–277. doi:10.1037/1082-989X.2.3.261

Humphreys, L. G. (1986). An analysis and evaluation of test and item bias in the prediction context. *Journal of Applied Psychology, 71*, 327–333. doi:10.1037/0021-9010.71.2.327

Irwin, D. E., Stucky, B. D., Langer, M. M., Thissen, D., DeWitt, E. M., Lai, J. S., . . . DeWalt, D. A. (2010). An item response analysis of the pediatric PROMIS anxiety and depressive symptoms scales. *Quality of Life Research, 19*, 595–607.

Jöreskog, K. G. (1969). A general approach to confirmatory maximum likelihood factor analysis. *Psychometrika, 34*, 183–202. doi:10.1007/BF02289343

Jöreskog, K. G. (1970). A general method for analysis of covariance structures. *Biometrika, 57*, 239–251.

Jöreskog, K. G. (1990). New developments in LISREL: Analysis of ordinal variables using polychoric correlations and weighted least squares. *Quality and Quantity, 24*, 387–404. doi:10.1007/BF00152012

Jöreskog, K. G., & Moustaki, I. (2001). Factor analysis of ordinal variables: A comparison of three approaches. *Multivariate Behavioral Research, 36*, 347–387. doi:10.1207/S15327906347-387

Jöreskog, K. G., & Sörbom, D. (2001). *LISREL user's guide*. Chicago, IL: Scientific Software International.

Krosnick, J. A. (1999). Survey research. *Annual Review of Psychology, 50*, 537–567. doi:10.1146/annurev.psych.50.1.537

Lazarsfeld, P. F. (1950). The logical and mathematical foundation of latent structure analysis. In S. A. Stouffer (Ed.), *Measurement and prediction*. Princeton, NJ: Princeton University Press.

Little, T. D., Cunningham, W. A., Shahar, G., & Widaman, K. F. (2002). To parcel or not to parcel: Exploring the question, weighing the merits. *Structural Equation Modeling, 9*, 151–173. doi:10.1207/S15328007SEM0902_1

Little, T. D., Lindenberger, U., & Nesselroade, J. R. (1999). On selecting indicators for multivariate measurement and modeling with latent variables. *Psychological Methods, 4*, 192–211. doi:10.1037/1082-989X.4.2.192

Lord, F. M. (1952). *A theory of test scores*. New York, NY: Psychometric Society.

Lord, F. M., & Novick, M. R. (1968). *Statistical theories of mental test scores*. Reading, MA: Addison-Wesley.

McArdle, J. J. (2007). Five steps in the structural factor analysis of longitudinal data. In R. Cudeck & R. C. MacCallum (Eds.), *Factor analysis at 100: Historical developments and future directions* (pp. 99–130). Mahwah, NJ: Erlbaum.

McDonald, R. P. (1967). Nonlinear factor analysis. *Psychometric Monograph, J5.*

McDonald, R. P. (1999). *Test theory: A unified treatment*. Mahwah, NJ: Erlbaum.

McDonald, R. P., & Ahlawat, K. S. (1974). Difficulty factors in binary data. *British Journal of Mathematical and Statistical Psychology, 27*, 82–99.

Meredith, W. (1993). Measurement invariance, factor analysis and factorial invariance. *Psychometrika, 58*, 525–543. doi:10.1007/BF02294825

Meredith, W., & Horn, J. L. (2001). The role of factorial invariance in modeling growth and change. In A. G. Sayer & L. M. Collins (Eds.), *New methods for the analysis of change* (pp. 203–240). Washington, DC: American Psychological Association. doi:10.1037/10409-007

Millsap, R. E. (1997). Invariance in measurement and prediction: Their relationship in the single-factor case. *Psychological Methods, 2*, 248–260. doi:10.1037/1082-989X.2.3.248

Millsap, R. E. (1998). Group differences in regression intercepts: Implications for factorial invariance. *Multivariate Behavioral Research, 33*, 403–424. doi:10.1207/s15327906mbr3303_5

Millsap, R. E., & Kwok, O. (2004). Evaluating the impact of partial factorial invariance on selection in two populations. *Psychological Methods, 9*, 93–115. doi:10.1037/1082-989X.9.1.93

Millsap, R. E., & Meredith, W. (2007). Factorial invariance: Historical perspectives and new problems. In R. Cudeck & R. C. MacCallum (Eds.), *Factor analysis at 100: Historical developments and future directions* (pp. 131–152). Mahwah, NJ: Erlbaum.

Millsap, R. E., & Tein, J. Y. (2004). Assessing factorial invariance in ordered-categorical measures. *Multivariate Behavioral Research, 39*, 479–515. doi:10.1207/S15327906MBR3903_4

Mislevy, R. J. (1986). Recent developments in the factor analysis of categorical variables. *Journal of Educational Statistics, 11*, 3–31. doi:10.2307/1164846

Muraki, E. (1992). A generalized partial credit model: Application of an EM algorithm. *Applied Psychological Measurement, 16*, 159–176. doi:10.1177/014662169201600206

Muthén, B. O. (1978). Contributions to factor analysis of dichotomous variables. *Psychometrika, 43*, 551–560. doi:10.1007/BF02293813

Muthén, B. (1983). Latent variable structural equation modeling with categorical data. *Journal of Econometrics, 22,* 43–65. doi:10.1016/0304-4076(83)90093-3

Muthén, B. O. (1984). A general structural equation model with dichotomous, ordered categorical, and continuous latent variable indicators. *Psychometrika, 49,* 115–132. doi:10.1007/BF02294210

Muthén, B. O., & Asparouhov, T. (2002). Latent variable analysis with categorical outcomes: Multiple-group and growth modeling in M*plus*. M*plus Web Note No. 4.* Retrieved from http://www.statmodel.com/examples/webnote.shtml

Muthén, B. O., du Toit, S. H. C., & Spisic, D. (1997). *Robust inference using weighted least squares and quadratic estimating equations in latent variable modeling with categorical and continuous outcomes.* Unpublished manuscript. Retrieved from http://www.gseis.ucla.edu/faculty/muthen/psychometrics.htm

Muthén, B. O., & Lehman, J. (1985). Multiple group IRT modeling: Application to item bias analysis. *Journal of Educational Statistics, 10,* 133–142. doi:10.2307/1164840

Muthén, L. K., & Muthén, B. O. (1998–2007). M*plus user's guide* (5th ed.). Los Angeles, CA: Muthén & Muthén.

Panter, A. T., Swygert, K., Dahlstrom, W. G., & Tanaka, J. S. (1997). Factor analytic models for item-level personality data. *Journal of Personality Assessment, 68,* 561–589. doi:10.1207/s15327752jpa6803_6

Panter, A. T., & Tanaka, J. S. (1987, April). *Statistically appropriate methods for analyzing dichotomous data: Assessing self-monitoring.* Paper presented at the Eastern Psychological Association, Arlington, VA.

Panter, A. T., Tanaka, J. S., & Wellens, T. R. (1992). The psychometrics of order effects. In S. Sudman & N. Schwarz (Eds.), *Context effects in social and psychological research* (pp. 249–264). New York, NY: Springer-Verlag.

Rasch, G. (1960). *Probabilistic models for some intelligence and attainment tests.* Chicago, IL: University of Chicago Press.

Reckase, M. D. (1979). Unifactor latent trait models applied to multifactor tests: Results and implications. *Journal of Educational Statistics, 4,* 207–230. doi:10.2307/1164671

Reckase, M. D. (2009). *Multidimensional item response theory.* New York, NY: Springer.

Reise, S. P., & Waller, N. G. (1990). Fitting the two-parameter model to personality data. *Applied Psychological Measurement, 14,* 45–58. doi:10.1177/014662169001400105

Reise, S. P., Widaman, K. F., & Pugh, R. H. (1993). Confirmatory factor analysis and item response theory: Two approaches for exploring measurement invariance. *Psychological Bulletin, 114,* 552–566. doi:10.1037/0033-2909.114.3.552

Robbins, H., & Monro, S. (1951). A stochastic approximation method. *Annals of Mathematical Statistics, 22,* 400–407. doi:10.1214/aoms/1177729586

Samejima, F. (1969). Estimation of latent ability using a response pattern of graded scores, *Psychometrika, Monograph No. 17.*

Satorra, A., & Bentler, P. M. (1994). Corrections to test statistic and standard errors in covariance structure analysis. In A. von Eye & C. C. Clogg (Eds.), *Analysis of latent variables in developmental research* (pp. 399–419). Newbury Park, CA: Sage.

Schaeffer, N. C. (1988). An application of the item response theory to the measurement of depression. In C. C. Clogg (Ed.), *Sociological methodology* (pp. 271–307). Washington, DC: American Sociological Association.

Schilling, S., & Bock, R. D. (2005). High-dimensional maximum marginal likelihood item factor analysis by adaptive quadrature. *Psychometrika, 70,* 533–555.

Steenkamp, J. E. M., & Baumgartner, H. (1998). Assessing measurement invariance in cross-national consumer research. *Journal of Consumer Research, 25,* 78–107. doi:10.1086/209528

Steinberg, L. (1994). Context and serial-order effects in personality measurement: Limits on the generality of measuring changes the measure. *Journal of Personality and Social Psychology, 66,* 341–349. doi:10.1037/0022-3514.66.2.341

Steinberg, L., & Thissen, D. (1995). Item response theory in personality research. In P. E. Shrout & S. Fiske (Eds.), *Personality research, methods, and theory: A Festschrift honoring Donald W. Fiske* (pp. 161–181). Hillsdale, NJ: Erlbaum.

Stout, W. F. (1987). A nonparametric approach for assessing latent trait dimensionality. *Psychometrika, 52,* 589–617. doi:10.1007/BF02294821

Takane, Y., & de Leeuw, J. (1987). On the relationship between item response theory and factor analysis of discretized variables. *Psychometrika, 52,* 393–408. doi:10.1007/BF02294363

Tanaka, J. S., Panter, A. T., & Winborne, W. C. (1988). Dimensions of the need for cognition: Subscales and gender differences. *Multivariate Behavioral Research, 23,* 35–50. doi:10.1207/s15327906mbr2301_2

Thissen, D. (1992, August). *Item response theory in psychological research.* Invited address at the 100th Annual Convention of the American Psychological Association, Washington, DC.

Thissen, D. (2003). *MULTILOG 7 user's guide.* Chicago, IL: Scientific Software International.

Thissen, D., & Steinberg, L. (1986). A taxonomy of item response models. *Psychometrika, 51,* 567–577. doi:10.1007/BF02295596

Thissen, D., Steinberg, L., & Mooney, J. (1989). Trace lines for testlets: A use of multiple-categorical response models. *Journal of Educational Measurement, 26*, 247–260. doi:10.1111/j.1745-3984.1989.tb00331.x

Thurstone, L. L. (1947). *Multiple factor analysis.* Chicago, IL: University of Chicago Press.

Wainer, H., Bradlow, E. T., & Wang, X. (2007). *Testlet response theory and its applications.* New York, NY: Cambridge University Press.

Wainer, H., & Kiely, G. L. (1987). Item clusters and computerized adaptive testing: A case for testlets. *Journal of Educational Measurement, 24*, 185–201. doi:10.1111/j.1745-3984.1987.tb00274.x

Waller, N. G., & Reise, S. P. (1989). Computerized adaptive personality assessment: An illustration with the absorption scale. *Journal of Personality and Social Psychology, 57*, 1051–1058. doi:10.1037/0022-3514.57.6.1051

West, S. G., Finch, J. F., & Curran, P. J. (1995). Structural equation models with non-normal variables: Problems and remedies. In R. Hoyle (Ed.), *Structural equation modeling: Concepts, issues, and applications* (pp. 56–75). Newbury Park, CA: Sage.

Widaman, K. F., & Reise, S. P. (1997). Exploring the measurement invariance of psychological instruments: Applications in the substance use domain. In K. J. Bryant, M. Windle, & S. G. West (Eds.), *The science of prevention: Methodological advances from alcohol and substance abuse research* (pp. 281–324). Washington, DC: American Psychological Association. doi:10.1037/10222-009

Wirth, R. J., & Edwards, M. C. (2007). Item factor analysis: Current approaches and future directions. *Psychological Methods, 12*, 58–79. doi:10.1037/1082-989X.12.1.58

Yen, W. M. (1984). Effects of local item dependence on the fit and equating performance of the three-parameter logistic model. *Applied Psychological Measurement, 8*, 125–145. doi:10.1177/0146621 68400800201

Zimowski, M. F., Muraki, E., Mislevy, R. J., & Bock, R. D. (2003). *BILOG-MG3 user's guide.* Chicago, IL: Scientific Software International.

AN INTRODUCTION TO ITEM RESPONSE THEORY MODELS AND THEIR APPLICATION IN THE ASSESSMENT OF NONCOGNITIVE TRAITS

Steven P. Reise and Tyler M. Moore

Item response theory (IRT; Embretson & Reise, 2000; Hambleton, Swaminathan, & Rogers, 1991; de Ayala, 2009) refers to a class of mathematical models relating individual differences on one or more latent variables to the probability of responding to a scale item in a specific way. A response of "3" on a 5-point personality item, a correct answer on a college entrance exam item, and a clinician's rating of an adolescent's anxiety are all item responses that can potentially be related (probabilistically) to a latent psychological variable. IRT models, which focus on characterizing how individual differences on a latent variable interact with item properties to produce a response, contrast sharply with classical test theory (Lord & Novick, 1968) procedures, which focus on understanding the statistical properties of a composite scale score (e.g., estimating reliability).

Development of IRT models and associated methods was originally motivated by applied problems in large-scale multiple-choice aptitude testing (e.g., how to efficiently administer different test items to individuals but still compare them on the same scale, how to link different sets of items measuring the same construct onto the same scale). Lately, however, applications of IRT models to personality, psychopathology, and patient-reported outcomes measurement have been increasing (see Reise & Waller, 2009, for review). Given the authors' interests and expertise, this chapter describes IRT models mostly through the lens of these latter, noncognitive measurement contexts.

Regardless of context, researchers from a variety of fields have been keenly interested in the potential of IRT modeling as an alternative to traditional psychometric approaches to scale construction, item analysis, scale administration, and scoring individual differences. As reviewed in Reise, Ainsworth, and Haviland (2005), IRT models potentially offer many attractive features. For example, through inspection of item and scale information functions, a researcher can gain a better understanding of how well an item, or scale, functions (e.g., measurement precision) across different ranges of a latent variable. This inspection is often done graphically. Moreover, because of the IRT item and person parameter invariance properties, IRT models can be used to either place items from different instruments onto a common scale, or place individuals who responded to different items onto a common scale. In turn, this facilitates the analysis of differential item functioning across demographic groups (i.e., do the items measure the same latent variable in the same way across different groups?) as well as the creation of

This work was supported by the Consortium for Neuropsychiatric Phenomics and National Institutes of Health (NIH) Roadmap for Medical Research Grants UL1-DE019580 (Robert Bilder, Principal Investigator [PI]) and RL1DA024853 (Edythe London, PI). Additional research support was obtained through NIH Roadmap for Medical Research Grant AR052177 (David Cella, PI), National Cancer Institute (NCI) Grant 4R44CA137841-03 (Patrick Mair, PI) for item response theory software development for health outcomes and behavioral cancer research, and through Institute of Educational Sciences Grant 00362556 (Noreen Webb, Program Director). The content is solely the responsibility of the authors and does not necessarily represent the official views of the NCI or the NIH.

DOI: 10.1037/13619-037
APA Handbook of Research Methods in Psychology: Vol. 1. Foundations, Planning, Measures, and Psychometrics, H. Cooper (Editor-in-Chief)

item banks that can be administered efficiently via computerized adaptive testing (Wainer, 2000).

Nevertheless, this chapter neither focuses on the virtues of IRT nor compares IRT with traditional psychometric procedures. Such articles are plentiful (see, e.g., Embretson, 1996; Reise & Henson, 2003). Rather, this chapter is divided into two sections. In the first, we describe commonly applied *unidimensional* IRT models that are appropriate for dichotomous or polytomous item response data; space considerations prevent us from extending these models to the multidimensional case. Our primary goal in this section is to inform readers of the most popular IRT models, their origin, and the interpretation of parameters. In short, this first section is oriented toward researchers who are relatively unfamiliar with modern measurement theory and who desire a basic understanding of IRT modeling options.

In the second section, we discuss conceptual and technical issues that arise in the application of IRT models to psychological data. Among the topics we consider are (a) the applicability of IRT models across various types of constructs and domains, (b) sample size and model selections issues, and (c) some lessons learned thus far from the research literature on application of IRT to noncognitive measures. This second section is oriented toward both novice researchers who are considering applying IRT to their data and to more experienced investigators who may not have considered some of the issues raised herein.

Many key topics are not addressed. For example, technical topics (such as item and person parameter estimation) and applications of IRT models are not covered, including using IRT (a) to score individuals on a latent variable, (b) to evaluate measures for differential item functioning, or (c) as a basis for computerized adaptive testing. Interested readers are referred to Embretson and Reise (2000); Hambleton, Swaminathan, and Rogers (1991); and de Ayala (2009) for treatment of these topics. Finally, given space constraints, we cannot do justice to the seemingly endless variety of alternative IRT models, such as nonparametric (Sijtsma & Molenaar, 2002), unfolding (Roberts, Donoghue, & Laughlin, 2000), explanatory (De Boeck & Wilson, 2004), hierarchical

(Fox & Glas, 2001), or sequential-steps models (Tutz, 1990).

UNIDIMENSIONAL DICHOTOMOUS IRT MODELS

IRT modeling begins with a Person ($i = 1 \ldots I$) × Item ($j = 1 \ldots J$) matrix of item responses (X). When items are dichotomously scored, such as correct versus incorrect or endorsed versus not endorsed, the item response matrix consists entirely of zeros and ones. Given this matrix, the chief objective of IRT modeling is to fit a mathematical function that characterizes the relation between individual differences on an assumed latent variable (labeled θ) and the probability of endorsing an item. Herein, for dichotomous items, this function will be termed an item response curve (IRC). The goal of fitting IRT models is to find a model such that the estimated IRC *best represents* or *fits* the observed item response data. In this section, we provide detailed review of the most commonly observed unidimensional IRT models for describing dichotomous item response data. We proceed slowly in developing these models for the sake of audiences with little prior exposure to IRT.

As noted, the basic goal of IRT modeling is to find a function that relates an individual's standing on a latent variable with the probability of endorsing an item. One such IRC must be found for each scale item. In considering an appropriate model, note that as individual trait levels increase, the probability of item endorsement should increase monotonically. Stated differently, groups of individuals who are higher on the latent variable measured by an item should have higher item endorsement rates relative to groups of individuals who are lower on the latent variable.

At first blush, the above observation may suggest that a straight-line function could be used to describe the relation between the latent variable and item endorsement probability. However, a straight-line function will not suffice because probabilities are bounded between zero and one, and any line will eventually predict values above one as the latent variable increases and predict values below zero as the latent variable decreases. Alternatively, a function that increases monotonically and is bounded between zero and one is the cumulative function of the normal distribution:

$$P(x=1\mid\theta)=\Phi(\theta)=\int_{-Z=-(\theta-\mu)/\sigma}^{\infty}\frac{1}{\sqrt{2\pi}}e^{-[1/2]z^2}dz. \quad (1)$$

Equation 1 states that to find the probability of endorsement, conditional on a latent variable, we need to integrate (find the area under the curve) between –Z and infinity. As –Z becomes more negative, proportions increase; as –Z becomes more positive, proportions decrease. To clarify, in Equation 1, θ represents individual differences on a latent variable. (For now, think of θ as a standardized raw scale score.) The μ and σ parameters in Equation 1 are the population mean and standard deviation of a normal distribution. The term $(\theta-\mu)/\sigma$ thus indicates how many standard deviation units an individual's level on the latent variable is relative to the mean. When different values of μ or σ are plugged into Equation 1, the resulting cumulative distribution takes different forms. By decreasing the standard deviation, we can produce a steeper curve, or by increasing the standard deviation, we can decrease the acceleration of the ogive. In turn, the mean always corresponds to the point on the latent continuum at which the proportion is .50.

To illustrate, we examined a large set of item response data drawn from a 24-item measure of adolescent Social Discomfort (Williams, Butcher, Ben-Porath, & Graham, 1992) administered to a large sample. Parts of this data set were previously analyzed in Reise and Waller (2003). For each item, we began our analysis by simply summing raw item responses (not including the item under study) and then standardizing those raw scale scores. We then plotted item endorsement proportions (i.e., means) for groups of individuals with similar Z-scores. These *empirical* IRCs are shown for items 16, 22, and 18 in the three panels of Figure 36.1, top, middle, and bottom, respectively. We then estimated best-fitting two-parameter cumulative normal ogives (2PNO), and these *estimated* IRCs are shown as solid lines in the figures. Clearly, these lines appear to describe the data quite nicely. Specifically, the three curves are cumulative ogives from three different normal distributions with means and standard devi-

ations of .17, .66 (top panel); .58, 2.17 (middle panel); and 2.19, 1.78 (bottom panel).

This example illustrates simple use of the cumulative normal distribution to model the proportions of individuals endorsing an item as a function of the latent variable. By using different normal distributions and their associated cumulative ogives, we can accommodate items regardless of difficulty or strength of relationship to the latent variable. Yet, Equation 1 is not the actual normal-ogive model referred to in the IRT literature. For that, we need to rearrange and redefine some terms. We start by relabeling the mean (μ) as an item location parameter (b) and defining a slope parameter (a; sometimes called a *discrimination parameter*) as the reciprocal of the standard deviation: $a=1/\sigma$. Replacing and rearranging terms leaves us with Equation 2:

$$P(x_{ij}=1\mid\theta)=\Phi(\theta)=\int_{-Z=-[a(\theta-b)]}^{\infty}\frac{1}{\sqrt{2\pi}}e^{-[1/2]z^2}dz. \quad (2)$$

Equation 2 makes clear that the probability of endorsing an item is now a function of an individual's standing on a latent variable, and two item properties, location and slope (to be defined more sharply in the following paragraphs). Individuals with trait level values above the item location will have high probabilities of endorsing the item, and conversely, individuals with trait levels below the item location will have low probabilities of item endorsement.

Finally, note that Equation 2 is in *slope and location* form, meaning, to find the probability of item endorsement given θ, we must know this particular item's slope (a) and location (b). We can rewrite Equation 2 to be in *slope and intercept* form by defining an intercept d as $-ab$:

$$P(x_{ij}=1\mid\theta)=\Phi(\theta)=\int_{-Z=-(a\theta+d)}^{\infty}\frac{1}{\sqrt{2\pi}}e^{-[1/2]z^2}dz. \quad (3)$$

Equations 2 and 3 express exactly the same thing; both are two-parameter normal-ogive IRT (2PNO) models. Equation 2 is the parameterization most frequently reported and discussed, but Equation 3 is critically important to understand because (a) it is the model that is most easily transformed in a factor analytic model (i.e., slopes transformed into factor loadings and intercepts transformed into factor thresholds;

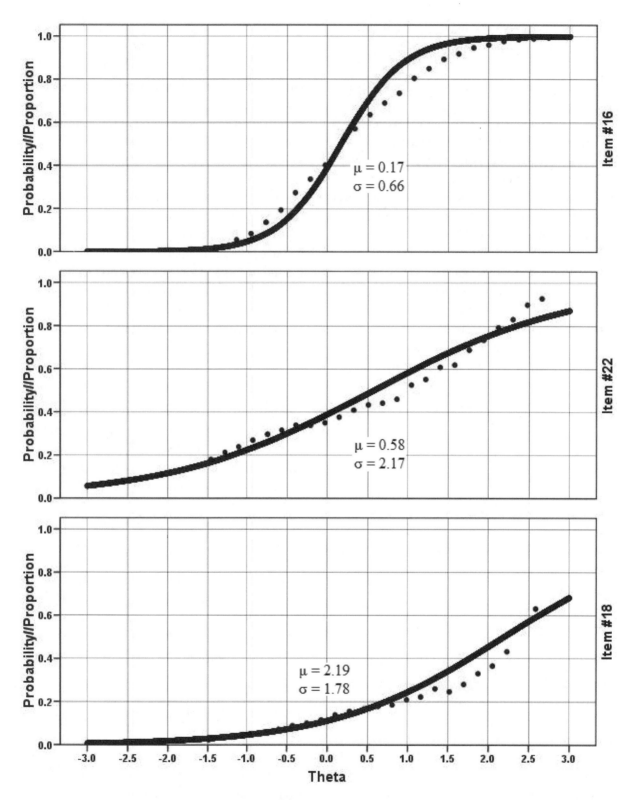

FIGURE 36.1.   Empirical (dots) and estimated (solid lines) item response curves for three social discomfort items.

McLeod, Swygert, & Thissen, 2001, p. 199), and thus (b) it is the model that generalizes most easily to multidimensional models (i.e., models with more than one latent variable), and (c) it is the parameterization

of the model that is estimated in most popular IRT software programs (Baker & Kim, 2004).

Thus far, we have been thinking of θ as a standardized scale score. Of course, in IRT applications, θ is a latent variable with an arbitrary scale, and an individual's position on that latent variable needs to be estimated. In most IRT applications, the scale of the latent variable is identified by specifying that the mean in the population is zero and the standard deviation is one. As a consequence, a person's standing on the latent variable is like a *z* score (if we assume normality of the latent variable), and importantly, the item parameters (location and slope) are estimated in reference to this latent trait scale. If we identified the latent variable in a different way, say using a mean of 500 and standard deviation of 100, the scale for the item parameters would change accordingly.

To illustrate and better define the 2PNO, Table 36.1 shows item parameter estimates for the 24 Adolescent Social Discomfort items noted earlier. Item parameters were estimated using marginal maximum likelihood as implemented by the BILOG-MG software program (Zimowski, Muraki, Mislevy, & Bock, 2003). The first two columns of Table 36.1 report the item–test correlations and the item means (proportions endorsed). Clearly, items do not vary greatly in their response rates—there are no highly endorsed items—but they do vary in item–test correlation. We note that the raw score distribution was highly skewed positively; most people score low on the measure.

The third column of Table 36.1 reports the estimated item intercepts ($-ab$). Generally speaking, intercepts tend to range between –3 and 3 with high values representing easy (high proportion endorsed) items and negative values reflecting difficult items (low proportion endorsed). Technically, the intercept corresponds to the *z* score on a normal distribution that cuts off the predicted proportion of endorsements for individuals at θ = 0. If the latent variable is perfectly normally distributed, the

TABLE 36.1

Descriptive Statistics and Two-Parameter IRT Parameter Estimates of the 24-Item Social Discomfort Scale

Item	Item–test correlation	Proportion endorsed	Normal ogive (IRT)			Logistic (IRT)		
			Int.	Location	Slope	Int.	Location	Slope
1	.44	.31	−.53	.72	.74	−.90	.72	1.26
2	.61	.35	−.51	.36	1.41	−.87	.36	2.39
3	.36	.51	.08	−.13	.59	.13	−.13	1.00
4	.35	.56	.22	−.40	.54	.37	−.40	.92
5	.56	.41	−.23	.20	1.13	−.39	.20	1.92
6	.45	.41	−.21	.27	.77	−.36	.27	1.32
7	.42	.29	−.62	.88	.70	−1.05	.88	1.19
8	.52	.37	−.38	.38	.98	−.64	.38	1.67
9	.39	.54	.18	−.27	.65	.30	−.27	1.10
10	.53	.26	−.84	.79	1.06	−1.43	.79	1.80
11	.43	.11	−1.67	1.64	1.02	−2.84	1.64	1.74
12	.29	.20	−.90	1.86	.48	−1.53	1.86	.82
13	.60	.29	−.82	.59	1.40	−1.40	.59	2.39
14	.43	.38	−.31	.43	.71	−.52	.43	1.21
15	.57	.33	−.55	.46	1.21	−.94	.46	2.06
16	.62	.41	−.26	.17	1.51	−.44	.17	2.57
17	.35	.50	.04	−.07	.56	.07	−.07	.95
18	.29	.14	−1.22	2.19	.56	−2.08	2.19	.95
19	.54	.33	−.56	.52	1.09	−.96	.52	1.86
20	.50	.39	−.29	.31	.93	−.49	.31	1.58
21	.52	.23	−1.00	.94	1.07	−1.70	.94	1.81
22	.31	.39	−.27	.58	.46	−.45	.58	.79
23	.36	.44	−.12	.22	.56	−.21	.22	.96
24	.45	.40	−.24	.31	.76	−.41	.31	1.30

Note. Int. = intercept; IRT = item response theory.

intercept is nothing more than the *z*-score cutpoint corresponding to the proportion who endorsed the item in the calibration sample. Consider, for example, that the intercepts in Table 36.1 are very close to the *z*-score cutpoints that correspond to the proportions endorsed. For example, for Item 1, the proportion endorsed is 31%. The *z* score that cuts off 31% from 69% is –0.49, very close to the estimated intercept of –.53. For Item 4, the endorsement rate is 56%. The *z* score that cuts off 56% from 44% is .16, which is again close to the estimated intercept of .22.

The fourth column of Table 36.1 shows the estimated item location parameters. These parameters are expressed on the same scale as the latent variable and typically range between –3 and 3. In this two-parameter model, the location parameter reflects the point on the latent variable continuum at which the endorsement rate is .50. Finally, the fifth column shows the estimated slope or *discrimination* parameters. Slope parameters indicate the steepness of the IRC in the area around the item location; higher slopes indicate more *discriminating* items. More technically, Equation 4 reveals that the slope in the normal-ogive metric, which typically ranges between .5 and 1.2, determines how fast –*Z* changes as the latent variable changes. Finally, observe that the slope is nearly perfectly correlated with the item-test correlation.

Before moving on, a few comments are in order regarding the intercept and location parameters. First, as noted, the intercept is essentially a simple transformation of the observed proportion endorsed into a *z*-score metric. In turn, because $b = -(d/a)$, items can have equal intercepts but different locations if the items have different slopes. This observation calls into question the use of the common label *difficulty* for the location parameter, *b*; it appears more reasonable to consider the intercepts as the difficulty of an item. Moreover, even if item parameters from multiple groups are linked on a common metric, a researcher cannot simply compare estimated location parameters across two or more groups without first establishing that the slopes are invariant. This is much like multiple-group confirmatory factor analysis, which requires first establishing loading invariance before investigating threshold invariance.

The normal-ogive model has the advantages of being familiar and easily related to the factor analysis of ordinal items, and it can be extended to multiple dimensions. However, there are some well-known mathematical difficulties in estimating model parameters. For this reason, most IRT applications estimate the IRC using a logistic-ogive model in place of the normal ogive. In fact, some statistical estimation software (MULTILOG; Thissen, 2003) only includes logistic models. Equations 4 and 5 show the two-parameter logistic model (2PLM) in both slope-and-location and slope-and-intercept forms, respectively.

$$P(x=1 \mid \theta) = \psi(\theta) = \frac{\exp[1.7a(\theta-b)]}{1+\exp[1.7a(\theta-b)]}. \quad (4)$$

$$P(x=1 \mid \theta) = \psi(\theta) = \frac{\exp(1.7a\theta+d)}{1+\exp(1.7a\theta+d)}. \quad (5)$$

As written in Equations 4 and 5, because of the inclusion of the constant 1.7 in the model, these are actually two-parameter logistic approximations of the normal-ogive model. The purpose of including this scaling factor is so that the slope parameter estimated in the logistic model is the same as its value estimated in the normal-ogive model. If the 1.7 scaling factor were not included in the model, the slope parameter in the pure logistic model would be 1.7 times higher than its value in the normal ogive. To demonstrate the equivalence of the logistic and normal-ogive models, in Table 36.1, we also display the estimated parameters from the logistic model using BILOG-MG (Zimowski et al., 2003).

Interpretation of the item parameters under the 2PLM remains essentially the same as under the 2PNO model. As usual, the scale for the latent variable is arbitrary and must be identified by setting the mean and standard deviation. Values of zero and one are typically chosen. The location parameter remains the point on the latent continuum at which the proportion endorsed is .50; these values are the same in the 2PNO and 2PLM. The slope indicates how rapidly response rates change as a function of the latent variable in the area of the item location. The slopes in a pure logistic model (no $D = 1.7$) are 1.7 times higher than in the normal ogive.

Reduced and Expanded Dichotomous Models

The 2PLM and 2PNO allow IRCs to vary in two ways: location and slope. Other IRT models for dichotomous responses can be viewed as either expansions of these models or as nested models derived by placing restrictions on the item slopes. For example, if we retain the identification constraint that the mean of the latent variable is zero with standard deviation of one in the population, we can impose the constraint that all the items have the same slope parameter. In Table 36.2, we show the Social Discomfort items under a logistic model with the equal slope constraint. This is called the one-parameter logistic model (1PLM). In this model, the IRCs will not intersect because they all constrained to have the same slope. Moreover, in the 1PLM, the probability of endorsement is solely a function of

the difference between an individual's trait standing and the item's location, weighted by a constant (the item slope).

The 1PLM, although similar, is not to be confused with the Rasch model (Bond & Fox, 2007). In a Rasch model, it is customary to impose the constraint that all the slopes are equal to one, and thus the slope parameter disappears from the model. In turn, to accommodate this constraint, one needs to free up the variance of the latent variable by estimating it rather than fixing its value (a variety of other identification constraints are possible). Over the past 30 years, many researchers have been championing the potential virtues of Rasch models (e.g., sufficient statistics for estimating item parameters, nonintersecting IRCs, specific objectivity) and an equal number have been questioning their utility in real-world psychological data. Such debates are

TABLE 36.2

1PLM and 3PLM Parameter Estimates for the Social Discomfort Scale

Item	1PLM			3PLM			
	Intercept	Slope	Location	Intercept	Slope	Location	c-P
1	−0.92	1.34	0.69	−0.63	0.85	0.74	0.00
2	−0.69	1.34	0.51	−0.99	1.96	0.51	0.03
3	0.18	1.34	−0.14	−1.63	2.47	0.66	0.34
4	0.46	1.34	−0.34	−0.34	0.90	0.38	0.27
5	−0.35	1.34	0.26	−0.40	1.24	0.32	0.00
6	−0.35	1.34	0.26	−0.30	0.86	0.35	0.00
7	−1.09	1.34	0.82	−0.71	0.80	0.88	0.00
8	−0.59	1.34	0.44	−0.52	1.10	0.47	0.00
9	0.35	1.34	−0.26	0.10	0.66	−0.16	0.01
10	−1.28	1.34	0.96	−1.04	1.28	0.81	0.00
11	−2.58	1.34	1.93	−1.98	1.44	1.37	0.00
12	−1.75	1.34	1.31	−0.96	0.58	1.66	0.00
13	−1.09	1.34	0.82	−1.95	2.98	0.65	0.04
14	−0.53	1.34	0.40	−0.48	0.86	0.55	0.03
15	−0.80	1.34	0.60	−1.22	2.05	0.59	0.05
16	−0.35	1.34	0.27	−0.77	2.08	0.37	0.04
17	0.11	1.34	−0.08	−1.07	1.60	0.67	0.30
18	−2.31	1.34	1.73	−1.31	0.70	1.87	0.00
19	−0.85	1.34	0.64	−1.82	2.74	0.67	0.09
20	−0.47	1.34	0.35	−1.39	2.29	0.61	0.15
21	−1.52	1.34	1.14	−1.28	1.40	0.92	0.01
22	−0.48	1.34	0.36	−1.58	1.61	0.98	0.25
23	−0.20	1.34	0.15	−0.36	0.74	0.48	0.09
24	−0.40	1.34	0.30	−0.53	1.04	0.51	0.07

Note. 1PLM = one-parameter logistic model; 3PLM = three-parameter logistic model; c-P = c parameter.

beyond the present treatment (see Borsboom, 2005, for extended discussion), but two features of Rasch modeling are worth noting.

First, Rasch modeling, by its nature, emphasizes the meaningfulness and interpretability of the latent variable metric and items arrayed along that dimension. This is a laudable goal and contrasts sharply with most psychometric work in its consideration of the unit of measurement. Second, as a general philosophy, following the factor analytic tradition, IRT modeling typically focuses on finding a model that *best fits* the data. On the other hand, a Rasch model is usually considered the only *real* measurement model, and the goal of research is to find a set of items that provide responses fitting that model. In short, the philosophies underlying application of Rasch and non-Rasch models can be very different (Wilson, 2005).

Moving beyond restricted models, we now consider models that *add* parameters to the 2PLM (or 2PNO). Consider that on multiple-choice tests, it is arguable that the 2PLM is inadequate to describe the item response process because individuals may produce a correct response by chance, regardless of their levels on the latent variable. Notice that in a two-parameter model, the IRC has a lower asymptote of zero (very low-scoring individuals have zero chance of answering the item correctly) and an upper asymptote of one (very high scoring individuals always get the item right). Thus, the model may be unrealistic in describing certain types of multiple-choice tests. Moreover, some personality researchers have argued that a two-parameter model is inadequate because individuals at low levels of the latent variable may have a nonzero probability of endorsing the item (Rouse, Finger, & Butcher, 1999). To accommodate this fact in either cognitive or noncognitive measurement, the canonical 2PLM can be expanded to include a lower-asymptote or *pseudoguessing* parameter, as in Equation 6.

$$P(x_{ij} = 1 \mid \theta) = \psi(\theta) = c + (1-c)\frac{\exp[a(\theta - b)]}{1 + \exp[a(\theta - b)]}. \quad (6)$$

In this three-parameter logistic model (3PLM), the lower asymptote parameter (c) places a lower boundary on the IRF. For example, if c is estimated to be .20, then regardless of how low an individual's

standing is on the latent variable, the IRC will go no lower than .20. The location (b) in Equation 6 is no longer the point on the latent trait continuum at which the probability of endorsing is .50. Rather, the probability of endorsing at $\theta = b$ is $(100 + c)/2$ (Hambleton & Swaminathan, 1985).

To illustrate, the last set of columns in Table 36.2 shows the 3PLM parameters estimated for the Adolescent Social Discomfort data (logistic model). For most items, there is no c parameter, indicating that as levels on the latent variable decrease, response probabilities go to zero. However, there are several items for which there is evidence for a c parameter (i.e., Items 3, 4, 17—three items with relatively high proportion endorsed—and 22). For example, Item 22 is interesting in that it has somewhat extreme content, abbreviated as "spend most of spare time alone" (Ben-Porath, Tellegen, & Kaemmer, 2005), which is keyed positively for Social Discomfort. Thus, the 3PLM tells us that even individuals low on Social Discomfort will say "yes" to this item approximately 25% of the time.

Moving beyond the 3PLM, Reise and Waller (2003) and Waller and Reise (2010) considered a 4PLM model that includes an upper asymptote parameter (γ) as well as a lower asymptote for psychopathology items.

$$P(x = 1 \mid \theta) = \psi(\theta) = c + (\gamma - c)\frac{\exp[a(\theta - b)]}{1 + \exp[a(\theta - b)]}. \quad (7)$$

This model was motivated by inspection of empirical IRCs and by theoretical considerations. For example, even in clinical populations (such as depressed populations), it would be unrealistic to expect that 100% of patients display any one symptom (e.g., suicide ideation, hopelessness). Hence, the upper asymptote for an item may not be 100%, as in the 2PLM or 3PLM, but rather some smaller value. Relative to the 2PLM, the interpretation of the item parameters in this 4PLM model changes slightly. Specifically, the location (b) is now the point on the latent scale at which the response proportion is $(100 + c - \gamma)/2$. We will not attempt to estimate and display parameters for the 4PLM herein. Instead, we refer readers to the original articles for discussion of the possible causes and consequences of upper and lower asymptote parameters in personality and psychopathology data.

Unidimensional Polytomous Item Response Models

Although dichotomously scored multiple-choice tests continue to dominate cognitive assessment, the fields of personality, psychopathology, and patient-reported outcomes assessment rely heavily on measures with ordered multicategory response options. Over the past 10 years, the application of polytomous IRT models has increased, especially in the field of patient-reported outcomes assessment (see Cella et al., 2007, 2010; Reise & Waller, 2009). The goals of this section are to introduce the logic of polytomous IRT models and to highlight important differences. There are many important polytomous models, but here, we focus discussion on only a small subset. In addition, we limit the description to only the logistic versions of each model. Readers interested in fuller treatment of the diverse family of polytomous IRT models should consult Nering and Ostini (2010) and Ostini and Nering (2006).

Just as the basic goal of IRT modeling for dichotomous items is to estimate an IRC that *best* represents the data, the chief objective of polytomous IRT models is to estimate a set of *best-fitting* category response curve (CRC). These CRCs model the relation between level on a latent variable and the probability of responding in a particular response category for an item. A central distinction between polytomous IRT models is the distinction between difference models and divide-by-total models (Thissen & Steinberg, 1986). As shown in the next section, difference models require a two-step computation procedure to derive CRCs, whereas in divide-by-total models, only a single equation is needed to derive the CRCs.

Graded-Response Model

We begin by describing the iconic graded-response model (GRM; Samejima, 1969), which appears to be the most frequently applied polytomous IRT model in the noncognitive assessment domain (Reise & Waller, 2009). One way to view the GRM is to think of it as an extension of the 2PLM to the polytomous response case. Consider that, with a dichotomous item, there are only two response options, and thus there is only a single boundary or threshold between a response of zero and one. As a consequence, only a

single IRC is needed to describe how increases on the latent variable increase the chances of an individual endorsing the item (i.e., responding one instead of zero).

Now consider an item with four ordered response options (0, 1, 2, 3). This item can be thought of as containing three (number of categories minus one) dichotomies: 0 versus 1, 2, 3; 0, 1 versus 2, 3; and 0, 1, 2 versus 3. When represented in this way, it is easy to understand that the first step in estimating a GRM is to estimate the number of categories minus one threshold response curve (TRC), one for each of the possible dichotomizations. These TRCs, shown in Equation 8, are simply 2PLM IRCs with equal slopes within an item (but not necessarily between items):

$$P_x^*(\theta) = \frac{\exp\left[\alpha\left(\theta - b_j\right)\right]}{1 + \exp\left[\alpha\left(\theta - b_j\right)\right]}, \tag{8}$$

where, $j = 1 \ldots$ number of response categories minus one.

Given that they are 2PLM functions, the TRCs indicate how the probability of responding in or above a given category changes as a function of the latent variable. In other words, for a four-category item, in the GRM, each item is described by one item slope parameter (a) and the number of categories minus one location parameter (b_j)—one for each threshold between the response categories. The TRCs are important, but they do not directly yield the desired CRCs. Rather, once the parameters of the TRCs are estimated, computing the conditional category response probabilities for $x = 0 \ldots 3$ requires a second step that is done by subtraction:

$$P_x(\theta) = P_{(x)}^*(\theta) - P_{(x+1)}^*(\theta). \tag{9}$$

By definition, the probability of responding in or above the lowest response category is $P_{(x=0)}^*(\theta) = 1.0$, and the probability of responding above the highest response category is $P_{(x=4)}^*(\theta) = 0.0$. The CRCs derived from Equation 9 represent the probability of an individual responding in a particular category conditional on the latent variable.

The item parameters in the GRM dictate the shape and location of the TRCs (and thus the CRCs). The higher the slope parameters (α), the steeper the TRCs, and the more narrow and peaked the CRCs, indicating that the response categories differentiate among individuals at different levels of the latent variable well. The location parameters (b_j) determine the location of the TRCs along the latent variable continuum and the point at which each of the CRCs for the middle response options peak. Specifically, the CRCs peak in the middle of two adjacent location parameters. To illustrate the model, Table 36.3 displays the estimated item parameters for a set of Depression items scored with four response options. These items were drawn from the National Institutes of Health (NIH) PROMIS project (Cella et al., 2007) and item parameters are based on a small subsample drawn from a much larger project (Pilkonis et al., 2011). The darker lines in Figure 36.2 show the TRCs and the CRCs for two items, namely,

the two items with the highest estimated (Item 21, "I felt hopeless") and lowest (Item 27, "I felt guilty") slopes.

Nominal Response Model

We now turn our attention to a set of nested models that belong to a distinct class of divide-by-total polytomous IRT models. We begin by introducing the most general direct model, namely, Bock's (1972) nominal response model (NRM). It is called a "nominal" response because the model does not assume that category responses are ordered within an item. Rather, the model treats category ordering as a property to be discovered, as we will see. In contrast, the GRM assumed that response categories are strictly ordered.

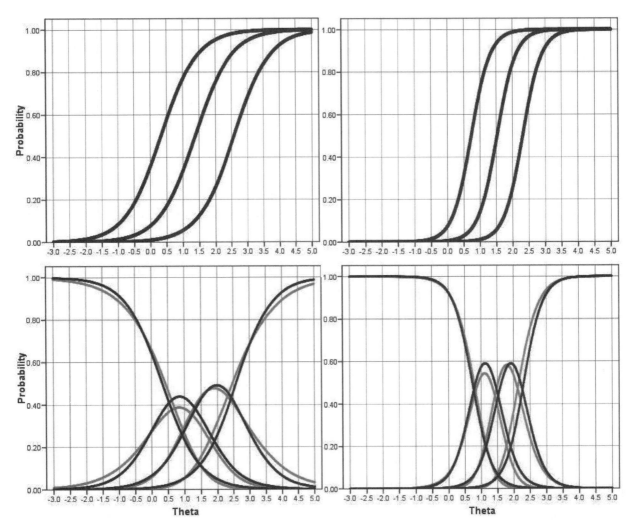

FIGURE 36.2. Threshold response curves (top) for the most and least discriminating depression items under the GRM, and CRCs (bottom) for these same items under the GRM (darker lines) and GPCM (lighter lines).

TABLE 36.3

Graded-Response Model and Generalized Partial Credit Model Parameter Estimates for an Example Depression Scale

Item	Graded-response model				Generalized partial credit model			
	α	b1	b2	b3	α	δ1	δ2	δ3
1	3.13	0.81	1.55	2.35	2.99	0.97	1.45	2.12
2	2.64	0.65	1.35	2.28	2.49	0.89	1.19	2.11
3	2.80	0.70	1.47	2.45	3.08	0.90	1.29	2.28
4	1.98	0.29	1.19	2.24	1.58	0.67	1.02	1.93
5	2.73	0.67	1.48	2.58	2.42	0.84	1.31	2.42
6	2.11	0.43	1.30	2.40	1.93	0.77	1.14	2.13
7	2.50	−0.37	0.72	1.94	2.11	−0.27	0.73	1.79
8	2.67	0.97	1.67	2.60	2.46	1.22	1.43	2.39
9	2.16	0.21	1.20	2.42	2.05	0.43	1.09	2.24
10	2.91	0.49	1.17	2.35	2.74	0.70	1.01	2.23
11	2.07	0.08	0.95	2.07	1.96	0.38	0.79	1.86
12	2.40	−0.21	0.74	1.94	2.20	−0.03	0.70	1.80
13	2.34	0.52	1.35	2.32	1.93	0.78	1.21	2.09
14	2.03	0.12	1.00	2.11	1.43	0.45	0.86	1.87
15	2.89	0.09	1.02	1.95	2.80	0.21	1.00	1.76
16	1.88	0.03	1.24	2.49	1.89	0.24	1.16	2.25
17	2.27	−0.10	0.72	1.99	1.98	0.16	0.57	1.88
18	2.30	0.13	1.01	2.20	2.02	0.38	0.87	2.07
19	3.08	−0.27	0.77	1.88	3.23	−0.20	0.76	1.75
20	2.37	1.46	2.20	2.89	2.13	1.77	1.99	2.49
21	3.43	0.73	1.52	2.31	3.16	0.83	1.42	2.12
22	1.86	0.15	1.20	2.44	1.69	0.46	1.08	2.19
23	2.02	0.56	1.48	2.75	2.12	0.88	1.26	2.57
24	2.08	0.32	1.41	2.81	2.18	0.51	1.26	2.65
25	2.04	−0.14	0.86	2.06	1.61	0.10	0.77	1.87
26	2.47	0.60	1.20	2.33	3.11	0.98	0.88	2.20
27	1.79	0.33	1.38	2.58	1.52	0.70	1.19	2.31
28	2.33	−0.01	0.90	1.94	2.03	0.21	0.83	1.74

Note. α denotes an item discrimination parameter, b denotes a threshold, and δ denotes an intersection.

In the NRM, the probability of an individual responding in category x ($x = 0$ . . . number of categories minus one) on an item, conditional on the latent variable (θ) is

$$P_x(\theta) = \frac{\exp(a_x \theta + c_x)}{\sum\limits_{x=0}^{NCAT-1} \exp(a_x \theta + c_x)}. \tag{10}$$

To identify the model, some constraint must be set: $\Sigma a_x = \Sigma c_x = 0$. This constraint forces one response option (the one with the highest a) to have a monotonically increasing CRC and one response option (the one with the lowest a) to have a monotonically decreasing CRC. In Equation 10, c_x is an

intercept parameter for category x, and the a_x is the slope of the linear regression of the latent variable on the log-odds of the probability of responding in a particular category. The c_x parameters reflect the *popularity* of a particular response category, where larger values reflect more popular options (Thissen, Steinberg, & Fitzpatrick, 1989).

Simply stated, Equation 10 is called a divide-by-total model because the numerator contains a single conditional probability and the denominator contains a scaling factor, which is the sum of conditional probabilities for each response distinction. In short, the denominator ensures that the sum of the probabilities of each category response conditional on the latent trait equals one. In other divide-by-total models to follow, the denominator will become more complicated but will always serve the exact same purpose.

This description of the NRM does not readily reveal some of its most intriguing properties. However, Thissen et al. (1989) and Thissen, Cai, and Bock (2010) have shown how the NRM can be thought of in terms of the choice between two adjacent response categories. Specifically, if one thinks of an item response as a choice between two options x and $x - 1$ (3 vs. 2), then the NRM for this choice can be written in the form of the 2PLM:

$$P_x \mid x = x \text{ or } x-1 = \frac{1}{1+\exp[-a^*(\theta-\delta)]}, \quad (11)$$

where $a^* = a_x - a_{x-1}$ and $\delta = c_{x-1} - c_x/(a_x - a_{x-1})$.

That is, the difference between the category slope parameters for adjacent categories functions is like a slope parameter in a two-parameter model (Equation 8), indicating how discriminating the choice between two adjacent categories is. Clearly, if a_x is larger than a_{x-1}, then a^* is positive, and the response categories are ordered along the latent variable; higher levels of the latent variable mean one is more likely to select x than $x - 1$.

Thus, inspection of the a^* parameters in the NRM allows an empirical test of the ordering of response categories. Preston, Reise, Cai, and Hays (2011) called the a^* parameters *category boundary discriminations* (CBDs). They argued that inspection of these values is important not only to test for the ordering of categories but also to determine whether the item contains too many response categories (e.g., when an a^* is near zero). It can also be used to evaluate whether the response categories are equally differentiating. For example, they cited examples of multipoint items for which the CBD between the first and second category is very high but the remaining CBDs are very low, suggesting that only the first response distinction is meaningful.

Finally, they argued that a lack of consistency between the CBDs within an item may call into question the application of models that specify only a single item slope parameter (e.g., the generalized partial credit model to be described shortly, or the GRM). For example, Table 36.4 displays the category slopes (a) and the CBDs (a^*) for the example Depression items estimated using MULTILOG (Thissen, 2003). In the present data, it appears that all categories (1 = *never*, 2 = *rarely*, 3 = *sometimes*, 4 = *often*) provide some useful discrimination. However, for some items, such as 3, 11, and 16, there appears to be a trend for the first CBD to be significantly higher than the second or third. If statistical tests (e.g., a Wald test) indicated that the a^* within an item varied significantly, one would have to question whether any model that proposed a single item slope is appropriate.

Finally, it can be shown that the category intercepts in the NRM can be transformed into useful and interpretable information by taking $c^* = (c_{x-1} - c_x)/a_j^*$ to obtain category intersection parameters. These intersection parameters, of which there are the number of categories minus one, indicate the point on the latent variable scale at which two CRCs intersect. These parameters contrast sharply with the location parameters in the GRM. Specifically, locations in the GRM indicate where the probability of responding in and above a category is .50, whereas intersections indicate where the selection of one response category becomes more likely than the previous category. Moreover, category intersections are not necessarily ordered, but locations in the GRM must be. Unordered category intersections do not indicate that the response options are unordered but rather merely that one response category is never the most likely response for any value of the latent trait.

Generalized Partial Credit Model

It may seem odd to describe Muraki's (1992) generalization of the partial credit model (GPCM) before describing the partial credit model (PCM; Masters, 1982).Our decision to include this model here is based on the fact that the NRM highlighted in the previous section is the most general direct polytomous IRT model. In turn, our goal is to emphasize that Muraki's model is simply a restricted version of the NRM, where item responses are assumed ordered, and CBD parameters (a^*) are set equal within an item. Thus, although the NRM allows within-item response category distinctions to vary in slope, the GPCM assumes that CBDs are equally

TABLE 36.4

Nominal Response Model (NRM) and Generalized Partial Credit Model (GPCM) Slope/Discrimination Parameter Estimates for Depression Items

Item	NRM slope (*a*) and CBD (*a**) estimates							GPCM slopes
	a_1	a_2	a_3	a_4	a^*_1	a^*_2	a^*_3	
1	−4.54	−1.62	1.53	4.64	2.92	3.15	3.11	2.99
2	−3.54	−0.77	0.69	3.62	2.77	1.46	2.93	2.49
3	−3.82	−0.63	1.26	3.19	3.19	1.89	1.93	3.08
4	−2.48	−0.58	0.93	2.13	1.90	1.51	1.20	1.58
5	−3.86	−0.86	1.24	3.49	3.00	2.10	2.25	2.42
6	−2.73	−0.91	0.92	2.72	1.82	1.83	1.80	1.93
7	−3.65	−1.66	1.14	4.16	1.99	2.80	3.02	2.11
8	−3.43	−0.74	0.95	3.21	2.69	1.69	2.26	2.46
9	−2.94	−0.70	0.76	2.88	2.24	1.46	2.12	2.05
10	−4.15	−1.24	1.15	4.24	2.91	2.39	3.09	2.74
11	−2.75	−0.50	0.83	2.42	2.25	1.33	1.59	1.96
12	−3.17	−1.22	0.94	3.45	1.95	2.16	2.51	2.20
13	−3.18	−0.76	0.93	3.00	2.42	1.69	2.07	1.93
14	−2.55	−0.68	0.85	2.37	1.87	1.53	1.52	1.43
15	−4.24	−1.33	1.65	3.92	2.91	2.98	2.27	2.80
16	−2.66	−0.47	0.82	2.31	2.19	1.29	1.49	1.89
17	−2.97	−0.80	0.74	3.03	2.17	1.54	2.29	1.98
18	−3.13	−0.65	0.94	2.85	2.48	1.59	1.91	2.02
19	−4.89	−1.79	1.69	4.99	3.10	3.48	3.30	3.23
20	−2.83	−0.28	0.41	2.70	2.55	0.69	2.29	2.13
21	−5.19	−1.09	1.68	4.59	4.10	2.77	2.91	3.16
22	−2.37	−0.76	0.79	2.34	1.61	1.55	1.55	1.69
23	−2.60	−0.61	0.93	2.28	1.99	1.54	1.35	2.12
24	−2.92	−0.62	0.72	2.82	2.30	1.34	2.10	2.18
25	−2.74	−0.74	0.80	2.67	2.00	1.54	1.87	1.61
26	−3.32	−0.75	1.05	3.02	2.57	1.80	1.97	3.11
27	−2.21	−0.41	0.78	1.84	1.80	1.19	1.06	1.52
28	−3.19	−0.79	1.14	2.84	2.40	1.93	1.70	2.03

Note. a denotes category slopes and *a** denotes category boundary discriminations. CBD = category boundary discrimination.

differentiating within an item but that items can vary in their overall discrimination. The GPCM can be written as

$$P_x(\theta) = \frac{EXP\sum_{j=0}^{x}\alpha(\theta-\delta_j)}{\sum_{x=0}^{NCAT-1}\left[EXP\sum_{j=0}^{x}\alpha(\theta-\delta_j)\right]}, \quad (12)$$

where $\sum_{j=0}^{0}\alpha(\theta-\delta_j) \equiv 0$.

For the GPCM (see Table 36.3), one unique slope parameter (α) and one minus the number of categories intersection parameters (δ) are estimated

for each item. The category intersection parameters (δ) in this model are interpreted in the same way as the c^* parameters in the NRM—as the intersection point of two adjacent CRCs. They are the points on the latent variable scale at which one category response becomes relatively more likely than the preceding response. The slope (α_i) parameters have the usual interpretation as a kind of *discrimination* parameter, that is, they "indicate the degree to which categorical responses vary among items as θ level changes" (Muraki, 1992, p. 162).

The GPCM and the GRM are very similar models but are derived from two different families (and thus are not *nested* models or comparable using a likelihood ratio test). Models like the GPCM are built by considering the choice between two adjacent response categories *x* and *x – 1*—ignoring all other categories—and then deriving how the latent variable interacts with item slope and intersection parameters to determine the response choice. This is certainly different than the GRM for which all response options are considered in deriving each within-item TRC. For comparison sake, the estimated parameters from the GPCM are shown in Table 36.3 alongside the GRM. Although the values look different, the two bottom graphs in Figure 36.2 show examples in which the CRCs estimated under the GRM (dark lines) and GPCM (lighter lines) are almost visually indistinguishable.

A Polytomous Rasch Model

The PCM (Masters, 1982) is the prototypical Rasch model suitable for analyzing ordered polytomous items. Recall that the GRM is built around dichotomizing items at the boundaries between the response categories (e.g., 1, 2 vs. 3, 4) and then fitting 2PLMs to each of the number of categories minus one of the *boundaries* between categories. The PCM is also built around dichotomizing items at the boundaries between categories, but this process differs from the GRM in important ways. Specifically, the PCM is based on fitting Rasch's 1PLM to the number of categories minus one ordered dichotomies but considering only two response categories at a time. Thus, with a four-category item, the PCM fits a Rasch model considering the dichotomy 0 versus 1; 1 versus 2; and 2 versus 3, as opposed to a GRM where the dichotomies are 0 versus 1, 2, 3; 0, 1 versus 2, 3; and 0, 1, 2, versus 3.

Interestingly, it is easy to show that the PCM is simply Equation 12 without the slope parameter. Thus, in the PCM, the probability of response is determined solely by the difference between an individual's level on the latent variable and the category intersections. An interesting feature of the PCM is that the category intersections are not necessarily ordered. Recall that in the GRM, locations (*b*) must be ordered. When the intersection parameters are not ordered, this phenomena is known as a "reversal" (Dodd & Koch, 1987). As a rule, if the intersection

parameters are ordered within an item, then there is at least one location on the latent variable where every response option is most likely (Andrich, 1988).

Thus, the divide-by-total or direct polytomous IRT models are a nested family going from least restricted NRM, to allowing items to vary in slope (GPCM), to allowing items to vary only in category intersection parameters (PCM). Of course, only the PCM has features associated with Rasch models (specific objectivity). We note that the model hierarchy considered here did not include the well-known rating scale version of the PCM (Andrich, 1978). We believe this model to be more of theoretical interest and thus was not detailed here.

PRACTICAL APPLICATIONS AND CONSIDERATIONS

The first section was dedicated to introducing key IRT models, their properties, and their interpretation. Understanding the mechanics of these models is crucial because all applications of IRT (e.g., computerized adaptive testing, analysis of item and scale information functions, linking distinct measures onto a common scale, analysis of differential item functioning) rest squarely on the validity of these representations. By validity of the model, we mean that term in the broadest sense to include the viability of IRT model assumptions, the accuracy of item parameter estimates, and the proper representation of the construct (i.e., is there really a latent variable that accounts for the relations among the items?). With this in mind, the following section is geared toward applied research. Specifically, we consider (a) the applicability of IRT models across various types of constructs and domains, (b) sample size and model selection issues, and (c) some lessons learned thus far from the research literature on the application of IRT to noncognitive measures.

The Applicability of IRT Models

As noted by many authors, IRT models developed in the context of large-scale cognitive testing; applications outside this domain emerged slowly and are only now starting to fully blossom. In considering the application of IRT models across a broad range of constructs, we consider the following three issues: (a) latent versus emergent variables, (b) cognitive versus noncognitive applications, and (c) the measurement of narrow versus broadband constructs. First, we point out that IRT models can be viewed as latent factor models (not components) that are applied to item-level data. As such, IRT models are clearly latent variable models for which the items are effect indicators in the Bollen and Lennox (1991) sense. In short, it makes little sense to apply IRT models unless one has reason to believe that a single common latent variable is causing variation in item responses and thus causing items to be intercorrelated.

Second, although it is challenging to cite any specific author, we have observed that some researchers are hesitant to embrace the application of IRT models to measures of noncognitive constructs (i.e., achievement, ability, competence). In this regard, we agree with the following: (a) noncognitive constructs, such as personality traits, psychopathology, attitudes, values, health outcomes, and so on, are conceptually different than such constructs as nursing competency, eighth-grade spelling knowledge, or verbal ability; and in turn (b) the psychometric properties of noncognitive measures are often very different than what is typically seen in the measurement of cognitive constructs (see concluding section for examples); and, finally, (c) the measurement context (i.e., the goals of measurement) between noncognitive and cognitive assessment is often dramatically different (see Reise, 2009, for further commentary).

Yet, despite these differences, we see little if any reason to question the application of IRT models to measures of well-examined personality, psychopathology, or health outcomes constructs. Latent variables models are justified when one can propose that the empirical relations among a set of content-diverse items is explained by individual differences on a common psychological process (a latent trait). In this regard, we see no empirical evidence that data derived from noncognitive measures are more multidimensional than cognitive measures or that a dominance response process (higher trait levels lead to higher item scores) does not apply. In fact, the history of factor analysis, both exploratory and confirmatory, leads us to believe that many noncognitive

measures should be entirely consistent with the assumptions of IRT (i.e., unidimensionality, monotonicity of response).

Finally, we note that researchers in both cognitive and noncognitive domains have long recognized the hierarchical nature of psychological constructs. Accordingly, it has long been recognized that constructs and their associated measures vary in conceptual bandwidth, ranging from narrow (physical attractiveness self-esteem, tooth brushing self-efficacy, test anxiety) to broad (general self-esteem, neuroticism). Commonly applied IRT models are unidimensional—they assume the existence of a single common variable affecting item responses. As pointed out by multiple authors over the years (see Humphreys, 1970; Gustafsson & Aberg-Bengtsson, 2010), attempting to create pure "unidimensional" scales can create quite a quandary and actually lead to poor measurement.

The way to achieve unidimensionality, and thus be consistent with IRT modeling, is to focus on a narrow construct and write items that are essentially replicates (this can increase coefficient alpha as well). Yet, it is questionable whether we really need the power of IRT to measure such conceptually narrow constructs in cases in which the correlation between the items can be explained merely by the semantic similarity of the items, rather than by the need to postulate an underlying psychological trait. On the other hand, the measurement of broadband constructs demands the inclusion of content diverse indicators. In turn, this almost guarantees violations of the IRT unidimensionality assumption. Yet, it appears to us that for these types of substantively complex constructs, this is exactly where the power of IRT and other latent variable methods are most needed and interestingly applied.

We raise this issue because it is important for future directions of IRT modeling. Specifically, we see the future as rejecting the unidimensional model as an appropriate foundation for IRT modeling and for defining good measurement in general. Nevertheless, we do not necessarily see the future as moving toward multidimensional *correlated traits* IRT models either (see Reckase, 2010) but rather as recognizing a broader definition of what the common latent variable is in IRT modeling.

For example, the bifactor model described by Gibbons and Hedeker (1992) has seen increased use as a tool for exploring the applicability of IRT models (e.g., Reise, Moore, & Haviland, 2010; Reise, Morizot, & Hays, 2007). This model allows each item to reflect a single common latent variable and one additional latent variable caused by clusters of items that share item content (i.e., sometimes referred to as content parcels). Thus, when a measure consists of multiple content parcels necessary to validly measure complex constructs, the bifactor model can easily accommodate such a structure. In other words, a bifactor framework affords the ability to use multidimensional item response data to achieve unidimensional measurement. Thus, we view the bifactor model not only as a tool for evaluating the distorting effects of forcing multidimensional data into a unidimensional model (Reise et al., 2007) but also for expanding the range of constructs that can be accommodated by IRT models (see also Chapter 35 of this volume).

Sample Size and Model Choice

A common question in seminars and workshops is "how many subjects do I need to estimate IRT model parameters?" This is a fundamental question, but unfortunately there is no simple rule-of-thumb answer. The needed sample size for reasonably accurate item parameter estimates depends on the interplay among a variety of intertwined factors, including (a) the model selected (constrained models are easier to estimate); (b) how large the item slope parameters are expected to be (higher is better); (c) how well the data fit the model (if the data do not fit the model, then parameter accuracy is meaningless); (d) the underlying latent trait distribution (normal vs. skewed); (e) sample heterogeneity (more is better); and, importantly, (f) what the ultimate research goal is (high-stakes testing vs. research-only scale).

There may be applications where accuracy of item parameter estimation is not critically important (e.g., in exploring basic item functioning). Moreover, given reasonable scale length (e.g., 20 items), minor biases in item parameter estimates or even estimating the wrong model may not greatly affect model outcomes, such as the scale response curve or

the relative order of trait level estimates (e.g., Wainer & Thissen, 1987). On the other hand, in some contexts, such as the evaluation of different CRCs or IRCs across different groups of individuals (e.g., men versus woman), high-stakes testing in health care settings, or large-scale computerized adaptive testing, item parameter accuracy is paramount.

To clarify the *number of subjects* issue, some researchers have conducted Monte Carlo simulation studies. For example, Reise and Yu (1990) showed that the GRM can be estimated with MULTILOG (Thissen, 2003) with as few as 250 examinees, but they recommend around 500 (the number of items is not critical with marginal maximum likelihood estimation). Yet simulation studies are useful only if the real data match the simulated data, and they should not be relied on to judge the viability of a particular application. Rather than suggesting some citable magic N or subjects-to-parameters ratio, we recommend the following.

First, thoroughly explore the data using nonparametric methods (Sijtsma & Molenaar, 2002). If the data considered at the nonparametric level do not reasonably conform to a parametric model, a large sample size is pointless—there is no sense precisely estimating parameters that do not exist. Second, evaluate model assumptions (dimensionality, monotonicity) carefully, even if sample size is small. Again, item parameter estimation accuracy is moot if the data are not appropriate for the model in the first place. Third, for models that include item slopes, consider their magnitude as being the key influence on parameter estimation. Research (MacCallum, Widaman, Zhang, & Hong, 1999) has shown that the size of a factor loading is a key factor in how many subjects are needed to conduct a factor analysis (i.e., high loadings can be estimated with fewer subjects). The IRT slope parameter is analogous to a factor loading, and the same principle should apply.

Finally, it is important to recognize the location parameters in the GRM are, generally speaking, easier to estimate than intersection parameters in divide-by-total models. Assuming that the items have a reasonable degree of slope, and that there are sufficient responses in each category, location parameters are relatively easy to estimate because all the data are used. An intersection parameter, on the other hand, is relatively harder to estimate than a location because the intersection considers only responses in x and $x - 1$. Thus, it is particularly important to have sufficient responses in every category for models like the NRM, GPCM, and PCM.

Finally, having decided to pursue IRT modeling, a critical question is which model should be estimated. Although the choice of model is often dictated by what software an individual has access to, for the sake of argument, we assume that any model described herein can be estimated. With this in mind, we note that from a statistical perspective, the 4, 3, 2, and 1 parameter logistic models for dichotomous item responses are nested, and thus a likelihood ratio test may be useful in model comparisons. Moreover, the same likelihood-ratio test also applies to divide-by-total models where the NRM, GPCM, and PCM also form a nested series. Unfortunately, comparison of the GRM with the GPCM cannot be made on the basis of a likelihood-ratio test, but rather it must be made on the basis of other statistical criteria (e.g., the Akaike information criterion) as well as substantive considerations.

Conversely, researchers seldom are concerned with overall model fit but rather are concerned with a comparison between the observed and estimated IRC or CRCs on an item-by-item basis. In considering the various modeling options in IRT, we feel that researchers spend too much effort worrying about relative model fit and item parameter accuracy rather than model outcomes. In any particular data set, it may be the case that a model can be shown to provide a better relative fit than another, but in terms of outcomes, model choice is inconsequential. Ostini and Nering (2006) pointed out that although the polytomous IRT models may differ in a variety of ways, few researchers have attempted to compare the models in terms of outcomes as opposed to fit. It is arguable that in terms of ultimate outcomes, such as scale-response curves or individuals trait-level estimates, the impact of model choice (or even poor parameter estimation) is minimal. Similar arguments were made by Embretson and Reise (2000), who fitted a personality scale to a number of different polytomous models and found that trait-level estimates were above .90 regardless of model. This demonstration should not be taken to mean that the

model never makes a difference. In fact, recent work has argued that model accuracy is important in scaling individuals correctly in certain trait ranges (Waller & Reise, 2010).

Lessons Learned From the Application of IRT to Noncognitive Measures

IRT modeling and its by-products (e.g., computerized adaptive testing) can be considered standard practice in education measurement, large-scale abilities testing, and licensure testing. Although this trend is by no means true in noncognitive assessment, even in those domains, IRT modeling has moved well beyond the stage of didactic articles and proof-of-concept demonstrations. In fact, there is now quite a substantial body of research that has considered IRT modeling outside the cognitive domain (see Cella et al., 2007, 2010; Reise & Waller, 2009). In this section, we consider some observations we have made regarding this research. In turn these observations may suggest future research issues and directions.

We have observed that several interesting phenomena occur relatively frequently when polytomous IRT models are applied to personality, health outcomes, and psychopathology measures, namely the following: (a) extreme item locations, (b) extremely high item slopes, (c) bunched item locations, and (d) an unusually large range of item slopes. In this section, we discuss each of these phenomena in turn and propose reasons why they occur. For simplicity and continuity, we discuss these issues in the context of the slope and location parameters resulting from the application of the GRM. These same issues arise in application of any model.

We begin with the phenomena of extremely high item slope parameters. To be conservative, we define high slopes as any value larger than 3 (logistic metric), but note that even a slope of two is relatively large compared with what is typically found in dichotomous IRT models. It is easy to demonstrate that as an item slope parameter moves beyond 3, the response categories are providing a high degree of discrimination among individuals. In other words, with a slope of three in the GRM, if a researcher knew an individual's trait level, he or she could predict which the individual's likely response category with high accuracy. Another way of thinking about this issue is as follows. As item slopes increase beyond three, the TRCs begin to look more like Guttman step functions than monotonically increasing ogives. Do such high slopes mean good measurement, or is there something wrong?

We argue that the answer to this question depends on understanding the causes of the high slope parameters. To begin, it is well known that one possible source of a high item slope is a problem known as *local dependency*. Local dependency means that two (or more) items share common variance above and beyond that because of the latent trait being measured. Local dependence can be caused by item content redundancy (i.e., asking essentially the same question twice) and results in inflated item slope parameters (Steinberg & Thissen, 1996). To the extent that slopes are inflated by local dependencies, the slope parameter estimates provide a misleading gauge of measurement precision. However, local dependence is not an explanation for high slopes when all or most of the items on a scale display exceptionally high slopes. In this situation, we need to turn to other explanations.

A second possible explanation for high slopes is that the measured construct has a narrow conceptual bandwidth (e.g., "knee joint pain"). Sparing the reader the technical details, in IRT, the magnitude of an item's average correlation with other items determines the item's slope (or factor loading in factor analysis). In measures of narrowband constructs, homogeneous item content is expected. In addition, because of a lack of diverse trait manifestations, in measures of narrowband constructs the conceptual distance between the item and the construct is often very small (e.g., "I experience pain when bending my knee"). These factors result in narrow measures containing items with very high intercorrelations, which in turn result in high IRT slope parameters. This is especially true if a 5-, 7-, or 9-point rating scale is used for each item because the more response options, the more room is left for individual differences in response style to operate, further inflating correlations.

When high item slopes are caused by the narrowband nature of the measured construct, their values are perfectly valid indicators of measurement precision. However, there is one big caveat. Namely, that measurement precision should not be viewed as resulting from quality measurement, but rather as resulting from the narrow construct that is being measured. It is unsurprising to observe high slopes on narrowband measures because individual differences are much easier to discriminate in that context. Consider this example: The items *3 + 4 = ?, 2 + 6 = ?,* and *1 + 3 = ?* would form a highly discriminating set of indicators of the construct of "adding two single digits." In short, the fewer and more homogeneous the trait (or ability) manifestations, the easier it is to discriminate between those that are high or low on the trait with high precision.

A narrow construct and the resulting item content homogeneity can explain some cases of extremely high slopes, but it is irrelevant when high slopes are observed on measures of complex and multifaceted broadband constructs that contain diverse item content. In this situation, we propose two additional sources as possible explanations, namely, (a) a mixture of extreme groups (e.g., clinical and nonclinical) included in the calibration sample, and (b) a skewed or quasi-trait. These latter two concepts are not synonyms, but discussion of them is joined because in practice we argue that it is very difficult to differentiate between a highly skewed latent distribution and a quasi-dimensional trait.

In the measurement of psychopathology or health outcomes, psychometricians have long warned against the use of combined clinical and nonclinical samples in judging the psychometric properties of instruments. The obvious danger is that if a nonclinical group with a floor effect is combined with a clinical group with a ceiling effect, an instrument can look deceptively good in terms of item intercorrelations, item-test correlations, factor loadings, and coefficient alpha. In short, in mixed clinical and nonclinical samples, strong psychometrics reflect merely the fact that the item differentiates between extreme groups rather than indicating a good measure of a dimensional construct across the entire range of the construct. Because IRT slope parameters are complex transformations of item intercorrelations, a mixed clinical and nonclinical sample can easily result in very high slope parameter estimates.

Finally, we propose that a second possible cause of unusually high slopes on broadband measures is a highly skewed or a quasi-trait. Although these concepts are difficult to differentiate in practice, we consider a skewed trait to be a fully continuous trait, conceptually definable at both ends, but with a strong floor or ceiling effect (e.g., an optimism–pessimism scale applied in a culture in which almost everyone is an optimist). A quasi-trait is a dimensional construct that is defined only on one end of the scale (i.e., meaningful individual differences exist only on one end of the scale). Many constructs in psychology, although assumed dimensional (e.g., aggression, self-esteem, spirituality), are possibly only quasi-traits.

For example, in our work on psychopathology (Reise & Waller, 2003; Waller & Reise, 2010), we noted that the low end of our measures, say depression, is not happiness or well-being but rather is lack of depression (i.e., no symptoms). In working with either highly skewed traits or quasi-traits, caution must be used in interpreting high slope parameters. For the same reasons as articulated for mixed samples, item slopes may be artificially inflated because of either the non-normality or quasi-trait status of the construct. In such cases, a high slope may indicate that the item differentiates between not-traited (not depressed) and traited (depressed) individuals, but it may not necessarily provide a precise differentiation among people along a meaningful continuous latent dimension.

The discussion of skewed traits or quasi-traits leads directly to the next topic, namely, the issue of *bunched* item location parameters. By bunched item location parameters, we mean location parameters (e.g., in the GRM) that are clumped closely together along the latent variable (usually at the trait extremes) rather than spread out over the trait continuum. When location parameters are bunched together, this implies that the instrument affords measurement precision in only a narrow trait range. This is an interesting occurrence given that the only legitimate purpose of having a multipoint response format is to allow people to *validly* make discriminations across the continuum. If a researcher uses a multipoint response scale in a diverse sample, and location parameters still clump together, this is evidence that either respondents cannot differentiate among response options, or more likely, that what is

being measured is a highly skewed trait or quasi-trait that is not a fully dimensional construct.

It appears that many researchers are operating under the assumption that all constructs are fully continuous, defined at both ends of the construct, and that items can be found that measure (have location parameters) across an entire trait range. For example, in a different context, Andrich (1995) conveyed the following sentiments:

> Although measuring instruments have operating ranges, a measurement is not taken to be a function of the operating range of any instrument—instead, if a measurement is contaminated by the operating range of the instrument (e.g., floor or ceiling effects), another instrument with a range more compatible with the location of the entity or object is sought. (p. 101)

Such a statement assumes that, in theory, a researcher could find an alternative instrument that would not produce a floor or ceiling effect. For another example, Fraley, Waller and Brennan (2000), on observing that in attachment measures item locations are highly bunched together on one end of the trait, suggested that new items be written to better spread out the measurement precision over the complete range of the latent variable. But what if such a search for new items or measures is fruitless?

With a highly skewed construct or a quasi-trait, it may not be possible to find items with location parameters spread out across the range. Consider a research study by Gray-Little, Williams, and Hancock (1997), who applied the GRM to a 5-point version of the Rosenberg Self-Esteem Scale (Rosenberg, 1989). This study is fascinating because although the items contain five response options, the four location parameters per item are closely bunched at the low end of the latent trait (i.e., low self-esteem). For example, even the third location ($x = 1, 2, 3$, vs. 4, 5) was in the negative range for 8 out of the 10 items. To make this more concrete, the third location parameter for Item 1 ("On the whole, I am satisfied with myself") was $b = -1.48$, implying that even individuals who are a standard deviation and a half below the mean on the trait are most likely to respond in the highest fourth or fifth category. In other words, even people far below the mean on self-esteem rate themselves highly self-satisfied. Although reasonable minds can disagree, one explanation for this effect is that it is not due to poor items or poor choice of response options. Rather, it is due to the nature of the self-esteem construct; items only differentiate people with low self-esteem because that is the only end of the construct that is meaningful.

Related to the topic of bunched item location parameters is the topic of extreme item locations. By extreme we mean that the location parameters that do not fall within a reasonable range of values, say –2 to 2 (assuming that the latent variable has a mean of zero and standard deviation of one). As mentioned, one reason why an extreme location may occur is if an item has a relatively low slope parameter (recall that the location is a function of the intercept divided by the slope). A second obvious reason is that either the lowest or highest response category is too extreme given the content of the item. A third, more interesting reason is that the latent variable is either highly skewed or is a quasi-trait.

We again use the results of the Gray-Little et al. (1997) study to illustrate the phenomena. In their calibration of the Rosenberg self-esteem scale, the category locations not only were bunched in the low end of the latent variable but also were very extreme. For example, for all 10 items the first category location (x = 1 vs. 2, 3, 4, 5) was an absurdly low value. For example, for Item 1 ("On the whole, I am satisfied with myself"), the estimated location was $b = -3.45$, suggesting that even individuals who are nearly three and a half standard deviations below the mean will be likely to respond in at least category 2. Moreover, for many items, even the fourth location (x = 1, 2, 3, 4 vs. 5) is barely above the trait mean. For example, for Item 3 ("I feel that I have a number of good qualities") the fourth location is only $b = 0.22$. Thus, even people barely above the mean on self-esteem are most likely to respond in the highest category on this item. The only item that displayed a more reasonable fourth location was Item 9 ("All in all I am inclined to feel that I am a failure"—reversed) that had a fourth threshold

of 2.13. This item has very low slope ($a = 1.16$), however, relative to the high slope items that have slopes ranging from 2.0 to 2.5. It is thus plausible that this item is not measuring the same common trait as the high slope items.

Our final practical issue in applying IRT models to noncognitive data is the observation that on some measures we have noticed a very wide spread of item slopes. For example, Van Der Ark (2001) reported slopes of 0.8, 3.6, 0.4, 6.4, and 0.2 for a measure of coping strategy to industrial odor annoyance. We call this a *steep descent pattern*, where one or two items have a relatively high slope, and then the value of the slope parameter decreases rapidly for the remainder of the items. Although it is reasonable that different trait indicators can be related to the latent trait to different degrees, a wide variance in slopes may also be a sign of problems. For example, in Hall, Reise, and Haviland (2007), a nine-item spiritual instability measure had GRM slopes ranging from 2.63 ("When I sin, I am afraid of what God will do to me") to 0.74 ("When I sin, I tend to withdraw from God"). The remaining items had slopes of 1.9, 1.9, 1.5, 1.5, 1.4, 1.0, and 0.9, respectively.

Such a variable pattern of slopes is troubling in a number of respects. First, one could argue that the construct is so narrow that one item essentially defines the latent variable and the other items are only tangentially related. If that were true, one could argue that the remaining items are unnecessary. More technically, a second potential problem is that if IRT methods were used to estimate standing on the construct, then in this example the best item has 3.7 times the influence compared with the worst item because the sufficient statistic for the latent trait estimate is the raw item response times the item slope. Moreover, because an item contributes to measurement precision by the square of the slope parameter, such results argue that the best item contributes 12.7 times more error reduction than the worst item; that is, it takes almost 13 items like the worst item to equal one item like the best.

This wide-ranging slope phenomenon is not unique to spirituality constructs and their associated measures. In fact, this phenomena is rather easy to observe in the IRT literature and non-IRT literature (in the form of variable item–test correlations or factor loadings). Ignoring multidimensionality as a possible cause, we propose that this phenomena is due to a combination of narrowband constructs (where one or two good items essentially define the construct), combined with limited item pools. Many constructs in personality, health, and psychopathology have an extremely limited indicator pool (e.g., how many ways are there to react to industrial odor?). Even a relatively complex and multifaceted construct such as depression has a finite set of indicators (e.g., sad moods, social isolation, suicide cognitions, feelings of hopelessness, and somatic disturbances). Importantly, when only a few items have high slopes and the remainder has much lower slopes, a researcher must be cautious in interpreting the latent variable. It could well be that the latent variable does not reflect variance on a common latent variable shared by all the items, but rather it merely reflects individual differences on the item with the highest slope.

In sum, this section is not meant to disparage or discourage IRT applications to typical performance constructs. Our goal is merely to draw attention to some interesting challenges that researchers may face in applying polytomous models to noncognitive constructs. As we stated, IRT emerged in the context of large-scale cognitive ability testing. In that context, it is relatively easy to conceive of normally distributed continuous traits and unlimited item pools. For example, it is easy to envision an endless number of spelling, algebra, analogy, constitutional law, or nursing skills questions. In turn, it is relatively easy to envision these items as varying in their location across the trait range. Moreover, large-scale cognitive ability researchers are typically working with broadband constructs (verbal ability, algebra, knowledge of the law, nursing expertise) for which domains of item content (learning or skill domains) are well articulated.

In contrast, as the IRT technology is transported from the cognitive abilities realm into the broader world of performance assessment, special issues and problems are bound to emerge (Reise, 2009). This is especially true given that noncognitive researchers have to work with constructs of varying conceptual breath, for which a set of limited indicators exist, and for which the underlying distribution cannot

possibly be standard normal. To the degree that IRT applications in noncognitive settings raise issues that have not caught the attention of previous researchers (e.g., the Gray-Little et al., 1997, study), or call into question the quality of legacy measures developed under traditional coefficient alpha–centric scale construction practices, this is a positive development for the field of psychometrics. Indeed, part of the excitement of current IRT research lies in identifying new problems and working toward their solutions.

References

Andrich, D. (1978). A rating formulation for ordered response categories. *Psychometrika, 43*, 561–573. doi:10.1007/BF02293814

Andrich, D. (1988). A general form of Rasch's extended logistic model for partial credit scoring. *Applied Measurement in Education, 1*, 363–378. doi:10.1207/s15324818ame0104_7

Andrich, D. (1995). Distinctive and incompatible properties of two common classes of IRT models for graded responses. *Applied Psychological Measurement, 19*, 101–119. doi:10.1177/014662169501900111

Baker, F. B., & Kim, S.-H. (2004). *Item response theory: Parameter estimation techniques* (2nd ed.). New York, NY: Marcel Dekker.

Ben-Porath, Y. S., Tellegen, A. T., & Kaemmer, B. (2005). *MMPI–A: Minnesota Multiphasic Personality Inventory—Adolescent™: Booklet of abbreviated items.* Minneapolis: University of Minnesota Press.

Bock, R. D. (1972). Estimating item parameters and latent ability when responses are scored in two or more latent categories. *Psychometrika, 37*, 29–51. doi:10.1007/BF02291411

Bollen, K., & Lennox, R. (1991). Conventional wisdom on measurement: A structural equation perspective. *Psychological Bulletin, 110*, 305–314. doi:10.1037/0033-2909.110.2.305

Bond, T. G., & Fox, C. M. (2007). *Applying the Rasch model: Fundamental measurement in the human sciences* (2nd ed.). Mahwah, NJ: Erlbaum.

Borsboom, D. (2005). *Measuring the mind: Conceptual issues in contemporary psychometrics.* Cambridge, England: Cambridge University Press. doi:10.1017/CBO9780511490026

Cella, D., Riley, W., Stone, A., Rothrock, N., Reeve, B., Yount, S., . . . Hays, R. D. (2010). Initial item banks and first wave testing of the Patient-Reported Outcomes Measurement Information System (PROMIS) network: 2005–2008. *Journal of Clinical Epidemiology, 63*, 1179–1194.

Cella, D., Yount, S., Rothrock, N., Gershon, R., Cook, K., Reeve, B., & Rose, M. (2007). The Patient-Reported Outcomes Measurement Information System (PROMIS): Progress of an NIH Roadmap Cooperative Group during its first two years. *Medical Care, 45*(5, Suppl. 1), S3–S11. doi:10.1097/01.mlr.0000258615.42478.55

de Ayala, R. J. (2009). *The theory and practice of item response theory*. New York, NY: Guilford Press.

De Boeck, P., & Wilson, M. (Eds.). (2004). *Explanatory item response models: A generalized linear and nonlinear approach*. New York, NY: Springer.

Dodd, B. G., & Koch, W. R. (1987). Effects of variations in item step values on item and test information in the partial credit model. *Applied Psychological Measurement, 11*, 371–384. doi:10.1177/014662168701100403

Embretson, S. E. (1996). The new rules of measurement. *Psychological Assessment, 8*, 341–349. doi:10.1037/1040-3590.8.4.341

Embretson, S. E., & Reise, S. P. (2000). *Psychometric methods: Item response theory for psychologists*. Mahwah, NJ: Erlbaum.

Fox, J-P., & Glas, C. A. W. (2001). Bayesian estimation of a multilevel IRT model using Gibbs sampling. *Psychometrika, 66*, 271–288. doi:10.1007/BF02294839

Fraley, R. C., Waller, N. G., & Brennan, K. A. (2000). An item response theory analysis of self- report measures of adult attachment. *Journal of Personality and Social Psychology, 78*, 350–365. doi:10.1037/0022-3514.78.2.350

Gibbons, R. D., & Hedeker, D. (1992). Full-information item bi-factor analysis. *Psychometrika, 57*, 423–436. doi:10.1007/BF02295430

Gray-Little, B., Williams, V. S. L., & Hancock, T. D. (1997). An item response theory analysis of the Rosenberg Self-Esteem Scale. *Personality and Social Psychology Bulletin, 23*, 443–451. doi:10.1177/0146167297235001

Gustafsson, J. E., & Aberg-Bengtsson, L. (2010). Unidimensionality and the interpretability of psychological instruments. In S. E. Embretson (Ed.), *Measuring psychological constructs* (pp. 97–121). Washington, DC: American Psychological Association. doi:10.1037/12074-005

Hall, T. W., Reise, S. P., & Haviland, M. G. (2007). An item response theory analysis of the spirituality assessment inventory. *International Journal for the Psychology of Religion, 17*, 157–178.

Hambleton, R. K., & Swaminathan, H. (1985). *Item response theory*. Boston, MA: Kluwer-Nijhoff.

Hambleton, R. K., Swaminathan, H., & Rogers, H. J. (1991). *Fundamentals of item response theory*. Newbury Park, CA: Sage.

Humphreys, L. G. (1970). A skeptical look at the factor pure test. In C. E. Lunneborg (Ed.) *Current problems and techniques in multivariate psychology: Proceedings of a conference honoring Professor Paul Horst* (pp. 23–32). Seattle: University of Washington.

Lord, F. M., & Novick, M. R. (1968). *Statistical theories of mental test scores*. Reading, PA: Addison-Wesley.

MacCallum, R. C., Widaman, K. F., Zhang, S., & Hong, S. (1999). Sample size in factor analysis. *Psychological Methods, 4*, 84–99. doi:10.1037/1082-989X.4.1.84

Masters, G. N. (1982). A Rasch model for partial credit scoring. *Psychometrika, 47*, 149–174. doi:10.1007/BF02296272

McLeod, L. D., Swygert, K. A., & Thissen, D. (2001). Factor analysis for items scored in two categories. In D. Thissen & H. Wainer (Eds.), *Test scoring* (pp. 189–216). Mahwah, NJ: Erlbaum.

Muraki, E. (1992). A generalized partial credit model: Application of an EM algorithm. *Applied Psychological Measurement, 16*, 159–176. doi:10.1177/014662169201600206

Nering, M. L., & Ostini, R. (Eds.). (2010). *Handbook of polytomous item response theory models*. New York, NY: Taylor & Francis.

Ostini, R., & Nering, M. L. (2006). *Polytomous item response theory models*. Thousand Oaks, CA: Sage.

Pilkonis, P. A., Choi, S. W., Reise, S. P., Stover, A. M., Riley, W. T., & Cella, D. (2011). Item banks for measuring emotional distress from the Patient-Reported Outcomes Measurement Information System (PROMIS): Depression, anxiety, and anger. *Assessment, 18*, 263–283.

Preston, K. S. J., Reise, S. P., Cai, L., & Hays, R. D. (2011). Using the nominal response model to evaluate response category discrimination in the PROMIS emotional distress item pools. *Educational and Psychological Measurement, 71*, 523–550.

Reckase, M. D. (2010). *Multidimensional item response theory*. New York, NY: Springer.

Reise, S. P. (2009). The emergence of item response theory (IRT) models and the Patient-Reported Outcomes Measurement Information System (PROMIS). *Austrian Journal of Statistics, 38*, 211–220.

Reise, S. P., Ainsworth, A. T., & Haviland, M. G. (2005). Item response theory: Fundamentals, applications, and promise in psychological research. *Current Directions in Psychological Science, 14*, 95–101. doi:10.1111/j.0963-7214.2005.00342.x

Reise, S. P., & Henson, J. M. (2003). A discussion of modern versus traditional psychometrics as applied to personality assessment scales. *Journal of Personality Assessment, 81*, 93–103. doi:10.1207/S15327752JPA8102_01

Reise, S. P., Moore, T. M., & Haviland, M. G. (2010). Bifactor models and rotations: Exploring the extent to which multidimensional data yield univocal scale scores. *Journal of Personality Assessment, 92*, 544–559.

Reise, S. P., Morizot, J., & Hays, R. D. (2007). The role of the bifactor model in resolving dimensionality issues in health outcomes measures. *Quality of Life Research, 16*, 19–31.

Reise, S. P., & Waller, N. G. (2003). How many IRT parameters does it take to model psychopathology items. *Psychological Methods, 8*, 164–184. doi:10.1037/1082-989X.8.2.164

Reise, S. P., & Waller, N. G. (2009). Item response theory and clinical measurement. *Annual Review of Clinical Psychology, 5*, 27–48. doi:10.1146/annurev.clinpsy.032408.153553

Reise, S. P., & Yu, J. (1990). Parameter recovery in the graded response model using MULTILOG. *Journal of Educational Measurement, 27*, 133–144. doi:10.1111/j.1745-3984.1990.tb00738.x

Roberts, J. S., Donoghue, J. R., & Laughlin, J. E. (2000). A general item response theory model for unfolding unidimensional polytomous responses. *Applied Psychological Measurement, 24*, 3–32. doi:10.1177/01466216000241001

Rosenberg, M. (1989). *Society and the adolescent self-image* (rev. ed.). Middletown, CT: Wesleyan University Press.

Rouse, S. V., Finger, M. S., & Butcher, J. N. (1999). Advances in clinical personality measurement: An item response theory analysis of the MMPI-2 PSY-5 scales. *Journal of Personality Assessment, 72*, 282–307. doi:10.1207/S15327752JP720212

Samejima, F. (1969). Estimation of latent ability using a response pattern of graded scores. *Psychometrika, Monograph Supplement 17*.

Sijtsma, K., & Molenaar, I. W. (2002). *Introduction to nonparametric item response theory*. Thousand Oaks, CA: Sage.

Steinberg, L., & Thissen, D. (1996). Uses of item response theory and the testlet concept in the measurement of psychopathology. *Psychological Methods, 1*, 81–97. doi:10.1037/1082-989X.1.1.81

Thissen, D. (2003). MULTILOG 7: Multiple categorical item analysis and test scoring using item response theory [Computer software]. Chicago, IL: SSI.

Thissen, D., Cai, L., & Bock, R. D. (2010). The nominal categories item response model. In M. Nering & R. Ostini (Eds.), *Handbook of item response theory models* (pp. 43–75). Philadelphia, PA: Taylor & Francis.

Thissen, D., & Steinberg, L. (1986). A taxonomy of item response models. *Psychometrika, 51*, 567–577. doi:10.1007/BF02295596

Thissen, D., Steinberg, L., & Fitzpatrick, A. R. (1989). Multiple-choice models: The distractors are also part of the item. *Journal of Educational Measurement, 26*, 161–176. doi:10.1111/j.1745-3984.1989.tb00326.x

Tutz, G. (1990). Sequential item response models with an ordered response. *British Journal of Mathematical and Statistical Psychology, 43*, 39–55.

Van Der Ark, L. A. (2001). Relationships and properties of polytomous item response theory models. *Applied Psychological Measurement, 25*, 273–282. doi:10.1177/01466210122032073

Wainer, H. (2000). *Computerized adaptive testing: A primer* (2nd ed.). Mahwah, NJ: Erlbaum.

Wainer, H., & Thissen, D. (1987). Estimating ability with the wrong model. *Journal of Educational Statistics, 12*, 339–368. doi:10.2307/1165054

Waller, N. G., & Reise, S. P. (2010). Measuring psychopathology with nonstandard item response theory models: Fitting the four-parameter model to the Minnesota Multiphasic Personality Inventory. In S. Embretson (Ed.), *Measuring psychological constructs: Advances in model-based approaches* (pp. 147–173). Washington, DC: American Psychological Association. doi:10.1037/12074-007

Williams, C. L., Butcher, J. N., Ben-Porath, Y. S., & Graham, J. R. (1992). *MMPI-A content scales: Assessing psychopathology in adolescents*. Minneapolis: University of Minnesota Press.

Wilson, M. (2005). *Constructing measures: An item response modeling approach*. Mahwah, NJ: Erlbaum.

Zimowski, M., Muraki, E., Mislevy, R., & Bock, R. D. (2003). BILOG-MG (Version 3) [Computer software]. Lincolnwood, IL: SSI.

CHAPTER 37

MEASURING TEST PERFORMANCE WITH SIGNAL DETECTION THEORY TECHNIQUES

Teresa A. Treat and Richard J. Viken

The development and evaluation of assessment and prediction strategies designed to distinguish two mutually exclusive states are central enterprises in psychological science. For example, we might want to assess diagnostic status (present or absent) or child maltreatment (present or absent). Alternatively, we might be interested in predicting whether violence is likely or whether treatment relapse will occur. Once classic psychometric methods have been used to develop one or more assessment devices, the predictive or criterion validity of the measurement strategies must be evaluated (see Clark & Watson, 1995; Smith, 2005). Widely used indexes of test performance include Sensitivity (the proportion of positive cases correctly classified as positive), Specificity (the proportion of negative cases correctly classified as negative), Positive Predictive Power (the proportion of cases classified as positive who actually are positive), and Negative Predictive Power (the proportion of cases classified as negative who actually are negative). However, these indexes vary widely as a function of cutoff scores, the base rates (BRs) of the phenomenon of interest, and the costs and benefits associated with a particular assessment or prediction context, as we will see.

As a result, researchers increasingly are relying on the methods of signal detection theory, particularly receiver operating characteristic (ROC) analysis and utility-based decision theory approaches. ROC methods can be used to quantify and compare the discriminative power of measurement devices independently of cutoff scores, BRs, and costs and benefits. Decision theory methods then can be used to determine optimal cutoff scores for particular contexts, given specification of the BRs and the values placed on different kinds of correct and incorrect decisions.

After presenting background on the role of BRs in assessment and prediction as well as traditional accuracy indexes, we provide an overview of the use of ROC and decision-theory approaches for examination and enhancement of decision making in psychology. We close with recommendations regarding the reporting of the development of new measures, especially with regard to optimal cutoff values for a range of BRs and several common decision goals.

TRADITIONAL INDEXES OF TEST PERFORMANCE

In this chapter, we will illustrate issues in evaluating test performance with a data set from the National Comorbidity Survey Replication (NCS-R; Kessler & Merikangas, 2004; Kessler et al., 2004). The NCS-R is a nationally representative survey of English-speaking adults in the United States that was conducted from 2001 to 2003. *Diagnostic and Statistical Manual of Mental Disorders* (4th ed.; *DSM–IV*; American Psychiatric Association, 1994) diagnoses were determined for 9,282 respondents by the World Mental Health Composite International Diagnostic Interview, a structured diagnostic interview administered by lay persons (see Kessler & Üstün, 2004). The K6 is six-item screening scale that was completed by 6,656 of the participants in the data set, which we use as our predictive test. The K6 contains questions

DOI: 10.1037/13619-038
APA Handbook of Research Methods in Psychology: Vol. 1. Foundations, Planning, Measures, and Psychometrics, H. Cooper (Editor-in-Chief)

about the frequency with which various aspects of psychological distress were experienced during the respondent's worst month emotionally in the past year (Kessler et al., 2002, 2003). Respondents indicated how often they felt worthless, depressed, restless, hopeless, nervous, and that everything was an effort. Responses were made on a five-point scale ranging from 1 = *all the time* to 5 = *none of the time*. Responses were summed to obtain a total score on both scales, with lower scores indicating greater psychological distress. The large size and the high quality of the NCS-R sample make it an excellent database to provide examples for the methods described in this chapter. The K6 data in the sample are not missing at random with respect to the full sample, so the results of the analyses in this paper should be considered illustrative only.

Evaluating the performance of the K6 screening scale requires selection of a "gold standard" of psychological distress. The gold standards used in test evaluation typically are higher quality or more expensive indicators of the phenomenon of interest,

although they still may contain error (Swets, Dawes, & Monahan, 2000). In the current analyses, we used the presence or absence of the 12-month *DSM–IV* anxiety and mood disorders that were assessed for all respondents and included in the current public release of the NCS-R data set: agoraphobia with or without panic disorder, generalized anxiety disorder, panic disorder, specific phobia, social phobia, major depression, dysthymia, and bipolar I and II disorders. We considered participants to be positive for a disorder if they met criteria for at least one of these disorders. This chapter examines the extent to which the K6 scale provides far lower cost and less time-intensive assessments of psychological distress than the gold standard.

Figure 37.1 provides an initial look at the association between the interview-based diagnostic outcomes and the K6 screen. The two interview-based outcomes (Disorder Present or Absent) are depicted in the rows of the figure. The two K6-based predictions (Disorder Present or Absent) are depicted in the columns of the figure. Of the 6,656 subjects with

		K6-Based Classification		
		Disorder Present (K6 < 22)	Disorder Absent (K6 > 22)	
Interview-Based Classification ("Truth")	Disorder Present	Valid Positives (Hits) Frequency = 911 Percent = 13.7%	False Negatives (Misses) Frequency = 988 Percent = 14.8%	Base Rate Frequency = 1,899 Percent = 28.5%
	Disorder Absent	False Positives (False Alarms) Frequency = 509 Percent = 7.7%	Valid Negatives (Correct Rejections) Frequency = 4,248 Percent = 63.8%	100 – Base Rate Frequency = 4,757 Percent = 71.5%
		Selection Ratio Frequency = 1,420 Percent = 21.3%	100 – Selection Ratio Frequency = 5,236 Percent = 78.7%	Frequency = 6,656 Percent = 100%

FIGURE 37.1. Matrix of interview-based classifications by K6-based classifications for National Comorbidity Survey Replication data set. The percentages in the figure do not sum perfectly because of rounding issues.

data on both the screen and the interview, 1,899 (28.5%) met criteria for at least one of the disorders. The percentage (or proportion) of the sample meeting criteria for a disorder according to the gold-standard interview is referred to as the *base rate* (BR) or, in conventional clinical terms, the prevalence of the disorder. This BR is reflected in the BR entry to the far right in the Disorder Present row of the figure. With 28.5% of the sample meeting criteria for a disorder, this means that 71.5% (100 – BR) did not. All technical terms used in the chapter are listed chronologically with a brief definition in Exhibit 37.1.

The columns of Figure 37.1 depict the predictions made on the basis of the K6. In this example, we used a cutoff value on the K6 of 22: Anyone with a score of 22 or lower (recall that lower K6 scores indicate more distress) is predicted to have a disorder. This value was selected for illustrative purposes because it optimizes the percentage of correct classifications in the current sample. The last entry in the first column shows that 1,420 (21.3%) of K6

respondents were predicted to have a disorder. The percentage (or proportion) of a sample predicted to have the characteristic of interest is often called the Selection Ratio because in many practical applications of test prediction this group is being selected for further action. In the current context, for example, respondents scoring at or below 22 might receive further evaluation or referrals for treatment. The remaining 78.7% of the sample (100 – Selection Ratio) is predicted not to have a disorder.

The shaded cells of Figure 37.1 provide the core information about test performance. In this sample, 911 (13.7%) persons were predicted to have a disorder on the basis of the K6 *and* were found to have a disorder on the basis of the interview-based "truth." In clinical prediction contexts, such persons would be referred to as the Valid Positive, or True Positive, cases, and in the signal detection theory context, they would be referred to as Hits. The remaining 509 respondents who were predicted to have a disorder on the basis of the K6 did not, in truth, have a disorder. In clinical prediction contexts, these

---

Exhibit 37.1
Glossary of Technical Terminology

Base rate (or Prevalence): Percentage (or proportion) of cases identified by the gold standard as positive.
Cutoff (or Threshold): Value of assessment or prediction measure that distinguishes cases classified as positive and negative.
Selection ratio: Percentage (or proportion) of cases classified as positive.
Valid positives (or Hits): Cases identified by the gold standard as positive who are classified as positive.
Valid negatives (or Correct rejections): Cases identified by the gold standard as negative who are classified as negative.
False negatives (or Misses): Cases identified by the gold standard as positive who are classified as negative.
False positives (or False alarms): Cases identified by the gold standard as negative who are classified as positive.
Percent correct: Percentage of correctly classified cases.
Percent correct by chance: Percentage of cases that can be classified correctly by chance.
Predicting from the base rate: Predicting the more frequently occurring outcome for all cases.
Sensitivity: Proportion (or percentage) of positive cases correctly classified as positive.
Specificity: Proportion (or percentage) of negative cases correctly classified as negative.
Positive predictive power: Proportion of cases classified as positive who actually are positive.
Negative predictive power: Proportion of cases classified as negative who actually are negative.
Hit rate (or Valid positive rate): Probability of correctly classifying a positive case as positive.
False alarm rate (or False positive rate): Probability of correctly classifying a negative case as positive.
Area under the curve: The probability that a randomly selected pair of positive and negative cases will be ranked correctly by the assessment method.
Utility: Value placed on a specific decision-making outcome (i.e., user-perceived benefit or cost).
Overall utility: A utilities-weighted sum of the probabilities of the four decision-making outcomes.
Utility ratio: User-perceived relative importance of decisions about negative versus positive cases.
Information gain: The reduction of uncertainty about the true classification of a case that results from administering an assessment or prediction measure.

respondents would be referred to as the False Positive cases, and in signal detection theory contexts, they are referred to as False Alarms. Among those predicted to have no disorder on the basis of the K6, 988 (14.8%) were found actually to have a disorder present on the basis of the interview. In clinical prediction contexts, such persons are referred to as False Negatives, whereas in signal detection theory, they would be referred to as Misses. The 4,248 remaining people who were predicted to have no disorder on the basis of the K6 (63.8%) were indeed found to have no disorder as judged by the interview. These respondents are referred to as Valid Negative or True Negative cases in clinical prediction, and as Correct Rejections in signal detection theory.

One of the first things to evaluate in a table like this is the percentage of cases for which the K6-predicted classification was correct. There are two ways to be correct: Valid Positive and Valid Negative classifications. We can add the percentage of respondents in these two cells (13.7 and 63.8) to find that the K6-based prediction was correct 77.5% of the time. Although 77.5% accuracy sounds pretty good, it is important to compare percentage correct when using the K6 predictor to the percentage correct expected by chance. Conceptually, percentage correct by chance would be equivalent to making our predictions on the basis of a random process like a set of coin tosses rather than on the basis of the predictor. How often would we be correct if we randomly assigned 21.3% (the same percentage reflected in the Selection Ratio used for the K6) of participants to a prediction of Disorder Present? We can compute this expected percentage correct by considering the marginal percentages associated with each of the two ways of being correct. The percentage of Valid Positives expected by chance will be the product of the BR and Selection Ratio (i.e., 28.5% × 21.3% = 6.1%) because the BR and Selection Ratio are the marginal percentages associated with the Valid Positive cell in Figure 37.1. The percentage of Valid Negative cases expected by chance is the product of (100 – BR) and (100 – Selection Ratio; i.e., 71.5% × 78.7% = 56.2%). Summing these two ways of being correct (6.1 + 56.2) gives us an expected percent correct by chance of 62.3%. Thus, in our example, it does appear that the K6 is

modestly more accurate than expected by chance (77.5% versus 62.3%). As first discussed by Meehl and Rosen (1955), the lower the BR is the more difficult it will be to make predictions that are better than chance. For instance, if the actual BR or prevalence of Disorder in the current example were 5% rather than 28.5%, then the expected percent correct by chance would be 75.9% [i.e., (5% × 21.3%) + (95% × 78.7%)]. Expected percent correct by chance is an important baseline against which to judge test performance.

There is another way to consider the effects of BR on our success in making accurate predictions on the basis of tests (Meehl & Rosen, 1955). As the BR of an outcome decreases, it becomes easier to obtain a high degree of accuracy just by predicting that no one will be in the affected group. In our current example, we would be accurate 71.5% of the time just by predicting that the disorder will never be present (in essence, setting the Selection Ratio to zero). We will always be wrong for respondents who do develop a disorder (the percentage of Valid Positive cases will be zero, because no positive cases are predicted to develop a disorder), but we will always be right for the far more numerous respondents who do not have a disorder (the percentage of Valid Negative cases will be 71.5, because all negative cases are predicted not to develop a disorder). This strategy is sometimes called *predicting from the base rate*. If the BR of the disorder were 5%, then we could achieve 95% accuracy just by predicting that no one will develop the disorder. It will be difficult to find a real predictor that can match the 95% accuracy obtained by predicting from the BR. This BR problem is a particular challenge in psychology, where many of the phenomena of interest have low BRs (e.g., violence, abuse, dementia, resilience), frequently prompting researchers to conduct studies with high-risk populations for which the BRs are higher.

The problem with measures of overall percentage correct (whether observed or expected by chance) is that they treat different kinds of correct predictions and different kinds of errors as though they are equal in importance. This assumption of equal importance will rarely be true. For instance, in a clinical prediction setting, because successfully recognizing a disorder can lead to appropriate treatment, we might place high value on maximizing the percentage of Valid Positive cases and minimizing the percentage of False Negative cases. At the same time, we may view the cost of False Positives to be relatively low, consisting primarily of the time and expense it takes to follow up with our gold standard assessment. Once we begin placing different values on the four cells in the Prediction × Outcome matrix, overall percentage correct is no longer a good index of our success. In the example in Figure 37.1, 13.7% of the sample are Valid Positive cases, more than twice the 6.1% that would be expected by chance and much more than 0% we would identify by assuming that no one will have a disorder (i.e., setting the Selection Ratio to zero). If maximizing Valid Positives is important to us, then the test will do much better than the other strategies, because a far greater percentage of Valid Positive cases will be identified. Thus, even when low BRs make it difficult to achieve better than chance accuracy, or better accuracy than predicting from the BR, a test can still be useful if it can help us to exchange certain types of errors for others. In most assessment and prediction settings, it is the *profile* of correct predictions and errors that matters most, not overall percentage correct.

There are several indexes of test performance that recognize our interest in particular types of correct predictions and particular types of errors. *Sensitivity* (expressed as either a proportion or a percentage) is an index that focuses attention on our accuracy in correctly predicting disorder among those who have a disorder. It is based on the Disorder Present row of the matrix for the interview-based classification, and it is computed as the Valid Positive Percent / BR Percent. In the current example, Sensitivity is relatively low: less than half (48.1%) of the individuals who had a disorder according to the interview were predicted to have a disorder on the basis of a K6 score of 22 or below. *Specificity* (expressed as either a proportion or a percentage) is an index that focuses attention on our ability to avoid mistaken predictions of disorders among individuals in whom disorders are absent. Specificity is based on the Disorder Absent row of the matrix and is computed as Valid Negative Percent/(100 – BR Percent). With a cutoff of 22 or lower on the K6, Specificity in this example is very high at .892.

Although Sensitivity and Specificity reflect, in part, the accuracy of a predictive instrument, they are also strongly influenced by the cutoff or threshold at which we predict that a disorder will be present. If we were to increase the cutoff score in our example from a K6 score of 22 or less to a score of 26 or less (thereby including individuals with less severe K6 scores among those predicted to have a disorder), our Sensitivity will increase, and our Specificity will decrease. To see why this is so, consider Figure 37.2, which shows frequency distributions of K6 scores for the sample described in Figure 37.1, split into people with no diagnosis (white bars) and people with at least one mood or anxiety disorder (black bars). Consider the cutoff of 22 or lower, which is the basis of Figure 37.1. Clearly, most individuals without a diagnosis have scores higher than 22, which is reflected in the high Specificity of the K6 using this cutoff. Although individuals with diagnoses predominate in the part of the distribution at or below 22, it is obvious that about half of diagnosed individuals actually have K6 scores higher than 22. This is reflected in the relatively low Sensitivity of the K6 at this cutoff level. If we were to raise our cutoff to 26 (moving to the right on the *x*-axis and including individuals who show less extreme responses to the K6), we would increase Sensitivity from .481 to .758. The reason is obvious in Figure 37.2. By moving our cutoff to the right, we include all of the additional diagnosed individuals with scores between 22 and 26 on the K6. These individuals, who previously were False Negatives, now are converted to Valid Positives. But this increase in true positives comes at a cost, because setting the cutoff K6 score to 26 means that we are also including many individuals who do not have diagnoses. Indeed, most of the people added by moving our cutoff from 22 to 26 are not diagnosed. Those individuals were previously Valid Negatives and are converted to False Positives. Accordingly, Specificity drops from .892 to .649. In general, as we make our threshold for predicting diagnosis more liberal (i.e., as we increase the Selection Ratio), Sensitivity will increase, and Specificity will decrease.

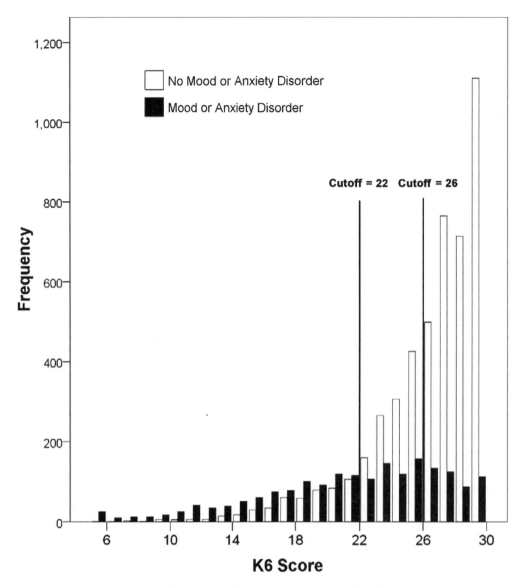

FIGURE 37.2.   Histograms of K6 scores for respondents who did and did not receive a mood or anxiety disorder diagnosis. Lower scores indicate greater psychological distress.

Figure 37.3 shows this inverse relationship across a wide range of cutoff values. If we set a conservative threshold that demands strong evidence of problems (in the case of the K6, this means a low score) before predicting disorder, then Specificity will be high and Sensitivity will be low. As we make our threshold more liberal, requiring less evidence of problems before we predict disorder, Specificity will decrease and Sensitivity will increase. It should be clear that general statements like "the Sensitivity of this scale when predicting depression is .8" are not very informative, given that Sensitivity depends on the cutoff that we choose.

Sensitivity and Specificity are conditional on outcomes (the interview-based classifications of present and absent expressed as the rows in Figure 37.1). Two additional indexes of test performance are conditional on our predictions (the columns of Figure 37.1). Positive Predictive Power is the probability that someone we predict to have a disorder actually has a disorder. It is computed as Valid Positive Percent/Selection Ratio, which in the current example equals .643. Negative Predictive Power is the probability that someone we predict not to have a disorder in fact does not have a disorder. It is computed as Valid Negative Percent/(100 – Selection

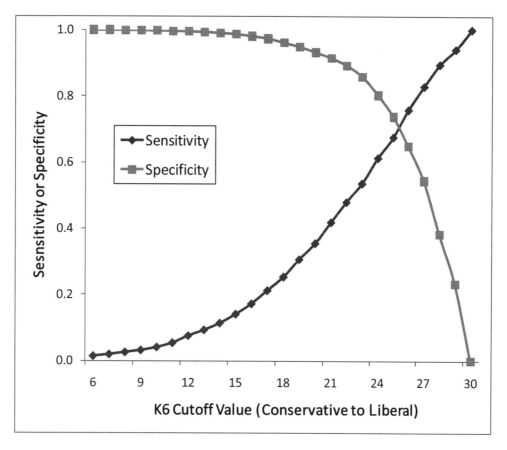

FIGURE 37.3.　Sensitivity and Specificity as a function of K6 cutoff values.

Ratio), which in the current example equals .811. Like Sensitivity and Specificity, Predictive Power is influenced by our cutoff for predicting disorder. Making a cutoff more liberal usually will decrease Positive Predictive Power because as we move toward the not-disordered side of the distribution (the right side of Figure 37.2), we will usually pick up more not-disordered individuals relative to those with disorders. This will increase the percentage of False Positives more than the percentage of Valid Positives. The same change to a more liberal threshold will usually result in an increase in Negative Predictive Power because as we move toward the not-disordered end of the distribution, we will lose a higher percentage of False Negative individuals than Valid Negative individuals. Figure 37.4 shows the empirical relationship between the selected cutoff and both Positive and Negative Predictive Power for the current sample.

Positive and Negative Predictive Power are also strongly influenced by the BR or prevalence of a phenomenon. At a given threshold, increasing prevalence implies relatively more Valid Positive than False Positive cases, and relatively fewer Valid Negative than False Positive cases. Thus, as prevalence increases, Positive Predictive Power will increase and Negative Predictive Power will decrease. Figure 37.5 shows the expected change in Positive and Negative Predictive Power with increasing prevalence in the current sample.

The discussion thus far shows why Sensitivity, Specificity, Positive Predictive Power, and Negative Predictive Power provide better information about test performance than an overall measure of percent correct. They focus our attention on specific goals (e.g., finding people who need help versus not squandering resources on people who do not need help) rather than on a general goal of overall accuracy. But because these indexes refer to test performance at only one of many possible criteria or thresholds, and because they refer to test performance at only one observed BR, their generalizability to

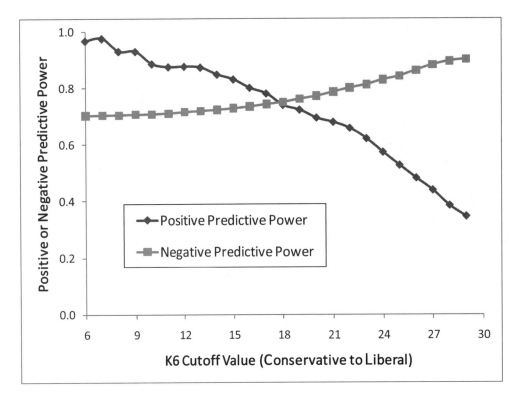

FIGURE 37.4.   Positive and Negative Predictive Power as a function of K6 cutoff values.

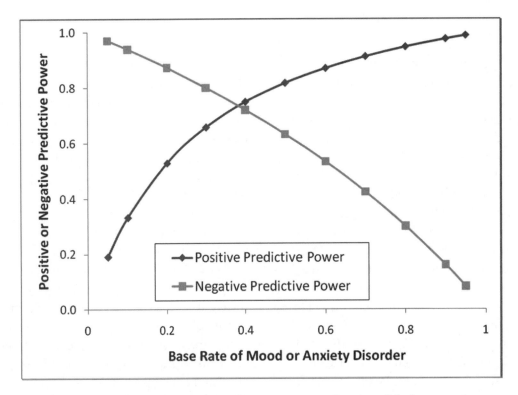

FIGURE 37.5.   Positive and Negative Predictive Power as a function of the base rate (or prevalence) of a mood or anxiety disorder, assuming a cutoff of 22 on the K6.

new samples and applications is questionable. If the relative importance of avoiding False Negative versus False Positive mistakes differs in a new setting, thereby implying a different cutoff score, or if the prevalence differs in the new setting, then it will be difficult to predict how a scale will function in the new setting on the basis of reports of Sensitivity, Specificity, Positive Predictive Power, and Negative Predictive Power in previous studies. It would be far more useful to have a measure of test performance that better generalizes across samples and thresholds. Next, we provide an overview of just such an index, the area under the ROC curve. Subsequently, we describe how decision-theory methods can be used to select a threshold or cutoff value that optimizes practical utility in a context characterized by a particular BR and set of values.

QUANTIFYING DISCRIMINATORY POWER: APPLICATION OF ROC ANALYSIS

ROC analysis, an analytic approach based on signal detection theory, yields a quantitative index of how well an assessment strategy detects or predicts a signal of interest or discriminates two signals of interest (e.g., the presence of a disorder, the occurrence of violence, response to treatment, recidivism, and so on). Originally, engineers developed ROC analysis to quantify how well a human receiver detected electronic signals in the presence of noise, and ROC analysis acquired its name from its application to radar-detection problems during World War II (Pierce, 1980). Unlike the indexes of test performance reviewed thus far, the ROC-based index is independent of the BRs or prevalence of a phenomenon, the selected cutoff score, and the values or utilities placed on the four potential decision-making outcomes. Subsequent decision-theory approaches then can be used to optimize cutoff selection for the assessment strategy with maximal discriminatory power in a particular context, which necessarily will be influenced by phenomenon BRs and user-specified values. The sequential employment of ROC analysis and decision-theory approaches provides psychologists with a powerful pair of tools for the selection and application of valid and practically

useful assessment and prediction methods (e.g., Swets, 1996; Swets et al., 2000).

We illustrate the use of ROC methods by continuing our analysis of the K6 screen for psychological distress and illness. We now will use the language of signal detection theory to refer to the four cells in Figure 37.1 (e.g., Hits, Misses, False Alarms, and Correct Rejections, rather than Valid Positives, False Negatives, False Positives, and Valid Negatives). Figure 37.6 presents the ROC curve for the K6 scale as a predictor of the interview-based diagnostic outcome discussed thus far. The axes of the ROC plot are the hit and false alarm rates (i.e., the proportions of Valid Positives and False Positives, respectively), and each point on the ROC curve corresponds to a pair of hit and false alarm rates that results from the use of a specific cutoff value. The hit rate can be computed as Hits/(Hits + Misses), and the false alarm rate corresponds to False Alarms/(False Alarms + Correct Rejections). In more traditional language, the ROC curve is a plot of Sensitivity against 1 – Specificity at all possible cutoff values. A few pairs of false alarm and hit rates are indicated by their associated K6 cutoff values. For example, counting K6 scores less than or equal to 22 as positive cases (because lower scores indicate more distress on the K6) produces a false alarm rate of .107 and a hit rate of .480, and a cutoff score of 28 produces false alarm and hit rates of .616 and .895, respectively. The cutoff value of 28 corresponds here to a liberal criterion or cutoff, which results in a substantial hit rate but also a high false alarm rate. In contrast, the markedly conservative cutoff value of 19 results in a very low false alarm rate (.050) but also an unimpressive hit rate (.307). Thus, the cutoff changes from maximally conservative to maximally liberal as one moves along an ROC curve from the lower left corner (where false alarm and hit rates both are 0.0) to the upper right corner (where false alarm and hit rates both are 1.0). Because lower K6 scores indicate greater pathology, lower scores index more conservative cutoffs. On other measures in which higher scores indicate greater pathology, however, higher scores correspond to more conservative cutoffs because fewer positive cases are identified by high cutoff scores.

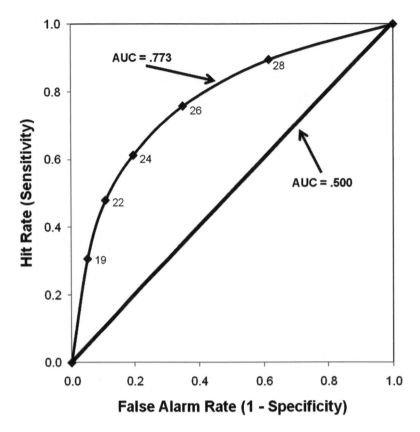

FIGURE 37.6. Receiver operating characteristic curve for K6 scale, with five labeled cutoff values ranging from conservative (19) to liberal (28). AUC = area under the curve.

The area under the ROC curve (AUC) quantifies the discriminative power of an assessment or prediction method independently of the cutoff value, unlike traditional accuracy indexes. The values for AUC can range from 0.0 (when the ROC curve passes from the lower left corner through the lower right corner to the upper right corner) to 1.0 (when the ROC curve passes from the lower left corner through the upper left corner to the upper right corner). An ROC curve that lies on the main diagonal (see Figure 37.6) indicates that the diagnostic system is operating at the level of chance because the hit and false alarm rates are equal across the range of possible cutoff values. Chance performance corresponds to an AUC of 0.5. As the performance of the diagnostic system increases, the distance of the observed ROC curve from the chance line increases.

The AUC for the K6 as a predictor of mood or anxiety disorder diagnoses in the current illustrative data set is .773, with a standard error of .007 and a 95% confidence interval estimate ranging from .763 to .783. The AUC value has a readily interpretable probabilistic meaning: It corresponds to the probability that a randomly selected pair of observations drawn from the two underlying distributions will be ranked correctly by the assessment method (Green & Swets, 1966; Hanley & McNeil, 1982). In the current context, this value indicates that the K6 score will be lower 77.3% of the time for a randomly selected individual with a mood or anxiety disorder than for a randomly selected individual without a mood or anxiety disorder. A z test demonstrates that the observed AUC value is significantly greater than the chance value of .500 ($z = 41.949$, $p < .0001$), indicating that K6 scores are a significant signal of the presence of a mood or anxiety disorder.

Figure 37.7 juxtaposes the ROC curve for the K6 with that for the K10, a 10-item screen that includes four additional items (Kessler et al., 2002, 2003).

The AUC value for the K10 is .782 (*SE* = .006, 95% confidence interval [CI] = .772–.792), and it is significantly greater than the chance value of .50, *z* = 44.373, *p* < .0001. The difference between the AUC values for the K10 and K6 is .008 (*SE* = .002, 95% CI = .005–.012) and is significantly greater than 0, *z* = 5.004, *p* < .001. This set of results indicates that the K10 shows a statistically but not practically significant advantage over the K6 for detection of the presence of a mood or anxiety disorder. Inspection of Figure 37.7 suggests that the K10 may have a small advantage over the K6 when more liberal cutoff values are employed (e.g., 24 and greater). Thus, when the practical goal in a particular context is to use a screening device to distinguish those with very few symptoms from those with more than very few symptoms, the K10 may be slightly preferable to the K6, in spite of the inclusion of four addition items. When the goal instead is to distinguish those reporting significant symptoms from the remainder of respondents, the K6 and K10 perform very similarly.

Formal methods are available to compare two ROC curves either (a) at a single hit or false alarm rate point on the curve (McNeil & Hanley, 1984) or (b) across a range of user-specified false alarm rate values (e.g., Y. He & Escobar, 2008; McClish, 1989). For example, we could use these methods to evaluate whether the Sensitivity of the K10 is significantly greater than the Sensitivity of the K6 at a false alarm rate of .500. Or, we could evaluate whether the discriminatory power of the K10 is significantly greater than that of the K6 for false alarm rate values ranging from .500 to .800.

In their initial report on the psychometric properties of the K6 and K10, Kessler et al. (2002) reported AUC values of .876 and .879, respectively. The notably higher values presumably reflect in part their use of a broader gold standard index: the 12-month diagnosis of any anxiety disorder, any mood disorder, or any nonaffective psychosis as well as a Global Assessment of Functioning score between 0 and 70. Similar to the present findings,

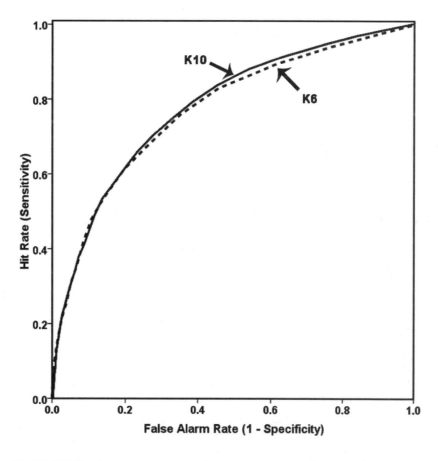

FIGURE 37.7.   Receiver operating characteristic curves for K6 and K10 scales.

however, administration of the K10 did not enhance substantially the information acquired from administering the K6. Given the negligible increase in discriminatory power associated with use of the longer K10 in both Kessler et al.'s initial report and the current illustrative analyses, we hereafter use the K6 in all analyses.

Of course, the AUC value for a scale will depend on the outcome that it is predicting. For illustrative purposes, Figure 37.8 presents K6 ROC curves for four of the six anxiety disorder diagnoses that currently are available in the NCS-R: generalized anxiety disorder, panic disorder, specific phobia, and social phobia. Table 37.1 lists the AUC values, standard errors, 95% CIs, and z statistics and evaluates whether discriminatory power is significant for each diagnosis. The discriminatory power of the K6 is significantly greater than chance for all four diagnoses.

Not surprisingly, the performance of this six-item screening measure varies across diagnoses; it is significantly worse for detection of specific phobia than for the other three diagnoses, all $p < .001$, and it is significantly better for detection of generalized anxiety disorder than for panic disorder, social phobia, and specific phobia, all $p < .05$.

ROC methods initially were parametric and assumed to be appropriate only when the underlying distributions were normal and showed homogeneous variances. Fortunately, parametric estimation appears to be robust to violations of these assumptions (Hanley, 1988), and nonparametric estimation methods also are available when either or both of these assumptions are violated (e.g., Hanley & McNeil, 1982). Both parametric and nonparametric methods allow the user to compare AUC values with chance performance values and to compare

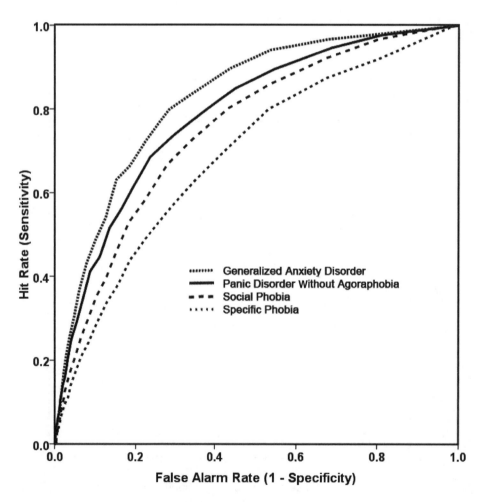

FIGURE 37.8. Receiver operating characteristic curves for K6-based detection of four anxiety disorders.

TABLE 37.1

Receiver Operating Characteristic Analysis Results for K6 Screening of Four Anxiety Disorders

Disorder	AUC	*SE*	*z*	*p*	95% CI
Generalized anxiety disorder	.825	.0102	31.899	.0001	.815–.834
Panic disorder	.788	.0141	20.430	.0001	.778–.797
Social phobia	.751	.00985	25.454	.0001	.740–.761
Specific phobia	.686	.0100	18.608	.0001	.675–.698

Note. AUC = area under the curve; CI = confidence interval.

two independent or dependent AUC values (e.g., DeLong, DeLong, & Clarke-Pearson, 1988; Hanley & McNeil, 1982, 1983; Metz, Wang, & Kronman, 1984).

ROC curves can be generated in a variety of ways. First, multiple pairs of hit and false alarm rates can be calculated from a single data set by varying the cutoff. Second, the assessment method may be used repeatedly with different decision criteria employed on each occasion (i.e., from conservative to liberal). Each occasion provides a unique set of hit and false alarm rates. Third, a rating scale method may be used, in which raters not only classify the person (or other stimulus) into one of two categories but also indicate their confidence level for the accuracy of their classification, typically on a 5- or 7-point scale. In this case, multiple pairs of hit and false alarm rates can be obtained by treating each confidence level as a separate cutoff value (see Macmillan & Creelman, 1991). When ROC analysis is used to quantify the performance of assessment and prediction strategies, the first strategy most commonly is employed.

ROC approaches typically have been applied only to dichotomous classification decisions, although diagnosticians often are called on to make classifications into more than two discrete categories. Fortunately, Scurfield (1996) generalized signal detection theory (SDT) analysis to account for unidimensional classifications into three or more categories, and recently there has been a flurry of developments on this front (e.g., X. He, Gallas, & Frey, 2010; Li & Zhou, 2009). DeCarlo (1998) also has shown how conventional SDT models are special cases of the generalized linear model, suggesting a wide variety of potential extensions, including

incorporation of predictors and covariates into ROC analyses.

A variety of software programs are available for ROC analysis. In a review, Stephan, Wesseling, Schink, and Jung (2003) recommended the use of Analyse-It Software (available for purchase at http://www.analyse-it.com), AccuROC (which no longer is available), or MedCalc (available for purchase at www.medcalc.be). Both Analyse-It and MedCalc have user-friendly interfaces and nice graphics, and they report results for both single AUC values and for the difference in two AUC values as well as associated standard errors, confidence intervals, and statistical tests. SPSS, in contrast, currently does not provide an evaluation of the difference between two AUC values. SAS, which was not included in the Stephan et al. (2003) review, provides a macro as well as several statements within the logistic procedure relevant to ROC analysis. Gönen (2007) detailed how other features of SAS can be employed to conduct far more extensive ROC analyses. STATA also provides a number of parametric and nonparametric ROC analysis options, including comparison of two AUC values. All analyses for this chapter were conducted using MedCalc version 11.2.1.0; parametric and nonparametric findings were nearly identical.

SELECTING A CUTOFF: APPLICATION OF DECISION AND INFORMATION THEORY

Although ROC analysis provides an index of discriminatory power that is independent of cutoff values, BRs, and the values or utilities placed on the four decision-making outcomes, it does not provide the optimal cutoff value or illustrate how the ideal cutoff value varies as a function of the hit and false alarm rates, BRs, and values (Hsiao, Bartko, & Potter, 1989; Mossman & Somoza, 1989; Murphy et al., 1987; Somoza et al., 1994; Swets et al., 2000). Having first used ROC methods to identify the assessment or prediction strategy with the greatest discriminatory power, users next must select an optimal cutoff value, which necessarily involves specification of a function to be maximized. Thus, there is no true and unique optimal cutoff value, and the usefulness of a diagnostic test can vary widely across the contexts in which it is employed as a function of cutoff selection. In the next section, we provide an overview of two common approaches to selecting optimal cutoff values that incorporate hit and false alarm rates, BRs, and utilities in their criterion function.

Decision Theory Approach to Cutoff Specification

Meehl and Rosen (1955) and Somoza and Mossman (1991), among others, have advocated the use of an approach that combines an SDT analysis with utility-based decision theory (see also Metz, 1978; Swets, 1992). This approach allows the user to place a differential value on (i.e., to specify the differential utility of) hits (H), false alarms (FA), correct rejections (CR), and misses (M). Frequently, the user does not value these four possible outcomes equally because of their differential implications (i.e., variation in the perceived benefits and costs associated with the four outcomes). As summarized in the following equation, the overall utility of a specific cutoff value is a function of the hit rates and false alarm rates (HR and FAR) that result from a given cutoff value, a BR estimate (expressed as a proportion), and the values or utilities placed on each of the four decision-making outcomes (UH = utility for hits, UM = utility for misses, UFA = utility for false alarms, and UCR = utility for correct rejections):

$$U_{overall} = (BR)(HR)(UH) + (BR)(1 - HR)(UM) \\ + (1 - BR)(FAR)(UFA) + (1 - BR) \\ (1 - FAR)(UCR). \quad (1)$$

Each term in $U_{overall}$ is the product of the probability of a particular outcome (e.g., the probability of

a Hit is $BR*HR$) and the utility of that outcome (e.g., UH). Thus, $U_{overall}$ is a utilities-weighted sum of the probabilities of the four decision-making outcomes. Utilities typically range between 0 and 1, where a value of 0 represents the least desired outcome and a value of 1 indicates the most desired outcome. Typically, therefore, hits and correct rejections are assigned utilities $\geq .5$, whereas misses and false alarms are assigned utilities $\leq .5$. Suppose, for example, that we wanted to instantiate the common decision goal of maximizing percent correct in the previous example. We would assign the maximal value of 1 to correct detection of individuals with an anxiety or mood disorder (i.e., UH = 1) and to correct rejection of individuals without an anxiety or mood disorder (i.e., UCR = 1). The minimal value of 0 would be assigned to failure to detect individuals with an anxiety or mood disorder (i.e., UM = 0) and to failure to reject individuals without an anxiety or mood disorder (i.e., UFA = 0). We then would compute $U_{overall}$ for all possible cutoff values (e.g., the 25 potential K6 cutoff scores) and a range of prevalence rates. These steps readily can be instantiated in Excel.

Figure 37.9 depicts how the overall utility of various K6 cutoff values changes as a function of phenomenon BRs in a specific decision context, assuming that the decision goal is to maximize percent correct. As the BR of either a mood or anxiety disorder increases from .100 to .900, the optimal cutoff value increases markedly from 13 to 30. More generally, whenever the decision goal is to maximize percent correct, the ideal cutoff value necessarily becomes more conservative and results in fewer positive classifications as the BR of a phenomenon decreases, so that false alarms do not become too frequent.

The potentially marked influence of changes in BRs on the utility of cut scores commonly is ignored in both research and applied contexts. Cutoff scores determined to be *optimal* during scale development may be reified and used without modification across contexts in which BRs vary widely. For example, an optimal cutscore might be determined in an initial study in which the BRs for the phenomenon of interest are higher (perhaps because of oversampling persons with disorders) than in the context in which the resulting measure and cutscore commonly are applied. As a result, the cutscore that was

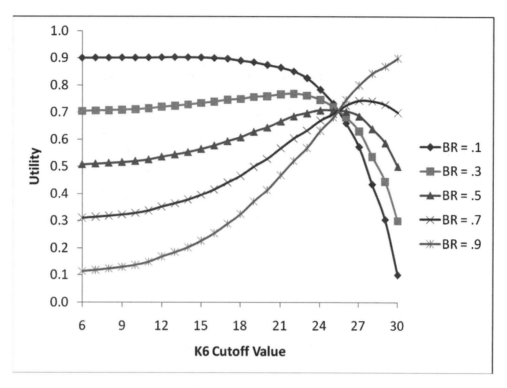

FIGURE 37.9.   Utility of K6 cutoff values as a function of the base rate (BR) of mood or anxiety disorders while maximizing percent correct.

optimal in the higher BR context is too liberal in the lower BR context, resulting in a notable increase in the relative frequency of false alarms. Alternatively, the ideal cutoff score for a measure that emerges from work with a large community sample might be unacceptably conservative when applied within a clinical context.

Exhibit 37.2 illustrates the potential impact of ignoring the influence of disorder prevalence on the practical utility of the K6. Exhibit 37.2A presents the classification results for the 6,656 individuals in the current sample, given two assumptions. First, the BR of a mood or anxiety disorder is assumed to be .285, the observed value for the current sample. Second, the cutoff score is 22, the optimal value assuming that the proportion correct is being maximized for the given prevalence. This cutoff is associated with a hit rate of .480 and a false alarm rate of .107. Overall proportion correct is .775 [i.e., (911 + 4248)/6656)]. Exhibit 37.2B then presents the results if the same cutoff value of 22 is employed in a context in which the BR of mood or anxiety disorders is .500, rather than .285. This might occur in a clinical context, for example. Overall proportion

correct drops to .686. Finally, Exhibit 37.2C presents the results if the ideal cutoff value is used for a context in which the BR of mood or anxiety disorders is .500. This cutoff value is higher (24), as would be expected when the proportion of positive cases increases, and it is associated with a hit rate of .613 and a false alarm rate of .197. Notably, overall proportion correct now increases to .708, and a significantly greater proportion of positive cases is detected. Thus, it is critical for researchers both to provide and to make use of BR-specific guidance on the cutoff values that optimally balance correct and incorrect decisions.

A decision goal of maximizing percent or proportion correct frequently is selected to sidestep the need to specify values or utilities for each of the four decision-making outcomes. This default approach makes equally strong implicit assumptions, however. In the present context, choosing to maximize percent correct is predicated on the assumption that correctly identifying those *without* mood or anxiety disorders is just as important as correctly identifying those *with* mood or anxiety disorders, although some might argue the latter is more valuable.

Exhibit 37.2

Influence of Base Rates on Proportion Correct

Classification of Mood or Anxiety Disorders on the Basis

of K6 Scores, Using a Cutoff of 22

		K6-based classification		
		Disorder present	Disorder absent	Total
A: Base rate = .285, cutoff = 22 (*HR* = .480, *FAR* = .107), proportion correct = .775				
Interview-based	Disorder present	911	988	1,899
classification ("Truth")	Disorder absent	509	4,248	4,757
	Total	1,420	5,236	6,656
B: Base rate = .500, cutoff = 22 (*HR* = .480, *FAR* = .107), proportion correct = .686				
Interview-based	Disorder present	1,597	1,731	3,328
classification ("Truth")	Disorder absent	356	2,972	3,328
	Total	1,953	4,703	6,656
C: Base rate = .500, cutoff = 24 (*HR* = .613, *FAR* = .197), proportion correct = .708				
Interview-based	Disorder present	2,040	1,288	3,328
classification ("Truth")	Disorder absent	654	2,674	3,328
	Total	2,694	3,962	6,656

Note. HR = hit rate; FAR = false alarm rate.

Analogously, this approach stipulates that erroneously classifying a person as having a mood or anxiety disorder is just as problematic as failing to identify a person with a mood or anxiety disorder, although some might perceive the latter to be more serious. Consideration of plausible value specifications is facilitated by inspection of the following utility ratio (Somoza & Mossman, 1991):

$$\text{Utility Ratio} = (UCR - UFA) / (UH - UM). \quad (2)$$

Maximizing percent correct essentially specifies a utility ratio of 1.0, whereby the difference between the values placed on correct versus incorrect decisions about negative cases in the numerator is the same as the difference between the values placed on correct versus incorrect decisions about positive cases in the denominator. Alternative value specifications could capture the greater perceived importance of decisions about positive cases than negative cases, however. For example, we might stipulate that $UH = 1$, $UCR = .75$, $UM = 0$, and $UFA = .25$, resulting in a utility ratio of .5 (i.e., we care twice as much about decisions regarding positive cases than

negative cases). Alternatively, pronounced concerns about the negative consequences or side effects of case identification or treatment might lead one to place greater value on decisions about negative cases ($UH = .75$, $UM = .25$, $UCR = 1$, $UFA = 0$), thereby specifying a utility ratio of 2.0 (i.e., we care twice as much about decisions regarding negative than positive cases). Thus, value configurations that weight decisions about positive and negative cases equally correspond to a utility ratio of 1.0, configurations that weight decisions about positive cases far more than negative cases produce utility ratios less than 1.0, and configurations that weight decisions about negative cases far more than positive cases produce utility ratios greater than 1.0.

Figure 37.10 illustrates how the overall utility of various K6 cutoff values changes as a function of the utility ratio, or the relative value placed on decisions about positive versus negative cases. The BR is held fixed at .285 for all computations, as this is the probability of a mood or anxiety disorder in the current data set. As greater importance is placed on decisions about positive cases (i.e., as the utility

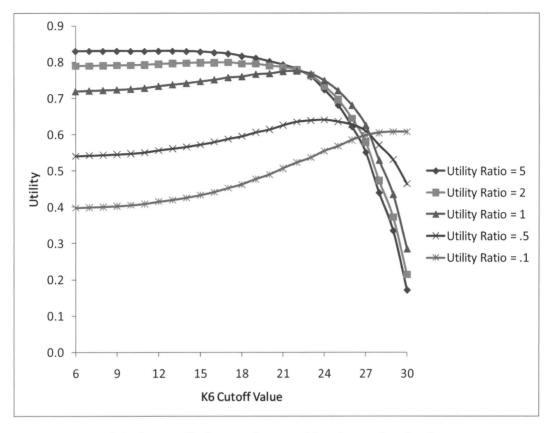

FIGURE 37.10.   Utility of K6 cutoff values as a function of the relative value placed on positive versus negative cases, assuming the base rate of mood or anxiety disorders is .285. See text for more information.

ratio decreases), the most useful threshold increases in value from 13 for a utility ratio of 5.0 (decisions about negative cases more important) to 30 for a utility ratio of 0.1 (decisions about positive cases more important). When decisions about positive and negative cases are valued equally (i.e., the utility ratio = 1.0), the optimal cutoff value is 22. Not surprisingly, as the value placed on positive cases increases, the cutoff becomes more liberal.

Exhibit 37.3 illustrates how ignoring implicit assumptions about the equal importance placed on decisions about positive and negative cases when maximizing proportion correct may result in the selection of unnecessarily conservative cutoff scores. Exhibit 37.3A presents the classification results for the 6,656 individuals in the current sample, given two assumptions. First, the prevalence of a mood or anxiety disorder is assumed to be .285, the observed value for the current sample. Second, the cutoff score is 22, which is the optimal value assuming that proportion correct is being maximized for the given prevalence rate (i.e., $UH = 1$, $UCR = 1$, $UM = 0$, and

$UFA = 0$; the utility ratio = 1.0). Using a cutoff of 22 produces a hit rate of .480 and a false alarm rate of .107. Under these conditions, the proportion correct for positive cases (Sensitivity) is .480, and the proportion correct for negative cases (Specificity) is .893. Exhibit 37.3B then presents the results if the cutoff score is 24, which is ideal in a context in which accurate decisions about those with a mood or anxiety disorder are construed as twice as important as accurate decisions about those without a mood or anxiety disorder (i.e., $UH = 1$, $UCR = .75$, $UM = 0$, and $UFA = .25$; the utility ratio = .5). The cutoff score of 24 is associated with a hit rate of .613 and a false alarm rate of .197. Under these conditions, the proportion correct for positive cases increases to .613 (an increase of 13 percentage points), whereas the proportion correct for negative cases declines to .803 (a decrease of 9 percentage points). This example highlights how implicitly placing equal importance on decisions about positive and negative cases when one in actuality places far greater importance on positive than negative

Exhibit 37.3
Influence of Relative Value Placed on Positive and Negative Cases on Proportion Correct Classification of Presence or Absence of Mood/Anxiety Disorders on the Basis of K6 Scores

		K6-based classification		
		Disorder present	Disorder absent	Total
A: Cutoff = 22 (*HR* = .480, *FAR* = .107), proportion correct (positive case) = .480, proportion correct (negative case) = .893				
Interview-based	Disorder present	911	988	1,899
classification ("Truth")	Disorder absent	509	4,248	4,757
	Total	1,420	5,236	6,656
B: Cutoff = 24 (*HR* = .613, *FAR* = .197), proportion correct (positive case) = .613, proportion correct (negative case) = .803				
Interview-based	Disorder present	1,164	735	1,899
classification ("Truth")	Disorder absent	935	3,822	4,757
	Total	2,099	4,557	6,656

Note. HR = hit rate; FAR = false alarm rate.

decisions may result in the use of unnecessarily conservative cutoff scores, resulting in decreased accuracy for positive cases.

More generally, the practical utility of assessment and prediction devices could be enhanced greatly if researchers routinely provided optimal cutoff scores for a range of BRs and utility ratios during measure development. Although the utility approach has been criticized because it requires the user to quantify both BRs and utility ratios,[1] it is important to recognize that proceeding instead by ignoring BR effects and maximizing percent correct also makes stringent assumptions that can exert marked influences on overall accuracy. In other words, no absolute optimal cutoff value exists in the absence of prevalence information and assumptions about the meaning of optimal.

Information Theory Approach to Cutoff Specification

To finesse the use of subjective utilities, Metz, Goodenough, and Rossmann (1973) proposed that an information theory (Shannon & Weaver, 1949) analysis of the ROC curve provides a natural optimization function (information gain, or I_{gain}) for the selection of an optimal threshold (see also Mossman & Somoza, 1989; Somoza, Soutullo-Esperon, & Mossman, 1989; Somoza, Steer, Beck, & Clark, 1994):

$$I_{gain} = (BR)(HR)(log2(HR/G)) + (BR)(1 - HR)(log2[(1 - HR)/(1 - G)]) + (1 - BR)(FAR)(log2(FAR/G)) + (1 - BR)(1 - FAR)(log2[(1 - FAR)/(1 - G)]), \quad (3)$$

where G = Selection Ratio (expressed as a proportion).

According to Metz et al.'s (1973) approach, information gain refers to the reduction of uncertainty about the true classification of a person that results from administering the diagnostic measure. For our example, information gain refers to the difference between the uncertainties about the mood or anxiety disorder status of an individual before and after knowing the individual's K6 score.

Inspection of the criterion functions specified by decision theorists ($U_{overall}$) and information

---

[1]In some settings, there may be data available on the relative cost (time, expense, productivity) of false positives and false negatives that can be used to facilitate utility specification. When such data are not available, expert ratings may provide subjective utilities that are useful as a starting point.

theorists (I_{gain}) reveals that both incorporate the false alarm rate, the hit rate, and the BR (expressed as a proportion). I_{gain} maximizes information gain, however, whereas $U_{overall}$ maximizes utility. Interestingly, $U_{overall}$ is a general case of I_{gain}, because I_{gain} provides an alternative specification of the utilities of the four outcomes (Metz et al., 1973; Somoza & Mossman, 1992a, 1992b). Thus, Metz et al.'s (1973) approach to criterion selection sidesteps the necessity of explicitly specifying the outcome utilities. Variability in prevalence continues to exert an influence on cutoff selection in the information theory approach, however.

Figure 37.11 depicts the influence of BRs on information gain for K6 cutoff values. Two effects are visible in the figure. First, information gain from administering the K6 is maximal for a BR of .5 and declines markedly when BRs are extremely low or high. This reflects the far greater a priori uncertainty about a case in which both positive and negative outcomes are equally likely. In contrast, markedly unequal BRs for positive and negative outcomes

provide extensive a priori information about the most likely outcome (i.e., one could simply predict the more prevalent category for each case and be correct the overwhelming majority of the time). Second, the optimal cutoff becomes more liberal as BRs increase. For the K6, ideal cutoffs range from 22, when the prevalence of a mood or anxiety disorder is 5%, to 26, when the prevalence is 95%. Ignoring the influence of BRs on information gain has similarly deleterious effects to those illustrated in Exhibit 37.2 for overall utility.

Comparison of Two Approaches and Recommendations

Table 37.2 contrasts the optimal K6 cutoff scores for varying BRs for four optimization functions: I_{gain}, $U_{overall}$ assuming decisions about positive cases are twice as important as decisions about negative cases, $U_{overall}$ assuming decisions about positive and negative cases are equivalent in value, and $U_{overall}$ assuming decisions about negative cases are twice as important as decisions about positive cases. These values range from 7 to 30, making it

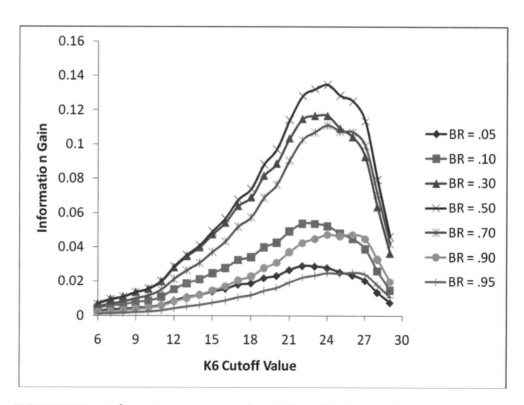

FIGURE 37.11.   Information gain associated with K6 cutoff values as a function of the base rate (BR) of a mood or anxiety disorder.

TABLE 37.2

Optimal K6 Cutoff Values as a Function of Base Rates and Optimization Function

Optimization function	Base rate						
	.05	.10	.30	.50	.70	.90	.95
Maximizing I_{gain}	22	22	23	24	24	26	26
Maximizing $U_{overall}$: Decisions about positive cases twice as important as decisions about negative cases	13	17	24	27	30	30	30
Maximizing $U_{overall}$: Decisions about positive and negative cases equal in importance	7	13	22	24	27	30	30
Maximizing $U_{overall}$: Decisions about negative cases twice as important as decisions about positive cases	7	9	17	22	26	30	30

Note. I_{gain} = information gain; $U_{overall}$ = overall utility.

---

evident that both users and developers of assessment and prediction devices will benefit from attending to three factors when selecting a cutoff score that maximizes practical utility: (a) the BRs of the phenomenon in the context in which the device is employed, (b) whether maximizing utility or information is preferred, and (c) the relative importance of decisions about positive versus negative cases of the phenomenon if maximizing utility is preferred. It is not critical to the profitable use of this information that either exact BRs be known or utility ratios be specified precisely. If the user is wholly unable to specify even an approximate utility ratio, then the cutoff value that maximizes information for the approximate prevalence rate should be selected. We suspect that most users will be in a position to articulate a clear preference between the three options provided in the table, however. In this case, cutoffs predicated on utility maximization are recommended. More generally, we urge those developing assessment and prediction devices to provide a similar table of ideal cutoff values rather than a single cutoff value that may not be robust to variations in BRs and utility ratios.

CONCLUSION

Contemporary evaluation of the performance of assessment and prediction strategies in psychological science entails the completion of a two-step strategy

that distinguishes the discriminative and decisional aspects of psychological measurement. First, ROC methods can be used to quantify the power of our measures to discriminate between two mutually exclusive states of interest. Indexes drawn from signal detection theory, such as AUC, assess performance independently of the selected cutoff value, the BRs of the phenomenon of interest, and the values placed on the four decision-making outcomes, unlike traditional indexes such as Sensitivity, Specificity, Positive Predictive Power, and Negative Predictive Power. Second, decision-theory methods can be employed to select a cutoff value that maximizes either the practical utility of or the information gained by test administration in a particular decision-making context, as defined by both BRs and the relative values or utilities placed on the different outcomes. This approach highlights the context specificity of optimal cutoffs or thresholds, prompting a recommendation that researchers who develop new measurement strategies routinely report optimal cutoff values for a range of potential BRs and four potential decision-making goals. Notably, precise specification of local BRs or utilities is not critical to the profitable use of this information, which will obviate the need to make stringent assumptions about the generalizability of BRs and utilities across decision-making contexts and will enhance the practical applicability of our measurement strategies.

References

American Psychiatric Association. (1994). *Diagnostic and statistical manual of mental disorders* (4th ed.). Washington, DC: Author.

Clark, L. A., & Watson, D. (1995). Constructing validity: Basic issues in objective scale development. *Psychological Assessment, 7*, 309–319. doi:10.1037/1040-3590.7.3.309

DeCarlo, L. T. (1998). Signal detection theory and generalized linear models. *Psychological Methods, 3*, 186–205.

DeLong, E. R., DeLong, D. M., & Clarke-Pearson, D. L. (1988). Comparing the areas under two or more correlated receiver operating characteristic curves: A nonparametric approach. *Biometrics, 44*, 837–845. doi:10.2307/2531595

Gönen, M. (2007). *Analyzing receiver operating characteristic curves with SAS.* Cary, NC: SAS Institute Inc.

Green, D. M., & Swets, J. A. (1966). *Signal detection theory and psychophysics.* New York, NY: Wiley.

Hanley, J. A. (1988). The robustness of the "binormal" assumptions in fitting ROC curves. *Medical Decision Making, 8*, 197–203. doi:10.1177/0272989X 8800800308

Hanley, J. A., & McNeil, B. J. (1982). The meaning and use of the area under a receiver operating characteristic (ROC) curve. *Radiology, 143*, 29–36.

Hanley, J. A., & McNeil, B. J. (1983). Method for comparing the area under two ROC curves derived from the same cases. *Radiology, 148*, 839–843.

He, X., Gallas, B. D., & Frey, E. C. (2010). Three-class ROC analysis-toward a general decision theoretic solution. *IEEE Transactions on Medical Imaging, 29*, 206–215. doi:10.1109/TMI.2009.2034516

He, Y., & Escobar, M. (2008). Nonparametric statistical inference method for partial areas under receiver operating characteristic curves, with application to genomic studies. *Statistics in Medicine, 27*, 5291–5308. doi:10.1002/sim.3335

Hsiao, J. K., Bartko, J. J., & Potter, W. Z. (1989). Diagnosing diagnoses. *Archives of General Psychiatry, 46*, 664–667.

Kessler, R. C., Andrews, G., Colpe, L. J., Hiripi, E., Mroczek, D. K., Normand, S.-L. T., . . . Zaslavsky, A. M. (2002). Short screening scales to monitor population prevalences and trends in nonspecific psychological distress. *Psychological Medicine, 32*, 959–976. doi:10.1017/S0033291702006074

Kessler, R. C., Barker, P. R., Colpe, L. J., Epstein, J. F., Gfroerer, J. C., Hiripi, E., . . . Zaslavsky, A. M. (2003). Screening for serious mental illness in the general population. *Archives of General Psychiatry, 60*, 184–189. doi:10.1001/archpsyc.60.2.184

Kessler, R. C., Berglund, P., Chiu, W-T., Demler, O., Heeringa, S., Hiripi, E., . . . Zheng, H. (2004). The US National Comorbidity Survey Replication (NCS-R): Design and field procedures. *International Journal of Methods in Psychiatric Research, 13*, 69–92. doi:10.1002/mpr.167

Kessler, R. C., & Merikangas, K. R. (2004). The National Comorbidity Survey Replication (NCSR): Background and aims. *International Journal of Methods in Psychiatric Research, 13*, 60–68. doi:10.1002/mpr.166

Kessler, R. C., & Üstün, T. B. (2004). The World Mental Health (WMH) survey initiative version of the World Health Organization (WHO) Composite International Diagnostic Interview (CIDI). *International Journal of Methods in Psychiatric Research, 13*, 93–121. doi:10.1002/mpr.168

Li, J. L., & Zhou, X. H. (2009). Nonparametric and semiparametric estimation of the three way receiver operating characteristic surface. *Journal of Statistical Planning and Inference, 139*, 4133–4142. doi:10.1016/j.jspi.2009.05.043

Macmillan, N. A., & Creelman, C. D. (1991). *Detection theory: A user's guide.* Cambridge, England: Cambridge University Press.

McClish, D. K. (1989). Analyzing a portion of the ROC curve. *Medical Decision Making, 9*, 190–195.

McNeil, B. J., & Hanley, J. A. (1984). Statistical approaches to the analysis of receiving operating characteristic (ROC) curves. *Medical Decision Making, 4*, 137–150. doi:10.1177/0272989X 8400400203

Meehl, P. E., & Rosen, A. (1955). Antecedent probability and the efficiency of psychometric signs, patterns, or cutting scores. *Psychological Bulletin, 52*, 194–216. doi:10.1037/h0048070

Metz, C. E. (1978). Basic principles of ROC analysis. *Seminars in Nuclear Medicine, 8*, 283–298. doi:10.1016/S0001-2998(78)80014-2

Metz, C. E., Goodenough, D. J., & Rossmann, K. (1973). Evaluation of receiver operating characteristic curve data in terms of information theory, with applications in radiography. *Radiology, 109*, 297–303.

Metz, C. E., Wang, P. L., & Kronman, H. B. (1984). A new approach for testing the significance of differences between ROC curves measured from correlated data. In F. Deconinck (Eds.), *Information processing in medical imaging* (pp. 432–445). The Hague, the Netherlands: Nijhoff.

Mossman, D., & Somoza, E. (1989). Maximizing diagnostic information from the dexamethasone suppression test: An approach to criterion selection using receiver operating characteristic analysis. *Archives of General Psychiatry, 46*, 653–660.

Murphy, J. M., Berwick, D. M., Weinstein, M. C., Borus, J. F., Budman, S. H., & Klerman, G. L. (1987). Performance of screening and diagnostic tests. *Archives of General Psychiatry, 44,* 550–555.

Pierce, J. R. (1980). *An introduction to information theory: Symbols, signals, and noise* (2nd ed.). New York, NY: Dover.

Scurfield, B. K. (1996). Multiple-event forced-choice tasks in the theory of signal detectability. *Journal of Mathematical Psychology, 40,* 253–296.

Shannon, C. E., & Weaver, W. (1949). *The mathematical theory of communication.* Urbana: University of Illinois Press.

Smith, G. T. (2005). On construct validity: Issues of method and measurement. *Psychological Assessment, 17,* 396–408. doi:10.1037/1040-3590.17.4.396

Somoza, E., & Mossman, D. (1991). "Biological markers" and psychiatric diagnosis: Risk-benefit balancing using ROC analysis. *Biological Psychiatry, 29,* 811–826. doi:10.1016/0006-3223(91)90200-6

Somoza, E., & Mossman, D. (1992a). Comparing and optimizing diagnostic tests: An information-theoretical approach. *Medical Decision Making, 12,* 179–188.

Somoza, E., & Mossman, D. (1992b). Comparing diagnostic tests using information theory: The INFO-ROC technique. *Journal of Neuropsychiatry and Clinical Neurosciences, 4,* 214–219.

Somoza, E., Soutullo-Esperon, L., & Mossman, D. (1989). Evaluation and optimization of diagnostic tests using receiver operating characteristic analysis and information theory. *International Journal of Bio-Medical Computing, 24,* 153–189. doi:10.1016/0020-7101(89)90029-9

Somoza, E., Steer, R. A., Beck, A. T., & Clark, D. A. (1994). Differentiating major depression and panic disorders by self-report and clinical rating scales: ROC analysis and information theory. *Behaviour Research and Therapy, 32,* 771–782. doi:10.1016/0005-7967(94)90035-3

Stephan, C., Wesseling, S., Schink, T., & Jung, K. (2003). Comparison of eight computer programs for receiver-operating characteristic analysis. *Clinical Chemistry, 49,* 433–439. doi:10.1373/49.3.433

Swets, J. A. (1992). The science of choosing the right decision threshold in high-stakes diagnostics. *American Psychologist, 47,* 522–532. doi:10.1037/0003-066X.47.4.522

Swets, J. A. (1996). *Signal detection theory and ROC analysis in psychological diagnostics: Collected papers.* Mahwah, NJ: Erlbaum.

Swets, J. A., Dawes, R. M., & Monahan, J. (2000). Psychological science can improve diagnostic decisions. *Psychological Science in the Public Interest, 1,* 1–26. doi:10.1111/1529-1006.001